C

HOW TO PROGRAM

EIGHTH EDITION

with an introduction to C++

Deitel® Series Page

How to Program Series

Android™ How to Program, 2/E
C++ How to Program, 9/E
C How to Program, 7/E
Java™ How to Program, Early Objects Version, 10/E
Java™ How to Program, Late Objects Version, 10/E
Internet & World Wide Web How to Program, 5/E
Visual Basic® 2012 How to Program, 6/E
Visual C#® 2012 How to Program, 5/E

Deitel® Developer Series

Android™ for Programmers: An App-Driven
    Approach, 2/E, Volume 1
C for Programmers with an Introduction to C11
C++11 for Programmers
C# 2012 for Programmers
iOS® 8 for Programmers: An App-Driven
    Approach with Swift™, Volume 1
Java™ for Programmers, 3/E
JavaScript for Programmers
Swift™ for Programmers

Simply Series

Simply C++: An App-Driven Tutorial Approach
Simply Java™ Programming: An App-Driven
    Tutorial Approach
(continued in next column)

(continued from previous column)
Simply C#: An App-Driven Tutorial Approach
Simply Visual Basic® 2010: An App-Driven
    Approach, 4/E

CourseSmart Web Books

www.deitel.com/books/CourseSmart/

C++ How to Program, 8/E and 9/E
Simply C++: An App-Driven Tutorial Approach
Java™ How to Program, 9/E and 10/E
Simply Visual Basic® 2010: An App-Driven
    Approach, 4/E
Visual Basic® 2012 How to Program, 6/E
Visual Basic® 2010 How to Program, 5/E
Visual C#® 2012 How to Program, 5/E
Visual C#® 2010 How to Program, 4/E

LiveLessons Video Learning Products

www.deitel.com/books/LiveLessons/

Android™ App Development Fundamentals, 2/e
C++ Fundamentals
Java™ Fundamentals, 2/e
C# 2012 Fundamentals
C# 2010 Fundamentals
iOS® 8 App Development Fundamentals, 3/e
JavaScript Fundamentals
Swift™ Fundamentals

To receive updates on Deitel publications, Resource Centers, training courses, partner offers and more, please join the Deitel communities on

- Facebook®—facebook.com/DeitelFan
- Twitter®—@deitel
- Google+™—google.com/+DeitelFan
- YouTube™—youtube.com/DeitelTV
- LinkedIn®—linkedin.com/company/deitel-&-associates

and register for the free *Deitel® Buzz Online* e-mail newsletter at:

www.deitel.com/newsletter/subscribe.html

To communicate with the authors, send e-mail to:

deitel@deitel.com

For information on *Dive-Into® Series* on-site seminars offered by Deitel & Associates, Inc. worldwide, write to us at deitel@deitel.com or visit:

www.deitel.com/training/

For continuing updates on Pearson/Deitel publications visit:

www.deitel.com
www.pearsonhighered.com/deitel/

Visit the Deitel Resource Centers that will help you master programming languages, software development, Android™ and iOS® app development, and Internet- and web-related topics:

www.deitel.com/ResourceCenters.html

C

HOW TO PROGRAM

EIGHTH EDITION

with an introduction to C++

Paul Deitel
Deitel & Associates, Inc.

Harvey Deitel
Deitel & Associates, Inc.

DEITEL®

PEARSON

Boston Columbus Hoboken Indianapolis New York San Francisco
Amsterdam Cape Town Dubai London Madrid Milan Munich Paris Montreal
Toronto Delhi Mexico City São Paulo Sydney Hong Kong Seoul Singapore Taipei Tokyo

Vice President and Editorial Director, ECS: Marcia J. Horton
Executive Editor: Tracy Johnson (Dunkelberger)
Editorial Assistant: Kelsey Loanes
Program Manager: Carole Snyder
Project Manager: Robert Engelhardt
Media Team Lead: Steve Wright
R&P Manager: Rachel Youdelman
R&P Senior Project Manager: William Opaluch
Senior Operations Specialist: Maura Zaldivar-Garcia
Inventory Manager: Bruce Boundy
Marketing Manager: Demetrius Hall
Product Marketing Manager: Bram Van Kempen
Marketing Assistant: Jon Bryant
Cover Designer: Chuti Prasertsith / Michael Rutkowski / Marta Samsel
Cover Art: © Willyam Bradberry / Shutterstock

Pearson Education Ltd., London
Pearson Education Australia Ply. Ltd., Sydney
Pearson Education Singapore, Pte. Ltd.
Pearson Education North Asia Ltd., Hong Kong
Pearson Education Canada, Inc., Toronto
Pearson Education de Mexico, S.A. de C.V.
Pearson Education-Japan, Tokyo
Pearson Education Malaysia, Pte. Ltd.
Pearson Education, Inc., Hoboken, New Jersey

Library of Congress Cataloging-in-Publication Data
On file

7 2019

www.pearsonhighered.com

ISBN-10: 0-13-397689-0
ISBN-13: 978-0-13-397689-2

NC 08.01.2019 1341

In memory of Dennis Ritchie,
*   creator of the C programming language*
*   and co-creator of the UNIX operating system.*

Paul and Harvey Deitel

Trademarks

Contents

Appendices F, G and H are PDF documents posted online at the book's Companion Website (located at www.pearsonhighered.com/deitel).

2 Introduction to C Programming — 39

3 Structured Program Development in C — 69

4 C Program Control — 113

5 C Functions 157

6 C Arrays 214

7 C Pointers

274

8   C Characters and Strings   333

9   C Formatted Input/Output   377

10 C Structures, Unions, Bit Manipulation and Enumerations   404

11 C File Processing   441

12 C Data Structures 477

13 C Preprocessor 518

16   Introduction to Classes, Objects and Strings   589

20 Object-Oriented Programming: Polymorphism   767

21 Stream Input/Output: A Deeper Look   812

22 Exception Handling: A Deeper Look 849

23 Introduction to Custom Templates 874

Appendices F, G and H are PDF documents posted online at the book's Companion Website (located at www.pearsonhighered.com/deitel).

F   Using the Visual Studio Debugger

G   Using the GNU gdb Debugger

H   Using the Xcode Debugger

Preface

Welcome to the C programming language and to *C How to Program, Eighth Edition*! This book presents leading-edge computing technologies for college students, instructors and software-development professionals.

At the heart of the book is the Deitel signature "live-code approach"—we present concepts in the context of complete working programs, rather than in code snippets. Each code example is followed by one or more sample executions. Read the online Before You Begin section at

```
http://www.deitel.com/books/chtp8/chtp8_BYB.pdf
```

to learn how to set up your computer to run the hundreds of code examples. All the source code is available at

```
http://www.deitel.com/books/chtp8
```

and

```
http://www.pearsonhighered.com/deitel
```

Use the source code we provide to run every program as you study it.

We believe that this book and its support materials will give you an informative, challenging and entertaining introduction to C. As you read the book, if you have questions, send an e-mail to deitel@deitel.com—we'll respond promptly. For book updates, visit www.deitel.com/books/chtp8/, join our social media communities:

- Facebook®—http://facebook.com/DeitelFan
- Twitter®—@deitel
- LinkedIn®—http://linkedin.com/company/deitel-&-associates
- YouTube™—http://youtube.com/DeitelTV
- Google+™—http://google.com/+DeitelFan

and register for the *Deitel® Buzz Online* e-mail newsletter at:

```
http://www.deitel.com/newsletter/subscribe.html
```

New and Updated Features

Here are some key features of *C How to Program, 8/e*:

- *Integrated More Capabilities of the C11 and C99 standards.* Support for the C11 and C99 standards varies by compiler. Microsoft Visual C++ supports a subset of the features that were added to C in C99 and C11—primarily the features that are also required by the C++ standard. We incorporated several widely supported C11 and C99 features into the book's early chapters, as appropriate for introductory courses and for the compilers we used in this book. Appendix E, Multithreading and Other C11 and C99 Topics, presents more advanced features (such as multithreading for today's increasingly popular multi-core architectures) and various other features that are not widely supported by today's C compilers.

- *All Code Tested on Linux, Windows and OS X.* We retested all the example and exercise code using GNU gcc on Linux, Visual C++ on Windows (in Visual Studio 2013 Community Edition) and LLVM in Xcode on OS X.

- *Updated Chapter 1.* The new Chapter 1 engages students with updated intriguing facts and figures to get them excited about studying computers and computer programming. The chapter includes current technology trends and hardware discussions, the data hierarchy, social networking and a table of business and technology publications and websites that will help you stay up to date with the latest technology news and trends. We've included updated test-drives that show how to run a command-line C program on Linux, Microsoft Windows and OS X. We also updated the discussions of the Internet and web, and the introduction to object technology.

- *Updated Coverage of C++ and Object-Oriented Programming.* We updated Chapters 15–23 on object-oriented programming in C++ with material from our textbook *C++ How to Program, 9/e*, which is up-to-date with the C++11 standard.

- *Updated Code Style.* We removed the spacing inside parentheses and square brackets, and toned down our use of comments a bit. We also added parentheses to certain compound conditions for clarity.

- *Variable Declarations.* Because of improved compiler support, we were able to move variable declarations closer to where they're first used and define for-loop counter-control variables in each for's initialization section.

- *Summary Bullets.* We removed the end-of-chapter terminology lists and updated the detailed section-by-section, bullet-list summaries with **bolded** key terms and, for most, page references to their defining occurrences.

- *Use of Standard Terminology.* To help students prepare to work in industry worldwide, we audited the book against the C standard and upgraded our terminology to use C standard terms in preference to general programming terms.

- *Online Debugger Appendices.* We've updated the online GNU gdb and Visual C++® debugging appendices, and added an Xcode® debugging appendix.

- *Additional Exercises.* We updated various exercises and added some new ones, including one for the Fisher-Yates unbiased shuffling algorithm in Chapter 10.

Other Features

Other features of *C How to Program, 8/e* include:

- *Secure C Programming Sections.* Many of the C chapters end with a Secure C Programming Section. We've also posted a Secure C Programming Resource Center at www.deitel.com/SecureC/. For more details, see the section "A Note About Secure C Programming" on the next page.

- *Focus on Performance Issues.* C (and C++) are favored by designers of performance-intensive systems such as operating systems, real-time systems, embedded systems and communications systems, so we focus intensively on performance issues.

- *"Making a Difference" Contemporary Exercises.* We encourage you to use computers and the Internet to research and solve significant problems. These exercises are meant to increase awareness of important issues the world is facing. We hope you'll approach them with your own values, politics and beliefs.

- *Sorting: A Deeper Look.* Sorting places data in order, based on one or more sort keys. We begin our sorting presentation in Chapter 6 with a simple algorithm—in Appendix D, we present a deeper look. We consider several algorithms and compare them with regard to their memory consumption and processor demands. For this purpose, we present a friendly introduction to Big O notation, which indicates how hard an algorithm may have to work to solve a problem. Through examples and exercises, Appendix D discusses the selection sort, insertion sort, recursive merge sort, recursive selection sort, bucket sort and recursive Quicksort. Sorting is an intriguing problem because different sorting techniques achieve the same final result but they can vary hugely in their consumption of memory, CPU time and other system resources.

- *Titled Programming Exercises.* Most of the programming exercises are titled to help instructors conveniently choose assignments appropriate for their students.

- *Order of Evaluation.* We caution the reader about subtle order of evaluation issues.

- *C++-Style // Comments.* We use the newer, more concise C++-style // comments in preference to C's older style /*...*/ comments.

A Note About Secure C Programming

Throughout this book, we focus on C programming *fundamentals*. When we write each *How to Program* book, we search the corresponding language's standards document for the features that we feel novices need to learn in a first programming course, and features that professional programmers need to know to begin working in that language. We also cover computer-science and software-engineering fundamentals for novices—our core audience.

Industrial-strength coding techniques in any programming language are beyond the scope of an introductory textbook. For that reason, our Secure C Programming sections present some key issues and techniques, and provide links and references so you can continue learning.

Experience has shown that it's difficult to build industrial-strength systems that stand up to attacks from viruses, worms, etc. Today, via the Internet, such attacks can be instantaneous and global in scope. Software vulnerabilities often come from simple programming issues. Building security into software from the start of the development cycle can greatly reduce costs and vulnerabilities.

The CERT® Coordination Center (www.cert.org) was created to analyze and respond promptly to attacks. CERT—the Computer Emergency Response Team—publishes and promotes secure coding standards to help C programmers and others implement industrial-strength systems that avoid the programming practices that leave systems vulnerable to attacks. The CERT standards evolve as new security issues arise.

We've upgraded our code (as appropriate for an introductory book) to conform to various CERT recommendations. If you'll be building C systems in industry, consider reading *The CERT C Secure Coding Standard, 2/e* (Robert Seacord, Addison-Wesley Professional, 2014) and *Secure Coding in C and C++, 2/e* (Robert Seacord, Addison-Wesley Professional, 2013). The CERT guidelines are available free online at

```
https://www.securecoding.cert.org/confluence/display/seccode/
        CERT+C+Coding+Standard
```

Mr. Seacord, a technical reviewer for the C portion of the last edition of this book, provided specific recommendations on each of our Secure C Programming sections. Mr. Seacord is the Secure Coding Manager at CERT at Carnegie Mellon University's Software Engineering Institute (SEI) and an adjunct professor in the Carnegie Mellon University School of Computer Science.

The Secure C Programming sections at the ends of Chapters 2–13 discuss many important topics, including:

- testing for arithmetic overflows
- using unsigned integer types
- the more secure functions in the C standard's Annex K
- the importance of checking the status information returned by standard-library functions
- range checking
- secure random-number generation
- array bounds checking

- preventing buffer overflows
- input validation
- avoiding undefined behaviors
- choosing functions that return status information vs. using similar functions that do not
- ensuring that pointers are always NULL or contain valid addresses
- using C functions vs. using preprocessor macros, and more.

Web-Based Materials

The book's open access Companion Website (http://www.pearsonhighered.com/deitel) contains source code for all the code examples and the following appendices in PDF format:

- Appendix F, Using the Visual Studio Debugger
- Appendix G, Using the GNU gdb Debugger
- Appendix H, Using the Xcode Debugger

Dependency Charts

Figures 1 and 2 on the next two pages show the dependencies among the chapters to help instructors plan their syllabi. *C How to Program, 8/e* is appropriate for CS1 and many CS2 courses, and for intermediate-level C and C++ programming courses. The C++ part of the book assumes that you've studied C Chapters 1–10.

Teaching Approach

C How to Program, 8/e, contains a rich collection of examples. We focus on good software engineering, program clarity, preventing common errors, program portability and performance issues.

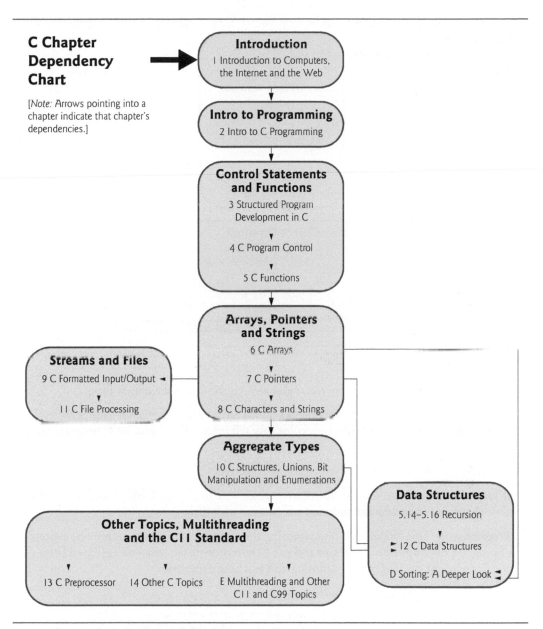

Fig. 1 | C chapter dependency chart.

Syntax Shading. For readability, we syntax shade the code, similar to the way most IDEs and code editors syntax color code. Our syntax-shading conventions are:

```
comments appear like this in gray
keywords appear like this in dark blue
constants and literal values appear like this in light blue
all other code appears in black
```

C++ Chapter Dependency Chart

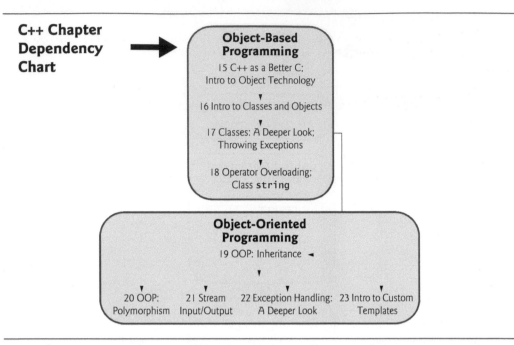

Fig. 2 | C++ chapter dependency chart.

Code Highlighting. We place gray rectangles around the key code in each program.

Using Fonts for Emphasis. We place the key terms and the index's page reference for each defining occurrence in **bold colored** text for easy reference. We emphasize C program text in the Lucida font (for example, int x = 5;).

Objectives. Each chapter begins with a list of objectives.

Illustrations/Figures. Abundant flowcharts, tables, line drawings, UML diagrams (in the C++ chapters), programs and program outputs are included.

Programming Tips. We include programming tips to help you focus on important aspects of program development. These tips and practices represent the best we've gleaned from a combined eight decades of programming and teaching experience.

Good Programming Practices

The Good Programming Practices *call attention to techniques that will help you produce programs that are clearer, more understandable and more maintainable.*

Common Programming Errors

Pointing out these Common Programming Errors *reduces the likelihood that you'll make them.*

Error-Prevention Tips

These tips contain suggestions for exposing and removing bugs from your programs and for avoiding bugs in the first place.

Performance Tips

These tips highlight opportunities for making your programs run faster or minimizing the amount of memory that they occupy.

Portability Tips

The Portability Tips *help you write code that will run on a variety of platforms.*

Software Engineering Observations

The Software Engineering Observations *highlight architectural and design issues that affect the construction of software systems, especially large-scale systems.*

Summary Bullets. We present a detailed section-by-section, bullet-list summary of each chapter with **bolded** key terms. For easy reference, most of the key terms are followed by the page number of their defining occurrences.

Self-Review Exercises and Answers. Extensive self-review exercises *and* answers are included for self-study.

Exercises. Each chapter concludes with a substantial set of exercises including:

- simple recall of important terminology and concepts
- identifying the errors in code samples
- writing individual program statements
- writing small portions of C functions (and C++ member functions and classes)
- writing complete programs
- implementing major projects

Index. We've included an extensive index, which is especially helpful when you use the book as a reference. Defining occurrences of key terms are highlighted in the index with a **bold colored** page number.

Software Used in *C How to Program, 8/e*

We tested the programs in *C How to Program, 8/e* using the following free compilers:

- GNU C and C++ (http://gcc.gnu.org/install/binaries.html), which are already installed on most Linux systems and can be installed on OS X and Windows systems.
- Microsoft's Visual C++ in Visual Studio 2013 Community edition, which you can download from http://go.microsoft.com/?linkid=9863608
- LLVM in Apple's Xcode IDE, which OS X users can download from the Mac App Store.

For other free C and C++ compilers, visit:

```
http://www.thefreecountry.com/compilers/cpp.shtml
http://www.compilers.net/Dir/Compilers/CCpp.htm
http://www.freebyte.com/programming/cpp/#cppcompilers
http://en.wikipedia.org/wiki/List_of_compilers#C.2B.2B_compilers
```

CourseSmart Web Books

Today's students and instructors have increasing demands on their time and money. Pearson has responded to that need by offering various digital texts and course materials online through CourseSmart. Faculty can review course materials online, saving time and costs. It offers students a high-quality digital version of the text for less than the cost of a print copy. Students receive the same content offered in the print textbook enhanced by search, note-taking and printing tools. For more information, visit http://www.coursesmart.com.

Instructor Resources

The following supplements are available to *qualified instructors only* through Pearson Education's password-protected Instructor Resource Center (www.pearsonhighered.com/irc):

- *PowerPoint® slides* containing all the code and figures in the text, plus bulleted items that summarize key points.

- *Test Item File* of multiple-choice questions (approximately two per top-level book section)

- *Solutions Manual* with solutions to *most* (but not all) of the end-of-chapter exercises. Please check the Instructor Resource Center to determine which exercises have solutions.

Please do not write to us requesting access to the Instructor Resource Center. Access is restricted to college instructors teaching from the book. Instructors may obtain access only through their Pearson representatives. If you're not a registered faculty member, contact your Pearson representative or visit http://www.pearsonhighered.com/replocator/.

Solutions are *not* provided for "project" exercises. Check out our Programming Projects Resource Center for lots of additional exercise and project possibilities (http://www.deitel.com/ProgrammingProjects/).

Acknowledgments

We'd like to thank Abbey Deitel and Barbara Deitel for long hours devoted to this project. Abbey co-authored Chapter 1. We're fortunate to have worked with the dedicated team of publishing professionals at Pearson. We appreciate the guidance, savvy and energy of Tracy Johnson, Executive Editor, Computer Science. Kelsey Loanes and Bob Engelhardt did a marvelous job managing the review and production processes, respectively.

C How to Program, 8/e *Reviewers*

We wish to acknowledge the efforts of our reviewers. Under tight deadlines, they scrutinized the text and the programs and provided countless suggestions for improving the presentation: Dr. Brandon Invergo (GNU/European Bioinformatics Institute), Danny Kalev (A Certified System Analyst, C Expert and Former Member of the C++ Standards Committee), Jim Hogg (Program Manager, C/C++ Compiler Team, Microsoft Corporation), José Antonio González Seco (Parliament of Andalusia), Sebnem Onsay (Special Instructor, Oakland University School of Engineering and Computer Science), Alan Bunning (Purdue University), Paul Clingan (Ohio State University), Michael Geiger (University of Massachusetts, Lowell), Jeonghwa Lee (Shippensburg University), Susan Mengel (Texas Tech University), Judith O'Rourke (SUNY at Albany) and Chen-Chi Shin (Radford University).

Other Recent Editions Reviewers

William Albrecht (University of South Florida), Ian Barland (Radford University), Ed James Beckham (Altera), John Benito (Blue Pilot Consulting, Inc. and Convener of ISO WG14—the Working Group responsible for the C Programming Language Standard), Dr. John F. Doyle (Indiana University Southeast), Alireza Fazelpour (Palm Beach Community College), Mahesh Hariharan (Microsoft), Hemanth H.M. (Software Engineer at SonicWALL), Kevin Mark Jones (Hewlett Packard), Lawrence Jones, (UGS Corp.), Don Kostuch (Independent Consultant), Vytautus Leonavicius (Microsoft), Xiaolong Li (Indiana State University), William Mike Miller (Edison Design Group, Inc.), Tom Rethard (The University of Texas at Arlington), Robert Seacord (Secure Coding Manager at SEI/CERT, author of *The CERT C Secure Coding Standard* and technical expert for the international standardization working group for the programming language C), José Antonio González Seco (Parliament of Andalusia), Benjamin Seyfarth (University of Southern Mississippi), Gary Sibbitts (St. Louis Community College at Meramec), William Smith (Tulsa Community College) and Douglas Walls (Senior Staff Engineer, C compiler, Sun Microsystems—now part of Oracle).

A Special Thank You to Brandon Invergo and Jim Hogg

We were privileged to have Brandon Invergo (GNU/European Bioinformatics Institute) and Jim Hogg (Program Manager, C/C++ Compiler Team, Microsoft Corporation) do full-book reviews. They scrutinized the C portion of the book, providing numerous insights and constructive comments. The largest part of our audience uses either the GNU gcc compiler or Microsoft's Visual C++ compiler (which also compiles C). Brandon and Jim helped us ensure that our content was accurate for the GNU and Microsoft compilers, respectively. Their comments conveyed a love of software engineering, computer science and education that we share.

Well, there you have it! C is a powerful programming language that will help you write high-performance, portable programs quickly and effectively. It scales nicely into the realm of enterprise systems development to help organizations build their business-critical and mission-critical information systems. As you read the book, we would sincerely appreciate your comments, criticisms, corrections and suggestions for improving the text. Please address all correspondence—including questions—to:

```
deitel@deitel.com
```

We'll respond promptly, and post corrections and clarifications on:

```
www.deitel.com/books/chtp8/
```

We hope you enjoy working with *C How to Program, Eighth Edition* as much as we enjoyed writing it!

Paul Deitel
Harvey Deitel

About the Authors

Paul Deitel, CEO and Chief Technical Officer of Deitel & Associates, Inc., is a graduate of MIT, where he studied Information Technology. Through Deitel & Associates, Inc., he has delivered hundreds of programming courses to industry clients, including Cisco, IBM, Siemens, Sun Microsystems, Dell, Lucent Technologies, Fidelity, NASA at the Kennedy Space Center, the National Severe Storm Laboratory, White Sands Missile Range, Hospital Sisters Health System, Rogue Wave Software, Boeing, SunGard Higher Education, Stratus, Cambridge Technology Partners, One Wave, Hyperion Software, Adra Systems, Entergy, CableData Systems, Nortel Networks, Puma, iRobot, Invensys and many more. He and his co-author, Dr. Harvey M. Deitel, are the world's best-selling programming-language textbook/professional book/video authors.

Dr. Harvey M. Deitel, Chairman and Chief Strategy Officer of Deitel & Associates, Inc., has 54 years of experience in the computer field. Dr. Deitel earned B.S. and M.S. degrees in electrical engineering from MIT and a Ph.D. in mathematics from Boston University (all with a focus on computing). He has extensive college teaching experience, including earning tenure and serving as the Chairman of the Computer Science Department at Boston College before founding Deitel & Associates in 1991 with his son, Paul Deitel. The Deitels' publications have earned international recognition, with translations published in Chinese, Korean, Japanese, German, Russian, Spanish, French, Polish, Italian, Portuguese, Greek, Urdu and Turkish. Dr. Deitel has delivered hundreds of programming courses to academic institutions, major corporations, government organizations and the military.

About Deitel & Associates, Inc.

Deitel & Associates, Inc., founded by Paul Deitel and Harvey Deitel, is an internationally recognized authoring and corporate training organization, specializing in computer programming languages, object technology, mobile app development and Internet and web software technology. The company's training clients include many of the world's largest companies, government agencies, branches of the military, and academic institutions. The company offers instructor-led training courses delivered at client sites worldwide on major programming languages and platforms, including C, C++, Java™, Android app development, Swift™ and iOS® app development, Visual C#®, Visual Basic®, Visual C++®, Python®, object technology, Internet and web programming and a growing list of additional programming and software development courses.

Through its 40-year publishing partnership with Pearson/Prentice Hall, Deitel & Associates, Inc., publishes leading-edge programming textbooks and professional books in print and popular e-book formats, and *LiveLessons* video courses (available on Safari Books Online and other video platforms). Deitel & Associates, Inc. and the authors can be reached at:

    deitel@deitel.com

To learn more about Deitel's *Dive-Into*® *Series* Corporate Training curriculum delivered to groups of software engineers at client sites worldwide, visit:

    http://www.deitel.com/training

To request a proposal for on-site, instructor-led training at your organization, e-mail deitel@deitel.com.

Individuals wishing to purchase Deitel books and *LiveLessons* video training can do so through www.deitel.com. Bulk orders by corporations, the government, the military and academic institutions should be placed directly with Pearson. For more information, visit

    http://www.informit.com/store/sales.aspx

Introduction to Computers, the Internet and the Web

1

Objectives

In this chapter, you'll learn:

- Basic computer concepts.

- The different types of programming languages.

- The history of the C programming language.

- The purpose of the C Standard Library.

- The basics of object technology.

- A typical C program-development environment.

- To test-drive a C application in Windows, Linux and Mac OS X.

- Some basics of the Internet and the World Wide Web.

1.1 Introduction

Welcome to C and C++! C is a concise yet powerful computer programming language that's appropriate for technically oriented people with little or no programming experience and for experienced programmers to use in building substantial software systems. *C How to Program, Eighth Edition*, is an effective learning tool for each of these audiences.

The core of the book emphasizes software engineering through the proven methodologies of *structured programming* in C and *object-oriented programming* in C++. The book presents hundreds of complete working programs and shows the outputs produced when those programs are run on a computer. We call this the "live-code approach." All of these example programs may be downloaded from our website www.deitel.com/books/chtp8/.

Most people are familiar with the exciting tasks that computers perform. Using this textbook, you'll learn how to command computers to perform those tasks. It's **software** (i.e., the instructions you write to command computers to perform **actions** and make **decisions**) that controls computers (often referred to as **hardware**).

1.2 Hardware and Software

Computers can perform calculations and make logical decisions phenomenally faster than human beings can. Many of today's personal computers can perform billions of calculations in one second—more than a human can perform in a lifetime. *Supercomputers* are already performing *thousands of trillions (quadrillions)* of instructions per second! China's National University of Defense Technology's Tianhe-2 supercomputer can perform over 33 quadrillion calculations per second (33.86 *petaflops*)![1] To put that in perspective, *the Tianhe-2 supercomputer can perform in one second about 3 million calculations for every person on the planet!* And supercomputing "upper limits" are growing quickly.

Computers process data under the control of sequences of instructions called **computer programs**. These software programs guide the computer through ordered actions specified by people called computer **programmers**.

A computer consists of various devices referred to as hardware (e.g., the keyboard, screen, mouse, hard disks, memory, DVD drives and processing units). Computing costs are dropping dramatically, owing to rapid developments in hardware and software technologies. Computers that might have filled large rooms and cost millions of dollars decades ago are now inscribed on silicon chips smaller than a fingernail, costing perhaps a few dollars each. Ironically, silicon is one of the most abundant materials on Earth—it's an ingredient in common sand. Silicon-chip technology has made computing so economical that computers have become a commodity.

1.2.1 Moore's Law

Every year, you probably expect to pay at least a little more for most products and services. The opposite has been the case in the computer and communications fields, especially with regard to the hardware supporting these technologies. For many decades, hardware costs have fallen rapidly.

Every year or two, the capacities of computers have approximately *doubled* inexpensively. This remarkable trend often is called **Moore's Law**, named for the person who identified it in the 1960s, Gordon Moore, co-founder of Intel—the leading manufacturer of the processors in today's computers and embedded systems. Moore's Law and *related* observations apply especially to the amount of memory that computers have for programs, the amount of secondary storage (such as disk storage) they have to hold programs and data over longer periods of time, and their processor speeds—the speeds at which they *execute* their programs (i.e., do their work).

Similar growth has occurred in the communications field—costs have plummeted as enormous demand for communications *bandwidth* (i.e., information-carrying capacity) has attracted intense competition. We know of no other fields in which technology improves so quickly and costs fall so rapidly. Such phenomenal improvement is truly fostering the *Information Revolution*.

---

1. http://www.top500.org.

1.2.2 Computer Organization

Regardless of differences in *physical* appearance, computers can be envisioned as divided into various **logical units** or sections (Fig. 1.1).

Logical unit	Description
Input unit	This "receiving" section obtains information (data and computer programs) from **input devices** and places it at the disposal of the other units for processing. Most user input is entered into computers through keyboards, touch screens and mouse devices. Other forms of input include receiving voice commands, scanning images and barcodes, reading from secondary storage devices (such as hard drives, DVD drives, Blu-ray Disc™ drives and USB flash drives—also called "thumb drives" or "memory sticks"), receiving video from a webcam and having your computer receive information from the Internet (such as when you stream videos from YouTube® or download e-books from Amazon). Newer forms of input include position data from a GPS device, and motion and orientation information from an *accelerometer* (a device that responds to up/down, left/right and forward/backward acceleration) in a smartphone or game controller (such as Microsoft® Kinect® for Xbox®, Wii™ Remote and Sony® PlayStation® Move).
Output unit	This "shipping" section takes information the computer has processed and places it on various **output devices** to make it available for use outside the computer. Most information that's output from computers today is displayed on screens (including touch screens), printed on paper ("going green" discourages this), played as audio or video on PCs and media players (such as Apple's iPods) and giant screens in sports stadiums, transmitted over the Internet or used to control other devices, such as robots and "intelligent" appliances. Information is also commonly output to secondary storage devices, such as hard drives, DVD drives and USB flash drives. Popular recent forms of output are smartphone and game controller vibration, and virtual reality devices like Oculus Rift.
Memory unit	This rapid-access, relatively low-capacity "warehouse" section retains information that has been entered through the input unit, making it immediately available for processing when needed. The memory unit also retains processed information until it can be placed on output devices by the output unit. Information in the memory unit is *volatile*—it's typically lost when the computer's power is turned off. The memory unit is often called either **memory, primary memory** or **RAM** (Random Access Memory). Main memories on desktop and notebook computers contain as much as 128 GB of RAM, though 2 to 16 GB is most common. GB stands for gigabytes; a gigabyte is approximately one billion bytes. A **byte** is eight bits. A **bit** is either a 0 or a 1.
Arithmetic and logic unit (ALU)	This "manufacturing" section performs *calculations*, such as addition, subtraction, multiplication and division. It also contains the *decision* mechanisms that allow the computer, for example, to compare two items from the memory unit to determine whether they're equal. In today's systems, the ALU is implemented as part of the next logical unit, the CPU.

Fig. 1.1 | Logical units of a computer. (Part 1 of 2.)

Logical unit	Description
Central processing unit (CPU)	This "administrative" section coordinates and supervises the operation of the other sections. The CPU tells the input unit when information should be read into the memory unit, tells the ALU when information from the memory unit should be used in calculations and tells the output unit when to send information from the memory unit to certain output devices. Many of today's computers have multiple CPUs and, hence, can perform many operations simultaneously. A **multi-core processor** implements multiple processors on a single integrated-circuit chip—a *dual-core processor* has two CPUs and a *quad-core processor* has four CPUs. Today's desktop computers have processors that can execute billions of instructions per second.
Secondary storage unit	This is the long-term, high-capacity "warehousing" section. Programs or data not actively being used by the other units normally are placed on secondary storage devices (e.g., your *hard drive*) until they're again needed, possibly hours, days, months or even years later. Information on secondary storage devices is *persistent*—it's preserved even when the computer's power is turned off. Secondary storage information takes much longer to access than information in primary memory, but its cost per unit is much less. Examples of secondary storage devices include hard drives, DVD drives and USB flash drives, some of which can hold over 2 TB (TB stands for terabytes; a terabyte is approximately one trillion bytes). Typical hard drives on desktop and notebook computers hold up to 2 TB, and some desktop hard drives can hold up to 6 TB.

Fig. 1.1 | Logical units of a computer. (Part 2 of 2.)

1.3 Data Hierarchy

Data items processed by computers form a **data hierarchy** that becomes larger and more complex in structure as we progress from the simplest data items (called "bits") to richer ones, such as characters and fields. Figure 1.2 illustrates a portion of the data hierarchy.

Bits
The smallest data item in a computer can assume the value 0 or the value 1. It's called a **bit** (short for "binary digit"—a digit that can assume one of *two* values). Remarkably, the impressive functions performed by computers involve only the simplest manipulations of 0s and 1s—*examining a bit's value*, *setting a bit's value* and *reversing a bit's value* (from 1 to 0 or from 0 to 1).

Characters
It's tedious for people to work with data in the low-level form of bits. Instead, they prefer to work with *decimal digits* (0–9), *letters* (A–Z and a–z), and *special symbols* (e.g., $, @, %, &, *, (,), –, +, ", :, ? and /). Digits, letters and special symbols are known as **characters**. The computer's **character set** is the set of all the characters used to write programs and represent data items. Computers process only 1s and 0s, so a computer's character set represents every character as a pattern of 1s and 0s. C supports various character sets (including **Unicode®**) that are composed of characters containing one, two or four bytes (8, 16 or 32 bits). Unicode contains characters for many of the world's languages. See Appendix B for more information on

the ASCII (**American Standard Code for Information Interchange**) character set—the popular subset of Unicode that represents uppercase and lowercase letters, digits and some common special characters.

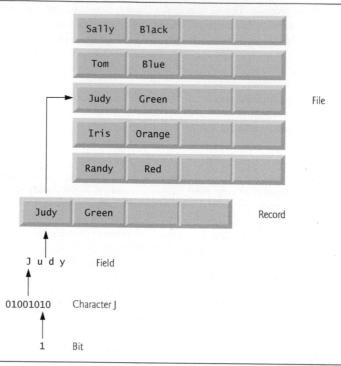

Fig. 1.2 | Data hierarchy.

Fields
Just as characters are composed of bits, **fields** are composed of characters or bytes. A field is a group of characters or bytes that conveys meaning. For example, a field consisting of uppercase and lowercase letters can be used to represent a person's name, and a field consisting of decimal digits could represent a person's age.

Records
Several related fields can be used to compose a **record**. In a payroll system, for example, the record for an employee might consist of the following fields (possible types for these fields are shown in parentheses):

- Employee identification number (a whole number)
- Name (a string of characters)
- Address (a string of characters)
- Hourly pay rate (a number with a decimal point)
- Year-to-date earnings (a number with a decimal point)
- Amount of taxes withheld (a number with a decimal point)

Thus, a record is a group of related fields. In the preceding example, all the fields belong to the *same* employee. A company might have many employees and a payroll record for each.

Files

A **file** is a group of related records. [*Note:* More generally, a file contains arbitrary data in arbitrary formats. In some operating systems, a file is viewed simply as a *sequence of bytes*—any organization of the bytes in a file, such as organizing the data into records, is a view created by the application programmer.] It's not unusual for an organization to have many files, some containing billions, or even trillions, of characters of information.

Database

A **database** is a collection of data organized for easy access and manipulation. The most popular model is the *relational database*, in which data is stored in simple *tables*. A table includes *records* and *fields*. For example, a table of students might include first name, last name, major, year, student ID number and grade point average fields. The data for each student is a record, and the individual pieces of information in each record are the fields. You can *search*, *sort* and otherwise manipulate the data based on its relationship to multiple tables or databases. For example, a university might use data from the student database in combination with data from databases of courses, on-campus housing, meal plans, etc.

Big Data

The amount of data being produced worldwide is enormous and growing quickly. According to IBM, approximately 2.5 quintillion bytes (2.5 *exabytes*) of data are created daily and 90% of the world's data was created in just the past two years![2] According to an IDC study, the global data supply will reach 40 *zettabytes* (equal to 40 trillion **gigabytes**) annually by 2020.[3] Figure 1.3 shows some common byte measurements. **Big data** applications deal with massive amounts of data and this field is growing quickly, creating lots of opportunity for software developers. According to a study by Gartner Group, over 4 million IT jobs globally will support big data by 2015.[4]

Unit	Bytes	Which is approximately
1 kilobyte (KB)	1024 bytes	10^3 (1024 bytes exactly)
1 megabyte (MB)	1024 kilobytes	10^6 (1,000,000 bytes)
1 gigabyte (GB)	1024 megabytes	10^9 (1,000,000,000 bytes)
1 terabyte (TB)	1024 gigabytes	10^{12} (1,000,000,000,000 bytes)
1 petabyte (PB)	1024 terabytes	10^{15} (1,000,000,000,000,000 bytes)
1 exabyte (EB)	1024 petabytes	10^{18} (1,000,000,000,000,000,000 bytes)
1 zettabyte (ZB)	1024 exabytes	10^{21} (1,000,000,000,000,000,000,000 bytes)

Fig. 1.3 | Byte measurements.

---

2. `http://www.ibm.com/smarterplanet/us/en/business_analytics/article/`
   `it_business_intelligence.html`.
3. `http://recode.net/2014/01/10/stuffed-why-data-storage-is-hot-again-really/`.
4. `http://tech.fortune.cnn.com/2013/09/04/big-data-employment-boom/`.

1.4 Machine Languages, Assembly Languages and High-Level Languages

Programmers write instructions in various programming languages, some directly understandable by computers and others requiring intermediate *translation* steps. Hundreds of such languages are in use today. These may be divided into three general types:

1. Machine languages
2. Assembly languages
3. High-level languages

Machine Languages

Any computer can directly understand only its own **machine language**, defined by its hardware design. Machine languages generally consist of strings of numbers (ultimately reduced to 1s and 0s) that instruct computers to perform their most elementary operations one at a time. Machine languages are *machine dependent* (a particular machine language can be used on only one type of computer). Such languages are cumbersome for humans. For example, here's a section of an early machine-language payroll program that adds overtime pay to base pay and stores the result in gross pay:

```
+1300042774
+1400593419
+1200274027
```

Assembly Languages and Assemblers

Programming in machine language was simply too slow and tedious for most programmers. Instead of using the strings of numbers that computers could directly understand, programmers began using English-like abbreviations to represent elementary operations. These abbreviations formed the basis of **assembly languages**. *Translator programs* called **assemblers** were developed to convert early assembly-language programs to machine language at computer speeds. The following section of an assembly-language payroll program also adds overtime pay to base pay and stores the result in gross pay:

```
load    basepay
add     overpay
store   grosspay
```

Although such code is clearer to humans, it's incomprehensible to computers until translated to machine language.

High-Level Languages and Compilers

With the advent of assembly languages, computer usage increased rapidly, but programmers still had to use numerous instructions to accomplish even the simplest tasks. To speed the programming process, **high-level languages** were developed in which single statements could be written to accomplish substantial tasks. Translator programs called **compilers** convert high-level language programs into machine language. High-level languages allow you to write instructions that look almost like everyday English and contain commonly used mathematical notations. A payroll program written in a high-level language might contain a *single* statement such as

```
grossPay = basePay + overTimePay
```

From the programmer's standpoint, high-level languages are preferable to machine and assembly languages. C is one of the most widely used high-level programming languages.

Interpreters

Compiling a large high-level language program into machine language can take considerable computer time. *Interpreter* programs, developed to execute high-level language programs directly, avoid the delay of compilation, although they run slower than compiled programs.

1.5 The C Programming Language

C evolved from two previous languages, BCPL and B. BCPL was developed in 1967 by Martin Richards as a language for writing operating systems and compilers. Ken Thompson modeled many features in his B language after their counterparts in BCPL, and in 1970 he used B to create early versions of the UNIX operating system at Bell Laboratories.

The C language was evolved from B by Dennis Ritchie at Bell Laboratories and was originally implemented in 1972. C initially became widely known as the development language of the UNIX operating system. Many of today's leading operating systems are written in C and/or C++. C is mostly hardware independent—with careful design, it's possible to write C programs that are **portable** to most computers.

Built for Performance

C is widely used to develop systems that demand performance, such as operating systems, embedded systems, real-time systems and communications systems (Figure 1.4).

Application	Description
Operating systems	C's portability and performance make it desirable for implementing operating systems, such as Linux and portions of Microsoft's Windows and Google's Android. Apple's OS X is built in Objective-C, which was derived from C. We discuss some key popular desktop/notebook operating systems and mobile operating systems in Section 1.11.
Embedded systems	The vast majority of the microprocessors produced each year are embedded in devices other than general-purpose computers. These embedded systems include navigation systems, smart home appliances, home security systems, smartphones, tablets, robots, intelligent traffic intersections and more. C is one of the most popular programming languages for developing embedded systems, which typically need to run as fast as possible and conserve memory. For example, a car's antilock brakes must respond immediately to slow or stop the car without skidding; game controllers used for video games should respond instantaneously to prevent any lag between the controller and the action in the game, and to ensure smooth animations.

Fig. 1.4 | Some popular performance-oriented C applications. (Part 1 of 2.)

Application	Description
Real-time systems	Real-time systems are often used for "mission-critical" applications that require nearly instantaneous and predictable response times. Real-time systems need to work continuously—for example, an air-traffic-control system must constantly monitor the positions and velocities of the planes and report that information to air-traffic controllers without delay so that they can alert the planes to change course if there's a possibility of a collision.
Communications systems	Communications systems need to route massive amounts of data to their destinations quickly to ensure that things such as audio and video are delivered smoothly and without delay.

Fig. 1.4 | Some popular performance-oriented C applications. (Part 2 of 2.)

By the late 1970s, C had evolved into what's now referred to as "traditional C." The publication in 1978 of Kernighan and Ritchie's book, *The C Programming Language,* drew wide attention to the language. This became one of the most successful computer science books of all time.

Standardization

The rapid expansion of C over various types of computers (sometimes called **hardware platforms**) led to many variations that were similar but often incompatible. This was a serious problem for programmers who needed to develop code that would run on several platforms. It became clear that a standard version of C was needed. In 1983, the X3J11 technical committee was created under the American National Standards Committee on Computers and Information Processing (X3) to "provide an unambiguous and machine-independent definition of the language." In 1989, the standard was approved as ANSI X3.159-1989 in the United States through the **American National Standards Institute (ANSI)**, then worldwide through the **International Standards Organization (ISO)**. We call this simply Standard C. This standard was updated in 1999—its standards document is referred to as *INCITS/ISO/IEC 9899-1999* and often referred to simply as C99. Copies may be ordered from the American National Standards Institute (www.ansi.org) at webstore.ansi.org/ansidocstore.

The C11 Standard

We also discuss the latest C standard (referred to as C11), which was approved in 2011. C11 refines and expands C's capabilities. We've integrated into the text and Appendix E (in easy-to-include-or-omit sections) many of the new features implemented in leading C compilers.

Portability Tip 1.1

Because C is a hardware-independent, widely available language, applications written in C often can run with little or no modification on a wide range of computer systems.

1.6 C Standard Library

As you'll learn in Chapter 5, C programs consist of pieces called **functions**. You can program all the functions that you need to form a C program, but most C programmers take advantage of the rich collection of existing functions called the **C Standard Library**. Thus, there are really two parts to learning how to program in C—learning the C language itself and learning how to use the functions in the C Standard Library. Throughout the book, we discuss many of these functions. P. J. Plauger's book *The Standard C Library* is must reading for programmers who need a deep understanding of the library functions, how to implement them and how to use them to write portable code. We use and explain many C library functions throughout this text.

C How to Program, 8/e encourages a *building-block approach* to creating programs. Avoid "reinventing the wheel." Instead, use existing pieces—this is called **software reuse**. When programming in C you'll typically use the following building blocks:

- C Standard Library functions

- Functions you create yourself

- Functions other people (whom you trust) have created and made available to you

The advantage of creating your own functions is that you'll know exactly how they work. You'll be able to examine the C code. The disadvantage is the time-consuming effort that goes into designing, developing, debugging and performance-tuning new functions.

Performance Tip 1.1
Using C Standard Library functions instead of writing your own versions can improve program performance, because these functions are carefully written to perform efficiently.

Portability Tip 1.2
Using C Standard Library functions instead of writing your own comparable versions can improve program portability, because these functions are used in virtually all Standard C implementations.

1.7 C++ and Other C-Based Languages

C++ was developed by Bjarne Stroustrup at Bell Laboratories. It has its roots in C, providing a number of features that "spruce up" the C language. More important, it provides capabilities for **object-oriented programming**. **Objects** are essentially reusable software **components** that model items in the real world. Using a modular, object-oriented design-and-implementation approach can make software-development groups more productive. Chapters 15–23 present a condensed treatment of C++ selected from our book *C++ How to Program*. Figure 1.5 introduces several other popular C-based programming languages.

Programming language	Description
Objective-C	Objective-C is an object-oriented language based on C. It was developed in the early 1980s and later acquired by NeXT, which in turn was acquired by Apple. It has become the key programming language for the OS X operating system and all iOS-powered devices (such as iPods, iPhones and iPads).

Fig. 1.5 | Popular C-based programming languages. (Part 1 of 2.)

Programming language	Description
Java	Sun Microsystems in 1991 funded an internal corporate research project which resulted in the C++-based object-oriented programming language called Java. A key goal of Java is to enable the writing of programs that will run on a broad variety of computer systems and computer-controlled devices. This is sometimes called "write once, run anywhere." Java is used to develop large-scale enterprise applications, to enhance the functionality of web servers (the computers that provide the content we see in our web browsers), to provide applications for consumer devices (smartphones, television set-top boxes and more) and for many other purposes. Java is also the language of Android app development.
C#	Microsoft's three primary object-oriented programming languages are Visual Basic (based on the original Basic), Visual C++ (based on C++) and Visual C# (based on C++ and Java, and developed for integrating the Internet and the web into computer applications). Non-Microsoft versions of C# are also available.
PHP	PHP, an object-oriented, open-source scripting language supported by a community of users and developers, is used by millions of websites. PHP is platform independent—implementations exist for all major UNIX, Linux, Mac and Windows operating systems. PHP also supports many databases, including the popular open-source MySQL.
Python	Python, another object-oriented scripting language, was released publicly in 1991. Developed by Guido van Rossum of the National Research Institute for Mathematics and Computer Science in Amsterdam (CWI), Python draws heavily from Modula-3—a systems programming language. Python is "extensible"—it can be extended through classes and programming interfaces.
JavaScript	JavaScript is the most widely used scripting language. It's primarily used to add dynamic behavior to web pages—for example, animations and improved interactivity with the user. It's provided with all major web browsers.
Swift	Swift, Apple's new programming language for developing iOS and Mac apps, was announced at the Apple World Wide Developer Conference (WWDC) in June 2014. Although apps can still be developed and maintained with Objective-C, Swift is Apple's app-development language of the future. It's a modern language that eliminates some of the complexity of Objective-C, making it easier for beginners and those transitioning from other high-level languages such as Java, C#, C++ and C. Swift emphasizes performance and security, and has full access to the iOS and Mac programming capabilities.

Fig. 1.5 | Popular C-based programming languages. (Part 2 of 2.)

1.8 Object Technology

This section is intended for readers who will be studying C++ in the later part of this book. Building software quickly, correctly and economically remains an elusive goal at a time when demands for new and more powerful software are soaring. *Objects*, or more precisely the *classes* objects come from, are essentially *reusable* software components. There are date objects, time objects, audio objects, video objects, automobile objects, people objects, etc. Almost any *noun* can be reasonably represented as a software object in terms of *attributes* (e.g., name, color and size) and *behaviors* (e.g., calculating, moving and communicating). Software developers are discovering that using a modular, object-oriented design-and-implementation approach can make software-development groups much more productive than was possible with earlier techniques—object-oriented programs are often easier to understand, correct and modify.

1.8.1 The Automobile as an Object

To help you understand objects and their contents, let's begin with a simple analogy. Suppose you want to *drive a car and make it go faster by pressing its accelerator pedal*. What must happen before you can do this? Well, before you can drive a car, someone has to *design* it. A car typically begins as engineering drawings, similar to the *blueprints* that describe the design of a house. These drawings include the design for an accelerator pedal. The pedal *hides* from the driver the complex mechanisms that actually make the car go faster, just as the brake pedal "hides" the mechanisms that slow the car, and the steering wheel "hides" the mechanisms that turn the car. This enables people with little or no knowledge of how engines, braking and steering mechanisms work to drive a car easily.

Just as you cannot cook meals in the kitchen of a blueprint, you cannot drive a car's engineering drawings. Before you can drive a car, it must be *built* from the engineering drawings that describe it. A completed car has an *actual* accelerator pedal to make it go faster, but even that's not enough—the car won't accelerate on its own (hopefully!), so the driver must *press* the pedal to accelerate the car.

1.8.2 Methods and Classes

Let's use our car example to introduce some key object-oriented programming concepts. Performing a task in a program requires a **method**. The method houses the program statements that actually perform its tasks. It hides these statements from its user, just as a car's accelerator pedal hides from the driver the mechanisms of making the car go faster. In object-oriented programming languages, we create a program unit called a **class** to house the set of methods that perform the class's tasks. For example, a class that represents a bank account might contain one method to *deposit* money to an account, another to *withdraw* money from an account and a third to *inquire* what the account's current balance is. A class is similar in concept to a car's engineering drawings, which house the design of an accelerator pedal, steering wheel, and so on.

1.8.3 Instantiation

Just as someone has to *build a car* from its engineering drawings before you can actually drive a car, you must *build an object* of a class before a program can perform the tasks that the class's methods define. The process of doing this is called *instantiation*. An object is then referred to as an **instance** of its class.

1.8.4 Reuse

Just as a car's engineering drawings can be *reused* many times to build many cars, you can *reuse* a class many times to build many objects. Reuse of existing classes when building new classes and programs saves time and effort. Reuse also helps you build more reliable and effective systems, because existing classes and components often have undergone extensive *testing*, *debugging* and *performance* tuning. Just as the notion of *interchangeable parts* was crucial to the Industrial Revolution, reusable classes are crucial to the software revolution that has been spurred by object technology.

Software Engineering Observation 1.1
Use a building-block approach to creating your programs. Avoid reinventing the wheel—use existing high-quality pieces wherever possible. Such software reuse is a key benefit of object-oriented programming.

1.8.5 Messages and Method Calls

When you drive a car, pressing its gas pedal sends a *message* to the car to perform a task—that is, to go faster. Similarly, you *send messages to an object*. Each message is implemented as a **method call** that tells a method of the object to perform its task. For example, a program might call a particular bank-account object's *deposit* method to increase the account's balance.

1.8.6 Attributes and Instance Variables

A car, besides having capabilities to accomplish tasks, also has *attributes*, such as its color, its number of doors, the amount of gas in its tank, its current speed and its record of total miles driven (i.e., its odometer reading). Like its capabilities, the car's attributes are represented as part of its design in its engineering diagrams (which, for example, include an odometer and a fuel gauge). As you drive an actual car, these attributes are carried along with the car. Every car maintains its *own* attributes. For example, each car knows how much gas is in its own gas tank, but *not* how much is in the tanks of *other* cars.

An object, similarly, has attributes that it carries along as it's used in a program. These attributes are specified as part of the object's class. For example, a bank-account object has a *balance attribute* that represents the amount of money in the account. Each bank-account object knows the balance in the account it represents, but *not* the balances of the *other* accounts in the bank. Attributes are specified by the class's **instance variables**.

1.8.7 Encapsulation and Information Hiding

Classes (and their objects) **encapsulate**, i.e., encase, their attributes and methods. A class's (and its objects) attributes and methods are intimately related. Objects may communicate with one another, but they're normally not allowed to know how other objects are implemented—implementation details are *hidden* within the objects themselves. This **information hiding**, as we'll see, is crucial to good software engineering.

1.8.8 Inheritance

A new class of objects can be created conveniently by **inheritance**—the new class (called the **subclass**) starts with the characteristics of an existing class (called the **superclass**), possibly customizing them and adding unique characteristics of its own. In our car analogy, an object of class "convertible" certainly *is an* object of the more *general* class "automobile," but more *specifically*, the roof can be raised or lowered.

1.9 Typical C Program-Development Environment

C systems generally consist of several parts: a program-development environment, the language and the C Standard Library. The following discussion explains the typical C development environment shown in Fig. 1.6.

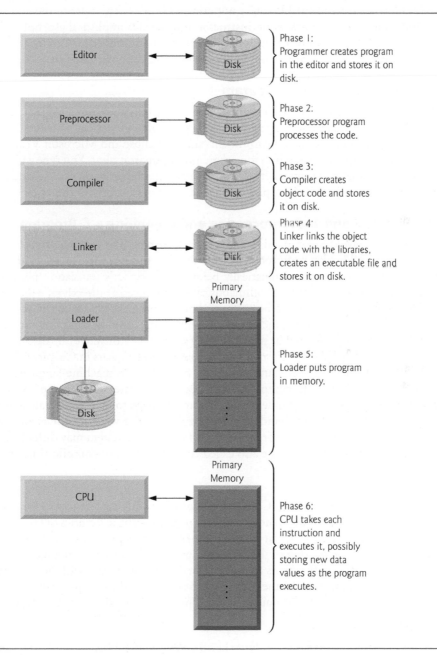

Fig. 1.6 | Typical C development environment.

C programs typically go through six phases to be executed (Fig. 1.6). These are: **edit, preprocess, compile, link, load** and **execute.** Although *C How to Program, 8/e,* is a generic C textbook (written independently of the details of any particular operating system), we concentrate in this section on a typical Linux-based C system. [*Note:* The programs in this book will run with little or no modification on most current C systems, including Microsoft Windows-based systems.] If you're not using a Linux system, refer to the documentation for your system or ask your instructor how to accomplish these tasks in your environment. Check out our C Resource Center at www.deitel.com/C to locate "getting started" tutorials for popular C compilers and development environments.

1.9.1 Phase 1: Creating a Program

Phase 1 consists of editing a file. This is accomplished with an **editor program.** Two editors widely used on Linux systems are vi and emacs. Software packages for the C/C++ integrated program development environments such as Eclipse and Microsoft Visual Studio have editors that are integrated into the programming environment. You type a C program with the editor, make corrections if necessary, then store the program on a secondary storage device such as a hard disk. C program filenames should end with the .c extension.

1.9.2 Phases 2 and 3: Preprocessing and Compiling a C Program

In Phase 2, you give the command to **compile** the program. The compiler translates the C program into machine-language code (also referred to as **object code**). In a C system, a **preprocessor** program executes automatically before the compiler's translation phase begins. The C **preprocessor** obeys special commands called **preprocessor directives**, which indicate that certain manipulations are to be performed on the program before compilation. These manipulations usually consist of including other files in the file to be compiled and performing various text replacements. The most common preprocessor directives are discussed in the early chapters; a detailed discussion of preprocessor features appears in Chapter 13.

In Phase 3, the compiler translates the C program into machine-language code. A **syntax error** occurs when the compiler cannot recognize a statement because it violates the rules of the language. The compiler issues an error message to help you locate and fix the incorrect statement. The C Standard does not specify the wording for error messages issued by the compiler, so the error messages you see on your system may differ from those on other systems. Syntax errors are also called **compile errors**, or **compile-time errors**.

1.9.3 Phase 4: Linking

The next phase is called **linking.** C programs typically contain references to functions defined elsewhere, such as in the standard libraries or in the private libraries of groups of programmers working on a particular project. The object code produced by the C compiler typically contains "holes" due to these missing parts. A **linker** links the object code with the code for the missing functions to produce an **executable image** (with no missing pieces). On a typical Linux system, the command to compile and link a program is called **gcc** (the GNU C compiler). To compile and link a program named welcome.c, type

```
gcc welcome.c
```

at the Linux prompt and press the *Enter* key (or *Return* key). [*Note:* Linux commands are case sensitive; make sure that each c is lowercase and that the letters in the filename are in the appropriate case.] If the program compiles and links correctly, a file called a.out (by default) is produced. This is the executable image of our welcome.c program.

1.9.4 Phase 5: Loading

The next phase is called **loading**. Before a program can be executed, the program must first be placed in memory. This is done by the **loader**, which takes the executable image from disk and transfers it to memory. Additional components from shared libraries that support the program are also loaded.

1.9.5 Phase 6: Execution

Finally, the computer, under the control of its CPU, **executes** the program one instruction at a time. To load and execute the program on a Linux system, type ./a.out at the Linux prompt and press *Enter*.

1.9.6 Problems That May Occur at Execution Time

Programs do not always work on the first try. Each of the preceding phases can fail because of various errors that we'll discuss. For example, an executing program might attempt to divide by zero (an illegal operation on computers just as in arithmetic). This would cause the computer to display an error message. You would then return to the edit phase, make the necessary corrections and proceed through the remaining phases again to determine that the corrections work properly.

Common Programming Error 1.1
Errors such as division-by-zero occur as a program runs, so they are called runtime errors or execution-time errors. Divide-by-zero is generally a fatal error, i.e., one that causes the program to terminate immediately without successfully performing its job. Nonfatal errors allow programs to run to completion, often producing incorrect results.

1.9.7 Standard Input, Standard Output and Standard Error Streams

Most C programs input and/or output data. Certain C functions take their input from stdin (the **standard input stream**), which is normally the keyboard, but stdin can be redirected to another stream. Data is often output to stdout (the **standard output stream**), which is normally the computer screen, but stdout can be redirected to another stream. When we say that a program prints a result, we normally mean that the result is displayed on a screen. Data may be output to devices such as disks and printers. There's also a **standard error stream** referred to as stderr. The stderr stream (normally connected to the screen) is used for displaying error messages. It's common to route regular output data, i.e., stdout, to a device other than the screen while keeping stderr assigned to the screen so that the user can be immediately informed of errors.

1.10 Test-Driving a C Application in Windows, Linux and Mac OS X

In this section, you'll run and interact with your first C application. You'll begin by running a guess-the-number game, which randomly picks a number from 1 to 1000 and prompts you to guess it. If your guess is correct, the game ends. If your guess is not correct, the application indicates it's higher or lower than the correct number. There's no limit on the number of guesses you can make but you should be able to guess any of the numbers in this range correctly in 10 or fewer tries. There's some nice computer science behind this game—in Section 6.10, Searching Arrays, you'll explore the *binary search* technique.

For this test-drive only, we've modified this application from the exercise you'll be asked to create in Chapter 5. Normally this application *randomly* selects the correct answers. The modified application uses the same sequence of correct answers every time you execute the program (though the particular sequence may vary by compiler), so you can use the same guesses we use in this section and see the same results.

We'll demonstrate running a C application using the Windows **Command Prompt**, a *shell* on Linux and a **Terminal** window in Mac OS X. The application runs similarly on all three platforms. After you perform the test-drive for your platform, you can try the *randomized* version of the game, which we've provided with each test drive's version of the example in a subfolder named `randomized_version`.

Many development environments are available in which you can compile, build and run C applications, such as GNU C, Dev C++, Microsoft Visual C++, CodeLite, NetBeans, Eclipse, Xcode, etc. Consult your instructor for information on your specific development environment. Most C++ development environments can compile both C and C++ programs.

In the following steps, you'll run the application and enter various numbers to guess the correct number. The elements and functionality that you see in this application are typical of those you'll learn to program in this book. We use fonts to distinguish between features you see on the screen (e.g., the **Command Prompt**) and elements that are not directly related to the screen. We emphasize screen features like titles and menus (e.g., the **File** menu) in a semibold **sans-serif Helvetica** font, and to emphasize filenames, text displayed by an application and values you should enter into an application (e.g., `Guess-Number` or `500`) we use a `sans-serif Lucida` font. As you've noticed, the **defining occurrence** of each key term is set in **bold blue** type.

For the Windows version of the test drive in this section, we've modified the background color of the **Command Prompt** window to make the **Command Prompt** windows more readable. To modify the **Command Prompt** colors on your system, open a **Command Prompt** by selecting **Start > All Programs > Accessories > Command Prompt**, then right click the title bar and select **Properties**. In the **"Command Prompt" Properties** dialog box that appears, click the **Colors** tab, and select your preferred text and background colors.

1.10.1 Running a C Application from the Windows Command Prompt

1. *Checking your setup.* It's important to read the Before You Begin section at `www.deitel.com/books/chtp8/` to make sure that you've copied the book's examples to your hard drive correctly.

2. *Locating the completed application.* Open a **Command Prompt** window. To change to the directory for the completed **GuessNumber** application, type `cd C:\examples\ch01\GuessNumber\Windows`, then press *Enter* (Fig. 1.7). The command `cd` is used to change directories.

Fig. 1.7 | Opening a **Command Prompt** window and changing the directory.

3. *Running the GuessNumber application.* Now that you are in the directory that contains the **GuessNumber** application, type the command GuessNumber (Fig. 1.8) and press *Enter*. [*Note:* GuessNumber.exe is the actual name of the application; however, Windows assumes the .exe extension by default.]

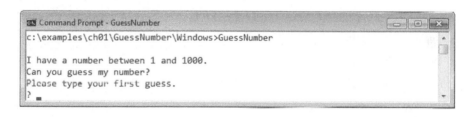

Fig. 1.8 | Running the **GuessNumber** application.

4. *Entering your first guess.* The application displays "Please type your first guess.", then displays a question mark (?) as a prompt on the next line (Fig. 1.8). At the prompt, enter 500 (Fig. 1.9).

Fig. 1.9 | Entering your first guess.

5. *Entering another guess.* The application displays "Too high. Try again.", meaning that the value you entered is greater than the number the application chose as the correct guess. So, you should enter a lower number for your next guess. At the prompt, enter 250 (Fig. 1.10). The application again displays "Too high. Try again.", because the value you entered is still greater than the number that the application chose.

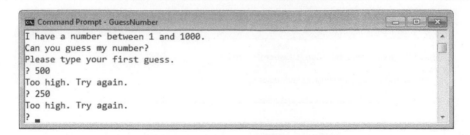

Fig. 1.10 | Entering a second guess and receiving feedback.

6. *Entering additional guesses.* Continue to play the game by entering values until you guess the correct number. The application will display "Excellent! You guessed the number!" (Fig. 1.11).

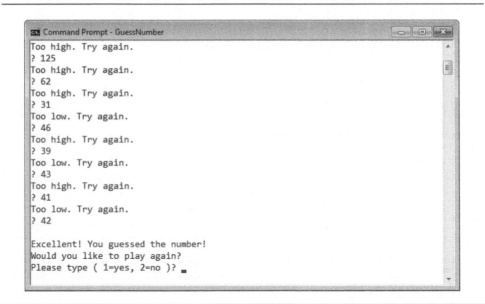

Fig. 1.11 | Entering additional guesses and guessing the correct number.

7. *Playing the game again or exiting the application.* After you guess correctly, the application asks if you'd like to play another game (Fig. 1.11). At the prompt, entering 1 causes the application to choose a new number and displays the message "Please type your first guess." followed by a question-mark prompt (Fig. 1.12), so you can make your first guess in the new game. Entering 2 ends the application and returns you to the application's directory at the **Command Prompt** (Fig. 1.13). Each time you execute this application from the beginning (i.e., *Step 3*), it will choose the same numbers for you to guess.

8. *Close the* **Command Prompt** *window.*

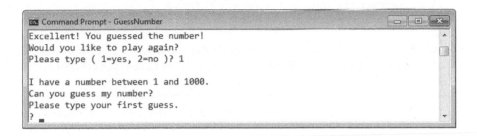

Fig. 1.12 | Playing the game again.

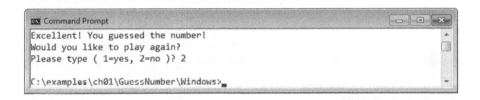

Fig. 1.13 | Exiting the game.

1.10.2 Running a C Application Using GNU C with Linux

For the figures in this section, we use a bold font to point out the user input required by each step. In this test drive, we assume that you know how to copy the examples into your home directory. Please see your instructor if you have any questions regarding copying the files to your Linux system. Also, for the figures in this section, we use a bold font to point out the user input required by each step. The prompt in the shell on our system uses the tilde (~) character to represent the home directory, and each prompt ends with the dollar-sign ($) character. The prompt will vary among Linux systems.

1. *Checking your setup.* It's important to read the Before You Begin section at www.deitel.com/books/chtp8/ to make sure that you've copied the book's examples to your hard drive correctly.

2. *Locating the completed application.* From a Linux shell, change to the completed **GuessNumber** application directory (Fig. 1.14) by typing

    ```
    cd examples/ch01/GuessNumber/GNU
    ```

    then pressing *Enter*. The command cd is used to change directories.

```
~$ cd examples/ch01/GuessNumber/GNU
~/examples/ch01/GuessNumber/GNU$
```

Fig. 1.14 | Changing to the **GuessNumber** application's directory.

3. *Compiling the GuessNumber application.* To run an application on the GNU C++ compiler, you must first compile it by typing

```
gcc GuessNumber.c -o GuessNumber
```

as in Fig. 1.15. This command compiles the application. The -o option is followed by the name you'd like the executable file to have—GuessNumber.

```
~/examples/ch01/GuessNumber/GNU$ gcc -std=c11 GuessNumber.c -o GuessNumber
~/examples/ch01/GuessNumber/GNU$
```

Fig. 1.15 | Compiling the **GuessNumber** application using the gcc command.

4. *Running the GuessNumber application.* To run the executable file GuessNumber, type ./GuessNumber at the next prompt, then press *Enter* (Fig. 1.16).

```
~/examples/ch01/GuessNumber/GNU$ ./GuessNumber

I have a number between 1 and 1000.
Can you guess my number?
Please type your first guess.
?
```

Fig. 1.16 | Running the **GuessNumber** application.

5. *Entering your first guess.* The application displays "Please type your first guess.", then displays a question mark (?) as a prompt on the next line (Fig. 1.16). At the prompt, enter 500 (Fig. 1.17).

```
~/examples/ch01/GuessNumber/GNU$ ./GuessNumber

I have a number between 1 and 1000.
Can you guess my number?
Please type your first guess.
? 500
Too high. Try again.
?
```

Fig. 1.17 | Entering an initial guess.

6. *Entering another guess.* The application displays "Too high. Try again.", meaning that the value you entered is greater than the number the application chose as the correct guess (Fig. 1.17). At the next prompt, enter 250 (Fig. 1.18). This time the application displays "Too low. Try again.", because the value you entered is less than the correct guess.

```
~/examples/ch01/GuessNumber/GNU$ ./GuessNumber

I have a number between 1 and 1000.
Can you guess my number?
Please type your first guess.
? 500
Too high. Try again.
? 250
Too low. Try again.
?
```

Fig. 1.18 | Entering a second guess and receiving feedback.

7. *Entering additional guesses.* Continue to play the game (Fig. 1.19) by entering values until you guess the correct number. When you guess correctly, the application displays "Excellent! You guessed the number!"

```
Too low. Try again.
? 375
Too low. Try again.
? 437
Too high. Try again.
? 406
Too high. Try again.
? 391
Too high. Try again.
? 383
Too low. Try again.
? 387
Too high. Try again.
? 385
Too high. Try again.
? 384

Excellent! You guessed the number!
Would you like to play again?
Please type ( 1=yes, 2=no )?
```

Fig. 1.19 | Entering additional guesses and guessing the correct number.

8. *Playing the game again or exiting the application.* After you guess the correct number, the application asks if you'd like to play another game. At the prompt, entering 1 causes the application to choose a new number and displays the message "Please type your first guess." followed by a question-mark prompt (Fig. 1.20) so that you can make your first guess in the new game. Entering 2 ends the application and returns you to the application's directory in the shell (Fig. 1.21). Each time you execute this application from the beginning (i.e., *Step 4*), it will choose the same numbers for you to guess.

```
Excellent! You guessed the number!
Would you like to play again?
Please type ( 1=yes, 2=no )? 1

I have a number between 1 and 1000.
Can you guess my number?
Please type your first guess.
?
```

Fig. 1.20 | Playing the game again.

```
Excellent! You guessed the number!
Would you like to play again?
Please type ( 1=yes, 2=no )? 2

~/examples/ch01/GuessNumber/GNU$
```

Fig. 1.21 | Exiting the game.

1.10.3 Running a C Application Using the Teminal on Mac OS X

For the figures in this section, we use a bold font to point out the user input required by each step. You'll use Mac OS X's **Terminal** window to perform this test-drive. To open a **Terminal** window, click the Spotlight Search icon in the upper-right corner of your screen, then type Terminal to locate the **Terminal** application. Under **Applications** in the Spotlight Search results, select **Terminal** to open a **Terminal** window. The prompt in a **Terminal** window has the form *hostName*:~ *userFolder*$ to represent your user directory. For the figures in this section, we removed the *hostName*: part and used the generic name *userFolder* to represent your user account's folder.

1. *Checking your setup.* It's important to read the Before You Begin section at www.deitel.com/books/chtp8/ to make sure that you've copied the book's examples to your hard drive correctly. We assume that the examples are located in your user account's Documents/examples folder.

2. *Locating the completed application.* In the **Terminal** window, change to the completed **GuessNumber** application directory (Fig. 1.22) by typing

   ```
   cd Documents/examples/ch01/GuessNumber/GNU
   ```

   then pressing *Enter*. The command cd is used to change directories.

```
hostName:~ userFolder$ cd Documents/examples/ch01/GuessNumber/GNU
hostName:GNU$
```

Fig. 1.22 | Changing to the **GuessNumber** application's directory.

3. *Compiling the GuessNumber application.* To run an application, you must first compile it by typing

   ```
   clang GuessNumber.c -o GuessNumber
   ```

as in Fig. 1.23. This command compiles the application and produces an executable file called GuessNumber.

```
hostName:GNU~ userFolder$ clang GuessNumber.c -o GuessNumber
hostName:GNU~ userFolder$
```

Fig. 1.23 | Compiling the **GuessNumber** application using the gcc command.

4. *Running the GuessNumber application.* To run the executable file GuessNumber, type ./GuessNumber at the next prompt, then press *Enter* (Fig. 1.24).

```
hostName:GNU~ userFolder$ ./GuessNumber

I have a number between 1 and 1000.
Can you guess my number?
Please type your first guess.
?
```

Fig. 1.24 | Running the **GuessNumber** application.

5. *Entering your first guess.* The application displays "Please type your first guess.", then displays a question mark (?) as a prompt on the next line (Fig. 1.24). At the prompt, enter 500 (Fig. 1.25).

```
hostName:GNU~ userFolder$ ./GuessNumber

I have a number between 1 and 1000.
Can you guess my number?
Please type your first guess.
? 500
Too low. Try again.
?
```

Fig. 1.25 | Entering an initial guess.

6. *Entering another guess.* The application displays "Too low. Try again." (Fig. 1.25), meaning that the value you entered is less than the number the application chose as the correct guess. At the next prompt, enter 750 (Fig. 1.26). Again the application displays "Too low. Try again.", because the value you entered is less than the correct guess.

7. *Entering additional guesses.* Continue to play the game (Fig. 1.27) by entering values until you guess the correct number. When you guess correctly, the application displays "Excellent! You guessed the number!"

```
hostName:GNU~ userFolder$ ./GuessNumber

I have a number between 1 and 1000.
Can you guess my number?
Please type your first guess.
? 500
Too low. Try again.
? 750
Too low. Try again.
?
```

Fig. 1.26 | Entering a second guess and receiving feedback.

```
? 825
Too high. Try again.
? 788
Too low. Try again.
? 806
Too low. Try again.
? 815
Too high. Try again.
? 811
Too high. Try again.
? 808

Excellent! You guessed the number!
Would you like to play again?
Please type ( 1=yes, 2=no )?
```

Fig. 1.27 | Entering additional guesses and guessing the correct number.

8. *Playing the game again or exiting the application.* After you guess the correct number, the application asks if you'd like to play another game. At the prompt, entering 1 causes the application to choose a new number and displays the message "Please type your first guess." followed by a question-mark prompt (Fig. 1.28) so you can make your first guess in the new game. Entering 2 ends the application and returns you to the application's folder in the **Terminal** window (Fig. 1.29). Each time you execute this application from the beginning (i.e., *Step 4*), it will choose the same numbers for you to guess.

```
Excellent! You guessed the number!
Would you like to play again?
Please type ( 1=yes, 2=no )? 1

I have a number between 1 and 1000.
Can you guess my number?
Please type your first guess.
?
```

Fig. 1.28 | Playing the game again.

```
Excellent! You guessed the number!
Would you like to play again?
Please type ( 1=yes, 2=no )? 2

hostName:GNU~ userFolder$
```

Fig. 1.29 | Exiting the game.

1.11 Operating Systems

Operating systems are software systems that make using computers more convenient for users, application developers and system administrators. They provide services that allow each application to execute safely, efficiently and *concurrently* (i.e., in parallel) with other applications. The software that contains the core components of the operating system is the **kernel**. Popular desktop operating systems include Linux, Windows and Mac OS X. Popular mobile operating systems used in smartphones and tablets include Google's Android, Apple's iOS (for its iPhone, iPad and iPod Touch devices), Windows Phone and BlackBerry OS.

1.11.1 Windows—A Proprietary Operating System

In the mid-1980s, Microsoft developed the Windows operating system, consisting of a graphical user interface built on top of DOS—an enormously popular personal-computer operating system that users interacted with by typing commands. Windows borrowed many concepts (such as icons, menus and windows) popularized by early Apple Macintosh operating systems and originally developed by Xerox PARC. Windows 8.1 is Microsoft's latest operating system—its features include PC and tablet support, a tiles-based user interface, security enhancements, touch-screen and multi-touch support, and more. Windows is a *proprietary* operating system—it's controlled by Microsoft exclusively. It's by far the world's most widely used operating system.

1.11.2 Linux—An Open-Source Operating System

The **Linux** operating system—which is popular in servers, personal computers and embedded systems—is perhaps the greatest success of the *open-source* movement. The **open-source software** development style departs from the *proprietary* development style (used, for example, with Microsoft's Windows and Apple's Mac OS X). With open-source development, individuals and companies—often worldwide—contribute their efforts in developing, maintaining and evolving software. Anyone can use and customize it for their own purposes, typically at no charge.

Some organizations in the open-source community are the *Eclipse Foundation* (the Eclipse Integrated Development Environment helps programmers conveniently develop software), the *Mozilla Foundation* (creators of the *Firefox web browser*), the *Apache Software Foundation* (creators of the *Apache web server* that delivers web pages over the Internet in response to web-browser requests) and *GitHub* and *SourceForge* (which provide the tools for managing open-source projects).

Rapid improvements to computing and communications, decreasing costs and open-source software have made it easier and more economical to create software-based businesses now than just a few decades ago. Facebook, which was launched from a college dorm room, was built with open-source software.[5]

A variety of issues—such as Microsoft's market power, the relatively small number of user-friendly Linux applications and the diversity of Linux distributions (Red Hat Linux, Ubuntu Linux and many others)—have prevented widespread Linux use on desktop computers. But Linux has become extremely popular on servers and in embedded systems, such as Google's Android-based smartphones.

1.11.3 Apple's Mac OS X; Apple's iOS for iPhone®, iPad® and iPod Touch® Devices

Apple, founded in 1976 by Steve Jobs and Steve Wozniak, quickly became a leader in personal computing. In 1979, Jobs and several Apple employees visited Xerox PARC (Palo Alto Research Center) to learn about Xerox's desktop computer that featured a graphical user interface (GUI). That GUI served as the inspiration for the Apple Macintosh, launched with much fanfare in a memorable Super Bowl ad in 1984.

The Objective-C programming language, created by Brad Cox and Tom Love at Stepstone in the early 1980s, added capabilities for object-oriented programming (OOP) to the C programming language. Steve Jobs left Apple in 1985 and founded NeXT Inc. In 1988, NeXT licensed Objective-C from StepStone and developed an Objective-C compiler and libraries which were used as the platform for the NeXTSTEP operating system's user interface and Interface Builder—used to construct graphical user interfaces.

Jobs returned to Apple in 1996 when Apple bought NeXT. Apple's Mac OS X operating system is a descendant of NeXTSTEP. Apple's proprietary operating system, **iOS**, is derived from Apple's Mac OS X and is used in the iPhone, iPad and iPod Touch devices.

1.11.4 Google's Android

Android—the fastest growing tablet and smartphone operating system—is based on the Linux kernel and Java as its primary programming language. One benefit of developing Android apps is the openness of the platform. The operating system is open source and free.

The Android operating system was developed by Android, Inc., which was acquired by Google in 2005. In 2007, the Open Handset Alliance™—which has 87 company members worldwide—was formed to develop, maintain and evolve Android, driving innovation in mobile technology and improving the user experience while reducing costs. As of April 2013, more than 1.5 million Android devices (smartphones, tablets, etc.) were being activated worldwide *daily*.[6] Android devices now include smartphones, tablets, e-readers, robots, jet engines, NASA satellites, game consoles, refrigerators, televisions, cameras, health-care devices, smartwatches, automobile in-vehicle infotainment systems (for controlling the radio, GPS, phone calls, thermostat, etc.) and more.[7] Android also executes on desktop and notebook computers.[8]

---

5. https://code.facebook.com/projects/.
6. http://www.technobuffalo.com/2013/04/16/google-daily-android-activations-1-5-million/.
7. http://www.businessweek.com/articles/2013-05-29/behind-the-internet-of-things-is-android-and-its-everywhere.
8. http://www.android-x86.org.

1.12 The Internet and World Wide Web

In the late 1960s, ARPA—the Advanced Research Projects Agency of the United States Department of Defense—rolled out plans for networking the main computer systems of approximately a dozen ARPA-funded universities and research institutions. The computers were to be connected with communications lines operating at speeds on the order of 50,000 bits per second, a stunning rate at a time when most people (of the few who even had networking access) were connecting over telephone lines to computers at a rate of 110 bits per second. Academic research was about to take a giant leap forward. ARPA proceeded to implement what quickly became known as the ARPANET, the precursor to today's **Internet**. Today's fastest Internet speeds are on the order of billions of bits per second with trillion-bits-per-second speeds on the horizon!

Things worked out differently from the original plan. Although the ARPANET enabled researchers to network their computers, its main benefit proved to be the capability for quick and easy communication via what came to be known as electronic mail (e-mail). This is true even on today's Internet, with e-mail, instant messaging, file transfer and social media such as Facebook and Twitter enabling billions of people worldwide to communicate quickly and easily.

The protocol (set of rules) for communicating over the ARPANET became known as the **Transmission Control Protocol** (TCP). TCP ensured that messages, consisting of sequentially numbered pieces called *packets*, were properly routed from sender to receiver, arrived intact and were assembled in the correct order.

1.12.1 The Internet: A Network of Networks

In parallel with the early evolution of the Internet, organizations worldwide were implementing their own networks for both intraorganization (that is, within an organization) and interorganization (that is, between organizations) communication. A huge variety of networking hardware and software appeared. One challenge was to enable these different networks to communicate with each other. ARPA accomplished this by developing the Internet Protocol (IP), which created a true "network of networks," the current architecture of the Internet. The combined set of protocols is now called **TCP/IP**.

Businesses rapidly realized that by using the Internet, they could improve their operations and offer new and better services to their clients. Companies started spending large amounts of money to develop and enhance their Internet presence. This generated fierce competition among communications carriers and hardware and software suppliers to meet the increased infrastructure demand. As a result, **bandwidth**—the information-carrying capacity of communications lines—on the Internet has increased tremendously, while hardware costs have plummeted.

1.12.2 The World Wide Web: Making the Internet User-Friendly

The **World Wide Web** (simply called "the web") is a collection of hardware and software associated with the Internet that allows computer users to locate and view multimedia-based documents (documents with various combinations of text, graphics, animations, audios and videos) on almost any subject. The introduction of the web was a relatively recent event. In 1989, Tim Berners-Lee of CERN (the European Organization for Nuclear Research) began to develop a technology for sharing information via "hyperlinked" text documents. Berners-Lee called his invention the **HyperText Markup Language** (HTML). He also wrote communication protocols such as **HyperText Transfer Protocol** (HTTP) to form the backbone of his new hypertext information system, which he referred to as the World Wide Web.

In 1994, Berners-Lee founded an organization, called the **World Wide Web Consortium** (W3C, http://www.w3.org), devoted to developing web technologies. One of the W3C's primary goals is to make the web universally accessible to everyone regardless of disabilities, language or culture.

1.12.3 Web Services

Web services are software components stored on one computer that can be accessed by an app (or other software component) on another computer over the Internet. With web services, you can create *mashups*, which enable you to rapidly develop apps by combining complementary web services, often from multiple organizations and possibly other forms of information feeds. For example, 100 Destinations (http://www.100destinations.co.uk) combines the photos and tweets from Twitter with the mapping capabilities of Google Maps to allow you to explore countries around the world through the photos of others.

Programmableweb (http://www.programmableweb.com/) provides a directory of over 11,150 APIs and 7,300 mashups, plus how-to guides and sample code for creating your own mashups. Figure 1.30 lists some popular web services. According to Programmableweb, the three most widely used APIs for mashups are Google Maps, Twitter and YouTube.

Web services source	How it's used
Google Maps	Mapping services
Twitter	Microblogging
YouTube	Video search
Facebook	Social networking
Instagram	Photo sharing
Foursquare	Mobile check-in
LinkedIn	Social networking for business
Groupon	Social commerce
Netflix	Movie rentals
eBay	Internet auctions
Wikipedia	Collaborative encyclopedia
PayPal	Payments
Last.fm	Internet radio
Amazon eCommerce	Shopping for books and lots of other products
Salesforce.com	Customer Relationship Management (CRM)
Skype	Internet telephony

Fig. 1.30 | Some popular web services (http://www.programmableweb.com/category/all/apis). (Part 1 of 2.)

Web services source	How it's used
Microsoft Bing	Search
Flickr	Photo sharing
Zillow	Real-estate pricing
Yahoo Search	Search
WeatherBug	Weather

Fig. 1.30 | Some popular web services (`http://www.programmableweb.com/category/all/apis`). (Part 2 of 2.)

Figure 1.31 lists directories where you'll find information about many of the most popular web services. Figure 1.32 lists a few popular web mashups.

Directory	URL
ProgrammableWeb	`www.programmableweb.com`
Google Code API Directory	`code.google.com/apis/qdata/docs/directory.html`

Fig. 1.31 | Web services directories.

URL	Description
`http://twikle.com/`	Twikle uses Twitter web services to aggregate popular news stories being shared online.
`http://trendsmap.com/`	TrendsMap uses Twitter and Google Maps. It allows you to track tweets by location and view them on a map in real time.
`http://www.coindesk.com/price/bitcoin-price-ticker-widget/`	The Bitcoin Price Ticker Widget uses CoinDesk's APIs to display the real-time Bitcoin price, the day's high and low prices and a graph of the price fluctuations over the last sixty minutes.
`http://www.dutranslation.com/`	The Double Translation mashup allows you to use Bing and Google translation services simultaneously to translate text to and from over 50 languages. You can then compare the results between the two.
`http://musicupdated.com/`	Music Updated uses Last.fm and YouTube web services. Use it to track album releases, concert information and more for your favorite artists.

Fig. 1.32 | A few popular web mashups.

1.12.4 Ajax

Ajax technology helps Internet-based applications perform like desktop applications—a difficult task, given that such applications suffer transmission delays as data is shuttled back and forth between your computer and server computers on the Internet. Using Ajax, applications like Google Maps have achieved excellent performance and approach the look-and-feel of desktop applications.

1.12.5 The Internet of Things

The Internet is no longer just a network of computers—it's an **Internet of Things**. A *thing* is any object with an IP address and the ability to send data automatically over the Internet—e.g., a car with a transponder for paying tolls, a heart monitor implanted in a human, a smart meter that reports energy usage, mobile apps that can track your movement and location, and smart thermostats that adjust room temperatures based on weather forecasts and activity in the home.

1.13 Some Key Software Terminology

Figure 1.33 lists a number of buzzwords that you'll hear in the software development community.

Technology	Description
Agile software development	**Agile software development** is a set of methodologies that try to get software implemented faster and using fewer resources. Check out the Agile Alliance (www.agilealliance.org) and the Agile Manifesto (www.agilemanifesto.org).
Refactoring	**Refactoring** involves reworking programs to make them clearer and easier to maintain while preserving their correctness and functionality. It's widely employed with agile development methodologies. Many IDEs contain built-in *refactoring tools* to do major portions of the reworking automatically.
Design patterns	**Design patterns** are proven architectures for constructing flexible and maintainable object-oriented software. The field of design patterns tries to enumerate those recurring patterns, encouraging software designers to *reuse* them to develop better-quality software using less time, money and effort.
LAMP	**LAMP** is an acronym for the open-source technologies that many developers use to build web applications inexpensively—it stands for *Linux, Apache, MySQL* and *PHP* (or *Perl* or *Python*—two other popular scripting languages). MySQL is an open-source database-management system. PHP is the most popular open-source server-side "scripting" language for developing web applications. Apache is the most popular web server software. The equivalent for Windows development is WAMP—*Windows, Apache, MySQL* and *PHP.*

Fig. 1.33 | Software technologies. (Part 1 of 2.)

Technology	Description
Software as a Service (SaaS)	Software has generally been viewed as a product; most software still is offered this way. If you want to run an application, you buy a software package from a software vendor—often a CD, DVD or web download. You then install that software on your computer and run it as needed. As new versions appear, you upgrade your software, often at considerable cost in time and money. This process can become cumbersome for organizations that must maintain tens of thousands of systems on a diverse array of computer equipment. With **Software as a Service (SaaS)**, the software runs on servers elsewhere on the Internet. When that server is updated, all clients worldwide see the new capabilities—no local installation is needed. You access the service through a browser. Browsers are quite portable, so you can run the same applications on a wide variety of computers from anywhere in the world. Salesforce.com, Google, and Microsoft's Office Live and Windows Live all offer SaaS.
Platform as a Service (PaaS)	**Platform as a Service (PaaS)** provides a computing platform for developing and running applications as a service over the web, rather than installing the tools on your computer. Some PaaS providers are Google App Engine, Amazon EC2 and Windows Azure™.
Cloud computing	SaaS and PaaS are examples of **cloud computing**. You can use software and data stored in the "cloud"—i.e., accessed on remote computers (or servers) via the Internet and available on demand—rather than having it stored locally on your desktop, notebook computer or mobile device. This allows you to increase or decrease computing resources to meet your needs at any given time, which is more cost effective than purchasing hardware to provide enough storage and processing power to meet occasional peak demands. Cloud computing also saves money by shifting to the service provider the burden of managing these apps (such as installing and upgrading the software, security, backups and disaster recovery).
Software Development Kit (SDK)	**Software Development Kits (SDKs)** include the tools and documentation developers use to program applications.

Fig. 1.33 | Software technologies. (Part 2 of 2.)

Software is complex. Large, real-world software applications can take many months or even years to design and implement. When large software products are under development, they typically are made available to the user communities as a series of releases, each more complete and polished than the last (Fig. 1.34).

Version	Description
Alpha	*Alpha* software is the earliest release of a software product that's still under active development. Alpha versions are often buggy, incomplete and unstable and are released to a relatively small number of developers for testing new features, getting early feedback, etc.

Fig. 1.34 | Software product-release terminology. (Part 1 of 2.)

Version	Description
Beta	*Beta* versions are released to a larger number of developers later in the development process after most major bugs have been fixed and new features are nearly complete. Beta software is more stable, but still subject to change.
Release candidates	*Release candidates* are generally *feature complete*, (mostly) bug free and ready for use by the community, which provides a diverse testing environment— the software is used on different systems, with varying constraints and for a variety of purposes.
Final release	Any bugs that appear in the release candidate are corrected, and eventually the final product is released to the general public. Software companies often distribute incremental updates over the Internet.
Continuous beta	Software that's developed using this approach (for example, Google search or Gmail) generally does not have version numbers. It's hosted in the *cloud* (not installed on your computer) and is constantly evolving so that users always have the latest version.

Fig. 1.34 | Software product-release terminology. (Part 2 of 2.)

1.14 Keeping Up-to-Date with Information Technologies

Figure 1.35 lists key technical and business publications that will help you stay up-to-date with the latest news and trends and technology. You can also find a growing list of Internet- and web-related Resource Centers at `www.deitel.com/ResourceCenters.html`.

Publication	URL
AllThingsD	`allthingsd.com`
Bloomberg BusinessWeek	`www.businessweek.com`
CNET	`news.cnet.com`
Communications of the ACM	`cacm.acm.org`
Computerworld	`www.computerworld.com`
Engadget	`www.engadget.com`
eWeek	`www.eweek.com`
Fast Company	`www.fastcompany.com`
Fortune	`money.cnn.com/magazines/fortune`
GigaOM	`gigaom.com`
Hacker News	`news.ycombinator.com`
IEEE Computer Magazine	`www.computer.org/portal/web/computingnow/computer`
InfoWorld	`www.infoworld.com`
Mashable	`mashable.com`
PCWorld	`www.pcworld.com`
SD Times	`www.sdtimes.com`

Fig. 1.35 | Technical and business publications. (Part 1 of 2.)

Publication	URL
Slashdot	slashdot.org
Stack Overflow	stackoverflow.com
Technology Review	technologyreview.com
Techcrunch	techcrunch.com
The Next Web	thenextweb.com
The Verge	www.theverge.com
Wired	www.wired.com

Fig. 1.35 | Technical and business publications. (Part 2 of 2.)

Self-Review Exercises

1.1 Fill in the blanks in each of the following statements:

a) Computers process data under the control of sets of instructions called _____.

b) The key logical units of the computer are the _____, _____, _____, _____, _____ and _____.

c) The three types of languages discussed in the chapter are _____, _____ and _____.

d) The programs that translate high-level-language programs into machine language are called _____.

e) _____ is an operating system for mobile devices based on the Linux kernel and Java.

f) _____ software is generally feature complete, (supposedly) bug free and ready for use by the community.

g) The Wii Remote, as well as many smartphones, use a(n) _____ which allows the device to respond to motion.

h) C is widely known as the development language of the _____ operating system.

i) _____ is the new programming language for developing iOS and Mac apps.

1.2 Fill in the blanks in each of the following sentences about the C environment.

a) C programs are normally typed into a computer using a(n) _____ program.

b) In a C system, a(n) _____ program automatically executes before the translation phase begins.

c) The two most common kinds of preprocessor directives are _____ and _____.

d) The _____ program combines the output of the compiler with various library functions to produce an executable image.

e) The _____ program transfers the executable image from disk to memory.

1.3 Fill in the blanks in each of the following statements (based on Section 1.8):

a) Objects have the property of _____—although objects may know how to communicate with one another across well-defined interfaces, they normally are not allowed to know how other objects are implemented.

b) In object-oriented programming languages, we create _____ to house the set of methods that perform tasks.

c) With _____, new classes of objects are derived by absorbing characteristics of existing classes, then adding unique characteristics of their own.

d) The size, shape, color and weight of an object are considered _____ of the object's class.

Answers to Self-Review Exercises

1.1   a) programs. b) input unit, output unit, memory unit, central processing unit, arithmetic and logic unit, secondary storage unit. c) machine languages, assembly languages, high-level languages. d) compilers. e) Android. f) Release candidate. g) acceleromoter. h) UNIX. i) Swift.

1.2   a) editor. b) preprocessor. c) including other files in the file to be compiled, performing various text replacements. d) linker. e) loader.

1.3   a) information hiding. b) classes. c) inheritance. d) attributes.

Exercises

1.4   Categorize each of the following items as either hardware or software:
  a) CPU
  b) C++ compiler
  c) ALU
  d) C++ preprocessor
  e) input unit
  f) an editor program

1.5   Fill in the blanks in each of the following statements:
  a) The logical unit that receives information from outside the computer for use by the computer is the _____.
  b) The process of instructing the computer to solve a problem is called _____.
  c) _____ is a type of computer language that uses Englishlike abbreviations for machine-language instructions.
  d) _____ is a logical unit that sends information which has already been processed by the computer to various devices so that it may be used outside the computer.
  e) _____ and _____ are logical units of the computer that retain information.
  f) _____ is a logical unit of the computer that performs calculations.
  g) _____ is a logical unit of the computer that makes logical decisions.
  h) _____ languages are most convenient to the programmer for writing programs quickly and easily.
  i) The only language a computer can directly understand is that computer's _____.
  j) The _____ is a logical unit of the computer that coordinates the activities of all the other logical units.

1.6   Fill in the blanks in each of the following statements:
  a) _____ is now used to develop large-scale enterprise applications, to enhance the functionality of web servers, to provide applications for consumer devices and for many other purposes.
  b) _____ initially became widely known as the development language of the UNIX operating system.
  c) The _____ programming language was developed by Bjarne Stroustrup in the early 1980s at Bell Laboratories.

1.7   Discuss the meaning of each of the following names:
  a) `stdin`
  b) `stdout`
  c) `stderr`

1.8   Why is so much attention today focused on object-oriented programming?

1.9 *(Internet Negatives)* Besides their numerous benefits, the Internet and the web have several downsides, such as privacy issues, identity theft, spam and malware. Research some of the negative aspects of the Internet. List five problems and describe what could possibly be done to help solve each.

1.10 *(Watch as an Object)* You are probably wearing on your wrist one of the most common types of objects—a watch. Discuss how each of the following terms and concepts applies to the notion of a watch: object, attributes, behaviors, class, inheritance (consider, for example, an alarm clock), messages, encapsulation and information hiding.

Making a Difference

Throughout the book we've included Making a Difference exercises in which you'll be asked to work on problems that really matter to individuals, communities, countries and the world.

1.11 *(Test-Drive: Carbon Footprint Calculator)* Some scientists believe that carbon emissions, especially from the burning of fossil fuels, contribute significantly to global warming and that this can be combatted if individuals take steps to limit their use of carbon-based fuels. Organizations and individuals are increasingly concerned about their "carbon footprints." Websites such as TerraPass

```
http://www.terrapass.com/carbon-footprint-calculator-2/
```

and Carbon Footprint

```
http://www.carbonfootprint.com/calculator.aspx
```

provide carbon-footprint calculators. Test drive these calculators to determine your carbon footprint. Exercises in later chapters will ask you to program your own carbon-footprint calculator. To prepare for this, use the web to research the formulas for calculating carbon footprints.

1.12 *(Test Drive: Body Mass Index Calculator)* Obesity causes significant increases in illnesses such as diabetes and heart disease. To determine whether a person is overweight or obese, you can use a measure called the body mass index (BMI). The United States Department of Health and Human Services provides a BMI calculator at http://www.nhlbi.nih.gov/guidelines/obesity/BMI/bmicalc.htm. Use it to calculate your own BMI. An exercise in Exercise 2.32 will ask you to program your own BMI calculator. To prepare for this, use the web to research the formulas for calculating BMI.

1.13 *(Attributes of Hybrid Vehicles)* In this chapter you learned some basics of classes. Now you'll "flesh out" aspects of a class called "Hybrid Vehicle." Hybrid vehicles are becoming increasingly popular, because they often get much better mileage than purely gasoline-powered vehicles. Browse the web and study the features of four or five of today's popular hybrid cars, then list as many of their hybrid-related attributes as you can. Some common attributes include city-miles-per-gallon and highway-miles-per-gallon. Also list the attributes of the batteries (type, weight, etc.).

1.14 *(Gender Neutrality)* Many people want to eliminate sexism in all forms of communication. You've been asked to create a program that can process a paragraph of text and replace gender-specific words with gender-neutral ones. Assuming that you've been given a list of gender-specific words and their gender-neutral replacements (e.g., replace "wife" with "spouse," "man" with "person," "daughter" with "child" and so on), explain the procedure you'd use to read through a paragraph of text and manually perform these replacements. How might your procedure generate a strange term like "woperchild?" In Chapter 4, you'll learn that a more formal term for "procedure" is "algorithm," and that an algorithm specifies the steps to be performed and the order in which to perform them.

1.15   *(Privacy)* Some online e-mail services save all e-mail correspondence for some period of time. Suppose a disgruntled employee were to post all of the e-mail correspondences for millions of people, including yours, on the Internet. Discuss the issues.

1.16   *(Programmer Responsibility and Liability)* As a programmer in industry, you may develop software that could affect people's health or even their lives. Suppose a software bug in one of your programs causes a cancer patient to receive an excessive dose during radiation therapy and that the person is severely injured or dies. Discuss the issues.

1.17   *(2010 "Flash Crash")* An example of the consequences of our excessive dependence on computers was the so-called "flash crash" which occurred on May 6, 2010, when the U.S. stock market fell precipitously in a matter of minutes, wiping out trillions of dollars of investments, and then recovered within minutes. Research online the causes of this crash and discuss the issues it raises.

Introduction to C Programming

2

Objectives

In this chapter, you'll:

- Write simple C programs.
- Use simple input and output statements.
- Use the fundamental data types.
- Learn computer memory concepts.
- Use arithmetic operators.
- Learn the precedence of arithmetic operators.
- Write simple decision-making statements.
- Begin focusing on secure C programming practices.

2.1 Introduction

The C language facilitates a structured and disciplined approach to computer-program design. In this chapter we introduce C programming and present several examples that illustrate many important features of C. Each example is analyzed one statement at a time. In Chapters 3 and 4 we present an introduction to structured programming in C. We then use the structured approach throughout the remainder of the C portion of the text. We provide the first of many "Secure C Programming" sections.

2.2 A Simple C Program: Printing a Line of Text

C uses some notations that may appear strange to people who have not programmed computers. We begin by considering a simple C program. Our first example prints a line of text. The program and its screen output are shown in Fig. 2.1.

```
1  // Fig. 2.1: fig02_01.c
2  // A first program in C.
3  #include <stdio.h>
4
5  // function main begins program execution
6  int main( void )
7  {
8     printf( "Welcome to C!\n" );
9  } // end function main
```

```
Welcome to C!
```

Fig. 2.1 | A first program in C.

Comments

Even though this program is simple, it illustrates several important features of the C language. Lines 1 and 2

```
// Fig. 2.1: fig02_01.c
// A first program in C
```

begin with //, indicating that these two lines are **comments**. You insert comments to **document programs** and improve program readability. Comments do *not* cause the computer to perform any action when the program is run—they're *ignored* by the C compiler and do *not* cause any machine-language object code to be generated. The preceding comment simply describes the figure number, filename and purpose of the program. Comments also help other people read and understand your program.

You can also use **/*...*/ multi-line comments** in which everything from /* on the first line to */ at the end of the last line is a comment. We prefer // comments because they're shorter and they eliminate common programming errors that occur with /*...*/ comments, especially when the closing */ is omitted.

#include *Preprocessor Directive*
Line 3

```
#include <stdio.h>
```

is a directive to the **C preprocessor**. Lines beginning with # are processed by the preprocessor *before* compilation. Line 3 tells the preprocessor to include the contents of the **standard input/output header** (**<stdio.h>**) in the program. This header contains information used by the compiler when compiling calls to standard input/output library functions such as printf (line 8). We explain the contents of headers in more detail in Chapter 5.

Blank Lines and White Space
Line 4 is simply a blank line. You use blank lines, space characters and tab characters (i.e., "tabs") to make programs easier to read. Together, these characters are known as **white space**. White-space characters are normally ignored by the compiler.

The main *Function*
Line 6

```
int main( void )
```

is a part of every C program. The parentheses after main indicate that main is a program building block called a **function**. C programs contain one or more functions, one of which *must* be main. Every program in C begins executing at the function main. Functions can *return* information. The keyword int to the left of main indicates that main "returns" an integer (whole-number) value. We'll explain what it means for a function to "return a value" when we demonstrate how to create your own functions in Chapter 5. For now, simply include the keyword int to the left of main in each of your programs.

Functions also can *receive* information when they're called upon to execute. The void in parentheses here means that main does *not* receive any information. In Chapter 14, we'll show an example of main receiving information.

Good Programming Practice 2.1

Every function should be preceded by a comment describing the function's purpose.

A left brace, {, begins the **body** of every function (line 7). A corresponding **right brace** ends each function (line 9). This pair of braces and the portion of the program between the braces is called a *block*. The block is an important program unit in C.

An Output Statement
Line 8

```
printf( "Welcome to C!\n" );
```

instructs the computer to perform an **action**, namely to print on the screen the **string** of characters marked by the quotation marks. A string is sometimes called a **character string**, a **message** or a **literal**. The entire line, including the printf function (the "f" stands for "formatted"), its **argument** within the parentheses and the semicolon (;), is called a **statement**. Every statement must end with a semicolon (also known as the **statement terminator**). When the preceding printf statement is executed, it prints the message Welcome to C! on the screen. The characters normally print exactly as they appear between the double quotes in the printf statement.

Escape Sequences

Notice that the characters \n were not printed on the screen. The backslash (\) as used here is called an **escape character**. It indicates that printf is supposed to do something out of the ordinary. When encountering a backslash in a string, the compiler looks ahead at the next character and combines it with the backslash to form an **escape sequence**. The escape sequence \n means **newline**. When a newline appears in the string output by a printf, the newline causes the cursor to position to the beginning of the next line on the screen. Some common escape sequences are listed in Fig. 2.2.

Escape sequence	Description
\n	Newline. Position the cursor at the beginning of the next line.
\t	Horizontal tab. Move the cursor to the next tab stop.
\a	Alert. Produces a sound or visible alert without changing the current cursor position.
\\	Backslash. Insert a backslash character in a string.
\"	Double quote. Insert a double-quote character in a string.

Fig. 2.2 | Some common escape sequences .

Because the backslash has special meaning in a string, i.e., the compiler recognizes it as an escape character, we use a *double* backslash (\\) to place a single backslash in a string. Printing a double quote also presents a problem because double quotes mark the boundaries of a string—such quotes are not printed. By using the escape sequence \" in a string to be output by printf, we indicate that printf should display a double quote. The right brace, }, (line 9) indicates that the end of main has been reached.

Good Programming Practice 2.2
Add a comment to the line containing the right brace, }, that closes every function, including main.

We said that printf causes the computer to perform an **action**. As any program executes, it performs a variety of actions and makes **decisions**. Section 2.6 discusses decision making. Chapter 3 discusses this **action/decision model** of programming in depth.

The Linker and Executables

Standard library functions like printf and scanf are *not* part of the C programming language. For example, the compiler *cannot* find a spelling error in printf or scanf. When the compiler compiles a `printf` statement, it merely provides space in the object program for a "call" to the library function. But the compiler does *not* know where the library functions are—the *linker* does. When the linker runs, it locates the library functions and inserts the proper calls to these library functions in the object program. Now the object program is complete and ready to be executed. For this reason, the linked program is called an **executable**. If the function name is misspelled, the *linker* will spot the error, because it will not be able to match the name in the C program with the name of any known function in the libraries.

Common Programming Error 2.1
Mistyping the name of the output function `printf` as `print` in a program.

Good Programming Practice 2.3
Indent the entire body of each function one level of indentation (we recommend three spaces) within the braces that define the body of the function. This indentation emphasizes the functional structure of programs and helps make them easier to read.

Good Programming Practice 2.4
Set a convention for the indent size you prefer and then uniformly apply that convention. The tab key may be used to create indents, but tab stops can vary. Professional style guides often recommend using spaces rather than tabs.

Using Multiple `printf`s
The `printf` function can print `Welcome to C!` several different ways. For example, the program of Fig. 2.3 produces the same output as the program of Fig. 2.1. This works because each `printf` resumes printing where the previous `printf` stopped printing. The first `printf` (line 8) prints `Welcome` followed by a space (but no newline), and the second `printf` (line 9) begins printing on the *same* line immediately following the space.

```
1   // Fig. 2.3: fig02_03.c
2   // Printing on one line with two printf statements.
3   #include <stdio.h>
4
5   // function main begins program execution
6   int main( void )
7   {
8      printf( "Welcome " );
9      printf( "to C!\n" );
10  } // end function main
```

```
Welcome to C!
```

Fig. 2.3 | Printing one line with two `printf` statements.

One `printf` can print *several* lines by using additional newline characters as in Fig. 2.4. Each time the \n (newline) escape sequence is encountered, output continues at the beginning of the next line.

```
1  // Fig. 2.4: fig02_04.c
2  // Printing multiple lines with a single printf.
3  #include <stdio.h>
4
5  // function main begins program execution
6  int main( void )
7  {
8     printf( "Welcome\nto\nC!\n" );
9  } // end function main
```

```
Welcome
to
C!
```

Fig. 2.4 | Printing multiple lines with a single `printf`.

2.3 Another Simple C Program: Adding Two Integers

Our next program uses the Standard Library function `scanf` to obtain two integers typed by a user at the keyboard, computes the sum of these values and prints the result using `printf`. The program and sample output are shown in Fig. 2.5. [In the input/output dialog of Fig. 2.5, we emphasize the numbers entered by the user in **bold**.]

```
1   // Fig. 2.5: fig02_05.c
2   // Addition program.
3   #include <stdio.h>
4
5   // function main begins program execution
6   int main( void )
7   {
8      int integer1; // first number to be entered by user
9      int integer2; // second number to be entered by user
10
11     printf( "Enter first integer\n" ); // prompt
12     scanf( "%d", &integer1 ); // read an integer
13
14     printf( "Enter second integer\n" ); // prompt
15     scanf( "%d", &integer2 ); // read an integer
16
17     int sum; // variable in which sum will be stored
18     sum = integer1 + integer2; // assign total to sum
19
20     printf( "Sum is %d\n", sum ); // print sum
21  } // end function main
```

```
Enter first integer
45
Enter second integer
72
Sum is 117
```

Fig. 2.5 | Addition program.

The comment in lines 1–2 states the purpose of the program. As we stated earlier, every program begins execution with main. The left brace { (line 7) marks the beginning of the body of main, and the corresponding right brace } (line 21) marks the end of main.

Variables and Variable Definitions
Lines 8–9

```
int integer1; // first number to be entered by user
int integer2; // second number to be entered by user
```

are **definitions**. The names integer1 and integer2 are the names of **variables**—locations in memory where values can be stored for use by a program. These definitions specify that variables integer1 and integer2 are of type **int**, which means that they'll hold *integer* values, i.e., whole numbers such as 7, –11, 0, 31914 and the like.

Define Variables Before They Are Used
All variables must be defined with a name and a data type *before* they can be used in a program. The C standard allows you to place each variable definition *anywhere* in main before that variable's first use in the code (though some older compilers do not allow this). You'll see later why you should define variables *close* to their first use.

Defining Multiple Variables of the Same Type in One Statement
The preceding definitions could be combined into a single definition as follows:

```
int integer1, integer2;
```

but that would have made it difficult to associate comments with each of the variables, as we did in lines 8–9.

Identifiers and Case Sensitivity
A variable name in C can be any valid **identifier**. An identifier is a series of characters consisting of letters, digits and underscores (_) that does *not* begin with a digit. C is **case sensitive**—uppercase and lowercase letters are *different* in C, so a1 and A1 are *different* identifiers.

Common Programming Error 2.2
Using a capital letter where a lowercase letter should be used (for example, typing Main *instead of* main*).*

Error-Prevention Tip 2.1
Avoid starting identifiers with the underscore character (_) to prevent conflicts with compiler-generated identifiers and standard library identifiers.

Good Programming Practice 2.5
Choosing meaningful variable names helps make a program self-documenting—that is, fewer comments are needed.

Good Programming Practice 2.6
The first letter of an identifier used as a simple variable name should be a lowercase letter. Later in the text we'll assign special significance to identifiers that begin with a capital letter and to identifiers that use all capital letters.

Good Programming Practice 2.7

Multiple-word variable names can help make a program more readable. Separate the words with underscores as in total_commissions, *or, if you run the words together, begin each word after the first with a capital letter as in* totalCommissions. *The latter style—often called camel casing because the pattern of uppercase and lowercase letters resembles the silhouette of a camel—is preferred.*

Prompting Messages
Line 11

```
    printf( "Enter first integer\n" ); // prompt
```

displays the literal "Enter first integer" and positions the cursor to the beginning of the next line. This message is called a **prompt** because it tells the user to take a specific action.

The scanf Function and Formatted Inputs
Line 12

```
    scanf( "%d", &integer1 ); // read an integer
```

uses **scanf** (the "f" stands for "formatted") to obtain a value from the user. The function reads from the *standard input*, which is usually the keyboard.

This scanf has two arguments, "%d" and &integer1. The first, the **format control string**, indicates the *type* of data that should be entered by the user. The **%d conversion specifier** indicates that the data should be an integer (the letter d stands for "decimal integer"). The % in this context is treated by scanf (and printf as we'll see) as a special character that begins a conversion specifier.

The second argument of scanf begins with an ampersand (&)—called the **address operator**—followed by the variable name. The &, when combined with the variable name, tells scanf the location (or address) in memory at which the variable integer1 is stored. The computer then stores the value that the user enters for integer1 at that location. The use of ampersand (&) is often confusing to novice programmers or to people who have programmed in other languages that do not require this notation. For now, just remember to precede each variable in every call to scanf with an ampersand. Some exceptions to this rule are discussed in Chapters 6 and 7. The use of the ampersand will become clear after we study *pointers* in Chapter 7.

Good Programming Practice 2.8

Place a space after each comma (,) to make programs more readable.

When the computer executes the preceding scanf, it waits for the user to enter a value for variable integer1. The user responds by typing an integer, then pressing the *Enter* key (sometimes labeled as the *Return* key) to send the number to the computer. The computer then assigns this number, or value, to the variable integer1. Any subsequent references to integer1 in this program will use this same value. Functions printf and scanf facilitate interaction between the user and the computer. This interaction resembles a dialogue and is often called **interactive computing**.

Prompting for and Inputting the Second Integer
Line 14

```
printf( "Enter second integer\n" ); // prompt
```

displays the message Enter second integer on the screen, then positions the cursor to the beginning of the next line. This printf also prompts the user to take action. Line 15

```
scanf( "%d", &integer2 ); // read an integer
```

obtains a value for variable integer2 from the user.

*Defining the **sum** Variable*
Line 17

```
int sum; // variable in which sum will be stored
```

defines the variable sum of type int just before its first use in line 18.

Assignment Statement
The **assignment statement** in line 18

```
sum = integer1 + integer2; // assign total to sum
```

calculates the total of variables integer1 and integer2 and assigns the result to variable sum using the **assignment operator** =. The statement is read as, "sum *gets* the value of the expression integer1 + integer2." Most calculations are performed in assignments. The = operator and the + operator are called *binary* operators because each has *two* **operands**. The + operator's operands are integer1 and integer2. The = operator's two operands are sum and the value of the expression integer1 + integer2.

Good Programming Practice 2.9
Place spaces on either side of a binary operator. This makes the operator stand out and makes the program more readable.

Common Programming Error 2.3
A calculation in an assignment statement must be on the right *side of the = operator. It's a compilation error to place a calculation on the* left *side of an assignment operator.*

Printing with a Format Control String
Line 20

```
printf( "Sum is %d\n", sum ); // print sum
```

calls function printf to print the literal Sum is followed by the numerical value of variable sum on the screen. This printf has two arguments, "Sum is %d\n" and sum. The first is the format control string. It contains some literal characters to be displayed and the conversion specifier %d indicating that an integer will be printed. The second argument specifies the value to be printed. The conversion specifier for an integer is the same in both printf and scanf—this is true for most C data types.

Combining a Variable Definition and Assignment Statement
You can assign a value to a variable in its definition—this is known as **initializing** the variable. For example, lines 17–18 can be combined into the statement

```
    int sum = integer1 + integer2; // assign total to sum
```

which adds `integer1` and `integer2`, then stores the result in the variable `sum`.

Calculations in *printf* Statements

Calculations can also be performed inside `printf` statements. For example, lines 17–20 can be replaced with the statement

```
    printf( "Sum is %d\n", integer1 + integer2 );
```

in which case the variable `sum` is not needed.

Common Programming Error 2.4

Forgetting to precede a variable in a `scanf` statement with an ampersand (&) when that variable should, in fact, be preceded by an ampersand results in an execution-time error. On many systems, this causes a "segmentation fault" or "access violation." Such an error occurs when a user's program attempts to access a part of the computer's memory to which it does not have access privileges. The precise cause of this error will be explained in Chapter 7.

Common Programming Error 2.5

Preceding a variable included in a `printf` statement with an ampersand when, in fact, that variable should not be preceded by an ampersand.

2.4 Memory Concepts

Variable names such as `integer1`, `integer2` and `sum` actually correspond to locations in the computer's memory. Every variable has a name, a type and a value.

In the addition program of Fig. 2.5, when the statement (line 12)

```
    scanf( "%d", &integer1 ); // read an integer
```

is executed, the value entered by the user is placed into a memory location to which the name `integer1` has been assigned. Suppose the user enters the number 45 as the value for `integer1`. The computer will place 45 into location `integer1`, as shown in Fig. 2.6. Whenever a value is placed in a memory location, the value *replaces* the previous value in that location and the previous value is lost; thus, this process is said to be **destructive**.

---

integer1	45

Fig. 2.6 | Memory location showing the name and value of a variable.

Returning to our addition program again, when the statement (line 15)

```
    scanf( "%d", &integer2 ); // read an integer
```

executes, suppose the user enters the value 72. This value is placed into the location `integer2`, and memory appears as in Fig. 2.7. These locations are not necessarily adjacent in memory.

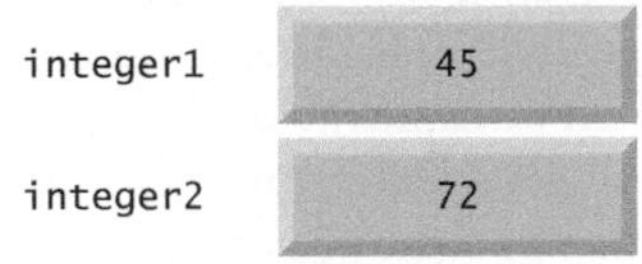

integer1   45

integer2   72

Fig. 2.7 | Memory locations after both variables are input.

Once the program has obtained values for integer1 and integer2, it adds these values and places the total into variable sum. The statement (line 18)

```
sum = integer1 + integer2; // assign total to sum
```

that performs the addition also *replaces* whatever value was stored in sum. This occurs when the calculated total of integer1 and integer2 is placed into location sum (destroying the value already in sum). After sum is calculated, memory appears as in Fig. 2.8. The values of integer1 and integer2 appear exactly as they did *before* they were used in the calculation. They were used, but not destroyed, as the computer performed the calculation. Thus, when a value is *read* from a memory location, the process is said to be **nondestructive**.

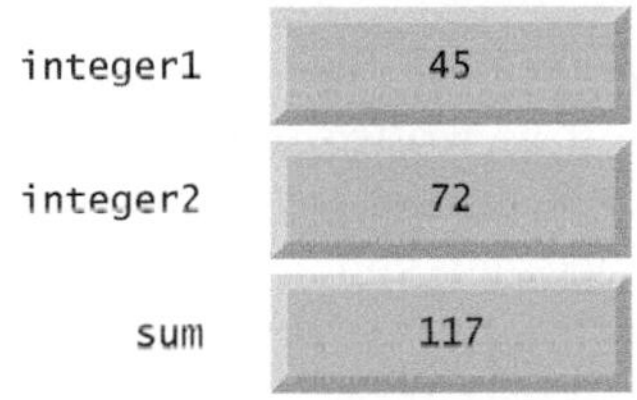

integer1   45

integer2   72

sum   117

Fig. 2.8 | Memory locations after a calculation.

2.5 Arithmetic in C

Most C programs perform calculations using the C **arithmetic operators** (Fig. 2.9).

C operation	Arithmetic operator	Algebraic expression	C expression
Addition	+	$f + 7$	f + 7
Subtraction	–	$p - c$	p - c
Multiplication	*	bm	b * m
Division	/	x / y or $\frac{x}{y}$ or $x \div y$	x / y
Remainder	%	$r \bmod s$	r % s

Fig. 2.9 | Arithmetic operators.

Note the use of various special symbols not used in algebra. The **asterisk** (*) indicates *multiplication* and the **percent sign** (%) denotes the *remainder operator*, which is introduced below. In algebra, to multiply *a* times *b*, we simply place these single-letter variable names side by side, as in *ab*. In C, however, if we were to do this, ab would be interpreted as a single, two-letter name (or identifier). Therefore, C (and many other programming languages) require that multiplication be explicitly denoted by using the * operator, as in a * b. The arithmetic operators are all *binary* operators. For example, the expression 3 + 7 contains the binary operator + and the operands 3 and 7.

Integer Division and the Remainder Operator

Integer division yields an integer result. For example, the expression 7 / 4 evaluates to 1 and the expression 17 / 5 evaluates to 3. C provides the **remainder operator, %,** which yields the *remainder* after integer division. The remainder operator is an integer operator that can be used only with integer operands. The expression x % y yields the remainder after x is divided by y. Thus, 7 % 4 yields 3 and 17 % 5 yields 2. We'll discuss several interesting applications of the remainder operator.

Common Programming Error 2.6

An attempt to divide by zero is normally undefined on computer systems and generally results in a fatal error *that causes the program to terminate immediately without having successfully performed its job.* Nonfatal errors *allow programs to run to completion, often producing incorrect results.*

Arithmetic Expressions in Straight-Line Form

Arithmetic expressions in C must be written in **straight-line form** to facilitate entering programs into the computer. Thus, expressions such as "a divided by b" must be written as a/b so that all operators and operands appear in a straight line. The algebraic notation

$$\frac{a}{b}$$

is generally not acceptable to compilers, although some special-purpose software packages do support more natural notation for complex mathematical expressions.

Parentheses for Grouping Subexpressions

Parentheses are used in C expressions in the same manner as in algebraic expressions. For example, to multiply a times the quantity b + c we write a * (b + c).

Rules of Operator Precedence

C applies the operators in arithmetic expressions in a precise sequence determined by the following **rules of operator precedence**, which are generally the same as those in algebra:

1. Operators in expressions contained within pairs of parentheses are evaluated first. Parentheses are said to be at the "highest level of precedence." In cases of **nested,** or **embedded, parentheses,** such as

   ((a + b) + c)

   the operators in the *innermost* pair of parentheses are applied first.

2. Multiplication, division and remainder operations are applied next. If an expression contains several multiplication, division and remainder operations, evaluation proceeds from left to right. Multiplication, division and remainder are said to be on the same level of precedence.

3. Addition and subtraction operations are evaluated next. If an expression contains several addition and subtraction operations, evaluation proceeds from left to right. Addition and subtraction also have the same level of precedence, which is lower than the precedence of the multiplication, division and remainder operations.

4. The assignment operator (=) is evaluated last.

The rules of operator precedence specify the order C uses to evaluate expressions.[1] When we say evaluation proceeds from left to right, we're referring to the **associativity** of the operators. We'll see that some operators associate from right to left. Figure 2.10 summarizes these rules of operator precedence for the operators we've seen so far.

Operator(s)	Operation(s)	Order of evaluation (precedence)
( )	Parentheses	Evaluated first. If the parentheses are nested, the expression in the *innermost* pair is evaluated first. If there are several pairs of parentheses "on the same level" (i.e., not nested), they're evaluated left to right.
* / %	Multiplication Division Remainder	Evaluated second. If there are several, they're evaluated left to right.
+ -	Addition Subtraction	Evaluated third. If there are several, they're evaluated left to right.
=	Assignment	Evaluated last.

Fig. 2.10 | Precedence of arithmetic operators.

Sample Algebraic and C Expressions

Now let's consider several expressions in light of the rules of operator precedence. Each example lists an algebraic expression and its C equivalent. The following expression calculates the arithmetic mean (average) of five terms.

Algebra: $m = \dfrac{a + b + c + d + e}{5}$

C: $\texttt{m = (a + b + c + d + e) / 5;}$

The parentheses here are *required* to group the additions because division has higher precedence than addition. The *entire* quantity (a + b + c + d + e) should be divided by 5. If the parentheses are erroneously omitted, we obtain a + b + c + d + e / 5, which evaluates incorrectly as

$$a + b + c + d + \frac{e}{5}$$

---

1. We use simple examples to explain the order of evaluation of expressions. Subtle issues occur in more complex expressions that you'll encounter later in the book. We'll discuss these issues as they arise.

The following expression is the equation of a straight line:

Algebra: $y = mx + b$

C: `y = m * x + b;`

No parentheses are required. The multiplication is evaluated first because multiplication has a higher precedence than addition.

The following expression contains remainder (%), multiplication, division, addition, subtraction and assignment operations:

Algebra: $z = pr \bmod q + w/x - y$

C: `z = p * r % q + w / x - y;`
              6   1   2   4   3   5

The circled numbers indicate the order in which C evaluates the operators. The multiplication, remainder and division are evaluated first in left-to-right order (i.e., they associate from left to right) because they have higher precedence than addition and subtraction. The addition and subtraction are evaluated next. They're also evaluated left to right. Finally, the result is assigned to the variable z.

Not all expressions with several pairs of parentheses contain nested parentheses. For example, the following expression does *not* contain nested parentheses—instead, the parentheses are said to be "on the same level."

`a * (b + c) + c * (d + e)`

Evaluation of a Second-Degree Polynomial

To develop a better understanding of the rules of operator precedence, let's see how C evaluates a second-degree polynomial.

`y = a * x * x + b * x + c;`
    6   1   2   4   3   5

The circled numbers under the statement indicate the order in which C performs the operations. There's no arithmetic operator for exponentiation in C, so we've represented x^2 as x * x. The C Standard Library includes the pow ("power") function to perform exponentiation. Because of some subtle issues related to the data types required by pow, we defer a detailed explanation of pow until Chapter 4.

Suppose variables a, b, c and x in the preceding second-degree polynomial are initialized as follows: a = 2, b = 3, c = 7 and x = 5. Figure 2.11 illustrates the order in which the operators are applied.

Using Parentheses for Clarity

As in algebra, it's acceptable to place unnecessary parentheses in an expression to make the expression clearer. These are called **redundant parentheses**. For example, the preceding statement could be parenthesized as follows:

`y = ( a * x * x ) + ( b * x ) + c;`

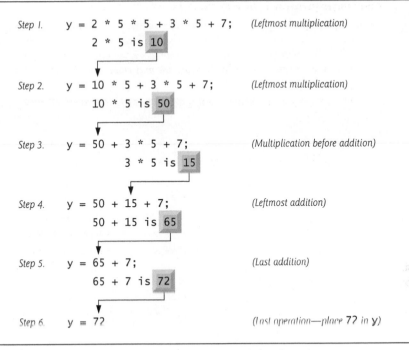

Fig. 2.11 | Order in which a second-degree polynomial is evaluated.

2.6 Decision Making: Equality and Relational Operators

Executable statements either perform actions (such as calculations or input or output of data) or make **decisions** (we'll soon see several examples of these). We might make a decision in a program, for example, to determine whether a person's grade on an exam is greater than or equal to 60 and whether the program should print the message "Congratulations! You passed." This section introduces a simple version of C's **if** statement that allows a program to make a decision based on the truth or falsity of a statement of fact called a **condition**. If the condition is **true** (i.e., the condition is met), the statement in the body of the if statement is executed. If the condition is **false** (i.e., the condition isn't met), the body statement isn't executed. Whether the body statement is executed or not, after the if statement completes, execution proceeds with the next statement in sequence after the if statement.

Conditions in if statements are formed by using the **equality operators** and **relational operators** summarized in Fig. 2.12. The relational operators all have the same level of precedence and they associate left to right. The equality operators have a lower level of precedence than the relational operators and they also associate left to right. [*Note:* In C, a condition may actually be *any expression that generates a zero (false) or nonzero (true) value.*]

Common Programming Error 2.7
A syntax error occurs if the two symbols in any of the operators ==, !=, >= and <= are separated by spaces.

Common Programming Error 2.8

Confusing the equality operator == with the assignment operator. To avoid this confusion, the equality operator should be read "double equals" and the assignment operator should be read "gets" or "is assigned the value of." As you'll see, confusing these operators may not cause an easy-to-recognize compilation error, but may cause extremely subtle logic errors.

Algebraic equality or relational operator	C equality or relational operator	Example of C condition	Meaning of C condition
Relational operators			
>	>	x > y	x is greater than y
<	<	x < y	x is less than y
≥	>=	x >= y	x is greater than or equal to y
≤	<=	x <= y	x is less than or equal to y
Equality operators			
=	==	x == y	x is equal to y
≠	!=	x != y	x is not equal to y

Fig. 2.12 | Equality and relational operators.

Figure 2.13 uses six if statements to compare two numbers entered by the user. If the condition in any of these if statements is true, the printf statement associated with that if executes. The program and three sample execution outputs are shown in the figure.

```
1   // Fig. 2.13: fig02_13.c
2   // Using if statements, relational
3   // operators, and equality operators.
4   #include <stdio.h>
5
6   // function main begins program execution
7   int main( void )
8   {
9      printf( "Enter two integers, and I will tell you\n" );
10     printf( "the relationships they satisfy: " );
11
12     int num1; // first number to be read from user
13     int num2; // second number to be read from user
14
15     scanf( "%d %d", &num1, &num2 ); // read two integers
16
17     if ( num1 == num2 ) {
18        printf( "%d is equal to %d\n", num1, num2 );
19     } // end if
20
```

Fig. 2.13 | Using if statements, relational operators, and equality operators. (Part 1 of 2.)

```
21      if ( num1 != num2 ) {
22         printf( "%d is not equal to %d\n", num1, num2 );
23      } // end if
24
25      if ( num1 < num2 ) {
26         printf( "%d is less than %d\n", num1, num2 );
27      } // end if
28
29      if ( num1 > num2 ) {
30         printf( "%d is greater than %d\n", num1, num2 );
31      } // end if
32
33      if ( num1 <= num2 ) {
34         printf( "%d is less than or equal to %d\n", num1, num2 );
35      } // end if
36
37      if ( num1 >= num2 ) {
38         printf( "%d is greater than or equal to %d\n", num1, num2 );
39      } // end if
40   } // end function main
```

```
Enter two integers, and I will tell you
the relationships they satisfy: 3 7
3 is not equal to 7
3 is less than 7
3 is less than or equal to 7
```

```
Enter two integers, and I will tell you
the relationships they satisfy: 22 12
22 is not equal to 12
22 is greater than 12
22 is greater than or equal to 12
```

```
Enter two integers, and I will tell you
the relationships they satisfy: 7 7
7 is equal to 7
7 is less than or equal to 7
7 is greater than or equal to 7
```

Fig. 2.13 | Using if statements, relational operators, and equality operators. (Part 2 of 2.)

The program uses scanf (line 15) to read two integers into the int variables num1 and num2. Each conversion specifier has a corresponding argument in which a value will be stored. The first %d converts a value to be stored in the variable num1, and the second %d converts a value to be stored in the variable num2.

Good Programming Practice 2.10

Although it's allowed, there should be no more than one statement per line in a program.

Common Programming Error 2.9

Placing commas (when none are needed) between conversion specifiers in the format control string of a scanf statement.

Comparing Numbers

The if statement in lines 17–19

```
if ( num1 == num2 ) {
   printf( "%d is equal to %d\n", num1, num2 );
} // end if
```

compares the values of variables num1 and num2 to test for equality. If the values are equal, the statement in line 18 displays a line of text indicating that the numbers are equal. If the conditions are true in one or more of the if statements starting in lines 21, 25, 29, 33 and 37, the corresponding body statement displays an appropriate line of text. Indenting the body of each if statement and placing blank lines above and below each if statement enhances program readability.

Common Programming Error 2.10

Placing a semicolon immediately to the right of the right parenthesis after the condition in an if statement.

A left brace, {, begins the body of each if statement (e.g., line 17). A corresponding right brace, }, ends each if statement's body (e.g., line 19). Any number of statements can be placed in the body of an if statement.[2]

Good Programming Practice 2.11

A lengthy statement may be spread over several lines. If a statement must be split across lines, choose breaking points that make sense (such as after a comma in a comma-separated list). If a statement is split across two or more lines, indent all subsequent lines. It's not correct to split identifiers.

Figure 2.14 lists from highest to lowest the precedence of the operators introduced in this chapter. Operators are shown top to bottom in decreasing order of precedence. The equals sign is also an operator. All these operators, with the exception of the assignment operator =, associate from left to right. The assignment operator (=) associates from right to left.

Good Programming Practice 2.12

Refer to the operator precedence chart when writing expressions containing many operators. Confirm that the operators in the expression are applied in the proper order. If you're uncertain about the order of evaluation in a complex expression, use parentheses to group expressions or break the statement into several simpler statements. Be sure to observe that some of C's operators such as the assignment operator (=) associate from right to left rather than from left to right.

---

2.   Using braces to delimit the body of an if statement is optional when the body contains only one statement. It's considered good practice to always use these braces. In Chapter 3, we'll explain the issues.

Operators				Associativity
( )				left to right
*	/	%		left to right
+	-			left to right
<	<=	>	>=	left to right
==	!=			left to right
=				right to left

Fig. 2.14 | Precedence and associativity of the operators discussed so far.

Some of the words we've used in the C programs in this chapter—in particular int, if and void—are **keywords** or reserved words of the language. Figure 2.15 contains the C keywords. These words have special meaning to the C compiler, so you must be careful not to use these as identifiers such as variable names.

In this chapter, we've introduced many important features of the C programming language, including displaying data on the screen, inputting data from the user, performing calculations and making decisions. In the next chapter, we build upon these techniques as we introduce structured programming. You'll become more familiar with indentation techniques. We'll study how to specify the *order in which statements are executed*—this is called **flow of control**.

Keywords				
auto	do	goto	signed	unsigned
break	double	if	sizeof	void
case	else	int	static	volatile
char	enum	long	struct	while
const	extern	register	switch	
continue	float	return	typedef	
default	for	short	union	
Keywords added in C99 standard				
_Bool _Complex _Imaginary inline restrict				
Keywords added in C11 standard				
_Alignas _Alignof _Atomic _Generic _Noreturn _Static_assert _Thread_local				

Fig. 2.15 | C's keywords.

2.7 Secure C Programming

We mentioned *The CERT C Secure Coding Standard* in the Preface and indicated that we would follow certain guidelines that will help you avoid programming practices that open systems to attacks.

Avoid Single-Argument printfs[3]

One such guideline is to *avoid using printf with a single string argument*. If you need to display a string that *terminates with a newline*, use the **puts function**, which displays its string argument followed by a newline character. For example, in Fig. 2.1, line 8

```
printf( "Welcome to C!\n" );
```

should be written as:

```
puts( "Welcome to C!" );
```

We did not include \n in the preceding string because puts adds it automatically.

If you need to display a string *without* a terminating newline character, use printf with *two* arguments—a "%s" format control string and the string to display. The **%s conversion specifier** is for displaying a string. For example, in Fig. 2.3, line 8

```
printf( "Welcome " );
```

should be written as:

```
printf( "%s", "Welcome " );
```

Although the printfs in this chapter as written are actually *not* insecure, these changes are responsible coding practices that will eliminate certain security vulnerabilities as we get deeper into C—we'll explain the rationale later in the book. From this point forward, we use these practices in the chapter examples and you should use them in your exercise solutions.

scanf *and* printf, scanf_s *and* printf_s

We introduced scanf and printf in this chapter. We'll be saying more about these in subsequent Secure C Coding Guidelines sections, beginning in Section 3.13. We'll also discuss scanf_s and printf_s, which were introduced in C11.

---

3. For more information, see CERT C Secure Coding rule FIO30-C (www.securecoding.cert.org/confluence/display/seccode/FIO30-C.+Exclude+user+input+from+format+strings). In Chapter 6's Secure C Programming section, we'll explain the notion of user input as referred to by this CERT guideline.

Summary

Section 2.1 Introduction
- The C language facilitates a structured and disciplined approach to computer-program design.

Section 2.2 A Simple C Program: Printing a Line of Text
- **Comments** (p. 40) begin with **//**. Comments **document programs** (p. 40) and improve program readability. C also supports **multi-line comments** that begin with **/*** and end with ***/** (p. 41).
- Comments do not cause the computer to perform any action when the program is run. They're ignored by the C compiler and do not cause any machine-language object code to be generated.
- Lines beginning with **#** are processed by the **preprocessor** before the program is compiled. The **#include directive** tells the preprocessor (p. 41) to include the contents of another file.

- The **<stdio.h> header** (p. 41) contains information used by the compiler when compiling calls to standard input/output library functions such as printf.

- The function **main** is a part of every C program. The parentheses after main indicate that main is a program building block called a **function** (p. 41). C programs contain one or more functions, one of which must be main. Every program in C begins executing at the function main.

- Functions can return information. The keyword **int** to the left of main indicates that main "returns" an integer (whole-number) value.

- Functions can receive information when they're called upon to execute. The **void** in parentheses after main indicates that main does not receive any information.

- A **left brace**, {, begins the **body** of every function (p. 41). A corresponding **right brace**, }, ends each function (p. 41). This pair of braces and the portion of the program between the braces is called a **block**.

- The **printf function** (p. 42) instructs the computer to display information on the screen.

- A **string** is sometimes called a **character string**, a **message** or a **literal** (p. 42).

- Every **statement** (p. 42) must end with a **semicolon** (also known as the **statement terminator**; p. 42).

- In \n (p. 42), the backslash (\) is called an **escape character** (p. 42). When encountering a backslash in a string, the compiler looks ahead at the next character and combines it with the backslash to form an **escape sequence** (p. 42). The escape sequence \n means newline.

- When a newline appears in the string output by a printf, the newline causes the cursor to position to the beginning of the next line on the screen.

- The **double backslash (\\) escape sequence** can be used to place a single backslash in a string.

- The escape sequence \" represents a literal double-quote character.

Section 2.3 Another Simple C Program: Adding Two Integers

- A **variable** (p. 45) is a location in memory where a value can be stored for use by a program.

- Variables of type **int** (p. 45) hold **integer values**, i.e., **whole numbers** such as 7, −11, 0, 31914.

- All variables must be defined with a name and a **data type** before they can be used in a program.

- A variable name in C is any valid **identifier**. An identifier (p. 45) is a series of characters consisting of letters, digits and underscores (_) that does not begin with a digit.

- C is **case sensitive** (p. 45)—uppercase and lowercase letters are different in C.

- Standard Library **function scanf** (p. 46) can be used to obtain input from the standard input, which is usually the keyboard.

- The **scanf format control string** (p. 46) indicates the type(s) of data that should be input.

- The **%d conversion specifier** (p. 46) indicates that the data should be an integer (the letter d stands for "decimal integer"). The % in this context is treated by scanf (and printf) as a special character that begins a conversion specifier.

- The arguments that follow scanf's format control string begin with an **ampersand (&)**—called the **address operator** (p. 46)—followed by a variable name. The ampersand, when combined with a variable name, tells scanf the location in memory at which the variable is located. The computer then stores the value for the variable at that location.

- Most calculations are performed in **assignment statements** (p. 47).

- The = operator and the + operator are **binary operators**—each has two operands (p. 47).

- In a printf that specifies a format control string as its first argument the conversion specifiers indicate placeholders for data to output.

Section 2.4 Memory Concepts

- Variable names correspond to locations in the computer's memory. Every **variable** has a **name**, a **type** and a **value**.

- Whenever a value is placed in a memory location, the value replaces the previous value in that location; thus, placing a new value into a memory location is said to be **destructive** (p. 48).

- When a value is read from a memory location, the process is said to be **nondestructive** (p. 49).

Section 2.5 Arithmetic in C

- In algebra, if we want to multiply *a* times *b*, we can simply place these single-letter variable names side by side, as in *ab*. In C, however, if we were to do this, ab would be interpreted as a single, two-letter name (or identifier). Therefore, C (like other programming languages, in general) requires that multiplication be explicitly denoted by using the * operator, as in a * b.

- **Arithmetic expressions** (p. 49) in C must be written in **straight-line form** (p. 50) to facilitate entering programs into the computer. Thus, expressions such as "a divided by b" must be written as a/b, so that all operators and operands appear in a straight line.

- **Parentheses** are used to group terms in C expressions in much the same manner as in algebraic expressions.

- C evaluates arithmetic expressions in a precise sequence determined by the following **rules of operator precedence** (p. 50), which are generally the same as those followed in algebra.

- **Multiplication**, **division** and **remainder** operations are applied first. If an expression contains several multiplication, division and remainder operations, evaluation proceeds from left to right. Multiplication, division and remainder are said to be on the same level of precedence.

- **Addition** and **subtraction** operations are evaluated next. If an expression contains several addition and subtraction operations, evaluation proceeds from left to right. Addition and subtraction also have the same level of precedence, which is lower than the precedence of the multiplication, division and remainder operators.

- The rules of operator precedence specify the order C uses to evaluate expressions. The **associativity** (p. 51) of the operators specifies whether they evaluate from left to right or from right to left.

Section 2.6 Decision Making: Equality and Relational Operators

- Executable C statements either perform **actions** or make **decisions**.

- C's **if statement** (p. 53) allows a program to make a decision based on the truth or falsity of a statement of fact called a condition (p. 53). If the condition is met (i.e., the condition is **true**; p. 53) the statement in the body of the if statement executes. If the condition isn't met (i.e., the condition is **false**; p. 53) the body statement does not execute. Whether the body statement is executed or not, after the if statement completes, execution proceeds with the next statement after the if statement.

- Conditions in if statements are formed by using the **equality** and **relational operators** (p. 53).

- The relational operators all have the same level of precedence and associate left to right. The equality operators have a lower level of precedence than the relational operators and they also associate left to right.

- To avoid confusing assignment (=) and equality (==), the assignment operator should be read "gets" and the equality operator should be read "double equals."

- In C programs, **white-space characters** such as tabs, newlines and spaces are normally **ignored**. So, statements may be split over several lines. It's not correct to split identifiers.

- **Keywords** (p. 57; or reserved words) have special meaning to the C compiler, so you cannot use them as identifiers such as variable names.

Section 2.7 Secure C Programming

- One practice to help avoid leaving systems open to attacks is to avoid using printf with a single string argument.
- To display a string followed by a newline character, use the **puts function** (p. 58), which displays its string argument followed by a newline character.
- To display a string without a trailing newline character, you can use printf with the "%s" conversion specifier (p. 58) as the first argument and the string to display as the second argument.

Self-Review Exercises

2.1 Fill in the blanks in each of the following.

a) Every C program begins execution at the function _____.

b) Every function's body begins with _____ and ends with _____.

c) Every statement ends with a(n) _____.

d) The _____ standard library function displays information on the screen.

e) The escape sequence \n represents the _____ character, which causes the cursor to position to the beginning of the next line on the screen.

f) The _____ Standard Library function is used to obtain data from the keyboard.

g) The conversion specifier _____ is used in a scanf format control string to indicate that an integer will be input and in a printf format control string to indicate that an integer will be output.

h) Whenever a new value is placed in a memory location, that value overrides the previous value in that location. This process is said to be _____.

i) When a value is read from a memory location, the value in that location is preserved; this process is said to be _____.

j) The _____ statement is used to make decisions.

2.2 State whether each of the following is *true* or *false*. If *false*, explain why.

a) Function printf always begins printing at the beginning of a new line.

b) Comments cause the computer to display the text after // on the screen when the program is executed.

c) The escape sequence \n when used in a printf format control string causes the cursor to position to the beginning of the next line on the screen.

d) All variables must be defined before they're used.

e) All variables must be given a type when they're defined.

f) C considers the variables number and NuMbEr to be identical.

g) Definitions can appear anywhere in the body of a function.

h) All arguments following the format control string in a printf function must be preceded by an ampersand (&).

i) The remainder operator (%) can be used only with integer operands.

j) The arithmetic operators *, /, %, + and - all have the same level of precedence.

k) A program that prints three lines of output must contain three printf statements.

2.3 Write a single C statement to accomplish each of the following:

a) Define the variables c, thisVariable, q76354 and number to be of type int.

b) Prompt the user to enter an integer. End your prompting message with a colon (:) followed by a space and leave the cursor positioned after the space.

c) Read an integer from the keyboard and store the value entered in integer variable a.

d) If number is not equal to 7, print "The variable number is not equal to 7."

e) Print the message "This is a C program." on one line.

f) Print the message "This is a C program." on two lines so that the first line ends with C.

g) Print the message "This is a C program." with each word on a separate line.

h) Print the message "This is a C program." with the words separated by tabs.

2.4 Write a statement (or comment) to accomplish each of the following:

a) State that a program will calculate the product of three integers.

b) Prompt the user to enter three integers.

c) Define the variables x, y and z to be of type int.

d) Read three integers from the keyboard and store them in the variables x, y and z.

e) Define the variable result, compute the product of the integers in the variables x, y and z, and use that product to initialize the variable result.

f) Print "The product is" followed by the value of the integer variable result.

2.5 Using the statements you wrote in Exercise 2.4, write a complete program that calculates the product of three integers.

2.6 Identify and correct the errors in each of the following statements:

a) `printf( "The value is %d\n", &number );`

b) `scanf( "%d%d", &number1, number2 );`

c)
```
if ( c < 7 );{
    printf( "C is less than 7\n" );
}
```

d)
```
if ( c => 7 ) {
    printf( "C is greater than or equal to 7\n" );
}
```

Answers to Self-Review Exercises

2.1 a) `main`. b) left brace ({), right brace (}). c) semicolon. d) `printf`. e) newline. f) `scanf`. g) %d. h) destructive. i) nondestructive. j) `if`.

2.2

a) False. Function `printf` always begins printing where the cursor is positioned, and this may be anywhere on a line of the screen.

b) False. Comments do not cause any action to be performed when the program is executed. They're used to document programs and improve their readability.

c) True.

d) True.

e) True.

f) False. C is case sensitive, so these variables are unique.

g) True.

h) False. Arguments in a `printf` function ordinarily should not be preceded by an ampersand. Arguments following the format control string in a `scanf` function ordinarily should be preceded by an ampersand. We'll discuss exceptions to these rules in Chapter 6 and Chapter 7.

i) True.

j) False. The operators *, / and % are on the same level of precedence, and the operators + and - are on a lower level of precedence.

k) False. A `printf` statement with multiple \n escape sequences can print several lines.

2.3

a) `int c, thisVariable, q76354, number;`

b) `printf( "Enter an integer: " );`

c) `scanf( "%d", &a );`

d)
```
if ( number != 7 ) {
    printf( "The variable number is not equal to 7.\n" );
}
```

　　　e) `printf( "This is a C program.\n" );`
　　　f) `printf( "This is a C\nprogram.\n" );`
　　　g) `printf( "This\nis\na\nC\nprogram.\n" );`
　　　h) `printf( "This\tis\ta\tC\tprogram.\n" );`

2.4　　a) `// Calculate the product of three integers`
　　　b) `printf( "Enter three integers: " );`
　　　c) `int x, y, z;`
　　　d) `scanf( "%d%d%d", &x, &y, &z );`
　　　e) `int result = x * y * z;`
　　　f) `printf( "The product is %d\n", result );`

2.5　　See below.

```
 1   // Calculate the product of three integers
 2   #include <stdio.h>
 3
 4   int main( void )
 5   {
 6      printf( "Enter three integers: " ); // prompt
 7
 8      int x, y, z; // declare variables
 9      scanf( "%d%d%d", &x, &y, &z ); // read three integers
10
11      int result = x * y * z; // multiply values
12      printf( "The product is %d\n", result ); // display result
13   } // end function main
```

2.6　　a) Error: &number.
　　　　　Correction: Eliminate the &. We discuss exceptions to this later.
　　　b) Error: number2 does not have an ampersand.
　　　　　Correction: number2 should be &number2. Later in the text we discuss exceptions to this.
　　　c) Error: Semicolon after the right parenthesis of the condition in the if statement.
　　　　　Correction: Remove the semicolon after the right parenthesis. [*Note:* The result of this error is that the printf statement will be executed whether or not the condition in the if statement is true. The semicolon after the right parenthesis is considered an empty statement—a statement that does nothing.]
　　　d) Error: => is not an operator in C.
　　　　　Correction: The relational operator => should be changed to >= (greater than or equal to).

Exercises

2.7　　Identify and correct the errors in each of the following statements. (*Note:* There may be more than one error per statement.)
　　　a) `scanf( "d", value );`
　　　b) `printf( "The product of %d and %d is %d"\n, x, y );`
　　　c) `firstNumber + secondNumber = sumOfNumbers`
　　　d) `if ( number => largest )`
　　　　　　`largest == number;`
　　　e) `*/ Program to determine the largest of three integers /*`
　　　f) `Scanf( "%d", anInteger );`
　　　g) `printf( "Remainder of %d divided by %d is\n", x, y, x % y );`
　　　h) `if ( x = y );`
　　　　　　`printf( %d is equal to %d\n", x, y );`

```
i)  print( "The sum is %d\n," x + y );
j)  Printf( "The value you entered is: %d\n, &value );
```

2.8   Fill in the blanks in each of the following:
a) _____ are used to document a program and improve its readability.
b) The function used to display information on the screen is _____.
c) A C statement that makes a decision is _____.
d) Calculations are normally performed by _____ statements.
e) The _____ function inputs values from the keyboard.

2.9   Write a single C statement or line that accomplishes each of the following:
a) Print the message "Enter two numbers."
b) Assign the product of variables b and c to variable a.
c) State that a program performs a sample payroll calculation (i.e., use text that helps to document a program).
d) Input three integer values from the keyboard and place them in int variables a, b and c.

2.10   State which of the following are *true* and which are *false*. If *false*, explain your answer.
a) C operators are evaluated from left to right.
b) The following are all valid variable names: _under_bar_, m928134, t5, j7, her_sales, his_account_total, a, b, c, z, z2.
c) The statement printf("a = 5;"); is a typical example of an assignment statement.
d) A valid arithmetic expression containing no parentheses is evaluated from left to right.
e) The following are all invalid variable names: 3g, 87, 67h2, h22, 2h.

2.11   Fill in the blanks in each of the following:
a) What arithmetic operations are on the same level of precedence as multiplication? _____.
b) When parentheses are nested, which set of parentheses is evaluated first in an arithmetic expression? _____.
c) A location in the computer's memory that may contain different values at various times throughout the execution of a program is called a _____.

2.12   What, if anything, prints when each of the following statements is performed? If nothing prints, then answer "Nothing." Assume x = 2 and y = 3.

```
a)  printf( "%d", x );
b)  printf( "%d", x + x );
c)  printf( "x=" );
d)  printf( "x=%d", x );
e)  printf( "%d = %d", x + y, y + x );
f)  z = x + y;
g)  scanf( "%d%d", &x, &y );
h)  // printf( "x + y = %d", x + y );
i)  printf( "\n" );
```

2.13   Which, if any, of the following C statements contain variables whose values are replaced?

```
a)  scanf( "%d%d%d%d%d", &b, &c, &d, &e, &f );
b)  p = i + j + k + 7;
c)  printf( "Values are replaced" );
d)  printf( "a = 5" );
```

2.14   Given the equation $y = ax^3 + 7$, which of the following, if any, are correct C statements for this equation?

```
a)  y = a * x * x * x + 7;
b)  y = a * x * x * ( x + 7 );
c)  y = ( a * x ) * x * ( x + 7 );
```

d) `y = ( a * x ) * x * x + 7;`
e) `y = a * ( x * x * x ) + 7;`
f) `y = a * x * ( x * x + 7 );`

2.15 State the order of evaluation of the operators in each of the following C statements and show the value of x after each statement is performed.

a) `x = 7 + 3 * 6 / 2 - 1;`
b) `x = 2 % 2 + 2 * 2 - 2 / 2;`
c) `x = ( 3 * 9 * ( 3 + ( 9 * 3 / ( 3 ) ) ) );`

2.16 *(Arithmetic)* Write a program that asks the user to enter two numbers, obtains them from the user and prints their sum, product, difference, quotient and remainder.

2.17 *(Printing Values with printf)* Write a program that prints the numbers 1 to 4 on the same line. Write the program using the following methods.

a) Using one `printf` statement with no conversion specifiers.
b) Using one `printf` statement with four conversion specifiers.
c) Using four `printf` statements.

2.18 *(Comparing Integers)* Write a program that asks the user to enter two integers, obtains the numbers from the user, then prints the larger number followed by the words "is larger." If the numbers are equal, print the message "These numbers are equal." Use only the single-selection form of the `if` statement you learned in this chapter.

2.19 *(Arithmetic, Largest Value and Smallest Value)* Write a program that inputs three different integers from the keyboard, then prints the sum, the average, the product, the smallest and the largest of these numbers. Use only the single-selection form of the `if` statement you learned in this chapter. The screen dialogue should appear as follows:

```
Enter three different integers: 13 27 14
Sum is 54
Average is 18
Product is 4914
Smallest is 13
Largest is 27
```

2.20 *(Diameter, Circumference and Area of a Circle)* Write a program that reads in the radius of a circle and prints the circle's diameter, circumference and area. Use the constant value 3.14159 for π. Perform each of these calculations inside the `printf` statement(s) and use the conversion specifier `%f`. [*Note:* In this chapter, we've discussed only integer constants and variables. In Chapter 3 we'll discuss floating-point numbers, i.e., values that can have decimal points.]

2.21 *(Shapes with Asterisks)* Write a program that prints the following shapes with asterisks.

```
*********        ***           *            *
*       *       *   *         ***          *   *
*       *      *     *       *****        *     *
*       *      *     *         *         *       *
*       *      *     *         *         *       *
*       *      *     *         *         *       *
*       *      *     *         *         *       *
*       *       *   *          *          *     *
*********        ***           *            *   *
                                              *
```

2.22 What does the following code print?

```
printf( "*\n**\n***\n****\n*****\n" );
```

2.23   *(Largest and Smallest Integers)* Write a program that reads in three integers and then determines and prints the largest and the smallest integers in the group. Use only the programming techniques you have learned in this chapter.

2.24   *(Odd or Even)* Write a program that reads an integer and determines and prints whether it's odd or even. [*Hint:* Use the remainder operator. An even number is a multiple of two. Any multiple of two leaves a remainder of zero when divided by 2.]

2.25   Print your initials in block letters down the page. Construct each block letter out of the letter it represents, as shown on the top of the next page:

```
PPPPPPPPP
    P    P
    P    P
    P    P
     P  P

  JJ
  J
J
  J
   JJJJJJJ

DDDDDDDDD
D        D
D        D
 D      D
  DDDDD
```

2.26   *(Multiples)* Write a program that reads in two integers and determines and prints whether the first is a multiple of the second. [*Hint:* Use the remainder operator.]

2.27   *(Checkerboard Pattern of Asterisks)* Display the following checkerboard pattern with eight `printf` statements and then display the same pattern with as few `printf` statements as possible.

```
* * * * * * * *
 * * * * * * * *
* * * * * * * *
 * * * * * * * *
* * * * * * * *
 * * * * * * * *
* * * * * * * *
 * * * * * * * *
```

2.28   Distinguish between the terms fatal error and nonfatal error. Why might you prefer to experience a fatal error rather than a nonfatal error?

2.29   *(Integer Value of a Character)* Here's a peek ahead. In this chapter you learned about integers and the type `int`. C can also represent uppercase letters, lowercase letters and a considerable variety of special symbols. C uses small integers internally to represent each different character. The set of characters a computer uses together with the corresponding integer representations for those characters is called that computer's character set. You can print the integer equivalent of uppercase A, for example, by executing the statement

```
printf( "%d", 'A' );
```

Write a C program that prints the integer equivalents of some uppercase letters, lowercase letters, digits and special symbols. As a minimum, determine the integer equivalents of the following: A B C a b c 0 1 2 $ * + / and the blank character.

2.30 *(Separating Digits in an Integer)* Write a program that inputs one five-digit number, separates the number into its individual digits and prints the digits separated from one another by three spaces each. [*Hint:* Use combinations of integer division and the remainder operation.] For example, if the user types in 42139, the program should print

```
4   2   1   3   9
```

2.31 *(Table of Squares and Cubes)* Using only the techniques you learned in this chapter, write a program that calculates the squares and cubes of the numbers from 0 to 10 and uses tabs to print the following table of values:

```
number  square  cube
0       0       0
1       1       1
2       4       8
3       9       27
4       16      64
5       25      125
6       36      216
7       49      343
8       64      512
9       81      729
10      100     1000
```

Making a Difference

2.32 *(Body Mass Index Calculator)* We introduced the body mass index (BMI) calculator in Exercise 1.12. The formulas for calculating BMI are

$$BMI = \frac{weightInPounds \times 703}{heightInInches \times heightInInches}$$

or

$$BMI = \frac{weightInKilograms}{heightInMeters \times heightInMeters}$$

Create a BMI calculator application that reads the user's weight in pounds and height in inches (or, if you prefer, the user's weight in kilograms and height in meters), then calculates and displays the user's body mass index. Also, the application should display the following information from the Department of Health and Human Services/National Institutes of Health so the user can evaluate his/her BMI:

```
BMI VALUES
Underweight:  less than 18.5
Normal:       between 18.5 and 24.9
Overweight:   between 25 and 29.9
Obese:        30 or greater
```

[*Note:* In this chapter, you learned to use the int type to represent whole numbers. The BMI calculations when done with int values will both produce whole-number results. In Chapter 4 you'll learn to use the double type to represent numbers with decimal points. When the BMI calculations are performed with doubles, they'll both produce numbers with decimal points—these are called "floating-point" numbers.]

2.33   *(Car-Pool Savings Calculator)* Research several car-pooling websites. Create an application that calculates your daily driving cost, so that you can estimate how much money could be saved by car pooling, which also has other advantages such as reducing carbon emissions and reducing traffic congestion. The application should input the following information and display the user's cost per day of driving to work:

a) Total miles driven per day.
b) Cost per gallon of gasoline.
c) Average miles per gallon.
d) Parking fees per day.
e) Tolls per day.

Structured Program Development in C

Objectives

In this chapter, you'll:

- Use basic problem-solving techniques.

- Develop algorithms through the process of top-down, stepwise refinement.

- Use the if selection statement and the if...else selection statement to select actions.

- Use the while iteration statement to execute statements in a program repeatedly.

- Use counter-controlled iteration and sentinel-controlled iteration.

- Learn structured programming.

- Use increment, decrement and assignment operators.

3.1 Introduction

Before writing a program to solve a particular problem, we must have a thorough understanding of the problem and a carefully planned solution approach. Chapters 3 and 4 discuss techniques that facilitate the development of structured computer programs. In Section 4.12, we present a summary of the structured programming techniques developed here and in Chapter 4.

3.2 Algorithms

The solution to any computing problem involves executing a series of actions in a specific order. A **procedure** for solving a problem in terms of

1. the **actions** to be executed, and
2. the **order** in which these actions are to be executed

is called an **algorithm**. The following example demonstrates that correctly specifying the order in which the actions are to be executed is important.

Consider the "rise-and-shine algorithm" followed by one junior executive for getting out of bed and going to work: (1) Get out of bed, (2) take off pajamas, (3) take a shower, (4) get dressed, (5) eat breakfast, (6) carpool to work. This routine gets the executive to work well prepared to make critical decisions. Suppose that the *same* steps are performed in a slightly different *order*: (1) Get out of bed, (2) take off pajamas, (3) get dressed, (4) take a shower, (5) eat breakfast, (6) carpool to work. In this case, our junior executive shows up for work soaking wet. Specifying the order in which statements are to be executed in a computer program is called **program control**. In this and the next chapter, we investigate C's program control capabilities.

3.3 Pseudocode

Pseudocode is an artificial and informal language that helps you develop algorithms. The pseudocode we present here is particularly useful for developing algorithms that will be converted to structured C programs. Pseudocode is similar to everyday *English*; it's convenient and user friendly although it's *not* an actual computer programming language.

Pseudocode programs are *not* executed on computers. Rather, they merely help you "think out" a program before attempting to write it in a programming language like C.

Pseudocode consists purely of characters, so you may conveniently type pseudocode programs into a computer using a text editor program. A carefully prepared pseudocode program can be easily converted to a corresponding C program. This is done in many cases simply by replacing pseudocode statements with their C equivalents.

Pseudocode consists only of *action* and *decision* statements—those that are executed when the program has been converted from pseudocode to C and is run in C. Definitions are *not* executable statements—they're simply messages to the compiler. For example, the definition

```
int i;
```

tells the compiler the type of variable i and instructs the compiler to reserve space in memory for the variable. But this definition does *not* cause any action—such as input, output, a calculation or a comparison—to occur when the program is executed. Some programmers choose to list each variable and briefly mention the purpose of each at the beginning of a pseudocode program.

3.4 Control Structures

Normally, statements in a program are executed one after the other in the order in which they're written. This is called **sequential execution**. Various C statements we'll soon discuss enable you to specify that the next statement to be executed may be *other* than the next one in sequence. This is called **transfer of control**.

During the 1960s, it became clear that the indiscriminate use of transfers of control was the root of a great deal of difficulty experienced by software-development groups. The finger of blame was pointed at the **goto statement** that allows you to specify a transfer of control to one of many possible destinations in a program. The notion of so-called structured programming became almost synonymous with "**goto elimination**."

The research of Bohm and Jacopini[1] had demonstrated that programs could be written *without* any goto statements. The challenge of the era was for programmers to shift their styles to "goto-less programming." It was not until well into the 1970s that the programming profession started taking structured programming seriously. The results were impressive, as software-development groups reported reduced development times, more frequent on-time delivery of systems and more frequent within-budget completion of software projects. Programs produced with structured techniques were clearer, easier to debug and modify and more likely to be bug free in the first place.[2]

Bohm and Jacopini's work demonstrated that all programs could be written in terms of only three **control structures**, namely the **sequence structure**, the **selection structure** and the **iteration structure**. The sequence structure is simple—unless directed otherwise, the computer executes C statements one after the other in the order in which they're written. The **flowchart** segment of Fig. 3.1 illustrates C's sequence structure.

---

1.   C. Bohm and G. Jacopini, "Flow Diagrams, Turing Machines, and Languages with Only Two Formation Rules," *Communications of the ACM*, Vol. 9, No. 5, May 1966, pp. 336–371.
2.   As you'll see in Section 14.10, there are some special cases in which the goto statement is useful.

Flowcharts

A flowchart is a *graphical* representation of an algorithm or of a portion of an algorithm. Flowcharts are drawn using certain special-purpose symbols such as *rectangles, diamonds, rounded rectaingles,* and *small circles*; these symbols are connected by arrows called **flowlines**.

Like pseudocode, flowcharts are useful for developing and representing algorithms, although pseudocode is preferred by most programmers. Flowcharts clearly show how control structures operate; that's what we use them for in this text.

Consider the flowchart for the sequence structure in Fig. 3.1. We use the **rectangle symbol**, also called the **action symbol**, to indicate any type of action including a calculation or an input/output operation. The flowlines in the figure indicate the *order* in which the actions are performed—first, grade is added to total, then 1 is added to counter. C allows us to have as many actions as we want in a sequence structure. As we'll soon see, *anywhere a single action may be placed, we may place several actions in sequence.*

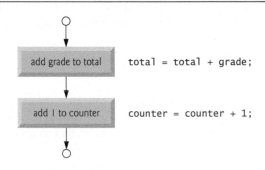

Fig. 3.1 | Flowcharting C's sequence structure.

When drawing a flowchart that represents a complete algorithm, the first symbol we use is a **rounded rectangle symbol** containing the word "Begin." The last symbol is a rounded rectangle containing the word "End." When drawing only a *portion* of an algorithm as in Fig. 3.1, we omit the rounded rectangle symbols in favor of using **small circle symbols**, also called **connector symbols**.

Perhaps the most important flowcharting symbol is the **diamond symbol**, also called the **decision symbol**, which indicates that a *decision* is to be made. We'll discuss the diamond symbol in the next section.

Selection Statements in C

C provides three types of selection structures in the form of statements. The if selection statement (Section 3.5) either *selects* (performs) an action if a condition is *true* or *skips* the action if the condition is *false*. The if...else selection statement (Section 3.6) performs an action if a condition is *true* and performs a different action if the condition is *false*. The switch selection statement (discussed in Chapter 4) performs one of *many* different actions, depending on the value of an expression. The if statement is called a **single-selection statement** because it selects or ignores a single action. The if...else statement is called a **double-selection statement** because it selects between two different actions. The switch statement is called a **multiple-selection statement** because it selects among many different actions.

Iteration Statements in C

C provides three types of *iteration structures* in the form of statements, namely while (Section 3.7), do...while, and for (both discussed in Chapter 4).

That's all there is. C has only seven control statements: sequence, three types of selection and three types of iteration. Each C program is formed by combining as many of each type of control statement as is appropriate for the algorithm the program implements. As with the sequence structure of Fig. 3.1, we'll see that the flowchart representation of each control statement has two small circle symbols, one at the *entry point* to the control statement and one at the *exit point*. These **single-entry/single-exit control statements** make it easy to build clear programs. We can attache the control-statement flowchart segments to one another by connecting the exit point of one control statement to the entry point of the next. This is much like the way in which a child stacks building blocks, so we call this **control-statement stacking**. We'll learn that there's only one other way control statements may be connected—a method called control-statement *nesting*. Thus, any C program we'll ever need to build can be constructed from only *seven* different types of control statements combined in only two ways. This is the essence of simplicity.

3.5 The if Selection Statement

Selection statements are used to choose among alternative courses of action. For example, suppose the passing grade on an exam is 60. The pseudocode statement

> *If student's grade is greater than or equal to 60*
> *Print "Passed"*

determines whether the condition "student's grade is greater than or equal to 60" is true or false. If the condition is true, then "Passed" is printed, and the next pseudocode statement in order is "performed" (remember that pseudocode isn't a real programming language). If the condition is false, the printing is ignored, and the next pseudocode statement in order is performed.

The preceding pseudocode *If* statement may be written in C as

```
if ( grade >= 60 ) {
   puts( "Passed" );
} // end if
```

Notice that the C code corresponds closely to the pseudocode (of course you'll also need to declare the int variable grade). This is one of the properties of pseudocode that makes it such a useful program-development tool. The second line of this selection statement is indented. Such indentation is optional, but it's highly recommended, as it helps emphasize the inherent structure of structured programs. The C compiler ignores **white-space characters** such as blanks, tabs and newlines used for indentation and vertical spacing.

The flowchart of Fig. 3.2 illustrates the single-selection if statement. This flowchart contains what is perhaps the most important flowcharting symbol—the diamond symbol, also called the decision symbol, which indicates that a decision is to be made. The decision symbol contains an expression, such as a condition, that can be either true or false. The decision symbol has *two* flowlines emerging from it. One indicates the direction to take when the expression in the symbol is true and the other the direction to take when the expression is false. Decisions can be based on conditions containing relational or equality operators. In fact, a decision can be based on *any* expression—if the expression evaluates to *zero*, it's treated as false, and if it evaluates to *nonzero*, it's treated as true.

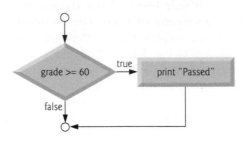

Fig. 3.2 | Flowcharting the single-selection `if` statement.

The `if` statement, too, is a *single-entry/single-exit* statement. We'll soon learn that the flowcharts for the remaining control structures can also contain (besides small circle symbols and flowlines) only rectangle symbols to indicate the actions to be performed, and diamond symbols to indicate decisions to be made. This is the *action/decision model of programming* we've been emphasizing.

We can envision seven bins, each containing only control-statement flowcharts of one of the seven types. These flowchart segments are empty—nothing is written in the rectangles and nothing in the diamonds. Your task, then, is assembling a program from as many of each type of control statement as the algorithm demands, combining them in only *two* possible ways (*stacking* or *nesting*), and then filling in the *actions* and *decisions* in a manner appropriate for the algorithm. We'll discuss the variety of ways in which actions and decisions may be written.

3.6 The `if...else` Selection Statement

The `if` selection statement performs an indicated action only when the condition is true; otherwise the action is skipped. The `if...else` selection statement allows you to specify that *different* actions are to be performed when the condition is true and when it's false. For example, the pseudocode statement

> *If student's grade is greater than or equal to 60*
> > *Print "Passed"*
> *else*
> > *Print "Failed"*

prints *Passed* if the student's grade is greater than or equal to 60 and *Failed* if the student's grade is less than 60. In either case, after printing occurs, the next pseudocode statement in sequence is "performed." The body of the *else* is also indented.

Good Programming Practice 3.1

Indent both body statements of an `if...else` statement (in both pseudocode and C).

Good Programming Practice 3.2

If there are several levels of indentation, each level should be indented the same additional amount of space.

The preceding pseudocode *If...else* statement may be written in C as

```
if ( grade >= 60 ) {
    puts( "Passed" );
} // end if
else {
    puts( "Failed" );
} // end else
```

The flowchart of Fig. 3.3 illustrates the flow of control in the if...else statement. Once again, besides small circles and arrows, the only symbols in the flowchart are rectangles (for actions) and a diamond (for a decision).

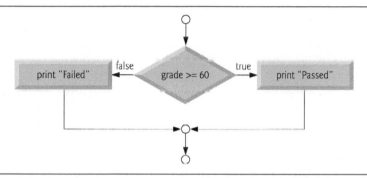

Fig. 3.3 | Flowcharting the double-selection if...else statement.

C provides the **conditional operator (?:)**, which is closely related to the if...else statement. The conditional operator is C's only *ternary* operator—it takes *three* operands. These together with the conditional operator form a **conditional expression**. The first operand is a *condition*. The second operand is the value for the entire conditional expression if the condition is *true* and the third operand is the value for the entire conditional expression if the condition is *false*. For example, the puts statement

```
puts( grade >= 60 ? "Passed" : "Failed" );
```

contains as its argument a conditional expression that evaluates to the string "Passed" if the condition grade >= 60 is true and to the string "Failed" if the condition is false. The puts statement performs in essentially the same way as the preceding if...else statement.

The second and third operands in a conditional expression can also be actions to be executed. For example, the conditional expression

```
grade >= 60 ? puts( "Passed" ) : puts( "Failed" );
```

is read, "If grade is greater than or equal to 60, then puts("Passed"), otherwise puts("Failed")." This, too, is comparable to the preceding if...else statement. Conditional operators can be used in places where if...else statements cannot, including expressions and arguments to functions (like printf).

Error-Prevention Tip 3.1

Use expressions of the same type for the second and third operands of the conditional operator (?:) to avoid subtle errors.

Nested if...else Statements

Nested **if...else statements** test for multiple cases by placing if...else statements *inside* if...else statements. For example, the following pseudocode statement will print A for exam grades greater than or equal to 90, B for grades greater than or equal to 80 (but less than 90), C for grades greater than or equal to 70 (but less than 80), D for grades greater than or equal to 60 (but less than 70), and F for all other grades.

> *If student's grade is greater than or equal to 90*
> > *Print "A"*
>
> *else*
> > *If student's grade is greater than or equal to 80*
> > > *Print "B"*
> >
> > *else*
> > > *If student's grade is greater than or equal to 70*
> > > > *Print "C"*
> > >
> > > *else*
> > > > *If student's grade is greater than or equal to 60*
> > > > > *Print "D"*
> > > >
> > > > *else*
> > > > > *Print "F"*

This pseudocode may be written in C as

```c
if ( grade >= 90 ) {
   puts( "A" );
} // end if
else {
   if ( grade >= 80 ) {
      puts( "B" );
   } // end if
   else {
      if ( grade >= 70 ) {
         puts( "C" );
      } // end if
      else {
         if ( grade >= 60 ) {
            puts( "D" );
         } // end if
         else {
            puts( "F" );
         } // end else
      } // end else
   } // end else
} // end else
```

If the variable grade is greater than or equal to 90, all four conditions will be true, but only the puts statement after the first test will be executed. After that puts is executed, the else part of the "outer" if...else statement is skipped.

You may prefer to write the preceding if statement as

```
if ( grade >= 90 ) {
   puts( "A" );
} // end if
else if ( grade >= 80 ) {
   puts( "B" );
} // end else if
else if ( grade >= 70 ) {
   puts( "C" );
} // end else if
else if ( grade >= 60 ) {
   puts( "D" );
} // end else if
else {
   puts( "F" );
} // end else
```

As far as the C compiler is concerned, both forms are equivalent. The latter form is popular because it avoids the deep indentation of the code to the right. Such indentation often leaves little room on a line, forcing lines to be split and decreasing program readability.

The if selection statement expects only one statement in its body—if you have only one statement in the if's body, you do not need to enclose it in braces. To include several statements in the body of an if, you must enclose the set of statements in braces ({ and }). A set of statements contained within a pair of braces is called a **compound statement** or a **block**.

 Software Engineering Observation 3.1
A compound statement can be placed anywhere in a program that a single statement can be placed.

The following example includes a compound statement in the else part of an if...else statement.

```
if ( grade >= 60 ) {
   puts( "Passed." );
} // end if
else {
   puts( "Failed." );
   puts( "You must take this course again." );
} // end else
```

In this case, if grade is less than 60, the program executes *both* puts statements in the body of the else and prints

```
Failed.
You must take this course again.
```

The braces surrounding the two statements in the else clause are important. Without them, the statement

```
puts( "You must take this course again." );
```

would be *outside* the body of the else part of the if and would execute regardless of whether the grade was less than 60, so even a passing student would have to take the course again!

Error-Prevention Tip 3.2
Always include your control statements' bodies in braces ({ and }), even if those bodies contain only a single statement. This solves the "dangling-else" problem, which we discuss in Exercises 3.30–3.31.

A *syntax error* is caught by the compiler. A *logic error* has its effect at execution time. A *fatal logic error* causes a program to fail and terminate prematurely. A *nonfatal logic error* allows a program to continue executing but to produce incorrect results.

Just as a compound statement can be placed anywhere a single statement can be placed, it's also possible to have no statement at all, i.e., the empty statement. The empty statement is represented by placing a semicolon (;) where a statement would normally be.

Common Programming Error 3.1
Placing a semicolon after the condition in an if statement as in if (grade >= 60); leads to a logic error in single-selection if statements and a syntax error in double-selection if statements.

Error-Prevention Tip 3.3
Typing the beginning and ending braces of compound statements before typing the individual statements within the braces helps avoid omitting one or both of the braces, preventing syntax errors and logic errors (where both braces are indeed required).

3.7 The while Iteration Statement

An **iteration statement** (also called an **repetition statement** or loop) allows you to specify that an action is to be repeated while some condition remains true. The pseudocode statement

> *While there are more items on my shopping list*
> *Purchase next item and cross it off my list*

describes the iteration that occurs during a shopping trip. The condition, "there are more items on my shopping list" may be true or false. If it's true, then the action, "Purchase next item and cross it off my list" is performed. This action will be performed *repeatedly* while the condition remains true. The statement(s) contained in the *while* iteration statement constitute the body of the *while*. The *while* statement body may be a single statement or a compound statement.

Eventually, the condition will become false (when the last item on the shopping list has been purchased and crossed off the list). At this point, the iteration terminates, and the first pseudocode statement *after* the iteration structure is executed.

Common Programming Error 3.2
Not providing in the body of a while statement an action that eventually causes the condition in the while to become false. Normally, such an iteration structure will never terminate—an error called an "infinite loop."

Common Programming Error 3.3

Spelling a keyword (such as while or if) with any uppercases letters (as in, While or If) is a compilation error. Remember C is case sensitive and keywords contain only lowercase letters.

As an example of a `while` statement, consider a program segment designed to find the first power of 3 larger than 100. The integer variable product has been initialized to 3. When the following code finishes executing, product will contain the desired answer:

```
product = 3;
while ( product <= 100 ) {
    product = 3 * product;
}
```

The flowchart of Fig. 3.4 illustrates the flow of control in the preceding `while` iteration statement. Once again, note that (besides small circles and arrows) the flowchart contains only a rectangle symbol and a diamond symbol. The flowchart clearly shows the iteration. The flowline emerging from the rectangle wraps back to the decision, which is tested each time through the loop until the decision eventually becomes false. At this point, the `while` statement is exited and control passes to the next statement in the program.

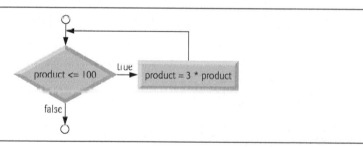

Fig. 3.4 | Flowcharting the `while` iteration statement.

When the `while` statement is entered, the value of product is 3. The variable product is repeatedly multiplied by 3, taking on the values 9, 27 and 81 successively. When product becomes 243, the condition in the `while` statement, product <= 100, becomes false. This terminates the iteration, and the final value of product is 243. Program execution continues with the next statement after the `while`.

3.8 Formulating Algorithms Case Study 1: Counter-Controlled Iteration

To illustrate how algorithms are developed, we solve several variations of a class-averaging problem. Consider the following problem statement:

> *A class of ten students took a quiz. The grades (integers in the range 0 to 100) for this quiz are available to you. Determine the class average on the quiz.*

The class average is equal to the sum of the grades divided by the number of students. The algorithm for solving this problem on a computer must input each of the grades, perform the averaging calculation, and print the result.

Let's use pseudocode to list the actions to execute and specify the order in which these actions should execute. We use **counter-controlled iteration** to input the grades one at a time. This technique uses a variable called a **counter** to specify the number of times a set of statements should execute. In this example, iteration terminates when the counter exceeds 10. In this case study we simply present the pseudocode algorithm (Fig. 3.5) and the corresponding C program (Fig. 3.6). In the next case study we show how pseudocode algorithms are *developed*. Counter-controlled iteration is often called **definite iteration** because the number of iterations is known *before* the loop begins executing.

1	*Set total to zero*
2	*Set grade counter to one*
3	
4	*While grade counter is less than or equal to ten*
5	*Input the next grade*
6	*Add the grade into the total*
7	*Add one to the grade counter*
8	
9	*Set the class average to the total divided by ten*
10	*Print the class average*

Fig. 3.5 | Pseudocode algorithm that uses counter-controlled iteration to solve the class-average problem.

```c
1   // Fig. 3.6: fig03_06.c
2   // Class average program with counter-controlled iteration.
3   #include <stdio.h>
4
5   // function main begins program execution
6   int main( void )
7   {
8      unsigned int counter; // number of grade to be entered next
9      int grade; // grade value
10     int total; // sum of grades entered by user
11     int average; // average of grades
12
13     // initialization phase
14     total = 0; // initialize total
15     counter = 1; // initialize loop counter
16
17     // processing phase
18     while ( counter <= 10 ) { // loop 10 times
19        printf( "%s", "Enter grade: " ); // prompt for input
20        scanf( "%d", &grade ); // read grade from user
21        total = total + grade; // add grade to total
22        counter = counter + 1; // increment counter
23     } // end while
24
```

Fig. 3.6 | Class-average problem with counter-controlled iteration. (Part 1 of 2.)

```
25       // termination phase
26       average = total / 10; // integer division
27
28       printf( "Class average is %d\n", average ); // display result
29   } // end function main
```

```
Enter grade: 98
Enter grade: 76
Enter grade: 71
Enter grade: 87
Enter grade: 83
Enter grade: 90
Enter grade: 57
Enter grade: 79
Enter grade: 82
Enter grade: 94
Class average is 81
```

Fig. 3.6 | Class-average problem with counter-controlled iteration. (Part 2 of 2.)

The algorithm mentions a total and a counter. A total is a variable used to accumulate the sum of a series of values. A counter is a variable (line 8) used to *count*—in this case, to count the number of grades entered. Because the counter variable is used to count from 1 to 10 in this program (all positive values), we declared the variable as an unsigned int, which can store only non-negative values (that is, 0 and higher). Variables used to store totals should be initialized to zero *before* being used in a program; otherwise the sum would include the previous value stored in the total's memory location. Counter variables are normally initialized to zero or one, depending on their use (we'll present examples of each). An uninitialized variable contains a "garbage" value—the value last stored in the memory location reserved for that variable.

Common Programming Error 3.4
If a counter or total isn't initialized, the results of your program will probably be incorrect. This is an example of a logic error.

Error-Prevention Tip 3.4
Initialize all counters and totals.

The averaging calculation in the program produced an integer result of 81. Actually, the sum of the grades in this example is 817, which when divided by 10 should yield 81.7, i.e., a number with a *decimal point*. We'll see how to deal with such numbers (called *floating-point* numbers) in the next section.

Important Note About the Placement of Variable Definitions
In Chapter 2, we mentioned that the C standard allows you to place each variable definition *anywhere* in main before that variable's first use in the code. In this chapter, we continue to group our variable definitions at the beginning of main to emphasize the initialization, processing and termination phases of simple programs. Beginning in Chapter 4, we'll place each variable definition just before that variable's first use. We'll see

in Chapter 5—when we discuss the *scope* of variables—how this practice helps you eliminate errors.

3.9 Formulating Algorithms with Top-Down, Stepwise Refinement Case Study 2: Sentinel-Controlled Iteration

Let's generalize the class-average problem. Consider the following problem:

> *Develop a class-averaging program that will process an* arbitrary *number of grades each time the program is run.*

In the first class-average example, the number of grades (10) was known in advance. In this example, no indication is given of how many grades are to be entered. The program must process an *arbitrary* number of grades. How can the program determine when to stop the input of grades? How will it know when to calculate and print the class average?

One way to solve this problem is to use a special value called a **sentinel value** (also called a **signal value**, a **dummy value**, or a **flag value**) to indicate "end of data entry." The user types grades until all *legitimate* grades have been entered. The user then types the sentinel value to indicate "the last grade has been entered." Sentinel-controlled iteration is often called **indefinite iteration** because the number of iterations isn't known *before* the loop begins executing.

Clearly, the sentinel value must be chosen so that it *cannot* be confused with an acceptable input value. Because grades on a quiz are normally *nonnegative* integers, –1 is an acceptable sentinel value for this problem. Thus, a run of the class-average program might process a stream of inputs such as 95, 96, 75, 74, 89 and –1. The program would then compute and print the class average for the grades 95, 96, 75, 74, and 89 (–1 is the sentinel value, so it should *not* enter into the averaging calculation).

Top-Down, Stepwise Refinement

We approach the class-average program with a technique called **top-down, stepwise refinement**, a technique that's essential to the development of well-structured programs. We begin with a pseudocode representation of the **top**:

> *Determine the class average for the quiz*

The top is a single statement that conveys the program's overall function. As such, the top is, in effect, a *complete* representation of a program. Unfortunately, the top rarely conveys a sufficient amount of detail for writing the C program. So we now begin the *refinement* process. We divide the top into a series of smaller tasks and list these in the order in which they need to be performed. This results in the following **first refinement**.

> *Initialize variables*
> *Input, sum, and count the quiz grades*
> *Calculate and print the class average*

Here, only the *sequence structure* has been used—the steps listed are to be executed in order, one after the other.

Software Engineering Observation 3.2

Each refinement, as well as the top itself, is a complete specification of the algorithm; only the level of detail varies.

Second Refinement

To proceed to the next level of refinement, i.e., the **second refinement**, we commit to specific variables. We need a running total of the numbers, a count of how many numbers have been processed, a variable to receive the value of each grade as it's input and a variable to hold the calculated average. The pseudocode statement

> *Initialize variables*

may be refined as follows:

> *Initialize total to zero*
> *Initialize counter to zero*

Only the total and counter need to be initialized; the variables average and grade (for the calculated average and the user input, respectively) need not be initialized because their values will be calulated and input from the user, respectively. The pseudocode statement

> *Input, sum, and count the quiz grades*

requires an *iteration structure* that successively inputs each grade. Because we do not know in advance how many grades are to be processed, we'll use sentinel-controlled iteration. The user will enter legitimate grades one at a time. After the last legitimate grade is typed, the user will type the sentinel value. The program will test for this value after each grade is input and will terminate the loop when the sentinel is entered. The refinement of the preceding pseudocode statement is then

> *Input the first grade (possibly the sentinel)*
> *While the user has not as yet entered the sentinel*
>   *Add this grade into the running total*
>   *Add one to the grade counter*
>   *Input the next grade (possibly the sentinel)*

Notice that in pseudocode, we do *not* use braces around the set of statements that form the body of the *while* statement. We simply indent all these statements under the *while* to show that they all belong to the *while*. Again, pseudocode is an informal program-development aid.

The pseudocode statement

> *Calculate and print the class average*

may be refined as follows:

> *If the counter is not equal to zero*
>   *Set the average to the total divided by the counter*
>   *Print the average*
> *else*
>   *Print "No grades were entered"*

Notice that we're being careful here to test for the possibility of *division by zero*—a **fatal error** that if undetected would cause the program to fail (often called "**crashing**"). The complete second refinement is shown in Fig. 3.7.

Common Programming Error 3.5

An attempt to divide by zero causes a fatal error.

Good Programming Practice 3.3

When performing division by an expression whose value could be zero, explicitly test for this case and handle it appropriately in your program (such as by printing an error message) rather than allowing the fatal error to occur.

In Fig. 3.5 and Fig. 3.7, we include some completely blank lines in the pseudocode for readability. Actually, the blank lines separate these programs into their various phases.

```
 1    Initialize total to zero
 2    Initialize counter to zero
 3
 4    Input the first grade (possibly the sentinel)
 5    While the user has not as yet entered the sentinel
 6        Add this grade into the running total
 7        Add one to the grade counter
 8        Input the next grade (possibly the sentinel)
 9
10    If the counter is not equal to zero
11        Set the average to the total divided by the counter
12        Print the average
13    else
14        Print "No grades were entered"
```

Fig. 3.7 | Pseudocode algorithm that uses sentinel-controlled iteration to solve the class-average problem.

Software Engineering Observation 3.3

Many programs can be divided logically into three phases: an initialization phase *that initializes the program variables; a* processing phase *that inputs data values and adjusts program variables accordingly; and a* termination phase *that calculates and prints the final results.*

The pseudocode algorithm in Fig. 3.7 solves the more general class-average problem. This algorithm was developed after only two levels of refinement. Sometimes more levels are necessary.

Software Engineering Observation 3.4

You terminate the top-down, stepwise refinement process when the pseudocode algorithm is specified in sufficient detail for you to be able to convert the pseudocode to C. Implementing the C program is then normally straightforward.

The C program and a sample execution are shown in Fig. 3.8. Although only integer grades are entered, the averaging calculation is likely to produce a number *with a decimal point.* The type int cannot represent such a number. The program introduces the data type **float** to handle numbers with decimal points (called **floating-point numbers**) and introduces a special operator called a *cast operator* to handle the averaging calculation. These features are explained after the program is presented.

```
 1   // Fig. 3.8: fig03_08.c
 2   // Class-average program with sentinel-controlled iteration.
 3   #include <stdio.h>
 4
 5   // function main begins program execution
 6   int main( void )
 7   {
 8      unsigned int counter; // number of grades entered
 9      int grade; // grade value
10      int total; // sum of grades
11
12      float average; // number with decimal point for average
13
14      // initialization phase
15      total = 0; // initialize total
16      counter = 0; // initialize loop counter
17
18      // processing phase
19      // get first grade from user
20      printf( "%s", "Enter grade, -1 to end: " ); // prompt for input
21      scanf( "%d", &grade ); // read grade from user
22
23      // loop while sentinel value not yet read from user
24      while ( grade != -1 ) {
25         total = total + grade; // add grade to total
26         counter = counter + 1; // increment counter
27
28         // get next grade from user
29         printf( "%s", "Enter grade, -1 to end: " ); // prompt for input
30         scanf("%d", &grade); // read next grade
31      } // end while
32
33      // termination phase
34      // if user entered at least one grade
35      if ( counter != 0 ) {
36
37         // calculate average of all grades entered
38         average = ( float ) total / counter; // avoid truncation
39
40         // display average with two digits of precision
41         printf( "Class average is %.2f\n", average );
42      } // end if
43      else { // if no grades were entered, output message
44         puts( "No grades were entered" );
45      } // end else
46   } // end function main
```

Fig. 3.8 | Class-average program with sentinel-controlled iteration. (Part 1 of 2.)

```
Enter grade, -1 to end: 75
Enter grade, -1 to end: 94
Enter grade, -1 to end: 97
Enter grade, -1 to end: 88
Enter grade, -1 to end: 70
Enter grade, -1 to end: 64
Enter grade, -1 to end: 83
Enter grade, -1 to end: 89
Enter grade, -1 to end: -1
Class average is 82.50
```

```
Enter grade, -1 to end: -1
No grades were entered
```

Fig. 3.8 | Class-average program with sentinel-controlled iteration. (Part 2 of 2.)

Notice the compound statement in the `while` loop (line 24) in Fig. 3.8. Once again, the braces are *necessary* to ensure that all four statements are executed within the loop. Without the braces, the last three statements in the body of the loop would fall *outside* the loop, causing the computer to interpret this code incorrectly as follows:

```
while ( grade != -1 )
    total = total + grade; // add grade to total
counter = counter + 1; // increment counter
printf( "%s", "Enter grade, -1 to end: " ); // prompt for input
scanf( "%d", &grade ); // read next grade
```

This would cause an *infinite loop* if the user did not input -1 for the first grade.

Error-Prevention Tip 3.5
In a sentinel-controlled loop, explicitly remind the user what the sentinel value is in prompts requesting data entry.

Converting Between Types Explicitly and Implicitly

Averages do not always evaluate to integer values. Often, an average is a value such as 7.2 or –93.5 that contains a fractional part. These values are referred to as floating-point numbers and can be represented by the data type `float`. The variable `average` is defined to be of type `float` (line 12) to capture the fractional result of our calculation. However, the result of the calculation `total / counter` is an integer because `total` and `counter` are *both* integer variables. Dividing two integers results in **integer division** in which any fractional part of the calculation is **truncated** (i.e., lost). Because the calculation is performed *first*, the fractional part is lost *before* the result is assigned to `average`. To produce a floating-point calculation with integer values, we must create temporary values that are floating-point numbers. C provides the unary **cast operator** to accomplish this task. Line 38

```
average = ( float ) total / counter;
```

includes the cast operator `(float)`, which creates a *temporary* floating-point copy of its operand, `total`. The value stored in `total` is still an integer. Using a cast operator in this manner is called **explicit conversion**. The calculation now consists of a floating-point value (the temporary `float` version of `total`) divided by the unsigned `int` value stored in `counter`. C evaluates arithmetic expressions only in which the data types of the operands are *identical*. To ensure that the operands are of the *same* type, the compiler performs an operation called **implicit conversion** on selected operands. For example, in an expression containing the data types `unsigned int` and `float`, copies of `unsigned int` operands are made and converted to `float`. In our example, after a copy of `counter` is made and converted to `float`, the calculation is performed and the result of the floating-point division is assigned to `average`. C provides a set of rules for conversion of operands of different types. We discuss this further in Chapter 5.

Cast operators are available for *most* data types—they're formed by placing parentheses around a type name. Each cast operator is a **unary operator**, i.e., an operator that takes only one operand. In Chapter 2, we studied the binary arithmetic operators. C also supports unary versions of the plus (+) and minus (-) operators, so you can write expressions such as -7 or +5. Cast operators associate from right to left and have the same precedence as other unary operators such as unary + and unary -. This precedence is one level higher than that of the **multiplicative operators *, /** and **%**.

Formatting Floating-Point Numbers

Figure 3.8 uses the `printf` conversion specifier `%.2f` (line 41) to print the value of `average`. The `f` specifies that a floating-point value will be printed. The `.2` is the **precision** with which the value will be displayed—with 2 digits to the right of the decimal point. If the `%f` conversion specifier is used (without specifying the precision), the **default precision** of 6 is used—exactly as if the conversion specifier `%.6f` had been used. When floating-point values are printed with precision, the printed value is **rounded** to the indicated number of decimal positions. The value in memory is unaltered. When the following statements are executed, the values 3.45 and 3.4 are printed.

```
printf( "%.2f\n", 3.446 ); // prints 3.45
printf( "%.1f\n", 3.446 ); // prints 3.4
```

Common Programming Error 3.6

Using precision in a conversion specification in the format control string of a `scanf` statement is an error. Precisions are used only in `printf` conversion specifications.

Notes on Floating-Point Numbers

Although floating-point numbers are not always "100% precise," they have numerous applications. For example, when we speak of a "normal" body temperature of 98.6 Fahrenheit, we do not need to be precise to a large number of digits. When we view the temperature on a thermometer and read it as 98.6, it may actually be 98.5999473210643. The point here is that calling this number simply 98.6 is fine for most applications. We'll say more about this issue later.

Another way floating-point numbers develop is through division. When we divide 10 by 3, the result is 3.3333333… with the sequence of 3s repeating infinitely. The computer allocates only a *fixed* amount of space to hold such a value, so the stored floating-point value can be only an *approximation*.

Common Programming Error 3.7

Using floating-point numbers in a manner that assumes they're represented precisely can lead to incorrect results. Floating-point numbers are represented only approximately by most computers.

Error-Prevention Tip 3.6

Do not compare floating-point values for equality.

3.10 Formulating Algorithms with Top-Down, Stepwise Refinement Case Study 3: Nested Control Statements

Let's work another complete problem. We'll once again formulate the algorithm using pseudocode and top-down, stepwise refinement, and write a corresponding C program. We've seen that control statements may be *stacked* on top of one another (in sequence) just as a child stacks building blocks. In this case study we'll see the only other structured way control statements may be connected in C, namely through **nesting** of one control statement *within* another. Consider the following problem statement:

> *A college offers a course that prepares students for the state licensing exam for real-estate brokers. Last year, 10 of the students who completed this course took the licensing examination. Naturally, the college wants to know how well its students did on the exam. You've been asked to write a program to summarize the results. You've been given a list of these 10 students. Next to each name a 1 is written if the student passed the exam or a 2 if the student failed.*

> *Your program should analyze the results of the exam as follows:*

> 1. *Input each test result (i.e., a 1 or a 2). Display the prompting message "Enter result" each time the program requests another test result.*

> 2. *Count the number of test results of each type.*

> 3. *Display a summary of the test results indicating the number of students who passed and the number who failed.*

> 4. *If more than eight students passed the exam, print the message "Bonus to instructor!"*

After reading the problem statement carefully, we make the following observations:

1. The program must process 10 test results. A counter-controlled loop will be used.

2. Each test result is a number—either a 1 or a 2. Each time the program reads a test result, the program must determine whether the number is a 1 or a 2. We test for a 1 in our algorithm. If the number is not a 1, we assume that it's a 2. (Exercise 3.27 asks you to ensure that every test result is a 1 or a 2.)

3. Two counters are used—one to count the number of students who passed the exam and one to count the number of students who failed the exam.

4. After the program has processed all the results, it must decide whether more than 8 students passed the exam.

Let's proceed with top-down, stepwise refinement. We begin with a pseudocode representation of the top:

Analyze exam results and decide whether instructor should receive a bonus

Once again, it's important to emphasize that the top is a *complete* representation of the program, but several refinements are likely to be needed before the pseudocode can be naturally evolved into a C program. Our first refinement is

> *Initialize variables*
> *Input the ten quiz grades and count passes and failures*
> *Print a summary of the exam results and decide whether instructor should receive a bonus*

Here, too, even though we have a *complete* representation of the entire program, further refinement is necessary. We now commit to specific variables. Counters are needed to record the passes and failures, a counter will be used to control the looping process, and a variable is needed to store the user input. The pseudocode statement

> *Initialize variables*

may be refined as follows:

> *Initialize passes to zero*
> *Initialize failures to zero*
> *Initialize student to one*

Notice that only the counter and totals are initialized. The pseudocode statement

> *Input the ten quiz grades and count passes and failures*

requires a loop that successively inputs the result of each exam. Here it's known *in advance* that there are precisely ten exam results, so counter-controlled looping is appropriate. Inside the loop (i.e., **nested** within the loop) a double-selection statement will determine whether each exam result is a pass or a failure and will increment the appropriate counters accordingly. The refinement of the preceding pseudocode statement is then

> *While student counter is less than or equal to ten*
>   *Input the next exam result*
>
>   *If the student passed*
>   *Add one to passes*
>   *else*
>   *Add one to failures*
>
>   *Add one to student counter*

Notice the use of blank lines to set off the *If...else* to improve program readability. The pseudocode statement

> *Print a summary of the exam results and decide whether instructor should receive a bonus*

may be refined as follows:

> *Print the number of passes*
> *Print the number of failures*
> *If more than eight students passed*
>   *Print "Bonus to instructor!"*

The complete second refinement appears in Fig. 3.9. We use blank lines to set off the while statement for program readability.

This pseudocode is now sufficiently refined for conversion to C. The C program and two sample executions are shown in Fig. 3.10. We've taken advantage of a feature of C that allows initialization to be incorporated into definitions (lines 9–11). Such initialization occurs at compile time. Also, notice that when you output an unsigned int you use the **%u conversion specifier** (lines 33–34).

1	*Initialize passes to zero*
2	*Initialize failures to zero*
3	*Initialize student to one*
4	
5	*While student counter is less than or equal to ten*
6	*Input the next exam result*
7	
8	*If the student passed*
9	*Add one to passes*
10	*else*
11	*Add one to failures*
12	
13	*Add one to student counter*
14	
15	*Print the number of passes*
16	*Print the number of failures*
17	*If more than eight students passed*
18	*Print "Bonus to instructor!"*

Fig. 3.9 | Pseudocode for examination-results problem.

Software Engineering Observation 3.5

Experience has shown that the most difficult part of solving a problem on a computer is developing the algorithm for the solution. Once a correct algorithm has been specified, the process of producing a working C program is normally straightforward.

Software Engineering Observation 3.6

Many programmers write programs without ever using program-development tools such as pseudocode. They feel that their ultimate goal is to solve the problem on a computer and that writing pseudocode merely delays the production of final outputs.

```
1   // Fig. 3.10: fig03_10.c
2   // Analysis of examination results.
3   #include <stdio.h>
4
```

Fig. 3.10 | Analysis of examination results. (Part 1 of 3.)

```
 5    // function main begins program execution
 6    int main( void )
 7    {
 8       // initialize variables in definitions
 9       unsigned int passes = 0; // number of passes
10       unsigned int failures = 0; // number of failures
11       unsigned int student = 1; // student counter
12       int result; // one exam result
13
14       // process 10 students using counter-controlled loop
15       while ( student <= 10 ) {
16
17          // prompt user for input and obtain value from user
18          printf( "%s", "Enter result ( 1=pass,2=fail ): " );
19          scanf( "%d", &result );
20
21          // if result 1, increment passes
22          if ( result == 1 ) {
23             passes = passes + 1;
24          } // end if
25          else { // otherwise, increment failures
26             failures = failures + 1;
27          } // end else
28
29          student = student + 1; // increment student counter
30       } // end while
31
32       // termination phase; display number of passes and failures
33       printf( "Passed %u\n", passes );
34       printf( "Failed %u\n", failures );
35
36       // if more than eight students passed, print "Bonus to instructor!"
37       if ( passes > 8 ) {
38          puts( "Bonus to instructor!" );
39       } // end if
40    } // end function main
```

```
Enter Result (1=pass,2=fail): 1
Enter Result (1=pass,2=fail): 2
Enter Result (1=pass,2=fail): 2
Enter Result (1=pass,2=fail): 1
Enter Result (1=pass,2=fail): 1
Enter Result (1=pass,2=fail): 1
Enter Result (1=pass,2=fail): 2
Enter Result (1=pass,2=fail): 1
Enter Result (1=pass,2=fail): 1
Enter Result (1=pass,2=fail): 2
Passed 6
Failed 4
```

Fig. 3.10 | Analysis of examination results. (Part 2 of 3.)

```
Enter Result (1=pass,2=fail): 1
Enter Result (1=pass,2=fail): 1
Enter Result (1=pass,2=fail): 1
Enter Result (1=pass,2=fail): 2
Enter Result (1=pass,2=fail): 1
Enter Result (1=pass,2=fail): 1
Enter Result (1=pass,2=fail): 1
Enter Result (1=pass,2=fail): 1
Enter Result (1=pass,2=fail): 1
Enter Result (1=pass,2=fail): 1
Passed 9
Failed 1
Bonus to instructor!
```

Fig. 3.10 | Analysis of examination results. (Part 3 of 3.)

3.11 Assignment Operators

C provides several assignment operators for abbreviating assignment expressions. For example, the statement

```
c = c + 3;
```

can be abbreviated with the **addition assignment operator** += as

```
c += 3;
```

The += operator adds the value of the expression on the *right* of the operator to the value of the variable on the *left* of the operator and stores the result in the variable on the *left* of the operator. Any statement of the form

variable = variable operator expression;

where *operator* is one of the binary operators +, -, *, / or % (or others we'll discuss in Chapter 10), can be written in the form

variable operator= expression;

Thus the assignment c += 3 adds 3 to c. Figure 3.11 shows the arithmetic assignment operators, sample expressions using these operators and explanations.

Assignment operator	Sample expression	Explanation	Assigns
Assume: int c = 3, d = 5, e = 4, f = 6, g = 12;			
+=	c += 7	c = c + 7	10 to c
-=	d -= 4	d = d - 4	1 to d
*=	e *= 5	e = e * 5	20 to e
/=	f /= 3	f = f / 3	2 to f
%=	g %= 9	g = g % 9	3 to g

Fig. 3.11 | Arithmetic assignment operators.

3.12 Increment and Decrement Operators

C also provides the unary **increment operator**, ++, and the unary **decrement operator**, --, which are summarized in Fig. 3.12. If a variable c is to be incremented by 1, the increment operator ++ can be used rather than the expressions c = c + 1 or c += 1. If increment or decrement operators are placed *before* a variable (i.e., *prefixed*), they're referred to as the **preincrement** or **predecrement operators**, respectively. If increment or decrement operators are placed *after* a variable (i.e., *postfixed*), they're referred to as the **postincrement** or **postdecrement operators**, respectively. Preincrementing (predecrementing) a variable causes the variable to be incremented (decremented) by 1, *then* its new value is used in the expression in which it appears. Postincrementing (postdecrementing) the variable causes the current value of the variable to be used in the expression in which it appears, *then* the variable value is incremented (decremented) by 1.

Operator	Sample expression	Explanation
++	++a	Increment a by 1, then use the new value of a in the expression in which a resides.
++	a++	Use the current value of a in the expression in which a resides, then increment a by 1.
--	--b	Decrement b by 1, then use the new value of b in the expression in which b resides.
--	b--	Use the current value of b in the expression in which b resides, then decrement b by 1.

Fig. 3.12 | Increment and decrement operators

Figure 3.13 demonstrates the difference between the preincrementing and the postincrementing versions of the ++ operator. Postincrementing the variable c causes it to be incremented *after* it's used in the printf statement. Preincrementing the variable c causes it to be incremented *before* it's used in the printf statement.

```
1   // Fig. 3.13: fig03_13.c
2   // Preincrementing and postincrementing.
3   #include <stdio.h>
4
5   // function main begins program execution
6   int main( void )
7   {
8      int c; // define variable
9
10     // demonstrate postincrement
11     c = 5; // assign 5 to c
12     printf( "%d\n", c ); // print 5
13     printf( "%d\n", c++ ); // print 5 then postincrement
14     printf( "%d\n\n", c ); // print 6
```

Fig. 3.13 | Preincrementing and postincrementing. (Part 1 of 2.)

```
15
16    // demonstrate preincrement
17    c = 5; // assign 5 to c
18    printf( "%d\n", c ); // print 5
19    printf( "%d\n", ++c ); // preincrement then print 6
20    printf( "%d\n", c ); // print 6
21  } // end function main
```

```
5
5
6

5
6
6
```

Fig. 3.13 | Preincrementing and postincrementing. (Part 2 of 2.)

The program displays the value of c before and after the ++ operator is used. The decrement operator (--) works similarly.

Good Programming Practice 3.4
Unary operators should be placed directly next to their operands with no intervening spaces.

The three assignment statements in Fig. 3.10

```
passes = passes + 1;
failures = failures + 1;
student = student + 1;
```

can be written more concisely with *assignment operators* as

```
passes += 1;
failures += 1;
student += 1;
```

with *preincrement operators* as

```
++passes;
++failures;
++student;
```

or with *postincrement operators* as

```
passes++;
failures++;
student++;
```

It's important to note here that when incrementing or decrementing a variable in a statement by *itself*, the preincrement and postincrement forms have the *same* effect. It's only when a variable appears in the context of a larger expression that preincrementing and postincrementing have *different* effects (and similarly for predecrementing and postdecrementing). Of the expressions we've studied thus far, only a simple variable name may be used as the operand of an increment or decrement operator.

Common Programming Error 3.8

Attempting to use the increment or decrement operator on an expression other than a simple variable name is a syntax error, e.g., writing ++(x + 1).

Error-Prevention Tip 3.7

C generally does not specify the order in which an operator's operands will be evaluated (although we'll see exceptions to this for a few operators in Chapter 4). Therefore you should use increment or decrement operators only in statements in which one variable is incremented or decremented by itself.

Figure 3.14 lists the precedence and associativity of the operators introduced to this point. The operators are shown top to bottom in decreasing order of precedence. The second column indicates the associativity of the operators at each level of precedence. Notice that the conditional operator (?:), the unary operators increment (++), decrement (--), plus (+), minus (-) and casts, and the assignment operators =, +=, -=, *=, /= and %= associate from right to left. The third column names the various groups of operators. All other operators in Fig. 3.14 associate from left to right.

Operators	Associativity	Type
++ *(postfix)* -- *(postfix)*	right to left	postfix
+ - *(type)* ++ *(prefix)* -- *(prefix)*	right to left	unary
* / %	left to right	multiplicative
+ -	left to right	additive
< <= > >=	left to right	relational
== !=	left to right	equality
?:	right to left	conditional
= += -= *= /= %=	right to left	assignment

Fig. 3.14 | Precedence and associativity of the operators encountered so far in the text.

3.13 Secure C Programming

Arithmetic Overflow

Figure 2.5 presented an addition program which calculated the sum of two int values (line 18) with the statement

```
sum = integer1 + integer2; // assign total to sum
```

Even this simple statement has a potential problem—adding the integers could result in a value that's *too large* to store in an int variable. This is known as **arithmetic overflow** and can cause undefined behavior, possibly leaving a system open to attack.

The platform-specific maximum and minimum values that can be stored in an int variable are represented by the constants INT_MAX and INT_MIN, respectively, which are defined in the header <limits.h>. There are similar constants for the other integral types that we'll be introducing in Chapter 4. You can see your platform's values for these constants by opening the header <limits.h> in a text editor.

It's considered a good practice to ensure that *before* you perform arithmetic calculations like the one in line 18 of Fig. 2.5, they will *not* overflow. The code for doing this is shown on the CERT website www.securecoding.cert.org—just search for guideline "INT32-C." The code uses the && (logical AND) and || (logical OR) operators, which we discuss in Chapter 4. In industrial-strength code, you should perform checks like these for *all* calculations. Later chapters show other programming techniques for handling such errors.

Unsigned Integers

In Fig. 3.6, line 8 declared as an unsigned int the variable counter because it's used to count *only non-negative values*. In general, counters that should store only non-negative values should be declared with unsigned before the integer type. Variables of unsigned types can represent values from 0 to approximately twice the positive range of the corresponding signed integer types. You can determine your platform's maximum unsigned int value with the constant UINT_MAX from <limits.h>.

The class-averaging program in Fig. 3.6 could have declared as unsigned int the variables grade, total and average. Grades are normally values from 0 to 100, so the total and average should each be greater than or equal to 0. We declared those variables as ints because we can't control what the user actually enters—the user could enter *negative* values. Worse yet, the user could enter a value that's not even a number. (We'll show how to deal with such inputs later in the book.)

Sometimes sentinel-controlled loops use invalid values to terminate a loop. For example, the class-averaging program of Fig. 3.8 terminates the loop when the user enters the sentinel -1 (an invalid grade), so it would be improper to declare variable grade as an unsigned int. As you'll see, the end-of-file (EOF) indicator—which is introduced in the next chapter and is often used to terminate sentinel-controlled loops—is also a negative number. For more information, see Chapter 5, "Integer Security," of Robert Seacord's book *Secure Coding in C and C++*, 2/e.

scanf_s and printf_s

The C11 standard's Annex K introduces more secure versions of printf and scanf called printf_s and scanf_s—we discuss these functions and the corresponding security issues Sections 6.13 and 7.13. Annex K is designated as *optional*, so not every C vendor will implement it. Microsoft implemented its own versions of printf_s and scanf_s prior to the publication of the C11 standard, and its compiler immediately began issuing warnings for every scanf call. The warnings say that scanf is *deprecated*—it should no longer be used—and that you should consider using scanf_s instead.

Many organizations have coding standards that require code to compile *without warning messages*. There are two ways to eliminate Visual C++'s scanf warnings—you can use scanf_s instead of scanf or you can disable these warnings. For the input statements we've used so far, Visual C++ users can simply replace scanf with scanf_s. You can disable the warning messages in Visual C++ as follows:

1. Type *Alt F7* to display the **Property Pages** dialog for your project.

2. In the left column, expand **Configuration Properties > C/C++** and select **Preprocessor**.

3. In the right column, at the end of the value for **Preprocessor Definitions**, insert

```
;_CRT_SECURE_NO_WARNINGS
```

4. Click **OK** to save the changes.

You'll no longer receive warnings on scanf (or any other functions that Microsoft has deprecated for similar reasons). For industrial-strength coding, disabling the warnings is discouraged. We'll say more about how to use scanf_s and printf_s in a later Secure C Coding Guidelines section.

Summary

Section 3.1 Introduction
- Before writing a program to solve a particular problem, you must have a thorough understanding of the problem and a carefully planned approach to solving the problem.

Section 3.2 Algorithms
- The solution to any computing problem involves executing a series of **actions** in a specific **order** (p. 70).
- A **procedure** (p. 70) for solving a problem in terms of the actions (p. 70) to be executed, and the order in which these actions are to be executed, is called an **algorithm** (p. 70).
- The order in which actions are to be executed is important.

Section 3.3 Pseudocode
- **Pseudocode** (p. 70) is an artificial and informal language that helps you develop algorithms.
- Pseudocode is similar to everyday English; it's not an actual computer programming language.
- Pseudocode programs help you "think out" a program.
- Pseudocode consists purely of characters; you may type pseudocode using a text editor.
- Carefully prepared pseudocode programs may be converted easily to corresponding C programs.
- Pseudocode consists only of action statements.

Section 3.4 Control Structures
- Normally, statements in a program execute one after the other in the order in which they're written. This is called **sequential execution** (p. 71).
- Various C statements enable you to specify that the next statement to execute may be other than the next one in sequence. This is called **transfer of control** (p. 71).
- **Structured programming** has become almost synonymous with "**goto elimination**" (p. 71).
- Structured programs are clearer, easier to debug and modify and more likely to be bug free.
- All programs can be written in terms of **sequence, selection** and **iteration control structures** (p. 71).
- Unless directed otherwise, the computer automatically executes C statements in sequence.
- A **flowchart** (p. 72) is a graphical representation of an algorithm. Flowcharts are drawn using **rectangles, diamonds, rounded rectangles** and **small circles**, connected by arrows called **flowlines** (p. 72).
- The **rectangle (action) symbol** (p. 72) indicates any type of action including a calculation or an input/output operation.
- **Flowlines** indicate the order in which the actions are performed.
- When drawing a flowchart that represents a complete algorithm, we use as the first symbol a rounded rectangle containing the word "Begin." We use as the last symbol a rounded rectangle

containing the word "End." When drawing only a portion of an algorithm, we omit the rounded rectangle symbols in favor of using small circle symbols, also called connector symbols (p. 72).

- The **diamond (decision) symbol** (p. 72) indicates that a decision is to be made.
- The **if single-selection statement** selects or ignores a single action.
- The **if...else double-selection statement** (p. 72) selects between two different actions.
- The **switch multiple-selection statement** (p. 72) selects among many different actions based on the value of an expression.
- C provides three types of **iteration statements** (also called repetition statements), namely **while**, **do...while** and **for**.
- Control-statement flowchart segments can be attached to one another with control-statement **stacking** (p. 73)—connecting the exit point of one control statement to the entry point of the next.
- There's only one other way control statements may be connected—control-statement **nesting**.

Section 3.5 The **if** Selection Statement
- Selection structures are used to choose among alternative courses of action.
- The **decision symbol** contains an expression, such as a condition, that can be either true or false. The decision symbol has two flowlines emerging from it. One indicates the direction to be taken when the expression is true; the other indicates the direction when the expression is false.
- A decision can be based on any expression—if the expression evaluates to zero, it's treated as **false**, and if it evaluates to nonzero, it's treated as **true**.
- The **if** statement is a **single-entry/single-exit structure** (p. 73).

Section 3.6 The **if...else** Selection Statement
- C provides the **conditional operator** (**?:**, p. 75) which is closely related to the **if...else** statement.
- The conditional operator is C's only **ternary operator**—it takes three operands. The first operand is a condition. The second operand is the value for the conditional expression (p. 75) if the condition is true, and the third operand is the value for the conditional expression if the condition is false.
- **Nested if...else statements** (p. 76) test for multiple cases by placing **if...else** statements inside **if...else** statements.
- The **if** selection statement expects only one statement in its body. To include several statements in the body of an **if**, you must enclose the set of statements in **braces** ({ and }).
- A set of statements contained within a pair of braces is called a **compound statement** or a **block** (p. 77).
- A **syntax error** is caught by the compiler. A **logic error** has its effect at **execution time**. A **fatal logic error** causes a program to fail and terminate prematurely. A **nonfatal logic error** allows a program to continue executing but to produce incorrect results.

Section 3.7 The **while** Iteration Statement
- The **while iteration statement** (p. 78) specifies that an action is to be repeated while a condition is true. Eventually, the condition will become false. At this point, the iteration terminates, and the first statement after the iteration statement executes.

Section 3.8 Formulating Algorithms Case Study 1: Counter-Controlled Iteration
- **Counter-controlled iteration** (p. 80) uses a variable called a counter (p. 80) to specify the number of times a set of statements should execute.
- Counter-controlled iteration is often called **definite iteration** (p. 80) because the number of iterations is known before the loop begins executing.

- A **total** is a variable used to accumulate the sum of a series of values. Variables used to store totals should normally be initialized to zero before being used in a program; otherwise the sum would include the previous value stored in the total's memory location.

- A **counter** is a variable used to count. Counter variables are normally initialized to zero or one, depending on their use.

- An **uninitialized variable** contains a "**garbage**" value (p. 81)—the value last stored in the memory location reserved for that variable.

Section 3.9 Formulating Algorithms with Top-Down, Stepwise Refinement Case Study 2: Sentinel-Controlled Iteration

- A **sentinel value** (p. 82; also called a **signal value**, a **dummy value**, or a **flag value**) is used in a sentinel-controlled loop to indicate the "**end of data entry.**"

- **Sentinel-controlled iteration** is often called **indefinite iteration** (p. 82) because the number of iterations is not known before the loop begins executing.

- The sentinel value must be chosen so that it cannot be confused with an acceptable input value.

- In **top-down, stepwise refinement** (p. 82), the **top** is a statement that conveys the program's overall function. It's a complete representation of a program. In the **refinement process**, we divide the top into smaller tasks and list these in execution order.

- The type **float** (p. 85) represents numbers with decimal points (called **floating-point numbers**).

- When two integers are divided, any fractional part of the result is **truncated** (p. 86).

- To produce a floating-point calculation with integer values, you must **cast** the integers to floating-point numbers. C provides the **unary cast operator** (float) to accomplish this task.

- **Cast operators** (p. 86) perform **explicit conversions**.

- Most computers can evaluate arithmetic expressions only in which the operands' data types are identical. To ensure this, the compiler performs an operation called **implicit conversion** (p. 87) on selected operands.

- A cast operator is formed by placing parentheses around a type name. The cast operator is a **unary operator**—it takes only one operand.

- **Cast operators associate from right to left** and have the same precedence as other unary operators such as unary + and unary -. This precedence is one level higher than that of *, / and %.

- The **printf** conversion specifier %.2f specifies that a floating-point value will be displayed with two digits to the right of the decimal point. If the %f conversion specifier is used (without specifying the precision), the default precision (p. 87) of 6 is used.

- When floating-point values are printed with precision, the printed value is rounded (p. 87) to the indicated number of decimal positions for display purposes.

Section 3.11 Assignment Operators

- C provides several assignment operators for **abbreviating assignment expressions** (p. 92).

- The += operator adds the value of the expression on the right of the operator to the value of the variable on the left of the operator and stores the result in the variable on the left of the operator.

- Any statement of the form

    variable = *variable operator expression*;

  where *operator* is one of the binary operators +, -, *, / or % (or others we'll discuss in Chapter 10), can be written in the form

    variable operator= *expression*;

Section 3.12 Increment and Decrement Operators

- C provides the **unary increment operator**, ++ (p. 93), and the **unary decrement operator**, -- (p. 93), for use with integral types.

- If increment or decrement operators are placed before a variable, they're referred to as the **preincrement** or **predecrement operators**, respectively. If increment or decrement operators are placed after a variable, they're referred to as the **postincrement** or **postdecrement operators**, respectively.

- Preincrementing (predecrementing) a variable causes it to be incremented (decremented) by 1, then the new value of the variable is used in the expression in which it appears.

- Postincrementing (postdecrementing) a variable uses the current value of the variable in the expression in which it appears, then the variable value is incremented (decremented) by 1.

- When incrementing or decrementing a variable in a statement by itself, the preincrement and postincrement forms have the same effect. When a variable appears in the context of a larger expression, preincrementing and postincrementing have different effects (and similarly for predecrementing and postdecrementing).

Section 3.13 Secure C Programming

- Adding integers can result in a value that's too large to store in an int variable. This is known as **arithmetic overflow** and can cause unpredictable runtime behavior, possibly leaving a system open to attack.

- The maximum and minimum values that can be stored in an int variable are represented by the constants `INT_MAX` and `INT_MIN`, respectively, from the **header <limits.h>**.

- It's considered a good practice to ensure that arithmetic calculations will not overflow before you perform the calculation. In industrial-strength code, you should perform checks for all calculations that can result in overflow or underflow (p. 95).

- In general, any integer variable that should store only non-negative values should be declared with **unsigned** before the integer type. Variables of unsigned types can represent values from 0 to approximately double the positive range of the corresponding signed integer type.

- You can determine your platform's maximum unsigned int value with the constant `UINT_MAX` from <limits.h>.

- The C11 standard's **Annex K** introduces **more secure versions of printf and scanf** called printf_s and scanf_s. Annex K is designated as optional, so not every C compiler vendor will implement it.

- Microsoft implemented its own versions of printf_s and scanf_s prior to the C11 standard's publication and immediately began issuing warnings for every scanf call. The warnings say that scanf is deprecated—it should no longer be used—and that you should consider using scanf_s instead.

- Many organizations have coding standards that require code to compile without warning messages. There are two ways to eliminate Visual C++'s scanf warnings. You can either start using scanf_s immediately or disable this warning message.

Self-Review Exercises

3.1 Fill in the blanks in each of the following questions.
    a) A procedure for solving a problem in terms of the actions to be executed and the order in which the actions should be executed is called a(n) _____.
    b) Specifying the execution order of statements by the computer is called _____.
    c) All programs can be written in terms of three types of control statements: _____, _____ and _____.

    d) The _____ selection statement is used to execute one action when a condition is true and another action when that condition is false.

    e) Several statements grouped together in braces ({ and }) are called a(n) _____.

    f) The _____ iteration statement specifies that a statement or group of statements is to be executed repeatedly while some condition remains true.

    g) Iteration of a set of instructions a specific number of times is called _____ iteration.

    h) When it's not known in advance how many times a set of statements will be repeated, a(n) _____ value can be used to terminate the iteration.

3.2 Write four different C statements that each add 1 to integer variable x.

3.3 Write a single C statement to accomplish each of the following:

    a) Multiply the variable product by 2 using the *= operator.

    b) Multiply the variable product by 2 using the = and * operators.

    c) Test whether the value of the variable count is greater than 10. If it is, print "Count is greater than 10."

    d) Calculate the remainder after q is divided by divisor and assign the result to q. Write this statement two different ways.

    e) Print the value 123.4567 with two digits of precision. What value is printed?

    f) Print the floating-point value 3.14159 with three digits to the right of the decimal point. What value is printed?

3.4 Write a C statement to accomplish each of the following tasks.

    a) Define variables sum and x to be of type int.

    b) Set variable x to 1.

    c) Set variable sum to 0.

    d) Add variable x to variable sum and assign the result to variable sum.

    e) Print "The sum is: " followed by the value of variable sum.

3.5 Combine the statements that you wrote in Exercise 3.4 into a program that calculates the sum of the integers from 1 to 10. Use the while statement to loop through the calculation and increment statements. The loop should terminate when the value of x becomes 11.

3.6 Write single C statements that

    a) Input unsigned integer variable x with scanf. Use the conversion specifier %u.

    b) Input unsigned integer variable y with scanf. Use the conversion specifier %u.

    c) Set unsigned integer variable i to 1.

    d) Set unsigned integer variable power to 1.

    e) Multiply unsigned integer variable power by x and assign the result to power.

    f) Increment variable i by 1.

    g) Test i to see if it's less than or equal to y in the condition of a while statement.

    h) Output unsigned integer variable power with printf. Use the conversion specifier %u.

3.7 Write a C program that uses the statements in Exercise 3.6 to calculate x raised to the y power. The program should have a while iteration control statement.

3.8 Identify and correct the errors in each of the following:

    a)
```
while ( c <= 5 ) {
    product *= c;
    ++c;
```

    b)
```
scanf( "%.4f", &value );
```

    c)
```
if ( gender == 1 )
    puts( "Woman" );
else;
    puts( "Man" );
```

3.9   What's wrong with the following while iteration statement (assume z has value 100), which is supposed to calculate the sum of the integers from 100 down to 1?

```
while ( z >= 0 )
    sum += z;
```

Answers to Self-Review Exercises

3.1   a) Algorithm. b) Program control. c) Sequence, selection, iteration. d) if...else. e) Compound statement or block. f) while. g) Counter-controlled or definite. h) Sentinel.

3.2
```
x = x + 1;
x += 1;
++x;
x++;
```

3.3
```
a)  product *= 2;
b)  product = product * 2;
c)  if ( count > 10 )
        puts( "Count is greater than 10." );
d)  q %= divisor;
    q = q % divisor;
e)  printf( "%.2f", 123.4567 );
```
123.46 is displayed.
```
f)  printf( "%.3f\n", 3.14159 );
```
3.142 is displayed.

3.4
```
a)  int sum, x;
b)  x = 1;
c)  sum = 0;
d)  sum += x; or sum = sum + x;
e)  printf( "The sum is: %d\n", sum );
```

3.5   See below.

```
1   // Calculate the sum of the integers from 1 to 10
2   #include <stdio.h>
3
4   int main( void )
5   {
6      unsigned int x = 1; // set x
7      unsigned int sum = 0; // set sum
8
9      while ( x <= 10 ) { // loop while x is less than or equal to 10
10        sum += x; // add x to sum
11        ++x; // increment x
12     } // end while
13
14     printf( "The sum is: %u\n", sum ); // display sum
15  } // end main function
```

3.6
```
a)  scanf( "%u", &x );
b)  scanf( "%u", &y );
c)  i = 1;
d)  power = 1;
e)  power *= x;
f)  ++i;
```

g) while (i <= y)
h) printf("%d", power);

3.7   See below.

```
 1    // raise x to the y power
 2    #include <stdio.h>
 3
 4    int main( void )
 5    {
 6       printf( "%s", "Enter first integer: " );
 7       unsigned int x;
 8       scanf( "%u", &x ); // read value for x from user
 9       printf( "%s", "Enter second integer: " );
10       unsigned int y;
11       scanf( "%u", &y ); // read value for y from user
12
13       unsigned int i = 1;
14       unsigned int power = 1; // set power
15
16       while ( i <= y ) { // loop while i is less than or equal to y
17          power *= x; // multiply power by x
18          ++i; // increment i
19       } // end while
20
21       printf( "%u\n", power ); // display power
22    } // end main function
```

3.8   a) Error: Missing the closing right brace of the while body.
Correction: Add closing right brace after the statement ++c;.
b) Error: Precision used in a scanf conversion specification.
Correction: Remove .4 from the conversion specification.
c) Error: Semicolon after the else part of the if...else statement results in a logic error.
The second puts will always be executed.
Correction: Remove the semicolon after else.

3.9   The value of the variable z is never changed in the while statement. Therefore, an infinite loop is created. To prevent the infinite loop, z must be decremented so that it eventually becomes 0.

Exercises

3.10   Identify and correct the errors in each of the following. [*Note:* There may be more than one error in each piece of code.]
a) if (age >= 65);
        puts("Age is greater than or equal to 65");
    else
        puts("Age is less than 65");
b) int x = 1, total;

    while (x <= 10) {
       total += x;
       ++x;
    }
c) While (x <= 100)
       total += x;
       ++x;

d) `while ( y > 0 ) {`
   `printf( "%d\n", y );`
   `++y;`
   `}`

3.11   Fill in the blanks in each of the following:
   a) The solution to any problem involves performing a series of actions in a specific _____.
   b) A synonym for procedure is _____.
   c) A variable that accumulates the sum of several numbers is a(n) _____.
   d) A special value used to indicate "end of data entry" is called a(n) _____, a(n) _____, a(n) _____ or a(n) _____ value.
   e) A(n) _____ is a graphical representation of an algorithm.
   f) In a flowchart, the order in which the steps should be performed is indicated by _____ symbols.
   g) Rectangle symbols correspond to calculations that are normally performed by statements and input/output operations that are normally performed by calls to the _____ and _____ Standard Library functions.
   h) The item written inside a decision symbol is called a(n) _____.

3.12   What does the following program print?

```
 1   #include <stdio.h>
 2
 3   int main( void )
 4   {
 5      unsigned int x = 1;
 6      unsigned int total = 0;
 7      unsigned int y;
 8
 9      while ( x <= 10 ) {
10         y = x * x;
11         printf( "%d\n", y );
12         total += y;
13         ++x;
14      } // end while
15
16      printf( "Total is %d\n", total );
17   } // end main
```

3.13   Write a single pseudocode statement that indicates each of the following:
   a) Display the message `"Enter two numbers"`.
   b) Assign the sum of variables x, y, and z to variable p.
   c) The following condition is to be tested in an `if...else` selection statement: The current value of variable m is greater than twice the current value of variable v.
   d) Obtain values for variables s, r, and t from the keyboard.

3.14   Formulate a pseudocode algorithm for each of the following:
   a) Obtain two numbers from the keyboard, compute their sum and display the result.
   b) Obtain two numbers from the keyboard, and determine and display which (if either) is the larger of the two numbers.
   c) Obtain a series of positive numbers from the keyboard, and determine and display their sum. Assume that the user types the sentinel value -1 to indicate "end of data entry."

3.15   State which of the following are *true* and which are *false*. If a statement is *false*, explain why.
   a) Experience has shown that the most difficult part of solving a problem on a computer is producing a working C program.
   b) A sentinel value must be a value that cannot be confused with a legitimate data value.
   c) Flowlines indicate the actions to be performed.
   d) Conditions written inside decision symbols always contain arithmetic operators (i.e., +, -, *, /, and %).
   e) In top-down, stepwise refinement, each refinement is a complete representation of the algorithm.

For Exercises 3.16–3.20, perform each of these steps:

   1. Read the problem statement.

   2. Formulate the algorithm using pseudocode and top-down, stepwise refinement.

   3. Write a C program.

   4. Test, debug and execute the C program.

3.16   *(Gas Mileage)* Drivers are concerned with the mileage obtained by their automobiles. One driver has kept track of several tankfuls of gasoline by recording miles driven and gallons used for each tankful. Develop a program that will input the miles driven and gallons used for each tankful. The program should calculate and display the miles per gallon obtained for each tankful. After processing all input information, the program should calculate and print the combined miles per gallon obtained for all tankfuls. Here is a sample input/output dialog:

```
Enter the gallons used (-1 to end): 12.8
Enter the miles driven: 287
The miles/gallon for this tank was 22,421875

Enter the gallons used (-1 to end): 10.3
Enter the miles driven: 200
The miles/gallon for this tank was 19.417475

Enter the gallons used (-1 to end): 5
Enter the miles driven: 120
The miles/gallon for this tank was 24.000000

Enter the gallons used (-1 to end): -1

The overall average miles/gallon was 21.601423
```

3.17   *(Credit-Limit Calculator)* Develop a C program that will determine whether a department store customer has exceeded the credit limit on a charge account. For each customer, the following facts are available:
   a) Account number
   b) Balance at the beginning of the month
   c) Total of all items charged by this customer this month
   d) Total of all credits applied to this customer's account this month
   e) Allowed credit limit

The program should input each fact, calculate the new balance (= *beginning balance* + *charges – credits*), and determine whether the new balance exceeds the customer's credit limit. For those customers whose credit limit is exceeded, the program should display the customer's account number, credit limit, new balance and the message "Credit limit exceeded." Here is a sample input/output dialog:

```
Enter account number (-1 to end): 100
Enter beginning balance: 5394.78
Enter total charges: 1000.00
Enter total credits: 500.00
Enter credit limit: 5500.00
Account:      100
Credit limit: 5500.00
Balance:      5894.78
Credit Limit Exceeded.

Enter account number (-1 to end): 200
Enter beginning balance: 1000.00
Enter total charges: 123.45
Enter total credits: 321.00
Enter credit limit: 1500.00

Enter account number (-1 to end): 300
Enter beginning balance: 500.00
Enter total charges: 274.73
Enter total credits: 100.00
Enter credit limit: 800.00

Enter account number (-1 to end): -1
```

3.18 *(Sales-Commission Calculator)* One large chemical company pays its salespeople on a commission basis. The salespeople receive $200 per week plus 9% of their gross sales for that week. For example, a salesperson who sells $5000 worth of chemicals in a week receives $200 plus 9% of $5000, or a total of $650. Develop a program that will input each salesperson's gross sales for last week and will calculate and display that salesperson's earnings. Process one salesperson's figures at a time. Here is a sample input/output dialog:

```
Enter sales in dollars (-1 to end): 5000.00
Salary is: $650.00

Enter sales in dollars (-1 to end): 1234.56
Salary is: $311.11

Enter sales in dollars (-1 to end): -1
```

3.19 *(Interest Calculator)* The simple interest on a loan is calculated by the formula

```
interest = principal * rate * days / 365;
```

The preceding formula assumes that rate is the annual interest rate, and therefore includes the division by 365 (days). Develop a program that will input principal, rate and days for several loans, and will calculate and display the simple interest for each loan, using the preceding formula. Here is a sample input/output dialog:

```
Enter loan principal (-1 to end): 1000.00
Enter interest rate: .1
Enter term of the loan in days: 365
The interest charge is $100.00

Enter loan principal (-1 to end): 1000.00
Enter interest rate: .08375
Enter term of the loan in days: 224
The interest charge is $51.40

Enter loan principal (-1 to end): -1
```

3.20 *(Salary Calculator)* Develop a program that will determine the gross pay for each of several employees. The company pays "straight time" for the first 40 hours worked by each employee and pays "time-and-a-half" for all hours worked in excess of 40 hours. You're given a list of the employees of the company, the number of hours each employee worked last week and the hourly rate of each employee. Your program should input this information for each employee and should determine and display the employee's gross pay. Here is a sample input/output dialog:

```
Enter # of hours worked (-1 to end): 39
Enter hourly rate of the worker ($00.00): 10.00
Salary is $390.00

Enter # of hours worked (-1 to end): 40
Enter hourly rate of the worker ($00.00): 10.00
Salary is $400.00

Enter # of hours worked (-1 to end): 41
Enter hourly rate of the worker ($00.00): 10.00
Salary is $415.00

Enter # of hours worked (-1 to end): -1
```

3.21 *(Predecrementing vs. Postdecrementing)* Write a program that demonstrates the difference between predecrementing and postdecrementing using the decrement operator --.

3.22 *(Printing Numbers from a Loop)* Write a program that utilizes looping to print the numbers from 1 to 10 side by side on the same line with three spaces between numbers.

3.23 *(Find the Largest Number)* The process of finding the largest number (i.e., the maximum of a group of numbers) is used frequently in computer applications. For example, a program that determines the winner of a sales contest would input the number of units sold by each salesperson. The salesperson who sells the most units wins the contest. Write a pseudocode program and then a program that inputs a series of 10 non-negative numbers and determines and prints the largest of the numbers. [*Hint:* Your program should use three variables as shown below.]

counter:	A counter to count to 10 (i.e., to keep track of how many numbers have been input and to determine when all 10 numbers have been processed)
number:	The current number input to the program
largest:	The largest number found so far

3.24 *(Tabular Output)* Write a program that uses looping to print the following table of values. Use the tab escape sequence, \t, in the printf statement to separate the columns with tabs.

N	10*N	100*N	1000*N
1	10	100	1000
2	20	200	2000
3	30	300	3000
4	40	400	4000
5	50	500	5000
6	60	600	6000
7	70	700	7000
8	80	800	8000
9	90	900	9000
10	100	1000	10000

3.25   *(Tabular Output)* Write a program that utilizes looping to produce the following table of values:

A	A+2	A+4	A+6
3	5	7	9
6	8	10	12
9	11	13	15
12	14	16	18
15	17	19	21

3.26   *(Find the Two Largest Numbers)* Using an approach similar to Exercise 3.23, find the *two* largest values of the 10 numbers. [*Note:* You may input each number only *once.*]

3.27   *(Validating User Input)* Modify the program in Figure 3.10 to validate its inputs. On any input, if the value entered is other than 1 or 2, keep looping until the user enters a correct value.

3.28   What does the following program print?

```
1   #include <stdio.h>
2
3   int main( void )
4   {
5      unsigned int count = 1; // initialize count
6
7      while ( count <= 10 ) { // loop 10 times
8
9         // output line of text
10        puts( count % 2 ? "****" : "++++++++" );
11        ++count; // increment count
12     } // end while
13  } // end function main
```

3.29   What does the following program print?

```
1   #include <stdio.h>
2
3   int main( void )
4   {
5      unsigned int row = 10; // initialize row
6
7      while ( row >= 1 ) { // loop until row < 1
8         unsigned int column = 1; // set column to 1 as iteration begins
9
10        while ( column <= 10 ) { // loop 10 times
11           printf( "%s", row % 2 ? "<": ">" ); // output
12           ++column; // increment column
13        } // end inner while
14
15        --row; // decrement row
16        puts( "" ); // begin new output line
17     } // end outer while
18  } // end function main
```

3.30   *(Dangling-Else Problem)* Determine the output for each of the following when x is 9 and y is 11, and when x is 11 and y is 9. The compiler ignores the indentation in a C program. Also, the compiler always associates an else with the previous if unless told to do otherwise by the placement of braces {}. Because, on first glance, you may not be sure which if an else matches, this is referred to as the "dangling else" problem. We eliminated the indentation from the following code to make the problem more challenging. [*Hint:* Apply indentation conventions you have learned.]

a)
```
if ( x < 10 )
if ( y > 10 )
puts( "*****" );
else
puts( "#####" );
puts( "$$$$$" );
```

b)
```
if ( x < 10 ) {
if ( y > 10 )
puts( "*****" );
}
else {
puts( "#####" );
puts( "$$$$$" );
}
```

3.31   *(Another Dangling-Else Problem)* Modify the following code to produce the output shown. Use proper indentation techniques. You may not make any changes other than inserting braces. The compiler ignores the indentation in a program. We eliminated the indentation from the following code to make the problem more challenging. [*Note:* It's possible that no modification is necessary.]

```
if ( y == 8 )
if ( x == 5 )
puts( "@@@@@" );
else
puts( "#####" );
puts( "$$$$$" );
puts( "&&&&&" );
```

a)   Assuming x = 5 and y = 8, the following output is produced.

```
@@@@@
$$$$$
&&&&&
```

b)   Assuming x = 5 and y = 8, the following output is produced.

```
@@@@@
```

c)   Assuming x = 5 and y = 8, the following output is produced.

```
@@@@@
&&&&&
```

d)   Assuming x = 5 and y = 7, the following output is produced.

```
#####
$$$$$
&&&&&
```

3.32 *(Square of Asterisks)* Write a program that reads in the side of a square and then prints that square out of asterisks. Your program should work for squares of all side sizes between 1 and 20. For example, if your program reads a size of 4, it should print

```
****
****
****
****
```

3.33 *(Hollow Square of Asterisks)* Modify the program you wrote in Exercise 3.32 so that it prints a hollow square. For example, if your program reads a size of 5, it should print

```
*****
*   *
*   *
*   *
*****
```

3.34 *(Palindrome Tester)* A palindrome is a number or a text phrase that reads the same backward as forward. For example, each of the following five-digit integers is a palindrome: 12321, 55555, 45554 and 11611. Write a program that reads in a five-digit integer and determines whether or not it's a palindrome. [*Hint*: Use the division and remainder operators to separate the number into its individual digits.]

3.35 *(Printing the Decimal Equivalent of a Binary Number)* Input an integer (5 digits or fewer) containing only 0s and 1s (i.e., a "binary" integer) and print its decimal equivalent. [*Hint*: Use the remainder and division operators to pick off the "binary" number's digits one at a time from right to left. Just as in the decimal number system, in which the rightmost digit has a positional value of 1, and the next digit left has a positional value of 10, then 100, then 1000, and so on, in the binary number system the rightmost digit has a positional value of 1, the next digit left has a positional value of 2, then 4, then 8, and so on. Thus the decimal number 234 can be interpreted as 4 * 1 + 3 * 10 + 2 * 100. The decimal equivalent of binary 1101 is 1 * 1 + 0 * 2 + 1 * 4 + 1 * 8 or 1 + 0 + 4 + 8 or 13.]

3.36 *(How Fast Is Your Computer?)* How can you determine how fast your own computer really operates? Write a program with a `while` loop that counts from 1 to 1,000,000,000 by 1s. Every time the count reaches a multiple of 100,000,000, print that number on the screen. Use your watch to time how long each 100 million iterations of the loop takes.

3.37 *(Detecting Multiples of 10)* Write a program that prints 100 asterisks, one at a time. After every tenth asterisk, your program should print a newline character. [*Hint*: Count from 1 to 100. Use the remainder operator to recognize each time the counter reaches a multiple of 10.]

3.38 *(Counting 7s)* Write a program that reads an integer (5 digits or fewer) and determines and prints how many digits in the integer are 7s.

3.39 *(Checkerboard Pattern of Asterisks)* Write a program that displays the following checkerboard pattern:

```
* * * * * * * *
 * * * * * * * *
* * * * * * * *
 * * * * * * * *
* * * * * * * *
 * * * * * * * *
* * * * * * * *
 * * * * * * * *
```

Your program must use only three output statements, one of each of the following forms:

```
printf( "%s", "* " );
printf( "%s", " " );
puts( "" ); // outputs a newline
```

3.40   *(Multiples of 2 with an Infinite Loop)* Write a program that keeps printing the multiples of the integer 2, namely 2, 4, 8, 16, 32, 64, and so on. Your loop should not terminate (i.e., you should create an infinite loop). What happens when you run this program?

3.41   *(Diameter, Circumference and Area of a Cirle)* Write a program that reads the radius of a circle (as a `float` value) and computes and prints the diameter, the circumference and the area. Use the value 3.14159 for π.

3.42   What's wrong with the following statement? Rewrite it to accomplish what the programmer was probably trying to do.

```
printf( "%d", ++( x + y ) );
```

3.43   *(Sides of a Triangle)* Write a program that reads three nonzero integer values and determines and prints whether they could represent the sides of a triangle.

3.44   *(Sides of a Right Triangle)* Write a program that reads three nonzero integers and determines and prints whether they could be the sides of a right triangle.

3.45   *(Factorial)* The factorial of a nonnegative integer n is written $n!$ (pronounced "n factorial") and is defined as follows:

$n! = n \cdot (n - 1) \cdot (n - 2) \cdot \ldots \cdot 1$ (for values of n greater than or equal to 1)

and

$n! = 1$ (for $n = 0$).

For example, $5! = 5 \cdot 4 \cdot 3 \cdot 2 \cdot 1$, which is 120.

a) Write a program that reads a nonnegative integer and computes and prints its factorial.
b) Write a program that estimates the value of the mathematical constant e by using the formula:

$$e = 1 + \frac{1}{1!} + \frac{1}{2!} + \frac{1}{3!} + \cdots$$

c) Write a program that computes the value of e^x by using the formula

$$e^x = 1 + \frac{x}{1!} + \frac{x^2}{2!} + \frac{x^3}{3!} + \cdots$$

Making a Difference

3.46   *(World-Population-Growth Calculator)* Use the web to determine the current world population and the annual world population growth rate. Write an application that inputs these values, then displays the estimated world population after one, two, three, four and five years.

3.47   *(Target-Heart-Rate Calculator)* While exercising, you can use a heart-rate monitor to see that your heart rate stays within a safe range suggested by your trainers and doctors. According to the American Heart Association (AHA), the formula for calculating your *maximum heart rate* in beats per minute is 220 minus your age in years. Your *target heart rate* is a range that's 50–85% of your maximum heart rate. [*Note:* These formulas are estimates provided by the AHA. Maximum and target heart rates may vary based on the health, fitness and gender of the individual. *Always consult a physician or qualified health-care professional before beginning or modifying an exercise program.*] Create a program that reads the user's birthday and the current day (each consisting of the month, day and year). Your program should calculate and display the person's age (in years), the person's maximum heart rate and the person's target-heart-rate range.

3.48   *(Enforcing Privacy with Cryptography)* The explosive growth of Internet communications and data storage on Internet-connected computers has greatly increased privacy concerns. The field of cryptography is concerned with coding data to make it difficult (and hopefully—with the most advanced schemes—impossible) for unauthorized users to read. In this exercise you'll investigate a simple scheme for *encrypting* and *decrypting* data. A company that wants to send data over the Internet has asked you to write a program that will encrypt it so that it may be transmitted more securely. All the data is transmitted as four-digit integers. Your application should read a four-digit integer entered by the user and *encrypt* it as follows: Replace each digit with the result of adding 7 to the digit and getting the remainder after dividing the new value by 10. Then swap the first digit with the third, and swap the second digit with the fourth. Then print the encrypted integer. Write a separate application that inputs an encrypted four-digit integer and *decrypts* it (by reversing the encryption scheme) to form the original number. [*Optional reading project:* In industrial-strength applications, you'll want to use much stronger encryption techniques than presented in this exercise. Research "public key cryptography" in general and the PGP (Pretty Good Privacy) specific public-key scheme. You may also want to investigate the RSA scheme, which is widely used in industrial-strength applications.]

C Program Control

Objectives

In this chapter, you'll learn:

- The essentials of counter-controlled iteration.

- To use the **for** and **do...while** iteration statements to execute statements repeatedly.

- To understand multiple selection using the **switch** selection statement.

- To use the **break** and **continue** statements to alter the flow of control.

- To use the logical operators to form complex conditional expressions in control statements.

- To avoid the consequences of confusing the equality and assignment operators.

Outline

4.1 Introduction

You should now be comfortable with writing simple, complete C programs. In this chapter, iteration is considered in greater detail, and additional iteration control statements, namely the `for` and the `do...while`, are presented. The `switch` multiple-selection statement is introduced. We discuss the `break` statement for exiting immediately from certain control statements, and the `continue` statement for skipping the remainder of the body of an iteration statement, then proceeding with the next iteration of the loop. The chapter discusses logical operators used for combining conditions, and summarizes the principles of structured programming as presented in Chapter 3 and this chapter.

4.2 Iteration Essentials

Most programs involve iteration, or looping. A loop is a group of instructions the computer executes repeatedly while some **loop-continuation condition** remains true. We've discussed two means of iteration:

1. Counter-controlled iteration
2. Sentinel-controlled iteration

Counter-controlled iteration is sometimes called *definite iteration* because we know *in advance* exactly how many times the loop will be executed. Sentinel-controlled iteration is sometimes called *indefinite iteration* because it's *not known* in advance how many times the loop will be executed.

In counter-controlled iteration, a **control variable** is used to count the number of iterations. The control variable is incremented (usually by 1) each time the group of instructions is performed. When the value of the control variable indicates that the correct number of iterations has been performed, the loop terminates and execution continues with the statement after the iteration statement.

Sentinel values are used to control iteration when:

1. The precise number of iterations isn't known in advance, and
2. The loop includes statements that obtain data each time the loop is performed.

The sentinel value indicates "end of data." The sentinel is entered after all regular data items have been supplied to the program. Sentinels must be distinct from regular data items.

4.3 Counter-Controlled Iteration

Counter-controlled iteration requires:

1. The **name** of a control variable (or loop counter).

2. The **initial value** of the control variable.

3. The **increment** (or **decrement**) by which the control variable is modified each time through the loop.

4. The condition that tests for the **final value** of the control variable (i.e., whether looping should continue).

Consider the simple program shown in Fig. 4.1, which prints the numbers from 1 to 10. The definition

```
unsigned int counter = 1; // initialization
```

names the control variable (counter), defines it to be an integer, reserves memory space for it, and sets its initial value to 1.

```c
1  // Fig. 4.1: fig04_01.c
2  // Counter-controlled iteration.
3  #include <stdio.h>
4
5  int main(void)
6  {
7     unsigned int counter = 1; // initialization
8
9     while (counter <= 10) { // iteration condition
10        printf ("%u\n", counter);
11        ++counter; // increment
12     }
13  }
```

```
1
2
3
4
5
6
7
8
9
10
```

Fig. 4.1 | Counter-controlled iteration.

The definition and initialization of counter also could have been written as

```
unsigned int counter;
counter = 1;
```

The definition is *not* executable, but the assignment *is*. We'll use both methods of setting the values of variables.

The statement

```
++counter; // increment
```

increments the loop counter by 1 each time the loop is performed. The loop-continuation condition in the `while` statement tests whether the value of the control variable is less than or equal to 10 (the last value for which the condition is true). The body of this `while` is performed even when the control variable is 10. The loop terminates when the control variable *exceeds* 10 (i.e., counter becomes 11).

You could make the program in Fig. 4.1 more concise by initializing counter to 0 and by replacing the `while` statement with

```
while (++counter <= 10) {
    printf("%u\n", counter);
}
```

This code saves a statement because the incrementing is done directly in the `while` condition before the condition is tested. Coding in such a condensed fashion takes some practice. Some programmers feel that this makes the code too cryptic and error prone.

Common Programming Error 4.1

Floating-point values may be approximate, so controlling counting loops with floating-point variables may result in imprecise counter values and inaccurate termination tests.

Error-Prevention Tip 4.1

Control counting loops with integer values.

Good Programming Practice 4.1

Too many levels of nesting can make a program difficult to understand. As a rule, try to avoid using more than three levels of nesting.

Good Programming Practice 4.2

The combination of vertical spacing before and after control statements and indentation of the bodies of control statements within the control-statement headers gives programs a two-dimensional appearance that greatly improves program readability.

4.4 for Iteration Statement

The `for` iteration statement handles all the details of counter-controlled iteration. To illustrate its power, let's rewrite the program of Fig. 4.1. The result is shown in Fig. 4.2. The program operates as follows. When the `for` statement begins executing, the control variable counter is defined and initialized to 1. Then, the loop-continuation condition counter <= 10 is checked. Because the initial value of counter is 1, the condition is satisfied, so the `printf` statement (line 10) prints the value of counter, namely 1. The control variable counter is then incremented by the expression ++counter, and the loop begins again with the loop-continuation test. Because the control variable is now equal to 2, the final value is not exceeded, so the program performs the `printf` statement again. This process continues until the control variable counter is incremented to its final value of 11—this causes the loop-continuation test to fail, and iteration terminates. The program continues by performing the first statement after the `for` statement (in this case, the program simply ends).

```
 1   // Fig. 4.2: fig04_02.c
 2   // Counter-controlled iteration with the for statement.
 3   #include <stdio.h>
 4
 5   int main(void)
 6   {
 7      // initialization, iteration condition, and increment
 8      //  are all included in the for statement header.
 9      for (unsigned int counter = 1; counter <= 10; ++counter) {
10         printf("%u\n", counter);
11      }
12   }
```

Fig. 4.2 | Counter-controlled iteration with the for statement.

for Statement Header Components

Figure 4.3 takes a closer look at the for statement of Fig. 4.2. Notice that the for statement "does it all"—it specifies each of the items needed for counter-controlled iteration with a control variable. If there's more than one statement in the body of the for, braces are required to define the body of the loop—as we discussed in Section 3.6, you should always place a control statement's body in braces, even if it has only one statement.

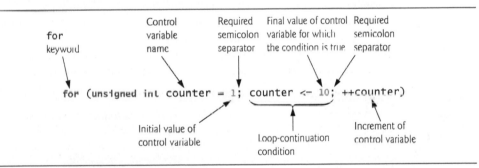

Fig. 4.3 | for statement header components.

Control Variables Defined in a for Header Exist Only Until the Loop Terminates

When you define the control variable in the for header before the first semicolon (;), as in line 9 of Fig. 4.2:

```
    for (unsigned int counter = 1; counter <= 10; ++counter) {
```

the control variable exists only until the loop terminates.

 Common Programming Error 4.2

For a control variable defined in a for statement's header, attempting to access the control variable after the for statement's closing right brace (}) is a compilation error.

Off-By-One Errors

Notice that Fig. 4.2 uses the loop-continuation condition counter <= 10. If you incorrectly wrote counter < 10, then the loop would be executed only 9 times. This is a common logic error called an **off-by-one error**.

Error-Prevention Tip 4.2

Using the final value in the condition of a while *or* for *statement and using the* <= *relational operator can help avoid off-by-one errors. For a loop used to print the values 1 to 10, for example, the loop-continuation condition should be* counter <= 10 *rather than* counter < 11 *or* counter < 10.

General Format of a **for** Statement

The general format of the for statement is

```
for (initialization; condition; increment) {
    statement
}
```

where the *initialization* expression initializes the loop-control variable (and might define it, as we did in Fig. 4.2), the *condition* expression is the loop-continuation condition and the *increment* expression increments the control variable.

Comma-Separated Lists of Expressions

Often, the *initialization* expression and the *increment* expression are comma-separated lists of expressions. The commas as used here are actually **comma operators** which guarantee that lists of expressions evaluate from left to right. The value and type of a comma-separated list of expressions are the value and type of the *rightmost* expression in the list. The comma operator is most often used in the for statement. Its primary use is to enable you to use multiple initialization and/or multiple increment expressions. For example, there may be two control variables in a single for statement that must be initialized and incremented.

Software Engineering Observation 4.1

Place only expressions involving the control variables in the initialization and increment sections of a for *statement. Manipulations of other variables should appear either before the loop (if they execute only once, like initialization statements) or in the loop body (if they execute once per iteration, like incrementing or decrementing statements).*

Expressions in the **for** Statement's Header Are Optional

The three expressions in the for statement are *optional*. If the *condition* expression is omitted, C *assumes* that the loop-continuation condition is *true*, thus creating an *infinite loop*. You may omit the *initialization* expression if the control variable is initialized before the for statement. The *increment* expression may be omitted if the increment is calculated by statements in the for statement's body or if no increment is needed.

Increment Expression Acts Like a Standalone Statement

The *increment* expression in the for statement acts like a standalone C statement at the end of the body of the for. Therefore, the expressions

```
counter = counter + 1
counter += 1
++counter
counter++
```

are all equivalent in the increment part of the for statement. Some C programmers prefer the form counter++ because the incrementing occurs *after* the loop body executes, and the postincrementing form *seems* more natural. Because the variable being preincremented or postincremented here does *not* appear in a larger expression, both forms of incrementing have the *same* effect. The two semicolons in the for statement are required.

Common Programming Error 4.3
Using commas instead of semicolons in a for header is a syntax error.

Error-Prevention Tip 4.3
Infinite loops are caused when the loop-continuation condition in an iteration statement never becomes false. To prevent infinite loops, ensure that you do not place a semicolon immediately after a while statement's header. In a counter-controlled loop, make sure the control variable is incremented (or decremented) in the loop. In a sentinel-controlled loop, make sure the sentinel value is eventually input.

4.5 for Statement: Notes and Observations

1. The initialization, loop-continuation condition and increment can contain arithmetic expressions. For example, if x = 2 and y = 10, the statement

    ```
    for (j = x; j <= 4 * x * y; j += y / x)
    ```

    is equivalent to the statement

    ```
    for (j = 2; j <= 80; j += 5)
    ```

2. The "increment" may be negative (in which case it's really a *decrement* and the loop actually counts *downward*).

3. If the loop-continuation condition is initially *false*, the loop body does *not* execute. Instead, execution proceeds with the statement following the for statement.

4. The control variable is frequently printed or used in calculations in the body of a loop, but it need not be. It's common to use the control variable for controlling iteration while never mentioning it in the body of the loop.

5. The for statement is flowcharted much like the while statement. For example, Fig. 4.4 shows the flowchart of the for statement

    ```
    for (unsigned int counter = 1; counter <= 10; ++counter) {
        printf("%u", counter);
    }
    ```

    This flowchart makes it clear that the initialization occurs only once and that incrementing occurs *after* the body statement each time it's performed.

Error-Prevention Tip 4.4
Although the value of the control variable can be changed in the body of a for loop, this can lead to subtle errors. It's best not to change it.

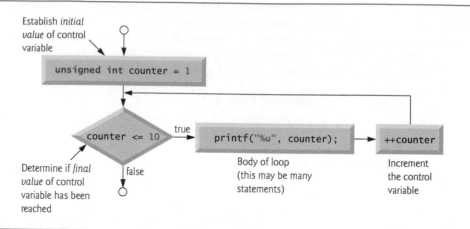

Establish *initial value* of control variable

```
unsigned int counter = 1
```

Determine if *final value* of control variable has been reached

counter <= 10

false

true

```
printf("%u", counter);
```

Body of loop (this may be many statements)

```
++counter
```

Increment the control variable

Fig. 4.4 | Flowcharting a typical for iteration statement.

4.6 Examples Using the for Statement

The following examples show methods of varying the control variable in a for statement.

1. Vary the control variable from 1 to 100 in increments of 1.

```
for (unsigned int i = 1; i <= 100; ++i)
```

2. Vary the control variable from 100 to 1 in increments of -1 (i.e., *decrements* of 1).

```
for (unsigned int i = 100; i >= 1; --i)
```

3. Vary the control variable from 7 to 77 in increments of 7.

```
for (unsigned int i = 7; i <= 77; i += 7)
```

4. Vary the control variable from 20 to 2 in increments of -2.

```
for (unsigned int i = 20; i >= 2; i -= 2)
```

5. Vary the control variable over the following sequence of values: 2, 5, 8, 11, 14, 17.

```
for (unsigned int j = 2; j <= 17; j += 3)
```

6. Vary the control variable over the following sequence of values: 44, 33, 22, 11, 0.

```
for (unsigned int j = 44; j >= 0; j -= 11)
```

Application: Summing the Even Integers from 2 to 100

Figure 4.5 uses the for statement to sum all the even integers from 2 to 100. Each iteration of the loop (lines 9–11) adds control variable number's value to variable sum.

Good Programming Practice 4.3

Limit the size of control-statement headers to a single line if possible.

```
 1   // Fig. 4.5: fig04_05.c
 2   // Summation with for.
 3   #include <stdio.h>
 4
 5   int main(void)
 6   {
 7      unsigned int sum = 0; // initialize sum
 8
 9      for (unsigned int number = 2; number <= 100; number += 2) {
10         sum += number; // add number to sum
11      }
12
13      printf("Sum is %u\n", sum);
14   }
```

```
Sum is 2550
```

Fig. 4.5 | Summation with for.

Application: Compound-Interest Calculations

The next example computes compound interest using the for statement. Consider the following problem statement:

> *A person invests $1000.00 in a savings account yielding 5% interest. Assuming that all interest is left on deposit in the account, calculate and print the amount of money in the account at the end of each year for 10 years. Use the following formula for determining these amounts:*
>
> $$a = p(1 + r)^n$$
>
> *where*
>
> *p is the original amount invested (i.e., the principal)*
> *r is the annual interest rate (for example, .05 for 5%)*
> *n is the number of years*
> *a is the amount on deposit at the end of the nth year.*

This problem involves a loop that performs the indicated calculation for each of the 10 years the money remains on deposit. The solution is shown in Fig. 4.6.

```
 1   // Fig. 4.6: fig04_06.c
 2   // Calculating compound interest.
 3   #include <stdio.h>
 4   #include <math.h>
 5
 6   int main(void)
 7   {
 8      double principal = 1000.0; // starting principal
 9      double rate = .05; // annual interest rate
10
11      // output table column heads
12      printf("%4s%21s\n", "Year", "Amount on deposit");
```

Fig. 4.6 | Calculating compound interest. (Part 1 of 2.)

```
13
14      // calculate amount on deposit for each of ten years
15      for (unsigned int year = 1; year <= 10; ++year) {
16
17          // calculate new amount for specified year
18          double amount = principal * pow(1.0 + rate, year);
19
20          // output one table row
21          printf("%4u%21.2f\n", year, amount);
22      }
23   }
```

```
Year     Amount on deposit
   1              1050.00
   2              1102.50
   3              1157.63
   4              1215.51
   5              1276.28
   6              1340.10
   7              1407.10
   8              1477.46
   9              1551.33
  10              1628.89
```

Fig. 4.6 | Calculating compound interest. (Part 2 of 2.)

The for statement executes the body of the loop 10 times, varying a control variable from 1 to 10 in increments of 1. Although C does *not* include an exponentiation operator, we can use the Standard Library function pow (line 18) for this purpose. The function pow(x, y) calculates the value of x raised to the yth power. It takes two arguments of type double and returns a double value.

Software Engineering Observation 4.2

Type double is a floating-point type like float, but typically a variable of type double can store a value of much greater magnitude with greater precision than float. Variables of type double occupy more memory than those of type float. For all but the most memory-intensive applications, professional programmers generally prefer double to float.

The header <math.h> (line 4) should be included whenever a math function such as pow is used. This program would malfunction without the inclusion of math.h, as the linker would be unable to find the pow function.[1] Function **pow** requires two double arguments, but variable year is an integer. The math.h file includes information that tells the compiler to convert the value of year to a temporary double representation *before* calling the function. This information is contained in pow's **function prototype**. These are

---

1.   On many Linux/UNIX C compilers, you must include the -lm option (e.g., gcc -lm fig04_06.c) when compiling Fig. 4.6. This links the math library to the program.

explained in Chapter 5, where we also provide a summary of the pow function and other math library functions.

A Caution about Using Type* float *or* double *for Monetary Amounts
Notice that we defined the variables amount, principal and rate to be of type double. We did this for simplicity because we're dealing with fractional parts of dollars.

> **Error-Prevention Tip 4.5**
>
> *Do not use variables of type* float *or* double *to perform monetary calculations. The impreciseness of floating-point numbers can cause errors that will result in incorrect monetary values. [In Exercise 4.23, we explore the use of integer numbers of pennies to perform precise monetary calculations.]*

Here is a simple explanation of what can go wrong when using float or double to represent dollar amounts. Two float dollar amounts stored in the machine could be 14.234 (which with %.2f prints as 14.23) and 18.673 (which with %.2f prints as 18.67). When these amounts are added, they produce the sum 32.907, which with %.2f prints as 32.91. Thus your printout could appear as

```
   14.23
 + 18.67
 -------
   32.91
```

Clearly the sum of the individual numbers as printed should be 32.90! You've been warned!

Formatting Numeric Output
The conversion specifier %21.2f is used to print the value of the variable amount in the program. The 21 in the conversion specifier denotes the *field width* in which the value will be printed. A field width of 21 specifies that the value printed will appear in 21 print positions. The 2 specifies the *precision* (i.e., the number of decimal positions). If the number of characters displayed is *less than* the field width, then the value will automatically be *right justified* with leading spaces in the field. This is particularly useful for aligning floating-point values with the same precision (so that their decimal points align vertically). To *left justify* a value in a field, place a - (minus sign) between the % and the field width. The minus sign may also be used to left justify integers (such as in %-6d) and character strings (such as in %-8s). We'll discuss the powerful formatting capabilities of printf and scanf in detail in Chapter 9.

4.7 switch Multiple-Selection Statement

In Chapter 3, we discussed the if single-selection statement and the if...else double-selection statement. Occasionally, an algorithm will contain a *series of decisions* in which a variable or expression is tested separately for each of the constant integral values it may assume, and different actions are taken. This is called *multiple selection*. C provides the switch multiple-selection statement to handle such decision making.

The switch statement consists of a series of case labels, an optional default case and statements to execute for each case. Figure 4.7 uses switch to count the number of each different letter grade students earned on an exam.

```
 1   // Fig. 4.7: fig04_07.c
 2   // Counting letter grades with switch.
 3   #include <stdio.h>
 4
 5   int main(void)
 6   {
 7      unsigned int aCount = 0;
 8      unsigned int bCount = 0;
 9      unsigned int cCount = 0;
10      unsigned int dCount = 0;
11      unsigned int fCount = 0;
12
13      puts("Enter the letter grades.");
14      puts("Enter the EOF character to end input.");
15      int grade; // one grade
16
17      // loop until user types end-of-file key sequence
18      while ((grade = getchar()) != EOF) {
19
20         // determine which grade was input
21         switch (grade) { // switch nested in while
22
23            case 'A': // grade was uppercase A
24            case 'a': // or lowercase a
25               ++aCount;
26               break; // necessary to exit switch
27
28            case 'B': // grade was uppercase B
29            case 'b': // or lowercase b
30               ++bCount;
31               break;
32
33            case 'C': // grade was uppercase C
34            case 'c': // or lowercase c
35               ++cCount;
36               break;
37
38            case 'D': // grade was uppercase D
39            case 'd': // or lowercase d
40               ++dCount;
41               break;
42
43            case 'F': // grade was uppercase F
44            case 'f': // or lowercase f
45               ++fCount;
46               break;
47
48            case '\n': // ignore newlines,
49            case '\t': // tabs,
50            case ' ': // and spaces in input
51               break;
```

Fig. 4.7 | Counting letter grades with switch. (Part 1 of 2.)

```
52
53              default: // catch all other characters
54                  printf("%s", "Incorrect letter grade entered.");
55                  puts(" Enter a new grade.");
56                  break; // optional; will exit switch anyway
57          }
58      } // end while
59
60      // output summary of results
61      puts("\nTotals for each letter grade are:");
62      printf("A: %u\n", aCount);
63      printf("B: %u\n", bCount);
64      printf("C: %u\n", cCount);
65      printf("D: %u\n", dCount);
66      printf("F: %u\n", fCount);
67  }
```

```
Enter the letter grades.
Enter the EOF character to end input.
a
b
c
c
A
d
f
C
E
Incorrect letter grade entered. Enter a new grade.
D
A
b
^Z ———————— Not all systems display a representation of the EOF character

Totals for each letter grade are:
A: 3
B: 2
C: 3
D: 2
F: 1
```

Fig. 4.7 | Counting letter grades with switch. (Part 2 of 2.)

Reading Character Input

In the program, the user enters letter grades for a class. In the while header (line 18),

```
while ((grade = getchar()) != EOF)
```

the parenthesized assignment (grade = getchar()) executes first. The getchar function (from <stdio.h>) reads one character from the keyboard and stores that character in the integer variable grade. Characters are normally stored in variables of type **char**. However, an important feature of C is that characters can be stored in any integer data type because they're usually represented as one-byte integers in the computer. Function getchar returns as an int the character that the user entered. We can treat a character as either an integer or a character, depending on its use. For example, the statement

```
printf("The character (%c) has the value %d.\n", 'a', 'a');
```

uses the conversion specifiers %c and %d to print the character 'a' and its integer value, respectively. The result is

```
The character (a) has the value 97.
```

ASCII

The integer 97 is the character's numerical representation in the computer. Many computers today use the **ASCII (American Standard Code for Information Interchange) character set** in which 97 represents the lowercase letter 'a'. A list of the ASCII characters and their decimal values is presented in Appendix B. Characters can be read with scanf by using the conversion specifier %c.

Assignments Have Values

Assignments as a whole actually have a value. This value is assigned to the variable on the left side of the =. The value of the assignment expression grade = getchar() is the character that's returned by getchar and assigned to the variable grade.

The fact that assignments have values can be useful for setting several variables to the same value. For example,

```
a = b = c = 0;
```

first evaluates the assignment c = 0 (because the = operator associates from right to left). The variable b is then assigned the value of the assignment c = 0 (which is 0). Then, the variable a is assigned the value of the assignment b = (c = 0) (which is also 0). In the program, the value of the assignment grade = getchar() is compared with the value of EOF (a symbol whose acronym stands for "end of file"). We use EOF (which normally has the value -1) as the sentinel value. The user types a system-dependent keystroke combination to mean "end of file"—i.e., "I have no more data to enter." EOF is a symbolic integer constant defined in the <stdio.h> header (we'll see in Chapter 6 how symbolic constants are defined). If the value assigned to grade is equal to EOF, the program terminates. We've chosen to represent characters in this program as ints because EOF has an integer value (again, normally -1).

Portability Tip 4.1
The keystroke combinations for entering EOF (end of file) are system dependent.

Portability Tip 4.2
Testing for the symbolic constant EOF (rather than −1) makes programs more portable. The C standard states that EOF is a negative integral value (but not necessarily −1). Thus, EOF could have different values on different systems.

Entering the EOF Indicator
On Linux/UNIX/Mac OS X systems, the EOF indicator is entered by typing

    <Ctrl> d

on a line by itself. This notation *<Ctrl> d* means to simultaneously press both the *Ctrl* key and the *d* key. On other systems, such as Microsoft Windows, the EOF indicator can be entered by typing

> *<Ctrl> z*

You also need to press *Enter* on Windows.

The user enters grades at the keyboard. When the *Enter* key is pressed, the characters are read by function getchar one at a time. If the character entered is not equal to EOF, the switch statement (lines 21–57) is entered.

switch Statement Details

Keyword switch is followed by the variable name grade in parentheses. This is called the **controlling expression.** The value of this expression is compared with each of the **case labels.** Assume the user has entered the letter C as a grade. C is automatically compared to each case in the switch. If a match occurs (case 'C':), the statements for that case are executed. In the case of the letter C, cCount is incremented by 1 (line 35), and the switch statement is exited immediately with the break statement.

The break statement causes program control to continue with the first statement after the switch statement. The break statement is used because the cases in a switch statement would otherwise run together. If break is *not* used anywhere in a switch statement, then each time a match occurs in the statement, the statements for *all* the remaining cases will be executed. (This feature—called fall-through—is rarely useful, although it's perfect for programming Exercise 4.38—the iterative song "The Twelve Days of Christmas"!) If no match occurs, the default case is executed, and an error message is printed.

switch Statement Flowchart

Each case can have one or more actions. The switch statement is different from all other control statements in that braces are *not* required around multiple actions in a case of a switch. The general switch multiple-selection statement (using a break in each case) is flowcharted in Fig. 4.8. The flowchart makes it clear that each break statement at the end of a case causes control to immediately exit the switch statement.

Common Programming Error 4.4

Forgetting a break statement when one is needed in a switch statement is a logic error.

Error-Prevention Tip 4.6

Provide a default case in switch statements. Values not explicitly tested in a switch would normally be ignored. The default case helps prevent this by focusing you on the need to process exceptional conditions. Sometimes no default processing is needed.

Good Programming Practice 4.4

Although the case clauses and the default case clause in a switch statement can occur in any order, it's common to place the default clause last.

Good Programming Practice 4.5

In a switch statement, when the default clause is last, the break statement isn't required. You may prefer to include this break for clarity and symmetry with other cases.

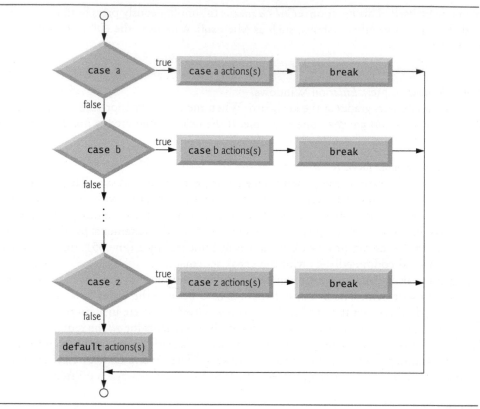

Fig. 4.8 | switch multiple-selection statement with breaks.

Ignoring Newline, Tab and Blank Characters in Input

In the switch statement of Fig. 4.7, the lines

```
case '\n': // ignore newlines,
case '\t': // tabs,
case ' ': // and spaces in input
    break;
```

cause the program to skip newline, tab and blank characters. Reading characters one at a time can cause problems. To have the program read the characters, you must send them to the computer by pressing *Enter*. This causes the newline character to be placed in the input after the character we wish to process. Often, this newline must be specifically ignored to make the program work correctly. The preceding cases in our switch statement prevent the error message in the default case from being printed each time a newline, tab or space is encountered in the input. So each input causes two iterations of the loop—the first for the letter grade and the second for '\n'. Listing several case labels together (such as case 'D': case 'd': in Fig. 4.7) simply means that the *same* set of actions is to occur for each of the cases.

Error-Prevention Tip 4.7

Remember to provide processing capabilities for newline (and possibly other white-space) characters in the input when processing characters one at a time.

Constant Integral Expressions

When using the switch statement, remember that each individual case can test only a **constant integral expression**—i.e., any combination of character constants and integer constants that evaluates to a constant integer value. A character constant can be represented as the specific character in single quotes, such as 'A'. Characters *must* be enclosed within single quotes to be recognized as character constants—characters in double quotes are recognized as strings. Integer constants are simply integer values. In our example, we've used character constants. Remember that characters are represented as small integer values.

Notes on Integral Types

Portable languages like C must have flexible data-type sizes. Different applications may need integers of different sizes. C provides several data types to represent integers. In addition to int and char, C provides types short int (which can be abbreviated as short) and long int (which can be abbreviated as long), as well as unsigned variations of all the integral types. In Section 5.14, we'll see that C also provides type long long int. The C standard specifies the minimum range of values for each integer type, but the actual range may be greater and depends on the implementation. For short ints the minimum range is −32767 to +32767. For most integer calculations, long ints are sufficient. The minimum range of values for long ints is −2147483647 to +2147483647. The range of values for an int is greater than or equal to that of a short int and less than or equal to that of a long int. On many of today's platforms, ints and long ints represent the same range of values. The data type signed char can be used to represent integers in the range −127 to +127 or any of the characters in the computer's character set. See Section 5.2.4.2 of the C standard document for the complete list of signed and unsigned integer-type ranges.

4.8 do...while Iteration Statement

The do...while iteration statement is similar to the while statement. In the while statement, the loop-continuation condition is tested at the *beginning* of the loop *before* the body of the loop is performed. The do...while statement tests the loop-continuation condition *after* the loop body is performed. Therefore, the loop body will always execute *at least once*. When a do...while terminates, execution continues with the statement after the while clause. The do...while statement is written as follows:

```
do {
    statements
} while (condition); // semicolon is required here
```

Figure 4.9 uses a do...while statement to print the numbers from 1 to 10. We chose to preincrement the control variable counter in the loop-continuation test (line 11).

```
1   // Fig. 4.9: fig04_09.c
2   // Using the do...while iteration statement.
3   #include <stdio.h>
4
5   int main(void)
6   {
```

Fig. 4.9 | Using the do...while iteration statement. (Part 1 of 2.)

```
 7      unsigned int counter = 1; // initialize counter
 8
 9      do {
10         printf("%u  ", counter);
11      } while (++counter <= 10);
12   }
```

```
1  2  3  4  5  6  7  8  9  10
```

Fig. 4.9 | Using the do...while iteration statement. (Part 2 of 2.)

do...while Statement Flowchart

Figure 4.10 shows the do...while statement flowchart, which makes it clear that the loop-continuation condition does not execute until after the action is performed *at least once*.

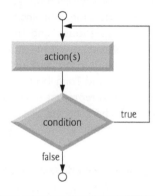

Fig. 4.10 | Flowcharting the do...while iteration statement.

4.9 break and continue Statements

The break and continue statements are used to alter the flow of control. Section 4.7 showed how break can be used to terminate a switch statement's execution. This section discusses how to use break in an iteration statement.

break Statement

The break statement, when executed in a while, for, do...while or switch statement, causes an *immediate exit* from that statement. Program execution continues with the next statement after that while, for, do...while or switch. Common uses of break are to escape early from a loop or to skip the remainder of a switch (as in Fig. 4.7). Figure 4.11 demonstrates the break statement (line 14) in a for iteration statement. When the if statement detects that x has become 5, break is executed. This terminates the for statement, and the program continues with the printf after the for. The loop fully executes only four times. We declared x before the loop in this example, so that we could use its final value after the loop terminates. Recall that when you declare the control variable in a for loop's *initialization* expression, the variable no longer exists after the loop terminates.

```
 1   // Fig. 4.11: fig04_11.c
 2   // Using the break statement in a for statement.
 3   #include <stdio.h>
 4
 5   int main(void)
 6   {
 7      unsigned int x; // declared here so it can be used after loop
 8
 9      // loop 10 times
10      for (x = 1; x <= 10; ++x) {
11
12         // if x is 5, terminate loop
13         if (x == 5) {
14            break; // break loop only if x is 5
15         }
16
17         printf("%u ", x);
18      }
19
20      printf("\nBroke out of loop at x == %u\n", x);
21   }
```

```
1 2 3 4
Broke out of loop at x == 5
```

Fig. 4.11 | Using the break statement in a for statement.

continue *Statement*

The continue statement, when executed in a while, for or do...while statement, skips the remaining statements in that control statement's body and performs the next iteration of the loop. In while and do...while statements, the loop-continuation test is evaluated immediately *after* the continue statement executes. In the for statement, the increment expression executes, then the loop-continuation test is evaluated. Figure 4.12 uses continue (line 12) in the for statement to skip the printf statement and begin the next iteration of the loop.

```
 1   // Fig. 4.12: fig04_12.c
 2   // Using the continue statement in a for statement.
 3   #include <stdio.h>
 4
 5   int main(void)
 6   {
 7      // loop 10 times
 8      for (unsigned int x = 1; x <= 10; ++x) {
 9
10         // if x is 5, continue with next iteration of loop
11         if (x == 5) {
12            continue; // skip remaining code in loop body
13         }
14
15         printf("%u ", x);
16      }
```

Fig. 4.12 | Using the continue statement in a for statement. (Part 1 of 2.)

```
17
18      puts("\nUsed continue to skip printing the value 5");
19  }
```

```
1 2 3 4 6 7 8 9 10
Used continue to skip printing the value 5
```

Fig. 4.12 | Using the `continue` statement in a `for` statement. (Part 2 of 2.)

Software Engineering Observation 4.3

Some programmers feel that `break` *and* `continue` *violate the norms of structured programming. The effects of these statements can be achieved by structured programming techniques we'll soon discuss, so these programmers do not use* `break` *and* `continue`.

Performance Tip 4.1

The `break` *and* `continue` *statements, when used properly, perform faster than the corresponding structured techniques that we'll soon learn.*

Software Engineering Observation 4.4

There's a tension between achieving quality software engineering and achieving the best-performing software. Often one of these goals is achieved at the expense of the other. For all but the most performance-intensive situations, apply the following guidelines: First, make your code simple and correct; then make it fast and small, but only if necessary.

4.10 Logical Operators

So far we've studied only simple conditions, such as `counter <= 10`, `total > 1000`, and `number != sentinelValue`. We've expressed these conditions in terms of the *relational operators*, `>`, `<`, `>=` and `<=`, and the *equality operators*, `==` and `!=`. Each decision tested precisely *one* condition. To test multiple conditions in the process of making a decision, we had to perform these tests in separate statements or in nested `if` or `if...else` statements. C provides *logical operators* that may be used to form more complex conditions by combining simple conditions. The logical operators are `&&` (**logical AND**), `||` (**logical OR**) and `!` (**logical NOT**, also called **logical negation**). We'll consider examples of each of these operators.

Logical AND (&&) Operator

Suppose we wish to ensure that two conditions are *both* true before we choose a certain path of execution. In this case, we can use the logical operator `&&` as follows:

```
if (gender == 1 && age >= 65) {
    ++seniorFemales;
}
```

This `if` statement contains two *simple* conditions. The condition `gender == 1` might be evaluated, for example, to determine whether a person is a female. The condition `age >= 65` is evaluated to determine whether a person is a senior citizen. The two simple conditions are evaluated first because `==` and `>=` each have *higher* precedence than `&&`. The `if` statement then considers the combined condition `gender == 1 && age >= 65`, which is *true* if and only if *both* of the simple conditions are *true*. Finally, if this combined condition is true, then the count of `seniorFemales` is incremented by 1. If *either or both* of the simple conditions are *false*, then the program skips the incrementing and proceeds to the statement following the `if`.

Figure 4.13 summarizes the **&& operator**. The table shows all four possible combinations of zero (false) and nonzero (true) values for expression1 and expression2. Such tables are often called **truth tables**. *C evaluates all expressions that include relational operators, equality operators, and/or logical operators to 0 or 1.* Although C *sets* a true value to 1, it accepts *any* nonzero value as true.

expression1	expression2	expression1 && expression2
0	0	0
0	nonzero	0
nonzero	0	0
nonzero	nonzero	1

Fig. 4.13 | Truth table for the logical AND (&&) operator.

Logical OR (||) Operator

Now let's consider the || (logical OR) operator. Suppose we wish to ensure at some point in a program that *either or both* of two conditions are *true* before we choose a certain path of execution. In this case, we use the || operator, as in the following program segment:

```
if (semesterAverage >= 90 || finalExam >= 90) {
    puts("Student grade is A");
}
```

This statement also contains two simple conditions. The condition `semesterAverage >= 90` is evaluated to determine whether the student deserves an "A" in the course because of a solid performance throughout the semester. The condition `finalExam >= 90` is evaluated to determine whether the student deserves an "A" in the course because of an outstanding performance on the final exam. The `if` statement then considers the combined condition

```
semesterAverage >= 90 || finalExam >= 90
```

and awards the student an "A" if *either or both* of the simple conditions are *true*. The message "Student grade is A" is *not* printed only when *both* of the simple conditions are *false* (zero). Figure 4.14 is a truth table for the logical OR operator (||).

expression1	expression2	expression1 || expression2
0	0	0
0	nonzero	1
nonzero	0	1
nonzero	nonzero	1

Fig. 4.14 | Truth table for the logical OR (||) operator.

Short-Circuit Evaluation

The && operator has a *higher* precedence than ||. Both operators associate from left to right. An expression containing && or || operators is evaluated *only* until truth or falsehood is known. Thus, evaluation of the condition

```
gender == 1 && age >= 65
```

will stop if gender is not equal to 1 (i.e., the entire expression is *guaranteed* to be false), and continue if gender is equal to 1 (i.e., the entire expression *could* still be true if age >= 65). This performance feature for the evaluation of logical AND and logical OR expressions is called **short-circuit evaluation**.

Performance Tip 4.2

In expressions using operator && , make the condition that's most likely to be false the leftmost condition. In expressions using operator || , make the condition that's most likely to be true the leftmost condition. This can reduce a program's execution time.

Logical Negation (!) Operator

C provides the ! (logical negation) operator to enable you to "reverse" the meaning of a condition. Unlike operators && and ||, which combine *two* conditions (and are therefore *binary* operators), the logical negation operator has only a *single* condition as an operand (and is therefore a *unary* operator). The logical negation operator is placed before a condition when we're interested in choosing a path of execution if the original condition (without the logical negation operator) is *false*, such as in the following program segment:

```
if (!(grade == sentinelValue)) {
    printf("The next grade is %f\n", grade);
}
```

The parentheses around the condition grade == sentinelValue are needed because the logical negation operator has a higher precedence than the equality operator. Figure 4.15 is a truth table for the logical negation operator.

expression	!expression
0	1
nonzero	0

Fig. 4.15 | Truth table for operator ! (logical negation).

In most cases, you can avoid using logical negation by expressing the condition differently with an appropriate relational operator. For example, the preceding statement may also be written as:

```
if (grade != sentinelValue) {
    printf("The next grade is %f\n", grade);
}
```

Summary of Operator Precedence and Associativity

Figure 4.16 shows the precedence and associativity of the operators introduced to this point. The operators are shown from top to bottom in decreasing order of precedence.

Operators						Associativity	Type
++ *(postfix)*	-- *(postfix)*					right to left	postfix
+	-	!	++ *(prefix)*	-- *(prefix)*	*(type)*	right to left	unary
*	/	%				left to right	multiplicative
+	-					left to right	additive
<	<=	>	>=			left to right	relational
==	!=					left to right	equality
&&						left to right	logical AND
||						left to right	logical OR
?:						right to left	conditional
=	+=	-=	*=	/=	%=	right to left	assignment
,						left to right	comma

Fig. 4.16 | Operator precedence and associativity.

The _Bool Data Type

The C standard includes a boolean type—represented by the keyword **_Bool**—which can hold only the values 0 or 1. Recall C's convention of using zero and nonzero values to represent false and true— the value 0 in a condition evaluates to false, while any nonzero value evaluates to true. Assigning any nonzero value to a _Bool sets it to 1. The standard also includes the **<stdbool.h>** header, which defines **bool** as a shorthand for the type _Bool, and **true** and **false** as named representations of 1 and 0, respectively. At preprocessor time, bool, true and false are replaced with _Bool, 1 and 0. Section E.4 presents an example that uses bool, true and false. The example uses a programmer-defined function, a concept we introduce in Chapter 5. You can study the example now, but you might wish to revisit it after reading Chapter 5.

4.11 Confusing Equality (==) and Assignment (=) Operators

There's one type of error that C programmers, no matter how experienced, tend to make so frequently that we feel it is worth a separate section. That error is accidentally swapping the operators == (equality) and = (assignment). What makes these swaps so damaging is the fact that they do *not* ordinarily cause *compilation errors*. Rather, statements with these errors ordinarily compile correctly, allowing programs to run to completion while likely generating incorrect results through *runtime logic errors*.

Two aspects of C cause these problems. One is that any expression that produces a value can be used in the decision portion of any control statement. If the value is 0, it's treated as false, and if the value is nonzero, it's treated as true. The second is that assignments in C produce a value, namely the value that's assigned to the variable on the left side of the assignment operator.

For example, suppose we intend to write

```
if (payCode == 4) {
    printf("%s", "You get a bonus!");
}
```

but we accidentally write

```
if (payCode = 4) {
    printf("%s", "You get a bonus!");
}
```

The first if statement properly awards a bonus to the person whose paycode is equal to 4. The second if statement—the one with the error—evaluates the assignment expression in the if condition. This expression is a simple assignment whose value is the constant 4. Because any nonzero value is interpreted as "true," the condition in this if statement is always true, and not only is the value of payCode inadvertently set to 4, but the person *always* receives a bonus regardless of what the actual paycode is!

Common Programming Error 4.5

Using operator == for assignment or using operator = for equality is a logic error.

lvalues *and* rvalues

You'll probably be inclined to write conditions such as x == 7 with the variable name on the left and the constant on the right. By reversing these terms so that the constant is on the left and the variable name is on the right, as in 7 == x, then if you accidentally replace the == operator with =, you'll be protected by the compiler. The compiler will treat this as a *syntax error*, because only a variable name can be placed on the left-hand side of an assignment expression. This will prevent the potential devastation of a runtime logic error.

Variable names are said to be *lvalues* (for "left values") because they can be used on the *left* side of an assignment operator. Constants are said to be *rvalues* (for "right values") because they can be used only on the *right* side of an assignment operator. *lvalues* can also be used as *rvalues*, but not vice versa.

Error-Prevention Tip 4.8

When an equality expression has a variable and a constant, as in x == 1, you may prefer to write it with the constant on the left and the variable name on the right (i.e., 1 == x) as protection against the logic error that occurs when you accidentally replace operator == with =.

Confusing == and = in Standalone Statements

The other side of the coin can be equally unpleasant. Suppose you want to assign a value to a variable with a simple statement such as

```
x = 1;
```

but instead write

```
x == 1;
```

Here, too, this is not a syntax error. Rather the compiler simply evaluates the conditional expression. If x is equal to 1, the condition is true and the expression returns the value 1. If x is not equal to 1, the condition is false and the expression returns the value 0. Regardless of what value is returned, there's no assignment operator, so the value is simply *lost*, and the value of x remains *unaltered*, probably causing an execution-time logic error. Unfortunately, we do not have a handy trick available to help you with this problem! Many compilers, however, will issue a *warning* on such a statement.

> **Error-Prevention Tip 4.9**
> *After you write a program, text search it for every = and check that it's used properly. This can help you prevent subtle bugs.*

4.12 Structured Programming Summary

Just as architects design buildings by employing the collective wisdom of their profession, so should programmers design programs. Our field is younger than architecture is, and our collective wisdom is considerably sparser. We've learned a great deal in a mere eight decades. Perhaps most important, we've learned that structured programming produces programs that are easier (than unstructured programs) to understand and therefore are easier to test, debug, modify, and even prove correct in a mathematical sense.

Chapters 3 and 4 have concentrated on C's control statements. Each statement has been presented, flowcharted and discussed separately with examples. Now, we summarize the results of Chapters 3 and 4 and introduce a simple set of rules for the formation and properties of structured programs.

Figure 4.17 summarizes the control statements discussed in Chapters 3 and 4. Small circles are used in the figure to indicate the *single entry point* and the *single exit point* of each statement. Connecting individual flowchart symbols arbitrarily can lead to unstructured programs. Therefore, the programming profession has chosen to combine flowchart symbols to form a limited set of control statements, and to build only properly structured programs by combining control statements in two simple ways. For simplicity, only *single-entry/single-exit* control statements are used—there's only one way to enter and only one way to exit each control statement. Connecting control statements in sequence to form structured programs is simple—the exit point of one control statement is connected to the entry point of the next—i.e., the control statements are simply placed one after another in a program—we've called this "control-statement stacking." Control statements also can be nested.

Figure 4.18 shows the rules for forming structured programs. The rules assume that the rectangle flowchart symbol may be used to indicate *any* action including input/output. Figure 4.19 shows the *simplest flowchart*.

Applying the rules of Fig. 4.18 always results in a structured flowchart with a neat, building-block appearance. Repeatedly applying Rule 2 to the simplest flowchart (Fig. 4.19) results in a structured flowchart containing many rectangles *in sequence* (Fig. 4.20). Rule 2 generates a stack of control statements; so we call Rule 2 the **stacking rule**.

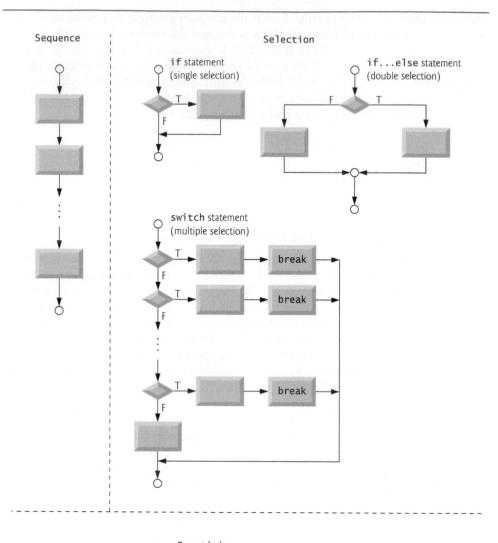

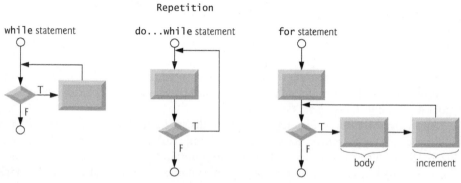

Fig. 4.17 | C's single-entry/single-exit sequence, selection and iteration statements.

Rules for forming structured programs

1. Begin with the "simplest flowchart" (Fig. 4.19).
2. ("Stacking" rule) Any rectangle (action) can be replaced by *two* rectangles (actions) in sequence.
3. ("Nesting" rule) Any rectangle (action) can be replaced by *any* control statement (sequence, if, if...else, switch, while, do...while or for).
4. Rules 2 and 3 may be applied as often as you like and in *any* order.

Fig. 4.18 | Rules for forming structured programs.

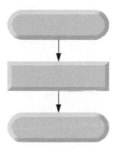

Fig. 4.19 | Simplest flowchart.

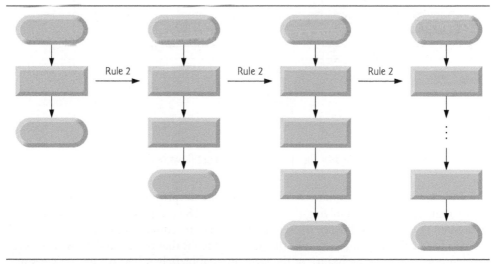

Fig. 4.20 | Repeatedly applying Rule 2 of Fig. 4.18 to the simplest flowchart.

Rule 3 is called the **nesting rule**. Repeatedly applying Rule 3 to the simplest flowchart results in a flowchart with neatly nested control statements. For example, in Fig. 4.21, the rectangle in the simplest flowchart is first replaced with a double-selection (if...else) statement. Then Rule 3 is applied again to both of the rectangles in the double-selection statement, replacing each of these rectangles with double-selection statements. The dashed box around each of the double-selection statements represents the rectangle that was replaced in the original flowchart.

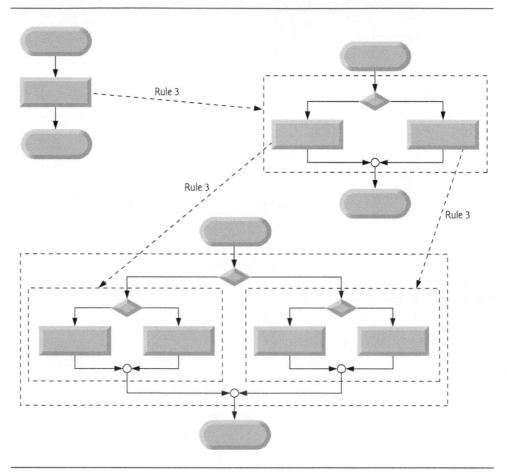

Fig. 4.21 | Applying Rule 3 of Fig. 4.18 to the simplest flowchart.

Rule 4 generates larger, more involved, and more deeply nested structures. The flowcharts that emerge from applying the rules in Fig. 4.18 constitute the set of all possible structured flowcharts and hence the set of all possible structured programs.

It's because of the elimination of the goto statement that these building blocks never overlap one another. The beauty of the structured approach is that we use only a small number of simple *single-entry/single-exit* pieces, and we assemble them in only *two* simple ways. Figure 4.22 shows the kinds of stacked building blocks that emerge from applying Rule 2 and the kinds of nested building blocks that emerge from applying Rule 3. The figure also shows the kind of overlapped building blocks that *cannot* appear in structured flowcharts (because of the elimination of the goto statement).

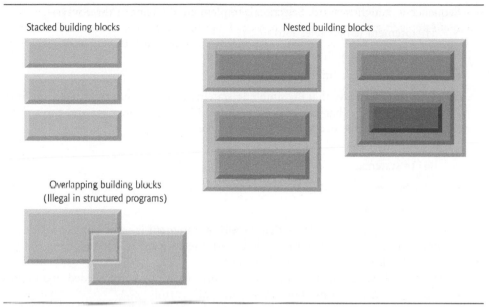

Stacked building blocks

Nested building blocks

Overlapping building blocks
(Illegal in structured programs)

Fig. 4.22 | Stacked, nested and overlapped building blocks.

If the rules in Fig. 4.18 are followed, an unstructured flowchart (such as that in Fig. 4.23) *cannot* be created. If you're uncertain whether a particular flowchart is structured, apply the rules of Fig. 4.18 in reverse to try to *reduce* the flowchart to the simplest flowchart. If you succeed, the original flowchart is structured; otherwise, it's not.

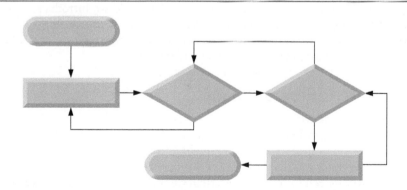

Fig. 4.23 | An unstructured flowchart.

Structured programming promotes simplicity. Bohm and Jacopini showed that only three forms of control are needed:

- Sequence
- Selection
- Iteration

Sequence is straightforward. Selection is implemented in one of three ways:

- `if` statement (single selection)
- `if...else` statement (double selection)
- `switch` statement (multiple selection)

It's straightforward to prove that the simple `if` statement is sufficient to provide *any* form of selection—everything that can be done with the `if...else` statement and the `switch` statement can be implemented with one or more `if` statements.

Iteration is implemented in one of three ways:

- `while` statement
- `do...while` statement
- `for` statement

It's also straightforward to prove that the `while` statement is sufficient to provide *any* form of iteration. Everything that can be done with the `do...while` statement and the `for` statement can be done with the `while` statement.

Combining these results illustrates that any form of control ever needed in a C program can be expressed in terms of only *three* forms of control:

- sequence
- `if` statement (selection)
- `while` statement (iteration)

And these control statements can be combined in only *two* ways—*stacking* and *nesting*. Indeed, structured programming promotes simplicity.

In Chapters 3 and 4, we've discussed how to compose programs from control statements containing only actions and decisions. In Chapter 5, we introduce another program-structuring unit called the function. We'll learn to compose large programs by combining functions, which, in turn, can be composed of control statements. We'll also discuss how using functions promotes software reusability.

4.13 Secure C Programming

*Checking Function **scanf**'s Return Value*
Figure 4.6 used the math library function pow, which calculates the value of its first argument raised to the power of its second argument and *returns* the result as a `double` value. The calculation's result was then used in the statement that called pow.

Many functions return values indicating whether they executed successfully. For example, function scanf returns an `int` indicating whether the input operation was successful. If an input failure occurs, scanf returns the value EOF (defined in `<stdio.h>`); otherwise, it returns the number of items that were read. If this value does *not* match the number you intended to read, then scanf was unable to complete the input operation.

Consider the following statement from Fig. 3.6:

```
scanf("%d", &grade); // read grade from user
```

which expects to read one `int` value. If the user enters an integer, scanf returns 1 indicating that one value was indeed read. If the user enters a string, such as `"hello"`, scanf returns 0 indicating that it was unable to read the input as an integer. In this case, the variable grade does *not* receive a value.

Function scanf can read multiple inputs, as in

```
scanf("%d%d", &number1, &number2); // read two integers
```

If the input is successful, scanf will return 2, indicating that two values were read. If the user enters a string for the first value, scanf will return 0 and neither number1 nor number2 will receive a value. If the user enters an integer followed by a string, scanf will return 1 and only number1 will receive a value.

Error-Prevention Tip 4.10
To make your input processing more robust, check scanf's return value to ensure that the number of inputs read matches the number of inputs expected. Otherwise, your program will use the values of the variables as if scanf completed successfully. This could lead to logic errors, program crashes or even attacks.

Range Checking

Even if a scanf operates successfully, the values read might still be *invalid*. For example, grades are typically integers in the range 0–100. In a program that inputs such grades, you should validate the grades by using **range checking** to ensure that they are values from 0 to 100. You can then ask the user to reenter any value that's out of range. If a program requires inputs from a specific set of values (e.g., nonsequential product codes), you can ensure that each input matches a value in the set. For more information, see Chapter 5, "Integer Security," of Robert Seacord's book *Secure Coding in C and C++, 2/e.*

Summary

Section 4.2 Iteration Essentials

- Most programs involve iteration, or looping. A loop is a group of instructions the computer executes repeatedly while some **loop-continuation condition** (p. 114) remains true.
- **Counter-controlled iteration** is sometimes called **definite iteration** (p. 114) because we know in advance exactly how many times the loop will execute.
- **Sentinel-controlled iteration** is sometimes called **indefinite iteration** (p. 114) because it's not known in advance how many times the loop will execute; the loop includes statements that obtain data each time the loop is performed.
- In counter-controlled iteration, a **control variable** (p. 114) is used to count the number of iterations. The control variable is **incremented** (or **decremented**) each time the group of instructions is performed (p. 115). When the correct number of iterations has been performed, the loop terminates, and the program resumes execution with the statement after the iteration statement.
- The **sentinel value** indicates "end of data." The sentinel is entered after all regular data items have been supplied to the program. Sentinels must be distinct from regular data items.

Section 4.3 Counter-Controlled Iteration

- Counter-controlled iteration requires the **name** (p. 115) of a control variable (or loop counter), the **initial value** (p. 115) of the control variable, the **increment** (or **decrement**) by which the control variable is modified each time through the loop, and the condition that tests for the **final value** (p. 115) of the control variable (i.e., whether looping should continue).

Section 4.4 **for** *Iteration Statement*

- The **for iteration statement** handles all the details of counter-controlled iteration.

- When the for statement begins executing, its control variable is initialized. Then, the loop-continuation condition is checked. If the condition is true, the loop's body executes. The control variable is then incremented, and the loop begins again with the loop-continuation condition. This process continues until the loop-continuation condition fails.

- The general format of the for statement is

  ```
  for (initialization; condition; increment) {
      statements
  }
  ```

  where the *initialization* expression initializes (and possibly defines) the control variable, the *condition* expression is the loop-continuation condition, and the *increment* expression increments the control variable.

- The **comma operator** (p. 118) guarantees that lists of expressions evaluate from left to right. The value of the entire expression is that of the rightmost expression.

- The three expressions in the for statement are optional. If the *condition* expression is omitted, C assumes that the condition is true, thus creating an infinite loop. One might omit the *initialization* expression if the control variable is initialized before the loop. The *increment* expression might be omitted if the increment is calculated by statements in the for statement's body or if no increment is needed.

- The *increment* expression in the for statement acts like a standalone C statement at the end of the body of the for.

- The two semicolons in the for statement are required.

Section 4.5 **for** *Statement: Notes and Observations*

- The initialization, loop-continuation condition and increment can contain arithmetic expressions.

- The "increment" may be negative (in which case it's really a decrement and the loop actually counts downward).

- If the loop-continuation condition is initially false, the body portion of the loop isn't performed. Instead, execution proceeds with the statement following the for statement.

Section 4.6 *Examples Using the* **for** *Statement*

- **Function pow** (p. 122) performs exponentiation. The function pow(x, y) calculates the value of x raised to the yth power. It takes two arguments of type double and returns a double value.

- Type **double** is a floating-point type much like float, but typically a variable of type double can store a value of much **greater magnitude** with **greater precision** than float.

- The **header <math.h>** (p. 122) should be included whenever a math function such as pow is used.

- The conversion specifier %21.2f denotes that a floating-point value will be displayed **right justified** in a field of 21 characters with two digits to the right of the decimal point.

- To **left justify** a value in a field, place a - (minus sign) between the % and the field width.

Section 4.7 **switch** *Multiple-Selection Statement*

- Occasionally, an algorithm will contain a series of decisions in which a variable or expression is tested separately for each of the constant integral values it may assume, and different actions are taken. This is called **multiple selection**. C provides the **switch statement** to handle this.

- The switch statement consists of a series of **case labels** (p. 127), an optional **default case** and statements to execute for each case.

- The **getchar function** (from the standard input/output library) reads and returns as an int one character from the keyboard.

- Characters are normally stored in variables of type **char** (p. 125). Characters can be stored in any integer data type because they're usually represented as one-byte integers in the computer. Thus, we can treat a character as either an integer or a character, depending on its use.

- Many computers today use the **ASCII** (**American Standard Code for Information Interchange**; p. 126) character set in which 97 represents the lowercase letter 'a'.

- Characters can be read with scanf by using the conversion specifier **%c**.

- **Assignment expressions** as a whole actually **have a value**. This value is assigned to the variable on the left side of the =.

- The fact that assignment statements have values can be useful for setting several variables to the same value, as in a = b = c = 0;.

- **EOF** is often used as a sentinel value. EOF is a symbolic integer constant defined in <stdio.h>.

- On Linux/UNIX systems and many others, the EOF indicator is entered by typing *<Ctrl> d* . On other systems, such as Microsoft Windows, the EOF indicator can be entered by typing *<Ctrl> z*.

- Keyword switch is followed by the **controlling expression** (p. 127) in parentheses. The value of this expression is compared with each of the case labels. If a match occurs, the statements for that case execute. If no match occurs, the default case executes.

- The **break statement** causes program control to continue with the statement after the switch. The break statement prevents the cases in a switch statement from running together.

- Each case can have one or more actions. The switch statement is different from all other control statements in that braces are not required around multiple actions in a case of a switch.

- **Listing several case labels together** simply means that the same set of actions is to occur for any of these cases.

- Remember that the switch statement can be used only for testing a **constant integral expression** (p. 129)—i.e., any combination of character constants and integer constants that evaluates to a constant integer value. A character constant can be represented as the specific character in single quotes, such as 'A'. Characters must be enclosed within single quotes to be recognized as character constants. Integer constants are simply integer values.

- In addition to integer types int and char, C provides types **short int** (which can be abbreviated as **short**) and **long int** (which can be abbreviated as **long**), as well as **unsigned** versions of all the integral types. The C standard specifies the minimum value range for each type, but the actual range may be greater, depending on the implementation. For short ints the minimum range is –32767 to +32767. The minimum range of values for long ints is –2147483647 to +2147483647. The range of values for an int is greater than or equal to that of a short int and less than or equal to that of a long int. On many of today's platforms, ints and long ints represent the same range of values. The data type signed char can be used to represent integers in the range –127 to +127 or any of the characters in the computer's character set. See Section 5.2.4.2 of the C standard document for the complete list of signed and unsigned integer-type ranges.

Section 4.8 **do...while** *Iteration Statement*
- The **do...while statement** tests the loop-continuation condition *after* the loop body is performed. Therefore, the loop body executes at least once. When a do...while terminates, execution continues with the statement after the while clause.

Section 4.9 **break** *and* **continue** *Statements*
- The **break statement**, when executed in a while, for, do...while or switch statement, causes immediate exit from that statement. Program execution continues with the next statement.

- The **continue statement**, when executed in a while, for or do...while statement, skips the remaining statements in the body and performs the next loop iteration. In while and do...while, the loop-continuation test is evaluated immediately after the continue statement is executed. In a for, the increment expression is executed, then the loop-continuation test is evaluated.

Section 4.10 Logical Operators
- **Logical operators** may be used to form complex conditions by combining simple conditions. The logical operators are && (logical AND), || (logical OR) and ! (logical NOT, or logical negation).
- A condition containing the **&& (logical AND**; p. 132) operator is true if and only if both of the simple conditions are true.
- C evaluates all expressions that include relational operators, equality operators, and/or logical operators to 0 or 1. Although C sets a **true value** to 1, it accepts *any* **nonzero** value as **true**.
- A condition containing the || (**logical OR**; p. 132) operator is true if either or both of the simple conditions are true.
- The && operator has a higher precedence than ||. Both operators associate from left to right.
- An expression containing && or || operators is evaluated only until truth or falsehood is known.
- C provides the ! (**logical negation**; p. 132) operator to enable you to "reverse" the meaning of a condition. Unlike the binary operators && and ||, which combine two conditions, the unary logical negation operator has only a single condition as an operand.
- The logical negation operator is placed before a condition when we're interested in choosing a path of execution if the original condition (without the logical negation operator) is false.
- In most cases, you can avoid using logical negation by expressing the condition differently with an appropriate relational operator.

Section 4.11 Confusing Equality (==) and Assignment (=) Operators
- Programmers often accidentally swap the operators == (equality) and = (assignment). What makes these swaps so damaging is that they do not ordinarily cause syntax errors. Rather, statements with these errors ordinarily compile correctly, allowing programs to run to completion while likely generating incorrect results through runtime logic errors.
- You may be inclined to write conditions such as x == 7 with the variable name on the left and the constant on the right. By reversing these terms so that the constant is on the left and the variable name is on the right, as in 7 == x, then if you accidentally replace the == operator with =, you'll be protected by the compiler. The compiler will treat this as a syntax error, because only a variable name can be placed on the left-hand side of an assignment statement.
- Variable names are said to be *lvalues* (for "**left values**"; p. 136) because they *can* be used on the left side of an assignment operator.
- Constants are said to be *rvalues* (for "**right values**"; p. 136) because they can be used *only* on the right side of an assignment operator. *lvalues* can also be used as *rvalues*, but not vice versa.

Self-Review Exercises
4.1   Fill in the blanks in each of the following statements.
   a) Counter-controlled iteration is also known as _____ iteration because it's known in advance how many times the loop will be executed.
   b) Sentinel-controlled iteration is also known as _____ iteration because it's not known in advance how many times the loop will be executed.
   c) In counter-controlled iteration, a(n) _____ is used to count the number of times a group of instructions should be repeated.

d) The _____ statement, when executed in an iteration statement, causes the next iteration of the loop to be performed immediately.

e) The _____ statement, when executed in an iteration statement or a switch, causes an immediate exit from the statement.

f) The _____ is used to test a particular variable or expression for each of the constant integral values it may assume.

4.2 State whether the following are *true* or *false*. If the answer is *false*, explain why.

a) The default case is required in the switch selection statement.

b) The break statement is required in the default case of a switch selection statement.

c) The expression (x > y && a < b) is true if either x > y is true or a < b is true.

d) An expression containing the || operator is true if either or both of its operands is true.

4.3 Write a statement or a set of statements to accomplish each of the following tasks:

a) Sum the odd integers between 1 and 99 using a for statement. Use the unsigned integer variables sum and count.

b) Print the value 333.546372 in a field width of 15 characters with precisions of 1, 2, 3, 4 and 5. Left justify the output. What are the five values that print?

c) Calculate the value of 2.5 raised to the power of 3 using the pow function. Print the result with a precision of 2 in a field width of 10 positions. What is the value that prints?

d) Print the integers from 1 to 20 using a while loop and the counter variable x. Print only five integers per line. [*Hint:* Use the calculation x % 5. When the value of this is 0, print a newline character, otherwise print a tab character.]

e) Repeat Exercise 4.3(d) using a for statement.

4.4 Find the error in each of the following code segments and explain how to correct it.

a)
```
x = 1;
while (x <= 10);
    ++x;
}
```

b)
```
for (double y = .1; y != 1.0; y += .1) {
    printf("%f\n", y);
}
```

c)
```
switch (n) {
    case 1:
        puts("The number is 1");
    case 2:
        puts("The number is 2");
        break;
    default:
        puts("The number is not 1 or 2");
        break;
}
```

d) The following code should print the values 1 to 10.
```
n = 1;
while (n < 10) {
    printf("%d ", n++);
}
```

Answers to Self-Review Exercises

4.1 a) definite. b) indefinite. c) control variable or counter. d) continue. e) break. f) switch selection statement.

4.2   a) False. The `default` case is optional. If no default action is needed, then there's no need for a `default` case.

      b) False. The `break` statement is used to exit the `switch` statement. The `break` statement is not required in *any* case.

      c) False. Both of the relational expressions must be true in order for the entire expression to be true when using the `&&` operator.

      d) True.

4.3   a)
```c
unsigned int sum = 0;
for (unsigned int count = 1; count <= 99; count += 2) {
   sum += count;
}
```

      b)
```c
printf("%-15.1f\n", 333.546372); // prints 333.5
printf("%-15.2f\n", 333.546372); // prints 333.55
printf("%-15.3f\n", 333.546372); // prints 333.546
printf("%-15.4f\n", 333.546372); // prints 333.5464
printf("%-15.5f\n", 333.546372); // prints 333.54637
```

      c)
```c
printf("%10.2f\n", pow(2.5, 3)); // prints 15.63
```

      d)
```c
unsigned int x = 1;
while (x <= 20) {
   printf("%d", x);
   if (x % 5 == 0) {
      puts("");
   }
   else {
      printf("%s", "\t");
   }
   ++x;
}
```
or
```c
unsigned int x = 1;
while (x <= 20) {
   if (x % 5 == 0) {
      printf("%u\n", x++);
   }
   else {
      printf("%u\t", x++);
   }
}
```
or
```c
unsigned int x = 0;
while (++x <= 20) {
   if (x % 5 == 0) {
      printf("%u\n", x);
   }
   else {
      printf("%u\t", x);
   }
}
```

e)
```
for (unsigned int x = 1; x <= 20; ++x) {
    printf("%u", x);
    if (x % 5 == 0) {
        puts("");
    }
    else {
        printf("%s", "\t");
    }
}
```

or

```
for (unsigned int x = 1; x <= 20; ++x) {
    if (x % 5 == 0) {
        printf("%u\n", x);
    }
    else {
        printf("%u\t", x);
    }
}
```

4.4   a) Error: The semicolon after the `while` header causes an infinite loop.
Correction: Replace the semicolon with a { or remove both the ; and the }.

b) Error: Using a floating-point number to control a `for` iteration statement.
Correction: Use an integer, and perform the proper calculation to get the values you desire.

```
for (int y = 1; y != 10; ++y) {
    printf("%f\n", (float) y / 10);
}
```

c) Error: Missing `break` statement in the statements for the first `case`.
Correction: Add a `break` statement at the end of the statements for the first `case`. This is not necessarily an error if you want the statement of `case 2:` to execute every time the `case 1:` statement executes.

d) Error: Improper relational operator used in the `while` iteration-continuation condition.
Correction: Use <= rather than <.

Exercises

4.5   Find the error in each of the following. (*Note:* There may be more than one error.)

a)
```
For (x = 100, x >= 1, ++x) {
    printf("%d\n", x);
}
```

b) The following code should print whether a given integer is odd or even:
```
switch (value % 2) {
    case 0:
    puts("Even integer");
    case 1:
    puts("Odd integer");
}
```

c) The following code should input an integer and a character and print them. Assume the user types as input 100 A.

```
scanf("%d", &intVal);
charVal = getchar();
printf("Integer: %d\nCharacter: %c\n", intVal, charVal);
```

d)
```
for (x = .000001; x == .0001; x += .000001) {
    printf("%.7f\n", x);
}
```

e) The following code should output the odd integers from 999 to 1:

```
for (x = 999; x >= 1; x += 2) {
    printf("%d\n", x);
}
```

f) The following code should output the even integers from 2 to 100:

```
counter = 2;

Do {
    if (counter % 2 == 0) {
        printf("%u\n", counter);
    }

    counter += 2;
} While (counter < 100);
```

g) The following code should sum the integers from 100 to 150 (assume total is initialized to 0):

```
for (x = 100; x <= 150; ++x); {
    total += x;
}
```

4.6   State which values of the control variable x are printed by each of the following for statements:

a)
```
for (x = 2; x <= 13; x += 2) {
    printf("%u\n", x);
}
```

b)
```
for (x = 5; x <= 22; x += 7) {
    printf("%u\n", x);
}
```

c)
```
for (x = 3; x <= 15; x += 3) {
    printf("%u\n", x);
}
```

d)
```
for (x = 1; x <= 5; x += 7) {
    printf("%u\n", x);
}
```

e)
```
for (x = 12; x >= 2; x -= 3) {
    printf("%d\n", x);
}
```

4.7   Write for statements that print the following sequences of values:
a) 1, 2, 3, 4, 5, 6, 7
b) 3, 8, 13, 18, 23
c) 20, 14, 8, 2, –4, –10
d) 19, 27, 35, 43, 51

4.8 What does the following program do?

```
1   #include <stdio.h>
2
3   int main(void)
4   {
5      unsigned int x;
6      unsigned int y;
7
8      // prompt user for input
9      printf("%s", "Enter two unsigned integers in the range 1-20: ");
10     scanf("%u%u", &x, &y); // read values for x and y
11
12     for (unsigned int i = 1; i <= y; ++i) { // count from 1 to y
13
14        for (unsigned int j = 1; j <= x; ++j) { // count from 1 to x
15           printf("%s", "@");
16        }
17
18        puts(""); // begin new line
19     }
20  }
```

4.9 *(Sum a Sequence of Integers)* Write a program that sums a sequence of integers. Assume that the first integer read with scanf specifies the number of values remaining to be entered. Your program should read only one value each time scanf is executed. A typical input sequence might be

    5 100 200 300 400 500

where the 5 indicates that the subsequent five values are to be summed.

4.10 *(Average a Sequence of Integers)* Write a program that calculates and prints the average of several integers. Assume the last value read with scanf is the sentinel 9999. A typical input sequence might be

    10 8 11 7 9 9999

indicating that the average of all the values preceding 9999 is to be calculated.

4.11 *(Find the Smallest)* Write a program that finds the smallest of several integers. Assume that the first value read specifies the number of values remaining.

4.12 *(Calculating the Sum of Even Integers)* Write a program that calculates and prints the sum of the even integers from 2 to 30.

4.13 *(Calculating the Product of Odd Integers)* Write a program that calculates and prints the product of the odd integers from 1 to 15.

4.14 *(Factorials)* The *factorial* function is used frequently in probability problems. The factorial of a positive integer *n* (written *n*! and pronounced "*n* factorial") is equal to the product of the positive integers from 1 to *n*. Write a program that evaluates the factorials of the integers from 1 to 5. Print the results in tabular format. What difficulty might prevent you from calculating the factorial of 20?

4.15 *(Modified Compound-Interest Program)* Modify the compound-interest program of Section 4.6 to repeat its steps for interest rates of 5%, 6%, 7%, 8%, 9%, and 10%. Use a for loop to vary the interest rate.

4.16 *(Triangle-Printing Program)* Write a program that prints the following patterns separately, one below the other. Use for loops to generate the patterns. All asterisks (*) should be printed by a single `printf` statement of the form `printf("%s", "*");` (this causes the asterisks to print side by side). [*Hint:* The last two patterns require that each line begin with an appropriate number of blanks.]

```
(A)                 (B)              (C)              (D)
*                   **********       **********                    *
**                  *********        *********                    **
***                 ********         ********                    ***
****                *******          *******                    ****
*****               ******           ******                    *****
******              *****            *****                    ******
*******             ****             ****                    *******
********            ***              ***                    ********
*********           **               **                    *********
**********          *                *                     **********
```

4.17 *(Calculating Credit Limits)* Collecting money becomes increasingly difficult during periods of recession, so companies may tighten their credit limits to prevent their accounts receivable (money owed to them) from becoming too large. In response to a prolonged recession, one company has cut its customers' credit limits in half. Thus, if a particular customer had a credit limit of $2000, it's now $1000. If a customer had a credit limit of $5000, it's now $2500. Write a program that analyzes the credit status of three customers of this company. For each customer you're given:

  a) The customer's account number.
  b) The customer's credit limit before the recession.
  c) The customer's current balance (i.e., the amount the customer owes the company).

  Your program should calculate and print the new credit limit for each customer and should determine (and print) which customers have current balances that exceed their new credit limits.

4.18 *(Bar-Chart Printing Program)* One interesting application of computers is drawing graphs and bar charts. Write a program that reads five numbers (each between 1 and 30). For each number read, your program should print a line containing that number of adjacent asterisks. For example, if your program reads the number seven, it should print `*******`.

4.19 *(Calculating Sales)* An online retailer sells five different products whose retail prices are shown in the following table:

Product number	Retail price
1	$ 2.98
2	$ 4.50
3	$ 9.98
4	$ 4.49
5	$ 6.87

Write a program that reads a series of pairs of numbers as follows:

  a) Product number
  b) Quantity sold for one day

Your program should use a `switch` statement to help determine the retail price for each product. Your program should calculate and display the total retail value of all products sold last week.

4.20 *(Truth Tables)* Complete the following truth tables by filling in each blank with 0 or 1.

Condition1	Condition2	Condition1 && Condition2
0	0	0
0	nonzero	0
nonzero	0	_____
nonzero	nonzero	_____

Condition1	Condition2	Condition1 || Condition2
0	0	0
0	nonzero	1
nonzero	0	_____
nonzero	nonzero	_____

Condition1	! Condition1
0	1
nonzero	_____

4.21 Rewrite the program of Fig. 4.2 so that the definition and initialization of the variable counter is peformed before the for statement, the output the value of counter after the loop terminates.

4.22 *(Average Grade)* Modify the program of Fig. 4.7 so that it calculates the average grade for the class.

4.23 *(Calculating the Compound Interest with Integers)* Modify the program of Fig. 4.6 so that it uses only integers to calculate the compound interest. [*Hint:* Treat all monetary amounts as integral numbers of pennies. Then "break" the result into its dollar portion and cents portion by using the division and remainder operations, respectively. Insert a period.]

4.24 Assume i = 1, j = 2, k = 3 and m = 2. What does each of the following statements print?

    a) printf("%d", i == 1);
    b) printf("%d", j == 3);
    c) printf("%d", i >= 1 && j < 4);
    d) printf("%d", m < = 99 && k < m);
    e) printf("%d", j >= i || k == m);
    f) printf("%d", k + m < j || 3 - j >= k);
    g) printf("%d", !m);
    h) printf("%d", !(j - m));
    i) printf("%d", !(k > m));
    j) printf("%d", !(j > k));

4.25 *(Table of Decimal, Binary, Octal and Hexadecimal Equivalents)* Write a program that prints a table of the binary, octal and hexadecimal equivalents of the decimal numbers in the range

1 through 256. If you're not familiar with these number systems, read Appendix C before you attempt this exercise. [*Note:* You can display an integer as an octal or hexadecimal value with the conversion specifiers %o and %X, respectively.]

4.26   *(Calculating the Value of π)* Calculate the value of π from the infinite series

$$\pi = 4 - \frac{4}{3} + \frac{4}{5} - \frac{4}{7} + \frac{4}{9} - \frac{4}{11} + \cdots$$

Print a table that shows the value of π approximated by one term of this series, by two terms, by three terms, and so on. How many terms of this series do you have to use before you first get 3.14? 3.141? 3.1415? 3.14159?

4.27   *(Pythagorean Triples)* A right triangle can have sides that are all integers. The set of three integer values for the sides of a right triangle is called a Pythagorean triple. These three sides must satisfy the relationship that the sum of the squares of two of the sides is equal to the square of the hypotenuse. Find all Pythagorean triples for side1, side2, and the hypotenuse all no larger than 500. Use a triple-nested for loop that simply tries all possibilities. This is an example of "brute-force" computing. It's not aesthetically pleasing to many people. But there are many reasons why these techniques are important. First, with computing power increasing at such a phenomenal pace, solutions that would have taken years or even centuries of computer time to produce with the technology of just a few years ago can now be produced in hours, minutes or even seconds. Recent microprocessor chips can process a billion instructions per second! Second, as you'll learn in more advanced computer science courses, there are large numbers of interesting problems for which there's no known algorithmic approach other than sheer brute force. We investigate many kinds of problem-solving methodologies in this book. We'll consider many brute-force approaches to various interesting problems.

4.28   *(Calculating Weekly Pay)* A company pays its employees as managers (who receive a fixed weekly salary), hourly workers (who receive a fixed hourly wage for up to the first 40 hours they work and "time-and-a-half"—i.e., 1.5 times their hourly wage—for overtime hours worked), commission workers (who receive $250 plus 5.7% of their gross weekly sales), or pieceworkers (who receive a fixed amount of money for each of the items they produce—each pieceworker in this company works on only one type of item). Write a program to compute the weekly pay for each employee. You do not know the number of employees in advance. Each type of employee has its own pay code: Managers have paycode 1, hourly workers have code 2, commission workers have code 3 and pieceworkers have code 4. Use a switch to compute each employee's pay based on that employee's paycode. Within the switch, prompt the user (i.e., the payroll clerk) to enter the appropriate facts your program needs to calculate each employee's pay based on that employee's paycode. [*Note:* You can input values of type double using the conversion specifier %lf with scanf.]

4.29   *(De Morgan's Laws)* In this chapter, we discussed the logical operators &&, ||, and !. De Morgan's Laws can sometimes make it more convenient for us to express a logical expression. These laws state that the expression !(*condition1* && *condition2*) is logically equivalent to the expression (!*condition1* || !*condition2*). Also, the expression !(*condition1* || *condition2*) is logically equivalent to the expression (!*condition1* && !*condition2*). Use De Morgan's Laws to write equivalent expressions for each of the following, and then write a program to show that both the original expression and the new expression in each case are equivalent.

    a) !(x < 5) && !(y >= 7)
    b) !(a == b) || !(g != 5)
    c) !((x <= 8) && (y > 4))
    d) !((i > 4) || (j <= 6))

4.30   *(Replacing switch with if...else)* Rewrite the program of Fig. 4.7 by replacing the switch statement with a nested if...else statement; be careful to deal with the default case properly. Then rewrite this new version by replacing the nested if...else statement with a series of if statements; here, too, be careful to deal with the default case properly (this is more difficult than in the nested if...else version). This exercise demonstrates that switch is a convenience and that any switch statement can be written with only single-selection statements.

4.31 *(Diamond-Printing Program)* Write a program that prints the following diamond shape. You may use printf statements that print either a single asterisk (*) or a single blank. Maximize your use of iteration (with nested for statements) and minimize the number of printf statements.

```
    *
   ***
  *****
 *******
*********
 *******
  *****
   ***
    *
```

4.32 *(Modified Diamond-Printing Program)* Modify the program you wrote in Exercise 4.31 to read an odd number in the range 1 to 19 to specify the number of rows in the diamond. Your program should then display a diamond of the appropriate size.

4.33 *(Roman-Numeral Equivalent of Decimal Values)* Write a program that prints a table of all the Roman-numeral equivalents of the decimal numbers in the range 1 to 100.

4.34 Describe the process you would use to replace a do...while loop with an equivalent while loop. What problem occurs when you try to replace a while loop with an equivalent do...while loop? Suppose you've been told that you must remove a while loop and replace it with a do...while. What additional control statement would you need to use and how would you use it to ensure that the resulting program behaves exactly as the original?

4.35 A criticism of the break statement and the continue statement is that each is unstructured. Actually, break statements and continue statements can always be replaced by structured statements, although doing so can be awkward. Describe in general how you would remove any break statement from a loop in a program and replace that statement with some structured equivalent. [*Hint:* The break statement leaves a loop from within the body of the loop. The other way to leave is by failing the loop-continuation test. Consider using in the loop-continuation test a second test that indicates "early exit because of a 'break' condition."] Use the technique you developed here to remove the break statement from the program of Fig. 4.11.

4.36 What does the following program segment do?

```
1   for (unsigned int i = 1; i <= 5; ++i) {
2       for (unsigned int j = 1; j <= 3; ++j) {
3           for (unsigned int k = 1; k <= 4; ++k) {
4               printf("%s", "*");
5           }
6           puts("");
7       }
8       puts("");
9   }
```

4.37 Describe in general how you would remove any continue statement from a loop in a program and replace that statement with some structured equivalent. Use the technique you developed here to remove the continue statement from the program of Fig. 4.12.

4.38 *("The Twelve Days of Christmas" Song)* Write a program that uses iteration and switch statements to print the song "The Twelve Days of Christmas." One switch statement should be used to print the day (i.e., "first," "second," etc.). A separate switch statement should be used to print the remainder of each verse.

4.39 *(Limitations of Floating-Point Numbers for Monetary Amounts)* Section 4.6 cautioned about using floating-point values for monetary calculations. Try this experiment: Create a float variable with the value 1000000.00. Next add to that variable the literal float value 0.12f. Display the result using printf and the conversion specifier "%.2f". What do you get?

Making a Difference

4.40 *(World Population Growth)* World population has grown considerably over the centuries. Continued growth could eventually challenge the limits of breathable air, drinkable water, arable cropland and other limited resources. There's evidence that growth has been slowing in recent years and that world population could peak some time this century, then start to decline.

For this exercise, research world population growth issues online. *Be sure to investigate various viewpoints.* Get estimates for the current world population and its growth rate (the percentage by which it's likely to increase this year). Write a program that calculates world population growth each year for the next 75 years, *using the simplifying assumption that the current growth rate will stay constant.* Print the results in a table. The first column should display the year from year 1 to year 75. The second column should display the anticipated world population at the end of that year. The third column should display the numerical increase in the world population that would occur that year. Using your results, determine the year in which the population would be double what it is today, if this year's growth rate were to persist.

4.41 *(Tax Plan Alternatives; The "FairTax")* There are many proposals to make taxation fairer. Check out the FairTax initiative in the United States at

    www.fairtax.org

Research how the proposed FairTax works. One suggestion is to eliminate income taxes and most other taxes in favor of a 23% consumption tax on all products and services that you buy. Some FairTax opponents question the 23% figure and say that because of the way the tax is calculated, it would be more accurate to say the rate is 30%—check this carefully. Write a program that prompts the user to enter expenses in various categories (e.g., housing, food, clothing, transportation, education, health care, vacations), then prints the estimated FairTax that person would pay.

C Functions

5

Objectives

In this chapter, you'll:

- Construct programs modularly from small pieces called functions.

- Use common math functions in the C standard library.

- Create new functions.

- Use the mechanisms that pass information between functions.

- Learn how the function call/ return mechanism is supported by the function call stack and stack frames.

- Use simulation techniques based on random number generation.

- Write and use functions that call themselves.

5.1 Introduction

Most computer programs that solve real-world problems are much larger than the programs presented in the first few chapters. Experience has shown that the best way to develop and maintain a large program is to construct it from smaller pieces, each of which is more manageable than the original program. This technique is called **divide and conquer**. This chapter describes some key features of the C language that facilitate the design, implementation, operation and maintenance of large programs.

5.2 Modularizing Programs in C

In C, **functions** are used to modularize programs. Programs are typically written by combining new functions you write with *prepackaged* functions available in the **C standard library**. We discuss both kinds of functions in this chapter. The C standard library provides a rich collection of functions for performing common *mathematical calculations*, *string manipulations*, *character manipulations*, *input/output*, and many other useful operations. This makes your job easier, because these functions provide many of the capabilities you need.

Good Programming Practice 5.1
Familiarize yourself with the rich collection of functions in the C standard library.

Software Engineering Observation 5.1
Avoid reinventing the wheel. When possible, use C standard library functions instead of writing new functions. This can reduce program development time. These functions are written by experts, well-tested and efficient.

Portability Tip 5.1
Using the functions in the C standard library helps make programs more portable.

The C language and the standard library are *both* specified by the C standard, and they're both provided with standard C systems (with the exception that some of the libraries are designated as optional). The functions printf, scanf and pow that we've used in previous chapters are standard library functions.

You can write functions to define specific tasks that may be used at many points in a program. These are sometimes referred to as **programmer-defined functions**. The actual statements defining the function are written only once, and the statements are hidden from other functions.

Functions are **invoked** by a **function call**, which specifies the function name and provides information (as arguments) that the function needs to perform its designated task. A common analogy for this is the hierarchical form of management. A boss (the **calling function** or **caller**) asks a worker (the **called function**) to perform a task and report back when the task is done (Fig. 5.1). For example, a function needing to display information on the screen calls the worker function printf to perform that task, then printf displays the information and reports back—or **returns**—to the calling function when its task is completed. The boss function does *not* know how the worker function performs its designated tasks. The worker may call other worker functions, and the boss will be unaware of this. We'll soon see how this "hiding" of implementation details promotes good software engineering. Figure 5.1 shows a boss function communicating with several worker functions in a hierarchical manner. Note that Worker1 acts as a boss function to Worker4 and Worker5. Relationships among functions may differ from the hierarchical structure shown in this figure.

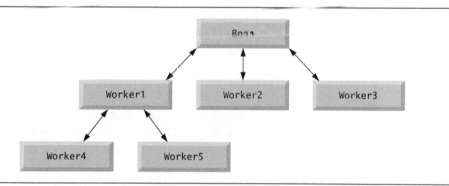

Fig. 5.1 | Hierarchical boss-function/worker-function relationship.

5.3 Math Library Functions

Math library functions allow you to perform certain common mathematical calculations. We use some of them here to introduce the concept of functions. Later in the book, we'll discuss many of the other functions in the C standard library.

Functions are normally used in a program by writing the name of the function followed by a left parenthesis followed by the **argument** (or a comma-separated list of arguments) of the function followed by a right parenthesis. For example, to calculate and print the square root of 900.0 you might write

```
printf("%.2f", sqrt(900.0));
```

When this statement executes, the math library function sqrt is *called* to calculate the square root of the number contained in the parentheses (900.0). The number 900.0 is the *argument* of the sqrt function. The preceding statement would print 30.00. The sqrt function takes an argument of type double and returns a result of type double. All functions in the math library that return floating-point values return the data type double. Note that double values, like float values, can be output using the %f conversion specification. You may also store a function call's result in a variable for later use as in:

```
double result = sqrt(900.0);
```

Error-Prevention Tip 5.1

Include the math header by using the preprocessor directive #include <math.h> when using functions in the math library.

Function arguments may be constants, variables, or expressions. If c1 = 13.0, d = 3.0 and f = 4.0, then the statement

```
printf("%.2f", sqrt(c1 + d * f));
```

calculates and prints the square root of 13.0 + 3.0 * 4.0 = 25.0, namely 5.00.

Figure 5.2 summarizes a small sample of the C math library functions. In the figure, the variables x and y are of type double. The C11 standard adds a wide range of floating-point and complex-number capabilities.

Function	Description	Example
sqrt(x)	square root of x	sqrt(900.0) is 30.0 sqrt(9.0) is 3.0
cbrt(x)	cube root of x (C99 and C11 only)	cbrt(27.0) is 3.0 cbrt(-8.0) is -2.0
exp(x)	exponential function e^x	exp(1.0) is 2.718282 exp(2.0) is 7.389056
log(x)	natural logarithm of x (base e)	log(2.718282) is 1.0 log(7.389056) is 2.0
log10(x)	logarithm of x (base 10)	log10(1.0) is 0.0 log10(10.0) is 1.0 log10(100.0) is 2.0
fabs(x)	absolute value of x as a floating-point number	fabs(13.5) is 13.5 fabs(0.0) is 0.0 fabs(-13.5) is 13.5
ceil(x)	rounds x to the smallest integer not less than x	ceil(9.2) is 10.0 ceil(-9.8) is -9.0
floor(x)	rounds x to the largest integer not greater than x	floor(9.2) is 9.0 floor(-9.8) is -10.0
pow(x, y)	x raised to power y (x^y)	pow(2, 7) is 128.0 pow(9, .5) is 3.0

Fig. 5.2 | Commonly used math library functions. (Part 1 of 2.)

Function	Description	Example
fmod(x, y)	remainder of *x*/*y* as a floating-point number	fmod(13.657, 2.333) is 1.992
sin(x)	trigonometric sine of *x* (*x* in radians)	sin(0.0) is 0.0
cos(x)	trigonometric cosine of *x* (*x* in radians)	cos(0.0) is 1.0
tan(x)	trigonometric tangent of *x* (*x* in radians)	tan(0.0) is 0.0

Fig. 5.2 | Commonly used math library functions. (Part 2 of 2.)

5.4 Functions

Functions allow you to modularize a program. All variables defined in function definitions are **local variables**—they can be accessed *only* in the function in which they're defined. Most functions have a list of **parameters** that provide the means for communicating information between functions via arguments in function calls. A function's parameters are also *local variables* of that function.

Software Engineering Observation 5.2

In programs containing many functions, main is often implemented as a group of calls to functions that perform the bulk of the program's work.

There are several motivations for "functionalizing" a program. The *divide-and-conquer* approach makes program development more manageable. Another motivation is **software reusability**— using existing functions as *building blocks* to create new programs. Software reusability is a major factor in the *object-oriented programming* movement that you'll learn more about when you study languages derived from C, such as C++, Objective-C, Java, C# (pronounced "C sharp") and Swift. With good function naming and definition, programs can be created from standardized functions that accomplish specific tasks, rather than being built by using customized code. This is known as **abstraction**. We use abstraction each time we use standard library functions like printf, scanf and pow. A third motivation is to avoid repeating code in a program. Packaging code as a function allows it to be executed from other locations in a program simply by calling the function.

Software Engineering Observation 5.3

Each function should be limited to performing a single, well-defined task, and the function name should express that task. This facilitates abstraction and promotes software reusability.

Software Engineering Observation 5.4

If you cannot choose a concise name that expresses what the function does, it's possible that your function is attempting to perform too many diverse tasks. It's usually best to break such a function into smaller functions—this is sometimes called decomposition.

5.5 Function Definitions

Each program we've presented has consisted of a function called main that called standard library functions to accomplish its tasks. We now consider how to write *custom* functions.

5.5.1 square Function

Consider a program that uses a function square to calculate and print the squares of the integers from 1 to 10 (Fig. 5.3).

```c
1   // Fig. 5.3: fig05_03.c
2   // Creating and using a programmer-defined function.
3   #include <stdio.h>
4
5   int square(int y); // function prototype
6
7   int main(void)
8   {
9      // loop 10 times and calculate and output square of x each time
10     for (int x = 1; x <= 10; ++x) {
11        printf("%d  ", square(x)); // function call
12     }
13
14     puts("");
15  }
16
17  // square function definition returns the square of its parameter
18  int square(int y) // y is a copy of the argument to the function
19  {
20     return y * y; // returns the square of y as an int
21  }
```

```
1   4   9   16   25   36   49   64   81   100
```

Fig. 5.3 | Creating and using a programmer-defined function.

Calling Function square
Function square is **invoked** or **called** in main within the printf statement (line 11)

```c
printf("%d  ", square(x)); // function call
```

Function square receives a *copy* of the *argument* x's value in the *parameter* y (line 18). Then square calculates y * y and passes the result back to line 11 in main where square was invoked (line 11). Line 11 continues by passing the square result to function printf, which displays the result on the screen. This process repeats 10 times—once for each iteration of the for statement.

square Function Definition
The definition of function square (lines 18–21) shows that square expects an integer parameter y. The keyword int preceding the function name (line 18) indicates that square *returns* an integer result. The **return statement** in square passes the value of the expression y * y (that is, the result of the calculation) back to the calling function.

square Function Prototype
Line 5

```c
int square(int y); // function prototype
```

is a **function prototype** (also called a **function declaration**). The int in parentheses informs the compiler that square expects to *receive* an integer value from the caller. The int to the *left* of the function name square informs the compiler that square *returns* an integer result to the caller. The compiler compares the calls to square (line 11) to the function prototype to ensure that:

- the number of arguments is correct,
- the arguments are of the correct type,
- the argument types are in the correct order, and
- the return type is consistent with the context in which the function is called.

Function prototypes are discussed in detail in Section 5.6.

Format of a Function Definition

The format of a function definition is

```
return-value-type function-name(parameter-list)
{
    statements
}
```

The *function-name* is any valid identifier. The ***return-value-type*** is the data type of the result returned to the caller. The *return-value-type* void indicates that a function does *not* return a value. Together, the *return-value-type*, *function-name* and *parameter-list* are sometimes referred to as the function **header**.

Error-Prevention Tip 5.2

Check that your functions that are supposed to return values do so. Check that your functions that are not supposed to return values do not.

The *parameter-list* is a comma-separated list that specifies the parameters received by the function when it's called. If a function does *not* receive any values, *parameter-list* is void. A type *must* be listed *explicitly* for each parameter.

Common Programming Error 5.1

Specifying function parameters of the same type as double x, y instead of double x, double y results in a compilation error.

Common Programming Error 5.2

Placing a semicolon after the right parenthesis enclosing the parameter list of a function definition is a syntax error.

Common Programming Error 5.3

Redefining a parameter as a local variable in a function is a compilation error.

Good Programming Practice 5.2

Although it's not incorrect to do so, do not use the same names for a function's arguments and the corresponding parameters in the function definition. This helps avoid ambiguity.

Function Body

The *statements* within braces form the **function body**, which is also a *block*. Variables can be declared in any block, and blocks can be nested (but functions connot be nested).

Common Programming Error 5.4

Defining a function inside another function is a syntax error.

Good Programming Practice 5.3

Choosing meaningful function names and meaningful parameter names makes programs more readable and helps avoid excessive use of comments.

Software Engineering Observation 5.5

Small functions promote software reusability.

Software Engineering Observation 5.6

Programs should be written as collections of small functions. This makes programs easier to write, debug, maintain and modify.

Software Engineering Observation 5.7

A function requiring a large number of parameters may be performing too many tasks. Consider dividing the function into smaller functions that perform the separate tasks. The function header should fit on one line if possible.

Software Engineering Observation 5.8

The function prototype, function header and function calls should all agree in the number, type, and order of arguments and parameters, and in the type of return value.

Returning Control from a Function

There are three ways to return control from a called function to the point at which a function was invoked. If the function does *not* return a result, control is returned simply when the function-ending right brace is reached, or by executing the statement

```
return;
```

If the function *does* return a result, the statement

```
return expression;
```

returns the value of *expression* to the caller.

main's *Return Type*

Notice that main has an int return type. The return value of main is used to indicate whether the program executed correctly. In earlier versions of C, we'd explicitly place

```
return 0;
```

at the end of main—0 indicates that a program ran successfully. The C standard indicates that main implicitly returns 0 if you to omit the preceding statement—as we've done throughout this book. You can explicitly return non-zero values from main to indicate that a problem occured during your program's execution. For information on how to report a program failure, see the documentation for your particular operating-system environment.

5.5.2 maximum Function

Our second example uses a programmer-defined function maximum to determine and return the largest of three integers (Fig. 5.4). The integers are input with scanf (line 14). Next, they're passed to maximum (line 18), which determines the largest integer. This value is returned to main by the return statement in maximum (line 35). The printf statement in line 18 then prints the value returned by maximum.

```c
1   // Fig. 5.4: fig05_04.c
2   // Finding the maximum of three integers.
3   #include <stdio.h>
4
5   int maximum(int x, int y, int z); // function prototype
6
7   int main(void)
8   {
9      int number1; // first integer entered by the user
10     int number2; // second integer entered by the user
11     int number3; // third integer entered by the user
12
13     printf("%s", "Enter three integers: ");
14     scanf("%d%d%d", &number1, &number2, &number3);
15
16     // number1, number2 and number3 are arguments
17     // to the maximum function call
18     printf("Maximum is: %d\n", maximum(number1, number2, number3));
19  }
20
21  // Function maximum definition
22  // x, y and z are parameters
23  int maximum(int x, int y, int z)
24  {
25     int max = x; // assume x is largest
26
27     if (y > max) { // if y is larger than max,
28        max = y; // assign y to max
29     }
30
31     if (z > max) { // if z is larger than max,
32        max = z; // assign z to max
33     }
34
35     return max; // max is largest value
36  }
```

```
Enter three integers: 22 85 17
Maximum is: 85
```

Fig. 5.4 | Finding the maximum of three integers. (Part 1 of 2.)

```
Enter three integers: 47 32 14
Maximum is: 47
```

```
Enter three integers: 35 8 79
Maximum is: 79
```

Fig. 5.4 | Finding the maximum of three integers. (Part 2 of 2.)

The function initially assumes that its first argument (stored in the parameter x) is the largest and assigns it to max (line 25). Next, the if statement at lines 27–29 determines whether y is greater than max and, if so, assigns y to max. Then, the if statement at lines 31–33 determines whether z is greater than max and, if so, assigns z to max. Finally, line 35 returns max to the caller.

5.6 Function Prototypes: A Deeper Look

An important C feature is the function prototype, which was borrowed from C++. The compiler uses function prototypes to validate function calls. Pre-standard C did *not* perform this kind of checking, so it was possible to call functions improperly without the compiler detecting the errors. Such calls could result in fatal execution-time errors or nonfatal errors that caused subtle, difficult-to-detect problems. Function prototypes correct this deficiency.

Good Programming Practice 5.4

Include function prototypes for all functions to take advantage of C's type-checking capabilities. Use #include preprocessor directives to obtain function prototypes for the standard library functions from the headers for the appropriate libraries, or to obtain headers containing function prototypes for functions developed by you and/or your group members.

The function prototype for maximum in Fig. 5.4 (line 5) is

```
int maximum(int x, int y, int z); // function prototype
```

It states that maximum takes three arguments of type int and returns a result of type int. Notice that the function prototype is the same as the first line of maximum's definition.

Good Programming Practice 5.5

Include parameter names in function prototypes for documentation purposes. The compiler ignores these names, so the prototype int maximum(int, int, int); is valid.

Common Programming Error 5.5

Forgetting the semicolon at the end of a function prototype is a syntax error.

Compilation Errors
A function call that does not match the function prototype is a *compilation* error. An error is also generated if the function prototype and the function definition disagree. For example, in Fig. 5.4, if the function prototype had been written

```
void maximum(int x, int y, int z);
```

the compiler would generate an error because the void return type in the function prototype would differ from the int return type in the function header.

Argument Coercion and "Usual Arithmetic Conversion Rules"

Another important feature of function prototypes is the **coercion of arguments,** i.e., the forcing of arguments to the appropriate type. For example, the math library function sqrt can be called with an integer argument even though the function prototype in <math.h> specifies a double parameter, and the function will still work correctly. The statement

```
printf("%.3f\n", sqrt(4));
```

correctly evaluates sqrt(4) and prints the 2.000. The function prototype causes the compiler to convert a *copy* of the int value 4 to the double value 4.0 before the *copy* is passed to sqrt. In general, *argument values that do not correspond precisely to the parameter types in the function prototype are converted to the proper type before the function is called.* These conversions can lead to incorrect results if C's **usual arithmetic conversion rules** are not followed. These specify how values can be converted to other types without losing data. In our sqrt example, an int is automatically converted to a double without changing its value (because double can represent a much larger range of values than int). However, a double converted to an int *truncates* the double's fractional part, thus changing the original value. Converting large integer types to small integer types (e.g., long to short) can also result in changed values.

The usual arithmetic conversion rules automatically apply to expressions containing values of two data types (also referred to as **mixed-type expressions**), and are handled by the compiler. In a mixed-type expression, the compiler makes a temporary copy of the value that needs to be converted, then converts the *copy* to the "highest" type in the expression—this is known as **promotion**. The usual arithmetic conversion rules for a mixed-type expression containing at least one floating-point value are:

- If one of the values is a long double, the other is converted to a long double.
- If one of the values is a double, the other is converted to a double.
- If one of the values is a float, the other is converted to a float.

If the mixed-type expression contains only integer types, then the usual arithmetic conversions specify a set of integer promotion rules. In *most* cases, the integer types lower in Fig. 5.5 are converted to types higher in the figure. Section 6.3.1 of the C standard document specifies the complete details of arithmetic operands and the usual arithmetic conversion rules. Figure 5.5 lists the floating-point and integer data types with each type's printf and scanf conversion specifications.

Data type	printf conversion specification	scanf conversion specification
Floating-point types		
long double	%Lf	%Lf
double	%f	%lf
float	%f	%f

Fig. 5.5 | Arithmetic data types and their conversion specifications. (Part 1 of 2.)

Data type	printf conversion specification	scanf conversion specification
Integer types		
unsigned long long int	%llu	%llu
long long int	%lld	%lld
unsigned long int	%lu	%lu
long int	%ld	%ld
unsigned int	%u	%u
int	%d	%d
unsigned short	%hu	%hu
short	%hd	%hd
char	%c	%c

Fig. 5.5 | Arithmetic data types and their conversion specifications. (Part 2 of 2.)

A value can be converted to a *lower* type *only* by explicitly assigning the value to a variable of lower type or by using a *cast* operator. Arguments in a function call are converted to the parameter types specified in a function prototype as if the arguments were being assigned directly to variables of those types. If our square function that uses an int parameter (Fig. 5.3) is called with a floating-point argument, the argument is converted to int (a lower type), and square usually returns an incorrect value. For example, square(4.5) returns 16, not 20.25.

Common Programming Error 5.6
Converting from a higher data type in the promotion hierarchy to a lower type can change the data value. Many compilers issue warnings in such cases.

If there's no function prototype for a function, the compiler forms its own function prototype using the first occurrence of the function—either the function definition or a call to the function. This typically leads to warnings or errors, depending on the compiler.

Error-Prevention Tip 5.3
Always include function prototypes for the functions you define or use in your program to help prevent compilation errors and warnings.

Software Engineering Observation 5.9
A function prototype placed outside any function definition applies to all calls to the function appearing after the function prototype in the file. A function prototype placed in a function body applies only to calls made in that function.

5.7 Function Call Stack and Stack Frames

To understand how C performs function calls, we first need to consider a data structure (i.e., collection of related data items) known as a **stack**. Think of a stack as analogous to a pile of dishes. When a dish is placed on the pile, it's normally placed at the *top* (referred to as **pushing** the dish onto the stack). Similarly, when a dish is removed from the pile, it's normally removed from the *top* (referred to as **popping** the dish off the stack). Stacks are known as **last-in, first-out (LIFO) data structures**—the *last* item pushed (inserted) on the stack is the *first* item popped (removed) from the stack.

An important mechanism for computer science students to understand is the **function call stack** (sometimes referred to as the **program execution stack**). This data structure— working "behind the scenes"—supports the function call/return mechanism. It also supports the creation, maintenance and destruction of each called function's local variables (also called *automatic variables*). We explained the last-in, first-out (LIFO) behavior of stacks with our dish-stacking example. As we'll see in Figs. 5.7–5.9, this LIFO behavior is *exactly* what a function does when returning to the function that called it.

As each function is called, it may call other functions, which may call other functions—all *before* any function returns. Each function eventually must return control to the function that called it. So, we must keep track of the return addresses that each function needs to return control to the function that called it. The function call stack is the perfect data structure for handling this information. Each time a function calls another function, an entry is *pushed* onto the stack. This entry, called a **stack frame**, contains the *return address* that the called function needs in order to return to the calling function. It also contains some additional information we'll soon discuss. If the called function returns, instead of calling another function before returning, the stack frame for the function call is *popped*, and control transfers to the return address in the popped stack frame.

Each called function *always* finds the information it needs to return to its caller at the *top* of the call stack. And, if a function makes a call to another function, a stack frame for the new function call is simply pushed onto the call stack. Thus, the return address required by the newly called function to return to its caller is now located at the *top* of the stack.

The stack frames have another important responsibility. Most functions have local (automatic) variables—parameters and some or all of their local variables. Automatic variables need to exist while a function is executing. They need to remain active if the function makes calls to other functions. But when a called function returns to its caller, the called function's automatic variables need to "go away." The called function's stack frame is a perfect place to reserve the memory for automatic variables. That stack frame exists only as long as the called function is active. When that function returns—and no longer needs its local automatic variables—its stack frame is *popped* from the stack, and those local automatic variables are no longer known to the program.

Of course, the amount of memory in a computer is finite, so only a certain amount of memory can be used to store stack frames on the function call stack. If more function calls occur than can have their stack frames stored on the function call stack, a *fatal* error known as **stack overflow** occurs.

Function Call Stack in Action

Now let's consider how the call stack supports the operation of a square function called by main (lines 8–13 of Fig. 5.6). First the operating system calls main—this pushes a stack frame onto the stack (shown in Fig. 5.7). The stack frame tells main how to return to the operating system (i.e., transfer to return address R1) and contains the space for main's automatic variable (i.e., a, which is initialized to 10).

```
1   // Fig. 5.6: fig05_06.c
2   // Demonstrating the function call stack
3   // and stack frames using a function square.
4   #include <stdio.h>
5
6   int square(int); // prototype for function square
7
8   int main()
9   {
10      int a = 10; // value to square (local automatic variable in main)
11
12      printf("%d squared: %d\n", a, square(a)); // display a squared
13  }
14
15  // returns the square of an integer
16  int square(int x) // x is a local variable
17  {
18      return x * x; // calculate square and return result
19  }
```

```
10 squared: 100
```

Fig. 5.6 | Demonstrating the function call stack and stack frames using a function square.

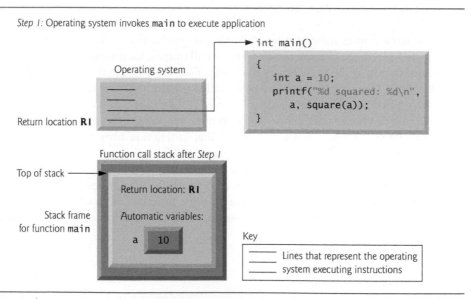

Step 1: Operating system invokes **main** to execute application

Fig. 5.7 | Function call stack after the operating system invokes main to execute the program.

Function main—before returning to the operating system—now calls function square in line 12 of Fig. 5.6. This causes a stack frame for square (lines 16–19) to be pushed onto the function call stack (Fig. 5.8). This stack frame contains the return address that square needs to return to main (i.e., R2) and the memory for square's automatic variable (i.e., x).

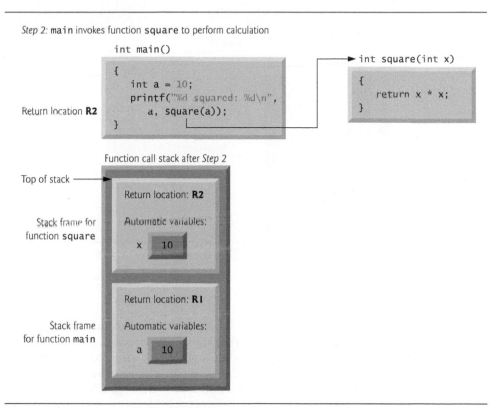

Fig. 5.8 | Function call stack after main invokes square to perform the calculation.

After square calculates the square of its argument, it needs to return to main—and no longer needs the memory for its automatic variable x. So the stack is popped—giving square the return location in main (i.e., R2) and losing square's automatic variable. Figure 5.9 shows the function call stack *after* square's stack frame has been popped.

Function main now displays the result of calling square (line 12 in Fig. 5.6). Reaching the closing right brace of main causes its stack frame to be popped from the stack, gives main the address it needs to return to the operating system (i.e., R1 in Fig. 5.7) and causes the memory for main's automatic variable (i.e., a) to become unavailable.

You've now seen how valuable the stack data structure is in implementing a key mechanism that supports program execution. Data structures have many important applications in computer science. We discuss stacks, queues, lists, trees and other data structures in Chapter 12.

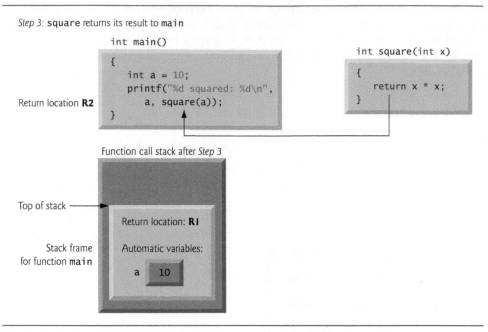

Fig. 5.9 | Function call stack after function `square` returns to `main`.

5.8 Headers

Each standard library has a corresponding **header** containing the function prototypes for all the functions in that library and definitions of various *data types* and constants needed by those functions. Figure 5.10 lists alphabetically some of the standard library headers that may be included in programs. The C standard includes additional headers. The term "macros" that's used several times in Fig. 5.10 is discussed in detail in Chapter 13.

Header	Explanation
`<assert.h>`	Contains information for adding diagnostics that aid program debugging.
`<ctype.h>`	Contains function prototypes for functions that test characters for certain properties, and function prototypes for functions that can be used to convert lowercase letters to uppercase letters and vice versa.
`<errno.h>`	Defines macros that are useful for reporting error conditions.
`<float.h>`	Contains the floating-point size limits of the system.
`<limits.h>`	Contains the integral size limits of the system.
`<locale.h>`	Contains function prototypes and other information that enables a program to be modified for the current locale on which it's running. The notion of locale enables the computer system to handle different conventions for expressing data such as dates, times, currency amounts and large numbers throughout the world.

Fig. 5.10 | Some of the standard library headers. (Part 1 of 2.)

Header	Explanation
`<math.h>`	Contains function prototypes for math library functions.
`<setjmp.h>`	Contains function prototypes for functions that allow bypassing of the usual function call and return sequence.
`<signal.h>`	Contains function prototypes and macros to handle various conditions that may arise during program execution.
`<stdarg.h>`	Defines macros for dealing with a list of arguments to a function whose number and types are unknown.
`<stddef.h>`	Contains common type definitions used by C for performing calculations.
`<stdio.h>`	Contains function prototypes for the standard input/output library functions, and information used by them.
`<stdlib.h>`	Contains function prototypes for conversions of numbers to text and text to numbers, memory allocation, random numbers and other utility functions.
`<string.h>`	Contains function prototypes for string-processing functions.
`<time.h>`	Contains function prototypes and types for manipulating the time and date.

Fig. 5.10 | Some of the standard library headers. (Part 2 of 2.)

You can create custom headers. Programmer-defined headers should also use the .h filename extension. A programmer-defined header can be included by using the `#include` preprocessor directive. For example, if the prototype for our square function was located in the header `square.h`, we'd include that header in our program by using the following directive at the top of the program:

```
#include "square.h"
```

Section 13.2 presents additional information on including headers, such as why programmer-defined headers are enclosed in quotes (" ") rather than angle brackets (<>).

5.9 Passing Arguments By Value and By Reference

In many programming languages, there are two ways to pass arguments—**pass-by-value** and **pass-by-reference**. When arguments are *passed by value*, a *copy* of the argument's value is made and passed to the called function. Changes to the copy do *not* affect an original variable's value in the caller. When an argument is *passed by reference*, the caller allows the called function to *modify* the original variable's value.

Pass-by-value should be used whenever the called function does not need to modify the value of the caller's original variable. This prevents the accidental **side effects** (variable modifications) that so greatly hinder the development of correct and reliable software systems. Pass-by-reference should be used only with *trusted* called functions that need to modify the original variable.

In C, all arguments are passed by value. As we'll see in Chapter 7, C Pointers, it's possible to achieve pass-by-reference by using the *address operator* and the *indirection operator*. In Chapter 6, we'll see that array arguments are automatically passed by reference for performance reasons. We'll see in Chapter 7 that this is *not* a contradiction. For now, we concentrate on pass-by-value.

5.10 Random Number Generation

We now take a brief and, hopefully, entertaining diversion into *simulation* and *game playing*. In this and the next section, we'll develop a nicely structured game-playing program that includes multiple functions. The program uses functions and several of the control statements we've studied. The *element of chance* can be introduced into computer applications by using the C standard library function rand from the <stdlib.h> header.

Obtaining a Random Integer Value
Consider the following statement:

```
i = rand();
```

The rand function generates an integer between 0 and RAND_MAX (a symbolic constant defined in the <stdlib.h> header). Standard C states that the value of RAND_MAX must be at least 32767, which is the maximum value for a two-byte (i.e., 16-bit) integer. The programs in this section were tested on Microsoft Visual C++ with a maximum RAND_MAX value of 32767, and on GNU gcc and Xcode LLVM with a maximum RAND_MAX value of 2147483647. If rand truly produces integers *at random*, every number between 0 and RAND_MAX has an equal chance (or probability) of being chosen each time rand is called.

The range of values produced directly by rand is often different from what's needed in a specific application. For example, a program that simulates coin tossing might require only 0 for "heads" and 1 for "tails." A dice-rolling program that simulates a six-sided die would require random integers from 1 to 6.

Rolling a Six-Sided Die
To demonstrate rand, let's develop a program (Fig. 5.11) to simulate 20 rolls of a six-sided die and print the value of each roll.

```
1   // Fig. 5.11: fig05_11.c
2   // Shifted, scaled random integers produced by 1 + rand() % 6.
3   #include <stdio.h>
4   #include <stdlib.h>
5
6   int main(void)
7   {
8      // loop 20 times
9      for (unsigned int i = 1; i <= 20; ++i) {
10
11         // pick random number from 1 to 6 and output it
12         printf("%10d", 1 + (rand() % 6));
13
14         // if counter is divisible by 5, begin new line of output
15         if (i % 5 == 0) {
16            puts("");
17         }
18      }
19   }
```

Fig. 5.11 | Shifted, scaled random integers produced by 1 + rand() % 6. (Part 1 of 2.)

6	6	5	5	6
5	1	1	5	3
6	6	2	4	2
6	2	3	4	1

Fig. 5.11 | Shifted, scaled random integers produced by 1 + rand() % 6. (Part 2 of 2.)

The function prototype for function rand is in <stdlib.h>. We use the remainder operator (%) in conjunction with rand as follows

```
rand() % 6
```

to produce integers in the range 0 to 5. This is called **scaling**. The number 6 is called the **scaling factor**. We then **shift** the range of numbers produced by adding 1 to our previous result. The output confirms that the results are in the range 1 to 6—the actual random values chosen might vary by compiler.

Rolling a Six-Sided Die 60,000,000 Times

To show that these numbers occur approximately with *equal likelihood*, let's simulate 60,000,000 rolls of a die with the program of Fig. 5.12. Each integer from 1 to 6 should appear approximately 10,000,000 times.

```c
1   // Fig. 5.12: fig05_12.c
2   // Rolling a six-sided die 60,000,000 times.
3   #include <stdio.h>
4   #include <stdlib.h>
5
6   int main(void)
7   {
8      unsigned int frequency1 = 0; // rolled 1 counter
9      unsigned int frequency2 = 0; // rolled 2 counter
10     unsigned int frequency3 = 0; // rolled 3 counter
11     unsigned int frequency4 = 0; // rolled 4 counter
12     unsigned int frequency5 = 0; // rolled 5 counter
13     unsigned int frequency6 = 0; // rolled 6 counter
14
15     // loop 60000000 times and summarize results
16     for (unsigned int roll = 1; roll <= 60000000; ++roll) {
17        int face = 1 + rand() % 6; // random number from 1 to 6
18
19        // determine face value and increment appropriate counter
20        switch (face) {
21
22           case 1: // rolled 1
23              ++frequency1;
24              break;
25
26           case 2: // rolled 2
27              ++frequency2;
28              break;
```

Fig. 5.12 | Rolling a six-sided die 60,000,000 times. (Part 1 of 2.)

```
29
30              case 3: // rolled 3
31                  ++frequency3;
32                  break;
33
34              case 4: // rolled 4
35                  ++frequency4;
36                  break;
37
38              case 5: // rolled 5
39                  ++frequency5;
40                  break;
41
42              case 6: // rolled 6
43                  ++frequency6;
44                  break; // optional
45          }
46      }
47
48      // display results in tabular format
49      printf("%s%13s\n", "Face", "Frequency");
50      printf("    1%13u\n", frequency1);
51      printf("    2%13u\n", frequency2);
52      printf("    3%13u\n", frequency3);
53      printf("    4%13u\n", frequency4);
54      printf("    5%13u\n", frequency5);
55      printf("    6%13u\n", frequency6);
56  }
```

```
Face     Frequency
   1       9999294
   2      10002929
   3       9995360
   4      10000409
   5      10005206
   6       9996802
```

Fig. 5.12 | Rolling a six-sided die 60,000,000 times. (Part 2 of 2.)

As the program output shows, by scaling and shifting we've used the rand function to realistically simulate the rolling of a six-sided die. Note the use of the %s conversion specifier to print the character strings "Face" and "Frequency" as column headers (line 49). After we study arrays in Chapter 6, we'll show how to replace this 26-line switch statement elegantly with a single-line statement.

Randomizing the Random Number Generator
Executing the program of Fig. 5.11 again produces

```
        6           6           5           5           6
        5           1           1           5           3
        6           6           2           4           2
        6           2           3           4           1
```

Notice that *exactly the same sequence of values* was printed. How can these be *random* numbers? Ironically, this *repeatability* is an important characteristic of function rand. When *debugging* a program, this repeatability is essential for proving that corrections to a program work properly.

Function rand actually generates **pseudorandom numbers**. Calling rand repeatedly produces a sequence of numbers that *appears* to be random. However, the sequence repeats itself each time the program is executed. Once a program has been thoroughly debugged, it can be conditioned to produce a *different* sequence of random numbers for each execution. This is called **randomizing** and is accomplished with the standard library function **srand**. Function srand takes an unsigned int argument and **seeds** function rand to produce a different sequence of random numbers for each execution of the program.

We demonstrate function srand in Fig. 5.13. The conversion specifier %u is used to read an unsigned int value with scanf. The function prototype for srand is found in <stdlib.h>.

```c
1   // Fig. 5.13: fig05_13.c
2   // Randomizing the die-rolling program.
3   #include <stdlib.h>
4   #include <stdio.h>
5
6   int main(void)
7   {
8       unsigned int seed; // number used to seed the random number generator
9
10      printf("%s", "Enter seed: ");
11      scanf("%u", &seed); // note %u for unsigned int
12
13      srand(seed); // seed the random number generator
14
15      // loop 10 times
16      for (unsigned int i = 1; i <= 10; ++i) {
17
18          // pick a random number from 1 to 6 and output it
19          printf("%10d", 1 + (rand() % 6));
20
21          // if counter is divisible by 5, begin a new line of output
22          if (i % 5 == 0) {
23              puts("");
24          }
25      }
26  }
```

```
Enter seed: 67
         6         1         4         6         2
         1         6         1         6         4
```

```
Enter seed: 867
         2         4         6         1         6
         1         1         3         6         2
```

Fig. 5.13 | Randomizing the die-rolling program. (Part 1 of 2.)

```
Enter seed: 67
        6           1           4           6           2
        1           6           1           6           4
```

Fig. 5.13 | Randomizing the die-rolling program. (Part 2 of 2.)

Let's run the program several times and observe the results. Notice that a *different* sequence of random numbers is obtained each time the program is run, provided that a *different* seed is supplied. The first and last outputs use the *same* seed value, so they show the same results.

To randomize *without* entering a seed each time, use a statement like

```
srand(time(NULL));
```

This causes the computer to read its clock to obtain the value for the seed automatically. Function time returns the number of seconds that have passed since midnight on January 1, 1970. This value is converted to an unsigned integer and used as the seed to the random number generator. The function prototype for time is in <time.h>. We'll say more about NULL in Chapter 7.

Generalized Scaling and Shifting of Random Numbers

The values produced directly by rand are always in the range:

```
0 ≤ rand() ≤ RAND_MAX
```

As you know, the following statement simulates rolling a six-sided die:

```
face = 1 + rand() % 6;
```

This statement always assigns an integer value (at random) to the variable face in the range 1 ≤ face ≤ 6. The *width* of this range (i.e., the number of consecutive integers in the range) is 6 and the *starting number* in the range is 1. Referring to the preceding statement, we see that the width of the range is determined by the number used to *scale* rand with the *remainder operator* (i.e., 6), and the *starting number* of the range is equal to the number (i.e., 1) that's added to rand % 6. We can generalize this result as follows:

```
n = a + rand() % b;
```

where a is the **shifting value** (which is equal to the *first* number in the desired range of consecutive integers) and b is the *scaling factor* (which is equal to the *width* of the desired range of consecutive integers). In the exercises, we'll see that it's possible to choose integers at random from sets of values other than ranges of consecutive integers.

5.11 Example: A Game of Chance; Introducing enum

One of the most popular games of chance is a dice game known as "craps," which is played in casinos and back alleys throughout the world. The rules of the game are straightforward:

A player rolls two dice. Each die has six faces. These faces contain 1, 2, 3, 4, 5, and 6 spots. After the dice have come to rest, the sum of the spots on the two upward faces is calculated. If the sum is 7 or 11 on the first throw, the player wins. If the sum is 2, 3, or 12 on the first throw (called "craps"), the player loses (i.e., the "house" wins). If the sum is 4, 5, 6, 8, 9, or 10 on the first throw, then that sum becomes the player's "point." To win, you must continue rolling the dice until you "make your point." The player loses by rolling a 7 before making the point.

Figure 5.14 simulates the game of craps and Fig. 5.15 shows several sample executions.

```c
1   // Fig. 5.14: fig05_14.c
2   // Simulating the game of craps.
3   #include <stdio.h>
4   #include <stdlib.h>
5   #include <time.h> // contains prototype for function time
6
7   // enumeration constants represent game status
8   enum Status { CONTINUE, WON, LOST };
9
10  int rollDice(void); // function prototype
11
12  int main(void)
13  {
14     // randomize random number generator using current time
15     srand(time(NULL));
16
17     int myPoint; // player must make this point to win
18     enum Status gameStatus; // can contain CONTINUE, WON, or LOST
19     int sum = rollDice(); // first roll of the dice
20
21     // determine game status based on sum of dice
22     switch(sum) {
23
24        // win on first roll
25        case 7: // 7 is a winner
26        case 11: // 11 is a winner
27           gameStatus = WON;
28           break;
29
30        // lose on first roll
31        case 2: // 2 is a loser
32        case 3: // 3 is a loser
33        case 12: // 12 is a loser
34           gameStatus = LOST;
35           break;
36
37        // remember point
38        default:
39           gameStatus = CONTINUE; // player should keep rolling
40           myPoint = sum; // remember the point
41           printf("Point is %d\n", myPoint);
42           break; // optional
43     }
44
```

Fig. 5.14 | Simulating the game of craps. (Part 1 of 2.)

```
45      // while game not complete
46      while (CONTINUE == gameStatus) { // player should keep rolling
47         sum = rollDice(); // roll dice again
48
49         // determine game status
50         if (sum == myPoint) { // win by making point
51            gameStatus = WON;
52         }
53         else {
54            if (7 == sum) { // lose by rolling 7
55               gameStatus = LOST;
56            }
57         }
58      }
59
60      // display won or lost message
61      if (WON == gameStatus) { // did player win?
62         puts("Player wins");
63      }
64      else { // player lost
65         puts("Player loses");
66      }
67   }
68
69   // roll dice, calculate sum and display results
70   int rollDice(void)
71   {
72      int die1 = 1 + (rand() % 6); // pick random die1 value
73      int die2 = 1 + (rand() % 6); // pick random die2 value
74
75      // display results of this roll
76      printf("Player rolled %d + %d = %d\n", die1, die2, die1 + die2);
77      return die1 + die2; // return sum of dice
78   }
```

Fig. 5.14 | Simulating the game of craps. (Part 2 of 2.)

Player wins on the first roll

```
Player rolled 5 + 6 = 11
Player wins
```

Player wins on a subsequent roll

```
Player rolled 4 + 1 = 5
Point is 5
Player rolled 6 + 2 = 8
Player rolled 2 + 1 = 3
Player rolled 3 + 2 = 5
Player wins
```

Fig. 5.15 | Sample runs for the game of craps. (Part 1 of 2.)

Player loses on the first roll

```
Player rolled 1 + 1 = 2
Player loses
```

Player loses on a subsequent roll

```
Player rolled 6 + 4 = 10
Point is 10
Player rolled 3 + 4 = 7
Player loses
```

Fig. 5.15 | Sample runs for the game of craps. (Part 2 of 2.)

In the rules of the game, notice that the player must roll *two* dice on the first roll, and must do so later on all subsequent rolls. We define a function rollDice to roll the dice and compute and print their sum. Function rollDice is defined *once*, but it's called from *two* places in the program (lines 19 and 47). The function takes no arguments, so we've indicated void in the parameter list (line 70) and in the function prototype. Function rollDice does return the sum of the two dice, so a return type of int is indicated in its function header and in its function prototype.

Enumerations

The game is reasonably involved. The player may win or lose on the first roll, or may win or lose on any subsequent roll. Variable gameStatus, defined to be of a new type—enum Status—stores the current status. Line 8 creates a programmer-defined type called an **enumeration**. An enumeration, introduced by the keyword **enum**, is a set of integer constants represented by identifiers. **Enumeration constants** help make programs more readable and easier to maintain. Values in an enum start with 0 and are incremented by 1. In line 8, the constant CONTINUE has the value 0, WON has the value 1 and LOST has the value 2. It's also possible to assign an integer value to each identifier in an enum (see Chapter 10). The *identifiers* in an enumeration must be *unique*, but the *values* may be *duplicated*.

Common Programming Error 5.7
Assigning a value to an enumeration constant after it has been defined is a syntax error.

Good Programming Practice 5.6
Use only uppercase letters in the names of enumeration constants to make these constants stand out in a program and to indicate that enumeration constants are not *variables.*

When the game is won, either on the first roll or on a subsequent roll, gameStatus is set to WON. When the game is lost, either on the first roll or on a subsequent roll, gameStatus is set to LOST. Otherwise gameStatus is set to CONTINUE and the game continues.

Game Ends on First Roll

After the first roll, if the game is over, the while statement (lines 46–58) is skipped because gameStatus is not CONTINUE. The program proceeds to the if...else statement at lines 61–66, which prints "Player wins" if gameStatus is WON and "Player loses" otherwise.

Game Ends on a Subsequent Roll

After the first roll, if the game is *not* over, then sum is saved in myPoint. Execution proceeds with the while statement because gameStatus is CONTINUE. Each time through the while, rollDice is called to produce a new sum. If sum matches myPoint, gameStatus is set to WON to indicate that the player won, the while-test fails, the if...else statement prints "Player wins" and execution terminates. If sum is equal to 7 (line 54), gameStatus is set to LOST to indicate that the player lost, the while-test fails, the if...else statement prints "Player loses" and execution terminates.

Control Architecture

Note the program's interesting control architecture. We've used two functions—main and rollDice—and the switch, while, nested if...else and nested if statements. In this chapter's exercises, we'll investigate various interesting characteristics of the game of craps.

5.12 Storage Classes

In Chapters 2–4, we used identifiers for variable names. The attributes of variables include *name, type, size* and *value*. In this chapter, we also use identifiers as names for user-defined functions. Actually, each identifier in a program has other attributes, including storage class, storage duration, scope and linkage.

C provides the **storage class specifiers** auto, register,[1] extern and **static**.[2] An identifier's **storage class** determines its storage duration, scope and linkage. An identifier's **storage duration** is the period during which the identifier *exists in memory*. Some exist briefly, some are repeatedly created and destroyed, and others exist for the program's entire execution. An identifier's **scope** is *where* the identifier can be referenced in a program. Some can be referenced throughout a program, others from only portions of a program. An identifier's **linkage** determines for a multiple-source-file program whether the identifier is known *only* in the current source file or in *any* source file with proper declarations. This section discusses storage classes and storage duration. Section 5.13 discusses scope. Chapter 14 discusses identifier linkage and programming with multiple source files.

The storage-class specifiers can be split between **automatic storage duration** and **static storage duration**. Keyword **auto** is used to declare variables of automatic storage duration. Variables with automatic storage duration are created when program control enters the block in which they're defined; they exist while the block is active, and they're destroyed when program control exits the block.

Local Variables

Only variables can have automatic storage duration. A function's local variables (those declared in the parameter list or function body) normally have automatic storage duration. Keyword auto explicitly declares variables of automatic storage duration. Local variables have automatic storage duration by *default*, so keyword auto is rarely used. For the remainder of the text, we'll refer to variables with automatic storage duration simply as **automatic variables**.

---

1. Keyword register is archaic and should not be used.
2. The C11 standard adds the storage class specifier _Thread_local, which is beyond this book's scope.

Performance Tip 5.1

Automatic storage is a means of conserving memory, because automatic variables exist only when they're needed. They're created when a function is entered and destroyed when the function is exited.

Static Storage Class

Keywords `extern` and `static` are used in the declarations of identifiers for variables and functions of *static storage duration*. Identifiers of static storage duration exist from the time at which the program begins execution until the program terminates. For `static` variables, storage is allocated and initialized *only once, before the program begins execution*. For functions, the name of the function exists when the program begins execution. However, even though the variables and the function names exist from the start of program execution, this does *not* mean that these identifiers can be accessed throughout the program. Storage duration and scope (*where* a name can be used) are separate issues, as we'll see in Section 5.13.

There are several types of identifiers with static storage duration: *external identifiers* (such as global variables and function names) and local variables declared with the storage-class specifier `static`. Global variables and function names are of storage class `extern` by default. Global variables are created by placing variable declarations *outside* any function definition, and they retain their values throughout the execution of the program. Global variables and functions can be referenced by any function that follows their declarations or definitions in the file. This is one reason for using function prototypes—when we include `stdio.h` in a program that calls `printf`, the function prototype is placed at the start of our file to make the name `printf` known to the rest of the file.

Software Engineering Observation 5.10

Defining a variable as global rather than local allows unintended side effects to occur when a function that does not need access to the variable accidentally or maliciously modifies it. In general, global variables should be avoided except in certain situations with unique performance requirements (as discussed in Chapter 14).

Software Engineering Observation 5.11

Variables used only in a particular function should be defined as local variables in that function rather than as external variables.

Local variables declared with the keyword `static` are still known *only* in the function in which they're defined, but unlike automatic variables, `static` local variables *retain* their value when the function is exited. The next time the function is called, the `static` local variable contains the value it had when the function last exited. The following statement declares local variable `count` to be `static` and initializes it to 1.

```
static int count = 1;
```

All numeric variables of static storage duration are initialized to zero by default if you do not explicitly initialize them.

Keywords `extern` and `static` have special meaning when explicitly applied to external identifiers. In Chapter 14 we discuss the explicit use of `extern` and `static` with external identifiers and multiple-source-file programs.

5.13 Scope Rules

The **scope of an identifier** is the portion of the program in which the identifier can be referenced. For example, when we define a local variable in a block, it can be referenced *only* following its definition in that block or in blocks nested within that block. The four identifier scopes are function scope, file scope, block scope, and function-prototype scope.

Labels (identifiers followed by a colon such as start:) are the *only* identifiers with **function scope**. Labels can be used *anywhere* in the function in which they appear, but cannot be referenced outside the function body. Labels are used in switch statements (as case labels) and in goto statements (see Chapter 14). Labels are hidden in the function in which they're defined. This hiding—more formally called **information hiding**—is a means of implementing the **principle of least privilege**—a fundamental principle of good software engineering. In the context of an application, the principle states that code should be granted *only* the amount of privilege and access that it needs to accomplish its designated task, but no more.

An identifier declared outside any function has **file scope**. Such an identifier is "known" (i.e., accessible) in all functions from the point at which the identifier is declared until the end of the file. Global variables, function definitions, and function prototypes placed outside a function all have file scope.

Identifiers defined inside a block have **block scope**. Block scope ends at the terminating right brace (}) of the block. Local variables defined at the beginning of a function have block scope, as do function parameters, which are considered local variables by the function. *Any block may contain variable definitions.* When blocks are nested, and an identifier in an outer block has the *same* name as an identifier in an inner block, the identifier in the outer block is *hidden* until the inner block terminates. This means that while executing in the inner block, the inner block sees the value of its own local identifier and *not* the value of the identically named identifier in the enclosing block. Local variables declared static still have block scope, even though they exist from before program startup. Thus, storage duration does *not* affect the scope of an identifier.

The only identifiers with **function-prototype scope** are those used in the parameter list of a function prototype. As mentioned previously, function prototypes do *not* require *names* in the parameter list—only *types* are required. If a name is used in the parameter list of a function prototype, the compiler *ignores* the name. Identifiers used in a function prototype can be reused elsewhere in the program without ambiguity.

Common Programming Error 5.8

Accidentally using the same name for an identifier in an inner block as is used for an identifier in an outer block, when in fact you want the identifier in the outer *block to be active for the duration of the inner block.*

Error-Prevention Tip 5.4

Avoid variable names that hide names in outer scopes.

Figure 5.16 demonstrates scoping issues with global variables, automatic local variables and static local variables. A global variable x is defined and initialized to 1 (line 9). This global variable is hidden in any block (or function) in which a variable named x is defined. In main, a local variable x is defined and initialized to 5 (line 13). This variable is then printed to show that the global x is hidden in main. Next, a new block is defined in main with another local variable x initialized to 7 (line 18). This variable is printed to show that it hides x in the outer block of main. The variable x with value 7 is automatically destroyed when the block is exited, and the local variable x in the outer block of main is printed again to show that it's no longer hidden.

```c
1   // Fig. 5.16: fig05_16.c
2   // Scoping.
3   #include <stdio.h>
4
5   void useLocal(void); // function prototype
6   void useStaticLocal(void); // function prototype
7   void useGlobal(void); // function prototype
8
9   int x = 1; // global variable
10
11  int main(void)
12  {
13     int x = 5; // local variable to main
14
15     printf("local x in outer scope of main is %d\n", x);
16
17     { // start new scope
18        int x = 7; // local variable to new scope
19
20        printf("local x in inner scope of main is %d\n", x);
21     } // end new scope
22
23     printf("local x in outer scope of main is %d\n", x);
24
25     useLocal(); // useLocal has automatic local x
26     useStaticLocal(); // useStaticLocal has static local x
27     useGlobal(); // useGlobal uses global x
28     useLocal(); // useLocal reinitializes automatic local x
29     useStaticLocal(); // static local x retains its prior value
30     useGlobal(); // global x also retains its value
31
32     printf("\nlocal x in main is %d\n", x);
33  }
34
35  // useLocal reinitializes local variable x during each call
36  void useLocal(void)
37  {
38     int x = 25; // initialized each time useLocal is called
39
40     printf("\nlocal x in useLocal is %d after entering useLocal\n", x);
41     ++x;
42     printf("local x in useLocal is %d before exiting useLocal\n", x);
43  }
44
```

Fig. 5.16 | Scoping. (Part 1 of 2.)

```
45   // useStaticLocal initializes static local variable x only the first time
46   // the function is called; value of x is saved between calls to this
47   // function
48   void useStaticLocal(void)
49   {
50       // initialized once
51       static int x = 50;
52
53       printf("\nlocal static x is %d on entering useStaticLocal\n", x);
54       ++x;
55       printf("local static x is %d on exiting useStaticLocal\n", x);
56   }
57
58   // function useGlobal modifies global variable x during each call
59   void useGlobal(void)
60   {
61       printf("\nglobal x is %d on entering useGlobal\n", x);
62       x *= 10;
63       printf("global x is %d on exiting useGlobal\n", x);
64   }
```

```
local x in outer scope of main is 5
local x in inner scope of main is 7
local x in outer scope of main is 5

local x in useLocal is 25 after entering useLocal
local x in useLocal is 26 before exiting useLocal

local static x is 50 on entering useStaticLocal
local static x is 51 on exiting useStaticLocal

global x is 1 on entering useGlobal
global x is 10 on exiting useGlobal

local x in useLocal is 25 after entering useLocal
local x in useLocal is 26 before exiting useLocal

local static x is 51 on entering useStaticLocal
local static x is 52 on exiting useStaticLocal

global x is 10 on entering useGlobal
global x is 100 on exiting useGlobal

local x in main is 5
```

Fig. 5.16 | Scoping. (Part 2 of 2.)

The program defines three functions that each take no arguments and return nothing. Function useLocal defines an automatic variable x and initializes it to 25 (line 38). When useLocal is called, the variable is printed, incremented, and printed again before exiting the function. Each time this function is called, the automatic variable x is *reinitialized* to 25.

Function useStaticLocal defines a static variable x and initializes it to 50 in line 51 (recall that the storage for static variables is allocated and initialized *only once, before the program begins execution*). Local variables declared as static *retain* their values even when they're out of scope. When useStaticLocal is called, x is printed, incremented, and printed again before exiting the function. In the next call to this function, the static local variable x will contain the previously incremented value 51.

Function useGlobal does not define any variables. Therefore, when it refers to variable x, the global x (line 9) is used. When useGlobal is called, the global variable is printed, multiplied by 10, and printed again before exiting the function. The next time function useGlobal is called, the global variable still has its modified value, 10. Finally, the program prints the local variable x in main again (line 32) to show that none of the function calls modified the value of x because the functions all referred to variables in other scopes.

5.14 Recursion

For some types of problems, it's useful to have functions call themselves. A **recursive function** is one that *calls itself* either directly or indirectly through another function. Recursion is a complex topic discussed at length in upper-level computer science courses. In this section and the next, we present simple examples of recursion. This book contains an extensive treatment of recursion, which is spread throughout Chapters 5–8 and 12 and Appendices D and E. Figure 5.21, in Section 5.16, summarizes the book's recursion examples and exercises.

We consider recursion conceptually first, then examine several programs containing recursive functions. Recursive problem-solving approaches have a number of elements in common. A recursive function is called to solve a problem. The function actually knows how to solve only the *simplest* case(s), or so-called **base case(s)**. If the function is called with a base case, the function simply returns a result. If the function is called with a more complex problem, the function typically divides the problem into two conceptual pieces: a piece that the function knows how to do and a piece that it does not know how to do. To make recursion feasible, the latter piece must resemble the original problem, but be a slightly simpler or smaller version. Because this new problem looks like the original problem, the function launches (calls) a fresh copy of itself to work on the smaller problem—this is referred to as a **recursive call** or the **recursion step**. The recursion step also includes a return statement, because its result will be combined with the portion of the problem the function knew how to solve to form a result that will be passed back to the original caller.

The recursion step executes while the original call to the function is paused, waiting for the result from the recursion step. The recursion step can result in many more such recursive calls, as the function keeps dividing each problem with which it's called into two conceptual pieces. For the recursion to terminate, each time the function calls itself with a slightly simpler version of the original problem, this sequence of smaller problems must eventually *converge on the base case.* When the function recognizes the base case, it returns a result to the previous copy of the function, and a sequence of returns ensues all the way up the line until the original call of the function eventually returns the final result to its caller. As an example of these concepts at work, let's write a recursive program to perform a popular mathematical calculation.

Recursively Calculating Factorials

The factorial of a nonnegative integer n, written $n!$ (pronounced "n factorial"), is the product

$$n \cdot (n-1) \cdot (n-2) \cdot \ldots \cdot 1$$

with 1! equal to 1, and 0! defined to be 1. For example, 5! is the product 5 * 4 * 3 * 2 * 1, which is equal to 120.

The factorial of an integer, number, greater than or equal to 0 can be calculated *iteratively* (nonrecursively) using a for statement as follows:

```
factorial = 1;

for (counter = number; counter >= 1; --counter)
    factorial *= counter;
```

A *recursive* definition of the factorial function is arrived at by observing the following relationship:

$$n! = n \cdot (n-1)!$$

For example, 5! is clearly equal to 5 * 4! as shown by the following:

```
5! = 5 · 4 · 3 · 2 · 1
5! = 5 · (4 · 3 · 2 · 1)
5! = 5 · (4!)
```

The evaluation of 5! would proceed as shown in Fig. 5.17. Figure 5.17(a) shows how the succession of recursive calls proceeds until 1! is evaluated to be 1 (i.e., the *base case*), which terminates the recursion. Figure 5.17(b) shows the values returned from each recursive call to its caller until the final value is calculated and returned.

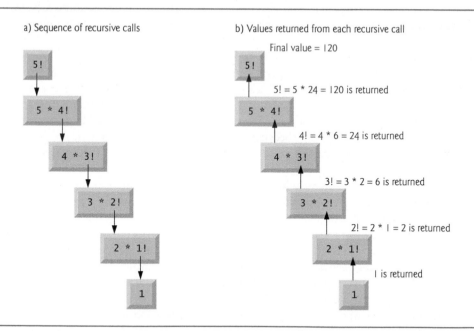

Fig. 5.17 | Recursive evaluation of 5!.

Figure 5.18 uses recursion to calculate and print the factorials of the integers 0–21 (the choice of the type unsigned long long int will be explained momentarily).

```
 1   // Fig. 5.18: fig05_18.c
 2   // Recursive factorial function.
 3   #include <stdio.h>
 4
 5   unsigned long long int factorial(unsigned int number);
 6
 7   int main(void)
 8   {
 9      // during each iteration, calculate
10      // factorial(i) and display result
11      for (unsigned int i = 0; i <= 21; ++i) {
12         printf("%u! = %llu\n", i, factorial(i));
13      }
14   }
15
16   // recursive definition of function factorial
17   unsigned long long int factorial(unsigned int number)
18   {
19      // base case
20      if (number <= 1) {
21         return 1;
22      }
23      else { // recursive step
24         return (number * factorial(number - 1));
25      }
26   }
```

```
0! = 1
1! = 1
2! = 2
3! = 6
4! = 24
5! = 120
6! = 720
7! = 5040
8! = 40320
9! = 362880
10! = 3628800
11! = 39916800
12! = 479001600
13! = 6227020800
14! = 87178291200
15! = 1307674368000
16! = 20922789888000
17! = 355687428096000
18! = 6402373705728000
19! = 121645100408832000
20! = 2432902008176640000
21! = 14197454024290336768
```

Fig. 5.18 | Recursive factorial function.

The recursive `factorial` function first tests whether a *terminating condition* is true, i.e., whether `number` is less than or equal to 1. If `number` is indeed less than or equal to 1, `factorial` returns 1, no further recursion is necessary, and the program terminates. If `number` is greater than 1, the statement

```
return number * factorial(number - 1);
```

expresses the problem as the product of `number` and a recursive call to `factorial` evaluating the factorial of `number - 1`. The call `factorial(number - 1)` is a slightly simpler problem than the original calculation `factorial(number)`.

Function `factorial` (lines 17–26) receives an `unsigned int` and returns a result of type `unsigned long long int`. The C standard specifies that a variable of type `unsigned long long int` can hold a value at least as large as 18,446,744,073,709,551,615. As can be seen in Fig. 5.18, factorial values become large quickly. We've chosen the data type `unsigned long long int` so the program can calculate larger factorial values. The conversion specifier `%llu` is used to print `unsigned long long int` values. Unfortunately, the `factorial` function produces large values so quickly that even `unsigned long long int` does not help us print very many factorial values before the maximum value of a `unsigned long long int` variable is exceeded.

Even when we use `unsigned long long int`, we still can't calculate factorials beyond 21! This points to a weakness in C (and most other procedural programming languages)—namely that the language is not easily *extended* to handle the unique requirements of various applications. As we'll see later in the book, C++ is an *extensible* language that, through "classes," allows us to create new data types, including ones that could hold arbitrarily large integers if we wish.

Common Programming Error 5.9
Forgetting to return a value from a recursive function when one is needed.

Common Programming Error 5.10
Either omitting the base case, or writing the recursion step incorrectly so that it does not converge on the base case, will cause infinite recursion, eventually exhausting memory. This is analogous to the problem of an infinite loop in an iterative (nonrecursive) solution.

5.15 Example Using Recursion: Fibonacci Series

The Fibonacci series

0, 1, 1, 2, 3, 5, 8, 13, 21, ...

begins with 0 and 1 and has the property that each subsequent Fibonacci number is the sum of the previous two Fibonacci numbers.

The series occurs in nature and, in particular, describes a form of spiral. The ratio of successive Fibonacci numbers converges to a constant value of 1.618.... This number, too, repeatedly occurs in nature and has been called the *golden ratio* or the *golden mean*. Humans tend to find the golden mean aesthetically pleasing. Architects often design windows, rooms, and buildings whose length and width are in the ratio of the golden mean. Postcards are often designed with a golden mean length/width ratio.

The Fibonacci series may be defined recursively as follows:

fibonacci(0) = 0
fibonacci(1) = 1
fibonacci(n) = fibonacci(n − 1) + fibonacci(n − 2)

Figure 5.19 calculates the nth Fibonacci number recursively using function `fibonacci`. Notice that Fibonacci numbers tend to become large quickly. Therefore, we've chosen the data type `unsigned int` for the parameter type and the data type `unsigned long long int` for the return type in function `fibonacci`. In Fig. 5.19, each pair of output lines shows a separate run of the program.

```
1   // Fig. 5.19: fig05_19.c
2   // Recursive fibonacci function
3   #include <stdio.h>
4
5   unsigned long long int fibonacci(unsigned int n); // function prototype
6
7   int main(void)
8   {
9      unsigned int number; // number input by user
10
11     // obtain integer from user
12     printf("%s", "Enter an integer: ");
13     scanf("%u", &number);
14
15     // calculate fibonacci value for number input by user
16     unsigned long long int result = fibonacci(number);
17
18     // display result
19     printf("Fibonacci(%u) = %llu\n", number, result);
20  }
21
22  // Recursive definition of function fibonacci
23  unsigned long long int fibonacci(unsigned int n)
24  {
25     // base case
26     if (0 == n || 1 == n) {
27        return n;
28     }
29     else { // recursive step
30        return fibonacci(n - 1) + fibonacci(n - 2);
31     }
32  }
```

```
Enter an integer: 0
Fibonacci(0) = 0
```

```
Enter an integer: 1
Fibonacci(1) = 1
```

Fig. 5.19 | Recursive fibonacci function. (Part 1 of 2.)

```
Enter an integer: 2
Fibonacci(2) = 1
```

```
Enter an integer: 3
Fibonacci(3) = 2
```

```
Enter an integer: 10
Fibonacci(10) = 55
```

```
Enter an integer: 20
Fibonacci(20) = 6765
```

```
Enter an integer: 30
Fibonacci(30) = 832040
```

```
Enter an integer: 40
Fibonacci(40) = 102334155
```

Fig. 5.19 | Recursive fibonacci function. (Part 2 of 2.)

The call to fibonacci from main is *not* a recursive call (line 16), but all subsequent calls to fibonacci are recursive (line 30). Each time fibonacci is invoked, it immediately tests for the *base case*—n is equal to 0 or 1. If this is true, n is returned. Interestingly, if n is greater than 1, the recursion step generates *two* recursive calls, each a slightly simpler problem than the original call to fibonacci. Figure 5.20 shows how function fibonacci would evaluate fibonacci(3).

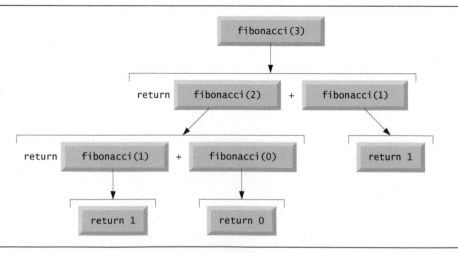

Fig. 5.20 | Set of recursive calls for fibonacci(3).

Order of Evaluation of Operands

This figure raises some interesting issues about the *order* in which C compilers will evaluate the operands of operators. This is a different issue from the order in which operators are applied to their operands, namely the order dictated by the rules of operator precedence abd associativity. Figure 5.20 shows that while evaluating fibonacci(3), *two* recursive calls will be made, namely fibonacci(2) and fibonacci(1). But in what order will these calls be made? You might simply assume the operands will be evaluated left to right. For optimization reasons, C does *not* specify the order in which the operands of most operators (including +) are to be evaluated. Therefore, you should make no assumption about the order in which these calls will execute. The calls could execute fibonacci(2) first and then fibonacci(1), or the calls could execute in the reverse order, fibonacci(1) then fibonacci(2). In this and most other programs, the final result would be the same. But in some programs the evaluation of an operand may have *side effects* that could affect the final result of the expression.

C specifies the order of evaluation of the operands of *only four* operators—&&, ||, the comma (,) operator and ?:. The first three of these are binary operators whose operands are guaranteed to be evaluated *left to right*. [*Note:* The commas used to separate the arguments in a function call are *not* comma operators.] The last operator is C's only *ternary* operator. Its leftmost operand is *always* evaluated *first*; if the leftmost operand evaluates to nonzero (true), the middle operand is evaluated next and the last operand is ignored; if the leftmost operand evaluates to zero (false), the third operand is evaluated next and the middle operand is ignored.

Common Programming Error 5.11

Writing programs that depend on the order of evaluation of the operands of operators other than &&, ||, ?:, and the comma (,) operator can lead to errors because compilers may not necessarily evaluate the operands in the order you expect.

Portability Tip 5.2

Programs that depend on the order of evaluation of the operands of operators other than &&, ||, ?:, and the comma (,) operator can function differently on different compilers.

Exponential Complexity

A word of caution is in order about recursive programs like the one we use here to generate Fibonacci numbers. Each level of recursion in the fibonacci function has a *doubling* effect on the number of calls—the number of recursive calls that will be executed to calculate the nth Fibonacci number is on the order of 2^n. This rapidly gets out of hand. Calculating only the 20th Fibonacci number would require on the order of 2^{20} or about a million calls, calculating the 30th Fibonacci number would require on the order of 2^{30} or about a billion calls, and so on. Computer scientists refer to this as *exponential complexity*. Problems of this nature humble even the world's most powerful computers! Complexity issues in general, and exponential complexity in particular, are discussed in detail in the upper-level computer science course generally called "Algorithms."

The example we showed in this section used an intuitively appealing solution to calculate Fibonacci numbers, but there are better approaches. Exercise 5.48 asks you to investigate recursion in more depth and propose alternate approaches to implementing the recursive Fibonacci algorithm.

5.16 Recursion vs. Iteration

In the previous sections, we studied two functions that can easily be implemented either recursively or iteratively. In this section, we compare the two approaches and discuss why you might choose one approach over the other in a particular situation.

- Both iteration and recursion are based on a *control statement*: Iteration uses an *iteration statement*; recursion uses a *selection statement*.

- Both iteration and recursion involve *repetition*: Iteration uses an *iteration statement*; recursion achieves repetition through *repeated function calls*.

- Iteration and recursion each involve a *termination test*: Iteration terminates when the *loop-continuation condition fails*; recursion when a *base case is recognized*.

- Iteration with counter-controlled iteration and recursion each *gradually approach termination*: Iteration keeps modifying a counter until the counter assumes a value that makes the *loop-continuation condition fail*; recursion keeps producing simpler versions of the original problem until the *base case is reached*.

- Both iteration and recursion can occur *infinitely*: An *infinite loop* occurs with iteration if the loop-continuation test *never* becomes false; *infinite recursion* occurs if the recursion step does *not* reduce the problem each time in a manner that *converges on the base case*. Infinite iteration and recursion typically occur as a result of errors in a program's logic.

Recursion has many negatives. It *repeatedly* invokes the mechanism, and consequently the *overhead, of function calls*. This can be expensive in both processor time and memory space. Each recursive call causes *another copy* of the function (actually only the function's variables) to be created; this can *consume considerable memory*. Iteration normally occurs within a function, so the overhead of repeated function calls and extra memory assignment is omitted. So why choose recursion?

Software Engineering Observation 5.12

Any problem that can be solved recursively can also be solved iteratively (nonrecursively). A recursive approach is normally chosen in preference to an iterative approach when the recursive approach more naturally mirrors the problem and results in a program that's easier to understand and debug. Another reason to choose a recursive solution is that an iterative solution may not be apparent.

Most programming textbooks introduce recursion much later than we've done here. We feel that recursion is a sufficiently rich and complex topic that it's better to introduce it earlier and spread the examples over the remainder of the text. Figure 5.21 summarizes by chapter the 30 recursion examples and exercises in the text.

Let's close this chapter with some observations that we make repeatedly throughout the book. Good software engineering is important. High performance is important. Unfortunately, these goals are often at odds with one another. Good software engineering is key to making more manageable the task of developing the larger and more complex software systems we need. High performance is key to realizing the systems of the future that will place ever greater computing demands on hardware. Where do functions fit in here?

Recursion examples and exercises

Chapter 5
Factorial function
Fibonacci function
Greatest common divisor
Multiply two integers
Raising an integer to an integer power
Towers of Hanoi
Recursive main
Visualizing recursion

Chapter 6
Sum the elements of an array
Print an array
Print an array backward
Print a string backward
Check whether a string is a palindrome
Minimum value in an array
Linear search
Binary search
Eight Queens

Chapter 7
Maze traversal

Chapter 8
Printing a string input at the keyboard backward

Chapter 12
Search a linked list
Print a linked list backward
Binary tree insert
Preorder traversal of a binary tree
Inorder traversal of a binary tree
Postorder traversal of a binary tree
Printing trees

Appendix D
Selection sort
Quicksort

Appendix E
Fibonacci function

Fig. 5.21 | Recursion examples and exercises in the text.

Performance Tip 5.2
Dividing a large program into functions promotes good software engineering. But it has a price. A heavily functionalized program—as compared to a monolithic (i.e., one-piece) program without functions—makes potentially large numbers of function calls, and these consume execution time on a computer's processor(s). Although monolithic programs may perform better, they're more difficult to program, test, debug, maintain, and evolve.

Performance Tip 5.3
Today's hardware architectures are tuned to make function calls efficient, C compilers help optimize your code and today's hardware processors are incredibly fast. For the vast majority of applications and software systems you'll build, concentrating on good software engineering will be more important than programming for high performance. Nevertheless, in many C applications and systems, such as game programming, real-time systems, operating systems and embedded systems, performance is crucial, so we include performance tips throughout the book.

5.17 Secure C Programming

Secure Random Numbers
In Section 5.10, we introduced the rand function for generating pseudorandom numbers. The C standard library does not provide a secure random-number generator. According to the C standard document's description of function rand, "There are no guarantees as to the

quality of the random sequence produced and some implementations are known to produce sequences with *distressingly* non-random low-order bits." The CERT guideline MSC30-C indicates that implementation-specific random-number generation functions must be used to ensure that the random numbers produced are *not predictable*—this is extremely important, for example, in cryptography and other security applications. The guideline presents several platform-specific random-number generators that are considered to be secure. For example, Microsoft Windows provides the `CryptGenRandom` function, and POSIX based systems (such as Linux) provide a `random` function that produces more secure results. For more information, see guideline MSC30-C at `https://www.securecoding.cert.org`. If you're building industrial-strength applications that require random numbers, you should investigate for your platform the recommended function(s) to use.

Summary

Section 5.1 Introduction

- The best way to develop and maintain a large program is to **divide** (p. 158) it into several smaller pieces, each more manageable than the original program.

Section 5.2 Modularizing Programs in C

- A **function** (p. 158) is invoked by a **function call** (p. 159). The function call specifies the function by name and provides information (as arguments) that the called function needs to perform its task.

- The purpose of **information hiding** is to give functions access only to the information they need to complete their tasks. This is a means of implementing the **principle of least privilege**, one of the most important principles of good software engineering.

Section 5.3 Math Library Functions

- A function is normally invoked in a program by writing the function's name followed by a left parenthesis followed by the argument (or a comma-separated list of arguments) of the function followed by a right parenthesis.

- Each argument of a function may be a constant, a variable, or an expression.

Section 5.4 Functions

- A **local variable** (p. 161) is known only in a function definition. Other functions are not allowed to know the names of a function's local variables, nor is any function allowed to know the implementation details of any other function.

Section 5.5 Function Definitions

- The general **format for a function definition** is

    return-value-type function-name(*parameter-list*)
    {
        statements
    }

  The *return-value-type* states the type of the value returned to the calling function. If a function does not return a value, the *return-value-type* is declared as void. The *function-name* is any valid identifier. The *parameter-list* (p. 163) is a comma-separated list containing the definitions of the variables that will be passed to the function. If a function does not receive any values, *parameter-list* is declared as void.

- The arguments passed to a function should match in number, type and order with the **parameters** (p. 161) in the function definition.
- When a program encounters a function call, control transfers from the point of invocation to the called function, the statements of that function execute then control returns to the caller.
- A **called function** can **return control** to the caller in one of three ways. If the function does not return a value, control is returned when the function-ending right brace is reached, or by executing the statement

      return;

  If the function does return a value, the statement

      return *expression*;

  returns the value of *expression*.

Section 5.6 Function Prototypes: A Deeper Look
- A **function prototype** (p. 163) declares the function's name, return type and declares the number, types, and order of the parameters the function expects to receive.
- Function prototypes enable the compiler to verify that functions are called correctly.
- The compiler ignores variable names mentioned in the function prototype.
- Arguments in a **mixed-type expression** (p. 167) are converted to the same type via the C standard's **usual arithmetic conversion rules** (p. 167).

Section 5.7 Function Call Stack and Stack Frames
- **Stacks** (p. 169) are known as **last-in, first-out** (**LIFO**; p. 169) data structures—the last item pushed (inserted) on the stack is the first item popped (removed) from the stack.
- A called function must know how to return to its caller, so the return address of the calling function is pushed onto the **program execution stack** (p. 169) when the function is called. If a series of function calls occurs, the successive return addresses are pushed onto the stack in last-in, first-out order so that the last function to execute will be the first to return to its caller.
- The program execution stack contains the **memory for the local variables** used in each invocation of a function during a program's execution. This data is known as the **stack frame** (p. 169) of the function call. When a function call is made, the stack frame for that function call is pushed onto the program execution stack. When the function returns to its caller, the stack frame for this function call is popped off the stack and those local variables are no longer known to the program.
- The amount of memory in a computer is finite, so only a certain amount of memory can be used to store stack frames on the program execution stack. If there are more function calls than can have their stack frames stored on the program execution stack, an error known as a **stack overflow** occurs. The application will compile correctly, but its execution will fail with a stack overflow.

Section 5.8 Headers
- Each standard library has a corresponding **header** (p. 172) containing the function prototypes for all of that library's functions, and definitions of various symbolic constants needed by those functions.
- You can create and include your own headers.

Section 5.9 Passing Arguments By Value and By Reference
- When an argument is **passed by value** (p. 173), a copy of its value is made and passed to the called function. Changes to the copy in the called function do not affect the original variable's value.

- When an argument is **passed by reference** (p. 173), the caller allows the called function to modify the original variable's value.
- All calls in C are call-by-value.
- It's possible to achieve call-by-reference by using address operators and indirection operators.

Section 5.10 Random Number Generation

- Function **rand** generates an integer between 0 and RAND_MAX which is defined by the C standard to be at least 32767.
- Values produced by rand can be **scaled** and **shifted** to produce values in a specific range (p. 175).
- To **randomize** a program, use the C standard library function srand.
- The **srand function** seeds (p. 177) the random number generator. An srand call is ordinarily inserted in a program only after it has been thoroughly debugged. While debugging, it's better to omit srand. This ensures repeatability, which is essential to proving that corrections to a random number generation program work properly.
- The function prototypes for rand and srand are contained in <stdlib.h>.
- To randomize without the need for entering a seed each time, we use **srand(time(NULL))**.
- The general equation for scaling and shifting a random number is

    ```
    n = a + rand() % b;
    ```

where a is the shifting value (i.e., the first number in the desired range of consecutive integers) and b is the scaling factor (i.e,. the width of the desired range of consecutive integers).

Section 5.11 Example: A Game of Chance; Introducing **enum**

- An **enumeration** (p. 181), introduced by the keyword **enum**, is a set of integer constants represented by identifiers. Values in an enum **start with 0** and are **incremented by 1**. It's also possible to assign an integer value to each identifier in an enum. The identifiers in an enumeration must be unique, but the values may be duplicated.

Section 5.12 Storage Classes

- Each identifier in a program has the attributes **storage class**, **storage duration**, **scope** and **linkage** (p. 182).
- C provides four **storage classes** indicated by the **storage class specifiers: auto**, **register**, **extern** and **static** (p. 182).
- An identifier's **storage duration** is when that identifier exists in memory.
- An identifier's **linkage** (p. 182) determines for a multiple-source-file program whether an identifier is known only in the current source file or in any source file with proper declarations.
- Variables with **automatic storage duration** (p. 182) are created when the block in which they're defined is entered, exist while the block is active and are destroyed when the block is exited. A function's local variables normally have automatic storage duration.
- Keywords **extern** and **static** are used to declare identifiers for variables and functions of static storage duration.
- **Static storage duration** (p. 182) variables are allocated and initialized once, before the program begins execution.
- There are two types of **identifiers with static storage duration**: external identifiers (such as global variables and function names) and **local variables declared with the storage-class specifier static**.
- **Global variables** are created by placing variable definitions outside any function definition. Global variables retain their values throughout the execution of the program.

- **Local static variables** retain their value between calls to the function in which they're defined.
- All numeric variables of static storage duration are initialized to zero if you do not explicitly initialize them.

Section 5.13 Scope Rules
- An identifier's **scope** (p. 184) is where the identifier can be referenced in a program.
- An identifier can have **function scope**, **file scope**, **block scope** or **function-prototype scope** (p. 184).
- **Labels** are the only identifiers with function scope. Labels can be used anywhere in the function in which they appear but cannot be referenced outside the function body.
- An identifier declared outside any function has file scope. Such an identifier is "known" in all functions from the point at which it's declared until the end of the file.
- Identifiers defined inside a block have block scope. Block scope ends at the terminating right brace (}) of the block.
- Local variables defined at the beginning of a function have block scope, as do function parameters, which are considered local variables by the function.
- Any block may contain variable definitions. When blocks are nested, and an identifier in an outer block has the same name as an identifier in an inner block, the identifier in the outer block is "hidden" until the inner block terminates.
- The only identifiers with function-prototype scope are those used in the parameter list of a function prototype. Identifiers used in a function prototype can be reused elsewhere in the program without ambiguity.

Section 5.14 Recursion
- A **recursive function** (p. 187) is a function that calls itself either directly or indirectly.
- If a recursive function is called with a **base case** (p. 187), the function simply returns a result. If it's called with a more complex problem, the function divides the problem into two conceptual pieces: a piece that the function knows how to do and a slightly smaller version of the original problem. Because this new problem looks like the original problem, the function launches a recursive call to work on the smaller problem.
- For recursion to terminate, each time the recursive function calls itself with a slightly simpler version of the original problem, the sequence of smaller and smaller problems must converge on the **base case**. When the function recognizes the base case, the result is returned to the previous function call, and a sequence of returns ensues all the way up the line until the original call of the function eventually returns the final result.
- Standard C does not specify the order in which the operands of most operators (including +) are to be evaluated. Of C's many operators, the standard specifies the order of evaluation of the operands of only the operators &&, ||, the comma (,) operator and ?:. The first three of these are binary operators whose two operands are evaluated left to right. The last operator is C's only ternary operator. Its leftmost operand is evaluated first; if it evaluates to nonzero, the middle operand is evaluated next and the last operand is ignored; if the leftmost operand evaluates to zero, the third operand is evaluated next and the middle operand is ignored.

Section 5.16 Recursion vs. Iteration
- Both iteration and recursion are based on a control structure: Iteration uses an iteration statement; recursion uses a selection statement.

- Both iteration and recursion involve repetition: Iteration uses an iteration statement; recursion achieves repetition through repeated function calls.

- Iteration and recursion each involve a termination test: Iteration terminates when the loop-continuation condition fails; recursion terminates when a base case is recognized.

- Iteration and recursion can occur infinitely: An infinite loop occurs with iteration if the loop-continuation test never becomes false; infinite recursion occurs if the recursion step does not reduce the problem in a manner that converges on the base case.

- Recursion repeatedly invokes the mechanism, and consequently the overhead, of function calls. This can be expensive in both processor time and memory space.

Self-Review Exercises

5.1 Answer each of the following:

a) _____ are used to modularize programs.

b) A function is invoked with a(n) _____.

c) A variable known only within the function in which it's defined is called a(n) _____.

d) The _____ statement in a called function is used to pass the value of an expression back to the calling function.

e) Keyword _____ is used in a function header to indicate that a function does not return a value or to indicate that a function contains no parameters.

f) The _____ of an identifier is the portion of the program in which the identifier can be used.

g) The three ways to return control from a called function to a caller are _____, _____ and _____.

h) A(n) _____ allows the compiler to check the number, types, and order of the arguments passed to a function.

i) The _____ function is used to produce random numbers.

j) The _____ function is used to set the random number seed to randomize a program.

k) The storage-class specifiers are _____, _____, _____ and _____.

l) Variables declared in a block or in the parameter list of a function are assumed to be of storage class _____ unless specified otherwise.

m) A non-static variable defined outside any block or function is a(n) _____ variable.

n) For a local variable in a function to retain its value between calls to the function, it must be declared with the _____ storage-class specifier.

o) The four possible scopes of an identifier are _____, _____, _____ and _____.

p) A function that calls itself either directly or indirectly is a(n) _____ function.

q) A recursive function typically has two components: one that provides a means for the recursion to terminate by testing for a(n) _____ case, and one that expresses the problem as a recursive call for a slightly simpler problem than the original call.

5.2 For the following program, state the scope (either function scope, file scope, block scope or function-prototype scope) of each of the following elements.

a) The variable x in main.

b) The variable y in cube.

c) The function cube.

d) The function main.

e) The function prototype for cube.

f) The identifier y in the function prototype for cube.

```
 1    #include <stdio.h>
 2    int cube(int y);
 3
 4    int main(void)
 5    {
 6        for (int x = 1; x <= 10; ++x)
 7            printf("%u\n", cube(x));
 8    }
 9
10    int cube(int y)
11    {
12        return y * y * y;
13    }
```

5.3   Write a program that tests whether the examples of the math library function calls shown in Fig. 5.2 actually produce the indicated results.

5.4   Give the function header for each of the following functions.

   a) Function hypotenuse that takes two double-precision floating-point arguments, side1 and side2, and returns a double-precision floating-point result.
   b) Function smallest that takes three integers, x, y, z, and returns an integer.
   c) Function instructions that does not receive any arguments and does not return a value. [*Note:* Such functions are commonly used to display instructions to a user.]
   d) Function intToFloat that takes an integer argument, number, and returns a floating-point result.

5.5   Give the function prototype for each of the following:

   a) The function described in Exercise 5.4(a).
   b) The function described in Exercise 5.4(b).
   c) The function described in Exercise 5.4(c).
   d) The function described in Exercise 5.4(d).

5.6   Write a declaration for floating-point variable lastVal that's to retain its value between calls to the function in which it's defined.

5.7   Find the error in each of the following program segments and explain how the error can be corrected (see also Exercise 5.46):

   a) ```
       int g(void)
       {
           printf("%s", Inside function g\n");
           int h(void)
           {
               printf("%s", Inside function h\n");
           }
       }
       ```
   b)  ```
       int sum(int x, int y)
       {
           int result = x + y;
       }
       ```
   c) ```
       void f(float a);
       {
           float a;
           printf("%f", a);
       }
       ```
       ```

```
d) int sum(int n)
   {
      if (0 == n) {
         return 0; //
      }
      else {
         n + sum(n - 1);
      }
   }
e) void product(void)
   {
      printf("%s", "Enter three integers: ")
      int a, b, c;
      scanf("%d%d%d", &a, &b, &c);
      int result = a * b * c;
      printf("Result is %d", result);
      return result;
   }
```

Answers to Self-Review Exercises

5.1 a) functions. b) function call. c) local variable. d) return. e) void. f) ccope. g) return; or return expression; or encountering the closing right brace of a function. h) function prototype. i) rand. j) srand. k) auto, register, extern, static. l) auto. m) external, global. n) static. o) function scope, file scope, block scope, function-prototype scope. p) recursive. q) base.

5.2 a) Block scope. b) Block scope. c) File scope. d) File scope. e) File scope. f) Function-prototyp scope.

5.3 See below. [*Note:* On most Linux systems, you must use the -lm option when compiling this program.]

```
1   // ex05_03.c
2   // Testing the math library functions
3   #include <stdio.h>
4   #include <math.h>
5
6   int main(void)
7   {
8      // calculates and outputs the square root
9      printf("sqrt(%.1f) = %.1f\n", 900.0, sqrt(900.0));
10     printf("sqrt(%.1f) = %.1f\n", 9.0, sqrt(9.0));
11
12     // calculates and outputs the cube root
13     printf("cbrt(%.1f) = %.1f\n", 27.0, cbrt(27.0));
14     printf("cbrt(%.1f) = %.1f\n", -8.0, cbrt(-8.0));
15
16     // calculates and outputs the exponential function e to the x
17     printf("exp(%.1f) = %f\n", 1.0, exp(1.0));
18     printf("exp(%.1f) = %f\n", 2.0, exp(2.0));
19
20     // calculates and outputs the logarithm (base e)
21     printf("log(%f) = %.1f\n", 2.718282, log(2.718282));
22     printf("log(%f) = %.1f\n", 7.389056, log(7.389056));
23
```

```
24        // calculates and outputs the logarithm (base 10)
25        printf("log10(%.1f) = %.1f\n", 1.0, log10(1.0));
26        printf("log10(%.1f) = %.1f\n", 10.0, log10(10.0));
27        printf("log10(%.1f) = %.1f\n", 100.0, log10(100.0));
28
29        // calculates and outputs the absolute value
30        printf("fabs(%.1f) = %.1f\n", 13.5, fabs(13.5));
31        printf("fabs(%.1f) = %.1f\n", 0.0, fabs(0.0));
32        printf("fabs(%.1f) = %.1f\n", -13.5, fabs(-13.5));
33
34        // calculates and outputs ceil(x)
35        printf("ceil(%.1f) = %.1f\n", 9.2, ceil(9.2));
36        printf("ceil(%.1f) = %.1f\n", -9.8, ceil(-9.8));
37
38        // calculates and outputs floor(x)
39        printf("floor(%.1f) = %.1f\n", 9.2, floor(9.2));
40        printf("floor(%.1f) = %.1f\n", -9.8, floor(-9.8));
41
42        // calculates and outputs pow(x, y)
43        printf("pow(%.1f, %.1f) = %.1f\n", 2.0, 7.0, pow(2.0, 7.0));
44        printf("pow(%.1f, %.1f) = %.1f\n", 9.0, 0.5, pow(9.0, 0.5));
45
46        // calculates and outputs fmod(x, y)
47        printf("fmod(%.3f/%.3f) = %.3f\n", 13.657, 2.333,
48           fmod(13.657, 2.333));
49
50        // calculates and outputs sin(x)
51        printf("sin(%.1f) = %.1f\n", 0.0, sin(0.0));
52
53        // calculates and outputs cos(x)
54        printf("cos(%.1f) = %.1f\n", 0.0, cos(0.0));
55
56        // calculates and outputs tan(x)
57        printf("tan(%.1f) = %.1f\n", 0.0, tan(0.0));
58     }
```

```
sqrt(900.0) = 30.0
sqrt(9.0) = 3.0
cbrt(27.0) = 3.0
cbrt(-8.0) = -2.0
exp(1.0) = 2.718282
exp(2.0) = 7.389056
log(2.718282) = 1.0
log(7.389056) = 2.0
log10(1.0) = 0.0
log10(10.0) = 1.0
log10(100.0) = 2.0
fabs(13.5) = 13.5
fabs(0.0) = 0.0
fabs(-13.5) = 13.5
ceil(9.2) = 10.0
ceil(-9.8) = -9.0
floor(9.2) = 9.0
floor(-9.8) = -10.0
pow(2.0, 7.0) = 128.0
pow(9.0, 0.5) = 3.0
fmod(13.657/2.333) = 1.992
sin(0.0) = 0.0
cos(0.0) = 1.0
tan(0.0) = 0.0
```

5.4   a) `double hypotenuse(double side1, double side2)`
       b) `int smallest(int x, int y, int z)`
       c) `void instructions(void)`
       d) `float intToFloat(int number)`

5.5   a) `double hypotenuse(double side1, double side2);`
       b) `int smallest(int x, int y, int z);`
       c) `void instructions(void);`
       d) `float intToFloat(int number);`

5.6   `static float lastVal;`

5.7   a) Error: Function h is defined in function g.
         Correction: Move the definition of h out of the definition of g.
       b) Error: The body of the function is supposed to return an integer, but does not.
         Correction: Replace the statement in the function body with:

```
return x + y;
```

       c) Error: Semicolon after the right parenthesis that encloses the parameter list, and re-defining the parameter a in the function definition.
         Correction: Delete the semicolon after the right parenthesis of the parameter list, and delete the declaration float a; in the function body.
       d) Error: The result of n + sum(n - 1) is not returned; sum returns an improper result.
         Correction: Rewrite the statement in the else clause as

```
return n + sum(n - 1);
```

       e) Error: The function returns a value when it's not supposed to.
         Correction: Eliminate the return statement.

Exercises

5.8   Show the value of x after each of the following statements is performed:
       a) `x = fabs(7.5);`
       b) `x = floor(7.5);`
       c) `x = fabs(0.0);`
       d) `x = ceil(0.0);`
       e) `x = fabs(-6.4);`
       f) `x = ceil(-6.4);`
       g) `x = ceil(-fabs(-8 + floor(-5.5)));`

5.9   *(Parking Charges)* A parking garage charges a $2.00 minimum fee to park for up to three hours and an additional $0.50 per hour for each hour *or part thereof* over three hours. The maximum charge for any given 24-hour period is $10.00. Assume that no car parks for longer than 24 hours at a time. Write a program that will calculate and print the parking charges for each of three customers who parked their cars in this garage yesterday. You should enter the hours parked for each customer. Your program should print the results in a tabular format, and should calculate and print the total of yesterday's receipts. The program should use the function `calculateCharges` to determine the charge for each customer. Your outputs should appear in the following format:

```
Car      Hours      Charge
1          1.5        2.00
2          4.0        2.50
3         24.0       10.00
TOTAL     29.5       14.50
```

5.10 *(Rounding Numbers)* An application of function floor is rounding a value to the nearest integer. The statement

```
y = floor(x + .5);
```

will round the number x to the nearest integer and assign the result to y. Write a program that reads several numbers and uses the preceding statement to round each of these numbers to the nearest integer. For each number processed, print both the original number and the rounded number.

5.11 *(Rounding Numbers)* Function floor may be used to round a number to a specific decimal place. The statement

```
y = floor(x * 10 + .5) / 10;
```

rounds x to the tenths position (the first position to the right of the decimal point). The statement

```
y = floor(x * 100 + .5) / 100;
```

rounds x to the hundredths position (the second position to the right of the decimal point). Write a program that defines four functions to round a number x in various ways

a) roundToInteger(number)
b) roundToTenths(number)
c) roundToHundreths(number)
d) roundToThousandths(number)

For each value read, your program should print the original value, the number rounded to the nearest integer, the number rounded to the nearest tenth, the number rounded to the nearest hundredth, and the number rounded to the nearest thousandth.

5.12 Answer each of the following questions.

a) What does it mean to choose numbers "at random"?
b) Why is the rand function useful for simulating games of chance?
c) Why would you randomize a program by using srand? Under what circumstances is it desirable not to randomize?
d) Why is it often necessary to scale and/or shift the values produced by rand?

5.13 Write statements that assign random integers to the variable *n* in the following ranges:

a) $1 \le n \le 2$
b) $1 \le n \le 100$
c) $0 \le n \le 9$
d) $1000 \le n \le 1112$
e) $-1 \le n \le 1$
f) $-3 \le n \le 11$

5.14 For each of the following sets of integers, write a single statement that will print a number at random from the set.

a) 2, 4, 6, 8, 10.
b) 3, 5, 7, 9, 11.
c) 6, 10, 14, 18, 22.

5.15 *(Hypotenuse Calculations)* Define a function called hypotenuse that calculates the length of the hypotenuse of a right triangle when the other two sides are given. The function should take two arguments of type double and return the hypotenuse as a double. Test your program with the side values specified in Fig. 5.22.

5.16 *(Exponentiation)* Write a function integerPower(base, exponent) that returns the value of

$$base^{exponent}$$

For example, integerPower(3, 4) = 3 * 3 * 3 * 3. Assume that exponent is a positive, nonzero integer, and base is an integer. Function integerPower should use for to control the calculation. Do not use any math library functions.

Triangle	Side 1	Side 2
1	3.0	4.0
2	5.0	12.0
3	8.0	15.0

Fig. 5.22 | Sample triangle side values for Exercise 5.15.

5.17 *(Multiples)* Write a function isMultiple that determines for a pair of integers whether the second integer is a multiple of the first. The function should take two integer arguments and return 1 (true) if the second is a multiple of the first, and 0 (false) otherwise. Use this function in a program that inputs a series of pairs of integers.

5.18 *(Even or Odd)* Write a program that inputs a series of integers and passes them one at a time to function isEven, which uses the remainder operator to determine whether an integer is even. The function should take an integer argument and return 1 if the integer is even and 0 otherwise.

5.19 *(Square of Asterisks)* Write a function that displays a solid square of asterisks whose side is specified in integer parameter side. For example, if side is 4, the function displays:

```
****
****
****
****
```

5.20 *(Displaying a Square of Any Character)* Modify the function created in Exercise 5.19 to form the square out of whatever character is contained in character parameter fillCharacter. Thus if side is 5 and fillCharacter is "#", then this function should print:

```
#####
#####
#####
#####
#####
```

5.21 *(Project: Drawing Shapes with Characters)* Use techniques similar to those developed in Exercises 5.19–5.20 to produce a program that graphs a wide range of shapes.

5.22 *(Separating Digits)* Write program segments that accomplish each of the following:
   a) Calculate the integer part of the quotient when integer a is divided by integer b.
   b) Calculate the integer remainder when integer a is divided by integer b.
   c) Use the program pieces developed in a) and b) to write a function that inputs an integer between 1 and 32767 and prints it as a series of digits, with two spaces between each digit. For example, the integer 4562 should be printed as:

```
4  5  6  2
```

5.23 *(Time in Seconds)* Write a function that takes the time as three integer arguments (for hours, minutes, and seconds) and returns the number of seconds since the last time the clock "struck 12." Use this function to calculate the amount of time in seconds between two times, both of which are within one 12-hour cycle of the clock.

5.24   *(Temperature Conversions)* Implement the following integer functions:
   a)   Function toCelsius returns the Celsius equivalent of a Fahrenheit temperature.
   b)   Function toFahrenheit returns the Fahrenheit equivalent of a Celsius temperature.
   c)   Use these functions to write a program that prints charts showing the Fahrenheit equivalents of all Celsius temperatures from 0 to 100 degrees, and the Celsius equivalents of all Fahrenheit temperatures from 32 to 212 degrees. Print the outputs in a tabular format that minimizes the number of lines of output while remaining readable.

5.25   *(Find the Minimum)* Write a function that returns the smallest of three floating-point numbers.

5.26   *(Perfect Numbers)* An integer number is said to be a *perfect number* if its factors, including 1 (but not the number itself), sum to the number. For example, 6 is a perfect number because 6 = 1 + 2 + 3. Write a function isPerfect that determines whether parameter number is a perfect number. Use this function in a program that determines and prints all the perfect numbers between 1 and 1000. Print the factors of each perfect number to confirm that the number is indeed perfect. Challenge the power of your computer by testing numbers much larger than 1000.

5.27   *(Prime Numbers)* An integer is said to be *prime* if it's divisible by only 1 and itself. For example, 2, 3, 5 and 7 are prime, but 4, 6, 8 and 9 are not.
   a)   Write a function that determines whether a number is prime.
   b)   Use this function in a program that determines and prints all the prime numbers between 1 and 10,000. How many of these 10,000 numbers do you really have to test before being sure that you have found all the primes?
   c)   Initially you might think that $n/2$ is the upper limit for which you must test to see whether a number is prime, but you need go only as high as the square root of n. Rewrite the program, and run it both ways. Estimate the performance improvement.

5.28   *(Reversing Digits)* Write a function that takes an integer value and returns the number with its digits reversed. For example, given the number 7631, the function should return 1367.

5.29   *(Greatest Common Divisor)* The *greatest common divisor* (GCD) of two integers is the largest integer that evenly divides each of the two numbers. Write a function gcd that returns the greatest common divisor of two integers.

5.30   *(Quality Points for Student's Grades)* Write a function toQualityPoints that inputs a student's average and returns 4 it's 90–100, 3 if it's 80–89, 2 if it's 70–79, 1 if it's 60–69, and 0 if the average is lower than 60.

5.31   *(Coin Tossing)* Write a program that simulates coin tossing. For each toss of the coin the program should print Heads or Tails. Let the program toss the coin 100 times, and count the number of times each side of the coin appears. Print the results. The program should call a separate function flip that takes no arguments and returns 0 for tails and 1 for heads. [*Note:* If the program realistically simulates the coin tossing, then each side of the coin should appear approximately half the time for a total of approximately 50 heads and 50 tails.]

5.32   *(Guess the Number)* Write a C program that plays the game of "guess the number" as follows: Your program chooses the number to be guessed by selecting an integer at random in the range 1 to 1000. The program then types:

```
I have a number between 1 and 1000.
Can you guess my number?
Please type your first guess.
```

The player then types a first guess. The program responds with one of the following:

```
1. Excellent! You guessed the number!
   Would you like to play again (y or n)?
2. Too low. Try again.
3. Too high. Try again.
```

If the player's guess is incorrect, your program should loop until the player finally gets the number right. Your program should keep telling the player Too high or Too low to help the player "zero in" on the correct answer. [*Note:* The searching technique employed in this problem is called binary search. We'll say more about this in the next problem.]

5.33   *(Guess the Number Modification)* Modify the program of Exercise 5.32 to count the number of guesses the player makes. If the number is 10 or fewer, print Either you know the secret or you got lucky! If the player guesses the number in 10 tries, then print Ahah! You know the secret! If the player makes more than 10 guesses, then print You should be able to do better! Why should it take no more than 10 guesses? Well, with each "good guess" the player should be able to eliminate half of the numbers. Now show why any number 1 to 1000 can be guessed in 10 or fewer tries.

5.34   *(Recursive Exponentiation)* Write a recursive function power(base, exponent) that when invoked returns

$$base^{exponent}$$

For example, power(3, 4) = 3 * 3 * 3 * 3. Assume that exponent is an integer greater than or equal to 1. *Hint:* The recursion step would use the relationship

$$base^{exponent} = base * base^{exponent-1}$$

and the terminating condition occurs when exponent is equal to 1 because

$$base^1 = base$$

5.35   *(Fibonacci)* The Fibonacci series

0, 1, 1, 2, 3, 5, 8, 13, 21, ...

begins with the terms 0 and 1 and has the property that each succeeding term is the sum of the two preceding terms. a) Write a *nonrecursive* function fibonacci(n) that calculates the nth Fibonacci number. Use unsigned int for the function's parameter and unsigned long long int for its return type. b) Determine the largest Fibonacci number that can be printed on your system.

5.36   *(Towers of Hanoi)* Every budding computer scientist must grapple with certain classic problems, and the Towers of Hanoi (see Fig. 5.23) is one of the most famous of these. Legend has it that in a temple in the Far East, priests are attempting to move a stack of disks from one peg to another. The initial stack had 64 disks threaded onto one peg and arranged from bottom to top by decreasing size. The priests are attempting to move the stack from this peg to a second peg under the constraints that exactly one disk is moved at a time, and at no time may a larger disk be placed above a smaller disk. A third peg is available for temporarily holding the disks. Supposedly the world will end when the priests complete their task, so there's little incentive for us to facilitate their efforts.

Let's assume that the priests are attempting to move the disks from peg 1 to peg 3. We wish to develop an algorithm that will print the precise sequence of disk-to-disk peg transfers.

If we were to approach this problem with conventional methods, we'd rapidly find ourselves hopelessly knotted up in managing the disks. Instead, if we attack the problem with recursion in mind, it immediately becomes tractable. Moving *n* disks can be viewed in terms of moving only *n* − 1 disks (and hence the recursion) as follows:

a)   Move *n* − 1 disks from peg 1 to peg 2, using peg 3 as a temporary holding area.

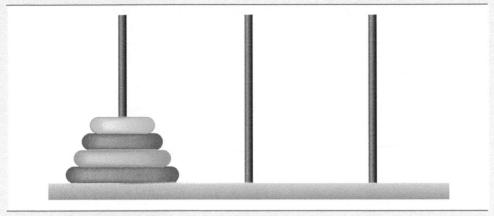

Fig. 5.23 | Towers of Hanoi for the case with four disks.

  b) Move the last disk (the largest) from peg 1 to peg 3.
  c) Move the $n - 1$ disks from peg 2 to peg 3, using peg 1 as a temporary holding area.
The process ends when the last task involves moving $n = 1$ disk, i.e., the base case. This is accomplished by trivially moving the disk without the need for a temporary holding area.
  Write a program to solve the Towers of Hanoi problem. Use a recursive function with four parameters:
  a) The number of disks to be moved
  b) The peg on which these disks are initially threaded
  c) The peg to which this stack of disks is to be moved
  d) The peg to be used as a temporary holding area
  Your program should print the precise instructions it will take to move the disks from the starting peg to the destination peg. For example, to move a stack of three disks from peg 1 to peg 3, your program should print the following series of moves:
       $1 \rightarrow 3$ (This means move one disk from peg 1 to peg 3.)
       $1 \rightarrow 2$
       $3 \rightarrow 2$
       $1 \rightarrow 3$
       $2 \rightarrow 1$
       $2 \rightarrow 3$
       $1 \rightarrow 3$

5.37   *(Towers of Hanoi: Iterative Solution)* Any program that can be implemented recursively can be implemented iteratively, although sometimes with considerably more difficulty and considerably less clarity. Try writing an iterative version of the Towers of Hanoi. If you succeed, compare your iterative version with the recursive version you developed in Exercise 5.36. Investigate issues of performance, clarity, and your ability to demonstrate the correctness of the programs.

5.38   *(Visualizing Recursion)* It's interesting to watch recursion "in action." Modify the factorial function of Fig. 5.18 to print its local variable and recursive call parameter. For each recursive call, display the outputs on a separate line and add a level of indentation. Do your utmost to make the outputs clear, interesting and meaningful. Your goal here is to design and implement an output format that helps a person understand recursion better. You may want to add such display capabilities to the many other recursion examples and exercises throughout the text.

5.39   *(Recursive Greatest Common Divisor)* The greatest common divisor of integers x and y is the largest integer that evenly divides both x and y. Write a recursive function gcd that returns the greatest common divisor of x and y. The gcd of x and y is defined recursively as follows: If y is equal to 0, then gcd(x, y) is x; otherwise gcd(x, y) is gcd(y, x % y), where % is the remainder operator.

5.40   *(Recursive main)* Can main be called recursively? Write a program containing a function main. Include static local variable count initialized to 1. Postincrement and print the value of count each time main is called. Run your program. What happens?

5.41   *(Distance Between Points)* Write a function distance that calculates the distance between two points *(x1, y1)* and *(x2, y2)*. All numbers and return values should be of type double.

5.42   What does the following program do? What happens if you exchange lines 8 and 9?

```
1   #include <stdio.h>
2
3   int main(void)
4   {
5      int c; // variable to hold character input by user
6
7      if ((c = getchar()) != EOF) {
8         main();
9         printf("%c", c);
10     }
11  }
```

5.43   What does the following program do?

```
1   #include <stdio.h>
2
3   unsigned int mystery(unsigned int a, unsigned int b); // function prototype
4
5   int main(void)
6   {
7      printf("%s", "Enter two positive integers: ");
8      unsigned int x; // first integer
9      unsigned int y; // second integer
10     scanf("%u%u", &x, &y);
11
12     printf("The result is %u\n", mystery(x, y));
13  }
14
15  // Parameter b must be a positive integer
16  // to prevent infinite recursion
17  unsigned int mystery(unsigned int a, unsigned int b)
18  {
19     // base case
20     if (1 == b) {
21        return a;
22     }
23     else { // recursive step
24        return a + mystery(a, b - 1);
25     }
26  }
```

5.44   After you determine what the program of Exercise 5.43 does, modify the program to function properly after removing the restriction of the second argument's being nonnegative.

5.45   *(Testing Math Library Functions)* Write a program that tests the math library functions in Fig. 5.2. Exercise each of these functions by having your program print out tables of return values for a diversity of argument values.

5.46 Find the error in each of the following program segments and explain how to correct it:

a)
```
double cube(float); // function prototype
cube(float number) // function definition
{
    return number * number * number;
}
```
b)
```
int randomNumber = srand();
```
c)
```
double y = 123.45678;
int x;
x = y;
printf("%f\n", (double) x);
```
d)
```
double square(double number)
{
    double number;
    return number * number;
}
```
e)
```
int sum(int n)
{
    if (0 == n) {
        return 0;
    }
    else {
        return n + sum(n);
    }
}
```

5.47 *(Craps Game Modification)* Modify the craps program of Fig. 5.14 to allow *wagering*. Package as a function the portion of the program that runs one game of craps. Initialize variable bankBalance to 1000 dollars. Prompt the player to enter a wager. Use a while loop to check that wager is less than or equal to bankBalance, and if not, prompt the user to reenter wager until a valid wager is entered. After a correct wager is entered, run one game of craps. If the player wins, increase bankBalance by wager and print the new bankBalance. If the player loses, decrease bankBalance by wager, print the new bankBalance, check whether bankBalance has become zero, and if so print the message, "Sorry. You busted!" As the game progresses, print various messages to create some "chatter" such as, "Oh, you're going for broke, huh?" or "Aw cmon, take a chance!" or "You're up big. Now's the time to cash in your chips!"

5.48 *(Research Project: Improving the Recursive Fibonacci Implementation)* In Section 5.15, the recursive algorithm we used to calculate Fibonacci numbers was intuitively appealing. However, recall that the algorithm resulted in the exponential explosion of recursive function calls. Research the recursive Fibonacci implementation online. Study the various approaches, including the iterative version in Exercise 5.35 and versions that use only so-called "tail recursion." Discuss the relative merits of each.

Making a Difference

5.49 *(Global Warming Facts Quiz)* The controversial issue of global warming has been widely publicized by the film *An Inconvenient Truth*, featuring former Vice President Al Gore. Mr. Gore and a U.N. network of scientists, the Intergovernmental Panel on Climate Change, shared the 2007 Nobel Peace Prize in recognition of "their efforts to build up and disseminate greater knowledge about man-made climate change." Research *both* sides of the global warming issue online (you might want to search for phrases like "global warming skeptics"). Create a five-question multiple-choice quiz on global warming, each question having four possible answers (numbered 1–4). Be objective and try to fairly represent both sides of the issue. Next, write an application that administers the quiz, calculates the number of correct answers (zero through five) and returns a message to the user. If the user correctly answers five questions, print "Excellent"; if four, print "Very good"; if three or fewer, print "Time to brush up on your knowledge of global warming," and include a list of some of the websites where you found your facts.

Computer-Assisted Instruction

As computer costs decline, it becomes feasible for every student, regardless of economic circumstance, to have a computer and use it in school. This creates exciting possibilities for improving the educational experience of all students worldwide as suggested by the next five exercises. [*Note:* Check out initiatives such as the One Laptop Per Child Project (www.laptop.org). Also, research "green" laptops—what are some key "going green" characteristics of these devices? Look into the Electronic Product Environmental Assessment Tool (www.epeat.net) which can help you assess the "greenness" of desktops, notebooks and monitors to help you decide which products to purchase.]

5.50 *(Computer-Assisted Instruction)* The use of computers in education is referred to as *computer-assisted instruction* (*CAI*). Write a program that will help an elementary school student learn multiplication. Use the rand function to produce two positive one-digit integers. The program should then prompt the user with a question, such as

```
How much is 6 times 7?
```

The student then inputs the answer. Next, the program checks the student's answer. If it's correct, display the message "Very good!" and ask another multiplication question. If the answer is wrong, display the message "No. Please try again." and let the student try the same question repeatedly until the student finally gets it right. A separate function should be used to generate each new question. This function should be called once when the application begins execution and each time the user answers the question correctly.

5.51 *(Computer-Assisted Instruction: Reducing Student Fatigue)* One problem in CAI environments is student fatigue. This can be reduced by varying the computer's responses to hold the student's attention. Modify the program of Exercise 5.50 so that various comments are displayed for each answer as follows:

Possible responses to a correct answer:

```
Very good!
Excellent!
Nice work!
Keep up the good work!
```

Possible responses to an incorrect answer:

```
No. Please try again.
Wrong. Try once more.
Don't give up!
No. Keep trying.
```

Use random-number generation to choose a number from 1 to 4 that will be used to select one of the four appropriate responses to each correct or incorrect answer. Use a switch statement to issue the responses.

5.52 *(Computer-Assisted Instruction: Monitoring Student Performance)* More sophisticated computer-assisted instruction systems monitor the student's performance over a period of time. The decision to begin a new topic is often based on the student's success with previous topics. Modify the program of Exercise 5.51 to count the number of correct and incorrect responses typed by the student. After the student types 10 answers, your program should calculate the percentage that are correct. If the percentage is lower than 75%, display "Please ask your teacher for extra help.", then reset the program so another student can try it. If the percentage is 75% or higher, display "Congratulations, you are ready to go to the next level!", then reset the program so another student can try it.

5.53   *(Computer-Assisted Instruction: Difficulty Levels)* Exercises 5.50 through Exercise 5.52 developed a computer-assisted instruction program to help teach an elementary-school student multiplication. Modify the program to allow the user to enter a difficulty level. At a difficulty level of 1, the program should use only single-digit numbers in the problems; at a difficulty level of 2, numbers as large as two digits, and so on.

5.54   *(Computer-Assisted Instruction: Varying the Types of Problems)* Modify the program of Exercise 5.53 to allow the user to pick a type of arithmetic problem to study. An option of 1 means addition problems only, 2 means subtraction problems only, 3 means multiplication problems only and 4 means a random mixture of all these types.

6

C Arrays

Objectives

In this chapter, you'll:

- Use the array data structure to represent lists and tables of values.

- Define an array, initialize an array and refer to individual elements of an array.

- Define symbolic constants.

- Pass arrays to functions.

- Use arrays to store, sort and search lists and tables of values.

- Define and manipulate multidimensional arrays.

- Create variable-length arrays whose size is determined at execution time.

- Understand security issues related to input with `scanf`, output with `printf` and arrays.

6.1 Introduction

This chapter introduces data structures. **Arrays** are data structures consisting of related data items of the same type. In Chapter 10, we discuss C's notion of struct—a data structure consisting of related data items of possibly different types. Arrays and structs are "static" entities in that they remain the same size throughout program execution (they may, of course, be of automatic storage class and hence created and destroyed each time the blocks in which they're defined are entered and exited).

6.2 Arrays

An array is a group of *contiguous* memory locations that all have the *same type*. To refer to a particular location or element in the array, we specify the array's name and the **position number** of the particular element in the array.

Figure 6.1 shows an integer array called c, containing 12 **elements**. Any one of these elements may be referred to by giving the array's name followed by the *position number* of the particular element in square brackets ([]). The first element in every array is the **zeroth element** (i.e., the one with position number 0). An array name, like other identifiers, can contain only letters, digits and underscores and cannot begin with a digit.

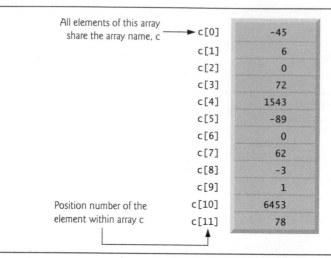

All elements of this array share the array name, c

Position number of the element within array c

Fig. 6.1 | 12-element array.

The position number in square brackets is called the element's **index** or **subscript**. An index must be an integer or an integer expression. For example, the statement

```
c[2] = 1000;
```

assigns 1000 to array element c[2]. Similarly, if a = 5 and b = 6, then the statement

```
c[a + b] += 2;
```

adds 2 to array element c[11]. An indexed array name is an *lvalue*—it can be used on the left side of an assignment.

Let's examine array c (Fig. 6.1) more closely. The array's **name** is c. Its 12 elements are referred to as c[0], c[1], c[2], ..., c[10] and c[11]. The **value** stored in c[0] is –45, the value of c[1] is 6, c[2] is 0, c[7] is 62 and c[11] is 78. To print the sum of the values contained in the first three elements of array c, we'd write

```
printf("%d", c[0] + c[1] + c[2]);
```

To divide the value of element 6 of array c by 2 and assign the result to the variable x, write

```
x = c[6] / 2;
```

The brackets used to enclose an array's index are actually considered to be an *operator* in C. They have the same level of precedence as the *function call operator* (i.e., the parentheses that are placed after a function name to call that function). Figure 6.2 shows the precedence and associativity of the operators introduced to this point in the text.

Operators	Associativity	Type
[] () ++ *(postfix)* -- *(postfix)*	left to right	highest
+ - ! ++ *(prefix)* -- *(prefix)* *(type)*	right to left	unary

Fig. 6.2 | Operator precedence and associativity. (Part 1 of 2.)

Operators	Associativity	Type
* / %	left to right	multiplicative
+ -	left to right	additive
< <= > >=	left to right	relational
== !=	left to right	equality
&&	left to right	logical AND
||	left to right	logical OR
?:	right to left	conditional
= += -= *= /= %=	right to left	assignment
,	left to right	comma

Fig. 6.2 | Operator precedence and associativity. (Part 2 of 2.)

6.3 Defining Arrays

Arrays occupy space in memory. You specify the type of each element and the number of elements each array requires so that the computer may reserve the appropriate amount of memory. The following definition reserves 12 elements for integer array c, which has indices in the range 0–11.

```
int c[12];
```

The definition

```
int b[100], x[27];
```

reserves 100 elements for integer array b and 27 elements for integer array x. These arrays have indices in the ranges 0–99 and 0–26, respectively. Though you can define multiple arrays at once, defining only one per line is preferred, so you can add a comment explaining each array's purpose.

Arrays may contain other data types. For example, an array of type char can store a character string. Character strings and their similarity to arrays are discussed in Chapter 8. The relationship between pointers and arrays is discussed in Chapter 7.

6.4 Array Examples

This section presents several examples that demonstrate how to define and initialize arrays, and how to perform many common array manipulations.

6.4.1 Defining an Array and Using a Loop to Set the Array's Element Values

Like any other variables, uninitialized array elements contain garbage values. Figure 6.3 uses for statements to set the elements of a five-element integer array n to zeros (lines 11–13) and print the array in tabular format (lines 18–20). The first printf statement (line 15) displays the column heads for the two columns printed in the subsequent for statement.

```
 1   // Fig. 6.3: fig06_03.c
 2   // Initializing the elements of an array to zeros.
 3   #include <stdio.h>
 4
 5   // function main begins program execution
 6   int main(void)
 7   {
 8      int n[5]; // n is an array of five integers
 9
10      // set elements of array n to 0
11      for (size_t i = 0; i < 5; ++i) {
12         n[i] = 0; // set element at location i to 0
13      }
14
15      printf("%s%13s\n", "Element", "Value");
16
17      // output contents of array n in tabular format
18      for (size_t i = 0; i < 5; ++i) {
19         printf("%7u%13d\n", i, n[i]);
20      }
21   }
```

```
Element        Value
      0            0
      1            0
      2            0
      3            0
      4            0
```

Fig. 6.3 | Initializing the elements of an array to zeros.

Notice that the counter-control variable i is declared to be of type size_t in each for statement (lines 11 and 18), which according to the C standard represents an unsigned integral type.[1] This type is recommended for any variable that represents an array's size or indices. Type size_t is defined in header <stddef.h>, which is often included by other headers (such as <stdio.h>). [*Note:* If you attempt to compile Fig. 6.3 and receive errors, simply include <stddef.h> in your program.]

6.4.2 Initializing an Array in a Definition with an Initializer List

The elements of an array can also be initialized when the array is defined by following the definition with an equals sign and braces, {}, containing a comma-separated list of **array initializers**. Figure 6.4 initializes an integer array with five values (line 9) and prints the array in tabular format.

---

1. On some compilers, size_t represents unsigned int and on others it represents unsigned long. Compilers that use unsigned long typically generate a warning on line 19 of Fig. 6.3, because %u is for displaying unsigned ints, not unsigned longs. To eliminate this warning, replace the format specification %u with %lu.

```
 1   // Fig. 6.4: fig06_04.c
 2   // Initializing the elements of an array with an initializer list.
 3   #include <stdio.h>
 4
 5   // function main begins program execution
 6   int main(void)
 7   {
 8      // use initializer list to initialize array n
 9      int n[5] = {32, 27, 64, 18, 95};
10
11      printf("%s%13s\n", "Element", "Value");
12
13      // output contents of array in tabular format
14      for (size_t i = 0; i < 5; ++i) {
15         printf("%7u%13d\n", i, n[i]);
16      }
17   }
```

Element	Value
0	32
1	27
2	64
3	18
4	95

Fig. 6.4 | Initializing the elements of an array with an initializer list.

If there are *fewer* initializers than elements in the array, the remaining elements are initialized to zero. For example, the elements of the array n in Fig. 6.3 could have been initialized to zero as follows:

```
int n[10] = {0}; // initializes entire array to zeros
```

This *explicitly* initializes the first element to zero and initializes the remaining nine elements to zero because there are fewer initializers than there are elements in the array. Arrays are *not* automatically initialized to zero. You must at least initialize the first element to zero for the remaining elements to be automatically zeroed. Array elements are initialized before program startup for static arrays and at runtime for *automatic* arrays.

Common Programming Error 6.1
Forgetting to initialize the elements of an array.

Common Programming Error 6.2
It's a syntax error to provide more initializers in an array initializer list than there are elements in the array—for example, int n[3] = {32, 27, 64, 18}; *is a syntax error, because there are four initializers but only three array elements.*

If the array size is *omitted* from a definition with an initializer list, the number of elements in the array will be the number of elements in the initializer list. For example,

```
int n[] = {1, 2, 3, 4, 5};
```

would create a five-element array initialized with the indicated values.

6.4.3 Specifying an Array's Size with a Symbolic Constant and Initializing Array Elements with Calculations

Figure 6.5 initializes the elements of a five-element array s to the values 2, 4, 6, ..., 10 and prints the array in tabular format. The values are generated by multiplying the loop counter by 2 and adding 2.

```c
1   // Fig. 6.5: fig06_05.c
2   // Initializing the elements of array s to the even integers from 2 to 10.
3   #include <stdio.h>
4   #define SIZE 5 // maximum size of array
5
6   // function main begins program execution
7   int main(void)
8   {
9       // symbolic constant SIZE can be used to specify array size
10      int s[SIZE]; // array s has SIZE elements
11
12      for (size_t j = 0; j < SIZE; ++j) { // set the values
13          s[j] = 2 + 2 * j;
14      }
15
16      printf("%s%13s\n", "Element", "Value");
17
18      // output contents of array s in tabular format
19      for (size_t j = 0; j < SIZE; ++j) {
20          printf("%7u%13d\n", j, s[j]);
21      }
22  }
```

```
Element        Value
      0            2
      1            4
      2            6
      3            8
      4           10
```

Fig. 6.5 | Initializing the elements of array s to the even integers from 2 to 10.

The **#define preprocessor directive** is introduced in this program. Line 4

```c
    #define SIZE 5
```

defines a **symbolic constant** SIZE whose value is 5. A symbolic constant is an identifier that's replaced with **replacement text** by the C preprocessor before the program is compiled. When the program is preprocessed, all occurrences of the symbolic constant SIZE are replaced with the replacement text 5. Using symbolic constants to specify array sizes makes programs more **modifiable**. In Fig. 6.5, we could have the first for loop (line 12) fill a 1000-element array by simply changing the value of SIZE in the #define directive from 5 to 1000. If the symbolic constant SIZE had not been used, we'd have to change the program in lines 10, 12 and 19. As programs get larger, this technique becomes more useful for writing clear, easy to read, maintainable programs—a symbolic constant (like SIZE) is easier to understand than the numeric value 5, which could have different meanings throughout the code.

Common Programming Error 6.3

Ending a #define or #include preprocessor directive with a semicolon. Remember that preprocessor directives are not C statements.

If you terminate the #define preprocessor directive in line 4 with a semicolon, the preprocessor replaces all occurrences of the symbolic constant SIZE in the program with the text "5;". This may lead to syntax errors at compile time, or logic errors at execution time. Remember that the preprocessor is *not* the C compiler.

Software Engineering Observation 6.1

Defining the size of each array as a symbolic constant makes programs more modifiable.

Common Programming Error 6.4

Assigning a value to a symbolic constant in an executable statement is a syntax error. The compiler does not reserve space for symbolic constants as it does for variables that hold values at execution time.

Good Programming Practice 6.1

Use only uppercase letters for symbolic constant names. This makes these constants stand out in a program and reminds you that symbolic constants are not variables.

Good Programming Practice 6.2

In multiword symbolic constant names, separate the words with underscores for readability.

6.4.4 Summing the Elements of an Array

Figure 6.6 sums the values contained in the 12-element integer array a. The for statement's body (line 15) does the totaling.

```c
1  // Fig. 6.6: fig06_06.c
2  // Computing the sum of the elements of an array.
3  #include <stdio.h>
4  #define SIZE 12
5
6  // function main begins program execution
7  int main(void)
8  {
9     // use an initializer list to initialize the array
10    int a[SIZE] = {1, 3, 5, 4, 7, 2, 99, 16, 45, 67, 89, 45};
11    int total = 0; // sum of array
12
13    // sum contents of array a
14    for (size_t i = 0; i < SIZE; ++i) {
15       total += a[i];
16    }
17
18    printf("Total of array element values is %d\n", total);
19 }
```

Fig. 6.6 | Computing the sum of the elements of an array. (Part 1 of 2.)

```
Total of array element values is 383
```

Fig. 6.6 | Computing the sum of the elements of an array. (Part 2 of 2.)

6.4.5 Using Arrays to Summarize Survey Results

Our next example uses arrays to summarize the results of data collected in a survey. Consider the problem statement.

> *Forty students were asked to rate the quality of the food in the student cafeteria on a scale of 1 to 10 (1 means awful and 10 means excellent). Place the 40 responses in an integer array and summarize the results of the poll.*

This is a typical array application (Fig. 6.7). We wish to summarize the number of responses of each type (i.e., 1 through 10). The 40-element array responses (lines 14–16) contains the students' responses. We use an 11-element array frequency (line 11) to count the number of occurrences of each response. We ignore frequency[0] because it's logical to have response 1 increment frequency[1] rather than frequency[0]. This allows us to use each response directly as the index in the frequency array.

```c
1   // Fig. 6.7: fig06_07.c
2   // Analyzing a student poll.
3   #include <stdio.h>
4   #define RESPONSES_SIZE 40 // define array sizes
5   #define FREQUENCY_SIZE 11
6
7   // function main begins program execution
8   int main(void)
9   {
10      // initialize frequency counters to 0
11      int frequency[FREQUENCY_SIZE] = {0};
12
13      // place the survey responses in the responses array
14      int responses[RESPONSES_SIZE] = {1, 2, 6, 4, 8, 5, 9, 7, 8, 10,
15          1, 6, 3, 8, 6, 10, 3, 8, 2, 7, 6, 5, 7, 6, 8, 6, 7, 5, 6, 6,
16          5, 6, 7, 5, 6, 4, 8, 6, 8, 10};
17
18      // for each answer, select value of an element of array responses
19      // and use that value as an index in array frequency to
20      // determine element to increment
21      for (size_t answer = 0; answer < RESPONSES_SIZE; ++answer) {
22          ++frequency[responses[answer]];
23      }
24
25      // display results
26      printf("%s%17s\n", "Rating", "Frequency");
27
28      // output the frequencies in a tabular format
29      for (size_t rating = 1; rating < FREQUENCY_SIZE; ++rating) {
30          printf("%6d%17d\n", rating, frequency[rating]);
31      }
32  }
```

Fig. 6.7 | Analyzing a student poll. (Part 1 of 2.)

Rating	Frequency
1	2
2	2
3	2
4	2
5	5
6	11
7	5
8	7
9	1
10	3

Fig. 6.7 | Analyzing a student poll. (Part 2 of 2.)

Good Programming Practice 6.3

Strive for program clarity. Sometimes it may be worthwhile to trade off the most efficient use of memory or processor time in favor of writing clearer programs.

Performance Tip 6.1

Sometimes performance considerations far outweigh clarity considerations.

The for loop (lines 21–23) takes the responses one at a time from the array responses and increments one of the 10 counters (frequency[1] to frequency[10]) in the frequency array. The key statement in the loop is line 22

```
++frequency[responses[answer]];
```

which increments the appropriate frequency counter depending on the value of the expression responses[answer]. When the counter variable answer is 0, responses[answer] is 1, so ++frequency[responses[answer]]; is interpreted as

```
++frequency[1];
```

which increments array element 1. When answer is 1, the value of responses[answer] is 2, so ++frequency[responses[answer]]; is interpreted as

```
++frequency[2];
```

which increments array element 2. When answer is 2, the value of responses[answer] is 6, so ++frequency[responses[answer]]; is interpreted as

```
++frequency[6];
```

which increments array element 6, and so on. Regardless of the number of responses processed in the survey, only an 11-element array is required (ignoring element zero) to summarize the results. If the data contained invalid values such as 13, the program would attempt to add 1 to frequency[13]. This would be outside the bounds of the array. *C has no array bounds checking to prevent the program from referring to an element that does not exist.* Thus, an executing program can "walk off" either end of an array without warning—a security problem that we discuss in Section 6.13. You should ensure that all array references remain within the bounds of the array.

Common Programming Error 6.5

Referring to an element outside the array bounds.

Error-Prevention Tip 6.1

When looping through an array, the array index should never go below 0 and should always be less than the total number of elements in the array (size − 1). Make sure the loop-continuation condition prevents accessing elements outside this range.

Error-Prevention Tip 6.2

Programs should validate the correctness of all input values to prevent erroneous information from affecting a program's calculations.

6.4.6 Graphing Array Element Values with Histograms

Our next example (Fig. 6.8) reads numbers from an array and graphs the information in the form of a bar chart or histogram—each number is printed, then a bar consisting of that many asterisks is printed beside the number. The nested for statement (lines 18–20) draws the bars. Note the use of puts("") to end each histogram bar (line 22).

```c
1   // Fig. 6.8: fig06_08.c
2   // Displaying a histogram.
3   #include <stdio.h>
4   #define SIZE 5
5
6   // function main begins program execution
7   int main(void)
8   {
9      // use initializer list to initialize array n
10     int n[SIZE] = {19, 3, 15, 7, 11};
11
12     printf("%s%13s%17s\n", "Element", "Value", "Histogram");
13
14     // for each element of array n, output a bar of the histogram
15     for (size_t i = 0; i < SIZE; ++i) {
16        printf("%7u%13d        ", i, n[i]);
17
18        for (int j = 1; j <= n[i]; ++j) { // print one bar
19           printf("%c", '*');
20        }
21
22        puts(""); // end a histogram bar with a newline
23     }
24  }
```

```
Element        Value        Histogram
      0           19        *******************
      1            3        ***
      2           15        ***************
      3            7        *******
      4           11        ***********
```

Fig. 6.8 | Displaying a histogram.

6.4.7 Rolling a Die 60,000,000 Times and Summarizing the Results in an Array

In Chapter 5, we stated that we'd show a more elegant method of writing the dice-rolling program of Fig. 5.12. Recall that the program rolled a single six-sided die 60,000,000 times to test whether the random number generator actually produces random numbers. An array version of this program is shown in Fig. 6.9. Line 18 replaces Fig. 5.12's entire switch statement.

```c
 1  // Fig. 6.9: fig06_09.c
 2  // Roll a six-sided die 60,000,000 times
 3  #include <stdio.h>
 4  #include <stdlib.h>
 5  #include <time.h>
 6  #define SIZE 7
 7
 8  // function main begins program execution
 9  int main(void)
10  {
11     unsigned int frequency[SIZE] = {0}; // clear counts
12
13     srand(time(NULL)); // seed random number generator
14
15     // roll die 60,000,000 times
16     for (unsigned int roll = 1; roll <= 60000000; ++roll) {
17        size_t face = 1 + rand() % 6;
18        ++frequency[face]; // replaces entire switch of Fig. 5.12
19     }
20
21     printf("%s%17s\n", "Face", "Frequency");
22
23     // output frequency elements 1-6 in tabular format
24     for (size_t face = 1; face < SIZE; ++face) {
25        printf("%4d%17d\n", face, frequency[face]);
26     }
27  }
```

```
Face        Frequency
   1          9997167
   2         10003506
   3         10001940
   4          9995833
   5         10000843
   6         10000711
```

Fig. 6.9 | Roll a six-sided die 60,000,000 times.

6.5 Using Character Arrays to Store and Manipulate Strings

We've discussed only integer arrays. However, arrays are capable of holding data of *any* type. We now discuss storing *strings* in character arrays. So far, the only string-processing capability we have is outputting a string with printf. A string such as "hello" is really an array of individual characters in C.

6.5.1 Initializing a Character Array with a String

Character arrays have several unique features. A character array can be initialized using a string literal. For example,

```
char string1[] = "first";
```

initializes the elements of array string1 to the individual characters in the string literal "first". In this case, the size of array string1 is determined by the compiler based on the length of the string. The string "first" contains five characters *plus* a special *string-termination character* called the **null character**. Thus, array string1 actually contains *six* elements. The escape sequence representing the null character is '\0'. All strings in C end with this character. A character array representing a string should always be defined large enough to hold the number of characters in the string and the terminating null character.

6.5.2 Initializing a Character Array with an Intializer List of Characters

Character arrays also can be initialized with individual character constants in an initializer list, but this can be tedious. The preceding definition is equivalent to

```
char string1[] = {'f', 'i', 'r', 's', 't', '\0'};
```

6.5.3 Accessing the Characters in a String

Because a string is really an array of characters, we can access individual characters in a string directly using array index notation. For example, string1[0] is the character 'f' and string1[3] is the character 's'.

6.5.4 Inputting into a Character Array

We also can input a string directly into a character array from the keyboard using scanf and the conversion specifier %s. For example,

```
char string2[20];
```

creates a character array capable of storing a string of *at most 19 characters* and a *terminating null character*. The statement

```
scanf("%19s", string2);
```

reads a string from the keyboard into string2. The name of the array is passed to scanf without the preceding & used with nonstring variables. The & is normally used to provide scanf with a variable's *location* in memory so that a value can be stored there. In Section 6.7, when we discuss passing arrays to functions, we'll see that the value of an array name *is the address of the start of the array*; therefore, the & is not necessary. Function scanf will read characters until a *space, tab, newline* or *end-of-file indicator* is encountered. The string string2 should be no longer than 19 characters to leave room for the terminating null character. If the user types 20 or more characters, your program may crash or create a security vulnerability called buffer overflow. For this reason, we used the conversion specifier %19s so that scanf reads a maximum of 19 characters and does not write characters into memory beyond the end of the array string2. (In Section 6.13, we revisit the potential security issue raised by inputting into a character array and discuss the C standard's scanf_s function.)

It's your responsibility to ensure that the array into which the string is read is capable of holding any string that the user types at the keyboard. Function scanf does *not* check how large the array is. Thus, scanf can write beyond the end of the array.

6.5.5 Outputting a Character Array That Represents a String

A character array representing a string can be output with printf and the %s conversion specifier. The array string2 is printed with the statement

```
printf("%s\n", string2);
```

Function printf, like scanf, does *not* check how large the character array is. The characters of the string are printed until a terminating null character is encountered. [Consider what would print if, for some reason, the terminating null character were missing.]

6.5.6 Demonstrating Character Arrays

Figure 6.10 demonstrates initializing a character array with a string literal, reading a string into a character array, printing a character array as a string and accessing individual characters of a string. The program uses a for statement (lines 22–24) to loop through the string1 array and print the individual characters separated by spaces, using the %c conversion specifier. The condition in the for statement is true while the counter is less than the size of the array and the terminating null character has *not* been encountered in the string. In this program, we read only strings that do not contain whitespace characters. We'll show how to read strings with whitespace characters in Chapter 8. Notice that lines 17–18 contain two string literals separated only by whitespace. The compiler automatically *combines* such string literals into one—this is helpful for making long string literals more readable.

```
1   // Fig. 6.10: fig06_10.c
2   // Treating character arrays as strings.
3   #include <stdio.h>
4   #define SIZE 20
5
6   // function main begins program execution
7   int main(void)
8   {
9       char string1[SIZE]; // reserves 20 characters
10      char string2[] = "string literal"; // reserves 15 characters
11
12      // read string from user into array string1
13      printf("%s", "Enter a string (no longer than 19 characters): ");
14      scanf("%19s", string1); // input no more than 19 characters
15
16      // output strings
17      printf("string1 is: %s\nstring2 is: %s\n"
18             "string1 with spaces between characters is:\n",
19             string1, string2);
```

Fig. 6.10 | Treating character arrays as strings. (Part 1 of 2.)

```
20
21     // output characters until null character is reached
22     for (size_t i = 0; i < SIZE && string1[i] != '\0'; ++i) {
23        printf("%c ", string1[i]);
24     }
25
26     puts("");
27  }
```

```
Enter a string (no longer than 19 characters): Hello there
string1 is: Hello
string2 is: string literal
string1 with spaces between characters is:
H e l l o
```

Fig. 6.10 | Treating character arrays as strings. (Part 2 of 2.)

6.6 Static Local Arrays and Automatic Local Arrays

Chapter 5 discussed the storage-class specifier static. A static local variable exists for the *duration* of the program but is *visible* only in the function body. We can apply static to a local array definition so the array is *not* created and initialized each time the function is called and the array is *not* destroyed each time the function is exited in the program. This reduces program execution time, particularly for programs with frequently called functions that contain large arrays.

Performance Tip 6.2

In functions that contain automatic arrays where the function is in and out of scope frequently, make the array static so it's not created each time the function is called.

Arrays that are static are initialized once at program startup. If you do not explicitly initialize a static array, that array's elements are initialized to *zero* by default.

Figure 6.11 demonstrates function staticArrayInit (lines 21–39) with a local static array (line 24) and function automaticArrayInit (lines 42–60) with a local automatic array (line 45). Function staticArrayInit is called twice (lines 12 and 16). The local static array in the function is initialized to zero before program startup (line 24). The function prints the array, adds 5 to each element and prints the array again. The second time the function is called, the static array contains the values stored during the first function call.

Function automaticArrayInit is also called twice (lines 13 and 17). The elements of the automatic local array in the function are initialized with the values 1, 2 and 3 (line 45). The function prints the array, adds 5 to each element and prints the array again. The second time the function is called, the array elements are initialized to 1, 2 and 3 again because the array has automatic storage duration.

Common Programming Error 6.6

Assuming that elements of a local static array are initialized to zero every time the function in which it is defined is called.

```
 1   // Fig. 6.11: fig06_11.c
 2   // Static arrays are initialized to zero if not explicitly initialized.
 3   #include <stdio.h>
 4
 5   void staticArrayInit(void); // function prototype
 6   void automaticArrayInit(void); // function prototype
 7
 8   // function main begins program execution
 9   int main(void)
10   {
11      puts("First call to each function:");
12      staticArrayInit();
13      automaticArrayInit();
14
15      puts("\n\nSecond call to each function:");
16      staticArrayInit();
17      automaticArrayInit();
18   }
19
20   // function to demonstrate a static local array
21   void staticArrayInit(void)
22   {
23      // initializes elements to 0 before the function is called
24      static int array1[3];
25
26      puts("\nValues on entering staticArrayInit:");
27
28      // output contents of array1
29      for (size_t i = 0; i <= 2; ++i) {
30         printf("array1[%u] = %d   ", i, array1[i]);
31      }
32
33      puts("\nValues on exiting staticArrayInit:");
34
35      // modify and output contents of array1
36      for (size_t i = 0; i <= 2; ++i) {
37         printf("array1[%u] = %d   ", i, array1[i] += 5);
38      }
39   }
40
41   // function to demonstrate an automatic local array
42   void automaticArrayInit(void)
43   {
44      // initializes elements each time function is called
45      int array2[3] = {1, 2, 3};
46
47      puts("\n\nValues on entering automaticArrayInit:");
48
49      // output contents of array2
50      for (size_t i = 0; i <= 2; ++i) {
51         printf("array2[%u] = %d   ", i, array2[i]);
52      }
53
```

Fig. 6.11 | Static arrays are initialized to zero if not explicitly initialized. (Part 1 of 2.)

```
54          puts("\nValues on exiting automaticArrayInit:");
55
56          // modify and output contents of array2
57          for (size_t i = 0; i <= 2; ++i) {
58             printf("array2[%u] = %d  ", i, array2[i] += 5);
59          }
60      }
```

```
First call to each function:

Values on entering staticArrayInit:
array1[0] = 0   array1[1] = 0   array1[2] = 0
Values on exiting staticArrayInit:
array1[0] = 5   array1[1] = 5   array1[2] = 5

Values on entering automaticArrayInit:
array2[0] = 1   array2[1] = 2   array2[2] = 3
Values on exiting automaticArrayInit:
array2[0] = 6   array2[1] = 7   array2[2] = 8

Second call to each function:

Values on entering staticArrayInit:
array1[0] = 5   array1[1] = 5   array1[2] = 5 ── values preserved from last call
Values on exiting staticArrayInit:
array1[0] = 10  array1[1] = 10  array1[2] = 10

Values on entering automaticArrayInit:
array2[0] = 1   array2[1] = 2   array2[2] = 3 ── values reinitialized after last call
Values on exiting automaticArrayInit:
array2[0] = 6   array2[1] = 7   array2[2] = 8
```

Fig. 6.11 | Static arrays are initialized to zero if not explicitly initialized. (Part 2 of 2.)

6.7 Passing Arrays to Functions

To pass an array argument to a function, specify the array's name without any brackets. For example, if array hourlyTemperatures has been defined as

```
int hourlyTemperatures[HOURS_IN_A_DAY];
```

the function call

```
modifyArray(hourlyTemperatures, HOURS_IN_A_DAY)
```

passes array hourlyTemperatures and its size to function modifyArray.

Recall that all arguments in C are passed *by value*. C automatically passes arrays to functions *by reference* (again, we'll see in Chapter 7 that this is *not* a contradiction)—the called functions can modify the element values in the callers' original arrays. The array's name evaluates to the *address* of the array's first element. Because the starting address of the array is passed, the called function knows precisely where the array is stored. Therefore, when the called function modifies array elements in its function body, it's modifying the actual elements of the array in their *original* memory locations.

Figure 6.12 demonstrates that "the value of an array name" is really the *address* of the first element of the array by printing array, &array[0] and &array using the %p conversion specifier for printing addresses. The %p conversion specifier normally outputs addresses as hexadecimal numbers, but this is compiler dependent. Hexadecimal (base 16) numbers consist of the digits 0 through 9 and the letters A through F (these letters are the hexadecimal equivalents of the decimal numbers 10–15). Appendix C provides an in-depth discussion of the relationships among binary (base 2), octal (base 8), decimal (base 10; standard integers) and hexadecimal integers. The output shows that array, &array and &array[0] have the same value, namely 0031F930. The output of this program is system dependent, but the addresses are always identical for a particular execution of this program on a particular computer.

Performance Tip 6.3

Passing arrays by reference makes sense for performance reasons. If arrays were passed by value, a copy of each element would be passed. For large, frequently passed arrays, this would be time consuming and would consume storage for the copies of the arrays.

```
1   // Fig. 6.12: fig06_12.c
2   // Array name is the same as the address of the array's first element.
3   #include <stdio.h>
4
5   // function main begins program execution
6   int main(void)
7   {
8       char array[5]; // define an array of size 5
9
10      printf("    array = %p\n&array[0] = %p\n    &array = %p\n",
11          array, &array[0], &array);
12  }
```

```
    array = 0031F930
&array[0] = 0031F930
   &array = 0031F930
```

Fig. 6.12 | Array name is the same as the address of the array's first element.

Software Engineering Observation 6.2

It's possible to pass an array by value (by placing it in a struct as we explain in Chapter 10, C Structures, Unions, Bit Manipulation and Enumerations).

Although entire arrays are passed by reference, individual array elements are passed by *value* exactly as simple variables are. Such simple single pieces of data (such as individual ints, floats and chars) are called **scalars**. To pass an element of an array to a function, use the indexed name of the array element as an argument in the function call. In Chapter 7, we show how to pass scalars (i.e., individual variables and array elements) to functions by reference.

For a function to receive an array through a function call, the function's parameter list must specify that an array will be received. For example, the function header for function modifyArray (that we called earlier in this section) might be written as

```
void modifyArray(int b[], size_t size)
```

indicating that modifyArray expects to receive an array of integers in parameter b and the number of array elements in parameter size. The size of the array is not required between the array brackets. If it's included, the compiler checks that it's greater than zero, then ignores it. Specifying a negative size is a compilation error. Because arrays are automatically passed by reference, when the called function uses the array name b, it will be referring to the array in the caller (array hourlyTemperatures in the preceding call). In Chapter 7, we introduce other notations for indicating that an array is being received by a function. As we'll see, these notations are based on the intimate relationship between arrays and pointers.

Difference Between Passing an Entire Array and Passing an Array Element

Figure 6.13 demonstrates the difference between passing an entire array and passing an individual array element. The program first prints the five elements of integer array a (lines 19–21). Next, a and its size are passed to function modifyArray (line 25), where each of a's elements is multiplied by 2 (lines 48–50). Then a is reprinted in main (lines 29–31). As the output shows, the elements of a are indeed modified by modifyArray. Now the program prints the value of a[3] (line 35) and passes it to function modifyElement (line 37). Function modifyElement multiplies its argument by 2 (line 58) and prints the new value. When a[3] is reprinted in main (line 40), it has *not* been modified, because individual array elements are passed by value.

```
1   // Fig. 6.13: fig06_13.c
2   // Passing arrays and individual array elements to functions.
3   #include <stdio.h>
4   #define SIZE 5
5
6   // function prototypes
7   void modifyArray(int b[], size_t size);
8   void modifyElement(int e);
9
10  // function main begins program execution
11  int main(void)
12  {
13     int a[SIZE] = {0, 1, 2, 3, 4}; // initialize array a
14
15     puts("Effects of passing entire array by reference:\n\nThe "
16        "values of the original array are:");
17
18     // output original array
19     for (size_t i = 0; i < SIZE; ++i) {
20        printf("%3d", a[i]);
21     }
22
23     puts(""); // outputs a newline
24
25     modifyArray(a, SIZE); // pass array a to modifyArray by reference
26     puts("The values of the modified array are:");
27
```

Fig. 6.13 | Passing arrays and individual array elements to functions. (Part 1 of 2.)

```
28      // output modified array
29      for (size_t i = 0; i < SIZE; ++i) {
30         printf("%3d", a[i]);
31      }
32
33      // output value of a[3]
34      printf("\n\n\nEffects of passing array element "
35         "by value:\n\nThe value of a[3] is %d\n", a[3]);
36
37      modifyElement(a[3]); // pass array element a[3] by value
38
39      // output value of a[3]
40      printf("The value of a[3] is %d\n", a[3]);
41   }
42
43   // in function modifyArray, "b" points to the original array "a"
44   // in memory
45   void modifyArray(int b[], size_t size)
46   {
47      // multiply each array element by 2
48      for (size_t j = 0; j < size; ++j) {
49         b[j] *= 2; // actually modifies original array
50      }
51   }
52
53   // in function modifyElement, "e" is a local copy of array element
54   // a[3] passed from main
55   void modifyElement(int e)
56   {
57      // multiply parameter by 2
58      printf("Value in modifyElement is %d\n", e *= 2);
59   }
```

```
Effects of passing entire array by reference:

The values of the original array are:
  0  1  2  3  4
The values of the modified array are:
  0  2  4  6  8


Effects of passing array element by value:

The value of a[3] is 6
Value in modifyElement is 12
The value of a[3] is 6
```

Fig. 6.13 | Passing arrays and individual array elements to functions. (Part 2 of 2.)

There may be situations in your programs in which a function should *not* be allowed to modify array elements. C provides the type qualifier **const** (for "constant") that can be used to prevent modification of array values in a function. When an array parameter is preceded by the const qualifier, the array elements become constant in the function body—

any attempt to modify an element of the array in the function body results in a compile-time error.

Using the const Qualifier with Array Parameters

Figure 6.14 shows the definition of a function named tryToModifyArray that's defined with the parameter const int b[] (line 3). This specifies that array b is *constant* and *cannot* be modified. Each of the function's attempts to modify array elements results in a compiler error. The const qualifier is discussed in additional contexts in Chapter 7.

Software Engineering Observation 6.3

The const type qualifier can be applied to an array parameter in a function definition to prevent the original array from being modified in the function body. This is another example of the principle of least privilege. A function should not be given the capability to modify an array in the caller unless it's absolutely necessary.

```
1   // in function tryToModifyArray, array b is const, so it cannot be
2   // used to modify its array argument in the caller
3   void tryToModifyArray(const int b[])
4   {
5      b[0] /= 2; // error
6      b[1] /= 2; // error
7      b[2] /= 2; // error
8   }
```

Fig. 6.14 | Using the const type qualifier with arrays.

6.8 Sorting Arrays

Sorting data (i.e., placing the data into ascending or descending order) is one of the most important computing applications. A bank sorts all checks by account number so that it can prepare individual bank statements at the end of each month. Telephone companies sort their lists of accounts by last name and, within that, by first name to make it easy to find phone numbers. Virtually every organization must sort some data, and in many cases massive amounts of it. Sorting data is an intriguing problem which has attracted some of the most intense research efforts in the field of computer science. In this chapter we discuss a simple sorting scheme. In Chapter 12 and Appendix D, we investigate more complex schemes that yield better performance.

Performance Tip 6.4

Often, the simplest algorithms perform poorly. Their virtue is that they're easy to write, test and debug. More complex algorithms are often needed to realize maximum performance.

Figure 6.15 sorts the values in the elements of the 10-element array a (line 10) into ascending order. The technique we use is called the **bubble sort** or the **sinking sort** because the smaller values gradually "bubble" their way upward to the top of the array like air bubbles rising in water, while the larger values sink to the bottom of the array. The technique is to make several passes through the array. On each pass, successive pairs of elements (element 0 and element 1, then element 1 and element 2, etc.) are compared. If a pair is in increasing order (or if the values are identical), we leave the values as they are. If a pair is in decreasing order, their values are swapped in the array.

```c
// Fig. 6.15: fig06_15.c
// Sorting an array's values into ascending order.
#include <stdio.h>
#define SIZE 10

// function main begins program execution
int main(void)
{
    // initialize a
    int a[SIZE] = {2, 6, 4, 8, 10, 12, 89, 68, 45, 37};

    puts("Data items in original order");

    // output original array
    for (size_t i = 0; i < SIZE; ++i) {
        printf("%4d", a[i]);
    }

    // bubble sort
    // loop to control number of passes
    for (unsigned int pass = 1; pass < SIZE; ++pass) {

        // loop to control number of comparisons per pass
        for (size_t i = 0; i < SIZE - 1; ++i) {

            // compare adjacent elements and swap them if first
            // element is greater than second element.
            if (a[i] > a[i + 1]) {
                int hold = a[i];
                a[i] = a[i + 1];
                a[i + 1] = hold;
            }
        }
    }

    puts("\nData items in ascending order");

    // output sorted array
    for (size_t i = 0; i < SIZE; ++i) {
        printf("%4d", a[i]);
    }

    puts("");
}
```

```
Data items in original order
   2   6   4   8  10  12  89  68  45  37
Data items in ascending order
   2   4   6   8  10  12  37  45  68  89
```

Fig. 6.15 | Sorting an array's values into ascending order.

First the program compares a[0] to a[1], then a[1] to a[2], then a[2] to a[3], and so on until it completes the pass by comparing a[8] to a[9]. Although there are 10 elements, only nine comparisons are performed. Because of the way the successive comparisons are made, a large value may move down the array many positions on a single pass, but a small value may move up only one position.

On the first pass, the largest value is guaranteed to sink to the bottom element of the array, a[9]. On the second pass, the second-largest value is guaranteed to sink to a[8]. On the ninth pass, the ninth-largest value sinks to a[1]. This leaves the smallest value in a[0], so only *nine* passes of the array are needed to sort the array, even though there are *ten* elements.

The sorting is performed by the nested for loops (lines 21–34). If a swap is necessary, it's performed by the three assignments

```
hold = a[i];
a[i] = a[i + 1];
a[i + 1] = hold;
```

where the extra variable hold *temporarily* stores one of the two values being swapped. The swap cannot be performed with only the two assignments

```
a[i] = a[i + 1];
a[i + 1] = a[i];
```

If, for example, a[i] is 7 and a[i + 1] is 5, after the first assignment both values will be 5 and the value 7 will be lost—hence the need for the extra variable hold.

The chief virtue of the bubble sort is that it's easy to program. However, it runs slowly because every exchange moves an element only one position closer to its final destination. This becomes apparent when sorting large arrays. In the exercises, we'll develop more efficient versions of the bubble sort. Far more efficient sorts than the bubble sort have been developed. We'll investigate other algorithms in Appendix D. More advanced courses investigate sorting and searching in greater depth.

6.9 Case Study: Computing Mean, Median and Mode Using Arrays

We now consider a larger example. Computers are commonly used for **survey data analysis** to compile and analyze the results of surveys and opinion polls. Figure 6.16 uses array response initialized with 99 responses to a survey. Each response is a number from 1 to 9. The program computes the mean, median and mode of the 99 values. Figure 6.17 contains a sample run of this program. This example includes most of the common manipulations usually required in array problems, including passing arrays to functions.

```
1  // Fig. 6.16: fig06_16.c
2  // Survey data analysis with arrays:
3  // computing the mean, median and mode of the data.
4  #include <stdio.h>
5  #define SIZE 99
```

Fig. 6.16 | Survey data analysis with arrays: computing the mean, median and mode of the data. (Part 1 of 4.)

```
6
7    // function prototypes
8    void mean(const unsigned int answer[]);
9    void median(unsigned int answer[]);
10   void mode(unsigned int freq[], unsigned const int answer[]) ;
11   void bubbleSort(int a[]);
12   void printArray(unsigned const int a[]);
13
14   // function main begins program execution
15   int main(void)
16   {
17      unsigned int frequency[10] = {0}; // initialize array frequency
18
19      // initialize array response
20      unsigned int response[SIZE] =
21         {6, 7, 8, 9, 8, 7, 8, 9, 8, 9,
22          7, 8, 9, 5, 9, 8, 7, 8, 7, 8,
23          6, 7, 8, 9, 3, 9, 8, 7, 8, 7,
24          7, 8, 9, 8, 9, 8, 9, 7, 8, 9,
25          6, 7, 8, 7, 8, 7, 9, 8, 9, 2,
26          7, 8, 9, 8, 9, 8, 9, 7, 5, 3,
27          5, 6, 7, 2, 5, 3, 9, 4, 6, 4,
28          7, 8, 9, 6, 8, 7, 8, 9, 7, 8,
29          7, 4, 4, 2, 5, 3, 8, 7, 5, 6,
30          4, 5, 6, 1, 6, 5, 7, 8, 7};
31
32      // process responses
33      mean(response);
34      median(response);
35      mode(frequency, response);
36   }
37
38   // calculate average of all response values
39   void mean(const unsigned int answer[])
40   {
41      printf("%s\n%s\n%s\n", "********", "  Mean", "********");
42
43      unsigned int total = 0; // variable to hold sum of array elements
44
45      // total response values
46      for (size_t j = 0; j < SIZE; ++j) {
47         total += answer[j];
48      }
49
50      printf("The mean is the average value of the data\n"
51             "items. The mean is equal to the total of\n"
52             "all the data items divided by the number\n"
53             "of data items (%u). The mean value for\n"
54             "this run is: %u / %u = %.4f\n\n",
55             SIZE, total, SIZE, (double) total / SIZE);
56   }
```

Fig. 6.16 | Survey data analysis with arrays: computing the mean, median and mode of the data. (Part 2 of 4.)

```
57
58   // sort array and determine median element's value
59   void median(unsigned int answer[])
60   {
61      printf("\n%s\n%s\n%s\n%s",
62              "********", " Median", "********",
63              "The unsorted array of responses is");
64
65      printArray(answer); // output unsorted array
66
67      bubbleSort(answer); // sort array
68
69      printf("%s", "\n\nThe sorted array is");
70      printArray(answer); // output sorted array
71
72      // display median element
73      printf("\n\nThe median is element %u of\n"
74              "the sorted %u element array.\n"
75              "For this run the median is %u\n\n",
76              SIZE / 2, SIZE, answer[SIZE / 2]);
77   }
78
79   // determine most frequent response
80   void mode(unsigned int freq[], const unsigned int answer[])
81   {
82      printf("\n%s\n%s\n%s\n","********", "  Mode", "********");
83
84      // initialize frequencies to 0
85      for (size_t rating = 1; rating <= 9; ++rating) {
86         freq[rating] = 0;
87      }
88
89      // summarize frequencies
90      for (size_t j = 0; j < SIZE; ++j) {
91         ++freq[answer[j]];
92      }
93
94      // output headers for result columns
95      printf("%s%11s%19s\n\n%54s\n%54s\n\n",
96              "Response", "Frequency", "Histogram",
97              "1    1    2    2", "5    0    5    0    5");
98
99      // output results
100     unsigned int largest = 0; // represents largest frequency
101     unsigned int modeValue = 0; // represents most frequent response
102
103     for (rating = 1; rating <= 9; ++rating) {
104        printf("%8u%11u          ", rating, freq[rating]);
105
```

Fig. 6.16 | Survey data analysis with arrays: computing the mean, median and mode of the data. (Part 3 of 4.)

```
106            // keep track of mode value and largest frequency value
107            if (freq[rating] > largest) {
108                largest = freq[rating];
109                modeValue = rating;
110            }
111
112            // output histogram bar representing frequency value
113            for (unsigned int h = 1; h <= freq[rating]; ++h) {
114                printf("%s", "*");
115            }
116
117            puts(""); // being new line of output
118        }
119
120        // display the mode value
121        printf("\nThe mode is the most frequent value.\n"
122               "For this run the mode is %u which occurred"
123               " %u times.\n", modeValue, largest);
124    }
125
126    // function that sorts an array with bubble sort algorithm
127    void bubbleSort(unsigned int a[])
128    {
129        // loop to control number of passes
130        for (unsigned int pass = 1; pass < SIZE; ++pass) {
131
132            // loop to control number of comparisons per pass
133            for (size_t j = 0; j < SIZE - 1; ++j) {
134
135                // swap elements if out of order
136                if (a[j] > a[j + 1]) {
137                    unsigned int hold = a[j];
138                    a[j] = a[j + 1];
139                    a[j + 1] = hold;
140                }
141            }
142        }
143    }
144
145    // output array contents (20 values per row)
146    void printArray(const unsigned int a[])
147    {
148        // output array contents
149        for (size_t j = 0; j < SIZE; ++j) {
150
151            if (j % 20 == 0) { // begin new line every 20 values
152                puts("");
153            }
154
155            printf("%2u", a[j]);
156        }
157    }
```

Fig. 6.16 | Survey data analysis with arrays: computing the mean, median and mode of the data. (Part 4 of 4.)

```
********
  Mean
********
The mean is the average value of the data
items. The mean is equal to the total of
all the data items divided by the number
of data items (99). The mean value for
this run is: 681 / 99 = 6.8788


********
  Median
********
The unsorted array of responses is
6 7 8 9 8 7 8 9 8 9 7 8 9 5 9 8 7 8 7 8
6 7 8 9 3 9 8 7 8 7 7 8 9 8 9 8 9 7 8 9
6 7 8 7 8 7 9 8 9 2 7 8 9 8 9 8 9 7 5 3
5 6 7 2 5 3 9 4 6 4 7 8 9 6 8 7 8 9 7 8
7 4 4 2 5 3 8 7 5 6 4 5 6 1 6 5 7 8 7

The sorted array is
1 2 2 2 3 3 3 3 4 4 4 4 5 5 5 5 5 5 5 5
5 6 6 6 6 6 6 6 6 6 7 7 7 7 7 7 7 7 7 7
7 7 7 7 7 7 7 7 7 7 7 7 7 8 8 8 8 8 8 8
8 8 8 8 8 8 8 8 8 8 8 8 8 8 8 8 8 8 8 8
9 9 9 9 9 9 9 9 9 9 9 9 9 9 9 9 9 9 9

The median is element 49 of
the sorted 99 element array.
For this run the median is 7


********
  Mode
********
Response  Frequency        Histogram

                           1     1     2     2
                     5     0     5     0     5

    1          1     *
    2          3     ***
    3          4     ****
    4          5     *****
    5          8     ********
    6          9     *********
    7         23     ***********************
    8         27     ***************************
    9         19     *******************

The mode is the most frequent value.
For this run the mode is 8 which occurred 27 times.
```

Fig. 6.17 | Sample run for the survey data analysis program.

Mean

The *mean* is the *arithmetic average* of the 99 values. Function mean (Fig. 6.16, lines 39–56) computes the mean by totaling the 99 elements and dividing the result by 99.

Median

The median is the *middle* value. Function median (lines 59–77) determines the median by calling function bubbleSort (defined in lines 127–143) to sort the array of responses into ascending order, then picking answer[SIZE / 2] (the middle element) of the sorted array. When the number of elements is even, the median should be calculated as the mean of the two middle elements. Function median does not currently provide this capability. Function printArray (lines 146–157) is called to output the response array.

Mode

The *mode* is the *value that occurs most frequently* among the 99 responses. Function mode (lines 80–124) determines the mode by counting the number of responses of each type, then selecting the value with the greatest count. This version of function mode does not handle a tie (see Exercise 6.14). Function mode also produces a histogram to aid in determining the mode graphically.

6.10 Searching Arrays

You'll often work with large amounts of data stored in arrays. It may be necessary to determine whether an array contains a value that matches a certain **key value**. The process of finding a particular element of an array is called **searching**. In this section we discuss two searching techniques—the simple **linear search** technique and the more efficient (but more complex) **binary search** technique. Exercises 6.32 and 6.33 ask you to implement *recursive* versions of the linear search and the binary search, respectively.

6.10.1 Searching an Array with Linear Search

The linear search (Fig. 6.18) compares each element of the array with the **search key**. Because the array is not in any particular order, it's just as likely that the value will be found in the first element as in the last. On average, therefore, the program will have to compare the search key with *half* the elements of the array.

```
1   // Fig. 6.18: fig06_18.c
2   // Linear search of an array.
3   #include <stdio.h>
4   #define SIZE 100
5
6   // function prototype
7   size_t linearSearch(const int array[], int key, size_t size);
8
9   // function main begins program execution
10  int main(void)
11  {
12     int a[SIZE]; // create array a
13
```

Fig. 6.18 | Linear search of an array. (Part 1 of 2.)

```
14      // create some data
15      for (size_t x = 0; x < SIZE; ++x) {
16         a[x] = 2 * x;
17      }
18
19      printf("Enter integer search key: ");
20      int searchKey; // value to locate in array a
21      scanf("%d", &searchKey);
22
23      // attempt to locate searchKey in array a
24      size_t index = linearSearch(a, searchKey, SIZE);
25
26      // display results
27      if (index != -1) {
28         printf("Found value at index %d\n", index);
29      }
30      else {
31         puts("Value not found");
32      }
33   }
34
35   // compare key to every element of array until the location is found
36   // or until the end of array is reached; return index of element
37   // if key is found or -1 if key is not found
38   size_t linearSearch(const int array[], int key, size_t size)
39   {
40      // loop through array
41      for (size_t n = 0; n < size; ++n) {
42
43         if (array[n] == key) {
44            return n; // return location of key
45         }
46      }
47
48      return -1; // key not found
49   }
```

```
Enter integer search key: 36
Found value at index 18
```

```
Enter integer search key: 37
Value not found
```

Fig. 6.18 | Linear search of an array. (Part 2 of 2.)

6.10.2 Searching an Array with Binary Search

The linear searching method works well for *small* or *unsorted* arrays. However, for *large* arrays linear searching is *inefficient*. If the array is sorted, the high-speed binary search technique can be used.

The binary search algorithm eliminates from consideration *one-half* of the elements in a sorted array after each comparison. The algorithm locates the *middle* element of the array and compares it to the search key. If they're equal, the search key is found and the array index of that element is returned. If they're not equal, the problem is reduced to searching *one-half* of the array. If the search key is less than the middle element of the array, the algorithm searches the *first half* of the array, otherwise the algorithm searches the *second half*. If the search key is not the middle element in the specified subarray (piece of the original array), the algorithm repeats on one-quarter of the original array. The search continues until the search key is equal to the middle element of a subarray, or until the subarray consists of one element that's not equal to the search key (i.e., the search key is not found).

In a worst case-scenario, searching a sorted array of 1023 elements takes *only* 10 comparisons using a binary search. Repeatedly dividing 1,024 by 2 yields the values 512, 256, 128, 64, 32, 16, 8, 4, 2 and 1. The number 1,024 (2^{10}) is divided by 2 only 10 times to get the value 1. Dividing by 2 is equivalent to one comparison in the binary search algorithm. An array of 1,048,576 (2^{20}) elements takes a maximum of *only* 20 comparisons to find the search key. A sorted array of one billion elements takes a maximum of *only* 30 comparisons to find the search key. This is a tremendous increase in performance over a linear search of a sorted array, which requires comparing the search key to an average of half of the array elements. For a one-billion-element array, this is a difference between an average of 500 million comparisons and a maximum of 30 comparisons! The maximum comparisons for any array can be determined by finding the first power of 2 greater than the number of array elements.

Figure 6.19 presents the *iterative* version of function binarySearch (lines 40–68). The function receives four arguments—an integer array b to be searched, an integer searchKey, the low array index and the high array index (these define the portion of the array to be searched). If the search key does *not* match the middle element of a subarray, the low index or high index is modified so that a smaller subarray can be searched. If the search key is *less than* the middle element, the high index is set to middle - 1 and the search is continued on the elements from low to middle - 1. If the search key is *greater than* the middle element, the low index is set to middle + 1 and the search is continued on the elements from middle + 1 to high. The program uses an array of 15 elements. The first power of 2 greater than the number of elements in this array is 16 (2^4), so no more than 4 comparisons are required to find the search key. The program uses function printHeader (lines 71–88) to output the array indices and function printRow (lines 92–110) to output each subarray during the binary search process. The middle element in each subarray is marked with an asterisk (*) to indicate the element to which the search key is compared.

```
1   // Fig. 6.19: fig06_19.c
2   // Binary search of a sorted array.
3   #include <stdio.h>
4   #define SIZE 15
5
6   // function prototypes
7   size_t binarySearch(const int b[], int searchKey, size_t low, size_t high);
```

Fig. 6.19 | Binary search of a sorted array. (Part 1 of 4.)

```
 8   void printHeader(void);
 9   void printRow(const int b[], size_t low, size_t mid, size_t high);
10
11   // function main begins program execution
12   int main(void)
13   {
14      int a[SIZE]; // create array a
15
16      // create data
17      for (size_t i = 0; i < SIZE; ++i) {
18         a[i] = 2 * i;
19      }
20
21      printf("%s", "Enter a number between 0 and 28: ");
22      int key; // value to locate in array a
23      scanf("%d", &key);
24
25      printHeader();
26
27      // search for key in array a
28      size_t result = binarySearch(a, key, 0, SIZE - 1);
29
30      // display results
31      if (result != -1) {
32         printf("\n%d found at index %d\n", key, result);
33      }
34      else {
35         printf("\n%d not found\n", key);
36      }
37   }
38
39   // function to perform binary search of an array
40   size_t binarySearch(const int b[], int searchKey, size_t low, size_t high)
41   {
42      // loop until low index is greater than high index
43      while (low <= high) {
44
45         // determine middle element of subarray being searched
46         size_t middle = (low + high) / 2;
47
48         // display subarray used in this loop iteration
49         printRow(b, low, middle, high);
50
51         // if searchKey matched middle element, return middle
52         if (searchKey == b[middle]) {
53            return middle;
54         }
55
56         // if searchKey is less than middle element, set new high
57         else if (searchKey < b[middle]) {
58            high = middle - 1; // search low end of array
59         } // if
```

Fig. 6.19 | Binary search of a sorted array. (Part 2 of 4.)

```c
60
61          // if searchKey is greater than middle element, set new low
62          else {
63             low = middle + 1; // search high end of array
64          }
65       } // end while
66
67       return -1; // searchKey not found
68    }
69
70    // Print a header for the output
71    void printHeader(void)
72    {
73       puts("\nIndices:");
74
75       // output column head
76       for (unsigned int i = 0; i < SIZE; ++i) {
77          printf("%3u ", i);
78       }
79
80       puts(""); // start new line of output
81
82       // output line of - characters
83       for (unsigned int i = 1; i <= 4 * SIZE; ++i) {
84          printf("%s", "-");
85       }
86
87       puts(""); // start new line of output
88    }
89
90    // Print one row of output showing the current
91    // part of the array being processed.
92    void printRow(const int b[], size_t low, size_t mid, size_t high)
93    {
94       // loop through entire array
95       for (size_t i = 0; i < SIZE; ++i) {
96
97          // display spaces if outside current subarray range
98          if (i < low || i > high) {
99             printf("%s", "    ");
100         }
101         else if (i == mid) { // display middle element
102            printf("%3d*", b[i]); // mark middle value
103         }
104         else { // display other elements in subarray
105            printf("%3d ", b[i]);
106         }
107      }
108
109      puts(""); // start new line of output
110   }
```

Fig. 6.19 | Binary search of a sorted array. (Part 3 of 4.)

```
Enter a number between 0 and 28: 25

Indices:
 0   1   2   3   4   5   6    7    8    9   10   11   12   13   14
------------------------------------------------------------------
 0   2   4   6   8  10  12  14*  16   18   20   22   24   26   28
                                16   18   20  22*  24   26   28
                                               24  26*  28
                                              24*

25 not found
```

```
Enter a number between 0 and 28: 8

Indices:
 0   1   2   3   4   5   6    7    8    9   10   11   12   13   14
------------------------------------------------------------------
 0   2   4   6   8  10  12  14*  16   18   20   22   24   26   28
 0   2   4  6*   8  10  12
             8  10*  12
             8*

8 found at index 4
```

```
Enter a number between 0 and 28: 6

Indices:
 0   1   2   3   4   5   6    7    8    9   10   11   12   13   14
------------------------------------------------------------------
 0   2   4   6   8  10  12  14*  16   18   20   22   24   26   28
 0   2   4  6*   8  10  12

6 found at index 3
```

Fig. 6.19 | Binary search of a sorted array. (Part 4 of 4.)

6.11 Multidimensional Arrays

Arrays in C can have multiple indices. A common use of multidimensional arrays, which the C standard refers to as **multidimensional arrays**, is to represent tables of values consisting of information arranged in *rows* and *columns*. To identify a particular table element, we must specify two indices: The *first* (by convention) identifies the element's *row* and the *second* (by convention) identifies the element's *column*. Tables or arrays that require two indices to identify a particular element are called **two-dimensional arrays**. Multidimensional arrays can have more than two indices.

6.11.1 Illustrating a Double-Subscripted Array

Figure 6.20 illustrates a two-dimensional array, a. The array contains three rows and four columns, so it's said to be a 3-by-4 array. In general, an array with *m* rows and *n* columns is called an *m*-by-*n* **array**.

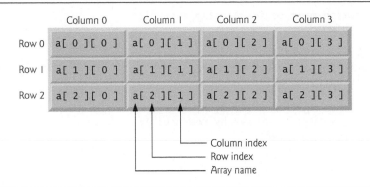

Fig. 6.20 | Two-dimensional array with three rows and four columns.

Every element in array a is identified in Fig. 6.20 by an element name of the form a[i][j]; a is the name of the array, and i and j are the indices that uniquely identify each element in a. The names of the elements in row 0 all have a first index of 0; the names of the elements in column 3 all have a second index of 3.

Common Programming Error 6.7

Referencing a two-dimensional array element as a[x, y] instead of a[x][y] is a logic error. C interprets a[x, y] as a[y] (because the comma in this context is treated as a comma operator), so this programmer error is not a syntax error.

6.11.2 Initializing a Double-Subscripted Array

A multidimensional array can be initialized when it's defined. For example, a two-dimensional array int b[2][2] could be defined and initialized with

```
int b[2][2] = {{1, 2}, {3, 4}};
```

The values are grouped by row in braces. The values in the first set of braces initialize row 0 and the values in the second set of braces initialize row 1. So, the values 1 and 2 initialize elements b[0][0] and b[0][1], respectively, and the values 3 and 4 initialize elements b[1][0] and b[1][1], respectively. *If there are not enough initializers for a given row, the remaining elements of that row are initialized to 0.* Thus,

```
int b[2][2] = {{1}, {3, 4}};
```

would initialize b[0][0] to 1, b[0][1] to 0, b[1][0] to 3 and b[1][1] to 4. Figure 6.21 demonstrates defining and initializing two-dimensional arrays.

```
1   // Fig. 6.21: fig06_21.c
2   // Initializing multidimensional arrays.
3   #include <stdio.h>
4
5   void printArray(int a[][3]); // function prototype
6
```

Fig. 6.21 | Initializing multidimensional arrays. (Part 1 of 2.)

```
7    // function main begins program execution
8    int main(void)
9    {
10       int array1[2][3] = {{1, 2, 3}, {4, 5, 6}};
11       puts("Values in array1 by row are:");
12       printArray(array1);
13
14       int array2[2][3] = {1, 2, 3, 4, 5};
15       puts("Values in array2 by row are:");
16       printArray(array2);
17
18       int array3[2][3] = {{1, 2}, {4}};
19       puts("Values in array3 by row are:");
20       printArray(array3);
21    }
22
23    // function to output array with two rows and three columns
24    void printArray(int a[][3])
25    {
26       // loop through rows
27       for (size_t i = 0; i <= 1; ++i) {
28
29          // output column values
30          for (size_t j = 0; j <= 2; ++j) {
31             printf("%d ", a[i][j]);
32          }
33
34          printf("\n"); // start new line of output
35       }
36    }
```

```
Values in array1 by row are:
1 2 3
4 5 6
Values in array2 by row are:
1 2 3
4 5 0
Values in array3 by row are:
1 2 0
4 0 0
```

Fig. 6.21 | Initializing multidimensional arrays. (Part 2 of 2.)

array1 *Definition*

The program defines three arrays of two rows and three columns (six elements each). The definition of array1 (line 10) provides six initializers in two sublists. The first sublist initializes *row 0* of the array to the values 1, 2 and 3; and the second sublist initializes *row 1* of the array to the values 4, 5 and 6.

array2 *Definition*

If the braces around each sublist are removed from the array1 initializer list, the compiler initializes the elements of the first row followed by the elements of the second row. The definition of array2 (line 14) provides five initializers. The initializers are assigned to the first row, then the second row. Any elements that do *not* have an explicit initializer are initialized to zero automatically, so array2[1][2] is initialized to 0.

array3 *Definition*
The definition of array3 (line 18) provides three initializers in two sublists. The sublist for the first row *explicitly* initializes the first two elements of the first row to 1 and 2. The third element is initialized to *zero*. The sublist for the second row explicitly initializes the first element to 4. The last two elements are initialized to *zero*.

printArray *Function*
The program calls printArray (lines 24–36) to output each array's elements. The function definition specifies the array parameter as int a[][3]. In a one-dimensional array parameter, the array brackets are *empty*. The first index of a multidimensional array is not required, but all subsequent indices are required. The compiler uses these indices to determine the locations in memory of elements in multidimensional arrays. All array elements are stored consecutively in memory regardless of the number of indices. In a two-dimensional array, the first row is stored in memory followed by the second row.

Providing the index values in a parameter declaration enables the compiler to tell the function how to locate an element in the array. In a two-dimensional array, each row is basically a one-dimensional array. To locate an element in a particular row, the compiler must know *how many elements are in each row* so that it can skip the proper number of memory locations when accessing the array. Thus, when accessing a[1][2] in our example, the compiler knows to skip the three elements of the first row to get to the second row (row 1). Then, the compiler accesses element 2 of that row.

6.11.3 Setting the Elements in One Row
Many common array manipulations use for iteration statements. For example, the following statement sets all the elements in row 2 of array a in Fig. 6.20 to zero:

```
for (column = 0; column <= 3; ++column) {
   a[2][column] = 0;
}
```

We specified row 2, so the first index is always 2. The loop varies only the second (column) index. The preceding for statement is equivalent to the assignment statements:

```
a[2][0] = 0;
a[2][1] = 0;
a[2][2] = 0;
a[2][3] = 0;
```

6.11.4 Totaling the Elements in a Two-Dimensional Array
The following nested for statement determines the total of all the elements in array a.

```
total = 0;

for (row = 0; row <= 2; ++row) {
   for (column = 0; column <= 3; ++column) {
      total += a[row][column];
   }
}
```

The `for` statement totals the elements of the array one row at a time. The outer `for` statement begins by setting row (i.e., the row index) to 0 so that the elements of that row may be totaled by the inner `for` statement. The outer `for` statement then increments row to 1, so the elements of that row can be totaled. Then, the outer `for` statement increments row to 2, so the elements of the third row can be totaled. When the nested `for` statement terminates, `total` contains the sum of all the elements in the array a.

6.11.5 Two-Dimensonal Array Manipulations

Figure 6.22 performs several other common array manipulations on a 3-by-4 array studentGrades using `for` statements. Each row of the array represents a student and each column represents a grade on one of the four exams the students took during the semester. The array manipulations are performed by four functions. Function `minimum` (lines 39–56) determines the lowest grade of any student for the semester. Function `maximum` (lines 59–76) determines the highest grade of any student for the semester. Function `average` (lines 79–89) determines a particular student's semester average. Function `printArray` (lines 92–108) outputs the two-dimensional array in a neat, tabular format.

```
1   // Fig. 6.22: fig06_22.c
2   // Two-dimensional array manipulations.
3   #include <stdio.h>
4   #define STUDENTS 3
5   #define EXAMS 4
6
7   // function prototypes
8   int minimum(const int grades[][EXAMS], size_t pupils, size_t tests);
9   int maximum(const int grades[][EXAMS], size_t pupils, size_t tests);
10  double average(const int setOfGrades[], size_t tests);
11  void printArray(const int grades[][EXAMS], size_t pupils, size_t tests);
12
13  // function main begins program execution
14  int main(void)
15  {
16     // initialize student grades for three students (rows)
17     int studentGrades[STUDENTS][EXAMS] =
18        { { 77, 68, 86, 73 },
19          { 96, 87, 89, 78 },
20          { 70, 90, 86, 81 } };
21
22     // output array studentGrades
23     puts("The array is:");
24     printArray(studentGrades, STUDENTS, EXAMS);
25
26     // determine smallest and largest grade values
27     printf("\n\nLowest grade: %d\nHighest grade: %d\n",
28        minimum(studentGrades, STUDENTS, EXAMS),
29        maximum(studentGrades, STUDENTS, EXAMS));
```

Fig. 6.22 | Two-dimensional array manipulations. (Part 1 of 3.)

```
30
31       // calculate average grade for each student
32       for (size_t student = 0; student < STUDENTS; ++student) {
33          printf("The average grade for student %u is %.2f\n",
34             student, average(studentGrades[student], EXAMS));
35       }
36    }
37
38    // Find the minimum grade
39    int minimum(const int grades[][EXAMS], size_t pupils, size_t tests)
40    {
41       int lowGrade = 100; // initialize to highest possible grade
42
43       // loop through rows of grades
44       for (size_t i = 0; i < pupils; ++i) {
45
46          // loop through columns of grades
47          for (size_t j = 0; j < tests; ++j) {
48
49             if (grades[i][j] < lowGrade) {
50                lowGrade = grades[i][j];
51             }
52          }
53       }
54
55       return lowGrade; // return minimum grade
56    }
57
58    // Find the maximum grade
59    int maximum(const int grades[][EXAMS], size_t pupils, size_t tests)
60    {
61       int highGrade = 0; // initialize to lowest possible grade
62
63       // loop through rows of grades
64       for (size_t i = 0; i < pupils; ++i) {
65
66          // loop through columns of grades
67          for (size_t j = 0; j < tests; ++j) {
68
69             if (grades[i][j] > highGrade) {
70                highGrade = grades[i][j];
71             }
72          }
73       }
74
75       return highGrade; // return maximum grade
76    }
77
```

Fig. 6.22 | Two-dimensional array manipulations. (Part 2 of 3.)

```
78   // Determine the average grade for a particular student
79   double average(const int setOfGrades[], size_t tests)
80   {
81      int total = 0; // sum of test grades
82
83      // total all grades for one student
84      for (size_t i = 0; i < tests; ++i) {
85         total += setOfGrades[i];
86      }
87
88      return (double) total / tests; // average
89   }
90
91   // Print the array
92   void printArray(const int grades[][EXAMS], size_t pupils, size_t tests)
93   {
94      // output column heads
95      printf("%s", "                       [0]  [1]  [2]  [3]");
96
97      // output grades in tabular format
98      for (size_t i = 0; i < pupils; ++i) {
99
100        // output label for row
101        printf("\nstudentGrades[%u] ", i);
102
103        // output grades for one student
104        for (size_t j = 0; j < tests; ++j) {
105           printf("%-5d", grades[i][j]);
106        }
107     }
108  }
```

```
The array is:
                  [0]  [1]  [2]  [3]
studentGrades[0]  77   68   86   73
studentGrades[1]  96   87   89   78
studentGrades[2]  70   90   86   81

Lowest grade: 68
Highest grade: 96
The average grade for student 0 is 76.00
The average grade for student 1 is 87.50
The average grade for student 2 is 81.75
```

Fig. 6.22 | Two-dimensional array manipulations. (Part 3 of 3.)

Functions minimum, maximum and printArray each receive three arguments—the studentGrades array (called grades in each function), the number of students (rows of the array) and the number of exams (columns of the array). Each function loops through array grades using nested for statements. The following nested for statement is from the function minimum definition:

```
      // loop through rows of grades
      for (i = 0; i < pupils; ++i) {
         // loop through columns of grades
         for (j = 0; j < tests; ++j) {
            if (grades[i][j] < lowGrade) {
               lowGrade = grades[i][j];
            }
         }
      }
```

The outer for statement begins by setting i (i.e., the row index) to 0 so the elements of that row (i.e., the grades of the first student) can be compared to variable lowGrade in the body of the inner for statement. The inner for statement loops through the four grades of a particular row and compares each grade to lowGrade. If a grade is less than lowGrade, lowGrade is set to that grade. The outer for statement then increments the row index to 1. The elements of that row are compared to variable lowGrade. The outer for statement then increments the row index to 2. The elements of that row are compared to variable lowGrade. When execution of the nested statement is complete, lowGrade contains the smallest grade in the two-dimensional array. Function maximum works similarly to function minimum.

Function average (lines 79–89) takes two arguments—a two-dimensional array of test results for a particular student called setOfGrades and the number of test results in the array. When average is called, the first argument studentGrades[student] is passed. This causes the address of one row of the two-dimensional array to be passed to average. The argument studentGrades[1] is the starting address of row 1 of the array. Remember that a two-dimensional array is basically an array of one-dimensional arrays and that the name of a one-dimensional array is the address of the array in memory. Function average calculates the sum of the array elements, divides the total by the number of test results and returns the floating-point result.

6.12 Variable-Length Arrays[2]

For each array you've defined so far, you've specified its size at compilation time. But what if you cannot determine an array's size until *execution time*? In the past, to handle this, you had to use dynamic memory allocation (introduced in Chapter 12, C Data Structures). For cases in which an array's size is not known at compilation time, C has **variable-length arrays** (VLAs)—that is, arrays whose lengths are defined in terms of expressions evaluated at *execution time*. The program of Fig. 6.23 declares and prints several VLAs.

```
1   // Fig. 6.23: fig06_23.c
2   // Using variable-length arrays in C99
3   #include <stdio.h>
4
5   // function prototypes
6   void print1DArray(size_t size, int array[size]);
```

Fig. 6.23 | Using variable-length arrays in C99. (Part I of 3.)

---

2. This feature is not supported in Microsoft Visual C++.

```
7   void print2DArray(int row, int col, int array[row][col]);
8
9   int main(void)
10  {
11     printf("%s", "Enter size of a one-dimensional array: ");
12     int arraySize; // size of 1-D array
13     scanf("%d", &arraySize);
14
15     int array[arraySize]; // declare 1-D variable-length array
16
17     printf("%s", "Enter number of rows and columns in a 2-D array: ");
18     int row1, col1; // number of rows and columns in a 2-D array
19     scanf("%d %d", &row1, &col1);
20
21     int array2D1[row1][col1]; // declare 2-D variable-length array
22
23     printf("%s",
24        "Enter number of rows and columns in another 2-D array: ");
25     int row2, col2; // number of rows and columns in another 2-D array
26     scanf("%d %d", &row2, &col2);
27
28     int array2D2[row2][col2]; // declare 2-D variable-length array
29
30     // test sizeof operator on VLA
31     printf("\nsizeof(array) yields array size of %d bytes\n",
32        sizeof(array));
33
34     // assign elements of 1-D VLA
35     for (size_t i = 0; i < arraySize; ++i) {
36        array[i] = i * i;
37     }
38
39     // assign elements of first 2-D VLA
40     for (size_t i = 0; i < row1; ++i) {
41        for (size_t j = 0; j < col1; ++j) {
42           array2D1[i][j] = i + j;
43        }
44     }
45
46     // assign elements of second 2-D VLA
47     for (size_t i = 0; i < row2; ++i) {
48        for (size_t j = 0; j < col2; ++j) {
49           array2D2[i][j] = i + j;
50        }
51     }
52
53     puts("\nOne-dimensional array:");
54     print1DArray(arraySize, array); // pass 1-D VLA to function
55
56     puts("\nFirst two-dimensional array:");
57     print2DArray(row1, col1, array2D1); // pass 2-D VLA to function
58
```

Fig. 6.23 | Using variable-length arrays in C99. (Part 2 of 3.)

```
59      puts("\nSecond two-dimensional array:");
60      print2DArray(row2, col2, array2D2); // pass other 2-D VLA to function
61   }
62
63   void print1DArray(size_t size, int array[size])
64   {
65      // output contents of array
66      for (size_t i = 0; i < size; i++) {
67         printf("array[%d] = %d\n", i, array[i]);
68      }
69   }
70
71   void print2DArray(size_t row, size_t col, int array[row][col])
72   {
73      // output contents of array
74      for (size_t i = 0; i < row; ++i) {
75         for (size_t j = 0; j < col; ++j) {
76            printf("%5d", array[i][j]);
77         }
78
79         puts("");
80      }
81   }
```

```
Enter size of a one-dimensional array: 6
Enter number of rows and columns in a 2-D array: 2 5
Enter number of rows and columns in another 2-D array: 4 3

sizeof(array) yields array size of 24 bytes

One-dimensional array:
array[0] = 0
array[1] = 1
array[2] = 4
array[3] = 9
array[4] = 16
array[5] = 25

First two-dimensional array:
    0    1    2    3    4
    1    2    3    4    5

Second two-dimensional array:
    0    1    2
    1    2    3
    2    3    4
    3    4    5
```

Fig. 6.23 | Using variable-length arrays in C99. (Part 3 of 3.)

Creating the VLAs

Lines 11–28 prompt the user for the desired sizes for a one-dimensional array and two two-dimensional arrays and use the input values in lines 15, 21 and 28 to create VLAs. Lines 15, 21 and 28 are valid as long as the variables representing the array sizes are of an integral type.

sizeof *Operator with VLAs*

After creating the arrays, we use the sizeof operator in lines 31–32 to ensure that our one-dimensional VLA is of the proper length. In early versions of C sizeof was always a compile-time operation, but when applied to a VLA, sizeof operates at runtime. The output window shows that the sizeof operator returns a size of 24 bytes—four times that of the number we entered because the size of an int on our machine is 4 bytes.

Assigning Values to VLA Elements

Next we assign values to the elements of our VLAs (lines 35–51). We use the loop-continuation condition i < arraySize when filling the one-dimensional array. As with fixed-length arrays, *there is no protection against stepping outside the array bounds.*

Function print1DArray

Lines 63–69 define function print1DArray that takes a *one-dimensional VLA* and displays it. The syntax for passing VLAs as parameters to functions is the same as with regular arrays. We use the variable size in the declaration of the array parameter, but it's purely documentation for the programmer.

Function print2DArray

Function print2DArray (lines 71–81) takes a *two-dimensional VLA* and displays it. Recall from Section 6.11.2 that you must specify a size for all but the first index in a multidimensional array parameter. The same restriction holds true for VLAs, except that the sizes can be specified by variables. The initial value of col passed to the function is used to determine where each row begins in memory, just as with a fixed-size array. Changing the value of col inside the function will not cause any changes to the indexing, but passing an incorrect value to the function will.

6.13 Secure C Programming

Bounds Checking for Array Indices

It's important to ensure that every index you use to access an array element is within the array's bounds. A one-dimensional array's indices must be greater than or equal to 0 and less than the number of array elements. A two-dimensional array's row and column indices must be greater than or equal to 0 and less than the numbers of rows and columns, respectively. This extends to arrays with additional dimensions as well.

Allowing programs to read from or write to array elements outside the bounds of arrays are common security flaws. Reading from out-of-bounds array elements can cause a program to crash or even appear to execute correctly while using bad data. Writing to an out-of-bounds element (known as a *buffer overflow*) can corrupt a program's data in memory, crash a program and allow attackers to exploit the system and execute their own code.

As we stated in the chapter, *C provides no automatic bounds checking for arrays*, so you must provide your own. For techniques that help you prevent such problems, see CERT guideline ARR30-C at www.securecoding.cert.org.

scanf_s

Bounds checking is also important in string processing. When reading a string into a char array, scanf does *not* prevent buffer overflows. If the number of characters input is greater than or equal to the array's length, scanf will write characters—including the string's terminating null character ('\0')—beyond the end of the array. This might *overwrite* other variables' values. In addition, if the program writes to those other variables, it might overwrite the string's '\0'.

A function determines where a string ends by looking for its terminating '\0' character. For example, recall that function printf outputs a string by reading characters from the beginning of the string in memory and continuing until it encounters the string's '\0'. If the '\0' is missing, printf continues reading from memory until it encounters some later '\0' in memory. This can lead to strange results or cause a program to crash.

The C11 standard's *optional* Annex K provides new, more secure, versions of many string-processing and input/output functions. When reading a string into a character array function scanf_s performs additional checks to ensure that it *does not* write beyond the end of the array. Assuming that myString is a 20-character array, the statement

```
scanf_s("%19s", myString, 20);
```

reads a string into myString. Function scanf_s requires two arguments for *each* %s in the format string:

- a character array in which to place the input string and
- the array's number of elements.

The function uses the number of elements to prevent buffer overflows. For example, it's possible to supply a field width for %s that's too long for the underlying character array, or to simply omit the field width entirely. With scanf_s, if the number of characters input plus the terminating null character is *larger* than the number of array elements specified, the %s conversion *fails*. For the preceding statement, which contains only one conversion specifier, scanf_s would return 0 indicating that no conversions were performed, and the array myString would be unaltered.

In general, if your compiler supports the functions from the C standard's optional Annex K, you should use them. We discuss additional Annex K functions in later Secure C Programming sections.

Portability Tip 6.1

Not all compilers support the C11 standard's Annex K functions. For programs that must compile on multiple platforms and compilers, you might have to edit your code to use the versions of scanf_s or scanf available on each platform. Your compiler might also require a specific setting to enable you to use the Annex K functions.

Don't Use Strings Read from the User as Format-Control Strings
You might have noticed that throughout this book, we do not use single-argument printf statements. Instead we use one of the following forms:

- When we need to output a '\n' after the string, we use function puts (which automatically outputs a '\n' after its single string argument), as in

```
puts("Welcome to C!");
```

- When we need the cursor to remain on the same line as the string, we use function printf, as in

```
printf("%s", "Enter first integer: ");
```

Because we were displaying *string literals*, we certainly could have used the one-argument form of printf, as in

```
printf("Welcome to C!\n");
printf("Enter first integer: ");
```

When printf evaluates the format-control string in its first (and possibly its only) argument, the function performs tasks based on the conversion specifier(s) in that string. If the format-control string were obtained from the user, an attacker could supply malicious conversion specifiers that would be "executed" by the formatted output function. Now that you know how to read strings into *character arrays*, it's important to note that you should *never* use as a printf's format-control string a character array that might contain user input. For more information, see CERT guideline FIO30-C at www.securecoding.cert.org.

Summary

Section 6.1 Introduction
- **Arrays** (p. 215) are data structures consisting of related data items of the same type.
- Arrays are "static" entities in that they remain the same size throughout program execution.

Section 6.2 Arrays
- An array is a **contiguous group of memory locations** related by the fact that they all have the same name and the same type.
- To refer to a particular **location** or **element** (p. 215) in the array, specify the array's name and the **position number** (p. 215) of the particular element in the array.
- The first element in every array is the **zeroth element** (p. 215), i.e., the one with position number 0. Thus, the first element of array c is referred to as c[0], the second element is referred to as c[1], the seventh element is referred to as c[6], and, in general, the *i*th element is referred to as c[i - 1].
- An **array name**, like other variable names, can contain only letters, digits and underscores and cannot begin with a digit.
- The position number contained within square brackets is more formally called an **index** or **subscript** (p. 216). An index must be an integer or an integer expression.
- The **brackets** used to enclose the index of an array are actually considered to be an operator in C. They have the same level of precedence as the function call operator.

Section 6.3 Defining Arrays
- Arrays occupy space in memory. You specify the type of each element and the **number of elements** in the array so that the computer may reserve the appropriate amount of memory.
- An **array of type char** can be used to store a **character string**.

Section 6.4 Array Examples
- Type size_t represents an **unsigned integral type**. This type is recommended for any variable that represents an array's size or an array's indices. The **header <stddef.h>** defines size_t and is often included by other headers (such as <stdio.h>).

- The elements of an array can be initialized when the array is defined by following the definition with an equals sign and braces, {}, containing a comma-separated **list of initializers** (p. 218). If there are fewer initializers than elements in the array, the remaining elements are initialized to zero.

- The statement int n[10] = {0}; explicitly initializes the first element to zero and initializes the remaining nine elements to zero because there are fewer initializers than there are elements in the array. It's important to remember that automatic arrays are not automatically initialized to zero. You must at least initialize the first element to zero for the remaining elements to be automatically zeroed. This method of initializing the array elements to 0 is performed before program startup for static arrays and at runtime for automatic arrays.

- If the array size is omitted from a definition with an initializer list, the number of elements in the array will be the number of elements in the initializer list.

- The **#define preprocessor directive** can be used to define a **symbolic constant**—an identifier that the preprocessor replaces with replacement text before the program is compiled. When the program is preprocessed, all occurrences of the symbolic constant are replaced with the replacement text (p. 220). Using symbolic constants to specify array sizes makes programs more **modifiable**.

- C has **no array bounds checking** to prevent a program from referring to an element that does not exist. Thus, an executing program can "walk off" the end of an array without warning. You should ensure that all array references remain within the bounds of the array.

Section 6.5 Using Character Arrays to Store and Manipulate Strings
- A string literal such as "hello" is really an array of individual characters in C.

- A **character array** can be initialized using a **string literal**. In this case, the size of the array is determined by the compiler based on the length of the string.

- Every string contains a special **string-termination character called the null character** (p. 226). The character constant representing the null character is '\0'.

- A character array representing a string should always be defined large enough to hold the number of characters in the string and the terminating null character.

- Character arrays also can be initialized with individual character constants in an initializer list.

- Because a string is really an array of characters, we can access individual characters in a string directly using array index notation.

- You can input a string directly into a character array from the keyboard using scanf and the **conversion specifier %s**. The name of the character array is passed to scanf without the preceding & used with non-array variables.

- Function scanf reads characters from the keyboard until the first white-space character is encountered—it does not check the array size. Thus, scanf can write beyond the end of the array.

- A character array representing a string can be output with printf and the %s conversion specifier. The characters of the string are printed until a terminating null character is encountered.

Section 6.6 Static Local Arrays and Automatic Local Arrays
- A **static local variable** exists for the duration of the program but is visible only in the function body. We can apply static to a local array definition so that the array is not created and initialized each time the function is called and the array is not destroyed each time the function is exited in the program. This reduces program execution time, particularly for programs with frequently called functions that contain large arrays.

- Arrays that are static are automatically initialized once before program startup. If you do not explicitly initialize a static array, that array's elements are initialized to zero by the compiler.

Section 6.7 Passing Arrays to Functions

- To pass an array argument to a function, specify the name of the array without any brackets.

- Unlike char arrays that contain strings, other array types do not have a special terminator. For this reason, the size of an array is passed to a function, so that the function can process the proper number of elements.

- **C automatically passes arrays to functions by reference**—the called functions can modify the element values in the callers' original arrays. The name of the array evaluates to the address of the first element of the array. Because the starting address of the array is passed, the called function knows precisely where the array is stored. Therefore, when the called function modifies array elements in its function body, it's modifying the actual elements of the array in their original memory locations.

- Although entire arrays are passed by reference, **individual array elements are passed by value** exactly as simple variables are.

- Such simple single pieces of data (such as individual ints, floats and chars) are called **scalars** (p. 231).

- To pass an element of an array to a function, use the indexed name of the array element as an argument in the function call.

- For a function to receive an array through a function call, the function's parameter list must specify that an array will be received. The size of the array is not required between the array brackets. If it's included, the compiler checks that it's greater than zero, then ignores it.

- When an array parameter is preceded by the **const qualifier** (p. 233), the elements of the array become constant in the function body, and any attempt to modify an element of the array in the function body results in a compile-time error.

Section 6.8 Sorting Arrays

- **Sorting** data (i.e., placing the data into a particular order such as ascending or descending) is one of the most important computing applications.

- One sorting technique is called the **bubble sort** (p. 234) or the **sinking sort**, because the smaller values gradually "bubble" their way upward to the top of the array like air bubbles rising in water, while the larger values sink to the bottom of the array. The technique is to make several passes through the array. On each pass, successive pairs of elements are compared. If a pair is in increasing order (or if the values are identical), we leave the values as they are. If a pair is in decreasing order, their values are swapped in the array.

- Because of the way the successive comparisons are made, a large value may move down the array many positions on a single pass, but a small value may move up only one position.

- The chief virtue of the bubble sort is that it's easy to program. However, the bubble sort runs slowly. This becomes apparent when sorting large arrays.

Section 6.9 Case Study: Computing Mean, Median and Mode Using Arrays

- The **mean** is the arithmetic average of a set of values.

- The **median** is the "middle value" in a sorted set of values.

- The **mode** is the value that occurs most frequently in a set of values.

Section 6.10 Searching Arrays

- The process of finding a particular element of an array is called **searching** (p. 241).

- The **linear search** compares each element of the array with the search key (p. 241). Because the array is not in any particular order, it's just as likely that the value will be found in the first element as in the last. On average, therefore, the search key will be compared with half the elements of the array.

- The linear search algoritm (p. 241) works well for small or unsorted arrays. For sorted arrays, the high-speed binary search algorithm can be used.

- The **binary search** algorithm (p. 241) eliminates from consideration one-half of the elements in a sorted array after each comparison. The algorithm locates the middle element of the array and compares it to the search key. If they're equal, the search key is found and the array index of that element is returned. If they're not equal, the problem is reduced to searching one-half of the array. If the search key is less than the middle element of the array, the first half of the array is searched, otherwise the second half is searched. If the search key is not found in the specified subarray (piece of the original array), the algorithm is repeated on one-quarter of the original array. The search continues until the search key is equal to the middle element of a subarray, or until the subarray consists of one element that's not equal to the search key (i.e., the search key is not found).

- When using a binary search, the maximum number of comparisons required for any array can be determined by finding the first power of 2 greater than the number of array elements.

Section 6.11 Multidimensional Arrays

- A common use of **multidimensional arrays** (p. 246) is to represent **tables** of values consisting of information arranged in **rows** and **columns.** To identify a particular table element, we must specify two indices: The first (by convention) identifies the element's row and the second (by convention) identifies the element's column.

- Tables or arrays that require two indices to identify a particular element are called **two-dimensional arrays** (p. 246).

- Multidimensional arrays can have more than two indices.

- A multidimensional array can be initialized when it's defined, much like a one-dimensional array. The values in a two-dimensional array are grouped by row in braces. If there are not enough initializers for a given row, the remaining elements of that row are initialized to 0.

- The first index of a multidimensional array parameter declaration is not required, but all subsequent indices are required. The compiler uses these indices to determine the locations in memory of elements in multidimensional arrays. All array elements are stored consecutively in memory regardless of the number of indices. In a two-dimensional array, the first row is stored in memory followed by the second row.

- Providing the index values in a parameter declaration enables the compiler to tell the function how to locate an array element. In a two-dimensional array, each row is basically a two-dimensional array. To locate an element in a particular row, the compiler must know how many elements are in each row so that it can skip the proper number of memory locations when accessing the array.

Section 6.12 Variable-Length Arrays

- A **variable-length array** (p. 253) is an array whose size is defined by an expression evaluated at execution time.

- When applied to a variable-length array, `sizeof` operates at runtime.

- As with fixed-length arrays, there is no protection against stepping outside the array bounds of variable-length arrays.

- The syntax for passing variable-length arrays as parameters to functions is the same as with a normal, fixed-length array.

Self-Review Exercises

6.1   Answer each of the following:
   a) Lists and tables of values are stored in _____.
   b) The number used to refer to a particular element of an array is called its _____.
   c) A(n) _____ should be used to specify the size of an array because it makes the program more modifiable.
   d) The process of placing the elements of an array in order is called _____ the array.
   e) Determining whether an array contains a certain key value is called _____ the array.
   f) An array that uses two indices is referred to as a(n) _____ array.

6.2   State whether the following are *true* or *false*. If the answer is *false*, explain why.
   a) An array can store many different types of values.
   b) An array index can be of data type `double`.
   c) If there are fewer initializers in an initializer list than the number of elements in the array, C automatically initializes the remaining elements to the last value in the list of initializers.
   d) It's an error if an initializer list contains more initializers than there are array elements.
   e) An individual array element that's passed to a function as an argument of the form `a[i]` and modified in the called function will contain the modified value in the calling function.

6.3   Follow the instructions below regarding an array called `fractions`.
   a) Define a symbolic constant `SIZE` to be replaced with the replacement text 10.
   b) Define an array with `SIZE` elements of type `double` and initialize the elements to 0.
   c) Refer to array element 4.
   d) Assign the value `1.667` to array element nine.
   e) Assign the value `3.333` to the seventh element of the array.
   f) Print array elements 6 and 9 with two digits of precision to the right of the decimal point, and show the output that's displayed on the screen.
   g) Print all the elements of the array, using a `for` iteration statement. Assume the integer variable x has been defined as a control variable for the loop. Show the output.

6.4   Write statements to accomplish the following:
   a) Define `table` to be an integer array and to have 3 rows and 3 columns. Assume the symbolic constant `SIZE` has been defined to be 3.
   b) How many elements does the array `table` contain? Print the total number of elements.
   c) Use a `for` iteration statement to initialize each element of `table` to the sum of its indices. Assume the integer variables x and y are defined as control variables.
   d) Print the values of each element of array `table`. Assume the array was initialized with the definition:

```
int table[SIZE][SIZE] =
   { { 1, 8 }, { 2, 4, 6 }, { 5 } };
```

6.5   Find the error in each of the following program segments and correct the error.
   a) `#define SIZE 100;`
   b) `SIZE = 10;`
   c) *Assume* `int b[10] = { 0 }, i;`

```
      for (i = 0; i <= 10; ++i) {
         b[i] = 1;
      }
```

   d) `#include <stdio.h>;`
   e) *Assume* `int a[2][2] = { { 1, 2 }, { 3, 4 } };`
      `a[1, 1] = 5;`
   f) `#define VALUE = 120`

Answers to Self-Review Exercises

6.1 a) arrays. b) index. c) symbolic constant. d) sorting. e) searching. f) two-dimensional.

6.2 a) False. An array can store only values of the same type.
b) False. An array index must be an integer or an integer expression.
c) False. C automatically initializes the remaining elements to zero.
d) True.
e) False. Individual elements of an array are passed by value. If the entire array is passed to a function, then any modifications to the elements will be reflected in the original.

6.3 a) `#define SIZE 10`
b) `double fractions[SIZE] = { 0.0 };`
c) `fractions[4]`
d) `fractions[9] = 1.667;`
e) `fractions[6] = 3.333;`
f) `printf("%.2f %.2f\n", fractions[6], fractions[9]);`
Output: 3.33 1.67.
g)
```
for (x = 0; x < SIZE; ++x) {
    printf("fractions[%u] = %f\n", x, fractions[x]);
}
```

Output:
```
fractions[0] = 0.000000
fractions[1] = 0.000000
fractions[2] = 0.000000
fractions[3] = 0.000000
fractions[4] = 0.000000
fractions[5] = 0.000000
fractions[6] = 3.333000
fractions[7] = 0.000000
fractions[8] = 0.000000
fractions[9] = 1.667000
```

6.4 a) `int table[SIZE][SIZE];`
b) Nine elements. `printf("%d\n", SIZE * SIZE);`
c)
```
for (x = 0; x < SIZE; ++x) {
    for (y = 0; y < SIZE; ++y) {
        table[x][y] = x + y;
    }
}
```
d)
```
for (x = 0; x < SIZE; ++x) {
    for (y = 0; y < SIZE; ++y) {
        printf("table[%d][%d] = %d\n", x, y, table[x][y]);
    }
}
```

Output:
```
table[0][0] = 1
table[0][1] = 8
table[0][2] = 0
table[1][0] = 2
table[1][1] = 4
table[1][2] = 6
table[2][0] = 5
table[2][1] = 0
table[2][2] = 0
```

6.5 a) Error: Semicolon at the end of the #define preprocessor directive.
Correction: Eliminate semicolon.

b) Error: Assigning a value to a symbolic constant using an assignment statement.
Correction: Assign a value to the symbolic constant in a #define preprocessor directive without using the assignment operator as in #define SIZE 10.

c) Error: Referencing an array element outside the bounds of the array (b[10]).
Correction: Change the final value of the control variable to 9.

d) Error: Semicolon at the end of the #include preprocessor directive.
Correction: Eliminate semicolon.

e) Error: Array indexing done incorrectly.
Correction: Change the statement to a[1][1] = 5;

f) Error: Assigning a value to a symbolic constant using an assignment statement.
Correction: Assign a value to the symbolic constant in a #define preprocessor directive without using the assignment operator as in #define VALUE 120.

Exercises

6.6 Fill in the blanks in each of the following:

a) C stores lists of values in _____.

b) The elements of an array are related by the fact that they _____.

c) When referring to an array element, the position number contained within square brackets is called a(n) _____.

d) The names of the five elements of array p are _____, _____, _____, _____ and _____.

e) The contents of a particular element of an array is called the _____ of that element.

f) Naming an array, stating its type and specifying the number of elements in the array is called _____ the array.

g) The process of placing the elements of an array into either ascending or descending order is called _____.

h) In a two-dimensional array, the first index identifies the _____ of an element and the second index identifies the _____ of an element.

i) An m-by-n array contains _____ rows, _____ columns and _____ elements.

j) The name of the element in row 3 and column 5 of array d is _____.

6.7 State which of the following are *true* and which are *false*. If *false*, explain why.

a) To refer to a particular location or element within an array, we specify the name of the array and the value of the particular element.

b) An array definition reserves space for the array.

c) To indicate that 100 locations should be reserved for integer array p, write

```
p[100];
```

d) A C program that initializes the elements of a 15-element array to zero must contain one for statement.

e) A C program that totals the elements of a two-dimensional array must contain nested for statements.

f) The mean, median and mode of the following set of values are 5, 6 and 7, respectively: 1, 2, 5, 6, 7, 7, 7.

6.8 Write statements to accomplish each of the following:

a) Display the value of the seventh element of character array f.

b) Input a value into element 4 of one-dimensional floating-point array b.

c) Initialize each of the five elements of one-dimensional integer array g to 8.

d) Total the elements of floating-point array c of 100 elements.

e) Copy array a into the first portion of array b. Assume `double a[11], b[34];`

f) Determine and print the smallest and largest values contained in 99-element floating-point array `w`.

6.9 Consider a 2-by-5 integer array `t`.

a) Write a definition for `t`.

b) How many rows does `t` have?

c) How many columns does `t` have?

d) How many elements does `t` have?

e) Write the names of all the elements in the second row of `t`.

f) Write the names of all the elements in the third column of `t`.

g) Write a single statement that sets the element of `t` in row 1 and column 2 to zero.

h) Write a series of statements that initialize each element of `t` to zero. Do not use an iteration statement.

i) Write a nested `for` statement that initializes each element of `t` to zero.

j) Write a statement that inputs the values for the elements of `t` from the terminal.

k) Write a series of statements that determine and print the smallest value in array `t`.

l) Write a statement that displays the elements of the first row of `t`.

m) Write a statement that totals the elements of the fourth column of `t`.

n) Write a series of statements that print the array `t` in tabular format. List the column indices as headings across the top and list the row indices at the left of each row.

6.10 *(Sales Commissions)* Use a one-dimensional array to solve the following problem. A company pays its salespeople on a commission basis. The salespeople receive $200 per week plus 9% of their gross sales for that week. For example, a salesperson who grosses $3,000 in sales in a week receives $200 plus 9% of $3,000, or a total of $470. Write a C program (using an array of counters) that determines how many of the salespeople earned salaries in each of the following ranges (assume that each salesperson's salary is truncated to an integer amount):

a) $200–299

b) $300–399

c) $400–499

d) $500–599

e) $600–699

f) $700–799

g) $800–899

h) $900–999

i) $1000 and over

6.11 *(Bubble Sort)* The bubble sort presented in Fig. 6.15 is inefficient for large arrays. Make the following simple modifications to improve its performance.

a) After the first pass, the largest number is guaranteed to be in the highest-numbered element of the array; after the second pass, the two highest numbers are "in place," and so on. Instead of making nine comparisons on every pass, modify the bubble sort to make eight comparisons on the second pass, seven on the third pass and so on.

b) The data in the array may already be in the proper or near-proper order, so why make nine passes if fewer will suffice? Modify the sort to check at the end of each pass whether any swaps have been made. If none has been made, then the data must already be in the proper order, so the program should terminate. If swaps have been made, then at least one more pass is needed.

6.12 Write loops that perform each of the following one-dimensional array operations:

a) Initialize the 10 elements of integer array `counts` to zeros.

b) Add 1 to each of the 15 elements of integer array `bonus`.

    c) Read the 12 values of floating-point array `monthlyTemperatures` from the keyboard.

    d) Print the five values of integer array `bestScores` in column format.

6.13 Find the error(s) in each of the following statements:

    a) Assume: `char str[5];`

```
scanf("%s", str); // User types hello
```

    b) Assume: `int a[3];`

```
printf("$d %d %d\n", a[1], a[2], a[3]);
```

    c) `double f[3] = { 1.1, 10.01, 100.001, 1000.0001 };`

    d) Assume: `double d[2][10];`

```
d[1, 9] = 2.345;
```

6.14 *(Mean, Median and Mode Program Modifications)* Modify the program of Fig. 6.16 so function `mode` is capable of handling a tie for the mode value. Also modify function `median` so the two middle elements are averaged in an array with an even number of elements.

6.15 *(Duplicate Elimination)* Use a one-dimensional array to solve the following problem. Read in 20 numbers, each of which is between 10 and 100, inclusive. As each number is read, print it only if it's not a duplicate of a number already read. Provide for the "worst case" in which all 20 numbers are different. Use the smallest possible array to solve this problem.

6.16 Label the elements of 3-by-5 two-dimensional array `sales` to indicate the order in which they're set to zero by the following program segment:

```
for (row = 0; row <= 2; ++row) {
    for (column = 0; column <= 4; ++column) {
        sales[row][column] = 0;
    }
}
```

6.17 What does the following program do?

```
1   // ex06_17.c
2   // What does this program do?
3   #include <stdio.h>
4   #define SIZE 10
5
6   int whatIsThis(const int b[], size_t p); // function prototype
7
8   // function main begins program execution
9   int main(void)
10  {
11      int x; // holds return value of function whatIsThis
12
13      // initialize array a
14      int a[SIZE] = { 1, 2, 3, 4, 5, 6, 7, 8, 9, 10 };
15
16      x = whatIsThis(a, SIZE);
17
18      printf("Result is %d\n", x);
19  }
20
21  // what does this function do?
22  int whatIsThis(const int b[], size_t p)
23  {
24      // base case
25      if (1 == p) {
26          return b[0];
27      }
```

```
28        else { // recursion step
29            return b[p - 1] + whatIsThis(b, p - 1);
30        }
31    }
```

6.18   What does the following program do?

```
1    // ex06_18.c
2    // What does this program do?
3    #include <stdio.h>
4    #define SIZE 10
5
6    // function prototype
7    void someFunction(const int b[], size_t startIndex, size_t size);
8
9    // function main begins program execution
10   int main(void)
11   {
12       int a[SIZE] = { 8, 3, 1, 2, 6, 0, 9, 7, 4, 5 }; // initialize a
13
14       puts("Answer is:");
15       someFunction(a, 0, SIZE);
16       puts("");
17   }
18
19   // What does this function do?
20   void someFunction(const int b[], size_t startIndex, size_t size)
21   {
22       if (startIndex < size) {
23           someFunction(b, startIndex + 1, size);
24           printf("%d  ", b[startIndex]);
25       }
26   }
```

6.19   *(Dice Rolling)* Write a program that simulates the rolling of two dice. The program should use rand twice to roll the first die and second die, respectively. The sum of the two values should then be calculated. [*Note:* Because each die can show an integer value from 1 to 6, then the sum of the two values will vary from 2 to 12, with 7 being the most frequent sum and 2 and 12 the least frequent sums.] Figure 6.24 shows the 36 possible combinations of the two dice. Your program should roll the two dice 36,000 times. Use a one-dimensional array to tally the numbers of times each possible sum appears. Print the results in a tabular format. Also, determine if the totals are reasonable; i.e., there are six ways to roll a 7, so approximately one-sixth of all the rolls should be 7.

	1	2	3	4	5	6
1	2	3	4	5	6	7
2	3	4	5	6	7	8
3	4	5	6	7	8	9
4	5	6	7	8	9	10
5	6	7	8	9	10	11
6	7	8	9	10	11	12

Fig. 6.24 | Dice-rolling outcomes.

6.20   *(Game of Craps)* Write a program that runs 1000 games of craps (without human intervention) and answers each of the following questions:

   a) How many games are won on the first roll, second roll, …, twentieth roll and after the twentieth roll?

   b) How many games are lost on the first roll, second roll, …, twentieth roll and after the twentieth roll?

   c) What are the chances of winning at craps? [*Note:* You should discover that craps is one of the fairest casino games. What do you suppose this means?]

   d) What's the average length of a game of craps?

   e) Do the chances of winning improve with the length of the game?

6.21   *(Airline Reservations System)* A small airline has just purchased a computer for its new automated reservations system. The president has asked you to program the new system. You'll write a program to assign seats on each flight of the airline's only plane (capacity: 10 seats).

Your program should display the following menu of alternatives:

```
Please type 1 for "first class"
Please type 2 for "economy"
```

If the person types 1, then your program should assign a seat in the first class section (seats 1–5). If the person types 2, then your program should assign a seat in the economy section (seats 6–10). Your program should then print a boarding pass indicating the person's seat number and whether it's in the first class or economy section of the plane.

Use a one-dimensional array to represent the seating chart of the plane. Initialize all the elements of the array to 0 to indicate that all seats are empty. As each seat is assigned, set the corresponding element of the array to 1 to indicate that the seat is no longer available.

Your program should, of course, never assign a seat that has already been assigned. When the first class section is full, your program should ask the person if it's acceptable to be placed in the economy section (and vice versa). If yes, then make the appropriate seat assignment. If no, then print the message `"Next flight leaves in 3 hours."`

6.22   *(Total Sales)* Use a two-dimensional array to solve the following problem. A company has four salespeople (1 to 4) who sell five different products (1 to 5). Once a day, each salesperson passes in a slip for each different type of product sold. Each slip contains:

   a) The salesperson number

   b) The product number

   c) The total dollar value of that product sold that day

Thus, each salesperson passes in between 0 and 5 sales slips per day. Assume that the information from all of the slips for last month is available. Write a program that will read all this information for last month's sales and summarize the total sales by salesperson by product. All totals should be stored in the two-dimensional array `sales`. After processing all the information for last month, print the results in tabular format with each column representing a particular salesperson and each row representing a particular product. Cross total each row to get the total sales of each product for last month; cross total each column to get the total sales by salesperson for last month. Your tabular printout should include these cross totals to the right of the totaled rows and to the bottom of the totaled columns.

6.23   *(Turtle Graphics)* The Logo language made the concept of *turtle graphics* famous. Imagine a mechanical turtle that walks around the room under the control of a C program. The turtle holds a pen in one of two positions, up or down. While the pen is down, the turtle traces out shapes as it moves; while the pen is up, the turtle moves about freely without writing anything. In this problem you'll simulate the operation of the turtle and create a computerized sketchpad as well.

Use a 50-by-50 array `floor` which is initialized to zeros. Read commands from an array that contains them. Keep track of the current turtle position at all times and whether the pen is currently up or down. Assume that the turtle always starts at position 0, 0 of the floor with its pen up. The set of turtle commands your program must process are shown in Fig. 6.25. Suppose that the turtle is somewhere near the center of the floor. The following "program" would draw and print a 12-by-12 square:

```
2
5,12
3
5,12
3
5,12
3
5,12
1
6
9
```

As the turtle moves with the pen down, set the appropriate elements of array floor to 1s. When the 6 command (print) is given, wherever there's a 1 in the array, display an asterisk, or some other character you choose. Wherever there's a zero, display a blank. Write a program to implement the turtle graphics capabilities discussed here. Write several turtle graphics programs to draw interesting shapes. Add other commands to increase the power of your turtle graphics language.

Command	Meaning
1	Pen up
2	Pen down
3	Turn right
4	Turn left
5, 10	Move forward 10 spaces (or a number other than 10)
6	Print the 50-by-50 array
9	End of data (sentinel)

Fig. 6.25 | Turtle commands.

6.24 *(Knight's Tour)* One of the more interesting puzzlers for chess buffs is the Knight's Tour problem, originally proposed by the mathematician Euler. The question is this: Can the chess piece called the knight move around an empty chessboard and touch each of the 64 squares once and only once? We study this intriguing problem in depth here.

The knight makes L-shaped moves (over two in one direction and then over one in a perpendicular direction). Thus, from a square in the middle of an empty chessboard, the knight can make eight different moves (numbered 0 through 7) as shown in Fig. 6.26.

    a) Draw an 8-by-8 chessboard on a sheet of paper and attempt a Knight's Tour by hand. Put a 1 in the first square you move to, a 2 in the second square, a 3 in the third, and so on. Before starting the tour, estimate how far you think you'll get, remembering that a full tour consists of 64 moves. How far did you get? Were you close to the estimate?

    b) Now let's develop a program that will move the knight around a chessboard. The board itself is represented by an 8-by-8 two-dimensional array board. Each square is initialized to zero. We describe each of the eight possible moves in terms of both its horizontal and vertical components. For example, a move of type 0 as shown in Fig. 6.26 consists of

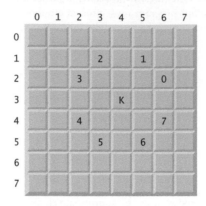

Fig. 6.26 | The eight possible moves of the knight.

moving two squares horizontally to the right and one square vertically upward. Move 2 consists of moving one square horizontally to the left and two squares vertically upward. Horizontal moves to the left and vertical moves upward are indicated with negative numbers. The eight moves may be described by two one-dimensional arrays, horizontal and vertical, as follows:

```
horizontal[0] = 2
horizontal[1] = 1
horizontal[2] = -1
horizontal[3] = -2
horizontal[4] = -2
horizontal[5] = -1
horizontal[6] = 1
horizontal[7] = 2

vertical[0] = -1
vertical[1] = -2
vertical[2] = -2
vertical[3] = -1
vertical[4] = 1
vertical[5] = 2
vertical[6] = 2
vertical[7] = 1
```

Let the variables currentRow and currentColumn indicate the row and column of the knight's current position on the board. To make a move of type moveNumber, where moveNumber is between 0 and 7, your program uses the statements

```
currentRow += vertical[moveNumber];
currentColumn += horizontal[moveNumber];
```

Keep a counter that varies from 1 to 64. Record the latest count in each square the knight moves to. Remember to test each potential move to see if the knight has already visited that square. And, of course, test every potential move to make sure that the knight does not land off the chessboard. Now write a program to move the knight around the chessboard. Run the program. How many moves did the knight make?

c) After attempting to write and run a Knight's Tour program, you have probably developed some valuable insights. We'll use these to develop a *heuristic* (or strategy) for moving the knight. Heuristics do not guarantee success, but a carefully developed heuristic greatly improves the chance of success. You may have observed that the outer squares are in some sense more troublesome than the squares nearer the center of the board. In fact, the most troublesome, or inaccessible, squares are the four corners.

Intuition may suggest that you should attempt to move the knight to the most troublesome squares first and leave open those that are easiest to get to, so that when the board gets congested near the end of the tour, there will be a greater chance of success.

We develop an "accessibility heuristic" by classifying each square according to how accessible it is and always moving the knight to the square (within the knight's L-shaped moves, of course) that's most inaccessible. We label a two-dimensional array `accessibility` with numbers indicating from how many squares each particular square is accessible. On a blank chessboard, the center squares are therefore rated as 8s, the corner squares are rated as 2s, and the other squares have accessibility numbers of 3, 4, or 6 as follows:

```
2  3  4  4  4  4  3  2
3  4  6  6  6  6  4  3
4  6  8  8  8  8  6  4
4  6  8  8  8  8  6  4
4  6  8  8  8  8  6  4
4  6  8  8  8  8  6  4
3  4  6  6  6  6  4  3
2  3  4  4  4  4  3  2
```

Now write a version of the Knight's Tour program using the accessibility heuristic. At any time, the knight should move to the square with the lowest accessibility number. In case of a tie, the knight may move to any of the tied squares. Therefore, the tour may begin in any of the four corners. [*Note:* As the knight moves around the chessboard, your program should reduce the accessibility numbers as more and more squares become occupied. In this way, at any given time during the tour, each available square's accessibility number will remain equal to precisely the number of squares from which that square may be reached.] Run this version of your program. Did you get a full tour? (*Optional:* Modify the program to run 64 tours, one from each square of the chessboard. How many full tours did you get?)

d) Write a version of the Knight's Tour program which, when encountering a tie between two or more squares, decides what square to choose by looking ahead to those squares reachable from the "tied" squares. Your program should move to the square for which the next move would arrive at a square with the lowest accessibility number.

6.25 *(Knight's Tour: Brute-Force Approaches)* In Exercise 6.24 we developed a solution to the Knight's Tour problem. The approach used, called the "accessibility heuristic," generates many solutions and executes efficiently.

As computers continue increasing in power, we'll be able to solve many problems with sheer computer power and relatively unsophisticated algorithms. Let's call this approach brute-force problem solving.

a) Use random number generation to enable the knight to walk around the chess board (in its legitimate L-shaped moves, of course) at random. Your program should run one tour and print the final chessboard. How far did the knight get?

b) Most likely, the preceding program produced a relatively short tour. Now modify your program to attempt 1,000 tours. Use a one-dimensional array to keep track of the number of tours of each length. When your program finishes attempting the 1000 tours, it should print this information in a tabular format. What was the best result?

c) Most likely, the preceding program gave you some "respectable" tours but no full tours. Now "pull all the stops out" and simply let your program run until it produces a full tour. [*Caution:* This version of the program could run for hours on a powerful computer.] Once again, keep a table of the number of tours of each length and print this table when the first full tour is found. How many tours did your program attempt before producing a full tour? How much time did it take?

d) Compare the brute-force version of the Knight's Tour with the accessibility-heuristic version. Which required a more careful study of the problem? Which algorithm was more difficult to develop? Which required more computer power? Could we be certain (in advance) of obtaining a full tour with the accessibility-heuristic approach? Could we be certain (in advance) of obtaining a full tour with the brute-force approach? Argue the pros and cons of brute-force problem solving in general.

6.26 *(Eight Queens)* Another puzzler for chess buffs is the Eight Queens problem. Simply stated: Is it possible to place eight queens on an empty chessboard so that no queen is "attacking" any other—that is, so that no two queens are in the same row, the same column, or along the same diagonal? Use the kind of thinking developed in Exercise 6.24 to formulate a heuristic for solving the Eight Queens problem. Run your program. [*Hint:* It's possible to assign a numeric value to each square of the chessboard indicating how many squares of an empty chessboard are "eliminated" once a queen is placed in that square. For example, each of the four corners would be assigned the value 22, as in Fig. 6.27.]

Once these "elimination numbers" are placed in all 64 squares, an appropriate heuristic might be: Place the next queen in the square with the smallest elimination number. Why is this strategy intuitively appealing?

6.27 *(Eight Queens: Brute-Force Approaches)* In this problem you'll develop several brute-force approaches to solving the Eight Queens problem introduced in Exercise 6.26.

a) Solve the Eight Queens problem, using the random brute-force technique developed in Exercise 6.25.

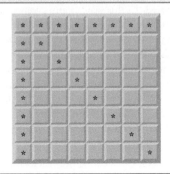

Fig. 6.27 | The 22 squares eliminated by placing a queen in the upper-left corner.

b) Use an exhaustive technique (i.e., try all possible combinations of eight queens on the chessboard).

c) Why do you suppose the exhaustive brute-force approach may not be appropriate for solving the Eight Queens problem?

d) Compare and contrast the random brute-force and exhaustive brute-force approaches in general.

6.28 *(Duplicate Elimination)* In Chapter 12, we explore the high-speed binary search tree data structure. One feature of a binary search tree is that duplicate values are discarded when insertions are made into the tree. This is referred to as duplicate elimination. Write a program that produces 20 random numbers between 1 and 20. The program should store all nonduplicate values in an array. Use the smallest possible array to accomplish this task.

6.29 *(Knight's Tour: Closed Tour Test)* In the Knight's Tour, a full tour occurs when the knight makes 64 moves touching each square of the chessboard once and only once. A closed tour occurs when the 64th move is one move away from the location in which the knight started the tour. Modify the Knight's Tour program you wrote in Exercise 6.24 to test for a closed tour if a full tour has occurred.

6.30 *(The Sieve of Eratosthenes)* A prime integer is any integer greater than 1 that can be divided evenly only by itself and 1. The Sieve of Eratosthenes is a method of finding prime numbers. It works as follows:

  a) Create an array with all elements initialized to 1 (true). Array elements with prime indices will remain 1. All other array elements will eventually be set to zero.
  b) Starting with array index 2 (index 1 is not prime), every time an array element is found whose value is 1, loop through the remainder of the array and set to zero every element whose index is a multiple of the index for the element with value 1. For array index 2, all elements beyond 2 in the array that are multiples of 2 will be set to zero (indices 4, 6, 8, 10, and so on.). For array index 3, all elements beyond 3 in the array that are multiples of 3 will be set to zero (indices 6, 9, 12, 15, and so on.).

When this process is complete, the array elements that are still set to 1 indicate that the index is a prime number. Write a program that uses an array of 1,000 elements to determine and print the prime numbers between 1 and 999. Ignore element 0 of the array.

Recursion Exercises

6.31 *(Palindromes)* A palindrome is a string that's spelled the same way forward and backward. Some examples of palindromes are: "radar," "able was i ere i saw elba," and, if you ignore blanks, "a man a plan a canal panama." Write a recursive function testPalindrome that returns 1 if the string stored in the array is a palindrome and 0 otherwise. The function should ignore spaces and punctuation in the string.

6.32 *(Linear Search)* Modify the program of Fig. 6.18 to use a recursive linearSearch function to perform the linear search of the array. The function should receive an integer array, the size of the array and the search key as arguments. If the search key is found, return the array index; otherwise, return –1.

6.33 *(Binary Search)* Modify the program of Fig. 6.19 to use a recursive binarySearch function to perform the binary search of the array. The function should receive an integer array, the starting index, the ending index and the search key as arguments. If the search key is found, return the array index; otherwise, return –1.

6.34 *(Eight Queens)* Modify the Eight Queens program you created in Exercise 6.26 to solve the problem recursively.

6.35 *(Print an Array)* Write a recursive function printArray that takes an array and the size of the array as arguments, prints the array, and returns nothing. The function should stop processing and return when it receives an array of size zero.

6.36 *(Print a String Backward)* Write a recursive function stringReverse that takes a character array as an argument, prints it back to front and returns nothing. The function should stop processing and return when the terminating null character of the string is encountered.

6.37 *(Find the Minimum Value in an Array)* Write a recursive function recursiveMinimum that takes an integer array and the array size as arguments and returns the smallest element of the array. The function should stop processing and return when it receives an array of one element.

7

C Pointers

Objectives

In this chapter, you'll:

■ Use pointers and pointer operators.

■ Pass arguments to functions by reference using pointers.

■ Understand the various placements of the `const` qualifier and how they affect what you can do with a variable.

■ Use the `sizeof` operator with variables and types.

■ Use pointer arithmetic to process the elements in arrays.

■ Understand the close relationships among pointers, arrays and strings.

■ Define and use arrays of strings.

■ Use pointers to functions.

■ Learn about secure C programming issues with regard to pointers.

7.1 Introduction

In this chapter, we discuss one of the most powerful features of the C programming language, the **pointer**.[1] Pointers are among C's most difficult capabilities to master. Pointers enable programs to accomplish pass-by-reference, to pass functions between functions, and to create and manipulate dynamic data structures—ones that can grow and shrink at execution time, such as linked lists, queues, stacks and trees. This chapter explains basic pointer concepts. In Section 7.13, we discuss various pointer-related security issues. Chapter 10 examines the use of pointers with structures. Chapter 12 introduces dynamic memory management techniques and presents examples of creating and using dynamic data structures.

---

1. Pointers and pointer-based entities such as arrays and strings, when misused intentionally or accidentally, can lead to errors and security breaches. See our Secure C Programming Resource Center (www.deitel.com/SecureC/) for articles, books, white papers and forums on this important topic.

7.2 Pointer Variable Definitions and Initialization

Pointers are variables whose values are *memory addresses*. Normally, a variable directly contains a specific value. A pointer, however, contains an *address* of a variable that contains a specific value. In this sense, a variable name *directly* references a value, and a pointer *indirectly* references a value (Fig. 7.1). Referencing a value through a pointer is called **indirection**.

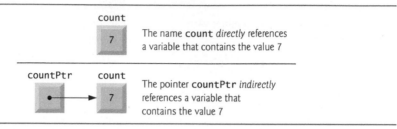

Fig. 7.1 | Directly and indirectly referencing a variable.

Declaring Pointers
Pointers, like all variables, must be defined before they can be used. The definition

```
int *countPtr, count;
```

specifies that variable countPtr is of type int * (i.e., a pointer to an integer) and is read (right to left), "countPtr is a pointer to int" or "countPtr points to an object[2] of type int." Also, the variable count is defined to be an int, *not* a pointer to an int. The * applies *only* to countPtr in the definition. When * is used in this manner in a definition, it indicates that the variable being defined is a pointer. Pointers can be defined to point to objects of any type. To prevent the ambiguity of declaring pointer and non-pointer variables in the same declaration as shown above, you should always declare only one variable per declaration.

Common Programming Error 7.1
The asterisk (*) notation used to declare pointer variables does not *distribute to all variable names in a declaration. Each pointer must be declared with the * prefixed to the name; e.g., if you wish to declare xPtr and yPtr as int pointers, use int *xPtr, *yPtr;.*

Good Programming Practice 7.1
We prefer to include the letters Ptr in pointer variable names to make it clear that these variables are pointers and need to be handled appropriately.

Initializing and Assigning Values to Pointers
Pointers should be initialized when they're defined, or they can be assigned a value. A pointer may be initialized to NULL, 0 or an address. A pointer with the value NULL points to *nothing*. NULL is a *symbolic constant* defined in the <stddef.h> header (and several other headers, such as <stdio.h>). Initializing a pointer to 0 is equivalent to initializing a pointer to NULL, but NULL is preferred, because it highlights the fact that the variable is of a pointer

---

2. In C, an "object" is a region of memory that can hold a value. So objects in C include primitive types such as ints, floats, chars and doubles, as well as aggregate types such as arrays and structs (which we discuss in Chapter 10).

type. When 0 is assigned, it's first converted to a pointer of the appropriate type. The value 0 is the *only* integer value that can be assigned directly to a pointer variable. Assigning a variable's address to a pointer is discussed in Section 7.3.

Error-Prevention Tip 7.1

Initialize pointers to prevent unexpected results.

7.3 Pointer Operators

In this section, we present the address (&) and indirection (*) operators, and the relationship between them.

The Address (&) Operator

The &, or **address operator**, is a unary operator that returns the *address* of its operand. For example, assuming the definitions

```
int y = 5;
int *yPtr;
```

the statement

```
yPtr = &y;
```

assigns the *address* of the variable y to pointer variable yPtr. Variable yPtr is then said to "point to" y. Figure 7.2 shows a schematic representation of memory after the preceding assignment is executed.

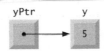

Fig. 7.2 | Graphical representation of a pointer pointing to an integer variable in memory.

Pointer Representation in Memory

Figure 7.3 shows the representation of the preceding pointer in memory, assuming that integer variable y is stored at location 600000, and pointer variable yPtr is stored at location 500000. The operand of the address operator must be a variable; the address operator *cannot* be applied to constants or expressions.

Fig. 7.3 | Representation of y and yPtr in memory.

The Indirection (*) Operator

The unary * operator, commonly referred to as the **indirection operator** or **dereferencing operator**, returns the *value* of the object to which its operand (i.e., a pointer) points. For example, the statement

```
        printf("%d", *yPtr);
```
prints the value of variable y (5). Using * in this manner is called **dereferencing a pointer**.

Common Programming Error 7.2

Dereferencing a pointer that has not been properly initialized or that has not been assigned to point to a specific location in memory is an error. This could cause a fatal execution-time error, or it could accidentally modify important data and allow the program to run to completion with incorrect results.

Demonstrating the & and * Operators

Figure 7.4 demonstrates the pointer operators & and *. The printf conversion specifier %p outputs the memory location as a *hexadecimal* integer on most platforms. (See Appendix C for more information on hexadecimal integers.) In the program's output, notice that the *address* of a and the *value* of aPtr are identical in the output, thus confirming that the address of a is indeed assigned to the pointer variable aPtr (line 8). The & and * operators are complements of one another—when they're both applied consecutively to aPtr in either order (line 18), the same result is printed. The addresses shown in the output will vary across systems. Figure 7.5 lists the precedence and associativity of the operators introduced to this point.

```
 1   // Fig. 7.4: fig07_04.c
 2   // Using the & and * pointer operators.
 3   #include <stdio.h>
 4
 5   int main(void)
 6   {
 7      int a = 7;
 8      int *aPtr = &a; // set aPtr to the address of a
 9
10      printf("The address of a is %p"
11             "\nThe value of aPtr is %p", &a, aPtr);
12
13      printf("\n\nThe value of a is %d"
14             "\nThe value of *aPtr is %d", a, *aPtr);
15
16      printf("\n\nShowing that * and & are complements of "
17             "each other\n&*aPtr = %p"
18             "\n*&aPtr = %p\n", &*aPtr, *&aPtr);
19   }
```

```
The address of a is 0028FEC0
The value of aPtr is 0028FEC0

The value of a is 7
The value of *aPtr is 7

Showing that * and & are complements of each other
&*aPtr = 0028FEC0
*&aPtr = 0028FEC0
```

Fig. 7.4 | Using the & and * pointer operators.

Operators								Associativity	Type
()	[]	++ *(postfix)*	-- *(postfix)*					left to right	postfix
+	-	++	--	!	*	&	*(type)*	right to left	unary
*	/	%						left to right	multiplicative
+	-							left to right	additive
<	<=	>	s>=					left to right	relational
==	!=							left to right	equality
&&								left to right	logical AND
||								left to right	logical OR
?:								right to left	conditional
=	+=	-=	*=	/=	%=			right to left	assignment
,								left to right	comma

Fig. 7.5 | Precedence and associativity of the operators discussed so far.

7.4 Passing Arguments to Functions by Reference

There are two ways to pass arguments to a function—**pass-by-value** and **pass-by-reference**. *However, all arguments in C are passed by value.* Functions often require the capability to *modify variables in the caller* or receive a pointer to a large data object to avoid the overhead of receiving the object by value (which incurs the time and memory overheads of making a copy of the object). As we saw in Chapter 5, return may be used to return *one* value from a called function to a caller (or to return control from a called function without passing back a value). Pass-by-reference also can be used to enable a function to "return" multiple values to its caller by modifying variables in the caller.

Use & and * to Accomplish Pass-By-Reference
In C, you use pointers and the indirection operator to accomplish pass-by-reference. When calling a function with arguments that should be modified, the *addresses* of the arguments are passed. This is normally accomplished by applying the address operator (&) to the variable (in the caller) whose value will be modified. As we saw in Chapter 6, arrays are *not* passed using operator & because C automatically passes the starting location in memory of the array (the name of an array is equivalent to &arrayName[0]). When the address of a variable is passed to a function, the indirection operator (*) may be used in the function to modify the value at that location in the caller's memory.

Pass-By-Value
The programs in Figs. 7.6 and 7.7 present two versions of a function that cubes an integer—cubeByValue and cubeByReference. Line 14 of Fig. 7.6 passes the variable number by value to function cubeByValue. The cubeByValue function cubes its argument and passes the new value back to main using a return statement. The new value is assigned to number in main (line 14).

```
1   // Fig. 7.6: fig07_06.c
2   // Cube a variable using pass-by-value.
3   #include <stdio.h>
4
5   int cubeByValue(int n); // prototype
6
7   int main(void)
8   {
9      int number = 5; // initialize number
10
11      printf("The original value of number is %d", number);
12
13      // pass number by value to cubeByValue
14      number = cubeByValue(number);
15
16      printf("\nThe new value of number is %d\n", number);
17   }
18
19   // calculate and return cube of integer argument
20   int cubeByValue(int n)
21   {
22      return n * n * n; // cube local variable n and return result
23   }
```

```
The original value of number is 5
The new value of number is 125
```

Fig. 7.6 | Cube a variable using pass-by-value.

Pass-By-Reference

Figure 7.7 passes the variable number by reference (line 15)—the address of number is passed—to function cubeByReference. Function cubeByReference takes as a parameter a pointer to an int called nPtr (line 21). The function *dereferences* the pointer and cubes the value to which nPtr points (line 23), then assigns the result to *nPtr (which is really number in main), thus changing the value of number in main. Figures 7.8 and 7.9 analyze graphically and step-by-step the programs in Figs. 7.6 and 7.7, respectively.

```
1   // Fig. 7.7: fig07_07.c
2   // Cube a variable using pass-by-reference with a pointer argument.
3
4   #include <stdio.h>
5
6   void cubeByReference(int *nPtr); // function prototype
7
8   int main(void)
9   {
```

Fig. 7.7 | Cube a variable using pass-by-reference with a pointer argument. (Part I of 2.)

```
10      int number = 5; // initialize number
11
12      printf("The original value of number is %d", number);
13
14      // pass address of number to cubeByReference
15      cubeByReference(&number);
16
17      printf("\nThe new value of number is %d\n", number);
18   }
19
20   // calculate cube of *nPtr; actually modifies number in main
21   void cubeByReference(int *nPtr)
22   {
23      *nPtr = *nPtr * *nPtr * *nPtr; // cube *nPtr
24   }
```

```
The original value of number is 5
The new value of number is 125
```

Fig. 7.7 | Cube a variable using pass-by-reference with a pointer argument. (Part 2 of 2.)

Use a Pointer Parameter to Receive an Address

A function receiving an *address* as an argument must define a *pointer parameter* to receive the address. For example, in Fig. 7.7 the header for function cubeByReference (line 21) is:

```
void cubeByReference(int *nPtr)
```

The header specifies that cubeByReference *receives* the *address* of an integer variable as an argument, stores the address locally in nPtr and does not return a value.

Pointer Parameters in Function Prototypes

The function prototype for cubeByReference (Fig. 7.7, line 6) specifies an int * parameter. As with other variable types, it's *not* necessary to include names of pointers in function prototypes. Names included for documentation purposes are ignored by the C compiler.

Functions That Receive One-Dimensional Arrays

For a function that expects a one-dimensional array as an argument, the function's prototype and header can use the pointer notation shown in the parameter list of function cubeByReference (line 21). The compiler does not differentiate between a function that receives a pointer and one that receives a one-dimensional array. This, of course, means that the function must "know" when it's receiving an array or simply a single variable for which it's to perform pass-by-reference. When the compiler encounters a function parameter for a one-dimensional array of the form int b[], the compiler converts the parameter to the pointer notation int *b. The two forms are interchangeable.

Error-Prevention Tip 7.2

Use pass-by-value to pass arguments to a function unless the caller explicitly requires the called function to modify the value of the argument variable in the caller's environment. This prevents accidental modification of the caller's arguments and is another example of the principle of least privilege.

Step 1: Before main calls cubeByValue:

```
int main(void)                              number      int cubeByValue(int n)
{                                                       {
    int number = 5;                           5             return n * n * n;
                                                        }
    number = cubeByValue(number);
}                                                                                 n

                                                                            undefined
```

Step 2: After cubeByValue receives the call:

```
int main(void)                              number      int cubeByValue( int n )
{                                                       {
    int number = 5;                           5             return n * n * n;
                                                        }
    number = cubeByValue(number);
}                                                                                 n

                                                                                  5
```

Step 3: After cubeByValue cubes parameter n and before cubeByValue returns to main:

```
int main(void)                              number      int cubeByValue(int n)
{                                                       {
    int number = 5;                           5                     125
                                                            return n * n * n;
    number = cubeByValue(number);                       }
}                                                                                 n

                                                                                  5
```

Step 4: After cubeByValue returns to main and before assigning the result to number:

```
int main(void)                              number      int cubeByValue(int n)
{                                                       {
    int number = 5;                           5             return n * n * n;
                        125                             }
    number = cubeByValue(number);                                                 n
}
                                                                            undefined
```

Step 5: After main completes the assignment to number:

```
int main(void)                              number      int cubeByValue(int n)
{                                                       {
    int number = 5;                          125            return n * n * n;
       125             125                              }
    number = cubeByValue(number);                                                 n
}
                                                                            undefined
```

Fig. 7.8 | Analysis of a typical pass-by-value.

Step 1: Before `main` calls `cubeByReference`:

```
int main(void)                    number
{
    int number = 5;                 5

    cubeByReference(&number);
}
```

```
void cubeByReference(int *nPtr)
{
    *nPtr = *nPtr * *nPtr * *nPtr;
}
                                   nPtr

                                undefined
```

Step 2: After `cubeByReference` receives the call and before `*nPtr` is cubed:

```
int main(void)                    number
{
    int number = 5;                 5

    cubeByReference(&number);
}
```

```
void cubeByReference( int *nPtr )
{
    *nPtr = *nPtr * *nPtr * *nPtr;
}
                                   nPtr

call establishes this pointer
```

Step 3: After `*nPtr` is cubed and before program control returns to `main`:

```
int main(void)                    number
{
    int number = 5;                125

    cubeByReference(&number);
}
```

```
void cubeByReference(int *nPtr)
{                            125

    *nPtr = *nPtr * *nPtr * *nPtr;
}
                                   nPtr
called function modifies caller's
variable
```

Fig. 7.9 | Analysis of a typical pass-by-reference with a pointer argument.

7.5 Using the `const` Qualifier with Pointers

The **const qualifier** enables you to inform the compiler that the value of a particular variable should not be modified.

Software Engineering Observation 7.1

The `const` qualifier can be used to enforce the principle of least privilege in software design. This can reduce debugging time and prevent unintentional side effects, making a program easier to modify and maintain.

Over the years, a large base of legacy code was written in early versions of C that did not use `const` because it was not available. For this reason, there are significant opportunities for improvement by reengineering old C code.

Six possibilities exist for using (or not using) `const` with function parameters—two with pass-by-value parameter passing and four with pass-by-reference parameter passing. How do you choose one of the six possibilities? Let the **principle of least privilege** be your guide—always award a function enough access to the data in its parameters to accomplish its specified task, but absolutely no more.

const *Values and Parameters*

In Chapter 5, we explained that *all function calls in C are pass-by-value*—a copy of the argument in the function call is made and passed to the function. If the copy is modified in the function, the original value in the caller does *not* change. In many cases, a value passed to a function is modified so the function can accomplish its task. However, in some instances, the value should *not* be altered in the called function, even though it manipulates only a *copy* of the original value.

Consider a function that takes a one-dimensional array and its size as arguments and prints the array. Such a function should loop through the array and output each array element individually. The size of the array is used in the function body to determine when the loop should terminate. Neither the size of the array nor its contents should change in the function body.

Error-Prevention Tip 7.3

If a variable does not (or should not) change in the body of a function to which it's passed, the variable should be declared const *to ensure that it's not accidentally modified.*

If an attempt is made to modify a value that's declared const, the compiler catches it and issues either a warning or an error, depending on the particular compiler.

Common Programming Error 7.3

Being unaware that a function is expecting pointers as arguments for pass-by-reference and passing arguments by value. Some compilers take the values assuming they're pointers and dereference the values as pointers. At runtime, memory-access violations or segmentation faults are often generated. Other compilers catch the mismatch in types between arguments and parameters and generate error messages.

There are four ways to pass a pointer to a function:

- a **non-constant pointer to non-constant data**.
- a **constant pointer to nonconstant data**.
- a **non-constant pointer to constant data**.
- a **constant pointer to constant data**.

Each of the four combinations provides different access privileges and is discussed in the next several examples.

7.5.1 Converting a String to Uppercase Using a Non-Constant Pointer to Non-Constant Data

The highest level of data access is granted by a **non-constant pointer to non-constant data**. In this case, the data can be modified through the dereferenced pointer, and the pointer can be modified to point to other data items. A declaration for a non-constant pointer to non-constant data does not include const. Such a pointer might be used to receive a string as an argument to a function that processes (and possibly modifies) each character in the string. Function convertToUppercase of Fig. 7.10 declares its parameter, a *non-constant pointer to non-constant data* called sPtr (char *sPtr), in line 19. The function processes the array string (pointed to by sPtr) one character at a time. C standard library function toupper (line 22) from the <ctype.h> header is called to convert each character to its corresponding uppercase letter—if the original character is not a letter or is already uppercase, toupper returns the original character. Line 23 moves the pointer to the next character in the string. Chapter 8 presents many C standard library character- and string-processing functions.

```c
 1   // Fig. 7.10: fig07_10.c
 2   // Converting a string to uppercase using a
 3   // non-constant pointer to non-constant data.
 4   #include <stdio.h>
 5   #include <ctype.h>
 6
 7   void convertToUppercase(char *sPtr); // prototype
 8
 9   int main(void)
10   {
11      char string[] = "cHaRaCters and $32.98"; // initialize char array
12
13      printf("The string before conversion is: %s", string);
14      convertToUppercase(string);
15      printf("\nThe string after conversion is: %s\n", string);
16   }
17
18   // convert string to uppercase letters
19   void convertToUppercase(char *sPtr)
20   {
21      while (*sPtr != '\0') { // current character is not '\0'
22         *sPtr = toupper(*sPtr); // convert to uppercase
23         ++sPtr; // make sPtr point to the next character
24      }
25   }
```

```
The string before conversion is: cHaRaCters and $32.98
The string after conversion is: CHARACTERS AND $32.98
```

Fig. 7.10 | Converting a string to uppercase using a non-constant pointer to non-constant data.

7.5.2 Printing a String One Character at a Time Using a Non-Constant Pointer to Constant Data

A **non-constant pointer to constant data** *can be modified* to point to any data item of the appropriate type, but the *data* to which it points *cannot be modified*. Such a pointer might be used to receive an array argument to a function that will process each element without modifying that element. For example, function printCharacters (Fig. 7.11) declares parameter sPtr to be of type const char * (line 21). The declaration is read from *right to left* as "sPtr is a pointer to a character constant." The function uses a for statement to output each character in the string until the null character is encountered. After each character is printed, pointer sPtr is incremented—this makes the pointer move to the next character in the string.

```
1    // Fig. 7.11: fig07_11.c
2    // Printing a string one character at a time using
3    // a non-constant pointer to constant data.
4
5    #include <stdio.h>
6
7    void printCharacters(const char *sPtr);
8
9    int main(void)
10   {
11      // initialize char array
12      char string[] = "print characters of a string";
13
14      puts("The string is:");
15      printCharacters(string);
16      puts("");
17   }
18
19   // sPtr cannot be used to modify the character to which it points,
20   // i.e., sPtr is a "read-only" pointer
21   void printCharacters(const char *sPtr)
22   {
23      // loop through entire string
24      for (; *sPtr != '\0'; ++sPtr) { // no initialization
25         printf("%c", *sPtr);
26      }
27   }
```

```
The string is:
print characters of a string
```

Fig. 7.11 | Printing a string one character at a time using a non-constant pointer to constant data.

Figure 7.12 illustrates the attempt to compile a function that receives a non-constant pointer (xPtr) to constant data. This function attempts to modify the data pointed to by xPtr in line 18—which results in a compilation error. The error shown is from the Visual C++ compiler. The actual error message you receive (in this and other examples) is compiler specific—for example, Xcode's LLVM compiler reports the error:

```
Read-only variable is not assignable"
```

and the GNU gcc compiler reports the error:

```
error: assignment of read-only location '*xPtr'
```

```
1    // Fig. 7.12: fig07_12.c
2    // Attempting to modify data through a
3    // non-constant pointer to constant data.
```

Fig. 7.12 | Attempting to modify data through a non-constant pointer to constant data. (Part 1 of 2.)

```
4    #include <stdio.h>
5    void f(const int *xPtr); // prototype
6
7    int main(void)
8    {
9        int y; // define y
10
11       f(&y); // f attempts illegal modification
12   }
13
14   // xPtr cannot be used to modify the
15   // value of the variable to which it points
16   void f(const int *xPtr)
17   {
18       *xPtr = 100; // error: cannot modify a const object
19   }
```

```
error C2166: l-value specifies const object
```

Fig. 7.12 | Attempting to modify data through a non-constant pointer to constant data. (Part 2 of 2.)

As you know, arrays are aggregate data types that store related data items of the same type under one name. In Chapter 10, we'll discuss another form of aggregate data type called a **structure** (sometimes called a **record** or tuple in other languages). A structure is capable of storing related data items of the same or *different* data types under one name (e.g., storing information about each employee of a company). When a function is called with an array as an argument, the array is automatically passed to the function *by reference*. However, structures are always passed *by value*—a *copy* of the entire structure is passed. This requires the execution-time overhead of making a copy of each data item in the structure and storing it on the computer's *function call stack*. When structure data must be passed to a function, we can use pointers to constant data to get the performance of pass-by-reference and the protection of pass-by-value. When a pointer to a structure is passed, only a copy of the *address* at which the structure is stored must be made. On a machine with four-byte addresses, a copy of four bytes of memory is made rather than a copy of a possibly large structure.

Performance Tip 7.1
Passing large objects such as structures by using pointers to constant data obtains the performance benefits of pass-by-reference and the security of pass-by-value.

If memory is low and execution efficiency is a concern, use pointers. If memory is in abundance and efficiency is not a major concern, pass data by value to enforce the principle of least privilege. Remember that some systems do not enforce const well, so pass-by-value is still the best way to prevent data from being modified.

7.5.3 Attempting to Modify a Constant Pointer to Non-Constant Data

A **constant pointer to non-constant data** always points to the *same* memory location, and the data at that location *can be modified* through the pointer. This is the default for an array name. An array name is a constant pointer to the beginning of the array. All data in the array can be accessed and changed by using the array name and array indexing. A constant pointer to non-constant data can be used to receive an array as an argument to a function that accesses array elements using only array index notation. Pointers that are declared const must be initialized when they're defined (if the pointer is a function parameter, it's initialized with a pointer that's passed to the function). Figure 7.13 attempts to modify a constant pointer. Pointer ptr is defined in line 12 to be of type int * const. The definition is read from *right to left* as "ptr is a constant pointer to an integer." The pointer is initialized (line 12) with the address of integer variable x. The program attempts to assign the address of y to ptr (line 15), but the compiler generates an error message.

```
1   // Fig. 7.13: fig07_13.c
2   // Attempting to modify a constant pointer to non-constant data.
3   #include <stdio.h>
4
5   int main(void)
6   {
7      int x; // define x
8      int y; // define y
9
10     // ptr is a constant pointer to an integer that can be modified
11     // through ptr, but ptr always points to the same memory location
12     int * const ptr = &x;
13
14     *ptr = 7; // allowed: *ptr is not const
15     ptr = &y; // error: ptr is const: cannot assign new address
16  }
```

```
c:\examples\ch07\fig07_13.c(15) : error C2166: l-value specifies const object
```

Fig. 7.13 | Attempting to modify a constant pointer to non-constant data.

7.5.4 Attempting to Modify a Constant Pointer to Constant Data

The *least* access privilege is granted by a **constant pointer to constant data**. Such a pointer always points to the *same* memory location, and the data at that memory location *cannot be modified*. This is how an array should be passed to a function that only looks at the array using array index notation and does *not* modify the array. Figure 7.14 defines pointer variable ptr (line 13) to be of type const int *const, which is read from *right to left* as "ptr is a constant pointer to an integer constant." The figure shows the error messages generated when an attempt is made to *modify* the *data* to which ptr points (line 16) and when an attempt is made to *modify* the *address* stored in the pointer variable (line 17).

```
1   // Fig. 7.14: fig07_14.c
2   // Attempting to modify a constant pointer to constant data.
3   #include <stdio.h>
4
```

Fig. 7.14 | Attempting to modify a constant pointer to constant data. (Part I of 2.)

```
5   int main(void)
6   {
7      int x = 5; // initialize x
8      int y; // define y
9
10     // ptr is a constant pointer to a constant integer. ptr always
11     // points to the same location; the integer at that location
12     // cannot be modified
13     const int *const ptr = &x; // initialization is OK
14
15     printf("%d\n", *ptr);
16     *ptr = 7; // error: *ptr is const; cannot assign new value
17     ptr = &y; // error: ptr is const; cannot assign new address
18  }
```

```
c:\examples\ch07\fig07_14.c(16) : error C2166: l-value specifies const object
c:\examples\ch07\fig07_14.c(17) : error C2166: l-value specifies const object
```

Fig. 7.14 | Attempting to modify a constant pointer to constant data. (Part 2 of 2.)

7.6 Bubble Sort[3] Using Pass-by-Reference

Let's improve the bubble sort program of Fig. 6.15 to use two functions—bubbleSort and swap (Fig. 7.15). Function bubbleSort sorts the array. It calls function swap (line 46) to exchange the array elements array[j] and array[j + 1].

```
1   // Fig. 7.15: fig07_15.c
2   // Putting values into an array, sorting the values into
3   // ascending order and printing the resulting array.
4   #include <stdio.h>
5   #define SIZE 10
6
7   void bubbleSort(int * const array, const size_t size); // prototype
8
9   int main(void)
10  {
11     // initialize array a
12     int a[SIZE] = { 2, 6, 4, 8, 10, 12, 89, 68, 45, 37 };
13
14     puts("Data items in original order");
15
16     // loop through array a
17     for (size_t i = 0; i < SIZE; ++i) {
18        printf("%4d", a[i]);
19     }
20
```

Fig. 7.15 | Putting values into an array, sorting the values into ascending order and printing the resulting array. (Part 1 of 2.)

---

3. In Chapter 12 and Appendix D, we investigate sorting schemes that yield better performance.

```
21        bubbleSort(a, SIZE); // sort the array
22
23        puts("\nData items in ascending order");
24
25        // loop through array a
26        for (size_t i = 0; i < SIZE; ++i) {
27            printf("%4d", a[i]);
28        }
29
30        puts("");
31   }
32
33   // sort an array of integers using bubble sort algorithm
34   void bubbleSort(int * const array, const size_t size)
35   {
36        void swap(int *element1Ptr, int *element2Ptr); // prototype
37
38        // loop to control passes
39        for (unsigned int pass = 0; pass < size - 1; ++pass) {
40
41            // loop to control comparisons during each pass
42            for (size_t j = 0; j < size - 1; ++j) {
43
44                // swap adjacent elements if they're out of order
45                if (array[j] > array[j + 1]) {
46                    swap(&array[j], &array[j + 1]);
47                }
48            }
49        }
50   }
51
52   // swap values at memory locations to which element1Ptr and
53   // element2Ptr point
54   void swap(int *element1Ptr, int *element2Ptr)
55   {
56        int hold = *element1Ptr;
57        *element1Ptr = *element2Ptr;
58        *element2Ptr = hold;
59   }
```

```
Data items in original order
   2   6   4   8  10  12  89  68  45  37
Data items in ascending order
   2   4   6   8  10  12  37  45  68  89
```

Fig. 7.15 | Putting values into an array, sorting the values into ascending order and printing the resulting array. (Part 2 of 2.)

Function swap

Remember that C enforces *information hiding* between functions, so swap does not have access to individual array elements in bubbleSort by default. Because bubbleSort *wants* swap to have access to the array elements to be swapped, bubbleSort passes each of these elements *by reference* to swap—the *address* of each array element is passed explicitly. Although entire arrays are automatically passed by reference, individual array elements are *scalars* and are ordinarily passed by value. Therefore, bubbleSort uses the address operator (&) on each of the array elements in the swap call (line 46) to effect pass-by-reference as follows

```
swap(&array[j], &array[j + 1]);
```

Function swap receives &array[j] in element1Ptr (line 54). Even though swap—because of information hiding—is *not* allowed to know the name array[j], swap may use *element1Ptr as a *synonym* for array[j]—when swap accesses *element1Ptr, it's *actually* referencing array[j] in bubbleSort. Similarly, when swap accesses *element2Ptr, it's *actually* referencing array[j + 1] in bubbleSort. Even though swap is not allowed to say

```
int hold = array[j];
array[j] = array[j + 1];
array[j + 1] = hold;
```

precisely the *same* effect is achieved by lines 56 through 58

```
int hold = *element1Ptr;
*element1Ptr = *element2Ptr;
*element2Ptr = hold;
```

Function *bubbleSort's* Array Parameter
Several features of function bubbleSort should be noted. The function header (line 34) declares array as int * const array rather than int array[] to indicate that bubbleSort receives a one-dimensional array array as an argument (again, these notations are interchangeable). Parameter size is declared const to enforce the principle of least privilege. Although parameter size receives a copy of a value in main, and modifying the copy cannot change the value in main, bubbleSort does *not* need to alter size to accomplish its task. The size of the array remains fixed during the execution of function bubbleSort. Therefore, size is declared const to ensure that it's *not* modified.

Function *swap's* Prototype in Function *bubbleSort's* Body
The prototype for function swap (line 36) is included in the body of function bubbleSort because bubbleSort is the only function that calls swap. Placing the prototype in bubbleSort restricts proper calls of swap to those made from bubbleSort (or any function that appears after swap in the source code). Other functions defined before swap that attempt to call swap do *not* have access to a proper function prototype, so the compiler generates one automatically. This normally results in a prototype that does *not* match the function header (and generates a compilation warning or error) because the compiler assumes int for the return type and the parameter types.

Software Engineering Observation 7.2
Placing function prototypes in the definitions of other functions enforces the principle of least privilege by restricting proper function calls to the functions in which the prototypes appear.

Function *bubbleSort's* size Parameter
Function bubbleSort receives the size of the array as a parameter (line 34). The function must know the size of the array to sort the array. When an array is passed to a function,

the memory address of the first element of the array is received by the function. The address, of course, does *not* convey the number of elements in the array. Therefore, you must pass the array size to the function. Another common practice is to pass a pointer to the beginning of the array and a pointer to the location just beyond the end of the array—as you'll learn in Section 7.8, the difference of the two pointers is the length of the array and the resulting code is simpler.

In the program, the size of the array is explicitly passed to function bubbleSort. There are two main benefits to this approach—*software reusability* and *proper software engineering*. By defining the function to receive the array size as an argument, we enable the function to be used by any program that sorts one-dimensional integer arrays of any size.

Software Engineering Observation 7.3

When passing an array to a function, also pass the size of the array. This helps make the function reusable in many programs.

We could have stored the array's size in a global variable that's accessible to the entire program. This would be more efficient, because a copy of the size is not made to pass to the function. However, other programs that require an integer array-sorting capability may not have the same global variable, so the function cannot be used in those programs.

Software Engineering Observation 7.4

Global variables usually violate the principle of least privilege and can lead to poor software engineering. Global variables should be used only to represent truly shared resources, such as the time of day.

The size of the array could have been programmed directly into the function. This restricts the use of the function to an array of a specific size and significantly reduces its reusability. Only programs processing one-dimensional integer arrays of the specific size coded into the function can use the function.

7.7 sizeof Operator

C provides the special unary operator sizeof to determine the size in bytes of an array (or any other data type). This operator is applied at compilation time, unless its operand is a variable-length array (Section 6.12). When applied to the name of an array as in Fig. 7.16 (line 15), the sizeof operator returns the total number of bytes in the array as type size_t.[4] Variables of type float on this computer are stored in 4 bytes of memory, and array is defined to have 20 elements. Therefore, there are a total of 80 bytes in array.

Performance Tip 7.2

sizeof is a compile-time operator, so it does not incur any execution-time overhead.

---

4. Recall that on a Mac size_t represents unsigned long. Xcode reports warnings when you display an unsigned long using "%u" in a printf. To eliminate the warnings, use "%lu" instead.

```
1   // Fig. 7.16: fig07_16.c
2   // Applying sizeof to an array name returns
3   // the number of bytes in the array.
4   #include <stdio.h>
5   #define SIZE 20
6
7   size_t getSize(float *ptr); // prototype
8
9   int main(void)
10  {
11     float array[SIZE]; // create array
12
13     printf("The number of bytes in the array is %u"
14            "\nThe number of bytes returned by getSize is %u\n",
15            sizeof(array), getSize(array));
16  }
17
18  // return size of ptr
19  size_t getSize(float *ptr)
20  {
21     return sizeof(ptr);
22  }
```

```
The number of bytes in the array is 80
The number of bytes returned by getSize is 4
```

Fig. 7.16 | Applying sizeof to an array name returns the number of bytes in the array.

The number of elements in an array also can be determined with sizeof. For example, consider the following array definition:

```
double real[22];
```

Variables of type double normally are stored in 8 bytes of memory. Thus, array real contains a total of 176 bytes. To determine the number of elements in the array, the following expression can be used:

```
sizeof(real) / sizeof(real[0])
```

The expression determines the number of bytes in array real and divides that value by the number of bytes used in memory to store the first element of array real (a double value). Even though function getSize receives an array of 20 elements as an argument, the function's parameter ptr is simply a pointer to the array's first element. When you use sizeof with a pointer, it returns the *size of the pointer*, not the size of the item to which it points. On our Windows and Linux test systems, the size of a pointer is 4 bytes, so getSize returns 4; on our Mac, the size of a pointer is 8 bytes, so getSize returns 8. Also, the calculation shown above for determining the number of array elements using sizeof works *only* when using the actual array, *not* when using a pointer to the array.

Determining the Sizes of the Standard Types, an Array and a Pointer

Figure 7.17 calculates the number of bytes used to store each of the standard data types. *The results of this program are implementation dependent and often differ across platforms and sometimes across different compilers on the same platform.* The output shows the results from our Windows system using the Visual C++ compiler. The size of a `long double` was 12 bytes on our Linux system using the GNU gcc compiler. The size of a `long` was 8 bytes and the size of a `long double` was 16 bytes on our Mac system using Xcode's LLVM compiler.

```c
1   // Fig. 7.17: fig07_17.c
2   // Using operator sizeof to determine standard data type sizes.
3   #include <stdio.h>
4
5   int main(void)
6   {
7      char c;
8      short s;
9      int i;
10     long l;
11     long long ll;
12     float f;
13     double d;
14     long double ld;
15     int array[20]; // create array of 20 int elements
16     int *ptr = array; // create pointer to array
17
18     printf("      sizeof c = %u\tsizeof(char)   = %u"
19            "\n      sizeof s = %u\tsizeof(short) = %u"
20            "\n      sizeof i = %u\tsizeof(int) = %u"
21            "\n      sizeof l = %u\tsizeof(long) = %u"
22            "\n     sizeof ll = %u\tsizeof(long long) = %u"
23            "\n      sizeof f = %u\tsizeof(float) = %u"
24            "\n      sizeof d = %u\tsizeof(double) = %u"
25            "\n     sizeof ld = %u\tsizeof(long double) = %u"
26          "\n sizeof array = %u"
27          "\n   sizeof ptr = %u\n",
28          sizeof c, sizeof(char), sizeof s, sizeof(short), sizeof i,
29          sizeof(int), sizeof l, sizeof(long), sizeof ll,
30          sizeof(long long), sizeof f, sizeof(float), sizeof d,
31          sizeof(double), sizeof ld, sizeof(long double),
32          sizeof array, sizeof ptr);
33  }
```

```
    sizeof c = 1      sizeof(char)   = 1
    sizeof s = 2      sizeof(short) = 2
    sizeof i = 4      sizeof(int) = 4
    sizeof l = 4      sizeof(long) = 4
   sizeof ll = 8      sizeof(long long) = 8
    sizeof f = 4      sizeof(float) = 4
    sizeof d = 8      sizeof(double) = 8
   sizeof ld = 8      sizeof(long double) = 8
sizeof array = 80
  sizeof ptr = 4
```

Fig. 7.17 | Using operator `sizeof` to determine standard data type sizes.

Portability Tip 7.1

The number of bytes used to store a particular data type may vary between systems. When writing programs that depend on data type sizes and that will run on several computer systems, use sizeof *to determine the number of bytes used to store the data types.*

Operator sizeof can be applied to any variable name, type or value (including the value of an expression). When applied to a variable name (that's *not* an array name) or a constant, the number of bytes used to store the specific type of variable or constant is returned. The parentheses are required when a type is supplied as sizeof's operand.

7.8 Pointer Expressions and Pointer Arithmetic

Pointers are valid operands in arithmetic expressions, assignment expressions and comparison expressions. However, not all the operators normally used in these expressions are valid in conjunction with pointer variables. This section describes the operators that can have pointers as operands, and how these operators are used.

7.8.1 Allowed Operators for Pointer Arithmetic

A pointer may be *incremented* (++) or *decremented* (--), an integer may be *added* to a pointer (+ or +=), an integer may be *subtracted* from a pointer (- or -=) and one pointer may be subtracted from another—this last operation is meaningful only when *both* pointers point to elements of the *same* array.

7.8.2 Aiming a Pointer at an Array

Assume that array int v[5] has been defined and its first element is at location 3000 in memory. Assume pointer vPtr has been initialized to point to v[0]—i.e., the value of vPtr is 3000. Figure 7.18 illustrates this situation for a machine with 4-byte integers. Variable vPtr can be initialized to point to array v with either of the statements

```
vPtr = v;
vPtr = &v[0];
```

Portability Tip 7.2

Because the results of pointer arithmetic depend on the size of the objects a pointer points to, pointer arithmetic is machine and compiler dependent.

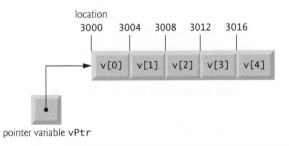

Fig. 7.18 | Array v and a pointer variable vPtr that points to v.

7.8.3 Adding an Integer to a Pointer

In conventional arithmetic, 3000 + 2 yields the value 3002. This is normally *not* the case with pointer arithmetic. When an integer is added to or subtracted from a pointer, the pointer is *not* incremented or decremented simply by that integer, but by that integer times the size of the object to which the pointer refers. The number of bytes depends on the object's data type. For example, the statement

```
vPtr += 2;
```

would produce 3008 (3000 + 2 * 4), assuming an integer is stored in 4 bytes of memory. In the array v, vPtr would now point to v[2] (Fig. 7.19). If an integer is stored in 2 bytes of memory, then the preceding calculation would result in memory location 3004 (3000 + 2 * 2). If the array were of a different data type, the preceding statement would increment the pointer by twice the number of bytes that it takes to store an object of that data type. When performing pointer arithmetic on a character array, the results will be consistent with regular arithmetic, because each character is 1 byte long.

 Common Programming Error 7.4
Using pointer arithmetic on a pointer that does not refer to an element in an array.

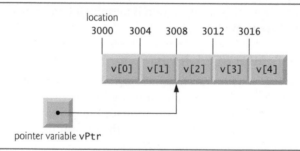

Fig. 7.19 | The pointer vPtr after pointer arithmetic.

7.8.4 Subtracting an Integer from a Pointer

If vPtr had been incremented to 3016, which points to v[4], the statement

```
vPtr -= 4;
```

would set vPtr back to 3000—the beginning of the array.

 Common Programming Error 7.5
Running off either end of an array when using pointer arithmetic.

7.8.5 Incrementing and Decrementing a Pointer

If a pointer is being incremented or decremented by one, the increment (++) and decrement (--) operators can be used. Either of the statements

```
++vPtr;
vPtr++;
```

increments the pointer to point to the *next* location in the array. Either of the statements

```
--vPtr;
vPtr--;
```

decrements the pointer to point to the *previous* element of the array.

7.8.6 Subtracting One Pointer from Another

Pointer variables may be subtracted from one another. For example, if vPtr contains the location 3000, and v2Ptr contains the address 3008, the statement

```
x = v2Ptr - vPtr;
```

would assign to x the *number of array elements* from vPtr to v2Ptr, in this case 2 (not 8). Pointer arithmetic is undefined unless performed on an array. We cannot assume that two variables of the same type are stored contiguously in memory unless they're adjacent elements of an array.

Common Programming Error 7.6
Subtracting two pointers that do not refer to elements in the same *array.*

7.8.7 Assigning Pointers to One Another

A pointer can be assigned to another pointer if both have the *same* type. The exception to this rule is the **pointer to void** (i.e., **void ***), which is a generic pointer that can represent *any* pointer type. All pointer types can be assigned a pointer to void, and a pointer to void can be assigned a pointer of any type (including another pointer to void). In both cases, a cast operation is *not* required.

7.8.8 Pointer to void

A pointer to void *cannot* be dereferenced. Consider this: The compiler knows that a pointer to int refers to 4 bytes of memory on a machine with 4-byte integers, but a pointer to void simply contains a memory location for an *unknown* data type—the precise number of bytes to which the pointer refers is *not* known by the compiler. The compiler *must* know the data type to determine the number of bytes that represent the referenced value.

Common Programming Error 7.7
Assigning a pointer of one type to a pointer of another type if neither is of type void * is a syntax error.

Common Programming Error 7.8
Dereferencing a void * pointer is a syntax error.

7.8.9 Comparing Pointers

Pointers can be compared using equality and relational operators, but such comparisons are meaningless unless the pointers point to elements of the *same* array. Pointer comparisons compare the addresses stored in the pointers. A comparison of two pointers pointing to elements in the same array could show, for example, that one pointer points to a higher-numbered element of the array than the other pointer does. A common use of pointer comparison is determining whether a pointer is NULL.

 Common Programming Error 7.9
Comparing two pointers that do not refer to elements in the same *array.*

7.9 Relationship between Pointers and Arrays

Arrays and pointers are intimately related in C and often may be used interchangeably. An *array name* can be thought of as a *constant pointer*. Pointers can be used to do any operation involving array indexing.

Assume the following definitions:

```
int b[5];
int *bPtr;
```

Because the array name b (without an index) is a pointer to the array's first element, we can set bPtr equal to the address of the array b's first element with the statement

```
bPtr = b;
```

This statement is equivalent to taking the address of array b's first element as follows:

```
bPtr = &b[0];
```

7.9.1 Pointer/Offset Notation

Array element b[3] can alternatively be referenced with the pointer expression

```
*(bPtr + 3)
```

The 3 in the expression is the **offset** to the pointer. When bPtr points to the array's first element, the offset indicates which array element to reference, and the offset value is identical to the array index. This notation is referred to as **pointer/offset notation**. The parentheses are necessary because the precedence of * is *higher* than the precedence of +. Without the parentheses, the above expression would add 3 to the value of the expression *bPtr (i.e., 3 would be added to b[0], assuming bPtr points to the beginning of the array). Just as the array element can be referenced with a pointer expression, the address

```
&b[3]
```

can be written with the pointer expression

```
bPtr + 3
```

The array itself can be treated as a pointer and used in pointer arithmetic. For example, the expression

```
*(b + 3)
```

also refers to the array element b[3]. In general, all indexed array expressions can be written with a pointer and an offset. In this case, pointer/offset notation was used with the name of the array as a pointer. The preceding statement does not modify the array name in any way; b still points to the first element in the array.

7.9.2 Pointer/Index Notation

Pointers can be indexed like arrays. If bPtr has the value b, the expression

```
bPtr[1]
```

refers to the array element b[1]. This is referred to as **pointer/index notation**.

7.9.3 Cannot Modify an Array Name with Pointer Arithmetic

Remember that an array name always points to the beginning of the array—so the array name is like a constant pointer. Thus, the expression

```
b += 3
```

is *invalid* because it attempts to modify the array name's value with pointer arithmetic.

 Common Programming Error 7.10
Attempting to modify the value of an array name with pointer arithmetic is a compilation error.

7.9.4 Demonstrating Pointer Indexing and Offsets

Figure 7.20 uses the four methods we've discussed for referring to array elements—array indexing, pointer/offset with the array name as a pointer, **pointer indexing**, and pointer/offset with a pointer—to print the four elements of the integer array b.

```c
1   // Fig. 7.20: fig07_20.cpp
2   // Using indexing and pointer notations with arrays.
3   #include <stdio.h>
4   #define ARRAY_SIZE 4
5
6   int main(void)
7   {
8      int b[] = {10, 20, 30, 40}; // create and initialize array b
9      int *bPtr = b; // create bPtr and point it to array b
10
11     // output array b using array index notation
12     puts("Array b printed with:\nArray index notation");
13
14     // loop through array b
15     for (size_t i = 0; i < ARRAY_SIZE; ++i) {
16        printf("b[%u] = %d\n", i, b[i]);
17     }
18
19     // output array b using array name and pointer/offset notation
20     puts("\nPointer/offset notation where\n"
21          "the pointer is the array name");
22
23     // loop through array b
24     for (size_t offset = 0; offset < ARRAY_SIZE; ++offset) {
25        printf("*(b + %u) = %d\n", offset, *(b + offset));
26     }
```

Fig. 7.20 | Using indexing and pointer notations with arrays. (Part 1 of 2.)

```
27
28      // output array b using bPtr and array index notation
29      puts("\nPointer index notation");
30
31      // loop through array b
32      for (size_t i = 0; i < ARRAY_SIZE; ++i) {
33         printf("bPtr[%u] = %d\n", i, bPtr[i]);
34      }
35
36      // output array b using bPtr and pointer/offset notation
37      puts("\nPointer/offset notation");
38
39      // loop through array b
40      for (size_t offset = 0; offset < ARRAY_SIZE; ++offset) {
41         printf("*(bPtr + %u) = %d\n", offset, *(bPtr + offset));
42      }
43   }
```

```
Array b printed with:
Array index notation
b[0] = 10
b[1] = 20
b[2] = 30
b[3] = 40

Pointer/offset notation where
the pointer is the array name
*(b + 0) = 10
*(b + 1) = 20
*(b + 2) = 30
*(b + 3) = 40

Pointer index notation
bPtr[0] = 10
bPtr[1] = 20
bPtr[2] = 30
bPtr[3] = 40

Pointer/offset notation
*(bPtr + 0) = 10
*(bPtr + 1) = 20
*(bPtr + 2) = 30
*(bPtr + 3) = 40
```

Fig. 7.20 | Using indexing and pointer notations with arrays. (Part 2 of 2.)

7.9.5 String Copying with Arrays and Pointers

To further illustrate the interchangeability of arrays and pointers, let's look at the two string-copying functions—copy1 and copy2—in the program of Fig. 7.21. Both functions copy a string into a character array. After a comparison of the function prototypes for copy1 and copy2, the functions appear identical. They accomplish the same task, but they're implemented differently.

```
 1    // Fig. 7.21: fig07_21.c
 2    // Copying a string using array notation and pointer notation.
 3    #include <stdio.h>
 4    #define SIZE 10
 5
 6    void copy1(char * const s1, const char * const s2); // prototype
 7    void copy2(char *s1, const char *s2); // prototype
 8
 9    int main(void)
10    {
11        char string1[SIZE]; // create array string1
12        char *string2 = "Hello"; // create a pointer to a string
13
14        copy1(string1, string2);
15        printf("string1 = %s\n", string1);
16
17        char string3[SIZE]; // create array string3
18        char string4[] = "Good Bye"; // create an array containing a string
19
20        copy2(string3, string4);
21        printf("string3 = %s\n", string3);
22    }
23
24    // copy s2 to s1 using array notation
25    void copy1(char * const s1, const char * const s2)
26    {
27        // loop through strings
28        for (size_t i = 0; (s1[i] = s2[i]) != '\0'; ++i) {
29            ; // do nothing in body
30        }
31    }
32
33    // copy s2 to s1 using pointer notation
34    void copy2(char *s1, const char *s2)
35    {
36        // loop through strings
37        for (; (*s1 = *s2) != '\0'; ++s1, ++s2) {
38            ; // do nothing in body
39        }
40    }
```

```
string1 = Hello
string3 = Good Bye
```

Fig. 7.21 | Copying a string using array notation and pointer notation.

Copying with Array Index Notation

Function copy1 uses *array index notation* to copy the string in s2 to the character array s1. The function defines counter variable i as the array index. The for statement header (line 28) performs the entire copy operation—its body is the empty statement. The header specifies that i is initialized to zero and incremented by one on each iteration of the loop. The expression s1[i] = s2[i] copies one character from s2 to s1. When the null character is encountered in s2, it's assigned to s1, and the value of the assignment becomes the value assigned to the left operand (s1). The loop terminates when the null character is assigned from s2 to s1 (false).

Copying with Pointers and Pointer Arithmetic

Function copy2 uses *pointers and pointer arithmetic* to copy the string in s2 to the character array s1. Again, the for statement header (line 37) performs the entire copy operation. The header does not include any variable initialization. As in function copy1, the expression (*s1 = *s2) performs the copy operation. Pointer s2 is dereferenced, and the resulting character is assigned to the dereferenced pointer *s1. After the assignment in the condition, the pointers are incremented to point to the next character in the array s1 and the next character in the string s2, respectively. When the null character is encountered in s2, it's assigned to the dereferenced pointer s1 and the loop terminates.

Notes Regarding Functions copy1 and copy2

The first argument to both copy1 and copy2 must be an array large enough to hold the string in the second argument. Otherwise, an error may occur when an attempt is made to write into a memory location that's not part of the array. Also, the second parameter of each function is declared as const char * const (a constant string). In both functions, the second argument is copied into the first argument—characters are read from it one at a time, but the characters are *never modified*. Therefore, the second parameter is declared to point to a constant value so that the *principle of least privilege* is enforced—neither function requires the capability of modifying the string in the second argument.

7.10 Arrays of Pointers

Arrays may contain pointers. A common use of an **array of pointers** is to form an **array of strings**, referred to simply as a **string array**. Each entry in the array is a string, but in C a string is essentially a pointer to its first character. So each entry in an array of strings is actually a pointer to the first character of a string. Consider the definition of string array suit, which might be useful in representing a deck of cards.

```
const char *suit[4] = {"Hearts", "Diamonds", "Clubs", "Spades"};
```

The suit[4] portion of the definition indicates an array of 4 elements. The char * portion of the declaration indicates that each element of array suit is of type "pointer to char." Qualifier const indicates that the strings pointed to by each element will not be modified. The four values to be placed in the array are "Hearts", "Diamonds", "Clubs" and "Spades". Each is stored in memory as a *null-terminated character string* that's one character longer than the number of characters between the quotes. The four strings are 7, 9, 6 and 7 characters long, respectively. Although it appears these strings are being placed in the suit array, only pointers are actually stored in the array (Fig. 7.22). Each pointer points to the first character of its corresponding string. Thus, even though the suit array is *fixed* in size, it provides access to character strings of *any length*. This flexibility is one example of C's powerful data-structuring capabilities.

The suits could have been placed in a two-dimensional array, in which each row would represent a suit and each column would represent a letter from a suit name. Such a data structure would have to have a fixed number of columns per row, and that number

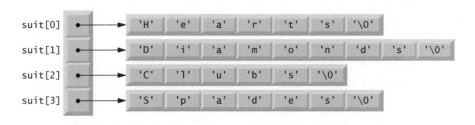

Fig. 7.22 | Graphical representation of the suit array.

would have to be as large as the largest string. Therefore, considerable memory could be wasted when storing a large number of strings of which most were shorter than the longest string. We use string arrays to represent a deck of cards in the next section.

7.11 Case Study: Card Shuffling and Dealing Simulation

In this section, we use random number generation to develop a card shuffling and dealing simulation program. This program can then be used to implement programs that play specific card games. To reveal some subtle performance problems, we've intentionally used suboptimal shuffling and dealing algorithms. In this chapter's exercises and in Chapter 10, we develop more efficient algorithms.

Using the top-down, stepwise refinement approach, we develop a program that will shuffle a deck of 52 playing cards and then deal each of the 52 cards. The top-down approach is particularly useful in attacking larger, more complex problems than you've seen in earlier chapters.

Representing a Deck of Cards as a Two-Dimensional Array
We use 4-by-13 two-dimensional array deck to represent the deck of playing cards (Fig. 7.23). The rows correspond to the *suits*—row 0 corresponds to hearts, row 1 to diamonds, row 2 to clubs and row 3 to spades. The columns correspond to the *face* values of the cards—columns 0 through 9 correspond to ace through ten respectively, and columns 10 through 12 correspond to jack, queen and king. We shall load string array suit with character strings representing the four suits, and string array face with character strings representing the thirteen face values.

Shuffling the Two-Dimensional Array
This simulated deck of cards may be *shuffled* as follows. First the array deck is cleared to zeros. Then, a row (0–3) and a column (0–12) are each chosen *at random*. The number 1 is inserted in array element deck[row][column] to indicate that this card will be the first one dealt from the shuffled deck. This process continues with the numbers 2, 3, ..., 52 being randomly inserted in the deck array to indicate which cards are to be placed second, third, ..., and fifty-second in the shuffled deck. As the deck array begins to fill with card numbers, it's possible that a card will be selected again—i.e., deck[row][column] will be nonzero when it's selected. This selection is simply ignored and other rows and columns are repeatedly chosen at random until an *unselected* card is found. Eventually, the numbers 1 through 52 will occupy the 52 slots of the deck array. At this point, the deck of cards is fully shuffled.

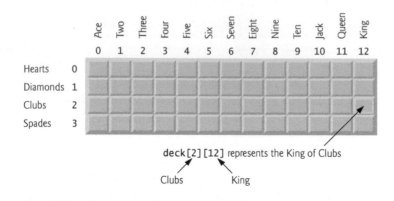

Fig. 7.23 | Two-dimensional array representation of a deck of cards.

Possibility of Indefinite Postponement

This shuffling algorithm can execute *indefinitely* if cards that have already been shuffled are repeatedly selected at random. This phenomenon is known as **indefinite postponement**. In this chapter's exercises, we discuss a better shuffling algorithm that eliminates the possibility of indefinite postponement.

Performance Tip 7.3

Sometimes an algorithm that emerges in a "natural" way can contain subtle performance problems, such as indefinite postponement. Seek algorithms that avoid indefinite postponement.

Dealing Cards from the Two-Dimensional Array

To deal the first card, we search the array for deck[row][column] equal to 1. This is accomplished with nested for statements that vary row from 0 to 3 and column from 0 to 12. What card does that element of the array correspond to? The suit array has been preloaded with the four suits, so to get the suit, we print the character string suit[row]. Similarly, to get the face value of the card, we print the character string face[column]. We also print the character string " of ". Printing this information in the proper order enables us to print each card in the form "King of Clubs", "Ace of Diamonds" and so on.

Developing the Program's Logic with Top-Down, Stepwise Refinement

Let's proceed with the top-down, stepwise refinement process. The *top* is simply

> *Shuffle and deal 52 cards*

Our *first refinement* yields:

> *Initialize the suit array*
> *Initialize the face array*
> *Initialize the deck array*
> *Shuffle the deck*
> *Deal 52 cards*

"Shuffle the deck" may be expanded as follows:

> *For each of the 52 cards*
> > *Place card number in randomly selected unoccupied element of deck*

"Deal 52 cards" may be expanded as follows:

> *For each of the 52 cards*
> > *Find card number in deck array and print face and suit of card*

Incorporating these expansions yields our complete *second refinement*:

> *Initialize the suit array*
> *Initialize the face array*
> *Initialize the deck array*
>
> *For each of the 52 cards*
> > *Place card number in randomly selected unoccupied slot of deck*
>
> *For each of the 52 cards*
> > *Find card number in deck array and print face and suit of card*

"Place card number in randomly selected unoccupied slot of deck" may be expanded as:

> *Choose slot of deck randomly*
>
> *While chosen slot of deck has been previously chosen*
> > *Choose slot of deck randomly*
>
> *Place card number in chosen slot of deck*

"Find card number in deck array and print face and suit of card" may be expanded as:

> *For each slot of the deck array*
> > *If slot contains card number*
> > > *Print the face and suit of the card*

Incorporating these expansions yields our *third refinement*:

> *Initialize the suit array*
> *Initialize the face array*
> *Initialize the deck array*
>
> *For each of the 52 cards*
> > *Choose slot of deck randomly*
> >
> > *While slot of deck has been previously chosen*
> > > *Choose slot of deck randomly*
> >
> > *Place card number in chosen slot of deck*
>
> *For each of the 52 cards*
> > *For each slot of deck array*
> > > *If slot contains desired card number*
> > > > *Print the face and suit of the card*

This completes the refinement process. This program is more efficient if the shuffle and deal portions of the algorithm are combined so that each card is dealt as it's placed in the deck. We've chosen to program these operations separately because normally cards are dealt after they're shuffled (not while they're being shuffled).

Implementing the Card Shuffling and Dealing Program

The card shuffling and dealing program is shown in Fig. 7.24, and a sample execution is shown in Fig. 7.25. Conversion specifier %s is used to print strings of characters in the calls to printf. The corresponding argument in the printf call must be a pointer to char (or a char array). The format specification "%5s of %-8s" (line 68) prints a character string *right justified* in a field of five characters followed by " of " and a character string *left justified* in a field of eight characters. The *minus sign* in %-8s signifies left justification.

There's a weakness in the dealing algorithm. Once a match is found, the two inner for statements continue searching the remaining elements of deck for a match. We correct this deficiency in this chapter's exercises and in a Chapter 10 case study.

```
1   // Fig. 7.24: fig07_24.c
2   // Card shuffling and dealing.
3   #include <stdio.h>
4   #include <stdlib.h>
5   #include <time.h>
6
7   #define SUITS 4
8   #define FACES 13
9   #define CARDS 52
10
11  // prototypes
12  void shuffle(unsigned int wDeck[][FACES]); // shuffling modifies wDeck
13  void deal(unsigned int wDeck[][FACES], const char *wFace[],
14     const char *wSuit[]); // dealing doesn't modify the arrays
15
16  int main(void)
17  {
18     // initialize deck array
19     unsigned int deck[SUITS][FACES] = {0};
20
21     srand(time(NULL)); // seed random-number generator
22     shuffle(deck); // shuffle the deck
23
24     // initialize suit array
25     const char *suit[SUITS] =
26        {"Hearts", "Diamonds", "Clubs", "Spades"};
27
28     // initialize face array
29     const char *face[FACES] =
30        {"Ace", "Deuce", "Three", "Four",
31         "Five", "Six", "Seven", "Eight",
32         "Nine", "Ten", "Jack", "Queen", "King"};
33
34     deal(deck, face, suit); // deal the deck
35  }
36
```

Fig. 7.24 | Card shuffling and dealing. (Part 1 of 2.)

```
37   // shuffle cards in deck
38   void shuffle(unsigned int wDeck[][FACES])
39   {
40      // for each of the cards, choose slot of deck randomly
41      for (size_t card = 1; card <= CARDS; ++card) {
42         size_t row; // row number
43         size_t column; // column number
44
45         // choose new random location until unoccupied slot found
46         do {
47            row = rand() % SUITS;
48            column = rand() % FACES;
49         } while(wDeck[row][column] != 0);
50
51         // place card number in chosen slot of deck
52         wDeck[row][column] = card;
53      }
54   }
55
56   // deal cards in deck
57   void deal(unsigned int wDeck[][FACES], const char *wFace[],
58      const char *wSuit[])
59   {
60      // deal each of the cards
61      for (size_t card = 1; card <= CARDS; ++card) {
62         // loop through rows of wDeck
63         for (size_t row = 0; row < SUITS; ++row) {
64            // loop through columns of wDeck for current row
65            for (size_t column = 0; column < FACES; ++column) {
66               // if slot contains current card, display card
67               if (wDeck[row][column] == card) {
68                  printf("%5s of %-8s%c", wFace[column], wSuit[row],
69                     card % 2 == 0 ? '\n' : '\t'); // 2-column format
70               }
71            }
72         }
73      }
74   }
```

Fig. 7.24 | Card shuffling and dealing. (Part 2 of 2.)

```
 Nine of Hearts        Five of Clubs
Queen of Spades       Three of Spades
Queen of Hearts         Ace of Clubs
 King of Hearts         Six of Spades
 Jack of Diamonds      Five of Spades
Seven of Hearts       King of Clubs
Three of Clubs        Eight of Hearts
Three of Diamonds      Four of Diamonds
Queen of Diamonds     Five of Diamonds
```

Fig. 7.25 | Sample run of card dealing program. (Part 1 of 2.)

```
Six of Diamonds       Five of Hearts
   Ace of Spades         Six of Hearts
  Nine of Diamonds     Queen of Clubs
 Eight of Spades        Nine of Clubs
 Deuce of Clubs          Six of Clubs
 Deuce of Spades        Jack of Clubs
  Four of Clubs        Eight of Clubs
  Four of Spades       Seven of Spades
 Seven of Diamonds     Seven of Clubs
  King of Spades         Ten of Diamonds
  Jack of Hearts         Ace of Hearts
  Jack of Spades         Ten of Clubs
 Eight of Diamonds     Deuce of Diamonds
   Ace of Diamonds      Nine of Spades
  Four of Hearts       Deuce of Hearts
  King of Diamonds       Ten of Spades
 Three of Hearts         Ten of Hearts
```

Fig. 7.25 | Sample run of card dealing program. (Part 2 of 2.)

7.12 Pointers to Functions

A **pointer to a function** contains the *address* of the function in memory. In Chapter 6, we saw that an array name is really the address in memory of the first element of the array. Similarly, a function name is really the starting address in memory of the code that performs the function's task. Pointers to functions can be *passed* to functions, *returned* from functions, *stored* in arrays and *assigned* to other function pointers.

7.12.1 Sorting in Ascending or Descending Order

To illustrate the use of pointers to functions, Fig. 7.26 presents a modified version of the bubble sort program in Fig. 7.15. The new version consists of main and functions bubble, swap, ascending and descending. Function bubbleSort receives a pointer to a function—either function ascending or function descending—as an *argument*, in addition to an integer array and the size of the array. The program prompts the user to choose whether the array should be sorted in *ascending* or in *descending* order. If the user enters 1, a pointer to function ascending is passed to function bubble, causing the array to be sorted into *increasing* order. If the user enters 2, a pointer to function descending is passed to function bubble, causing the array to be sorted into *decreasing* order. The output of the program is shown in Fig. 7.27.

```
1   // Fig. 7.26: fig07_26.c
2   // Multipurpose sorting program using function pointers.
3   #include <stdio.h>
4   #define SIZE 10
5
```

Fig. 7.26 | Multipurpose sorting program using function pointers. (Part 1 of 3.)

```
 6    // prototypes
 7    void bubble(int work[], size_t size, int (*compare)(int a, int b) );
 8    int ascending(int a, int b);
 9    int descending(int a, int b);
10
11    int main(void)
12    {
13        // initialize unordered array a
14        int a[SIZE] = { 2, 6, 4, 8, 10, 12, 89, 68, 45, 37 };
15
16        printf("%s", "Enter 1 to sort in ascending order,\n"
17               "Enter 2 to sort in descending order: ");
18        int order; // 1 for ascending order or 2 for descending order
19        scanf("%d", &order);
20
21        puts("\nData items in original order");
22
23        // output original array
24        for (size_t counter = 0; counter < SIZE; ++counter) {
25            printf("%5d", a[counter]);
26        }
27
28        // sort array in ascending order; pass function ascending as an
29        // argument to specify ascending sorting order
30        if (order == 1) {
31            bubble(a, SIZE, ascending);
32            puts("\nData items in ascending order");
33        }
34        else { // pass function descending
35            bubble(a, SIZE, descending);
36            puts("\nData items in descending order");
37        }
38
39        // output sorted array
40        for (size_t counter = 0; counter < SIZE; ++counter) {
41            printf("%5d", a[counter]);
42        }
43
44        puts("\n");
45    }
46
47    // multipurpose bubble sort; parameter compare is a pointer to
48    // the comparison function that determines sorting order
49    void bubble(int work[], size_t size, int (*compare)(int a, int b))
50    {
51        void swap(int *element1Ptr, int *element2ptr); // prototype
52
53        // loop to control passes
54        for (unsigned int pass = 1; pass < size; ++pass) {
55
56            // loop to control number of comparisons per pass
57            for (size_t count = 0; count < size - 1; ++count) {
58
```

Fig. 7.26 | Multipurpose sorting program using function pointers. (Part 2 of 3.)

```
59              // if adjacent elements are out of order, swap them
60              if ((*compare)(work[count], work[count + 1])) {
61                  swap(&work[count], &work[count + 1]);
62              }
63          }
64      }
65  }
66
67  // swap values at memory locations to which element1Ptr and
68  // element2Ptr point
69  void swap(int *element1Ptr, int *element2Ptr)
70  {
71      int hold = *element1Ptr;
72      *element1Ptr = *element2Ptr;
73      *element2Ptr = hold;
74  }
75
76  // determine whether elements are out of order for an ascending
77  // order sort
78  int ascending(int a, int b)
79  {
80      return b < a; // should swap if b is less than a
81  }
82
83  // determine whether elements are out of order for a descending
84  // order sort
85  int descending(int a, int b)
86  {
87      return b > a; // should swap if b is greater than a
88  }
```

Fig. 7.26 | Multipurpose sorting program using function pointers. (Part 3 of 3.)

```
Enter 1 to sort in ascending order,
Enter 2 to sort in descending order: 1

Data items in original order
    2    6    4    8   10   12   89   68   45   37
Data items in ascending order
    2    4    6    8   10   12   37   45   68   89
```

```
Enter 1 to sort in ascending order,
Enter 2 to sort in descending order: 2

Data items in original order
    2    6    4    8   10   12   89   68   45   37
Data items in descending order
   89   68   45   37   12   10    8    6    4    2
```

Fig. 7.27 | The outputs of the bubble sort program in Fig. 7.26.

The following parameter appears in the function header for `bubble` (line 49)

```
int (*compare)(int a, int b)
```

This tells `bubble` to expect a parameter (`compare`) that's a pointer to a function that receives two integer parameters and returns an integer result. Parentheses are needed around `*compare` to group the `*` with `compare` to indicate that `compare` is a *pointer*. If we had not included the parentheses, the declaration would have been

```
int *compare(int a, int b)
```

which declares a function that receives two integers as parameters and returns a pointer to an integer.

The function prototype for `bubble` is shown in line 7. The third parameter in the prototype could have been written as

```
int (*)(int, int);
```

without the function-pointer name and parameter names.

The function passed to `bubble` is called in an `if` statement (line 60) as follows:

```
if ((*compare)(work[count], work[count + 1]))
```

Just as a pointer to a variable is dereferenced to access the value of the variable, *a pointer to a function is dereferenced to use the function.*

The call to the function could have been made without dereferencing the pointer as in

```
if (compare(work[count], work[count + 1]))
```

which uses the pointer directly as the function name. We prefer the first method of calling a function through a pointer because it explicitly illustrates that `compare` is a pointer to a function that's dereferenced to call the function. The second method of calling a function through a pointer makes it appear as if `compare` is an *actual* function. This may be confusing to a programmer reading the code who would like to see the definition of function `compare` and finds that it's *never defined* in the file.

7.12.2 Using Function Pointers to Create a Menu-Driven System

A common use of **function pointers** is in text-based *menu-driven systems*. A user is prompted to select an option from a menu (possibly from 1 to 5) by typing the menu item's number. Each option is serviced by a different function. Pointers to each function are stored in an array of pointers to functions. The user's choice is used as a index in the array, and the pointer in the array is used to call the function.

Figure 7.28 provides a generic example of the mechanics of defining and using an array of pointers to functions. We define three functions—`function1`, `function2` and `function3`—that each take an integer argument and return nothing. We store pointers to these three functions in array `f`, which is defined in line 14. The definition is read beginning at the leftmost set of parentheses, "`f` is an array of 3 pointers to functions that each take an `int` as an argument and return `void`." The array is initialized with the names of the three functions. When the user enters a value between 0 and 2, the value is used as the index into the array of pointers to functions. In the function call (line 25), `f[choice]` selects the pointer at location `choice` in the array. The *pointer is dereferenced to call the func-*

tion, and choice is passed as the argument to the function. Each function prints its argument's value and its function name to demonstrate that the function is called correctly. In this chapter's exercises, you'll develop several text-based, menu-driven systems.

```c
 1   // Fig. 7.28: fig07_28.c
 2   // Demonstrating an array of pointers to functions.
 3   #include <stdio.h>
 4
 5   // prototypes
 6   void function1(int a);
 7   void function2(int b);
 8   void function3(int c);
 9
10   int main(void)
11   {
12      // initialize array of 3 pointers to functions that each take an
13      // int argument and return void
14      void (*f[3])(int) = { function1, function2, function3 };
15
16      printf("%s", "Enter a number between 0 and 2, 3 to end: ");
17      size_t choice; // variable to hold user's choice
18      scanf("%u", &choice);
19
20      // process user's choice
21      while (choice >= 0 && choice < 3) {
22
23         // invoke function at location choice in array f and pass
24         // choice as an argument
25         (*f[choice])(choice);
26
27         printf("%s", "Enter a number between 0 and 2, 3 to end: ");
28         scanf("%u", &choice);
29      }
30
31      puts("Program execution completed.");
32   }
33
34   void function1(int a)
35   {
36      printf("You entered %d so function1 was called\n\n", a);
37   }
38
39   void function2(int b)
40   {
41      printf("You entered %d so function2 was called\n\n", b);
42   }
43
44   void function3(int c)
45   {
46      printf("You entered %d so function3 was called\n\n", c);
47   }
```

Fig. 7.28 | Demonstrating an array of pointers to functions. (Part 1 of 2.)

```
Enter a number between 0 and 2, 3 to end: 0
You entered 0 so function1 was called

Enter a number between 0 and 2, 3 to end: 1
You entered 1 so function2 was called

Enter a number between 0 and 2, 3 to end: 2
You entered 2 so function3 was called

Enter a number between 0 and 2, 3 to end: 3
Program execution completed.
```

Fig. 7.28 | Demonstrating an array of pointers to functions. (Part 2 of 2.)

7.13 Secure C Programming

printf_s, scanf_s and Other Secure Functions

Earlier Secure C Programming sections presented printf_s and scanf_s, and mentioned other more secure versions of standard library functions that are described by Annex K of the C standard. A key feature of functions like printf_s and scanf_s that makes them more secure is that they have *runtime constraints* requiring their pointer arguments to be non-NULL. The functions check these runtime constraints *before* attempting to use the pointers. Any NULL pointer argument is considered to be a *constraint violation* and causes the function to fail and return a status notification. In a scanf_s, if any of the pointer arguments (including the format-control string) are NULL, the function returns EOF. In a printf_s, if the format-control string or any argument that corresponds to a %s is NULL, the function stops outputting data and returns a negative number. For complete details of the Annex K functions, see the C standard document or your compiler's library documentation.

Other CERT Guidelines Regarding Pointers

Misused pointers lead to many of the most common security vulnerabilities in systems today. CERT provides various guidelines to help you prevent such problems. If you're building industrial-strength C systems, you should familiarize yourself with the *CERT C Secure Coding Standard* at www.securecoding.cert.org. The following guidelines apply to pointer programming techniques that we presented in this chapter:

- EXP34-C: Dereferencing NULL pointers typically causes programs to crash, but CERT has encountered cases in which dereferencing NULL pointers can allow attackers to execute code.

- DCL13-C: Section 7.5 discussed uses of const with pointers. If a function parameter points to a value that will not be changed by the function, const should be used to indicate that the data is constant. For example, to represent a pointer to a string that will not be modified, use const char * as the pointer parameter's type, as in line 21 of Fig. 7.11.

- MSC16-C: This guideline discusses techniques for encrypting function pointers to help prevent attackers from overwriting them and executing attack code.

Summary

Section 7.2 Pointer Variable Definitions and Initialization

- A **pointer** (p. 275) contains an address of another variable that contains a value. In this sense, a variable name *directly* references a value, and a pointer *indirectly* references a value.

- Referencing a value through a pointer is called **indirection** (p. 276).

- Pointers can be defined to point to objects of any type.

- Pointers should be initialized either when they're defined or in an assignment statement. A pointer may be initialized to NULL, **0** or **an address**. A pointer with the value NULL points to nothing. Initializing a pointer to 0 is equivalent to initializing a pointer to NULL, but NULL is preferred for clarity. The value 0 is the only integer value that can be assigned directly to a pointer variable.

- NULL is a symbolic constant defined in the <stddef.h> header (and several other headers).

Section 7.3 Pointer Operators

- The **&**, or **address operator** (p. 277), is a unary operator that returns the address of its operand.

- The operand of the address operator must be a variable.

- The **indirection operator** * (p. 277) returns the value of the object to which its operand points.

- The printf **conversion specifier %p** outputs a memory location as a hexadecimal integer on most platforms.

Section 7.4 Passing Arguments to Functions by Reference

- All arguments in C are **passed by value** (p. 279).

- C programs accomplish **pass-by-reference** (p. 279) by using pointers and the indirection operator. To pass a variable by reference, apply the address operator (**&**) to the variable's name.

- When the address of a variable is passed to a function, the indirection operator (*) may be used in the function to read and/or modify the value at that location in the caller's memory.

- A function receiving an address as an argument must define a **pointer parameter** to receive the address.

- The compiler does not differentiate between a function that receives a pointer and one that receives a **one-dimensional array**. A function must "know" when it's receiving an array vs. a single variable passed by reference.

- When the compiler encounters a function parameter for a one-dimensional array of the form int b[], the compiler converts the parameter to the pointer notation int *b.

Section 7.5 Using the **const** Qualifier with Pointers

- The **const qualifier** (p. 283) indicates that the value of a particular variable should not be modified.

- If an attempt is made to modify a value that's declared const, the compiler catches it and issues either a warning or an error, depending on the particular compiler.

- There are four ways to pass a pointer to a function (p. 284): a **non-constant pointer to non-constant data**, a **constant pointer to non-constant data**, a **non-constant pointer to constant data**, and a **constant pointer to constant data**.

- With a non-constant pointer to non-constant data, the data can be modified through the dereferenced pointer, and the pointer can be modified to point to other data items.

- A non-constant pointer to constant data can be modified to point to any data item of the appropriate type, but the data to which it points cannot be modified.

- A constant pointer to non-constant data always points to the same memory location, and the data at that location can be modified through the pointer. This is the default for an array name.

- A constant pointer to constant data always points to the same memory location, and the data at that memory location cannot be modified.

Section 7.7 sizeof Operator
- Unary **operator** sizeof (p. 292) determine the size in bytes of a variable or type at compilation time.
- When applied to the name of an array, sizeof returns the total number of bytes in the array.
- Operator sizeof can be applied to any variable name, type or value.
- The parentheses used with sizeof are required if a type name is supplied as its operand.

Section 7.8 Pointer Expressions and Pointer Arithmetic
- A limited set of **arithmetic operations** (p. 296) **may be performed on pointers.** A pointer may be **incremented** (++) or **decremented** (--), an integer may be **added** to a pointer (+ or +=), an integer may be **subtracted** from a pointer (- or -=) and **one pointer may be subtracted from another.**
- When an integer is added to or subtracted from a pointer, the pointer is incremented or decremented by that integer times the size of the object to which the pointer refers.
- Two pointers to elements of the same array may be subtracted from one another to determine the number of elements between them.
- A pointer can be assigned to another pointer if both have the same type. An exception is the pointer of type void * (p. 297) which can represent any pointer type. All pointer types can be assigned a void * pointer, and a void * pointer can be assigned a pointer of any type.
- A void * pointer cannot be dereferenced.
- **Pointers can be compared** using equality and relational operators, but such comparisons are meaningless unless the pointers point to elements of the same array. Pointer comparisons compare the addresses stored in the pointers.
- A common use of pointer comparison is **determining whether a pointer is NULL.**

Section 7.9 Relationship between Pointers and Arrays
- Arrays and pointers are intimately related in C and often may be used interchangeably.
- An **array name** can be thought of as a **constant pointer.**
- Pointers can be used to do any operation involving array indexing.
- When a pointer points to the beginning of an array, adding an **offset** (p. 298) to the pointer indicates which element of the array should be referenced, and the offset value is identical to the array index. This is referred to as pointer/offset notation.
- An **array name can be treated as a pointer** and used in pointer arithmetic expressions that do not attempt to modify the address of the pointer.
- **Pointers can be indexed** (p. 299) exactly as arrays can. This is referred to as pointer/index notation.
- A parameter of type const char * typically represents a constant string.

Section 7.10 Arrays of Pointers
- **Arrays may contain pointers** (p. 302). A common use of an array of pointers is to form an **array of strings** (p. 302). Each entry in the array is a string, but in C a string is essentially a pointer to its first character. So, each entry in an array of strings is actually a pointer to the first character of a string.

Section 7.12 Pointers to Functions
- A **function pointer** (p. 311) contains the address of the function in memory. A function name is really the starting address in memory of the code that performs the function's task.
- Pointers to functions can be **passed to functions, returned from functions, stored in arrays** and **assigned to other function pointers.**
- A pointer to a function is dereferenced to call the function. A function pointer can be used directly as the function name when calling the function.
- A common use of function pointers is in text-based, **menu-driven systems.**

Self-Review Exercises

7.1   Answer each of the following:
   a) A pointer variable contains as its value the _____ of another variable.
   b) The three values that can be used to initialize a pointer are _____, _____ and _____.
   c) The only integer that can be assigned to a pointer is _____.

7.2   State whether the following are *true* or *false*. If the answer is *false*, explain why.
   a) A pointer that's declared to be void can be dereferenced.
   b) Pointers of different types may not be assigned to one another without a cast operation.

7.3   Answer each of the following. Assume that single-precision floating-point numbers are stored in 4 bytes, and that the starting address of the array is at location 1002500 in memory. Each part of the exercise should use the results of previous parts where appropriate.
   a) Define an array of type float called numbers with 10 elements, and initialize the elements to the values 0.0, 1.1, 2.2, ..., 9.9. Assume the symbolic constant SIZE has been defined as 10.
   b) Define a pointer, nPtr, that points to an object of type float.
   c) Print the elements of array numbers using array index notation. Use a for statement. Print each number with 1 position of precision to the right of the decimal point.
   d) Give two separate statements that assign the starting address of array numbers to the pointer variable nPtr.
   e) Print the elements of array numbers using pointer/offset notation with the pointer nPtr.
   f) Print the elements of array numbers using pointer/offset notation with the array name as the pointer.
   g) Print the elements of array numbers by indexing pointer nPtr.
   h) Refer to element 4 of array numbers using array index notation, pointer/offset notation with the array name as the pointer, pointer index notation with nPtr and pointer/offset notation with nPtr.
   i) Assuming that nPtr points to the beginning of array numbers, what address is referenced by nPtr + 8? What value is stored at that location?
   j) Assuming that nPtr points to numbers[5], what address is referenced by nPtr -= 4? What's the value stored at that location?

7.4   For each of the following, write a statement that performs the indicated task. Assume that floating-point variables number1 and number2 are defined and that number1 is initialized to 7.3.
   a) Define the variable fPtr to be a pointer to an object of type float.
   b) Assign the address of variable number1 to pointer variable fPtr.
   c) Print the value of the object pointed to by fPtr.
   d) Assign the value of the object pointed to by fPtr to variable number2.
   e) Print the value of number2.

  f) Print the address of number1. Use the %p conversion specifier.
  g) Print the address stored in fPtr. Use the %p conversion specifier. Is the value printed the same as the address of number1?

7.5   Do each of the following:
  a) Write the function header for a function called exchange that takes two pointers to floating-point numbers x and y as parameters and does not return a value.
  b) Write the function prototype for the function in part (a).
  c) Write the function header for a function called evaluate that returns an integer and that takes as parameters integer x and a pointer to function poly. Function poly takes an integer parameter and returns an integer.
  d) Write the function prototype for the function in part (c).

7.6   Find the error in each of the following program segments. Assume

```
int *zPtr; // zPtr will reference array z
int *aPtr = NULL;
void *sPtr = NULL;
int number;
int z[5] = {1, 2, 3, 4, 5};
sPtr = z;
```

  a) ++zptr;
  b) // use pointer to get first value of array; assume zPtr is initialized
     number = zPtr;
  c) // assign array element 2 (the value 3) to number;
     assume zPtr is initialized
     number = *zPtr[2];
  d) // print entire array z; assume zPtr is initialized
     for (size_t i = 0; i <= 5; ++i) {
        printf("%d ", zPtr[i]);
     }
  e) // assign the value pointed to by sPtr to number
     number = *sPtr;
  f) ++z;

Answers to Self-Review Exercises

7.1   a) address. b) 0, NULL, an address. c) 0.

7.2   a) False. A pointer to void cannot be dereferenced, because there's no way to know exactly how many bytes of memory to dereference. b) False. Pointers of type void can be assigned pointers of other types, and pointers of type void can be assigned to pointers of other types.

7.3   a) float numbers[SIZE] = {0.0, 1.1, 2.2, 3.3, 4.4, 5.5, 6.6, 7.7, 8.8, 9.9};
  b) float *nPtr;
  c) for (size_t i = 0; i < SIZE; ++i) {
        printf("%.1f ", numbers[i]);
     }
  d) nPtr = numbers;
     nPtr = &numbers[0];
  e) for (size_t i = 0; i < SIZE; ++i) {
        printf("%.1f ", *(nPtr + i));
     }

f) ```
    for (size_t i = 0; i < SIZE; ++i) {
        printf("%.1f ", *(numbers + i));
    }
    ```
g)  ```
    for (size_t i = 0; i < SIZE; ++i) {
        printf("%.1f ", nPtr[i]);
    }
    ```
h) ```
    numbers[4]
    *(numbers + 4)
    nPtr[4]
    *(nPtr + 4)
    ```
i)  The address is 1002500 + 8 * 4 = 1002532. The value is 8.8.
j)  The address of numbers[5] is 1002500 + 5 * 4 = 1002520.
    The address of nPtr -= 4 is 1002520 - 4 * 4 = 1002504.
    The value at that location is 1.1.

**7.4**  
a)  `float *fPtr;`
b)  `fPtr = &number1;`
c)  `printf("The value of *fPtr is %f\n", *fPtr);`
d)  `number2 = *fPtr;`
e)  `printf("The value of number2 is %f\n", number2);`
f)  `printf("The address of number1 is %p\n", &number1);`
g)  `printf("The address stored in fptr is %p\n", fPtr);`
    Yes, the value is the same.

**7.5**  
a)  `void exchange(float *x, float *y)`
b)  `void exchange(float *x, float *y);`
c)  `int evaluate(int x, int (*poly)(int))`
d)  `int evaluate(int x, int (*poly)(int));`

**7.6**  
a)  Error: zPtr has not been initialized.
    Correction: Initialize zPtr with zPtr = z; before performing the pointer arithmetic.
b)  Error: The pointer is not dereferenced.
    Correction: Change the statement to number = *zPtr;
c)  Error: zPtr[2] is not a pointer and should not be dereferenced.
    Correction: Change *zPtr[2] to zPtr[2].
d)  Error: Referring to an array element outside the array bounds with pointer indexing.
    Correction: Change the operator <= in the for condition to <.
e)  Error: Dereferencing a void pointer.
    Correction: To dereference the pointer, it must first be cast to an integer pointer.
    Change the statement to number = *((int *) sPtr);
f)  Error: Trying to modify an array name with pointer arithmetic.
    Correction: Use a pointer variable instead of the array name to accomplish pointer
    arithmetic, or index the array name to refer to a specific element.

## Exercises

**7.7**   Answer each of the following:
a)  The _____ operator returns the location in memory where its operand is stored.
b)  The _____ operator returns the value of the object to which its operand points.
c)  To accomplish pass-by-reference when passing a nonarray variable to a function, it's
    necessary to pass the _____ of the variable to the function.

**7.8**   State whether the following are *true* or *false*. If *false*, explain why.
    ```

a) Two pointers that point to different arrays cannot be compared meaningfully.

b) Because the name of an array is a pointer to the first element of the array, array names may be manipulated in precisely the same manner as pointers.

7.9   Answer each of the following. Assume that unsigned integers are stored in 2 bytes and that the starting address of the array is at location 1002500 in memory.

a) Define an array of type unsigned int called values with five elements, and initialize the elements to the even integers from 2 to 10. Assume the symbolic constant SIZE has been defined as 5.

b) Define a pointer vPtr that points to an object of type unsigned int.

c) Print the elements of array values using array index notation. Use a for statement and assume integer control variable i has been defined.

d) Give two separate statements that assign the starting address of array values to pointer variable vPtr.

e) Print the elements of array values using pointer/offset notation.

f) Print the elements of array values using pointer/offset notation with the array name as the pointer.

g) Print the elements of array values by indexing the pointer to the array.

h) Refer to element 5 of array values using array index notation, pointer/offset notation with the array name as the pointer, pointer index notation, and pointer/offset notation.

i) What address is referenced by vPtr + 3? What value is stored at that location?

j) Assuming vPtr points to values[4], what address is referenced by vPtr - 4? What value is stored at that location?

7.10   For each of the following, write a single statement that performs the indicated task. Assume that long integer variables value1 and value2 have been defined and that value1 has been initialized to 200000.

a) Define the variable lPtr to be a pointer to an object of type long.

b) Assign the address of variable value1 to pointer variable lPtr.

c) Print the value of the object pointed to by lPtr.

d) Assign the value of the object pointed to by lPtr to variable value2.

e) Print the value of value2.

f) Print the address of value1.

g) Print the address stored in lPtr. Is the value printed the same as the address of value1?

7.11   Do each of the following:

a) Write the function header for function zero, which takes a long integer array parameter bigIntegers and does not return a value.

b) Write the function prototype for the function in part (a).

c) Write the function header for function add1AndSum, which takes an integer array parameter oneTooSmall and returns an integer.

d) Write the function prototype for the function described in part (c).

Note: Exercises 7.12–7.15 are reasonably challenging. Once you have done these problems, you ought to be able to implement most popular card games easily.

7.12   *(Card Shuffling and Dealing)* Modify the program in Fig. 7.24 so that the card-dealing function deals a five-card poker hand. Then write the following additional functions:

a) Determine whether the hand contains a pair.

b) Determine whether the hand contains two pairs.

   c) Determine whether the hand contains three of a kind (e.g., three jacks).
   d) Determine whether the hand contains four of a kind (e.g., four aces).
   e) Determine whether the hand contains a flush (i.e., all five cards of the same suit).
   f) Determine whether the hand contains a straight (i.e., five cards of consecutive face values).

7.13 *(Project: Card Shuffling and Dealing)* Use the functions developed in Exercise 7.12 to write a program that deals two five-card poker hands, evaluates each, and determines which is the better hand.

7.14 *(Project: Card Shuffling and Dealing)* Modify the program developed in Exercise 7.13 so that it can simulate the dealer. The dealer's five-card hand is dealt "face down" so the player cannot see it. The program should then evaluate the dealer's hand, and based on the quality of the hand, the dealer should draw one, two or three more cards to replace the corresponding number of unneeded cards in the original hand. The program should then reevaluate the dealer's hand. [*Caution:* This is a difficult problem!]

7.15 *(Project: Card Shuffling and Dealing)* Modify the program developed in Exercise 7.14 so that it can handle the dealer's hand automatically, but the player is allowed to decide which cards of the player's hand to replace. The program should then evaluate both hands and determine who wins. Now use this new program to play 20 games against the computer. Who wins more games, you or the computer? Have one of your friends play 20 games against the computer. Who wins more games? Based on the results of these games, make appropriate modifications to refine your poker-playing program (this, too, is a difficult problem). Play 20 more games. Does your modified program play a better game?

7.16 *(Card Shuffling and Dealing Modification)* In the card shuffling and dealing program of Fig. 7.24, we intentionally used an inefficient shuffling algorithm that introduced the possibility of indefinite postponement. In this problem, you'll create a high-performance shuffling algorithm that avoids indefinite postponement.
   Modify the program of Fig. 7.24 as follows. Begin by initializing the deck array as shown in Fig. 7.29. Modify the shuffle function to loop row-by-row and column-by-column through the array, touching every element once. Each element should be swapped with a randomly selected element of the array. Print the resulting array to determine whether the deck is satisfactorily shuffled (as in Fig. 7.30, for example). You may want your program to call the shuffle function several times to ensure a satisfactory shuffle.

Unshuffled deck array												
	0	1	2	3	4	5	6	7	8	9	10	11	12
0	1	2	3	4	5	6	7	8	9	10	11	12	13
1	14	15	16	17	18	19	20	21	22	23	24	25	26
2	27	28	29	30	31	32	33	34	35	36	37	38	39
3	40	41	42	43	44	45	46	47	48	49	50	51	52

Fig. 7.29 | Unshuffled deck array.

Sample shuffled deck array												
	0	1	2	3	4	5	6	7	8	9	10	11	12
0	19	40	27	25	36	46	10	34	35	41	18	2	44
1	13	28	14	16	21	30	8	11	31	17	24	7	1
2	12	33	15	42	43	23	45	3	29	32	4	47	26
3	50	38	52	39	48	51	9	5	37	49	22	6	20

Fig. 7.30 | Sample shuffled deck array.

Although the approach in this problem improves the shuffling algorithm, the dealing algorithm still requires searching the deck array for card 1, then card 2, then card 3, and so on. Worse yet, even after the dealing algorithm locates and deals the card, the algorithm still searches through the remainder of the deck. Modify the program of Fig. 7.24 so that once a card is dealt, no further attempts are made to match that card number, and the program immediately proceeds with dealing the next card. In Chapter 10, we develop a dealing algorithm that requires only one operation per card.

7.17 *(Simulation: The Tortoise and the Hare)* In this problem, you'll recreate one of the truly great moments in history, namely the classic race of the tortoise and the hare. You'll use random number generation to develop a simulation of this memorable event.

Our contenders begin the race at "square 1" of 70 squares. Each square represents a possible position along the race course. The finish line is at square 70. The first contender to reach or pass square 70 is rewarded with a pail of fresh carrots and lettuce. The course weaves its way up the side of a slippery mountain, so occasionally the contenders lose ground.

There's a clock that ticks once per second. With each tick of the clock, your program should adjust the position of the animals according to the rules of Fig. 7.31.

Animal	Move type	Percentage of the time	Actual move
Tortoise	Fast plod	50%	3 squares forward
	Slip	20%	6 squares backward
	Slow plod	30%	1 square forward
Hare	Sleep	20%	No move at all
	Big hop	20%	9 squares forward
	Big slip	10%	12 squares backward
	Small hop	30%	1 square forward
	Small slip	20%	2 squares backward

Fig. 7.31 | Tortoise and hare rules for adjusting positions.

Use variables to keep track of the positions of the animals (i.e., position numbers are 1–70). Start each animal at position 1 (i.e., the "starting gate"). If an animal slips left before square 1, move the animal back to square 1. Generate the percentages in the preceding table by producing a random integer, i, in the range $1 \le i \le 10$. For the tortoise, perform a "fast plod" when $1 \le i \le 5$, a "slip" when $6 \le i \le 7$, or a "slow plod" when $8 \le i \le 10$. Use a similar technique to move the hare.

Begin the race by printing

```
BANG !!!!!
AND THEY'RE OFF !!!!!
```

Then, for each tick of the clock (i.e., each iteration of a loop), print a 70-position line showing the letter T in the position of the tortoise and the letter H in the position of the hare. Occasionally, the contenders will land on the same square. In this case, the tortoise bites the hare and your program should print OUCH!!! beginning at that position. All print positions other than the T, the H, or the OUCH!!! (in case of a tie) should be blank.

After each line is printed, test whether either animal has reached or passed square 70. If so, then print the winner and terminate the simulation. If the tortoise wins, print TORTOISE WINS!!! YAY!!! If the hare wins, print Hare wins. Yuch. If both animals win on the same tick of the clock, you may want to favor the turtle (the "underdog"), or you may want to print It's a tie. If neither animal wins, perform the loop again to simulate the next tick of the clock. When you're ready to run your program, assemble a group of fans to watch the race. You'll be amazed at how involved your audience gets!

7.18   *(Card Shuffling and Dealing Modification)* Modify the card shuffling and dealing program of Fig. 7.24 so the shuffling and dealing operations are performed by the same function (shuffle-AndDeal). The function should contain one nested looping structure that's similar to function shuffle in Fig. 7.24.

7.19   What does this program do, assuming that the user enters two strings of the same length?

```c
1   // ex07_19.c
2   // What does this program do?
3   #include <stdio.h>
4   #define SIZE 80
5
6   void mystery1(char *s1, const char *s2); // prototype
7
8   int main(void)
9   {
10     char string1[SIZE]; // create char array
11     char string2[SIZE]; // create char array
12
13     puts("Enter two strings: ");
14     scanf("%79s%79s" , string1, string2);
15     mystery1(string1, string2);
16     printf("%s", string1);
17  }
18
19  // What does this function do?
20  void mystery1(char *s1, const char *s2)
21  {
22     while (*s1 != '\0') {
23        ++s1;
24     }
25
26     for (; *s1 = *s2; ++s1, ++s2) {
27        ; // empty statement
28     }
29  }
```

7.20   What does this program do?

```
 1   // ex07_20.c
 2   // what does this program do?
 3   #include <stdio.h>
 4   #define SIZE 80
 5
 6   size_t mystery2(const char *s); // prototype
 7
 8   int main(void)
 9   {
10      char string[SIZE]; // create char array
11
12      puts("Enter a string: ");
13      scanf("%79s", string);
14      printf("%d\n", mystery2(string));
15   }
16
17   // What does this function do?
18   size_t mystery2(const char *s)
19   {
20      size_t x;
21
22      // loop through string
23      for (x = 0; *s != '\0'; ++s) {
24         ++x;
25      }
26
27      return x;
28   }
```

7.21   Find the error in each of the following program segments. If the error can be corrected, explain how.

a) `int *number;`
    `printf("%d\n", *number);`

b) `float *realPtr;`
    `long *integerPtr;`
    `integerPtr = realPtr;`

c) `int * x, y;`
    `x = y;`

d) `char s[] = "this is a character array";`
    `int count;`
    `for (; *s != '\0'; ++s)`
    `   printf("%c ", *s);`

e) `short *numPtr, result;`
    `void *genericPtr = numPtr;`
    `result = *genericPtr + 7;`

f) `float x = 19.34;`
    `float xPtr = &x;`
    `printf("%f\n", xPtr);`

g) `char *s;`
    `printf("%s\n", s);`

7.22 *(Maze Traversal)* The following grid is a two-dimensional array representation of a maze.

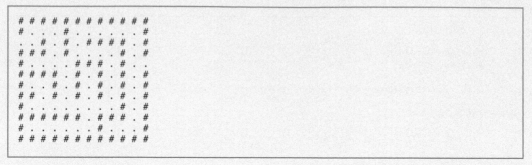

The # symbols represent the walls of the maze, and the periods (.) represent squares in the possible paths through the maze.

There's a simple algorithm for walking through a maze that guarantees finding the exit (assuming there's an exit). If there's not an exit, you'll arrive at the starting location again. Place your right hand on the wall to your right and begin walking forward. Never remove your hand from the wall. If the maze turns to the right, you follow the wall to the right. As long as you do not remove your hand from the wall, eventually you'll arrive at the exit of the maze. There may be a shorter path than the one you have taken, but you're guaranteed to get out of the maze.

Write recursive function mazeTraverse to walk through the maze. The function should receive as arguments a 12-by-12 character array representing the maze and the starting location of the maze. As mazeTraverse attempts to locate the exit from the maze, it should place the character X in each square in the path. The function should display the maze after each move so the user can watch as the maze is solved.

7.23 *(Generating Mazes Randomly)* Write a function mazeGenerator that takes as an argument a two-dimensional 12-by-12 character array and randomly produces a maze. The function should also provide the starting and ending locations of the maze. Try your function mazeTraverse from Exercise 7.22 using several randomly generated mazes.

7.24 *(Mazes of Any Size)* Generalize functions mazeTraverse and mazeGenerator of Exercises 7.22–7.23 to process mazes of any width and height.

7.25 *(Arrays of Pointers to Functions)* Rewrite the program of Fig. 6.22 to use a menu-driven interface. The program should offer the user four options as follows:

```
Enter a choice:
   0  Print the array of grades
   1  Find the minimum grade
   2  Find the maximum grade
   3  Print the average on all tests for each student
   4  End program
```

One restriction on using arrays of pointers to functions is that all the pointers must have the same type. The pointers must be to functions of the same return type that receive arguments of the same type. For this reason, the functions in Fig. 6.22 must be modified so that they each return the same type and take the same parameters. Modify functions minimum and maximum to print the minimum or maximum value and return nothing. For option 3, modify function average of Fig. 6.22 to output the average for each student (not a specific student). Function average should return nothing and take the same parameters as printArray, minimum and maximum. Store the pointers to the four functions in array processGrades and use the choice made by the user as the index into the array for calling each function.

7.26   What does this program do, assuming that the user enters two strings of the same length?

```c
 1  // ex07_26.c
 2  // What does this program do?
 3  #include <stdio.h>
 4  #define SIZE 80
 5
 6  int mystery3(const char *s1, const char *s2); // prototype
 7
 8  int main(void)
 9  {
10     char string1[SIZE]; // create char array
11     char string2[SIZE]; // create char array
12
13     puts("Enter two strings: ");
14     scanf("%79s%79s", string1 , string2);
15     printf("The result is %d\n", mystery3(string1, string2));
16  }
17
18  int mystery3(const char *s1, const char *s2)
19  {
20     int result = 1;
21
22     for (; *s1 != '\0' && *s2 != '\0'; ++s1, ++s2) {
23        if (*s1 != *s2) {
24           result = 0;
25        }
26     }
27
28     return result;
29  }
```

Special Section: Building Your Own Computer

In the next several exercises, we take a temporary diversion away from the world of high-level language programming. We "peel open" a computer and look at its internal structure. We introduce machine-language programming and write several machine-language programs. To make this an especially valuable experience, we then build a computer (through the technique of software-based *simulation*) on which you can execute your machine-language programs!

7.27   *(Machine-Language Programming)* Let's create a computer we'll call the Simpletron. As its name implies, it's a simple machine, but as we'll soon see, it's a powerful one as well. The Simpletron runs programs written in the only language it directly understands—that is, Simpletron Machine Language, or SML for short.

The Simpletron contains an *accumulator*—a "special register" in which information is put before the Simpletron uses that information in calculations or examines it in various ways. All information in the Simpletron is handled in terms of *words*. A word is a signed four-digit decimal number such as +3364, -1293, +0007, -0001 and so on. The Simpletron is equipped with a 100-word memory, and these words are referenced by their location numbers 00, 01, ..., 99.

Before running an SML program, we must *load* or place the program into memory. The first instruction (or statement) of every SML program is always placed in location 00.

Each instruction written in SML occupies one word of the Simpletron's memory, so instructions are signed four-digit decimal numbers. We assume that the sign of an SML instruction is always plus, but the sign of a data word may be either plus or minus. Each location in the Simpletron's memory may contain either an instruction, a data value used by a program or an unused (and hence undefined) area of memory. The first two digits of each SML instruction are the *opera-*

tion code, which specifies the operation to be performed. SML operation codes are summarized in Fig. 7.32.

Operation code	Meaning
Input/output operations:	
#define READ 10	Read a word from the terminal into a specific location in memory.
#define WRITE 11	Write a word from a specific location in memory to the terminal.
Load/store operations:	
#define LOAD 20	Load a word from a specific location in memory into the accumulator.
#define STORE 21	Store a word from the accumulator into a specific location in memory.
Arithmetic operations:	
#define ADD 30	Add a word from a specific location in memory to the word in the accumulator (leave result in accumulator).
#define SUBTRACT 31	Subtract a word from a specific location in memory from the word in the accumulator (leave result in accumulator).
#define DIVIDE 32	Divide a word from a specific location in memory into the word in the accumulator (leave result in accumulator).
#define MULTIPLY 33	Multiply a word from a specific location in memory by the word in the accumulator (leave result in accumulator).
Transfer-of-control operations:	
#define BRANCH 40	Branch to a specific location in memory.
#define BRANCHNEG 41	Branch to a specific location in memory if the accumulator is negative.
#define BRANCHZERO 42	Branch to a specific location in memory if the accumulator is zero.
#define HALT 43	Halt—i.e., the program has completed its task.

Fig. 7.32 | Simpletron Machine Language (SML) operation codes.

The last two digits of an SML instruction are the *operand*, which is the address of the memory location containing the word to which the operation applies. Now let's consider several simple SML programs. The following SML program reads two numbers from the keyboard, and computes and prints their sum. The instruction +1007 reads the first number from the keyboard and places it into location 07 (which has been initialized to zero). Then +1008 reads the next number into location 08. The *load* instruction, +2007, puts the first number into the accumulator, and the *add* instruction, +3008, adds the second number to the number in the accumulator. *All SML arithmetic instructions leave their results in the accumulator.* The *store* instruction, +2109, places the result back into memory location 09, from which the *write* instruction, +1109, takes the number and prints it (as a signed four-digit decimal number). The *halt* instruction, +4300, terminates execution.

Example 1 Location	Number	Instruction
00	+1007	(Read A)
01	+1008	(Read B)
02	+2007	(Load A)
03	+3008	(Add B)
04	+2109	(Store C)
05	+1109	(Write C)
06	+4300	(Halt)
07	+0000	(Variable A)
08	+0000	(Variable B)
09	+0000	(Result C)

The following SML program reads two numbers from the keyboard, and determines and prints the larger value. Note the use of the instruction +4107 as a conditional transfer of control, much the same as C's if statement.

Example 2 Location	Number	Instruction
00	+1009	(Read A)
01	+1010	(Read B)
02	+2009	(Load A)
03	+3110	(Subtract B)
04	+4107	(Branch negative to 07)
05	+1109	(Write A)
06	+4300	(Halt)
07	+1110	(Write B)
08	+4300	(Halt)
09	+0000	(Variable A)
10	+0000	(Variable B)

Now write SML programs to accomplish each of the following tasks.
a) Use a sentinel-controlled loop to read positive integers and compute and print their sum.
b) Use a counter-controlled loop to read seven numbers, some positive and some negative, and compute and print their average.
c) Read a series of numbers and determine and print the largest number. The first number read indicates how many numbers should be processed.

7.28 *(A Computer Simulator)* It may at first seem outrageous, but in this problem you're going to build your own computer. No, you won't be soldering components together. Rather, you'll use the powerful technique of *software-based simulation* to create a *software model* of the Simpletron. You'll not be disappointed. Your Simpletron simulator will turn the computer you're using into a Simpletron, and you'll actually be able to run, test and debug the SML programs you wrote in Exercise 7.27.

When you run your Simpletron simulator, it should begin by printing:

```
*** Welcome to Simpletron! ***
*** Please enter your program one instruction ***
*** (or data word) at a time. I will type the ***
*** location number and a question mark (?).  ***
*** You then type the word for that location. ***
*** Type the sentinel -99999 to stop entering ***
*** your program. ***
```

Simulate the memory of the Simpletron with a one-dimensional array `memory` that has 100 elements. Now assume that the simulator is running, and let's examine the dialog as we enter the program of Example 2 of Exercise 7.27:

```
00 ? +1009
01 ? +1010
02 ? +2009
03 ? +3110
04 ? +4107
05 ? +1109
06 ? +4300
07 ? +1110
08 ? +4300
09 ? +0000
10 ? +0000
11 ? -99999
*** Program loading completed ***
*** Program execution begins  ***
```

The SML program has now been placed (or loaded) into the array `memory`. Now the Simpletron executes the SML program. It begins with the instruction in location 00 and continues sequentially, unless directed to some other part of the program by a transfer of control.

Use the variable `accumulator` to represent the accumulator register. Use the variable `instructionCounter` to keep track of the location in memory that contains the instruction being performed. Use the variable `operationCode` to indicate the operation currently being performed—i.e., the left two digits of the instruction word. Use the variable `operand` to indicate the memory location on which the current instruction operates. Thus, if an instrucion has an `operand`, it's the rightmost two digits of the instruction currently being performed. Do not execute instructions directly from memory. Rather, transfer the next instruction to be performed from memory to a variable called `instructionRegister`. Then "pick off" the left two digits and place them in the variable `operationCode`, and "pick off" the right two digits and place them in `operand`.

When Simpletron begins execution, the special registers are initialized as follows:

accumulator	+0000
instructionCounter	00
instructionRegister	+0000
operationCode	00
operand	00

Now let's "walk through" the execution of the first SML instruction, +1009 in memory location 00. This is called an *instruction execution cycle.*

The `instructionCounter` tells us the location of the next instruction to be performed. We *fetch* the contents of that location from `memory` by using the C statement

```
instructionRegister = memory[instructionCounter];
```

The operation code and the operand are extracted from the instruction register by the statements

```
operationCode = instructionRegister / 100;
operand = instructionRegister % 100;
```

Now the Simpletron must determine that the operation code is actually a *read* (versus a *write*, a *load*, and so on). A `switch` differentiates among the twelve operations of SML.

The `switch` statement simulates the behavior of various SML instructions as follows (we leave the others to the reader):

read: `scanf("%d", &memory[operand]);`
load: `accumulator = memory[operand];`
add: `accumulator += memory[operand];`
Various branch instructions: We'll discuss these shortly.
halt: This instruction prints the message

```
        *** Simpletron execution terminated ***
```

then prints the name and contents of each register as well as the complete contents of memory. Such a printout is often called a *computer dump*. To help you program your dump function, a sample dump format is shown in Fig. 7.33. A dump after executing a Simpletron program would show the actual values of instructions and data values at the moment execution terminated. You can print leading 0s in front of an integer that is shorter than its field width by placing the 0 formatting flag before the field width in the format specifier as in "%02d". You can place a + or - sign before a value with the + formatting flag. So to produce a number of the form +0000, you can use the format specifier "%+05d".

```
REGISTERS:
accumulator             +0000
instructionCounter         00
instructionRegister     +0000
operationCode              00
operand                    00

MEMORY:
       0      1      2      3      4      5      6      7      8      9
 0  +0000  +0000  +0000  +0000  +0000  +0000  +0000  +0000  +0000  +0000
10  +0000  +0000  +0000  +0000  +0000  +0000  +0000  +0000  +0000  +0000
20  +0000  +0000  +0000  +0000  +0000  +0000  +0000  +0000  +0000  +0000
30  +0000  +0000  +0000  +0000  +0000  +0000  +0000  +0000  +0000  +0000
40  +0000  +0000  +0000  +0000  +0000  +0000  +0000  +0000  +0000  +0000
50  +0000  +0000  +0000  +0000  +0000  +0000  +0000  +0000  +0000  +0000
60  +0000  +0000  +0000  +0000  +0000  +0000  +0000  +0000  +0000  +0000
70  +0000  +0000  +0000  +0000  +0000  +0000  +0000  +0000  +0000  +0000
80  +0000  +0000  +0000  +0000  +0000  +0000  +0000  +0000  +0000  +0000
90  +0000  +0000  +0000  +0000  +0000  +0000  +0000  +0000  +0000  +0000
```

Fig. 7.33 | Sample Simpletron dump format.

Let's proceed with the execution of our program's first instruction, namely the +1009 in location 00. As we've indicated, the `switch` statement simulates this by performing the C statement

```
scanf("%d", &memory[operand]);
```

A question mark (?) should be displayed on the screen before the `scanf` is executed to prompt the user for input. The Simpletron waits for the user to type a value and then press the *Return* key. The value is then read into location 09.

At this point, simulation of the first instruction is completed. All that remains is to prepare the Simpletron to execute the next instruction. Because the instruction just performed was not a transfer of control, we need merely increment the instruction counter register as follows:

```
++instructionCounter;
```

This completes the simulated execution of the first instruction. The entire process (i.e., the instruction execution cycle) begins anew with the fetch of the next instruction to be executed.

Now let's consider how the branching instructions—the transfers of control—are simulated. All we need to do is adjust the value in the instruction counter appropriately. Therefore, the unconditional branch instruction (40) is simulated within the switch as

```
instructionCounter = operand;
```

The conditional "branch if accumulator is zero" instruction is simulated as

```
if (accumulator == 0) {
   instructionCounter = operand;
}
```

At this point, you should implement your Simpletron simulator and run the SML programs you wrote in Exercise 7.27. You may embellish SML with additional features and provide for these in your simulator.

Your simulator should check for various types of errors. During the program loading phase, for example, each number the user types into the Simpletron's memory must be in the range -9999 to +9999. Your simulator should use a while loop to test that each number entered is in this range, and, if not, keep prompting the user to reenter the number until a correct number is entered.

During the execution phase, your simulator should check for serious errors, such as attempts to divide by zero, attempts to execute invalid operation codes and accumulator overflows (i.e., arithmetic operations resulting in values larger than +9999 or smaller than -9999). Such serious errors are called *fatal errors*. When a fatal error is detected, print an error message such as:

```
*** Attempt to divide by zero ***
*** Simpletron execution abnormally terminated ***
```

and print a full computer dump in the format we've discussed previously. This will help the user locate the error in the program.

Implementation Note: When you implement the Simpletron Simulator, define the memory array and all the registers as variables in main. The program should contain three other functions—load, execute and dump. Function load reads the SML instructions from the user at the keyboard. (Once you study file processing in Chapter 11, you'll be able to read the SML instruction from a file.) Function execute executes the SML program currently loaded in the memory array. Function dump displays the contents of memory and all of the registers stored in main's variables. Pass the memory array and registers to the other functions as necessary to complete their tasks. Functions load and execute need to modify variables that are defined in main, so you'll need to pass those variables to the functions by reference using pointers. So, you'll need to modify the statements we showed throughout this problem description to use the appropriate pointer notations.

7.29   *(Modifications to the Simpletron Simulator)* In Exercise 7.28, you wrote a software simulation of a computer that executes programs written in Simpletron Machine Language (SML). In this exercise, we propose several modifications and enhancements to the Simpletron Simulator. In Exercises 12.25 and 12.26, we propose building a compiler that converts programs written in a high-level programming language (a variation of BASIC) to Simpletron Machine Language. Some of the following modifications and enhancements may be required to execute the programs produced by the compiler.

   a) Extend the Simpletron Simulator's memory to contain 1000 memory locations to enable the Simpletron to handle larger programs.

b) Allow the simulator to perform remainder calculations. This requires an additional Simpletron Machine Language instruction.

c) Allow the simulator to perform exponentiation calculations. This requires an additional Simpletron Machine Language instruction.

d) Modify the simulator to use hexadecimal values rather than integer values to represent Simpletron Machine Language instructions.

e) Modify the simulator to allow output of a newline. This requires an additional Simpletron Machine Language instruction.

f) Modify the simulator to process floating-point values in addition to integer values.

g) Modify the simulator to handle string input. [*Hint:* Each Simpletron word can be divided into two groups, each holding a two-digit integer. Each two-digit integer represents the ASCII decimal equivalent of a character. Add a machine-language instruction that will input a string and store it beginning at a specific Simpletron memory location. The first half of the word at that location will be a count of the number of characters in the string (i.e., the length of the string). Each succeeding half word contains one ASCII character expressed as two decimal digits. The machine-language instruction converts each character into its ASCII equivalent and assigns it to a half word.]

h) Modify the simulator to handle output of strings stored in the format of part (g). [*Hint:* Add a machine-language instruction that prints a string beginning at a specified Simpletron memory location. The first half of the word at that location is the length of the string in characters. Each succeeding half word contains one ASCII character expressed as two decimal digits. The machine-language instruction checks the length and prints the string by translating each two-digit number into its equivalent character.]

Array of Function Pointer Exercises

7.30 *(Calculating Circle Circumference, Circle Area or Sphere Volume Using Function Pointers)* Using the techniques you learned in Fig. 7.28, create a text-based, menu-driven program that allows the user to choose whether to calculate the circumference of a circle, the area of a circle or the volume of a sphere. The program should then input a radius from the user, perform the appropriate calculation and display the result. Use an array of function pointers in which each pointer represents a function that returns void and receives a double parameter. The corresponding functions should each display messages indicating which calculation was performed, the value of the radius and the result of the calculation.

7.31 *(Calculator Using Function Pointers)* Using the techniques you learned in Fig. 7.28, create a text-based, menu-driven program that allows the user to choose whether to add, subtract, multiply or divide two numbers. The program should then input two double values from the user, perform the appropriate calculation and display the result. Use an array of function pointers in which each pointer represents a function that returns void and receives two double parameters. The corresponding functions should each display messages indicating which calculation was performed, the values of the parameters and the result of the calculation.

Making a Difference

7.32 *(Polling)* The Internet and the web are enabling more people to network, join a cause, voice opinions, and so on. The U.S. presidential candidates in 2008 used the Internet intensively to get out their messages and raise money for their campaigns. In this exercise, you'll write a simple polling program that allows users to rate five social-consciousness issues from 1 (least important) to 10 (most important). Pick five causes that are important to you (e.g., political issues, global environmental issues). Use a one-dimensional array topics (of type char *) to store the five causes. To summarize the survey responses, use a 5-row, 10-column two-dimensional array responses (of type int), each row corresponding to an element in the topics array. When the program runs, it should ask the user to rate each issue. Have your friends and family respond to the survey. Then have the program display a summary of the results, including:

    a) A tabular report with the five topics down the left side and the 10 ratings across the top, listing in each column the number of ratings received for each topic.

    b) To the right of each row, show the average of the ratings for that issue.

    c) Which issue received the highest point total? Display both the issue and the point total.

    d) Which issue received the lowest point total? Display both the issue and the point total.

7.33 *(Carbon Footprint Calculator: Arrays of Function Pointers)* Using arrays of function pointers, as you learned in this chapter, you can specify a set of functions that are called with the same types of arguments and return the same type of data. Governments and companies worldwide are becoming increasingly concerned with carbon footprints (annual releases of carbon dioxide into the atmosphere) from buildings burning various types of fuels for heat, vehicles burning fuels for power, and the like. Many scientists blame these greenhouse gases for the phenomenon called global warming. Create three functions that help calculate the carbon footprint of a building, a car and a bicycle, respectively. Each function should input appropriate data from the user, then calculate and display the carbon footprint. (Check out a few websites that explain how to calculate carbon footprints.) Each function should receive no parameters and return void. Write a program that prompts the user to enter the type of carbon footprint to calculate, then calls the corresponding function in the array of function pointers. For each type of carbon footprint, display some identifying information and the object's carbon footprint.

C Characters and Strings

8

8.1 Introduction

This chapter introduces the C standard library functions that help us process strings and characters. The functions enable programs to process characters, strings, lines of text and blocks of memory. The chapter discusses the techniques used to develop editors, word processors, page-layout software, computerized typesetting systems and other kinds of text-processing software. The text manipulations performed by formatted input/output functions like printf and scanf can be implemented using the functions discussed in this chapter.

C11 Annex K Functions

As we discuss in Section 8.11, C11's *optional* Annex K describes more secure versions of many functions that we present in this chapter. As with printf_s and scanf_s for printf and scanf, the more secure Annex K versions should be used, if available for your compiler.

8.2 Fundamentals of Strings and Characters

Characters are the fundamental building blocks of source programs. Every program is composed of a sequence of characters that—when grouped together meaningfully—is interpreted by the computer as a series of instructions used to accomplish a task. A program may contain **character constants**. A character constant is an `int` value represented as a character in single quotes. The value of a character constant is the integer value of the character in the machine's **character set**. For example, `'z'` represents the integer value of the letter z, and `'\n'` the integer value of newline (122 and 10 in ASCII, respectively).

A **string** is a series of characters treated as a single unit. A string may include letters, digits and various **special characters** such as +, -, *, / and $. **String literals**, or **string constants**, in C are written in double quotation marks as follows:

`"John Q. Doe"`	(a name)
`"99999 Main Street"`	(a street address)
`"Waltham, Massachusetts"`	(a city and state)
`"(201) 555-1212"`	(a telephone number)

A string in C is an array of characters ending with the **null character** (`'\0'`). A string is accessed via a *pointer* to the first character in the string. The value of a string is the address of its first character. Thus, in C, it's appropriate to say that a **string is a pointer**—in fact, a pointer to the string's first character. This is just like arrays, because strings are simply arrays of characters.

A *character array* or a *variable of type char ** can be initialized with a string in a definition. The definitions

```
char color[] = "blue";
const char *colorPtr = "blue";
```

each initialize a variable to the string "blue". The first definition creates a 5-element array color containing the characters `'b'`, `'l'`, `'u'`, `'e'` and `'\0'`. The second definition creates pointer variable colorPtr that points to the string "blue" somewhere in read-only memory.

Portability Tip 8.1

The C standard indicates that a string literal is immutable (i.e., not modifiable), but some compilers do not enforce this. If you might need to modify a string literal, it must be stored in a character array.

The preceding array definition could also have been written

```
char color[] = { 'b', 'l', 'u', 'e', '\0' };
```

When defining a character array to contain a string, the array must be large enough to store the string *and* its terminating null character. The preceding definition automatically determines the size of the array based on the number of initializers (5) in the initializer list.

Common Programming Error 8.1

Not allocating sufficient space in a character array to store the null character that terminates a string is an error.

Common Programming Error 8.2

Printing a "string" that does not contain a terminating null character is an error. Printing will continue past the end of the "string" until a null character is encountered.

Error-Prevention Tip 8.1

When storing a string of characters in a character array, be sure that the array is large enough to hold the largest string that will be stored. C allows strings of any length to be stored. If a string is longer than the character array in which it's to be stored, characters beyond the end of the array will overwrite data in memory following the array.

A string can be stored in an array using scanf. For example, the following statement stores a string in character array word[20]:

```
scanf("%19s", word);
```

The string entered by the user is stored in word. Variable word is an array, which is a pointer, so the & is not needed with argument word. Recall from Section 6.5.4 that function scanf will read characters until a space, tab, newline or end-of-file indicator is encountered. So, it's possible that, without the field width 19 in the conversion specifier %19s, the user input could exceed 19 characters and that your program might crash! For this reason, you should *always* use a field width when using *scanf* to read into a char array. The field width 19 in the preceding statement ensures that scanf reads a *maximum* of 19 characters and saves the last character for the string's terminating null character. This prevents scanf from writing characters into memory beyond the end of the character array. (For reading input lines of arbitrary length, there's a nonstandard—yet widely supported—function readline, usually included in stdio.h.) For a character array to be printed properly as a string, the array must contain a terminating null character.

Common Programming Error 8.3

Processing a single character as a string. A string is a pointer—probably a respectably large integer. However, a character is a small integer (ASCII values range 0–255). On many systems this causes an error, because low memory addresses are reserved for special purposes such as operating-system interrupt handlers—so "access violations" occur.

Common Programming Error 8.4

Passing a character as an argument to a function when a string is expected (and vice versa) is a compilation error.

8.3 Character-Handling Library

The **character-handling library** (<ctype.h>) includes several functions that perform useful tests and manipulations of character data. Each function receives an unsigned char (represented as an int) or EOF as an argument. As we discussed in Chapter 4, characters are often manipulated as integers, because a character in C is a one-byte integer. EOF normally has the value −1. Figure 8.1 summarizes the functions of the character-handling library.

8.3.1 Functions isdigit, isalpha, isalnum and isxdigit

Figure 8.2 demonstrates functions isdigit, isalpha, isalnum and isxdigit. Function isdigit determines whether its argument is a digit (0–9). Function isalpha determines whether its argument is an uppercase (A–Z) or lowercase letter (a–z). Function isalnum

Prototype	Function description
int isblank(int c);	Returns a true value if c is a *blank character* that separates words in a line of text and 0 (false) otherwise. [*Note:* This function is not available in Microsoft Visual C++.]
int isdigit(int c);	Returns a true value if c is a *digit* and 0 (false) otherwise.
int isalpha(int c);	Returns a true value if c is a *letter* and 0 (false) otherwise.
int isalnum(int c);	Returns a true value if c is a *digit* or a *letter* and 0 (false) otherwise.
int isxdigit(int c);	Returns a true value if c is a *hexadecimal digit character* and 0 (false) otherwise. (See Appendix C for a detailed explanation of binary numbers, octal numbers, decimal numbers and hexadecimal numbers.)
int islower(int c);	Returns a true value if c is a *lowercase letter* and 0 (false) otherwise.
int isupper(int c);	Returns a true value if c is an *uppercase letter* and 0 (false) otherwise.
int tolower(int c);	If c is an *uppercase letter*, tolower returns c as a *lowercase letter*. Otherwise, tolower returns the argument unchanged.
int toupper(int c);	If c is a *lowercase letter*, toupper returns c as an *uppercase letter*. Otherwise, toupper returns the argument unchanged.
int isspace(int c);	Returns a true value if c is a *whitespace character*—newline ('\n'), space (' '), form feed ('\f'), carriage return ('\r'), horizontal tab ('\t') or vertical tab ('\v')—and 0 (false) otherwise.
int iscntrl(int c);	Returns a true value if c is a *control character*—horizontal tab ('\t'), vertical tab ('\v'), form feed ('\f'), alert ('\a'), backspace ('\b'), carriage return ('\r'), newline ('\n') and others— and 0 (false) otherwise.
int ispunct(int c);	Returns a true value if c is a *printing character other than a space, a digit, or a letter*—such as $, #, (,), [,], {, }, ;, : or %—and returns 0 otherwise.
int isprint(int c);	Returns a true value if c is a *printing character* (i.e., a character that's visible on the screen) *including a space* and returns 0 (false) otherwise.
int isgraph(int c);	Returns a true value if c is a *printing character other than a space* and returns 0 (false) otherwise.

Fig. 8.1 | Character-handling library (<ctype.h>) functions.

determines whether its argument is an uppercase letter, a lowercase letter or a digit. Function isxdigit determines whether its argument is a **hexadecimal digit** (A–F, a–f, 0–9).

```
1   // Fig. 8.2: fig08_02.c
2   // Using functions isdigit, isalpha, isalnum, and isxdigit
3   #include <stdio.h>
4   #include <ctype.h>
5
6   int main(void)
7   {
```

Fig. 8.2 | Using functions isdigit, isalpha, isalnum and isxdigit. (Part 1 of 2.)

```
8      printf("%s\n%s%s\n%s%s\n\n", "According to isdigit: ",
9         isdigit('8')   ? "8 is a " : "8 is not a ", "digit",
10        isdigit('#')   ? "# is a " : "# is not a ", "digit");
11
12     printf("%s\n%s%s\n%s%s\n%s%s\n%s%s\n\n",
13        "According to isalpha:",
14        isalpha('A')   ? "A is a " : "A is not a ", "letter",
15        isalpha('b')   ? "b is a " : "b is not a ", "letter",
16        isalpha('&')   ? "& is a " : "& is not a ", "letter",
17        isalpha('4')   ? "4 is a " : "4 is not a ", "letter");
18
19     printf("%s\n%s%s\n%s%s\n%s%s\n\n",
20        "According to isalnum:",
21        isalnum('A')   ? "A is a " : "A is not a ",
22        "digit or a letter",
23        isalnum('8')   ? "8 is a " : "8 is not a ",
24        "digit or a letter",
25        isalnum('#')   ? "# is a " : "# is not a ",
26        "digit or a letter");
27
28     printf("%s\n%s%s\n%s%s\n%s%s\n%s%s\n%s%s\n",
29        "According to isxdigit:",
30        isxdigit('F')   ? "F is a " : "F is not a ",
31        "hexadecimal digit",
32        isxdigit('J')   ? "J is a " : "J is not a ",
33        "hexadecimal digit",
34        isxdigit('7')   ? "7 is a " : "7 is not a ",
35        "hexadecimal digit",
36        isxdigit('$')   ? "$ is a " : "$ is not a ",
37        "hexadecimal digit",
38        isxdigit('f')   ? "f is a " : "f is not a ",
39        "hexadecimal digit");
40  }
```

```
According to isdigit:
8 is a digit
# is not a digit

According to isalpha:
A is a letter
b is a letter
& is not a letter
4 is not a letter

According to isalnum:
A is a digit or a letter
8 is a digit or a letter
# is not a digit or a letter

According to isxdigit:
F is a hexadecimal digit
J is not a hexadecimal digit
7 is a hexadecimal digit
$ is not a hexadecimal digit
f is a hexadecimal digit
```

Fig. 8.2 | Using functions isdigit, isalpha, isalnum and isxdigit. (Part 2 of 2.)

Figure 8.2 uses the conditional operator (?:) to determine whether the string " is a " or the string " is not a " should be printed in the output for each character tested. For example, the expression

```
isdigit('8') ? "8 is a " : "8 is not a "
```

indicates that if '8' is a digit, the string "8 is a " is printed, and if '8' is not a digit (i.e., isdigit returns 0), the string "8 is not a " is printed.

8.3.2 Functions islower, isupper, tolower and toupper

Figure 8.3 demonstrates functions **islower**, **isupper**, **tolower** and **toupper**. Function islower determines whether its argument is a lowercase letter (a–z). Function isupper determines whether its argument is an uppercase letter (A–Z). Function tolower converts an uppercase letter to a lowercase letter and returns the lowercase letter. If the argument is *not* an uppercase letter, tolower returns the argument *unchanged*. Function toupper converts a lowercase letter to an uppercase letter and returns the uppercase letter. If the argument is *not* a lowercase letter, toupper returns the argument *unchanged*.

```
1   // Fig. 8.3: fig08_03.c
2   // Using functions islower, isupper, tolower and toupper
3   #include <stdio.h>
4   #include <ctype.h>
5
6   int main(void)
7   {
8      printf("%s\n%s%s\n%s%s\n%s%s\n%s%s\n\n",
9         "According to islower:",
10        islower('p')   ? "p is a " : "p is not a ",
11        "lowercase letter",
12        islower('P')   ? "P is a " : "P is not a ",
13        "lowercase letter",
14        islower('5')   ? "5 is a " : "5 is not a ",
15        "lowercase letter",
16        islower('!')   ? "! is a " : "! is not a ",
17        "lowercase letter");
18
19     printf("%s\n%s%s\n%s%s\n%s%s\n%s%s\n\n",
20        "According to isupper:",
21        isupper('D')   ? "D is an " : "D is not an ",
22        "uppercase letter",
23        isupper('d')   ? "d is an " : "d is not an ",
24        "uppercase letter",
25        isupper('8')   ? "8 is an " : "8 is not an ",
26        "uppercase letter",
27        isupper('$')   ? "$ is an " : "$ is not an ",
28        "uppercase letter");
29
30     printf("%s%c\n%s%c\n%s%c\n%s%c\n",
31        "u converted to uppercase is ", toupper('u') ,
32        "7 converted to uppercase is ", toupper('7') ,
```

Fig. 8.3 | Using functions islower, isupper, tolower and toupper. (Part 1 of 2.)

```
33          "$ converted to uppercase is ", toupper('$') ,
34          "L converted to lowercase is ", tolower('L') );
35   }
```

```
According to islower:
p is a lowercase letter
P is not a lowercase letter
5 is not a lowercase letter
! is not a lowercase letter

According to isupper:
D is an uppercase letter
d is not an uppercase letter
8 is not an uppercase letter
$ is not an uppercase letter

u converted to uppercase is U
7 converted to uppercase is 7
$ converted to uppercase is $
L converted to lowercase is l
```

Fig. 8.3 | Using functions islower, isupper, tolower and toupper. (Part 2 of 2.)

8.3.3 Functions isspace, iscntrl, ispunct, isprint and isgraph

Figure 8.4 demonstrates functions isspace, iscntrl, ispunct, isprint and isgraph. Function isspace determines whether a character is one of the following whitespace characters: space (' '), form feed ('\f'), newline ('\n'), carriage return ('\r'), horizontal tab ('\t') or vertical tab ('\v'). Function iscntrl determines whether a character is one of the following **control characters**: horizontal tab ('\t'), vertical tab ('\v'), form feed ('\f'), alert ('\a'), backspace ('\b'), carriage return ('\r') or newline ('\n'). Function ispunct determines whether a character is a **printing character** other than a space, a digit or a letter, such as $, #, (,), [,], {, }, ;, : or %. Function isprint determines whether a character can be displayed on the screen (including the space character). Function isgraph is the same as isprint, except that the space character is not included.

```
1   // Fig. 8.4: fig08_04.c
2   // Using functions isspace, iscntrl, ispunct, isprint and isgraph
3   #include <stdio.h>
4   #include <ctype.h>
5
6   int main(void)
7   {
8      printf("%s\n%s%s%s\n%s%s%s\n%s%s\n\n",
9         "According to isspace:",
10        "Newline", isspace('\n')  ? " is a " : " is not a ",
11        "whitespace character", "Horizontal tab",
12        isspace('\t')  ? " is a " : " is not a ",
13        "whitespace character",
```

Fig. 8.4 | Using functions isspace, iscntrl, ispunct, isprint and isgraph. (Part 1 of 2.)

```
14              isspace('%')    ? "% is a " : "% is not a ",
15          "whitespace character");
16
17      printf("%s\n%s%s%s\n%s%s\n\n", "According to iscntrl:",
18          "Newline", iscntrl('\n')   ? " is a " : " is not a ",
19          "control character", iscntrl('$')   ? "$ is a " :
20          "$ is not a ", "control character");
21
22      printf("%s\n%s%s\n%s%s\n%s%s\n\n",
23          "According to ispunct:",
24          ispunct(';')    ? "; is a " : "; is not a ",
25          "punctuation character",
26          ispunct('Y')    ? "Y is a " : "Y is not a ",
27          "punctuation character",
28          ispunct('#')    ? "# is a " : "# is not a ",
29          "punctuation character");
30
31      printf("%s\n%s%s\n%s%s%s\n\n", "According to isprint:",
32          isprint('$')    ? "$ is a " : "$ is not a ",
33          "printing character",
34          "Alert", isprint('\a')   ? " is a " : " is not a ",
35          "printing character");
36
37      printf("%s\n%s%s\n%s%s%s\n",  "According to isgraph:",
38          isgraph('Q')    ? "Q is a " : "Q is not a ",
39          "printing character other than a space",
40          "Space", isgraph(' ')    ? " is a " : " is not a ",
41          "printing character other than a space");
42  }
```

```
According to isspace:
Newline is a whitespace character
Horizontal tab is a whitespace character
% is not a whitespace character

According to iscntrl:
Newline is a control character
$ is not a control character

According to ispunct:
; is a punctuation character
Y is not a punctuation character
# is a punctuation character

According to isprint:
$ is a printing character
Alert is not a printing character

According to isgraph:
Q is a printing character other than a space
Space is not a printing character other than a space
```

Fig. 8.4 | Using functions isspace, iscntrl, ispunct, isprint and isgraph. (Part 2 of 2.)

8.4 String-Conversion Functions

This section presents the **string-conversion functions** from the **general utilities library** (**<stdlib.h>**). These functions convert strings of digits to integer and floating-point values. Figure 8.5 summarizes the string-conversion functions. The C standard also includes strtoll and strtoull for converting strings to long long int and unsigned long long int, respectively. Note the use of const to declare variable nPtr in the function headers (read from right to left as "nPtr is a pointer to a character constant"); const specifies that the argument value will not be modified.

Function prototype	Function description
`double strtod(const char *nPtr, char **endPtr);`	
	Converts the string nPtr to double.
`long strtol(const char *nPtr, char **endPtr, int base);`	
	Converts the string nPtr to long.
`unsigned long strtoul(const char *nPtr, char **endPtr, int base);`	
	Converts the string nPtr to unsigned long.

Fig. 8.5 | String-conversion functions of the general utilities library.

8.4.1 Function strtod

Function **strtod** (Fig. 8.6) converts a sequence of characters representing a floating-point value to double. The function returns 0 if it's unable to convert any portion of its first argument to double. The function receives two arguments—a string (char *) and a pointer to a string (char **). The string argument contains the character sequence to be converted to double—any whitespace characters at the beginning of the string are ignored. The function uses the char ** argument to modify a char * in the calling function (stringPtr) so that it points to the *location of the first character after the converted portion of the string* or to the entire string if no portion can be converted. Line 11 indicates that d is assigned the double value converted from string, and stringPtr is assigned the location of the first character after the converted value (51.2) in string.

```
 1   // Fig. 8.6: fig08_06.c
 2   // Using function strtod
 3   #include <stdio.h>
 4   #include <stdlib.h>
 5
 6   int main(void)
 7   {
 8      const char *string = "51.2% are admitted"; // initialize string
 9      char *stringPtr; // create char pointer
10
11      double d = strtod(string, &stringPtr);
12
```

Fig. 8.6 | Using function strtod. (Part 1 of 2.)

```
13      printf("The string \"%s\" is converted to the\n", string);
14      printf("double value %.2f and the string \"%s\"\n", d, stringPtr);
15  }
```

```
The string "51.2% are admitted" is converted to the
double value 51.20 and the string "% are admitted"
```

Fig. 8.6 | Using function strtod. (Part 2 of 2.)

8.4.2 Function strtol

Function **strtol** (Fig. 8.7) converts to long int a sequence of characters representing an integer. The function returns 0 if it's unable to convert any portion of its first argument to long int. The function's three arguments are a string (char *), a pointer to a string and an integer. The string contains the character sequence to be converted to long—any whitespace characters at the beginning of the string are ignored. The function uses the char ** argument to modify a char * in the calling function (remainderPtr) so that it points to the *location of the first character after the converted portion of the string* or to the entire string if no portion can be converted. The integer specifies the *base* of the value being converted.

```
1   // Fig. 8.7: fig08_07.c
2   // Using function strtol
3   #include <stdio.h>
4   #include <stdlib.h>
5
6   int main(void)
7   {
8       const char *string = "-1234567abc"; // initialize string pointer
9       char *remainderPtr; // create char pointer
10
11      long x = strtol(string, &remainderPtr, 0);
12
13      printf("%s\"%s\"\n%s%ld\n%s\"%s\"\n%s%ld\n",
14          "The original string is ", string,
15          "The converted value is ", x,
16          "The remainder of the original string is ",
17          remainderPtr,
18          "The converted value plus 567 is ", x + 567);
19  }
```

```
The original string is "-1234567abc"
The converted value is -1234567
The remainder of the original string is "abc"
The converted value plus 567 is -1234000
```

Fig. 8.7 | Using function strtol.

Line 11 indicates that x is assigned the long value converted from string. The second argument, remainderPtr, is assigned the remainder of string after the conversion. Using NULL for the second argument causes the *remainder of the string to be ignored*. The third argument, 0, indicates that the value to be converted can be in octal (base 8), decimal (base 10) or hexadecimal (base 16) format. The base can be specified as 0 or any value between 2 and 36. (See Appendix C for a detailed explanation of the octal, decimal and hexadecimal number systems.) Numeric representations of integers from base 11 to base 36 use the characters A–Z to represent the values 10 to 35. For example, hexadecimal values can consist of the digits 0–9 and the characters A–F. A base-11 integer can consist of the digits 0–9 and the character A. A base-24 integer can consist of the digits 0–9 and the characters A–N. A base-36 integer can consist of the digits 0–9 and the characters A–Z.

8.4.3 Function `strtoul`

Function **strtoul** (Fig. 8.8) converts to unsigned long int a sequence of characters representing an unsigned long int value. The function works identically to function strtol. Line 11 indicates that x is assigned the unsigned long int value converted from string. The second argument, &remainderPtr, is assigned the remainder of string after the conversion. The third argument, 0, indicates that the value to be converted can be in octal, decimal or hexadecimal format.

```
1   // Fig. 8.8: fig08_08.c
2   // Using function strtoul
3   #include <stdio.h>
4   #include <stdlib.h>
5
6   int main(void)
7   {
8      const char *string = "1234567abc"; // initialize string pointer
9      char *remainderPtr; // create char pointer
10
11     unsigned long int x = strtoul(string, &remainderPtr, 0);
12
13     printf("%s\"%s\"\n%s%lu\n%s\"%s\"\n%s%lu\n",
14        "The original string is ", string,
15        "The converted value is ", x,
16        "The remainder of the original string is ",
17        remainderPtr,
18        "The converted value minus 567 is ", x - 567);
19   }
```

```
The original string is "1234567abc"
The converted value is 1234567
The remainder of the original string is "abc"
The converted value minus 567 is 1234000
```

Fig. 8.8 | Using function `strtoul`.

8.5 Standard Input/Output Library Functions

This section presents several functions from the standard input/output library (**<stdio.h>**) specifically for manipulating character and string data. Figure 8.9 summarizes the character and string input/output functions of the standard input/output library.

Function prototype	Function description
`int getchar(void);`	Inputs the next character from the standard input and returns it as an integer.
`char *fgets(char *s, int n, FILE *stream);`	
	Inputs characters from the specified stream into the array s until a *newline* or *end-of-file* character is encountered, or until n - 1 bytes are read. In this chapter, we specify the stream as `stdin`—the *standard input stream*, which is typically used to read characters from the keyboard. A *terminating null character* is appended to the array. Returns the string that was read into s. If a newline is encountered, it's included in the string stored in s.
`int putchar(int c);`	Prints the character stored in c and returns it as an integer.
`int puts(const char *s);`	Prints the string s followed by a *newline* character. Returns a non-zero integer if successful, or EOF if an error occurs.
`int sprintf(char *s, const char *format, ...);`	
	Equivalent to `printf`, except the output is stored in the array s instead of printed on the screen. Returns the number of characters written to s, or EOF if an error occurs. [*Note:* We mention the more secure related functions in the Secure C Programming section of this chapter.]
`int sscanf(char *s, const char *format, ...);`	
	Equivalent to `scanf`, except the input is read from the array s rather than from the keyboard. Returns the number of items successfully read by the function, or EOF if an error occurs. [*Note:* We mention the more secure related functions in the Secure C Programming section of this chapter.]

Fig. 8.9 | Standard input/output library character and string functions.

8.5.1 Functions fgets and putchar

Figure 8.10 uses functions **fgets** and **putchar** to read a line of text from the standard input (keyboard) and recursively output the characters of the line in reverse order. Function fgets reads characters from the *standard input* into its first argument—an array of chars—until a *newline* or the *end-of-file* indicator is encountered, or until the maximum number of characters is read. The maximum number of characters is one fewer than the value specified in fgets's second argument. The third argument specifies the *stream* from which to read characters—in this case, we use the *standard input stream* (stdin). A null character ('\0') is appended to the array when reading terminates. Function putchar prints its character argument. The program calls *recursive* function reverse[1] to print the line of text backward. If the first character of the array received by reverse is the null character '\0', reverse returns. Otherwise, reverse is called again with the address of the subarray be-

---

1. We use recursion here for demonstration purposes. It's usually more efficient to use a loop to iterate from a string's last character (the one at the position one less than the string's length) to its first character (the one at position 0).

ginning at element sPtr[1], and character sPtr[0] is output with putchar when the recursive call is completed. The order of the two statements in the else portion of the if statement causes reverse to walk to the terminating null character of the string *before* a character is printed. As the recursive calls are completed, the characters are output in reverse order.

```c
1   // Fig. 8.10: fig08_10.c
2   // Using functions fgets and putchar
3   #include <stdio.h>
4   #define SIZE 80
5
6   void reverse(const char * const sPtr); // prototype
7
8   int main(void)
9   {
10     char sentence[SIZE]; // create char array
11
12     puts("Enter a line of text:");
13
14     // use fgets to read line of text
15     fgets(sentence, SIZE, stdin);
16
17     printf("\n%s", "The line printed backward is:");
18     reverse(sentence);
19  }
20
21  // recursively outputs characters in string in reverse order
22  void reverse(const char * const sPtr)
23  {
24     // if end of the string
25     if ('\0' == sPtr[0]) { // base case
26        return;
27     }
28     else { // if not end of the string
29        reverse(&sPtr[1]); // recursion step
30        putchar(sPtr[0]); // use putchar to display character
31     }
32  }
```

```
Enter a line of text:
Characters and Strings

The line printed backward is:
sgnirtS dna sretcarahC
```

Fig. 8.10 | Using functions fgets and putchar.

8.5.2 Function getchar

Figure 8.11 uses functions **getchar** and puts to read characters from the standard input into character array sentence and display the characters as a string. Function getchar reads a character from the *standard input* and returns the character as an integer—recall from Section 4.7 that an integer is returned to support the end-of-file indicator. As you know, function `puts` takes a string as an argument and displays the string followed by a newline character. The program stops inputting characters either when 79 characters have been read or when `getchar` reads the *newline* character entered by the user to end the line of text. A *null character* is appended to array `sentence` (line 20) so that the array may be treated as a string. Then line 24 uses `puts` to display the string contained in `sentence`.

```c
1  // Fig. 8.11: fig08_11.c
2  // Using function getchar.
3  #include <stdio.h>
4  #define SIZE 80
5
6  int main(void)
7  {
8     int c; // variable to hold character input by user
9     char sentence[SIZE]; // create char array
10    int i = 0; // initialize counter i
11
12    // prompt user to enter line of text
13    puts("Enter a line of text:");
14
15    // use getchar to read each character
16    while ((i < SIZE - 1) && (c = getchar()) != '\n') {
17       sentence[i++] = c;
18    }
19
20    sentence[i] = '\0'; // terminate string
21
22    // use puts to display sentence
23    puts("\nThe line entered was:");
24    puts(sentence);
25 }
```

```
Enter a line of text:
This is a test.

The line entered was:
This is a test.
```

Fig. 8.11 | Using function getchar.

8.5.3 Function sprintf

Figure 8.12 uses function **sprintf** to print formatted data into array s—an array of characters. The function uses the same conversion specifiers as printf (see Chapter 9 for a detailed discussion of formatting). The program inputs an int value and a double value to be formatted and printed to array s. Array s is the first argument of sprintf. [*Note:* If your system supports C11's snprintf_s, then use that in preference to sprintf. If your system doesn't support snprintf_s but does support snprintf, then use that in preference to sprintf.]

```
 1   // Fig. 8.12: fig08_12.c
 2   // Using function sprintf
 3   #include <stdio.h>
 4   #define SIZE 80
 5
 6   int main(void)
 7   {
 8      int x; // x value to be input
 9      double y; // y value to be input
10
11      puts("Enter an integer and a double:");
12      scanf("%d%lf", &x, &y);
13
14      char s[SIZE]; // create char array
15      sprintf(s, "integer:%6d\ndouble:%7.2f", x, y);
16
17      printf("%s\n%s\n", "The formatted output stored in array s is:", s);
18
19   }
```

```
Enter an integer and a double:
298 87.375
The formatted output stored in array s is:
integer:   298
double:  87.38
```

Fig. 8.12 | Using function sprintf.

8.5.4 Function sscanf

Figure 8.13 uses function **sscanf** to read formatted data from character array s. The function uses the same conversion specifiers as scanf. The program reads an int and a double from array s and stores the values in x and y, respectively. The values of x and y are printed. Array s is the first argument of sscanf.

```
 1   // Fig. 8.13: fig08_13.c
 2   // Using function sscanf
 3   #include <stdio.h>
 4
 5   int main(void)
 6   {
 7      char s[] = "31298 87.375"; // initialize array s
 8      int x; // x value to be input
 9      double y; // y value to be input
10
11      sscanf(s, "%d%lf", &x, &y);
12      printf("%s\n%s%6d\n%s%8.3f\n",
13          "The values stored in character array s are:",
14          "integer:", x, "double:", y);
15   }
```

Fig. 8.13 | Using function sscanf. (Part 1 of 2.)

```
The values stored in character array s are:
integer: 31298
double:  87.375
```

Fig. 8.13 | Using function sscanf. (Part 2 of 2.)

8.6 String-Manipulation Functions of the String-Handling Library

The string-handling library (<string.h>) provides many useful functions for manipulating string data (**copying strings** and **concatenating strings**), **comparing strings**, searching strings for characters and other strings, **tokenizing strings** (separating strings into logical pieces) and determining the **length of strings**. This section presents the string-manipulation functions of the string-handling library. The functions are summarized in Fig. 8.14. Every function—except for strncpy—appends the *null character* to its result. [*Note:* Each of these functions has a more secure version described in the optional Annex K of the C11 standard. We mention these in the Secure C Programming section of this chapter.]

Function prototype	Function description
char *strcpy(char *s1, const char *s2)	*Copies* string s2 into array s1. The value of s1 is returned.
char *strncpy(char *s1, const char *s2, size_t n)	*Copies* at most n characters of string s2 into array s1 and returns s1.
char *strcat(char *s1, const char *s2)	*Appends* string s2 to array s1. The first character of s2 *overwrites the terminating null character* of s1. The value of s1 is returned.
char *strncat(char *s1, const char *s2, size_t n)	*Appends at most n characters* of string s2 to array s1. The first character of s2 *overwrites the terminating null character* of s1. The value of s1 is returned.

Fig. 8.14 | String-manipulation functions of the string-handling library.

Functions **strncpy** and **strncat** specify a parameter of type size_t. Function strcpy copies its second argument (a string) into its first argument—a character array that *you must ensure is large enough* to store the string and its terminating null character, which is also copied. Function strncpy is equivalent to strcpy, except that strncpy specifies the number of characters to be copied from the string into the array. *Function strncpy does not necessarily copy the terminating null character of its second argument. This occurs only if the number of characters to be copied is more than the length of the string.* For example, if "test" is the second argument, a *terminating null character* is written only if the third argument to strncpy is at least 5 (four characters in "test" plus a terminating null character). If the third argument is larger than 5, some implementations append null characters to the array until the total number of characters specified by the third argument are written and others stop after writing the first null character.

Common Programming Error 8.5

Not appending a terminating null character to the first argument of a strncpy when the third argument is less than or equal to the length of the string in the second argument.

8.6.1 Functions strcpy and strncpy

Figure 8.15 uses strcpy to copy the entire string in array x into array y and uses strncpy to copy the first 14 characters of array x into array z. A *null character* ('\0') is appended to array z, because the call to strncpy in the program *does not write a terminating null character* (the third argument is less than the string length of the second argument).

```
 1   // Fig. 8.15: fig08_15.c
 2   // Using functions strcpy and strncpy
 3   #include <stdio.h>
 4   #include <string.h>
 5   #define SIZE1 25
 6   #define SIZE2 15
 7
 8   int main(void)
 9   {
10      char x[] = "Happy Birthday to You"; // initialize char array x
11      char y[SIZE1]; // create char array y
12      char z[SIZE2]; // create char array z
13
14      // copy contents of x into y
15      printf("%s%s\n%s%s\n",
16         "The string in array x is: ", x,
17         "The string in array y is: ", strcpy(y, x));
18
19      // copy first 14 characters of x into z. Does not copy null
20      // character
21      strncpy(z, x, SIZE2 - 1);
22
23      z[SIZE2 - 1] = '\0'; // terminate string in z
24      printf("The string in array z is: %s\n", z);
25   }
```

```
The string in array x is: Happy Birthday to You
The string in array y is: Happy Birthday to You
The string in array z is: Happy Birthday
```

Fig. 8.15 | Using functions strcpy and strncpy.

8.6.2 Functions strcat and strncat

Function **strcat** appends its second argument (a string) to its first argument (a character array containing a string). The first character of the second argument replaces the null ('\0') that terminates the string in the first argument. *You must ensure that the array used to store the first string is large enough to store the first string, the second string and the terminating null character copied from the second string.* Function strncat appends a specified number of characters from the second string to the first string. A terminating null character is automatically appended to the result. Figure 8.16 demonstrates function strcat and function strncat.

```
 1   // Fig. 8.16: fig08_16.c
 2   // Using functions strcat and strncat
 3   #include <stdio.h>
 4   #include <string.h>
 5
 6   int main(void)
 7   {
 8      char s1[20] = "Happy "; // initialize char array s1
 9      char s2[] = "New Year "; // initialize char array s2
10      char s3[40] = ""; // initialize char array s3 to empty
11
12      printf("s1 = %s\ns2 = %s\n", s1, s2);
13
14      // concatenate s2 to s1
15      printf("strcat(s1, s2) = %s\n", strcat(s1, s2)  );
16
17      // concatenate first 6 characters of s1 to s3. Place '\0'
18      // after last character
19      printf("strncat(s3, s1, 6) = %s\n", strncat(s3, s1, 6));
20
21      // concatenate s1 to s3
22      printf("strcat(s3, s1) = %s\n", strcat(s3, s1)  );
23   }
```

```
s1 = Happy
s2 = New Year
strcat(s1, s2) = Happy New Year
strncat(s3, s1, 6) = Happy
strcat(s3, s1) = Happy Happy New Year
```

Fig. 8.16 | Using functions strcat and strncat.

8.7 Comparison Functions of the String-Handling Library

This section presents the string-handling library's **string-comparison functions, strcmp** and **strncmp**. Figure 8.17 contains their prototypes and a brief description of each function.

Function prototype	Function description
`int strcmp(const char *s1, const char *s2);`	
	Compares the string s1 with the string s2. The function returns 0, less than 0 or greater than 0 if s1 is equal to, less than or greater than s2, respectively.
`int strncmp(const char *s1, const char *s2, size_t n);`	
	Compares up to n characters of the string s1 with the string s2. The function returns 0, less than 0 or greater than 0 if s1 is equal to, less than or greater than s2, respectively.

Fig. 8.17 | String-comparison functions of the string-handling library.

Figure 8.18 compares three strings using strcmp and strncmp. Function strcmp compares its first string argument with its second string argument, character by character. The function returns 0 if the strings are equal, a *negative value* if the first string is less than the second string and a *positive value* if the first string is greater than the second string. Function strncmp is equivalent to strcmp, except that strncmp compares up to a specified number of characters. Function strncmp does *not* compare characters following a null character in a string. The program prints the integer value returned by each function call.

```c
 1  // Fig. 8.18: fig08_18.c
 2  // Using functions strcmp and strncmp
 3  #include <stdio.h>
 4  #include <string.h>
 5
 6  int main(void)
 7  {
 8     const char *s1 = "Happy New Year"; // initialize char pointer
 9     const char *s2 = "Happy New Year"; // initialize char pointer
10     const char *s3 = "Happy Holidays"; // initialize char pointer
11
12     printf("%s%s\n%s%s\n%s%s\n\n%s%2d\n%s%2d\n%s%2d\n\n",
13        "s1 = ", s1, "s2 = ", s2, "s3 = ", s3,
14        "strcmp(s1, s2) = ", strcmp(s1, s2) ,
15        "strcmp(s1, s3) = ", strcmp(s1, s3) ,
16        "strcmp(s3, s1) = ", strcmp(s3, s1) );
17
18     printf("%s%2d\n%s%2d\n%s%2d\n",
19        "strncmp(s1, s3, 6) = ", strncmp(s1, s3, 6) ,
20        "strncmp(s1, s3, 7) = ", strncmp(s1, s3, 7) ,
21        "strncmp(s3, s1, 7) = ", strncmp(s3, s1, 7) );
22  }
```

```
s1 = Happy New Year
s2 = Happy New Year
s3 = Happy Holidays

strcmp(s1, s2) =  0
strcmp(s1, s3) =  1
strcmp(s3, s1) = -1

strncmp(s1, s3, 6) =  0
strncmp(s1, s3, 7) =  1
strncmp(s3, s1, 7) = -1
```

Fig. 8.18 | Using functions strcmp and strncmp.

Common Programming Error 8.6
Assuming that strcmp and strncmp return 1 when their arguments are equal is a logic error. Both functions return 0 (strangely, the equivalent of C's false value) for equality. Therefore, when comparing two strings for equality, the result of function strcmp or strncmp should be compared with 0 to determine whether the strings are equal.

To understand just what it means for one string to be "greater than" or "less than" another, consider the process of alphabetizing a series of last names. The reader would, no doubt, place "Jones" before "Smith," because the first letter of "Jones" comes before the first letter of "Smith" in the alphabet. But the alphabet is more than just a list of 26 letters—it's an ordered list of characters. Each letter occurs in a specific position within the list. "Z" is more than merely a letter of the alphabet; "Z" is specifically the 26th letter of the alphabet.

How do the string-comparison functions know that one particular letter comes before another? All characters are represented inside the computer as **numeric codes** in character sets such as ASCII and Unicode; when the computer compares two strings, it actually compares the numeric codes of the characters in the strings—this is called a lexicographical comparison. See Appendix B for the numeric values of ASCII characters.

The negative and positive values returned by functions `strcmp` and `strncmp` *differ by compiler*. For some (e.g, Visual C++ and GNU gcc), these values are `-1` or `1` (as shown in Fig. 8.18). For other compilers (e.g., Xcode LLVM), the values returned represent the difference between the numeric codes of the first characters that differ in each string. For the comparisons in this program, that's the difference betweeen the numeric codes of "N" in "New" and "H" in "Happy" (6 or -6, depending on which string is the first argument in each call).

8.8 Search Functions of the String-Handling Library

This section presents the functions of the string-handling library used to *search strings* for characters and other strings. The functions are summarized in Fig. 8.19. The functions `strcspn` and `strspn` return `size_t`. [*Note:* Function `strtok` has a more secure version described in optional Annex K of the C11 standard. We mention this in the Secure C Programming section of this chapter.]

Function prototypes and descriptions
`char *strchr(const char *s, int c);`
Locates the first occurrence of character c in string s. If c is found, a pointer to c in s is returned. Otherwise, a NULL pointer is returned.
`size_t strcspn(const char *s1, const char *s2);`
Determines and returns the length of the initial segment of string s1 consisting of characters *not* contained in string s2.
`size_t strspn(const char *s1, const char *s2);`
Determines and returns the length of the initial segment of string s1 consisting *only* of characters contained in string s2.
`char *strpbrk(const char *s1, const char *s2);`
Locates the first occurrence in string s1 of any character in string s2. If a character from string s2 is found, a pointer to the character in string s1 is returned. Otherwise, a NULL pointer is returned.
`char *strrchr(const char *s, int c);`
Locates the last occurrence of c in string s. If c is found, a pointer to c in string s is returned. Otherwise, a NULL pointer is returned.

Fig. 8.19 | Search functions of the string-handling library. (Part 1 of 2.)

Function prototypes and descriptions

```
char *strstr(const char *s1, const char *s2);
```
> *Locates the first occurrence* in string s1 of string s2. If the string is found, a pointer to the string in s1 is returned. Otherwise, a NULL pointer is returned.

```
char *strtok(char *s1, const char *s2);
```
> A sequence of calls to strtok breaks string s1 into *tokens*—logical pieces such as words in a line of text—separated by characters contained in string s2. The first call contains s1 as the first argument, and subsequent calls to continue tokenizing the same string contain NULL as the first argument. A pointer to the current token is returned by each call. If there are no more tokens when the function is called, NULL is returned.

Fig. 8.19 | Search functions of the string-handling library. (Part 2 of 2.)

8.8.1 Function strchr

Function **strchr** searches for the *first occurrence* of a character in a string. If the character is found, strchr returns a pointer to the character in the string; otherwise, strchr returns NULL. Figure 8.20 searches for the first occurrences of 'a' and 'z' in "This is a test".

```c
 1  // Fig. 8.20: fig08_20.c
 2  // Using function strchr
 3  #include <stdio.h>
 4  #include <string.h>
 5
 6  int main(void)
 7  {
 8     const char *string = "This is a test"; // initialize char pointer
 9     char character1 = 'a'; // initialize character1
10     char character2 = 'z'; // initialize character2
11
12     // if character1 was found in string
13     if (strchr(string, character1) != NULL) { // can remove "!= NULL"
14        printf("\'%c\' was found in \"%s\".\n",
15           character1, string);
16     }
17     else { // if character1 was not found
18        printf("\'%c\' was not found in \"%s\".\n",
19           character1, string);
20     }
21
22     // if character2 was found in string
23     if (strchr(string, character2) != NULL) { // can remove "!= NULL"
24        printf("\'%c\' was found in \"%s\".\n",
25           character2, string);
26     }
27     else { // if character2 was not found
```

Fig. 8.20 | Using function strchr. (Part 1 of 2.)

```
28              printf("\'%c\' was not found in \"%s\".\n",
29                  character2, string);
30          }
31   }
```

```
'a' was found in "This is a test".
'z' was not found in "This is a test".
```

Fig. 8.20 | Using function strchr. (Part 2 of 2.)

8.8.2 Function strcspn

Function **strcspn** (Fig. 8.21) determines the length of the initial part of the string in its first argument that does *not* contain any characters from the string in its second argument. The function returns the length of the segment.

```
1    // Fig. 8.21: fig08_21.c
2    // Using function strcspn
3    #include <stdio.h>
4    #include <string.h>
5
6    int main(void)
7    {
8        // initialize two char pointers
9        const char *string1 = "The value is 3.14159";
10       const char *string2 = "1234567890";
11
12       printf("%s%s\n%s%s\n\n%s\n%s%u\n",
13           "string1 = ", string1, "string2 = ", string2,
14           "The length of the initial segment of string1",
15           "containing no characters from string2 = ",
16           strcspn(string1, string2)  );
17   }
```

```
string1 = The value is 3.14159
string2 = 1234567890

The length of the initial segment of string1
containing no characters from string2 = 13
```

Fig. 8.21 | Using function strcspn.

8.8.3 Function strpbrk

Function **strpbrk** searches its first string argument for the *first occurrence* of any character in its second string argument. If a character from the second argument is found, strpbrk returns a pointer to the character in the first argument; otherwise, strpbrk returns NULL. Figure 8.22 shows a program that locates the first occurrence in string1 of any character from string2.

```
1   // Fig. 8.22: fig08_22.c
2   // Using function strpbrk
3   #include <stdio.h>
4   #include <string.h>
5
6   int main(void)
7   {
8      const char *string1 = "This is a test"; // initialize char pointer
9      const char *string2 = "beware"; // initialize char pointer
10
11     printf("%s\"%s\"\n'%c'%s\n\"%s\"\n",
12        "Of the characters in ", string2,
13        *strpbrk(string1, string2)  ,
14        " appears earliest in ", string1);
15  }
```

```
Of the characters in "beware"
'a' appears earliest in
"This is a test"
```

Fig. 8.22 | Using function strpbrk.

8.8.4 Function strrchr

Function **strrchr** searches for the *last occurrence* of the specified character in a string. If the character is found, strrchr returns a pointer to the character in the string; otherwise, strrchr returns NULL. Figure 8.23 shows a program that searches for the last occurrence of the character 'z' in the string "A zoo has many animals including zebras".

```
1   // Fig. 8.23: fig08_23.c
2   // Using function strrchr
3   #include <stdio.h>
4   #include <string.h>
5
6   int main(void)
7   {
8      // initialize char pointer
9      const char *string1 = "A zoo has many animals including zebras";
10
11     int c = 'z'; // character to search for
12
13     printf("%s\n%s'%c'%s\"%s\"\n",
14        "The remainder of string1 beginning with the",
15        "last occurrence of character ", c,
16        " is: ", strrchr(string1, c)  );
17  }
```

```
The remainder of string1 beginning with the
last occurrence of character 'z' is: "zebras"
```

Fig. 8.23 | Using function strrchr.

8.8.5 Function strspn

Function strspn (Fig. 8.24) determines the length of the *initial part* of the string in its first argument that contains only characters from the string in its second argument. The function returns the length of the segment.

```
 1   // Fig. 8.24: fig08_24.c
 2   // Using function strspn
 3   #include <stdio.h>
 4   #include <string.h>
 5
 6   int main(void)
 7   {
 8      // initialize two char pointers
 9      const char *string1 = "The value is 3.14159";
10      const char *string2 = "aehi lsTuv";
11
12      printf("%s%s\n%s%s\n\n%s\n%s%u\n",
13         "string1 = ", string1, "string2 = ", string2,
14         "The length of the initial segment of string1",
15         "containing only characters from string? = ",
16         strspn(string1, string2) );
17   }
```

```
string1 = The value is 3.14159
string2 = aehi lsTuv

The length of the initial segment of string1
containing only characters from string2 = 13
```

Fig. 8.24 | Using function strspn.

8.8.6 Function strstr

Function **strstr** searches for the *first occurrence* of its second string argument in its first string argument. If the second string is found in the first string, a pointer to the location of the string in the first argument is returned. Figure 8.25 uses strstr to find the string "def" in the string "abcdefabcdef".

```
 1   // Fig. 8.25: fig08_25.c
 2   // Using function strstr
 3   #include <stdio.h>
 4   #include <string.h>
 5
 6   int main(void)
 7   {
 8      const char *string1 = "abcdefabcdef"; // string to search
 9      const char *string2 = "def"; // string to search for
10
```

Fig. 8.25 | Using function strstr. (Part 1 of 2.)

```
11    printf("%s%s\n%s%s\n\n%s\n%s%s\n",
12        "string1 = ", string1, "string2 = ", string2,
13        "The remainder of string1 beginning with the",
14        "first occurrence of string2 is: ",
15        strstr(string1, string2) );
16    }
```

```
string1 = abcdefabcdef
string2 = def

The remainder of string1 beginning with the
first occurrence of string2 is: defabcdef
```

Fig. 8.25 | Using function `strstr`. (Part 2 of 2.)

8.8.7 Function `strtok`

Function **strtok** (Fig. 8.26) is used to break a string into a series of **tokens**. A token is a sequence of characters separated by **delimiters** (usually *spaces* or *punctuation marks*, but a delimiter can be *any character*). For example, in a line of text, each word can be considered a token, and the spaces and punctuation separating the words can be considered delimiters.

```c
1    // Fig. 8.26: fig08_26.c
2    // Using function strtok
3    #include <stdio.h>
4    #include <string.h>
5
6    int main(void)
7    {
8        // initialize array string
9        char string[] = "This is a sentence with 7 tokens";
10
11        printf("%s\n%s\n\n%s\n",
12            "The string to be tokenized is:", string,
13            "The tokens are:");
14
15        char *tokenPtr = strtok(string, " "); // begin tokenizing sentence
16
17        // continue tokenizing sentence until tokenPtr becomes NULL
18        while (tokenPtr != NULL) {
19            printf("%s\n", tokenPtr);
20            tokenPtr = strtok(NULL, " "); // get next token
21        }
22    }
```

```
The string to be tokenized is:
This is a sentence with 7 tokens
```

Fig. 8.26 | Using function `strtok`. (Part 1 of 2.)

```
The tokens are:
This
is
a
sentence
with
7
tokens
```

Fig. 8.26 | Using function `strtok`. (Part 2 of 2.)

Multiple calls to `strtok` are required to *tokenize a string*—i.e., break it into tokens (assuming that the string contains more than one token). The first call to `strtok` (line 15) contains two arguments: a string to be tokenized, and a string containing characters that separate the tokens. In line 15, the statement

```
char * tokenPtr = strtok(string, " "); // begin tokenizing sentence
```

assigns `tokenPtr` a pointer to the first token in `string`. The second argument, `" "`, indicates that tokens are separated by spaces. Function `strtok` searches for the first character in string that's not a delimiting character (space). This begins the first token. The function then finds the next delimiting character in the string and *replaces it with a null (`'\0'`) character* to terminate the current token. Function `strtok` saves a pointer to the next character following the token in `string` and returns a pointer to the current token.

Subsequent `strtok` calls in line 20 continue tokenizing `string`. These calls *contain NULL as their first argument.* The `NULL` argument indicates that the call to `strtok` should continue tokenizing from the location in `string` saved by the last call to `strtok`. If no tokens remain when `strtok` is called, `strtok` returns `NULL`. You can change the delimiter string in each new call to `strtok`. Figure 8.26 uses `strtok` to tokenize the string `"This is a sentence with 7 tokens"`. Each token is printed separately. Function `strtok` *modifies the input string* by placing `'\0'` at the end of each token; therefore, a *copy* of the string should be made if the string will be used after the calls to `strtok`. [*Note:* Also see CERT recommendation STR06-C, which discusses the problems with assuming that `strtok` does not modify the string in its first argument.]

8.9 Memory Functions of the String-Handling Library

The string-handling library functions presented in this section manipulate, compare and search blocks of memory. The functions treat blocks of memory as character arrays and can manipulate any block of data. Figure 8.27 summarizes the memory functions of the string-handling library. In the function discussions, "object" refers to a block of data. [*Note:* Each of these functions has a more secure version described in optional Annex K of the C11 standard. We mention these in the Secure C Programming section of this chapter.]

The pointer parameters are declared `void *` so they can be used to manipulate memory for *any* data type. Recall from Chapter 7 that any pointer can be assigned directly to a pointer of type `void *`, and a pointer of type `void *` can be assigned directly to a pointer of any other type. Because a `void *` pointer cannot be dereferenced, each function receives a size argument that specifies the number of bytes the function will process. For

Function prototype	Function description
`void *memcpy(void *s1, const void *s2, size_t n);`	
	Copies n bytes from the object pointed to by s2 into the object pointed to by s1. A pointer to the resulting object is returned.
`void *memmove(void *s1, const void *s2, size_t n);`	
	Copies n bytes from the object pointed to by s2 into the object pointed to by s1. The copy is performed as if the bytes were first copied from the object pointed to by s2 into a *temporary array* and then from the temporary array into the object pointed to by s1. A pointer to the resulting object is returned.
`int memcmp(const void *s1, const void *s2, size_t n);`	
	Compares the first n bytes of the objects pointed to by s1 and s2. The function returns 0, less than 0 or greater than 0 if s1 is equal to, less than or greater than s2.
`void *memchr(const void *s, int c, size_t n);`	
	Locates the first occurrence of c (converted to unsigned char) in the first n bytes of the object pointed to by s. If c is found, a pointer to c in the object is returned. Otherwise, NULL is returned.
`void *memset(void *s, int c, size_t n);`	
	Copies c (converted to unsigned char) into the *first n bytes* of the object pointed to by s. A pointer to the result is returned.

Fig. 8.27 | Memory functions of the string-handling library.

simplicity, the examples in this section manipulate character arrays (blocks of characters). The functions in Fig. 8.27 *do not* check for terminating null characters, because they manipulate blocks of memory that are not necessarily strings.

8.9.1 Function memcpy

Function **memcpy** copies a specified number of bytes from the object pointed to by its second argument into the object pointed to by its first argument. The function can receive a pointer to any type of object. The result of this function is *undefined* if the two objects overlap in memory (i.e., if they are parts of the same object)—in such cases, use memmove. Figure 8.28 uses memcpy to copy the string in array s2 to array s1.

Performance Tip 8.1
memcpy is more efficient than strcpy when you know the size of the string you are copying.

```
1   // Fig. 8.28: fig08_28.c
2   // Using function memcpy
3   #include <stdio.h>
4   #include <string.h>
```

Fig. 8.28 | Using function memcpy. (Part 1 of 2.)

```
5
6   int main(void)
7   {
8      char s1[17]; // create char array s1
9      char s2[] = "Copy this string"; // initialize char array s2
10
11     memcpy(s1, s2, 17);
12     printf("%s\n%s\"%s\"\n",
13        "After s2 is copied into s1 with memcpy,",
14        "s1 contains ", s1);
15  }
```

```
After s2 is copied into s1 with memcpy,
s1 contains "Copy this string"
```

Fig. 8.28 | Using function memcpy. (Part 2 of 2.)

8.9.2 Function memmove

Function memmove, like memcpy, *copies a specified number of bytes* from the object pointed to by its second argument into the object pointed to by its first argument. Copying is performed as if the bytes were copied from the second argument into a temporary array, then copied from the temporary array into the first argument. This allows bytes from one part of a string to be copied into another part of the *same* string, even if the two portions overlap. Figure 8.29 uses memmove to copy the last 10 bytes of array x into the first 10 bytes of array x.

 Common Programming Error 8.7
String-manipulation functions other than memmove *that copy characters have undefined results when copying takes place between parts of the* same *string.*

```
1   // Fig. 8.29: fig08_29.c
2   // Using function memmove
3   #include <stdio.h>
4   #include <string.h>
5
6   int main(void)
7   {
8      char x[] = "Home Sweet Home"; // initialize char array x
9
10     printf("%s%s\n", "The string in array x before memmove is: ", x);
11     printf("%s%s\n", "The string in array x after memmove is: ",
12        (char *) memmove(x, &x[5], 10));
13  }
```

```
The string in array x before memmove is: Home Sweet Home
The string in array x after memmove is: Sweet Home Home
```

Fig. 8.29 | Using function memmove.

8.9.3 Function memcmp

Function memcmp (Fig. 8.30) *compares the specified number of bytes* of its first argument with the corresponding bytes of its second argument. The function returns a value greater than 0 if the first argument is *greater than* the second, returns 0 if the arguments are equal and returns a value less than 0 if the first argument is less than the second.

```c
1   // Fig. 8.30: fig08_30.c
2   // Using function memcmp
3   #include <stdio.h>
4   #include <string.h>
5
6   int main(void)
7   {
8      char s1[] = "ABCDEFG"; // initialize char array s1
9      char s2[] = "ABCDXYZ"; // initialize char array s2
10
11     printf("%s%s\n%s%s\n\n%s%2d\n%s%2d\n%s%2d\n",
12        "s1 = ", s1, "s2 = ", s2,
13        "memcmp(s1, s2, 4) = ", memcmp(s1, s2, 4),
14        "memcmp(s1, s2, 7) = ", memcmp(s1, s2, 7),
15        "memcmp(s2, s1, 7) = ", memcmp(s2, s1, 7));
16  }
```

```
s1 = ABCDEFG
s2 = ABCDXYZ

memcmp(s1, s2, 4) =  0
memcmp(s1, s2, 7) = -1
memcmp(s2, s1, 7) =  1
```

Fig. 8.30 | Using function memcmp.

8.9.4 Function memchr

Function memchr searches for the *first occurrence of a byte*, represented as unsigned char, in the specified number of bytes of an object. If the byte is found, a pointer to the byte in the object is returned; otherwise, a NULL pointer is returned. Figure 8.31 searches for the byte containing 'r' in the string "This is a string".

```c
1   // Fig. 8.31: fig08_31.c
2   // Using function memchr
3   #include <stdio.h>
4   #include <string.h>
5
6   int main(void)
7   {
```

Fig. 8.31 | Using function memchr. (Part 1 of 2.)

```
8       const char *s = "This is a string"; // initialize char pointer
9
10      printf("%s\'%c\'%s\"%s\"\n",
11          "The remainder of s after character ", 'r',
12          " is found is ", (char *) memchr(s, 'r', 16));
13  }
```

```
The remainder of s after character 'r' is found is "ring"
```

Fig. 8.31 | Using function memchr. (Part 2 of 2.)

8.9.5 Function memset

Function **memset** copies the value of the byte in its second argument into the first *n* bytes of the object pointed to by its first argument, where *n* is specified by the third argument. Figure 8.32 uses memset to copy 'b' into the first 7 bytes of string1.

Performance Tip 8.2

Use memset to set an array's elements to 0 rather than looping through them and assigning 0 to each element. For example, Fig. 6.3 could have initialized the five-element array n with memset(n, 0, 5);. Many hardware architectures have a block copy or clear instruction that the compiler can use to optimize memset for high-performance zeroing of memory.

```
1   // Fig. 8.32: fig08_32.c
2   // Using function memset
3   #include <stdio.h>
4   #include <string.h>
5
6   int main(void)
7   {
8       char string1[15] = "BBBBBBBBBBBBBB"; // initialize string1
9
10      printf("string1 = %s\n", string1);
11      printf("string1 after memset = %s\n",
12          (char *) memset(string1, 'b', 7));
13  }
```

```
string1 = BBBBBBBBBBBBBB
string1 after memset = bbbbbbbBBBBBBB
```

Fig. 8.32 | Using function memset.

8.10 Other Functions of the String-Handling Library

The two remaining functions of the string-handling library are strerror and strlen. Figure 8.33 summarizes the strerror and strlen functions.

Function prototype	Function description
`char *strerror(int errornum);`	
	Maps errornum into a full text string in a compiler- and locale-specific manner (e.g. the message may appear in different spoken languages based on the computer's locale). A pointer to the string is returned. Error numbers are defined in `errno.h`.
`size_t strlen(const char *s);`	
	Determines the length of string s. The number of characters preceding the terminating null character is returned.

Fig. 8.33 | Other functions of the string-handling library.

8.10.1 Function `strerror`

Function **strerror** takes an error number and creates an error message string. A pointer to the string is returned. Figure 8.34 demonstrates `strerror`.

```
1   // Fig. 8.34: fig08_34.c
2   // Using function strerror
3   #include <stdio.h>
4   #include <string.h>
5
6   int main(void)
7   {
8      printf("%s\n", strerror(2));
9   }
```

```
No such file or directory
```

Fig. 8.34 | Using function `strerror`.

8.10.2 Function `strlen`

Function **strlen** takes a string as an argument and returns the number of characters in the string—the terminating null character is not included in the length. Figure 8.35 demonstrates function `strlen`.

```
1   // Fig. 8.35: fig08_35.c
2   // Using function strlen
3   #include <stdio.h>
4   #include <string.h>
5
6   int main(void)
7   {
8      // initialize 3 char pointers
9      const char *string1 = "abcdefghijklmnopqrstuvwxyz";
```

Fig. 8.35 | Using function `strlen`. (Part 1 of 2.)

```
10        const char *string2 = "four";
11        const char *string3 = "Boston";
12
13        printf("%s\"%s\"%s%u\n%s\"%s\"%s%u\n%s\"%s\"%s%u\n",
14            "The length of ", string1, " is ", strlen(string1),
15            "The length of ", string2, " is ", strlen(string2),
16            "The length of ", string3, " is ", strlen(string3));
17   }
```

```
The length of "abcdefghijklmnopqrstuvwxyz" is 26
The length of "four" is 4
The length of "Boston" is 6
```

Fig. 8.35 | Using function strlen. (Part 2 of 2.)

8.11 Secure C Programming

Secure String-Processing Functions

Earlier Secure C Programming sections in this book covered C11's more secure functions
printf_s and scanf_s. In this chapter, we presented functions sprintf, strcpy,
strncpy, strcat, strncat, strtok, strlen, memcpy, memmove and memset. More secure
versions of these and many other string-processing and input/output functions are described by the C11 standard's *optional* Annex K. If your C compiler supports Annex K,
you should use the secure versions of these functions. Among other things, the more secure
versions help prevent buffer overflows by requiring additional parameters that specify the
number of elements in a target array and by ensuring that pointer arguments are non-NULL.

Reading Numeric Inputs and Input Validation

It's important to validate the data that you input into a program. For example, when you
ask the user to enter an int in the range 1–100, then attempt to read that int using scanf,
there are several possible problems. The user could enter:

- an int that's outside the program's required range (such as 102).
- an int that's outside the allowed range for ints on that computer (such as
  8,000,000,000 on a machine with 32-bit ints).
- a noninteger numeric value (such as 27.43).
- a nonnumeric value (such as FOVR).

You can use various functions that you learned in this chapter to fully validate such
input. For example, you could

- use fgets to read the input as a line of text,
- convert the string to a number using strtol and ensure that the conversion was
  successful, then
- ensure that the value is in range.

For more information and techniques for converting input to numeric values, see CERT
guideline INT05-C at www.securecoding.cert.org.

Summary

Section 8.2 Fundamentals of Strings and Characters

- **Characters** are the fundamental building blocks of source programs. Every program is composed of a sequence of characters that—when grouped together meaningfully—is interpreted by the computer as a series of instructions used to accomplish a task.

- A **character constant** (p. 335) is an int value represented as a character in single quotes. The value of a character constant is the character's integer value in the machine's **character set** (p. 335).

- A **string** (p. 335) is a series of characters treated as a single unit. A string may include letters, digits and various special characters (p. 335) such as +, -, *, / and $. String literals, or string constants, in C are written in double quotation marks.

- A string in C is an **array of characters** ending in the **null character** (p. 335; '\0').

- A string is accessed via a **pointer** to its first character (p. 335). The value of a string is the **address** of its first character.

- A **character array** or a **variable of type char** * can be initialized with a string in a definition.

- When defining a character array to contain a string, the array must be large enough to store the string and its terminating null character.

- A string can be stored in an array using scanf. Function scanf will read characters until a space, tab, newline or end-of-file indicator is encountered.

- For a character array to be printed as a string, the array must contain a terminating null character.

Section 8.3 Character-Handling Library

- Function **isdigit** (p. 336) determines whether its argument is a **digit** (0–9).

- Function **isalpha** (p. 336) determines whether its argument is an **uppercase letter** (A–Z) or a **lowercase letter** (a–z).

- Function **isalnum** (p. 336) determines whether its argument is an **uppercase letter** (A–Z), a **lowercase letter** (a–z) or a **digit** (0–9).

- Function **isxdigit** (p. 336) determines whether its argument is a **hexadecimal digit** (p. 337; A–F, a–f, 0–9).

- Function **islower** (p. 339) determines whether its argument is a **lowercase letter** (a–z).

- Function **isupper** (p. 339) determines whether its argument is an **uppercase letter** (A–Z).

- Function **toupper** (p. 339) converts a lowercase letter to uppercase and returns the uppercase letter.

- Function **tolower** (p. 339) converts an uppercase letter to lowercase and returns the lowercase letter.

- Function **isspace** (p. 340) determines whether its argument is one of the following **whitespace characters**: ' ' (space), '\f', '\n', '\r', '\t' or '\v'.

- Function **iscntrl** (p. 340) determines whether its argument is one of the following **control characters**: '\t', '\v', '\f', '\a', '\b', '\r' or '\n'.

- Function **ispunct** (p. 340) determines whether its argument is a **printing character** other than a space, a digit or a letter.

- Function **isprint** (p. 340) determines whether its argument is any printing character including the space character.

- Function **isgraph** (p. 340) determines whether its argument is a printing character other than the space character.

Section 8.4 String-Conversion Functions

- Function **strtod** (p. 342) converts a sequence of characters representing a floating-point value to double. The function receives two arguments—a string (char *) and a pointer to char *. The string contains the character sequence to be converted, and the location specified by the pointer to char * is assigned the address of the remainder of the string after the conversion, or to the entire string if no portion of the string can be converted.

- Function **strtol** (p. 343) converts a sequence of characters representing an integer to long. The function receives three arguments—a string (char *), a pointer to char * and an integer. The string contains the character sequence to be converted, the location specified by the pointer to char * is assigned the address of the remainder of the string after the conversion, or to the entire string if no portion of the string can be converted. The integer specifies the base of the value being converted.

- Function **strtoul** (p. 344) converts a sequence of characters representing an integer to unsigned long int. The function works identically to strtol.

Section 8.5 Standard Input/Output Library Functions

- Function **fgets** (p. 345) reads characters until a newline character or the end-of-file indicator is encountered. The arguments to fgets are an array of type char, the maximum number of characters that can be read and the stream from which to read. A null character ('\0') is appended to the array after reading terminates. If a newline is encountered, it's included in the input string.

- Function **putchar** (p. 345) prints its character argument.

- Function **getchar** (p. 346) reads a single character from the standard input and returns it as an integer. If the end-of-file indicator is encountered, getchar returns EOF.

- Function **puts** (p. 347) takes a string (char *) as an argument and prints the string followed by a newline character.

- Function **sprintf** (p. 347) uses the same conversion specifications as function printf to print formatted data into an array of type char.

- Function **sscanf** (p. 348) uses the same conversion specifications as function scanf to read formatted data from a string.

Section 8.6 String-Manipulation Functions of the String-Handling Library

- Function **strcpy** copies its second argument (a string) into its first argument (a character array). You must ensure that the array is large enough to store the string and its terminating null character.

- Function **strncpy** (p. 349) is equivalent to strcpy, except that strncpy specifies the maximum number of characters to be copied from the string into the array. The terminating null character will be copied only if the number of characters to be copied is one more than the length of the string.

- Function **strcat** (p. 350) appends its second string argument—including the terminating null character—to its first string argument. The first character of the second string replaces the null ('\0') character of the first string. You must ensure that the array used to store the first string is large enough to store both the first string and the second string.

- Function **strncat** (p. 349) appends a specified number of characters from the second string to the first string. A terminating null character is appended to the result.

Section 8.7 Comparison Functions of the String-Handling Library

- Function **strcmp** (p. 351) compares its first string argument to its second string argument, character by character. It returns 0 if the strings are equal, returns a negative value if the first string is less than the second and returns a positive value if the first string is greater than the second.

- Function `strncmp` (p. 351) is equivalent to `strcmp`, except that `strncmp` compares a specified number of characters. If one of the strings is shorter than the number of characters specified, `strncmp` compares characters until the null character in the shorter string is encountered.

Section 8.8 Search Functions of the String-Handling Library

- Function `strchr` (p. 354) searches for the first occurrence of a character in a string. If the character is found, `strchr` returns a pointer to the character in the string; otherwise, `strchr` returns `NULL`.

- Function `strcspn` (p. 355) determines the length of the initial part of the string in its first argument that does not contain any characters from the string in its second argument. The function returns the length of the segment.

- Function `strpbrk` (p. 355) searches for the first occurrence in its first argument of any character in its second argument. If a character from the second argument is found, `strpbrk` returns a pointer to the character; otherwise, `strpbrk` returns `NULL`.

- Function `strrchr` (p. 356) searches for the last occurrence of a character in a string. If the character is found, `strrchr` returns a pointer to the character in the string; otherwise, `strrchr` returns `NULL`.

- Function `strspn` (p. 357) determines the length of the initial part of the string in its first argument that contains only characters from the string in its second argument. The function returns the length of the segment.

- Function `strstr` (p. 357) searches for the first occurrence of its second string argument in its first string argument. If the second string is found in the first string, a pointer to the location of the string in the first argument is returned.

- A sequence of calls to `strtok` (p. 358) breaks the first string `s1` into tokens (p. 358) that are separated by characters contained in the second string `s2`. The first call contains `s1` as the first argument, and subsequent calls to continue tokenizing the same string contain `NULL` as the first argument. A pointer to the current token is returned by each call. If there are no more tokens when the function is called, a `NULL` pointer is returned.

Section 8.9 Memory Functions of the String-Handling Library

- Function `memcpy` (p. 360) copies a specified number of bytes from the object to which its second argument points into the object to which its first argument points. The function can receive a pointer to any type of object.

- Function `memmove` (p. 361) copies a specified number of bytes from the object pointed to by its second argument to the object pointed to by its first argument. Copying is accomplished as if the bytes were copied from the second argument to a temporary array and then copied from the temporary array to the first argument.

- Function `memcmp` (p. 362) compares the specified number of bytes of its first and second arguments.

- Function `memchr` (p. 362) searches for the first occurrence of a byte, represented as `unsigned char`, in the specified number of bytes of an object. If the byte is found, a pointer to the byte is returned; otherwise, a `NULL` pointer is returned.

- Function `memset` (p. 363) copies its second argument, treated as an `unsigned char`, to a specified number of bytes of the object pointed to by the first argument.

Section 8.10 Other Functions of the String-Handling Library

- Function `strerror` (p. 364) maps an integer error number into a full text string in a locale specific manner. A pointer to the string is returned.

- Function `strlen` (p. 364) takes a string as an argument and returns the **number of characters** in the string—the terminating null character is not included in the length of the string.

Self-Review Exercises

8.1 Write a single statement to accomplish each of the following. Assume that variables c (which stores a character), x, y and z are of type int, variables d, e and f are of type double, variable ptr is of type char * and arrays s1[100] and s2[100] are of type char.

a) Convert the character stored in variable c to an uppercase letter. Assign the result to variable c.

b) Determine whether the value of variable c is a digit. Use the conditional operator as shown in Figs. 8.2–8.4 to print " is a " or " is not a " when the result is displayed.

c) Determine whether the value of variable c is a control character. Use the conditional operator to print " is a " or " is not a " when the result is displayed.

d) Read a line of text into array s1 from the keyboard. Do not use scanf.

e) Print the line of text stored in array s1. Do not use printf.

f) Assign ptr the location of the last occurrence of c in s1.

g) Print the value of variable c. Do not use printf.

h) Determine whether the value of c is a letter. Use the conditional operator to print " is a " or " is not a " when the result is displayed.

i) Read a character from the keyboard and store the character in variable c.

j) Assign ptr the location of the first occurrence of s2 in s1.

k) Determine whether the value of variable c is a printing character. Use the conditional operator to print " is a " or " is not a " when the result is displayed.

l) Read three double values into variables d, e and f from the string "1.27 10.3 9.432".

m) Copy the string stored in array s2 into array s1.

n) Assign ptr the location of the first occurrence in s1 of any character from s2.

o) Compare the string in s1 with the string in s2. Print the result.

p) Assign ptr the location of the first occurrence of c in s1.

q) Use sprintf to print the values of integer variables x, y and z into array s1. Each value should be printed with a field width of 7.

r) Append 10 characters from the string in s2 to the string in s1.

s) Determine the length of the string in s1. Print the result.

t) Assign ptr to the location of the first token in s2. Tokens in the string s2 are separated by commas (,).

8.2 Show two different ways to initialize character array vowel with the string of vowels "AEIOU".

8.3 What, if anything, prints when each of the following C statements is performed? If the statement contains an error, describe the error and indicate how to correct it. Assume the following variable definitions:

```
char s1[50] = "jack", s2[50] = "jill", s3[50];
```

a) printf("%c%s", toupper(s1[0]), &s1[1]);

b) printf("%s", strcpy(s3, s2));

c) printf("%s", strcat(strcat(strcpy(s3, s1), " and "), s2));

d) printf("%u", strlen(s1) + strlen(s2));

e) printf("%u", strlen(s3)); // using s3 after part (c) executes

8.4 Find the error in each of the following program segments and explain how to correct it:

a) char s[10];
   strncpy(s, "hello", 5);
   printf("%s\n", s);

b) printf("%s", 'a');

c) char s[12];
   strcpy(s, "Welcome Home");

```
d) if (strcmp(string1, string2)) {
      puts("The strings are equal");
   }
```

Answers to Self-Review Exercises

8.1
 a) `c = toupper(c);`
 b) `printf("'%c'%sdigit\n", c, isdigit(c) ? " is a " : " is not a ");`
 c) `printf("'%c'%scontrol character\n",`
   `c, iscntrl(c) ? " is a " : " is not a ");`
 d) `fgets(s1, 100, stdin);`
 e) `puts(s1);`
 f) `ptr = strrchr(s1, c);`
 g) `putchar(c);`
 h) `printf("'%c'%sletter\n", c, isalpha(c) ? " is a " : " is not a ");`
 i) `c = getchar();`
 j) `ptr = strstr(s1, s2);`
 k) `printf("'%c'%sprinting character\n",`
   `c, isprint(c) ? " is a " : " is not a ");`
 l) `sscanf("1.27 10.3 9.432", "%f%f%f", &d, &e, &f);`
 m) `strcpy(s1, s2);`
 n) `ptr = strpbrk(s1, s2);`
 o) `printf("strcmp(s1, s2) = %d\n", strcmp(s1, s2));`
 p) `ptr = strchr(s1, c);`
 q) `sprintf(s1, "%7d%7d%7d", x, y, z);`
 r) `strncat(s1, s2, 10);`
 s) `printf("strlen(s1) = %u\n", strlen(s1));`
 t) `ptr = strtok(s2, ",");`

8.2 `char vowel[] = "AEIOU";`
  `char vowel[] = { 'A', 'E', 'I', 'O', 'U', '\0' };`

8.3
 a) `Jack`
 b) `jill`
 c) `jack and jill`
 d) `8`
 e) `13`

8.4
 a) Error: Function `strncpy` does not write a terminating null character to array `s`, because its third argument is equal to the length of the string `"hello"`.
  Correction: Make the third argument of `strncpy` 6, or assign `'\0'` to `s[5]`.
 b) Error: Attempting to print a character constant as a string.
  Correction: Use `%c` to output the character, or replace `'a'` with `"a"`.
 c) Error: Character array `s` is not large enough to store the terminating null character.
  Correction: Declare the array with more elements.
 d) Error: Function `strcmp` returns 0 if the strings are equal; therefore, the condition in the `if` statement is false, and the `printf` will not be executed.
  Correction: Compare the result of `strcmp` with 0 in the condition.

Exercises

8.5 *(Character Testing)* Write a program that inputs a character from the keyboard and tests it with each of the functions in the character-handling library. The program should print the value returned by each function.

8.6 *(Displaying Strings in Uppercase and Lowercase)* Write a program that inputs a line of text into char array s[100]. Output the line in uppercase letters and in lowercase letters.

8.7 *(Converting Strings to Integers for Calculations)* Write a program that inputs four strings that represent integers, converts the strings to integers, sums the values and prints the total of the four values.

8.8 *(Converting Strings to Floating Point for Calculations)* Write a program that inputs four strings that represent floating-point values, converts the strings to double values, sums the values and prints the total of the four values.

8.9 *(Comparing Strings)* Write a program that uses function strcmp to compare two strings input by the user. The program should state whether the first string is less than, equal to or greater than the second string.

8.10 *(Comparing Portions of Strings)* Write a program that uses function strncmp to compare two strings input by the user. The program should input the number of characters to be compared, then display whether the first string is less than, equal to or greater than the second string.

8.11 *(Random Sentences)* Write a program that uses random-number generation to create sentences. The program should use four arrays of pointers to char called article, noun, verb and preposition. The program should create a sentence by selecting a word at random from each array in the following order: article, noun, verb, preposition, article and noun. As each word is picked, it should be concatenated to the previous words in an array large enough to hold the entire sentence. The words should be separated by spaces. When the final sentence is output, it should start with a capital letter and end with a period. The program should generate 20 such sentences. The arrays should be filled as follows: The article array should contain the articles "the", "a", "one", "some" and "any"; the noun array should contain the nouns "boy", "girl", "dog", "town" and "car"; the verb array should contain the verbs "drove", "jumped", "ran", "walked" and "skipped"; the preposition array should contain the prepositions "to", "from", "over", "under" and "on".

After the preceding program is written and working, modify it to produce a short story consisting of several of these sentences. (How about the possibility of a random term-paper writer?)

8.12 *(Limericks)* A limerick is a humorous five-line verse in which the first and second lines rhyme with the fifth, and the third line rhymes with the fourth. Using techniques similar to those developed in Exercise 8.11, write a program that produces random limericks. Polishing this program to produce good limericks is a challenging problem, but the result will be worth the effort!

8.13 *(Pig Latin)* Write a program that encodes English-language phrases into pig Latin. Pig Latin is a form of coded language often used for amusement. Many variations exist in the methods used to form pig-Latin phrases. For simplicity, use the following algorithm:

To form a pig-Latin phrase from an English-language phrase, tokenize the phrase into words with function strtok. To translate each English word into a pig-Latin word, place the first letter of the English word at the end of the English word and add the letters "ay". Thus the word "jump" becomes "umpjay", the word "the" becomes "hetay" and the word "computer" becomes "omputercay". Blanks between words remain as blanks. Assume the following: The English phrase consists of words separated by blanks, there are no punctuation marks, and all words have two or more letters. Function printLatinWord should display each word. [*Hint:* Each time a token is found in a call to strtok, pass the token pointer to function printLatinWord, and print the pig-Latin word. *Note:* We've provided simplified rules for converting words to pig Latin here. For more detailed rules and variations, visit en.wikipedia.org/wiki/Pig_latin.]

8.14 *(Tokenizing Telephone Numbers)* Write a program that inputs a telephone number as a string in the form (555) 555-5555. The program should use function strtok to extract the area code as a token, the first three digits of the phone number as a token and the last four digits of the phone number as a token. The seven digits of the phone number should be concatenated into one string.

The program should convert the area-code string to `int` and convert the phone-number string to `long`. Both the area code and the phone number should be printed.

8.15 *(Displaying a Sentence with Its Words Reversed)* Write a program that inputs a line of text, tokenizes the line with function `strtok` and outputs the tokens in reverse order.

8.16 *(Searching for Substrings)* Write a program that inputs a line of text and a search string from the keyboard. Using function `strstr`, locate the first occurrence of the search string in the line of text, and assign the location to variable `searchPtr` of type `char *`. If the search string is found, print the remainder of the line of text beginning with the search string. Then, use `strstr` again to locate the next occurrence of the search string in the line of text. If a second occurrence is found, print the remainder of the line of text beginning with the second occurrence. [*Hint:* The second call to `strstr` should contain `searchPtr + 1` as its first argument.]

8.17 *(Counting the Occurrences of a Substring)* Write a program based on the program of Exercise 8.16 that inputs several lines of text and a search string and uses function `strstr` to determine the total occurrences of the string in the lines of text. Print the result.

8.18 *(Counting the Occurrences of a Character)* Write a program that inputs several lines of text and a search character and uses function `strchr` to determine the total occurrences of the character in the lines of text.

8.19 *(Counting the Letters of the Alphabet in a String)* Write a program based on the program of Exercise 8.18 that inputs several lines of text and uses function `strchr` to determine the total occurrences of each letter of the alphabet in the lines of text. Uppercase and lowercase letters should be counted together. Store the totals for each letter in an array and print the values in tabular format after the totals have been determined.

8.20 *(Counting the Number of Words in a String)* Write a program that inputs several lines of text and uses `strtok` to count the total number of words. Assume that the words are separated by either spaces or newline characters.

8.21 *(Alphabetizing a List of Strings)* Use the string-comparison functions and the techniques for sorting arrays to write a program that alphabetizes a list of strings. Use the names of 10 or 15 towns in your area as data for your program.

8.22 The chart in Appendix B shows the numeric code representations for the characters in the ASCII character set. Study this chart and then state whether each of the following is *true* or *false*.
   a) The letter "A" comes before the letter "B".
   b) The digit "9" comes before the digit "0".
   c) The commonly used symbols for addition, subtraction, multiplication and division all come before any of the digits.
   d) The digits come before the letters.
   e) If a sort program sorts strings into ascending sequence, then the program will place the symbol for a right parenthesis before the symbol for a left parenthesis.

8.23 *(Strings Starting with "b")* Write a program that reads a series of strings and prints only those beginning with the letter "b".

8.24 *(Strings Ending with "ed")* Write a program that reads a series of strings and prints only those that end with the letters "ed".

8.25 *(Printing Letters for Various ASCII Codes)* Write a program that inputs an ASCII code and prints the corresponding character.

8.26 *(Write Your Own Character-Handling Functions)* Using the ASCII character chart in Appendix B as a guide, write your own versions of the character-handling functions in Fig. 8.1.

8.27 *(Write Your String-Conversion Functions)* Write your own versions of the functions in Fig. 8.5 for converting strings to numbers.

8.28 *(Write Your Own String-Copy and String-Concatenation Functions)* Write two versions of each of the string-copy and string-concatenation functions in Fig. 8.14. The first version should use array indexing, and the second should use pointers and pointer arithmetic.

8.29 *(Write Your Own String-Comparison Functions)* Write two versions of each string-comparison function in Fig. 8.17. The first version should use array indexing, and the second should use pointers and pointer arithmetic.

8.30 *(Write Your Own String-Length Function)* Write two versions of function `strlen` in Fig. 8.33. The first version should use array indexing, and the second should use pointers and pointer arithmetic.

Special Section: Advanced String-Manipulation Exercises

The preceding exercises are keyed to the text and designed to test the reader's understanding of fundamental string-manipulation concepts. This section contains intermediate and advanced problems that you should find challenging yet enjoyable. They vary considerably in difficulty. Some require an hour or two of programming. Others are useful for lab assignments that might require two or three weeks of study and implementation. Some are challenging term projects.

8.31 *(Text Analysis)* The availability of computers with string-manipulation capabilities has resulted in some rather interesting approaches to analyzing the writings of great authors. Much attention has been focused on whether William Shakespeare ever lived. Some scholars find substantial evidence that Christopher Marlowe actually penned the masterpieces attributed to Shakespeare. Researchers have used computers to find similarities in the writings of these two authors. This exercise examines three methods for analyzing texts with a computer.

  a) Write a program that reads several lines of text and prints a table indicating the number of occurrences of each letter of the alphabet in the text. For example, the phrase

```
To be, or not to be: that is the question:
```

  contains one "a," two "b's," no "c's," and so on.

  b) Write a program that reads several lines of text and prints a table indicating the number of one-letter words, two-letter words, three-letter words, and so on, appearing in the text. For example, the phrase

```
Whether 'tis nobler in the mind to suffer
```

  contains

Word length	Occurrences
1	0
2	2
3	1
4	2 (including 'tis)
5	0
6	2
7	1

c) Write a program that reads several lines of text and prints a table indicating the number of occurrences of each different word in the text. The program should include the words in the table in the same order in which they appear in the text. For example, the lines

```
To be, or not to be: that is the question:
Whether 'tis nobler in the mind to suffer
```

contain the words "to" three times, "be" two times, "or" once, and so on.

8.32   *(Printing Dates in Various Formats)* Dates are commonly printed in several different formats in business correspondence. Two of the more common formats are

07/21/2003 and July 21, 2003

Write a program that reads a date in the first format and prints it in the second format.

8.33   *(Check Protection)* Computers are frequently used in check-writing systems, such as payroll and accounts payable applications. Many stories circulate regarding weekly paychecks being printed (by mistake) for amounts in excess of $1 million. Weird amounts are printed by computerized check-writing systems because of human error and/or machine failure. Systems designers, of course, make every effort to build controls into their systems to prevent erroneous checks from being issued.

Another serious problem is the intentional alteration of a check amount by someone who intends to cash it fraudulently. To prevent a dollar amount from being altered, most computerized check-writing systems employ a technique called *check protection*.

Checks designed for imprinting by computer contain a fixed number of spaces in which the computer may print an amount. Suppose a paycheck contains nine blank spaces in which the computer is supposed to print the amount of a weekly paycheck. If the amount is large, then all nine of those spaces will be filled—for example:

```
11,230.60  (check amount)
---------
123456789  (position numbers)
```

On the other hand, if the amount is less than $1,000, then several of the spaces will ordinarily be left blank—for example,

```
    99.87
---------
123456789
```

contains four blank spaces. If a check is printed with blank spaces, it's easier for someone to alter the amount of the check. To prevent such alteration, many check-writing systems insert *leading asterisks* to protect the amount as follows:

```
****99.87
---------
123456789
```

Write a program that inputs a dollar amount to be printed on a check and then prints the amount in check-protected format with leading asterisks if necessary. Assume that nine spaces are available for printing an amount.

8.34   *(Writing the Word Equivalent of a Check Amount)* Continuing the discussion of the previous exercise, we reiterate the importance of designing check-writing systems to prevent alteration of check amounts. One common security method requires that the check amount be both written in numbers and "spelled out" in words. Even if someone is able to alter the numerical amount of the check, it's extremely difficult to change the amount in words. Write a program that inputs a numeric check amount and writes the word equivalent of the amount. For example, the amount 52.43 should be written as

FIFTY TWO and 43/100

8.35   *(Project: A Metric Conversion Program)* Write a program that will assist the user with metric conversions. Your program should allow the user to specify the names of the units as strings (i.e., centimeters, liters, grams, and so on for the metric system and inches, quarts, pounds, and so on for the English system) and should respond to simple questions such as

```
"How many inches are in 2 meters?"
"How many liters are in 10 quarts?"
```

Your program should recognize invalid conversions. For example, the question

```
"How many feet are in 5 kilograms?"
```

is not meaningful, because `"feet"` are units of length while `"kilograms"` are units of mass.

A Challenging String-Manipulation Project

8.36   *(Project: A Crossword-Puzzle Generator)* Most people have worked a crossword puzzle at one time or another, but few have ever attempted to generate one. Generating a crossword puzzle is a difficult problem. It's suggested here as a string-manipulation project requiring substantial sophistication and effort. There are many issues you must resolve to get even the simplest crossword-puzzle generator program working. For example, how does one represent the grid of a crossword puzzle inside the computer? Should one use a series of strings, or perhaps two-dimensional arrays? You need a source of words (i.e., a computerized dictionary) that can be directly referenced by the program. In what form should these words be stored to facilitate the complex manipulations required by the program? The really ambitious reader will want to generate the "clues" portion of the puzzle in which the brief hints for each "across" word and each "down" word are printed for the puzzle worker. Merely printing a version of the blank puzzle itself is not a simple problem.

Making a Difference

8.37   *(Cooking with Healthier Ingredients)* Obesity in the United States is increasing at an alarming rate. Check the Centers for Disease Control and Prevention (CDC) webpage at www.cdc.gov/obesity/data/index.html, which contains United States obesity data and facts. As obesity increases, so do occurrences of related problems (e.g., heart disease, high blood pressure, high cholesterol, type 2 diabetes). Write a program that helps users choose healthier ingredients when cooking, and helps those allergic to certain foods (e.g., nuts, gluten) find substitutes. The program should read a recipe from the user and suggest healthier replacements for some of the ingredients. For simplicity, your program should assume the recipe has no abbreviations for measures such as teaspoons, cups, and tablespoons, and uses numerical digits for quantities (e.g., 1 egg, 2 cups) rather than spelling them out (one egg, two cups). Some common substitutions are shown in Fig. 8.36. Your program should display a warning such as, "Always consult your physician before making significant changes to your diet."

   Your program should take into consideration that replacements are not always one-for-one. For example, if a cake recipe calls for three eggs, it might reasonably use six egg whites instead. Conversion data for measurements and substitutes can be obtained at websites such as:

```
chinesefood.about.com/od/recipeconversionfaqs/f/usmetricrecipes.htm
www.pioneerthinking.com/eggsub.html
www.gourmetsleuth.com/conversions.htm
```

Your program should consider the user's health concerns, such as high cholesterol, high blood pressure, weight loss, gluten allergy, and so on. For high cholesterol, the program should suggest substitutes for eggs and dairy products; if the user wishes to lose weight, low-calorie substitutes for ingredients such as sugar should be suggested.

Ingredient	Substitution
1 cup sour cream	1 cup yogurt
1 cup milk	1/2 cup evaporated milk and 1/2 cup water
1 teaspoon lemon juice	1/2 teaspoon vinegar
1 cup sugar	1/2 cup honey, 1 cup molasses or 1/4 cup agave nectar
1 cup butter	1 cup margarine or yogurt
1 cup flour	1 cup rye or rice flour
1 cup mayonnaise	1 cup cottage cheese or 1/8 cup mayonnaise and 7/8 cup yogurt
1 egg	2 tablespoons cornstarch, arrowroot flour or potato starch or 2 egg whites or 1/2 of a large banana (mashed)
1 cup milk	1 cup soy milk
1/4 cup oil	1/4 cup applesauce
white bread	whole-grain bread

Fig. 8.36 | Common ingredient substitutions.

8.38 *(Spam Scanner)* Spam (or junk e-mail) costs U.S. organizations billions of dollars a year in spam-prevention software, equipment, network resources, bandwidth, and lost productivity. Research online some of the most common spam e-mail messages and words, and check your own junk e-mail folder. Create a list of 30 words and phrases commonly found in spam messages. Write a program in which the user enters an e-mail message. Read the message into a large character array and ensure that the program does not attempt to insert characters past the end of the array. Then scan the message for each of the 30 keywords or phrases. For each occurrence of one of these within the message, add a point to the message's "spam score." Next, rate the likelihood that the message is spam, based on the number of points it received.

8.39 *(SMS Language)* Short Message Service (SMS) is a communications service that allows sending text messages of 160 or fewer characters between mobile phones. With the proliferation of mobile phone use worldwide, SMS is being used in many developing nations for political purposes (e.g., voicing opinions and opposition), reporting news about natural disasters, and so on. For example, check out comunica.org/radio2.0/archives/87. Because the length of SMS messages is limited, SMS Language—abbreviations of common words and phrases in mobile text messages, e-mails, instant messages, etc.—is often used. For example, "in my opinion" is "IMO" in SMS Language. Research SMS Language online. Write a program that lets the user enter a message using SMS Language, then translates it into English (or your own language). Also provide a mechanism to translate text written in English (or your own language) into SMS Language. One potential problem is that one SMS abbreviation could expand into a variety of phrases. For example, IMO (as used above) could also stand for "International Maritime Organization," "in memory of," etc.

8.40 *(Gender Neutrality)* In Exercise 1.14, you researched eliminating sexism in all forms of communication. You then described the algorithm you'd use to read through a paragraph of text and replace gender-specific words with gender-neutral equivalents. Create a program that reads a paragraph of text, then replaces gender-specific words with gender-neutral ones. Display the resulting gender-neutral text.

C Formatted Input/Output

Objectives

In this chapter, you'll:

- Use input and output streams.

- Use print formatting capabilities.

- Use input formatting capabilities.

- Print integers, floating-point numbers, strings and characters.

- Print with field widths and precisions.

- Use formatting flags in the `printf` format control string.

- Output literals and escape sequences.

- Read formatted input using `scanf`.

9.1 Introduction

An important part of the solution to any problem is the *presentation* of the results. In this chapter, we discuss in depth the formatting features of **printf** and **scanf**, which input data from the standard input stream and output data to the standard output stream, respectively. Include the header **<stdio.h>** in programs that call these functions. Chapter 11 discusses several additional functions included in the standard input/output (<stdio.h>) library.

9.2 Streams

All input and output is performed with **streams**, which are sequences of bytes. In *input* operations, the bytes flow *from a device* (e.g., a keyboard, a hard disk, a network connection) *to main memory*. In *output* operations, bytes flow *from main memory to a device* (e.g., a display screen, a printer, a hard disk, a network connection, and so on).

When program execution begins, three streams are connected to the program automatically. Normally, the *standard input stream* is connected to the *keyboard* and the *standard output stream* is connected to the *screen*. A third stream, the **standard error stream**, also is connected to the *screen*. Operating systems often allow these streams to be *redirected* to other devices. We'll show how to output error messages to the *standard error stream* in Chapter 11. Streams are also discussed in detail in Chapter 11.

9.3 Formatting Output with `printf`

Precise output formatting is accomplished with `printf`. Every `printf` call contains a **format control string** that describes the output format. The format control string consists of

conversion specifiers, **flags**, **field widths**, **precisions** and **literal characters**. Together with the percent sign (%), these form **conversion specifications**. Function printf can perform the following formatting capabilities, each of which is discussed in this chapter:

1. **Rounding** floating-point values to an indicated number of decimal places.
2. Aligning a column of numbers with decimal points appearing one above the other.
3. **Right justification** and **left justification** of outputs.
4. Inserting literal characters at precise locations in a line of output.
5. Representing floating-point numbers in exponential format.
6. Representing unsigned integers in octal and hexadecimal format. See Appendix C for more information on octal and hexadecimal values.
7. Displaying all types of data with fixed-size field widths and precisions.

The printf function has the form

```
printf(format-control-string, other-arguments);
```

format-control-string describes the output format, and *other-arguments* (which are optional) correspond to each conversion specification in *format-control-string*. Each conversion specification begins with a percent sign and ends with a conversion specifier. There can be many conversion specifications in one format control string.

Common Programming Error 9.1

Forgetting to enclose a format-control-string in quotation marks is a syntax error.

9.4 Printing Integers

An integer is a whole number, such as 776, 0 or −52. Integer values are displayed in one of several formats. Figure 9.1 describes the **integer conversion specifiers**.

Conversion specifier	Description
d	Display as a *signed decimal integer*.
i	Display as a *signed decimal integer*. [*Note:* The i and d specifiers are *different* when used with scanf.]
o	Display as an *unsigned octal integer*.
u	Display as an *unsigned decimal integer*.
x or X	Display as an *unsigned hexadecimal integer*. X causes the digits 0-9 and the *uppercase* letters A-F to be used in the display and x causes the digits 0-9 and the *lowercase* letters a-f to be used in the display.
h, l or ll (letter "ell")	Place *before* any integer conversion specifier to indicate that a short, long or long long integer is displayed, respectively. These are called length modifiers.

Fig. 9.1 | Integer conversion specifiers.

Figure 9.2 prints an integer using each of the integer conversion specifiers. Only the minus sign prints; plus signs are normally suppressed—we'll see how to force plus signs to print. Also, the value -455, when printed with **%u** (line 15), is interpreted as an unsigned value 4294966841.

Common Programming Error 9.2

Printing a negative value with a conversion specifier that expects an unsigned *value.*

```
1   // Fig. 9.2: fig09_02.c
2   // Using the integer conversion specifiers
3   #include <stdio.h>
4
5   int main(void)
6   {
7      printf("%d\n", 455);
8      printf("%i\n", 455); // i same as d in printf
9      printf("%d\n", +455); // plus sign does not print
10     printf("%d\n", -455); // minus sign prints
11     printf("%hd\n", 32000);
12     printf("%ld\n", 2000000000L); // L suffix makes literal a long int
13     printf("%o\n", 455); // octal
14     printf("%u\n", 455);
15     printf("%u\n", -455);
16     printf("%x\n", 455); // hexadecimal with lowercase letters
17     printf("%X\n", 455); // hexadecimal with uppercase letters
18  }
```

```
455
455
455
-455
32000
2000000000
707
455
4294966841
1c7
1C7
```

Fig. 9.2 | Using the integer conversion specifiers.

9.5 Printing Floating-Point Numbers

A floating-point value contains a decimal point as in 33.5, 0.0 or -657.983. Floating-point values are displayed in one of several formats. Figure 9.3 describes the floating-point conversion specifiers. The **conversion specifiers e and E** display floating-point values in **exponential notation**—the computer equivalent of **scientific notation** used in mathematics. For example, the value 150.4582 is represented in scientific notation as

$$1.504582 \times 10^2$$

and in exponential notation as

```
1.504582E+02
```

by the computer. This notation indicates that 1.504582 is multiplied by 10 raised to the second power (E+02). The E stands for "exponent."

Conversion specifier	Description
e or E	Display a floating-point value in *exponential notation.*
f or F	Display floating-point values in *fixed-point notation* (F is supported in the Microsoft Visual C++ compiler in Visual Studio 2015 and higher).
g or G	Display a floating-point value in either the *floating-point form* f or the exponential form e (or E), based on the magnitude of the value.
L	Place before any floating-point conversion specifier to indicate that a long double floating-point value should be displayed.

Fig. 9.3 | Floating point conversion specifiers.

9.5.1 Conversion Specifiers e, E and f

Values displayed with the conversion specifiers e, E and f show *six digits of precision* to the right of the decimal point by default (e.g., 1.045927); other precisions can be specified explicitly. Conversion specifier f always prints at least one digit to the *left* of the decimal point. Conversion specifiers e and E print *lowercase* e and *uppercase* E, respectively, preceding the exponent, and print *exactly one* digit to the left of the decimal point.

9.5.2 Conversion Specifiers g and G

Conversion specifier g (or G) prints in either e (E) or f format with *no trailing zeros* (1.234000 is printed as 1.234). Values are printed with e (E) if, after conversion to exponential notation, the value's exponent is less than -4, or the exponent is greater than or equal to the specified precision (*six significant digits* by default for g and G). Otherwise, conversion specifier f is used to print the value. At least one decimal digit is required for the decimal point to be output. For example, the values 0.0000875, 8750000.0, 8.75 and 87.50 are printed as 8.75e-05, 8.75e+06, 8.75 and 87.5 with the conversion specifier g. The value 0.0000875 uses e notation because, when it's converted to exponential notation, its exponent (-5) is less than -4. The value 8750000.0 uses e notation because its exponent (6) is equal to the default precision.

The precision for conversion specifiers g and G indicates the maximum number of significant digits printed, *including* the digit to the *left* of the decimal point. The value 1234567.0 is printed as 1.23457e+06, using conversion specifier %g (remember that all floating-point conversion specifiers have a *default precision of 6*). There are six significant digits in the result. The difference between g and G is identical to the difference between e and E when the value is printed in exponential notation—*lowercase* g causes a *lowercase* e to be output, and *uppercase* G causes an *uppercase* E to be output.

Error-Prevention Tip 9.1

When outputting data, be sure that the user is aware of situations in which data may be imprecise due to formatting (e.g., rounding errors from specifying precisions).

9.5.3 Demonstrating Floating-Point Conversion Specifiers

Figure 9.4 demonstrates each of the floating-point conversion specifiers. The **%E**, **%e** and %g conversion specifiers cause the value to be *rounded* in the output and the conversion specifier %f does *not*.

Portability Tip 9.1

With some compilers, the exponent in the outputs will be shown with two digits to the right of the + sign.

```
1   // Fig. 9.4: fig09_04.c
2   // Using the floating-point conversion specifiers
3   #include <stdio.h>
4
5   int main(void)
6   {
7       printf("%e\n", 1234567.89);
8       printf("%e\n", +1234567.89); // plus does not print
9       printf("%e\n", -1234567.89); // minus prints
10      printf("%E\n", 1234567.89);
11      printf("%f\n", 1234567.89); // six digits to right of decimal point
12      printf("%g\n", 1234567.89); // prints with lowercase e
13      printf("%G\n", 1234567.89); // prints with uppercase E
14  }
```

```
1.234568e+006
1.234568e+006
-1.234568e+006
1.234568E+006
1234567.890000
1.23457e+006
1.23457E+006
```

Fig. 9.4 | Using the floating-point conversion specifiers.

9.6 Printing Strings and Characters

The c and s conversion specifiers are used to print individual characters and strings, respectively. **Conversion specifier** c requires a char argument. **Conversion specifier** s requires a pointer to char as an argument. Conversion specifier s causes characters to be printed until a terminating null ('\0') character is encountered. If for some reason the string being printed does not have a null terminator, the printf will continue printing until it is eventually stopped by a zero byte. The program in Fig. 9.5 displays characters and strings with conversion specifiers c and s.

```
 1   // Fig. 9.5: fig09_05c
 2   // Using the character and string conversion specifiers
 3   #include <stdio.h>
 4
 5   int main(void)
 6   {
 7      char character = 'A'; // initialize char
 8      printf("%c\n", character);
 9
10      printf("%s\n", "This is a string");
11
12      char string[] = "This is a string"; // initialize char array
13      printf("%s\n", string);
14
15      const char *stringPtr = "This is also a string"; // char pointer
16      printf("%s\n", stringPtr);
17   }
```

```
A
This is a string
This is a string
This is also a string
```

Fig. 9.5 | Using the character and string conversion specifiers.

Most compilers do not catch errors in the format-control string, so you typically will not become aware of such errors until a program produces incorrect results at runtime.

Common Programming Error 9.3
*Using %c to print a string is an error. The conversion specifier %c expects a char argument. A string is a pointer to char (i.e., a char *).*

Common Programming Error 9.4
Using %s to print a char argument often causes a fatal execution-time error called an access violation. The conversion specifier %s expects an argument of type pointer to char.

Common Programming Error 9.5
Using single quotes around the characters you want to form into a string is a syntax error. Character strings must be enclosed in double quotes.

Common Programming Error 9.6
Using double quotes around a character constant creates a pointer to a string consisting of two characters, the second of which is the terminating null.

9.7 Other Conversion Specifiers

Figure 9.6 shows the p and % conversion specifiers. Figure 9.7's **%p** prints the value of ptr and the address of x; these values are identical because ptr is assigned the address of x. The last printf statement uses **%%** to print the % character in a character string.

Portability Tip 9.2

The conversion specifier p displays an address in an implementation-defined manner (on many systems, hexadecimal notation is used rather than decimal notation).

Common Programming Error 9.7

Trying to print a literal percent character using % rather than %% in the format control string—when % appears in a format control string, it must be followed by a conversion specifier.

Conversion specifier	Description
p	Display a pointer value in an implementation-defined manner.
%	Display the percent character.

Fig. 9.6 | Other conversion specifiers.

```
1   // Fig. 9.7: fig09_07.c
2   // Using the p and % conversion specifiers
3   #include <stdio.h>
4
5   int main(void)
6   {
7      int x = 12345; // initialize int x
8      int *ptr = &x; // assign address of x to ptr
9
10     printf("The value of ptr is %p\n", ptr);
11     printf("The address of x is %p\n\n", &x);
12
13     printf("Printing a %% in a format control string\n");
14  }
```

```
The value of ptr is 002EF778
The address of x is 002EF778

Printing a % in a format control string
```

Fig. 9.7 | Using the p and % conversion specifiers.

9.8 Printing with Field Widths and Precision

The exact size of a field in which data is printed is specified by a **field width**. If the field width is larger than the data being printed, the data will normally be *right justified* within that field. An integer representing the field width is inserted between the percent sign (%) and the conversion specifier (e.g., %4d).

9.8.1 Specifying Field Widths for Printing Integers

Figure 9.8 prints two groups of five numbers each, *right justifying* those numbers that contain fewer digits than the field width. The field width is increased to print values wider than the field. Note that the minus sign for a negative value uses one character position in the field width. Field widths can be used with all conversion specifiers.

> **Common Programming Error 9.8**
> *Not providing a sufficiently large field width to handle a value to be printed can offset other data being printed, producing confusing outputs. Know your data!*

```
1   // Fig. 9.8: fig09_08.c
2   // Right justifying integers in a field
3   #include <stdio.h>
4
5   int main(void)
6   {
7      printf("%4d\n", 1);
8      printf("%4d\n", 12);
9      printf("%4d\n", 123);
10     printf("%4d\n", 1234);
11     printf("%4d\n\n", 12345);
12
13     printf("%4d\n", -1);
14     printf("%4d\n", -12);
15     printf("%4d\n", -123);
16     printf("%4d\n", 1234),
17     printf("%4d\n", -12345);
18  }
```

```
   1
  12
 123
1234
12345

  -1
 -12
-123
-1234
-12345
```

Fig. 9.8 | Right justifying integers in a field.

9.8.2 Specifying Precisions for Integers, Floating-Point Numbers and Strings

Function printf also enables you to specify the *precision* with which data is printed. Precision has different meanings for different data types. When used with integer conversion specifiers, precision indicates the *minimum number of digits to be printed*. If the printed value contains fewer digits than the specified precision and the precision value has a leading zero or decimal point, zeros are prefixed to the printed value until the total number of digits is equivalent to the precision. If neither a zero nor a decimal point is present in the precision value, spaces are inserted instead. The default precision for integers is 1. When used with floating-point conversion specifiers e, E and f, the precision is the *number of digits to appear after the decimal point*. When used with conversion specifiers g and G, the precision is the *maximum number of significant digits to be printed*. When used with conversion specifier s, the precision is the *maximum number of characters to be written from the beginning of the string*.

To use precision, place a decimal point (.), followed by an integer representing the precision between the percent sign and the conversion specifier. Figure 9.9 demonstrates the use of precision in format control strings. When a floating-point value is printed with a precision smaller than the original number of decimal places in the value, the value is *rounded*.

```
1   // Fig. 9.9: fig09_09.c
2   // Printing integers, floating-point numbers and strings with precisions
3   #include <stdio.h>
4
5   int main(void)
6   {
7      puts("Using precision for integers");
8      int i = 873; // initialize int i
9      printf("\t%.4d\n\t%.9d\n\n", i, i);
10
11     puts("Using precision for floating-point numbers");
12     double f = 123.94536; // initialize double f
13     printf("\t%.3f\n\t%.3e\n\t%.3g\n\n", f, f, f);
14
15     puts("Using precision for strings");
16     char s[] = "Happy Birthday"; // initialize char array s
17     printf("\t%.11s\n", s);
18  }
```

```
Using precision for integers
        0873
        000000873

Using precision for floating-point numbers
        123.945
        1.239e+002
        124

Using precision for strings
        Happy Birth
```

Fig. 9.9 | Printing integers, floating-point numbers and strings with precisions.

9.8.3 Combining Field Widths and Precisions

The field width and the precision can be combined by placing the field width, followed by a decimal point, followed by a precision between the percent sign and the conversion specifier, as in the statement

```
printf("%9.3f", 123.456789);
```

which displays 123.457 with three digits to the right of the decimal point right justified in a nine-digit field.

It's possible to specify the field width and the precision using integer expressions in the argument list following the format control string. To use this feature, insert an asterisk (*) in place of the field width or precision (or both). The matching `int` argument in the argument list is evaluated and used in place of the asterisk. A field width's value may be either positive or negative (which causes the output to be left justified in the field, as described in the next section). The statement

```
printf("%*.*f", 7, 2, 98.736);
```

uses 7 for the field width, 2 for the precision and outputs the value 98.74 right justified.

9.9 Using Flags in the `printf` Format Control String

Function `printf` also provides *flags* to supplement its output formatting capabilities. Five flags are available for use in format control strings (Fig. 9.10). To use a flag in a format control string, place the flag immediately to the right of the percent sign. Several flags may be combined in one conversion specifier.

Flag	Description
- (minus sign)	*Left justify* the output within the specified field.
+	Display a *plus sign* preceding positive values and a *minus sign* preceding negative values.
space	Print a space before a positive value not printed with the + flag.
#	Prefix 0 to the output value when used with the octal conversion specifier o.
	Prefix 0x or 0X to the output value when used with the hexadecimal conversion specifiers x or X.
	Force a decimal point for a floating-point number printed with e, E, f, g or G that does *not* contain a fractional part. (Normally the decimal point is printed *only* if a digit follows it.) For g and G specifiers, trailing zeros are not eliminated.
0 (zero)	Pad a field with *leading zeros*.

Fig. 9.10 | Format-control-string flags.

9.9.1 Right and Left Justification

Figure 9.11 demonstrates right justification and left justification of a string, an integer, a character and a floating-point number. Line 7 outputs a line of numbers representing the column positions, so you can confirm that the right and left justification worked correctly.

```
1   // Fig. 9.11: fig09_11.c
2   // Right justifying and left justifying values
3   #include <stdio.h>
4
```

Fig. 9.11 | Right justifying and left justifying values. (Part 1 of 2.)

```
5   int main(void)
6   {
7       puts("12345678901234567890123456789012345678901234567890\n");
8       printf("%10s%10d%10c%10f\n\n", "hello", 7, 'a', 1.23);
9       printf("%-10s%-10d%-10c%-10f\n", "hello", 7, 'a', 1.23);
10  }
```

```
12345678901234567890123456789012345678901234567890
     hello         7         a  1.230000

hello     7         a          1.230000
```

Fig. 9.11 | Right justifying and left justifying values. (Part 2 of 2.)

9.9.2 Printing Positive and Negative Numbers with and without the + Flag

Figure 9.12 prints a positive number and a negative number, each with and without the + flag. The minus sign is displayed in both cases, but the plus sign is displayed only when the + flag is used.

```
1   // Fig. 9.12: fig09_12.c
2   // Printing positive and negative numbers with and without the + flag
3   #include <stdio.h>
4
5   int main(void)
6   {
7       printf("%d\n%d\n", 786, -786);
8       printf("%+d\n%+d\n", 786, -786);
9   }
```

```
786
-786
+786
-786
```

Fig. 9.12 | Printing positive and negative numbers with and without the + flag.

9.9.3 Using the Space Flag

Figure 9.13 prefixes a space to the positive number with the **space flag**. This is useful for aligning positive and negative numbers with the same number of digits. The value -547 is not preceded by a space in the output because of its minus sign.

```
1   // Fig. 9.13: fig09_13.c
2   // Using the space flag
3   // not preceded by + or -
4   #include <stdio.h>
5
```

Fig. 9.13 | Using the space flag. (Part 1 of 2.)

```
6   int main(void)
7   {
8       printf("% d\n% d\n", 547, -547);
9   }
```

```
547
-547
```

Fig. 9.13 | Using the space flag. (Part 2 of 2.)

9.9.4 Using the # Flag

Figure 9.14 uses the # flag to prefix 0 to the octal value and 0x and 0X to the hexadecimal values, and to force the decimal point on a value printed with g.

```
1   // Fig. 9.14: fig09_14.c
2   // Using the # flag with conversion specifiers
3   // o, x, X and any floating-point specifier
4   #include <stdio.h>
5
6   int main(void)
7   {
8       int c = 1427; // initialize c
9       printf("%#o\n", c);
10      printf("%#x\n", c);
11      printf("%#X\n", c);
12
13      double p = 1427.0; // initialize p
14      printf("\n%g\n", p);
15      printf("%#g\n", p);
16  }
```

```
02623
0x593
0X593

1427
1427.00
```

Fig. 9.14 | Using the # flag with conversion specifiers.

9.9.5 Using the 0 Flag

Figure 9.15 combines the + flag and the 0 (zero) flag to print 452 in a nine-space field with a + sign and leading zeros, then prints 452 again using only the 0 flag and a nine-space field.

```
1   // Fig. 9.15: fig09_15.c
2   // Using the 0 (zero) flag
3   #include <stdio.h>
```

Fig. 9.15 | Using the 0 (zero) flag. (Part 1 of 2.)

```
4
5   int main(void)
6   {
7      printf("%+09d\n", 452);
8      printf("%09d\n", 452);
9   }
```

```
+00000452
000000452
```

Fig. 9.15 | Using the 0 (zero) flag. (Part 2 of 2.)

9.10 Printing Literals and Escape Sequences

As you've seen throughout the book, literal characters included in the format control string are simply output by printf. However, there are several "problem" characters, such as the *quotation mark* (") that delimits the format control string itself. Various control characters, such as *newline* and *tab*, must be represented by escape sequences. An escape sequence is represented by a backslash (\), followed by a particular escape character. Figure 9.16 lists the escape sequences and the actions they cause.

Escape sequence	Description
\' (single quote)	Output the single quote (') character.
\" (double quote)	Output the double quote (") character.
\? (question mark)	Output the question mark (?) character.
\\ (backslash)	Output the backslash (\) character.
\a (alert or bell)	Cause an audible (bell) or visual alert (typically, flashing the window in which the program is running).
\b (backspace)	Move the cursor back one position on the current line.
\f (new page or form feed)	Move the cursor to the start of the next logical page.
\n (newline)	Move the cursor to the beginning of the *next* line.
\r (carriage return)	Move the cursor to the beginning of the *current* line.
\t (horizontal tab)	Move the cursor to the next horizontal tab position.
\v (vertical tab)	Move the cursor to the next vertical tab position.

Fig. 9.16 | Escape sequences.

9.11 Reading Formatted Input with scanf

Precise *input formatting* can be accomplished with scanf. Every scanf statement contains a format control string that describes the format of the data to be input. The format control string consists of conversion specifiers and literal characters. Function scanf has the following input formatting capabilities:

1. Inputting all types of data.

2. Inputting specific characters from an input stream.

3. Skipping specific characters in the input stream.

9.11.1 scanf Syntax

Function scanf is written in the following form:

scanf(*format-control-string*, *other-arguments*);

format-control-string describes the formats of the input, and *other-arguments* are pointers to variables in which the input will be stored.

Good Programming Practice 9.1

When inputting data, prompt the user for one data item or a few data items at a time. Avoid asking the user to enter many data items in response to a single prompt.

Good Programming Practice 9.2

Always consider what the user and your program will do when (not if) incorrect data is entered—for example, a value for an integer that's nonsensical in a program's context, or a string with missing punctuation or spaces.

9.11.2 scanf Conversion Specifiers

Figure 9.17 summarizes the conversion specifiers used to input all types of data. The remainder of this section provides programs that demonstrate reading data with the various scanf conversion specifiers. Note that the d and i conversion specifiers have different meanings for input with scanf, whereas they're interchangeable for output with printf.

Conversion specifier	Description
Integers	
d	Read an *optionally signed decimal integer*. The corresponding argument is a pointer to an int.
i	Read an *optionally signed decimal, octal or hexadecimal integer*. The corresponding argument is a pointer to an int.
o	Read an *octal integer*. The corresponding argument is a pointer to an unsigned int.
u	Read an *unsigned decimal integer*. The corresponding argument is a pointer to an unsigned int.
x or X	Read a *hexadecimal integer*. The corresponding argument is a pointer to an unsigned int.
h, 1 and 11	Place *before* any of the integer conversion specifiers to indicate that a short, long or long long integer is to be input, respectively.
Floating-point numbers	
e, E, f, g or G	Read a *floating-point value*. The corresponding argument is a pointer to a floating-point variable.

Fig. 9.17 | Conversion specifiers for scanf. (Part 1 of 2.)

Conversion specifier	Description
l or L	Place before any of the floating-point conversion specifiers to indicate that a double or long double value is to be input. The corresponding argument is a pointer to a double or long double variable.
Characters and strings	
c	Read a *character*. The corresponding argument is a pointer to a char; no null ('\0') is added.
s	Read a *string*. The corresponding argument is a pointer to an array of type char that's large enough to hold the string and a terminating null ('\0') character—which is automatically added.
Scan set	
[*scan characters*]	Scan a string for a set of characters that are stored in an array.
Miscellaneous	
p	Read an *address* of the same form produced when an address is output with %p in a printf statement.
n	Store the number of characters input so far in this call to scanf. The corresponding argument must be a pointer to an int.
%	Skip a percent sign (%) in the input.

Fig. 9.17 | Conversion specifiers for scanf. (Part 2 of 2.)

9.11.3 Reading Integers with scanf

Figure 9.18 reads integers with the various integer conversion specifiers and displays the integers as decimal numbers. Conversion specifier %i can input decimal, octal and hexadecimal integers.

```
1   // Fig. 9.18: fig09_18.c
2   // Reading input with integer conversion specifiers
3   #include <stdio.h>
4
5   int main(void)
6   {
7      int a;
8      int b;
9      int c;
10     int d;
11     int e;
12     int f;
13     int g;
14
15     puts("Enter seven integers: ");
16     scanf("%d%i%i%i%o%u%x", &a, &b, &c, &d, &e, &f, &g);
17
18     puts("\nThe input displayed as decimal integers is:");
```

Fig. 9.18 | Reading input with integer conversion specifiers. (Part 1 of 2.)

```
19        printf("%d %d %d %d %d %d %d\n", a, b, c, d, e, f, g);
20    }
```

```
Enter seven integers:
-70 -70 070 0x70 70 70 70

The input displayed as decimal integers is:
-70 -70 56 112 56 70 112
```

Fig. 9.18 | Reading input with integer conversion specifiers. (Part 2 of 2.)

9.11.4 Reading Floating-Point Numbers with scanf

When inputting floating-point numbers, any of the floating-point conversion specifiers e, E, f, g or G can be used. Figure 9.19 reads three floating-point numbers, one with each of the three types of floating conversion specifiers, and displays all three numbers with conversion specifier f.

```
1    // Fig. 9.19: fig09_19.c
2    // Reading input with floating-point conversion specifiers
3    #include <stdio.h>
4
5    // function main begins program execution
6    int main(void)
7    {
8        double a;
9        double b;
10       double c;
11
12       puts("Enter three floating-point numbers:");
13       scanf("%le%lf%lg", &a, &b, &c);
14
15       printf("\nHere are the numbers entered in plain:");
16       puts("floating-point notation:\n");
17       printf("%f\n%f\n%f\n", a, b, c);
18   }
```

```
Enter three floating-point numbers:
1.27987 1.27987e+03 3.38476e-06

Here are the numbers entered in plain floating-point notation:
1.279870
1279.870000
0.000003
```

Fig. 9.19 | Reading input with floating-point conversion specifiers.

9.11.5 Reading Characters and Strings with scanf

Characters and strings are input using the conversion specifiers c and s, respectively. Figure 9.20 prompts the user to enter a string. The program inputs the first character of the string with **%c** and stores it in the character variable x, then inputs the remainder of the string with **%s** and stores it in character array y.

```
1   // Fig. 9.20: fig09_20.c
2   // Reading characters and strings
3   #include <stdio.h>
4
5   int main(void)
6   {
7      char x;
8      char y[9];
9
10     printf("%s", "Enter a string: ");
11     scanf("%c%8s", &x, y);
12
13     puts("The input was:\n");
14     printf("the character \"%c\" and the string \"%s\"\n", x, y);
15  }
```

```
Enter a string: Sunday
The input was:
the character "S" and the string "unday"
```

Fig. 9.20 | Reading characters and strings.

9.11.6 Using Scan Sets with scanf

A sequence of characters can be input using a **scan set**. A scan set is a set of characters enclosed in square brackets, [], and preceded by a percent sign in the format control string. A scan set scans the characters in the input stream, looking only for those characters that match characters contained in the scan set. Each time a character is matched, it's stored in the scan set's corresponding argument—a pointer to a character array. The scan set stops inputting characters when a character that's *not* contained in the scan set is encountered. If the first character in the input stream does *not* match a character in the scan set, the array is not modified. Figure 9.21 uses the scan set [aeiou] to scan the input stream for vowels. Notice that the first seven letters of the input are read. The eighth letter (h) is not in the scan set and therefore the scanning is terminated.

```
1   // Fig. 9.21: fig09_21.c
2   // Using a scan set
3   #include <stdio.h>
4
5   // function main begins program execution
6   int main(void)
7   {
8      char z[9]; // define array z
9
10     printf("%s", "Enter string: ");
11     scanf("%8[aeiou]", z); // search for set of characters
```

Fig. 9.21 | Using a scan set. (Part 1 of 2.)

```
12
13      printf("The input was \"%s\"\n", z);
14   }
```

```
Enter string: ooeeooahah
The input was "ooeeooa"
```

Fig. 9.21 | Using a scan set. (Part 2 of 2.)

The scan set can also be used to scan for characters *not* contained in the scan set by using an **inverted scan set**. To create an inverted scan set, place a **caret** (^) in the square brackets before the scan characters. This causes characters not appearing in the scan set to be stored. When a character contained in the inverted scan set is encountered, input terminates. Figure 9.22 uses the inverted scan set [^aeiou] to search for consonants—more properly to search for "nonvowels."

```
1   // Fig. 9.22: fig09_22.c
2   // Using an inverted scan set
3   #include <stdio.h>
4
5   int main(void)
6   {
7      char z[9];
8
9      printf("%s", "Enter a string: ");
10     scanf("%8[^aeiou]", z); // inverted scan set
11
12     printf("The input was \"%s\"\n", z);
13   }
```

```
Enter a string: String
The input was "Str"
```

Fig. 9.22 | Using an inverted scan set.

9.11.7 Using Field Widths with scanf

A field width can be used in a scanf conversion specifier to *read a specific number of characters* from the input stream. Figure 9.23 inputs a series of consecutive digits as a two-digit integer and an integer consisting of the remaining digits in the input stream.

```
1   // Fig. 9.23: fig09_23.c
2   // inputting data with a field width
3   #include <stdio.h>
4
5   int main(void)
6   {
```

Fig. 9.23 | Inputting data with a field width. (Part 1 of 2.)

```
 7      int x;
 8      int y;
 9
10      printf("%s", "Enter a six digit integer: ");
11      scanf("%2d%d", &x, &y);
12
13      printf("The integers input were %d and %d\n", x, y);
14  }
```

```
Enter a six digit integer: 123456
The integers input were 12 and 3456
```

Fig. 9.23 | Inputting data with a field width. (Part 2 of 2.)

9.11.8 Skipping Characters in an Input Stream

Often it's necessary to *skip* certain characters in the input stream. For example, a date could be entered as

```
11-10-1999
```

Each number in the date needs to be stored, but the dashes that separate the numbers can be discarded. To eliminate unnecessary characters, include them in the format control string of scanf—whitespace characters, such as space, newline and tab, skip all leading whitespace. For example, to discard the dashes in the input, use the statement

```
scanf("%d-%d-%d", &month, &day, &year);
```

Although this scanf *does* eliminate the dashes in the preceding input, it's possible that the date could be entered as

```
10/11/1999
```

In this case, the preceding scanf would *not* eliminate the unnecessary characters. For this reason, scanf provides the **assignment suppression character** *. This character enables scanf to read any type of data from the input and discard it without assigning it to a variable. Figure 9.24 uses the assignment suppression character in the %c conversion specifier to indicate that a character appearing in the input stream should be read and discarded. Only the month, day and year are stored. The values of the variables are printed to demonstrate that they're in fact input correctly. The argument lists for each scanf call do not contain variables for the conversion specifiers that use the assignment suppression character. The corresponding characters are simply *discarded*.

```
 1  // Fig. 9.24: fig09_24.c
 2  // Reading and discarding characters from the input stream
 3  #include <stdio.h>
 4
 5  int main(void)
 6  {
 7     int month = 0;
```

Fig. 9.24 | Reading and discarding characters from the input stream. (Part 1 of 2.)

```
8       int day = 0;
9       int year = 0;
10      printf("%s", "Enter a date in the form mm-dd-yyyy: ");
11      scanf("%d%*c%d%*c%d", &month, &day, &year);
12      printf("month = %d   day = %d   year = %d\n\n", month, day, year);
13
14      printf("%s", "Enter a date in the form mm/dd/yyyy: ");
15      scanf("%d%*c%d%*c%d", &month, &day, &year);
16      printf("month = %d   day = %d   year = %d\n", month, day, year);
17  }
```

```
Enter a date in the form mm-dd-yyyy: 11-18-2012
month = 11   day = 18   year = 2012

Enter a date in the form mm/dd/yyyy: 11/18/2012
month = 11   day = 18   year = 2012
```

Fig. 9.24 | Reading and discarding characters from the input stream. (Part 2 of 2.)

9.12 Secure C Programming

The C standard lists many cases in which using incorrect library-function arguments can result in *undefined behaviors*. These can cause security vulnerabilities, so they should be avoided. Such problems can occur when using printf (or any of its variants, such as sprintf, fprintf, printf_s, etc.) with improperly formed conversion specifications. CERT rule FIO00-C (www.securecoding.cert.org) discusses these issues and presents a table showing the valid combinations of formatting flags, length modifiers and conversion-specifier characters that can be used to form conversion specifications. The table also shows the proper argument type for each valid conversion specification. In general, as you study *any* programming language, if the language specification says that doing something can lead to undefined behavior, avoid doing it to prevent security vulnerabilities.

Summary

Section 9.2 Streams
- All input and output is performed with **streams** (p. 378)—which are sequences of bytes.
- Normally, the **standard input stream** is connected to the keyboard, and the **standard output and error streams** are connected to the computer screen (p. 378).
- Operating systems often allow the standard input and standard output streams to be **redirected** to other devices.

Section 9.3 Formatting Output with printf
- A **format control string** (p. 378) describes the formats in which the output values appear. The format control string consists of **conversion specifiers**, **flags**, **field widths**, **precisions** and **literal characters**.
- A **conversion specification** (p. 379) consists of a **%** (p. 379) and a conversion specifier.

Section 9.4 Printing Integers
- Integers are printed with the following conversion specifiers (p. 379): **d** or **i** for optionally signed integers, **o** for unsigned integers in octal form, **u** for unsigned integers in decimal form and **x** or **X** for unsigned integers in hexadecimal form. The modifier **h**, **l** or **ll** is prefixed to the preceding conversion specifiers to indicate a short, long or long long integer, respectively.

Section 9.5 Printing Floating-Point Numbers
- Floating-point values are printed with the following conversion specifiers: **e** or **E** (p. 380) for exponential notation, **f** (p. 381) for regular floating-point notation, and **g** or **G** for either e (or E) notation or f notation. When the g (or G, p. 381) conversion specifier is indicated, the e (or E) conversion specifier is used if the value's exponent is less than -4 or greater than or equal to the precision with which the value is printed.
- The **precision** for the g and G conversion specifiers indicates the maximum number of significant digits printed.

Section 9.6 Printing Strings and Characters
- The conversion specifier **c** (p. 382) prints a **character**.
- The conversion specifier **s** (p. 382) prints a **string of characters** ending in the null character.

Section 9.7 Other Conversion Specifiers
- The conversion specifier **p** (p. 383) displays an **address** in an implementation-defined manner (on many systems, hexadecimal notation is used).
- The conversion specifier **%%** (p. 384) causes a literal % to be output.

Section 9.8 Printing with Field Widths and Precision
- If the **field width** (p. 379) is larger than the object being printed, the object is **right justified** by default.
- **Field widths** can be used with all conversion specifiers.
- **Precision** used with integer conversion specifiers indicates the minimum number of digits printed. Zeros are prefixed to the printed value until the number of digits is equivalent to the precision.
- **Precision** used with floating-point conversion specifiers e, E and f indicates the number of digits that appear after the decimal point. Precision used with floating-point conversion specifiers g and G indicates the number of significant digits to appear.
- **Precision** used with conversion specifier s indicates the number of characters to be printed.
- The **field width** and the **precision** can be combined by placing the field width, followed by a decimal point, followed by the precision between the percent sign and the conversion specifier.
- It's possible to specify the **field width** and the **precision** through **integer expressions** in the argument list following the format control string. To do so, use an asterisk (*) for the field width or precision. The matching argument in the argument list is used in place of the asterisk.

Section 9.9 Using Flags in the **printf** Format Control String
- The - **flag** left justifies its argument in a field.
- The + **flag** (p. 388) prints a plus sign for positive values and a minus sign for negative values.
- The **space flag** (p. 388) prints a space preceding a positive value that's not displayed with the + flag.
- The # **flag** (p. 389) prefixes 0 to octal values and 0x or 0X to hexadecimal values and forces the decimal point to be printed for floating-point values printed with e, E, f, g or G.

- The **0 flag** (p. 389) prints leading zeros for a value that does not occupy its entire field width.

Section 9.10 Printing Literals and Escape Sequences
- Most **literal characters** to be printed in a printf statement can simply be included in the format control string. However, there are several "problem" characters, such as the quotation mark (", p. 390) that delimits the format control string itself. Various **control characters**, such as newline and tab, must be represented by **escape sequences**. An escape sequence is represented by a backslash (\), followed by a particular escape character.

Section 9.11 Reading Formatted Input with **scanf**
- **Input formatting** is accomplished with the **scanf** library function.
- Integers are input with scanf with the conversion specifiers **d** and **i** (p. 392) for optionally signed integers and **o**, **u**, **x** or **X** for unsigned integers. The modifiers **h**, **l** and **ll** are placed before an integer conversion specifier to input a short, long and long long integer, respectively.
- Floating-point values are input with scanf with the conversion specifiers **e**, **E**, **f**, **g** or **G**. The modifiers **l** and **L** are placed before any of the floating-point conversion specifiers to indicate that the input value is a double or long double value, respectively.
- Characters are input with scanf with the conversion specifier **c** (p. 394).
- Strings are input with scanf with the conversion specifier **s** (p. 394).
- A scanf with a **scan set** (p. 394) scans the characters in the input, looking only for those characters that match characters contained in the scan set. When a character is matched, it's stored in a character array. The scan set stops inputting characters when a character not contained in the scan set is encountered.
- To create an **inverted scan set** (p. 395), place a caret (∧) in the square brackets before the scan characters. This causes characters input with scanf and not appearing in the scan set to be stored until a character contained in the inverted scan set is encountered.
- **Address values** are input with scanf with the conversion specifier **p**.
- Conversion specifier **n** stores the **number of characters input** so far in the current scanf. The corresponding argument is a pointer to int.
- The **assignment suppression character** (*, p. 396) reads data from the input stream and discards the data.
- A **field width** is used in scanf to read a specific number of characters from the input stream.

Self-Review Exercises
9.1 Fill in the blanks in each of the following:
   a) All input and output is dealt with in the form of _____.
   b) The _____ stream is normally connected to the keyboard.
   c) The _____ stream is normally connected to the computer screen.
   d) Precise output formatting is accomplished with the _____ function.
   e) The format control string may contain _____, _____, _____, _____ and _____.
   f) The conversion specifier _____ or _____ may be used to output a signed decimal integer.
   g) The conversion specifiers _____, _____ and _____ are used to display unsigned integers in octal, decimal and hexadecimal form, respectively.
   h) The modifiers _____ and _____ are placed before the integer conversion specifiers to indicate that short or long integer values are to be displayed.

i) The conversion specifier _____ is used to display a floating-point value in exponential notation.

j) The modifier _____ is placed before any floating-point conversion specifier to indicate that a `long double` value is to be displayed.

k) The conversion specifiers `e`, `E` and `f` are displayed with _____ digits of precision to the right of the decimal point if no precision is specified.

l) The conversion specifiers _____ and _____ are used to print strings and characters, respectively.

m) All strings end in the _____ character.

n) The field width and precision in a `printf` conversion specifier can be controlled with integer expressions by substituting a(n) _____ for the field width or for the precision and placing an integer expression in the corresponding argument of the argument list.

o) The _____ flag causes output to be left justified in a field.

p) The _____ flag causes values to be displayed with either a plus sign or a minus sign.

q) Precise input formatting is accomplished with the _____ function.

r) A(n) _____ is used to scan a string for specific characters and store the characters in an array.

s) The conversion specifier _____ can be used to input optionally signed octal, decimal and hexadecimal integers.

t) The conversion specifiers _____ can be used to input a `double` value.

u) The _____ is used to read data from the input stream and discard it without assigning it to a variable.

v) A(n) _____ can be used in a `scanf` conversion specifier to indicate that a specific number of characters or digits should be read from the input stream.

9.2 Find the error in each of the following and explain how it can be corrected.

a) The following statement should print the character `'c'`.
```
printf("%s\n", 'c');
```

b) The following statement should print 9.375%.
```
printf("%.3f%", 9.375);
```

c) The following statement should print the first character of the string `"Monday"`.
```
printf("%c\n", "Monday");
```

d) `puts(""A string in quotes"");`

e) `printf(%d%d, 12, 20);`

f) `printf("%c", "x");`

g) `printf("%s\n", 'Richard');`

9.3 Write a statement for each of the following:

a) Print 1234 right justified in a 10-digit field.

b) Print 123.456789 in exponential notation with a sign (+ or -) and 3 digits of precision.

c) Read a `double` value into variable `number`.

d) Print 100 in octal form preceded by 0.

e) Read a string into character array `string`.

f) Read characters into array `n` until a nondigit character is encountered.

g) Use integer variables `x` and `y` to specify the field width and precision used to display the `double` value 87.4573.

h) Read a value of the form 3.5%. Store the percentage in `float` variable `percent` and eliminate the % from the input stream. Do not use the assignment suppression character.

i) Print 3.333333 as a `long double` value with a sign (+ or -) in a field of 20 characters with a precision of 3.

Answers to Self-Review Exercises

9.1   a) streams. b) standard input. c) standard output. d) `printf`. e) conversion specifiers, flags, field widths, precisions, literal characters. f) d, i. g) o, u, x (or X). h) h, 1. i) e (or E). j) L. k) 6. l) s, c. m) NULL (`'\0'`). n) asterisk (*). o) - (minus). p) + (plus). q) `scanf`. r) scan set. s) i. t) 1e, 1E, 1f, 1g or 1G. u) assignment suppression character (*). v) field width.

9.2   a) Error: Conversion specifier s expects an argument of type pointer to `char`.
Correction: To print the character `'c'`, use the conversion specifier %c or change `'c'` to `"c"`.
b) Error: Trying to print the literal character % without using the conversion specifier %%.
Correction: Use %% to print a literal % character.
c) Error: Conversion specifier c expects an argument of type `char`.
Correction: To print the first character of `"Monday"` use the conversion specifier %1s.
d) Error: Trying to print the literal character " without using the \" escape sequence.
Correction: Replace each quote in the inner set of quotes with \".
e) Error: The format control string is not enclosed in double quotes.
Correction: Enclose %d%d in double quotes.
f) Error: The character x is enclosed in double quotes.
Correction: Character constants to be printed with %c must be enclosed in single quotes.
g) Error: The string to be printed is enclosed in single quotes.
Correction: Use double quotes instead of single quotes to represent a string.

9.3   a) `printf("%10d\n", 1234);`
b) `printf("%+.3e\n", 123.456789);`
c) `scanf("%1f", &number);`
d) `printf("%#o\n", 100);`
e) `scanf("%s", string);`
f) `scanf("%[0123456789]", n);`
g) `printf("%*.*f\n", x, y, 87.4573);`
h) `scanf("%f%%", &percent);`
i) `printf("%+20.3Lf\n", 3.333333);`

Exercises

9.4   Write a `printf` or `scanf` statement for each of the following:
a) Print unsigned integer 40000 left justified in a 15-digit field with 8 digits.
b) Read a hexadecimal value into variable `hex`.
c) Print 200 with and without a sign.
d) Print 100 in hexadecimal form preceded by `0x`.
e) Read characters into array `s` until the letter p is encountered.
f) Print 1.234 in a 9-digit field with preceding zeros.
g) Read a time of the form hh:mm:ss, storing the parts of the time in the integer variables `hour`, `minute` and `second`. Skip the colons (:) in the input stream. Use the assignment suppression character.
h) Read a string of the form `"characters"` from the standard input. Store the string in character array `s`. Eliminate the quotation marks from the input stream.
i) Read a time of the form hh:mm:ss, storing the parts of the time in the integer variables `hour`, `minute` and `second`. Skip the colons (:) in the input stream. Do not use the assignment suppression character.

9.5   Show what each of the following statements prints. If a statement is incorrect, indicate why.

```
a)  printf("%-10d\n", 10000);
b)  printf("%c\n", "This is a string");
c)  printf("%*.*lf\n", 8, 3, 1024.987654);
d)  printf("%#o\n%#X\n%#e\n", 17, 17, 1008.83689);
e)  printf("% ld\n%+ld\n", 1000000, 1000000);
f)  printf("%10.2E\n", 444.93738);
g)  printf("%10.2g\n", 444.93738);
h)  printf("%d\n", 10.987);
```

9.6 Find the error(s) in each of the following program segments. Explain how each error can be corrected.

```
a)  printf("%s\n", 'Happy Birthday');
b)  printf("%c\n", 'Hello');
c)  printf("%c\n", "This is a string");
```
d) The following statement should print "Bon Voyage":
```
    printf(""%s"", "Bon Voyage");
```
e)
```
    char day[] = "Sunday";
    printf("%s\n", day[3]);
```
f)
```
    puts('Enter your name: ');
```
g)
```
    printf(%f, 123.456);
```
h) The following statement should print the characters 'O' and 'K':
```
    printf("%s%s\n", 'O', 'K');
```
i)
```
    char s[10];
    scanf("%c", s[7]);
```

9.7 *(Differences Between %d and %i)* Write a program to test the difference between the %d and %i conversion specifiers when used in scanf statements. Ask the user to enter two integers separated by a space. Use the statements

```
scanf("%i%d", &x, &y);
printf("%d %d\n", x, y);
```

to input and print the values. Test the program with the following sets of input data:

```
    10      10
   -10     -10
    010     010
    0x10    0x10
```

9.8 *(Printing Numbers in Various Field Widths)* Write a program to test the results of printing the integer value 12345 and the floating-point value 1.2345 in fields of various sizes. What happens when the values are printed in fields containing fewer digits than the values?

9.9 *(Rounding Floating-Point Numbers)* Write a program that prints the value 100.453627 rounded to the nearest digit, tenth, hundredth, thousandth and ten-thousandth.

9.10 *(Temperature Conversions)* Write a program that converts integer Fahrenheit temperatures from 0 to 212 degrees to floating-point Celsius temperatures with 3 digits of precision. Perform the calculation using the formula

```
celsius = 5.0 / 9.0 * (fahrenheit - 32);
```

The output should be printed in two right-justified columns of 10 characters each, and the Celsius temperatures should be preceded by a sign for both positive and negative values.

9.11   *(Escape Sequences)* Write a program to test the escape sequences \', \", \?, \\, \a, \b, \n, \r and \t. For the escape sequences that move the cursor, print a character before and after printing the escape sequence so it's clear where the cursor has moved.

9.12   *(Printing a Question Mark)* Write a program that determines whether ? can be printed as part of a printf format control string as a literal character rather than using the \? escape sequence.

9.13   *(Reading an Integer with Each scanf Conversion Specifier)* Write a program that inputs the value 437 using each of the scanf integer conversion specifiers. Print each input value using all the integer conversion specifiers.

9.14   *(Outputting a Number with the Floating-Point Conversion Specifiers)* Write a program that uses each of the conversion specifiers e, f and g to input the value 1.2345. Print the values of each variable to prove that each conversion specifier can be used to input this same value.

9.15   *(Reading Strings in Quotes)* In some programming languages, strings are entered surrounded by either single *or* double quotation marks. Write a program that reads the three strings suzy, "suzy" and 'suzy'. Are the single and double quotes ignored by C or read as part of the string?

9.16   *(Printing a Question Mark as a Character Constant)* Write a program that determines whether ? can be printed as the character constant '?' rather than the character constant escape sequence '\?' using conversion specifier %c in the format control string of a printf statement.

9.17   *(Using %g with Various Precisions)* Write a program that uses the conversion specifier g to output the value 9876.12345. Print the value with precisions ranging from 1 to 9.

10

C Structures, Unions, Bit Manipulation and Enumerations

Objectives

In this chapter, you'll:

- Create and use **struct**s, **union**s and **enum**s.

- Understand self-referential **struct**s.

- Learn about the operations that can be performed on **struct** instances.

- Initialize **struct** members.

- Access **struct** members.

- Pass **struct** instances to functions by value and by reference.

- Use **typedef**s to create aliases for existing type names.

- Learn about the operations that can be performed on **union**s.

- Initialize **union**s.

- Manipulate integer data with the bitwise operators.

- Create bit fields for storing data compactly.

- Use **enum** constants.

- Consider the security issues of working with **struct**s, bit manipulation and **enum**s.

10.1 Introduction

Structures—sometimes referred to as **aggregates** in the C standard—are collections of related variables under one name. Structures may contain variables of many different data types—in contrast to arrays, which contain only elements of the *same* data type. Structures are commonly used to define *records* to be stored in files (see Chapter 11). Pointers and structures facilitate the formation of more complex data structures such as linked lists, queues, stacks and trees (see Chapter 12). We'll also discuss:

- typedefs—for creating *aliases* for previously defined data types.

- unions—similar to structures, but with members that *share* the *same* storage space.

- bitwise operators—for manipulating the bits of integral operands.

- bit fields—unsigned int or int members of structures or unions for which you specify the number of bits in which the members are stored, helping you pack information tightly.

- enumerations—sets of integer constants represented by identifiers.

10.2 Structure Definitions

Structures are **derived data types**—they're constructed using objects of other types. Consider the following structure definition:

```
struct card {
   char *face;
   char *suit;
};
```

Keyword **struct** introduces a structure definition. The identifier card is the **structure tag,** which names the structure definition and is used with struct to declare variables of the **structure type**—e.g., struct card. Variables declared within the braces of the structure definition are the structure's **members.** Members of the same structure type must have unique names, but two different structure types may contain members of the same name without conflict (we'll soon see why). Each structure definition *must* end with a semicolon.

Common Programming Error 10.1
Forgetting the semicolon that terminates a structure definition is a syntax error.

The definition of struct card contains members face and suit, each of type char *. Structure members can be variables of the primitive data types (e.g., int, float, etc.), or aggregates, such as arrays and other structures. As we saw in Chapter 6, each element of an array must be of the *same* type. Structure members, however, can be of *different* types. For example, the following struct contains character array members for an employee's first and last names, an unsigned int member for the employee's age, a char member that would contain 'M' or 'F' for the employee's gender and a double member for the employee's hourly salary:

```
struct employee {
    char firstName[20];
    char lastName[20];
    unsigned int age;
    char gender;
    double hourlySalary;
};
```

10.2.1 Self-Referential Structures

A variable of a struct type cannot be declared in the definition of that same struct type. A pointer to that struct type, however, may be included. For example, in struct employee2:

```
struct employee2 {
    char firstName[20];
    char lastName[20];
    unsigned int age;
    char gender;
    double hourlySalary;
    struct employee2 teamLeader; // ERROR
    struct employee2 *teamLeaderPtr; // pointer
};
```

the instance of itself (teamLeader) is an error. Because teamLeaderPtr is a pointer (to type struct employee2), it's permitted in the definition. A structure containing a member that's a pointer to the *same* structure type is referred to as a **self-referential structure.** Self-referential structures are used in Chapter 12, to build linked data structures.

Common Programming Error 10.2
A structure cannot contain an instance of itself.

10.2.2 Defining Variables of Structure Types

Structure definitions do *not* reserve any space in memory; rather, each definition creates a new data type that's used to define variables—like a blueprint of how to build instances of that struct. Structure variables are defined like variables of other types. The definition

```
struct card aCard, deck[52], *cardPtr;
```

declares aCard to be a variable of type struct card, declares deck to be an array with 52 elements of type struct card and declares cardPtr to be a pointer to struct card. After the preceding statement, we've reserved memory for one struct card object named aCard, 52 struct card objects in the deck array and an uninitialized pointer of type struct card. Variables of a given structure type may also be declared by placing a comma-separated list of the variable names between the closing brace of the structure definition and the semicolon that ends the structure definition. For example, the preceding definition could have been incorporated into the struct card definition as follows:

```
struct card {
    char *face;
    char *suit;
} aCard, deck[52], *cardPtr;
```

10.2.3 Structure Tag Names

The structure tag name is optional. If a structure definition does not contain a structure tag name, variables of the structure type may be declared *only* in the structure definition— *not* in a separate declaration.

Good Programming Practice 10.1

Always provide a structure tag name when creating a structure type. The structure tag name is required for declaring new variables of the structure type later in the program.

10.2.4 Operations That Can Be Performed on Structures

The only valid operations that may be performed on structures are:

- assigning struct variables to struct variables of the *same* type (see Section 10.7)— for a pointer member, this copies only the address stored in the pointer.

- taking the address (&) of a struct variable (see Section 10.4).

- accessing the members of a struct variable (see Section 10.4).

- using the sizeof operator to determine the size of a struct variable.

Common Programming Error 10.3

Assigning a structure of one type to a structure of a different type is a compilation error.

Structures may *not* be compared using operators == and !=, because structure members are not necessarily stored in consecutive bytes of memory. Sometimes there are "holes" in a structure, because computers may store specific data types only on certain memory boundaries such as half-word, word or double-word boundaries. A word is a memory unit used to store data in a computer—usually 4 bytes or 8 bytes. Consider the following structure definition, in which sample1 and sample2 of type struct example are declared:

```
struct example {
   char c;
   int i;
} sample1, sample2;
```

A computer with 4-byte words might require that each member of struct example be aligned on a word boundary, i.e., at the beginning of a word—this is machine dependent. Figure 10.1 shows a sample storage alignment for a variable of type struct example that has been assigned the character 'a' and the integer 97 (the bit representations of the values are shown). If the members are stored beginning at word boundaries, there's a three-byte hole (bytes 1–3 in the figure) in the storage for variables of type struct example. The value in the three-byte hole is *undefined*. Even if the member values of sample1 and sample2 are in fact equal, the structures are not necessarily equal, because the undefined three-byte holes are not likely to contain identical values.

Fig. 10.1 | Possible storage alignment for a variable of type struct example showing an undefined area in memory.

Portability Tip 10.1

Because the size of data items of a particular type is machine dependent and because storage alignment considerations are machine dependent, so too is the representation of a structure.

10.3 Initializing Structures

Structures can be initialized using initializer lists as with arrays. To initialize a structure, follow the variable name in the definition with an equals sign and a brace-enclosed, comma-separated list of initializers. For example, the declaration

```
struct card aCard = { "Three", "Hearts" };
```

creates variable aCard to be of type struct card (as defined in Section 10.2) and initializes member face to "Three" and member suit to "Hearts". If there are *fewer* initializers in the list than members in the structure, the remaining members are automatically initialized to 0 (or NULL if the member is a pointer). Structure variables defined outside a function definition (i.e., externally) are initialized to 0 or NULL if they're not explicitly initialized in the external definition. Structure variables may also be initialized in assignment statements by assigning a structure variable of the *same* type, or by assigning values to the *individual* members of the structure.

10.4 Accessing Structure Members with . and ->

Two operators are used to access members of structures: the **structure member operator** (.)—also called the **dot operator**—and the **structure pointer operator** (->)—also called the **arrow operator**. The structure member operator accesses a structure member via the structure variable name. For example, to print member suit of structure variable aCard defined in Section 10.3, use the statement

```
printf("%s", aCard.suit); // displays Hearts
```

The structure pointer operator—consisting of a minus (-) sign and a greater than (>) sign with no intervening spaces—accesses a structure member via a **pointer to the structure**. Assume that the pointer cardPtr has been declared to point to struct card and that the address of structure aCard has been assigned to cardPtr. To print member suit of structure aCard with pointer cardPtr, use the statement

```
printf("%s", cardPtr->suit); // displays Hearts
```

The expression cardPtr->suit is equivalent to (*cardPtr).suit, which dereferences the pointer and accesses the member suit using the structure member operator. The parentheses are needed here because the structure member operator (.) has a higher precedence than the pointer dereferencing operator (*). The structure pointer operator and structure member operator, along with parentheses (for calling functions) and brackets ([]) used for array indexing, have the highest operator precedence and associate from left to right.

Good Programming Practice 10.2
Do not put spaces around the -> and . operators. Omitting spaces helps emphasize that the expressions the operators are contained in are essentially single variable names.

Common Programming Error 10.4
Inserting space between the - and > components of the structure pointer operator or between the components of any other multiple-keystroke operator except ?: is a syntax error.

Common Programming Error 10.5
Attempting to refer to a structure member by using only the member's name is a syntax error.

Common Programming Error 10.6
*Not using parentheses when referring to a structure member that uses a pointer and the structure member operator (e.g., *cardPtr.suit) is a syntax error. To prevent this problem use the arrow (->) operator instead.*

The program of Fig. 10.2 demonstrates the use of the structure member and structure pointer operators. Using the structure member operator, the members of structure aCard are assigned the values "Ace" and "Spades", respectively (lines 17 and 18). Pointer cardPtr is assigned the address of structure aCard (line 20). Function printf prints the members of structure variable aCard using the structure member operator with variable name aCard, the structure pointer operator with pointer cardPtr and the structure member operator with dereferenced pointer cardPtr (lines 22–24).

```
1   // Fig. 10.2: fig10_02.c
2   // Structure member operator and
3   // structure pointer operator
```

Fig. 10.2 | Structure member operator and structure pointer operator. (Part 1 of 2.)

```
 4    #include <stdio.h>
 5
 6    // card structure definition
 7    struct card {
 8       char *face; // define pointer face
 9       char *suit; // define pointer suit
10    };
11
12    int main(void)
13    {
14       struct card aCard; // define one struct card variable
15
16       // place strings into aCard
17       aCard.face = "Ace";
18       aCard.suit = "Spades";
19
20       struct card *cardPtr = &aCard; // assign address of aCard to cardPtr
21
22       printf("%s%s%s\n%s%s%s\n%s%s%s\n", aCard.face, " of ", aCard.suit,
23          cardPtr->face, " of ", cardPtr->suit,
24          (*cardPtr).face, " of ", (*cardPtr).suit);
25    }
```

```
Ace of Spades
Ace of Spades
Ace of Spades
```

Fig. 10.2 | Structure member operator and structure pointer operator. (Part 2 of 2.)

10.5 Using Structures with Functions

Structures may be passed to functions by

- passing individual structure members.
- passing an entire structure.
- passing a pointer to a structure.

When structures or individual structure members are passed to a function, they're passed by value. Therefore, the members of a caller's structure cannot be modified by the called function. To pass a structure by reference, pass the address of the structure variable. Arrays of structures—like all other arrays—are automatically passed by reference.

In Chapter 6, we stated that you can use a structure to pass an array by value. To do so, create a structure with the array as a member. Structures are passed by value, so the array is passed by value.

Common Programming Error 10.7

Assuming that structures, like arrays, are automatically passed by reference and trying to modify the caller's structure values in the called function is a logic error.

Performance Tip 10.1

Passing structures by reference is more efficient than passing structures by value (which requires the entire structure to be copied).

10.6 typedef

The keyword **typedef** provides a mechanism for creating synonyms (or aliases) for previously defined data types. Names for structure types are often defined with typedef to create shorter type names. For example, the statement

```
typedef struct card Card;
```

defines the new type name Card as a synonym for type struct card. C programmers often use typedef to define a structure type, so a structure tag is not required. For example, the following definition

```
typedef struct {
    char *face;
    char *suit;
} Card;
```

creates the structure type Card without the need for a separate typedef statement.

Good Programming Practice 10.3
Capitalize the first letter of typedef names to emphasize that they're synonyms for other type names.

Card can now be used to declare variables of type struct card. The declaration

```
Card deck[52];
```

declares an array of 52 Card structures (i.e., variables of type struct card). Creating a new name with typedef does *not* create a new type; typedef simply creates a new *type name*, which may be used as an *alias* for an existing type name. A meaningful name helps make the program self-documenting. For example, when we read the previous declaration, we know "deck is an array of 52 Cards."

Often, typedef is used to create synonyms for the basic data types. For example, a program requiring four-byte integers may use type int on one system and type long on another. Programs designed for portability often use typedef to create an alias for four-byte integers, such as Integer. The alias Integer can be changed once in the program to make the program work on both systems.

Portability Tip 10.2
Use typedef to help make a program more portable.

Good Programming Practice 10.4
Using typedefs can help make a program more readable and maintainable.

10.7 Example: High-Performance Card Shuffling and Dealing Simulation

The program in Fig. 10.3 is based on the card shuffling and dealing simulation discussed in Chapter 7. The program represents the deck of cards as an array of structures and uses high-performance shuffling and dealing algorithms. The program output is shown in Fig. 10.4.

```c
1  // Fig. 10.3: fig10_03.c
2  // Card shuffling and dealing program using structures
3  #include <stdio.h>
4  #include <stdlib.h>
5  #include <time.h>
6
7  #define CARDS 52
8  #define FACES 13
9
10 // card structure definition
11 struct card {
12    const char *face; // define pointer face
13    const char *suit; // define pointer suit
14 };
15
16 typedef struct card Card; // new type name for struct card
17
18 // prototypes
19 void fillDeck(Card * const wDeck, const char * wFace[],
20    const char * wSuit[]);
21 void shuffle(Card * const wDeck);
22 void deal(const Card * const wDeck);
23
24 int main(void)
25 {
26    Card deck[CARDS]; // define array of Cards
27
28    // initialize array of pointers
29    const char *face[] = { "Ace", "Deuce", "Three", "Four", "Five",
30       "Six", "Seven", "Eight", "Nine", "Ten",
31       "Jack", "Queen", "King"};
32
33    // initialize array of pointers
34    const char *suit[] = { "Hearts", "Diamonds", "Clubs", "Spades"};
35
36    srand(time(NULL)); // randomize
37
38    fillDeck(deck, face, suit); // load the deck with Cards
39    shuffle(deck); // put Cards in random order
40    deal(deck); // deal all 52 Cards
41 }
42
43 // place strings into Card structures
44 void fillDeck(Card * const wDeck, const char * wFace[],
45    const char * wSuit[])
46 {
47    // loop through wDeck
48    for (size_t i = 0; i < CARDS; ++i) {
49       wDeck[i].face = wFace[i % FACES];
```

Fig. 10.3 | Card shuffling and dealing program using structures. (Part 1 of 2.)

```
50          wDeck[i].suit = wSuit[i / FACES];
51      }
52  }
53
54  // shuffle cards
55  void shuffle(Card * const wDeck)
56  {
57      // loop through wDeck randomly swapping Cards
58      for (size_t i = 0; i < CARDS; ++i) {
59          size_t j = rand() % CARDS;
60          Card temp = wDeck[i];
61          wDeck[i] = wDeck[j];
62          wDeck[j] = temp;
63      }
64  }
65
66  // deal cards
67  void deal(const Card * const wDeck)
68  {
69      // loop through wDeck
70      for (size_t i = 0; i < CARDS; ++i) {
71          printf("%5s of %-8s%s", wDeck[i].face , wDeck[i].suit ,
72              (i + 1) % 4 ? "  " : "\n");
73      }
74  }
```

Fig. 10.3 | Card shuffling and dealing program using structures. (Part 2 of 2.)

Three of Hearts	Jack of Clubs	Three of Spades	Six of Diamonds
Five of Hearts	Eight of Spades	Three of Clubs	Deuce of Spades
Jack of Spades	Four of Hearts	Deuce of Hearts	Six of Clubs
Queen of Clubs	Three of Diamonds	Eight of Diamonds	King of Clubs
King of Hearts	Eight of Hearts	Queen of Hearts	Seven of Clubs
Seven of Diamonds	Nine of Spades	Five of Clubs	Eight of Clubs
Six of Hearts	Deuce of Diamonds	Five of Spades	Four of Clubs
Deuce of Clubs	Nine of Hearts	Seven of Hearts	Four of Spades
Ten of Spades	King of Diamonds	Ten of Hearts	Jack of Diamonds
Four of Diamonds	Six of Spades	Five of Diamonds	Ace of Diamonds
Ace of Clubs	Jack of Hearts	Ten of Clubs	Queen of Diamonds
Ace of Hearts	Ten of Diamonds	Nine of Clubs	King of Spades
Ace of Spades	Nine of Diamonds	Seven of Spades	Queen of Spades

Fig. 10.4 | Output for the high-performance card shuffling and dealing simulation.

In the program, function fillDeck (lines 44–52) initializes the Card array in order with "Ace" through "King" of each suit. The Card array is passed (in line 39) to function shuffle (lines 55–64), where the high-performance shuffling algorithm is implemented. Function shuffle takes an array of 52 Cards as an argument. The function loops through the 52 Cards (lines 58–63). For each Card, a number between 0 and 51 is picked randomly. Next, the current Card and the randomly selected Card are swapped in the array (lines 60–62). A total of 52 swaps are made in a single pass of the entire array, and the array of Cards is shuffled! This algorithm *cannot* suffer from *indefinite postponement* like the shuffling algorithm presented in Chapter 7. Because the Cards were swapped in place in the array, the high-performance dealing algorithm implemented in function deal (lines 67–74) requires only *one* pass of the array to deal the shuffled Cards.

Common Programming Error 10.8

Forgetting to include the array index when referring to individual structures in an array of structures is a syntax error.

Fisher-Yates Shuffling Algorithm

It's recommended that you use a so-called *unbiased* shuffling algorithm for real card games. Such an algorithm ensures that all possible shuffled card sequences are equally likely to occur. Exercise 10.18 asks you to research the popular unbiased Fisher-Yates shuffling algorithm and use it to reimplement the DeckOfCards method shuffle in Fig. 10.3.

10.8 Unions

Like a structure, a **union** also is a *derived data type*, but with members that *share the same storage space*. For different situations in a program, some variables may not be relevant, but other variables are—so a union *shares* the space instead of wasting storage on variables that are not being used. The members of a union can be of *any* data type. The number of bytes used to store a union must be at least enough to hold the *largest* member. In most cases, unions contain two or more data types. Only one member, and thus one data type, can be referenced at a time. It's your responsibility to ensure that the data in a union is referenced with the proper data type.

Common Programming Error 10.9

Referencing data in a union with a variable of the wrong type is a logic error.

Portability Tip 10.3

If data is stored in a union as one type and referenced as another type, the results are implementation dependent.

10.8.1 Union Declarations

A union definition has the same format as a structure definition. The union definition

```
union number {
    int x;
    double y;
};
```

indicates that number is a union type with members int x and double y. The union definition is normally placed in a header and included in all source files that use the union type.

Software Engineering Observation 10.1

As with a struct definition, a union definition simply creates a new type. Placing a union or struct definition outside any function does not create a global variable.

10.8.2 Operations That Can Be Performed on Unions

The operations that can be performed on a union are:

- assigning a union to another union of the same type.

- taking the address (&) of a union variable.

- accessing union members using the structure member operator and the structure pointer operator.

Unions may not be compared using operators == and != for the same reasons that structures cannot be compared.

10.8.3 Initializing Unions in Declarations

In a declaration, *a union may be initialized with a value of the same type as the first union member.* For example, with the union in Section 10.8.1, the statement

```
union number value = { 10 };
```

is a valid initialization of union variable value because the union is initialized with an int, but the following declaration would truncate the initializer value's floating-point part (some compilers will issue a warning about this):

```
union number value = { 1.43 };
```

Portability Tip 10.4

The amount of storage required to store a union is implementation dependent but will always be at least as large as the largest member of the union.

Portability Tip 10.5

Some unions may not port easily among computer systems. Whether a union is portable or not often depends on the storage alignment requirements for the union member data types on a given system.

10.8.4 Demonstrating Unions

The program in Fig. 10.5 uses the variable value (line 13) of type union number (lines 6–9) to display the value stored in the union as both an int and a double. The program output is *implementation dependent*. The program output shows that the internal representation of a double value can be quite different from the representation of int.

```c
1   // Fig. 10.5: fig10_05.c
2   // Displaying the value of a union in both member data types
3   #include <stdio.h>
4
5   // number union definition
6   union number {
7      int x;
8      double y;
9   };
```

Fig. 10.5 | Displaying the value of a union in both member data types. (Part 1 of 2.)

```
10
11   int main(void)
12   {
13      union number value; // define union variable
14
15      value.x = 100; // put an integer into the union
16      printf("%s\n%s\n%s\n  %d\n%s\n  %f\n\n\n",
17         "Put 100 in the integer member",
18         "and print both members.",
19         "int:", value.x,
20         "double:", value.y);
21
22      value.y = 100.0; // put a double into the same union
23      printf("%s\n%s\n%s\n  %d\n%s\n  %f\n",
24         "Put 100.0 in the floating member",
25         "and print both members.",
26         "int:", value.x,
27         "double:", value.y);
28   }
```

```
Put 100 in the integer member
and print both members.
int:
  100

double:
  -9255959211743313600000000000000000000000000000000000000000000000.000000

Put 100.0 in the floating member
and print both members.
int:
  0

double:
  100.000000
```

Fig. 10.5 | Displaying the value of a union in both member data types. (Part 2 of 2.)

10.9 Bitwise Operators

Computers represent all data internally as sequences of bits. Each bit can assume the value 0 or the value 1. On most systems, a sequence of eight bits forms a byte—the typical storage unit for a variable of type char. Other data types are stored in larger numbers of bytes. The bitwise operators are used to manipulate the bits of integral operands, both signed and unsigned. Unsigned integers are normally used with the bitwise operators, which are summarized in Fig. 10.6.

Portability Tip 10.6
Bitwise data manipulations are machine dependent.

The bitwise AND, bitwise inclusive OR and bitwise exclusive OR operators compare their two operands bit by bit. The *bitwise AND operator* sets each bit in the result to 1 if the corresponding bit in both operands is 1. The *bitwise inclusive OR operator* sets each bit in the result to 1 if the corresponding bit in either (or both) operand(s) is 1. The *bitwise exclusive OR operator* sets each bit in the result to 1 if the corresponding bits in each operand are different. The *left-shift operator* shifts the bits of its left operand to the left by the number of bits specified in its right operand. The *right-shift operator* shifts the bits in its left operand to the right by the number of bits specified in its right operand. The *bitwise complement operator* sets all 0 bits in its operand to 1 in the result and sets all 1 bits to 0 in the result—often called *toggling* the bits. Detailed discussions of each bitwise operator appear in the examples that follow. The bitwise operators are summarized in Fig. 10.6.

Operator		Description
&	bitwise AND	Compares its two operands bit by bit. The bits in the result are set to 1 if the corresponding bits in the two operands are *both* 1.
|	bitwise inclusive OR	Compares its two operands bit by bit. The bits in the result are set to 1 if *at least one* of the corresponding bits in the two operands is 1.
^	bitwise exclusive OR (also known as bitwise XOR)	Compares its two operands bit by bit. The bits in the result are set to 1 if the corresponding bits in the two operands are different.
<<	left shift	Shifts the bits of the first operand left by the number of bits specified by the second operand; fill from the right with 0 bits.
>>	right shift	Shifts the bits of the first operand right by the number of bits specified by the second operand; the method of filling from the left is machine dependent when the left operand is negative.
~	complement	All 0 bits are set to 1 and all 1 bits are set to 0.

Fig. 10.6 | Bitwise operators.

The bitwise operator discussions in this section show the binary representations of the integer operands. For a detailed explanation of the binary (also called base-2) number system see Appendix C. Because of the machine-dependent nature of bitwise manipulations, these programs might not work correctly or might work differently on your system.

10.9.1 Displaying an Unsigned Integer in Bits

When using the bitwise operators, it's useful to display values in binary to show the precise effects of these operators. The program of Fig. 10.7 prints an unsigned int in its binary representation in groups of eight bits each for readability. For the examples in this section, we assume an implementation where unsigned ints are stored in 4 bytes (32 bits) of memory.

```
1   // Fig. 10.7: fig10_07.c
2   // Displaying an unsigned int in bits
3   #include <stdio.h>
```

Fig. 10.7 | Displaying an unsigned int in bits. (Part 1 of 2.)

```
 4
 5    void displayBits(unsigned int value); // prototype
 6
 7    int main(void)
 8    {
 9       unsigned int x; // variable to hold user input
10
11       printf("%s", "Enter a nonnegative int: ");
12       scanf("%u", &x);
13
14       displayBits(x);
15    }
16
17    // display bits of an unsigned int value
18    void displayBits(unsigned int value)
19    {
20       // define displayMask and left shift 31 bits
21       unsigned int displayMask = 1 << 31;
22
23       printf("%10u = ", value);
24
25       // loop through bits
26       for (unsigned int c = 1; c <= 32; ++c) {
27          putchar(value & displayMask ? '1' : '0');
28          value <<= 1; // shift value left by 1
29
30          if (c % 8 == 0) { // output space after 8 bits
31             putchar(' ');
32          }
33       }
34
35       putchar('\n');
36    }
```

```
Enter a nonnegative int: 65000
    65000 = 00000000 00000000 11111101 11101000
```

Fig. 10.7 | Displaying an unsigned int in bits. (Part 2 of 2.)

Function displayBits (lines 18–36) uses the bitwise AND operator to combine variable value with variable displayMask (line 27). Often, the bitwise AND operator is used with an operand called a **mask**—an integer value with specific bits set to 1. Masks are used to *hide* some bits in a value while *selecting* other bits. In function displayBits, mask variable displayMask is assigned the value

```
    1 << 31         (10000000 00000000 00000000 00000000)
```

The left-shift operator shifts the value 1 from the low-order (rightmost) bit to the high-order (leftmost) bit in displayMask and fills in 0 bits from the right. Line 27

```
    putchar(value & displayMask ? '1' : '0');
```

determines whether a 1 or a 0 should be printed for the current leftmost bit of variable value. When value and displayMask are combined using &, all the bits except the high-order bit in variable value are "masked off" (hidden), because any bit "ANDed" with 0 yields 0. If the leftmost bit is 1, value & displayMask evaluates to a nonzero (true) value and 1 is printed—otherwise, 0 is printed. Variable value is then left shifted one bit by the expression value <<= 1 (this is equivalent to value = value << 1). These steps are repeated for each bit in unsigned variable value. Figure 10.8 summarizes the results of combining two bits with the bitwise AND operator.

Common Programming Error 10.10
Using the logical AND operator (&&) for the bitwise AND operator (&)—and vice versa—is an error.

Bit 1	Bit 2	Bit 1 & Bit 2
0	0	0
0	1	0
1	0	0
1	1	1

Fig. 10.8 | Results of combining two bits with the bitwise AND operator &.

10.9.2 Making Function displayBits More Generic and Portable

In line 21 of Fig. 10.7, we hard coded the integer 31 to indicate that the value 1 should be shifted to the leftmost bit in the variable displayMask. Similarly, in line 26, we hard coded the integer 32 to indicate that the loop should iterate 32 times—once for each bit in variable value. We assumed that unsigned ints are always stored in 32 bits (four bytes) of memory. Today's popular computers generally use 32-bit- or 64-bit-word hardware architectures. As a C programmer, you'll tend to work across many hardware architectures, and sometimes unsigned ints will be stored in smaller or larger numbers of bits.

Portability Tip 10.7
*Figure 10.7 can be made more generic and portable by replacing the integers 31 (line 21) and 32 (line 26) with expressions that calculate these integers, based on the size of an unsigned int for the platform on which the program executes. The symbolic constant CHAR_BIT (defined in <limits.h>) represents the number of bits in a byte (normally 8). Recall sizeof determines the number of bytes used to store an object or type. The expression sizeof(unsigned int) evaluates to 4 for 32-bit unsigned ints and 8 for 64-bit unsigned ints. You can replace 31 with CHAR_BIT * sizeof(unsigned int) - 1 and replace 32 with CHAR_BIT * sizeof(unsigned int). For 32-bit unsigned ints, these expressions evaluate to 31 and 32, respectively. For 64-bit unsigned ints, they evaluate to 63 and 64.*

10.9.3 Using the Bitwise AND, Inclusive OR, Exclusive OR and Complement Operators

Figure 10.9 demonstrates the use of the bitwise AND operator, the bitwise inclusive OR operator, the bitwise exclusive OR operator and the bitwise complement operator. The program uses function displayBits (lines 46–64) to print the unsigned int values. The output is shown in Fig. 10.10.

```c
1   // Fig. 10.9: fig10_09.c
2   // Using the bitwise AND, bitwise inclusive OR, bitwise
3   // exclusive OR and bitwise complement operators
4   #include <stdio.h>
5
6   void displayBits(unsigned int value); // prototype
7
8   int main(void)
9   {
10      // demonstrate bitwise AND (&)
11      unsigned int number1 = 65535;
12      unsigned int mask = 1;
13      puts("The result of combining the following");
14      displayBits(number1);
15      displayBits(mask);
16      puts("using the bitwise AND operator & is");
17      displayBits(number1 & mask);
18
19      // demonstrate bitwise inclusive OR (|)
20      number1 = 15;
21      unsigned int setBits = 241;
22      puts("\nThe result of combining the following");
23      displayBits(number1);
24      displayBits(setBits);
25      puts("using the bitwise inclusive OR operator | is");
26      displayBits(number1 | setBits);
27
28      // demonstrate bitwise exclusive OR (^)
29      number1 = 139;
30      unsigned int number2 = 199;
31      puts("\nThe result of combining the following");
32      displayBits(number1);
33      displayBits(number2);
34      puts("using the bitwise exclusive OR operator ^ is");
35      displayBits(number1 ^ number2);
36
37      // demonstrate bitwise complement (~)
38      number1 = 21845;
39      puts("\nThe one's complement of");
40      displayBits(number1);
41      puts("is");
42      displayBits(~number1);
43   }
```

Fig. 10.9 | Using the bitwise AND, bitwise inclusive OR, bitwise exclusive OR and bitwise complement operators. (Part 1 of 2.)

```
44
45   // display bits of an unsigned int value
46   void displayBits(unsigned int value)
47   {
48      // declare displayMask and left shift 31 bits
49      unsigned int displayMask = 1 << 31;
50
51      printf("%10u = ", value);
52
53      // loop through bits
54      for (unsigned int c = 1; c <= 32; ++c) {
55         putchar(value & displayMask ? '1' : '0');
56         value <<= 1; // shift value left by 1
57
58         if (c % 8 == 0) { // output a space after 8 bits
59            putchar(' ');
60         }
61      }
62
63      putchar('\n');
64   }
```

Fig. 10.9 | Using the bitwise AND, bitwise inclusive OR, bitwise exclusive OR and bitwise complement operators. (Part 2 of 2.)

```
The result of combining the following
     65535 = 00000000 00000000 11111111 11111111
         1 = 00000000 00000000 00000000 00000001
using the bitwise AND operator & is
         1 = 00000000 00000000 00000000 00000001

The result of combining the following
        15 = 00000000 00000000 00000000 00001111
       241 = 00000000 00000000 00000000 11110001
using the bitwise inclusive OR operator | is
       255 = 00000000 00000000 00000000 11111111

The result of combining the following
       139 = 00000000 00000000 00000000 10001011
       199 = 00000000 00000000 00000000 11000111
using the bitwise exclusive OR operator ^ is
        76 = 00000000 00000000 00000000 01001100

The one's complement of
     21845 = 00000000 00000000 01010101 01010101
is
4294945450 = 11111111 11111111 10101010 10101010
```

Fig. 10.10 | Output for the program of Fig. 10.9.

Bitwise AND Operator (&)

In Fig. 10.9, integer variable `number1` is assigned value 65535 (00000000 00000000 11111111 11111111) in line 11 and variable `mask` is assigned the value 1 (00000000

00000000 00000000 00000001) in line 12. When number1 and mask are combined using the *bitwise AND operator (&)* in the expression number1 & mask (line 17), the result is 00000000 00000000 00000000 00000001. All the bits except the low-order bit in variable number1 are "masked off" (hidden) by "ANDing" with variable mask.

Bitwise Inclusive OR Operator (|)

The *bitwise inclusive OR operator* is used to set specific bits to 1 in an operand. In Fig. 10.9, variable number1 is assigned 15 (00000000 00000000 00000000 00001111) in line 20, and variable setBits is assigned 241 (00000000 00000000 00000000 11110001) in line 21. When number1 and setBits are combined using the *bitwise inclusive OR operator* in the expression number1 | setBits (line 26), the result is 255 (00000000 00000000 00000000 11111111). Figure 10.11 summarizes the results of combining two bits with the *bitwise inclusive OR operator*.

Bit 1	Bit 2	Bit 1 | Bit 2
0	0	0
0	1	1
1	0	1
1	1	1

Fig. 10.11 | Results of combining two bits with the bitwise inclusive OR operator |.

Bitwise Exclusive OR Operator (^)

The *bitwise exclusive OR operator (^)* sets each bit in the result to 1 if *exactly* one of the corresponding bits in its two operands is 1. In Fig. 10.9, variables number1 and number2 are assigned the values 139 (00000000 00000000 00000000 10001011) and 199 (00000000 00000000 00000000 11000111) in lines 29–30. When these variables are combined with the *bitwise exclusive OR operator* in the expression number1 ^ number2 (line 35), the result is 00000000 00000000 00000000 01001100. Figure 10.12 summarizes the results of combining two bits with the *bitwise exclusive OR operator*.

Bit 1	Bit 2	Bit 1 ^ Bit 2
0	0	0
0	1	1
1	0	1
1	1	0

Fig. 10.12 | Results of combining two bits with the bitwise exclusive OR operator ^.

Bitwise Complement Operator (~)

The *bitwise complement operator (~)* sets all 1 bits in its operand to 0 in the result and sets all 0 bits to 1 in the result—otherwise referred to as "taking the **one's complement** of the value." In Fig. 10.9, variable number1 is assigned the value 21845 (00000000 00000000 01010101 01010101) in line 38. When the expression ~number1 (line 42) is evaluated, the result is 11111111 11111111 10101010 10101010.

10.9.4 Using the Bitwise Left- and Right-Shift Operators

The program of Fig. 10.13 demonstrates the *left-shift operator (<<)* and the *right-shift operator (>>)*. Function displayBits is used to print the unsigned int values.

```c
1   // Fig. 10.13: fig10_13.c
2   // Using the bitwise shift operators
3   #include <stdio.h>
4
5   void displayBits(unsigned int value); // prototype
6
7   int main(void)
8   {
9      unsigned int number1 = 960; // initialize number1
10
11     // demonstrate bitwise left shift
12     puts("\nThe result of left shifting"),
13     displayBits(number1);
14     puts("8 bit positions using the left shift operator << is");
15     displayBits(number1 << 8);
16
17     // demonstrate bitwise right shift
18     puts("\nThe result of right shifting");
19     displayBits(number1);
20     puts("8 bit positions using the right shift operator >> is");
21     displayBits(number1 >> 8);
22  }
23
24  // display bits of an unsigned int value
25  void displayBits(unsigned int value)
26  {
27     // declare displayMask and left shift 31 bits
28     unsigned int displayMask = 1 << 31;
29
30     printf("%7u = ", value);
31
32     // loop through bits
33     for (unsigned int c = 1; c <= 32; ++c) {
34        putchar(value & displayMask ? '1' : '0');
35        value <<= 1; // shift value left by 1
36
37        if (c % 8 == 0) { // output a space after 8 bits
38           putchar(' ');
39        }
40     }
41
42     putchar('\n');
43  }
```

Fig. 10.13 | Using the bitwise shift operators. (Part 1 of 2.)

```
The result of left shifting
    960 = 00000000 00000000 00000011 11000000
8 bit positions using the left shift operator << is
 245760 = 00000000 00000011 11000000 00000000

The result of right shifting
    960 = 00000000 00000000 00000011 11000000
8 bit positions using the right shift operator >> is
      3 = 00000000 00000000 00000000 00000011
```

Fig. 10.13 | Using the bitwise shift operators. (Part 2 of 2.)

Left-Shift Operator (<<)

The *left-shift operator (<<)* shifts the bits of its left operand to the left by the number of bits specified in its right operand. Bits vacated to the right are replaced with 0s; bits shifted off the left are lost. In Fig. 10.13, variable number1 is assigned the value 960 (00000000 00000000 00000011 11000000) in line 9. The result of left shifting variable number1 8 bits in the expression number1 << 8 (line 15) is 245760 (00000000 00000011 11000000 00000000).

Right-Shift Operator (>>)

The *right-shift operator (>>)* shifts the bits of its left operand to the right by the number of bits specified in its right operand. Performing a right shift on an unsigned int causes the vacated bits at the left to be replaced by 0s; bits shifted off the right are lost. In Fig. 10.13, the result of right shifting number1 in the expression number1 >> 8 (line 21) is 3 (00000000 00000000 00000000 00000011).

Common Programming Error 10.11

The result of right or left shifting a value is undefined if the right operand is negative or if the right operand is larger than the number of bits in which the left operand is stored.

Portability Tip 10.8

The result of right shifting a negative number is implementation defined.

10.9.5 Bitwise Assignment Operators

Each binary bitwise operator has a corresponding assignment operator. These **bitwise assignment operators** are shown in Fig. 10.14 and are used in a manner similar to the arithmetic assignment operators introduced in Chapter 3.

Bitwise assignment operators	
&=	Bitwise AND assignment operator.
|=	Bitwise inclusive OR assignment operator.
^=	Bitwise exclusive OR assignment operator.
<<=	Left-shift assignment operator.
>>=	Right-shift assignment operator.

Fig. 10.14 | The bitwise assignment operators.

Figure 10.15 shows the precedence and associativity of the various operators introduced to this point in the text. They're shown top to bottom in decreasing order of precedence.

Operator							Associativity	Type
() [] . -> ++ *(postfix)* -- *(postfix)*							left to right	highest
+ - ++ -- ! & * ~ sizeof *(type)*							right to left	unary
* / %							left to right	multiplicative
+ -							left to right	additive
<< >>							left to right	shifting
< <= > >=							left to right	relational
== !=							left to right	equality
&							left to right	bitwise AND
^							left to right	bitwise XOR
								left to right	bitwise OR
&&							left to right	logical AND
||							left to right	logical OR
?:							right to left	conditional
= += -= *= /= &= |= ^= <<= >>= %=							right to left	assignment
,							left to right	comma

Fig. 10.15 | Operator precedence and associativity.

10.10 Bit Fields

C enables you to specify the number of bits in which an unsigned or signed integral member of a structure or union is stored. This is referred to as a **bit field**. Bit fields enable better memory utilization by storing data in the minimum number of bits required. Bit field members *must* be declared as int or unsigned int.

10.10.1 Defining Bit Fields

Consider the following structure definition:

```
struct bitCard {
    unsigned int face : 4;
    unsigned int suit : 2;
    unsigned int color : 1;
};
```

which contains three unsigned int bit fields—face, suit and color—used to represent a card from a deck of 52 cards. A bit field is declared by following an unsigned or signed integral **member name** with a colon (:) and an integer constant representing the **width** of the field (i.e., the number of bits in which the member is stored). The constant representing the width must be an integer between 0 (discussed in Section 10.10.3) and the total number of bits used to store an int on your system, inclusive. Our examples were tested on a computer with 4-byte (32-bit) integers.

The preceding structure definition indicates that member face is stored in 4 bits, member suit is stored in 2 bits and member color is stored in 1 bit. The number of bits is based on the desired range of values for each structure member. Member face stores values from 0 (Ace) through 12 (King)—4 bits can store values in the range 0–15. Member suit stores values from 0 through 3 (0 = Hearts, 1 = Diamonds, 2 = Clubs, 3 = Spades)— 2 bits can store values in the range 0–3. Finally, member color stores either 0 (Red) or 1 (Black)—1 bit can store either 0 or 1.

10.10.2 Using Bit Fields to Represent a Card's Face, Suit and Color

Figure 10.16 (output shown in Fig. 10.17) creates array deck containing 52 struct bit-Card structures in line 20. Function fillDeck (lines 31–39) inserts the 52 cards in the deck array and function deal (lines 43–55) prints the 52 cards. Notice that bit field members of structures are accessed exactly as any other structure member. Member color is included as a means of indicating the card color on a system that allows color displays.

```
1   // Fig. 10.16: fig10_16.c
2   // Representing cards with bit fields in a struct
3   #include <stdio.h>
4   #define CARDS 52
5
6   // bitCard structure definition with bit fields
7   struct bitCard {
8      unsigned int face : 4; // 4 bits; 0-15
9      unsigned int suit : 2; // 2 bits; 0-3
10     unsigned int color : 1; // 1 bit; 0-1
11  };
12
13  typedef struct bitCard Card; // new type name for struct bitCard
14
15  void fillDeck(Card * const wDeck); // prototype
16  void deal(const Card * const wDeck); // prototype
17
18  int main(void)
19  {
20     Card deck[CARDS]; // create array of Cards
21
22     fillDeck(deck);
23
24     puts("Card values 0-12 correspond to Ace through King");
25     puts("Suit values 0-3 correspond Hearts, Diamonds, Clubs and Spades");
26     puts("Color values 0-1 correspond to red and black\n");
27     deal(deck);
28  }
29
30  // initialize Cards
31  void fillDeck(Card * const wDeck)
32  {
33     // loop through wDeck
34     for (size_t i = 0; i < CARDS; ++i) {
35        wDeck[i].face = i % (CARDS / 4);
```

Fig. 10.16 | Representing cards with bit fields in a struct. (Part 1 of 2.)

```
36            wDeck[i].suit = i / (CARDS / 4);
37            wDeck[i].color = i / (CARDS / 2);
38        }
39    }
40
41    // output cards in two-column format; cards 0-25 indexed with
42    // k1 (column 1); cards 26-51 indexed with k2 (column 2)
43    void deal(const Card * const wDeck)
44    {
45        printf("%-6s%-6s%-15s%-6s%-6s%s\n", "Card", "Suit", "Color",
46            "Card", "Suit", "Color");
47
48        // loop through wDeck
49        for (size_t k1 = 0, k2 = k1 + 26; k1 < CARDS / 2; ++k1, ++k2) {
50            printf("Card:%3d  Suit:%2d  Color:%2d    ",
51                wDeck[k1].face, wDeck[k1].suit, wDeck[k1].color);
52            printf("Card:%3d  Suit:%2d  Color:%2d\n",
53                wDeck[k2].face, wDeck[k2].suit, wDeck[k2].color);
54        }
55    }
```

Fig. 10.16 | Representing cards with bit fields in a struct. (Part 2 of 2.)

```
Card values 0-12 correspond to Ace through King
Suit values 0-3 correspond Hearts, Diamonds, Clubs and Spades
Color values 0-1 correspond to red and black

Card  Suit  Color          Card  Suit  Color
0     0     0              0     2     1
1     0     0              1     2     1
2     0     0              2     2     1
3     0     0              3     2     1
4     0     0              4     2     1
5     0     0              5     2     1
6     0     0              6     2     1
7     0     0              7     2     1
8     0     0              8     2     1
9     0     0              9     2     1
10    0     0              10    2     1
11    0     0              11    2     1
12    0     0              12    2     1
0     1     0              0     3     1
1     1     0              1     3     1
2     1     0              2     3     1
3     1     0              3     3     1
4     1     0              4     3     1
5     1     0              5     3     1
6     1     0              6     3     1
7     1     0              7     3     1
8     1     0              8     3     1
9     1     0              9     3     1
10    1     0              10    3     1
11    1     0              11    3     1
12    1     0              12    3     1
```

Fig. 10.17 | Output of the program in Fig. 10.16.

Performance Tip 10.2

Bit fields help reduce the amount of memory a program needs.

Portability Tip 10.9

Bit-field manipulations are machine dependent.

Common Programming Error 10.12

Attempting to access individual bits of a bit field as if they were elements of an array is a syntax error. Bit fields are not "arrays of bits."

Common Programming Error 10.13

Attempting to take the address of a bit field (the & operator may not be used with bit fields because they do not have addresses).

Performance Tip 10.3

Although bit fields save space, using them can cause the compiler to generate slower-executing machine-language code. This occurs because it takes extra machine-language operations to access only portions of an addressable storage unit. This is one of many examples of the kinds of space–time trade-offs that occur in computer science.

10.10.3 Unnamed Bit Fields

It's possible to specify an **unnamed bit field** to be used as **padding** in the structure. For example, the structure definition

```
struct example {
    unsigned int a : 13;
    unsigned int   : 19;
    unsigned int b : 4;
};
```

uses an unnamed 19-bit field as padding—nothing can be stored in those 19 bits. Member b (on our 4-byte-word computer) is stored in another storage unit.

An **unnamed bit field with a zero width** is used to align the next bit field on a new *storage-unit boundary*. For example, the structure definition

```
struct example {
    unsigned int a : 13;
    unsigned int   : 0;
    unsigned int : 4;
};
```

uses an unnamed 0-bit field to skip the remaining bits (as many as there are) of the storage unit in which a is stored and to align b on the next storage-unit boundary.

10.11 Enumeration Constants

An enumeration (discussed briefly in Section 5.11), introduced by the keyword enum, is a set of integer **enumeration constants** represented by identifiers. Values in an enum start with 0, unless specified otherwise, and are incremented by 1. For example, the enumeration

```
enum months {
    JAN, FEB, MAR, APR, MAY, JUN, JUL, AUG, SEP, OCT, NOV, DEC
};
```

creates a new type, enum months, in which the identifiers are set to the integers 0 to 11, respectively. To number the months 1 to 12, use:

```
enum months {
    JAN = 1, FEB, MAR, APR, MAY, JUN, JUL, AUG, SEP, OCT, NOV, DEC
};
```

Because the first value in the preceding enumeration is explicitly set to 1, the remaining values are incremented from 1, resulting in the values 1 through 12. The *identifiers* in any enumeration accessible in the same scope *must be unique*. The value of each enumeration constant of an enumeration can be set explicitly in the definition by assigning a value to the identifier. Multiple members of an enumeration *can* have the *same* constant value. In the program of Fig. 10.18, the enumeration variable month is used in a for statement to print the months of the year from the array monthName. We've made monthName[0] the empty string "". You could set monthName[0] to a value such as ***ERROR*** to indicate that a logic error occurred.

Common Programming Error 10.14

Assigning a value to an enumeration constant after it's been defined is a syntax error.

Good Programming Practice 10.5

Use only uppercase letters in enumeration constant names. This makes these constants stand out in a program and reminds you that enumeration constants are not variables.

```
 1  // Fig. 10.18: fig10_18.c
 2  // Using an enumeration
 3  #include <stdio.h>
 4
 5  // enumeration constants represent months of the year
 6  enum months {
 7      JAN = 1, FEB, MAR, APR, MAY, JUN, JUL, AUG, SEP, OCT, NOV, DEC
 8  };
 9
10  int main(void)
11  {
12      // initialize array of pointers
13      const char *monthName[] = { "", "January", "February", "March",
14          "April", "May", "June", "July", "August", "September", "October",
15          "November", "December" };
16
17      // loop through months
18      for (enum months month = JAN; month <= DEC; ++month) {
19          printf("%2d%11s\n", month, monthName[month]);
20      }
21  }
```

Fig. 10.18 | Using an enumeration. (Part 1 of 2.)

```
 1     January
 2    February
 3     March
 4     April
 5      May
 6     June
 7     July
 8    August
 9   September
10    October
11   November
12   December
```

Fig. 10.18 | Using an enumeration. (Part 2 of 2.)

10.12 Anonymous Structures and Unions

Earlier in this chapter we introduced structs and unions. C11 now supports anonymous structs and unions that can be nested in named structs and unions. The members in a nested anonymous struct or union are considered to be members of the enclosing struct or union and can be accessed directly through an object of the enclosing type. For example, consider the following struct declaration:

```
struct MyStruct {
    int member1;
    int member2;

    struct {
        int nestedMember1;
        int nestedMember2;
    }; // end nested struct
}; // end outer struct
```

For a variable myStruct of type struct MyStruct, you can access the members as:

```
myStruct.member1;
myStruct.member2;
myStruct.nestedMember1;
myStruct.nestedMember2;
```

10.13 Secure C Programming

Various CERT guidelines and rules apply to this chapter's topics. For more information on each, visit www.securecoding.cert.org.

CERT Guidelines for structs

As we discussed in Section 10.2.4, the boundary alignment requirements for struct members may result in extra bytes containing undefined data for each struct variable you create. Each of the following guidelines is related to this issue:

- EXP03-C: Because of *boundary alignment* requirements, the size of a struct variable is *not* necessarily the sum of its members' sizes. Always use sizeof to determine the number of bytes in a struct variable. As you'll see, we use this technique to manipulate fixed-length records that are written to and read from files in Chapter 11, and to create so-called dynamic data structures in Chapter 12.

- EXP04-C: As we discussed in Section 10.2.4, struct variables cannot be compared for equality or inequality, because they might contain bytes of undefined data. Therefore, you must compare their individual members.

- DCL39-C: In a struct variable, the undefined extra bytes could contain secure data—left over from prior use of those memory locations—that should *not* be accessible. This CERT guideline discusses compiler-specific mechanisms for *packing the data* to eliminate these extra bytes.

CERT Guideline for typedef

- DCL05-C: Complex type declarations, such as those for function pointers, can be difficult to read. You should use typedef to create self-documenting type names that make your programs more readable.

CERT Guidelines for Bit Manipulation

- INT02-C: As a result of the integer promotion rules (discussed in Section 5.6), performing bitwise operations on integer types smaller than int can lead to unexpected results. Explicit casts are required to ensure correct results.

- INT13-C: Some bitwise operations on *signed* integer types are *implementation defined*—this means that the operations may have different results across C compilers. For this reason, *unsigned* integer types should be used with the bitwise operators.

- EXP46-C: The logical operators && and || are frequently confused with the bitwise operators & and |, respectively. Using & and | in the condition of a conditional expression (?:) can lead to unexpected behavior, because the & and | operators do not use short-circuit evaluation.

CERT Guideline for enum

- INT09-C: Allowing multiple enumeration constants to have the *same* value can result in difficult-to-find logic errors. In most cases, an enum's enumeration constants should each have *unique* values to help prevent such logic errors.

Summary

Section 10.1 Introduction
- **Structures** (p. 405) are collections of related variables under one name. They may contain variables of many different data types.
- Structures are commonly used to define records to be stored in files.
- Pointers and structures facilitate the formation of more complex data structures such as linked lists, queues, stacks and trees.

Section 10.2 Structure Definitions
- Keyword **struct** introduces a structure definition (p. 406).

- The identifier following keyword struct is the **structure tag** (p. 406), which names the structure definition. The structure tag is used with the keyword struct to declare variables of the structure type (p. 406).
- Variables declared within the braces of the structure definition are the structure's **members**.
- Members of the same structure type must have unique names.
- Each structure definition must end with a semicolon.
- Structure members can have primitive or aggregates data types.
- A structure cannot contain an instance of itself but may include a pointer to its type.
- A structure containing a member that's a pointer to the same structure type is referred to as a **self-referential structure**. Self-referential structures (p. 406) are used to build linked data structures.
- Structure definitions create new data types that are used to define variables.
- Variables of a given structure type can be declared by placing a comma-separated list of variable names between the closing brace of the structure definition and its ending semicolon.
- The structure tag name is optional. If a structure definition does not contain a structure tag name, variables of the structure type may be declared only in the structure definition.
- The only valid operations that may be performed on structures are assigning structure variables to variables of the same type, taking the address (&) of a structure variable, accessing the members of a structure variable and using the sizeof operator to determine the size of a structure variable.

Section 10.3 Initializing Structures
- Structures can be initialized using **initializer lists**.
- If there are fewer initializers in the list than members in the structure, the remaining members are automatically initialized to 0 (or NULL if the member is a pointer).
- Members of structure variables defined outside a function definition are initialized to 0 or NULL if they're not explicitly initialized in the external definition.
- Structure variables may be initialized in assignment statements by assigning a structure variable of the same type, or by assigning values to the individual members of the structure.

Section 10.4 Accessing Structure Members with . and ->
- The **structure member operator** (.) and the **structure pointer operator** (->) are used to access structure members (p. 408).
- The structure member operator accesses a structure member via the structure variable name.
- The structure pointer operator accesses a structure member via a pointer to the structure (p. 409).

Section 10.5 Using Structures with Functions
- Structures may be passed to functions by passing individual structure members, by passing an entire structure or by passing a pointer to a structure.
- Stucture variables are **passed by value by default**.
- To pass a structure by reference, pass its address. Arrays of structures—like all other arrays—are automatically passed by reference.
- To **pass an array by value**, create a structure with the array as a member. Structures are passed by value, so the array is passed by value.

Section 10.6 typedef
- The keyword **typedef** (p. 411) provides a mechanism for creating synonyms for previously defined types.

- Names for structure types are often defined with typedef to create shorter type names.

- Often, typedef is used to create synonyms for the basic data types. For example, a program requiring 4-byte integers may use type int on one system and type long on another. Programs designed for portability often use typedef to create an alias for 4-byte integers such as Integer. The alias Integer can be changed once in the program to make the program work on both systems.

Section 10.8 Unions
- A **union** (p. 414) is declared with keyword **union** in the same format as a structure. Its members share the same storage space.

- The members of a union can be of any data type. The number of bytes used to store a union must be at least enough to hold the largest member.

- Only one member of a union can be referenced at a time. It's your responsibility to ensure that the data in a union is referenced with the proper data type.

- The operations that can be performed on a union are assigning a union to another of the same type, taking the address (&) of a union variable, and accessing union members using the structure member operator and the structure pointer operator.

- A union may be initialized in a declaration with a value of the same type as the first union member.

Section 10.9 Bitwise Operators
- Computers represent all data internally as sequences of bits with the values 0 or 1.

- On most systems, a sequence of **8 bits form a byte**—the standard storage unit for a variable of type char. Other data types are stored in larger numbers of bytes.

- The **bitwise operators** are used to manipulate the bits of integral operands (char, short, int and long; both signed and unsigned). Unsigned integers are normally used.

- The bitwise operators (p. 417) are **bitwise AND (&)**, **bitwise inclusive OR (|)**, **bitwise exclusive OR (^)**, **left shift (<<)**, **right shift (>>)** and **complement (~)**.

- The bitwise AND, bitwise inclusive OR and bitwise exclusive OR operators compare their two operands bit by bit. The **bitwise AND operator** (p. 417) sets each bit in the result to 1 if the corresponding bit in both operands is 1. The **bitwise inclusive OR operator** (p. 417) sets each bit in the result to 1 if the corresponding bit in either (or both) operand(s) is 1. The **bitwise exclusive OR operator** (p. 417) sets each bit in the result to 1 if the corresponding bits both operands are different.

- The **left-shift operator** (p. 417) shifts the bits of its left operand to the left by the number of bits specified in its right operand. Bits vacated to the right are replaced with 0s; bits shifted off the left are lost.

- The **right-shift operator** (p. 417) shifts the bits in its left operand to the right by the number of bits specified in its right operand. Performing a right shift on an unsigned int causes the vacated bits at the left to be replaced by 0s; bits shifted off the right are lost.

- The **bitwise complement operator** (p. 417) sets all 0 bits in its operand to 1 and all 1 bits to 0 in the result.

- Often, the bitwise AND operator is used with an operand called a **mask** (p. 418)—an integer value with specific bits set to 1. Masks are used to hide some bits in a value while selecting other bits.

- The symbolic constant CHAR_BIT (p. 419; defined in <limits.h>) represents the number of bits in a byte (normally 8). It can be used to make a bit-manipulation program more generic and portable.

- Each binary bitwise operator has a corresponding **bitwise assignment operator** (p. 424).

Section 10.10 Bit Fields

- C enables you to specify the number of bits in which an unsigned or signed integral member of a structure or union is stored. This is referred to as a **bit field** (p. 425). Bit fields enable better memory utilization by storing data in the minimum number of bits required.

- A bit field is declared by following an unsigned int or int member name (p. 425) with a colon (:) and an integer constant representing the width of the field (p. 425). The constant must be an integer between 0 and the total number of bits used to store an int on your system, inclusive.

- Bit-field members of structures are accessed exactly as any other structure member.

- It's possible to specify an **unnamed bit field** (p. 428) to be used as **padding** in the structure (p. 428).

- An **unnamed bit field with a zero width** (p. 428) aligns the next bit field on a new storage-unit boundary.

Section 10.11 Enumeration Constants

- An **enum** defines a set of integer constants represented by identifiers (p. 428). Values in an enum start with 0, unless specified otherwise, and are incremented by 1.

- The identifiers in an enum must be unique.

- The value of an enum constant can be set explicitly via assignment in the enum definition.

Self-Review Exercises

10.1 Fill in the blanks in each of the following:
  a) A(n) _____ is a collection of related variables under one name.
  b) A(n) _____ is a collection of variables under one name in which the variables share the same storage.
  c) The bits in the result of an expression using the _____ operator are set to 1 if the corresponding bits in each operand are set to 1. Otherwise, the bits are set to zero.
  d) The variables declared in a structure definition are called its _____ .
  e) In an expression using the _____ operator, bits are set to 1 if at least one of the corresponding bits in either operand is set to 1. Otherwise, the bits are set to zero.
  f) Keyword _____ introduces a structure declaration.
  g) Keyword _____ is used to create a synonym for a previously defined data type.
  h) In an expression using the _____ operator, bits are set to 1 if exactly one of the corresponding bits in either operand is set to 1. Otherwise, the bits are set to zero.
  i) The bitwise AND operator (&) is often used to _____ bits—that is, to select certain bits while zeroing others.
  j) Keyword _____ is used to introduce a union definition.
  k) The name of the structure is referred to as the structure _____.
  l) A structure member is accessed with either the _____ or the _____ operator.
  m) The _____ and _____ operators are used to shift the bits of a value to the left or to the right, respectively.
  n) A(n) _____ is a set of integers represented by identifiers.

10.2 State whether each of the following is *true* or *false*. If *false*, explain why.
  a) Structures may contain variables of only one data type.
  b) Two unions can be compared (using ==) to determine whether they're equal.
  c) The tag name of a structure is optional.
  d) Members of different structures must have unique names.
  e) Keyword typedef is used to define new data types.

f) Structures are always passed to functions by reference.

g) Structures may not be compared by using operators == and !=.

10.3 Write code to accomplish each of the following:

a) Define a structure called part containing unsigned int variable partNumber and char array partName with values that may be as long as 25 characters (including the terminating null character).

b) Define Part to be a synonym for the type struct part.

c) Use Part to declare variable a to be of type struct part, array b[10] to be of type struct part and variable ptr to be of type pointer to struct part.

d) Read a part number and a part name from the keyboard into the individual members of variable a.

e) Assign the member values of variable a to element 3 of array b.

f) Assign the address of array b to the pointer variable ptr.

g) Print the member values of element 3 of array b using the variable ptr and the structure pointer operator to refer to the members.

10.4 Find the error in each of the following:

a) Assume that struct card has been defined containing two pointers to type char, namely face and suit. Also, the variable c has been defined to be of type struct card and the variable cPtr has been defined to be of type pointer to struct card. Variable cPtr has been assigned the address of c.

```
printf("%s\n", *cPtr->face);
```

b) Assume that struct card has been defined containing two pointers to type char, namely face and suit. Also, the array hearts[13] has been defined to be of type struct card. The following statement should print the member face of array element 10.

```
printf("%s\n", hearts.face);
```

c)
```
union values {
    char w;
    float x;
    double y;
};
union values v = { 1.27 };
```

d)
```
struct person {
    char lastName[15];
    char firstName[15];
    unsigned int age;
}
```

e) Assume struct person has been defined as in part (d) but with the appropriate correction.

```
person d;
```

f) Assume variable p has been declared as type struct person and variable c has been declared as type struct card.

```
p = c;
```

Answers to Self-Review Exercises

10.1 a) structure. b) union. c) bitwise AND (&). d) members. e) bitwise inclusive OR (|). f) struct. g) typedef. h) bitwise exclusive OR (^). i) mask. j) union. k) tag name. l) structure member, structure pointer. m) left-shift operator (<<), right-shift operator (>>). n) enumeration.

10.2   a)   False. A structure can contain variables of many data types.
        b)   False. Unions cannot be compared, because there might be bytes of undefined data with different values in union variables that are otherwise identical.
        c)   True.
        d)   False. The members of separate structures can have the same names, but the members of the same structure must have unique names.
        e)   False. Keyword `typedef` is used to define new names (synonyms) for previously defined data types.
        f)   False. Structures are always passed to functions by value.
        g)   True, because of alignment problems.

10.3   a)
```
struct part {
    unsigned int partNumber;
    char partName[25];
};
```
        b)   `typedef struct part Part;`
        c)   `Part a, b[10], *ptr;`
        d)   `scanf("%d%24s", &a.partNumber, a.partName);`
        e)   `b[3] = a;`
        f)   `ptr = b;`
        g)   `printf("%d %s\n", (ptr + 3)->partNumber, (ptr + 3)->partName);`

10.4   a)   The parentheses that should enclose `*cPtr` have been omitted, causing the order of evaluation of the expression to be incorrect. The expression should be
```
    cPtr->face
```
          or
```
    (*cPtr).face
```
        b)   The array index has been omitted. The expression should be
```
    hearts[10].face
```
        c)   A union can be initialized only with a value that has the same type as the union's first member.
        d)   A semicolon is required to end a structure definition.
        e)   Keyword `struct` was omitted from the variable declaration. The declaration should be
```
    struct person d;
```
        f)   Variables of different structure types cannot be assigned to one another.

Exercises

10.5   Provide the definition for each of the following structures and unions:
        a)   Structure `inventory` containing character array `partName[30]`, integer `partNumber`, floating-point `price`, integer `stock` and integer `reorder`.
        b)   Union `data` containing `char c`, `short s`, `long b`, `float f` and `double d`.
        c)   A structure called `address` that contains character arrays `streetAddress[25]`, `city[20]`, `state[3]` and `zipCode[6]`.
        d)   Structure `student` that contains arrays `firstName[15]` and `lastName[15]` and variable `homeAddress` of type `struct address` from part (c).
        e)   Structure `test` containing 16 bit fields with widths of 1 bit. The names of the bit fields are the letters a to p.

10.6   Given the following structure and variable definitions,
```
struct customer {
    char lastName[15];
```

```
        char firstName[15];
        unsigned int customerNumber;

        struct {
            char phoneNumber[11];
            char address[50];
            char city[15];
            char state[3];
            char zipCode[6];
        } personal;

    } customerRecord, *customerPtr;

    customerPtr = &customerRecord;
```

write an expression that can be used to access the structure members in each of the following parts:

a) Member lastName of structure customerRecord.
b) Member lastName of the structure pointed to by customerPtr.
c) Member firstName of structure customerRecord.
d) Member firstName of the structure pointed to by customerPtr.
e) Member customerNumber of structure customerRecord.
f) Member customerNumber of the structure pointed to by customerPtr.
g) Member phoneNumber of member personal of structure customerRecord.
h) Member phoneNumber of member personal of the structure pointed to by customerPtr.
i) Member address of member personal of structure customerRecord.
j) Member address of member personal of the structure pointed to by customerPtr.
k) Member city of member personal of structure customerRecord.
l) Member city of member personal of the structure pointed to by customerPtr.
m) Member state of member personal of structure customerRecord.
n) Member state of member personal of the structure pointed to by customerPtr.
o) Member zipCode of member personal of structure customerRecord.
p) Member zipCode of member personal of the structure pointed to by customerPtr.

10.7 *(Card Shuffling and Dealing Modification)* Modify the program of Fig. 10.16 to shuffle the cards using a high-performance shuffle (as shown in Fig. 10.3). Print the resulting deck in a two-column format that uses the face and suit names. Precede each card with its color.

10.8 *(Using Unions)* Create union integer with members char c, short s, int i and long b. Write a program that inputs values of type char, short, int and long and stores the values in union variables of type union integer. Each union variable should be printed as a char, a short, an int and a long. Do the values always print correctly?

10.9 *(Using Unions)* Create union floatingPoint with members float f, double d and long double x. Write a program that inputs values of type float, double and long double and stores the values in union variables of type union floatingPoint. Each union variable should be printed as a float, a double and a long double. Do the values always print correctly?

10.10 *(Right Shifting Integers)* Write a program that right shifts an integer variable 4 bits. The program should print the integer in bits before and after the shift operation. Does your system place 0s or 1s in the vacated bits?

10.11 *(Left Shifting Integers)* Left shifting an unsigned int by 1 bit is equivalent to multiplying the value by 2. Write function power2 that takes two integer arguments number and pow and calculates

number * 2^{pow}

Use the shift operator to calculate the result. Print the values as integers and as bits.

10.12 *(Packing Characters into an Integer)* The left-shift operator can be used to pack four character values into a four-byte unsigned int variable. Write a program that inputs four characters from the keyboard and passes them to function packCharacters. To pack four characters into an unsigned int variable, assign the first character to the unsigned int variable, shift the unsigned int variable left by 8 bit positions and combine the unsigned variable with the second character using the bitwise inclusive OR operator. Repeat this process for the third and fourth characters. The program should output the characters in their bit format before and after they're packed into the unsigned int to prove that the characters are in fact packed correctly in the unsigned int variable.

10.13 *(Unpacking Characters from an Integer)* Using the right-shift operator, the bitwise AND operator and a mask, write function unpackCharacters that takes the unsigned int from Exercise 10.12 and unpacks it into four characters. To unpack characters from a four-byte unsigned int, combine the unsigned int with the mask 4278190080 (11111111 00000000 00000000 00000000) and right shift the result 8 bits. Assign the resulting value to a char variable. Then combine the unsigned int with the mask 16711680 (00000000 11111111 00000000 00000000). Assign the result to another char variable. Continue this process with the masks 65280 and 255. The program should print the unsigned int in bits before it's unpacked, then print the characters in bits to confirm that they were unpacked correctly.

10.14 *(Reversing the Order of an Integer's Bits)* Write a program that reverses the order of the bits in an unsigned int value. The program should input the value from the user and call function reverseBits to print the bits in reverse order. Print the value in bits both before and after the bits are reversed to confirm that the bits are reversed properly.

10.15 *(Portable displayBits Function)* Modify function displayBits of Fig. 10.7 so it's portable between systems using 2-byte integers and systems using 4-byte integers. [*Hint:* Use the sizeof operator to determine the size of an integer on a particular machine.]

10.16 *(What's the Value of X?)* The following program uses function multiple to determine if the integer entered from the keyboard is a multiple of some integer X. Examine the function multiple, then determine X's value.

```c
 1   // ex10_16.c
 2   // This program determines whether a value is a multiple of X.
 3   #include <stdio.h>
 4
 5   int multiple(int num); // prototype
 6
 7   int main(void)
 8   {
 9      int y; // y will hold an integer entered by the user
10
11      puts("Enter an integer between 1 and 32000: ");
12      scanf("%d", &y);
13
14      // if y is a multiple of X
15      if (multiple(y)) {
16         printf("%d is a multiple of X\n", y);
17      }
18      else {
19         printf("%d is not a multiple of X\n", y);
20      }
21   }
22
23   // determine whether num is a multiple of X
24   int multiple(int num)
25   {
```

```
26      int mask = 1; // initialize mask
27      int mult = 1; // initialize mult
28
29      for (int i = 1; i <= 10; ++i, mask <<= 1) {
30
31         if ((num & mask) != 0) {
32            mult = 0;
33            break;
34         }
35      }
36
37      return mult;
38   }
```

10.17 What does the following program do?

```
1    // ex10_17.c
2    #include <stdio.h>
3
4    int mystery(unsigned int bits); // prototype
5
6    int main(void)
7    {
8       unsigned int x; // x will hold an integer entered by the user
9
10      puts("Enter an integer: ");
11      scanf("%u", &x);
12
13      printf("The result is %d\n", mystery(x));
14   }
15
16   // What does this function do?
17   int mystery(unsigned int bits)
18   {
19      unsigned int mask = 1 << 31; // initialize mask
20      unsigned int total = 0; // initialize total
21
22      for (unsigned int i = 1; i <= 32; ++i, bits <<= 1) {
23
24         if ((bits & mask) == mask) {
25            ++total;
26         }
27      }
28
29      return !(total % 2) ? 1 : 0;
30   }
```

10.18 *(Fisher-Yates Shuffling Algorithm)* Research the Fisher-Yates shuffling algorithm online, then use it to reimplement the shuffle method in Fig. 10.3.

Making a Difference

10.19 *(Computerization of Health Records)* A health care issue that has been in the news lately is the computerization of health records. This possibility is being approached cautiously because of sensitive privacy and security concerns, among others. Computerizing health records could make it easier for patients to share their health profiles and histories among their various health care professionals. This could improve the quality of health care, help avoid drug conflicts and erroneous drug prescriptions, reduce costs and in emergencies could save lives. In this exercise, you'll design a "starter" HealthProfile structure for a person. The structure's members should include the person's first name, last name, gender, date of birth (consisting of separate attributes for the month, day and year of birth), height (in inches) and weight (in pounds). Your program should have a function that receives this data and uses it to set the members of a HealthProfile variable. The program also should include functions that calculate and return the user's age in years, maximum heart rate and target-heart-rate range (see Exercise 3.47), and body mass index (BMI; see Exercise 2.32). The program should prompt for the person's information, create a HealthProfile variable for that person and display the information from that variable—including the person's first name, last name, gender, date of birth, height and weight—then calculate and display the person's age in years, BMI, maximum heart rate and target-heart-rate range. It should also display the "BMI values" chart from Exercise 2.32.

11

C File Processing

Objectives

In this chapter, you'll:

- Understand the concepts of files and streams.

- Create and read data using sequential-access file processing.

- Create, read and update data using random-access file processing.

- Develop a substantial transaction-processing program.

- Study Secure C programming in the context of file processing.

11.1 Introduction

You studied the *data hierarchy* in Chapter 1. Storage of data in variables and arrays is *temporary*—such data is *lost* when a program terminates. **Files** are used for long-term retention of data. Computers store files on secondary storage devices, such as hard drives, solid-state drives, flash drives and DVDs. In this chapter, we explain how data files are created, updated and processed by C programs. We consider both sequential-access and random-access file processing.

11.2 Files and Streams

C views each file simply as a *sequential stream of bytes* (Fig. 11.1). Each file ends either with an **end-of-file marker** or at a specific byte number recorded in a system-maintained, administrative data structure—this is determined by each platform and is hidden from you.

Fig. 11.1 | C's view of a file of *n* bytes.

Standard Streams in Every Program

When a file is *opened*, a **stream** is associated with it. Three streams are automatically opened when program execution begins:

- the **standard input** (which receives input from the keyboard),
- the **standard output** (which displays output on the screen) and
- the **standard error** (which displays error messages on the screen).

Communication Channels

Streams provide communication channels between files and programs. For example, the standard input stream enables a program to read data from the keyboard, and the standard output stream enables a program to print data on the screen.

FILE Structure

Opening a file returns a pointer to a FILE structure (defined in <stdio.h>) that contains information used to process the file. In some operating systems, this structure includes a **file descriptor**, i.e., an integer index into an operating-system array called the **open file table**. Each array element contains a **file control block (FCB)**—information that the operating system uses to administer a particular file. The standard input, standard output and standard error are manipulated using **stdin**, **stdout** and **stderr**.

File-Processing Function fgetc

The standard library provides many functions for reading data from files and for writing data to files. Function **fgetc**, like getchar, reads one character from a file. Function fgetc receives as an argument a **FILE** pointer for the file from which a character will be read. The call fgetc(stdin) reads one character from stdin—the standard input. This call is equivalent to the call getchar().

File-Processing Function fputc

Function **fputc**, like putchar, writes one character to a file. Function fputc receives as arguments a character to be written and a pointer for the file to which the character will be written. The function call fputc('a', stdout) writes the character 'a' to stdout—the standard output. This call is equivalent to putchar('a').

Other File-Processing Functions

Several other functions used to read data from standard input and write data to standard output have similarly named file-processing functions. The **fgets** and **fputs** functions, for example, can be used to *read a line from a file* and *write a line to a file*, respectively. In the next several sections, we introduce the file-processing equivalents of functions scanf and **printf**—**fscanf** and **fprintf**. Later in the chapter we discuss functions **fread** and **fwrite**.

11.3 Creating a Sequential-Access File

C imposes no structure on a file. Thus, notions such as a *record* of a file are not part of the C language. The following example shows how you can impose your own record structure on a file.

Figure 11.2 creates a simple sequential-access file that might be used in an accounts receivable system to keep track of the amounts owed by a company's credit clients. For each client, the program obtains an *account number*, the *client's name* and the *client's balance* (i.e., the amount the client owes the company for goods and services received in the past). The data obtained for each client constitutes a "record" for that client. The account number is used as the *record key* in this application—the file will be created and maintained in account-number order. This program assumes the user enters the records in account-number order. In a comprehensive accounts receivable system, a sorting capability would be provided so the user could enter the records in any order. The records would then be sorted and written to the file. [*Note:* Figures 11.6–11.7 use the data file created in Fig. 11.2, so you must run the program in Fig. 11.2 before the programs in Figs. 11.6–11.7.]

```
1   // Fig. 11.2: fig11_02.c
2   // Creating a sequential file
3   #include <stdio.h>
4
5   int main(void)
6   {
7      FILE *cfPtr; // cfPtr = clients.txt file pointer
8
9      // fopen opens file. Exit program if unable to create file
10     if ((cfPtr = fopen("clients.txt", "w")) == NULL) {
11        puts("File could not be opened");
12     }
13     else {
14        puts("Enter the account, name, and balance.");
15        puts("Enter EOF to end input.");
16        printf("%s", "? ");
17
18        unsigned int account; // account number
19        char name[30]; // account name
20        double balance; // account balance
21
22        scanf("%d%29s%lf", &account, name, &balance);
23
24        // write account, name and balance into file with fprintf
25        while (!feof(stdin) ) {
26           fprintf(cfPtr, "%d %s %.2f\n", account, name, balance);
27           printf("%s", "? ");
28           scanf("%d%29s%lf", &account, name, &balance);
29        }
30
31        fclose(cfPtr); // fclose closes file
32     }
33  }
```

```
Enter the account, name, and balance.
Enter EOF to end input.
? 100 Jones 24.98
? 200 Doe 345.67
? 300 White 0.00
? 400 Stone -42.16
? 500 Rich 224.62
? ^Z
```

Fig. 11.2 | Creating a sequential file.

11.3.1 Pointer to a FILE

Now let's examine this program. Line 7 states that cfPtr is a *pointer to a FILE structure*. A C program administers each file with a separate FILE structure. Each open file must have a separately declared pointer of type FILE that's used to refer to the file. You need not know the specifics of the FILE structure to use files, but you can study the declaration in stdio.h if you like. We'll soon see precisely how the FILE structure leads *indirectly* to the operating system's file control block (FCB) for a file.

11.3.2 Using fopen to Open the File

Line 10 names the file—"clients.txt"—to be used by the program and establishes a "line of communication" with the file. The file pointer cfPtr is assigned a *pointer to the FILE structure* for the file opened with fopen. Function fopen takes two arguments:

- a filename (which can include path information leading to the file's location) and
- a file open mode.

The file open mode "w" indicates that the file is to be opened for writing. If a file *does not exist* and it's opened for writing, fopen *creates the file*. If an existing file is opened for writing, the contents of the file are *discarded without warning*. In the program, the if statement is used to determine whether the file pointer cfPtr is NULL (i.e., the file is not opened because it does not exist or the user does not have permission to open the file). If it's NULL, the program prints an error message and terminates. Otherwise, the program processes the input and writes it to the file.

Common Programming Error 11.1
Opening an existing file for writing ("w") when, in fact, the user wants to preserve the file, discards the contents of the file without warning.

Common Programming Error 11.2
Forgetting to open a file before attempting to reference it in a program is a logic error.

11.3.3 Using feof to Check for the End-of-File Indicator

The program prompts the user to enter the various fields for each record or to enter *end-of-file* when data entry is complete. Figure 11.3 lists the key combinations for entering end-of-file for various computer systems.

Operating system	Key combination
Linux/Mac OS X/UNIX	*<Ctrl> d*
Windows	*<Ctrl> z* then press *Enter*

Fig. 11.3 | End-of-file key combinations for various popular operating systems.

Line 25 uses function **feof** to determine whether the end-of-file indicator is set for stdin. The *end-of-file indicator* informs the program that there's no more data to be processed. In Fig. 11.2, the end-of-file indicator is set for the standard input when the user enters the *end-of-file key combination*. The argument to function feof is a pointer to the file being tested for the end-of-file indicator (stdin in this case). The function returns a nonzero (true) value when the end-of-file indicator has been set; otherwise, the function returns zero. The while statement that includes the feof call in this program continues executing while the end-of-file indicator is not set.

11.3.4 Using `fprintf` to Write to the File

Line 26 writes data to the file clients.txt. The data may be retrieved later by a program designed to read the file (see Section 11.4). Function fprintf is equivalent to printf except that fprintf also receives as an argument a file pointer for the file to which the data will be written. Function fprintf can output data to the standard output by using stdout as the file pointer, as in:

```
fprintf(stdout, "%d %s %.2f\n", account, name, balance);
```

11.3.5 Using `fclose` to Close the File

After the user enters end-of-file, the program closes the clients.txt file with **fclose** (line 31) and terminates. Function fclose also receives the file pointer (rather than the filename) as an argument. *If function fclose is not called explicitly, the operating system normally will close the file when program execution terminates.* This is an example of operating-system "housekeeping."

Performance Tip 11.1
Closing a file can free resources for which other users or programs may be waiting, so you should close each file as soon as it's no longer needed rather than waiting for the operating system to close it at program termination.

In the sample execution for the program of Fig. 11.2, the user enters information for five accounts, then enters end-of-file to signal that data entry is complete. The sample execution does not show how the data records actually appear in the file. To verify that the file has been created successfully, in the next section we present a program that reads the file and prints its contents.

Relationship Betweeen FILE Pointers, FILE Structures and FCBs

Figure 11.4 illustrates the relationship between FILE pointers, FILE structures and FCBs. When the file "clients.txt" is opened, an FCB for the file is copied into memory. The figure shows the connection between the file pointer returned by fopen and the FCB used by the operating system to administer the file. Programs may process no files, one file or several files. Each file used in a program will have a different file pointer returned by fopen. *All subsequent file-processing functions after the file is opened must refer to the file with the appropriate file pointer.*

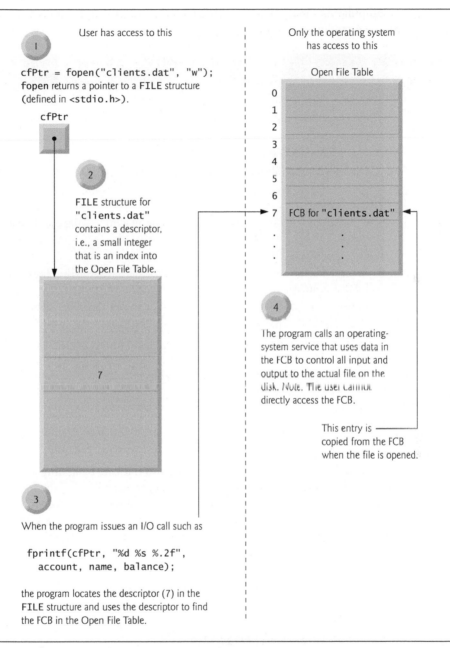

Fig. 11.4 | Relationship between FILE pointers, FILE structures and FCBs.

11.3.6 File Open Modes

Files may be opened in one of several modes, which are summarized in Fig. 11.5. Each file open mode in the first half of the table has a corresponding *binary* mode (containing the letter b) for manipulating binary files. The binary modes are used in Sections 11.5–11.9 when we introduce random-access files.

Mode	Description
r	Open an existing file for reading.
w	Create a file for writing. If the file already exists, *discard* the current contents.
a	Open or create a file for writing at the end of the file—i.e., write operations *append* data to the file.
r+	Open an existing file for update (reading and writing).
w+	Create a file for reading and writing. If the file already exists, *discard* the current contents.
a+	Open or create a file for reading and updating; all writing is done at the end of the file—i.e., write operations *append* data to the file.
rb	Open an existing file for reading in binary mode.
wb	Create a file for writing in binary mode. If the file already exists, discard the current contents.
ab	Append: open or create a file for writing at the end of the file in binary mode.
rb+	Open an existing file for update (reading and writing) in binary mode.
wb+	Create a file for update in binary mode. If the file already exists, discard the current contents.
ab+	Append: open or create a file for update in binary mode; writing is done at the end of the file.

Fig. 11.5 | File opening modes.

C11 Exclusive Write Mode

In addition, C11 provides *exclusive* write mode, which you indicate by adding an x to the end of the w, w+, wb or wb+ modes. In exclusive write mode, fopen will fail if the file already exists or cannot be created. If opening a file in exclusive write mode is successful and the underlying system supports exclusive file access, then *only* your program can access the file while it's open. (Some compilers and platforms do not support exclusive write mode.) If an error occurs while opening a file in any mode, **fopen** returns NULL.

Common Programming Error 11.3
Opening a nonexistent file for reading is an error.

Common Programming Error 11.4
Opening a file for reading or writing without having been granted the appropriate access rights to the file (this is operating-system dependent) is an error.

Common Programming Error 11.5
Opening a file for writing when no space is available is a runtime error.

Common Programming Error 11.6

Opening a file in write mode ("w") when it should be opened in update mode ("r+") causes the contents of the file to be discarded.

Error-Prevention Tip 11.1

Open a file only for reading (and not updating) if its contents should not be modified. This prevents unintentional modification of the file's contents. This is another example of the principle of least privilege.

11.4 Reading Data from a Sequential-Access File

Data is stored in files so that it can be retrieved for processing when needed. The previous section demonstrated how to create a file for sequential access. This section shows how to read data sequentially from a file.

Figure 11.6 reads records from the file "clients.txt" created by the program of Fig. 11.2 and prints their contents. Line 7 indicates that cfPtr is a *pointer to a FILE*. Line 10 attempts to open the file "clients.txt" for reading ("r") and determines whether it opened successfully (i.e., fopen does *not* return NULL). Line 19 reads a "record" from the file. Function fscanf is equivalent to function scanf, except fscanf receives as an argument a file pointer for the file from which the data is read. After this statement executes the first time, account will have the value 100, name will have the value "Jones" and balance will have the value 24.98. Each time the *second* fscanf statement (line 24) executes, the program reads another record from the file and account, name and balance take on new values. When the program reaches the end of the file, the file is closed (line 27) and the program terminates. Function feof returns true only *after* the program attempts to read the nonexistent data following the last line.

```c
1   // Fig. 11.6: fig11_06.c
2   // Reading and printing a sequential file
3   #include <stdio.h>
4
5   int main(void)
6   {
7      FILE *cfPtr; // cfPtr = clients.txt file pointer
8
9      // fopen opens file; exits program if file cannot be opened
10     if ((cfPtr = fopen("clients.txt", "r")) == NULL) {
11        puts("File could not be opened");
12     }
13     else { // read account, name and balance from file
14        unsigned int account; // account number
15        char name[30]; // account name
16        double balance; // account balance
17
18        printf("%-10s%-13s%s\n", "Account", "Name", "Balance");
19        fscanf(cfPtr, "%d%29s%lf", &account, name, &balance);
20
```

Fig. 11.6 | Reading and printing a sequential file. (Part 1 of 2.)

```
21              // while not end of file
22              while (!feof(cfPtr)  ) {
23                  printf("%-10d%-13s%7.2f\n", account, name, balance);
24                  fscanf(cfPtr, "%d%29s%lf", &account, name, &balance);
25              }
26
27              fclose(cfPtr); // fclose closes the file
28          }
29      }
```

```
Account  Name         Balance
100      Jones          24.98
200      Doe           345.67
300      White           0.00
400      Stone         -42.16
500      Rich          224.62
```

Fig. 11.6 | Reading and printing a sequential file. (Part 2 of 2.)

11.4.1 Resetting the File Position Pointer

To retrieve data sequentially from a file, a program normally starts reading from the beginning of the file and reads all data consecutively until the desired data is found. It may be desirable to process the data sequentially in a file several times (from the beginning of the file) during the execution of a program. The statement

```
rewind(cfPtr);
```

causes a program's **file position pointer**—which indicates the number of the next byte in the file to be read or written—to be repositioned to the *beginning* of the file (i.e., byte 0) pointed to by cfPtr. The file position pointer is *not* really a pointer. Rather it's an integer value that specifies the byte in the file at which the next read or write is to occur. This is sometimes referred to as the **file offset**. The file position pointer is a member of the FILE structure associated with each file.

11.4.2 Credit Inquiry Program

The program of Fig. 11.7 allows a credit manager to obtain lists of customers with zero balances (i.e., customers who do not owe any money), customers with credit balances (i.e., customers to whom the company owes money) and customers with debit balances (i.e., customers who owe the company money for goods and services received). A credit balance is a *negative* amount; a debit balance is a *positive* amount.

The program displays a menu and allows the credit manager to enter one of four options:

- Option 1 produces a list of accounts with zero balances.
- Option 2 produces a list of accounts with *credit balances*.
- Option 3 produces a list of accounts with *debit balances*.
- Option 4 terminates program execution.

A sample output is shown in Fig. 11.8.

```
1   // Fig. 11.7: fig11_07.c
2   // Credit inquiry program
3   #include <stdio.h>
4
5   // function main begins program execution
6   int main(void)
7   {
8      FILE *cfPtr; // clients.txt file pointer
9
10     // fopen opens the file; exits program if file cannot be opened
11     if ((cfPtr = fopen("clients.txt", "r")) == NULL) {
12        puts("File could not be opened");
13     }
14     else {
15
16        // display request options
17        printf("%s", "Enter request\n"
18           " 1 - List accounts with zero balances\n"
19           " 2 - List accounts with credit balances\n"
20           " 3 - List accounts with debit balances\n"
21           " 4 - End of run\n? ");
22        unsigned int request; // request number
23        scanf("%u", &request);
24
25        // process user's request
26        while (request != 4) {
27           unsigned int account; // account number
28           double balance; // account balance
29           char name[30]; // account name
30
31           // read account, name and balance from file
32           fscanf(cfPtr, "%d%29s%1f", &account, name, &balance);
33
34           switch (request) {
35              case 1:
36                 puts("\nAccounts with zero balances:");
37
38                 // read file contents (until eof)
39                 while (!feof(cfPtr)) {
40                    // output only if balance is 0
41                    if (balance == 0) {
42                       printf("%-10d%-13s%7.2f\n",
43                          account, name, balance);
44                    }
45
46                    // read account, name and balance from file
47                    fscanf(cfPtr, "%d%29s%1f",
48                       &account, name, &balance);
49                 }
50
51                 break;
```

Fig. 11.7 | Credit inquiry program. (Part 1 of 2.)

```
52              case 2:
53                  puts("\nAccounts with credit balances:\n");
54
55                  // read file contents (until eof)
56                  while (!feof(cfPtr)) {
57                      // output only if balance is less than 0
58                      if (balance < 0) {
59                          printf("%-10d%-13s%7.2f\n",
60                              account, name, balance);
61                      }
62
63                      // read account, name and balance from file
64                      fscanf(cfPtr, "%d%29s%lf",
65                          &account, name, &balance);
66                  }
67
68                  break;
69              case 3:
70                  puts("\nAccounts with debit balances:\n");
71
72                  // read file contents (until eof)
73                  while (!feof(cfPtr)) {
74                      // output only if balance is greater than 0
75                      if (balance > 0) {
76                          printf("%-10d%-13s%7.2f\n",
77                              account, name, balance);
78                      }
79
80                      // read account, name and balance from file
81                      fscanf(cfPtr, "%d%29s%lf",
82                          &account, name, &balance);
83                  }
84
85                  break;
86          }
87
88          rewind(cfPtr); // return cfPtr to beginning of file
89
90          printf("%s", "\n? ");
91          scanf("%d", &request);
92      }
93
94      puts("End of run.");
95      fclose(cfPtr); // fclose closes the file
96   }
97 }
```

Fig. 11.7 | Credit inquiry program. (Part 2 of 2.)

```
Enter request
 1 - List accounts with zero balances
 2 - List accounts with credit balances
 3 - List accounts with debit balances
 4 - End of run
? 1

Accounts with zero balances:
300        White              0.00

? 2

Accounts with credit balances:
400        Stone            -42.16

? 3

Accounts with debit balances:
100        Jones             24.98
200        Doe              345.67
500        Rich             224.62

? 4
End of run.
```

Fig. 11.8 | Sample output of the credit inquiry program of Fig. 11.7.

Updating a Sequential File

Data in this type of sequential file cannot be modified without the risk of destroying other data. For example, if the name "White" needs to be changed to "Worthington," the old name cannot simply be overwritten. The record for White was written to the file as

    300 White 0.00

If the record is rewritten beginning at the same location in the file using the new name, the record will be

    300 Worthington 0.00

The new record is *larger* (has more characters) than the original record. The characters beyond the second "o" in "Worthington" will *overwrite* the beginning of the next sequential record in the file. The problem here is that in the **formatted input/output model** using fprintf and fscanf, fields—and hence records—can *vary* in size. For example, the values 7, 14, –117, 2074 and 27383 are all ints stored in the same number of bytes internally, but they're different-sized fields when displayed on the screen or written to a file as text.

Therefore, sequential access with fprintf and fscanf is *not* usually used to *update records in place*. Instead, the entire file is usually *rewritten*. To make the preceding name change, the records before 300 White 0.00 in such a sequential-access file would be copied to a new file, the new record would be written and the records after 300 White 0.00 would be copied to the new file. This requires processing *every* record in the file to update *one* record.

11.5 Random-Access Files

As we stated previously, records in a file created with the formatted output function fprintf are not necessarily of the same length. However, individual records that you write to and read from a **random-access file** are normally *fixed in length* and may be accessed directly (and thus quickly) without searching through other records. This makes random-access files appropriate for airline reservation systems, banking systems, point-of-sale systems, and other kinds of **transaction-processing systems** that require rapid access to specific data. There are other ways of implementing random-access files, but we'll limit our discussion to this straightforward approach using fixed-length records.

Because every record in a random-access file normally has the same length, the exact location of a record relative to the beginning of the file can be calculated as a function of the record key. We'll soon see how this facilitates *immediate* access to specific records, even in large files.

Figure 11.9 illustrates one way to implement a random-access file. Such a file is like a freight train with many cars—some empty and some with cargo. Each car in the train has the same length.

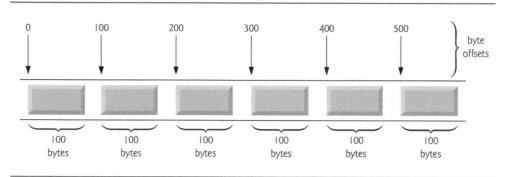

Fig. 11.9 | C's view of a random-access file.

Fixed-length records enable data to be inserted in a random-access file *without destroying other data in the file*. Data stored previously can also be updated or deleted without rewriting the entire file. In the following sections we explain how to

- create a random-access file,
- enter data,
- read the data both sequentially and randomly,
- update the data,
- and delete data no longer needed.

11.6 Creating a Random-Access File

Function fwrite transfers a specified number of bytes beginning at a specified location in memory to a file. The data is written beginning at the location in the file indicated by the file position pointer. Function fread transfers a specified number of bytes from the location in the file specified by the file position pointer to an area in memory beginning with a specified address. Now, when writing a four-byte integer, instead of using

```
fprintf(fPtr, "%d", number);
```

which could print a single digit or as many as 11 digits (10 digits plus a sign, each of which requires at least one byte of storage, based on the character set for the locale), we can use

```
fwrite(&number, sizeof(int), 1, fPtr);
```

which *always* writes *four* bytes on a system with four-byte integers from a variable number to the file represented by fPtr (we'll explain the 1 argument shortly). Later, fread can be used to read those four bytes into an integer variable number. Although fread and fwrite read and write data, such as integers, in fixed-size rather than variable-size format, the data they handle are processed in computer "raw data" format (i.e., bytes of data) rather than in printf's and scanf's human-readable text format. Because the "raw" representation of data is system dependent, "raw data" may not be readable on other systems, or by programs produced by other compilers or with other compiler options.

fwrite and fread Can Write and Read Arrays

Functions fwrite and fread are capable of reading and writing arrays of data to and from files. The third argument of both fread and fwrite is the number of elements in the array that should be read from or written to a file. The preceding fwrite function call writes a single integer to a file, so the third argument is 1 (as if one element of an array were being written). File-processing programs rarely write a single field to a file. Normally, they write one struct at a time, as we show in the following examples.

Problem Statement

Consider the following problem statement:

> *Create a transaction-processing system capable of storing up to 100 fixed-length records. Each record should consist of an account number that will be used as the record key, a last name, a first name and a balance. The resulting program should be able to update an account, insert a new account record, delete an account and list all the account records in a formatted text file for printing. Use a random-access file.*

The next several sections introduce the techniques necessary to create the transaction-processing program. Figure 11.10 shows how to open a random-access file, define a record format using a struct, write data to the file and close the file. This program initializes all 100 records of the file "accounts.dat" with empty structs using the function fwrite. Each empty struct contains 0 for the account number, "" (the empty string) for the last name, "" for the first name and 0.0 for the balance. The file is initialized in this manner to create the space in which the file will be stored and to make it possible to determine whether a record contains data.

```
1   // Fig. 11.10: fig11_10.c
2   // Creating a random-access file sequentially
3   #include <stdio.h>
4
```

Fig. 11.10 | Creating a random-access file sequentially. (Part 1 of 2.)

```
5    // clientData structure definition
6    struct clientData {
7       unsigned int acctNum; // account number
8       char lastName[15]; // account last name
9       char firstName[10]; // account first name
10      double balance; // account balance
11   };
12
13   int main(void)
14   {
15      FILE *cfPtr; // accounts.dat file pointer
16
17      // fopen opens the file; exits if file cannot be opened
18      if ((cfPtr = fopen("accounts.dat", "wb")) == NULL) {
19         puts("File could not be opened.");
20      }
21      else {
22         // create clientData with default information
23         struct clientData blankClient = {0, "", "", 0.0};
24
25         // output 100 blank records to file
26         for (unsigned int i = 1; i <= 100; ++i) {
27            fwrite(&blankClient, sizeof(struct clientData), 1, cfPtr);
28         }
29
30         fclose (cfPtr); // fclose closes the file
31      }
32   }
```

Fig. 11.10 | Creating a random-access file sequentially. (Part 2 of 2.)

Function fwrite writes a block of bytes to a file. Line 27 causes the structure blank-Client of size sizeof(struct clientData) to be written to the file pointed to by cfPtr. The operator sizeof returns the size in bytes of its operand in parentheses (in this case struct clientData).

Function fwrite can actually be used to write several elements of an array of objects. To do so, supply in the call to fwrite a pointer to an array as the first argument and the number of elements to be written as the third argument. In the preceding statement, fwrite was used to write a single object that was not an array element. Writing a single object is equivalent to writing one element of an array, hence the 1 in the fwrite call. [*Note:* Figures 11.11, 11.14 and 11.15 use the data file created in Fig. 11.10, so you must run Fig. 11.10 before Figs. 11.11, 11.14 and 11.15.]

11.7 Writing Data Randomly to a Random-Access File

Figure 11.11 writes data to the file "accounts.dat". It uses the combination of fseek and fwrite to store data at specific locations in the file. Function fseek sets the file position pointer to a specific position in the file, then fwrite writes the data. A sample execution is shown in Fig. 11.12.

```
 1    // Fig. 11.11: fig11_11.c
 2    // Writing data randomly to a random-access file
 3    #include <stdio.h>
 4
 5    // clientData structure definition
 6    struct clientData {
 7       unsigned int acctNum; // account number
 8       char lastName[15]; // account last name
 9       char firstName[10]; // account first name
10       double balance; // account balance
11    }; // end structure clientData
12
13    int main(void)
14    {
15       FILE *cfPtr; // accounts.dat file pointer
16
17       // fopen opens the file; exits if file cannot be opened
18       if ((cfPtr = fopen("accounts.dat", "rb+")) == NULL) {
19          puts("File could not be opened.");
20       }
21       else {
22          // create clientData with default information
23          struct clientData client = {0, "", "", 0.0};
24
25          // require user to specify account number
26          printf("%s", "Enter account number"
27             " (1 to 100, 0 to end input): ");
28          scanf("%d", &client.acctNum);
29
30          // user enters information, which is copied into file
31          while (client.acctNum != 0) {
32             // user enters last name, first name and balance
33             printf("%s", "\nEnter lastname, firstname, balance: ");
34
35             // set record lastName, firstName and balance value
36             fscanf(stdin, "%14s%9s%lf", client.lastName,
37                client.firstName, &client.balance);
38
39             // seek position in file to user-specified record
40             fseek(cfPtr, (client.acctNum - 1) *
41                sizeof(struct clientData), SEEK_SET);
42
43             // write user-specified information in file
44             fwrite(&client, sizeof(struct clientData), 1, cfPtr);
45
46             // enable user to input another account number
47             printf("%s", "\nEnter account number: ");
48             scanf("%d", &client.acctNum);
49          }
50
51          fclose(cfPtr); // fclose closes the file
52       }
53    }
```

Fig. 11.11 | Writing data randomly to a random-access file.

```
Enter account number (1 to 100, 0 to end input): 37

Enter lastname, firstname, balance: Barker Doug 0.00

Enter account number: 29

Enter lastname, firstname, balance: Brown Nancy -24.54

Enter account number: 96

Enter lastname, firstname, balance: Stone Sam 34.98

Enter account number: 88

Enter lastname, firstname, balance: Smith Dave 258.34

Enter account number: 33

Enter lastname, firstname, balance: Dunn Stacey 314.33

Enter account number: 0
```

Fig. 11.12 | Sample execution of the program in Fig. 11.11.

11.7.1 Positioning the File Position Pointer with `fseek`

Lines 40–41 position the file position pointer for the file referenced by `cfPtr` to the byte location calculated by `(client.accountNum - 1) * sizeof(struct clientData)`. The value of this expression is called the **offset** or the **displacement**. Because the account number is between 1 and 100 but the byte positions in the file start with 0, 1 is subtracted from the account number when calculating the byte location of the record. Thus, for record 1, the file position pointer is set to byte 0 of the file. The symbolic constant **SEEK_SET** indicates that the file position pointer is positioned relative to the beginning of the file by the amount of the offset. As the above statement indicates, a seek for account number 1 in the file sets the file position pointer to the beginning of the file because the byte location calculated is 0.

Figure 11.13 illustrates the file pointer referring to a FILE structure in memory. The file position pointer in this diagram indicates that the next byte to be read or written is 5 bytes from the beginning of the file.

fseek Function Prototype
The function prototype for `fseek` is

```
int fseek(FILE *stream, long int offset, int whence);
```

where `offset` is the number of bytes to seek from `whence` in the file pointed to by `stream`—a positive `offset` seeks forward and a negative one seeks backward. Argument `whence` is one of the values SEEK_SET, **SEEK_CUR** or **SEEK_END** (all defined in <stdio.h>), which indicate the location from which the seek begins. SEEK_SET indicates that the seek starts at the *beginning* of the file; SEEK_CUR indicates that the seek starts at the *current location* in the file; and SEEK_END indicates that the seek is measured from at the *end* of the file.

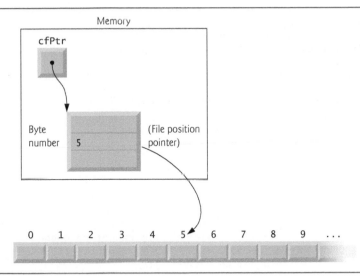

Fig. 11.13 | File position pointer indicating an offset of 5 bytes from the beginning of the file.

11.7.2 Error Checking

For simplicity, the programs in this chapter do *not* perform error checking. Industrial-strength programs should determine whether functions such as fscanf (Fig. 11.11, lines 36–37), fseek (lines 40–41) and fwrite (line 44) operate correctly by checking their return values. Function fscanf returns the number of data items successfully read or the value EOF if a problem occurs while reading data. Function fseek returns a nonzero value if the seek operation cannot be performed (e.g., attempting to seek to a position before the start of the file). Function fwrite returns the number of items it successfully output. If this number is less than the *third argument* in the function call, then a write error occurred.

11.8 Reading Data from a Random-Access File

Function fread reads a specified number of bytes from a file into memory. For example,

```
fread(&client, sizeof(struct clientData), 1, cfPtr);
```

reads the number of bytes determined by sizeof(struct clientData) from the file referenced by cfPtr, stores the data in client and returns the number of bytes read. The bytes are read from the location specified by the file position pointer. Function fread can read several fixed-size array elements by providing a pointer to the array in which the elements will be stored and by indicating the number of elements to be read. The preceding statement reads *one* element. To read *more than one*, specify the number of elements as fread's third argument. Function fread returns the number of items it successfully input. If this number is less than the third argument in the function call, then a read error occurred.

Figure 11.14 reads sequentially every record in the "accounts.dat" file, determines whether each record contains data and displays the formatted data for records containing data. Function feof determines when the end of the file is reached, and the fread function transfers data from the file to the clientData structure client.

```
 1   // Fig. 11.14: fig11_14.c
 2   // Reading a random-access file sequentially
 3   #include <stdio.h>
 4
 5   // clientData structure definition
 6   struct clientData {
 7      unsigned int acctNum; // account number
 8      char lastName[15]; // account last name
 9      char firstName[10]; // account first name
10      double balance; // account balance
11   };
12
13   int main(void)
14   {
15      FILE *cfPtr; // accounts.dat file pointer
16
17      // fopen opens the file; exits if file cannot be opened
18      if ((cfPtr = fopen("credit.txt", "rb")) == NULL) {
19         puts("File could not be opened.");
20      }
21      else {
22         printf("%-6s%-16s%-11s%10s\n", "Acct", "Last Name",
23            "First Name", "Balance");
24
25         // read all records from file (until eof)
26         while (!feof(cfPtr)) {
27            // create clientData with default information
28            struct clientData client = {0, "", "", 0.0};
29
30            int result = fread(&client, sizeof(struct clientData), 1, cfPtr);
31
32            // display record
33            if (result != 0 && client.acctNum != 0) {
34               printf("%-6d%-16s%-11s%10.2f\n",
35                  client.acctNum, client.lastName,
36                  client.firstName, client.balance);
37            }
38         }
39
40         fclose(cfPtr); // fclose closes the file
41      }
42   }
```

```
Acct   Last Name        First Name     Balance
29     Brown            Nancy           -24.54
33     Dunn             Stacey          314.33
37     Barker           Doug              0.00
88     Smith            Dave            258.34
96     Stone            Sam              34.98
```

Fig. 11.14 | Reading a random-access file sequentially.

11.9 Case Study: Transaction-Processing Program

We now present a substantial transaction-processing program (Fig. 11.15) using random-access files. The program maintains a bank's account information—updating existing accounts, adding new accounts, deleting accounts and storing a listing of all the current accounts in a text file for printing. We assume that the program of Fig. 11.10 has been executed to create the file accounts.dat.

Option 1: Create a Formatted List of Accounts

The program has five options—option 5 terminates the program. Option 1 calls function textFile (lines 64–94) to store a formatted list of all the accounts (typically called a report) in a text file called accounts.txt that may be printed later. The function uses fread and the sequential file-access techniques used in the program of Fig. 11.14. After option 1, accounts.txt contains:

```
Acct   Last Name        First Name        Balance
29     Brown            Nancy             -24.54
33     Dunn             Stacey            314.33
37     Barker           Doug                0.00
88     Smith            Dave              258.34
96     Stone            Sam                34.98
```

Option 2: Update an Account

Option 2 calls the function updateRecord (lines 97–140) to update an account. The function will update only a record that already exists, so the function first checks whether the record specified by the user is empty. The record is read into structure client with fread, then member acctNum is compared to 0. If it's 0, the record contains no information, and a message is printed stating that the record is empty. Then the menu choices are displayed. If the record contains information, function updateRecord inputs the transaction amount, calculates the new balance and rewrites the record to the file. A typical output for option 2 is

```
Enter account to update (1 - 100): 37
37     Barker           Doug                0.00

Enter charge (+) or payment (-): +87.99
37     Barker           Doug               87.99
```

Option 3: Create a New Account

Option 3 calls the function newRecord (lines 177–215) to add a new account to the file. If the user enters an account number for an existing account, newRecord displays an error message indicating that the record already contains information, and the menu choices are printed again. This function uses the same process to add a new account as does the program in Fig. 11.11. A typical output for option 3 is

```
Enter new account number (1 - 100): 22
Enter lastname, firstname, balance
? Johnston Sarah 247.45
```

Option 4: Delete an Account

Option 4 calls function deleteRecord (lines 143–174) to delete a record from the file. Deletion is accomplished by asking the user for the account number and reinitializing the record. If the account contains no information, deleteRecord displays an error message indicating that the account does not exist.

Code for the Transaction-Processing Program

The program is shown in Fig. 11.15. The file "accounts.dat" is opened for update (reading and writing) using "rb+" mode.

```c
1   // Fig. 11.15: fig11_15.c
2   // Transaction-processing program reads a random-access file sequentially,
3   // updates data already written to the file, creates new data to
4   // be placed in the file, and deletes data previously stored in the file.
5   #include <stdio.h>
6
7   // clientData structure definition
8   struct clientData {
9      unsigned int acctNum; // account number
10     char lastName[15]; // account last name
11     char firstName[10]; // account first name
12     double balance; // account balance
13  };
14
15  // prototypes
16  unsigned int enterChoice(void);
17  void textFile(FILE *readPtr);
18  void updateRecord(FILE *fPtr);
19  void newRecord(FILE *fPtr);
20  void deleteRecord(FILE *fPtr);
21
22  int main(void)
23  {
24     FILE *cfPtr; // accounts.dat file pointer
25
26     // fopen opens the file; exits if file cannot be opened
27     if ((cfPtr = fopen("accounts.dat", "rb+")) == NULL) {
28        puts("File could not be opened.");
29     }
30     else {
31        unsigned int choice; // user's choice
32
33        // enable user to specify action
34        while ((choice = enterChoice()) != 5) {
35           switch (choice) {
36              // create text file from record file
37              case 1:
38                 textFile(cfPtr);
39                 break;
```

Fig. 11.15 | Transaction-processing program. (Part 1 of 5.)

```
40                    // update record
41                    case 2:
42                       updateRecord(cfPtr);
43                       break;
44                    // create record
45                    case 3:
46                       newRecord(cfPtr);
47                       break;
48                    // delete existing record
49                    case 4:
50                       deleteRecord(cfPtr);
51                       break;
52                    // display message if user does not select valid choice
53                    default:
54                       puts("Incorrect choice");
55                       break;
56              }
57           }
58
59        fclose(cfPtr); // fclose closes the file
60     }
61  }
62
63  // create formatted text file for printing
64  void textFile(FILE *readPtr)
65  {
66     FILE *writePtr; // accounts.txt file pointer
67
68     // fopen opens the file; exits if file cannot be opened
69     if ((writePtr = fopen("accounts.txt", "w")  ) == NULL) {
70        puts("File could not be opened.");
71     }
72     else {
73        rewind(readPtr); // sets pointer to beginning of file
74        fprintf(writePtr, "%-6s%-16s%-11s%10s\n",
75           "Acct", "Last Name", "First Name","Balance");
76
77        // copy all records from random-access file into text file
78        while (!feof(readPtr)) {
79           // create clientData with default information
80           struct clientData client = { 0, "", "", 0.0 };
81           int result =
82              fread(&client, sizeof(struct clientData), 1, readPtr);
83
84           // write single record to text file
85           if (result != 0 && client.acctNum != 0) {
86              fprintf(writePtr, "%-6d%-16s%-11s%10.2f\n",
87                 client.acctNum, client.lastName,
88                 client.firstName, client.balance);
89           }
90        }
```

Fig. 11.15 | Transaction-processing program. (Part 2 of 5.)

```
91
92          fclose(writePtr); // fclose closes the file
93      }
94  }
95
96  // update balance in record
97  void updateRecord(FILE *fPtr)
98  {
99      // obtain number of account to update
100     printf("%s", "Enter account to update (1 - 100): ");
101     unsigned int account; // account number
102     scanf("%d", &account);
103
104     // move file pointer to correct record in file
105     fseek(fPtr, (account - 1) * sizeof(struct clientData),
106         SEEK_SET);
107
108     // create clientData with no information
109     struct clientData client = {0, "", "", 0.0};
110
111     // read record from file
112     fread(&client, sizeof(struct clientData), 1, fPtr);
113
114     // display error if account does not exist
115     if (client.acctNum == 0) {
116         printf("Account #%d has no information.\n", account);
117     }
118     else { // update record
119         printf("%-6d%-16s%-11s%10.2f\n\n",
120             client.acctNum, client.lastName,
121             client.firstName, client.balance);
122
123         // request transaction amount from user
124         printf("%s", "Enter charge (+) or payment (-): ");
125         double transaction; // transaction amount
126         scanf("%lf", &transaction);
127         client.balance += transaction; // update record balance
128
129         printf("%-6d%-16s%-11s%10.2f\n",
130             client.acctNum, client.lastName,
131             client.firstName, client.balance);
132
133         // move file pointer to correct record in file
134         fseek(fPtr, (account - 1) * sizeof(struct clientData),
135             SEEK_SET);
136
137         // write updated record over old record in file
138         fwrite(&client, sizeof(struct clientData), 1, fPtr);
139     }
140 }
141
```

Fig. 11.15 | Transaction-processing program. (Part 3 of 5.)

```
142  // delete an existing record
143  void deleteRecord(FILE *fPtr)
144  {
145     // obtain number of account to delete
146     printf("%s", "Enter account number to delete (1 - 100): ");
147     unsigned int accountNum; // account number
148     scanf("%d", &accountNum);
149
150     // move file pointer to correct record in file
151     fseek(fPtr, (accountNum - 1) * sizeof(struct clientData),
152        SEEK_SET);
153
154     struct clientData client; // stores record read from file
155
156     // read record from file
157     fread(&client, sizeof(struct clientData), 1, fPtr);
158
159     // display error if record does not exist
160     if (client.acctNum == 0) {
161        printf("Account %d does not exist.\n", accountNum);
162     }
163     else { // delete record
164        // move file pointer to correct record in file
165        fseek(fPtr, (accountNum - 1) * sizeof(struct clientData),
166           SEEK_SET);
167
168        struct clientData blankClient = {0, "", "", 0}; // blank client
169
170        // replace existing record with blank record
171        fwrite(&blankClient,
172           sizeof(struct clientData), 1, fPtr);
173     }
174  }
175
176  // create and insert record
177  void newRecord(FILE *fPtr)
178  {
179     // obtain number of account to create
180     printf("%s", "Enter new account number (1 - 100): ");
181     unsigned int accountNum; // account number
182     scanf("%d", &accountNum);
183
184     // move file pointer to correct record in file
185     fseek(fPtr, (accountNum - 1) * sizeof(struct clientData),
186        SEEK_SET);
187
188     // create clientData with default information
189     struct clientData client = { 0, "", "", 0.0 };
190
191     // read record from file
192     fread(&client, sizeof(struct clientData), 1, fPtr);
193
```

Fig. 11.15 | Transaction-processing program. (Part 4 of 5.)

```
194     // display error if account already exists
195     if (client.acctNum != 0) {
196        printf("Account #%d already contains information.\n",
197           client.acctNum);
198     }
199     else { // create record
200        // user enters last name, first name and balance
201        printf("%s", "Enter lastname, firstname, balance\n? ");
202        scanf("%14s%9s%lf", &client.lastName, &client.firstName,
203           &client.balance);
204
205        client.acctNum = accountNum;
206
207        // move file pointer to correct record in file
208        fseek(fPtr, (client.acctNum - 1) *
209           sizeof(struct clientData), SEEK_SET);
210
211        // insert record in file
212        fwrite(&client,
213           sizeof(struct clientData), 1, fPtr);
214     }
215  }
216
217  // enable user to input menu choice
218  unsigned int enterChoice(void)
219  {
220     // display available options
221     printf("%s", "\nEnter your choice\n"
222        "1 - store a formatted text file of accounts called\n"
223        "     \"accounts.txt\" for printing\n"
224        "2 - update an account\n"
225        "3 - add a new account\n"
226        "4 - delete an account\n"
227        "5 - end program\n? ");
228
229     unsigned int menuChoice; // variable to store user's choice
230     scanf("%u", &menuChoice); // receive choice from user
231     return menuChoice;
232  }
```

Fig. 11.15 | Transaction-processing program. (Part 5 of 5.)

11.10 Secure C Programming

fprintf_s *and* fscanf_s

The examples in Sections 11.3–11.4 used functions fprintf and fscanf to write text to and read text from files, respectively. The new standard's Annex K provides more secure versions of these functions named fprintf_s and fscanf_s that are identical to the printf_s and scanf_s functions we've previously introduced, except that you also specify a FILE pointer argument indicating the file to manipulate. If your C compiler's standard libraries include these functions, you should use them instead of fprintf and fscanf. As with scanf_s and printf_s, Microsoft's versions of fprintf_s and fscanf_s differ from those in Annex K.

Chapter 9 of the CERT Secure C Coding Standard

Chapter 9 of the *CERT Secure C Coding Standard* is dedicated to input/output recommendations and rules—many apply to file processing in general and several of these apply to the file-processing functions presented in this chapter. For more information on each, visit www.securecoding.cert.org.

- FIO03-C: When opening a file for writing using the nonexclusive file-open modes (Fig. 11.5), if the file exists, function fopen opens it and truncates its contents, providing no indication of whether the file existed before the fopen call. To ensure that an existing file is *not* opened and truncated, you can use C11's new *exclusive write mode* (discussed in Section 11.3), which allows fopen to open the file *only* if it does *not* already exist.

- FIO04-C: In industrial-strength code, you should always check the return values of file-processing functions that return error indicators to ensure that the functions performed their tasks correctly.

- FIO07-C. Function rewind does not return a value, so you cannot test whether the operation was successful. It's recommended instead that you use function fseek, because it returns a nonzero value if it fails.

- FIO09-C. We demonstrated both text files and binary files in this chapter. Due to differences in binary data representations across platforms, files written in binary format often are *not* portable. For more portable file representations, consider using text files or a function library that can handle the differences in binary file representations across platforms.

- FIO14-C. Some library functions do not operate identically on text files and binary files. In particular, function fseek is *not* guaranteed to work correctly with binary files if you seek from SEEK_END, so SEEK_SET should be used.

- FIO42-C. On many platforms, you can have only a limited number of files open at once. For this reason, you should always close a file as soon as it's no longer needed by your program.

Summary

Section 11.1 Introduction
- **Files** (p. 442) are used for permanent retention of large amounts of data.
- Computers store files on **secondary storage devices**, such as hard drives, solid-state drives, flash drives and DVDs.

Section 11.2 Files and Streams
- C views each file as a sequential **stream of bytes** (p. 442). When a file is opened, a stream is associated with the file.
- Three streams are automatically opened when program execution begins—the **standard input** (p. 442), the **standard output** (p. 442) and the **standard error** (p. 442).
- Streams provide **communication channels** between files and programs.

- The **standard input stream** enables a program to **read data from the keyboard**, and the **standard output stream** enables a program to **print data on the screen**.

- Opening a file returns a pointer to a **FILE structure** (defined in <stdio.h>; p. 443) that contains information used to process the file. This structure includes a **file descriptor** (p. 443), i.e., an index into an operating-system array called the **open file table** (p. 443). Each array element contains a **file control block** (**FCB**; p. 443) that the operating system uses to administer a particular file.

- The standard input, standard output and standard error are manipulated using the predefined file pointers **stdin**, **stdout** and **stderr**.

- Function **fgetc** (p. 443) **reads one character** from a file. It receives as an argument a FILE pointer for the file from which a character will be read.

- Function **fputc** (p. 443) **writes one character** to a file. It receives as arguments a character to be written and a FILE pointer for the file to which the character will be written.

- The **fgets** and **fputs** functions (p. 443) **read a line from a file** or **write a line to a file**, respectively.

Section 11.3 Creating a Sequential-Access File

- C imposes no structure on a file. You must provide a file structure to meet the requirements of a particular application.

- A C program administers each file with a separate FILE structure.

- Each open file must have a separately declared **pointer of type FILE** that's used to refer to the file.

- Function **fopen** (p. 448) takes as arguments a filename and a **file open mode** (p. 445) and returns a pointer to the FILE structure for the file opened.

- The **file open mode "w"** indicates that the file is to be opened for writing. If the file does not exist, fopen creates it. If the file exists, the contents are discarded without warning.

- Function fopen returns NULL if it's unable to open a file.

- Function **feof** (p. 446) receives a pointer to a FILE and returns a nonzero (true) value when the end-of-file indicator has been set; otherwise, the function returns zero. Any attempt to read from a file for which feof returns true will fail.

- Function **fprintf** (p. 443) is equivalent to printf except that fprintf also receives as an argument a file pointer for the file to which the data will be written.

- Function **fclose** (p. 446) receives a file pointer as an argument and closes the specified file.

- When a file is opened, the file control block (FCB) for the file is copied into memory. The FCB is used by the operating system to administer the file.

- To create a new file, or to discard an existing file's contents before writing data, open the file for **writing ("w")**.

- To read an existing file, open it for **reading ("r")**.

- To add records to the end of an existing file, open the file for **appending ("a")**.

- To open a file so that it may be written to and read from, open the file for updating in one of the three **update modes**—**"r+"**, **"w+"** or **"a+"**. Mode "r+" opens a file for reading and writing. Mode "w+" creates a file for reading and writing. If the file already exists, it's opened and its contents are discarded. Mode "a+" opens a file for reading and writing—all writing is done at the end of the file. If the file does not exist, it's created.

- Each file open mode has a corresponding **binary mode** (containing the letter **b**) for manipulating **binary files**.

- C11 also supports **exclusive write mode** by appending **x** to the w, w+, wb and wb+ modes.

Section 11.4 Reading Data from a Sequential-Access File

- Function **fscanf** (p. 443) is equivalent to function scanf except fscanf receives as an argument a file pointer for the file from which the data is read.

- To retrieve data sequentially from a file, a program normally starts reading from the beginning of the file and reads all data consecutively until the desired data is found.

- Function **rewind** causes a program's **file position pointer** (p. 450) to be repositioned to the beginning of the file (i.e., byte 0) pointed to its argument.

- The file position pointer is an integer value that specifies the byte location in the file at which the next read or write is to occur. This is sometimes referred to as the **file offset** (p. 450). The file position pointer is a member of the FILE structure associated with each file.

- The data in a sequential file typically cannot be modified without the risk of destroying other data in the file.

Section 11.5 Random-Access Files

- Individual records of a **random-access file** (p. 454) are normally **fixed in length** and may be accessed directly (and thus quickly) without searching through other records.

- Because every record in a random-access file normally has the same length, the exact location of a record relative to the beginning of the file can be calculated as a function of the **record key**.

- Fixed-length records enable data to be inserted in a random-access file without destroying other data. Data stored previously can also be updated or deleted without rewriting the entire file.

Section 11.6 Creating a Random-Access File

- Function **fwrite** (p. 454) transfers a specified number of bytes beginning at a specified location in memory to a file. The data is written beginning at the file position pointer's location.

- Function **fread** (p. 454) transfers a specified number of bytes from the location in the file specified by the file position pointer to an area in memory beginning with a specified address.

- Functions fwrite and fread are capable of **reading and writing arrays of data** from and to files. The third argument of both fread and fwrite is the number of elements to process.

- File-processing programs normally write one struct at a time.

- Function fwrite writes a **block** (specific number of bytes) of data to a file.

- To write several array elements, supply in the call to fwrite a pointer to an array as the first argument and the number of elements to be written as the third argument.

Section 11.7 Writing Data Randomly to a Random-Access File

- Function **fseek** (p. 456) sets the file position pointer for a given file to a specific position in the file. Its second argument indicates the number of bytes to seek and its third argument indicates the location from which to seek. The third argument can have one of three values—SEEK_SET, SEEK_CUR or SEEK_END (all defined in <stdio.h>). **SEEK_SET** (p. 458) indicates that the seek starts at the beginning of the file; **SEEK_CUR** (p. 458) indicates that the seek starts at the current location in the file; and **SEEK_END** (p. 458) indicates that the seek is measured from at the end of the file.

- Industrial-strength programs should determine whether functions such as fscanf, fseek and fwrite operate correctly by checking their return values.

- Function fscanf returns the number of fields successfully read or the value EOF if a problem occurs while reading data.

- Function fseek returns a nonzero value if the seek operation cannot be performed.

- Function fwrite returns the number of items it successfully output. If this number is less than the third argument in the function call, then a write error occurred.

Section 11.8 Reading Data from a Random-Access File

- Function `fread` reads a specified number of bytes from a file into memory.

- Function `fread` can be used to read several fixed-size array elements by providing a pointer to the array in which the elements will be stored and by indicating the number of elements to be read.

- Function `fread` returns the number of items it successfully input. If this number is less than the third argument in the function call, then a read error occurred.

Self-Review Exercises

11.1   Fill in the blanks in each of the following:
   a) Function _____ closes a file.
   b) The _____ function reads data from a file in a manner similar to how `scanf` reads from `stdin`.
   c) Function _____ reads a character from a specified file.
   d) Function _____ reads a line from a specified file.
   e) Function _____ opens a file.
   f) Function _____ is normally used when reading data from a file in random-access applications.
   g) Function _____ repositions the file position pointer to a specific location in the file.

11.2   State which of the following are *true* and which are *false*. If *false*, explain why.
   a) Function `fscanf` cannot be used to read data from the standard input.
   b) You must explicitly use `fopen` to open the standard input, standard output and standard error streams.
   c) A program must explicitly call function `fclose` to close a file.
   d) If the file position pointer points to a location in a sequential file other than the beginning of the file, the file must be closed and reopened to read from the beginning of the file.
   e) Function `fprintf` can write to the standard output.
   f) Data in sequential-access files is always updated without overwriting other data.
   g) It's not necessary to search through all the records in a random-access file to find a specific record.
   h) Records in random-access files are not of uniform length.
   i) Function `fseek` may seek only relative to the beginning of a file.

11.3   Write a single statement to accomplish each of the following. Assume that each of these statements applies to the same program.
   a) Write a statement that opens the file `"oldmast.dat"` for reading and assigns the returned file pointer to `ofPtr`.
   b) Write a statement that opens the file `"trans.dat"` for reading and assigns the returned file pointer to `tfPtr`.
   c) Write a statement that opens the file `"newmast.dat"` for writing (and creation) and assigns the returned file pointer to `nfPtr`.
   d) Write a statement that reads a record from the file `"oldmast.dat"`. The record consists of integer `accountNum`, string `name` and floating-point `currentBalance`.
   e) Write a statement that reads a record from the file `"trans.dat"`. The record consists of the integer `accountNum` and floating-point `dollarAmount`.
   f) Write a statement that writes a record to the file `"newmast.dat"`. The record consists of the integer `accountNum`, string `name` and floating-point `currentBalance`.

11.4   Find the error in each of the following program segments and explain how to correct it.
   a) The file referred to by `fPtr` (`"payables.dat"`) has not been opened.

```
printf(fPtr, "%d%s%d\n", account, company, amount);
```

b) `open("receive.dat", "r+");`
c) The following statement should read a record from the file "`payables.dat`". File pointer `payPtr` refers to this file, and file pointer `recPtr` refers to the file "`receive.dat`":

    `scanf(recPtr, "%d%s%d\n", &account, company, &amount);`

d) The file "`tools.dat`" should be opened to add data to the file without discarding the current data.

    `if ((tfPtr = fopen("tools.dat", "w")) != NULL)`

e) The file "`courses.dat`" should be opened for appending without modifying the current contents of the file.

    `if ((cfPtr = fopen("courses.dat", "w+")) != NULL)`

Answers to Self-Review Exercises

11.1 a) `fclose`. b) `fscanf`. c) `fgetc`. d) `fgets`. e) `fopen`. f) `fread`. g) `fseek`.

11.2 a) False. Function `fscanf` can be used to read from the standard input by including the pointer to the standard input stream, `stdin`, in the call to `fscanf`.
   b) False. These three streams are opened automatically by C when program execution begins.
   c) False. The files will be closed when program execution terminates, but all files should be explicitly closed with `fclose`.
   d) False. Function `rewind` can be used to reposition the file position pointer to the beginning of the file.
   e) True.
   f) False. In most cases, sequential file records are not of uniform length. Therefore, it's possible that updating a record will cause other data to be overwritten.
   g) True.
   h) False. Records in a random-access file are normally of uniform length.
   i) False. It's possible to seek from the beginning of the file, from the end of the file and from the current location in the file.

11.3 a) `ofPtr = fopen("oldmast.dat", "r");`
   b) `tfPtr = fopen("trans.dat", "r");`
   c) `nfPtr = fopen("newmast.dat", "w");`
   d) `fscanf(ofPtr, "%d%s%f", &accountNum, name, &currentBalance);`
   e) `fscanf(tfPtr, "%d%f", &accountNum, &dollarAmount);`
   f) `fprintf(nfPtr, "%d %s %.2f", accountNum, name, currentBalance);`

11.4 a) Error: The file "`payables.dat`" has not been opened before the reference to its file pointer.
      Correction: Use `fopen` to open "`payables.dat`" for writing, appending or updating.
   b) Error: Function `open` is not a Standard C function.
      Correction: Use function `fopen`.
   c) Error: The function `scanf` should be `fscanf`. Function `fscanf` uses the incorrect file pointer to refer to file "`payables.dat`".
      Correction: Use file pointer `payPtr` to refer to "`payables.dat`" and use `fscanf`.
   d) Error: The contents of the file are discarded because the file is opened for writing ("w").
      Correction: To add data to the file, either open the file for updating ("r+") or open the file for appending ("a" or "a+").
   e) Error: File "`courses.dat`" is opened for updating in "w+" mode, which discards the current contents of the file.
      Correction: Open the file in "a" or "a+" mode.

Exercises

11.5 Fill in the blanks in each of the following:
a) Computers store large amounts of data on secondary storage devices as _____.
b) A(n) _____ is composed of several fields.
c) To facilitate the retrieval of specific records from a file, one field in each record is chosen as a(n) _____.
d) A group of related characters that conveys meaning is called a(n) _____.
e) The file pointers for the three streams that are opened automatically when program execution begins are named _____, _____ and _____.
f) Function _____ writes a character to a specified file.
g) Function _____ writes a line to a specified file.
h) Function _____ is generally used to write data to a random-access file.
i) Function _____ repositions the file position pointer to the beginning of the file.

11.6 State which of the following are *true* and which are *false*. If *false*, explain why.
a) The impressive functions performed by computers essentially involve the manipulation of zeros and ones.
b) People prefer to manipulate bits instead of characters and fields because bits are more compact.
c) People specify programs and data items as characters; computers then manipulate and process these characters as groups of zeros and ones.
d) A person's zip code is an example of a numeric field.
e) Data items processed by a computer form a data hierarchy in which data items become larger and more complex as we progress from fields to characters to bits, and so on.
f) A record key identifies a record as belonging to a particular field.
g) Most companies store their information in a single file to facilitate computer processing.
h) Files are always referred to by name in C programs.
i) When a program creates a file, the file is automatically retained by the computer for future reference.

11.7 *(Creating Data for a File-Matching Program)* Write a simple program to create some test data for checking out the program of Exercise 11.8. Use the following sample account data:

Master File: Account number	Name	Balance
100	Alan Jones	348.17
300	Mary Smith	27.19
500	Sam Sharp	0.00
700	Suzy Green	-14.22

Transaction File: Account number	Dollar amount
100	27.14
300	62.11
400	100.56
900	82.17

11.8 *(File Matching)* Exercise 11.3 asked the reader to write a series of single statements. Actually, these statements form the core of an important type of file-processing program, namely, a file-matching program. In commercial data processing, it's common to have several files in each system. In an accounts receivable system, for example, there's generally a master file containing detailed information about each customer such as the customer's name, address, telephone number, outstanding balance, credit limit, discount terms, contract arrangements and possibly a condensed history of recent purchases and cash payments.

As transactions occur (i.e., sales are made and cash payments arrive in the mail), they're entered into a file. At the end of each business period (i.e., a month for some companies, a week for others and a day in some cases) the file of transactions (called "trans.dat" in Exercise 11.3) is applied to the master file (called "oldmast.dat" in Exercise 11.3), thus updating each account's record of purchases and payments. After each of these updates runs, the master file is rewritten as a new file ("newmast.dat"), which is then used at the end of the next business period to begin the updating process again.

File-matching programs must deal with certain problems that do not exist in single-file programs. For example, a match does not always occur. A customer on the master file might not have made any purchases or cash payments in the current business period, and therefore no record for this customer will appear on the transaction file. Similarly, a customer who did make some purchases or cash payments might have just moved to this community, and the company may not have had a chance to create a master record for this customer.

Use the statements written in Exercise 11.3 as the basis for a complete file-matching accounts receivable program. Use the account number on each file as the record key for matching purposes. Assume that each file is a sequential file with records stored in increasing account-number order.

When a match occurs (i.e., records with the same account number appear on both the master file and the transaction file), add the dollar amount on the transaction file to the current balance on the master file and write the "newmast.dat" record. (Assume that purchases are indicated by positive amounts on the transaction file, and that payments are indicated by negative amounts.) When there's a master record for a particular account but no corresponding transaction record, merely write the master record to "newmast.dat". When there's a transaction record but no corresponding master record, print the message "Unmatched transaction record for account number …" (fill in the account number from the transaction record).

11.9 *(Testing the File-Matching Exercises)* Run the program of Exercise 11.8 using the files of test data created in Exercise 11.7. Check the results carefully.

11.10 *(File Matching with Multiple Transactions)* It's possible (actually common) to have several transaction records with the same record key. This occurs because a particular customer might make several purchases and cash payments during a business period. Rewrite your accounts receivable file-matching program of Exercise 11.8 to provide for the possibility of handling several transaction records with the same record key. Modify the test data of Exercise 11.7 to include the following additional transaction records:

Account number	Dollar amount
300	83.89
700	80.78
700	1.53

11.11 *(Write Statements to Accomplish a Task)* Write statements that accomplish each of the following. Assume that the structure

```
struct person {
   char lastName[15];
   char firstName[15];
   char age[4];
};
```

has been defined and that the file is already open for writing.

a) Initialize the file "nameage.dat" so that there are 100 records with lastName = "unas-signed", firstname = "" and age = "0".

b) Input 10 last names, first names and ages, and write them to the file.

c) Update a record; if there's no information in the record, tell the user "No info".

d) Delete a record that has information by reinitializing that particular record.

11.12 *(Hardware Inventory)* You're the owner of a hardware store and need to keep an inventory that can tell you what tools you have, how many you have and the cost of each one. Write a program that initializes the file "hardware.dat" to 100 empty records, lets you input the data concerning each tool, enables you to list all your tools, lets you delete a record for a tool that you no longer have and lets you update *any* information in the file. The tool identification number should be the record number. Use the following information to start your file:

Record #	Tool name	Quantity	Cost
3	Electric sander	7	57.98
17	Hammer	76	11.99
24	Jig saw	21	11.00
39	Lawn mower	3	79.50
56	Power saw	18	99.99
68	Screwdriver	106	6.99
77	Sledge hammer	11	21.50
83	Wrench	34	7.50

11.13 *(Telephone-Number Word Generator)* Standard telephone keypads contain the digits 0–9. The numbers 2–9 each have three letters associated with them, as is indicated by the following table:

Digit	Letter	Digit	Letter
2	A B C	6	M N O
3	D E F	7	P R S
4	G H I	8	T U V
5	J K L	9	W X Y

Many people find it difficult to memorize phone numbers, so they use the correspondence between digits and letters to develop seven-letter words that correspond to their phone numbers. For example, a person whose telephone number is 686-2377 might use the correspondence indicated in the above table to develop the seven-letter word "NUMBERS."

Businesses frequently attempt to get telephone numbers that are easy for their clients to remember. If a business can advertise a simple word for its customers to dial, then, no doubt, the business will receive a few more calls.

Each seven-letter word corresponds to exactly one seven-digit telephone number. The restaurant wishing to increase its take-home business could surely do so with the number 825-3688 (i.e., "TAKEOUT").

Each seven-digit phone number corresponds to many separate seven-letter words. Unfortunately, most of these represent unrecognizable juxtapositions of letters. It's possible, however, that the owner of a barber shop would be pleased to know that the shop's telephone number, 424-7288, corresponds to "HAIRCUT." The owner of a liquor store would, no doubt, be delighted to find that the store's telephone number, 233-7226, corresponds to "BEERCAN." A veterinarian with the phone number 738-2273 would be pleased to know that the number corresponds to the letters "PETCARE."

Write a C program that, given a seven-digit number, writes to a file every possible seven-letter word corresponding to that number. There are 2187 (3 to the seventh power) such words. Avoid phone numbers with the digits 0 and 1.

11.14 *(Project: Telephone-Number Word Generator Modification)* If you have a computerized dictionary available, modify the program you wrote in Exercise 11.13 to look up the words in the dictionary. Some seven-letter combinations created by this program consist of two or more words (e.g., the phone number 843-2677 produces "THEBOSS").

11.15 *(Using File-Processing Functions with Standard Input/Output Streams)* Modify the example of Fig. 8.11 to use functions `fgetc` and `fputs` rather than `getchar` and `puts`. The program should give the user the option to read from the standard input and write to the standard output or to read from a specified file and write to a specified file. If the user chooses the second option, have the user enter the filenames for the input and output files.

11.16 *(Outputting Type Sizes to a File)* Write a program that uses the `sizeof` operator to determine the sizes in bytes of the various data types on your computer system. Write the results to the file "data-size.dat" so you may print the results later. The format for the results in the file should be as follows (the type sizes on your computer might be different from those shown in the sample output):

Data type	Size
char	1
unsigned char	1
short int	2
unsigned short int	2
int	4
unsigned int	4
long int	4
unsigned long int	4
float	4
double	8
long double	16

11.17 *(Simpletron with File Processing)* In Exercise 7.28, you wrote a software simulation of a computer that used a special machine language called Simpletron Machine Language (SML). In the simulation, each time you wanted to run an SML program, you entered the program into the simulator from the keyboard. If you made a mistake while typing the SML program, the simulator was restarted and the SML code was reentered. It would be nice to be able to read the SML program from a file rather than type it each time. This would reduce time and mistakes in preparing to run SML programs.

a) Modify the simulator you wrote in Exercise 7.28 to read SML programs from a file specified by the user at the keyboard.

b) After the Simpletron executes, it outputs the contents of its registers and memory on the screen. It would be nice to capture the output in a file, so modify the simulator to write its output to a file in addition to displaying it on the screen.

11.18 *(Modified Transaction-Processing Program)* Modify the program of Section 11.9 to include an option that displays the list of accounts on the screen. Consider modifying function textFile to use either the standard output or a text file based on an additional function parameter that specifies where the output should be written.

Making a Difference

11.19 *(Project: Phishing Scanner)* Phishing is a form of identity theft in which, in an e-mail, a sender posing as a trustworthy source attempts to acquire private information, such as your user names, passwords, credit-card numbers and social security number. Phishing e-mails claiming to be from popular banks, credit-card companies, auction sites, social networks and online payment services may look quite legitimate. These fraudulent messages often provide links to spoofed (fake) websites where you're asked to enter sensitive information.

Visit http://www.snopes.com and other websites to find lists of the top phishing scams. Also check out the Anti-Phishing Working Group (http://www.antiphishing.org/), and the FBI's Cyber Investigations website (http://www.fbi.gov/about-us/investigate/cyber/cyber), where you'll find information about the latest scams and how to protect yourself.

Create a list of 30 words, phrases and company names commonly found in phishing messages. Assign a point value to each based on your estimate of its likeliness to be in a phishing message (e.g., one point if it's somewhat likely, two points if moderately likely, or three points if highly likely). Write a program that scans a file of text for these terms and phrases. For each occurrence of a keyword or phrase within the text file, add the assigned point value to the total points for that word or phrase. For each keyword or phrase found, output one line with the word or phrase, the number of occurrences and the point total. Then show the point total for the entire message. Does your program assign a high point total to some actual phishing e-mails you've received? Does it assign a high point total to some legitimate e-mails you've received?

C Data Structures

12

Objectives

In this chapter, you'll:

- Allocate and free memory dynamically for data objects.

- Form linked data structures using pointers, self-referential structures and recursion.

- Create and manipulate linked lists, queues, stacks and binary trees.

- Learn important applications of linked data structures.

- Study Secure C programming recommendations for pointers and dynamic memory allocation.

- Optionally build your own compiler in the exercises.

12.1 Introduction

We've studied fixed-size data structures such as one-dimensional arrays, two-dimensional arrays and structs. This chapter introduces **dynamic data structures** that can grow and shrink at execution time.

- **Linked lists** are collections of data items "lined up in a row"—insertions and deletions are made *anywhere* in a linked list.

- **Stacks** are important in compilers and operating systems—insertions and deletions are made *only at one end* of a stack—its **top**.

- **Queues** represent waiting lines; insertions are made *only at the back* (also referred to as the **tail**) of a queue and deletions are made *only from the front* (also referred to as the **head**) of a queue.

- **Binary trees** facilitate high-speed searching and sorting of data, efficiently eliminating duplicate data items and compiling expressions into machine language.

Each of these data structures has many other interesting applications.

We'll discuss each of the major types of data structures and implement programs that create and manipulate them. In the C++ part of the book—which introduces object-oriented programming—we'll study data abstraction. This technique will enable us to build these data structures in a dramatically different manner designed for producing software that's easier to maintain and reuse.

Optional Project: Building Your Own Compiler

We hope that you'll attempt the optional major project described in the special section entitled Building Your Own Compiler. You have been using a compiler to translate your C programs to machine language so that you could execute your programs on your computer. In this project, you'll actually build your own compiler. It will read a file of statements written in a simple, yet powerful, high-level language. Your compiler will translate these statements into a file of Simpletron Machine Language (SML) instructions. SML is the (Deitel-created) language you learned in the Chapter 7 special section, Building Your Own Computer. Your Simpletron Simulator program will then execute the SML program produced by your compiler! This project will give you a wonderful opportunity to exercise most of what you've learned in this book. The special section carefully walks you through the specifications of the high-level language and describes the algorithms you'll need to convert each type of high-level language statement into machine-language instructions. If you enjoy being challenged, you might attempt the many enhancements to both the compiler and the Simpletron Simulator suggested in the exercises.

12.2 Self-Referential Structures

Recall that a *self-referential structure* contains a pointer member that points to a structure of the *same* structure type. For example, the definition

```
struct node {
    int data;
    struct node *nextPtr;
};
```

defines a type, struct node. A structure of type struct node has two members—integer member data and pointer member nextPtr. Member nextPtr points to a structure of type struct node—a structure of the *same* type as the one being declared here, hence the term *self-referential structure*. Member nextPtr is referred to as a link—i.e., it can be used to "tie" (i.e., link) a structure of type struct node to another structure of the same type. Self-referential structures can be *linked* together to form useful data structures such as lists, queues, stacks and trees. Figure 12.1 illustrates two self-referential structure objects linked together to form a list. A slash—representing a NULL pointer—is placed in the link member of the second self-referential structure to indicate that the link does not point to another structure. [*Note:* The slash is only for illustration purposes; it does not correspond to the backslash character in C.] A NULL pointer normally indicates the *end* of a data structure just as the null character indicates the end of a string.

Common Programming Error 12.1
Not setting the link in the last node of a list to NULL can lead to runtime errors.

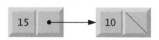

Fig. 12.1 | Self-referential structures linked together.

12.3 Dynamic Memory Allocation

Creating and maintaining dynamic data structures that can grow and shrink as the program runs requires **dynamic memory allocation**—the ability for a program to *obtain more memory space at execution time* to hold new nodes, and to *release space no longer needed*.

Functions **malloc** and **free**, and operator sizeof, are essential to dynamic memory allocation. Function malloc takes as an argument the number of bytes to be allocated and returns a pointer of type void * (pointer to void) to the allocated memory. As you recall, a void * pointer may be assigned to a variable of *any* pointer type. Function malloc is normally used with the sizeof operator. For example, the statement

```
newPtr = malloc(sizeof(struct node));
```

evaluates `sizeof(struct node)` to determine a `struct node` object's size in bytes, *allocates a new area in memory* of that number of bytes and stores a pointer to the allocated memory in `newPtr`. The memory is *not* guaranteed to be initialized, though many implementations initialize it for security. If no memory is available, `malloc` returns `NULL`.

Function `free` *deallocates* memory—i.e., the memory is *returned* to the system so that it can be reallocated in the future. To *free* memory dynamically allocated by the preceding `malloc` call, use the statement

```
free(newPtr);
```

C also provides functions `calloc` and `realloc` for creating and modifying *dynamic arrays*. These functions are discussed in Section 14.9. The sections that follow discuss lists, stacks, queues and trees, each of which is created and maintained with dynamic memory allocation and self-referential structures.

Portability Tip 12.1

A structure's size is not necessarily the sum of the sizes of its members. This is so because of various machine-dependent boundary alignment requirements (see Chapter 10).

Error-Prevention Tip 12.1

When using `malloc`, test for a `NULL` pointer return value, which indicates that the memory was not allocated.

Common Programming Error 12.2

Not freeing dynamically allocated memory when it's no longer needed can cause the system to run out of memory prematurely. This is sometimes called a "memory leak."

Error-Prevention Tip 12.2

When memory that was dynamically allocated is no longer needed, use `free` to return the memory to the system immediately. Then set the pointer to `NULL` to eliminate the possibility that the program could refer to memory that's been reclaimed and which may have already been allocated for another purpose.

Common Programming Error 12.3

Freeing memory not allocated dynamically with `malloc` is an error.

Common Programming Error 12.4

Referring to memory that has been freed is an error that typically results in the program crashing.

12.4 Linked Lists

A **linked list** is a linear collection of self-referential structures, called **nodes**, connected by pointer **links**—hence, the term "linked" list. A linked list is accessed via a pointer to the *first* node of the list. Subsequent nodes are accessed via the *link pointer member* stored in each node. By convention, the link pointer in the last node of a list is set to `NULL` to mark the *end* of the list. Data is stored in a linked list dynamically—each node is created as necessary. A node can contain data of *any* type including other `struct`s. Stacks and queues are also linear data structures, and, as we'll see, are constrained versions of linked lists. Trees are *nonlinear* data structures.

Lists of data can be stored in arrays, but linked lists provide several advantages. A linked list is appropriate when the number of data elements to be represented in the data structure is *unpredictable*. Linked lists are dynamic, so the length of a list can increase or decrease at *execution time* as necessary. The size of an array created at compile time, however, cannot be altered. Arrays can become full. Linked lists become full only when the system has *insufficient memory* to satisfy dynamic storage allocation requests.

 Performance Tip 12.1
An array can be declared to contain more elements than the number of data items expected, but this can waste memory. Linked lists can provide better memory utilization in these situations.

Linked lists can be maintained in sorted order by inserting each new element at the proper point in the list.

 Performance Tip 12.2
Insertion and deletion in a sorted array can be time consuming—all the elements following the inserted or deleted element must be shifted appropriately.

 Performance Tip 12.3
The elements of an array are stored contiguously in memory. This allows immediate access to any array element because the address of any element can be calculated directly based on its position relative to the beginning of the array. Linked lists do not afford such immediate access to their elements.

Linked-list nodes are normally *not* stored contiguously in memory. Logically, however, the nodes of a linked list *appear* to be contiguous. Figure 12.2 illustrates a linked list with several nodes.

 Performance Tip 12.4
Using dynamic memory allocation (instead of arrays) for data structures that grow and shrink at execution time can save memory. Keep in mind, however, that the pointers take up space, and that dynamic memory allocation incurs the overhead of function calls.

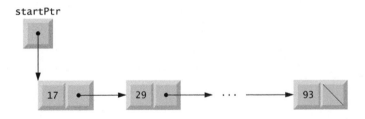

Fig. 12.2 | Linked-list graphical representation.

Figure 12.3 (output shown in Fig. 12.4) manipulates a list of characters. You can insert a character in the list in alphabetical order (function `insert`) or delete a character from the list (function `delete`). A detailed discussion of the program follows.

```c
1   // Fig. 12.3: fig12_03.c
2   // Inserting and deleting nodes in a list
3   #include <stdio.h>
4   #include <stdlib.h>
5
6   // self-referential structure
7   struct listNode {
8      char data; // each listNode contains a character
9      struct listNode *nextPtr; // pointer to next node
10  };
11
12  typedef struct listNode ListNode; // synonym for struct listNode
13  typedef ListNode *ListNodePtr; // synonym for ListNode*
14
15  // prototypes
16  void insert(ListNodePtr *sPtr, char value);
17  char delete(ListNodePtr *sPtr, char value);
18  int isEmpty(ListNodePtr sPtr);
19  void printList(ListNodePtr currentPtr);
20  void instructions(void);
21
22  int main(void)
23  {
24     ListNodePtr startPtr = NULL; // initially there are no nodes
25     char item; // char entered by user
26
27     instructions(); // display the menu
28     printf("%s", "? ");
29     unsigned int choice; // user's choice
30     scanf("%u", &choice);
31
32     // loop while user does not choose 3
33     while (choice != 3) {
34
35        switch (choice) {
36           case 1:
37              printf("%s", "Enter a character: ");
38              scanf("\n%c", &item);
39              insert(&startPtr, item); // insert item in list
40              printList(startPtr);
41              break;
42           case 2: // delete an element
43              // if list is not empty
44              if (!isEmpty(startPtr)) {
45                 printf("%s", "Enter character to be deleted: ");
46                 scanf("\n%c", &item);
47
```

Fig. 12.3 | Inserting and deleting nodes in a list. (Part 1 of 4.)

```
48                    // if character is found, remove it
49                    if (delete(&startPtr, item)) { // remove item
50                        printf("%c deleted.\n", item);
51                        printList(startPtr);
52                    }
53                    else {
54                        printf("%c not found.\n\n", item);
55                    }
56                }
57                else {
58                    puts("List is empty.\n");
59                }
60
61                break;
62            default:
63                puts("Invalid choice.\n");
64                instructions();
65                break;
66        }
67
68        printf("%s", "? ");
69        scanf("%u", &choice);
70    }
71
72    puts("End of run.");
73 }
74
75 // display program instructions to user
76 void instructions(void)
77 {
78    puts("Enter your choice:\n"
79        "   1 to insert an element into the list.\n"
80        "   2 to delete an element from the list.\n"
81        "   3 to end.");
82 }
83
84 // insert a new value into the list in sorted order
85 void insert(ListNodePtr *sPtr, char value)
86 {
87    ListNodePtr newPtr = malloc(sizeof(ListNode)); // create node
88
89    if (newPtr != NULL) { // is space available?
90        newPtr->data = value; // place value in node
91        newPtr->nextPtr = NULL; // node does not link to another node
92
93        ListNodePtr previousPtr = NULL;
94        ListNodePtr currentPtr = *sPtr;
95
96        // loop to find the correct location in the list
97        while (currentPtr != NULL && value > currentPtr->data) {
98            previousPtr = currentPtr; // walk to ...
99            currentPtr = currentPtr->nextPtr; // ... next node
100       }
```

Fig. 12.3 | Inserting and deleting nodes in a list. (Part 2 of 4.)

```
101
102        // insert new node at beginning of list
103        if (previousPtr == NULL) {
104           newPtr->nextPtr = *sPtr;
105           *sPtr = newPtr;
106        }
107        else { // insert new node between previousPtr and currentPtr
108           previousPtr->nextPtr = newPtr;
109           newPtr->nextPtr = currentPtr;
110        }
111     }
112     else {
113        printf("%c not inserted. No memory available.\n", value);
114     }
115  }
116
117  // delete a list element
118  char delete(ListNodePtr *sPtr, char value)
119  {
120     // delete first node if a match is found
121     if (value == (*sPtr)->data) {
122        ListNodePtr tempPtr = *sPtr; // hold onto node being removed
123        *sPtr = (*sPtr)->nextPtr; // de-thread the node
124        free(tempPtr); // free the de-threaded node
125        return value;
126     }
127     else {
128        ListNodePtr previousPtr = *sPtr;
129        ListNodePtr currentPtr = (*sPtr)->nextPtr;
130
131        // loop to find the correct location in the list
132        while (currentPtr != NULL && currentPtr->data != value) {
133           previousPtr = currentPtr; // walk to ..,
134           currentPtr = currentPtr->nextPtr; // ... next node
135        }
136
137        // delete node at currentPtr
138        if (currentPtr != NULL) {
139           ListNodePtr tempPtr = currentPtr;
140           previousPtr->nextPtr = currentPtr->nextPtr;
141           free(tempPtr);
142           return value;
143        }
144     }
145
146     return '\0';
147  }
148
149  // return 1 if the list is empty, 0 otherwise
150  int isEmpty(ListNodePtr sPtr)
151  {
152     return sPtr == NULL;
153  }
```

Fig. 12.3 | Inserting and deleting nodes in a list. (Part 3 of 4.)

```
154
155  // print the list
156  void printList(ListNodePtr currentPtr)
157  {
158     // if list is empty
159     if (isEmpty(currentPtr)) {
160        puts("List is empty.\n");
161     }
162     else {
163        puts("The list is:");
164
165        // while not the end of the list
166        while (currentPtr != NULL) {
167           printf("%c --> ", currentPtr->data);
168           currentPtr = currentPtr->nextPtr;
169        }
170
171        puts("NULL\n");
172     }
173  }
```

Fig. 12.3 | Inserting and deleting nodes in a list. (Part 4 of 4.)

```
Enter your choice:
   1 to insert an element into the list.
   2 to delete an element from the list.
   3 to end.
? 1
Enter a character: B
The list is:
B --> NULL

? 1
Enter a character: A

The list is:
A --> B --> NULL

? 1
Enter a character: C
The list is:
A --> B --> C --> NULL

? 2
Enter character to be deleted: D
D not found.

? 2
Enter character to be deleted: B
B deleted.
The list is:
A --> C --> NULL
```

Fig. 12.4 | Sample output for the program of Fig. 12.3. (Part 1 of 2.)

```
? 2
Enter character to be deleted: C
C deleted.
The list is:
A --> NULL

? 2
Enter character to be deleted: A
A deleted.
List is empty.

? 4
Invalid choice.

Enter your choice:
   1 to insert an element into the list.
   2 to delete an element from the list.
   3 to end.
? 3
End of run.
```

Fig. 12.4 | Sample output for the program of Fig. 12.3. (Part 2 of 2.)

The primary functions of linked lists are insert (lines 85–115) and delete (lines 118–147). Function isEmpty (lines 150–153) is called a **predicate function**—it does *not* alter the list in any way; rather it determines whether the list is empty (i.e., the pointer to the first node of the list is NULL). If the list is empty, 1 is returned; otherwise, 0 is returned. [*Note:* If you're using a compiler that's compliant with the C99 standard, you can use the _Bool type (Section 4.10) rather than int.] Function printList (lines 156–173) prints the list.

12.4.1 Function insert

Characters are inserted in the list in *alphabetical order*. Function insert (lines 85–115) receives the address of the list and a character to be inserted. The list's address is necessary when a value is to be inserted at the *start* of the list. Providing the address enables the list (i.e., the pointer to the first node of the list) to be *modified* via a call by reference. Because the list itself is a pointer (to its first element), passing its address creates a **pointer to a pointer** (i.e., **double indirection**). This is a complex notion and requires careful programming. The steps for inserting a character in the list are as follows (see Fig. 12.5):

1. *Create a node* by calling malloc, assigning to newPtr the address of the allocated memory (line 87), assigning the character to be inserted to newPtr->data (line 90), and assigning NULL to newPtr->nextPtr (line 91).

2. Initialize previousPtr to NULL (line 93) and currentPtr to *sPtr (line 94)—the pointer to the start of the list. Pointers previousPtr and currentPtr store the locations of the node *preceding* and *after* the insertion point, respectively.

3. While currentPtr is not NULL and the value to be inserted is greater than currentPtr->data (line 97), assign currentPtr to previousPtr (line 98) and advance currentPtr to the next node in the list (line 99). This locates the *insertion point* for the value.

4. If previousPtr is NULL (line 103), insert the new node as the *first* in the list (lines 104–105). Assign *sPtr to newPtr->nextPtr (the *new node link* points to the *for-*

mer first node) and assign newPtr to *sPtr (*sPtr points to the *new node*). Otherwise, if previousPtr is not NULL, insert the new node in place (lines 108–109). Assign newPtr to previousPtr->nextPtr (the *previous* node points to the *new* node) and assign currentPtr to newPtr->nextPtr (the *new* node link points to the *current* node).

Error-Prevention Tip 12.3

Assign NULL to a new node's link member. Pointers should be initialized before they're used.

Figure 12.5 illustrates the insertion of a node containing the character 'C' into an ordered list. Part (a) of the figure shows the list and the new node just before the insertion. Part (b) of the figure shows the result of inserting the new node. The reassigned pointers are dotted arrows. For simplicity, we implemented function insert (and other similar functions in this chapter) with a void return type. It's possible that function malloc will *fail* to allocate the requested memory. In this case, it would be better for our insert function to return a status that indicates whether the operation was successful.

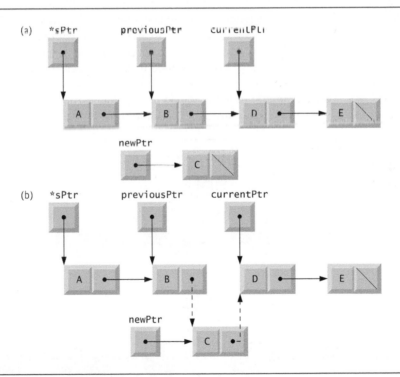

Fig. 12.5 | Inserting a node in order in a list.

12.4.2 Function delete

Function delete (lines 118–147) receives the address of the pointer to the start of the list and a character to be deleted. The steps for deleting a character from the list are as follows (see Fig. 12.6):

1. If the character to be deleted matches the character in the *first* node of the list (line 121), assign *sPtr to tempPtr (tempPtr will be used to free the unneeded memory), assign (*sPtr)->nextPtr to *sPtr (*sPtr now points to the *second* node in the list), free the memory pointed to by tempPtr, and return the character that was deleted.

2. Otherwise, initialize previousPtr with *sPtr and initialize currentPtr with (*sPtr)->nextPtr (lines 128–129) to advance to the second node.

3. While currentPtr is not NULL and the value to be deleted is not equal to currentPtr->data (line 132), assign currentPtr to previousPtr (line 133) and assign currentPtr->nextPtr to currentPtr (line 134). This locates the character to be deleted if it's contained in the list.

4. If currentPtr is not NULL (line 138), assign currentPtr to tempPtr (line 139), assign currentPtr->nextPtr to previousPtr->nextPtr (line 140), *free* the node pointed to by tempPtr (line 141), and return the character that was deleted from the list (line 142). If currentPtr is NULL, return the null character ('\0') to signify that the character to be deleted was *not* found in the list (line 146).

Figure 12.6 illustrates the deletion of the node containing the character 'C' from a linked list. Part (a) of the figure shows the linked list after the preceding insert operation. Part (b) shows the reassignment of the link element of previousPtr and the assignment of currentPtr to tempPtr. Pointer tempPtr is used to *free* the memory allocated to the node that stores 'C'. Note that in lines 124 and 141 we free tempPtr. Recall that we recommended setting a freed pointer to NULL. We do not do that in these two cases, because tempPtr is a local automatic variable and the function returns immediately.

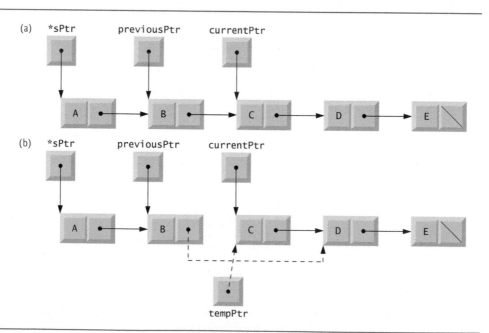

Fig. 12.6 | Deleting a node from a list.

12.4.3 Function `printList`

Function `printList` (lines 156–173) receives a pointer to the start of the list as an argument and refers to the pointer as `currentPtr`. The function first determines whether the list is *empty* (lines 159–161) and, if so, prints "`List is empty.`" and terminates. Otherwise, it prints the data in the list (lines 162–172). While `currentPtr` is not `NULL`, the value of `currentPtr->data` is printed by the function, and `currentPtr->nextPtr` is assigned to `currentPtr` to advance to the next node. If the link in the last node of the list is not `NULL`, the printing algorithm will try to print *past the end of the list*, and an error will occur. The printing algorithm is identical for linked lists, stacks and queues.

Exercise 12.20 asks you to implement a recursive function that prints a list backward. Exercise 12.21 asks the reader to implement a recursive function that searches a linked list for a particular data item.

12.5 Stacks

A **stack** can be implemented as a constrained version of a linked list. New nodes can be added to a stack and removed from a stack *only* at the *top*. For this reason, a stack is referred to as a **last-in, first-out (LIFO)** data structure. A stack is referenced via a pointer to the top element of the stack. The link member in the last node of the stack is set to `NULL` to indicate the bottom of the stack.

Figure 12.7 illustrates a stack with several nodes—`stackPtr` points to the stack's top element. We represent stacks and linked lists in these figures identically. The difference between stacks and linked lists is that insertions and deletions may occur *anywhere* in a linked list, but *only* at the *top* of a stack.

Common Programming Error 12.5
Not setting the link in the bottom node of a stack to `NULL` can lead to runtime errors.

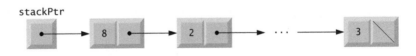

Fig. 12.7 | Stack graphical representation.

Primary Stack Operations
The primary functions used to manipulate a stack are push and pop. Function push creates a new node and places it on *top* of the stack. Function pop *removes* a node from the *top* of the stack, *frees* the memory that was allocated to the popped node and *returns the popped value.*

Implementing a Stack
Figure 12.8 (output shown in Fig. 12.9) implements a simple stack of integers. The program provides three options: 1) push a value onto the stack (function push), 2) pop a value off the stack (function pop) and 3) terminate the program.

```
1   // Fig. 12.8: fig12_08.c
2   // A simple stack program
3   #include <stdio.h>
4   #include <stdlib.h>
5
6   // self-referential structure
7   struct stackNode {
8      int data; // define data as an int
9      struct stackNode *nextPtr; // stackNode pointer
10  };
11
12  typedef struct stackNode StackNode; // synonym for struct stackNode
13  typedef StackNode *StackNodePtr; // synonym for StackNode*
14
15  // prototypes
16  void push(StackNodePtr *topPtr, int info);
17  int pop(StackNodePtr *topPtr);
18  int isEmpty(StackNodePtr topPtr);
19  void printStack(StackNodePtr currentPtr);
20  void instructions(void);
21
22  // function main begins program execution
23  int main(void)
24  {
25     StackNodePtr stackPtr = NULL; // points to stack top
26     int value; // int input by user
27
28     instructions(); // display the menu
29     printf("%s", "? ");
30     unsigned int choice; // user's menu choice
31     scanf("%u", &choice);
32
33     // while user does not enter 3
34     while (choice != 3) {
35
36        switch (choice) {
37           // push value onto stack
38           case 1:
39              printf("%s", "Enter an integer: ");
40              scanf("%d", &value);
41              push(&stackPtr, value);
42              printStack(stackPtr);
43              break;
44           // pop value off stack
45           case 2:
46              // if stack is not empty
47              if (!isEmpty(stackPtr)) {
48                 printf("The popped value is %d.\n", pop(&stackPtr));
49              }
50
51              printStack(stackPtr);
52              break;
```

Fig. 12.8 | A simple stack program. (Part 1 of 3.)

```
53              default:
54                  puts("Invalid choice.\n");
55                  instructions();
56                  break;
57          }
58
59          printf("%s", "? ");
60          scanf("%u", &choice);
61      }
62
63      puts("End of run.");
64  }
65
66  // display program instructions to user
67  void instructions(void)
68  {
69      puts("Enter choice:\n"
70          "1 to push a value on the stack\n"
71          "2 to pop a value off the stack\n"
72          "3 to end program");
73  }
74
75  // insert a node at the stack top
76  void push(StackNodePtr *topPtr, int info)
77  {
78      StackNodePtr newPtr = malloc(sizeof(StackNode));
79
80      // insert the node at stack top
81      if (newPtr != NULL) {
82          newPtr->data = info;
83          newPtr->nextPtr = *topPtr;
84          *topPtr = newPtr;
85      }
86      else { // no space available
87          printf("%d not inserted. No memory available.\n", info);
88      }
89  }
90
91  // remove a node from the stack top
92  int pop(StackNodePtr *topPtr)
93  {
94      StackNodePtr tempPtr = *topPtr;
95      int popValue = (*topPtr)->data;
96      *topPtr = (*topPtr)->nextPtr;
97      free(tempPtr);
98      return popValue;
99  }
100
101 // print the stack
102 void printStack(StackNodePtr currentPtr)
103 {
```

Fig. 12.8 | A simple stack program. (Part 2 of 3.)

```
104     // if stack is empty
105     if (currentPtr == NULL) {
106        puts("The stack is empty.\n");
107     }
108     else {
109        puts("The stack is:");
110
111        // while not the end of the stack
112        while (currentPtr != NULL) {
113           printf("%d --> ", currentPtr->data);
114           currentPtr = currentPtr->nextPtr;
115        }
116
117        puts("NULL\n");
118     }
119  }
120
121  // return 1 if the stack is empty, 0 otherwise
122  int isEmpty(StackNodePtr topPtr)
123  {
124     return topPtr == NULL;
125  }
```

Fig. 12.8 | A simple stack program. (Part 3 of 3.)

```
Enter choice:
1 to push a value on the stack
2 to pop a value off the stack
3 to end program
? 1
Enter an integer: 5
The stack is:
5 --> NULL

? 1
Enter an integer: 6
The stack is:
6 --> 5 --> NULL

? 1
Enter an integer: 4
The stack is:
4 --> 6 --> 5 --> NULL

? 2
The popped value is 4.
The stack is:
6 --> 5 --> NULL

? 2
The popped value is 6.
The stack is:
5 --> NULL
```

Fig. 12.9 | Sample output from the program of Fig. 12.8. (Part 1 of 2.)

```
? 2
The popped value is 5.
The stack is empty.

? 2
The stack is empty.

? 4
Invalid choice.

Enter choice:
1 to push a value on the stack
2 to pop a value off the stack
3 to end program
? 3
End of run.
```

Fig. 12.9 | Sample output from the program of Fig. 12.8. (Part 2 of 2.)

12.5.1 Function push

Function push (lines 76–89) places a new node at the top of the stack. The function consists of three steps:

1. Create a *new node* by calling malloc and assign the location of the allocated memory to newPtr (line 78).

2. Assign to newPtr->data the value to be placed on the stack (line 82) and assign *topPtr (the *stack top pointer*) to newPtr->nextPtr (line 83)—the *link member* of newPtr now points to the *previous* top node.

3. Assign newPtr to *topPtr (line 84)—*topPtr now points to the *new* stack top.

Manipulations involving *topPtr change the value of stackPtr in main. Figure 12.10 illustrates function push. Part (a) of the figure shows the stack and the new node *before* the

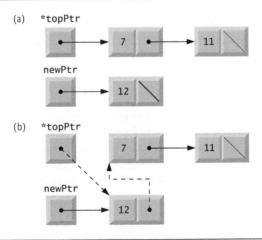

Fig. 12.10 | push operation.

push operation. The dotted arrows in part (b) illustrate *Steps 2* and *3* of the push operation that enable the node containing 12 to become the new stack top.

12.5.2 Function pop

Function pop (lines 92–99) removes the node at the top of the stack. Function main determines whether the stack is empty before calling pop. The pop operation consists of five steps:

1. Assign *topPtr to tempPtr (line 94); tempPtr will be used to *free* the unneeded memory.

2. Assign (*topPtr)->data to popValue (line 95) to *save* the value in the top node.

3. Assign (*topPtr)->nextPtr to *topPtr (line 96) so *topPtr contains *address of the new top node*.

4. *Free the memory* pointed to by tempPtr (line 97).

5. *Return popValue* to the caller (line 98).

Figure 12.11 illustrates function pop. Part (a) shows the stack *after* the previous push operation. Part (b) shows tempPtr pointing to the *first node* of the stack and topPtr pointing to the *second node* of the stack. Function **free** is used to *free the memory* pointed to by tempPtr.

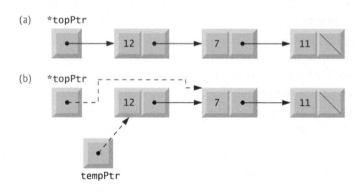

Fig. 12.11 | pop operation.

12.5.3 Applications of Stacks

Stacks have many interesting applications. For example, whenever a *function call* is made, the called function must know how to *return* to its caller, so the *return address* is pushed onto a stack (Section 5.7). In a series of function calls, the successive return addresses are pushed onto the stack in *last-in, first-out order* so that each function can return to its caller. Stacks support recursive function calls in the same manner as conventional nonrecursive calls.

Stacks contain the space created for *automatic variables* on each invocation of a function. When the function returns to its caller, the space for that function's automatic variables is popped off the stack, and these variables no longer are known to the program. Stacks also are sometimes used by compilers in the process of evaluating expressions and generating machine-language code. The exercises explore several applications of stacks.

12.6 Queues

Another common data structure is the **queue**. A queue is similar to a checkout line in a grocery store—the *first* person in line is *serviced first,* and other customers enter the line only at the *end* and *wait* to be serviced. Queue nodes are removed *only* from the **head of the queue** and are inserted *only* at the **tail of the queue.** For this reason, a queue is referred to as a **first-in, first-out (FIFO)** data structure. The *insert* and *remove* operations are known as enqueue (pronounced "en-cue") and dequeue (pronounced "dee-cue"), respectively.

Queues have many applications in computer systems. For computers that have only a single processor, only one user at a time may be serviced. Entries for the other users are placed in a queue. Each entry gradually advances to the front of the queue as users receive service. The entry at the *front* of the queue is the *next to receive service*. Similarly, for today's multicore systems, there could be more users than there are processors, so the users not currently running are placed in a queue until a currently busy processor becomes available. In Appendix E, we discuss multithreading. When a user's work is divided into multiple threads capable of executing in parallel, there could be more threads than there are processors, so the threads not currently running need to be waiting in a queue.

Queues are also used to support *print spooling*. A multiuser environment may have only a single printer. Many users may be generating outputs to be printed. If the printer is busy, other outputs may still be generated. These are *spooled* (just as sewing thread is wrapped around a spool until it's needed) to disk where they *wait* in a *queue* until the printer becomes available.

Information packets also wait in queues in computer networks. Each time a packet arrives at a network node, it must be routed to the next node on the network along the path to its final destination. The routing node routes one packet at a time, so additional packets are enqueued until the router can route them. Figure 12.12 illustrates a queue with several nodes. Note the pointers to the head of the queue and the tail of the queue.

Common Programming Error 12.6
Not setting the link in the last node of a queue to NULL can lead to runtime errors.

Figure 12.13 (output in Fig. 12.14) performs queue manipulations. The program provides several options: *insert* a node in the queue (function **enqueue**), *remove* a node from the queue (function **dequeue**) and terminate the program.

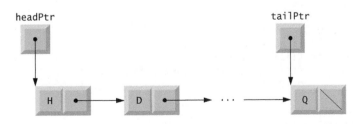

Fig. 12.12 | Queue graphical representation.

```
 1   // Fig. 12.13: fig12_13.c
 2   // Operating and maintaining a queue
 3   #include <stdio.h>
 4   #include <stdlib.h>
 5
 6   // self-referential structure
 7   struct queueNode {
 8      char data; // define data as a char
 9      struct queueNode *nextPtr; // queueNode pointer
10   };
11
12   typedef struct queueNode QueueNode;
13   typedef QueueNode *QueueNodePtr;
14
15   // function prototypes
16   void printQueue(QueueNodePtr currentPtr);
17   int isEmpty(QueueNodePtr headPtr);
18   char dequeue(QueueNodePtr *headPtr, QueueNodePtr *tailPtr);
19   void enqueue(QueueNodePtr *headPtr, QueueNodePtr *tailPtr, char value);
20   void instructions(void);
21
22   // function main begins program execution
23   int main(void)
24   {
25      QueueNodePtr headPtr = NULL; // initialize headPtr
26      QueueNodePtr tailPtr = NULL; // initialize tailPtr
27      char item; // char input by user
28
29      instructions(); // display the menu
30      printf("%s", "? ");
31      unsigned int choice; // user's menu choice
32      scanf("%u", &choice);
33
34      // while user does not enter 3
35      while (choice != 3) {
36
37         switch(choice) {
38            // enqueue value
39            case 1:
40               printf("%s", "Enter a character: ");
41               scanf("\n%c", &item);
42               enqueue(&headPtr, &tailPtr, item);
43               printQueue(headPtr);
44               break;
45            // dequeue value
46            case 2:
47               // if queue is not empty
48               if (!isEmpty(headPtr)) {
49                  item = dequeue(&headPtr, &tailPtr);
50                  printf("%c has been dequeued.\n", item);
51               }
```

Fig. 12.13 | Operating and maintaining a queue. (Part 1 of 3.)

```
52
53                    printQueue(headPtr);
54                    break;
55                default:
56                    puts("Invalid choice.\n");
57                    instructions();
58                    break;
59          }
60
61          printf("%s", "? ");
62          scanf("%u", &choice);
63      }
64
65      puts("End of run.");
66  }
67
68  // display program instructions to user
69  void instructions(void)
70  {
71      printf ("Enter your choice:\n"
72              "   1 to add an item to the queue\n"
73              "   2 to remove an item from the queue\n"
74              "   3 to end\n");
75  }
76
77  // insert a node at queue tail
78  void enqueue(QueueNodePtr *headPtr, QueueNodePtr *tailPtr, char value)
79  {
80      QueueNodePtr newPtr = malloc(sizeof(QueueNode));
81
82      if (newPtr != NULL) { // is space available?
83          newPtr->data = value;
84          newPtr->nextPtr = NULL;
85
86          // if empty, insert node at head
87          if (isEmpty(*headPtr)) {
88              *headPtr = newPtr;
89          }
90          else {
91              (*tailPtr)->nextPtr = newPtr;
92          }
93
94          *tailPtr = newPtr;
95      }
96      else {
97          printf("%c not inserted. No memory available.\n", value);
98      }
99  }
100
101 // remove node from queue head
102 char dequeue(QueueNodePtr *headPtr, QueueNodePtr *tailPtr)
103 {
```

Fig. 12.13 | Operating and maintaining a queue. (Part 2 of 3.)

```
104        char value = (*headPtr)->data;
105        QueueNodePtr tempPtr = *headPtr;
106        *headPtr = (*headPtr)->nextPtr;
107
108        // if queue is empty
109        if (*headPtr == NULL) {
110            *tailPtr = NULL;
111        }
112
113        free(tempPtr);
114        return value;
115    }
116
117    // return 1 if the queue is empty, 0 otherwise
118    int isEmpty(QueueNodePtr headPtr)
119    {
120        return headPtr == NULL;
121    }
122
123    // print the queue
124    void printQueue(QueueNodePtr currentPtr)
125    {
126        // if queue is empty
127        if (currentPtr == NULL) {
128            puts("Queue is empty.\n");
129        }
130        else {
131            puts("The queue is:");
132
133            // while not end of queue
134            while (currentPtr != NULL) {
135                printf("%c --> ", currentPtr->data);
136                currentPtr = currentPtr->nextPtr;
137            }
138
139            puts("NULL\n");
140        }
141    }
```

Fig. 12.13 | Operating and maintaining a queue. (Part 3 of 3.)

```
Enter your choice:
   1 to add an item to the queue
   2 to remove an item from the queue
   3 to end

? 1
Enter a character: A
The queue is:
A --> NULL
```

Fig. 12.14 | Sample output from the program in Fig. 12.13. (Part 1 of 2.)

```
? 1
Enter a character: B
The queue is:
A --> B --> NULL

? 1
Enter a character: C
The queue is:
A --> B --> C --> NULL

? 2
A has been dequeued.
The queue is:
B --> C --> NULL

? 2
B has been dequeued.
The queue is:
C --> NULL

? 2
C has been dequeued.
Queue is empty.

? 2
Queue is empty.

? 4
Invalid choice.

Enter your choice:
    1 to add an item to the queue
    2 to remove an item from the queue
    3 to end
? 3
End of run.
```

Fig. 12.14 | Sample output from the program in Fig. 12.13. (Part 2 of 2.)

12.6.1 Function enqueue

Function enqueue (lines 78–99) receives three arguments from main: the *address* of the *pointer to the head of the queue*, the *address* of the *pointer to the tail of the queue* and the *value* to be inserted in the queue. The function consists of three steps:

1. To create a new node: Call malloc, assign the allocated memory location to newPtr (line 80), assign the value to be inserted in the queue to newPtr->data (line 83) and assign NULL to newPtr->nextPtr (line 84).

2. If the queue is empty (line 87), assign newPtr to *headPtr (line 88), because the new node will be both the head and tail of the queue; otherwise, assign pointer newPtr to (*tailPtr)->nextPtr (line 91), because the new node will be placed after the previous tail node.

3. Assign newPtr to *tailPtr (line 94), because the new node is the queue's tail.

Figure 12.15 illustrates an enqueue operation. Part (a) shows the queue and the new node *before* the operation. The dotted arrows in part (b) illustrate *Steps 2* and *3* of function enqueue that enable a new node to be added to the *end* of a queue that's not empty.

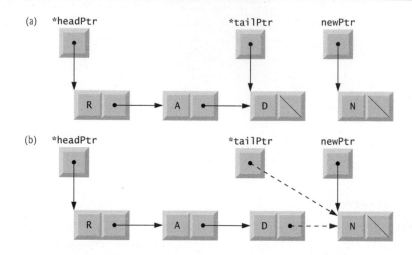

Fig. 12.15 | enqueue operation.

12.6.2 Function dequeue

Function dequeue (lines 102–115; illustrated in Fig. 12.16) receives the *address* of the *pointer to the head of the queue* and the *address* of the *pointer to the tail of the queue* as arguments and removes the *first* node from the queue. The dequeue operation consists of six steps:

1. Assign (*headPtr)->data to value to save the data (line 104).

2. Assign *headPtr to tempPtr (line 105), which will be used to free the unneeded memory.

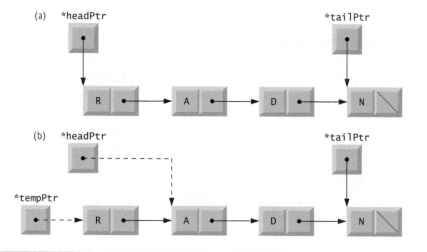

Fig. 12.16 | dequeue operation.

3. Assign (*headPtr)->nextPtr to *headPtr (line 106) so that *headPtr now points to the new first node in the queue.

4. If *headPtr is NULL (line 109), assign NULL to *tailPtr (line 110) because the queue is now empty.

5. Free the memory pointed to by tempPtr (line 113).

6. Return value to the caller (line 114).

Figure 12.16 illustrates function dequeue. Figure 12.16(a) shows the queue *after* the preceding enqueue operation. Part (b) shows tempPtr pointing to the *dequeued node*, and headPtr pointing to the *new first node* of the queue. Function free is used to *reclaim the memory* pointed to by tempPtr.

12.7 Trees

Linked lists, stacks and queues are **linear data structures**. A tree is a *nonlinear, two-dimensional data structure* with special properties. Tree nodes contain *two or more* links. This section discusses **binary trees** (Fig. 12.17)—trees whose nodes all contain *two* links (none, one, or both of which may be NULL). The root node is the *first* node in a tree. Each link in the root node refers to a **child**. The **left child** is the *first* node in the **left subtree**, and the **right child** is the *first* node in the **right subtree**. The children of a node are called **siblings**. A node with *no* children is called a **leaf node**. Computer scientists normally draw trees with the root node at the top—exactly the *opposite* of trees in nature.

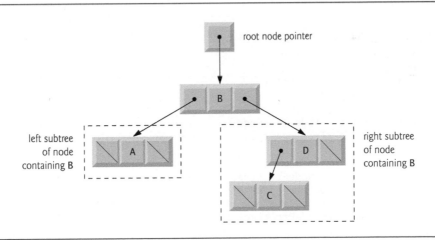

Fig. 12.17 | Binary tree graphical representation.

In this section, a special binary tree called a **binary search tree** is created. A binary search tree (with no duplicate node values) has the characteristic that the values in any *left* subtree are less than the value in its **parent node**, and the values in any *right* subtree are greater than the value in its parent node. Figure 12.18 illustrates a binary search tree with nine values. The shape of the binary search tree that corresponds to a set of data can *vary*, depending on the *order* in which the values are *inserted* into the tree.

Common Programming Error 12.7

Not setting to NULL the links in leaf nodes of a tree can lead to runtime errors.

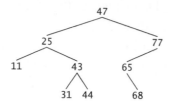

Fig. 12.18 | Binary search tree.

Figure 12.19 (output shown in Fig. 12.20) creates a binary search tree and *traverses* it three ways—**inorder**, **preorder** and **postorder**. The program generates 10 random numbers and inserts each in the tree, except that *duplicate* values are *discarded*.

```c
// Fig. 12.19: fig12_19.c
// Creating and traversing a binary tree
// preorder, inorder, and postorder
#include <stdio.h>
#include <stdlib.h>
#include <time.h>

// self-referential structure
struct treeNode {
   struct treeNode *leftPtr; // pointer to left subtree
   int data; // node value
   struct treeNode *rightPtr; // pointer to right subtree
};

typedef struct treeNode TreeNode; // synonym for struct treeNode
typedef TreeNode *TreeNodePtr; // synonym for TreeNode*

// prototypes
void insertNode(TreeNodePtr *treePtr, int value);
void inOrder(TreeNodePtr treePtr);
void preOrder(TreeNodePtr treePtr);
void postOrder(TreeNodePtr treePtr);

// function main begins program execution
int main(void)
{
   TreeNodePtr rootPtr = NULL; // tree initially empty

   srand(time(NULL));
   puts("The numbers being placed in the tree are:");

```

Fig. 12.19 | Creating and traversing a binary tree. (Part 1 of 3.)

```
32       // insert random values between 0 and 14 in the tree
33       for (unsigned int i = 1; i <= 10; ++i) {
34          int item = rand() % 15;
35          printf("%3d", item);
36          insertNode(&rootPtr, item);
37       }
38
39       // traverse the tree preOrder
40       puts("\n\nThe preOrder traversal is:");
41       preOrder(rootPtr);
42
43       // traverse the tree inOrder
44       puts("\n\nThe inOrder traversal is:");
45       inOrder(rootPtr);
46
47       // traverse the tree postOrder
48       puts("\n\nThe postOrder traversal is:");
49       postOrder(rootPtr);
50    }
51
52    // insert node into tree
53    void insertNode(TreeNodePtr *treePtr, int value)
54    {
55       // if tree is empty
56       if (*treePtr == NULL) {
57          *treePtr = malloc(sizeof(TreeNode));
58
59          // if memory was allocated, then assign data
60          if (*treePtr != NULL) {
61             (*treePtr)->data = value;
62             (*treePtr)->leftPtr = NULL;
63             (*treePtr)->rightPtr = NULL;
64          }
65          else {
66             printf("%d not inserted. No memory available.\n", value);
67          }
68       }
69       else { // tree is not empty
70          // data to insert is less than data in current node
71          if (value < (*treePtr)->data) {
72             insertNode(&((*treePtr)->leftPtr), value);
73          }
74
75          // data to insert is greater than data in current node
76          else if (value > (*treePtr)->data) {
77             insertNode(&((*treePtr)->rightPtr), value);
78          }
79          else { // duplicate data value ignored
80             printf("%s", "dup");
81          }
82       }
83    }
84
```

Fig. 12.19 | Creating and traversing a binary tree. (Part 2 of 3.)

```
85   // begin inorder traversal of tree
86   void inOrder(TreeNodePtr treePtr)
87   {
88      // if tree is not empty, then traverse
89      if (treePtr != NULL) {
90         inOrder(treePtr->leftPtr);
91         printf("%3d", treePtr->data);
92         inOrder(treePtr->rightPtr);
93      }
94   }
95
96   // begin preorder traversal of tree
97   void preOrder(TreeNodePtr treePtr)
98   {
99      // if tree is not empty, then traverse
100     if (treePtr != NULL) {
101        printf("%3d", treePtr->data);
102        preOrder(treePtr->leftPtr);
103        preOrder(treePtr->rightPtr);
104     }
105  }
106
107  // begin postorder traversal of tree
108  void postOrder(TreeNodePtr treePtr)
109  {
110     // if tree is not empty, then traverse
111     if (treePtr != NULL) {
112        postOrder(treePtr->leftPtr);
113        postOrder(treePtr->rightPtr);
114        printf("%3d", treePtr->data);
115     }
116  }
```

Fig. 12.19 | Creating and traversing a binary tree. (Part 3 of 3.)

```
The numbers being placed in the tree are:
  6   7   4  12   7dup   2   2dup   5   7dup  11

The preOrder traversal is:
  6   4   2   5   7  12  11

The inOrder traversal is:
  2   4   5   6   7  11  12

The postOrder traversal is:
  2   5   4  11  12   7   6
```

Fig. 12.20 | Sample output from the program of Fig. 12.19.

12.7.1 Function insertNode

The functions used in Fig. 12.19 to create a binary search tree and traverse it are *recursive*. Function insertNode (lines 53–83) receives the *address of the tree* and an integer to be stored in the tree as arguments. A node can be inserted only as a *leaf node* in a binary search tree. The steps for inserting a node in a binary search tree are as follows:

1. If *treePtr is NULL (line 56), create a new node (line 57). Call malloc, assign the *allocated memory* to *treePtr, assign to (*treePtr)->data the *integer to be stored* (line 61), assign to (*treePtr)->leftPtr and (*treePtr)->rightPtr the value NULL (lines 62–63, and return control to the caller (either main or a previous call to insertNode).

2. If the value of *treePtr is not NULL and the value to be inserted is *less than* (*treePtr)->data, function insertNode is called with the address of (*treePtr)->leftPtr (line 72) to insert the node in the *left* subtree of the node pointed to by treePtr. If the value to be inserted is *greater than* (*treePtr)-> data, function insertNode is called with the address of (*treePtr)->rightPtr (line 77) to insert the node in the *right* subtree of the node pointed to by treePtr.

The *recursive steps* continue until a NULL pointer is found, then *Step 1* inserts the new node.

12.7.2 Traversals: Functions inOrder, preOrder and postOrder

Functions inOrder (lines 86–94), preOrder (lines 97–105) and postOrder (lines 108–116) each receive a *tree* (i.e., the *pointer to the root node of the tree*) and *traverse* the tree.

The steps for an inOrder traversal are:

1. Traverse the *left* subtree inOrder.

2. Process the value in the node.

3. Traverse the *right* subtree inOrder.

The value in a node is not processed until the values in its *left* subtree are processed. The inOrder traversal of the tree in Fig. 12.21 is:

    6 13 17 27 33 42 48

The inOrder traversal of a binary search tree prints the node values in *ascending* order. The process of creating a binary search tree actually sorts the data—and thus this process is called the **binary tree sort**.

The steps for a preOrder traversal are:

1. Process the value in the node.

2. Traverse the *left* subtree preOrder.

3. Traverse the *right* subtree preOrder.

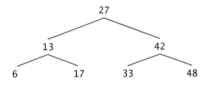

Fig. 12.21 | Binary search tree with seven nodes.

The value in each node is processed as the node is visited. After the value in a given node is processed, the values in the *left* subtree are processed, then those in the *right* subtree are processed. The preOrder traversal of the tree in Fig. 12.21 is:

```
27 13 6 17 42 33 48
```

The steps for a postOrder traversal are:

1. Traverse the *left* subtree postOrder.
2. Traverse the *right* subtree postOrder.
3. Process the value in the node.

The value in each node is not printed until the values of its children are printed. The postOrder traversal of the tree in Fig. 12.21 is:

```
6 17 13 33 48 42 27
```

12.7.3 Duplicate Elimination

The binary search tree facilitates **duplicate elimination**. As the tree is being created, an attempt to insert a duplicate value will be recognized because a duplicate will follow the *same* "go left" or "go right" decisions on each comparison as the original value did. Thus, the duplicate will eventually be compared with a node in the tree containing the *same* value. The duplicate value may simply be discarded at this point.

12.7.4 Binary Tree Search

Searching a binary tree for a value that matches a key value is also fast. If the tree is tightly packed, each level contains about *twice* as many elements as the previous level. So a binary search tree with n elements would have a maximum of $\log_2 n$ levels, and thus a *maximum* of $\log_2 n$ comparisons would have to be made either to find a match or to determine that no match exists. This means, for example, that when searching a (tightly packed) 1,000-element binary search tree, no more than 10 comparisons need to be made because $2^{10} > 1,000$. When searching a (tightly packed) 1,000,000-element binary search tree, no more than 20 comparisons need to be made because $2^{20} > 1,000,000$.

12.7.5 Other Binary Tree Operations

In the exercises, algorithms are presented for several other binary tree operations such as *printing* a binary tree in a two-dimensional tree format and performing a *level order traversal* of a binary tree. The level order traversal visits the nodes of the tree *row-by-row* starting at the root node level. On each level of the tree, the nodes are visited from left to right. Other binary tree exercises include allowing a binary search tree to contain duplicate values, inserting string values in a binary tree and determining how many levels are contained in a binary tree.

12.8 Secure C Programming

Chapter 8 of the *CERT Secure C Coding Standard* is dedicated to memory-management recommendations and rules—many apply to the uses of pointers and dynamic memory allocation presented in this chapter. For more information, visit www.securecoding.cert.org.

- MEM01-C/MEM30-C: Pointers should not be left uninitialized. Rather, they should be assigned either NULL or the address of a valid item in memory. When you use free to deallocate dynamically allocated memory, the pointer passed to free is *not* assigned a new value, so it still points to the memory location where the dynamically allocated memory *used* to be. Using such a "dangling" pointer can lead to program crashes and security vulnerabilities. When you free dynamically allocated memory, you should immediately assign the pointer either NULL or a valid address. We chose not to do this for local pointer variables that immediately go out of scope after a call to free.

- MEM01-C: Undefined behavior occurs when you attempt to use free to deallocate dynamic memory that was already deallocated—this is known as a "double free vulnerability." To ensure that you don't attempt to deallocate the same memory more than once, immediately set a pointer to NULL after the call to free—attempting to free a NULL pointer has no effect.

- ERR33-C: Most standard library functions return values that enable you to determine whether the functions performed their tasks correctly. Function malloc, for example, returns NULL if it's unable to allocate the requested memory. You should *always* ensure that malloc did not return NULL *before* attempting to use the pointer that stores malloc's return value.

Summary

Section 12.1 Introduction
- Dynamic data structures (p. 478) grow and shrink at execution time.
- Linked lists (p. 478) are collections of data items "lined up in a row"—insertions and deletions are made anywhere in a linked list.
- With stacks (p. 478), insertions and deletions are made only at the top (p. 478).
- Queues (p. 478) represent waiting lines; insertions are made at the back (also referred to as the tail; p. 478) of a queue and deletions are made from the front (also referred to as the head; p. 478) of a queue.
- Binary trees facilitate high-speed searching and sorting of data, efficient elimination of duplicate data items, representing file-system directories and compiling expressions into machine language.

Section 12.2 Self-Referential Structures
- A self-referential structure (p. 479) contains a pointer member that points to a structure of the same type.
- Self-referential structures can be linked together to form lists, queues, stacks and trees.
- A NULL pointer (p. 479) normally indicates the end of a data structure.

Section 12.3 Dynamic Memory Allocation
- Creating and maintaining dynamic data structures require dynamic memory allocation (p. 479).
- Functions malloc and free, and operator sizeof, are essential to dynamic memory allocation.
- Function malloc (p. 479) receives the number of bytes to be allocated and returns a void * pointer to the allocated memory. A void * pointer may be assigned to a variable of any pointer type.
- Function malloc is normally used with the sizeof operator.

- The memory allocated by malloc is not initialized.
- If no memory is available, malloc returns NULL.
- Function free (p. 479) deallocates memory so that it can be reallocated in the future.
- C also provides functions calloc and realloc for creating and modifying dynamic arrays.

Section 12.4 Linked Lists
- A linked list is a linear collection of self-referential structures, called nodes (p. 480), connected by pointer links (p. 480).
- A linked list is accessed via a pointer to the first node. Subsequent nodes are accessed via the link pointer member stored in each node.
- By convention, the link pointer in the last node of a list is set to NULL to mark the end of the list.
- Data is stored in a linked list dynamically—each node is created as necessary.
- A node can contain data of any type including other struct objects.
- Linked lists are dynamic, so the length of a list can increase or decrease as necessary.
- Linked-list nodes are normally not stored contiguously in memory. Logically, however, the nodes of a linked list appear to be contiguous.

Section 12.5 Stacks
- A stack (p. 489) can be implemented as a constrained version of a linked list. New nodes can be added to a stack and removed from a stack only at the top—referred to as a last-in, first-out (LIFO; p. 489) data structure.
- The primary functions used to manipulate a stack are push and pop. Function push creates a new node and places it on top of the stack. Function pop removes a node from the top of the stack, frees the memory that was allocated to the popped node and returns the popped value.
- Whenever a function call is made, the called function must know how to return to its caller, so the return address is pushed onto a stack. If a series of function calls occurs, the successive return values are pushed onto the stack in last-in, first-out order so that each function can return to its caller. Stacks support recursive function calls in the same manner as conventional nonrecursive calls.
- Stacks are used by compilers in the process of evaluating expressions and generating machine-language code.

Section 12.6 Queues
- Queue nodes are removed only from the head of the queue and inserted only at the tail of the queue—referred to as a first-in, first-out (FIFO; p. 495) data structure.
- The insert and remove operations for a queue are known as enqueue and dequeue (p. 495).

Section 12.7 Trees
- A tree (p. 501) is a nonlinear, two-dimensional data structure. Tree nodes contain two or more links.
- Binary trees (p. 501) are trees whose nodes all contain two links.
- The root node (p. 501) is the first node in a tree. Each link in the root node of a binary tree refers to a child (p. 501). The left child (p. 501) is the first node in the left subtree (p. 501), and the right child (p. 501) is the first node in the right subtree (p. 501). The children of a node are called siblings (p. 501).
- A node with no children is called a leaf node (p. 501).

- A binary search tree (with no duplicate node values; p. 501) has the characteristic that the values in any left subtree are less than the value in its parent node (p. 501), and the values in any right subtree are greater than the value in its parent node.

- A node can be inserted only as a leaf node in a binary search tree.

- The steps for an in-order traversal are: Traverse the left subtree in-order, process the value in the node, then traverse the right subtree in-order. The value in a node is not processed until the values in its left subtree are processed.

- The in-order traversal (p. 502) of a binary search tree processes the node values in ascending order. The process of creating a binary search tree actually sorts the data—and thus this process is called the binary tree sort (p. 505).

- The steps for a pre-order traversal (p. 502) are: Process the value in the node, traverse the left subtree pre-order, then traverse the right subtree pre-order. The value in each node is processed as the node is visited. After the value in a given node is processed, the values in the left subtree are processed, then the values in the right subtree are processed.

- The steps for a post-order traversal (p. 502) are: Traverse the left subtree post-order, traverse the right subtree post-order, then process the value in the node. The value in each node is not processed until the values of its children are processed.

- A binary search tree facilitates duplicate elimination (p. 506). As the tree is being created, an attempt to insert a duplicate value will be recognized because a duplicate will follow the same "go left" or "go right" decisions on each comparison as the original value did. Thus, the duplicate will eventually be compared with a node in the tree containing the same value. The duplicate value may simply be discarded at this point.

- Searching a binary tree for a value that matches a key value is fast. If the tree is tightly packed, each level contains about twice as many elements as the previous level. So a binary search tree with n elements would have a maximum of $\log_2 n$ levels, and thus a maximum of $\log_2 n$ comparisons would have to be made either to find a match or to determine that no match exists. This means that when searching a (tightly packed) 1,000-element binary search tree, no more than 10 comparisons need to be made because $2^{10} > 1{,}000$. When searching a (tightly packed) 1,000,000-element binary search tree, no more than 20 comparisons need to be made because $2^{20} > 1{,}000{,}000$.

Self-Review Exercises

12.1 Fill in the blanks in each of the following:
    a) A self-_____ structure is used to form dynamic data structures.
    b) Function _____ is used to dynamically allocate memory.
    c) A(n) _____ is a specialized version of a linked list in which nodes can be inserted and deleted only from the start of the list.
    d) Functions that look at a linked list but do not modify it are referred to as _____.
    e) A queue is referred to as a(n) _____ data structure.
    f) The pointer to the next node in a linked list is referred to as a(n) _____.
    g) Function _____ is used to reclaim dynamically allocated memory.
    h) A(n) _____ is a specialized version of a linked list in which nodes can be inserted only at the start of the list and deleted only from the end of the list.
    i) A(n) _____ is a nonlinear, two-dimensional data structure that contains nodes with two or more links.
    j) A stack is referred to as a(n) _____ data structure because the last node inserted is the first node removed.
    k) The nodes of a(n) _____ tree contain two link members.

l) The first node of a tree is the _____ node.

m) Each link in a tree node points to a(n) _____ or _____ of that node.

n) A tree node that has no children is called a(n) _____ node.

o) The three traversal algorithms (covered in this chapter) for a binary tree are _____, _____ and _____.

12.2 What are the differences between a linked list and a stack?

12.3 What are the differences between a stack and a queue?

12.4 Write a statement or set of statements to accomplish each of the following. Assume that all the manipulations occur in main (therefore, no addresses of pointer variables are needed), and assume the following definitions:

```
struct gradeNode {
   char lastName[ 20 ];
   double grade;
   struct gradeNode *nextPtr;
};

typedef struct gradeNode GradeNode;
typedef GradeNode *GradeNodePtr;
```

a) Create a pointer to the start of the list called startPtr. The list is empty.

b) Create a new node of type GradeNode that's pointed to by pointer newPtr of type Grade-NodePtr. Assign the string "Jones" to member lastName and the value 91.5 to member grade (use strcpy). Provide any necessary declarations and statements.

c) Assume that the list pointed to by startPtr currently consists of 2 nodes—one containing "Jones" and one containing "Smith". The nodes are in alphabetical order. Provide the statements necessary to insert in order nodes containing the following data for lastName and grade:

```
"Adams"        85.0
"Thompson"     73.5
"Pritchard"    66.5
```

Use pointers previousPtr, currentPtr and newPtr to perform the insertions. State what previousPtr and currentPtr point to before each insertion. Assume that newPtr always points to the new node, and that the new node has already been assigned the data.

d) Write a while loop that prints the data in each node of the list. Use pointer currentPtr to move along the list.

e) Write a while loop that deletes all the nodes in the list and frees the memory associated with each node. Use pointer currentPtr and pointer tempPtr to walk along the list and free memory, respectively.

12.5 *(Binary Search Tree Traversals)* Provide the in-order, pre-order and post-order traversals of the binary search tree of Fig. 12.22.

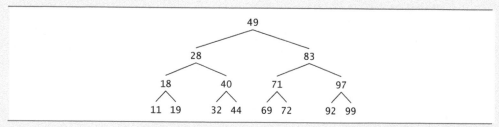

Fig. 12.22 | A 15-node binary search tree.

Answers to Self-Review Exercises

12.1 a) referential. b) `malloc`. c) stack. d) predicates. e) FIFO. f) link. g) `free`. h) queue.
i) tree. j) LIFO. k) binary. l) root. m) child, subtree. n) leaf. o) in-order, pre-order, post-order.

12.2 It's possible to insert a node anywhere in a linked list and remove a node from anywhere in
a linked list. However, nodes in a stack may be inserted only at the top of the stack and removed
only from the top of a stack.

12.3 A queue has pointers to both its head and its tail so that nodes may be inserted at the tail
and deleted from the head. A stack has a single pointer to the top of the stack where both insertion
and deletion of nodes is performed.

12.4
    a) `GradeNodePtr startPtr = NULL;`
    b) `GradeNodePtr newPtr;`
       `newPtr = malloc(sizeof(GradeNode));`
       `strcpy(newPtr->lastName, "Jones");`
       `newPtr->grade = 91.5;`
       `newPtr->nextPtr = NULL;`
    c) To insert "Adams":
       `previousPtr` is NULL, `currentPtr` points to the first element in the list.
       `newPtr->nextPtr = currentPtr;`
       `startPtr = newPtr;`
       To insert "Thompson":
       `previousPtr` points to the last element in the list (containing "Smith")
       `currentPtr` is NULL.
       `newPtr->nextPtr = currentPtr;`
       `previousPtr->nextPtr = newPtr;`
       To insert "Pritchard":
       `previousPtr` points to the node containing "Jones"
       `currentPtr` points to the node containing "Smith"
       `newPtr->nextPtr = currentPtr;`
       `previousPtr->nextPtr = newPtr;`

```
d) currentPtr = startPtr;
   while (currentPtr != NULL) {
       printf("Lastname = %s\nGrade = %6.2f\n",
               currentPtr->lastName, currentPtr->grade);
       currentPtr = currentPtr->nextPtr;
   }
e) currentPtr = startPtr;
   while (currentPtr != NULL) {
       tempPtr = currentPtr;
       currentPtr = currentPtr->nextPtr;
       free(tempPtr);
   }
   startPtr = NULL;
```

12.5 The *in-order* traversal is:
       11 18 19 28 32 40 44 49 69 71 72 83 92 97 99
    The *pre-order* traversal is:
       49 28 18 11 19 40 32 44 83 71 69 72 97 92 99

The *post-order* traversal is:
11 19 18 32 44 40 28 69 72 71 92 99 97 83 49

Exercises

12.6 *(Concatenating Lists)* Write a program that concatenates two linked lists of characters. The program should include function concatenate that takes pointers to both lists as arguments and concatenates the second list to the first list.

12.7 *(Merging Ordered Lists)* Write a program that merges two ordered lists of integers into a single ordered list of integers. Function merge should receive pointers to the first node of each of the lists to be merged and return a pointer to the first node of the merged list.

12.8 *(Inserting into an Ordered List)* Write a program that inserts 25 random integers from 0 to 100 in order in a linked list. The program should calculate the sum of the elements and the floating-point average of the elements.

12.9 *(Creating a Linked List, Then Reversing Its Elements)* Write a program that creates a linked list of 10 characters, then creates a copy of the list in reverse order.

12.10 *(Reversing the Words of a Sentence)* Write a program that inputs a line of text and uses a stack to print the line reversed.

12.11 *(Palindrome Tester)* Write a program that uses a stack to determine whether a string is a palindrome (i.e., the string is spelled identically backward and forward). The program should ignore spaces and punctuation.

12.12 *(Infix-to-Postfix Converter)* Stacks are used by compilers to help in the process of evaluating expressions and generating machine-language code. In this and the next exercise, we investigate how compilers evaluate arithmetic expressions consisting only of constants, operators and parentheses.

Humans generally write expressions like 3 + 4 and 7 / 9 in which the operator (+ or / here) is written between its operands—this is called infix notation. Computers "prefer" postfix notation in which the operator is written to the right of its two operands. The preceding infix expressions would appear in postfix notation as 3 4 + and 7 9 /, respectively.

To evaluate a complex infix expression, some compilers first convert the expression to postfix notation, and then evaluate the postfix version. Each of these algorithms requires only a single left-to-right pass of the expression. Each algorithm uses a stack in support of its operation, and in each the stack is used for a different purpose.

In this exercise, you'll write a version of the infix-to-postfix conversion algorithm. In the next exercise, you'll write a version of the postfix-expression evaluation algorithm.

Write a program that converts an ordinary infix arithmetic expression (assume a valid expression is entered) with single-digit integers such as

(6 + 2) * 5 - 8 / 4

to a postfix expression. The postfix version of the preceding infix expression is

6 2 + 5 * 8 4 / -

The program should read the expression into character array infix and use the stack functions implemented in this chapter to help create the postfix expression in character array postfix. The algorithm for creating a postfix expression is as follows:
1) Push a left parenthesis '(' onto the stack.
2) Append a right parenthesis ')' to the end of infix.

3) While the stack is not empty, read infix from left to right and do the following:

If the current character in infix is a digit, copy it to the next element of postfix.

If the current character in infix is a left parenthesis, push it onto the stack.

If the current character in infix is an operator,

Pop operators (if there are any) at the top of the stack while they have equal or higher precedence than the current operator, and insert the popped operators in postfix.

Push the current character in infix onto the stack.

If the current character in infix is a right parenthesis

Pop operators from the top of the stack and insert them in postfix until a left parenthesis is at the top of the stack.

Pop (and discard) the left parenthesis from the stack.

The following arithmetic operations are allowed in an expression:

+   addition
-   subtraction
*   multiplication
/   division
∧   exponentiation
%   remainder

The stack should be maintained with the following declarations:

```
struct stackNode {
    char data;
    struct stackNode *nextPtr;
};

typedef struct stackNode StackNode;
typedef StackNode *StackNodePtr;
```

The program should consist of main and eight other functions with the following function headers:

```
void convertToPostfix(char infix[], char postfix[])
```

Convert the infix expression to postfix notation.

```
int isOperator(char c)
```

Determine whether c is an operator.

```
int precedence(char operator1, char operator2)
```

Determine whether the precedence of operator1 is less than, equal to, or greater than the precedence of operator2. The function returns -1, 0 and 1, respectively.

```
void push(StackNodePtr *topPtr, char value)
```

Push a value on the stack.

```
char pop(StackNodePtr *topPtr)
```

Pop a value off the stack.

```
char stackTop(StackNodePtr topPtr)
```

Return the top value of the stack without popping the stack.

```
int isEmpty(StackNodePtr topPtr)
```

Determine whether the stack is empty.

```
void printStack(StackNodePtr topPtr)
```

Print the stack.

12.13 *(Postfix Evaluator)* Write a program that evaluates a postfix expression (assume it's valid) such as

```
6 2 + 5 * 8 4 / -
```

The program should read a postfix expression consisting of single digits and operators into a character array. Using the stack functions implemented earlier in this chapter, the program should scan the expression and evaluate it. The algorithm is as follows:

1) Append the null character ('\0') to the end of the postfix expression. When the null character is encountered, no further processing is necessary.
2) While '\0' has not been encountered, read the expression from left to right.

    If the current character is a digit,

        Push its integer value onto the stack (the integer value of a digit character is its value in the computer's character set minus the value of '0' in the computer's character set).

    Otherwise, if the current character is an *operator*,

        Pop the two top elements of the stack into variables x and y.

        Calculate y *operator* x.

        Push the result of the calculation onto the stack.

3) When the null character is encountered in the expression, pop the top value of the stack. This is the result of the postfix expression.

[*Note:* In 2) above, if the operator is '/', the top of the stack is 2, and the next element in the stack is 8, then pop 2 into x, pop 8 into y, evaluate 8 / 2, and push the result, 4, back onto the stack. This note also applies to the other binary operators.]

The arithmetic operations allowed in an expression are:

+   addition
-   subtraction
*   multiplication
/   division
∧   exponentiation
%   remainder

The stack should be maintained with the following declarations:

```
struct stackNode {
    int data;
    struct stackNode *nextPtr;
};

typedef struct stackNode StackNode;
typedef StackNode *StackNodePtr;
```

The program should consist of main and six other functions with the following function headers:

```
int evaluatePostfixExpression(char *expr)
```

Evaluate the postfix expression.

```
int calculate(int op1, int op2, char operator)
```

Evaluate the expression op1 operator op2.

```
void push(StackNodePtr *topPtr, int value)
```

Push a value on the stack.

```
int pop(StackNodePtr *topPtr)
```

Pop a value off the stack.

```
int isEmpty(StackNodePtr topPtr)
```

Determine whether the stack is empty.

```
void printStack(StackNodePtr topPtr)
```

Print the stack.

12.14 *(Postfix Evaluator Modification)* Modify the postfix evaluator program of Exercise 12.13 so that it can process integer operands larger than 9.

12.15 *(Supermarket Simulation)* Write a program that simulates a check-out line at a supermarket. The line is a queue. Customers arrive in random integer intervals of 1 to 4 minutes. Also, each customer is serviced in random integer intervals of 1 to 4 minutes. Obviously, the rates need to be balanced. If the average arrival rate is larger than the average service rate, the queue will grow infinitely. Even with balanced rates, randomness can still cause long lines. Run the supermarket simulation for a 12-hour day (720 minutes) using the following algorithm:

1) Choose a random integer between 1 and 4 to determine the minute at which the first customer arrives.
2) At the first customer's arrival time:
   Determine customer's service time (random integer from 1 to 4);
   Begin servicing the customer;
   Schedule arrival time of next customer (random integer 1 to 4 added to the current time).
3) For each minute of the day:
   If the next customer arrives,
       Say so;
       Enqueue the customer;
       Schedule the arrival time of the next customer.
   If service was completed for the last customer,
       Say so;
       Dequeue next customer to be serviced;
       Determine customer's service completion time
           (random integer from 1 to 4 added to the current time).

Now run your simulation for 720 minutes and answer each of the following:

a) What's the maximum number of customers in the queue at any time?
b) What's the longest wait any one customer experienced?
c) What happens if the arrival interval is changed from 1 to 4 minutes to 1 to 3 minutes?

12.16 *(Allowing Duplicates in a Binary Tree)* Modify the program of Fig. 12.19 to allow the binary tree to contain duplicate values.

12.17 *(Binary Search Tree of Strings)* Write a program based on the program of Fig. 12.19 that inputs a line of text, tokenizes the sentence into separate words, inserts the words in a binary search tree, and prints the in-order, pre-order, and post-order traversals of the tree.

   [*Hint:* Read the line of text into an array. Use `strtok` to tokenize the text. When a token is found, create a new node for the tree, assign the pointer returned by `strtok` to member `string` of the new node, and insert the node in the tree.]

12.18 *(Duplicate Elimination)* We've seen that duplicate elimination is straightforward when creating a binary search tree. Describe how you would perform duplicate elimination using only a one-dimensional array. Compare the performance of array-based duplicate elimination with the performance of binary-search-tree-based duplicate elimination.

12.19 *(Depth of a Binary Tree)* Write a function depth that receives a binary tree and determines how many levels it has.

12.20 *(Recursively Print a List Backward)* Write a function `printListBackward` that recursively outputs the items in a list in reverse order. Use your function in a test program that creates a sorted list of integers and prints the list in reverse order.

12.21 *(Recursively Search a List)* Write a function `searchList` that recursively searches a linked list for a specified value. The function should return a pointer to the value if it's found; otherwise, `NULL` should be returned. Use your function in a test program that creates a list of integers. The program should prompt the user for a value to locate in the list.

12.22 *(Binary Tree Search)* Write function `binaryTreeSearch` that attempts to locate a specified value in a binary search tree. The function should take as arguments a pointer to the root node of the binary tree and a search key to be located. If the node containing the search key is found, the function should return a pointer to that node; otherwise, the function should return a `NULL` pointer.

12.23 *(Level Order Binary Tree Traversal)* The program of Fig. 12.19 illustrated three recursive methods of traversing a binary tree—inorder traversal, preorder traversal, and postorder traversal. This exercise presents the level order traversal of a binary tree in which the node values are printed level-by-level starting at the root node level. The nodes on each level are printed from left to right. The level order traversal is not a recursive algorithm. It uses the queue data structure to control the output of the nodes. The algorithm is as follows:

    1) Insert the root node in the queue
    2) While there are nodes left in the queue,

            Get the next node in the queue
            Print the node's value
            If the pointer to the left child of the node is not `NULL`
                Insert the left child node in the queue
            If the pointer to the right child of the node is not `NULL`
                Insert the right child node in the queue.

Write function `levelOrder` to perform a level order traversal of a binary tree. The function should take as an argument a pointer to the root node of the binary tree. Modify the program of Fig. 12.19 to use this function. Compare the output from this function to the outputs of the other traversal algorithms to see that it worked correctly. [*Note:* You'll also need to modify and incorporate the queue-processing functions of Fig. 12.13 in this program.]

12.24 *(Printing Trees)* Write a recursive function `outputTree` to display a binary tree on the screen. The function should output the tree row-by-row with the top of the tree at the left of the screen and the bottom of the tree toward the right of the screen. Each row is output vertically. For example, the binary tree illustrated in Fig. 12.22 is output as follows:

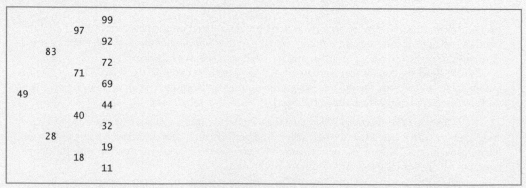

Note that the rightmost leaf node appears at the top of the output in the rightmost column, and the root node appears at the left of the output. Each column of output starts five spaces to the right of the previous column. Function outputTree should receive as arguments a pointer to the root node of the tree and an integer totalSpaces representing the number of spaces preceding the value to be output (this variable should start at zero so that the root node is output at the left of the screen). The function uses a modified inorder traversal to output the tree. The algorithm is as follows:

> While the pointer to the current node is not NULL
>> Recursively call outputTree with the current node's right subtree and totalSpaces + 5.
>> Use a for statement to count from 1 to totalSpaces and output spaces.
>> Output the value in the current node.
>> Recursively call outputTree with the current node's left subtree and totalSpaces + 5.

Special Section: Building Your Own Compiler

In Exercises 7.27–7.29, we introduced Simpletron Machine Language (SML), and you implemented a Simpletron computer simulator to execute SML programs. In Exercises 12.25–12.29, we build a compiler that converts programs written in a high-level programming language to SML. This section "ties" together the entire programming process. You'll write programs in this new high-level language, compile them on the compiler you build and run them on the simulator you built in Exercise 7.28. [*Note:* Due to the size of the descriptions for Exercises 12.25–12.29, we've posted them in a PDF document located at www.deitel.com/books/chtp8/.]

13

C Preprocessor

Objectives

In this chapter, you'll:

- Use #include to develop large programs.

- Use #define to create macros with and without arguments.

- Use conditional compilation to specify portions of a program that should not always be compiled (such as code that assists you in debugging).

- Display error messages during conditional compilation.

- Use assertions to test whether the values of expressions are correct.

Outline

13.1 Introduction

The C **preprocessor** executes *before* a program is compiled. Some actions it performs are.

- the inclusion of other files into the file being compiled,
- definition of **symbolic constants** and **macros**,
- **conditional compilation** of program code and
- **conditional execution of preprocessor directives**.

Preprocessor directives begin with #, and only whitespace characters and comments delimited by /* and */ may appear before a preprocessor directive on a line.

C has perhaps the largest installed base of "legacy code" of any modern programming language. It's been in active use for more than four decades. As a professional C programmer, you're likely to encounter code written many years ago using older programming techniques. To help you prepare for this, we discuss a number of those techniques in this chapter and recommend some newer techniques that can replace them.

13.2 #include Preprocessor Directive

The **#include preprocessor directive** has been used throughout this text. It causes a *copy* of a specified file to be included in place of the directive. The two forms of the #include directive are:

```
#include <filename>
#include "filename"
```

The difference between these is the location at which the preprocessor begins searches for the file to be included. If the filename is enclosed in angle brackets (< and >)—used for **standard library headers**—the search is performed in an *implementation-dependent* manner, normally through predesignated compiler and system directories. If the filename is enclosed in *quotes*, the preprocessor starts searches in the *same* directory as the file being compiled for the file to be included. This method is normally used to include programmer-defined headers. If the compiler cannot find the file in the current directory, then it will search through the predesignated compiler and system directories.

The `#include` directive is used to include standard library headers such as `stdio.h` and `stdlib.h` (see Fig. 5.10) and with programs consisting of *multiple source files* that are to be compiled together. A header containing declarations common to the separate program files is often created and included in the file. Examples of such declarations are:

- structure and union declarations,
- `typedefs`,
- enumerations and
- function prototypes.

13.3 #define Preprocessor Directive: Symbolic Constants

The **#define directive** creates *symbolic constants*—constants represented as symbols—and **macros**—operations defined as symbols. The `#define` directive format is

> `#define` *identifier   replacement-text*

When this line appears in a file, all subsequent occurrences of *identifier* that do *not* appear in string literals or comments will be replaced by *replacement text* automatically *before* the program is compiled. For example,

> `#define PI 3.14159`

replaces all subsequent occurrences of the symbolic constant PI with the numeric constant 3.14159. Symbolic constants enable you to create a name for a constant and use the name throughout the program.

Error-Prevention Tip 13.1
Everything to the right of the symbolic constant name replaces the symbolic constant. For example, #define PI = 3.14159 causes the preprocessor to replace every occurrence of the identifier PI with = 3.14159. This is the cause of many subtle logic and syntax errors. For this reason, you may prefer to use `const` variable declarations, such as `const double PI = 3.14159`; in preference to the preceding #define.

Common Programming Error 13.1
Attempting to redefine a symbolic constant with a new value is an error.

Software Engineering Observation 13.1
Using symbolic constants makes programs easier to modify. Rather than search for every occurrence of a value in your code, you modify a symbolic contant once in its #define directive. When the program is recompiled, all occurrences of that constant in the program are modified accordingly.

Good Programming Practice 13.1
Using meaningful names for symbolic constants helps make programs self-documenting.

Good Programming Practice 13.2
By convention, symbolic constants are defined using only uppercase letters and underscores.

13.4 #define Preprocessor Directive: Macros

A macro is an identifier defined in a #define preprocessor directive. As with symbolic constants, the **macro-identifier** is replaced with **replacement-text** before the program is compiled. Macros may be defined with or without **arguments**. A macro without arguments is processed like a symbolic constant. In a **macro with arguments**, the arguments are substituted in the replacement text, then the macro is **expanded**—the replacement-text replaces the identifier and argument list in the program. A symbolic constant is a type of macro.

13.4.1 Macro with One Argument

Consider the following one-argument *macro definition* that calculates the area of a circle:

```
#define CIRCLE_AREA(x) ((PI) * (x) * (x))
```

Expanding a Macro with an Argument

Wherever CIRCLE_AREA(y) appears in the file, the value of y is substituted for x in the replacement-text, the symbolic constant PI is replaced by its value (defined previously) and the macro is expanded in the program. For example, the statement

```
area = CIRCLE_AREA(4);
```

is expanded to

```
area = ((3.14159) * (4) * (4));
```

then, at compile time, the value of the expression is evaluated and assigned to variable area.

Importance of Parentheses

The *parentheses* around each x in the replacement-text force the proper order of evaluation when the macro argument is an expression. For example, the statement

```
area = CIRCLE_AREA(c + 2);
```

is expanded to

```
area = ((3.14159) * (c + 2) * (c + 2));
```

which evaluates *correctly* because the parentheses force the proper order of evaluation. If the parentheses in the macro definition are omitted, the macro expansion is

```
area = 3.14159 * c + 2 * c + 2;
```

which evaluates *incorrectly* as

```
area = (3.14159 * c) + (2 * c) + 2;
```

because of the rules of operator precedence.

Error-Prevention Tip 13.2
Enclose macro arguments in parentheses in the replacement-text to prevent logic errors.

Better to Use a Function

Macro CIRCLE_AREA could be defined more safely as a function. Function circleArea

```
double circleArea(double x)
{
    return 3.14159 * x * x;
}
```

performs the same calculation as macro CIRCLE_AREA, but the function's argument is evaluated only once when the function is called. Also, the compiler performs type checking on functions—the preprocessor does not support type checking.

Performance Tip 13.1

In the past, macros were often used to replace function calls with inline code to eliminate the function-call overhead. Today's optimizing compilers often inline function calls for you, so many programmers no longer use macros for this purpose. You can also use the C standard's inline keyword (see Appendix E).

13.4.2 Macro with Two Arguments

The following two-argument macro calculates the area of a rectangle:

```
#define RECTANGLE_AREA(x, y)  ((x) * (y))
```

Wherever RECTANGLE_AREA(x, y) appears in the program, the values of x and y are substituted in the macro replacement-text and the macro is expanded in place of the macro name. For example, the statement

```
rectArea = RECTANGLE_AREA(a + 4, b + 7);
```

is expanded to

```
rectArea = ((a + 4) * (b + 7));
```

The value of the expression is evaluated at runtime and assigned to variable rectArea.

13.4.3 Macro Continuation Character

The replacement-text for a macro or symbolic constant is normally any text on the line after the identifier in the #define directive. If the replacement-text for a macro or symbolic constant is longer than the remainder of the line, a **backslash** (\) continuation character must be placed at the end of the line, indicating that the replacement-text continues on the next line.

13.4.4 #undef Preprocessor Directive

Symbolic constants and macros can be discarded by using the **#undef preprocessor directive.** Directive #undef *"undefines"* a symbolic constant or macro name. The scope of a symbolic constant or macro is from its definition until it's undefined with #undef, or until the end of the file. Once undefined, a name can be redefined with #define.

13.4.5 Standard Library Functions and Macros

Functions in the standard library sometimes are defined as macros based on other library functions. A macro commonly defined in the <stdio.h> header is

```
#define getchar() getc(stdin)
```

The macro definition of getchar uses function getc to get one character from the standard input stream. Function putchar of the <stdio.h> header and the character-handling functions of the <ctype.h> header often are implemented as macros as well.

13.4.6 Do Not Place Expressions with Side Effects in Macros

Expressions with *side effects* (e.g., variable values are modified) should *not* be passed to a macro because macro arguments may be evaluated more than once. We'll show an example of this in Section 13.11.

13.5 Conditional Compilation

Conditional compilation enables you to control the execution of preprocessor directives and the compilation of program code. Each conditional preprocessor directive evaluates a constant integer expression. Cast expressions, sizeof expressions and enumeration constants *cannot* be evaluated in preprocessor directives.

13.5.1 #if…#endif Preprocessor Directive

The conditional preprocessor construct is much like the if selection statement. Consider the following preprocessor code:

```
#if !defined(MY_CONSTANT)
    #define MY_CONSTANT 0
#endif
```

which determines whether MY_CONSTANT is *defined*—that is, whether MY_CONSTANT has already appeared in an earlier #define directive. The expression defined(MY_CONSTANT) evaluates to 1 if MY_CONSTANT is defined and 0 otherwise. If the result is 0, !defined(MY_CONSTANT) evaluates to 1 and MY_CONSTANT is defined. Otherwise, the #define directive is skipped. Every **#if** construct ends with **#endif**. Directives **#ifdef** and **#ifndef** are shorthand for #if defined(*name*) and #if !defined(*name*). A multiple-part conditional preprocessor construct may be tested by using the **#elif** (the equivalent of else if in an if statement) and the **#else** (the equivalent of else in an if statement) directives. These directives are frequently used to *prevent header files from being included multiple times in the same source file*—we use this technique extensively in the C++ part of this book. These directives also are frequently used to enable and disable code that makes software compatible with a range of platforms.

13.5.2 Commenting Out Blocks of Code with #if…#endif

During program development, it's often helpful to "comment out" portions of code to prevent them from being compiled. If the code contains multiline comments, /* and */ cannot be used to accomplish this task, because such comments cannot be nested. Instead, you can use the following preprocessor construct:

```
#if 0
    code prevented from compiling
#endif
```

To enable the code to be compiled, replace the 0 in the preceding construct with 1.

13.5.3 Conditionally Compiling Debugging Code

Conditional compilation is sometimes used as a *debugging* aid. Debuggers provide much more powerful features than conditional compilation, but if a debugger is not available, `printf` statements can be used to print variable values and to confirm the flow of control. These `printf` statements can be enclosed in conditional preprocessor directives so the statements are compiled only while the debugging process is *not* completed. For example,

```
#ifdef DEBUG
    printf("Variable x = %d\n", x);
#endif
```

compiles the `printf` statement if the symbolic constant DEBUG is defined (`#define DEBUG`) before `#ifdef DEBUG`. When debugging is completed, you remove or comment out the `#define` directive from the source file and the `printf` statements inserted for debugging purposes are ignored during compilation. In larger programs, it may be desirable to define several symbolic constants that control the conditional compilation in separate sections of the source file. Many compilers allow you to define and undefine symbolic constants like DEBUG with a compiler flag that you supply each time you compile the code so that you do not need to change the code.

Error-Prevention Tip 13.3

When inserting conditionally compiled `printf` *statements in locations where C expects a single statement (e.g., the body of a control statement), ensure that the conditionally compiled statements are enclosed in blocks.*

13.6 #error and #pragma Preprocessor Directives

The **#error** directive

```
#error tokens
```

prints an implementation-dependent message including the *tokens* specified in the directive. The tokens are sequences of characters separated by spaces. For example,

```
#error 1 - Out of range error
```

contains 6 tokens. When a `#error` directive is processed on some systems, the tokens in the directive are displayed as an error message, preprocessing stops and the program does not compile.

The **#pragma** directive

```
#pragma tokens
```

causes an *implementation-defined* action. A pragma not recognized by the implementation is ignored. For more information on `#error` and `#pragma`, see the documentation for your C implementation.

13.7 # and ## Operators

The # operator causes a replacement-text token to be converted to a string surrounded by quotes. Consider the following macro definition:

```
#define HELLO(x) puts("Hello, " #x);
```

When HELLO(John) appears in a program file, it's expanded to

```
puts("Hello, " "John");
```

The string "John" replaces #x in the replacement-text. Strings separated by whitespace are concatenated during preprocessing, so the preceding statement is equivalent to

```
puts("Hello, John");
```

The # operator must be used in a macro with arguments because the operand of # refers to an argument of the macro.

The ## operator *concatenates two tokens*. Consider the following macro definition:

```
#define TOKENCONCAT(x, y)  x ## y
```

When TOKENCONCAT appears in the program, its arguments are concatenated and used to replace the macro. For example, TOKENCONCAT(O, K) is replaced by OK in the program. The ## operator must have two operands.

13.8 Line Numbers

The #line preprocessor directive causes the subsequent source code lines to be renumbered starting with the specified constant integer value. The directive

```
#line 100
```

starts line numbering from 100 beginning with the next source-code line. A filename can be included in the #line directive. The directive

```
#line 100 "file1.c"
```

indicates that lines are numbered from 100 beginning with the next source-code line and that the name of the file for the purpose of any compiler messages is "file1.c". The directive normally is used to help make the messages produced by syntax errors and compiler warnings more meaningful. The line numbers do not appear in the source file.

13.9 Predefined Symbolic Constants

Standard C provides **predefined symbolic constants,** several of which are shown in Fig. 13.1—the rest are in Section 6.10.8 of the C standard document. These identifiers begin and end with *two* underscores and often are useful to include additional information in error messages. These identifiers and the defined identifier (used in Section 13.5) cannot be used in #define or **#undef** directives.

Symbolic constant	Explanation
__LINE__	The line number of the current source-code line (an integer constant).
__FILE__	The name of the source file (a string).
__DATE__	The date the source file was compiled (a string of the form "Mmm dd yyyy" such as "Jan 19 2002").

Fig. 13.1 | Some predefined symbolic constants. (Part 1 of 2.)

Symbolic constant	Explanation
__TIME__	The time the source file was compiled (a string literal of the form "hh:mm:ss").
__STDC__	The value 1 if the compiler supports Standard C; 0 otherwise. Requires the compiler flag /Za in Visual C++.

Fig. 13.1 | Some predefined symbolic constants. (Part 2 of 2.)

13.10 Assertions

The **assert** macro—defined in **<assert.h>**—tests the value of an expression at execution time. If the value is false (0), assert prints an error message and calls function **abort** (of the general utilities library—**<stdlib.h>**) to terminate program execution. This is a useful debugging tool for testing whether a variable has a correct value. For example, suppose variable x should never be larger than 10 in a program. An assertion may be used to test the value of x and print an error message if the value of x is greater than 10. The statement would be

```
assert(x <= 10);
```

If x is greater than 10 when the preceding statement executes, the program displays an error message containing the line number and filename where the assert statement appears, then *terminates*. You then concentrate on this area of the code to find the error.

If the symbolic constant NDEBUG is defined, subsequent assertions will be *ignored*. Thus, when assertions are no longer needed, you can insert the line

```
#define NDEBUG
```

in the code file rather than delete each assertion manually. Many compilers have debug and release modes that automatically define and undefine NDEBUG, respectively.

Software Engineering Observation 13.2

Assertions are not meant as a substitute for error handling during normal runtime conditions. Their use should be limited to finding logic errors during program development.

[*Note:* The new C standard includes a capability called _Static_assert, which is essentially a compile-time version of assert that produces a *compilation error* if the assertion fails. We discuss _Static_assert in Appendix E.]

13.11 Secure C Programming

The CIRCLE_AREA macro defined in Section 13.4

```
#define CIRCLE_AREA(x) ((PI) * (x) * (x))
```

is considered to be an *unsafe* macro because it evaluates its argument x *more than once*. This can cause subtle errors. If the macro argument contains *side effects*—such as incrementing a variable or calling a function that modifies a variable's value—those side effects would be performed *multiple* times.

For example, if we call CIRCLE_AREA as follows:

```
result = CIRCLE_AREA(++radius);
```

the call to the macro CIRCLE_AREA is expanded to:

```
result = ((3.14159) * (++radius) * (++radius));
```

which increments radius *twice* in the statement. In addition, the result of the preceding statement is *undefined* because C allows a variable to be modified *only once* in a statement. In a function call, the argument is evaluated *only once before* it's passed to the function. So, functions are always preferred to unsafe macros.

Summary

Section 13.1 Introduction
- The **preprocessor** (p. 519) executes before a program is compiled.
- All **preprocessor directives** (p. 519) begin with #.
- Only whitespace characters and comments may appear before a preprocessor directive on a line.

Section 13.2 #include Presprocessor Directive
- The **#include directive** (p. 519) includes a copy of the specified file. If the filename is enclosed in quotes, the preprocessor begins searching in the same directory as the file being compiled for the file to be included. If the filename is enclosed in angle brackets (< and >), as is the case for C standard library headers, the search is performed in an implementation-defined manner.

Section 13.3 #define Preprocessor Directive: Symbolic Constants
- The **#define preprocessor directive** (p. 520) is used to create symbolic constants and macros.
- A **symbolic constant** (p. 520) is a name for a constant.

Section 13.4 #define Preprocessor Directive: Macros
- A **macro** is an operation defined in a #define preprocessor directive. Macros may be defined with or without **arguments** (p. 521).
- **Replacement-text** (p. 520) is specified after a symbolic constant's identifier or after the closing right parenthesis of a macro's argument list. If the replacement-text for a macro or symbolic constant is longer than the remainder of the line, a **backslash** (\; p. 522) is placed at the end of the line, indicating that the replacement-text continues on the next line.
- Symbolic constants and macros can be discarded by using the **#undef preprocessor directive** (p. 522). Directive #undef "undefines" the symbolic constant or macro name.
- The **scope** (p. 522) of a symbolic constant or macro is from its definition until it's undefined with #undef or until the end of the file.

Section 13.5 Conditional Compilation
- **Conditional compilation** (p. 523) enables you to control the execution of preprocessor directives and the compilation of program code.
- The **conditional preprocessor directives** evaluate constant integer expressions. Cast expressions, sizeof expressions and enumeration constants cannot be evaluated in preprocessor directives.
- Every **#if** construct ends with **#endif** (p. 523).
- Directives **#ifdef** and **#ifndef** (p. 523) are provided as shorthand for **#if defined(**name**)** and **#if !defined(**name**)**.
- **Multiple-part conditional preprocessor constructs** may be tested with directives **#elif** and **#else** (p. 523).

Section 13.6 #error and #pragma Preprocessor Directives

- The **#error** directive (p. 524) prints an implementation-dependent message that includes the tokens specified in the directive.

- The **#pragma** directive (p. 524) causes an implementation-defined action. If the pragma is not recognized by the implementation, the pragma is ignored.

Section 13.7 # and ## Operators

- The **#** operator causes a *replacement-text* token to be converted to a string surrounded by quotes. The # operator must be used in a macro with arguments, because the operand of # must be an argument of the macro.

- The **##** operator concatenates two tokens. The ## operator must have two operands.

Section 13.8 Line Numbers

- The **#line** preprocessor directive (p. 525) causes the subsequent source-code lines to be renumbered starting with the specified constant integer value.

Section 13.9 Predefined Symbolic Constants

- Constant **__LINE__** (p. 525) is the line number (an integer) of the current source-code line.
- Constant **__FILE__** (p. 525) is the name of the file (a string).
- Constant **__DATE__** (p. 525) is the date the source file is compiled (a string).
- Constant **__TIME__** (p. 525) is the time the source file is compiled (a string).
- Constant **__STDC__** (p. 525) indicates whether the compiler supports Standard C.
- Each of the predefined symbolic constants begins and ends with two underscores.

Section 13.10 Assertions

- Macro **assert** (p. 526; **<assert.h>** header) tests the value of an expression. If the value is 0 (false), assert prints an error message and calls **function abort** (p. 526) to terminate program execution.

Self-Review Exercises

13.1 Fill in the blanks in each of the following:
   a) Every preprocessor directive must begin with _____.
   b) The conditional compilation construct may be extended to test for multiple cases by using the _____ and _____ directives.
   c) The _____ directive creates macros and symbolic constants.
   d) Only _____ characters may appear before a preprocessor directive on a line.
   e) The _____ directive discards symbolic constant and macro names.
   f) The _____ and _____ directives are provided as shorthand notation for #if defined(*name*) and #if !defined(*name*).
   g) _____ enables you to control the execution of preprocessor directives and the compilation of program code.
   h) The _____ macro prints a message and terminates program execution if the value of the expression the macro evaluates is 0.
   i) The _____ directive inserts a file in another file.
   j) The _____ operator concatenates its two arguments.
   k) The _____ operator converts its operand to a string.
   l) The character _____ indicates that the replacement-text for a symbolic constant or macro continues on the next line.
   m) The _____ directive causes the source-code lines to be numbered from the indicated value beginning with the next source-code line.

13.2 Write a program to print the values of the predefined symbolic constants listed in Fig. 13.1.

13.3 Write a preprocessor directive to accomplish each of the following:
a) Define symbolic constant YES to have the value 1.
b) Define symbolic constant NO to have the value 0.
c) Include the header common.h. The header is found in the same directory as the file being compiled.
d) Renumber the remaining lines in the file beginning with line number 3000.
e) If symbolic constant TRUE is defined, undefine it and redefine it as 1. Do not use #ifdef.
f) If symbolic constant TRUE is defined, undefine it and redefine it as 1. Use the #ifdef preprocessor directive.
g) If symbolic constant TRUE is not equal to 0, define symbolic constant FALSE as 0. Otherwise define FALSE as 1.
h) Define macro CUBE_VOLUME that computes the volume of a cube. The macro takes one argument.

Answers to Self-Review Exercises

13.1 a) #. b) #elif, #else. c) #define. d) whitespace. e) #undef. f) #ifdef, #ifndef. g) Conditional compilation. h) assert. i) #include. j) ##. k) #. l) \. m) #line.

13.2 See below. [*Note:* __STDC__ works in Visual C++ only with the /Za compiler flag.]

```
1   // Print the values of the predefined macros
2   #include <stdio.h>
3   int main(void)
4   {
5      printf("__LINE__ = %d\n", __LINE__);
6      printf("__FILE__ = %s\n", __FILE__);
7      printf("__DATE__ = %s\n", __DATE__);
8      printf("__TIME__ = %s\n", __TIME__);
9      printf("__STDC__ = %s\n", __STDC__);
10  }
```

```
__LINE__ = 5
__FILE__ = ex13_02.c
__DATE__ = Jan  5 2012
__TIME__ = 09:38:58
__STDC__ = 1
```

13.3
a) #define YES 1
b) #define NO 0
c) #include "common.h"
d) #line 3000
e) #if defined(TRUE)
    #undef TRUE
    #define TRUE 1
  #endif
f) #ifdef TRUE
    #undef TRUE
    #define TRUE 1
  #endif

g) ```
    #if TRUE
        #define FALSE 0
    #else
        #define FALSE 1
    #endif
    ```
h)  `#define CUBE_VOLUME(x)  ((x) * (x) * (x))`

## Exercises

**13.4** *(Volume of a Sphere)* Write a program that defines a macro with one argument to compute the volume of a sphere. The program should compute the volume for spheres of radius 1 to 10 and print the results in tabular format. The formula for the volume of a sphere is

$$(4.0 / 3) * \pi * r^3$$

where $\pi$ is 3.14159.

**13.5** *(Adding Two Numbers)* Write a program that defines macro SUM with two arguments, x and y, and use SUM to produce the following output:

```
The sum of x and y is 13
```

13.6 *(Smallest of Two Numbers)* Write a program that defines and uses macro MINIMUM2 to determine the smallest of two numeric values. Input the values from the keyboard.

13.7 *(Smallest of Three Numbers)* Write a program that defines and uses macro MINIMUM3 to determine the smallest of three numeric values. Macro MINIMUM3 should use macro MINIMUM2 defined in Exercise 13.6 to determine the smallest number. Input the values from the keyboard.

13.8 *(Printing a String)* Write a program that defines and uses macro PRINT to print a string value.

13.9 *(Printing an Array)* Write a program that defines and uses macro PRINTARRAY to print an array of integers. The macro should receive the array and the number of elements in the array as arguments.

13.10 *(Totaling an Array's Contents)* Write a program that defines and uses macro SUMARRAY to sum the values in a numeric array. The macro should receive the array and the number of elements in the array as arguments.
```

Other C Topics

Objectives

In this chapter, you'll:

- Redirect program input to come from a file.

- Redirect program output to be placed in a file.

- Write functions that use variable-length argument lists.

- Process command-line arguments.

- Compile multiple-source-file programs.

- Assign specific types to numeric constants.

- Terminate programs with `exit` and `atexit`.

- Process external asynchronous events in a program.

- Dynamically allocate arrays and resize memory that was dynamically allocated previously.

14.1 Introduction

This chapter presents additional topics not ordinarily covered in introductory courses. Many of the capabilities discussed here are specific to particular operating systems, especially Linux/UNIX and Windows.

14.2 Redirecting I/O

In command-line applications, normally the input is received from the *keyboard* (standard input), and the output is displayed on the *screen* (standard output). On most computer systems—Linux/UNIX, Mac OS X and Windows systems in particular—it's possible to **redirect** inputs to come from a *file* rather than the keyboard and redirect outputs to be placed in a *file* rather than on the screen. Both forms of redirection can be accomplished without using the file-processing capabilities of the standard library (e.g., by changing your code to use fprintf rather than printf, etc.). Students often find it difficult to understand that redirection is an operating-system function, not another C feature.

14.2.1 Redirecting Input with <

There are several ways to redirect input and output from the command line—that is, a **Command Prompt** window in Windows, a shell in Linux or a **Terminal** window in Mac OS X. Consider the executable file sum (on Linux/UNIX systems) that inputs integers one at a time and keeps a running total of the values until the end-of-file indicator is set, then prints the result. Normally the user inputs integers from the keyboard and enters the end-of-file key combination to indicate that no further values will be input. With input redirection, the input can be read from a file. For example, if the data is stored in file input, the command line

```
$ sum < input
```

executes the program sum; the **redirect input symbol** (<) indicates that the data in file input is to be used as the program's input. Redirecting input on a Windows system or in a Terminal window on OS X is performed identically. The character $ shown in the line above is a typical Linux/UNIX command-line prompt (some systems use a % prompt or other symbol).

14.2.2 Redirecting Input with |

The second method of redirecting input is **piping**. A **pipe** (|) causes the output of one program to be redirected as the input to another. Suppose program random outputs a series of random integers; the output of random can be "piped" directly to program sum using the command line

```
$ random | sum
```

This causes the sum of the integers produced by random to be calculated. Piping is performed identically in Linux/UNIX, Windows and OS X.

14.2.3 Redirecting Output

The standard output stream can be redirected to a file by using the **redirect output symbol** (>). For example, to redirect the output of program random to file out, use

```
$ random > out
```

Finally, program output can be appended to the end of an existing file by using the **append output symbol** (>>). For example, to append the output from program random to file out created in the preceding command line, use the command line

```
$ random >> out
```

14.3 Variable-Length Argument Lists

It's possible to create functions that receive an *unspecified* number of arguments. Most programs in the text have used the standard library function printf, which, as you know, takes a variable number of arguments. As a minimum, printf must receive a string as its first argument, but printf can receive any number of additional arguments. The function prototype for printf is

```
int printf(const char *format, ...);
```

The **ellipsis** (...) in the function prototype indicates that the function receives a *variable number of arguments of any type*. The ellipsis must always be placed at the *end* of the parameter list.

The macros and definitions of the **variable arguments headers <stdarg.h>** (Fig. 14.1) provide the capabilities necessary to build functions with **variable-length argument lists**. Figure 14.2 demonstrates function average (lines 25–39) that receives a variable number of arguments. The first argument of average is always the number of values to be averaged.

Identifier	Explanation
va_list	A *type* suitable for holding information needed by macros va_start, va_arg and va_end. To access the arguments in a variable-length argument list, an object of type va_list must be defined.

Fig. 14.1 | stdarg.h variable-length argument-list type and macros. (Part 1 of 2.)

Identifier	Explanation
va_start	A *macro* that's invoked before the arguments of a variable-length argument list can be accessed. The macro initializes the object declared with va_list for use by the va_arg and va_end macros.
va_arg	A *macro* that expands to the value of the next argument in the variable-length argument list—the value has the type specified as the macro's second argument. Each invocation of va_arg modifies the object declared with va_list so that it points to the next argument in the list.
va_end	A *macro* that facilitates a normal return from a function whose variable-length argument list was referred to by the va_start macro.

Fig. 14.1 | stdarg.h variable-length argument-list type and macros. (Part 2 of 2.)

```
1   // Fig. 14.2: fig14_02.c
2   // Using variable-length argument lists
3   #include <stdio.h>
4   #include <stdarg.h>
5
6   double average(int i, ...); // prototype
7
8   int main(void)
9   {
10     double w = 37.5;
11     double x = 22.5;
12     double y = 1.7;
13     double z = 10.2;
14
15     printf("%s%.1f\n%s%.1f\n%s%.1f\n%s%.1f\n\n",
16        "w = ", w, "x = ", x, "y = ", y, "z = ", z);
17     printf("%s%.3f\n%s%.3f\n%s%.3f\n",
18        "The average of w and x is ", average(2, w, x),
19        "The average of w, x, and y is ", average(3, w, x, y),
20        "The average of w, x, y, and z is ",
21        average(4, w, x, y, z));
22   }
23
24   // calculate average
25   double average(int i, ...)
26   {
27     double total = 0; // initialize total
28     va_list ap; // stores information needed by va_start and va_end
29
30     va_start(ap, i); // initializes the va_list object
31
32     // process variable-length argument list
33     for (int j = 1; j <= i; ++j) {
34        total += va_arg(ap, double);
35     }
```

Fig. 14.2 | Using variable-length argument lists. (Part 1 of 2.)

```
36
37     va_end(ap); // clean up variable-length argument list
38     return total / i; // calculate average
39 }
```

```
w = 37.5
x = 22.5
y = 1.7
z = 10.2

The average of w and x is 30.000
The average of w, x, and y is 20.567
The average of w, x, y, and z is 17.975
```

Fig. 14.2 | Using variable-length argument lists. (Part 2 of 2.)

Function average (lines 25–39) uses all the definitions and macros of header <stdarg.h>, except va_copy (Section E.8.10), which was added in C11. Object ap, of type **va_list** (line 28), is used by macros **va_start**, **va_arg** and **va_end** to process the variable-length argument list of function average. The function begins by invoking macro va_start (line 30) to initialize object ap for use in va_arg and va_end. The macro receives two arguments—object ap and the identifier of the rightmost argument in the argument list *before* the ellipsis—i in this case (va_start uses i here to determine where the variable-length argument list begins). Next, function average repeatedly adds the arguments in the variable-length argument list to variable total (lines 33–35). The value to be added to total is retrieved from the argument list by invoking macro va_arg. Macro va_arg receives two arguments—object ap and the *type* of the value expected in the argument list—double in this case. The macro returns the value of the argument. Function average invokes macro va_end (line 37) with object ap as an argument to facilitate a normal return to main from average. Finally, the average is calculated and returned to main.

Common Programming Error 14.1

Placing an ellipsis in the middle of a function parameter list is a syntax error—an ellipsis may be placed only at the end of the parameter list.

You might wonder how functions with variable-length argument lists like printf and function scanf know what type to use in each va_arg macro. The answer is that, as the program executes, they scan the format conversion specifiers in the format control string to determine the type of the next argument to be processed.

14.4 Using Command-Line Arguments

On many systems, it's possible to pass arguments to main from a command line by including parameters int argc and char *argv[] in the parameter list of main. Parameter **argc** receives the number of command-line arguments that the user has entered. Parameter **argv** is an array of strings in which the actual command-line arguments are stored. Common uses of command-line arguments include passing options to a program and passing filenames to a program.

Figure 14.3 copies a file into another file one character at a time. We assume that the executable file for the program is called `mycopy`. A typical command line for the `mycopy` program on a Linux/UNIX system is

```
$ mycopy input output
```

This command line indicates that file `input` is to be copied to file `output`. When the program is executed, if `argc` is not 3 (`mycopy` counts as one of the arguments), the program prints an error message and terminates. Otherwise, array `argv` contains the strings `"mycopy"`, `"input"` and `"output"`. The second and third arguments on the command line are used as filenames by the program. The files are opened using function `fopen`. If both files are opened successfully, characters are read from file `input` and written to file `output` until the end-of-file indicator for file `input` is set. Then the program terminates. The result is an exact copy of file `input` (if no errors occur during processing). See your system documentation for more information on command-line arguments. [*Note:* In Visual C++, you specify command-line arguments by right clicking the project name in the Solution Explorer and selecting **Properties**, then expanding **Configuration Properties**, selecting **Debugging** and entering the arguments in the textbox to the right of **Command Arguments**.]

```c
1   // Fig. 14.3: fig14_03.c
2   // Using command-line arguments
3   #include <stdio.h>
4
5   int main(int argc, char *argv[])
6   {
7      // check number of command-line arguments
8      if (argc != 3) {
9         puts("Usage: mycopy infile outfile");
10     }
11     else {
12        FILE *inFilePtr; // input file pointer
13
14        // try to open the input file
15        if ((inFilePtr = fopen(argv[1], "r")) != NULL) {
16           FILE *outFilePtr; // output file pointer
17
18           // try to open the output file
19           if ((outFilePtr = fopen(argv[2], "w")) != NULL) {
20              int c; // holds characters read from source file
21
22              // read and output characters
23              while ((c = fgetc(inFilePtr)) != EOF) {
24                 fputc(c, outFilePtr);
25              }
26
27              fclose(outFilePtr); // close the output file
28           }
29           else { // output file could not be opened
30              printf("File \"%s\" could not be opened\n", argv[2]);
31           }
32
```

Fig. 14.3 | Using command-line arguments. (Part 1 of 2.)

```
33              fclose(inFilePtr); // close the input file
34         }
35         else { // input file could not be opened
36             printf("File \"%s\" could not be opened\n", argv[1]);
37         }
38     }
39  }
```

Fig. 14.3 | Using command-line arguments. (Part 2 of 2.)

14.5 Compiling Multiple-Source-File Programs

It's possible to build programs that consist of multiple source files. There are several considerations when creating programs in multiple files. For example, the definition of a function must be entirely contained in one file—it cannot span two or more files.

14.5.1 extern Declarations for Global Variables in Other Files

In Chapter 5, we introduced the concepts of storage class and scope. We learned that variables declared *outside* any function definition are referred to as *global variables*. Global variables are accessible to any function defined in the same file after the variable is declared. Global variables also are accessible to functions in other files. However, the global variables must be declared in each file in which they're used. For example, to refer to global integer variable flag in another file, you can use the declaration

```
extern int flag;
```

This declaration uses the storage-class specifier **extern** to indicate that variable flag is defined either *later in the same file or in a different file*. The compiler informs the linker that unresolved references to variable flag appear in the file. If the linker finds a proper global definition, the linker resolves the references by indicating where flag is located. If the linker cannot locate a definition of flag, it issues an error message and does not produce an executable file. Any identifier that's declared at file scope is extern by default.

Software Engineering Observation 14.1

Global variables should be avoided unless application performance is critical because they violate the principle of least privilege.

14.5.2 Function Prototypes

Just as extern declarations can be used to declare *global variables* to other program files, *function prototypes can extend the scope of a function beyond the file in which it's defined* (the extern specifier is not required in a function prototype). Simply include the function prototype in each file in which the function is invoked and compile the files together (see Section 13.2). Function prototypes indicate to the compiler that the specified function is defined either later in the *same* file or in a *different* file. Again, the compiler does *not* attempt to resolve references to such a function—that task is left to the linker. If the linker cannot locate a proper function definition, the linker issues an error message.

As an example of using function prototypes to extend the scope of a function, consider any program containing the preprocessor directive #include <stdio.h>, which includes a file containing the function prototypes for functions such as printf and scanf. Other functions in the file can use printf and scanf to accomplish their tasks. The printf and scanf functions are defined in other files. We do *not* need to know *where* they're defined. We're simply reusing their code in our programs. The linker resolves our references to these functions automatically. This process enables us to use the functions in the standard library.

Software Engineering Observation 14.2

Creating programs in multiple source files facilitates software reusability and good software engineering. Functions may be common to many applications. In such instances, those functions should be stored in their own source files, and each source file should have a corresponding header file containing function prototypes. This enables programmers of different applications to reuse the same code by including the proper header file and compiling their applications with the corresponding source file.

14.5.3 Restricting Scope with static

It's possible to restrict the scope of a global variable or a function to the file in which it's defined. The storage-class specifier static, when applied to a global variable or a function, prevents it from being used by any function that's not defined in the same file. This is referred to as **internal linkage**. Global variables and functions that are *not* preceded by static in their definitions have **external linkage**—they can be accessed in other files if those files contain proper declarations and/or function prototypes.

The global variable declaration

```
static const double PI = 3.14159;
```

creates constant variable PI of type double, initializes it to 3.14159 and indicates that PI is known *only* to functions in the file in which it's defined.

The static specifier is commonly used with utility functions that are called only by functions in a particular file. If a function is not required outside a particular file, the principle of least privilege should be enforced by applying static to both the function's definition and prototype.

14.5.4 Makefiles

When building large programs in multiple source files, compiling the program becomes tedious if small changes are made to one file and the entire program is needlessly recompiled. Many systems provide special utilities that recompile *only* the modified program files. On Linux/UNIX systems the utility is called **make**. Utility make reads a file called **makefile** that contains instructions for compiling and linking the program. Products such as Eclipse™ and Microsoft® Visual C++® provide similar utilities.

14.6 Program Termination with exit and atexit

The general utilities library (<stdlib.h>) provides methods of terminating program execution by means other than a conventional return from function main. Function **exit** causes a program to terminate immediately. The function often is used to terminate a program when an input error is detected, or when a file to be processed by the program cannot be opened. Function **atexit** registers a function that should be called when the program terminates by reaching the end of main or when exit is invoked.

Function atexit takes as an argument a pointer to a function (i.e., the *function name*). *Functions called at program termination cannot have arguments and cannot return a value.*

Function exit takes one argument. The argument is normally the symbolic constant **EXIT_SUCCESS** or the symbolic constant **EXIT_FAILURE**. If exit is called with EXIT_SUCCESS, the implementation-defined value for successful termination is returned to the calling environment. If exit is called with EXIT_FAILURE, the implementation-defined value for unsuccessful termination is returned. When function exit is invoked, any functions previously registered with atexit are invoked in the *reverse* order of their registration.

Figure 14.4 tests functions exit and atexit. The program prompts the user to determine whether the program should be terminated with exit or by reaching the end of main. Function print is executed at program termination in each case.

```c
1   // Fig. 14.4: fig14_04.c
2   // Using the exit and atexit functions
3   #include <stdio.h>
4   #include <stdlib.h>
5
6   void print(void); // prototype
7
8   int main(void)
9   {
10      atexit(print); // register function print
11      puts("Enter 1 to terminate program with function exit"
12         "\nEnter 2 to terminate program normally");
13      int answer; // user's menu choice
14      scanf("%d", &answer);
15
16      // call exit if answer is 1
17      if (answer == 1) {
18         puts("\nTerminating program with function exit");
19         exit(EXIT_SUCCESS);
20      }
21
22      puts("\nTerminating program by reaching the end of main");
23   }
24
25   // display message before termination
26   void print(void)
27   {
28      puts("Executing function print at program "
29         "termination\nProgram terminated");
30   }
```

Fig. 14.4 | Using the exit and atexit functions. (Part 1 of 2.)

```
Enter 1 to terminate program with function exit
Enter 2 to terminate program normally
1

Terminating program with function exit
Executing function print at program termination
Program terminated
```

```
Enter 1 to terminate program with function exit
Enter 2 to terminate program normally
2

Terminating program by reaching the end of main
Executing function print at program termination
Program terminated
```

Fig. 14.4 | Using the exit and atexit functions. (Part 2 of 2.)

14.7 Suffixes for Integer and Floating-Point Literals

C provides integer and floating-point *suffixes* for explicitly specifying the data types of integer and floating-point literal values. (The C standard refers to such literal values as constants). If an integer literal is *not* suffixed, its type is determined by the first type capable of storing a value of that size (first int, then long int, then unsigned long int, etc.). A floating-point literal that's *not* suffixed is automatically of type double.

The integer suffixes are: **u** or **U** for an unsigned int, **l** or **L** for a long int, and **ll** or **LL** for a long long int. You can combine u or U with those for long int and long long int to create unsigned literals for the larger integer types. The following literals are of type unsigned int, long int, unsigned long int and unsigned long long int, respectively:

```
174u
8358L
28373ul
9876543210llu
```

The floating-point suffixes are: **f** or **F** for a float, and **l** or **L** for a long double. The following constants are of type **float** and **long double**, respectively:

```
1.28f
3.14159L
```

14.8 Signal Handling

An *external asynchronous* event, or **signal**, can cause a program to terminate prematurely. Some events include interrupts (typing *<Ctrl> c* on a Linux/UNIX or Windows system or *<command> c* on OS X) and termination orders from the operating system. The **signal-handling library** (**<signal.h>**) provides the capability to **trap** unexpected events with function **signal**. Function signal receives two arguments—an integer *signal number* and a *pointer to the signal-handling function*. Signals can be generated by function **raise**, which takes an integer signal number as an argument. Figure 14.5 summarizes the *standard signals* defined in header file <signal.h>.

Signal	Explanation
SIGABRT	Abnormal termination of the program (such as a call to function abort).
SIGFPE	An erroneous arithmetic operation, such as a divide-by-zero or an operation resulting in overflow.
SIGILL	Detection of an illegal instruction.
SIGINT	Receipt of an interactive attention signal (*<Ctrl> c* or *<command> c*).
SIGSEGV	An attempt to access memory that is not allocated to a program.
SIGTERM	A termination request sent to the program.

Fig. 14.5 | signal.h standard signals.

Figure 14.6 uses function signal to *trap* a SIGINT. Line 12 calls signal with SIGINT and a pointer to function signalHandler (remember that the name of a function is a pointer to the function). When a signal of type SIGINT occurs, control passes to function signalHandler, which prints a message and gives the user the option to continue normal execution of the program. If the user wishes to continue execution, the signal handler is reinitialized by calling signal again and control returns to the point in the program at which the signal was detected.

In this program, function raise (line 21) is used to simulate a SIGINT. A random number between 1 and 50 is chosen. If the number is 25, raise is called to generate the signal. Normally, SIGINTs are initiated outside the program. For example, typing *<Ctrl> c* during program execution on a Linux/UNIX or Windows system generates a SIGINT that *terminates* program execution. Signal handling can be used to trap the SIGINT and prevent the program from being terminated.

```c
1   // Fig. 14.6: fig14_06.c
2   // Using signal handling
3   #include <stdio.h>
4   #include <signal.h>
5   #include <stdlib.h>
6   #include <time.h>
7
8   void signalHandler(int signalValue); // prototype
9
10  int main(void)
11  {
12     signal(SIGINT, signalHandler); // register signal handler
13     srand(time(NULL));
14
15     // output numbers 1 to 100
16     for (int i = 1; i <= 100; ++i) {
17        int x = 1 + rand() % 50; // generate random number to raise SIGINT
```

Fig. 14.6 | Using signal handling. (Part 1 of 3.)

```
18
19          // raise SIGINT when x is 25
20          if (x == 25) {
21              raise(SIGINT);
22          }
23
24          printf("%4d", i);
25
26          // output \n when i is a multiple of 10
27          if (i % 10 == 0) {
28              printf("%s", "\n");
29          }
30      }
31  }
32
33  // handles signal
34  void signalHandler(int signalValue)
35  {
36      printf("%s%d%s\n%s",
37          "\nInterrupt signal (", signalValue, ") received.",
38          "Do you wish to continue (1 = yes or 2 = no)? ");
39      int response; // user's response to signal (1 or 2)
40      scanf("%d", &response);
41
42      // check for invalid responses
43      while (response != 1 && response != 2) {
44          printf("%s", "(1 = yes or 2 = no)? ");
45          scanf("%d", &response);
46      }
47
48      // determine whether it's time to exit
49      if (response == 1) {
50          // reregister signal handler for next SIGINT
51          signal(SIGINT, signalHandler);
52      }
53      else {
54          exit(EXIT_SUCCESS);
55      }
56  }
```

```
   1   2   3   4   5   6   7   8   9  10
  11  12  13  14  15  16  17  18  19  20
  21  22  23  24  25  26  27  28  29  30
  31  32  33  34  35  36  37  38  39  40
  41  42  43  44  45  46  47  48  49  50
  51  52  53  54  55  56  57  58  59  60
  61  62  63  64  65  66  67  68  69  70
  71  72  73  74  75  76  77  78  79  80
  81  82  83  84  85  86  87  88  89  90
  91  92  93
Interrupt signal (2) received.
Do you wish to continue (1 = yes or 2 = no)? 1
```

Fig. 14.6 | Using signal handling. (Part 2 of 3.)

```
   94  95  96
Interrupt signal (2) received.
Do you wish to continue (1 = yes or 2 = no)? 2
```

Fig. 14.6 | Using signal handling. (Part 3 of 3.)

14.9 Dynamic Memory Allocation: Functions `calloc` and `realloc`

Chapter 12 introduced the notion of dynamically allocating memory using function `malloc`. As we stated in Chapter 12, arrays are better than linked lists for rapid sorting, searching and data access. However, arrays are normally **static data structures**. The general utilities library (**stdlib.h**) provides two other functions for dynamic memory allocation—**calloc** and **realloc**. These functions can be used to create and modify **dynamic arrays**. Function `calloc` dynamically allocates memory for an array. The prototype for `calloc` is

```
    void *calloc(size_t nmemb, size_t size);
```

Its two arguments represent the *number of elements* (nmemb) and the *size of each element* (size). Function `calloc` also initializes the elements of the array to zero. The function returns a pointer to the allocated memory, or a NULL pointer if the memory is *not* allocated. The primary difference between `malloc` and `calloc` is that `calloc` *clears the memory* it allocates and `malloc` *does not*.

Function `realloc` *changes the size* of an object allocated by a previous call to `malloc`, `calloc` or `realloc`. The original object's contents are *not modified* provided that the amount of memory allocated is *larger* than the amount allocated previously. Otherwise, the contents are unchanged up to the size of the new object. The prototype for `realloc` is

```
    void *realloc(void *ptr, size_t size);
```

The two arguments are a pointer to the original object (ptr) and the *new size* of the object (size). If ptr is NULL, `realloc` works identically to `malloc`. If ptr is not NULL and size is greater than zero, `realloc` tries to *allocate a new block of memory* for the object. If the new space *cannot* be allocated, the object pointed to by ptr is unchanged. Function `realloc` returns either a pointer to the reallocated memory, or a NULL pointer to indicate that the memory was not reallocated.

Error-Prevention Tip 14.1
Avoid zero-sized allocations in calls to `malloc`, `calloc` and `realloc`.

14.10 Unconditional Branching with `goto`

We've stressed the importance of using structured programming techniques to build reliable software that's easy to debug, maintain and modify. In some cases, performance is more important than strict adherence to structured programming techniques. In these cases, some unstructured programming techniques may be used. For example, we can use

break to terminate execution of an iteration statement before the loop-continuation condition becomes false. This saves unnecessary iterations of the loop if the task is completed
before loop termination.

Another instance of unstructured programming is the **goto statement**—an unconditional branch. The result of the goto statement is a change in the flow of control to the
first statement after the **label** specified in the goto statement. A label is an identifier followed by a colon. A label must appear in the *same* function as the goto statement that
refers to it. Labels need not be unique among functions. Figure 14.7 uses goto statements
to loop ten times and print the counter value each time. After initializing count to 1, line
11 tests count to determine whether it's greater than 10 (the label start: is skipped
because labels do not perform any action). If so, control is transferred from the goto to the
first statement after the label end: (which appears at line 20). Otherwise, lines 15–16 print
and increment count, and control transfers from the goto (line 18) to the first statement
after the label start: (which appears at line 9).

```c
1   // Fig. 14.7: fig14_07.c
2   // Using the goto statement
3   #include <stdio.h>
4
5   int main(void)
6   {
7       int count = 1; // initialize count
8
9       start: // label
10
11          if (count > 10) {
12              goto end;
13          }
14
15          printf("%d  ", count);
16          ++count;
17
18          goto start; // goto start on line 9
19
20      end: // label
21          putchar('\n');
22  }
```

```
1  2  3  4  5  6  7  8  9  10
```

Fig. 14.7 | Using the goto statement.

In Chapter 3, we stated that only three control structures are required to write any
program—sequence, selection and iteration. When the rules of structured programming
are followed, it's possible to create deeply nested control structures within a function from
which it's difficult to escape efficiently. Some programmers use goto statements in such
situations as a quick exit from a deeply nested structure. This eliminates the need to test
multiple conditions to escape from a control structure. There are some additional situations where goto is actually recommended—see, for example, CERT recommendation

MEM12-C, "Consider using a Goto-Chain when leaving a function on error when using and releasing resources."

Performance Tip 14.1

The goto statement can be used to exit from deeply nested control structures efficiently.

Software Engineering Observation 14.3

The goto statement is unstructured and can lead to programs that are more difficult to debug, maintain and modify.

Summary

Section 14.2 Redirecting I/O

- On many computer systems it's possible to **redirect input** (p. 532) to a program and **output** from a program.
- Input is redirected from the command line using the **redirect input symbol** (<; p. 532) or a pipe (|; p. 533).
- Output is redirected from the command line using the **redirect output symbol** (>; p. 533) or the **append output symbol** (>>; p. 533). The redirect output symbol simply stores the program output in a file, and the append output symbol appends the output to the end of a file.

Section 14.3 Variable-Length Argument Lists

- The macros and definitions of the variable arguments **header <stdarg.h>** (p. 533) provide the capabilities necessary to build functions with **variable-length argument lists** (p. 533).
- An **ellipsis** (...; p. 533) in a function prototype indicates a variable number of arguments.
- Type **va_list** (p. 535) is suitable for holding information needed by macros va_start, va_arg and va_end. To access the arguments in a variable-length argument list, an object of type va_list must be declared.
- Invoke macro **va_start** (p. 535) before accessing the arguments of a variable-length argument list. The macro initializes the object declared with va_list for use by the va_arg and va_end macros.
- Macro **va_arg** (p. 535) expands to an expression of the value and type of the next argument in the variable-length argument list. Each invocation of va_arg modifies the object declared with va_list so that the object points to the next argument in the list.
- Macro **va_end** (p. 535) facilitates a normal return from a function whose variable-length argument list was referred to by the va_start macro.

Section 14.4 Using Command-Line Arguments

- On many systems it's possible to pass arguments to main from the command line by including the parameters **int argc** (p. 535) and **char *argv[]** (p. 535) in the parameter list of main. Parameter argc receives the number of command-line arguments. Parameter argv is an array of strings in which the actual command-line arguments are stored.

Section 14.5 Compiling Multiple-Source-File Programs

- A function definition must be entirely contained in one file—it cannot span two or more files.
- The **storage-class specifier extern** (p. 537) indicates that a variable is defined either later in the same file or in a different file of the program.

- **Global variables** must be declared in each file in which they're used.
- **Function prototypes** can extend the scope of a function beyond the file in which it's defined. This is accomplished by including the function prototype in each file in which the function is invoked (often by using #include to include a header containing the prototype) and compiling the files together.
- The **storage-class specifier static**, when applied to a global variable or a function, prevents it from being used by any function that's not defined in the same file. This is referred to as **internal linkage** (p. 538). Global variables and functions that are not preceded by static in their definitions have **external linkage** (p. 538)—they can be accessed in other files if those files contain proper declarations or function prototypes.
- The static specifier is commonly used with utility functions that are called only by functions in a particular file. If a function is not required outside a particular file, the principle of least privilege should be enforced by applying static to the function's definition and prototype.
- When building large programs in multiple source files, compiling the program becomes tedious if small changes are made to one file and the entire program must be recompiled. Many systems provide special utilities that recompile only the modified program file. On Linux/UNIX systems the utility is called make. Utility **make** (p. 538) reads a file called **makefile** (p. 538) that contains instructions for compiling and linking the program, and recompiles only those files that have changed since the last time the project was built.

Section 14.6 Program Termination with `exit` and `atexit`
- Function **exit** (p. 538) forces a program to terminate.
- Function **atexit** (p. 539) registers a function to be called when the program terminates by reaching the end of main or when exit is invoked.
- Function atexit takes a pointer to a function as an argument. Functions called at program termination cannot have arguments and cannot return a value.
- Function exit takes one argument. The argument is normally the symbolic constant **EXIT_SUCCESS** (p. 539) or the symbolic constant **EXIT_FAILURE** (p. 539).
- When function exit is invoked, any functions registered with atexit are invoked in the reverse order of their registration.

Section 14.7 Suffixes for Integer and Floating-Point Literals
- C provides **integer** and **floating-point suffixes** for specifying the types of integer and floating-point constants. The integer suffixes are: u or U for an unsigned integer, l or L for a long integer, and ul or UL for an unsigned long integer. If an integer constant is not suffixed, its type is determined by the first type capable of storing a value of that size (first int, then long int, then unsigned long int, etc.). The floating-point suffixes are: f or F for a float, and l or L for a long double. A floating-point constant that's not suffixed is of type double.

Section 14.8 Signal Handling
- The **signal-handling library** (p. 540) enables trapping of unexpected events with function **signal** (p. 540). Function **signal** receives two arguments—an integer signal number and a pointer to the signal-handling function.
- Signals can also be generated with **function raise** (p. 540) and an integer argument.

Section 14.9 Dynamic Memory Allocation: Functions `calloc` and `realloc`
- The **general utilities library** (`<stdlib.h>`; p. 543) provides two functions for dynamic memory allocation—calloc and realloc. These functions can be used to create dynamic arrays (p. 543).

- Function **calloc** (p. 543) allocates memory for an array. It receives two arguments—the number of elements and the size of each element—and initializes the elements of the array to zero. The function returns either a pointer to the allocated memory, or a NULL pointer if the memory is not allocated.

- Function **realloc** changes the size of an object allocated by a previous call to malloc, calloc or realloc. The original object's contents are not modified, provided that the amount of memory allocated is larger than the amount allocated previously.

- Function realloc takes two arguments—a pointer to the original object and the new size of the object. If ptr is NULL, realloc works identically to malloc. Otherwise, if ptr is not NULL and size is greater than zero, realloc tries to allocate a new block of memory for the object. If the new space cannot be allocated, the object pointed to by ptr is unchanged. Function realloc returns either a pointer to the reallocated memory, or a NULL pointer to indicate that memory was not reallocated.

Section 14.10 Unconditional Branching with **goto**

- The result of the **goto statement** (p. 544) is a change in the flow of control of the program. Program execution continues at the first statement after the **label** (p. 544) specified in the goto statement.

- A label is an **identifier followed by a colon**. A label must appear in the same function as the goto statement that refers to it.

Self-Review Exercise

14.1   Fill in the blanks in each of the following:
   a) The _____ symbol redirects input data from a file rather than the keyboard.
   b) The _____ symbol is used to redirect the screen output so that it's placed in a file.
   c) The _____ symbol is used to append the output of a program to the end of a file.
   d) A(n) _____ directs the output of one program to be the input of another program.
   e) A(n) _____ in the parameter list of a function indicates that the function can receive a variable number of arguments.
   f) Macro _____ must be invoked before the arguments in a variable-length argument list can be accessed.
   g) Macro _____ accesses the individual arguments of a variable-length argument list.
   h) Macro _____ facilitates a normal return from a function whose variable-length argument list was referred to by macro va_start.
   i) Argument _____ of main receives the number of arguments in a command line.
   j) Argument _____ of main stores command-line arguments as character strings.
   k) Linux/UNIX utility _____ reads a file called _____ that contains instructions for compiling and linking a program consisting of multiple source files.
   l) Function _____ forces a program to terminate execution.
   m) Function _____ registers a function to be called upon normal program termination.
   n) An integer or floating-point _____ can be appended to an integer or floating-point constant to specify the exact type of the constant.
   o) Function _____ can be used to trap unexpected events.
   p) Function _____ generates a signal from within a program.
   q) Function _____ dynamically allocates memory for an array and initializes the elements to zero.
   r) Function _____ changes the size of a block of previously allocated dynamic memory.

Answers to Self-Review Exercise

14.1 a) redirect input (<). b) redirect output (>). c) append output (>>). d) pipe (|). e) ellipsis (...). f) va_start. g) va_arg. h) va_end. i) argc. j) argv. k) make, makefile. l) exit. m) atexit. n) suffix. o) signal. p) raise. q) calloc. r) realloc.

Exercises

14.2 *(Variable-Length Argument List: Calculating Products)* Write a program that calculates the product of a series of integers that are passed to function product using a variable-length argument list. Test your function with several calls, each with a different number of arguments.

14.3 *(Printing Command-Line Arguments)* Write a program that prints the command-line arguments of the program.

14.4 *(Sorting Integers)* Write a program that sorts an array of integers into ascending or descending order. Use command-line arguments to pass either argument -a for ascending order or -d for descending order. [*Note:* This is the standard format for passing options to a program in UNIX.]

14.5 *(Signal Handling)* Read the documentation for your compiler to determine what signals are supported by the signal-handling library (<signal.h>). Write a program that contains signal handlers for the standard signals SIGABRT and SIGINT. The program should test the trapping of these signals by calling function abort to generate a signal of type SIGABRT and by having the user type <Ctrl> c (<control> C on OS X) to generate a signal of type SIGINT.

14.6 *(Dynamic Array Allocation)* Write a program that dynamically allocates an array of integers. The size of the array should be input from the keyboard. The elements of the array should be assigned values input from the keyboard. Print the values of the array. Next, reallocate the memory for the array to half of the current number of elements. Print the values remaining in the array to confirm that they match the first half of the values in the original array.

14.7 *(Command-Line Arguments)* Write a program that takes two command-line arguments that are filenames, reads the characters from the first file one at a time and writes the characters in reverse order to the second file.

14.8 *(goto Statement)* Write a program that uses goto statements and only the following three printf statements to simulate a nested looping structure that prints a square of asterisks as shown below:

```
printf("%s", "*");
printf("%s", " ");
printf("%s", "\n");
```

```
*****
*   *
*   *
*   *
*****
```

C++ as a Better C; Introducing Object Technology

Objectives

In this chapter you'll:

- Learn key C++ enhancements to C.

- Learn the C++ Standard Library's header files.

- Use inline functions to improve performance.

- Use references to pass arguments to functions by reference.

- Use default arguments that the compiler passes to a function if the corresponding arguments are not provided in a function call.

- Use the unary scope resolution operator to access a global variable.

- Overload functions to create several functions of the same name that perform similar tasks, but on data of different types.

- Create and use function templates that perform identical operations on data of different types.

15.1 Introduction

We now begin the second section of this unique text. The first 14 chapters presented a thorough treatment of procedural programming and top-down program design with C. The C++ section (Chapters 15–23) introduces two additional programming paradigms— **object-oriented programming** (with classes, encapsulation, objects, operator overloading, inheritance and polymorphism) and **generic programming** (with function templates and class templates). These chapters emphasize "crafting valuable classes" to create reusable software componentry.

15.2 C++

C++ improves on many of C's features and provides object-oriented-programming (OOP) capabilities that increase software productivity, quality and reusability. This chapter discusses many of C++'s enhancements to C.

C's designers and early implementers never anticipated that the language would become such a phenomenon. When a programming language becomes as entrenched as C, new requirements demand that the language evolve rather than simply be displaced by a new language. C++ was developed by Bjarne Stroustrup at Bell Laboratories and was originally called "C with classes." The name C++ includes C's increment operator (++) to indicate that C++ is an enhanced version of C.

Chapters 15–23 provide an introduction to the version of C++11 standardized in the United States through the American National Standards Institute (ANSI) and worldwide through the International Standards Organization (ISO). We have done a careful walk-through of the ANSI/ISO C++ standard document and audited our presentation against it for completeness and accuracy. However, C++ is a rich language, and there are some subtleties in the language and some advanced subjects that we have not covered. If you need additional technical details on C++, we suggest that you read the C++ standard document "Programming languages—C++" (document number ISO/IEC 14882-2011), which can be purchased from various standards organization websites, such as ansi.org and iso.org. A near-final draft of the standard document can be found at:

```
http://www.open-std.org/jtc1/sc22/wg21/docs/papers/2011/n3242.pdf
```

15.3 A Simple Program: Adding Two Integers

This section revisits the addition program of Fig. 2.5 and illustrates several important features of the C++ language as well as some differences between C and C++. C file names have the .c (lowercase) extension. C++ file names can have one of several extensions, such as .cpp, .cxx or .C (uppercase). We use the extension .cpp.

15.3.1 Addition Program in C++

Figure 15.1 uses C++-style input and output to obtain two integers typed by a user at the keyboard, computes the sum of these values and outputs the result. Lines 1 and 2 each begin with //, indicating that the remainder of each line is a comment. You may also use /*...*/ comments, which can be more than one line long.

```cpp
1   // Fig. 15.1: fig15_01.cpp
2   // Addition program that displays the sum of two numbers.
3   #include <iostream> // allows program to perform input and output
4
5   int main()
6   {
7      std::cout << "Enter first integer: "; // prompt user for data
8      int number1;
9      std::cin >> number1; // read first integer from user into number1
10
11     std::cout << "Enter second integer: "; // prompt user for data
12     int number2;
13     std::cin >> number2; // read second integer from user into number2
14     int sum = number1 + number2; // add the numbers; store result in sum
15     std::cout << "Sum is " << sum << std::endl; // display sum; end line
16  }
```

```
Enter first integer: 45
Enter second integer: 72
Sum is 117
```

Fig. 15.1 | Addition program that displays the sum of two numbers.

15.3.2 <iostream> Header

The C++ preprocessor directive in line 3 exhibits the standard C++ style for including header files from the standard library. This line tells the C++ preprocessor to include the contents of the **input/output stream header** file **<iostream>**. This file must be included for any program that outputs data to the screen or inputs data from the keyboard using C++-style stream input/output. We discuss iostream's many features in detail in Chapter 21, Stream Input/Output: A Deeper Look.

15.3.3 main Function

As in C, every C++ program begins execution with function main (line 5). Keyword int to the left of main indicates that main returns an integer value. C++ requires you to specify the return type, possibly void, for all functions. In C++, specifying a parameter list with empty parentheses is equivalent to specifying a void parameter list in C. In C, using empty parentheses in a function definition or prototype is dangerous. It disables compile-time argument checking in function calls, which allows the caller to pass *any* arguments to the function. This could lead to runtime errors.

Common Programming Error 15.1
Omitting the return type in a C++ function definition is a syntax error.

15.3.4 Variable Declarations

Lines 8, 12 and 14 are familiar variable declarations. Declarations can be placed almost anywhere in a C++ program, but they must appear before their corresponding variables are used in the program.

15.3.5 Standard Output Stream and Standard Input Stream Objects

Line 7 uses the **standard output stream object**—**std::cout**—and the **stream insertion operator**, <<, to display the string "Enter first integer: ". Output and input in C++ are accomplished with streams of characters. Thus, when line 7 executes, it sends the stream of characters "Enter first integer: " to std::cout, which is normally "connected" to the screen. We like to pronounce the preceding statement as "std::cout *gets* the character string "Enter first integer: "."

Line 9 uses the **standard input stream object**—**std::cin**—and the **stream extraction operator**, >>, to obtain a value from the keyboard. Using the stream extraction operator with std::cin takes character input from the standard input stream, which is usually the keyboard. We like to pronounce the preceding statement as, "std::cin *gives* a value to number1" or simply "std::cin *gives* number1."

When the computer executes the statement in line 9, it waits for the user to enter a value for variable number1. The user responds by typing an integer (as characters), then pressing the *Enter* key. The computer converts the character representation of the number to an integer and assigns this value to the variable number1.

Line 11 displays "Enter second integer: " on the screen, prompting the user to take action. Line 13 obtains a value for variable number2 from the user.

15.3.6 `std::endl` Stream Manipulator

Line 14 calculates the sum of the variables `number1` and `number2` and assigns the result to variable `sum`. Line 15 displays the character string `Sum is` followed by the numerical value of variable `sum` followed by **`std::endl`**—a so-called **stream manipulator**. The name `endl` is an abbreviation for "end line." The `std::endl` stream manipulator outputs a newline, then "flushes the output buffer." This simply means that, on some systems where outputs accumulate in the machine until there are enough to "make it worthwhile" to display on the screen, `std::endl` forces any accumulated outputs to be displayed at that moment. This can be important when the outputs are prompting the user for an action, such as entering data.

15.3.7 `std::` Explained

We place `std::` before `cout`, `cin` and `endl`. This is required when we use standard C++ header files. The notation `std::cout` specifies that we're using a name, in this case `cout`, that belongs to "namespace" `std`. Namespaces are an advanced C++ feature that we do not discuss in detail. For now, you should simply remember to include `std::` before each mention of `cout`, `cin` and `endl` in a program. This can be cumbersome—in Fig. 15.3, we introduce the `using` statement, which will enable us to avoid placing `std::` before each use of a namespace `std` name.

15.3.8 Concatenated Stream Outputs

The statement in line 15 outputs values of different types. The stream insertion operator "knows" how to output each type of data. Using multiple stream insertion operators (`<<`) in a single statement is referred to as **concatenating, chaining** or **cascading stream insertion operations.**

Calculations can also be performed in output statements. We could have combined the statements in lines 14–15 into the statement

```
std::cout << "Sum is " << number1 + number2 << std::endl;
```

thus eliminating the need for the variable `sum`.

15.3.9 `return` Statement Not Required in `main`

You'll notice that we did not have a `return 0;` statement at the end of `main` in this example. According to the C++ standard, if program execution reaches the end of `main` without encountering a `return` statement, it's assumed that the program terminated successfully—exactly as when the last statement in main is a `return` statement with the value 0. For that reason, we omit the `return` statement at the end of `main` in our C++ programs.

15.3.10 Operator Overloading

A powerful C++ feature is that users can create their own types called classes (we introduce this capability in Chapter 16 and explore it in depth in Chapter 17). Users can then "teach" C++ how to input and output values of these new data types using the `>>` and `<<` operators (this is called **operator overloading**—a topic we explore in Chapter 18).

15.4 C++ Standard Library

C++ programs consist of pieces called **classes** and functions. You can program each piece that you need to form a C++ program. Instead, most C++ programmers take advantage of the rich collections of existing classes and functions in the **C++ Standard Library**. Thus, there are really two parts to learning the C++ "world." The first is learning the C++ language itself; the second is learning how to use the classes and functions in the C++ Standard Library. In the C++ part of this book, we discuss some of these classes and functions, and we cover more of them in our book *C++ How to Program, 9/e*. The standard class libraries generally are provided by compiler vendors. Many special-purpose class libraries are supplied by independent software vendors.

Software Engineering Observation 15.1

Use a "building-block" approach to create programs. Avoid reinventing the wheel. Use existing pieces wherever possible. Called software reuse, this practice is central to object-oriented programming.

Software Engineering Observation 15.2

When programming in C++, you typically will use the following building blocks: classes and functions from the C++ Standard Library, classes and functions you and your colleagues create and classes and functions from various popular third-party libraries.

The advantage of creating your own functions and classes is that you'll know exactly how they work. You'll be able to examine the C++ code. The disadvantage is the time-consuming and complex effort that goes into designing, developing and maintaining new functions and classes that are correct and that operate efficiently.

Performance Tip 15.1

Using C++ Standard Library functions and classes instead of writing your own versions can improve program performance, because they are written to perform efficiently. This technique also shortens program development time.

Portability Tip 15.1

Using C++ Standard Library functions and classes instead of writing your own improves program portability, because they are included in every C++ implementation.

15.5 Header Files

The C++ Standard Library is divided into many portions, each with its own header file. The header files contain the function prototypes for the related functions that form each portion of the library. The header files also contain definitions of various class types and functions, as well as constants needed by those functions. A header file "instructs" the compiler on how to interface with library and user-written components.

Figure 15.2 lists some common C++ Standard Library header files. Header file names ending in .h are "old-style" header files that have been superseded by the C++ Standard Library header files.

C++ Standard Library header file	Explanation
`<iostream>`	Contains function prototypes for the C++ standard input and output functions, introduced in Section 15.3, and is covered in more detail in Chapter 21, Stream Input/Output: A Deeper Look.
`<iomanip>`	Contains function prototypes for stream manipulators that format streams of data. This header is first used in Section 15.15 and is discussed in more detail in Chapter 21.
`<cmath>`	Contains function prototypes for the math library functions.
`<cstdlib>`	Contains function prototypes for conversions of numbers to text, text to numbers, memory allocation, random numbers and various other utility functions. Portions of the header are covered in Chapter 18, Operator Overloading; Class `string` and Chapter 22, Exception Handling: A Deeper Look.
`<ctime>`	Contains function prototypes and types for manipulating the time and date.
`<array>`, `<vector>`, `<list>`, `<forward_list>`, `<deque>`, `<queue>`, `<stack>`, `<map>`, `<unordered_map>`, `<unordered_set>`, `<set>`, `<bitset>`	These headers contain classes that implement the C++ Standard Library containers. Containers store data during a program's execution. The `<vector>` header is first introduced in Section 15.15.
`<cctype>`	Contains function prototypes for functions that test characters for certain properties (such as whether the character is a digit or a punctuation), and function prototypes for functions that can be used to convert lowercase letters to uppercase letters and vice versa.
`<cstring>`	Contains function prototypes for C-style string-processing functions. This header is used in Chapter 18.
`<typeinfo>`	Contains classes for runtime type identification (determining data types at execution time). This header is discussed in Section 20.8.
`<exception>`, `<stdexcept>`	These headers contain classes that are used for exception handling (discussed in Chapter 22).
`<memory>`	Contains classes and functions used by the C++ Standard Library to allocate memory to the C++ Standard Library containers. This header is used in Chapter 22.
`<fstream>`	Contains function prototypes for functions that perform input from and output to files on disk.
`<string>`	Contains the definition of class `string` from the C++ Standard Library.
`<sstream>`	Contains function prototypes for functions that perform input from strings in memory and output to strings in memory.
`<functional>`	Contains classes and functions used by C++ Standard Library algorithms.
`<iterator>`	Contains classes for accessing data in the C++ Standard Library containers.

Fig. 15.2 | C++ Standard Library header files. (Part 1 of 2.)

C++ Standard Library header file	Explanation
`<algorithm>`	Contains functions for manipulating data in C++ Standard Library containers.
`<cassert>`	Contains macros for adding diagnostics that aid program debugging.
`<cfloat>`	Contains the floating-point size limits of the system.
`<climits>`	Contains the integral size limits of the system.
`<cstdio>`	Contains function prototypes for the C's standard I/O functions.
`<locale>`	Contains classes and functions normally used by stream processing to process data in the natural form for different languages (e.g., monetary formats, sorting strings, character presentation, etc.).
`<limits>`	Contains classes for defining the numerical data type limits on each computer platform.
`<utility>`	Contains classes and functions that are used by many C++ Standard Library headers.

Fig. 15.2 | C++ Standard Library header files. (Part 2 of 2.)

You can create custom header files. Programmer-defined header files should end in .h. A programmer-defined header file can be included by using the #include preprocessor directive. For example, the header file square.h can be included in a program by placing the directive #include "square.h" at the beginning of the program.

15.6 Inline Functions

Implementing a program as a set of functions is good from a software engineering standpoint, but function calls involve execution-time overhead. C++ provides **inline functions** to help reduce function call overhead—especially for small functions. Placing the qualifier **inline** before a function's return type in the function definition "advises" the compiler to generate a copy of the function's code in place (when appropriate) to avoid a function call. The trade-off is that multiple copies of the function code are inserted in the program (often making the program larger) rather than there being a single copy of the function to which control is passed each time the function is called. The compiler can ignore the inline qualifier and typically does so for all but the smallest functions.

Software Engineering Observation 15.3
Changing to an inline function could require clients of the function to be recompiled. This can be significant in program development and maintenance situations.

Performance Tip 15.2
Using inline functions can reduce execution time but may increase program size.

Software Engineering Observation 15.4
The inline qualifier should be used only with small, frequently used functions.

*Defining an **inline** Function*

Figure 15.3 uses inline function cube (lines 11–14) to calculate the volume of a cube of side length side. Keyword const in the parameter list of function cube tells the compiler that the function does not modify variable side. This ensures that the value of side is not changed by the function when the calculation is performed. Notice that the complete definition of function cube appears before it's used in the program. This is required so that the compiler knows how to expand a cube function call into its inlined code. For this reason, reusable inline functions are typically placed in header files, so that their definitions can be included in each source file that uses them.

Software Engineering Observation 15.5

The const qualifier should be used to enforce the principle of least privilege. Using the principle of least privilege to properly design software can greatly reduce debugging time and improper side effects, and can make a program easier to modify and maintain.

Lines 4–6 are using statements that help us eliminate the need to repeat the std:: prefix. Once we include these using statements, we can write cout instead of std::cout, cin instead of std::cin and endl instead of std::endl, in the remainder of the program. From this point forward, every C++ example contains one or more using statements.

```cpp
1   // Fig. 15.3: fig15_03.cpp
2   // inline function that calculates the volume of a cube.
3   #include <iostream>
4   using std::cout;
5   using std::cin;
6   using std::endl;
7
8   // Definition of inline function cube. Definition of function appears
9   // before function is called, so a function prototype is not required.
10  // First line of function definition acts as the prototype.
11  inline double cube( const double side )
12  {
13     return side * side * side; // calculate the cube of side
14  }
15
16  int main()
17  {
18     double sideValue; // stores value entered by user
19
20     for ( int i = 1; i <= 3; i++ )
21     {
22        cout << "\nEnter the side length of your cube: ";
23        cin >> sideValue; // read value from user
24
25        // calculate cube of sideValue and display result
26        cout << "Volume of cube with side "
27           << sideValue << " is " << cube( sideValue ) << endl;
28     }
29  }
```

Fig. 15.3 | inline function that calculates the volume of a cube. (Part 1 of 2.)

```
Enter the side length of your cube: 1.0
Volume of cube with side 1 is 1

Enter the side length of your cube: 2.3
Volume of cube with side 2.3 is 12.167

Enter the side length of your cube: 5.4
Volume of cube with side 5.4 is 157.464
```

Fig. 15.3 | `inline` function that calculates the volume of a cube. (Part 2 of 2.)

In place of lines 4–6, many programmers prefer to use the declaration

```
using namespace std;
```

which enables a program to use all the names in any standard C++ header file (such as `<iostream>`) that a program might include. From this point forward in this chapter, we'll use the preceding declaration in our programs.

The `for` statement's condition (line 20) evaluates to either 0 (false) or nonzero (true). This is consistent with C. C++ also provides type **bool** for representing boolean (true/false) values. The two possible values of a `bool` are the keywords **true** and **false**. When `true` and `false` are converted to integers, they become the values 1 and 0, respectively. When non-boolean values are converted to type `bool`, non-zero values become `true`, and zero or null pointer values become `false`.

15.7 C++ Keywords

Figure 15.4 lists the keywords common to C and C++, the keywords unique to C++ and the keywords that were added to C++ in the C++11 standard.

C++ Keywords				
Keywords common to the C and C++ programming languages				
auto	break	case	char	const
continue	default	do	double	else
enum	extern	float	for	goto
if	int	long	register	return
short	signed	sizeof	static	struct
switch	typedef	union	unsigned	void
volatile	while			
C++-only keywords				
and	and_eq	asm	bitand	bitor
bool	catch	class	compl	const_cast
delete	dynamic_cast	explicit	export	false

Fig. 15.4 | C++ keywords. (Part 1 of 2.)

C++ Keywords				
friend	inline	mutable	namespace	new
not	not_eq	operator	or	or_eq
private	protected	public	reinterpret_cast	static_cast
template	this	throw	true	try
typeid	typename	using	virtual	wchar_t
xor	xor_eq			
C++11 keywords				
alignas	alignof	char16_t	char32_t	constexpr
decltype	noexcept	nullptr	static_assert	thread_local

Fig. 15.4 | C++ keywords. (Part 2 of 2.)

15.8 References and Reference Parameters

Two ways to pass arguments to functions in many programming languages are pass-by-value and pass-by-reference. When an argument is passed by value, a *copy* of the argument's value is made and passed (on the function call stack) to the called function. Changes to the copy do not affect the original variable's value in the caller. This prevents the accidental side effects that can greatly hinder the development of correct and reliable software systems. Each argument that has been passed in the programs in this chapter so far has been passed by value.

Performance Tip 15.3
One disadvantage of pass-by-value is that, if a large data item is being passed, copying that data can take a considerable amount of execution time and memory space.

15.8.1 Reference Parameters

This section introduces **reference parameters**—the first of two means that C++ provides for performing pass-by-reference. With pass-by-reference, the caller gives the called function the ability to access the caller's data directly, and to modify that data if the called function chooses to do so.

Performance Tip 15.4
Pass-by-reference is good for performance reasons, because it can eliminate the pass-by-value overhead of copying large amounts of data.

Software Engineering Observation 15.6
Pass-by-reference can weaken security; the called function can corrupt the caller's data.

Later, we'll show how to achieve the performance advantage of pass-by-reference while simultaneously achieving the software engineering advantage of protecting the caller's data from corruption.

A reference parameter is an alias for its corresponding argument in a function call. To indicate that a function parameter is passed by reference, simply follow the parameter's type in the function prototype and function definition by an ampersand (&). For example, the following parameter declaration

```
int &count
```

when read from right to left is pronounced "count is a reference to an int." In the function call, simply mention the variable by name to pass it by reference. Then, mentioning the variable by its parameter name in the body of the called function actually refers to the original variable in the calling function, and the original variable can be modified directly by the called function.

15.8.2 Passing Arguments by Value and by Reference

Figure 15.5 compares pass-by-value and pass-by-reference with reference parameters. The "styles" of the arguments in the calls to function squareByValue (line 15) and function squareByReference (line 21) are identical—both variables are simply mentioned by name in the function calls. Without checking the function prototypes or function definitions, it's not possible to tell from the calls alone whether either function can modify its arguments. Because function prototypes are mandatory, however, the compiler has no trouble resolving the ambiguity. Recall that a function prototype tells the compiler the type of data returned by the function, the number of parameters the function expects to receive, the types of the parameters, and the order in which they're expected. The compiler uses this information to validate function calls. In C, function prototypes are not required. Making them mandatory in C++ enables **type-safe linkage**, which ensures that the types of the arguments conform to the types of the parameters. Otherwise, the compiler reports an error. Locating such type errors at compile time helps prevent the runtime errors that can occur in C when arguments of incorrect data types are passed to functions.

```cpp
1   // Fig. 15.5: fig15_05.cpp
2   // Comparing pass-by-value and pass-by-reference with references.
3   #include <iostream>
4   using namespace std;
5
6   int squareByValue( int ); // function prototype (value pass)
7   void squareByReference( int & ); // function prototype (reference pass)
8
9   int main()
10  {
11     // demonstrate squareByValue
12     int x = 2;
13     cout << "x = " << x << " before squareByValue\n";
14     cout << "Value returned by squareByValue: "
15        << squareByValue( x ) << endl;
16     cout << "x = " << x << " after squareByValue\n" << endl;
17
18     // demonstrate squareByReference
19     int z = 4;
```

Fig. 15.5 | Comparing pass-by-value and pass-by-reference with references. (Part 1 of 2.)

```
20      cout << "z = " << z << " before squareByReference" << endl;
21      squareByReference( z );
22      cout << "z = " << z << " after squareByReference" << endl;
23   }
24
25   // squareByValue multiplies number by itself, stores the
26   // result in number and returns the new value of number
27   int squareByValue( int number )
28   {
29      return number *= number; // caller's argument not modified
30   }
31
32   // squareByReference multiplies numberRef by itself and stores the result
33   // in the variable to which numberRef refers in the caller
34   void squareByReference( int &numberRef )
35   {
36      numberRef *= numberRef; // caller's argument modified
37   }
```

```
x = 2 before squareByValue
Value returned by squareByValue: 4
x = 2 after squareByValue

z = 4 before squareByReference
z = 16 after squareByReference
```

Fig. 15.5 | Comparing pass-by-value and pass-by-reference with references. (Part 2 of 2.)

Common Programming Error 15.2
Because reference parameters are mentioned only by name in the body of the called function, you might inadvertently treat reference parameters as pass-by-value parameters. This can cause unexpected side effects if the original copies of the variables are changed by the function.

Performance Tip 15.5
For passing large objects efficiently, use a constant reference parameter to simulate the appearance and security of pass-by-value and avoid the overhead of passing a copy of the large object. The called function will not be able to modify the object in the caller.

Software Engineering Observation 15.7
Many programmers do not declare parameters passed by value as const, *even when the called function should not modify the passed argument. Keyword* const *in this context would protect only a copy of the original argument, not the original argument itself, which when passed by value is safe from modification by the called function.*

To specify a reference to a constant, place the const qualifier before the type specifier in the parameter declaration. Note in line 34 of Fig. 15.5 the placement of & in the parameter list of function squareByReference. Some C++ programmers prefer to write int& numberRef with the ampersand abutting int—both forms are equivalent to the compiler.

> ### Software Engineering Observation 15.8
> *For the combined reasons of clarity and performance, many C++ programmers prefer that modifiable arguments be passed to functions by using pointers, small nonmodifiable arguments be passed by value and large nonmodifiable arguments be passed by using references to constants.*

15.8.3 References as Aliases within a Function

References can also be used as aliases for other variables within a function (although they typically are used with functions as shown in Fig. 15.5). For example, the code

```
int count = 1; // declare integer variable count
int &cRef = count; // create cRef as an alias for count
cRef++; // increment count (using its alias cRef)
```

increments variable count by using its alias cRef. Reference variables must be initialized in their declarations, as we show in line 9 of both Fig. 15.6 and Fig. 15.7, and cannot be reassigned as aliases to other variables. Once a reference is declared as an alias for a variable, all operations "performed" on the alias (i.e., the reference) are actually performed on the original variable. The alias is simply another name for the original variable. Taking the address of a reference and comparing references do not cause syntax errors; rather, each operation occurs on the variable for which the reference is an alias. Unless it's a reference to a constant, a reference argument must be an *lvalue* (e.g., a variable name), not a constant or expression that returns an *rvalue* (e.g., the result of a calculation).

```
 1   // Fig. 15.6: fig15_06.cpp
 2   // Initializing and using a reference.
 3   #include <iostream>
 4   using namespace std;
 5
 6   int main()
 7   {
 8      int x = 3;
 9      int &y = x; // y refers to (is an alias for) x
10
11      cout << "x = " << x << endl << "y = " << y << endl;
12      y = 7; // actually modifies x
13      cout << "x = " << x << endl << "y = " << y << endl;
14   }
```

```
x = 3
y = 3
x = 7
y = 7
```

Fig. 15.6 | Initializing and using a reference.

```
 1   // Fig. 15.7: fig15_07.cpp
 2   // Uninitialized reference is a syntax error.
 3   #include <iostream>
 4   using namespace std;
 5
 6   int main()
 7   {
 8      int x = 3;
 9      int &y; // Error: y must be initialized
10
11      cout << "x = " << x << endl << "y = " << y << endl;
12      y = 7;
13      cout << "x = " << x << endl << "y = " << y << endl;
14   }
```

Microsoft Visual C++ compiler error message:

```
fig15_07.cpp(9) : error C2530: 'y' :
   references must be initialized
```

GNU C++ compiler error message:

```
fig15_07.cpp:9: error: 'y' declared as a reference but not initialized
```

Xcode LLVM compiler error message:

```
Declaration of reference variable 'y' requires an initializer
```

Fig. 15.7 | Uninitialized reference is a syntax error.

15.8.4 Returning a Reference from a Function

Returning references from functions can be dangerous. When returning a reference to a variable declared in the called function, the variable should be declared static within that function. Otherwise, the reference refers to an automatic variable that is discarded when the function terminates; such a variable is "undefined," and the program's behavior is unpredictable. References to undefined variables are called **dangling references**.

Common Programming Error 15.3

Not initializing a reference variable when it's declared is a compilation error, unless the declaration is part of a function's parameter list. Reference parameters are initialized when the function in which they're declared is called.

Common Programming Error 15.4

Attempting to reassign a previously declared reference to be an alias to another variable is a logic error. The value of the other variable is simply assigned to the variable for which the reference is already an alias.

Common Programming Error 15.5

Returning a reference to an automatic variable in a called function is a logic error. Some compilers issue a warning when this occurs.

15.8.5 Error Messages for Uninitialized References

The C++ standard does not specify the error messages that compilers use to indicate particular errors. For this reason, we show in Fig. 15.7 the error messages produced by several compilers when a reference is not initialized.

15.9 Empty Parameter Lists

C++, like C, allows you to define functions with no parameters. In C++, an empty parameter list is specified by writing either void or nothing at all in parentheses. The prototypes

```
void print();
void print( void );
```

each specify that function print does not take arguments and does not return a value. These prototypes are equivalent.

Portability Tip 15.2

The meaning of an empty function parameter list in C++ is dramatically different than in C. In C, it means all argument checking is disabled (i.e., the function call can pass any arguments it wants). In C++, it means that the function takes no arguments. Thus, C programs using this feature might cause compilation errors when compiled in C++.

15.10 Default Arguments

It's not uncommon for a program to invoke a function repeatedly with the same argument value for a particular parameter. In such cases, you can specify that such a parameter has a **default argument**, i.e., a default value to be passed to that parameter. When a program omits an argument for a parameter with a default argument in a function call, the compiler rewrites the function call and inserts the default value of that argument to be passed as an argument in the function call.

Default arguments must be the rightmost (trailing) arguments in a function's parameter list. When calling a function with two or more default arguments, if an omitted argument is not the rightmost argument in the argument list, then all arguments to the right of that argument also must be omitted. Default arguments should be specified with the first occurrence of the function name—typically, in the function prototype. If the function prototype is omitted because the function definition also serves as the prototype, then the default arguments should be specified in the function header. Default values can be any expression, including constants, global variables or function calls. Default arguments also can be used with inline functions.

Figure 15.8 demonstrates using default arguments in calculating the volume of a box. The function prototype for boxVolume (line 7) specifies that all three parameters have been given default values of 1. We provided variable names in the function prototype for readability, but these are not required.

Common Programming Error 15.6

It's a compilation error to specify default arguments in both a function's prototype and header.

```
1   // Fig. 15.8: fig15_08.cpp
2   // Using default arguments.
3   #include <iostream>
4   using namespace std;
5
6   // function prototype that specifies default arguments
7   int boxVolume( int length = 1, int width = 1, int height = 1 );
8
9   int main()
10  {
11     // no arguments--use default values for all dimensions
12     cout << "The default box volume is: " << boxVolume();
13
14     // specify length; default width and height
15     cout << "\n\nThe volume of a box with length 10,\n"
16        << "width 1 and height 1 is: " << boxVolume( 10 );
17
18     // specify length and width; default height
19     cout << "\n\nThe volume of a box with length 10,\n"
20        << "width 5 and height 1 is: " << boxVolume( 10, 5 );
21
22     // specify all arguments
23     cout << "\n\nThe volume of a box with length 10,\n"
24        << "width 5 and height 2 is: " << boxVolume( 10, 5, 2 )
25        << endl;
26  }
27
28  // function boxVolume calculates the volume of a box
29  int boxVolume( int length, int width, int height )
30  {
31     return length * width * height;
32  }
```

```
The default box volume is: 1

The volume of a box with length 10,
width 1 and height 1 is: 10

The volume of a box with length 10,
width 5 and height 1 is: 50

The volume of a box with length 10,
width 5 and height 2 is: 100
```

Fig. 15.8 | Using default arguments.

The first call to boxVolume (line 12) specifies no arguments, thus using all three default values of 1. The second call (line 16) passes a length argument, thus using default values of 1 for the width and height arguments. The third call (line 20) passes arguments for length and width, thus using a default value of 1 for the height argument. The last call (line 24) passes arguments for length, width and height, thus using no default values. Any arguments passed to the function explicitly are assigned to the function's parameters from left to right. Therefore, when boxVolume receives one argument, the function assigns the value of that argument to its length parameter (i.e., the leftmost parameter in the parameter list). When boxVolume receives two arguments, the function assigns the values of those arguments to its length and width parameters in that order. Finally, when box-Volume receives all three arguments, the function assigns the values of those arguments to its length, width and height parameters, respectively.

Good Programming Practice 15.1

Using default arguments can simplify writing function calls. However, some programmers feel that explicitly specifying all arguments is clearer.

Software Engineering Observation 15.9

If the default values for a function change, all client code must be recompiled.

Common Programming Error 15.7

In a function definition, specifying and attempting to use a default argument that is not a rightmost (trailing) argument (while not simultaneously defaulting all the rightmost arguments) is a syntax error.

15.11 Unary Scope Resolution Operator

It's possible to declare local and global variables of the same name. This causes the global variable to be "hidden" by the local variable in the local scope. C++ provides the **unary scope resolution operator** (::) to access a global variable when a local variable of the same name is in scope. The unary scope resolution operator cannot be used to access a local variable of the same name in an outer block. A global variable can be accessed directly without the unary scope resolution operator if the name of the global variable is not the same as that of a local variable in scope.

Figure 15.9 demonstrates the unary scope resolution operator with global and local variables of the same name (lines 6 and 10, respectively). To emphasize that the local and global versions of variable number are distinct, the program declares one variable of type int and the other double.

```
1   // Fig. 15.9: fig15_09.cpp
2   // Using the unary scope resolution operator.
3   #include <iostream>
4   using namespace std;
5
6   int number = 7; // global variable named number
7
8   int main()
9   {
10      double number = 10.5; // local variable named number
11
12      // display values of local and global variables
13      cout << "Local double value of number = " << number
14         << "\nGlobal int value of number = " << ::number << endl;
15  }
```

Fig. 15.9 | Using the unary scope resolution operator. (Part 1 of 2.)

```
Local double value of number = 10.5
Global int value of number = 7
```

Fig. 15.9 | Using the unary scope resolution operator. (Part 2 of 2.)

Using the unary scope resolution operator (::) with a given variable name is optional when the only variable with that name is a global variable.

Common Programming Error 15.8
It's an error to attempt to use the unary scope resolution operator (::) to access a nonglobal variable in an outer block. If no global variable with that name exists, a compilation error occurs. If a global variable with that name exists, this is a logic error, because the program will refer to the global variable when you intended to access the nonglobal variable in the outer block.

Good Programming Practice 15.2
Always using the unary scope resolution operator (::) to refer to global variables makes it clear that you intend to access a global variable rather than a nonglobal variable.

Software Engineering Observation 15.10
Always using the unary scope resolution operator (::) to refer to global variables makes programs easier to modify by reducing the risk of name collisions with nonglobal variables.

Error-Prevention Tip 15.1
Always using the unary scope resolution operator (::) to refer to a global variable eliminates logic errors that might occur if a nonglobal variable hides the global variable.

Error-Prevention Tip 15.2
Avoid using variables of the same name for different purposes in a program. Although this is allowed in various circumstances, it can lead to errors.

15.12 Function Overloading

C++ enables several functions of the same name to be defined, as long as these functions have different sets of parameters (at least as far as the parameter types or the number of parameters or the order of the parameter types are concerned). This capability is called **function overloading**. When an overloaded function is called, the C++ compiler selects the proper function by examining the number, types and order of the arguments in the call. Function overloading is commonly used to create several functions of the same name that perform similar tasks, but on data of different types. For example, many functions in the math library are overloaded for different numeric data types.[1]

Good Programming Practice 15.3
Overloading functions that perform closely related tasks can make programs more readable and understandable.

*Overloaded **square** Functions*

Figure 15.10 uses overloaded square functions to calculate the square of an int (lines 7–11) and the square of a double (lines 14–18). Line 22 invokes the int version of function square by passing the literal value 7. C++ treats whole-number literal values as type int by default. Similarly, line 24 invokes the double version of function square by passing the literal value 7.5, which C++ treats as a double value by default. In each case the compiler chooses the proper function to call, based on the type of the argument. The outputs confirm that the proper function was called in each case.

```cpp
1   // Fig. 15.10: fig15_10.cpp
2   // Overloaded square functions.
3   #include <iostream>
4   using namespace std;
5
6   // function square for int values
7   int square( int x )
8   {
9      cout << "square of integer " << x << " is ";
10     return x * x;
11  }
12
13  // function square for double values
14  double square( double y )
15  {
16     cout << "square of double " << y << " is ";
17     return y * y;
18  }
19
20  int main()
21  {
22     cout << square( 7 ); // calls int version
23     cout << endl;
24     cout << square( 7.5 ); // calls double version
25     cout << endl;
26  }
```

```
square of integer 7 is 49
square of double 7.5 is 56.25
```

Fig. 15.10 | Overloaded square functions.

How the Compiler Differentiates Overloaded Functions

Overloaded functions are distinguished by their **signatures**—a combination of a function's name and its parameter types in order (but not its return type). The compiler encodes each function identifier with the number and types of its parameters (sometimes referred to as **name mangling** or **name decoration**) to enable type-safe linkage. This ensures that the proper overloaded function is called and that the argument types conform to the parameter types.

---

1. The C++ standard requires float, double and long double overloaded versions of the math library functions discussed in Section 5.3.

Figure 15.11 was compiled with GNU C++. Rather than showing the execution output of the program (as we normally would), we show the mangled function names produced in assembly language by GNU C++. Each mangled name (other than main) begins with two underscores (__) followed by the letter Z, a number and the function name. The number that follows Z specifies how many characters are in the function's name. For example, function square has 6 characters in its name, so its mangled name is prefixed with __Z6.

Common Programming Error 15.9
Creating overloaded functions with identical parameter lists and different return types is a compilation error.

```
1   // Fig. 15.11: fig15_11.cpp
2   // Name mangling to enable type-safe linkage.
3
4   // function square for int values
5   int square( int x )
6   {
7      return x * x;
8   }
9
10  // function square for double values
11  double square( double y )
12  {
13     return y * y;
14  }
15
16  // function that receives arguments of types
17  // int, float, char and int &
18  void nothing1( int a, float b, char c, int &d )
19  {
20     // empty function body
21  }
22
23  // function that receives arguments of types
24  // char, int, float & and double &
25  int nothing2( char a, int b, float &c, double &d )
26  {
27     return 0;
28  }
29
30  int main()
31  {
32     return 0; // indicates successful termination
33  }
```

```
__Z6squarei
__Z6squared
__Z8nothing1ifcRi
__Z8nothing2ciRfRd
_main
```

Fig. 15.11 | Name mangling to enable type-safe linkage.

The function name is then followed by an encoding of its parameter list. In the parameter list for function nothing2 (line 25; see the fourth output line), c represents a char, i represents an int, Rf represents a float & (i.e., a reference to a float) and Rd represents a double & (i.e., a reference to a double). In the parameter list for function nothing1, i represents an int, f represents a float, c represents a char and Ri represents an int &. The two square functions are distinguished by their parameter lists; one specifies d for double and the other specifies i for int.

The return types of the functions are not specified in the mangled names. Overloaded functions can have different return types, but if they do, they must also have different parameter lists. Again, you cannot have two functions with the same signature and different return types. Function-name mangling is compiler specific. Also, function main is not mangled, because it cannot be overloaded.

The compiler uses only the parameter lists to distinguish between functions of the same name. Overloaded functions need not have the same number of parameters. Programmers should use caution when overloading functions with default parameters, because this may cause ambiguity.

Common Programming Error 15.10

A function with default arguments omitted might be called identically to another overloaded function; this is a compilation error. For example, having in a program both a function that explicitly takes no arguments and a function of the same name that contains all default arguments results in a compilation error when an attempt is made to call that function with no arguments. The compiler does not know which version of the function to choose.

Overloaded Operators

In Chapter 18, we discuss how to overload operators to define how they should operate on objects of user-defined data types. (In fact, we've been using overloaded operators, including the stream insertion operator << and the stream extraction operator >>, each of which is overloaded to be able to display data of all the fundamental types. We say more about overloading << and >> to be able to handle objects of user-defined types in Chapter 18.) Section 15.13 introduces function templates for automatically generating overloaded functions that perform identical tasks on data of different types.

15.13 Function Templates

Overloaded functions are typically used to perform similar operations that may involve different program logic on different data types. If the program logic and operations are identical for each data type, overloading may be performed more compactly and conveniently by using **function templates**. You write a single function template definition. Given the argument types provided in calls to this function, C++ automatically generates separate **function template specializations** to handle each type of call appropriately. Thus, defining a single function template essentially defines a whole family of overloaded functions.

15.13.1 Defining a Function Template

Figure 15.12 contains the definition of a function template (lines 4–18) for a maximum function that determines the largest of three values. All function template definitions begin with the template keyword (line 4) followed by a **template parameter list** to the function template enclosed in angle brackets (< and >). Every parameter in the template parameter list (each is referred to as a **formal type parameter**) is preceded by keyword typename or keyword class (which are synonyms). The formal type parameters are placeholders for fundamental types or user-defined types. These placeholders are used to specify the types of the function's parameters (line 5), to specify the function's return type and to declare variables within the body of the function definition (line 7). A function template is defined like any other function, but uses the formal type parameters as placeholders for actual data types.

```
1   // Fig. 15.12: maximum.h
2   // Function template maximum header file.
3
4   template < class T >   // or template< typename T >
5   T maximum( T value1, T value2, T value3 )
6   {
7       T maximumValue = value1; // assume value1 is maximum
8
9       // determine whether value2 is greater than maximumValue
10      if ( value2 > maximumValue )
11          maximumValue = value2;
12
13      // determine whether value3 is greater than maximumValue
14      if ( value3 > maximumValue )
15          maximumValue = value3;
16
17      return maximumValue;
18  }
```

Fig. 15.12 | Function template maximum header file.

The function template in Fig. 15.12 declares a single formal type parameter T (line 4) as a placeholder for the type of the data to be tested by function maximum. The name of a type parameter must be unique in the template parameter list for a particular template definition. When the compiler detects a maximum invocation in the program source code, the type of the data passed to maximum is substituted for T throughout the template definition, and C++ creates a complete source-code function for determining the maximum of three values of the specified data type. Then the newly created function is compiled. Thus, templates are a means of code generation for a range of similar functions.

Common Programming Error 15.11
Not placing keyword class or keyword typename before every formal type parameter of a function template (e.g., writing <class S, T> instead of <class S, class T>) is a syntax error.

15.13.2 Using a Function Template

Figure 15.13 uses the maximum function template (lines 18, 28 and 38) to determine the largest of three int values, three double values and three char values.

```
 1   // Fig. 15.13: fig15_13.cpp
 2   // Demonstrating function template maximum.
 3   #include <iostream>
 4   using namespace std;
 5
 6   #include "maximum.h" // include definition of function template maximum
 7
 8   int main()
 9   {
10      // demonstrate maximum with int values
11      int int1, int2, int3;
12
13      cout << "Input three integer values: ";
14      cin >> int1 >> int2 >> int3;
15
16      // invoke int version of maximum
17      cout << "The maximum integer value is: "
18         << maximum( int1, int2, int3 );
19
20      // demonstrate maximum with double values
21      double double1, double2, double3;
22
23      cout << "\n\nInput three double values: ";
24      cin >> double1 >> double2 >> double3;
25
26      // invoke double version of maximum
27      cout << "The maximum double value is: "
28         << maximum( double1, double2, double3 );
29
30      // demonstrate maximum with char values
31      char char1, char2, char3;
32
33      cout << "\n\nInput three characters: ";
34      cin >> char1 >> char2 >> char3;
35
36      // invoke char version of maximum
37      cout << "The maximum character value is: "
38         << maximum( char1, char2, char3 ) << endl;
39   }
```

```
Input three integer values: 1 2 3
The maximum integer value is: 3

Input three double values: 3.3 2.2 1.1
The maximum double value is: 3.3

Input three characters: A C B
The maximum character value is: C
```

Fig. 15.13 | Demonstrating function template maximum.

In Fig. 15.13, three functions are created as a result of the calls in lines 18, 28 and 38—expecting three int values, three double values and three char values, respectively.

For example, the function template specialization created for type int replaces each occurrence of T with int as follows:

```
int maximum( int value1, int value2, int value3 )
{
    int maximumValue = value1; // assume value1 is maximum

    // determine whether value2 is greater than maximumValue
    if ( value2 > maximumValue )
        maximumValue = value2;

    // determine whether value3 is greater than maximumValue
    if ( value3 > maximumValue )
        maximumValue = value3;

    return maximumValue;
}
```

15.14 Introduction to Object Technology and the UML

In this section, we discuss object orientation, a natural way of thinking about the world and writing computer programs. Our goal here is to help you develop an object-oriented way of thinking and to introduce you to the **Unified Modeling Language™ (UML™)**— a graphical language that allows people who design object-oriented software systems to use an industry-standard notation to represent them. Here, we'll first review some object-oriented programming concepts we introduced in Section 1.8, then introduce some additional terminology that we use in Section 15.15 and Chapters 16–23.

15.14.1 Basic Object Technology Concepts

Everywhere you look in the real world you see objects—people, animals, plants, cars, planes, buildings, computers and so on. Humans think in terms of objects. Telephones, houses, traffic lights, microwave ovens and water coolers are just a few more objects we see around us every day.

Attributes and Behaviors
Objects have some things in common. They all have **attributes** (e.g., size, shape, color and weight), and they all exhibit **behaviors** (e.g., a ball rolls, bounces, inflates and deflates; a baby cries, sleeps, crawls, walks and blinks; a car accelerates, brakes and turns; a towel absorbs water). Humans learn about existing objects by studying their attributes and observing their behaviors. Different objects can have similar attributes and can exhibit similar behaviors. Comparisons can be made, for example, between babies and adults and between humans and chimpanzees. We'll study the kinds of attributes and behaviors that software objects have.

Object-Oriented Design and Inheritance
Object-oriented design (OOD) models software in terms similar to those that people use to describe real-world objects. It takes advantage of class relationships, where objects of a certain class, such as a class of vehicles, have the same characteristics—cars, trucks, little red wagons and roller skates have much in common. OOD takes advantage of **inheritance** relationships, where new classes of objects are derived by absorbing characteristics of existing classes and adding unique characteristics of their own. An object of class "convertible"

certainly has the characteristics of the more general class "automobile," but more specifi-cally, the roof goes up and down.

Object-oriented design provides a natural and intuitive way to view the software design process—namely, modeling objects by their attributes, behaviors and interrelation-ships just as we describe real-world objects. OOD also models communication between objects. Just as people send messages to one another (e.g., a sergeant commands a soldier to stand at attention), objects also communicate via messages. A bank account object may receive a message to decrease its balance by a certain amount because the customer has withdrawn that amount of money.

Encapsulation and Information Hiding

OOD **encapsulates** (i.e., wraps) attributes and **operations** (behaviors) into objects—an object's attributes and operations are intimately tied together. Objects have the property of **information hiding**. This means that objects may know how to communicate with one another across well-defined **interfaces**, but normally they're not allowed to know how oth-er objects are implemented—implementation details are hidden within the objects them-selves. We can drive a car effectively, for instance, without knowing the details of how engines, transmissions, brakes and exhaust systems work internally—as long as we know how to use the accelerator pedal, the brake pedal, the steering wheel and so on. Informa-tion hiding, as we'll see, is crucial to good software engineering.

Object-Oriented Programming

Languages like C++ are **object oriented**. Programming in such a language is called **object-oriented programming** (OOP), and it allows you to implement an object-oriented design as a working software system. Languages like C, on the other hand, are **procedural**, so pro-gramming tends to be **action oriented**. In C, the unit of programming is the function. In C++, the unit of programming is the "class" from which objects are eventually **instantiated** (an OOP term for "created"). C++ classes contain functions that implement operations and data that implements attributes.

C programmers concentrate on writing functions. Programmers group actions that perform some common task into functions, and group functions to form programs. Data is certainly important in C, but the view is that data exists primarily in support of the actions that functions perform. The verbs in a system specification help you determine the set of functions that will work together to implement the system.

15.14.2 Classes, Data Members and Member Functions

C++ programmers concentrate on creating their own user-defined types called classes. Each class contains data as well as the set of functions that manipulate that data and pro-vide services to **clients** (i.e., other classes or functions that use the class). The data compo-nents of a class are called **data members**. For example, a bank account class might include an account number and a balance. The function components of a class are called **member functions** (typically called **methods** in other object-oriented programming languages such as Java). For example, a bank account class might include member functions to make a deposit (increasing the balance), make a withdrawal (decreasing the balance) and inquire what the current balance is. You use built-in types (and other user-defined types) as the "building blocks" for constructing new user-defined types (classes). The nouns in a system specification help the C++ programmer determine the set of classes from which objects are created that work together to implement the system.

Classes are to objects as blueprints are to houses—a class is a "plan" for building an object of the class. Just as we can build many houses from one blueprint, we can instantiate (create) many objects from one class. You cannot cook meals in the kitchen of a blueprint; you can cook meals in the kitchen of a house. You cannot sleep in the bedroom of a blueprint; you can sleep in the bedroom of a house.

Classes can have relationships with other classes. In an object-oriented design of a bank, the "bank teller" class relates to other classes, such as the "customer" class, the "cash drawer" class, the "safe" class, and so on. These relationships are called **associations**. Packaging software as classes makes it possible for future software systems to **reuse** the classes.

Software Engineering Observation 15.11

Reuse of existing classes when building new classes and programs saves time, money and effort. Reuse also helps you build more reliable and effective systems, because existing classes often have gone through extensive testing, debugging and performance tuning.

Indeed, with object technology, you can build much of the new software you'll need by combining existing classes, just as automobile manufacturers combine interchangeable parts. Each new class you create can become a valuable software asset that you and others can reuse to speed and enhance the quality of future software development efforts.

15.14.3 Object-Oriented Analysis and Design

Soon you'll be writing larger programs in C++. How will you create the code for your programs? Perhaps, like many beginning programmers, you'll simply turn on your computer and start typing. This approach may work for small programs, but what if you were asked to create a software system to control thousands of automated teller machines for a major bank? Or what if you were asked to work on a team of 1000 software developers building the next generation of the U.S. air traffic control system? For projects so large and complex, you could not simply sit down and start writing programs.

To create the best solutions, you should follow a detailed process for **analyzing** your project's **requirements** (i.e., determining *what* the system is supposed to do) and developing a **design** that satisfies them (i.e., deciding *how* the system should do it). Ideally, you would go through this process and carefully review the design (or have your design reviewed by other software professionals) before writing any code. If this process involves analyzing and designing your system from an object-oriented point of view, it's called **object-oriented analysis and design** (OOAD). Experienced programmers know that analysis and design can save many hours by helping avoid an ill-planned system development approach that has to be abandoned partway through its implementation, possibly wasting considerable time, money and effort.

OOAD is the generic term for the process of analyzing a problem and developing an approach for solving it. Small problems like the ones discussed in the next few chapters do not require an exhaustive OOAD process.

As problems and the groups of people solving them increase in size, the methods of OOAD quickly become more appropriate than pseudocode. Ideally, a group should agree on a strictly defined process for solving its problem and a uniform way of communicating the results of that process to one another. Although many different OOAD processes exist, a single graphical language for communicating the results of *any* OOAD process has come into wide use. This language, known as the Unified Modeling Language (UML), was developed in the mid-1990s under the initial direction of three software methodologists: Grady Booch, James Rumbaugh and Ivar Jacobson.

15.14.4 The Unified Modeling Language

In the 1980s, increasing numbers of organizations began using OOP to build their applications, and a need developed for a standard OOAD process. Many methodologists—including Booch, Rumbaugh and Jacobson—individually produced and promoted separate processes to satisfy this need. Each process had its own notation, or "language" (in the form of graphical diagrams), to convey the results of analysis and design.

In 1994, James Rumbaugh joined Grady Booch at Rational Software Corporation (now a division of IBM), and the two began working to unify their popular processes. They soon were joined by Ivar Jacobson. In 1996, the group released early versions of the UML to the software engineering community and requested feedback. Around the same time, an organization known as the **Object Management Group™ (OMG™)** invited submissions for a common modeling language. The OMG (www.omg.org) is a nonprofit organization that promotes the standardization of object-oriented technologies by issuing guidelines and specifications, such as the UML. Several corporations—among them HP, IBM, Microsoft, Oracle and Rational Software—had already recognized the need for a common modeling language. In response to the OMG's request for proposals, these companies formed **UML Partners**—the consortium that developed the UML version 1.1 and submitted it to the OMG. The OMG accepted the proposal and, in 1997, assumed responsibility for the continuing maintenance and revision of the UML. We present the terminology and notation of the current version of the UML—UML version 2— throughout the C++ section of this book.

The Unified Modeling Language is now the most widely used graphical representation scheme for modeling object-oriented systems. Those who design systems use the language (in the form of diagrams) to model their systems, as we do throughout the C++ section of this book. An attractive feature of the UML is its flexibility. The UML is **extensible** (i.e., capable of being enhanced with new features) and is independent of any particular OOAD process. UML modelers are free to use various processes in designing systems, but all developers can now express their designs with one standard set of graphical notations. For more information, visit our UML Resource Center at www.deitel.com/UML/.

15.15 Introduction to C++ Standard Library Class Template vector

We now introduce C++ Standard Library class template **vector**, which represents a more robust type of array featuring many additional capabilities.

15.15.1 Problems Associated with C-Style Pointer-Based Arrays

C-style pointer-based arrays (i.e., the type of arrays presented thus far) have great potential for errors. For example, as mentioned earlier, a program can easily "walk off" either end of an array, because neither C nor C++ check whether indices fall outside the range of an array.

Two arrays cannot be meaningfully compared with equality operators or relational operators. As you learned in Chapter 7, pointer variables (known more commonly as pointers) contain memory addresses as their values. Array names are simply *pointers* to where the arrays begin in memory, and, of course, two different arrays will always be at different memory locations.

When an array is passed to a general-purpose function designed to handle arrays of any size, the size of the array must be passed as an additional argument. Furthermore, one array cannot be assigned to another with the assignment operator(s)—array names are const pointers, so they cannot be used on the left side of an assignment operator.

These and other capabilities certainly seem like "naturals" for dealing with arrays, but C++ does not provide such capabilities. However, the C++ Standard Library provides class template vector to allow you to create a more powerful and less error-prone alternative to arrays. In Chapter 18, we present the means to implement such array capabilities as those provided by vector. You'll learn how to customize operators for use with your own classes (a technique known as *operator overloading*).

15.15.2 Using Class Template vector

The vector class template is available to anyone building C++ applications. The notations that the vector example uses might be unfamiliar to you, because vectors use template notation. In Section 15.13, we discussed function templates. In Chapter 23, we discuss creating your own class templates. For now, you should feel comfortable using class template vector by mimicking the syntax in the example we show in this section.

The program of Fig. 15.14 demonstrates capabilities provided by C++ Standard Library class template vector that are not available for C-style pointer-based arrays. Standard class template vector provides many of the same features as the Array class that we construct in Chapter 18. Standard class template vector is defined in header <vector> (line 5) and belongs to namespace std. At the end of this section, we'll demonstrate class vector's bounds checking capabilities and introduce C++'s exception-handling mechanism, which can be used to detect and handle an out-of-bounds vector index.

```cpp
1   // Fig. 15.14: fig15_14.cpp
2   // Demonstrating C++ Standard Library class template vector.
3   #include <iostream>
4   #include <iomanip>
5   #include <vector>
6   using namespace std;
7
8   void outputVector( const vector< int > & ); // display the vector
9   void inputVector( vector< int > & ); // input values into the vector
10
11  int main()
12  {
13     vector< int > integers1( 7 ); // 7-element vector< int >
14     vector< int > integers2( 10 ); // 10-element vector< int >
```

Fig. 15.14 | Demonstrating C++ Standard Library class template vector. (Part 1 of 4.)

```
15
16      // print integers1 size and contents
17      cout << "Size of vector integers1 is " << integers1.size()
18         << "\nvector after initialization:" << endl;
19      outputVector( integers1 );
20
21      // print integers2 size and contents
22      cout << "\nSize of vector integers2 is " << integers2.size()
23         << "\nvector after initialization:" << endl;
24      outputVector( integers2 );
25
26      // input and print integers1 and integers2
27      cout << "\nEnter 17 integers:" << endl;
28      inputVector( integers1 );
29      inputVector( integers2 );
30
31      cout << "\nAfter input, the vectors contain:\n"
32         << "integers1:" << endl;
33      outputVector( integers1 );
34      cout << "integers2:" << endl;
35      outputVector( integers2 );
36
37      // use inequality (!=) operator with vector objects
38      cout << "\nEvaluating: integers1 != integers2" << endl;
39
40      if ( integers1 != integers2 )
41         cout << "integers1 and integers2 are not equal" << endl;
42
43      // create vector integers3 using integers1 as an
44      // initializer; print size and contents
45      vector< int > integers3( integers1 ); // copy constructor
46
47      cout << "\nSize of vector integers3 is " << integers3.size()
48         << "\nvector after initialization:" << endl;
49      outputVector( integers3 );
50
51      // use overloaded assignment (=) operator
52      cout << "\nAssigning integers2 to integers1:" << endl;
53      integers1 = integers2; // assign integers2 to integers1
54
55      cout << "integers1:" << endl;
56      outputVector( integers1 );
57      cout << "integers2:" << endl;
58      outputVector( integers2 );
59
60      // use equality (==) operator with vector objects
61      cout << "\nEvaluating: integers1 == integers2" << endl;
62
63      if ( integers1 == integers2 )
64         cout << "integers1 and integers2 are equal" << endl;
65
66      // use square brackets to create rvalue
67      cout << "\nintegers1[5] is " << integers1[ 5 ];
```

Fig. 15.14 | Demonstrating C++ Standard Library class template vector. (Part 2 of 4.)

```
68
69      // use square brackets to create lvalue
70      cout << "\n\nAssigning 1000 to integers1[5]" << endl;
71      integers1[ 5 ] = 1000;
72      cout << "integers1:" << endl;
73      outputVector( integers1 );
74
75      // attempt to use out-of-range index
76      try
77      {
78         cout << "\nAttempt to display integers1.at( 15 )" << endl;
79         cout << integers1.at( 15 ) << endl; // ERROR: out of range
80      }
81      catch ( out_of_range &ex )
82      {
83         cout << "An exception occurred: " << ex.what() << endl;
84      }
85   }
86
87   // output vector contents
88   void outputVector( const vector< int > &array )
89   {
90      size_t i; // declare control variable
91
92      for ( i = 0; i < array.size(); ++i )
93      {
94         cout << setw( 12 ) << array[ i ];
95
96         if ( ( i + 1 ) % 4 == 0 ) // 4 numbers per row of output
97            cout << endl;
98      }
99
100     if ( i % 4 != 0 )
101        cout << endl;
102  }
103
104  // input vector contents
105  void inputVector( vector< int > &array )
106  {
107     for ( size_t i = 0; i < array.size(); ++i )
108        cin >> array[ i ];
109  }
```

```
Size of vector integers1 is 7
vector after initialization:
           0            0            0            0
           0            0            0

Size of vector integers2 is 10
vector after initialization:
           0            0            0            0
           0            0            0            0
           0            0
```

Fig. 15.14 | Demonstrating C++ Standard Library class template vector. (Part 3 of 4.)

```
Enter 17 integers:
1 2 3 4 5 6 7 8 9 10 11 12 13 14 15 16 17

After input, the vectors contain:
integers1:
             1             2             3             4
             5             6             7
integers2:
             8             9            10            11
            12            13            14            15
            16            17

Evaluating: integers1 != integers2
integers1 and integers2 are not equal

Size of vector integers3 is 7
vector after initialization:
             1             2             3             4
             5             6             7

Assigning integers2 to integers1:
integers1:
             8             9            10            11
            12            13            14            15
            16            17
integers2:
             8             9            10            11
            12            13            14            15
            16            17

Evaluating: integers1 == integers2
integers1 and integers2 are equal

integers1[5] is 13

Assigning 1000 to integers1[5]
integers1:
             8             9            10            11
            12          1000            14            15
            16            17

Attempt to display integers1.at( 15 )
An exception occurred: invalid vector<T> subscript
```

Fig. 15.14 | Demonstrating C++ Standard Library class template vector. (Part 4 of 4.)

Creating vector Objects

Lines 13–14 create two vector objects that store values of type int—integers1 contains seven elements, and integers2 contains 10 elements. By default, all the elements of each vector object are set to 0. Note that vectors can be defined to store *any* data type, by replacing int in vector<int> with the appropriate data type. This notation, which specifies the type stored in the vector, is similar to the template notation that Section 15.13 introduced with function templates.

vector Member Function size; Function outputVector

Line 17 uses vector member function **size** to obtain the size (i.e., the number of elements) of integers1. To invoke a member function, you access it with the dot (.) operator, just as you do with struct and union members. Line 19 passes integers1 to function outputVector (lines 88–102), which uses square brackets, [] (line 94), to obtain the value in each element of the vector for output. Note the resemblance of this notation to that used to access the value of an array element. Lines 22 and 24 perform the same tasks for integers2.

Member function size of class template vector returns the number of elements in a vector as a value of type size_t (which represents the type unsigned int on many systems). As a result, line 90 declares the control variable i to be of type size_t, too. On some compilers, declaring i as an int causes the compiler to issue a warning message, since the loop-continuation condition (line 92) would compare a signed value (i.e., int i) and an unsigned value (i.e., a value of type size_t returned by function size).

Function inputVector
Lines 28–29 pass integers1 and integers2 to function inputVector (lines 105–109) to read values for each vector's elements from the user. The function uses square brackets ([]) to form *lvalues* that are used to store the input values in each vector element.

Comparing vector Objects for Inequality
Line 40 demonstrates that vector objects can be compared with one another using the != operator. If the contents of two vectors are not equal, the operator returns true; otherwise, it returns false.

Initializing One vector with the Contents of Another
The C++ Standard Library class template vector allows you to create a new vector object that is initialized with the contents of an existing vector. Line 45 creates a vector object integers3 and initializes it with a copy of integers1. This invokes vector's so-called copy constructor to perform the copy operation. You'll learn how to create copy constructors in Chapter 18. Lines 47–49 output the size and contents of integers3 to demonstrate that it was initialized correctly.

Assigning vectors and Comparing vectors for Equality
Line 53 assigns integers2 to integers1, demonstrating that the assignment (=) operator can be used with vector objects. Lines 55–58 output the contents of both objects to show that they now contain identical values. Line 63 then compares integers1 to integers2 with the equality (==) operator to determine whether the contents of the two objects are equal after the assignment in line 53 (which they are).

Using the [] Operator to Access and Modify vector Elements
Lines 67 and 71 use square brackets ([]) to obtain a vector element as an *rvalue* and as an *lvalue*, respectively. An *rvalue* cannot be modified, but an *lvalue* can. As is the case with C-style pointer-based arrays, C++ *does not perform any bounds checking when vector elements are accessed with square brackets*. Therefore, you must ensure that operations using [] do not accidentally attempt to manipulate elements outside the bounds of the vector. Standard class template vector does, however, provide bounds checking in its member function at, which we use at line 79 and discuss shortly.

15.15.3 Exception Handling: Processing an Out-of-Range Index
An **exception** indicates a problem that occurs while a program executes. The name "exception" suggests that the problem occurs infrequently—if the "rule" is that a statement nor-

mally executes correctly, then the problem represents the "exception to the rule." **Exception handling** enables you to create **fault-tolerant programs** that can resolve (or handle) exceptions. In many cases, this allows a program to continue executing as if no problems were encountered. For example, Fig. 15.14 still runs to completion, even though an attempt was made to access an out-of-range index. More severe problems might prevent a program from continuing normal execution, instead requiring the program to notify the user of the problem, then terminate. When a function detects a problem, such as an invalid array index or an invalid argument, it **throws** an exception—that is, an exception occurs. Here we introduce exception handling briefly. We'll discuss it in detail in Chapter 22.

The **try** Statement

To handle an exception, place any code that might throw an exception in a **try statement** (lines 76–84). The **try block** (lines 76–80) contains the code that might *throw* an exception, and the **catch block** (lines 81–84) contains the code that *handles* the exception if one occurs. You can have many catch blocks to handle different types of exceptions that might be thrown in the corresponding try block. If the code in the try block executes successfully, lines 81–84 are ignored. The braces that delimit try and catch blocks' bodies are required.

The vector member function **at** provides bounds checking and throws an exception if its argument is an invalid index. By default, this causes a C++ program to terminate. If the index is valid, function at returns the element at the specified location as a modifiable *lvalue* or an unmodifiable *lvalue*, depending on the context in which the call appears. An unmodifiable *lvalue* is an expression that identifies an object in memory (such as an element in a vector), but cannot be used to modify that object.

Executing the **catch** Block

When the program calls vector member function at with the argument 15 (line 79), the function attempts to access the element at location 15, which is *outside* the vector's bounds—integers1 has only 10 elements at this point. Because bounds checking is performed at execution time, vector member function at generates an exception—specifically line 79 throws an **out_of_range** exception (from header <stdexcept>) to notify the program of this problem. At this point, the try block terminates immediately and the catch block begins executing—if you declared any variables in the try block, they're now out of scope and are not accessible in the catch block. [*Note:* To avoid compilation errors with GNU C++, you may need to include header <stdexcept> to use class out_of_range.]

The catch block declares a type (out_of_range) and an exception parameter (ex) that it receives as a reference. The catch block can handle exceptions of the specified type. Inside the block, you use the parameter's identifier to interact with a caught exception object.

what Member Function of the Exception Parameter

When lines 81–84 *catch* the exception, the program displays a message indicating the problem that occurred. Line 83 calls the exception object's **what** member function to get the error message that is stored in the exception object and display it. Once the message is displayed in this example, the exception is considered handled and the program continues with the next statement after the catch block's closing brace. In this example, the end of the program is reached, so the program terminates. We use exception handling throughout our treatment of C++; Chapter 22 presents a deeper look at exception handling.

Summary of This Example

In this section, we demonstrated the C++ Standard Library class template vector, a robust, reusable class that can replace C-style pointer-based arrays. In Chapter 18, you'll see that vector achieves many of its capabilities by "overloading" C++'s built-in operators, and you'll learn how to customize operators for use with your own classes in similar ways. For example, we create an Array class that, like class template vector, improves upon basic array capabilities. Our Array class also provides additional features, such as the ability to input and output entire arrays with operators >> and <<, respectively.

15.16 Wrap-Up

In this chapter, you learned several of C++'s enhancements to C. We presented basic C++-style input and output with cin and cout and overviewed the C++ Standard Library header files. We discussed inline functions for improving performance by eliminating the overhead of function calls. You learned how to use pass-by-reference with C++'s reference parameters, which enable you to create aliases for existing variables. You learned that multiple functions can be overloaded by providing functions with the same name and different signatures; such functions can be used to perform the same or similar tasks, using different types or different numbers of parameters. We then demonstrated a simpler way of overloading functions using function templates, where a function is defined once but can be used for several different types. You learned the basic terminology of object technology and were introduced to the UML—the most widely used graphical representation scheme for modeling OO systems. In Chapter 16, you'll learn how to implement your own classes and use objects of those classes in applications.

Summary

Section 15.2 C++

- C++ improves on many of C's features and provides **object-oriented-programming** (OOP; p. 550) capabilities that increase software productivity, quality and reusability.

- C++ was developed by Bjarne Stroustrup at Bell Labs and was originally called "C with classes."

Section 15.3 A Simple Program: Adding Two Integers

- C++ filenames can have one of several extensions, such as **.cpp**, **.cxx** or **.C** (uppercase).

- C++ allows you to begin a comment with // and use the remainder of the line as comment text. C++ programmers may also use comments delimited by /* and */.

- The input/output stream **header file <iostream>** (p. 552) must be included for any program that outputs data to the screen or inputs data from the keyboard using C++-style stream input/output.

- As in C, every C++ program begins execution with function **main**. Keyword int to the left of main indicates that main "returns" an integer value.

- In C, you need not specify a return type for functions. However, C++ requires you to specify the return type, possibly void, for all functions; otherwise, a syntax error occurs.

- Declarations can be placed almost anywhere in a C++ program, but they must appear before their corresponding variables are used in the program.

- The **standard output stream object** (**std::cout**; p. 552) and the **stream insertion operator** (<<; p. 552) are used to display text on the screen.

- The **standard input stream object** (**std::cin**; p. 552) and the **stream extraction operator** (**>>**; p. 552) are used to obtain values from the keyboard.

- The stream manipulator **std::endl** (p. 553) outputs a newline, then "flushes the output buffer."

- The notation **std::cout** specifies that cout belongs to "namespace" std.

- Using multiple stream insertion operators (**<<**) in a single statement is referred to as **concatenating, chaining** or **cascading stream insertion operations** (p. 553).

Section 15.4 C++ Standard Library
- C++ programs consist of pieces called classes and functions. You can program each piece you may need to form a C++ program. However, most C++ programmers take advantage of the rich collections of existing classes and functions in the **C++ Standard Library** (p. 554).

Section 15.5 Header Files
- The C++ Standard Library is divided into many portions, each with its own header file. The header files contain the function prototypes for the related functions that form each portion of the library. The header files also contain definitions of various class types and functions, as well as constants needed by those functions.

- Header file names ending in .h are "old-style" header files that have been superceded by the C++ Standard Library header files.

Section 15.6 Inline Functions
- C++ provides **inline functions** (p. 556) to help reduce function call overhead. Placing the qualifier **inline** (p. 556) before a function's return type in the function definition "advises" the compiler to generate a copy of the function's code in place to avoid a function call.

Section 15.8 References and Reference Parameters
- Two ways to pass arguments to functions in many programming languages are pass-by-value and pass-by-reference.

- When an argument is passed by value, a *copy* of its value is made and passed (on the function call stack) to the called function. Changes to the copy do not affect the original in the caller.

- With pass-by-reference, the caller gives the called function the ability to access the caller's data directly and to modify it if the called function chooses to do so.

- A **reference parameter** (p. 559) is an alias for its corresponding argument in a function call.

- **Type-safe linkage** ensures that the proper overloaded function is called and that the types of the arguments conform to the types of the parameters.

- To indicate that a function parameter is passed by reference, simply follow the parameter's type in the function prototype by an **ampersand** (**&**); use the same notation when listing the parameter's type in the function header.

- Once a reference is declared as an alias for another variable, all operations supposedly performed on the alias (i.e., the reference) are actually performed on the original variable. The alias is simply another name for the original variable.

Section 15.9 Empty Parameter Lists
- In C++, an **empty parameter list** is specified by writing either void or **nothing in parentheses**.

Section 15.10 Default Arguments
- It's not uncommon for a program to invoke a function repeatedly with the same argument value for a particular parameter. In such cases, the programmer can specify that such a parameter has a **default argument** (p. 564), i.e., a default value to be passed to that parameter.

- When a program omits an argument for a parameter with a default argument, the compiler inserts the default value of that argument to be passed as an argument in the function call.
- Default arguments must be the rightmost (trailing) arguments in a function's parameter list.
- Default arguments should be specified with the first occurrence of the function name—typically, in the function prototype.

Section 15.11 Unary Scope Resolution Operator
- C++ provides the **unary scope resolution operator** (::, p. 566) to access a global variable when a local variable of the same name is in scope.

Section 15.12 Function Overloading
- C++ enables several functions of the same name to be defined, as long as they have different sets of parameters (by number, type and/or order). This capability is called **function overloading** (p. 567).
- When an overloaded function is called, the C++ compiler selects the proper function by examining the number, types and order of the arguments in the call.
- Overloaded functions are distinguished by their **signatures** (p. 568).
- The compiler encodes each function identifier with the number and types of its parameters to enable type-safe linkage.

Section 15.13 Function Templates
- Overloaded functions are used to perform similar operations that may involve different program logic on data of different types. If the program logic and operations are identical for each data type, overloading may be performed more compactly and conveniently using **function templates** (p. 570).
- The programmer writes a single function template definition. Given the argument types provided in calls to this function, C++ automatically generates separate **function template specializations** (p. 570) to handle each type of call appropriately. Thus, defining a single function template essentially defines a family of overloaded functions.
- All function template definitions begin with the **template** keyword followed by a **template parameter list** (p. 571) to the function template enclosed in **angle brackets** (< and >).
- The **formal type parameters** (p. 571) are placeholders for fundamental types or user-defined types. These placeholders are used to specify the types of the function's parameters, to specify the function's return type and to declare variables within the body of the function definition.

Section 15.14 Introduction to Object Technology and the UML
- The **Unified Modeling Language** (UML; p. 573) is a graphical language that allows people who build systems to represent their object-oriented designs in a common notation.
- **Object-oriented design** (**OOD**; p. 573) models software components in terms of real-world objects. It takes advantage of class relationships, where **objects** (p. 573) of a certain class have the same characteristics. It also takes advantage of inheritance relationships, where newly created classes of objects are derived by absorbing characteristics of existing classes and adding unique characteristics of their own. OOD encapsulates data (**attributes**; p. 573) and functions (**behavior**; p. 573) into objects—the data and functions of an object are intimately tied together.
- Objects have the property of information hiding (p. 574)—objects normally are not allowed to know how other objects are implemented.
- **Object-oriented programming** (**OOP**) allows programmers to implement object-oriented designs as working systems.

- C++ programmers create their own user-defined types called classes. Each class contains data (known as **data members**; p. 574) and the set of functions (known as **member functions**; p. 574) that manipulate that data and provide services to clients.

- Classes can have relationships with other classes called **associations** (p. 575).

- Packaging software as classes makes it possible for future software systems to **reuse** (p. 575) the classes. Groups of related classes are often packaged as reusable components.

- An instance of a class is called an object.

- With object technology, programmers can build much of the software they will need by combining standardized, interchangeable parts called classes.

- The process of analyzing and designing a system from an object-oriented point of view is called **object-oriented analysis and design** (**OOAD**; p. 575).

Section 15.15 Introduction to C++ Standard Library Class Template `vector`

- C++ Standard Library **class template vector** (p. 576) represents a more robust alternative to arrays featuring many capabilities that are not provided for C-style pointer-based arrays.

- By default, all the elements of an integer `vector` object are set to 0.

- A `vector` can be defined to store any data type using a declaration of the form

        vector<*type*> *name*(*size*) ;

- Member function **size** (p. 580) of class template vector returns the number of elements in the vector on which it's invoked.

- The value of an element of a `vector` can be accessed or modified using **square brackets** (**[]**).

- Objects of standard class template vector can be compared directly with the equality (`==`) and inequality (`!=`) operators. The assignment (`=`) operator can also be used with `vector` objects.

- An **unmodifiable** *lvalue* is an expression that identifies an object in memory (such as an element in a vector), but cannot be used to modify that object. A **modifiable** *lvalue* also identifies an object in memory, but can be used to modify the object.

- An **exception** (p. 581) indicates a problem that occurs while a program executes. The name "exception" suggests that the problem occurs infrequently—if the "rule" is that a statement normally executes correctly, then the problem represents the "exception to the rule."

- **Exception handling** (p. 582) enables you to create **fault-tolerant programs** (p. 582) that can resolve exceptions.

- To handle an exception, place any code that might **throw an exception** (p. 582) in a **try statement**.

- The **try block** (p. 582) contains the code that might throw an exception, and the **catch block** (p. 582) contains the code that handles the exception if one occurs.

- When a `try` block terminates any variables declared in the `try` block go out of scope.

- A `catch` block declares a type and an exception parameter. Inside the `catch` block, you can use the parameter's identifier to interact with a caught exception object.

- An exception object's **what** method (p. 582) returns the exception's error message.

Self-Review Exercises

15.1   Answer each of the following:

     a) In C++, it's possible to have various functions with the same name that operate on different types or numbers of arguments. This is called function _____.

    b) The _____ enables access to a global variable with the same name as a variable in the current scope.

    c) A function _____ enables a single function to be defined to perform the same task on data of many different types.

    d) _____ is the most widely used graphical representation scheme for OO modeling.

    e) _____ models software components in terms of real-world objects.

    f) C++ programmers create their own user-defined types called _____.

15.2 Why would a function prototype contain a parameter type declaration such as double &?

15.3 (True/False) All arguments to function calls in C++ are passed by value.

15.4 Write a complete program that prompts the user for the radius of a sphere, and calculates and prints the volume of that sphere. Use an inline function sphereVolume that returns the result of the following expression: (4.0 / 3.0) * 3.14159 * pow(radius, 3).

Answers to Self-Review Exercises

15.1 a) overloading. b) unary scope resolution operator (::). c) template. d) The UML. e) Object-oriented design (OOD). f) classes.

15.2 This creates a reference parameter of type "reference to double" that enables the function to modify the original variable in the calling function.

15.3 False. C++ enables pass-by-reference using reference parameters.

15.4 See the following program:

```
1   // Exercise 15.4 Solution: Ex15_04.cpp
2   // Inline function that calculates the volume of a sphere.
3   #include <iostream>
4   #include <cmath>
5
6   const double PI = 3.14159; // define global constant PI
7
8   // calculates volume of a sphere
9   inline double sphereVolume( const double radius )
10  {
11     return 4.0 / 3.0 * PI * pow( radius, 3 );
12  }
13
14  int main()
15  {
16     double radiusValue;
17
18     // prompt user for radius
19     cout << "Enter the length of the radius of your sphere: ";
20     cin >> radiusValue; // input radius
21
22     // use radiusValue to calculate volume of sphere and display result
23     cout << "Volume of sphere with radius " << radiusValue
24        << " is " << sphereVolume( radiusValue ) << endl;
25  }
```

```
Enter the length of the radius of your sphere: 2
Volume of sphere with radius 2 is 33.5103
```

Exercises

15.5   Write a C++ program that prompts the user for the radius of a circle, then calls `inline` function `circleArea` to calculate the area of that circle.

15.6   Write a complete C++ program with the two alternate functions specified below, each of which simply triples the variable count defined in `main`. Then compare and contrast the two approaches. These two functions are

  a) function `tripleByValue` that passes a copy of count by value, triples the copy and returns the new value and

  b) function `tripleByReference` that passes count by reference via a reference parameter and triples the original value of count through its alias (i.e., the reference parameter).

15.7   What is the purpose of the unary scope resolution operator?

15.8   Write a program that uses a function template called `min` to determine the smaller of two arguments. Test the program using integer, character and floating-point number arguments.

15.9   Write a program that uses a function template called `max` to determine the larger of two arguments. Test the program using integer, character and floating-point number arguments.

15.10   Determine whether the following program segments contain errors. For each error, explain how to correct it. [*Note:* It's possible that no errors are present in the segment.]

  a)
```
template < class A >
int sum( int num1, int num2, int num3 )
{
    return num1 + num2 + num3;
}
```
  b)
```
void printResults( int x, int y )
{
    cout << "The sum is " << x + y << '\n';
    return x + y;
}
```
  c)
```
template < A >
A product( A num1, A num2, A num3 )
{
    return num1 * num2 * num3;
}
```
  d)
```
double cube( int );
int cube( int );
```

Introduction to Classes, Objects and Strings

16

16.1 Introduction

In this chapter, you'll begin writing programs that employ the basic concepts of *object-oriented programming* that we introduced in Sections 1.8 and 15.13. Typically, the programs you develop in this portion of the book will consist of function main and one or more *classes*, each containing *data members* and *member functions*. If you become part of a development team in industry, you might work on software systems that contain hundreds, or even thousands, of classes. In this chapter, we develop a simple, well-engineered framework for organizing object-oriented programs in C++.

We present a carefully paced sequence of complete working programs to demonstrate creating and using your own classes. These examples begin our integrated case study on developing a grade-book class that instructors can use to maintain student test scores. We also introduce the C++ standard library class string.

16.2 Defining a Class with a Member Function

We begin with an example (Fig. 16.1) that consists of class GradeBook (lines 8–16)—which will represent a grade book that an instructor can use to maintain student test scores—and a main function (lines 19–23) that creates a GradeBook object. Function main uses this object and its displayMessage member function (lines 12–15) to display a message on the screen welcoming the instructor to the grade-book program.

```
1   // Fig. 16.1: fig16_01.cpp
2   // Define class GradeBook with a member function displayMessage,
3   // create a GradeBook object, and call its displayMessage function.
4   #include <iostream>
5   using namespace std;
6
```

Fig. 16.1 | Define class GradeBook with a member function displayMessage, create a GradeBook object and call its displayMessage function. (Part 1 of 2.)

```
 7    // GradeBook class definition
 8    class GradeBook
 9    {
10    public:
11        // function that displays a welcome message to the GradeBook user
12        void displayMessage() const
13        {
14            cout << "Welcome to the Grade Book!" << endl;
15        } // end function displayMessage
16    }; // end class GradeBook
17
18    // function main begins program execution
19    int main()
20    {
21        GradeBook myGradeBook; // create a GradeBook object named myGradeBook
22        myGradeBook.displayMessage(); // call object's displayMessage function
23    } // end main
```

```
Welcome to the Grade Book!
```

Fig. 16.1 | Define class GradeBook with a member function displayMessage, create a GradeBook object and call its displayMessage function. (Part 2 of 2.)

Class *GradeBook*

Before function main (lines 19–23) can create a GradeBook object, we must tell the compiler what member functions and data members belong to the class. The GradeBook **class definition** (lines 8–16) contains a member function called displayMessage (lines 12–15) that displays a message on the screen (line 14). We need to make an object of class Grade-Book (line 21) and call its displayMessage member function (line 22) to get line 14 to execute and display the welcome message. We'll soon explain lines 21–22 in detail.

The class definition begins in line 8 with the keyword class followed by the class name GradeBook. By convention, the name of a user-defined class begins with a capital letter, and for readability, each subsequent word in the class name begins with a capital letter. This capitalization style is often referred to as **Pascal case**, because the convention was widely used in the Pascal programming language. The occasional uppercase letters resemble a camel's humps. More generally, **camel case** capitalization style allows the first letter to be either lowercase or uppercase (e.g., myGradeBook in line 21).

Every class's **body** is enclosed in a pair of left and right braces ({ and }), as in lines 9 and 16. The class definition terminates with a semicolon (line 16).

Common Programming Error 16.1

Forgetting the semicolon at the end of a class definition is a syntax error.

Recall that the function main is always called automatically when you execute a program. Most functions do *not* get called automatically. As you'll soon see, you must call member function displayMessage *explicitly* to tell it to perform its task.

Line 10 contains the keyword **public**, which is an **access specifier.** Lines 12–15 define member function displayMessage. This member function appears *after* access specifier public: to indicate that the function is "available to the public"—that is, it can be called by other functions in the program (such as main), and by member functions of other classes (if there are any). Access specifiers are always followed by a colon (:). For the remainder of the text, when we refer to the access specifier public in the text, we'll omit the colon as we did in this sentence. Section 16.4 introduces the access specifier private. Later in the book we'll study the access specifier protected.

Each function in a program performs a task and may *return a value* when it completes its task—for example, a function might perform a calculation, then return the result of that calculation. When you define a function, you must specify a **return type** to indicate the type of the value returned by the function when it completes its task. In line 12, keyword **void** to the left of the function name displayMessage is the function's return type. Return type void indicates that displayMessage will *not* return any data to its **calling function** (in this example, line 22 of main, as we'll see in a moment) when it completes its task. In Fig. 16.5, you'll see an example of a function that *does* return a value.

The name of the member function, displayMessage, follows the return type (line 12). By convention, our function names use the *camel case* style with a lowercase first letter. The parentheses after the member function name indicate that this is a *function.* An empty set of parentheses, as shown in line 12, indicates that this member function does *not* require additional data to perform its task. You'll see an example of a member function that *does* require additional data in Section 16.3.

We declared member function displayMessage **const** in line 12 because in the process of displaying "Welcome to the Grade Book!" the function *does not,* and *should not,* modify the GradeBook object on which it's called. Declaring displayMessage const tells the compiler, "this function should *not* modify the object on which it's called—if it does, please issue a compilation error." This can help you locate errors if you accidentally insert code in displayMessage that *would* modify the object. Line 12 is commonly referred to as a **function header.**

Every function's *body* is delimited by left and right braces ({ and }), as in lines 13 and 15. The *function body* contains statements that perform the function's task. In this case, member function displayMessage contains one statement (line 14) that displays the message "Welcome to the Grade Book!". After this statement executes, the function has completed its task.

Testing Class **GradeBook**

Next, we'd like to use class GradeBook in a program. The function main (lines 19–23) begins the program's execution. In this program, we'd like to call class GradeBook's displayMessage member function to display the welcome message. Typically, you cannot call a member function of a class until you *create an object* of that class. (As you'll learn in Section 17.14, static member functions are an exception.) Line 21 creates an object of class GradeBook called myGradeBook. The variable's type is GradeBook—the class we defined in lines 8–16. When we declare variables of type int, the compiler knows what int is—it's a *fundamental type* that's "built into" C++. In line 21, however, the compiler does *not* automatically know what type GradeBook is—it's a **user-defined type.** We tell the compiler what GradeBook is by including the *class definition* (lines 8–16). If we omitted these lines, the compiler would issue an error message. Each class you create becomes a new *type* that can be used to create objects. You can define new class types as needed; this is one reason why C++ is known as an **extensible programming language**.

Line 22 *calls* the member function displayMessage using variable myGradeBook followed by the **dot operator** (.), the function name displayMessage and an empty set of parentheses. This call causes the displayMessage function to perform its task. At the beginning of line 22, "myGradeBook." indicates that main should use the GradeBook object that was created in line 21. The *empty parentheses* in line 12 indicate that member function displayMessage does *not* require additional data to perform its task, which is why we called this function with empty parentheses in line 22. (In Section 16.3, you'll see how to pass data to a function.) When displayMessage completes its task, the program reaches the end of main (line 23) and terminates.

UML Class Diagram for Class *GradeBook*

Recall from Section 15.13 that the UML is a standardized graphical language used by software developers to represent their object-oriented systems. In the UML, each class is modeled in a **UML class diagram** as a *rectangle* with three *compartments*. Figure 16.2 presents a class diagram for class GradeBook (Fig. 16.1). The *top compartment* contains the class's name centered horizontally and in boldface type. The *middle compartment* contains the class's attributes, which correspond to data members in C++. This compartment is currently empty, because class GradeBook does not yet have any attributes. (Section 16.4 presents a version of class GradeBook with an attribute.) The *bottom compartment* contains the class's operations, which correspond to member functions in C++. The UML models operations by listing the operation name followed by a set of parentheses. Class GradeBook has only one member function, displayMessage, so the bottom compartment of Fig. 16.2 lists one operation with this name. Member function displayMessage does *not* require additional information to perform its tasks, so the parentheses following displayMessage in the class diagram are *empty*, just as they are in the member function's header in line 12 of Fig. 16.1. The *plus sign (+)* in front of the operation name indicates that displayMessage is a *public* operation in the UML (i.e., a public member function in C++).

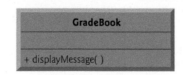

Fig. 16.2 | UML class diagram indicating that class GradeBook has a public displayMessage operation.

16.3 Defining a Member Function with a Parameter

In our car analogy from Section 1.8, we mentioned that pressing a car's gas pedal sends a *message* to the car to perform a task—make the car go faster. But *how fast* should the car accelerate? As you know, the farther down you press the pedal, the faster the car accelerates. So the message to the car includes *both* the *task to perform* and *additional information that helps the car perform the task*. This additional information is known as a **parameter**—

the *value* of the parameter helps the car determine how fast to accelerate. Similarly, a member function can require one or more parameters that represent additional data it needs to perform its task. A function call supplies values—called **arguments**—for each of the function's parameters. For example, to make a deposit into a bank account, suppose a deposit member function of an Account class specifies a parameter that represents the *deposit amount*. When the deposit member function is called, an argument value representing the deposit amount is copied to the member function's parameter. The member function then adds that amount to the account balance.

Defining and Testing Class *GradeBook*

Our next example (Fig. 16.3) redefines class GradeBook (lines 9–18) with a display-Message member function (lines 13–17) that displays the course name as part of the welcome message. The new version of displayMessage requires a *parameter* (courseName in line 13) that represents the course name to output.

```cpp
1   // Fig. 16.3: fig16_03.cpp
2   // Define class GradeBook with a member function that takes a parameter,
3   // create a GradeBook object and call its displayMessage function.
4   #include <iostream>
5   #include <string> // program uses C++ standard string class
6   using namespace std;
7
8   // GradeBook class definition
9   class GradeBook
10  {
11  public:
12     // function that displays a welcome message to the GradeBook user
13     void displayMessage( string courseName ) const
14     {
15        cout << "Welcome to the grade book for\n" << courseName << "!"
16           << endl;
17     } // end function displayMessage
18  }; // end class GradeBook
19
20  // function main begins program execution
21  int main()
22  {
23     string nameOfCourse; // string of characters to store the course name
24     GradeBook myGradeBook; // create a GradeBook object named myGradeBook
25
26     // prompt for and input course name
27     cout << "Please enter the course name:" << endl;
28     getline( cin, nameOfCourse ); // read a course name with blanks
29     cout << endl; // output a blank line
30
31     // call myGradeBook's displayMessage function
32     // and pass nameOfCourse as an argument
33     myGradeBook.displayMessage( nameOfCourse );
34  } // end main
```

Fig. 16.3 | Define class GradeBook with a member function that takes a parameter, create a GradeBook object and call its displayMessage function. (Part I of 2.)

```
Please enter the course name:
CS101 Introduction to C++ Programming

Welcome to the grade book for
CS101 Introduction to C++ Programming!
```

Fig. 16.3 | Define class GradeBook with a member function that takes a parameter, create a GradeBook object and call its displayMessage function. (Part 2 of 2.)

Before discussing the new features of class GradeBook, let's see how the new class is used in main (lines 21–34). Line 23 creates a variable of type **string** called nameOfCourse that will be used to store the course name entered by the user. A variable of type string represents a string of characters such as "CS101 Introduction to C++ Programming". A string is actually an *object* of the C++ Standard Library class string. This class is defined in **header <string>**, and the name string, like cout, belongs to namespace std. To enable lines 13 and 23 to compile, line 5 *includes* the <string> header. The using directive in line 6 allows us to simply write string in line 23 rather than std::string. For now, you can think of string variables like variables of other types such as int. You'll learn additional string capabilities in Section 16.8.

Line 24 creates an object of class GradeBook named myGradeBook. Line 27 prompts the user to enter a course name. Line 28 reads the name from the user and assigns it to the nameOfCourse variable, using the library function **getline** to perform the input. Before we explain this line of code, let's explain why we cannot simply write

```
cin >> nameOfCourse;
```

to obtain the course name.

In our sample program execution, we use the course name "CS101 Introduction to C++ Programming," which contains multiple words *separated by blanks*. (Recall that we highlight user-entered data in bold.) When reading a string with the stream extraction operator, cin reads characters *until the first white-space character is reached*. Thus, only "CS101" would be read by the preceding statement. The rest of the course name would have to be read by subsequent input operations.

In this example, we'd like the user to type the complete course name and press *Enter* to submit it to the program, and we'd like to store the *entire* course name in the string variable nameOfCourse. The function call getline(cin, nameOfCourse) in line 28 reads characters (*including* the space characters that separate the words in the input) from the standard input stream object cin (i.e., the keyboard) until the *newline* character is encountered, places the characters in the string variable nameOfCourse and *discards* the newline character. When you press *Enter* while entering data, a newline is inserted in the input stream. The <string> header must be included in the program to use function getline, which belongs to namespace std.

Line 33 calls myGradeBook's displayMessage member function. The nameOfCourse variable in parentheses is the *argument* that's passed to member function displayMessage so that it can perform its task. The value of variable nameOfCourse in main is *copied* to member function displayMessage's parameter courseName in line 13. When you execute this program, member function displayMessage outputs as part of the welcome message the course name you type (in our sample execution, CS101 Introduction to C++ Programming).

More on Arguments and Parameters

To specify in a function definition that the function requires data to perform its task, you place additional information in the function's **parameter list**, which is located in the parentheses following the function name. The parameter list may contain *any* number of parameters, including *none at all* (represented by empty parentheses as in Fig. 16.1, line 12) to indicate that a function does *not* require any parameters. The displayMessage member function's parameter list (Fig. 16.3, line 13) declares that the function requires one parameter. Each parameter specifies a *type* and an *identifier*. The type string and the identifier courseName indicate that member function displayMessage requires a string to perform its task. The member function body uses the parameter courseName to access the value that's passed to the function in the function call (line 33 in main). Lines 15–16 display parameter courseName's value as part of the welcome message.

A function can specify multiple parameters by separating each from the next with a comma. The number and order of arguments in a function call *must match* the number and order of parameters in the parameter list of the called member function's header. Also, the argument types in the function call must be consistent with the types of the corresponding parameters in the function header. (As you'll learn in subsequent chapters, an argument's type and its corresponding parameter's type need not always be *identical*, but they must be "consistent.") In our example, the one string argument in the function call (i.e., nameOfCourse) *exactly matches* the one string parameter in the member-function definition (i.e., courseName).

*Updated UML Class Diagram for Class **GradeBook***

The UML class diagram of Fig. 16.4 models class GradeBook of Fig. 16.3. Like the class GradeBook defined in Fig. 16.1, this GradeBook class contains public member function displayMessage. However, this version of displayMessage has a *parameter*. The UML models a parameter by listing the parameter name, followed by a colon and the parameter type in the parentheses following the operation name. The UML has its *own* data types *similar* to those of C++.

The UML is *language independent*—it's used with many different programming languages—so its terminology does not exactly match that of C++. For example, the UML type String corresponds to the C++ type string. Member function displayMessage of class GradeBook (Fig. 16.3, lines 13–17) has a string parameter named courseName, so Fig. 16.4 lists courseName : String between the parentheses following the operation name displayMessage. This version of the GradeBook class still does *not* have any data members.

Fig. 16.4 | UML class diagram indicating that class GradeBook has a public displayMessage operation with a courseName parameter of UML type String.

16.4 Data Members, *set* Member Functions and *get* Member Functions

As you know, variables declared in a function definition's body are known as local variables and can be used *only* from the line of their declaration in the function to the closing right brace (}) of the block in which they're declared. A local variable must be declared *before* it can be used in a function. A local variable cannot be accessed *outside* the function in which it's declared.

A class normally consists of one or more member functions that manipulate the attributes that belong to a particular object of the class. Attributes are represented as variables in a class definition. Such variables are called **data members** and are declared *inside* a class definition but *outside* the bodies of the class's member-function definitions. Each object of a class maintains its own attributes in memory. These attributes exist throughout the life of the object. The example in this section demonstrates a GradeBook class that contains a courseName data member to represent a particular GradeBook object's course name. If you create more than one GradeBook object, each will have its own courseName data member, and these can contain *different* values.

GradeBook *Class with a Data Member, and* set *and* get *Member Functions*

In our next example, class GradeBook (Fig. 16.5) maintains the course name as a *data member* so that it can be *used* or *modified* throughout a program's execution. The class contains member functions setCourseName, getCourseName and displayMessage. Member function setCourseName *stores* a course name in a GradeBook data member. Member function getCourseName *obtains* the course name from that data member. Member function displayMessage—which now specifies *no parameters*—still displays a welcome message that includes the course name. However, as you'll see, the function now *obtains* the course name by calling another function in the same class—getCourseName.

```
1   // Fig. 16.5: fig16_05.cpp
2   // Define class GradeBook that contains a courseName data member
3   // and member functions to set and get its value;
4   // Create and manipulate a GradeBook object with these functions.
5   #include <iostream>
6   #include <string> // program uses C++ standard string class
7   using namespace std;
8
9   // GradeBook class definition
10  class GradeBook
11  {
12  public:
13     // function that sets the course name
14     void setCourseName( string name )
15     {
16        courseName = name; // store the course name in the object
17     } // end function setCourseName
```

Fig. 16.5 | Defining and testing class GradeBook with a data member and *set* and *get* member functions. (Part 1 of 2.)

```
18
19    // function that gets the course name
20    string getCourseName() const
21    {
22       return courseName; // return the object's courseName
23    } // end function getCourseName
24
25    // function that displays a welcome message
26    void displayMessage() const
27    {
28       // this statement calls getCourseName to get the
29       // name of the course this GradeBook represents
30       cout << "Welcome to the grade book for\n" << getCourseName() << "!"
31          << endl;
32    } // end function displayMessage
33 private:
34    string courseName; // course name for this GradeBook
35 }; // end class GradeBook
36
37 // function main begins program execution
38 int main()
39 {
40    string nameOfCourse; // string of characters to store the course name
41    GradeBook myGradeBook; // create a GradeBook object named myGradeBook
42
43    // display initial value of courseName
44    cout << "Initial course name is: " << myGradeBook.getCourseName()
45       << endl;
46
47    // prompt for, input and set course name
48    cout << "\nPlease enter the course name:" << endl;
49    getline( cin, nameOfCourse ); // read a course name with blanks
50    myGradeBook.setCourseName( nameOfCourse ); // set the course name
51
52    cout << endl; // outputs a blank line
53    myGradeBook.displayMessage(); // display message with new course name
54 } // end main
```

```
Initial course name is:

Please enter the course name:
CS101 Introduction to C++ Programming

Welcome to the grade book for
CS101 Introduction to C++ Programming!
```

Fig. 16.5 | Defining and testing class GradeBook with a data member and *set* and *get* member functions. (Part 2 of 2.)

A typical instructor teaches *several* courses, each with its own course name. Line 34 declares that courseName is a variable of type string. Because the variable is declared in the class definition (lines 10–35) but outside the bodies of the class's member-function definitions (lines 14–17, 20–23 and 26–32), the variable is a *data member*. Every instance (i.e., object) of class GradeBook contains each of the class's data members—if there are two GradeBook objects, each has its *own* courseName (one per object), as you'll see in the example of Fig. 16.7. A benefit of making courseName a data member is that *all* the member functions of the class can manipulate any data members that appear in the class definition (in this case, courseName).

Access Specifiers *public and private*

Most data-member declarations appear after the **private** access specifier. Variables or functions declared after access specifier private (and *before* the next access specifier if there is one) are accessible only to member functions of the class for which they're declared (or to "friends" of the class, as you'll see in Chapter 17). Thus, data member courseName can be used *only* in member functions setCourseName, getCourseName and displayMessage of class GradeBook (or to "friends" of the class, if there are any).

> **Error-Prevention Tip 16.1**
> *Making the data members of a class private and the member functions of the class public facilitates debugging because problems with data manipulations are localized to either the class's member functions or the friends of the class.*

> **Common Programming Error 16.2**
> *An attempt by a function, which is not a member of a particular class (or a friend of that class) to access a private member of that class is a compilation error.*

The *default access* for class members is private so all members *after* the class header and *before* the first access specifier (if there are any) are private. The access specifiers public and private may be repeated, but this is unnecessary and can be confusing.

Declaring data members with access specifier private is known as **data hiding**. When a program creates a GradeBook object, data member courseName is *encapsulated* (hidden) in the object and can be accessed only by member functions of the object's class. In class GradeBook, member functions setCourseName and getCourseName manipulate the data member courseName directly.

Member Functions *setCourseName and getCourseName*

Member function setCourseName (lines 14–17) does not *return* any data when it completes its task, so its return type is void. The member function *receives* one parameter— name—which represents the course name that will be passed to it as an argument (as we'll see in line 50 of main). Line 16 assigns name to data member courseName, thus *modifying* the object—for this reason, we do *not* declare setCourseName const. In this example, set-CourseName does not *validate* the course name—i.e., the function does *not* check that the course name adheres to any particular format or follows any other rules regarding what a "valid" course name looks like. Suppose, for instance, that a university can print student transcripts containing course names of only 25 characters or fewer. In this case, we might want class GradeBook to ensure that its data member courseName never contains more than 25 characters. We discuss validation in Section 16.8.

Member function getCourseName (lines 20–23) *returns* a particular GradeBook object's courseName, *without* modifying the object—for this reason, we declare get-CourseName const. The member function has an *empty parameter list*, so it does *not* require additional data to perform its task. The function specifies that it returns a string. When a function that specifies a return type other than void is called and completes its task, the function uses a **return statement** (as in line 22) to *return a result* to its calling function. For example, when you go to an automated teller machine (ATM) and request your account balance, you expect the ATM to give you a value that represents your balance. Similarly, when a statement calls member function getCourseName on a GradeBook object, the statement expects to receive the GradeBook's course name (in this case, a string, as specified by the function's return type).

If you have a function square that returns the square of its argument, the statement

```
result = square( 2 );
```

returns 4 from function square and assigns to variable result the value 4. If you have a function maximum that returns the largest of three integer arguments, the statement

```
biggest = maximum( 27, 114, 51 );
```

returns 114 from function maximum and assigns this value to variable biggest.

The statements in lines 16 and 22 each use variable courseName (line 34) even though it was *not* declared in any of the member functions. We can do this because courseName is a *data member* of the class and data members are accessible from a class's member functions.

Member Function *displayMessage*

Member function displayMessage (lines 26–32) does *not* return any data when it completes its task, so its return type is void. The function does *not* receive parameters, so its parameter list is empty. Lines 30–31 output a welcome message that includes the value of data member courseName. Line 30 calls member function getCourseName to obtain the value of courseName. Member function displayMessage could also access data member courseName directly, just as member functions setCourseName and getCourseName do. We explain shortly why it's preferable from a software engineering perspective to call member function getCourseName to obtain the value of courseName.

Testing Class *GradeBook*

The main function (lines 38–54) creates one object of class GradeBook and uses each of its member functions. Line 41 creates a GradeBook object named myGradeBook. Lines 44–45 display the initial course name by calling the object's getCourseName member function. The first line of the output does not show a course name, because the object's courseName data member (i.e., a string) is initially empty—by default, the initial value of a string is the so-called **empty string**, i.e., a string that does not contain any characters. Nothing appears on the screen when an empty string is displayed.

Line 48 prompts the user to enter a course name. Local string variable nameOfCourse (declared in line 40) is set to the course name entered by the user, which is obtained by the call to the getline function (line 49). Line 50 calls object myGradeBook's setCourseName member function and supplies nameOfCourse as the function's argument. When the function is called, the argument's value is copied to parameter name (line 14) of member function setCourseName. Then the parameter's value is assigned to data member courseName (line 16). Line 52 skips a line; then line 53 calls object myGradeBook's displayMessage member function to display the welcome message containing the course name.

Software Engineering with Set *and* Get *Functions*

A class's private data members can be manipulated *only* by member functions of that class (and by "friends" of the class as you'll see in Chapter 17). So a **client of an object**—that is, any statement that calls the object's member functions from *outside* the object—calls the class's public member functions to request the class's services for particular objects of the class. This is why the statements in function main call member functions setCourse-Name, getCourseName and displayMessage on a GradeBook object. Classes often provide public member functions to allow clients of the class to *set* (i.e., assign values to) or *get* (i.e., obtain the values of) private data members. These member function names need not begin with set or get, but this naming convention is common. In this example, the member function that *sets* the courseName data member is called setCourseName, and the member function that *gets* the value of the courseName data member is called getCourseName. *Set* functions are sometimes called **mutators** (because they mutate, or change, values), and *get* functions are also called **accessors** (because they access values).

Recall that declaring data members with access specifier private enforces data hiding. Providing public *set* and *get* functions allows clients of a class to access the hidden data, but only *indirectly*. The client knows that it's attempting to modify or obtain an object's data, but the client does *not* know *how* the object performs these operations. In some cases, a class may *internally* represent a piece of data one way, but expose that data to clients in a different way. For example, suppose a Clock class represents the time of day as a private int data member time that stores the number of seconds since midnight. However, when a client calls a Clock object's getTime member function, the object could return the time with hours, minutes and seconds in a string in the format "HH:MM:SS". Similarly, suppose the Clock class provides a *set* function named setTime that takes a string parameter in the "HH:MM:SS" format. The setTime function could convert this string to a number of seconds, which the function stores in its private data member. The *set* function could also check that the value it receives represents a valid time (e.g., "12:30:45" is valid but "42:85:70" is not). The *set* and *get* functions allow a client to interact with an object, but the object's private data remains safely *encapsulated* (i.e., hidden) in the object itself.

The *set* and *get* functions of a class also should be used by other member functions *within* the class to manipulate the class's private data, even though these member functions *can* access the private data directly. In Fig. 16.5, member functions setCourseName and getCourseName are public member functions, so they're accessible to clients of the class, as well as to the class itself. Member function displayMessage calls member function getCourseName to obtain the value of data member courseName for display purposes, even though displayMessage can access courseName directly—accessing a data member via its *get* function creates a better, more robust class (i.e., a class that's easier to maintain and less likely to malfunction). If we decide to change the data member courseName in some way, the displayMessage definition will *not* require modification—only the bodies of the *get* and *set* functions that directly manipulate the data member will need to change. For example, suppose we want to represent the course name as two separate data members—courseNumber (e.g., "CS101") and courseTitle (e.g., "Introduction to C++ Programming"). Member function displayMessage can still issue a single call to member function getCourseName to obtain the full course name to display as part of the welcome message. In this case, getCourseName would need to build and return a string containing the courseNumber followed by the courseTitle. Member function displayMessage could continue to display the complete course title "CS101 Introduction to C++ Programming." The benefits of calling a *set* function from another member function of the same class will become clearer when we discuss validation in Section 16.8.

Good Programming Practice 16.1

Always try to localize *the effects of changes to a class's data members by accessing and manipulating the data members through their corresponding* get *and* set *functions.*

Software Engineering Observation 16.1

Write programs that are clear and easy to maintain. Change is the rule rather than the exception. You should anticipate that your code will be modified, and possibly often.

GradeBook's UML Class Diagram with a Data Member and set and get Functions

Figure 16.6 contains an updated UML class diagram for the version of class GradeBook in Fig. 16.5. This diagram models GradeBook's data member courseName as an attribute in the middle compartment. The UML represents data members as attributes by listing the attribute name, followed by a colon and the attribute type. The UML type of attribute courseName is String, which corresponds to string in C++. Data member courseName is private in C++, so the class diagram lists a *minus sign (–)* in front of the corresponding attribute's name. Class GradeBook contains three public member functions, so the class diagram lists three operations in the third compartment. Operation setCourseName has a String parameter called name. The UML indicates the *return type* of an operation by placing a colon and the return type after the parentheses following the operation name. Member function getCourseName of class GradeBook has a string return type in C++, so the class diagram shows a String return type in the UML. Operations setCourseName and displayMessage do not return values (i.e., they return void in C++), so the UML class diagram does not specify a return type after the parentheses of these operations.

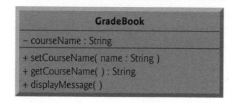

Fig. 16.6 | UML class diagram for class GradeBook with a private courseName attribute and public operations setCourseName, getCourseName and displayMessage.

16.5 Initializing Objects with Constructors

As mentioned in Section 16.4, when an object of class GradeBook (Fig. 16.5) is created, its data member courseName is initialized to the empty string by default. What if you want to provide a course name when you *create* a GradeBook object? Each class you declare can provide one or more **constructors** that can be used to initialize an object of the class when the object is created. A constructor is a special member function that must be defined with the *same name as the class*, so that the compiler can distinguish it from the class's other member functions. An important difference between constructors and other functions is that *constructors cannot return values*, so they *cannot* specify a return type (not even void). Normally, constructors are declared public. You also can create classes with more that one constructor using *function overloading*.

C++ automatically calls a constructor for each object that's created, which helps ensure that objects are initialized properly before they're used in a program. The constructor call occurs when the object is created. If a class does not *explicitly* include constructors, the compiler provides a **default constructor** with *no* parameters. For example, when line 41 of Fig. 16.5 creates a GradeBook object, the default constructor is called. The default constructor provided by the compiler creates a GradeBook object without giving any initial values to the object's fundamental type data members. For data members that are objects of other classes, the default constructor implicitly calls each data member's default constructor to ensure that the data member is initialized properly. This is why the string data member courseName (in Fig. 16.5) was initialized to the empty string—the default constructor for class string sets the string's value to the empty string.

In the example of Fig. 16.7, we specify a course name for a GradeBook object when the object is created (e.g., line 47). In this case, the argument "CS101 Introduction to C++ Programming" is passed to the GradeBook object's constructor (lines 14–18) and used to initialize the courseName. Figure 16.7 defines a modified GradeBook class containing a constructor with a string parameter that receives the initial course name.

```cpp
1   // Fig. 16.7: fig16_07.cpp
2   // Instantiating multiple objects of the GradeBook class and using
3   // the GradeBook constructor to specify the course name
4   // when each GradeBook object is created.
5   #include <iostream>
6   #include <string> // program uses C++ standard string class
7   using namespace std;
8
9   // GradeBook class definition
10  class GradeBook
11  {
12  public:
13     // constructor initializes courseName with string supplied as argument
14     explicit GradeBook( string name )
15        : courseName( name ) // member initializer to initialize courseName
16     {
17        // empty body
18     } // end GradeBook constructor
19
20     // function to set the course name
21     void setCourseName( string name )
22     {
23        courseName = name; // store the course name in the object
24     } // end function setCourseName
```

Fig. 16.7 | Instantiating multiple objects of the GradeBook class and using the GradeBook constructor to specify the course name when each GradeBook object is created. (Part 1 of 2.)

```
25
26      // function to get the course name
27      string getCourseName() const
28      {
29         return courseName; // return object's courseName
30      } // end function getCourseName
31
32      // display a welcome message to the GradeBook user
33      void displayMessage() const
34      {
35         // call getCourseName to get the courseName
36         cout << "Welcome to the grade book for\n" << getCourseName()
37            << "!" << endl;
38      } // end function displayMessage
39   private:
40      string courseName; // course name for this GradeBook
41   }; // end class GradeBook
42
43   // function main begins program execution
44   int main()
45   {
46      // create two GradeBook objects
47      GradeBook gradeBook1( "CS101 Introduction to C++ Programming" );
48      GradeBook gradeBook2( "CS102 Data Structures in C++" );
49
50      // display initial value of courseName for each GradeBook
51      cout << "gradeBook1 created for course: " << gradeBook1.getCourseName()
52         << "\ngradeBook2 created for course: " << gradeBook2.getCourseName()
53         << endl;
54   } // end main
```

```
gradeBook1 created for course: CS101 Introduction to C++ Programming
gradeBook2 created for course: CS102 Data Structures in C++
```

Fig. 16.7 | Instantiating multiple objects of the GradeBook class and using the GradeBook constructor to specify the course name when each GradeBook object is created. (Part 2 of 2.)

Defining a Constructor

Lines 14–18 of Fig. 16.7 define a constructor for class GradeBook. The constructor has the *same* name as its class, GradeBook. A constructor specifies in its parameter list the data it requires to perform its task. When you create a new object, you place this data in the parentheses that follow the object name (as we did in lines 47–48). Line 14 indicates that class GradeBook's constructor has a string parameter called name. We declared this constructor **explicit**, because it takes a *single* parameter—this is important for subtle reasons that you'll learn in Section 18.13. For now, just declare *all* single-parameter constructors explicit. Line 14 does *not* specify a return type, because constructors *cannot* return values (or even void). Also, constructors cannot be declared const (because initializing an object modifies it).

The constructor uses a **member-initializer list** (line 15) to initialize the courseName data member with the value of the constructor's parameter name. *Member initializers* appear between a constructor's parameter list and the left brace that begins the constructor's body. The member initializer list is separated from the parameter list with a *colon (:)*. A member initializer consists of a data member's *variable name* followed by parentheses containing the member's *initial value*. In this example, courseName is initialized with the value of the parameter name. If a class contains more than one data member, each data member's initializer is separated from the next by a comma. The member initializer list executes *before* the body of the constructor executes. You can perform initialization in the constructor's body, but as you'll learn later it's more efficient to do it with member initializers, and some types of data members must be initialized this way.

Notice that both the constructor (line 14) and the setCourseName function (line 21) use a parameter called name. You can use the *same* parameter names in *different* functions because the parameters are *local* to each function—they do *not* interfere with one another.

Testing Class *GradeBook*

Lines 44–54 of Fig. 16.7 define the main function that tests class GradeBook and demonstrates initializing GradeBook objects using a constructor. Line 47 creates and initializes GradeBook object gradeBook1. When this line executes, the GradeBook constructor (lines 14–18) is called with the argument "CS101 Introduction to C++ Programming" to initialize gradeBook1's course name. Line 48 repeats this process for GradeBook object gradeBook2, this time passing the argument "CS102 Data Structures in C++" to initialize gradeBook2's course name. Lines 51–52 use each object's getCourseName member function to obtain the course names and show that they were indeed initialized when the objects were created. The output confirms that each GradeBook object maintains its *own* data member courseName.

Ways to Provide a Default Constructor for a Class

Any constructor that takes *no* arguments is called a default constructor. A class can get a default constructor in one of several ways:

1. The compiler *implicitly* creates a default constructor in every class that does *not* have any user-defined constructors. The default constructor does *not* initialize the class's data members, but *does* call the default constructor for each data member that's an object of another class. An uninitialized variable contains an undefined ("garbage") value.

2. You *explicitly* define a constructor that takes no arguments. Such a default constructor will call the default constructor for each data member that's an object of another class and will perform additional initialization specified by you.

3. *If you define any constructors with arguments, C++ will not implicitly create a default constructor for that class.* We'll show later that C++11 allows you to force the compiler to create the default constructor even if you've defined non-default constructors.

For each version of class GradeBook in Fig. 16.1, Fig. 16.3 and Fig. 16.5 the compiler *implicitly* defined a default constructor.

Error-Prevention Tip 16.2

Unless no initialization of your class's data members is necessary (almost never), provide constructors to ensure that your class's data members are initialized with meaningful values when each new object of your class is created.

Software Engineering Observation 16.2

Data members can be initialized in a constructor, or their values may be set later after the object is created. However, it's a good software engineering practice to ensure that an object is fully initialized before the client code invokes the object's member functions. You should not rely on the client code to ensure that an object gets initialized properly.

*Adding the Constructor to Class **GradeBook**'s UML Class Diagram*

The UML class diagram of Fig. 16.8 models the GradeBook class of Fig. 16.7, which has a constructor with a `name` parameter of type `string` (represented by type `String` in the UML). Like operations, the UML models constructors in the third compartment of a class in a class diagram. To distinguish a constructor from a class's operations, the UML places the word "constructor" between guillemets (« and ») before the constructor's name. By convention, you list the class's constructor *before* other operations in the third compartment.

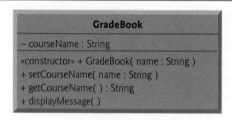

Fig. 16.8 | UML class diagram indicating that class GradeBook has a constructor with a name parameter of UML type String.

16.6 Placing a Class in a Separate File for Reusability

One of the benefits of creating class definitions is that, when packaged properly, your classes can be *reused* by other programmers. For example, you can *reuse* C++ Standard Library type `string` in any C++ program by including the header `<string>` (and, as you'll see, by being able to link to the library's object code).

Programmers who wish to use our GradeBook class cannot simply include the file from Fig. 16.7 in another program. As you know, function main begins the execution of every program, and every program must have *exactly one* main function. If other programmers include the code from Fig. 16.7, they get extra "baggage"—our main function—and their programs will then have two main functions. Attempting to compile a program with two main functions produces an error. So, placing main in the same file with a class definition *prevents that class from being reused* by other programs. In this section, we demonstrate how to make class GradeBook reusable by *separating it into another file* from the main function.

Headers

Each of the previous examples in the chapter consists of a single `.cpp` file, also known as a **source-code file**, that contains a GradeBook class definition and a main function. When building an object-oriented C++ program, it's customary to define *reusable* source code (such as a class) in a file that by convention has a `.h` filename extension—known as a **header**. Programs use `#include` preprocessing directives to include headers and take advantage of reusable software components, such as type string provided in the C++ Standard Library and user-defined types like class GradeBook.

Our next example separates the code from Fig. 16.7 into two files—GradeBook.h (Fig. 16.9) and fig16_10.cpp (Fig. 16.10). As you look at the header in Fig. 16.9, notice that it contains only the GradeBook class definition (lines 7–38) and the headers on which the class depends. The main function that *uses* class GradeBook is defined in the source-code file fig16_10.cpp (Fig. 16.10) in lines 8–18. To help you prepare for the larger programs you'll encounter later in this book and in industry, we often use a separate source-code file containing function main to test our classes (this is called a **driver program**). You'll soon learn how a source-code file with main can use the class definition found in a header to create objects of a class.

```cpp
1   // Fig. 16.9: GradeBook.h
2   // GradeBook class definition in a separate file from main.
3   #include <iostream>
4   #include <string> // class GradeBook uses C++ standard string class
5
6   // GradeBook class definition
7   class GradeBook
8   {
9   public:
10     // constructor initializes courseName with string supplied as argument
11     explicit GradeBook( std::string name )
12        : courseName( name ) // member initializer to initialize courseName
13     {
14        // empty body
15     } // end GradeBook constructor
16
17     // function to set the course name
18     void setCourseName( std::string name )
19     {
20        courseName = name; // store the course name in the object
21     } // end function setCourseName
22
23     // function to get the course name
24     std::string getCourseName() const
25     {
26        return courseName; // return object's courseName
27     } // end function getCourseName
28
29     // display a welcome message to the GradeBook user
30     void displayMessage() const
31     {
32        // call getCourseName to get the courseName
33        std::cout << "Welcome to the grade book for\n" << getCourseName()
34           << "!" << std::endl;
35     } // end function displayMessage
36   private:
37     std::string courseName; // course name for this GradeBook
38   }; // end class GradeBook
```

Fig. 16.9 | GradeBook class definition in a separate file from main.

```
 1   // Fig. 16.10: fig16_10.cpp
 2   // Including class GradeBook from file GradeBook.h for use in main.
 3   #include <iostream>
 4   #include "GradeBook.h" // include definition of class GradeBook
 5   using namespace std;
 6
 7   // function main begins program execution
 8   int main()
 9   {
10      // create two GradeBook objects
11      GradeBook gradeBook1( "CS101 Introduction to C++ Programming" );
12      GradeBook gradeBook2( "CS102 Data Structures in C++" );
13
14      // display initial value of courseName for each GradeBook
15      cout << "gradeBook1 created for course: " << gradeBook1.getCourseName()
16         << "\ngradeBook2 created for course: " << gradeBook2.getCourseName()
17         << endl;
18   } // end main
```

```
gradeBook1 created for course: CS101 Introduction to C++ Programming
gradeBook2 created for course: CS102 Data Structures in C++
```

Fig. 16.10 | Including class GradeBook from file GradeBook.h for use in main.

Use std:: with Standard Library Components in Headers

Throughout the header (Fig. 16.9), we use std:: when referring to string (lines 11, 18, 24 and 37), cout (line 33) and endl (line 34). For subtle reasons that we'll explain in a later chapter, headers should *never* contain using directives or using declarations.

Including a Header That Contains a User-Defined Class

A header such as GradeBook.h (Fig. 16.9) cannot be used as a complete program, because it does not contain a main function. To test class GradeBook (defined in Fig. 16.9), you must write a separate source-code file containing a main function (such as Fig. 16.10) that instantiates and uses objects of the class.

The compiler doesn't know what a GradeBook is because it's a user-defined type. In fact, the compiler doesn't even know the classes in the C++ Standard Library. To help it understand how to use a class, we must explicitly provide the compiler with the class's definition—that's why, for example, to use type string, a program must include the <string> header. This enables the compiler to determine the amount of memory that it must reserve for each string object and ensure that a program calls a string's member functions correctly.

To create GradeBook objects gradeBook1 and gradeBook2 in lines 11–12 of Fig. 16.10, the compiler must know the *size* of a GradeBook object. While objects conceptually contain data members and member functions, C++ objects actually contain *only* data. The compiler creates only *one* copy of the class's member functions and *shares* that copy among all the class's objects. Each object, of course, needs its own data members, because their contents can vary among objects (such as two different BankAccount objects having two different balances). The member-function code, however, is *not modifiable*, so it can be shared among all objects of the class. Therefore, the size of an object depends on the amount of memory required to store the class's data members. By including Grade-Book.h in line 4, we give the compiler access to the information it needs (Fig. 16.9, line 37) to determine the size of a GradeBook object and to determine whether objects of the class are used correctly (in lines 11–12 and 15–16 of Fig. 16.10).

Line 4 instructs the C++ preprocessor to replace the directive with a copy of the contents of GradeBook.h (i.e., the GradeBook class definition) *before* the program is compiled. When the source-code file fig16_10.cpp is compiled, it now contains the GradeBook class definition (because of the #include), and the compiler is able to determine how to create GradeBook objects and see that their member functions are called correctly. Now that the class definition is in a header (without a main function), we can include that header in *any* program that needs to reuse our GradeBook class.

How Headers Are Located

Notice that the name of the GradeBook.h header in line 4 of Fig. 16.10 is enclosed in quotes (" ") rather than angle brackets (< >). Normally, a program's source-code files and user-defined headers are placed in the *same* directory. When the preprocessor encounters a header name in quotes, it attempts to locate the header in the same directory as the file in which the #include directive appears. If the preprocessor cannot find the header in that directory, it searches for it in the same location(s) as the C++ Standard Library headers. When the preprocessor encounters a header name in angle brackets (e.g., <iostream>), it assumes that the header is part of the C++ Standard Library and does *not* look in the directory of the program that's being preprocessed.

Error-Prevention Tip 16.3

To ensure that the preprocessor can locate headers correctly, #include preprocessing directives should place user-defined headers names in quotes (e.g., "GradeBook.h") and place C++ Standard Library headers names in angle brackets (e.g., <iostream>).

Additional Software Engineering Issues

Now that class GradeBook is defined in a header, the class is *reusable*. Unfortunately, placing a class definition in a header as in Fig. 16.9 still *reveals the entire implementation of the class to the class's clients*—GradeBook.h is simply a text file that anyone can open and read. Conventional software engineering wisdom says that to use an object of a class, the client code needs to know only what member functions to call, what arguments to provide to each member function and what return type to expect from each member function. *The client code does not need to know how those functions are implemented.*

If client code *does* know how a class is implemented, the programmer might write client code based on the class's implementation details. Ideally, if that implementation changes, the class's clients should not have to change. *Hiding the class's implementation details makes it easier to change the class's implementation while minimizing, and hopefully eliminating, changes to client code.*

In Section 16.7, we show how to break up the GradeBook class into two files so that

1. the class is *reusable*,
2. the clients of the class know what member functions the class provides, how to call them and what return types to expect, and
3. the clients do *not* know how the class's member functions are implemented.

16.7 Separating Interface from Implementation

In the preceding section, we showed how to promote software reusability by separating a class definition from the client code (e.g., function main) that uses the class. We now introduce another fundamental principle of good software engineering—**separating interface from implementation**.

Interface of a Class

Interfaces define and standardize the ways in which things such as people and systems interact with one another. For example, a radio's controls serve as an interface between the radio's users and its internal components. The controls allow users to perform a limited set of operations (such as changing the station, adjusting the volume, and choosing between AM and FM stations). Various radios may implement these operations differently—some provide push buttons, some provide dials and some support voice commands. The interface specifies *what* operations a radio permits users to perform but does not specify *how* the operations are implemented inside the radio.

Similarly, the **interface of a class** describes *what* services a class's clients can use and how to *request* those services, but not *how* the class carries out the services. A class's public interface consists of the class's public member functions (also known as the class's **public services**). For example, class GradeBook's interface (Fig. 16.9) contains a constructor and member functions setCourseName, getCourseName and displayMessage. GradeBook's clients (e.g., main in Fig. 16.10) *use* these functions to request the class's services. As you'll soon see, you can specify a class's interface by writing a class definition that lists *only* the member-function names, return types and parameter types.

Separating the Interface from the Implementation

In our prior examples, each class definition contained the complete definitions of the class's public member functions and the declarations of its private data members. However, it's better software engineering to define member functions *outside* the class definition, so that their implementation details can be *hidden* from the client code. This practice *ensures* that you do not write client code that depends on the class's implementation details.

The program of Figs. 16.11–16.13 separates class GradeBook's interface from its implementation by splitting the class definition of Fig. 16.9 into two files—the header GradeBook.h (Fig. 16.11) in which class GradeBook is defined, and the source-code file GradeBook.cpp (Fig. 16.12) in which GradeBook's member functions are defined. By convention, member-function definitions are placed in a source-code file of the same base name (e.g., GradeBook) as the class's header but with a .cpp filename extension. The source-code file fig16_13.cpp (Fig. 16.13) defines function main (the client code). The code and output of Fig. 16.13 are identical to that of Fig. 16.10. Figure 16.14 shows how this three-file program is compiled from the perspectives of the GradeBook class programmer and the client-code programmer—we'll explain this figure in detail.

GradeBook.h: Defining a Class's Interface with Function Prototypes

Header GradeBook.h (Fig. 16.11) contains another version of GradeBook's class definition (lines 8–17). This version is similar to the one in Fig. 16.9, but the function definitions in Fig. 16.9 are replaced here with **function prototypes** (lines 11–14) that *describe the class's* *public interface without revealing the class's member-function implementations.* A function prototype is a *declaration* of a function that tells the compiler the function's name, its return type and the types of its parameters. Also, the header still specifies the class's private data member (line 16) as well. Again, the compiler *must* know the data members of the class to determine how much memory to reserve for each object of the class. Including the header GradeBook.h in the client code (line 5 of Fig. 16.13) provides the compiler with the information it needs to ensure that the client code calls the member functions of class GradeBook correctly.

```
1   // Fig. 16.11: GradeBook.h
2   // GradeBook class definition. This file presents GradeBook's public
3   // interface without revealing the implementations of GradeBook's member
4   // functions, which are defined in GradeBook.cpp.
5   #include <string> // class GradeBook uses C++ standard string class
6
7   // GradeBook class definition
8   class GradeBook
9   {
10  public:
11     explicit GradeBook( std::string ); // constructor initialize courseName
12     void setCourseName( std::string ); // sets the course name
13     std::string getCourseName() const; // gets the course name
14     void displayMessage() const; // displays a welcome message
15  private:
16     std::string courseName; // course name for this GradeBook
17  }; // end class GradeBook
```

Fig. 16.11 | GradeBook class definition containing function prototypes that specify the interface of the class.

The function prototype in line 11 (Fig. 16.11) indicates that the constructor requires one string parameter. Recall that constructors don't have return types, so no return type appears in the function prototype. Member function setCourseName's function prototype indicates that setCourseName requires a string parameter and does not return a value (i.e., its return type is void). Member function getCourseName's function prototype indicates that the function does not require parameters and returns a string. Finally, member function displayMessage's function prototype (line 14) specifies that displayMessage does not require parameters and does not return a value. These function prototypes are the same as the first lines of the corresponding function definitions in Fig. 16.9, except that the parameter names (which are *optional* in prototypes) are not included and each function prototype *must* end with a semicolon.

Good Programming Practice 16.2
Although parameter names in function prototypes are optional (they're ignored by the compiler), many programmers use these names for documentation purposes.

GradeBook.cpp: *Defining Member Functions in a Separate Source-Code File*
Source-code file GradeBook.cpp (Fig. 16.12) *defines* class GradeBook's member functions, which were *declared* in lines 11–14 of Fig. 16.11. The definitions appear in lines 9–33 and

are nearly identical to the member-function definitions in lines 11–35 of Fig. 16.9. Note that the const keyword *must* appear in *both* the function prototypes (Fig. 16.11, lines13–14) and the function definitions for functions getCourseName and displayMessage (lines 22 and 28).

```
1   // Fig. 16.12: GradeBook.cpp
2   // GradeBook member-function definitions. This file contains
3   // implementations of the member functions prototyped in GradeBook.h.
4   #include <iostream>
5   #include "GradeBook.h" // include definition of class GradeBook
6   using namespace std;
7
8   // constructor initializes courseName with string supplied as argument
9   GradeBook::GradeBook( string name )
10     : courseName( name ) // member initializer to initialize courseName
11  {
12     // empty body
13  } // end GradeBook constructor
14
15  // function to set the course name
16  void GradeBook::setCourseName( string name )
17  {
18     courseName = name; // store the course name in the object
19  } // end function setCourseName
20
21  // function to get the course name
22  string GradeBook::getCourseName() const
23  {
24     return courseName; // return object's courseName
25  } // end function getCourseName
26
27  // display a welcome message to the GradeBook user
28  void GradeBook::displayMessage() const
29  {
30     // call getCourseName to get the courseName
31     cout << "Welcome to the grade book for\n" << getCourseName()
32        << "!" << endl;
33  } // end function displayMessage
```

Fig. 16.12 | GradeBook member-function definitions represent the implementation of class GradeBook.

Each member-function name (lines 9, 16, 22 and 28) is preceded by the class name and ::, which is known as the **scope resolution operator**. This "ties" each member function to the (now separate) GradeBook class definition (Fig. 16.11), which declares the class's member functions and data members. Without "GradeBook::" preceding each function name, these functions would *not* be recognized by the compiler as member functions of class GradeBook—the compiler would consider them "free" or "loose" functions, like main. These are also called *global functions*. Such functions cannot access GradeBook's private data or call the class's member functions, without specifying an object. So, the compiler would *not* be able to compile these functions. For example, lines 18 and 24 in Fig. 16.12 that access variable courseName would cause compilation errors because courseName is not declared as a local variable in each function—the compiler would not know that courseName is already declared as a data member of class GradeBook.

Common Programming Error 16.3
When defining a class's member functions outside that class, omitting the class name and scope resolution operator (::) preceding the function names causes errors.

To indicate that the member functions in GradeBook.cpp are part of class GradeBook, we must first include the GradeBook.h header (line 5 of Fig. 16.12). This allows us to access the class name GradeBook in the GradeBook.cpp file. When compiling Grade-Book.cpp, the compiler uses the information in GradeBook.h to ensure that

1. the first line of each member function (lines 9, 16, 22 and 28) matches its prototype in the GradeBook.h file—for example, the compiler ensures that getCourse-Name accepts no parameters and returns a string, and that

2. each member function knows about the class's data members and other member functions—for example, lines 18 and 24 can access variable courseName because it's declared in GradeBook.h as a data member of class GradeBook, and line 31 can call function getCourseName, because it's declared as a member function of the class in GradeBook.h (and because the call conforms with the corresponding prototype).

Testing Class *GradeBook*
Figure 16.13 performs the same GradeBook object manipulations as Fig. 16.10. Separating GradeBook's interface from the implementation of its member functions does *not* affect the way that this client code uses the class. It affects only how the program is compiled and linked, which we discuss in detail shortly.

```cpp
1   // Fig. 16.13: fig16_13.cpp
2   // GradeBook class demonstration after separating
3   // its interface from its implementation.
4   #include <iostream>
5   #include "GradeBook.h" // include definition of class GradeBook
6   using namespace std;
7
8   // function main begins program execution
9   int main()
10  {
11      // create two GradeBook objects
12      GradeBook gradeBook1( "CS101 Introduction to C++ Programming" );
13      GradeBook gradeBook2( "CS102 Data Structures in C++" );
14
15      // display initial value of courseName for each GradeBook
16      cout << "gradeBook1 created for course: " << gradeBook1.getCourseName()
17          << "\ngradeBook2 created for course: " << gradeBook2.getCourseName()
18          << endl;
19  } // end main
```

Fig. 16.13 | GradeBook class demonstration after separating its interface from its implementation. (Part 1 of 2.)

```
gradeBook1 created for course: CS101 Introduction to C++ Programming
gradeBook2 created for course: CS102 Data Structures in C++
```

Fig. 16.13 | GradeBook class demonstration after separating its interface from its implementation. (Part 2 of 2.)

As in Fig. 16.10, line 5 of Fig. 16.13 includes the GradeBook.h header so that the compiler can ensure that GradeBook objects are created and manipulated correctly in the client code. Before executing this program, the source-code files in Fig. 16.12 and Fig. 16.13 must both be compiled, then linked together—that is, the member-function calls in the client code need to be tied to the implementations of the class's member functions—a job performed by the linker.

The Compilation and Linking Process

The diagram in Fig. 16.14 shows the compilation and linking process that results in an executable GradeBook application that can be used by instructors. Often a class's interface and implementation will be created and compiled by one programmer and used by a separate programmer who implements the client code that uses the class. So, the diagram shows what's required by both the class-implementation programmer and the client-code programmer. The dashed lines in the diagram show the pieces required by the class-implementation programmer, the client-code programmer and the GradeBook application user, respectively. [*Note:* Figure 16.14 is *not* a UML diagram.]

A class-implementation programmer responsible for creating a reusable GradeBook class creates the header GradeBook.h and the source-code file GradeBook.cpp that #includes the header, then compiles the source-code file to create GradeBook's object code. To hide the class's member-function implementation details, the class-implementation programmer would provide the client-code programmer with the header GradeBook.h (which specifies the class's interface and data members) and the GradeBook object code (i.e., the machine code instructions that represent GradeBook's member functions). The client-code programmer is *not* given GradeBook.cpp, so the client remains unaware of how GradeBook's member functions are implemented.

The client code programmer needs to know only GradeBook's interface to use the class and must be able to link its object code. Since the interface of the class is part of the class definition in the GradeBook.h header, the client-code programmer must have access to this file and must #include it in the client's source-code file. When the client code is compiled, the compiler uses the class definition in GradeBook.h to ensure that the main function creates and manipulates objects of class GradeBook correctly.

To create the executable GradeBook application, the last step is to link

1. the object code for the main function (i.e., the client code),

2. the object code for class GradeBook's member-function implementations and

3. the C++ Standard Library object code for the C++ classes (e.g., string) used by the class-implementation programmer and the client-code programmer.

The linker's output is the *executable* GradeBook application that instructors can use to manage their students' grades. Compilers and IDEs typically invoke the linker for you after compiling your code.

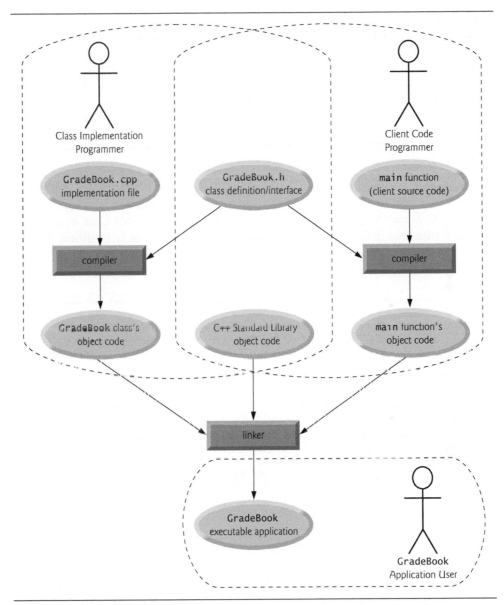

Fig. 16.14 | Compilation and linking process that produces an executable application.

For further information on compiling multiple-source-file programs, see your compiler's documentation. We provide links to various C++ compilers in our C++ Resource Center at www.deitel.com/cplusplus/.

16.8 Validating Data with *set* Functions

In Section 16.4, we introduced *set* functions for allowing clients of a class to modify the value of a private data member. In Fig. 16.5, class GradeBook defines member function setCourseName to simply assign a value received in its parameter name to data member courseName. This member function does not ensure that the course name adheres to any particular format or follows any other rules regarding what a "valid" course name looks like. Suppose that a university can print student transcripts containing course names of only 25 characters or less. If the university uses a system containing GradeBook objects to generate the transcripts, we might want class GradeBook to ensure that its data member courseName never contains more than 25 characters. The program of Figs. 16.15–16.17 enhances class GradeBook's member function setCourseName to perform this **validation** (also known as **validity checking**).

GradeBook Class Definition

GradeBook's class definition (Fig. 16.15)—and hence, its interface—is identical to that of Fig. 16.11. Since the interface remains unchanged, clients of this class need not be changed when the definition of member function setCourseName is modified. This enables clients to take advantage of the improved GradeBook class simply by linking the client code to the updated GradeBook's object code.

```
 1   // Fig. 16.15: GradeBook.h
 2   // GradeBook class definition presents the public interface of
 3   // the class. Member-function definitions appear in GradeBook.cpp.
 4   #include <string> // program uses C++ standard string class
 5
 6   // GradeBook class definition
 7   class GradeBook
 8   {
 9   public:
10      explicit GradeBook( std::string ); // constructor initialize courseName
11      void setCourseName( std::string ); // sets the course name
12      std::string getCourseName() const; // gets the course name
13      void displayMessage() const; // displays a welcome message
14   private:
15      std::string courseName; // course name for this GradeBook
16   }; // end class GradeBook
```

Fig. 16.15 | GradeBook class definition presents the public interface of the class.

Validating the Course Name with GradeBook Member Function setCourseName

The changes to class GradeBook are in the definitions of the constructor (Fig. 16.16, lines 9–12) and setCourseName (lines 16–29). Rather than using a member initializer, the constructor now calls setCourseName. In general, *all* data members should be initialized with *member initializers*. However, sometimes a constructor must also *validate* its argument(s)—often, this is handled in the constructor's body (line 11). The call to setCourseName *validates* the constructor's argument and *sets* the data member courseName. Initially, courseName's value will be set to the empty string *before* the constructor's body executes, then setCourseName will *modify* courseName's value.

In setCourseName, the if statement in lines 18–19 determines whether parameter name contains a *valid* course name (i.e., a string of 25 or fewer characters). If the course name is valid, line 19 stores it in data member courseName. Note the expression name.size() in line 18. This is a member-function call just like myGradeBook.display-Message(). The C++ Standard Library's string class defines a member function **size** that returns the number of characters in a string object. Parameter name is a string object, so the call name.size() returns the number of characters in name. If this value is less than or equal to 25, name is valid and line 19 executes.

```cpp
1   // Fig. 16.16: GradeBook.cpp
2   // Implementations of the GradeBook member-function definitions.
3   // The setCourseName function performs validation.
4   #include <iostream>
5   #include "GradeBook.h" // include definition of class GradeBook
6   using namespace std;
7
8   // constructor initializes courseName with string supplied as argument
9   GradeBook::GradeBook( string name )
10  {
11     setCourseName( name ); // validate and store courseName
12  } // end GradeBook constructor
13
14  // function that sets the course name;
15  // ensures that the course name has at most 25 characters
16  void GradeBook::setCourseName( string name )
17  {
18     if ( name.size() <= 25 ) // if name has 25 or fewer characters
19        courseName = name; // store the course name in the object
20
21     if ( name.size() > 25 ) // if name has more than 25 characters
22     {
23        // set courseName to first 25 characters of parameter name
24        courseName = name.substr( 0, 25 ); // start at 0, length of 25
25
26        cerr << "Name \"" << name << "\" exceeds maximum length (25).\n"
27           << "Limiting courseName to first 25 characters.\n" << endl;
28     } // end if
29  } // end function setCourseName
30
31  // function to get the course name
32  string GradeBook::getCourseName() const
33  {
34     return courseName; // return object's courseName
35  } // end function getCourseName
36
37  // display a welcome message to the GradeBook user
38  void GradeBook::displayMessage() const
39  {
40     // call getCourseName to get the courseName
41     cout << "Welcome to the grade book for\n" << getCourseName()
42        << "!" << endl;
43  } // end function displayMessage
```

Fig. 16.16 | Member-function definitions for class GradeBook with a *set* function that validates the length of data member courseName.

The if statement in lines 21–28 handles the case in which setCourseName receives an *invalid* course name (i.e., a name that is more than 25 characters long). Even if parameter name is too long, we still want to leave the GradeBook object in a **consistent state**—that is, a state in which the object's data member courseName contains a valid value (i.e., a string of 25 characters or less). Thus, we truncate the specified course name and assign the first 25 characters of name to the courseName data member (unfortunately, this could truncate the course name awkwardly). Standard class string provides member function **substr** (short for "substring") that returns a new string object created by copying part of an existing string object. The call in line 24 (i.e., name.substr(0, 25)) passes two integers (0 and 25) to name's member function substr. These arguments indicate the portion of the string name that substr should return. The first argument specifies the *starting position* in the original string from which characters are copied—the first character in every string is considered to be at position 0. The second argument specifies the *number of characters to copy*. Therefore, the call in line 24 returns a 25-character substring of name starting at position 0 (that is, the first 25 characters in name). For example, if name holds the value "CS101 Introduction to Programming in C++", substr returns "CS101 Introduction to Pro". After the call to substr, line 24 assigns the substring returned by substr to data member courseName. In this way, setCourseName ensures that courseName is always assigned a string containing 25 or fewer characters. If the member function has to truncate the course name to make it valid, lines 26–27 display a warning message using cerr.

The if statement in lines 21–28 contains two body statements—one to set the courseName to the first 25 characters of parameter name and one to print an accompanying message to the user.

The statement in lines 26–27 could also appear without a stream insertion operator at the start of the second line of the statement, as in:

```
cerr << "Name \"" << name << "\" exceeds maximum length (25).\n"
        "Limiting courseName to first 25 characters.\n" << endl;
```

The C++ compiler combines adjacent string literals, even if they appear on separate lines of a program. Thus, in the statement above, the C++ compiler would combine the string literals "\" exceeds maximum length (25).\n" and "Limiting courseName to first 25 charac-ters.\n" into a single string literal that produces output identical to that of lines 26–27 in Fig. 16.16. This behavior allows you to print lengthy strings by breaking them across lines in your program without including additional stream insertion operations.

Testing Class *GradeBook*

Figure 16.17 demonstrates the modified version of class GradeBook (Figs. 16.15–16.16) featuring validation. Line 12 creates a GradeBook object named gradeBook1. Recall that the GradeBook constructor calls setCourseName to initialize data member courseName. In previous versions of the class, the benefit of calling setCourseName in the constructor was not evident. Now, however, *the constructor takes advantage of the validation* provided by setCourseName. The constructor simply calls setCourseName, *rather than duplicating* its validation code. When line 12 of Fig. 16.17 passes an initial course name of "CS101 Introduction to Programming in C++" to the GradeBook constructor, the constructor passes this value to setCourseName, where the actual initialization occurs. Because this course name contains more than 25 characters, the body of the second if statement executes, causing courseName to be initialized to the truncated 25-character course name "CS101

Introduction to Pro" (the truncated part is highlighted in line 12). The output in Fig. 16.17 contains the warning message output by lines 26–27 of Fig. 16.16 in member function setCourseName. Line 13 creates another GradeBook object called gradeBook2—the valid course name passed to the constructor is exactly 25 characters.

```cpp
1   // Fig. 16.17: fig16_17.cpp
2   // Create and manipulate a GradeBook object; illustrate validation.
3   #include <iostream>
4   #include "GradeBook.h" // include definition of class GradeBook
5   using namespace std;
6
7   // function main begins program execution
8   int main()
9   {
10     // create two GradeBook objects;
11     // initial course name of gradeBook1 is too long
12     GradeBook gradeBook1( "CS101 Introduction to Programming in C++" );
13     GradeBook gradeBook2( "CS102 C++ Data Structures" );
14
15     // display each GradeBook's courseName
16     cout << "gradeBook1's initial course name is: "
17        << gradeBook1.getCourseName()
18        << "\ngradeBook2's initial course name is: "
19        << gradeBook2.getCourseName() << endl;
20
21     // modify gradeBook1's courseName (with a valid-length string)
22     gradeBook1.setCourseName( "CS101 C++ Programming" );
23
24     // display each GradeBook's courseName
25     cout << "\ngradeBook1's course name is: "
26        << gradeBook1.getCourseName()
27        << "\ngradeBook2's course name is: "
28        << gradeBook2.getCourseName() << endl;
29   } // end main
```

```
Name "CS101 Introduction to Programming in C++" exceeds maximum length (25).
Limiting courseName to first 25 characters.

gradeBook1's initial course name is: CS101 Introduction to Pro
gradeBook2's initial course name is: CS102 C++ Data Structures

gradeBook1's course name is: CS101 C++ Programming
gradeBook2's course name is: CS102 C++ Data Structures
```

Fig. 16.17 | Creating and manipulating a GradeBook object in which the course name is limited to 25 characters in length.

Lines 16–19 of Fig. 16.17 display the truncated course name for gradeBook1 (we highlight this in blue in the program output) and the course name for gradeBook2. Line 22 calls gradeBook1's setCourseName member function directly, to change the course name in the GradeBook object to a shorter name that does not need to be truncated. Then, lines 25–28 output the course names for the GradeBook objects again.

Additional Notes on Set *Functions*

A public *set* function such as setCourseName should carefully scrutinize any attempt to modify the value of a data member (e.g., courseName) to ensure that the new value is appropriate for that data item. For example, an attempt to *set* the day of the month to 37 should be rejected, an attempt to *set* a person's weight to zero or a negative value should be rejected, an attempt to *set* a grade on an exam to 185 (when the proper range is zero to 100) should be rejected, and so on.

Software Engineering Observation 16.3

Making data members private *and controlling access, especially write access, to those data members through* public *member functions helps ensure data integrity.*

Error-Prevention Tip 16.4

The benefits of data integrity are not automatic simply because data members are made private*—you must provide appropriate validity checking and report the errors.*

A *set* function could return a value indicating that an attempt was made to assign invalid data to an object of the class. A client could then test the return value of the *set* function to determine whether the attempt to modify the object was successful and to take appropriate action if not. We will do that in later chapters after we introduce a bit more programming technology. In C++, clients of objects also can be notified of problems via the *exception-handling mechanism*, which we present in-depth in Chapter 17.

16.9 Wrap-Up

In this chapter, you created user-defined classes, and created and used objects of those classes. We declared data members of a class to maintain data for each object of the class. We also defined member functions that operate on that data. You learned that member functions that do not modify a class's data should be declared const. We showed how to call an object's member functions to request the services the object provides and how to pass data to those member functions as arguments. We discussed the difference between a local variable of a member function and a data member of a class. We also showed how to use a constructor and a member-initializer list to ensure that every object is initialized properly. You learned that a single-parameter constructor should be declared explicit, and that a constructor cannot be declared const because it modifies the object being initialized.

We demonstrated how to separate the interface of a class from its implementation to promote good software engineering. You learned that using directives and using declarations should never be placed in headers. We presented a diagram that shows the files that class-implementation programmers and client-code programmers need to compile the code they write. We demonstrated how *set* functions can be used to validate an object's data and ensure that objects are maintained in a consistent state. UML class diagrams were used to model classes and their constructors, member functions and data members. In the next chapter, we begin our deeper treatment of classes.

Summary

Section 16.2 Defining a Class with a Member Function

- A class definition (p. 591) contains the data members and member functions that define the class's attributes and behaviors, respectively.
- A class definition begins with the keyword class followed immediately by the class name.
- By convention, the name of a user-defined class (p. 592) begins with a capital letter and, for readability, each subsequent word in the class name begins with a capital letter.
- Every class's body (p. 591) is enclosed in a pair of braces ({ and }) and ends with a semicolon.
- Member functions that appear after access specifier public (p. 591) can be called by other functions in a program and by member functions of other classes.
- Access specifiers are always followed by a colon (:).
- Keyword void (p. 592) is a special return type which indicates that a function will perform a task but will not return any data to its calling function when it completes its task.
- By convention, function names (p. 592) begin with a lowercase first letter and all subsequent words in the name begin with a capital letter.
- An empty set of parentheses after a function name indicates that the function does not require additional data to perform its task.
- A function that does not, and should not, modify the object on which it's called should be declared const.
- Typically, you cannot call a member function until you create an object of its class.
- Each new class you create becomes a new type in C++.
- In the UML, each class is modeled in a class diagram (p. 593) as a rectangle with three compartments, which (top to bottom) contain the class's name, attributes and operations, respectively.
- The UML models operations as the operation name followed by parentheses. A plus sign (+) preceding the name indicates a public operation (i.e., a public member function in C++).

Section 16.3 Defining a Member Function with a Parameter

- A member function can require one or more parameters (p. 593) that represent additional data it needs to perform its task. A function call supplies an argument (p. 594) for each function parameter.
- A member function is called by following the object name with a dot (.) operator (p. 593), the function name and a set of parentheses containing the function's arguments.
- A variable of C++ Standard Library class string (p. 595) represents a string of characters. This class is defined in header <string>, and the name string belongs to namespace std.
- Function getline (from header <string>, p. 595) reads characters from its first argument until a newline character is encountered, then places the characters (not including the newline) in the string variable specified as its second argument. The newline character is discarded.
- A parameter list (p. 596) may contain any number of parameters, including none at all (represented by empty parentheses) to indicate that a function does not require any parameters.
- The number of arguments in a function call must match the number of parameters in the parameter list of the called member function's header. Also, the argument types in the function call must be consistent with the types of the corresponding parameters in the function header.
- The UML models a parameter of an operation by listing the parameter name, followed by a colon and the parameter type between the parentheses following the operation name.

- The UML has its own data types. Not all the UML data types have the same names as the corresponding C++ types. The UML type String corresponds to the C++ type string.

Section 16.4 Data Members, set Member Functions and get Member Functions

- Variables declared in a function's body are local variables (p. 597) and can be used only from the point of their declaration to the closing right brace (}) of the block in which they are declared.

- A local variable must be declared before it can be used in a function. A local variable cannot be accessed outside the function in which it's declared.

- Data members (p. 597) normally are private (p. 599). Variables or functions declared private are accessible only to member functions of the class in which they're declared, or to friends of the class.

- When a program creates (instantiates) an object, its private data members are encapsulated (hidden, p. 599) in the object and can be accessed only by member functions of the object's class (or by "friends" of the class, as you'll see in Chapter 17).

- When a function that specifies a return type other than void is called and completes its task, the function returns a result to its calling function.

- By default, the initial value of a string is the empty string (p. 600)—i.e., a string that does not contain any characters. Nothing appears on the screen when an empty string is displayed.

- A class often provides public member functions to allow the class's clients to set or get (p. 601) private data members. The names of these member functions normally begin with set or get.

- Set and get functions allow clients of a class to indirectly access the hidden data. The client does not know how the object performs these operations.

- A class's set and get functions should be used by other member functions of the class to manipulate the class's private data. If the class's data representation is changed, member functions that access the data only via the set and get functions will not require modification.

- A public set function should carefully scrutinize any attempt to modify the value of a data member to ensure that the new value is appropriate for that data item.

- The UML represents data members as attributes by listing the attribute name, followed by a colon and the attribute type. Private attributes are preceded by a minus sign (–) in the UML.

- The UML indicates the return type of an operation by placing a colon and the return type after the parentheses following the operation name.

- UML class diagrams do not specify return types for operations that do not return values.

Section 16.5 Initializing Objects with Constructors

- Each class should provide one or more constructors (p. 602) to initialize an object of the class when the object is created. A constructor must be defined with the same name as the class.

- A difference between constructors and functions is that constructors cannot return values, so they cannot specify a return type (not even void). Normally, constructors are declared public.

- C++ automatically calls a constructor for each object that's created, which helps ensure that objects are initialized properly before they're used in a program.

- A constructor with no parameters is a default constructor (p. 603). If you do not provide a constructor, the compiler provides a default constructor. You can also define a default constructor explicitly. If you define any constructors for a class, C++ will not create a default constructor.

- A single-parameter constructor should be declared explicit.

- A constructor uses a member initializer list to initialize a class's data members. Member initializers appear between a constructor's parameter list and the left brace that begins the constructor's body. The member initializer list is separated from the parameter list with a colon (:). A member initializer consists of a data member's variable name followed by parentheses containing the member's initial value. You can perform initialization in the constructor's body, but you'll learn later in the book that it's more efficient to do it with member initializers, and some types of data members must be initialized this way.

- The UML models constructors as operations in a class diagram's third compartment with the word "constructor" between guillemets (« and ») before the constructor's name.

Section 16.6 Placing a Class in a Separate File for Reusability
- Class definitions, when packaged properly, can be reused by programmers worldwide.
- It's customary to define a class in a header (p. 606) that has a .h filename extension.

Section 16.7 Separating Interface from Implementation
- If the class's implementation changes, the class's clients should not be required to change.
- Interfaces define and standardize the ways in which things such as people and systems interact.
- A class's public interface (p. 610) describes the public member functions that are made available to the class's clients. The interface describes *what* services (p. 610) clients can use and how to *request* those services, but does not specify *how* the class carries out the services.
- Separating interface from implementation (p. 610) makes programs easier to modify. Changes in the class's implementation do not affect the client as long as the class's interface remains unchanged.
- You should never place using directives and using declarations in headers.
- A function prototype (p. 610) contains a function's name, its return type and the number, types and order of the parameters the function expects to receive.
- Once a class is defined and its member functions are declared (via function prototypes), the member functions should be defined in a separate source-code file.
- For each member function defined outside of its corresponding class definition, the function name must be preceded by the class name and the scope resolution operator (::, p. 612).

Section 16.8 Validating Data with set Functions
- Class string's size member function (p. 617) returns the number of characters in a string.
- Class string's member function substr (p. 618) returns a new string containing a copy of part of an existing string. The first argument specifies the starting position in the original string. The second specifies the number of characters to copy.

Self-Review Exercises

16.1 Fill in the blanks in each of the following:
    a) Every class definition contains the keyword _____ followed immediately by the class's name.
    b) A class definition is typically stored in a file with the _____ filename extension.
    c) Each parameter in a function header specifies both a(n) _____ and a(n) _____.
    d) When each object of a class maintains its own version of an attribute, the variable that represents the attribute is also known as a(n) _____.
    e) Keyword public is a(n) _____.
    f) Return type _____ indicates that a function will perform a task but will not return any information when it completes its task.
    g) Function _____ from the <string> library reads characters until a newline character is encountered, then copies those characters into the specified string.

    h) When a member function is defined outside the class definition, the function header must include the class name and the _____, followed by the function name to "tie" the member function to the class definition.

    i) The source-code file and any other files that use a class can include the class's header via a(n) _____ preprocessing directive.

16.2 State whether each of the following is *true* or *false*. If *false*, explain why.

    a) By convention, function names begin with a capital letter and all subsequent words in the name begin with a capital letter.

    b) Empty parentheses following a function name in a function prototype indicate that the function does not require any parameters to perform its task.

    c) Data members or member functions declared with access specifier private are accessible to member functions of the class in which they're declared.

    d) Variables declared in the body of a particular member function are known as data members and can be used in all member functions of the class.

    e) Every function's body is delimited by left and right braces ({ and }).

    f) Any source-code file that contains int main() can be used to execute a program.

    g) The types of arguments in a function call must be consistent with the types of the corresponding parameters in the function prototype's parameter list.

16.3 What is the difference between a local variable and a data member?

16.4 Explain the purpose of a function parameter. What's the difference between a parameter and an argument?

Answers to Self-Review Exercises

16.1 a) class. b) .h. c) type, name. d) data member. e) access specifier. f) void. g) getline. h) scope resolution operator (::). i) #include.

16.2 a) False. Function names begin with a lowercase letter and all subsequent words in the name begin with a capital letter. b) True. c) True. d) False. Such variables are local variables and can be used only in the member function in which they're declared. e) True. f) True. g) True.

16.3 A local variable is declared in the body of a function and can be used only from its declaration to the closing brace of the block in which it's declared. A data member is declared in a class, but not in the body of any of the class's member functions. Every object of a class has each of the class's data members. Data members are accessible to all member functions of the class.

16.4 A parameter represents additional information that a function requires to perform its task. Each parameter required by a function is specified in the function header. An argument is the value supplied in the function call. When the function is called, the argument value is passed into the function parameter so that the function can perform its task.

Exercises

16.5 *(Function Prototypes and Definitions)* Explain the difference between a function prototype and a function definition.

16.6 *(Default Constructor)* What's a default constructor? How are an object's data members initialized if a class has only an implicitly defined default constructor?

16.7 *(Data Members)* Explain the purpose of a data member.

16.8 *(Header and Source-Code Files)* What's a header? What's a source-code file? Discuss the purpose of each.

16.9 *(Using a Class Without a using Directive)* Explain how a program could use class string without inserting a using directive.

16.10 *(Set and Get Functions)* Explain why a class might provide a *set* function and a *get* function for a data member.

16.11 *(Modifying Class GradeBook)* Modify class GradeBook (Figs. 16.11–16.12) as follows:
   a) Include a second string data member that represents the course instructor's name.
   b) Provide a *set* function to change the instructor's name and a *get* function to retrieve it.
   c) Modify the constructor to specify course name and instructor name parameters.
   d) Modify function displayMessage to output the welcome message and course name, then the string "This course is presented by: " followed by the instructor's name.

Use your modified class in a test program that demonstrates the class's new capabilities.

16.12 *(Account Class)* Create an Account class that a bank might use to represent customers' bank accounts. Include a data member of type int to represent the account balance. Provide a constructor that receives an initial balance and uses it to initialize the data member. The constructor should validate the initial balance to ensure that it's greater than or equal to 0. If not, set the balance to 0 and display an error message indicating that the initial balance was invalid. Provide three member functions. Member function credit should add an amount to the current balance. Member function debit should withdraw money from the Account and ensure that the debit amount does not exceed the Account's balance. If it does, the balance should be left unchanged and the function should print a message indicating "Debit amount exceeded account balance." Member function getBalance should return the current balance. Create a program that creates two Account objects and tests the member functions of class Account.

16.13 *(Invoice Class)* Create a class called Invoice that a hardware store might use to represent an invoice for an item sold at the store. An Invoice should include four data members—a part number (type string), a part description (type string), a quantity of the item being purchased (type int) and a price per item (type int). Your class should have a constructor that initializes the four data members. A constructor that receives multiple arguments is defined with the form:

   ClassName(TypeName1 parameterName1, TypeName2 parameterName2, ...)

Provide a *set* and a *get* function for each data member. In addition, provide a member function named getInvoiceAmount that calculates the invoice amount (i.e., multiplies the quantity by the price per item), then returns the amount as an int value. If the quantity is not positive, it should be set to 0. If the price per item is not positive, it should be set to 0. Write a test program that demonstrates class Invoice's capabilities.

16.14 *(Employee Class)* Create a class called Employee that includes three pieces of information as data members—a first name (type string), a last name (type string) and a monthly salary (type int). Your class should have a constructor that initializes the three data members. Provide a *set* and a *get* function for each data member. If the monthly salary is not positive, set it to 0. Write a test program that demonstrates class Employee's capabilities. Create two Employee objects and display each object's *yearly* salary. Then give each Employee a 10 percent raise and display each Employee's yearly salary again.

16.15 *(Date Class)* Create a class called Date that includes three pieces of information as data members—a month (type int), a day (type int) and a year (type int). Your class should have a constructor with three parameters that uses the parameters to initialize the three data members. For the purpose of this exercise, assume that the values provided for the year and day are correct, but ensure that the month value is in the range 1–12; if it isn't, set the month to 1. Provide a *set* and a *get* function for each data member. Provide a member function displayDate that displays the month, day and year separated by forward slashes (/). Write a test program that demonstrates class Date's capabilities.

Making a Difference

16.16 *(Target-Heart-Rate Calculator)* While exercising, you can use a heart-rate monitor to see that your heart rate stays within a safe range suggested by your trainers and doctors. According to the American Heart Association (AHA) (www.americanheart.org/presenter.jhtml?identifier=4736), the formula for calculating your *maximum heart rate* in beats per minute is 220 minus your age in years. Your *target heart rate* is a range that is 50–85% of your maximum heart rate. [Note: *These formulas are estimates provided by the AHA. Maximum and target heart rates may vary based on the health, fitness and gender of the individual. Always consult a physician or qualified health care professional before beginning or modifying an exercise program.*] Create a class called HeartRates. The class attributes should include the person's first name, last name and date of birth (consisting of separate attributes for the month, day and year of birth). Your class should have a constructor that receives this data as parameters. For each attribute provide *set* and *get* functions. The class also should include a function getAge that calculates and returns the person's age (in years), a function getMaxiumumHeartRate that calculates and returns the person's maximum heart rate and a function getTargetHeartRate that calculates and returns the person's target heart rate. Since you do not yet know how to obtain the current date from the computer, function getAge should prompt the user to enter the current month, day and year before calculating the person's age. Write an application that prompts for the person's information, instantiates an object of class HeartRates and prints the information from that object—including the person's first name, last name and date of birth—then calculates and prints the person's age in (years), maximum heart rate and target-heart-rate range.

16.17 *(Computerization of Health Records)* A health care issue that has been in the news lately is the computerization of health records. This possibility is being approached cautiously because of sensitive privacy and security concerns, among others. Computerizing health records could make it easier for patients to share their health profiles and histories among their various health care professionals. This could improve the quality of health care, help avoid drug conflicts and erroneous drug prescriptions, reduce costs and in emergencies, could save lives. In this exercise, you'll design a "starter" HealthProfile class for a person. The class attributes should include the person's first name, last name, gender, date of birth (consisting of separate attributes for the month, day and year of birth), height (in inches) and weight (in pounds). Your class should have a constructor that receives this data. For each attribute, provide *set* and *get* functions. The class also should include functions that calculate and return the user's age in years, maximum heart rate and target-heart-rate range (see Exercise 16.16), and body mass index (BMI; see Exercise 2.32). Write an application that prompts for the person's information, instantiates an object of class HealthProfile for that person and prints the information from that object—including the person's first name, last name, gender, date of birth, height and weight—then calculates and prints the person's age in years, BMI, maximum heart rate and target-heart-rate range. It should also display the "BMI values" chart from Exercise 2.32. Use the same technique as Exercise 16.16 to calculate the person's age.

Classes: A Deeper Look;
Throwing Exceptions

17

Objectives
In this chapter you'll:

- Use an include guard.

- Access class members via an object's name, a reference or a pointer.

- Use destructors to perform "termination housekeeping."

- Learn the order of constructor and destructor calls.

- Learn about the dangers of returning a reference to `private` data.

- Assign the data members of one object to those of another object.

- Create objects composed of other objects.

- Use `friend` functions and `friend` classes.

- Use the `this` pointer in a member function to access a non-`static` class member.

- Use `static` data members and member functions.

17.1 Introduction

This chapter takes a deeper look at classes. We use an integrated Time class case study and other examples to demonstrate several class construction capabilities. We begin with a Time class that reviews several of the features presented in preceding chapters. The example also demonstrates using an *include guard* in headers to prevent header code from being included in the same source code file more than once.

We demonstrate how client code can access a class's public members via the name of an object, a reference to an object or a pointer to an object. As you'll see, object names and references can be used with the dot (.) member selection operator to access a public member, and pointers can be used with the arrow (->) member selection operator.

We discuss access functions that can read or write an object's data members. A common use of access functions is to test the truth or falsity of conditions—such functions are known as *predicate functions*. We also demonstrate the notion of a utility function (also called a *helper function*)—a private member function that supports the operation of the class's public member functions, but is *not* intended for use by clients of the class.

We show how to pass arguments to constructors and show how default arguments can be used in constructors to enable client code to initialize objects using a variety of arguments. Next, we discuss a special member function called a *destructor* that's part of every class and is used to perform "termination housekeeping" on an object before it's destroyed. We demonstrate the *order* in which constructors and destructors are called.

We show that returning a reference or pointer to private data *breaks the encapsulation of a class*, allowing client code to directly access an object's data. We use default memberwise assignment to assign an object of a class to another object of the same class.

We use const objects and const member functions to prevent modifications of objects and enforce the principle of least privilege. We discuss *composition*—a form of reuse in which a class can have objects of other classes as members. Next, we use *friendship* to specify that a nonmember function can also access a class's non-public members—a technique that's often used in operator overloading (Chapter 18) for performance reasons. We discuss the this pointer, which is an *implicit* argument in all calls to a class's non-static member functions, allowing them to access the correct object's data members and non-static member functions. We motivate the need for static class members and show how to use them in your own classes.

17.2 Time Class Case Study

Our first example creates class Time and tests the class. We demonstrate an important C++ software engineering concept—using an include guard in headers to prevent the code in the header from being included into the same source code file more than once. Since a class can be defined only once, using such preprocessing directives prevents multiple-definition errors.

Time Class Definition
The class definition (Fig. 17.1) contains prototypes (lines 13–16) for member functions Time, setTime, printUniversal and printStandard, and includes private unsigned int members hour, minute and second (lines 18–20). Class Time's private data members can be accessed *only* by its member functions. Chapter 19 introduces a third access specifier, protected, as we study inheritance and the part it plays in object-oriented programming.

Good Programming Practice 17.1

For clarity and readability, use each access specifier only once in a class definition. Place public members first, where they're easy to locate.

Software Engineering Observation 17.1

Each member of a class should have private visibility unless it can be proven that the element needs public visibility. This is another example of the principle of least privilege.

```cpp
1   // Fig. 17.1: Time.h
2   // Time class definition.
3   // Member functions are defined in Time.cpp
4
5   // prevent multiple inclusions of header
6   #ifndef TIME_H
7   #define TIME_H
8
9   // Time class definition
10  class Time
11  {
12  public:
13     Time(); // constructor
14     void setTime( int, int, int ); // set hour, minute and second
15     void printUniversal() const; // print time in universal-time format
16     void printStandard() const; // print time in standard-time format
17  private:
18     unsigned int hour; // 0 - 23 (24-hour clock format)
19     unsigned int minute; // 0 - 59
20     unsigned int second; // 0 - 59
21  }; // end class Time
22
23  #endif
```

Fig. 17.1 | Time class definition.

In Fig. 17.1, the class definition is enclosed in the following **include guard** (lines 6, 7 and 23):

```
// prevent multiple inclusions of header
#ifndef TIME_H
#define TIME_H
   ...
#endif
```

When we build larger programs, other definitions and declarations will also be placed in headers. The preceding include guard prevents the code between **#ifndef** (which means "if not defined") and **#endif** from being included if the name TIME_H has been defined. If the header has *not* been included previously in a file, the name TIME_H is defined by the **#define** directive and the header statements *are* included. If the header has been included previously, TIME_H *is defined* already and the header is *not* included again. Attempts to include a header multiple times (inadvertently) typically occur in large programs with many headers that may themselves include other headers.

Error-Prevention Tip 17.1

Use #ifndef, #define and #endif preprocessing directives to form an include guard that prevents headers from being included more than once in a source-code file.

Good Programming Practice 17.2

By convention, use the name of the header in uppercase with the period replaced by an underscore in the #ifndef and #define preprocessing directives of a header.

Time Class Member Functions
In Fig. 17.2, the Time constructor (lines 11–14) initializes the data members to 0—the universal-time equivalent of 12 AM. Invalid values cannot be stored in the data members of a Time object, because the constructor is called when the Time object is created, and all subsequent attempts by a client to modify the data members are scrutinized by function setTime (discussed shortly). Finally, it's important to note that you can define *overloaded constructors* for a class—we studied overloaded functions in Chapter 15.

```
1  // Fig. 17.2: Time.cpp
2  // Time class member-function definitions.
3  #include <iostream>
4  #include <iomanip>
5  #include <stdexcept> // for invalid_argument exception class
6  #include "Time.h" // include definition of class Time from Time.h
7
8  using namespace std;
9
10 // Time constructor initializes each data member to zero.
11 Time::Time()
12    : hour( 0 ), minute( 0 ), second( 0 )
13 {
14 } // end Time constructor
```

Fig. 17.2 | Time class member-function definitions. (Part 1 of 2.)

```
15
16    // set new Time value using universal time
17    void Time::setTime( int h, int m, int s )
18    {
19       // validate hour, minute and second
20       if ( ( h >= 0 && h < 24 ) && ( m >= 0 && m < 60 ) &&
21          ( s >= 0 && s < 60 ) )
22       {
23          hour = h;
24          minute = m;
25          second = s;
26       } // end if
27       else
28          throw invalid_argument(
29             "hour, minute and/or second was out of range" );
30    } // end function setTime
31
32    // print Time in universal-time format (HH:MM:SS)
33    void Time::printUniversal() const
34    {
35       cout << setfill( '0' ) << setw( 2 ) << hour << ":"
36          << setw( 2 ) << minute << ":" << setw( 2 ) << second;
37    } // end function printUniversal
38
39    // print Time in standard-time format (HH:MM:SS AM or PM)
40    void Time::printStandard() const
41    {
42       cout << ( ( hour == 0 || hour == 12 ) ? 12 : hour % 12 ) << ":"
43          << setfill( '0' ) << setw( 2 ) << minute << ":" << setw( 2 )
44          << second << ( hour < 12 ? " AM" : " PM" );
45    } // end function printStandard
```

Fig. 17.2 | Time class member-function definitions. (Part 2 of 2.)

Before C++11, only static const int data members could be initialized where they were declared in the class body. For this reason, data members typically should be initialized by the class's constructor as *there is no default initialization for fundamental-type data members*. As of C++11, you can now use an *in-class initializer* to initialize any data member where it's declared in the class definition.

Time Class Member Function setTime and Throwing Exceptions

Function setTime (lines 17–30) is a public function that declares three int parameters and uses them to set the time. Lines 20–21 test each argument to determine whether the value is in range, and, if so, lines 23–25 assign the values to the hour, minute and second data members. The hour value must be greater than or equal to 0 and less than 24, because universal-time format represents hours as integers from 0 to 23 (e.g., 1 PM is hour 13 and 11 PM is hour 23; midnight is hour 0 and noon is hour 12). Similarly, both minute and second must be greater than or equal to 0 and less than 60. For values outside these ranges, setTime **throws an exception** (lines 28–29) of type **invalid_argument** (from header <stdexcept>), which notifies the client code that an invalid argument was received. You can use try...catch to catch exceptions and attempt to recover from them, which we'll do in Fig. 17.3. The **throw statement** (lines 28–29) creates a new object of type invalid_argument. The parentheses following the class name indicate a call to the invalid_argument constructor that allows us to specify a custom error message string. After the exception object is created, the throw statement immediately terminates function setTime and the exception is returned to the code that attempted to set the time.

Time Class Member Function `printUniversal`
Function printUniversal (lines 33–37 of Fig. 17.2) takes no arguments and outputs the time in universal-time format, consisting of three colon-separated pairs of digits. If the time were 1:30:07 PM, function printUniversal would return 13:30:07. Line 35 uses parameterized stream manipulator **setfill** to specify the **fill character** that's displayed when an integer is output in a field *wider* than the number of digits in the value. The fill characters appear to the *left* of the digits in the number, because the number is *right aligned* by default—for *left aligned* values, the fill characters would appear to the right. In this example, if the minute value is 2, it will be displayed as 02, because the fill character is set to zero ('0'). If the number being output fills the specified field, the fill character will *not* be displayed. Once the fill character is specified with setfill, it applies for *all* subsequent values that are displayed in fields wider than the value being displayed—setfill is a "sticky" setting. This is in contrast to setw, which applies *only* to the next value displayed—setw is a "nonsticky" setting.

Error-Prevention Tip 17.2
Each sticky setting (such as a fill character or floating-point precision) should be restored to its previous setting when it's no longer needed. Failure to do so may result in incorrectly formatted output later in a program. Chapter 21, Stream Input/Output: A Deeper Look, discusses how to reset the fill character and precision.

Time Class Member Function `printStandard`
Function printStandard (lines 40–45) takes no arguments and outputs the date in standard-time format, consisting of the hour, minute and second values separated by colons and followed by an AM or PM indicator (e.g., 1:27:06 PM). Like function printUniversal, function printStandard uses setfill('0') to format the minute and second as two digit values with leading zeros if necessary. Line 42 uses the conditional operator (?:) to determine the value of hour to be displayed—if the hour is 0 or 12 (AM or PM), it appears as 12; otherwise, the hour appears as a value from 1 to 11. The conditional operator in line 44 determines whether AM or PM will be displayed.

Defining Member Functions Outside the Class Definition; Class Scope
Even though a member function declared in a class definition may be defined outside that class definition (and "tied" to the class via the *scope resolution operator*), that member function is still within that **class's scope**—that is, its name is known to other class members referred to via an object of the class, a reference to an object of the class, a pointer to an object of the class or the scope resolution operator. We'll say more about class scope shortly.

If a member function is defined in a class's body, the member function is implicitly declared *inline*. Remember that the compiler reserves the right not to inline any function.

Performance Tip 17.1

Defining a member function inside the class definition inlines the member function (if the compiler chooses to do so). This can improve performance.

Software Engineering Observation 17.2

Only the simplest and most stable member functions (i.e., whose implementations are unlikely to change) should be defined in the class header.

Member Functions vs. Global Functions (Also Called Free Functions)

The `printUniversal` and `printStandard` member functions take no arguments, because these member functions implicitly know that they're to print the data members of the particular `Time` object on which they're invoked. This can make member function calls more concise than conventional function calls in procedural programming.

Software Engineering Observation 17.3

Using an object-oriented programming approach often simplifies function calls by reducing the number of parameters. This benefit derives from the fact that encapsulating data members and member functions within a class gives the member functions the right to access the data members.

Software Engineering Observation 17.4

Member functions are usually shorter than functions in non-object-oriented programs, because the data stored in data members have ideally been validated by a constructor or by member functions that store new data. Because the data is already in the object, the member-function calls often have no arguments or fewer arguments than function calls in non-object-oriented languages. Thus, the calls, the function definitions and the function prototypes are shorter. This improves many aspects of program development.

Error-Prevention Tip 17.3

The fact that member function calls generally take either no arguments or substantially fewer arguments than conventional function calls in non-object-oriented languages reduces the likelihood of passing the wrong arguments, the wrong types of arguments or the wrong number of arguments.

Using Class Time

Once defined, `Time` can be used as a type in declarations as follows:

```
Time sunset; // object of type Time
array< Time, 5 > arrayOfTimes; // array of 5 Time objects
Time &dinnerTime = sunset; // reference to a Time object
Time *timePtr = &dinnerTime; // pointer to a Time object
```

Figure 17.3 uses class `Time`. Line 11 instantiates a single object of class `Time` called t. When the object is instantiated, the `Time` constructor is called to initialize each `private` data member to 0. Then, lines 15 and 17 print the time in universal and standard formats, respectively, to confirm that the members were initialized properly. Line 19 sets a new time by calling member function `setTime`, and lines 23 and 25 print the time again in both formats.

```cpp
1   // Fig. 17.3: fig17_03.cpp
2   // Program to test class Time.
3   // NOTE: This file must be compiled with Time.cpp.
4   #include <iostream>
5   #include <stdexcept> // for invalid_argument exception class
6   #include "Time.h" // include definition of class Time from Time.h
7   using namespace std;
8
9   int main()
10  {
11     Time t; // instantiate object t of class Time
12
13     // output Time object t's initial values
14     cout << "The initial universal time is ";
15     t.printUniversal(); // 00:00:00
16     cout << "\nThe initial standard time is ";
17     t.printStandard(); // 12:00:00 AM
18
19     t.setTime( 13, 27, 6 ); // change time
20
21     // output Time object t's new values
22     cout << "\n\nUniversal time after setTime is ";
23     t.printUniversal(); // 13:27:06
24     cout << "\nStandard time after setTime is ";
25     t.printStandard(); // 1:27:06 PM
26
27     // attempt to set the time with invalid values
28     try
29     {
30        t.setTime( 99, 99, 99 ); // all values out of range
31     } // end try
32     catch ( invalid_argument &e )
33     {
34        cout << "Exception: " << e.what() << endl;
35     } // end catch
36
37     // output t's values after specifying invalid values
38     cout << "\n\nAfter attempting invalid settings:"
39        << "\nUniversal time: ";
40     t.printUniversal(); // 13:27:06
41     cout << "\nStandard time: ";
42     t.printStandard(); // 1:27:06 PM
43     cout << endl;
44  } // end main
```

```
The initial universal time is 00:00:00
The initial standard time is 12:00:00 AM

Universal time after setTime is 13:27:06
Standard time after setTime is 1:27:06 PM

Exception: hour, minute and/or second was out of range
```

Fig. 17.3 | Program to test class Time. (Part 1 of 2.)

```
After attempting invalid settings:
Universal time: 13:27:06
Standard time: 1:27:06 PM
```

Fig. 17.3 | Program to test class Time. (Part 2 of 2.)

Calling setTime *with Invalid Values*

To illustrate that method setTime validates its arguments, line 30 calls setTime with invalid arguments of 99 for the hour, minute and second. This statement is placed in a try block (lines 28–31) in case setTime throws an invalid_argument exception, which it will do since the arguments are all invalid. When this occurs, the exception is caught at lines 32–35 and line 34 displays the exception's error message by calling its what member function. Lines 38–42 output the time again in both formats to confirm that setTime did not change the time when invalid arguments were supplied.

Looking Ahead to Composition and Inheritance

Often, classes do not have to be created "from scratch." Rather, they can *include objects of other classes as members* or they may be **derived** from other classes that provide attributes and behaviors the new classes can use. Such software reuse can greatly enhance productivity and simplify code maintenance. Including class objects as members of other classes is called **composition (or aggregation)** and is discussed in Section 17.11. Deriving new classes from existing classes is called **inheritance** and is discussed in Chapter 19.

Object Size

People new to object-oriented programming often suppose that objects must be quite large because they contain data members and member functions. *Logically*, this is true—you may think of objects as containing data and functions (and our discussion has certainly encouraged this view); *physically*, however, this is *not* true.

> **Performance Tip 17.2**
>
> *Objects contain only data, so objects are much smaller than if they also contained member functions. The compiler creates one copy (only) of the member functions separate from all objects of the class. All objects of the class share this one copy. Each object, of course, needs its own copy of the class's data, because the data can vary among the objects. The function code is nonmodifiable and, hence, can be shared among all objects of one class.*

17.3 Class Scope and Accessing Class Members

A class's data members and member functions belong to that class's scope. Nonmember functions are defined at *global namespace scope,* by default.

Within a class's scope, class members are immediately accessible by all of that class's member functions and can be referenced by name. Outside a class's scope, public class members are referenced through one of the **handles** on an object—an *object name*, a *reference* to an object or a *pointer* to an object. The type of the object, reference or pointer specifies the interface (e.g., the member functions) accessible to the client. [We'll see in Section 17.13 that an *implicit handle* is inserted by the compiler on every reference to a data member or member function from within an object.]

Class Scope and Block Scope
Variables declared in a member function have *block scope* and are known only to that function. If a member function defines a variable with the same name as a variable with class scope, the class-scope variable is *hidden* in the function by the block-scope variable. Such a hidden variable can be accessed by preceding the variable name with the class name followed by the scope resolution operator (::). Hidden global variables can be accessed with the scope resolution operator, as in ::*globalVariableName*.

Dot (.) and Arrow (->) Member Selection Operators
The dot member selection operator (.) is preceded by an object's name or with a reference to an object to access the object's members. The **arrow member selection operator (->)** is preceded by a pointer to an object to access the object's members.

Accessing **public** *Class Members Through Objects, References and Pointers*
Consider an Account class that has a public setBalance member function. Given the following declarations:

```
Account account; // an Account object

// accountRef refers to an Account object
Account &accountRef = account;

// accountPtr points to an Account object
Account *accountPtr = &account;
```

You can invoke member function setBalance using the dot (.) and arrow (->) member selection operators as follows:

```
// call setBalance via the Account object
account.setBalance( 123.45 );

// call setBalance via a reference to the Account object
accountRef.setBalance( 123.45 );

// call setBalance via a pointer to the Account object
accountPtr->setBalance( 123.45 );
```

17.4 Access Functions and Utility Functions

Access Functions
Access functions can read or display data. Another common use for access functions is to test the truth or falsity of conditions—such functions are often called **predicate functions**. An example of a predicate function would be an isEmpty function for any container class—a class capable of holding many objects, like a vector. A program might test isEmpty before attempting to read another item from the container object. An isFull predicate function might test a container-class object to determine whether it has no additional room. Useful predicate functions for our Time class might be isAM and isPM.

Utility Functions
A **utility function** (also called a **helper function**) is a private member function that supports the operation of a class's other member functions. Utility functions are declared private because they're not intended for use by the class's clients. A common use of a utility function would be to place in a function some common code that would otherwise be duplicated in several other member functions.

17.5 Time Class Case Study: Constructors with Default Arguments

The program of Figs. 17.4–17.6 enhances class Time to demonstrate how arguments are implicitly passed to a constructor. The constructor defined in Fig. 17.2 initialized hour, minute and second to 0 (i.e., midnight in universal time). Like other functions, constructors can specify *default arguments*. Line 13 of Fig. 17.4 declares the Time constructor to include default arguments, specifying a default value of zero for each argument passed to the constructor. The constructor is declared explicit because it can be called with one argument. We discuss explicit constructors in detail in Section 18.13.

```
1   // Fig. 17.4: Time.h
2   // Time class containing a constructor with default arguments.
3   // Member functions defined in Time.cpp.
4
5   // prevent multiple inclusions of header
6   #ifndef TIME_H
7   #define TIME_H
8
9   // Time class definition
10  class Time
11  {
12  public:
13     explicit Time( int = 0, int = 0, int = 0 ); // default constructor
14
15     // set functions
16     void setTime( int, int, int ); // set hour, minute, second
17     void setHour( int ); // set hour (after validation)
18     void setMinute( int ); // set minute (after validation)
19     void setSecond( int ); // set second (after validation)
20
21     // get functions
22     unsigned int getHour() const; // return hour
23     unsigned int getMinute() const; // return minute
24     unsigned int getSecond() const; // return second
25
26     void printUniversal() const; // output time in universal-time format
27     void printStandard() const; // output time in standard-time format
28  private:
29     unsigned int hour; // 0 - 23 (24-hour clock format)
30     unsigned int minute; // 0 - 59
31     unsigned int second; // 0 - 59
32  }; // end class Time
33
34  #endif
```

Fig. 17.4 | Time class containing a constructor with default arguments.

In Fig. 17.5, lines 10–13 define the new version of the Time constructor that receives values for parameters hour, minute and second that will be used to initialize private data members hour, minute and second, respectively. The default arguments to the constructor ensure that, even if no values are provided in a constructor call, the constructor still initializes the data members. *A constructor that defaults all its arguments is also a default constructor—that is, a constructor that can be invoked with no arguments. There can be at most one default constructor per class.* The version of class `Time` in this example provides *set* and *get* functions for each data member. The `Time` constructor now calls `setTime`, which calls the `setHour`, `setMinute` and `setSecond` functions to validate and assign values to the data members.

Software Engineering Observation 17.5

Any change to the default argument values of a function requires the client code to be recompiled (to ensure that the program still functions correctly).

```cpp
1   // Fig. 17.5: Time.cpp
2   // Member-function definitions for class Time.
3   #include <iostream>
4   #include <iomanip>
5   #include <stdexcept>
6   #include "Time.h" // include definition of class Time from Time.h
7   using namespace std;
8
9   // Time constructor initializes each data member
10  Time::Time( int hour, int minute, int second )
11  {
12     setTime( hour, minute, second ); // validate and set time
13  } // end Time constructor
14
15  // set new Time value using universal time
16  void Time::setTime( int h, int m, int s )
17  {
18     setHour( h ); // set private field hour
19     setMinute( m ); // set private field minute
20     setSecond( s ); // set private field second
21  } // end function setTime
22
23  // set hour value
24  void Time::setHour( int h )
25  {
26     if ( h >= 0 && h < 24 )
27        hour = h;
28     else
29        throw invalid_argument( "hour must be 0-23" );
30  } // end function setHour
31
32  // set minute value
33  void Time::setMinute( int m )
34  {
35     if ( m >= 0 && m < 60 )
36        minute = m;
37     else
38        throw invalid_argument( "minute must be 0-59" );
39  } // end function setMinute
```

Fig. 17.5 | Member-function definitions for class Time. (Part 1 of 2.)

```
40
41   // set second value
42   void Time::setSecond( int s )
43   {
44      if ( s >= 0 && s < 60 )
45         second = s;
46      else
47         throw invalid_argument( "second must be 0-59" );
48   } // end function setSecond
49
50   // return hour value
51   unsigned int Time::getHour() const
52   {
53      return hour;
54   } // end function getHour
55
56   // return minute value
57   unsigned Time::getMinute() const
58   {
59      return minute;
60   } // end function getMinute
61
62   // return second value
63   unsigned Time::getSecond() const
64   {
65      return second;
66   } // end function getSecond
67
68   // print Time in universal-time format (HH:MM:SS)
69   void Time::printUniversal() const
70   {
71      cout << setfill( '0' ) << setw( 2 ) << getHour() << ":"
72         << setw( 2 ) << getMinute() << ":" << setw( 2 ) << getSecond();
73   } // end function printUniversal
74
75   // print Time in standard-time format (HH:MM:SS AM or PM)
76   void Time::printStandard() const
77   {
78      cout << ( ( getHour() == 0 || getHour() == 12 ) ? 12 : getHour() % 12 )
79         << ":" << setfill( '0' ) << setw( 2 ) << getMinute()
80         << ":" << setw( 2 ) << getSecond() << ( hour < 12 ? " AM" : " PM" );
81   } // end function printStandard
```

Fig. 17.5 | Member-function definitions for class Time. (Part 2 of 2.)

In Fig. 17.5, line 12 of the constructor calls member function setTime with the values passed to the constructor (or the default values). Function setTime calls setHour to ensure that the value supplied for hour is in the range 0–23, then calls setMinute and setSecond to ensure that the values for minute and second are each in the range 0–59. Functions setHour (lines 24–30), setMinute (lines 33–39) and setSecond (lines 42–48) each throw an exception if an out-of-range argument is received.

Function main in Fig. 17.6 initializes five Time objects—one with all three arguments defaulted in the implicit constructor call (line 10), one with one argument specified (line 11), one with two arguments specified (line 12), one with three arguments specified (line 13) and one with three invalid arguments specified (line 38). The program displays each object in universal-time and standard-time formats. For Time object t5 (line 38), the program displays an error message because the constructor arguments are out of range.

```cpp
1   // Fig. 17.6: fig17_06.cpp
2   // Constructor with default arguments.
3   #include <iostream>
4   #include <stdexcept>
5   #include "Time.h" // include definition of class Time from Time.h
6   using namespace std;
7
8   int main()
9   {
10     Time t1; // all arguments defaulted
11     Time t2( 2 ); // hour specified; minute and second defaulted
12     Time t3( 21, 34 ); // hour and minute specified; second defaulted
13     Time t4( 12, 25, 42 ); // hour, minute and second specified
14
15     cout << "Constructed with:\n\nt1: all arguments defaulted\n   ";
16     t1.printUniversal(); // 00:00:00
17     cout << "\n   ";
18     t1.printStandard(); // 12:00:00 AM
19
20     cout << "\n\nt2: hour specified; minute and second defaulted\n   ";
21     t2.printUniversal(); // 02:00:00
22     cout << "\n   ";
23     t2.printStandard(); // 2:00:00 AM
24
25     cout << "\n\nt3: hour and minute specified; second defaulted\n   ";
26     t3.printUniversal(); // 21:34:00
27     cout << "\n   ";
28     t3.printStandard(); // 9:34:00 PM
29
30     cout << "\n\nt4: hour, minute and second specified\n   ";
31     t4.printUniversal(); // 12:25:42
32     cout << "\n   ";
33     t4.printStandard(); // 12:25:42 PM
34
35     // attempt to initialize t6 with invalid values
36     try
37     {
38        Time t5( 27, 74, 99 ); // all bad values specified
39     } // end try
40     catch ( invalid_argument &e )
41     {
42        cerr << "\n\nException while initializing t5: " << e.what() << endl;
43     } // end catch
44   } // end main
```

Fig. 17.6 | Constructor with default arguments. (Part 1 of 2.)

```
Constructed with:

t1: all arguments defaulted
   00:00:00
   12:00:00 AM

t2: hour specified; minute and second defaulted
   02:00:00
   2:00:00 AM

t3: hour and minute specified; second defaulted
   21:34:00
   9:34:00 PM

t4: hour, minute and second specified
   12:25:42
   12:25:42 PM

Exception while initializing t5: hour must be 0-23
```

Fig. 17.6 | Constructor with default arguments. (Part 2 of 2.)

Notes Regarding Class Time's Set and Get Functions and Constructor

Time's *set* and *get* functions are called throughout the class's body. In particular, function setTime (lines 16–21 of Fig. 17.5) calls functions setHour, setMinute and setSecond, and functions printUniversal and printStandard call functions getHour, getMinute and getSecond in line 71–72 and lines 78–80. In each case, these functions could have accessed the class's private data directly. However, consider changing the representation of the time from three int values (requiring 12 bytes of memory on systems with four-byte ints) to a single int value representing the total number of seconds that have elapsed since midnight (requiring only four bytes of memory). If we made such a change, only the bodies of the functions that access the private data directly would need to change—in particular, the individual *set* and *get* functions for the hour, minute and second. There would be no need to modify the bodies of functions setTime, printUniversal or printStandard, because they do *not* access the data directly. Designing the class in this manner reduces the likelihood of programming errors when altering the class's implementation.

Similarly, the Time constructor could be written to include a copy of the appropriate statements from function setTime. Doing so may be slightly more efficient, because the extra call to setTime is eliminated. However, duplicating statements in multiple functions or constructors makes changing the class's internal data representation more difficult. Having the Time constructor call setTime and having setTime call setHour, setMinute and setSecond enables us to limit the changes to code that validates the hour, minute or second to the corresponding *set* function. This reduces the likelihood of errors when altering the class's implementation.

Software Engineering Observation 17.6

If a member function of a class already provides all or part of the functionality required by a constructor (or other member function) of the class, call that member function from the constructor (or other member function). This simplifies the maintenance of the code and reduces the likelihood of an error if the implementation of the code is modified. As a general rule: Avoid repeating code.

Common Programming Error 17.1

A constructor can call other member functions of the class, such as set *or get functions, but because the constructor is initializing the object, the data members may not yet be initialized. Using data members before they have been properly initialized can cause logic errors.*

C++11: Using List Initializers to Call Constructors

C++11 now provides a uniform initialization syntax called list initializers that can be used to initialize any variable. Lines 11–13 of Fig. 17.6 can be written using list initializers as follows:

```
Time t2{ 2 }; // hour specified; minute and second defaulted
Time t3{ 21, 34 }; // hour and minute specified; second defaulted
Time t4{ 12, 25, 42 }; // hour, minute and second specified
```

or

```
Time t2 = { 2 }; // hour specified; minute and second defaulted
Time t3 = { 21, 34 }; // hour and minute specified; second defaulted
Time t4 = { 12, 25, 42 }; // hour, minute and second specified
```

The form without the = is preferred.

C++11: Overloaded Constructors and Delegating Constructors

Chapter 15 showed how to overload functions. A class's constructors and member functions can also be overloaded. Overloaded constructors typically allow objects to be initialized with different types and/or numbers of arguments. To overload a constructor, provide in the class definition a prototype for each version of the constructor, and provide a separate constructor definition for each overloaded version. This also applies to the class's member functions.

In Figs. 17.4–17.6, the Time constructor with three parameters had a default argument for each parameter. We could have defined that constructor instead as four overloaded constructors with the following prototypes:

```
Time(); // default hour, minute and second to 0
Time( int ); // initialize hour; default minute and second to 0
Time( int, int ); // initialize hour and minute; default second to 0
Time( int, int, int ); // initialize hour, minute and second
```

Just as a constructor can call a class's other member functions to perform tasks, C++11 now allows constructors to call other constructors in the same class. The calling constructor is known as a **delegating constructor**—it *delegates* its work to another constructor. This is useful when overloaded constructors have common code that previously would have been defined in a private utility function and called by all the constructors.

The first three of the four Time constructors declared above can delegate work to one with three int arguments, passing 0 as the default value for the extra parameters. To do so, you use a member initializer with the name of the class as follows:

```
Time::Time()
   : Time( 0, 0, 0 ) // delegate to Time( int, int, int )
{
} // end constructor with no arguments
```

```
Time::Time( int hour )
   : Time( hour, 0, 0 ) // delegate to Time( int, int, int )
{
} // end constructor with one argument
Time::Time( int hour, int minute )
   : Time( hour, minute, 0 ) // delegate to Time( int, int, int )
{
} // end constructor with two arguments
```

17.6 Destructors

A **destructor** is another type of special member function. The name of the destructor for a class is the **tilde character** (~) followed by the class name. This naming convention has intuitive appeal, because the tilde symnol is also used as the bitwise complement operator, and, in a sense, the destructor is the complement of the constructor. A destructor may not specify parameters or a return type.

A class's destructor is called *implicitly* when an object is destroyed. This occurs, for example, as an object is destroyed when program execution leaves the scope in which that object was instantiated. *The destructor itself does not actually release the object's memory*—it performs termination housekeeping before the object's memory is reclaimed, so the memory may be reused to hold new objects.

Even though destructors have not been defined for the classes presented so far, *every class has one destructor*. If you do not *explicitly* define a destructor, the compiler defines an "empty" destructor. [*Note:* We'll see that such an *implicitly* created destructor does, in fact, perform important operations on class-type objects that are created through composition (Section 17.11) and inheritance (Chapter 19).] In Chapter 18, we'll build destructors appropriate for classes whose objects contain dynamically allocated memory (e.g., for arrays and strings) or use other system resources (e.g., files on disk). We discuss how to dynamically allocate and deallocate memory in Chapter 18.

17.7 When Constructors and Destructors Are Called

Constructors and destructors are called *implicitly* by the compiler. The order in which these function calls occur depends on the order in which execution enters and leaves the scopes where the objects are instantiated. Generally, destructor calls are made in the *reverse order* of the corresponding constructor calls, but as we'll see in Figs. 17.7–17.9, the storage classes of objects can alter the order in which destructors are called.

Constructors and Destructors for Objects in Global Scope

Constructors are called for objects defined in global scope (also called global namespace scope) *before* any other function (including main) in that program begins execution (although the order of execution of global object constructors between files is *not* guaranteed). The corresponding destructors are called when main terminates. Function **exit** forces a program to terminate immediately and does *not* execute the destructors of local objects. The exit function often is used to terminate a program when a fatal unrecoverable error occurs. Function **abort** performs similarly to function exit but forces the program to terminate *immediately*, without allowing the destructors of any objects to be called. Function abort is usually used to indicate an *abnormal termination* of the program.

Constructors and Destructors for Local Objects

The constructor for an local object is called when execution reaches the point where that object is defined—the corresponding destructor is called when execution leaves the object's scope (i.e., the block in which that object is defined has finished executing). Constructors and destructors for local objects are called each time execution enters and leaves the scope of the object. Destructors are not called for local objects if the program terminates with a call to function exit or function abort.

Constructors and Destructors for **static** Local Objects

The constructor for a static local object is called only *once*, when execution first reaches the point where the object is defined—the corresponding destructor is called when main terminates or the program calls function exit. Global and static objects are destroyed in the *reverse* order of their creation. Destructors are *not* called for static objects if the program terminates with a call to function abort.

Demonstrating When Constructors and Destructors Are Called

The program of Figs. 17.7–17.9 demonstrates the order in which constructors and destructors are called for objects of class CreateAndDestroy (Fig. 17.7 and Fig. 17.8) of various storage classes in several scopes. Each object of class CreateAndDestroy contains an integer (objectID) and a string (message) that are used in the program's output to identify the object (Fig. 17.7, lines 16–17). This mechanical example is purely for pedagogic purposes. For this reason, line 19 of the destructor in Fig. 17.8 determines whether the object being destroyed has an objectID value 1 or 6 (line 19) and, if so, outputs a newline character. This line makes the program's output easier to follow.

```
1   // Fig. 17.7: CreateAndDestroy.h
2   // CreateAndDestroy class definition.
3   // Member functions defined in CreateAndDestroy.cpp.
4   #include <string>
5   using namespace std;
6
7   #ifndef CREATE_H
8   #define CREATE_H
9
10  class CreateAndDestroy
11  {
12  public:
13     CreateAndDestroy( int, string ); // constructor
14     ~CreateAndDestroy(); // destructor
15  private:
16     int objectID; // ID number for object
17     string message; // message describing object
18  }; // end class CreateAndDestroy
19
20  #endif
```

Fig. 17.7 | CreateAndDestroy class definition.

```
 I   // Fig. 17.8: CreateAndDestroy.cpp
 2   // CreateAndDestroy class member-function definitions.
 3   #include <iostream>
 4   #include "CreateAndDestroy.h"// include CreateAndDestroy class definition
 5   using namespace std;
 6
 7   // constructor sets object's ID number and descriptive message
 8   CreateAndDestroy::CreateAndDestroy( int ID, string messageString )
 9      : objectID( ID ), message( messageString )
10   {
11      cout << "Object " << objectID << "  constructor runs   "
12         << message << endl;
13   } // end CreateAndDestroy constructor
14
15   // destructor
16   CreateAndDestroy::~CreateAndDestroy()
17   {
18      // output newline for certain objects; helps readability
19      cout << ( objectID == 1 || objectID == 6 ? "\n" : "" );
20
21      cout << "Object " << objectID << "  destructor runs   "
22         << message << endl;
23   } // end ~CreateAndDestroy destructor
```

Fig. 17.8 | CreateAndDestroy class member-function definitions.

Figure 17.9 defines object first (line 10) in global scope. Its constructor is actually called *before* any statements in main execute and its destructor is called at program termination *after* the destructors for all objects with automatic storage duration have run.

```
 I   // Fig. 17.9: fig17_09.cpp
 2   // Order in which constructors and
 3   // destructors are called.
 4   #include <iostream>
 5   #include "CreateAndDestroy.h" // include CreateAndDestroy class definition
 6   using namespace std;
 7
 8   void create( void ); // prototype
 9
10   CreateAndDestroy first( 1, "(global before main)" ); // global object
11
12   int main()
13   {
14      cout << "\nMAIN FUNCTION: EXECUTION BEGINS" << endl;
15      CreateAndDestroy second( 2, "(local automatic in main)" );
16      static CreateAndDestroy third( 3, "(local static in main)" );
17
18      create(); // call function to create objects
19
20      cout << "\nMAIN FUNCTION: EXECUTION RESUMES" << endl;
21      CreateAndDestroy fourth( 4, "(local automatic in main)" );
```

Fig. 17.9 | Order in which constructors and destructors are called. (Part 1 of 2.)

```
22        cout << "\nMAIN FUNCTION: EXECUTION ENDS" << endl;
23    } // end main
24
25    // function to create objects
26    void create( void )
27    {
28        cout << "\nCREATE FUNCTION: EXECUTION BEGINS" << endl;
29        CreateAndDestroy fifth( 5, "(local automatic in create)" );
30        static CreateAndDestroy sixth( 6, "(local static in create)" );
31        CreateAndDestroy seventh( 7, "(local automatic in create)" );
32        cout << "\nCREATE FUNCTION: EXECUTION ENDS" << endl;
33    } // end function create
```

```
Object 1   constructor runs   (global before main)

MAIN FUNCTION: EXECUTION BEGINS
Object 2   constructor runs   (local automatic in main)
Object 3   constructor runs   (local static in main)

CREATE FUNCTION: EXECUTION BEGINS
Object 5   constructor runs   (local automatic in create)
Object 6   constructor runs   (local static in create)
Object 7   constructor runs   (local automatic in create)

CREATE FUNCTION: EXECUTION ENDS
Object 7   destructor runs    (local automatic in create)
Object 5   destructor runs    (local automatic in create)

MAIN FUNCTION: EXECUTION RESUMES
Object 4   constructor runs   (local automatic in main)

MAIN FUNCTION: EXECUTION ENDS
Object 4   destructor runs    (local automatic in main)
Object 2   destructor runs    (local automatic in main)

Object 6   destructor runs    (local static in create)
Object 3   destructor runs    (local static in main)

Object 1   destructor runs    (global before main)
```

Fig. 17.9 | Order in which constructors and destructors are called. (Part 2 of 2.)

Function main (lines 12–23) declares three objects. Objects second (line 15) and fourth (line 21) are local objects, and object third (line 16) is a static local object. The constructor for each of these objects is called when execution reaches the point where that object is declared. The destructors for objects fourth then second are called—in the *reverse* of the order in which their constructors were called—when execution reaches the end of main. Because object third is static, it exists until program termination. The destructor for object third is called *before* the destructor for global object first, but *after* all other objects are destroyed.

Function create (lines 26–33) declares three objects—fifth (line 29) and seventh (line 31) as local automatic objects, and sixth (line 30) as a static local object. The destructors for objects seventh then fifth are called—the *reverse* of the order in which their constructors were called—when create terminates. Because sixth is static, it exists until program termination. The destructor for sixth is called *before* the destructors for third and first, but *after* all other objects are destroyed.

17.8 Time Class Case Study: A Subtle Trap— Returning a Reference or a Pointer to a private Data Member

A reference to an object is an alias for the name of the object and, hence, may be used on the left side of an assignment statement. In this context, the reference makes a perfectly acceptable *lvalue* that can receive a value. One way to use this capability is to have a public member function of a class return a reference to a private data member of that class. If a function returns a reference that is declared const, the reference is a non-modifiable *lvalue* and cannot be used to modify the data.

The program of Figs. 17.10–17.12 uses a simplified Time class (Fig. 17.10 and Fig. 17.11) to demonstrate returning a reference to a private data member with member function badSetHour (declared in Fig. 17.10 in line 15 and defined in Fig. 17.11 in lines 37–45). Such a reference return actually makes a call to member function badSetHour an alias for private data member hour! The function call can be used in any way that the private data member can be used, including as an *lvalue* in an assignment statement, thus *enabling clients of the class to clobber the class's private data at will!* A similar problem would occur if a pointer to the private data were to be returned by the function.

```
 1   // Fig. 17.10: Time.h
 2   // Time class declaration.
 3   // Member functions defined in Time.cpp
 4
 5   // prevent multiple inclusions of header
 6   #ifndef TIME_H
 7   #define TIME_H
 8
 9   class Time
10   {
11   public:
12      explicit Time( int = 0, int = 0, int = 0 );
13      void setTime( int, int, int );
14      unsigned int getHour() const;
15      unsigned int &badSetHour( int ); // dangerous reference return
16   private:
17      unsigned int hour;
18      unsigned int minute;
19      unsigned int second;
20   }; // end class Time
21
22   #endif
```

Fig. 17.10 | Time class declaration.

```
1   // Fig. 17.11: Time.cpp
2   // Time class member-function definitions.
3   #include <stdexcept>
4   #include "Time.h" // include definition of class Time
5   using namespace std;
6
7   // constructor function to initialize private data; calls member function
8   // setTime to set variables; default values are 0 (see class definition)
9   Time::Time( int hr, int min, int sec )
10  {
11     setTime( hr, min, sec );
12  } // end Time constructor
13
14  // set values of hour, minute and second
15  void Time::setTime( int h, int m, int s )
16  {
17     // validate hour, minute and second
18     if ( ( h >= 0 && h < 24 ) && ( m >= 0 && m < 60 ) &&
19        ( s >= 0 && s < 60 ) )
20     {
21        hour = h;
22        minute = m;
23        second = s;
24     } // end if
25     else
26        throw invalid_argument(
27           "hour, minute and/or second was out of range" );
28  } // end function setTime
29
30  // return hour value
31  unsigned int Time::getHour()
32  {
33     return hour;
34  } // end function getHour
35
36  // poor practice: returning a reference to a private data member.
37  unsigned int &Time::badSetHour( int hh )
38  {
39     if ( hh >= 0 && hh < 24 )
40        hour = hh;
41     else
42        throw invalid_argument( "hour must be 0-23" );
43
44     return hour; // dangerous reference return
45  } // end function badSetHour
```

Fig. 17.11 | Time class member-function definitions.

Figure 17.12 declares Time object t (line 10) and reference hourRef (line 13), which is initialized with the reference returned by the call t.badSetHour(20). Line 15 displays the value of the alias hourRef. This shows how hourRef *breaks the encapsulation of the class*—statements in main should not have access to the private data of the class. Next, line 16 uses the alias to set the value of hour to 30 (an invalid value) and line 17 displays the value returned by function getHour to show that assigning a value to hourRef actually modifies the private data in the Time object t. Finally, line 21 uses the badSetHour function call itself as an *lvalue* and assigns 74 (another invalid value) to the reference returned by the function. Line 26 again displays the value returned by function getHour to show that assigning a value to the result of the function call in line 21 modifies the private data in the Time object t.

Software Engineering Observation 17.7

Returning a reference or a pointer to a private data member breaks the encapsulation of the class and makes the client code dependent on the representation of the class's data. There are cases where doing this is appropriate—we'll show an example of this when we build our custom Array class in Section 18.10.

```cpp
1   // Fig. 17.12: fig17_12.cpp
2   // Demonstrating a public member function that
3   // returns a reference to a private data member.
4   #include <iostream>
5   #include "Time.h" // include definition of class Time
6   using namespace std;
7
8   int main()
9   {
10     Time t; // create Time object
11
12     // initialize hourRef with the reference returned by badSetHour
13     int &hourRef = t.badSetHour( 20 ); // 20 is a valid hour
14
15     cout << "Valid hour before modification: " << hourRef;
16     hourRef = 30; // use hourRef to set invalid value in Time object t
17     cout << "\nInvalid hour after modification: " << t.getHour();
18
19     // Dangerous: Function call that returns
20     // a reference can be used as an lvalue!
21     t.badSetHour( 12 ) = 74; // assign another invalid value to hour
22
23     cout << "\n\n*****************************************************\n"
24        << "POOR PROGRAMMING PRACTICE!!!!!!!!\n"
25        << "t.badSetHour( 12 ) as an lvalue, invalid hour: "
26        << t.getHour()
27        << "\n*****************************************************" << endl;
28  } // end main
```

```
Valid hour before modification: 20
Invalid hour after modification: 30

*****************************************************
POOR PROGRAMMING PRACTICE!!!!!!!!
t.badSetHour( 12 ) as an lvalue, invalid hour: 74
*****************************************************
```

Fig. 17.12 | public member function that returns a reference to a private data member.

17.9 Default Memberwise Assignment

The assignment operator (=) can be used to assign an object to another object of the same class. By default, such assignment is performed by **memberwise assignment** (also called **copy assignment**)—each data member of the object on the *right* of the assignment operator is assigned individually to the *same* data member in the object on the *left* of the assignment operator. Figures 17.13–17.14 define a Date class. Line 18 of Fig. 17.15 uses **default memberwise assignment** to assign the data members of Date object date1 to the corresponding data members of Date object date2. In this case, the month member of date1 is assigned to the month member of date2, the day member of date1 is assigned to the day member of date2 and the year member of date1 is assigned to the year member of date2. [*Caution:* Memberwise assignment can cause serious problems when used with a class whose data members contain pointers to dynamically allocated memory; we discuss these problems in Chapter 18 and show how to deal with them.]

```
1   // Fig. 17.13: Date.h
2   // Date class declaration.  Member functions are defined in Date.cpp.
3
4   // prevent multiple inclusions of header
5   #ifndef DATE_H
6   #define DATE_H
7
8   // class Date definition
9   class Date
10  {
11  public:
12     explicit Date( int = 1, int = 1, int = 2000 ); // default constructor
13     void print();
14  private:
15     unsigned int month;
16     unsigned int day;
17     unsigned int year;
18  }; // end class Date
19
20  #endif
```

Fig. 17.13 | Date class declaration.

```
1   // Fig. 17.14: Date.cpp
2   // Date class member-function definitions.
3   #include <iostream>
4   #include "Date.h" // include definition of class Date from Date.h
5   using namespace std;
6
7   // Date constructor (should do range checking)
8   Date::Date( int m, int d, int y )
9      : month( m ), day( d ), year( y )
10  {
11  } // end constructor Date
```

Fig. 17.14 | Date class member-function definitions. (Part 1 of 2.)

```
12
13    // print Date in the format mm/dd/yyyy
14    void Date::print()
15    {
16       cout << month << '/' << day << '/' << year;
17    } // end function print
```

Fig. 17.14 | Date class member-function definitions. (Part 2 of 2.)

```
1    // Fig. 17.15: fig17_15.cpp
2    // Demonstrating that class objects can be assigned
3    // to each other using default memberwise assignment.
4    #include <iostream>
5    #include "Date.h" // include definition of class Date from Date.h
6    using namespace std;
7
8    int main()
9    {
10       Date date1( 7, 4, 2004 );
11       Date date2; // date2 defaults to 1/1/2000
12
13       cout << "date1 = ";
14       date1.print();
15       cout << "\ndate2 = ";
16       date2.print();
17
18       date2 = date1; // default memberwise assignment
19
20       cout << "\n\nAfter default memberwise assignment, date2 = ";
21       date2.print();
22       cout << endl;
23    } // end main
```

```
date1 = 7/4/2004
date2 = 1/1/2000

After default memberwise assignment, date2 = 7/4/2004
```

Fig. 17.15 | Class objects can be assigned to each other using default memberwise assignment.

Objects may be passed as function arguments and may be returned from functions. Such passing and returning is performed using pass-by-value by default—a *copy* of the object is passed or returned. In such cases, C++ creates a new object and uses a **copy constructor** to copy the original object's values into the new object. For each class, the compiler provides a default copy constructor that copies each member of the original object into the corresponding member of the new object. Like memberwise assignment, copy constructors can cause serious problems when used with a class whose data members contain pointers to dynamically allocated memory. Chapter 18 discusses how to define customized copy constructors that properly copy objects containing pointers to dynamically allocated memory.

17.10 const Objects and const Member Functions

Let's see how the principle of least privilege applies to objects. Some objects need to be modifiable and some do not. You may use keyword const to specify that an object *is not* modifiable and that any attempt to modify the object should result in a compilation error. The statement

```
const Time noon( 12, 0, 0 );
```

declares a const object noon of class Time and initializes it to 12 noon. It's possible to instantiate const and non-const objects of the same class.

Software Engineering Observation 17.8
Attempts to modify a const object are caught at compile time rather than causing execution-time errors.

Performance Tip 17.3
Declaring variables and objects const when appropriate can improve performance— compilers can perform optimizations on constants that cannot be performed on non-const variables.

C++ disallows member function calls for const objects unless the member functions themselves are also declared const. This is true even for *get* member functions that do *not* modify the object. *This is also a key reason that we've declared as const all member-functions that do not modify the objects on which they're called.*

As you saw starting with class GradeBook in Chapter 16, a member function is specified as const *both* in its prototype by inserting the keyword const *after* the function's parameter list and, in the case of the function definition, before the left brace that begins the function *body.*

Common Programming Error 17.2
Defining as const a member function that modifies a data member of the object is a compilation error.

Common Programming Error 17.3
Defining as const a member function that calls a non-const member function of the class on the same object is a compilation error.

Common Programming Error 17.4
Invoking a non-const member function on a const object is a compilation error.

An interesting problem arises for constructors and destructors, each of which typically modifies objects. A constructor *must* be allowed to modify an object so that the object can be initialized properly. A destructor must be able to perform its termination housekeeping chores before an object's memory is reclaimed by the system. Attempting to declare a constructor or destructor const is a compilation error. The "constness" of a const object is enforced from the time the constructor *completes* initialization of the object until that object's destructor is called.

*Using **const** and Non-**const** Member Functions*
The program of Fig. 17.16 uses class Time from Figs. 17.4–17.5, but removes const from function printStandard's prototype and definition so that we can show a compilation error. We instantiate two Time objects—non-const object wakeUp (line 7) and const object noon (line 8). The program attempts to invoke non-const member functions setHour (line 13) and printStandard (line 20) on the const object noon. In each case, the compiler generates an error message. The program also illustrates the three other member-function-call combinations on objects—a non-const member function on a non-const object (line 11), a const member function on a non-const object (line 15) and a const member function on a const object (lines 17–18). The error messages generated for non-const member functions called on a const object are shown in the output window.

```cpp
1   // Fig. 17.16: fig17_16.cpp
2   // const objects and const member functions.
3   #include "Time.h" // include Time class definition
4
5   int main()
6   {
7      Time wakeUp( 6, 45, 0 ); // non-constant object
8      const Time noon( 12, 0, 0 ); // constant object
9
10                                  // OBJECT       MEMBER FUNCTION
11     wakeUp.setHour( 18 );  // non-const    non-const
12
13     noon.setHour( 12 );      // const        non-const
14
15     wakeUp.getHour();        // non-const    const
16
17     noon.getMinute();        // const        const
18     noon.printUniversal(); // const        const
19
20     noon.printStandard();  // const        non-const
21  } // end main
```

Microsoft Visual C++ compiler error messages:

```
C:\examples\ch17\Fig17_16_18\fig17_18.cpp(13) : error C2662:
   'Time::setHour' : cannot convert 'this' pointer from 'const Time' to
   'Time &'
         Conversion loses qualifiers
C:\examples\ch17\Fig17_16_18\fig17_18.cpp(20) : error C2662:
   'Time::printStandard' : cannot convert 'this' pointer from 'const Time' to
   'Time &'
         Conversion loses qualifiers
```

Fig. 17.16 | const objects and const member functions.

A constructor must be a non-const member function, but it can still be used to initialize a const object (Fig. 17.16, line 8). Recall from Fig. 17.5 that the Time constructor's definition calls another non-const member function—setTime—to perform the initialization of a Time object. Invoking a non-const member function from the constructor call as part of the initialization of a const object is allowed.

Line 20 in Fig. 17.16 generates a compilation error even though member function printStandard of class Time *does not* modify the object on which it's invoked. The fact that a member function does not modify an object is *not* sufficient—the function must *explicitly* be declared const.

17.11 Composition: Objects as Members of Classes

An AlarmClock object needs to know when it's supposed to sound its alarm, so why not include a Time object as a member of the AlarmClock class? Such a capability is called **composition** and is sometimes referred to as a *has-a* relationship—*a class can have objects of other classes as members.*

Software Engineering Observation 17.9

A common form of software reusability is composition, in which a class has objects of other types as members.

Previously, we saw how to pass arguments to the constructor of an object we created in main. Now we show how *an class's constructor can pass arguments to member-object constructors via member initializers.*

Software Engineering Observation 17.10

Data members are constructed in the order in which they're declared in the class definition (not in the order they're listed in the constructor's member initializer list) and before their enclosing class objects (sometimes called host objects) are constructed.

The next program uses classes Date (Figs. 17.17–17.18) and Employee (Figs. 17.19–17.20) to demonstrate composition. Class Employee's definition (Fig. 17.19) contains private data members firstName, lastName, birthDate and hireDate. Members birthDate and hireDate are const objects of class Date, which contains private data members month, day and year. The Employee constructor's header (Fig. 17.20, lines 10–11) specifies that the constructor has four parameters (first, last, dateOfBirth and dateOfHire). The first two parameters are passed via member initializers to the string class constructor for the firstName and lastName data members. The last two are passed via member initializers to the Date class constructor for the birthDate and hireDate data members..

```
1   // Fig. 17.17: Date.h
2   // Date class definition; Member functions defined in Date.cpp
3   #ifndef DATE_H
4   #define DATE_H
5
6   class Date
7   {
8   public:
9      static const unsigned int monthsPerYear = 12; // months in a year
10     explicit Date( int = 1, int = 1, int = 1900 ); // default constructor
11     void print() const; // print date in month/day/year format
12     ~Date(); // provided to confirm destruction order
```

Fig. 17.17 | Date class definition. (Part 1 of 2.)

```
13   private:
14      unsigned int month; // 1-12 (January-December)
15      unsigned int day; // 1-31 based on month
16      unsigned int year; // any year
17
18      // utility function to check if day is proper for month and year
19      unsigned int checkDay( int ) const;
20   }; // end class Date
21
22   #endif
```

Fig. 17.17 | Date class definition. (Part 2 of 2.)

```
1    // Fig. 17.18: Date.cpp
2    // Date class member-function definitions.
3    #include <array>
4    #include <iostream>
5    #include <stdexcept>
6    #include "Date.h" // include Date class definition
7    using namespace std;
8
9    // constructor confirms proper value for month; calls
10   // utility function checkDay to confirm proper value for day
11   Date::Date( int mn, int dy, int yr )
12   {
13      if ( mn > 0 && mn <= monthsPerYear ) // validate the month
14         month = mn;
15      else
16         throw invalid_argument( "month must be 1-12" );
17
18      year = yr; // could validate yr
19      day = checkDay( dy ); // validate the day
20
21      // output Date object to show when its constructor is called
22      cout << "Date object constructor for date ";
23      print();
24      cout << endl;
25   } // end Date constructor
26
27   // print Date object in form month/day/year
28   void Date::print() const
29   {
30      cout << month << '/' << day << '/' << year;
31   } // end function print
32
33   // output Date object to show when its destructor is called
34   Date::~Date()
35   {
36      cout << "Date object destructor for date ";
37      print();
38      cout << endl;
39   } // end ~Date destructor
```

Fig. 17.18 | Date class member-function definitions. (Part 1 of 2.)

```
40
41   // utility function to confirm proper day value based on
42   // month and year; handles leap years, too
43   unsigned int Date::checkDay( int testDay ) const
44   {
45      static const array< int, monthsPerYear + 1 > daysPerMonth =
46         { 0, 31, 28, 31, 30, 31, 30, 31, 31, 30, 31, 30, 31 };
47
48      // determine whether testDay is valid for specified month
49      if ( testDay > 0 && testDay <= daysPerMonth[ month ] )
50         return testDay;
51
52      // February 29 check for leap year
53      if ( month == 2 && testDay == 29 && ( year % 400 == 0 ||
54         ( year % 4 == 0 && year % 100 != 0 ) ) )
55         return testDay;
56
57      throw invalid_argument( "Invalid day for current month and year" );
58   } // end function checkDay
```

Fig. 17.18 | Date class member-function definitions. (Part 2 of 2.)

```
1    // Fig. 17.19: Employee.h
2    // Employee class definition showing composition.
3    // Member functions defined in Employee.cpp.
4    #ifndef EMPLOYEE_H
5    #define EMPLOYEE_H
6
7    #include <string>
8    #include "Date.h" // include Date class definition
9
10   class Employee
11   {
12   public:
13      Employee( const std::string &, const std::string &,
14         const Date &, const Date & );
15      void print() const;
16      ~Employee(); // provided to confirm destruction order
17   private:
18      std::string firstName; // composition: member object
19      std::string lastName; // composition: member object
20      const Date birthDate; // composition: member object
21      const Date hireDate; // composition: member object
22   }; // end class Employee
23
24   #endif
```

Fig. 17.19 | Employee class definition showing composition.

```
1    // Fig. 17.20: Employee.cpp
2    // Employee class member-function definitions.
3    #include <iostream>
4    #include "Employee.h" // Employee class definition
5    #include "Date.h" // Date class definition
6    using namespace std;
7
8    // constructor uses member initializer list to pass initializer
9    // values to constructors of member objects
10   Employee::Employee( const string &first, const string &last,
11      const Date &dateOfBirth, const Date &dateOfHire )
12      : firstName( first ), // initialize firstName
13        lastName( last ), // initialize lastName
14        birthDate( dateOfBirth ), // initialize birthDate
15        hireDate( dateOfHire ) // initialize hireDate
16   {
17      // output Employee object to show when constructor is called
18      cout << "Employee object constructor: "
19         << firstName << ' ' << lastName << endl;
20   } // end Employee constructor
21
22   // print Employee object
23   void Employee::print() const
24   {
25      cout << lastName << ", " << firstName << "  Hired: ";
26      hireDate.print();
27      cout << "  Birthday: ";
28      birthDate.print();
29      cout << endl;
30   } // end function print
31
32   // output Employee object to show when its destructor is called
33   Employee::~Employee()
34   {
35      cout << "Employee object destructor: "
36         << lastName << ", " << firstName << endl;
37   } // end ~Employee destructor
```

Fig. 17.20 | Employee class member-function definitions.

Employee Constructor's Member Initializer List

The *colon (:)* following the constructor's header (Fig. 17.20, line 12) begins the *member initializer list.* The member initializers specify the Employee constructor parameters being passed to the constructors of the string and Date data members. Parameters first, last, dateOfBirth and dateOfHire are passed to the constructors for objects firstName (line 12), lastName (line 13), birthDate (line 14) and hireDate (line 15), respectively. Again, member initializers are separated by commas. The order of the member initializers does not matter. They're executed in the order that the member objects are declared in class Employee.

Good Programming Practice 17.3

For clarity, list member initializers in the order that the class's data members are declared.

Date Class's Default Copy Constructor

As you study class Date (Fig. 17.17), notice that the class does *not* provide a constructor that receives a parameter of type Date. So, why can the Employee constructor's member initializer list initialize the birthDate and hireDate objects by passing Date objects to their Date constructors? As we mentioned in Section 17.9, the compiler provides each class with a *default copy constructor* that copies each data member of the constructor's argument object into the corresponding member of the object being initialized. Chapter 18 discusses how you can define *customized* copy constructors.

Testing Classes Date and Employee

Figure 17.21 creates two Date objects (lines 10–11) and passes them as arguments to the constructor of the Employee object created in line 12. Line 15 outputs the Employee object's data. When each Date object is created in lines 10–11, the Date constructor defined in lines 11–25 of Fig. 17.18 displays a line of output to show that the constructor was called (see the first two lines of the sample output). [*Note:* Line 12 of Fig. 17.21 causes two additional Date constructor calls that do not appear in the program's output. When each of the Employee's Date member objects is initialized in the Employee constructor's member-initializer list (Fig. 17.20, lines 14–15), the default copy constructor for class Date is called. Since this constructor is defined implicitly by the compiler, it does not contain any output statements to demonstrate when it's called.]

```cpp
1   // Fig. 17.21: fig17_21.cpp
2   // Demonstrating composition--an object with member objects.
3   #include <iostream>
4   #include "Date.h" // Date class definition
5   #include "Employee.h" // Employee class definition
6   using namespace std;
7
8   int main()
9   {
10      Date birth( 7, 24, 1949 );
11      Date hire( 3, 12, 1988 );
12      Employee manager( "Bob", "Blue", birth, hire );
13
14      cout << endl;
15      manager.print();
16   } // end main
```

```
Date object constructor for date 7/24/1949
Date object constructor for date 3/12/1988
Employee object constructor: Bob Blue

Blue, Bob  Hired: 3/12/1988  Birthday: 7/24/1949
Employee object destructor: Blue, Bob
Date object destructor for date 3/12/1988
Date object destructor for date 7/24/1949
Date object destructor for date 3/12/1988
Date object destructor for date 7/24/1949
```

There are actually five constructor calls when an Employee is constructed—two calls to the string class's constructor (lines 12–13 of Fig. 17.20), two calls to the Date class's default copy constructor (lines 14–15 of Fig. 17.20) and the call to the Employee class's constructor.

Fig. 17.21 | Demonstrating composition—an object with member objects.

Class `Date` and class `Employee` each include a destructor (lines 34–39 of Fig. 17.18 and lines 33–37 of Fig. 17.20, respectively) that prints a message when an object of its class is destructed. This enables us to confirm in the program output that objects are constructed from the *inside out* and destroyed in the *reverse* order, from the *outside in* (i.e., the `Date` *member* objects are destroyed after the `Employee` object that *contains* them).

Notice the last four lines in the output of Fig. 17.21. The last two lines are the outputs of the `Date` destructor running on `Date` objects `hire` (Fig. 17.21, line 11) and `birth` (Fig. 17.21, line 10), respectively. These outputs confirm that the three objects created in `main` are destructed in the *reverse* of the order in which they were constructed. The `Employee` destructor output is five lines from the bottom. The fourth and third lines from the bottom of the output window show the destructors running for the `Employee`'s member objects `hireDate` (Fig. 17.19, line 21) and `birthDate` (Fig. 17.19, line 20). The last two lines of the output correspond to the `Date` objects created in lines 11 and 10 of Fig. 17.21.

These outputs confirm that the `Employee` object is destructed from the *outside in*— i.e., the `Employee` destructor runs first (output shown five lines from the bottom of the output window), then the member objects are destructed in the *reverse order* from which they were constructed. Class `string`'s destructor does not contain output statements, so we do *not* see the `firstName` and `lastName` objects being destructed. Again, Fig. 17.21's output did not show the constructors running for member objects `birthDate` and `hireDate`, because these objects were initialized with the *default* `Date` class copy constructors provided by the compiler.

What Happens When You Do Not Use the Member Initializer List?
If a member object is *not* initialized through a member initializer, the member object's *default constructor* will be called *implicitly*. Values, if any, established by the default constructor can be overridden by *set* functions. However, for complex initialization, this approach may require significant additional work and time.

Common Programming Error 17.5
A compilation error occurs if a member object is not initialized with a member initializer and the member object's class does not provide a default constructor (i.e., the member object's class defines one or more constructors, but none is a default constructor).

Performance Tip 17.4
Initialize member objects explicitly through member initializers. This eliminates the overhead of "doubly initializing" member objects—once when the member object's default constructor is called and again when set *functions are called in the constructor body (or later) to initialize the member object.*

Software Engineering Observation 17.11
If a data member is an object of another class, making that member object public *does not violate the encapsulation and hiding of that member object's* private *members. But, it does violate the encapsulation and hiding of the containing class's implementation, so member objects of class types should still be* private.

17.12 friend Functions and friend Classes

A **friend function** of a class is a non-member function that has the right to access the pub-lic *and* non-public class members. Standalone functions, entire classes or member func-tions of other classes may be declared to be *friends* of another class.

This section presents a mechanical example of how a friend function works. In Chapter 18 we'll show friend functions that overload operators for use with class objects—as you'll see, sometimes a member function cannot be used for certain over-loaded operators.

Declaring a friend

To declare a function as a friend of a class, precede the function prototype in the class definition with keyword friend. To declare all member functions of class ClassTwo as friends of class ClassOne, place a declaration of the form

```
friend class ClassTwo;
```

in the definition of class ClassOne.

Friendship is *granted, not taken*—for class B to be a friend of class A, class A must *explicitly* declare that class B is its friend. Friendship is not *symmetric*—if class A is a friend of class B, you cannot infer that class B is a friend of class A. Friendship is not *transitive*—if class A is a friend of class B and class B is a friend of class C, you cannot infer that class A is a friend of class C.

Modifying a Class's private Data with a Friend Function

Figure 17.22 is a mechanical example in which we define friend function setX to set the private data member x of class Count. As a convention, we place the friend declaration (line 9) *first* in the class definition, even before public member functions are declared. Again, this friend declaration can appear *anywhere* in the class.

Function setX (lines 29–32) is a stand-alone (global) function—it isn't a member function of class Count. For this reason, when setX is invoked for object counter, line 41 passes counter as an argument to setX rather than using a handle (such as the name of the object) to call the function, as in

```
counter.setX( 8 ); // error: setX not a member function
```

If you remove the friend declaration in line 9, you'll receive error messages indicating that function setX cannot modify class Count's private data member x.

```
1   //Fig. 17.22: fig17_22.cpp
2   // Friends can access private members of a class.
3   #include <iostream>
4   using namespace std;
5
6   // Count class definition
7   class Count
8   {
9      friend void setX( Count &, int ); // friend declaration
```

Fig. 17.22 | Friends can access private members of a class. (Part 1 of 2.)

```
10   public:
11      // constructor
12      Count()
13         : x( 0 ) // initialize x to 0
14      {
15         // empty body
16      } // end constructor Count
17
18      // output x
19      void print() const
20      {
21         cout << x << endl;
22      } // end function print
23   private:
24      int x; // data member
25   }; // end class Count
26
27   // function setX can modify private data of Count
28   // because setX is declared as a friend of Count (line 9)
29   void setX( Count &c, int val )
30   {
31      c.x = val; // allowed because setX is a friend of Count
32   } // end function setX
33
34   int main()
35   {
36      Count counter; // create Count object
37
38      cout << "counter.x after instantiation: ";
39      counter.print();
40
41      setX( counter, 8 ); // set x using a friend function
42      cout << "counter.x after call to setX friend function: ";
43      counter.print();
44   } // end main
```

```
counter.x after instantiation: 0
counter.x after call to setX friend function: 8
```

Fig. 17.22 | Friends can access private members of a class. (Part 2 of 2.)

As we mentioned, Fig. 17.22 is a mechanical example of using the friend construct. It would normally be appropriate to define function setX as a member function of class Count. It would also normally be appropriate to separate the program of Fig. 17.22 into three files:

1. A header (e.g., Count.h) containing the Count class definition, which in turn contains the prototype of friend function setX

2. An implementation file (e.g., Count.cpp) containing the definitions of class Count's member functions and the definition of friend function setX

3. A test program (e.g., fig17_22.cpp) with main.

Overloaded **friend** *Functions*

It's possible to specify overloaded functions as friends of a class. Each function intended to be a friend must be explicitly declared in the class definition as a friend of the class.

Software Engineering Observation 17.12

Even though the prototypes for friend functions appear in the class definition, friends are not member functions.

Software Engineering Observation 17.13

Member access notions of private, protected and public are not relevant to friend declarations, so friend declarations can be placed anywhere in a class definition.

Good Programming Practice 17.4

Place all friendship declarations first inside the class definition's body and do not precede them with any access specifier.

17.13 Using the this Pointer

We've seen that an object's member functions can manipulate the object's data. There can be *many* objects of a class, so how do member functions know *which* object's data members to manipulate? Every object has access to its own address through a pointer called **this** (a C++ keyword). The this pointer is *not* part of the object itself—i.e., the memory occupied by the this pointer is not reflected in the result of a sizeof operation on the object. Rather, the this pointer is passed (by the compiler) as an *implicit* argument to each of the object's non-static member functions. Section 17.14 introduces static class members and explains why the this pointer is *not* implicitly passed to static member functions.

Using the **this** *Pointer to Avoid Naming Collisions*

Member functions use the this pointer *implicitly* (as we've done so far) or *explicitly* to reference an object's data members and other member functions. A common *explicit* use of the this pointer is to avoid *naming conflicts* between a class's data members and member-function parameters (or other local variables). Consider the Time class's hour data member and setHour member function in Figs. 17.4–17.5. We could have defined setHour as:

```
// set hour value
void Time::setHour( int hour )
{
   if ( hour >= 0 && hour < 24 )
      this->hour = hour; // use this pointer to access data member
   else
      throw invalid_argument( "hour must be 0-23" );
} // end function setHour
```

In this function definition, setHour's parameter has the *same name* as the data member hour. In setHour's scope, the parameter hour *hides* the data member. However, you can still access the data member hour by qualifying its name with this->. So the following statement assigns the hour parameter's value to the data member hour

```
this->hour = hour; // use this pointer to access data member
```

Error-Prevention Tip 17.4

To make your code clearer and more maintainable, and to avoid errors, never hide data members with local variable names.

*Type of the **this** Pointer*
The type of the this pointer depends on the type of the object and whether the member function in which this is used is declared const. For example, in a non-const member function of class Employee, the this pointer has the type Employee *. In a const member function, the this pointer has the type const Employee *.

*Implicitly and Explicitly Using the **this** Pointer to Access an Object's Data Members*
Figure 17.23 demonstrates the implicit and explicit use of the this pointer to enable a member function of class Test to print the private data x of a Test object. In the next example and in Chapter 18, we show some substantial and subtle examples of using this.

```cpp
1   // Fig. 17.23: fig17_23.cpp
2   // Using the this pointer to refer to object members.
3   #include <iostream>
4   using namespace std;
5
6   class Test
7   {
8   public:
9      explicit Test( int = 0 ); // default constructor
10     void print() const;
11  private:
12     int x;
13  }; // end class Test
14
15  // constructor
16  Test::Test( int value )
17     : x( value ) // initialize x to value
18  {
19     // empty body
20  } // end constructor Test
21
22  // print x using implicit and explicit this pointers;
23  // the parentheses around *this are required
24  void Test::print() const
25  {
26     // implicitly use the this pointer to access the member x
27     cout << "        x = " << x;
28
29     // explicitly use the this pointer and the arrow operator
30     // to access the member x
31     cout << "\n  this->x = " << this->x;
32
```

Fig. 17.23 | using the this pointer to refer to object members. (Part 1 of 2.)

```
33          // explicitly use the dereferenced this pointer and
34          // the dot operator to access the member x
35          cout << "\n(*this).x = " << ( *this ).x << endl;
36      } // end function print
37
38      int main()
39      {
40          Test testObject( 12 ); // instantiate and initialize testObject
41
42          testObject.print();
43      } // end main
```

```
      x = 12
this->x = 12
(*this).x = 12
```

Fig. 17.23 | using the this pointer to refer to object members. (Part 2 of 2.)

For illustration purposes, member function print (lines 24–36) first prints x by using the this pointer *implicitly* (line 27)—only the name of the data member is specified. Then print uses two different notations to access x through the this pointer—the arrow operator (->) off the this pointer (line 31) and the dot operator (.) off the dereferenced this pointer (line 35). Note the parentheses around *this (line 35) when used with the dot member selection operator (.). The parentheses are required because the dot operator has *higher* precedence than the * operator. Without the parentheses, the expression *this.x would be evaluated as if it were parenthesized as *(this.x), which is a *compilation error*, because the dot operator cannot be used with a pointer.

One interesting use of the this pointer is to prevent an object from being assigned to itself. As we'll see in Chapter 18, *self-assignment* can cause serious errors when the object contains pointers to dynamically allocated storage.

Using the *this* Pointer to Enable Cascaded Function Calls

Another use of the this pointer is to enable **cascaded member-function calls**—that is, invoking multiple functions in the same statement (as in line 12 of Fig. 17.26). The program of Figs. 17.24–17.26 modifies class Time's *set* functions setTime, setHour, setMinute and setSecond such that each returns a reference to a Time object to enable cascaded member-function calls. Notice in Fig. 17.25 that the last statement in the body of each of these member functions returns *this (lines 23, 34, 45 and 56) into a return type of Time &.

The program of Fig. 17.26 creates Time object t (line 9), then uses it in *cascaded member-function calls* (lines 12 and 24). Why does the technique of returning *this as a reference work? The dot operator (.) associates from left to right, so line 12 first evaluates t.setHour(18), then returns a reference to object t as the value of this function call. The remaining expression is then interpreted as

```
    t.setMinute( 30 ).setSecond( 22 );
```

The t.setMinute(30) call executes and returns a reference to the object t. The remaining expression is interpreted as

```
    t.setSecond( 22 );
```

```
 1   // Fig. 17.24: Time.h
 2   // Cascading member function calls.
 3
 4   // Time class definition.
 5   // Member functions defined in Time.cpp.
 6   #ifndef TIME_H
 7   #define TIME_H
 8
 9   class Time
10   {
11   public:
12      explicit Time( int = 0, int = 0, int = 0 ); // default constructor
13
14      // set functions (the Time & return types enable cascading)
15      Time &setTime( int, int, int ); // set hour, minute, second
16      Time &setHour( int ); // set hour
17      Time &setMinute( int ); // set minute
18      Time &setSecond( int ); // set second
19
20      // get functions (normally declared const)
21      unsigned int getHour() const; // return hour
22      unsigned int getMinute() const; // return minute
23      unsigned int getSecond() const; // return second
24
25      // print functions (normally declared const)
26      void printUniversal() const; // print universal time
27      void printStandard() const; // print standard time
28   private:
29      unsigned int hour; // 0 - 23 (24-hour clock format)
30      unsigned int minute; // 0 - 59
31      unsigned int second; // 0 - 59
32   }; // end class Time
33
34   #endif
```

Fig. 17.24 | Time class modified to enable cascaded member-function calls.

```
 1   // Fig. 17.25: Time.cpp
 2   // Time class member-function definitions.
 3   #include <iostream>
 4   #include <iomanip>
 5   #include <stdexcept>
 6   #include "Time.h" // Time class definition
 7   using namespace std;
 8
 9   // constructor function to initialize private data;
10   // calls member function setTime to set variables;
11   // default values are 0 (see class definition)
12   Time::Time( int hr, int min, int sec )
13   {
```

Fig. 17.25 | Time class member-function definitions modified to enable cascaded member-function calls. (Part 1 of 3.)

```
14        setTime( hr, min, sec );
15     } // end Time constructor
16
17     // set values of hour, minute, and second
18     Time &Time::setTime( int h, int m, int s ) // note Time & return
19     {
20        setHour( h );
21        setMinute( m );
22        setSecond( s );
23        return *this; // enables cascading
24     } // end function setTime
25
26     // set hour value
27     Time &Time::setHour( int h ) // note Time & return
28     {
29        if ( h >= 0 && h < 24 )
30           hour = h;
31        else
32           throw invalid_argument( "hour must be 0-23" );
33
34        return *this; // enables cascading
35     } // end function setHour
36
37     // set minute value
38     Time &Time::setMinute( int m ) // note Time & return
39     {
40        if ( m >= 0 && m < 60 )
41           minute = m;
42        else
43           throw invalid_argument( "minute must be 0-59" );
44
45        return *this; // enables cascading
46     } // end function setMinute
47
48     // set second value
49     Time &Time::setSecond( int s ) // note Time & return
50     {
51        if ( s >= 0 && s < 60 )
52           second = s;
53        else
54           throw invalid_argument( "second must be 0-59" );
55
56        return *this; // enables cascading
57     } // end function setSecond
58
59     // get hour value
60     unsigned int Time::getHour() const
61     {
62        return hour;
63     } // end function getHour
64
```

Fig. 17.25 | Time class member-function definitions modified to enable cascaded member-function calls. (Part 2 of 3.)

```
65    // get minute value
66    unsigned int Time::getMinute() const
67    {
68       return minute;
69    } // end function getMinute
70
71    // get second value
72    unsigned int Time::getSecond() const
73    {
74       return second;
75    } // end function getSecond
76
77    // print Time in universal-time format (HH:MM:SS)
78    void Time::printUniversal() const
79    {
80       cout << setfill( '0' ) << setw( 2 ) << hour << ":"
81          << setw( 2 ) << minute << ":" << setw( 2 ) << second;
82    } // end function printUniversal
83
84    // print Time in standard-time format (HH:MM:SS AM or PM)
85    void Time::printStandard() const
86    {
87       cout << ( ( hour == 0 || hour == 12 ) ? 12 : hour % 12 )
88          << ":" << setfill( '0' ) << setw( 2 ) << minute
89          << ":" << setw( 2 ) << second << ( hour < 12 ? " AM" : " PM" );
90    } // end function printStandard
```

Fig. 17.25 | Time class member-function definitions modified to enable cascaded member-function calls. (Part 3 of 3.)

Line 24 (Fig. 17.26) also uses cascading. Note that we cannot chain another member-function call after printStandard here, because printStandard does *not* return a reference to t. Placing the call to printStandard before the call to setTime in line 24 results in a compilation error. Chapter 18 presents several practical examples of using cascaded function calls. One such example uses multiple << operators with cout to output multiple values in a single statement.

```
1    // Fig. 17.26: fig17_26.cpp
2    // Cascading member-function calls with the this pointer.
3    #include <iostream>
4    #include "Time.h" // Time class definition
5    using namespace std;
6
7    int main()
8    {
9       Time t; // create Time object
10
11      // cascaded function calls
12      t.setHour( 18 ).setMinute( 30 ).setSecond( 22 );
13
```

Fig. 17.26 | Cascading member-function calls with the this pointer. (Part 1 of 2.)

```
14      // output time in universal and standard formats
15      cout << "Universal time: ";
16      t.printUniversal();
17
18      cout << "\nStandard time: ";
19      t.printStandard();
20
21      cout << "\n\nNew standard time: ";
22
23      // cascaded function calls
24      t.setTime( 20, 20, 20 ).printStandard();
25      cout << endl;
26   } // end main
```

```
Universal time: 18:30:22
Standard time: 6:30:22 PM

New standard time: 8:20:20 PM
```

Fig. 17.26 | Cascading member-function calls with the this pointer. (Part 2 of 2.)

17.14 static Class Members

There is an important exception to the rule that each object of a class has its own copy of all the data members of the class. In certain cases, only *one* copy of a variable should be *shared* by *all* objects of a class. A **static data member** is used for these and other reasons. Such a variable represents "class-wide" information, i.e., data that is shared by *all* instances and is *not* specific to any one object of the class.

Motivating Class-Wide Data

Let's further motivate the need for static class-wide data with an example. Suppose that we have a video game with Martians and other space creatures. Each Martian tends to be brave and willing to attack other space creatures when the Martian is aware that there are at least five Martians present. If fewer than five are present, each Martian becomes cowardly. So each Martian needs to know the martianCount. We could endow each instance of class Martian with martianCount as a data member. If we do, every Martian will have a *separate* copy of the data member. Every time we create a new Martian, we'll have to update the data member martianCount in all Martian objects. Doing this would require every Martian object to have, or have access to, handles to all other Martian objects in memory. This wastes space with the redundant copies of the martianCount and wastes time in updating the separate copies. Instead, we declare martianCount to be static. This makes martianCount class-wide data. Every Martian can access martianCount as if it were a data member of the Martian, but only *one* copy of the static variable martianCount is maintained in the program. This saves space. We save time by having the Martian constructor increment static variable martianCount and having the Martian destructor decrement martianCount. Because there's only one copy, we do not have to increment or decrement separate copies of martianCount for each Martian object.

Performance Tip 17.5

Use static data members to save storage when a single copy of the data for all objects of a class will suffice.

Scope and Initialization of static Data Members

A class's static data members have *class scope*. A static data member *must* be initialized *exactly* once. Fundamental-type static data members are initialized by default to 0. Prior to C++11, a static const data member of int or enum type could be initialized in its declaration in the class definition and all other static data members had to be defined and intialized *at global namespace scope* (i.e., outside the body of the class definition). Again, C++11's in-class initializers also allow you to initialize these variables where they're declared in the class definition. If a static data member is an object of a class that provides a default constructor, the static data member need not be initialized because its default constructor will be called.

Accessing static Data Members

A class's private and protected static members are normally accessed through the class's public member functions or friends. *A class's static members exist even when no objects of that class exist.* To access a public static class member when no objects of the class exist, simply prefix the class name and the scope resolution operator (::) to the name of the data member. For example, if our preceding variable martianCount is public, it can be accessed with the expression Martian::martianCount, even when there are no Martian objects. (Of course, using public data is discouraged.)

To access a private or protected static class member when *no* objects of the class exist, provide a public **static member function** and call the function by prefixing its name with the class name and scope resolution operator. A static member function is a service of the *class*, *not* of a specific *object* of the class.

Software Engineering Observation 17.14

A class's static data members and static member functions exist and can be used even if no objects of that class have been instantiated.

Demonstrating static Data Members

The program of Figs. 17.27–17.29 demonstrates a private static data member called count (Fig. 17.27, line 24) and a public static member function called getCount (Fig. 17.27, line 18). In Fig. 17.28, line 8 defines and initializes the data member count to zero *at global namespace scope* and lines 12–15 define static member function getCount. Notice that neither line 8 nor line 12 includes keyword static, yet both lines define static class members. The static keyword cannot be applied to a member definition that appears outside the class definition. Data member count maintains a count of the number of objects of class Employee that have been instantiated. When objects of class Employee exist, member count can be referenced through *any* member function of an Employee object—in Fig. 17.28, count is referenced by both line 22 in the constructor and line 32 in the destructor.

```
1   // Fig. 17.27: Employee.h
2   // Employee class definition with a static data member to
3   // track the number of Employee objects in memory
4   #ifndef EMPLOYEE_H
5   #define EMPLOYEE_H
6
7   #include <string>
8
9   class Employee
10  {
11  public:
12     Employee( const std::string &, const std::string & ); // constructor
13     ~Employee(); // destructor
14     std::string getFirstName() const; // return first name
15     std::string getLastName() const; // return last name
16
17     // static member function
18     static unsigned int getCount(); // return # of objects instantiated
19  private:
20     std::string firstName;
21     std::string lastName;
22
23     // static data
24     static unsigned int count; // number of objects instantiated
25  }; // end class Employee
26
27  #endif
```

Fig. 17.27 | Employee class definition with a static data member to track the number of Employee objects in memory.

```
1   // Fig. 17.28: Employee.cpp
2   // Employee class member-function definitions.
3   #include <iostream>
4   #include "Employee.h" // Employee class definition
5   using namespace std;
6
7   // define and initialize static data member at global namespace scope
8   unsigned int Employee::count = 0; // cannot include keyword static
9
10  // define static member function that returns number of
11  // Employee objects instantiated (declared static in Employee.h)
12  unsigned int Employee::getCount()
13  {
14     return count;
15  } // end static function getCount
16
17  // constructor initializes non-static data members and
18  // increments static data member count
19  Employee::Employee( const string &first, const string &last )
20     : firstName( first ), lastName( last )
21  {
```

Fig. 17.28 | Employee class member-function definitions. (Part 1 of 2.)

```
22        ++count; // increment static count of employees
23        cout << "Employee constructor for " << firstName
24           << ' ' << lastName << " called." << endl;
25     } // end Employee constructor
26
27     // destructor deallocates dynamically allocated memory
28     Employee::~Employee()
29     {
30        cout << "~Employee() called for " << firstName
31           << ' ' << lastName << endl;
32        --count; // decrement static count of employees
33     } // end ~Employee destructor
34
35     // return first name of employee
36     string Employee::getFirstName() const
37     {
38        return firstName; // return copy of first name
39     } // end function getFirstName
40
41     // return last name of employee
42     string Employee::getLastName() const
43     {
44        return lastName; // return copy of last name
45     } // end function getLastName
```

Fig. 17.28 | Employee class member-function definitions. (Part 2 of 2.)

Figure 17.29 uses static member function getCount to determine the number of Employee objects in memory at various points in the program. The program calls Employee::getCount() before any Employee objects have been created (line 12), after two Employee objects have been created (line 23) and after those Employee objects have been destroyed (line 34). Lines 16–29 in main define a *nested scope*. Recall that local variables exist until the scope in which they're defined terminates. In this example, we create two Employee objects in lines 17–18 inside the nested scope. As each constructor executes, it increments class Employee's static data member count. These Employee objects are destroyed when the program reaches line 29. At that point, each object's destructor executes and decrements class Employee's static data member count.

```
1     // Fig. 17.29: fig17_29.cpp
2     // static data member tracking the number of objects of a class.
3     #include <iostream>
4     #include "Employee.h" // Employee class definition
5     using namespace std;
6
7     int main()
8     {
9        // no objects exist; use class name and binary scope resolution
10       // operator to access static member function getCount
11       cout << "Number of employees before instantiation of any objects is "
12          << Employee::getCount() << endl; // use class name
```

Fig. 17.29 | static data member tracking the number of objects of a class. (Part 1 of 2.)

```
13
14      // the following scope creates and destroys
15      // Employee objects before main terminates
16      {
17          Employee e1( "Susan", "Baker" );
18          Employee e2( "Robert", "Jones" );
19
20          // two objects exist; call static member function getCount again
21          // using the class name and the scope resolution operator
22          cout << "Number of employees after objects are instantiated is "
23              << Employee::getCount();
24
25          cout << "\n\nEmployee 1: "
26              << e1.getFirstName() << " " << e1.getLastName()
27              << "\nEmployee 2: "
28              << e2.getFirstName() << " " << e2.getLastName() << "\n\n";
29      } // end nested scope in main
30
31      // no objects exist, so call static member function getCount again
32      // using the class name and the scope resolution operator
33      cout << "\nNumber of employees after objects are deleted is "
34          << Employee::getCount() << endl;
35  } // end main
```

```
Number of employees before instantiation of any objects is 0
Employee constructor for Susan Baker called.
Employee constructor for Robert Jones called.
Number of employees after objects are instantiated is 2

Employee 1: Susan Baker
Employee 2: Robert Jones

~Employee() called for Robert Jones
~Employee() called for Susan Baker

Number of employees after objects are deleted is 0
```

Fig. 17.29 | static data member tracking the number of objects of a class. (Part 2 of 2.)

A member function should be declared static if it does *not* access non-static data members or non-static member functions of the class. Unlike non-static member functions, *a static member function does not have a this pointer, because static data members and static member functions exist independently of any objects of a class.* The this pointer *must* refer to a specific *object* of the class, and when a static member function is called, there might *not* be any objects of its class in memory.

Common Programming Error 17.6
Using the this pointer in a static member function is a compilation error.

Common Programming Error 17.7
Declaring a static member function const is a compilation error. The const qualifier indicates that a function cannot modify the contents of the object on which it operates, but static member functions exist and operate independently of any objects of the class.

17.15 Wrap-Up

This chapter deepened our coverage of classes, using a Time class case study to introduce several new features. We used an include guard to prevent the code in a header (.h) file from being included multiple times in the same source code (.cpp) file. You learned how to use the arrow operator to access an object's members via a pointer of the object's class type. You learned that member functions have class scope—the member function's name is known only to the class's other members unless referred to by a client of the class via an object name, a reference to an object of the class, a pointer to an object of the class or the scope resolution operator. We also discussed access functions (commonly used to retrieve the values of data members or to test the truth or falsity of conditions) and utility functions (private member functions that support the operation of the class's public member functions).

You learned that a constructor can specify default arguments that enable it to be called in a variety of ways. You also learned that any constructor that can be called with no arguments is a default constructor and that there can be at most one default constructor per class. We discussed destructors for performing termination housekeeping on an object of a class before that object is destroyed, and demonstrated the order in which an object's constructors and destructors are called.

We demonstrated the problems that can occur when a member function returns a reference or a pointer to a private data member, which breaks the encapsulation of the class. We also showed that objects of the same type can be assigned to one another using default memberwise assignment—in Chapter 18, we'll discuss how this can cause problems when an object contains pointer members.

You learned how to specify const objects and const member functions to prevent modifications to objects, thus enforcing the principle of least privilege. You also learned that, through composition, a class can have objects of other classes as members. We demonstrated how to use friend functions.

You learned that the this pointer is passed as an implicit argument to each of a class's non-static member functions, allowing them to access the correct object's data members and other non-static member functions. We used the this pointer explicitly to access the class's members and to enable cascaded member-function calls. We motivated the notion of static data members and member functions and demonstrated how to declare and use them in your own classes.

In Chapter 18, we continue our study of classes and objects by showing how to enable C++'s operators to work with *class-type objects*—a process called *operator overloading*. For example, you'll see how to overload the << operator so it can be used to output a complete array without explicitly using a repetition statement.

Summary

Section 17.2 Time Class Case Study

- Preprocessing directives #ifndef (which means "if not defined"; p. 630) and #endif (p. 630) are used to prevent multiple inclusions of a header. If the code between these directives has not previously been included in an application, #define (p. 630) defines a name that can be used to prevent future inclusions, and the code is included in the source code file.

- Before C++11, only static const int data members could be initialized where they were declared in the class body. For this reason, data members typically should be initialized by the class's constructor. As of C++11, you can now use an in-class initializer to initialize any data member where it's declared in the class definition.

- A class's functions can throw (p. 631) exceptions (such as `invalid_argument`; p. 631) to indicate invalid data.

- Stream manipulator `setfill` (p. 632) specifies the fill character (p. 632) that's displayed when an integer is output in a field that's wider than the number of digits in the value.

- If a member function defines a variable with the same name as a variable with class scope (p. 632), the class-scope variable is hidden in the function by the block-scope variable.

- By default, the fill characters appear before the digits in the number.

- Stream manipulator `setfill` is a "sticky" setting, meaning that once the fill character is set, it applies for all subsequent fields being printed.

- Even though a member function declared in a class definition may be defined outside that class definition (and "tied" to the class via the scope resolution operator), that member function is still within that class's scope.

- If a member function is defined in the body of a class definition, the member function is implicitly declared inline.

- Classes can include objects of other classes as members or they may be derived (p. 635) from other classes that provide attributes and behaviors the new classes can use.

Section 17.3 Class Scope and Accessing Class Members
- A class's data members and member functions belong to that class's scope.

- Nonmember functions are defined at global namespace scope.

- Within a class's scope, class members are immediately accessible by all of that class's member functions and can be referenced by name.

- Outside a class's scope, class members are referenced through one of the handles on an object— an object name, a reference to an object or a pointer to an object.

- Variables declared in a member function have block scope and are known only to that function.

- The dot member selection operator (`.`) is preceded by an object's name or by a reference to an object to access the object's `public` members.

- The arrow member selection operator (`->`; p. 636) is preceded by a pointer to an object to access that object's `public` members.

Section 17.4 Access Functions and Utility Functions
- Access functions (p. 636) read or display data. They can also be used to test the truth or falsity of conditions—such functions are often called predicate functions.

- A utility function (p. 636) is a `private` member function that supports the operation of the class's `public` member functions. Utility functions are not intended to be used by clients of a class.

Section 17.5 Time Class Case Study: Constructors with Default Arguments
- Like other functions, constructors can specify default arguments.

Section 17.6 Destructors
- A class's destructor (p. 643) is called implicitly when an object of the class is destroyed.

- The name of the destructor for a class is the tilde (~) character followed by the class name.

- A destructor does not release an object's storage—it performs termination housekeeping (p. 643) before the system reclaims an object's memory, so the memory may be reused to hold new objects.

- A destructor receives no parameters and returns no value. A class may have only one destructor.
- If you do not explicitly provide a destructor, the compiler creates an "empty" destructor, so every class has exactly one destructor.

Section 17.7 When Constructors and Destructors Are Called
- The order in which constructors and destructors are called depends on the order in which execution enters and leaves the scopes where the objects are instantiated.
- Generally, destructor calls are made in the reverse order of the corresponding constructor calls, but the storage classes of objects can alter the order in which destructors are called.

Section 17.8 Time Class Case Study: A Subtle Trap—Returning a Reference or a Pointer to a private Data Member
- A reference to an object is an alias for the name of the object and, hence, may be used on the left side of an assignment statement. In this context, the reference makes a perfectly acceptable *lvalue* that can receive a value.
- If the function returns a reference to const data, then the reference cannot be used as a modifiable *lvalue*.

Section 17.9 Default Memberwise Assignment
- The assignment operator (=) can be used to assign an object to another object of the same type. By default, such assignment is performed by memberwise assignment (p. 650).
- Objects may be passed by value to or returned by value from functions. C++ creates a new object and uses a copy constructor (p. 651) to copy the original object's values into the new object.
- For each class, the compiler provides a default copy constructor that copies each member of the original object into the corresponding member of the new object.

Section 17.10 const Objects and const Member Functions
- The keyword const can be used to specify that an object is not modifiable and that any attempt to modify the object should result in a compilation error.
- C++ compilers disallow non-const member function calls on const objects.
- An attempt by a const member function to modify an object of its class is a compilation error.
- A member function is specified as const both in its prototype and in its definition.
- A const object must be initialized.
- Constructors and destructors cannot be declared const.

Section 17.11 Composition: Objects as Members of Classes
- A class can have objects of other classes as members—this concept is called composition.
- Member objects are constructed in the order in which they're declared in the class definition and before their enclosing class objects are constructed.
- If a member initializer is not provided for a member object, the member object's default constructor (p. 654) will be called implicitly.

Section 17.12 friend Functions and friend Classes
- A friend function (p. 660) of a class is defined outside that class's scope, yet has the right to access all of the class's members. Stand-alone functions or entire classes may be declared to be friends.
- A friend declaration can appear anywhere in the class.
- The friendship relation is neither symmetric nor transitive.

Section 17.13 Using the this Pointer

- Every object has access to its own address through the this pointer (p. 662).

- An object's this pointer is not part of the object itself—i.e., the size of the memory occupied by the this pointer is not reflected in the result of a sizeof operation on the object.

- The this pointer is passed as an implicit argument to each non-static member function.

- Objects use the this pointer implicitly (as we've done to this point) or explicitly to reference their data members and member functions.

- The this pointer enables cascaded member-function calls (p. 664) in which multiple functions are invoked in the same statement.

Section 17.14 static Class Members

- A static data member (p. 668) represents "class-wide" information (i.e., a property of the class shared by all instances, not a property of a specific object of the class).

- static data members have class scope and can be declared public, private or protected.

- A class's static members exist even when no objects of that class exist.

- To access a public static class member when no objects of the class exist, simply prefix the class name and the scope resolution operator (::) to the name of the data member.

- The static keyword cannot be applied to a member definition that appears outside the class definition.

- A member function should be declared static (p. 669) if it does not access non-static data members or non-static member functions of the class. Unlike non-static member functions, a static member function does not have a this pointer, because static data members and static member functions exist independently of any objects of a class.

Self-Review Exercises

17.1 Fill in the blanks in each of the following:

a) Class members are accessed via the _____ operator in conjunction with the name of an object (or reference to an object) of the class or via the _____ operator in conjunction with a pointer to an object of the class.

b) Class members specified as _____ are accessible only to member functions of the class and friends of the class.

c) _____ class members are accessible anywhere an object of the class is in scope.

d) _____ can be used to assign an object of a class to another object of the same class.

e) A nonmember function must be declared as a(n) _____ of a class to have access to that class's private data members.

f) A constant object must be _____; it cannot be modified after it's created.

g) A(n) _____ data member represents class-wide information.

h) An object's non-static member functions have access to a "self pointer" to the object called the _____ pointer.

i) Keyword _____ specifies that an object or variable is not modifiable.

j) If a member initializer is not provided for a member object of a class, the object's _____ is called.

k) A member function should be static if it does not access _____ class members.

l) Member objects are constructed _____ their enclosing class object.

17.2 Find the error(s) in each of the following and explain how to correct it (them):

a) Assume the following prototype is declared in class Time:

```
void ~Time( int );
```

b) Assume the following prototype is declared in class `Employee`:

```
int Employee( string, string );
```

c) The following is a definition of class `Example`:

```
class Example
{
public:
   Example( int y = 10 )
      : data( y )
   {
      // empty body
   } // end Example constructor

   int getIncrementedData() const
   {
      return ++data;
   } // end function getIncrementedData

   static int getCount()
   {
      cout << "Data is " << data << endl;
      return count;
   } // end function getCount
private:
   int data;
   static int count;
}; // end class Example
```

Answers to Self-Review Exercises

17.1   a) dot (.), arrow (->). b) private. c) public. d) Default memberwise assignment (performed by the assignment operator). e) friend. f) initialized. g) static. h) this. i) const. j) default constructor. k) non-static. l) before.

17.2   a) *Error:* Destructors are not allowed to return values (or even specify a return type) or take arguments.
   Correction: Remove the return type void and the parameter int from the declaration.
   b) *Error:* Constructors are not allowed to return values.
   Correction: Remove the return type int from the declaration.
   c) *Error:* The class definition for Example has two errors. The first occurs in function getIncrementedData. The function is declared const, but it modifies the object.
   Correction: To correct the first error, remove the const keyword from the definition of getIncrementedData. [*Note:* It would also be appropriate to rename this member function as *get* functions are typically const member functions.]
   Error: The second error occurs in function getCount. This function is declared static, so it's not allowed to access any non-static class member (i.e., data).
   Correction: To correct the second error, remove the output line from the getCount definition.

Exercises

17.3   *(Scope Resolution Operator)* What's the purpose of the scope resolution operator?

17.4   *(Enhancing Class Time)* Provide a constructor that's capable of using the current time from the time and localtime functions—declared in the C++ Standard Library header <ctime>—to initialize an object of the Time class.

17.5   *(Complex Class)* Create a class called Complex for performing arithmetic with complex numbers. Write a program to test your class. Complex numbers have the form

```
realPart + imaginaryPart * i
```

where *i* is

$$\sqrt{-1}$$

Use double variables to represent the private data of the class. Provide a constructor that enables an object of this class to be initialized when it's declared. The constructor should contain default values in case no initializers are provided. Provide public member functions that perform the following tasks:

   a) Adding two Complex numbers: The real parts are added together and the imaginary parts are added together.

   b) Subtracting two Complex numbers: The real part of the right operand is subtracted from the real part of the left operand, and the imaginary part of the right operand is subtracted from the imaginary part of the left operand.

   c) Printing Complex numbers in the form (a, b), where a is the real part and b is the imaginary part.

17.6   *(Rational Class)* Create a class called Rational for performing arithmetic with fractions. Write a program to test your class. Use integer variables to represent the private data of the class—the numerator and the denominator. Provide a constructor that enables an object of this class to be initialized when it's declared. The constructor should contain default values in case no initializers are provided and should store the fraction in reduced form. For example, the fraction

$$\frac{2}{4}$$

would be stored in the object as 1 in the numerator and 2 in the denominator. Provide public member functions that perform each of the following tasks:

   a) Adding two Rational numbers. The result should be stored in reduced form.

   b) Subtracting two Rational numbers. The result should be stored in reduced form.

   c) Multiplying two Rational numbers. The result should be stored in reduced form.

   d) Dividing two Rational numbers. The result should be stored in reduced form.

   e) Printing Rational numbers in the form a/b, where a is the numerator and b is the denominator.

   f) Printing Rational numbers in floating-point format.

17.7   *(Enhancing Class Time)* Modify the Time class of Figs. 17.4–17.5 to include a tick member function that increments the time stored in a Time object by one second. Write a program that tests the tick member function in a loop that prints the time in standard format during each iteration of the loop to illustrate that the tick member function works correctly. Be sure to test the following cases:

   a) Incrementing into the next minute.

   b) Incrementing into the next hour.

   c) Incrementing into the next day (i.e., 11:59:59 PM to 12:00:00 AM).

17.8   *(Enhancing Class Date)* Modify the Date class of Figs. 17.13–17.14 to perform error checking on the initializer values for data members month, day and year. Also, provide a member function nextDay to increment the day by one. Write a program that tests function nextDay in a loop that prints the date during each iteration to illustrate that nextDay works correctly. Be sure to test the following cases:

   a) Incrementing into the next month.

   b) Incrementing into the next year.

17.9 *(Combining Class* Time *and Class* Date*)* Combine the modified Time class of Exercise 17.7 and the modified Date class of Exercise 17.8 into one class called DateAndTime. (In Chapter 19, we'll discuss inheritance, which will enable us to accomplish this task quickly without modifying the existing class definitions.) Modify the tick function to call the nextDay function if the time increments into the next day. Modify functions printStandard and printUniversal to output the date and time. Write a program to test the new class DateAndTime. Specifically, test incrementing the time into the next day.

17.10 *(Returning Error Indicators from Class* Time*'s* set *Functions)* Modify the *set* functions in the Time class of Figs. 17.4–17.5 to return appropriate error values if an attempt is made to *set* a data member of an object of class Time to an invalid value. Write a program that tests your new version of class Time. Display error messages when *set* functions return error values.

17.11 *(*Rectangle *Class)* Create a class Rectangle with attributes length and width, each of which defaults to 1. Provide member functions that calculate the perimeter and the area of the rectangle. Also, provide *set* and *get* functions for the length and width attributes. The *set* functions should verify that length and width are each floating-point numbers larger than 0.0 and less than 20.0.

17.12 *(Enhancing Class* Rectangle*)* Create a more sophisticated Rectangle class than the one you created in Exercise 17.11. This class stores only the Cartesian coordinates of the four corners of the rectangle. The constructor calls a *set* function that accepts four sets of coordinates and verifies that each of these is in the first quadrant with no single *x*- or *y*-coordinate larger than 20.0. The *set* function also verifies that the supplied coordinates do, in fact, specify a rectangle. Provide member functions that calculate the length, width, perimeter and area. The length is the larger of the two dimensions. Include a predicate function square that determines whether the rectangle is a square.

17.13 *(Enhancing Class* Rectangle*)* Modify class Rectangle from Exercise 17.12 to include a draw function that displays the rectangle inside a 25-by-25 box enclosing the portion of the first quadrant in which the rectangle resides. Include a setFillCharacter function to specify the character out of which the body of the rectangle will be drawn. Include a setPerimeterCharacter function to specify the character that will be used to draw the border of the rectangle. If you feel ambitious, you might include functions to scale the size of the rectangle, rotate it, and move it around within the designated portion of the first quadrant.

17.14 *(*HugeInteger *Class)* Create a class HugeInteger that uses a 40-element array of digits to store integers as large as 40 digits each. Provide member functions input, output, add and subtract. For comparing HugeInteger objects, provide functions isEqualTo, isNotEqualTo, isGreaterThan, isLessThan, isGreaterThanOrEqualTo and isLessThanOrEqualTo—each of these is a "predicate" function that simply returns true if the relationship holds between the two HugeIntegers and returns false if the relationship does not hold. Also, provide a predicate function isZero. If you feel ambitious, provide member functions multiply, divide and modulus.

17.15 *(*TicTacToe *Class)* Create a class TicTacToe that will enable you to write a complete program to play the game of tic-tac-toe. The class contains as private data a 3-by-3 two-dimensional array of integers. The constructor should initialize the empty board to all zeros. Allow two human players. Wherever the first player moves, place a 1 in the specified square. Place a 2 wherever the second player moves. Each move must be to an empty square. After each move, determine whether the game has been won or is a draw. If you feel ambitious, modify your program so that the computer makes the moves for one of the players. Also, allow the player to specify whether he or she wants to go first or second. If you feel exceptionally ambitious, develop a program that will play three-dimensional tic-tac-toe on a 4-by-4-by-4 board. [*Caution:* This is an extremely challenging project that could take many weeks of effort!]

17.16 *(Friendship)* Explain the notion of friendship. Explain the negative aspects of friendship as described in the text.

17.17   *(Constructor Overloading)* Can a `Time` class definition that includes *both* of the following constructors:

```
Time( int h = 0, int m = 0, int s = 0 );
Time();
```

be used to default construct a `Time` object? If not, explain why.

17.18   *(Constructors and Destructors)* What happens when a return type, even `void`, is specified for a constructor or destructor?

17.19   *(Date Class Modification)* Modify class `Date` in Fig. 17.17 to have the following capabilities:

a)   Output the date in multiple formats such as

```
DDD YYYY
MM/DD/YY
June 14, 1992
```

b)   Use overloaded constructors to create `Date` objects initialized with dates of the formats in part (a).

c)   Create a `Date` constructor that reads the system date using the standard library functions of the `<ctime>` header and sets the `Date` members. See your compiler's reference documentation or `en.cppreference.com/w/cpp/chrono/c` for information on the functions in header `<ctime>`. You might also want to check out C++11's new chrono library at `en.cppreference.com/w/cpp/chrono`.

In Chapter 18, we'll be able to create operators for testing the equality of two dates and for comparing dates to determine whether one date is prior to, or after, another.

17.20   *(SavingsAccount Class)* Create a `SavingsAccount` class. Use a `static` data member `annualInterestRate` to store the annual interest rate for each of the savers. Each member of the class contains a `private` data member `savingsBalance` indicating the amount the saver currently has on deposit. Provide member function `calculateMonthlyInterest` that calculates the monthly interest by multiplying the `savingsBalance` by `annualInterestRate` divided by 12; this interest should be added to `savingsBalance`. Provide a `static` member function `modifyInterestRate` that sets the `static annualInterestRate` to a new value. Write a driver program to test class `SavingsAccount`. Instantiate two different objects of class `SavingsAccount`, `saver1` and `saver2`, with balances of $2000.00 and $3000.00, respectively. Set the `annualInterestRate` to 3 percent. Then calculate the monthly interest and print the new balances for each of the savers. Then set the `annualInterestRate` to 4 percent, calculate the next month's interest and print the new balances for each of the savers.

17.21   *(IntegerSet Class)* Create class `IntegerSet` for which each object can hold integers in the range 0 through 100. Represent the set internally as a `vector` of `bool` values. Element `a[i]` is `true` if integer i is in the set. Element `a[j]` is `false` if integer j is not in the set. The default constructor initializes a set to the so-called "empty set," i.e., a set for which all elements contain `false`.

a)   Provide member functions for the common set operations. For example, provide a `unionOfSets` member function that creates a third set that is the set-theoretic union of two existing sets (i.e., an element of the result is set to `true` if that element is `true` in either or both of the existing sets, and an element of the result is set to `false` if that element is `false` in each of the existing sets).

b)   Provide an `intersectionOfSets` member function which creates a third set which is the set-theoretic intersection of two existing sets (i.e., an element of the result is set to `false` if that element is `false` in either or both of the existing sets, and an element of the result is set to `true` if that element is `true` in each of the existing sets).

c)   Provide an `insertElement` member function that places a new integer k into a set by setting `a[k]` to `true`. Provide a `deleteElement` member function that deletes integer m by setting `a[m]` to `false`.

d) Provide a printSet member function that prints a set as a list of numbers separated by spaces. Print only those elements that are present in the set (i.e., their position in the vector has a value of true). Print --- for an empty set.

e) Provide an isEqualTo member function that determines whether two sets are equal.

f) Provide an additional constructor that receives an array of integers and the size of that array and uses the array to initialize a set object.

Now write a driver program to test your IntegerSet class. Instantiate several IntegerSet objects. Test that all your member functions work properly.

17.22 *(Time Class Modification)* It would be perfectly reasonable for the Time class of Figs. 17.4–17.5 to represent the time internally as the number of seconds since midnight rather than the three integer values hour, minute and second. Clients could use the same public methods and get the same results. Modify the Time class of Fig. 17.4 to implement the time as the number of seconds since midnight and show that there is no visible change in functionality to the clients of the class. [*Note:* This exercise nicely demonstrates the virtues of implementation hiding.]

17.23 *(Card Shuffling and Dealing)* Create a program to shuffle and deal a deck of cards. The program should consist of class Card, class DeckOfCards and a driver program. Class Card should provide:

a) Data members face and suit of type int.

b) A constructor that receives two ints representing the face and suit and uses them to initialize the data members.

c) Two static arrays of strings representing the faces and suits.

d) A toString function that returns the Card as a string in the form "*face* of *suit*." You can use the + operator to concatenate strings.

Class DeckOfCards should contain:

a) An array of Cards named deck to store the Cards.

b) An integer currentCard representing the next card to deal.

c) A default constructor that initializes the Cards in the deck.

d) A shuffle function that shuffles the Cards in the deck. The shuffle algorithm should iterate through the array of Cards. For each Card, randomly select another Card in the deck and swap the two Cards.

e) A dealCard function that returns the next Card object from the deck.

f) A moreCards function that returns a bool value indicating whether there are more Cards to deal.

The driver program should create a DeckOfCards object, shuffle the cards, then deal the 52 cards.

17.24 *(Card Shuffling and Dealing)* Modify the program you developed in Exercise 17.23 so that it deals a five-card poker hand. Then write functions to accomplish each of the following:

a) Determine whether the hand contains a pair.

b) Determine whether the hand contains two pairs.

c) Determine whether the hand contains three of a kind (e.g., three jacks).

d) Determine whether the hand contains four of a kind (e.g., four aces).

e) Determine whether the hand contains a flush (i.e., all five cards of the same suit).

f) Determine whether the hand contains a straight (i.e., five cards of consecutive face values).

17.25 *(Project: Card Shuffling and Dealing)* Use the functions from Exercise 17.24 to write a program that deals two five-card poker hands, evaluates each hand and determines which is the better hand.

17.26 *(Project: Card Shuffling and Dealing)* Modify the program you developed in Exercise 17.25 so that it can simulate the dealer. The dealer's five-card hand is dealt "face down" so the player cannot see it. The program should then evaluate the dealer's hand, and, based on the quality of the hand, the dealer should draw one, two or three more cards to replace the corresponding number of unneeded cards in the original hand. The program should then reevaluate the dealer's hand.

17.27 *(Project: Card Shuffling and Dealing)* Modify the program you developed in Exercise 17.26 so that it handles the dealer's hand, but the player is allowed to decide which cards of the player's hand to replace. The program should then evaluate both hands and determine who wins. Now use this new program to play 20 games against the computer. Who wins more games, you or the computer? Have one of your friends play 20 games against the computer. Who wins more games? Based on the results of these games, make appropriate modifications to refine your poker-playing program. Play 20 more games. Does your modified program play a better game?

Making a Difference

17.28 *(Project: Emergency Response Class)* The North American emergency response service, *9-1-1*, connects callers to a *local* Public Service Answering Point (PSAP). Traditionally, the PSAP would ask the caller for identification information—including the caller's address, phone number and the nature of the emergency, then dispatch the appropriate emergency responders (such as the police, an ambulance or the fire department). *Enhanced 9-1-1 (or E9-1-1)* uses computers and databases to determine the caller's physical address, directs the call to the nearest PSAP, and displays the caller's phone number and address to the call taker. *Wireless Enhanced 9-1-1* provides call takers with identification information for wireless calls. Rolled out in two phases, the first phase required carriers to provide the wireless phone number and the location of the cell site or base station transmitting the call. The second phase required carriers to provide the location of the caller (using technologies such as GPS). To learn more about 9-1-1, visit www.fcc.gov/pshs/services/911-services/Welcome.html and people.howstuffworks.com/9-1-1.htm.

An important part of creating a class is determining the class's attributes (instance variables). For this class design exercise, research 9-1-1 services on the Internet. Then, design a class called Emergency that might be used in an object-oriented 9-1-1 emergency response system. List the attributes that an object of this class might use to represent the emergency. For example, the class might include information on who reported the emergency (including their phone number), the location of the emergency, the time of the report, the nature of the emergency, the type of response and the status of the response. The class attributes should completely describe the nature of the problem and what's happening to resolve that problem.

Operator Overloading; Class string

18

Objectives

In this chapter you'll:

- Learn how operator overloading can help you craft valuable classes.

- Overload unary and binary operators.

- Convert objects from one class to another class.

- Use overloaded operators and additional features of the string class.

- Create PhoneNumber, Date and Array classes that provide overloaded operators.

- Perform dynamic memory allocation with new and delete.

- Use keyword explicit to indicate that a constructor cannot be used for implicit conversions.

- Experience a "light-bulb moment" when you'll truly appreciate the elegance and beauty of the class concept.

18.1 Introduction

This chapter shows how to enable C++'s operators to work with class objects—a process called **operator overloading**. One example of an overloaded operator built into C++ is <<, which is used *both* as the stream insertion operator *and* as the bitwise left-shift operator (which we discussed in Chapter 10). Similarly, >> also is overloaded; it's used both as the stream extraction operator and the bitwise right-shift operator. Both of these operators are overloaded in the C++ Standard Library. You've already been using overloaded operators. The overloads are built into the base C++ language itself. For example, C++ overloads the addition operator (+) and the subtraction operator (-) to perform differently, depending on their context in integer, floating-point and pointer arithmetic with data of fundamental types.

You can overload *most* operators to be used with class objects—the compiler generates the appropriate code based on the *types* of the operands. The jobs performed by overloaded operators also can be performed by explicit function calls, but operator notation is often more natural.

Our examples start by demonstrating the C++ Standard Library's class `string`, which has lots of overloaded operators. This enables you to see overloaded operators in use before implementing your own overloaded operators. Next, we create a `PhoneNumber` class that enables us to use overloaded operators << and >> to conveniently output and input fully formatted, 10-digit phone numbers. We then present a `Date` class that overloads the prefix and postfix increment (++) operators to add one day to the value of a `Date`. The class also overloads the += operator to allow a program to increment a `Date` by the number of days specified on the right side of the operator.

Next, we present a capstone case study—an `Array` class that uses overloaded operators and other capabilities to solve various problems with pointer-based arrays. This is one of the most important case studies in the book. Many of our students have indicated that the `Array` case study is their "light bulb moment" in truly understanding what classes and object technology are all about. As part of this class, we'll overload stream insertion, stream extraction, assignment, equality, relational and subscript operators. Once you master this

Array class, you'll indeed understand the essence of object technology—crafting, using and reusing valuable classes.

The chapter concludes with discussions of how you can convert between types (incuding class types), problems with certain implicit conversions and how to prevent those problems.

18.2 Using the Overloaded Operators of Standard Library Class `string`

Figure 18.1 demonstrates many of class `string`'s overloaded operators and several other useful member functions, including `empty`, `substr` and `at`. Function `empty` determines whether a `string` is empty, function `substr` returns a `string` that represents a portion of an existing `string` and function `at` returns the character at a specific index in a `string` (after checking that the index is in range).

```cpp
1   // Fig. 18.1: fig18_01.cpp
2   // Standard Library string class test program.
3   #include <iostream>
4   #include <string>
5   using namespace std;
6
7   int main()
8   {
9      string s1( "happy" );
10     string s2( " birthday" );
11     string s3;
12
13     // test overloaded equality and relational operators
14     cout << "s1 is \"" << s1 << "\"; s2 is \"" << s2
15        << "\"; s3 is \"" << s3 << '\"'
16        << "\n\nThe results of comparing s2 and s1:"
17        << "\ns2 == s1 yields " << ( s2 == s1 ? "true" : "false" )
18        << "\ns2 != s1 yields " << ( s2 != s1 ? "true" : "false" )
19        << "\ns2 >  s1 yields " << ( s2 > s1 ? "true" : "false" )
20        << "\ns2 <  s1 yields " << ( s2 < s1 ? "true" : "false" )
21        << "\ns2 >= s1 yields " << ( s2 >= s1 ? "true" : "false" )
22        << "\ns2 <= s1 yields " << ( s2 <= s1 ? "true" : "false" );
23
24     // test string member-function empty
25     cout << "\n\nTesting s3.empty():" << endl;
26
27     if ( s3.empty() )
28     {
29        cout << "s3 is empty; assigning s1 to s3;" << endl;
30        s3 = s1; // assign s1 to s3
31        cout << "s3 is \"" << s3 << "\"";
32     } // end if
33
34     // test overloaded string concatenation operator
35     cout << "\n\ns1 += s2 yields s1 = ";
```

Fig. 18.1 | Standard Library `string` class test program. (Part 1 of 3.)

```
36        s1 += s2; // test overloaded concatenation
37        cout << s1;
38
39        // test overloaded string concatenation operator with a C string
40        cout << "\n\ns1 += \" to you\" yields" << endl;
41        s1 += " to you";
42        cout << "s1 = " << s1 << "\n\n";
43
44        // test string member function substr
45        cout << "The substring of s1 starting at location 0 for\n"
46           << "14 characters, s1.substr(0, 14), is:\n"
47           << s1.substr( 0, 14 ) << "\n\n";
48
49        // test substr "to-end-of-string" option
50        cout << "The substring of s1 starting at\n"
51           << "location 15, s1.substr(15), is:\n"
52           << s1.substr( 15 ) << endl;
53
54        // test copy constructor
55        string s4( s1 );
56        cout << "\ns4 = " << s4 << "\n\n";
57
58        // test overloaded copy assignment (=) operator with self-assignment
59        cout << "assigning s4 to s4" << endl;
60        s4 = s4;
61        cout << "s4 = " << s4 << endl;
62
63        // test using overloaded subscript operator to create lvalue
64        s1[ 0 ] = 'H';
65        s1[ 6 ] = 'B';
66        cout << "\ns1 after s1[0] = 'H' and s1[6] = 'B' is: "
67           << s1 << "\n\n";
68
69        // test subscript out of range with string member function "at"
70        try
71        {
72           cout << "Attempt to assign 'd' to s1.at( 30 ) yields:" << endl;
73           s1.at( 30 ) = 'd'; // ERROR: subscript out of range
74        } // end try
75        catch ( out_of_range &ex )
76        {
77           cout << "An exception occurred: " << ex.what() << endl;
78        } // end catch
79     } // end main
```

```
s1 is "happy"; s2 is " birthday"; s3 is ""

The results of comparing s2 and s1:
s2 == s1 yields false
s2 != s1 yields true
s2 >  s1 yields false
s2 <  s1 yields true
```

Fig. 18.1 | Standard Library `string` class test program. (Part 2 of 3.)

```
s2 >= s1 yields false
s2 <= s1 yields true

Testing s3.empty():
s3 is empty; assigning s1 to s3;
s3 is "happy"

s1 += s2 yields s1 = happy birthday

s1 += " to you" yields
s1 = happy birthday to you

The substring of s1 starting at location 0 for
14 characters, s1.substr(0, 14), is:
happy birthday

The substring of s1 starting at
location 15, s1.substr(15), is:
to you

s4 = happy birthday to you

assigning s4 to s4
s4 = happy birthday to you

s1 after s1[0] = 'H' and s1[6] = 'B' is: Happy Birthday to you

Attempt to assign 'd' to s1.at( 30 ) yields:
An exception occurred: invalid string position
```

Fig. 18.1 | Standard Library string class test program. (Part 3 of 3.)

Lines 9–11 create three string objects—s1 is initialized with the literal "happy", s2 is initialized with the literal " birthday" and s3 uses the default string constructor to create an empty string. Lines 14–15 output these three objects, using cout and operator <<, which the string class designers overloaded to handle string objects. Then lines 16–22 show the results of comparing s2 to s1 by using class string's overloaded equality and relational operators, which perform lexicographical comparisons (i.e., like a dictionary ordering) using the numerical values of the characters (see Appendix B, ASCII Character Set) in each string.

Class string provides member function **empty** to determine whether a string is empty, which we demonstrate in line 27. Member function empty returns true if the string is empty; otherwise, it returns false.

Line 30 demonstrates class string's overloaded copy assignment operator by assigning s1 to s3. Line 31 outputs s3 to demonstrate that the assignment worked correctly.

Line 36 demonstrates class string's overloaded += operator for *string concatenation*. In this case, the contents of s2 are appended to s1. Then line 37 outputs the resulting string that's stored in s1. Line 41 demonstrates that a string literal can be appended to a string object by using operator +=. Line 42 displays the result.

Class string provides member function **substr** (lines 47 and 52) to return a *portion* of a string as a string object. The call to substr in line 47 obtains a 14-character substring (specified by the second argument) of s1 starting at position 0 (specified by the first argument).The call to `substr` in line 52 obtains a substring starting from position 15 of `s1`. When the second argument is not specified, `substr` returns the *remainder* of the `string` on which it's called.

Line 55 creates `string` object `s4` and initializes it with a copy of `s1`. This results in a call to class `string`'s *copy constructor*. Line 60 uses class `string`'s overloaded copy assignment (=) operator to demonstrate that it handles *self-assignment* properly—we'll see when we build class `Array` later in the chapter that self-assignment can be dangerous and we'll show how to deal with the issues.

Lines 64–65 use class `string`'s overloaded [] operator to create *lvalues* that enable new characters to replace existing characters in `s1`. Line 67 outputs the new value of `s1`. *Class `string`'s overloaded [] operator does not perform any bounds checking.* Therefore, *you must ensure that operations using standard class `string`'s overloaded [] operator do not accidentally manipulate elements outside the bounds of the `string`.* Class `string` *does* provide bounds checking in its member function **at**, which throws an exception if its argument is an *invalid* subscript. If the subscript is valid, function `at` returns the character at the specified location as a modifiable *lvalue* or a nonmodifiable *lvalue* (e.g., a `const` reference), depending on the context in which the call appears. Line 73 demonstrates a call to function `at` with an invalid subscript; this throws an `out_of_range` exception.

18.3 Fundamentals of Operator Overloading

As you saw in Fig. 18.1, operators provide a concise notation for manipulating `string` objects. You can use operators with your own user-defined types as well. Although C++ does *not* allow *new* operators to be created, it *does* allow most existing operators to be overloaded so that, when they're used with objects, they have meaning appropriate to those objects.

Operator overloading is *not* automatic—you must write operator-overloading functions to perform the desired operations. An operator is overloaded by writing a non-`static` member function definition or non-member function definition as you normally would, except that the function name starts with the keyword `operator` followed by the symbol for the operator being overloaded. For example, the function name `operator+` would be used to overload the addition operator (+) for use with objects of a particular class (or enum). When operators are overloaded as member functions, they must be non-`static`, because *they must be called on an object of the class* and operate on that object.

To use an operator on an object of a class, you must define overloaded operator functions for that class—with three exceptions:

- The *assignment operator (=)* may be used with *most* classes to perform *memberwise assignment* of the data members—each data member is assigned from the assignment's "source" object (on the right) to the "target" object (on the left). *Memberwise assignment is dangerous for classes with pointer members*, so we'll explicitly overload the assignment operator for such classes.

- The *address (&) operator* returns a pointer to the object; this operator also can be overloaded.

- The *comma operator* evaluates the expression to its left then the expression to its right, and returns the value of the latter expression. This operator also can be overloaded.

Operators That Cannot Be Overloaded
Most of C++'s operators can be overloaded. Figure 18.2 shows the operators that cannot be overloaded.[1]

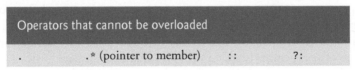

Operators that cannot be overloaded			
.	.* (pointer to member)	::	?:

Fig. 18.2 | Operators that cannot be overloaded.

Rules and Restrictions on Operator Overloading
As you prepare to overload operators for your own classes, there are several rules and restrictions you should keep in mind:

- *The precedence of an operator cannot be changed by overloading.* However, parentheses can be used to *force* the order of evaluation of overloaded operators in an expression.

- *The associativity of an operator cannot be changed by overloading*—if an operator normally associates from left to right, then so do all of its overloaded versions.

- *You cannot change the "arity" of an operator* (that is, the number of operands an operator takes)—overloaded unary operators remain unary operators; overloaded binary operators remain binary operators. Operators &, *, + and - all have both unary and binary versions; these unary and binary versions can be separately overloaded.

- *You cannot create new operators; only existing operators can be overloaded.*

- The meaning of how an operator works on values of fundamental types *cannot* be changed by operator overloading. For example, you cannot make the + operator subtract two ints. Operator overloading works only with *objects of user-defined types or with a mixture of an object of a user-defined type and an object of a fundamental type.*

- Related operators, like + and +=, must be overloaded separately.

- When overloading (), [], -> or any of the assignment operators, the operator overloading function *must* be declared as a class member. For all other overloadable operators, the operator overloading functions can be member functions or non-member functions.

Software Engineering Observation 18.1
Overload operators for class types so they work as closely as possible to the way built-in operators work on fundamental types.

18.4 Overloading Binary Operators

A binary operator can be overloaded as a non-static member function with one parameter or as a non-member function with two parameters (one of those parameters must be either a class

---

1. Although it's possible to overload the address (&), comma (,), && and || operators, you should avoid doing so to avoid subtle errors. For insights on this, see CERT guideline DCL10-CPP.

object or a reference to a class object). A non-member operator function is often declared as friend of a class for performance reasons.

Binary Overloaded Operators as Member Functions

Consider using < to compare two objects of a `String` class that you define. When overloading binary operator < as a non-`static` member function of a `String` class, if y and z are `String`-class objects, then y < z is treated as if y.operator<(z) had been written, invoking the `operator<` member function with one argument declared below:

```
class String
{
public:
    bool operator<( const String & ) const;
    ...
}; // end class String
```

Overloaded operator functions for binary operators can be member functions *only* when the *left* operand is an object of the class in which the function is a member.

Binary Overloaded Operators as Non-Member Functions

As a non-member function, binary operator < *must* take *two* arguments—*one* of which *must* be an object (or a reference to an object) of the class that the overloaded operator is associated with. If y and z are `String`-class objects or references to `String`-class objects, then y < z is treated as if the call operator<(y, z) had been written in the program, invoking function operator< which is declared as follows:

```
bool operator<( const String &, const String & );
```

18.5 Overloading the Binary Stream Insertion and Stream Extraction Operators

You can input and output fundamental-type data using the stream extraction operator >> and the stream insertion operator <<. The C++ class libraries overload these binary operators for each fundamental type, including pointers and char * strings. You can also overload these operators to perform input and output for your own types. The program of Figs. 18.3–18.5 overloads these operators to input and output PhoneNumber objects in the format "(000) 000-0000." The program assumes telephone numbers are input correctly.

```
1   // Fig. 18.3: PhoneNumber.h
2   // PhoneNumber class definition
3   #ifndef PHONENUMBER_H
4   #define PHONENUMBER_H
5
6   #include <iostream>
7   #include <string>
8
9   class PhoneNumber
10  {
```

Fig. 18.3 | PhoneNumber class with overloaded stream insertion and stream extraction operators as `friend` functions. (Part 1 of 2.)

```
11      friend std::ostream &operator<<( std::ostream &, const PhoneNumber & );
12      friend std::istream &operator>>( std::istream &, PhoneNumber & );
13   private:
14      std::string areaCode; // 3-digit area code
15      std::string exchange; // 3-digit exchange
16      std::string line; // 4-digit line
17   }; // end class PhoneNumber
18
19   #endif
```

Fig. 18.3 | PhoneNumber class with overloaded stream insertion and stream extraction operators as friend functions. (Part 2 of 2.)

```
1    // Fig. 18.4: PhoneNumber.cpp
2    // Overloaded stream insertion and stream extraction operators
3    // for class PhoneNumber.
4    #include <iomanip>
5    #include "PhoneNumber.h"
6    using namespace std;
7
8    // overloaded stream insertion operator; cannot be
9    // a member function if we would like to invoke it with
10   // cout << somePhoneNumber;
11   ostream &operator<<( ostream &output, const PhoneNumber &number )
12   {
13      output << "(" << number.areaCode << ") "
14         << number.exchange << "-" << number.line;
15      return output; // enables cout << a << b << c;
16   } // end function operator<<
17
18   // overloaded stream extraction operator; cannot be
19   // a member function if we would like to invoke it with
20   // cin >> somePhoneNumber;
21   istream &operator>>( istream &input, PhoneNumber &number )
22   {
23      input.ignore(); // skip (
24      input >> setw( 3 ) >> number.areaCode; // input area code
25      input.ignore( 2 ); // skip ) and space
26      input >> setw( 3 ) >> number.exchange; // input exchange
27      input.ignore(); // skip dash (-)
28      input >> setw( 4 ) >> number.line; // input line
29      return input; // enables cin >> a >> b >> c;
30   } // end function operator>>
```

Fig. 18.4 | Overloaded stream insertion and stream extraction operators for class PhoneNumber.

```
1    // Fig. 18.5: fig18_05.cpp
2    // Demonstrating class PhoneNumber's overloaded stream insertion
3    // and stream extraction operators.
4    #include <iostream>
```

Fig. 18.5 | Overloaded stream insertion and stream extraction operators. (Part 1 of 2.)

```
5    #include "PhoneNumber.h"
6    using namespace std;
7
8    int main()
9    {
10       PhoneNumber phone; // create object phone
11
12       cout << "Enter phone number in the form (123) 456-7890:" << endl;
13
14       // cin >> phone invokes operator>> by implicitly issuing
15       // the non-member function call operator>>( cin, phone )
16       cin >> phone;
17
18       cout << "The phone number entered was: ";
19
20       // cout << phone invokes operator<< by implicitly issuing
21       // the non-member function call operator<<( cout, phone )
22       cout << phone << endl;
23    } // end main
```

```
Enter phone number in the form (123) 456-7890:
(800) 555-1212
The phone number entered was: (800) 555-1212
```

Fig. 18.5 | Overloaded stream insertion and stream extraction operators. (Part 2 of 2.)

Overloading the Stream Extraction (>>) Operator

The stream extraction operator function `operator>>` (Fig. 18.4, lines 21–30) takes the `istream` reference `input` and the `PhoneNumber` reference `number` as arguments and returns an `istream` reference. Operator function `operator>>` inputs phone numbers of the form

    (800) 555-1212

into objects of class `PhoneNumber`. When the compiler sees the expression

    cin >> phone

in line 16 of Fig. 18.5, the compiler generates the *non-member function call*

    operator>>(cin, phone);

When this call executes, reference parameter `input` (Fig. 18.4, line 21) becomes an alias for `cin` and reference parameter `number` becomes an alias for `phone`. The operator function reads as `string`s the three parts of the telephone number into the `areaCode` (line 24), exchange (line 26) and `line` (line 28) members of the `PhoneNumber` object referenced by parameter `number`. Stream manipulator `setw` limits the number of characters read into each `string`. *When used with `cin` and `string`s, `setw` restricts the number of characters read to the number of characters specified by its argument* (i.e., `setw(3)` allows three characters to be read). The parentheses, space and dash characters are skipped by calling `istream` member function `ignore` (Fig. 18.4, lines 23, 25 and 27), which discards the specified number of characters in the input stream (one character by default). Function `operator>>` returns `istream` reference `input` (i.e., `cin`). This enables input operations on PhoneNumber objects to be *cascaded* with input operations on other PhoneNumber objects or other data types. For example, a program can input two PhoneNumber objects in one statement as follows:

```
cin >> phone1 >> phone2;
```

First, the expression cin >> phone1 executes by making the non-member function call

```
operator>>( cin, phone1 );
```

This call then returns a reference to cin as the value of cin >> phone1, so the remaining portion of the expression is interpreted simply as cin >> phone2. This executes by making the *non-member function call*

```
operator>>( cin, phone2 );
```

Good Programming Practice 18.1

Overloaded operators should mimic the functionality of their built-in counterparts—e.g., the + operator should perform addition, not subtraction. Avoid excessive or inconsistent use of operator overloading, as this can make a program cryptic and difficult to read.

Overloading the Stream Insertion (<<) Operator

The stream insertion operator function (Fig. 18.4, lines 11–16) takes an ostream reference (output) and a const PhoneNumber reference (number) as arguments and returns an ostream reference. Function operator<< displays objects of type PhoneNumber. When the compiler sees the expression

```
cout << phone
```

in line 22 of Fig. 18.5, the compiler generates the *non-member function call*

```
operator<<( cout, phone );
```

Function operator<< displays the parts of the telephone number as strings, because they're stored as string objects.

Overloaded Operators as Non-Member friend Functions

The functions operator>> and operator<< are declared in PhoneNumber as *non-member, friend functions* (Fig. 18.3, lines 11–12). They're *non-member functions* because the object of class PhoneNumber must be the operator's *right* operand. If these were to be PhoneNumber *member functions*, the following awkward statements would have to be used to output and input a PhoneNumber:

```
phone << cout;
phone >> cin;
```

Such statements would be confusing to most C++ programmers, who are familiar with cout and cin appearing as the *left* operands of << and >>, respectively.

Overloaded operator functions for binary operators can be member functions only when the *left* operand is an object of the class in which the function is a member. *Overloaded input and output operators are declared as friends if they need to access non-public class members directly or because the class may not offer appropriate get functions.* Also, the PhoneNumber reference in function operator<<'s parameter list (Fig. 18.4, line 11) is const, because the PhoneNumber will simply be output, and the PhoneNumber reference in function operator>>'s parameter list (line 21) is non-const, because the PhoneNumber object must be modified to store the input telephone number in the object.

Software Engineering Observation 18.2

New input/output capabilities for user-defined types are added to C++ without modifying standard input/output library classes. This is another example of C++'s extensibility.

Why Overloaded Stream Insertion and Stream Extraction Operators Are Overloaded as Non-Member Functions

The overloaded stream insertion operator (<<) is used in an expression in which the left operand has type ostream &, as in cout << classObject. To use the operator in this manner where the *right* operand is an object of a user-defined class, it must be overloaded as a *non-member function*. To be a member function, operator << would have to be a member of class ostream. This is *not* possible for user-defined classes, since we are *not allowed to modify C++ Standard Library classes*. Similarly, the overloaded stream extraction operator (>>) is used in an expression in which the *left* operand has the type istream &, as in cin >> classObject, and the *right* operand is an object of a user-defined class, so it, too, must be a *non-member function*. Also, each of these overloaded operator functions may require access to the private data members of the class object being output or input, so these overloaded operator functions can be made friend functions of the class for performance reasons.

18.6 Overloading Unary Operators

A unary operator for a class can be overloaded as a non-static member function with no arguments or as a non-member function with one argument that must be an object (or a reference to an object) of the class. Member functions that implement overloaded operators must be non-static so that they can access the non-static data in each object of the class.

Unary Overloaded Operators as Member Functions

Consider overloading unary operator ! to test whether an object of your own String class is empty. Such a function would return a bool result. When a unary operator such as ! is overloaded as a member function with no arguments and the compiler sees the expression !s (in which s is an object of class String), the compiler generates the function call s.operator!(). The operand s is the String object for which the String class member function operator! is being invoked. The function is declared as follows:

```
class String
{
public:
    bool operator!() const;
    ...
}; // end class String
```

Unary Overloaded Operators as Non-Member Functions

A unary operator such as ! may be overloaded as a *non-member function* with one parameter. If s is a String class object (or a reference to a String class object), then !s is treated as if the call operator!(s) had been written, invoking the *non-member* operator! function that's declared as follows:

```
bool operator!( const String & );
```

18.7 Overloading the Unary Prefix and Postfix ++ and –– Operators

The prefix and postfix versions of the increment and decrement operators can all be overloaded. We'll see how the compiler distinguishes between the prefix version and the postfix version of an increment or decrement operator.

To overload the prefix and postfix increment operators, each overloaded operator function must have a distinct signature, so that the compiler will be able to determine which version of ++ is intended. The prefix versions are overloaded exactly as any other prefix unary operator would be. Everything stated in this section for overloading prefix and postfix increment operators applies to overloading predecrement and postdecrement operators. In the next section, we examine a Date class with overloaded prefix and postfix increment operators.

Overloading the Prefix Increment Operator

Suppose that we want to add 1 to the day in Date object d1. When the compiler sees the preincrementing expression ++d1, the compiler generates the *member-function call*

```
d1.operator++()
```

The prototype for this operator member function would be

```
Date &operator++();
```

If the prefix increment operator is implemented as a *non-member function*, then, when the compiler sees the expression ++d1, the compiler generates the function call

```
operator++( d1 )
```

The prototype for this non-member operator function would be declared as

```
Date &operator++( Date & );
```

Overloading the Postfix Increment Operator

Overloading the postfix increment operator presents a challenge, because the compiler must be able to distinguish between the signatures of the overloaded prefix and postfix increment operator functions. The *convention* that has been adopted is that, when the compiler sees the postincrementing expression d1++, it generates the *member-function call*

```
d1.operator++( 0 )
```

The prototype for this operator member function is

```
Date operator++( int )
```

The argument 0 is strictly a *dummy value* that enables the compiler to distinguish between the prefix and postfix increment operator functions. The same syntax is used to differentiate between the prefix and postfix decrement operator functions.

If the postfix increment is implemented as a *non-member function*, then, when the compiler sees the expression d1++, the compiler generates the function call

```
operator++( d1, 0 )
```

The prototype for this function would be

```
Date operator++( Date &, int );
```

Once again, the 0 argument is used by the compiler to distinguish between the prefix and postfix increment operators implemented as non-member functions. Note that the *postfix increment operator* returns Date objects *by value*, whereas the prefix increment operator returns Date objects *by reference*—the postfix increment operator typically returns a temporary object that contains the original value of the object before the increment occurred. C++ treats such objects as *rvalues*, which *cannot be used on the left side of an assignment*. The prefix increment operator returns the actual incremented object with its new value. Such an object *can* be used as an *lvalue* in a continuing expression.

Performance Tip 18.1

The extra object that's created by the postfix *increment (or decrement) operator can result in a performance problem—especially when the operator is used in a loop. For this reason, you should prefer the overloaded* prefix *increment and decrement operators.*

18.8 Case Study: A Date Class

The program of Figs. 18.6–18.8 demonstrates a Date class, which uses overloaded prefix and postfix increment operators to add 1 to the day in a Date object, while causing appropriate increments to the month and year if necessary. The Date header (Fig. 18.6) specifies that Date's public interface includes an overloaded stream insertion operator (line 11), a default constructor (line 13), a setDate function (line 14), an overloaded prefix increment operator (line 15), an overloaded postfix increment operator (line 16), an overloaded += addition assignment operator (line 17), a function to test for leap years (line 18) and a function to determine whether a day is the last day of the month (line 19).

```cpp
1   // Fig. 18.6: Date.h
2   // Date class definition with overloaded increment operators.
3   #ifndef DATE_H
4   #define DATE_H
5
6   #include <array>
7   #include <iostream>
8
9   class Date
10  {
11     friend std::ostream &operator<<( std::ostream &, const Date & );
12  public:
13     Date( int m = 1, int d = 1, int y = 1900 ); // default constructor
14     void setDate( int, int, int ); // set month, day, year
15     Date &operator++(); // prefix increment operator
16     Date operator++( int ); // postfix increment operator
17     Date &operator+=( unsigned int ); // add days, modify object
18     static bool leapYear( int ); // is date in a leap year?
19     bool endOfMonth( int ) const; // is date at the end of month?
20  private:
21     unsigned int month;
22     unsigned int day;
23     unsigned int year;
```

Fig. 18.6 | Date class definition with overloaded increment operators. (Part 1 of 2.)

```
24
25      static const std::array< unsigned int, 13 > days; // days per month
26      void helpIncrement(); // utility function for incrementing date
27   }; // end class Date
28
29   #endif
```

Fig. 18.6 | Date class definition with overloaded increment operators. (Part 2 of 2.)

```
1    // Fig. 18.7: Date.cpp
2    // Date class member- and friend-function definitions.
3    #include <iostream>
4    #include <string>
5    #include "Date.h"
6    using namespace std;
7
8    // initialize static member; one classwide copy
9    const array< unsigned int, 13 > Date::days =
10      { 0, 31, 28, 31, 30, 31, 30, 31, 31, 30, 31, 30, 31 };
11
12   // Date constructor
13   Date::Date( int month, int day, int year )
14   {
15      setDate( month, day, year );
16   } // end Date constructor
17
18   // set month, day and year
19   void Date::setDate( int mm, int dd, int yy )
20   {
21      if ( mm >= 1 && mm <= 12 )
22         month = mm;
23      else
24         throw invalid_argument( "Month must be 1-12" );
25
26      if ( yy >= 1900 && yy <= 2100 )
27         year = yy;
28      else
29         throw invalid_argument( "Year must be >= 1900 and <= 2100" );
30
31      // test for a leap year
32      if ( ( month == 2 && leapYear( year ) && dd >= 1 && dd <= 29 ) ||
33         ( dd >= 1 && dd <= days[ month ] ) )
34         day = dd;
35      else
36         throw invalid_argument(
37            "Day is out of range for current month and year" );
38   } // end function setDate
39
40   // overloaded prefix increment operator
41   Date &Date::operator++()
42   {
```

Fig. 18.7 | Date class member- and friend-function definitions. (Part 1 of 3.)

```
43        helpIncrement(); // increment date
44        return *this; // reference return to create an lvalue
45     } // end function operator++
46
47     // overloaded postfix increment operator; note that the
48     // dummy integer parameter does not have a parameter name
49     Date Date::operator++( int )
50     {
51        Date temp = *this; // hold current state of object
52        helpIncrement();
53
54        // return unincremented, saved, temporary object
55        return temp; // value return; not a reference return
56     } // end function operator++
57
58     // add specified number of days to date
59     Date &Date::operator+=( unsigned int additionalDays )
60     {
61        for ( int i = 0; i < additionalDays; ++i )
62           helpIncrement();
63
64        return *this; // enables cascading
65     } // end function operator+=
66
67     // if the year is a leap year, return true; otherwise, return false
68     bool Date::leapYear( int testYear )
69     {
70        if ( testYear % 400 == 0 ||
71           ( testYear % 100 != 0 && testYear % 4 == 0 ) )
72           return true; // a leap year
73        else
74           return false; // not a leap year
75     } // end function leapYear
76
77     // determine whether the day is the last day of the month
78     bool Date::endOfMonth( int testDay ) const
79     {
80        if ( month == 2 && leapYear( year ) )
81           return testDay == 29; // last day of Feb. in leap year
82        else
83           return testDay == days[ month ];
84     } // end function endOfMonth
85
86     // function to help increment the date
87     void Date::helpIncrement()
88     {
89        // day is not end of month
90        if ( !endOfMonth( day ) )
91           ++day; // increment day
92        else
93           if ( month < 12 ) // day is end of month and month < 12
94           {
95              ++month; // increment month
```

Fig. 18.7 | Date class member- and `friend`-function definitions. (Part 2 of 3.)

```
96              day = 1; // first day of new month
97          } // end if
98          else // last day of year
99          {
100             ++year; // increment year
101             month = 1; // first month of new year
102             day = 1; // first day of new month
103         } // end else
104  } // end function helpIncrement
105
106  // overloaded output operator
107  ostream &operator<<( ostream &output, const Date &d )
108  {
109     static string monthName[ 13 ] = { "", "January", "February",
110         "March", "April", "May", "June", "July", "August",
111         "September", "October", "November", "December" };
112     output << monthName[ d.month ] << ' ' << d.day << ", " << d.year;
113     return output; // enables cascading
114  } // end function operator<<
```

Fig. 18.7 | Date class member- and `friend`-function definitions. (Part 3 of 3.)

```
1   // Fig. 18.8: fig18_08.cpp
2   // Date class test program.
3   #include <iostream>
4   #include "Date.h" // Date class definition
5   using namespace std;
6
7   int main()
8   {
9      Date d1( 12, 27, 2010 ); // December 27, 2010
10     Date d2; // defaults to January 1, 1900
11
12     cout << "d1 is " << d1 << "\nd2 is " << d2;
13     cout << "\n\nd1 += 7 is " << ( d1 += 7 );
14
15     d2.setDate( 2, 28, 2008 );
16     cout << "\n\n  d2 is " << d2;
17     cout << "\n++d2 is " << ++d2 << " (leap year allows 29th)";
18
19     Date d3( 7, 13, 2010 );
20
21     cout << "\n\nTesting the prefix increment operator:\n"
22        << "  d3 is " << d3 << endl;
23     cout << "++d3 is " << ++d3 << endl;
24     cout << "  d3 is " << d3;
25
26     cout << "\n\nTesting the postfix increment operator:\n"
27        << "  d3 is " << d3 << endl;
28     cout << "d3++ is " << d3++ << endl;
29     cout << "  d3 is " << d3 << endl;
30  } // end main
```

Fig. 18.8 | Date class test program. (Part 1 of 2.)

```
d1 is December 27, 2010
d2 is January 1, 1900

d1 += 7 is January 3, 2011

  d2 is February 28, 2008
++d2 is February 29, 2008 (leap year allows 29th)

Testing the prefix increment operator:
  d3 is July 13, 2010
++d3 is July 14, 2010
  d3 is July 14, 2010

Testing the postfix increment operator:
  d3 is July 14, 2010
d3++ is July 14, 2010
  d3 is July 15, 2010
```

Fig. 18.8 | Date class test program. (Part 2 of 2.)

Function `main` (Fig. 18.8) creates two `Date` objects (lines 9–10)—`d1` is initialized to December 27, 2010 and `d2` is initialized by default to January 1, 1900. The `Date` constructor (defined in Fig. 18.7, lines 13–16) calls `setDate` (defined in Fig. 18.7, lines 19–38) to validate the month, day and year specified. Invalid values for the month, day or year result in `invalid_argument` exceptions.

Line 12 of `main` (Fig. 18.8) outputs each of the `Date` objects, using the overloaded stream insertion operator (defined in Fig. 18.7, lines 107–114). Line 13 of `main` uses the overloaded operator `+=` (defined in Fig. 18.7, lines 59–65) to add seven days to `d1`. Line 15 in Fig. 18.8 uses function `setDate` to set `d2` to February 28, 2008, which is a leap year. Then, line 17 preincrements `d2` to show that the date increments properly to February 29. Next, line 19 creates a `Date` object, `d3`, which is initialized with the date July 13, 2010. Then line 23 increments `d3` by 1 with the overloaded prefix increment operator. Lines 21–24 output `d3` before and after the preincrement operation to confirm that it worked correctly. Finally, line 28 increments `d3` with the overloaded postfix increment operator. Lines 26–29 output `d3` before and after the postincrement operation to confirm that it worked correctly.

Date *Class Prefix Increment Operator*
Overloading the prefix increment operator is straightforward. The prefix increment operator (defined in Fig. 18.7, lines 41–45) calls utility function `helpIncrement` (defined in Fig. 18.7, lines 87–104) to increment the date. This function deals with "wraparounds" or "carries" that occur when we increment the last day of the month. These carries require incrementing the month. If the month is already 12, then the year must also be incremented and the month must be set to 1. Function `helpIncrement` uses function `endOfMonth` to determine whether the end of a month has been reached and increment the day correctly.

The overloaded prefix increment operator returns a reference to the current `Date` object (i.e., the one that was just incremented). This occurs because the current object, `*this`, is returned as a `Date &`. This enables a preincremented `Date` object to be used as an *lvalue*, which is how the built-in prefix increment operator works for fundamental types.

***Date* Class Postfix Increment Operator**
Overloading the postfix increment operator (defined in Fig. 18.7, lines 49–56) is trickier. To emulate the effect of the postincrement, we must return an *unincremented copy* of the Date object. For example, if int variable x has the value 7, the statement

```
cout << x++ << endl;
```

outputs the *original* value of variable x. So we'd like our postfix increment operator to operate the same way on a Date object. On entry to operator++, we save the current object (*this) in temp (line 51). Next, we call helpIncrement to increment the current Date object. Then, line 55 returns the *unincremented copy* of the object previously stored in temp. This function *cannot* return a reference to the local Date object temp, because a local variable is destroyed when the function in which it's declared exits. Thus, declaring the return type to this function as Date & would return a reference to an object that no longer exists.

Common Programming Error 18.1
Returning a reference (or a pointer) to a local variable is a common error for which most compilers will issue a warning.

18.9 Dynamic Memory Management

You can control the *allocation* and *deallocation* of memory in a program for objects and for arrays of any built-in or user-defined type. This is known as **dynamic memory management** and is performed with the operators **new** and **delete**. We'll use these capabilities to implement our Array class in the next section.

You can use the new operator to dynamically **allocate** (i.e., reserve) the exact amount of memory required to hold an object or built-in array at execution time. The object or built-in array is created in the **free store** (also called the **heap**)—*a region of memory assigned to each program for storing dynamically allocated objects.*[2] Once memory is allocated in the free store, you can access it via the pointer that operator new returns. When you no longer need the memory, you can *return* it to the free store by using the delete operator to **deallocate** (i.e., *release*) the memory, which can then be *reused* by future new operations.[3]

***Obtaining Dynamic Memory with* new**
Consider the following statement:

```
Time *timePtr = new Time();
```

The new operator allocates storage of the proper size for an object of type Time, calls the default constructor to initialize the object and returns a pointer to the type specified to the right of the new operator (i.e., a Time *). If new is unable to find sufficient space in memory for the object, it indicates that an error occurred by throwing an exception.

---

2. Operator new could fail to obtain the needed memory, in which case a bad_alloc exception will occur. Chapter 22 shows how to deal with failures when using new.
3. Operators new and delete *can* be overloaded, but this is beyond the scope of the book. If you do overload new, then you should overload delete in the *same scope* to avoid subtle dynamic memory management errors.

Releasing Dynamic Memory with **delete**

To destroy a dynamically allocated object and free the space for the object, use the `delete` operator as follows:

```
delete timePtr;
```

This statement first *calls the destructor for the object to which* `timePtr` *points, then deallocates the memory associated with the object, returning the memory to the free store.*

> **Common Programming Error 18.2**
>
> *Not releasing dynamically allocated memory when it's no longer needed can cause the system to run out of memory prematurely. This is sometimes called a "memory leak."*

> **Error-Prevention Tip 18.1**
>
> *Do not delete memory that was not allocated by* new. *Doing so results in undefined behavior.*

> **Error-Prevention Tip 18.2**
>
> *After you delete a block of dynamically allocated memory be sure not to delete the same block again. One way to guard against this is to immediately set the pointer to* nullptr. *Deleting a* nullptr *has no effect.*

Initializing Dynamic Memory

You can provide an initializer for a newly created fundamental-type variable, as in

```
double *ptr = new double( 3.14159 );
```

which initializes a newly created `double` to `3.14159` and assigns the resulting pointer to `ptr`. The same syntax can be used to specify a comma-separated list of arguments to the constructor of an object. For example,

```
Time *timePtr = new Time( 12, 45, 0 );
```

initializes a new `Time` object to 12:45 PM and assigns the resulting pointer to `timePtr`.

Dynamically Allocating Built-In Arrays with **new []**

You can also use the `new` operator to allocate built-in arrays dynamically. For example, a 10-element integer array can be allocated and assigned to `gradesArray` as follows:

```
int *gradesArray = new int[ 10 ]();
```

which declares `int` pointer `gradesArray` and assigns to it a pointer to the first element of a dynamically allocated 10-element array of `int`s. The parentheses following new int[10] value initialize the array's elements—fundamental numeric types are set to 0, `bool`s are set to `false`, pointers are set to `nullptr` and class objects are initialized by their default constructors. The size of an array created at compile time must be specified using an integral constant expression; however, a dynamically allocated array's size can be specified using *any* non-negative integral expression that can be evaluated at execution time.

C++11: Using a List Initializer with a Dynamically Allocated Built-In Array

Prior to C++11, when allocating a built-in array of objects dynamically, you *could not* pass arguments to each object's constructor—each object was initialized by its *default* constructor. In C++11, you can use a list initializer to initialize the elements of a dynamically allocated built-in array, as in

```
int *gradesArray = new int[ 10 ]{};
```

The empty set of braces as shown here indicates that *default initialization* should be used for each element—for fundamental types each element is set to 0. The braces may also contain a comma-separated list of initializers for the array's elements.

Releasing Dynamically Allocated Built-In Arrays with `delete []`
To deallocate the memory to which gradesArray points, use the statement

```
delete [] gradesArray;
```

If the pointer points to a built-in array of objects, the statement first calls the destructor for every object in the array, then deallocates the memory. If the preceding statement did *not* include the square brackets ([]) and gradesArray pointed to a built-in array of objects, the result is *undefined—some compilers call the destructor only for the first object in the array. Using delete or delete [] on a nullptr has no effect.*

Common Programming Error 18.3

Using delete instead of delete [] for built-in arrays of objects can lead to runtime logic errors. To ensure that every object in the array receives a destructor call, always delete memory allocated as an array with operator delete []. Similarly, always delete memory allocated as an individual element with operator delete —the result of deleting a single object with operator delete [] is undefined.

C++11: Managing Dynamically Allocated Memory with `unique_ptr`
C++11's new unique_ptr is a "smart pointer" for managing dynamically allocated memory. When a unique_ptr goes out of scope, its destructor *automatically* returns the managed memory to the free store. In Chapter 22, we introduce unique_ptr and show how to use it to manage dynamically allocated objects or a dynamically allocated built-in arrays.

18.10 Case Study: Array Class

We discussed built-in arrays in Chapter 6. Pointer-based arrays have many problems, including:

- A program can easily "walk off" either end of a built-in array, because *C++ does not check whether subscripts fall outside the range of the array* (though you can still do this explicitly).

- Built-in arrays of size *n* must number their elements 0, ..., $n-1$; alternate subscript ranges are *not* allowed.

- An entire built-in array cannot be input or output at once; each element must be read or written individually (unless the array is a null-terminated C string).

- Two built-in arrays cannot be meaningfully compared with equality or relational operators (because the array names are simply pointers to where the arrays begin in memory and two arrays will always be at different memory locations).

- When a built-in array is passed to a general-purpose function designed to handle arrays of any size, the array's *size* must be passed as an additional argument.

- One built-in array cannot be *assigned* to another with the assignment operator(s).

Class development is an interesting, creative and intellectually challenging activity—always with the goal of *crafting valuable classes*. With C++, you can implement more robust array capabilities via classes and operator overloading as has been done with class templates array and vector in the C++ Standard Library. In this section, we'll develop our own custom array class that's preferable to built-in arrays. When we refer to "arrays" in this case study, we mean built-in arrays.

In this example, we create a powerful Array class that performs range checking to ensure that subscripts remain within the bounds of the Array. The class allows one Array object to be assigned to another with the assignment operator. Array objects know their size, so the size does not need to be passed separately to functions that receive Array parameters. Entire Arrays can be input or output with the stream extraction and stream insertion operators, respectively. You can compare Arrays with the equality operators == and !=.

18.10.1 Using the Array Class

The program of Figs. 18.9–18.11 demonstrates class Array and its overloaded operators. First we walk through main (Fig. 18.9) and the program's output, then we consider the class definition (Fig. 18.10) and each of its member-function definitions (Fig. 18.11).

```cpp
1   // Fig. 18.9: fig18_09.cpp
2   // Array class test program.
3   #include <iostream>
4   #include <stdexcept>
5   #include "Array.h"
6   using namespace std;
7
8   int main()
9   {
10     Array integers1( 7 ); // seven-element Array
11     Array integers2; // 10-element Array by default
12
13     // print integers1 size and contents
14     cout << "Size of Array integers1 is "
15        << integers1.getSize()
16        << "\nArray after initialization:\n" << integers1;
17
18     // print integers2 size and contents
19     cout << "\nSize of Array integers2 is "
20        << integers2.getSize()
21        << "\nArray after initialization:\n" << integers2;
22
23     // input and print integers1 and integers2
24     cout << "\nEnter 17 integers:" << endl;
25     cin >> integers1 >> integers2;
```

Fig. 18.9 | Array class test program. (Part 1 of 3.)

```
26
27      cout << "\nAfter input, the Arrays contain:\n"
28         << "integers1:\n" << integers1
29         << "integers2:\n" << integers2;
30
31      // use overloaded inequality (!=) operator
32      cout << "\nEvaluating: integers1 != integers2" << endl;
33
34      if ( integers1 != integers2 )
35         cout << "integers1 and integers2 are not equal" << endl;
36
37      // create Array integers3 using integers1 as an
38      // initializer; print size and contents
39      Array integers3( integers1 ); // invokes copy constructor
40
41      cout << "\nSize of Array integers3 is "
42         << integers3.getSize()
43         << "\nArray after initialization:\n" << integers3;
44
45      // use overloaded assignment (=) operator
46      cout << "\nAssigning integers2 to integers1:" << endl;
47      integers1 = integers2; // note target Array is smaller
48
49      cout << "integers1:\n" << integers1
50         << "integers2:\n" << integers2;
51
52      // use overloaded equality (==) operator
53      cout << "\nEvaluating: integers1 == integers2" << endl;
54
55      if ( integers1 == integers2 )
56         cout << "integers1 and integers2 are equal" << endl;
57
58      // use overloaded subscript operator to create rvalue
59      cout << "\nintegers1[5] is " << integers1[ 5 ];
60
61      // use overloaded subscript operator to create lvalue
62      cout << "\n\nAssigning 1000 to integers1[5]" << endl;
63      integers1[ 5 ] = 1000;
64      cout << "integers1:\n" << integers1;
65
66      // attempt to use out-of-range subscript
67      try
68      {
69         cout << "\nAttempt to assign 1000 to integers1[15]" << endl;
70         integers1[ 15 ] = 1000; // ERROR: subscript out of range
71      } // end try
72      catch ( out_of_range &ex )
73      {
74         cout << "An exception occurred: " << ex.what() << endl;
75      } // end catch
76  } // end main
```

Fig. 18.9 | Array class test program. (Part 2 of 3.)

```
Size of Array integers1 is 7
Array after initialization:
           0              0             0             0
           0              0             0

Size of Array integers2 is 10
Array after initialization:
           0              0             0             0
           0              0             0             0
           0              0

Enter 17 integers:
1 2 3 4 5 6 7 8 9 10 11 12 13 14 15 16 17

After input, the Arrays contain:
integers1:
           1              2             3             4
           5              6             7
integers2:
           8              9            10            11
          12             13            14            15
          16             17

Evaluating: integers1 != integers2
integers1 and integers2 are not equal

Size of Array integers3 is 7
Array after initialization:
           1              2             3             4
           5              6             7

Assigning integers2 to integers1:
integers1:
           8              9            10            11
          12             13            14            15
          16             17

integers2:
           8              9            10            11
          12             13            14            15
          16             17

Evaluating: integers1 == integers2
integers1 and integers2 are equal

integers1[5] is 13

Assigning 1000 to integers1[5]
integers1:
           8              9            10            11
          12           1000            14            15
          16             17

Attempt to assign 1000 to integers1[15]
An exception occurred: Subscript out of range
```

Fig. 18.9 | Array class test program. (Part 3 of 3.)

Creating Arrays, Outputting Their Size and Displaying Their Contents

The program begins by instantiating two objects of class Array—integers1 (Fig. 18.9, line 10) with seven elements, and integers2 (line 11) with the default Array size—10 elements (specified by the Array default constructor's prototype in Fig. 18.10, line 14). Lines 14–16 in Fig. 18.9 use member function getSize to determine the size of integers1 then output integers1's contents, using the Array overloaded stream insertion operator. The sample output confirms that the Array elements were set correctly to zeros by the constructor. Next, lines 19–21 output the size of Array integers2 then output integers2's contents, using the Array overloaded stream insertion operator.

Using the Overloaded Stream Insertion Operator to Fill an Array

Line 24 prompts the user to input 17 integers. Line 25 uses the Array overloaded stream extraction operator to read the first seven values into integers1 and the remaining 10 values into integers2. Lines 27–29 output the two arrays with the overloaded Array stream insertion operator to confirm that the input was performed correctly.

Using the Overloaded Inequality Operator

Line 34 tests the overloaded inequality operator by evaluating the condition

```
integers1 != integers2
```

The program output shows that the Arrays are not equal.

Initializing a New Array with a Copy of an Existing Array's Contents

Line 39 instantiates a third Array called integers3 and initializes it with a copy of Array integers1. This invokes class Array's copy constructor to copy the elements of integers1 into integers3. We discuss the details of the copy constructor shortly. The copy constructor can also be invoked by writing line 39 as follows:

```
Array integers3 = integers1;
```

The equal sign in the preceding statement is *not* the assignment operator. When an equal sign appears in the declaration of an object, it invokes a constructor for that object. This form can be used to pass only a single argument to a constructor—specifically, the value on the right side of the = symbol.

Lines 41–43 output the size of integers3 then output integers3's contents, using the Array overloaded stream insertion operator to confirm that integers3's elements were set correctly by the copy constructor.

Using the Overloaded Assignment Operator

Line 47 tests the overloaded assignment operator (=) by assigning integers2 to integers1. Lines 49–50 display both Array objects' contents to confirm that the assignment was successful. Array integers1 originally held 7 integers, but was resized to hold a copy of the 10 elements in integers2. As we'll see, the overloaded assignment operator performs this resizing operation in a manner that's transparent to the client code.

Using the Overloaded Equality Operator

Line 55 uses the overloaded equality operator (==) to confirm that objects integers1 and integers2 are indeed *identical* after the assignment in line 47.

Using the Overloaded Subscript Operator

Line 59 uses the overloaded subscript operator to refer to `integers1[5]`—an in-range element of `integers1`. This subscripted name is used as an *rvalue* to print the value stored in `integers1[5]`. Line 63 uses `integers1[5]` as a modifiable *lvalue* on the left side of an assignment statement to assign a new value, 1000, to element 5 of `integers1`. We'll see that `operator[]` returns a reference to use as the modifiable *lvalue* after the operator confirms that 5 is a valid subscript for `integers1`.

Line 70 attempts to assign the value 1000 to `integers1[15]`—an *out-of-range* element. In this example, `operator[]` determines that the subscript is out of range and throws an `out_of_range` exception.

Interestingly, *the array subscript operator [] is not restricted for use only with arrays*; it also can be used, for example, to select elements from other kinds of *container classes*, such as `strings` and dictionaries. Also, when overloaded `operator[]` functions are defined, *subscripts no longer have to be integers*—characters, strings or even objects of user-defined classes also could be used.

18.10.2 Array Class Definition

Now that we've seen how this program operates, let's walk through the class header (Fig. 18.10). As we refer to each member function in the header, we discuss that function's implementation in Fig. 18.11. In Fig. 18.10, lines 34–35 represent the `private` data members of class `Array`. Each `Array` object consists of a `size` member indicating the number of elements in the `Array` and an `int` pointer—`ptr`—that points to the dynamically allocated pointer-based array of integers managed by the `Array` object.

```
 1   // Fig. 18.10: Array.h
 2   // Array class definition with overloaded operators.
 3   #ifndef ARRAY_H
 4   #define ARRAY_H
 5
 6   #include <iostream>
 7
 8   class Array
 9   {
10      friend std::ostream &operator<<( std::ostream &, const Array & );
11      friend std::istream &operator>>( std::istream &, Array & );
12
13   public:
14      explicit Array( int = 10 ); // default constructor
15      Array( const Array & ); // copy constructor
16      ~Array(); // destructor
17      size_t getSize() const; // return size
18
19      const Array &operator=( const Array & ); // assignment operator
20      bool operator==( const Array & ) const; // equality operator
21
```

Fig. 18.10 | Array class definition with overloaded operators. (Part 1 of 2.)

```
22       // inequality operator; returns opposite of == operator
23       bool operator!=( const Array &right ) const
24       {
25          return ! ( *this == right ); // invokes Array::operator==
26       } // end function operator!=
27
28       // subscript operator for non-const objects returns modifiable lvalue
29       int &operator[]( int );
30
31       // subscript operator for const objects returns rvalue
32       int operator[]( int ) const;
33    private:
34       size_t size; // pointer-based array size
35       int *ptr; // pointer to first element of pointer-based array
36    }; // end class Array
37
38    #endif
```

Fig. 18.10 | Array class definition with overloaded operators. (Part 2 of 2.)

```
1     // Fig. 18.11: Array.cpp
2     // Array class member- and friend-function definitions.
3     #include <iostream>
4     #include <iomanip>
5     #include <stdexcept>
6
7     #include "Array.h" // Array class definition
8     using namespace std;
9
10    // default constructor for class Array (default size 10)
11    Array::Array( int arraySize )
12       : size( arraySize > 0 ? arraySize :
13             throw invalid_argument( "Array size must be greater than 0" ) ),
14         ptr( new int[ size ] )
15    {
16       for ( size_t i = 0; i < size; ++i )
17          ptr[ i ] = 0; // set pointer-based array element
18    } // end Array default constructor
19
20    // copy constructor for class Array;
21    // must receive a reference to an Array
22    Array::Array( const Array &arrayToCopy )
23       : size( arrayToCopy.size ),
24         ptr( new int[ size ] )
25    {
26       for ( size_t i = 0; i < size; ++i )
27          ptr[ i ] = arrayToCopy.ptr[ i ]; // copy into object
28    } // end Array copy constructor
29
30    // destructor for class Array
31    Array::~Array()
32    {
```

Fig. 18.11 | Array class member- and friend-function definitions. (Part 1 of 3.)

```
33      delete [] ptr; // release pointer-based array space
34   } // end destructor
35
36   // return number of elements of Array
37   size_t Array::getSize() const
38   {
39      return size; // number of elements in Array
40   } // end function getSize
41
42   // overloaded assignment operator;
43   // const return avoids: ( a1 = a2 ) = a3
44   const Array &Array::operator=( const Array &right )
45   {
46      if ( &right != this ) // avoid self-assignment
47      {
48         // for Arrays of different sizes, deallocate original
49         // left-side Array, then allocate new left-side Array
50         if ( size != right.size )
51         {
52            delete [] ptr; // release space
53            size = right.size; // resize this object
54            ptr = new int[ size ]; // create space for Array copy
55         } // end inner if
56
57         for ( size_t i = 0; i < size; ++i )
58            ptr[ i ] = right.ptr[ i ]; // copy array into object
59      } // end outer if
60
61      return *this; // enables x = y = z, for example
62   } // end function operator=
63
64   // determine if two Arrays are equal and
65   // return true, otherwise return false
66   bool Array::operator==( const Array &right ) const
67   {
68      if ( size != right.size )
69         return false; // arrays of different number of elements
70
71      for ( size_t i = 0; i < size; ++i )
72         if ( ptr[ i ] != right.ptr[ i ] )
73            return false; // Array contents are not equal
74
75      return true; // Arrays are equal
76   } // end function operator==
77
78   // overloaded subscript operator for non-const Arrays;
79   // reference return creates a modifiable lvalue
80   int &Array::operator[]( int subscript )
81   {
82      // check for subscript out-of-range error
83      if ( subscript < 0 || subscript >= size )
84         throw out_of_range( "Subscript out of range" );
85
```

Fig. 18.11 | Array class member- and `friend`-function definitions. (Part 2 of 3.)

```
86      return ptr[ subscript ]; // reference return
87   } // end function operator[]
88
89   // overloaded subscript operator for const Arrays
90   // const reference return creates an rvalue
91   int Array::operator[]( int subscript ) const
92   {
93      // check for subscript out-of-range error
94      if ( subscript < 0 || subscript >= size )
95         throw out_of_range( "Subscript out of range" );
96
97      return ptr[ subscript ]; // returns copy of this element
98   } // end function operator[]
99
100  // overloaded input operator for class Array;
101  // inputs values for entire Array
102  istream &operator>>( istream &input, Array &a )
103  {
104     for ( size_t i = 0; i < a.size; ++i )
105        input >> a.ptr[ i ];
106
107     return input; // enables cin >> x >> y;
108  } // end function
109
110  // overloaded output operator for class Array
111  ostream &operator<<( ostream &output, const Array &a )
112  {
113     // output private ptr-based array
114     for ( size_t i = 0, i < a.size; ++i )
115     {
116        output << setw( 12 ) << a.ptr[ i ];
117
118        if ( ( i + 1 ) % 4 == 0 ) // 4 numbers per row of output
119           output << endl;
120     } // end for
121
122     if ( a.size % 4 != 0 ) // end last line of output
123        output << endl;
124
125     return output; // enables cout << x << y;
126  } // end function operator<<
```

Fig. 18.11 | Array class member- and friend-function definitions. (Part 3 of 3.)

Overloading the Stream Insertion and Stream Extraction Operators as friends
Lines 10–11 of Fig. 18.10 declare the overloaded stream insertion operator and the overloaded stream extraction operator as friends of class Array. When the compiler sees an expression like cout << arrayObject, it invokes *non-member function* operator<< with the call

```
operator<<( cout, arrayObject )
```

When the compiler sees an expression like cin >> arrayObject, it invokes *non-member function* operator>> with the call

```
operator>>( cin, arrayObject )
```

Again, these stream insertion and stream extraction operator functions *cannot* be members of class `Array`, because the `Array` object is always mentioned on the *right* side of the stream insertion or stream extraction operator.

Function `operator<<` (defined in Fig. 18.11, lines 111–126) prints the number of elements indicated by `size` from the integer array to which `ptr` points. Function `operator>>` (defined in Fig. 18.11, lines 102–108) inputs directly into the array to which `ptr` points. Each of these operator functions returns an appropriate reference to enable *cascaded* output or input statements, respectively. These functions have access to an `Array`'s `private` data because they're declared as `friends` of class `Array`. We could have used class `Array`'s `getSize` and `operator[]` functions in the bodies of `operator<<` and `operator>>`, in which case these operator functions would not need to be `friends` of class `Array`.

You might be tempted to replace the counter-controlled `for` statement in lines 104–105 and many of the other `for` statements in class `Array`'s implementation with the C++11 range-based `for` statement. Unfortunately, range-based `for` does *not* work with dynamically allocated built-in arrays.

Array Default Constructor

Line 14 of Fig. 18.10 declares the *default constructor* for the class and specifies a default size of 10 elements. When the compiler sees a declaration like line 11 in Fig. 18.9, it invokes class `Array`'s default constructor to set the size of the `Array` to 10 elements. The default constructor (defined in Fig. 18.11, lines 11–18) validates and assigns the argument to data member `size`, uses `new` to obtain the memory for the *internal pointer-based representation* of this `Array` and assigns the pointer returned by `new` to data member `ptr`. Then the constructor uses a `for` statement to set all the elements of the array to zero. It's possible to have an `Array` class that does not initialize its members if, for example, these members are to be read at some later time; but this is considered to be a poor programming practice. `Arrays`, and *objects in general, should be properly initialized as they're created.*

Array Copy Constructor

Line 15 of Fig. 18.10 declares a *copy constructor* (defined in Fig. 18.11, lines 22–28) that initializes an `Array` by making a copy of an existing `Array` object. *Such copying must be done carefully to avoid the pitfall of leaving both `Array` objects pointing to the same dynamically allocated memory.* This is exactly the problem that would occur with *default memberwise copying*, if the compiler is allowed to define a default copy constructor for this class. Copy constructors are invoked whenever a copy of an object is needed, such as in

- passing an object by value to a function,
- returning an object by value from a function or
- initializing an object with a copy of another object of the same class.

The copy constructor is called in a declaration when an object of class `Array` is instantiated and initialized with another object of class `Array`, as in the declaration in line 39 of Fig. 18.9.

The copy constructor for `Array` copies the `size` of the initializer `Array` into data member `size`, uses `new` to obtain the memory for the internal pointer-based representation of this `Array` and assigns the pointer returned by `new` to data member `ptr`. Then the copy constructor uses a `for` statement to copy all the elements of the initializer `Array` into the new `Array` object. An object of a class can look at the `private` data of any other object of that class (using a handle that indicates which object to access).

Software Engineering Observation 18.3

The argument to a copy constructor should be a const reference to allow a const object to be copied.

Common Programming Error 18.4

If the copy constructor simply copied the pointer in the source object to the target object's pointer, then both would point to the same dynamically allocated memory. The first destructor to execute would delete the dynamically allocated memory, and the other object's ptr would point to memory that's no longer allocated, a situation called a dangling pointer—this would likely result in a serious runtime error (such as early program termination) when the pointer was used.

Array Destructor

Line 16 of Fig. 18.10 declares the class's destructor (defined in Fig. 18.11, lines 31–34). The destructor is invoked when an object of class Array goes out of scope. The destructor uses delete [] to release the memory allocated dynamically by new in the constructor.

Error-Prevention Tip 18.3

If after deleting dynamically allocated memory, the pointer will continue to exist in memory, set the pointer's value to nullptr to indicate that the pointer no longer points to memory in the free store. By setting the pointer to nullptr, the program loses access to that free-store space, which could be reallocated for a different purpose. If you do not set the pointer to nullptr, your code could inadvertently access the reallocated memory, causing subtle, nonrepeatable logic errors. We did not set ptr to nullptr in line 33 of Fig. 18.11 because after the destructor executes, the Array object no longer exists in memory.

getSize Member Function

Line 17 of Fig. 18.10 declares function getSize (defined in Fig. 18.11, lines 37–40) that returns the number of elements in the Array.

Overloaded Assignment Operator

Line 19 of Fig. 18.10 declares the overloaded assignment operator function for the class. When the compiler sees the expression integers1 = integers2 in line 47 of Fig. 18.9, the compiler invokes member function operator= with the call

```
integers1.operator=( integers2 )
```

Member function operator='s implementation (Fig. 18.11, lines 44–62) tests for **self-assignment** (line 46) in which an Array object is being assigned to itself. When this is equal to the right operand's address, a *self-assignment* is being attempted, so the assignment is skipped (i.e., the object already is itself; in a moment we'll see why self-assignment is dangerous). If it isn't a self-assignment, then the function determines whether the sizes of the two Arrays are identical (line 50); in that case, the original array of integers in the left-side Array object is *not* reallocated. Otherwise, operator= uses delete [] (line 52) to release the memory originally allocated to the target Array, copies the size of the source Array to the size of the target Array (line 53), uses new to allocate the memory for the target Array and places the pointer returned by new into the Array's ptr member. Then the for statement in lines 57–58 copies the elements from the source Array to the target Array.

Regardless of whether this is a self-assignment, the member function returns the current object (i.e., *this in line 61) as a constant reference; this enables cascaded `Array` assignments such as x = y = z, but prevents ones like (x = y) = z because z cannot be assigned to the const `Array` reference that's returned by (x = y). If self-assignment occurs, and function operator= did not test for this case, operator= would unnecessarily copy the elements of the `Array` into itself.

Software Engineering Observation 18.4

A copy constructor, a destructor and an overloaded assignment operator are usually provided as a group for any class that uses dynamically allocated memory. With the addition of move semantics in C++11, other functions should also be provided, as we discuss in Chapter 24 of our book C++ How to Program, 9/e.

Common Programming Error 18.5

Not providing a copy constructor and overloaded assignment operator for a class when objects of that class contain pointers to dynamically allocated memory is a potential logic error.

C++11: Move Constructor and Move Assignment Operator

C++11 adds the notions of a *move constructor* and a *move assignment operator*. We discuss these new functions in Chapter 24, C++11: Additional Features, of our book *C++ How to Program, 9/e*.

C++11: Deleting Unwanted Member Functions from Your Class

Prior to C++11, you could prevent class objects from being *copied* or *assigned* by declaring as private the class's copy constructor and overloaded assignment operator. As of C++11, you can simply *delete* these functions from your class. To do so in class `Array`, replace the prototypes in lines 15 and 19 of Fig. 18.10 with:

```
Array( const Array & ) = delete;
const Array &operator=( const Array & ) = delete;
```

Though you can delete *any* member function, it's most commonly used with member functions that the compiler can *auto-generate*—the default constructor, copy constructor, assignment operator, and in C++11, the move constructor and move assignment operator.

Overloaded Equality and Inequality Operators

Line 20 of Fig. 18.10 declares the overloaded equality operator (==) for the class. When the compiler sees the expression integers1 == integers2 in line 55 of Fig. 18.9, the compiler invokes member function operator== with the call

```
integers1.operator==( integers2 )
```

Member function operator== (defined in Fig. 18.11, lines 66–76) immediately returns false if the size members of the `Array`s are not equal. Otherwise, operator== compares each pair of elements. If they're all equal, the function returns true. The first pair of elements to differ causes the function to return false immediately.

Lines 23–26 of Fig. 18.9 define the overloaded inequality operator (!=) for the class. Member function operator!= uses the overloaded operator== function to determine whether one `Array` is *equal* to another, then returns the *opposite* of that result. Writing operator!= in this manner enables you to *reuse* operator==, which *reduces the amount of code that must be written in the class.* Also, the full function definition for operator!= is in the Array header. This allows the compiler to *inline* the definition of operator!=.

Overloaded Subscript Operators

Lines 29 and 32 of Fig. 18.10 declare two overloaded subscript operators (defined in Fig. 18.11 in lines 80–87 and 91–98, respectively). When the compiler sees the expression integers1[5] (Fig. 18.9, line 59), it invokes the appropriate overloaded operator[] member function by generating the call

```
integers1.operator[]( 5 )
```

The compiler creates a call to the const version of operator[] (Fig. 18.11, lines 91–98) when the subscript operator is used on a const Array object. For example, if you pass an Array to a function that receives the Array as a const Array & named z, then the const version of operator[] is required to execute a statement such as

```
cout << z[ 3 ] << endl;
```

Remember, a program can invoke only the const member functions of a const object.

Each definition of operator[] determines whether the subscript it receives as an argument is *in range* and if not, each throws an out_of_range exception. If the subscript is in range, the non-const version of operator[] returns the appropriate Array element as a reference so that it may be used as a modifiable *lvalue* (e.g., on the *left* side of an assignment statement). If the subscript is in range, the const version of operator[] returns a copy of the appropriate element of the Array.

C++11: Managing Dynamically Allocated Memory with `unique_ptr`

In this case study, class Array's destructor used delete [] to return the dynamically allocated built-in array to the free store. As you recall, C++11 enables you to use unique_ptr to ensure that this dynamically allocated memory is deleted when the Array object goes out of scope. In Chapter 22, we introduce unique_ptr and show how to use it to manage a dynamically allocated objects or dynamically allocated built-in arrays.

C++11: Passing a List Initializer to a Constructor

You can initialize an array object with a comma-separated list of initializers in braces, as in

```
array< int, 5 > n = { 32, 27, 64, 18, 95 };
```

C++11 actually allows *any* object to be initialized with a *list initializer*. In addition, the preceding statement can also be written without the =, as in

```
array< int, 5 > n{ 32, 27, 64, 18, 95 };
```

C++11 also allows you to use list initializers when you declare objects of your own classes. For example, you can now provide an Array constructor that would enabled the following declarations:

```
Array integers = { 1, 2, 3, 4, 5 };
```

or

```
Array integers{ 1, 2, 3, 4, 5 };
```

each of which creates an Array object with five elements containing the integers from 1 to 5.

To support list initialization, you can define a constructor that receives an *object* of the class template `initializer_list`. For class `Array`, you'd include the `<initializer_list>` header. Then, you'd define a constructor with the first line:

```
Array::Array( initializer_list< int > list )
```

You can determine the number of elements in the `list` parameter by calling its `size` member function. To obtain each initializer and copy it into the `Array` object's dynamically allocated built-in array, you can use a range-based `for` as follows:

```
size_t i = 0;

for ( int item : list )
   ptr[ i++ ] = item;
```

18.11 Operators as Member vs. Non-Member Functions

Whether an operator function is implemented as a *member function* or as a *non-member function*, the operator is still used the same way in expressions. So which is best?

When an operator function is implemented as a *member function*, the *leftmost* (or only) operand must be an object (or a reference to an object) of the operator's class. If the left operand *must* be an object of a different class or a fundamental type, this operator function *must* be implemented as a *non-member function* (as we did in Section 18.5 when overloading `<<` and `>>` as the stream insertion and stream extraction operators, respectively). A *non-member operator function* can be made a `friend` of a class if that function must access `private` or `protected` members of that class directly.

Operator member functions of a specific class are called (*implicitly* by the compiler) only when the *left* operand of a binary operator is specifically an object of that class, or when the *single operand of a unary operator* is an object of that class.

Commutative Operators

Another reason why you might choose a non-member function to overload an operator is to enable the operator to be *commutative*. For example, suppose we have a *fundamental type variable*, number, of type `long int`, and an *object* bigInteger1, of class `HugeInt` (a class in which integers may be arbitrarily large rather than being limited by the machine word size of the underlying hardware; class `HugeInt` is developed in the chapter exercises). The addition operator (+) produces a *temporary* `HugeInt` object as the sum of a `HugeInt` and a `long int` (as in the expression bigInteger1 + number), *or* as the sum of a `long int` and a `HugeInt` (as in the expression number + bigInteger1). Thus, we require the addition operator to be *commutative* (exactly as it is with two fundamental-type operands). The problem is that the class object *must* appear on the *left* of the addition operator if that operator is to be overloaded as a *member function*. So, we *also* overload the operator as a *non-member function* to allow the `HugeInt` to appear on the *right* of the addition. The `operator+` function that deals with the `HugeInt` on the *left* can still be a *member function*. The *non-member function* can simply swap its arguments and call the *member function*.

18.12 Converting Between Types

Most programs process information of many types. Sometimes all the operations "stay within a type." For example, adding an `int` to an `int` produces an `int`. It's often necessary, however, to convert data of one type to data of another type. This can happen in assignments, in calculations, in passing values to functions and in returning values from functions. The compiler knows how to perform certain conversions among fundamental types. You can use *cast operators* to *force* conversions among fundamental types.

But what about user-defined types? The compiler cannot know in advance how to convert among user-defined types, and between user-defined types and fundamental types, so you must specify how to do this. Such conversions can be performed with **conversion constructors**—constructors that can be called with a single argument (we'll refer to these as *single-argument constructors*). Such constructors can turn objects of other types (including fundamental types) into objects of a particular class.

Conversion Operators

A **conversion operator** (also called a *cast operator*) can be used to convert an object of one class to another type. Such a conversion operator must be a *non-static member function*. The function prototype

```
MyClass::operator char *() const;
```

declares an overloaded cast operator function for converting an object of class MyClass into a temporary char * object. The operator function is declared const because it does *not* modify the original object. The return type of an overloaded **cast operator function** is implicitly the type to which the object is being converted. If s is a class object, when the compiler sees the expression static_cast<char *>(s), the compiler generates the call

```
s.operator char *()
```

to convert the operand s to a char *.

Overloaded Cast Operator Functions

Overloaded cast operator functions can be defined to convert objects of user-defined types into fundamental types or into objects of other user-defined types. The prototypes

```
MyClass::operator int() const;
MyClass::operator OtherClass() const;
```

declare *overloaded cast operator functions* that can convert an object of user-defined type MyClass into an integer or into an object of user-defined type OtherClass, respectively.

Implicit Calls to Cast Operators and Conversion Constructors

One of the nice features of cast operators and conversion constructors is that, when necessary, the compiler can call these functions *implicitly* to create *temporary* objects. For example, if an object s of a user-defined String class appears in a program at a location where an ordinary char * is expected, such as

```
cout << s;
```

the compiler can call the overloaded cast-operator function operator char * to convert the object into a char * and use the resulting char * in the expression. With this cast operator provided for a String class, the stream insertion operator does *not* have to be overloaded to output a String using cout.

Software Engineering Observation 18.5

When a conversion constructor or conversion operator is used to perform an implicit *conversion, C++ can apply only one* implicit constructor or operator function call *(i.e., a single user-defined conversion) to try to match the needs of another overloaded operator. The compiler will not satisfy an overloaded operator's needs by performing a series of implicit, user-defined conversions.*

18.13 `explicit` Constructors and Conversion Operators

Recall that we've been declaring as `explicit` every constructor that can be called with one argument. With the exception of copy constructors, any constructor that can be called with a *single argument* and is *not* declared `explicit` can be used by the compiler to perform an *implicit conversion*. The constructor's argument is converted to an object of the class in which the constructor is defined. The conversion is automatic and you need not use a cast operator. *In some situations, implicit conversions are undesirable or error-prone.* For example, our `Array` class in Fig. 18.10 defines a constructor that takes a single `int` argument. The intent of this constructor is to create an `Array` object containing the number of elements specified by the `int` argument. However, if this constructor were not declared `explicit` it could be misused by the compiler to perform an *implicit conversion*.

Common Programming Error 18.6

Unfortunately, the compiler might use implicit conversions in cases that you do not expect, resulting in ambiguous expressions that generate compilation errors or result in execution-time logic errors.

Accidentally Using a Single-Argument Constructor as a Conversion Constructor
The program (Fig. 18.12) uses the `Array` class of Figs. 18.10–18.11 to demonstrate an improper implicit conversion. To allow this implicit conversion, we removed the explicit keyword from line 14 in `Array.h` (Fig. 18.10).

Line 11 in `main` (Fig. 18.12) instantiates `Array` object `integers1` and calls the *single-argument constructor* with the `int` value 7 to specify the number of elements in the `Array`. Recall from Fig. 18.11 that the `Array` constructor that receives an `int` argument initializes all the `Array` elements to 0. Line 12 calls function `outputArray` (defined in lines 17–21), which receives as its argument a `const Array &` to an `Array`. The function outputs the number of elements in its `Array` argument and the contents of the `Array`. In this case, the size of the `Array` is 7, so seven 0s are output.

Line 13 calls function `outputArray` with the `int` value 3 as an argument. However, this program does *not* contain a function called `outputArray` that takes an `int` argument. So, the compiler determines whether class `Array` provides a *conversion constructor* that can convert an `int` into an `Array`. Since the `Array` constructor receives one `int` argument, the compiler assumes that the constructor is a conversion constructor that can be used to convert the argument 3 into a temporary `Array` object containing three elements. Then, the compiler passes the temporary `Array` object to function `outputArray` to output the `Array`'s contents. Thus, even though we do not *explicitly* provide an `outputArray` function that receives an `int` argument, the compiler is able to compile line 13. The output shows the contents of the three-element `Array` containing 0s.

```
1   // Fig. 18.12: fig18_12.cpp
2   // Single-argument constructors and implicit conversions.
3   #include <iostream>
4   #include "Array.h"
5   using namespace std;
6
7   void outputArray( const Array & ); // prototype
8
9   int main()
10  {
11     Array integers1( 7 ); // 7-element Array
12     outputArray( integers1 ); // output Array integers1
13     outputArray( 3 ); // convert 3 to an Array and output Array's contents
14  } // end main
15
16  // print Array contents
17  void outputArray( const Array &arrayToOutput )
18  {
19     cout << "The Array received has " << arrayToOutput.getSize()
20        << " elements. The contents are:\n" << arrayToOutput << endl;
21  } // end outputArray
```

```
The Array received has 7 elements. The contents are:
        0            0            0            0
        0            0            0

The Array received has 3 elements. The contents are:
        0            0            0
```

Fig. 18.12 | Single-argument constructors and implicit conversions.

Preventing Implicit Conversions with Single-Argument Constructors

The reason we've been declaring every single-argument contructor preceded by the keyword **explicit** is to *suppress implicit conversions via conversion constructors when such conversions should not be allowed.* A constructor that's declared explicit *cannot* be used in an *implicit* conversion. In the example of Figure 18.13, we use the original version of Array.h from Fig. 18.10, which included the keyword explicit in the declaration of the *single-argument constructor* in line 14

```
explicit Array( int = 10 ); // default constructor
```

Figure 18.13 presents a slightly modified version of the program in Fig. 18.12. When this program in Fig. 18.13 is compiled, the compiler produces an error message indicating that the integer value passed to outputArray in line 13 *cannot* be converted to a const Array &. The compiler error message (from Visual C++) is shown in the output window. Line 14 demonstrates how the explicit constructor can be used to create a temporary Array of 3 elements and pass it to function outputArray.

Error-Prevention Tip 18.4

Always use the explicit keyword on single-argument constructors unless they're intended to be used as conversion constructors.

```
 1   // Fig. 18.13: fig18_13.cpp
 2   // Demonstrating an explicit constructor.
 3   #include <iostream>
 4   #include "Array.h"
 5   using namespace std;
 6
 7   void outputArray( const Array & ); // prototype
 8
 9   int main()
10   {
11      Array integers1( 7 ); // 7-element Array
12      outputArray( integers1 ); // output Array integers1
13      outputArray( 3 ); // convert 3 to an Array and output Array's contents
14      outputArray( Array( 3 ) ); // explicit single-argument constructor call
15   } // end main
16
17   // print Array contents
18   void outputArray( const Array &arrayToOutput )
19   {
20      cout << "The Array received has " << arrayToOutput.getSize()
21         << " elements. The contents are:\n" << arrayToOutput << endl;
22   } // end outputArray
```

```
c:\examples\ch18\fig18_13\fig18_13.cpp(13): error C2664: 'outputArray' : can-
not convert parameter 1 from 'int' to 'const Array &'
         Reason: cannot convert from 'int' to 'const Array'
         Constructor for class 'Array' is declared 'explicit'
```

Fig. 18.13 | Demonstrating an `explicit` constructor.

C++11: explicit Conversion Operators

As of C++11, similar to declaring single-argument constructors `explicit`, you can declare conversion operators `explicit` to prevent the compiler from using them to perform implicit conversions. For example, the prototype:

```
explicit MyClass::operator char *() const;
```

declares `MyClass`'s `char *` cast operator `explicit`.

18.14 Overloading the Function Call Operator ()

Overloading the **function call operator ()** is powerful, because functions can take an *arbitrary* number of comma-separated parameters. In a *customized* `String` class, for example, you could overload this operator to select a substring from a `String`—the operator's two integer parameters could specify the *start location* and the *length of the substring to be selected*. The `operator()` function could check for such errors as a *start location out of range* or a *negative substring length*.

The overloaded function call operator must be a *non-static* member function and could be defined with the first line:

```
String String::operator()( size_t index, size_t length ) const
```

In this case, it should be a const member function because obtaining a substring should *not* modify the original String object.

Suppose string1 is a String object containing the string "AEIOU". When the compiler encounters the expression string1(2, 3), it generates the member-function call

```
string1.operator()( 2, 3 )
```

which returns a String containing "IOU".

Another possible use of the function call operator is to enable an alternate Array subscripting notation. Instead of using C++'s double-square-bracket notation, such as in chessBoard[row][column], you might prefer to overload the function call operator to enable the notation chessBoard(row, column), where chessBoard is an object of a modified two-dimensional Array class. Exercise 18.7 asks you to build this class. The primary use of the function call operator is to define function objects (discussed in Chapter 16 of our book *C++ How to Program, 9/e*).

18.15 Wrap-Up

In this chapter, you learned how to overload operators to work with class objects. We demonstrated standard C++ class string, which makes extensive use of overloaded operators to create a robust, reusable class that can replace C strings. Next, we discussed several restrictions that the C++ standard places on overloaded operators. We then presented a PhoneNumber class that overloaded operators << and >> to conveniently output and input phone numbers. You also saw a Date class that overloaded the prefix and postfix increment (++) operators and we showed a special syntax that's required to differentiate between the prefix and postfix versions of the increment (++) operator.

Next, we introduced the concept of dynamic memory management. You learned that you can create and destroy objects dynamically with the new and delete operators, respectively. Then, we presented a capstone Array class case study that used overloaded operators and other capabilities to solve various problems with pointer-based arrays. This case study helped you truly understand what classes and object technology are all about—crafting, using and reusing valuable classes. As part of this class, you saw overloaded stream insertion, stream extraction, assignment, equality and subscript operators.

You learned reasons for implementing overloaded operators as member functions or as non-member functions. The chapter concluded with discussions of converting between types (including class types), problems with certain implicit conversions defined by single-argument constructors and how to prevent those problems by using explicit constructors.

In the next chapter, we continue our discussion of classes by introducing a form of software reuse called inheritance. We'll see that when classes share common attributes and behaviors, it's possible to define those attributes and behaviors in a common "base" class and "inherit" those capabilities into new class definitions, enabling you to create the new classes with a minimal amount of code.

Summary

Section 18.1 Introduction
- C++ enables you to overload most operators to be sensitive to the context in which they're used—the compiler generates the appropriate code based on the types of the operands.

- One example of an overloaded operator built into C++ is operator <<, which is used both as the stream insertion operator and as the bitwise left-shift operator. Similarly, >> is also overloaded; it's used both as the stream extraction operator and as the bitwise right-shift operator. Both of these operators are overloaded in the C++ Standard Library.

- C++ overloads + and - to perform differently, depending on their context in integer arithmetic, floating-point arithmetic and pointer arithmetic.

- The jobs performed by overloaded operators can also be performed by explicit function calls, but operator notation is often more natural.

Section 18.2 Using the Overloaded Operators of Standard Library Class `string`

- Standard class `string` is defined in header <string> and belongs to namespace std.

- Class `string` provides many overloaded operators, including equality, relational, assignment, addition assignment (for concatenation) and subscript operators.

- Class `string` provides member function empty (p. 687), which returns true if the `string` is empty; otherwise, it returns false.

- Standard class `string` member function substr (p. 687) obtains a substring of a length specified by the second argument, starting at the position specified by the first argument. When the second argument is not specified, substr returns the remainder of the `string` on which it's called.

- Class `string`'s overloaded [] operator does not perform any bounds checking. Therefore, you must ensure that operations using standard class `string`'s overloaded [] operator do not accidentally manipulate elements outside the bounds of the `string`.

- Standard class `string` provides bounds checking with member function at (p. 688), which "throws an exception" if its argument is an invalid subscript. By default, this causes the program to terminate. If the subscript is valid, function at returns a reference or a const reference to the character at the specified location depending on the context.

Section 18.3 Fundamentals of Operator Overloading

- An operator is overloaded by writing a non-static member-function definition or non-member function definition in which the function name is the keyword operator followed by the symbol for the operator being overloaded.

- When operators are overloaded as member functions, they must be non-static, because they must be called on an object of the class and operate on that object.

- To use an operator on class objects, you must define an overloaded operator function, with three exceptions—the assignment operator (=), the address operator (&) and the comma operator (,).

- You cannot change the precedence and associativity of an operator by overloading.

- You cannot change the "arity" of an operator (i.e., the number of operands an operator takes).

- You cannot create new operators—only existing operators can be overloaded.

- You cannot change the meaning of how an operator works on objects of fundamental types.

- Overloading an assignment operator and an addition operator for a class does not imply that += is also overloaded. You must explicitly overload operator += for that class.

- Overloaded (), [], -> and assignment operators must be declared as class members. For the other operators, the operator overloading functions can be class members or non-member functions.

Section 18.4 Overloading Binary Operators

- A binary operator can be overloaded as a non-static member function with one argument or as a non-member function with two arguments (one of those arguments must be either a class object or a reference to a class object).

Section 18.5 Overloading the Binary Stream Insertion and Stream Extraction Operators

- The overloaded stream insertion operator (<<) is used in an expression in which the left operand has type ostream &. For this reason, it must be overloaded as a non-member function. Similarly, the overloaded stream extraction operator (>>) must be a non-member function.

- Another reason to choose a non-member function to overload an operator is to enable the operator to be commutative.

- When used with cin, setw restricts the number of characters read to the number of characters specified by its argument.

- istream member function ignore discards the specified number of characters in the input stream (one character by default).

- Overloaded input and output operators are declared as friends if they need to access non-public class members directly for performance reasons.

Section 18.6 Overloading Unary Operators

- A unary operator for a class can be overloaded as a non-static member function with no arguments or as a non-member function with one argument; that argument must be either an object of the class or a reference to an object of the class.

- Member functions that implement overloaded operators must be non-static so that they can access the non-static data in each object of the class.

Section 18.7 Overloading the Unary Prefix and Postfix ++ and -- Operators

- The prefix and postfix increment and decrement operators can all be overloaded.

- To overload the pre- and post-increment operators, each overloaded operator function must have a distinct signature. The prefix versions are overloaded like any other unary operator. The postfix increment operator's unique signature is accomplished by providing a second argument, which must be of type int. This argument is not supplied in the client code. It's used implicitly by the compiler to distinguish between the prefix and postfix versions of the increment operator. The same syntax is used to differentiate between the prefix and postfix decrement operator functions.

Section 18.9 Dynamic Memory Management

- Dynamic memory management (p. 701) enables you to control the allocation and deallocation of memory in a program for any built-in or user-defined type.

- The free store (sometimes called the heap; p. 701) is a region of memory assigned to each program for storing objects dynamically allocated at execution time.

- The new operator (p. 701) allocates storage of the proper size for an object, runs the object's constructor and returns a pointer of the correct type. If new is unable to find space in memory for the object, it indicates that an error occurred by "throwing" an "exception." This usually causes the program to terminate immediately, unless the exception is handled.

- To destroy a dynamically allocated object and free its space, use the delete operator (p. 701).

- A built-in array of objects can be allocated dynamically with new as in

```
int *ptr = new int[ 100 ]();
```

which allocates a built-in array of 100 integers, initializes each to 0 with value initialization and assigns the built-in array's starting location to ptr. The preceding built-in array is deleted (p. 703) with the statement

```
delete [] ptr;
```

Section 18.10 Case Study: **Array Class**

- A copy constructor initializes a new object of a class by copying the members of an existing one. Classes that contain dynamically allocated memory typically provide a copy constructor, a destructor and an overloaded assignment operator.

- The implementation of member function `operator=` should test for self-assignment (p. 713), in which an object is being assigned to itself.

- The compiler calls the `const` version of `operator[]` when the subscript operator is used on a `const` object and calls the non-`const` version of the operator when it's used on a non-`const` object.

- The subscript operator (`[]`) can be used to select elements from other types of containers. Also, with overloading, the index values no longer need to be integers.

Section 18.11 Operators as Member vs. Non-Member Functions

- Operator functions can be member functions or non-member functions—non-member functions are often made `friend`s for performance reasons. Member functions use the `this` pointer implicitly to obtain one of their class object arguments (the left operand for binary operators). Arguments for both operands of a binary operator must be explicitly listed in a non-member function call.

- When an operator function is implemented as a member function, the leftmost (or only) operand must be an object (or a reference to an object) of the operator's class.

- If the left operand must be an object of a different class or a fundamental type, this operator function must be implemented as a non-member function.

- A non-member operator function can be made a `friend` of a class if that function must access `private` or `protected` members of that class directly.

Section 18.12 Converting Between Types

- The compiler cannot know in advance how to convert among user-defined types, and between user-defined types and fundamental types, so you must specify how to do this. Such conversions can be performed with conversion constructors (p. 717)—single-argument constructors that turn objects of other types (including fundamental types) into objects of a particular class.

- A constructor that can be called with a single argument can be used as a conversion constructor.

- A conversion operator (p. 717) must be a non-`static` member function. Overloaded cast-operator functions (p. 717) can be defined for converting objects of user-defined types into fundamental types or into objects of other user-defined types.

- An overloaded cast operator function does not specify a return type—the return type is the type to which the object is being converted.

- When necessary, the compiler can call cast operators and conversion constructors implicitly.

Section 18.13 **explicit** Constructors and Conversion Operators

- A constructor that's declared `explicit` (p. 719) cannot be used in an implicit conversion.

Section 18.14 Overloading the Function Call Operator ()

- Overloading the function call operator () (p. 720) is powerful, because functions can have an arbitrary number of parameters.

Self-Review Exercises

18.1 Fill in the blanks in each of the following:

  a) Suppose a and b are integer variables and we form the sum a + b. Now suppose c and d are floating-point variables and we form the sum c + d. The two + operators here are clearly being used for different purposes. This is an example of _____.

b) Keyword _____ introduces an overloaded-operator function definition.

c) To use operators on class objects, they must be overloaded, with the exception of operators _____, _____ and _____.

d) The _____, _____ and _____ of an operator cannot be changed by overloading the operator.

e) The operators that cannot be overloaded are _____, _____, _____ and _____.

f) The _____ operator reclaims memory previously allocated by new.

g) The _____ operator dynamically allocates memory for an object of a specified type and returns a(n) _____ to that type.

18.2 Explain the multiple meanings of the operators << and >>.

18.3 In what context might the name operator/ be used?

18.4 (True/False) Only existing operators can be overloaded.

18.5 How does the precedence of an overloaded operator compare with the precedence of the original operator?

Answers to Self-Review Exercises

18.1 a) operator overloading. b) operator. c) assignment (=), address (&), comma (,). d) precedence, associativity, "arity." e) ., ?:, .*, and ::. f) delete. g) new, pointer.

18.2 Operator >> is both the right-shift operator and the stream extraction operator, depending on its context. Operator << is both the left-shift operator and the stream insertion operator, depending on its context.

18.3 For operator overloading: It would be the name of a function that would provide an overloaded version of the / operator for a specific class.

18.4 True.

18.5 The precedence is identical.

Exercises

18.6 *(Memory Allocation and Deallocation Operators)* Compare and contrast dynamic memory allocation and deallocation operators new, new [], delete and delete [].

18.7 *(Overloading the Parentheses Operator)* One nice example of overloading the function call operator () is to allow another form of double-array subscripting popular in some programming languages. Instead of saying

```
chessBoard[ row ][ column ]
```

for an array of objects, overload the function call operator to allow the alternate form

```
chessBoard( row, column )
```

Create a class DoubleSubscriptedArray that has similar features to class Array in Figs. 18.10–18.11. At construction time, the class should be able to create a DoubleSubscriptedArray of any number of rows and columns. The class should supply operator() to perform double-subscripting operations. For example, in a 3-by-5 DoubleSubscriptedArray called chessBoard, the user could write chessBoard(1, 3) to access the element at row 1 and column 3. Remember that operator() can receive *any* number of arguments. The underlying representation of the DoubleSubscriptedArray could be a one-dimensional array of integers with *rows * columns* number of elements. Function operator() should perform the proper pointer arithmetic to access each element of the underlying array. There should be *two* versions of operator()—one that returns int & (so that an element of a

DoubleSubscriptedArray can be used as an *lvalue*) and one that returns int. The class should also provide the following operators: ==, !=, =, << (for outputting the DoubleSubscriptedArray in row and column format) and >> (for inputting the entire DoubleSubscriptedArray contents).

18.8 *(Complex Class)* Consider class Complex shown in Figs. 18.14–18.16. The class enables operations on so-called *complex numbers*. These are numbers of the form realPart + imaginaryPart * i, where i has the value

$$\sqrt{-1}$$

a) Modify the class to enable input and output of complex numbers via overloaded >> and << operators, respectively (you should remove the print function from the class).
b) Overload the multiplication operator to enable multiplication of two complex numbers as in algebra.
c) Overload the == and != operators to allow comparisons of complex numbers.

After doing this exercise, you might want to read about the Standard Library's complex class (from header <complex>).

```
1   // Fig. 18.14: Complex.h
2   // Complex class definition.
3   #ifndef COMPLEX_H
4   #define COMPLEX_H
5
6   class Complex
7   {
8   public:
9      explicit Complex( double = 0.0, double = 0.0 ); // constructor
10     Complex operator+( const Complex & ) const; // addition
11     Complex operator-( const Complex & ) const; // subtraction
12     void print() const; // output
13  private:
14     double real; // real part
15     double imaginary; // imaginary part
16  }; // end class Complex
17
18  #endif
```

Fig. 18.14 | Complex class definition.

```
1   // Fig. 18.15: Complex.cpp
2   // Complex class member-function definitions.
3   #include <iostream>
4   #include "Complex.h" // Complex class definition
5   using namespace std;
6
7   // Constructor
8   Complex::Complex( double realPart, double imaginaryPart )
9      : real( realPart ),
10       imaginary( imaginaryPart )
11  {
12     // empty body
13  } // end Complex constructor
14
```

Fig. 18.15 | Complex class member-function definitions. (Part 1 of 2.)

```
15    // addition operator
16    Complex Complex::operator+( const Complex &operand2 ) const
17    {
18       return Complex( real + operand2.real,
19          imaginary + operand2.imaginary );
20    } // end function operator+
21
22    // subtraction operator
23    Complex Complex::operator-( const Complex &operand2 ) const
24    {
25       return Complex( real - operand2.real,
26          imaginary - operand2.imaginary );
27    } // end function operator-
28
29    // display a Complex object in the form: (a, b)
30    void Complex::print() const
31    {
32       cout << '(' << real << ", " << imaginary << ')';
33    } // end function print
```

Fig. 18.15 | Complex class member-function definitions. (Part 2 of 2.)

```
34    // Fig. 18.16: fig18_16.cpp
35    // Complex class test program.
36    #include <iostream>
37    #include "Complex.h"
38    using namespace std;
39
40    int main()
41    {
42       Complex x;
43       Complex y( 4.3, 8.2 );
44       Complex z( 3.3, 1.1 );
45
46       cout << "x: ";
47       x.print();
48       cout << "\ny: ";
49       y.print();
50       cout << "\nz: ";
51       z.print();
52
53       x = y + z;
54       cout << "\n\nx = y + z:" << endl;
55       x.print();
56       cout << " = ";
57       y.print();
58       cout << " + ";
59       z.print();
60
61       x = y - z;
62       cout << "\n\nx = y - z:" << endl;
63       x.print();
64       cout << " = ";
65       y.print();
66       cout << " - ";
67       z.print();
68       cout << endl;
69    } // end main
```

Fig. 18.16 | Complex class test program. (Part 1 of 2.)

```
x: (0, 0)
y: (4.3, 8.2)
z: (3.3, 1.1)

x = y + z:
(7.6, 9.3) = (4.3, 8.2) + (3.3, 1.1)

x = y - z:
(1, 7.1) = (4.3, 8.2) - (3.3, 1.1)
```

Fig. 18.16 | Complex class test program. (Part 2 of 2.)

18.9 *(HugeInt Class)* A machine with 32-bit integers can represent integers in the range of approximately –2 billion to +2 billion. This fixed-size restriction is rarely troublesome, but there are applications in which we would like to be able to use a much wider range of integers. This is what C++ was built to do, namely, create powerful new data types. Consider class `HugeInt` of Figs. 18.17–18.19. Study the class carefully, then answer the following:

    a) Describe precisely how it operates.
    b) What restrictions does the class have?
    c) Overload the * multiplication operator.
    d) Overload the / division operator.
    e) Overload all the relational and equality operators.

[*Note:* We do not show an assignment operator or copy constructor for class `HugeInt`, because the assignment operator and copy constructor provided by the compiler are capable of copying the entire array data member properly.]

```
1   // Fig. 18.17: Hugeint.h
2   // HugeInt class definition.
3   #ifndef HUGEINT_H
4   #define HUGEINT_H
5
6   #include <array>
7   #include <iostream>
8   #include <string>
9
10  class HugeInt
11  {
12     friend std::ostream &operator<<( std::ostream &, const HugeInt & );
13  public:
14     static const int digits = 30; // maximum digits in a HugeInt
15
16     HugeInt( long = 0 ); // conversion/default constructor
17     HugeInt( const std::string & ); // conversion constructor
18
19     // addition operator; HugeInt + HugeInt
20     HugeInt operator+( const HugeInt & ) const;
21
22     // addition operator; HugeInt + int
23     HugeInt operator+( int ) const;
24
25     // addition operator;
26     // HugeInt + string that represents large integer value
27     HugeInt operator+( const std::string & ) const;
```

Fig. 18.17 | HugeInt class definition. (Part 1 of 2.)

```
28    private:
29       std::array< short, digits > integer;
30    }; // end class HugetInt
31
32    #endif
```

Fig. 18.17 | HugeInt class definition. (Part 2 of 2.)

```
 1    // Fig. 18.18: Hugeint.cpp
 2    // HugeInt member-function and friend-function definitions.
 3    #include <cctype> // isdigit function prototype
 4    #include "Hugeint.h" // HugeInt class definition
 5    using namespace std;
 6
 7    // default constructor; conversion constructor that converts
 8    // a long integer into a HugeInt object
 9    HugeInt::HugeInt( long value )
10    {
11       // initialize array to zero
12       for ( short &element : integer )
13          element = 0;
14
15       // place digits of argument into array
16       for ( size_t j = digits - 1; value != 0 && j >= 0; j-- )
17       {
18          integer[ j ] = value % 10;
19          value /= 10;
20       } // end for
21    } // end HugeInt default/conversion constructor
22
23    // conversion constructor that converts a character string
24    // representing a large integer into a HugeInt object
25    HugeInt::HugeInt( const string &number )
26    {
27       // initialize array to zero
28       for ( short &element : integer )
29          element = 0;
30
31       // place digits of argument into array
32       size_t length = number.size();
33
34       for ( size_t j = digits - length, k = 0; j < digits; ++j, ++k )
35          if ( isdigit( number[ k ] ) ) // ensure that character is a digit
36             integer[ j ] = number[ k ] - '0';
37    } // end HugeInt conversion constructor
38
39    // addition operator; HugeInt + HugeInt
40    HugeInt HugeInt::operator+( const HugeInt &op2 ) const
41    {
42       HugeInt temp; // temporary result
43       int carry = 0;
44
45       for ( int i = digits - 1; i >= 0; i-- )
46       {
47          temp.integer[ i ] = integer[ i ] + op2.integer[ i ] + carry;
48
```

Fig. 18.18 | HugeInt member-function and friend-function definitions. (Part 1 of 2.)

```
49        // determine whether to carry a 1
50        if ( temp.integer[ i ] > 9 )
51        {
52           temp.integer[ i ] %= 10;   // reduce to 0-9
53           carry = 1;
54        } // end if
55        else // no carry
56           carry = 0;
57     } // end for
58
59     return temp; // return copy of temporary object
60  } // end function operator+
61
62  // addition operator; HugeInt + int
63  HugeInt HugeInt::operator+( int op2 ) const
64  {
65     // convert op2 to a HugeInt, then invoke
66     // operator+ for two HugeInt objects
67     return *this + HugeInt( op2 );
68  } // end function operator+
69
70  // addition operator;
71  // HugeInt + string that represents large integer value
72  HugeInt HugeInt::operator+( const string &op2 ) const
73  {
74     // convert op2 to a HugeInt, then invoke
75     // operator+ for two HugeInt objects
76     return *this + HugeInt( op2 );
77  } // end operator+
78
79  // overloaded output operator
80  ostream& operator<<( ostream &output, const HugeInt &num )
81  {
82     int i;
83
84     for ( i = 0; ( i < HugeInt::digits ) && ( 0 == num.integer[ i ] ); ++i )
85        ; // skip leading zeros
86
87     if ( i == HugeInt::digits )
88        output << 0;
89     else
90        for ( ; i < HugeInt::digits; ++i )
91           output << num.integer[ i ];
92
93     return output;
94  } // end function operator<<
```

Fig. 18.18 | HugeInt member-function and `friend`-function definitions. (Part 2 of 2.)

```
1   // Fig. 18.19: fig18_19.cpp
2   // HugeInt test program.
3   #include <iostream>
4   #include "Hugeint.h"
5   using namespace std;
6
7   int main()
8   {
```

Fig. 18.19 | HugeInt test program. (Part 1 of 2.)

```
9      HugeInt n1( 7654321 );
10     HugeInt n2( 7891234 );
11     HugeInt n3( "99999999999999999999999999999" );
12     HugeInt n4( "1" );
13     HugeInt n5;
14
15     cout << "n1 is " << n1 << "\nn2 is " << n2
16        << "\nn3 is " << n3 << "\nn4 is " << n4
17        << "\nn5 is " << n5 << "\n\n";
18
19     n5 = n1 + n2;
20     cout << n1 << " + " << n2 << " = " << n5 << "\n\n";
21
22     cout << n3 << " + " << n4 << "\n= " << ( n3 + n4 ) << "\n\n";
23
24     n5 = n1 + 9;
25     cout << n1 << " + " << 9 << " = " << n5 << "\n\n";
26
27     n5 = n2 + "10000";
28     cout << n2 << " + " << "10000" << " = " << n5 << endl;
29  } // end main
```

```
n1 is 7654321
n2 is 7891234
n3 is 99999999999999999999999999999
n4 is 1
n5 is 0

7654321 + 7891234 = 15545555

99999999999999999999999999999 + 1
= 100000000000000000000000000000

7654321 + 9 = 7654330

7891234 + 10000 = 7901234
```

Fig. 18.19 | HugeInt test program. (Part 2 of 2.)

18.10 *(RationalNumber Class)* Create a class RationalNumber (fractions) with these capabilities:
   a) Create a constructor that prevents a 0 denominator in a fraction, reduces or simplifies fractions that are not in reduced form and avoids negative denominators.
   b) Overload the addition, subtraction, multiplication and division operators for this class.
   c) Overload the relational and equality operators for this class.

18.11 *(Polynomial Class)* Develop class Polynomial. The internal representation of a Polynomial is an array of terms. Each term contains a coefficient and an exponent, e.g., the term

$2x^4$

has the coefficient 2 and the exponent 4. Develop a complete class containing proper constructor and destructor functions as well as *set* and *get* functions. The class should also provide the following overloaded operator capabilities:
   a) Overload the addition operator (+) to add two Polynomials.
   b) Overload the subtraction operator (-) to subtract two Polynomials.
   c) Overload the assignment operator to assign one Polynomial to another.
   d) Overload the multiplication operator (*) to multiply two Polynomials.
   e) Overload the addition assignment operator (+=), subtraction assignment operator (-=), and multiplication assignment operator (*=).

19

Object-Oriented Programming: Inheritance

Objectives

In this chapter you'll learn:

- What inheritance is and how it promotes software reuse.

- The notions of base classes and derived classes and the relationships between them.

- The **protected** member access specifier.

- The use of constructors and destructors in inheritance hierarchies.

- The order in which constructors and destructors are called in inheritance hierarchies.

- The differences between **public**, **protected** and **private** inheritance.

- To use inheritance to customize existing software.

19.1 Introduction

This chapter continues our discussion of object-oriented programming (OOP) by introducing **inheritance**—a form of software reuse in which you create a class that absorbs an existing class's capabilities, then *customizes* or enhances them. Software reuse saves time during program development by taking advantage of proven, high-quality software.

When creating a class, instead of writing completely new data members and member functions, you can specify that the new class should **inherit** the members of an existing class. This existing class is called the **base class**, and the new class is called the **derived class**. Other programming languages, such as Java and C#, refer to the base class as the **superclass** and the derived class as the **subclass**. A derived class represents a *more specialized* group of objects.

C++ offers public, protected and private inheritance. In this chapter, we concentrate on public inheritance and briefly explain the other two. *With public inheritance, every object of a derived class is also an object of that derived class's base class.* However, base-class objects are *not* objects of their derived classes. For example, if we have Vehicle as a base class and Car as a derived class, then all Cars are Vehicles, but not all Vehicles are Cars—for example, a Vehicle could also be a Truck or a Boat.

We distinguish between the *is-a* **relationship** and the *has-a* relationship. The *is-a* relationship represents inheritance. In an *is-a* relationship, an object of a derived class also can be treated as an object of its base class—for example, a Car *is a* Vehicle, so any attributes and behaviors of a Vehicle are also attributes and behaviors of a Car. By contrast, the *has-a* relationship represents *composition*, which was discussed in Chapter 17. In a *has-a* relationship, an object *contains* one or more objects of other classes as members. For example, a Car has many components—it *has a* steering wheel, *has a* brake pedal, *has a* transmission, etc.

19.2 Base Classes and Derived Classes

Figure 19.1 lists several simple examples of base classes and derived classes. Base classes tend to be *more general* and derived classes tend to be *more specific*.

Base class	Derived classes
Student	GraduateStudent, UndergraduateStudent
Shape	Circle, Triangle, Rectangle, Sphere, Cube
Loan	CarLoan, HomeImprovementLoan, MortgageLoan
Employee	Faculty, Staff
Account	CheckingAccount, SavingsAccount

Fig. 19.1 | Inheritance examples.

Because every derived-class object *is an* object of its base class, and one base class can have *many* derived classes, the set of objects represented by a base class typically is *larger* than the set of objects represented by any of its derived classes. For example, the base class Vehicle represents all vehicles, including cars, trucks, boats, airplanes, bicycles and so on. By contrast, derived class Car represents a *smaller, more specific* subset of all vehicles.

Inheritance relationships form **class hierarchies**. A base class exists in a hierarchical relationship with its derived classes. Although classes can exist independently, once they're employed in inheritance relationships, they become affiliated with other classes. A class becomes either a base class—supplying members to other classes, a derived class—inheriting its members from other classes, or *both*.

CommunityMember Class Hierarchy

Let's develop a simple inheritance hierarchy with five levels (represented by the UML class diagram in Fig. 19.2). A university community has thousands of CommunityMembers.

These CommunityMembers consist of Employees, Students and alumni (each of class Alumnus). Employees are either Faculty or Staff. Faculty are either Administrators or

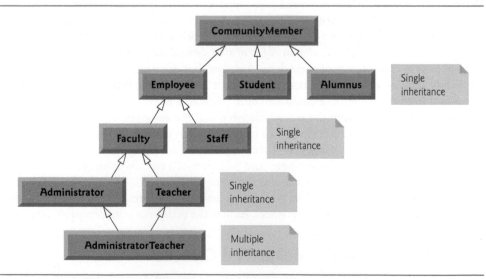

Fig. 19.2 | Inheritance hierarchy for university CommunityMembers.

Teachers. Some Administrators, however, are also Teachers. We've used *multiple inheritance* to form class AdministratorTeacher. With **single inheritance**, a class is derived from *one* base class. With **multiple inheritance**, a derived class inherits simultaneously from *two or more* (possibly unrelated) base classes. Multiple inheritance is generally discouraged.

Each arrow in the hierarchy (Fig. 19.2) represents an *is-a* relationship. For example, as we follow the arrows in this class hierarchy, we can state "an Employee *is a* CommunityMember" and "a Teacher *is a* Faculty member." CommunityMember is the **direct base class** of Employee, Student and Alumnus. In addition, CommunityMember is an **indirect base class** of all the other classes in the diagram. An indirect base class is inherited from two or more levels up the class hierarchy.

Starting from the bottom of the diagram, you can follow the arrows upwards and apply the *is-a* relationship to the topmost base class. For example, an AdministratorTeacher *is an* Administrator, *is a* Faculty member, *is an* Employee and *is a* CommunityMember.

Shape Class Hierarchy

Now consider the Shape inheritance hierarchy in Fig. 19.3. This hierarchy begins with base class Shape. Classes TwoDimensionalShape and ThreeDimensionalShape derive from base class Shape—a Shape *is a* TwoDimensionalShape or *is a* ThreeDimensionalShape. The third level of this hierarchy contains *more specific* types of TwoDimensionalShapes and ThreeDimensionalShapes. As in Fig. 19.2, we can follow the arrows from the bottom of the diagram upwards to the topmost base class in this hierarchy to identify several *is-a* relationships. For instance, a Triangle *is a* TwoDimensionalShape and *is a* Shape, while a Sphere *is a* ThreeDimensionalShape and *is a* Shape.

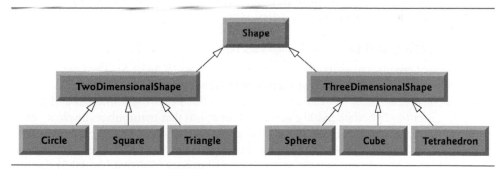

Fig. 19.3 | Inheritance hierarchy for Shapes.

To specify that class TwoDimensionalShape (Fig. 19.3) is derived from (or inherits from) class Shape, class TwoDimensionalShape's definition could begin as follows:

```
class TwoDimensionalShape : public Shape
```

This is an example of **public inheritance**, the most commonly used form. We'll also discuss **private inheritance** and **protected inheritance** (Section 19.5). With all forms of inheritance, private members of a base class are *not* accessible directly from that class's derived classes, but these private base-class members are still inherited (i.e., they're still considered parts of the derived classes). With public inheritance, all other base-class members retain their original member access when they become members of the derived class (e.g., public members of the base class become public members of the derived class, and, as we'll soon see, protected members of the base class become protected members of the derived class). Through inherited base-class member functions, the derived class can manipulate private members of the base class (if these inherited member functions provide such functionality in the base class). Note that friend functions are *not* inherited.

Inheritance is *not* appropriate for every class relationship. In Chapter 17, we discussed the *has-a* relationship, in which classes have members that are objects of other classes. Such relationships create classes by *composition* of existing classes. For example, given the classes Employee, BirthDate and TelephoneNumber, it's improper to say that an Employee *is a* BirthDate or that an Employee *is a* TelephoneNumber. However, it is appropriate to say that an Employee *has a* BirthDate and that an Employee *has a* TelephoneNumber.

It's possible to treat base-class objects and derived-class objects similarly; their commonalities are expressed in the members of the base class. Objects of all classes derived from a common base class can be treated as objects of that base class (i.e., such objects have an *is-a* relationship with the base class). In Chapter 20, we consider many examples that take advantage of this relationship.

19.3 Relationship between Base and Derived Classes

In this section, we use an inheritance hierarchy containing types of employees in a company's payroll application to discuss the relationship between a base class and a derived class. Commission employees (who will be represented as objects of a base class) are paid a percentage of their sales, while base-salaried commission employees (who will be represented as objects of a derived class) receive a base salary plus a percentage of their sales. We divide our discussion of the relationship between commission employees and base-salaried commission employees into a carefully paced series of five examples.

19.3.1 Creating and Using a CommissionEmployee Class

Let's examine CommissionEmployee's class definition (Figs. 19.4–19.5). The Commission-Employee header (Fig. 19.4) specifies class CommissionEmployee's public services, which include a constructor (lines 11–12) and member functions earnings (line 29) and print (line 30). Lines 14–27 declare public *get* and *set* functions that manipulate the class's data members (declared in lines 32–36) firstName, lastName, socialSecurityNumber, grossSales and commissionRate. Member functions setGrossSales (defined in lines 57–63 of Fig. 19.5) and setCommissionRate (defined in lines 72–78 of Fig. 19.5), for example, validate their arguments before assigning the values to data members grossSales and commissionRate, respectively.

```
 1   // Fig. 19.4: CommissionEmployee.h
 2   // CommissionEmployee class definition represents a commission employee.
 3   #ifndef COMMISSION_H
 4   #define COMMISSION_H
 5
 6   #include <string> // C++ standard string class
 7
```

Fig. 19.4 | CommissionEmployee class header. (Part 1 of 2.)

```
 8   class CommissionEmployee
 9   {
10   public:
11      CommissionEmployee( const std::string &, const std::string &,
12         const std::string &, double = 0.0, double = 0.0 );
13
14      void setFirstName( const std::string & ); // set first name
15      std::string getFirstName() const; // return first name
16
17      void setLastName( const std::string & ); // set last name
18      std::string getLastName() const; // return last name
19
20      void setSocialSecurityNumber( const std::string & ); // set SSN
21      std::string getSocialSecurityNumber() const; // return SSN
22
23      void setGrossSales( double ); // set gross sales amount
24      double getGrossSales() const; // return gross sales amount
25
26      void setCommissionRate( double ); // set commission rate (percentage)
27      double getCommissionRate() const; // return commission rate
28
29      double earnings() const; // calculate earnings
30      void print() const; // print CommissionEmployee object
31   private:
32      std::string firstName;
33      std::string lastName;
34      std::string socialSecurityNumber;
35      double grossSales; // gross weekly sales
36      double commissionRate; // commission percentage
37   }; // end class CommissionEmployee
38
39   #endif
```

Fig. 19.4 | CommissionEmployee class header. (Part 2 of 2.)

```
 1   // Fig. 19.5: CommissionEmployee.cpp
 2   // Class CommissionEmployee member-function definitions.
 3   #include <iostream>
 4   #include <stdexcept>
 5   #include "CommissionEmployee.h" // CommissionEmployee class definition
 6   using namespace std;
 7
 8   // constructor
 9   CommissionEmployee::CommissionEmployee(
10      const string &first, const string &last, const string &ssn,
11      double sales, double rate )
12   {
13      firstName = first; // should validate
14      lastName = last; // should validate
15      socialSecurityNumber = ssn; // should validate
16      setGrossSales( sales ); // validate and store gross sales
```

Fig. 19.5 | Implementation file for CommissionEmployee class that represents an employee who is paid a percentage of gross sales. (Part 1 of 3.)

```
17      setCommissionRate( rate ); // validate and store commission rate
18   } // end CommissionEmployee constructor
19
20   // set first name
21   void CommissionEmployee::setFirstName( const string &first )
22   {
23      firstName = first; // should validate
24   } // end function setFirstName
25
26   // return first name
27   string CommissionEmployee::getFirstName() const
28   {
29      return firstName;
30   } // end function getFirstName
31
32   // set last name
33   void CommissionEmployee::setLastName( const string &last )
34   {
35      lastName = last; // should validate
36   } // end function setLastName
37
38   // return last name
39   string CommissionEmployee::getLastName() const
40   {
41      return lastName;
42   } // end function getLastName
43
44   // set social security number
45   void CommissionEmployee::setSocialSecurityNumber( const string &ssn )
46   {
47      socialSecurityNumber = ssn; // should validate
48   } // end function setSocialSecurityNumber
49
50   // return social security number
51   string CommissionEmployee::getSocialSecurityNumber() const
52   {
53      return socialSecurityNumber;
54   } // end function getSocialSecurityNumber
55
56   // set gross sales amount
57   void CommissionEmployee::setGrossSales( double sales )
58   {
59      if ( sales >= 0.0 )
60         grossSales = sales;
61      else
62         throw invalid_argument( "Gross sales must be >= 0.0" );
63   } // end function setGrossSales
64
65   // return gross sales amount
66   double CommissionEmployee::getGrossSales() const
67   {
```

Fig. 19.5 | Implementation file for CommissionEmployee class that represents an employee who is paid a percentage of gross sales. (Part 2 of 3.)

```
68        return grossSales;
69    } // end function getGrossSales
70
71    // set commission rate
72    void CommissionEmployee::setCommissionRate( double rate )
73    {
74        if ( rate > 0.0 && rate < 1.0 )
75            commissionRate = rate;
76        else
77            throw invalid_argument( "Commission rate must be > 0.0 and < 1.0" );
78    } // end function setCommissionRate
79
80    // return commission rate
81    double CommissionEmployee::getCommissionRate() const
82    {
83        return commissionRate;
84    } // end function getCommissionRate
85
86    // calculate earnings
87    double CommissionEmployee::earnings() const
88    {
89        return commissionRate * grossSales;
90    } // end function earnings
91
92    // print CommissionEmployee object
93    void CommissionEmployee::print() const
94    {
95        cout << "commission employee: " << firstName << ' ' << lastName
96            << "\nsocial security number: " << socialSecurityNumber
97            << "\ngross sales: " << grossSales
98            << "\ncommission rate: " << commissionRate;
99    } // end function print
```

Fig. 19.5 | Implementation file for CommissionEmployee class that represents an employee who is paid a percentage of gross sales. (Part 3 of 3.)

CommissionEmployee *Constructor*

The CommissionEmployee constructor definition *purposely does not use member-initializer syntax* in the first several examples of this section, so that we can demonstrate how private and protected specifiers affect member access in derived classes. As shown in Fig. 19.5, lines 13–15, we assign values to data members firstName, lastName and socialSecurityNumber in the constructor body. Later in this section, we'll return to using member-initializer lists in the constructors.

We do not validate the values of the constructor's arguments first, last and ssn before assigning them to the corresponding data members. We certainly could validate the first and last names—perhaps by ensuring that they're of a reasonable length. Similarly, a social security number could be validated to ensure that it contains nine digits, with or without dashes (e.g., 123-45-6789 or 123456789).

CommissionEmployee *Member Functions* earnings *and* print

Member function earnings (lines 87–90) calculates a CommissionEmployee's earnings. Line 89 multiplies the commissionRate by the grossSales and returns the result. Member function print (lines 93–99) displays the values of a CommissionEmployee object's data members.

Testing Class *CommissionEmployee*

Figure 19.6 tests class CommissionEmployee. Lines 11–12 instantiate CommissionEmployee object employee and invoke the constructor to initialize the object with "Sue" as the first name, "Jones" as the last name, "222-22-2222" as the social security number, 10000 as the gross sales amount and .06 as the commission rate. Lines 19–24 use employee's *get* functions to display the values of its data members. Lines 26–27 invoke the object's member functions setGrossSales and setCommissionRate to change the values of data members grossSales and commissionRate, respectively. Line 31 then calls employee's print member function to output the updated CommissionEmployee information. Finally, line 34 displays the CommissionEmployee's earnings, calculated by the object's earnings member function using the updated values of data members grossSales and commissionRate.

```cpp
1   // Fig. 19.6: fig19_06.cpp
2   // CommissionEmployee class test program.
3   #include <iostream>
4   #include <iomanip>
5   #include "CommissionEmployee.h" // CommissionEmployee class definition
6   using namespace std;
7
8   int main()
9   {
10      // instantiate a CommissionEmployee object
11      CommissionEmployee employee(
12         "Sue", "Jones", "222-22-2222", 10000, .06 );
13
14      // set floating-point output formatting
15      cout << fixed << setprecision( 2 );
16
17      // get commission employee data
18      cout << "Employee information obtained by get functions: \n"
19         << "\nFirst name is " << employee.getFirstName()
20         << "\nLast name is " << employee.getLastName()
21         << "\nSocial security number is "
22         << employee.getSocialSecurityNumber()
23         << "\nGross sales is " << employee.getGrossSales()
24         << "\nCommission rate is " << employee.getCommissionRate() << endl;
25
26      employee.setGrossSales( 8000 ); // set gross sales
27      employee.setCommissionRate( .1 ); // set commission rate
28
29      cout << "\nUpdated employee information output by print function: \n"
30         << endl;
31      employee.print(); // display the new employee information
32
33      // display the employee's earnings
34      cout << "\n\nEmployee's earnings: $" << employee.earnings() << endl;
35   } // end main
```

Fig. 19.6 | CommissionEmployee class test program. (Part 1 of 2.)

```
Employee information obtained by get functions:

First name is Sue
Last name is Jones
Social security number is 222-22-2222
Gross sales is 10000.00
Commission rate is 0.06

Updated employee information output by print function:

commission employee: Sue Jones
social security number: 222-22-2222
gross sales: 8000.00
commission rate: 0.10

Employee's earnings: $800.00
```

Fig. 19.6 | CommissionEmployee class test program. (Part 2 of 2.)

19.3.2 Creating a BasePlusCommissionEmployee Class Without Using Inheritance

We now discuss the second part of our introduction to inheritance by creating and testing (a completely new and independent) class BasePlusCommissionEmployee (Figs. 19.7–19.8), which contains a first name, last name, social security number, gross sales amount, commission rate *and* base salary.

```
 1  // Fig. 19.7: BasePlusCommissionEmployee.h
 2  // BasePlusCommissionEmployee class definition represents an employee
 3  // that receives a base salary in addition to commission.
 4  #ifndef BASEPLUS_H
 5  #define BASEPLUS_H
 6
 7  #include <string> // C++ standard string class
 8
 9  class BasePlusCommissionEmployee
10  {
11  public:
12     BasePlusCommissionEmployee( const std::string &, const std::string &,
13        const std::string &, double = 0.0, double = 0.0, double = 0.0 );
14
15     void setFirstName( const std::string & ); // set first name
16     std::string getFirstName() const; // return first name
17
18     void setLastName( const std::string & ); // set last name
19     std::string getLastName() const; // return last name
20
21     void setSocialSecurityNumber( const std::string & ); // set SSN
22     std::string getSocialSecurityNumber() const; // return SSN
23
24     void setGrossSales( double ); // set gross sales amount
25     double getGrossSales() const; // return gross sales amount
```

Fig. 19.7 | BasePlusCommissionEmployee class header. (Part 1 of 2.)

```
26
27      void setCommissionRate( double ); // set commission rate
28      double getCommissionRate() const; // return commission rate
29
30      void setBaseSalary( double ); // set base salary
31      double getBaseSalary() const; // return base salary
32
33      double earnings() const; // calculate earnings
34      void print() const; // print BasePlusCommissionEmployee object
35  private:
36      std::string firstName;
37      std::string lastName;
38      std::string socialSecurityNumber;
39      double grossSales; // gross weekly sales
40      double commissionRate; // commission percentage
41      double baseSalary; // base salary
42  }; // end class BasePlusCommissionEmployee
43
44  #endif
```

Fig. 19.7 | BasePlusCommissionEmployee class header. (Part 2 of 2.)

```
1   // Fig. 19.8: BasePlusCommissionEmployee.cpp
2   // Class BasePlusCommissionEmployee member-function definitions.
3   #include <iostream>
4   #include <stdexcept>
5   #include "BasePlusCommissionEmployee.h"
6   using namespace std;
7
8   // constructor
9   BasePlusCommissionEmployee::BasePlusCommissionEmployee(
10      const string &first, const string &last, const string &ssn,
11      double sales, double rate, double salary )
12  {
13      firstName = first; // should validate
14      lastName = last; // should validate
15      socialSecurityNumber = ssn; // should validate
16      setGrossSales( sales ); // validate and store gross sales
17      setCommissionRate( rate ); // validate and store commission rate
18      setBaseSalary( salary ); // validate and store base salary
19  } // end BasePlusCommissionEmployee constructor
20
21  // set first name
22  void BasePlusCommissionEmployee::setFirstName( const string &first )
23  {
24      firstName = first; // should validate
25  } // end function setFirstName
26
27  // return first name
28  string BasePlusCommissionEmployee::getFirstName() const
29  {
```

Fig. 19.8 | BasePlusCommissionEmployee class represents an employee who receives a base salary in addition to a commission. (Part 1 of 3.)

```
30       return firstName;
31    } // end function getFirstName
32
33    // set last name
34    void BasePlusCommissionEmployee::setLastName( const string &last )
35    {
36       lastName = last; // should validate
37    } // end function setLastName
38
39    // return last name
40    string BasePlusCommissionEmployee::getLastName() const
41    {
42       return lastName;
43    } // end function getLastName
44
45    // set social security number
46    void BasePlusCommissionEmployee::setSocialSecurityNumber(
47       const string &ssn )
48    {
49       socialSecurityNumber = ssn; // should validate
50    } // end function setSocialSecurityNumber
51
52    // return social security number
53    string BasePlusCommissionEmployee::getSocialSecurityNumber() const
54    {
55       return socialSecurityNumber;
56    } // end function getSocialSecurityNumber
57
58    // set gross sales amount
59    void BasePlusCommissionEmployee::setGrossSales( double sales )
60    {
61       if ( sales >= 0.0 )
62          grossSales = sales;
63       else
64          throw invalid_argument( "Gross sales must be >= 0.0" );
65    } // end function setGrossSales
66
67    // return gross sales amount
68    double BasePlusCommissionEmployee::getGrossSales() const
69    {
70       return grossSales;
71    } // end function getGrossSales
72
73    // set commission rate
74    void BasePlusCommissionEmployee::setCommissionRate( double rate )
75    {
76       if ( rate > 0.0 && rate < 1.0 )
77          commissionRate = rate;
78       else
79          throw invalid_argument( "Commission rate must be > 0.0 and < 1.0" );
80    } // end function setCommissionRate
81
```

Fig. 19.8 | BasePlusCommissionEmployee class represents an employee who receives a base salary in addition to a commission. (Part 2 of 3.)

```
82   // return commission rate
83   double BasePlusCommissionEmployee::getCommissionRate() const
84   {
85      return commissionRate;
86   } // end function getCommissionRate
87
88   // set base salary
89   void BasePlusCommissionEmployee::setBaseSalary( double salary )
90   {
91      if ( salary >= 0.0 )
92         baseSalary = salary;
93      else
94         throw invalid_argument( "Salary must be >= 0.0" );
95   } // end function setBaseSalary
96
97   // return base salary
98   double BasePlusCommissionEmployee::getBaseSalary() const
99   {
100     return baseSalary;
101  } // end function getBaseSalary
102
103  // calculate earnings
104  double BasePlusCommissionEmployee::earnings() const
105  {
106     return baseSalary + ( commissionRate * grossSales );
107  } // end function earnings
108
109  // print BasePlusCommissionEmployee object
110  void BasePlusCommissionEmployee::print() const
111  {
112     cout << "base-salaried commission employee: " << firstName << ' '
113        << lastName << "\nsocial security number: " << socialSecurityNumber
114        << "\ngross sales: " << grossSales
115        << "\ncommission rate: " << commissionRate
116        << "\nbase salary: " << baseSalary;
117  } // end function print
```

Fig. 19.8 | BasePlusCommissionEmployee class represents an employee who receives a base salary in addition to a commission. (Part 3 of 3.)

Defining Class *BasePlusCommissionEmployee*

The BasePlusCommissionEmployee header (Fig. 19.7) specifies class BasePlusCommissionEmployee's public services, which include the BasePlusCommissionEmployee constructor (lines 12–13) and member functions earnings (line 33) and print (line 34). Lines 15–31 declare public *get* and *set* functions for the class's private data members (declared in lines 36–41) firstName, lastName, socialSecurityNumber, grossSales, commissionRate *and* baseSalary. These variables and member functions encapsulate all the necessary features of a base-salaried commission employee. Note the similarity between this class and class CommissionEmployee (Figs. 19.4–19.5)—in this example, we do *not* yet exploit that similarity.

Class BasePlusCommissionEmployee's earnings member function (defined in lines 104–107 of Fig. 19.8) computes the earnings of a base-salaried commission employee.

Line 106 returns the result of adding the employee's base salary to the product of the commission rate and the employee's gross sales.

Testing Class **BasePlusCommissionEmployee**

Figure 19.9 tests class BasePlusCommissionEmployee. Lines 11–12 instantiate object employee of class BasePlusCommissionEmployee, passing "Bob", "Lewis", "333-33-3333", 5000, .04 and 300 to the constructor as the first name, last name, social security number, gross sales, commission rate *and* base salary, respectively. Lines 19–25 use BasePlus-CommissionEmployee's *get* functions to retrieve the values of the object's data members for output. Line 27 invokes the object's setBaseSalary member function to change the base salary. Member function setBaseSalary (Fig. 19.8, lines 89–95) ensures that data member baseSalary is not assigned a negative value, because an employee's base salary cannot be negative. Line 31 of Fig. 19.9 invokes the object's print member function to output the updated BasePlusCommissionEmployee's information, and line 34 calls member function earnings to display the BasePlusCommissionEmployee's earnings.

```cpp
1   // Fig. 19.9: fig19_09.cpp
2   // BasePlusCommissionEmployee class test program.
3   #include <iostream>
4   #include <iomanip>
5   #include "BasePlusCommissionEmployee.h"
6   using namespace std;
7
8   int main()
9   {
10      // instantiate BasePlusCommissionEmployee object
11      BasePlusCommissionEmployee
12         employee( "Bob", "Lewis", "333-33-3333", 5000, .04, 300 );
13
14      // set floating-point output formatting
15      cout << fixed << setprecision( 2 );
16
17      // get commission employee data
18      cout << "Employee information obtained by get functions: \n"
19         << "\nFirst name is " << employee.getFirstName()
20         << "\nLast name is " << employee.getLastName()
21         << "\nSocial security number is "
22         << employee.getSocialSecurityNumber()
23         << "\nGross sales is " << employee.getGrossSales()
24         << "\nCommission rate is " << employee.getCommissionRate()
25         << "\nBase salary is " << employee.getBaseSalary() << endl;
26
27      employee.setBaseSalary( 1000 ); // set base salary
28
29      cout << "\nUpdated employee information output by print function: \n"
30         << endl;
31      employee.print(); // display the new employee information
32
33      // display the employee's earnings
34      cout << "\n\nEmployee's earnings: $" << employee.earnings() << endl;
35   } // end main
```

Fig. 19.9 | BasePlusCommissionEmployee class test program. (Part 1 of 2.)

```
Employee information obtained by get functions:

First name is Bob
Last name is Lewis
Social security number is 333-33-3333
Gross sales is 5000.00
Commission rate is 0.04
Base salary is 300.00

Updated employee information output by print function:

base-salaried commission employee: Bob Lewis
social security number: 333-33-3333
gross sales: 5000.00
commission rate: 0.04
base salary: 1000.00

Employee's earnings: $1200.00
```

Fig. 19.9 | BasePlusCommissionEmployee class test program. (Part 2 of 2.)

Exploring the Similarities Between Class BasePlusCommissionEmployee and Class CommissionEmployee

Most of the code for class BasePlusCommissionEmployee (Figs. 19.7–19.8) is *similar, if not identical,* to the code for class CommissionEmployee (Figs. 19.4–19.5). For example, in class BasePlusCommissionEmployee, private data members firstName and lastName and member functions setFirstName, getFirstName, setLastName and getLastName are identical to those of class CommissionEmployee. Classes CommissionEmployee and Base-PlusCommissionEmployee also both contain private data members socialSecurity-Number, commissionRate and grossSales, as well as *get* and *set* functions to manipulate these members. In addition, the BasePlusCommissionEmployee constructor is *almost* identical to that of class CommissionEmployee, except that BasePlusCommissionEmployee's constructor *also* sets the baseSalary. The other additions to class BasePlusCommission-Employee are private data member baseSalary *and* member functions setBaseSalary and getBaseSalary. Class BasePlusCommissionEmployee's print member function is *nearly identical* to that of class CommissionEmployee, except that BasePlusCommissionEmployee's print *also* outputs the value of data member baseSalary.

We literally *copied* code from class CommissionEmployee and *pasted* it into class Base-PlusCommissionEmployee, then modified class BasePlusCommissionEmployee to include a base salary and member functions that manipulate the base salary. This *copy-and-paste approach* is error prone and time consuming.

Software Engineering Observation 19.1

Copying and pasting code *from one class to another can spread many physical* copies of the same code *and can spread* errors *throughout a system, creating a code-maintenance nightmare. To avoid duplicating code (and possibly errors), use* inheritance, *rather than the "copy-and-paste" approach, in situations where you want one class to "absorb" the data members and member functions of another class.*

Software Engineering Observation 19.2

With inheritance, the common data members and member functions of all the classes in the hierarchy are declared in a base class. When changes are required for these common features, you need to make the changes only in the base class—derived classes then inherit the changes. Without inheritance, changes would need to be made to all *the source code files that contain a copy of the code in question.*

19.3.3 Creating a CommissionEmployee-BasePlusCommissionEmployee Inheritance Hierarchy

Now we create and test a new BasePlusCommissionEmployee class (Figs. 19.10–19.11) that *derives from* class CommissionEmployee (Figs. 19.4–19.5). In this example, a Base-PlusCommissionEmployee object *is a* CommissionEmployee (because inheritance passes on the capabilities of class CommissionEmployee), but class BasePlusCommissionEmployee *also* has data member baseSalary (Fig. 19.10, line 22). The *colon (:)* in line 10 of the class definition indicates inheritance. Keyword public indicates the *type of inheritance.* As a derived class (formed with public inheritance), BasePlusCommissionEmployee inherits *all* the members of class CommissionEmployee, *except* for the constructor—each class provides its *own* constructors that are specific to the class. (Destructors, too, are not inherited.) Thus, the public services of BasePlusCommissionEmployee include its constructor (lines 13–14) and the public member functions inherited from class CommissionEmployee—*although we cannot see these inherited member functions* in BasePlusCommissionEmployee's source code, they're nevertheless a part of derived class BasePlusCommissionEmployee. The derived class's public services also include member functions setBaseSalary, get-BaseSalary, earnings and print (lines 16–20).

```
1   // Fig. 19.10: BasePlusCommissionEmployee.h
2   // BasePlusCommissionEmployee class derived from class
3   // CommissionEmployee.
4   #ifndef BASEPLUS_H
5   #define BASEPLUS_H
6
7   #include <string> // C++ standard string class
8   #include "CommissionEmployee.h" // CommissionEmployee class declaration
9
10  class BasePlusCommissionEmployee : public CommissionEmployee
11  {
12  public:
13     BasePlusCommissionEmployee( const std::string &, const std::string &,
14        const std::string &, double = 0.0, double = 0.0, double = 0.0 );
15
16     void setBaseSalary( double ); // set base salary
17     double getBaseSalary() const; // return base salary
18
19     double earnings() const; // calculate earnings
20     void print() const; // print BasePlusCommissionEmployee object
```

Fig. 19.10 | BasePlusCommissionEmployee class definition indicating inheritance relationship with class CommissionEmployee. (Part 1 of 2.)

```
21   private:
22      double baseSalary; // base salary
23   }; // end class BasePlusCommissionEmployee
24
25   #endif
```

Fig. 19.10 | BasePlusCommissionEmployee class definition indicating inheritance relationship with class CommissionEmployee. (Part 2 of 2.)

```
1    // Fig. 19.11: BasePlusCommissionEmployee.cpp
2    // Class BasePlusCommissionEmployee member-function definitions.
3    #include <iostream>
4    #include <stdexcept>
5    #include "BasePlusCommissionEmployee.h"
6    using namespace std;
7
8    // constructor
9    BasePlusCommissionEmployee::BasePlusCommissionEmployee(
10      const string &first, const string &last, const string &ssn,
11      double sales, double rate, double salary )
12      // explicitly call base-class constructor
13      : CommissionEmployee( first, last, ssn, sales, rate )
14   {
15      setBaseSalary( salary ); // validate and store base salary
16   } // end BasePlusCommissionEmployee constructor
17
18   // set base salary
19   void BasePlusCommissionEmployee::setBaseSalary( double salary )
20   {
21      if ( salary >= 0.0 )
22         baseSalary = salary;
23      else
24         throw invalid_argument( "Salary must be >= 0.0" );
25   } // end function setBaseSalary
26
27   // return base salary
28   double BasePlusCommissionEmployee::getBaseSalary() const
29   {
30      return baseSalary;
31   } // end function getBaseSalary
32
33   // calculate earnings
34   double BasePlusCommissionEmployee::earnings() const
35   {
36      // derived class cannot access the base class's private data
37      return baseSalary + ( commissionRate * grossSales );
38   } // end function earnings
39
```

Fig. 19.11 | BasePlusCommissionEmployee implementation file: private base-class data cannot be accessed from derived class. (Part 1 of 2.)

```
40   // print BasePlusCommissionEmployee object
41   void BasePlusCommissionEmployee::print() const
42   {
43       // derived class cannot access the base class's private data
44       cout << "base-salaried commission employee: " << firstName << ' '
45           << lastName << "\nsocial security number: " << socialSecurityNumber
46           << "\ngross sales: " << grossSales
47           << "\ncommission rate: " << commissionRate
48           << "\nbase salary: " << baseSalary;
49   } // end function print
```

Compilation Errors from the LLVM Compiler in Xcode

```
BasePlusCommissionEmployee.cpp:37:26:
   'commissionRate' is a private member of 'CommissionEmployee'
BasePlusCommissionEmployee.cpp:37:43:
   'grossSales' is a private member of 'CommissionEmployee'
BasePlusCommissionEmployee.cpp:44:53:
   'firstName' is a private member of 'CommissionEmployee'
BasePlusCommissionEmployee.cpp:45:10:
   'lastName' is a private member of 'CommissionEmployee'
BasePlusCommissionEmployee.cpp:45:54:
   'socialSecurityNumber' is a private member of 'CommissionEmployee'
BasePlusCommissionEmployee.cpp:46:31:
   'grossSales' is a private member of 'CommissionEmployee'
BasePlusCommissionEmployee.cpp:47:35:
   'commissionRate' is a private member of 'CommissionEmployee'
```

Fig. 19.11 | BasePlusCommissionEmployee implementation file: private base-class data cannot be accessed from derived class. (Part 2 of 2.)

Figure 19.11 shows BasePlusCommissionEmployee's member-function implementations. The constructor (lines 9–16) introduces **base-class initializer syntax** (line 13), which uses a member initializer to pass arguments to the base-class (CommissionEmployee) constructor. C++ requires that a derived-class constructor call its base-class constructor to initialize the base-class data members that are inherited into the derived class. Line 13 does this by *explicitly* invoking the CommissionEmployee constructor by name, passing the constructor's parameters first, last, ssn, sales and rate as arguments to initialize the base-class data members firstName, lastName, socialSecurityNumber, grossSales and commissionRate, respectively. If BasePlusCommissionEmployee's constructor did *not* invoke class CommissionEmployee's constructor *explicitly*, C++ would attempt to invoke class CommissionEmployee's default constructor implicitly—but the class does *not* have such a constructor, so the compiler would issue an *error*. Recall from Chapter 16 that the compiler provides a default constructor with no parameters in any class that does *not* explicitly include a constructor. However, CommissionEmployee *does* explicitly include a constructor, so a default constructor is *not* provided.

Common Programming Error 19.1
When a derived-class constructor calls a base-class constructor, the arguments passed to the base-class constructor must be consistent with the number and types of parameters specified in one of the base-class constructors; otherwise, a compilation error occurs.

Performance Tip 19.1

In a derived-class constructor, invoking base-class constructors and initializing member objects explicitly in the member initializer list prevents duplicate initialization in which a default constructor is called, then data members are modified again in the derived-class constructor's body.

Compilation Errors from Accessing Base-Class *private* Members

The compiler generates errors for line 37 of Fig. 19.11 because base class CommissionEmployee's data members commissionRate and grossSales are private—derived class BasePlusCommissionEmployee's member functions are *not* allowed to access base class CommissionEmployee's private data. The compiler issues additional errors in lines 44–47 of BasePlusCommissionEmployee's print member function for the same reason. As you can see, C++ rigidly enforces restrictions on accessing private data members, so that *even a derived class (which is intimately related to its base class) cannot access the base class's private data.*

Preventing the Errors in *BasePlusCommissionEmployee*

We purposely included the erroneous code in Fig. 19.11 to emphasize that a derived class's member functions *cannot* access its base class's private data. The errors in BasePlusCommissionEmployee could have been prevented by using the *get* member functions inherited from class CommissionEmployee. For example, line 37 could have invoked getCommissionRate and getGrossSales to access CommissionEmployee's private data members commissionRate and grossSales, respectively. Similarly, lines 44–47 could have used appropriate *get* member functions to retrieve the values of the base class's data members. In the next example, we show how using protected data *also* allows us to avoid the errors encountered in this example.

Including the Base-Class Header in the Derived-Class Header with *#include*

Notice that we #include the base class's header in the derived class's header (line 8 of Fig. 19.10). This is necessary for three reasons. First, for the derived class to use the base class's name in line 10, we must tell the compiler that the base class exists—the class definition in CommissionEmployee.h does exactly that.

The second reason is that the compiler uses a class definition to determine the *size* of an object of that class (as we discussed in Section 16.6). A client program that creates an object of a class #includes the class definition to enable the compiler to reserve the proper amount of memory for the object. When using inheritance, a derived-class object's size depends on the data members declared explicitly in its class definition *and* the data members *inherited* from its direct and indirect base classes. Including the base class's definition in line 8 allows the compiler to determine the memory requirements for the base class's data members that become part of a derived-class object and thus contribute to the total size of the derived-class object.

The last reason for line 8 is to allow the compiler to determine whether the derived class uses the base class's inherited members properly. For example, in the program of Figs. 19.10–19.11, the compiler uses the base-class header to determine that the data members being accessed by the derived class are private in the base class. Since these are *inaccessible* to the derived class, the compiler generates errors. The compiler also uses the base class's *function prototypes* to *validate* function calls made by the derived class to the inherited base-class functions.

Linking Process in an Inheritance Hierarchy

In Section 16.7, we discussed the linking process for creating an executable GradeBook application. In that example, you saw that the client's object code was linked with the object code for class GradeBook, as well as the object code for any C++ Standard Library classes used in either the client code or in class GradeBook.

The linking process is similar for a program that uses classes in an inheritance hierarchy. The process requires the object code for all classes used in the program and the object code for the direct and indirect base classes of any derived classes used by the program. Suppose a client wants to create an application that uses class BasePlusCommission-Employee, which is a derived class of CommissionEmployee (we'll see an example of this in Section 19.3.4). When compiling the client application, the client's object code must be linked with the object code for classes BasePlusCommissionEmployee and Commission-Employee, because BasePlusCommissionEmployee inherits member functions from its base class CommissionEmployee. The code is also linked with the object code for any C++ Standard Library classes used in class CommissionEmployee, class BasePlusCommission-Employee or the client code. This provides the program with access to the implementations of all of the functionality that the program may use.

19.3.4 CommissionEmployee–BasePlusCommissionEmployee Inheritance Hierarchy Using protected Data

Chapter 16 introduced access specifiers public and private. A base class's public members are accessible within its body and anywhere that the program has a handle (i.e., a name, reference or pointer) to an object of that class or one of its derived classes. A base class's private members are accessible only within its body and to the friends of that base class. In this section, we introduce the access specifier **protected**.

Using protected access offers an intermediate level of protection between public and private access. To enable class BasePlusCommissionEmployee to *directly access* CommissionEmployee data members firstName, lastName, socialSecurityNumber, grossSales and commissionRate, we can declare those members as protected in the base class. A base class's protected members *can* be accessed within the body of that base class, by members and friends of that base class, and by members and friends of any classes derived from that base class.

Defining Base Class CommissionEmployee with protected Data

Class CommissionEmployee (Fig. 19.12) now declares data members firstName, last-Name, socialSecurityNumber, grossSales and commissionRate as protected (lines 31–36) rather than private. The member-function implementations are identical to those in Fig. 19.5, so CommissionEmployee.cpp is not shown here.

```
1   // Fig. 19.12: CommissionEmployee.h
2   // CommissionEmployee class definition with protected data.
3   #ifndef COMMISSION_H
4   #define COMMISSION_H
5
```

Fig. 19.12 | CommissionEmployee class definition that declares protected data to allow access by derived classes. (Part 1 of 2.)

```
6    #include <string> // C++ standard string class
7
8    class CommissionEmployee
9    {
10   public:
11      CommissionEmployee( const std::string &, const std::string &,
12         const std::string &, double = 0.0, double = 0.0 );
13
14      void setFirstName( const std::string & ); // set first name
15      std::string getFirstName() const; // return first name
16
17      void setLastName( const std::string & ); // set last name
18      std::string getLastName() const; // return last name
19
20      void setSocialSecurityNumber( const std::string & ); // set SSN
21      std::string getSocialSecurityNumber() const; // return SSN
22
23      void setGrossSales( double ); // set gross sales amount
24      double getGrossSales() const; // return gross sales amount
25
26      void setCommissionRate( double ); // set commission rate
27      double getCommissionRate() const; // return commission rate
28
29      double earnings() const; // calculate earnings
30      void print() const; // print CommissionEmployee object
31   protected:
32      std::string firstName;
33      std::string lastName;
34      std::string socialSecurityNumber;
35      double grossSales; // gross weekly sales
36      double commissionRate; // commission percentage
37   }; // end class CommissionEmployee
38
39   #endif
```

Fig. 19.12 | CommissionEmployee class definition that declares protected data to allow access by derived classes. (Part 2 of 2.)

Class *BasePlusCommissionEmployee*

The definition of class BasePlusCommissionEmployee from Figs. 19.10–19.11 remains *unchanged*, so we do *not* show it again here. Now that BasePlusCommissionEmployee inherits from the updated class CommissionEmployee (Fig. 19.12), BasePlusCommissionEmployee objects *can* access inherited data members that are declared protected in class CommissionEmployee (i.e., data members firstName, lastName, socialSecurityNumber, grossSales and commissionRate). As a result, the compiler does *not* generate errors when compiling the BasePlusCommissionEmployee earnings and print member-function definitions in Fig. 19.11 (lines 34–38 and 41–49, respectively). This shows the special privileges that a derived class is granted to access protected base-class data members. Objects of a derived class also can access protected members in *any* of that derived class's *indirect* base classes.

Class BasePlusCommissionEmployee does *not* inherit class CommissionEmployee's constructor. However, class BasePlusCommissionEmployee's constructor (Fig. 19.11, lines 9–16) calls class CommissionEmployee's constructor explicitly with member initializer syntax (line 13). Recall that BasePlusCommissionEmployee's constructor must *explicitly* call the constructor of class CommissionEmployee, because CommissionEmployee does *not* contain a default constructor that could be invoked implicitly.

Testing the Modified **BasePlusCommissionEmployee** *Class*
To test the updated class hierarchy, we reused the test program from Fig. 19.9. As shown in Fig. 19.13, the output is identical to that of Fig. 19.9. We created the first class Base-PlusCommissionEmployee *without using inheritance* and created this version of Base-PlusCommissionEmployee *using inheritance*; however, both classes provide the *same* functionality. The code for class BasePlusCommissionEmployee (i.e., the header and implementation files), which is 74 lines, is considerably *shorter* than the code for the noninherited version of the class, which is 161 lines, because the inherited version absorbs part of its functionality from CommissionEmployee, whereas the noninherited version does not absorb any functionality. Also, there is now only *one* copy of the CommissionEmployee functionality declared and defined in class CommissionEmployee. This makes the source code easier to maintain, modify and debug, because the source code related to a CommissionEmployee exists only in the files CommissionEmployee.h and CommissionEmployee.cpp.

```
Employee information obtained by get functions:

First name is Bob
Last name is Lewis
Social security number is 333-33-3333
Gross sales is 5000.00
Commission rate is 0.04
Base salary is 300.00

Updated employee information output by print function:

base-salaried commission employee: Bob Lewis
social security number: 333-33-3333
gross sales: 5000.00
commission rate: 0.04
base salary: 1000.00

Employee's earnings: $1200.00
```

Fig. 19.13 | protected base-class data can be accessed from derived class.

Notes on Using **protected** *Data*
In this example, we declared base-class data members as protected, so derived classes can modify the data directly. Inheriting protected data members slightly improves performance, because we can directly access the members without incurring the overhead of calls to *set* or *get* member functions.

Software Engineering Observation 19.3
In most cases, it's better to use private *data members to encourage proper software engineering, and leave code optimization issues to the compiler. Your code will be easier to maintain, modify and debug.*

Using protected data members creates two serious problems. First, the derived-class object does *not* have to use a member function to set the value of the base class's protected data member. An *invalid* value can easily be assigned to the protected data member, thus leaving the object in an *inconsistent* state—e.g., with CommissionEmployee's data member grossSales declared as protected, a derived-class object can assign a negative value to grossSales. The second problem with using protected data members is that derived-class member functions are more likely to be written so that they *depend on the base-class implementation*. Derived classes should depend only on the base-class services (i.e., non-private member functions) and *not* on the base-class implementation. With protected data members in the base class, if the base-class implementation changes, we may need to modify *all* derived classes of that base class. For example, if for some reason we were to change the names of data members firstName and lastName to first and last, then we'd have to do so for all occurrences in which a derived class references these base-class data members directly. Such software is said to be **fragile** or **brittle**, because a small change in the base class can "break" derived-class implementation. You should be able to change the base-class implementation while still providing the *same* services to derived classes. Of course, if the base-class services change, we must reimplement our derived classes—good object-oriented design attempts to prevent this.

Software Engineering Observation 19.4
It's appropriate to use the protected access specifier when a base class should provide a service (i.e., a non-private member function) only to its derived classes and friends.

Software Engineering Observation 19.5
Declaring base-class data members private (as opposed to declaring them protected) enables you to change the base-class implementation without having to change derived-class implementations.

19.3.5 CommissionEmployee–BasePlusCommissionEmployee Inheritance Hierarchy Using private Data

We now reexamine our hierarchy once more, this time using the *best software engineering practices*. Class CommissionEmployee now declares data members firstName, lastName, socialSecurityNumber, grossSales and commissionRate as private as shown previously in lines 31–36 of Fig. 19.4.

Changes to Class CommissionEmployee's Member Function Definitions
In the CommissionEmployee constructor implementation (Fig. 19.14, lines 9–16), we use member initializers (line 12) to set the values of the members firstName, lastName and socialSecurityNumber. We show how the derived-class BasePlusCommissionEmployee (Fig. 19.15) can invoke non-private base-class member functions (setFirstName, get-FirstName, setLastName, getLastName, setSocialSecurityNumber and getSocialSecurityNumber) to manipulate these data members.

In the body of the constructor and in the bodies of member function's earnings (Fig. 19.14, lines 85–88) and print (lines 91–98), we call the class's *set* and *get* member functions to access the class's private data members. If we decide to change the data member names, the earnings and print definitions will *not* require modification—only the definitions of the *get* and *set* member functions that directly manipulate the data members will need to change. *These changes occur solely within the base class—no changes to the derived class are needed.* Localizing the effects of changes like this is a good software engineering practice.

```cpp
 1  // Fig. 19.14: CommissionEmployee.cpp
 2  // Class CommissionEmployee member-function definitions.
 3  #include <iostream>
 4  #include <stdexcept>
 5  #include "CommissionEmployee.h" // CommissionEmployee class definition
 6  using namespace std;
 7
 8  // constructor
 9  CommissionEmployee::CommissionEmployee(
10     const string &first, const string &last, const string &ssn,
11     double sales, double rate )
12     : firstName( first ), lastName( last ), socialSecurityNumber( ssn )
13  {
14     setGrossSales( sales ); // validate and store gross sales
15     setCommissionRate( rate ); // validate and store commission rate
16  } // end CommissionEmployee constructor
17
18  // set first name
19  void CommissionEmployee::setFirstName( const string &first )
20  {
21     firstName = first; // should validate
22  } // end function setFirstName
23
24  // return first name
25  string CommissionEmployee::getFirstName() const
26  {
27     return firstName;
28  } // end function getFirstName
29
30  // set last name
31  void CommissionEmployee::setLastName( const string &last )
32  {
33     lastName = last; // should validate
34  } // end function setLastName
35
36  // return last name
37  string CommissionEmployee::getLastName() const
38  {
39     return lastName;
40  } // end function getLastName
41
42  // set social security number
43  void CommissionEmployee::setSocialSecurityNumber( const string &ssn )
44  {
45     socialSecurityNumber = ssn; // should validate
46  } // end function setSocialSecurityNumber
47
```

Fig. 19.14 | CommissionEmployee class implementation file: CommissionEmployee class uses member functions to manipulate its private data. (Part 1 of 2.)

```
48   // return social security number
49   string CommissionEmployee::getSocialSecurityNumber() const
50   {
51      return socialSecurityNumber;
52   } // end function getSocialSecurityNumber
53
54   // set gross sales amount
55   void CommissionEmployee::setGrossSales( double sales )
56   {
57      if ( sales >= 0.0 )
58         grossSales = sales;
59      else
60         throw invalid_argument( "Gross sales must be >= 0.0" );
61   } // end function setGrossSales
62
63   // return gross sales amount
64   double CommissionEmployee::getGrossSales() const
65   {
66      return grossSales;
67   } // end function getGrossSales
68
69   // set commission rate
70   void CommissionEmployee::setCommissionRate( double rate )
71   {
72      if ( rate > 0.0 && rate < 1.0 )
73         commissionRate = rate;
74      else
75         throw invalid_argument( "Commission rate must be > 0.0 and < 1.0" );
76   } // end function setCommissionRate
77
78   // return commission rate
79   double CommissionEmployee::getCommissionRate() const
80   {
81      return commissionRate;
82   } // end function getCommissionRate
83
84   // calculate earnings
85   double CommissionEmployee::earnings() const
86   {
87      return getCommissionRate() * getGrossSales();
88   } // end function earnings
89
90   // print CommissionEmployee object
91   void CommissionEmployee::print() const
92   {
93      cout << "commission employee: "
94         << getFirstName() << ' ' << getLastName()
95         << "\nsocial security number: " << getSocialSecurityNumber()
96         << "\ngross sales: " << getGrossSales()
97         << "\ncommission rate: " << getCommissionRate();
98   } // end function print
```

Fig. 19.14 | CommissionEmployee class implementation file: CommissionEmployee class uses member functions to manipulate its private data. (Part 2 of 2.)

Performance Tip 19.2

Using a member function to access a data member's value can be slightly slower than accessing the data directly. However, today's optimizing compilers are carefully designed to perform many optimizations implicitly (such as inlining set and get member-function calls). You should write code that adheres to proper software engineering principles, and leave optimization to the compiler. A good rule is, "Do not second-guess the compiler."

Changes to Class **BasePlusCommissionEmployee**'s *Member Function Definitions*

Class BasePlusCommissionEmployee inherits CommissionEmployee's public member functions and can access the private base-class members via the inherited member functions. The class's header remains unchanged from Fig. 19.10. The class has several changes to its member-function implementations (Fig. 19.15) that distinguish it from the previous version of the class (Figs. 19.10–19.11). Member functions earnings (Fig. 19.15, lines 34–37) and print (lines 40–48) each invoke member function getBaseSalary to obtain the base salary value, rather than accessing baseSalary directly. This insulates earnings and print from potential changes to the implementation of data member baseSalary. For example, if we decide to rename data member baseSalary or change its type, only member functions setBaseSalary and getBaseSalary will need to change.

```cpp
1   // Fig. 19.15: BasePlusCommissionEmployee.cpp
2   // Class BasePlusCommissionEmployee member function definitions.
3   #include <iostream>
4   #include <stdexcept>
5   #include "BasePlusCommissionEmployee.h"
6   using namespace std;
7
8   // constructor
9   BasePlusCommissionEmployee::BasePlusCommissionEmployee(
10      const string &first, const string &last, const string &ssn,
11      double sales, double rate, double salary )
12      // explicitly call base-class constructor
13      : CommissionEmployee( first, last, ssn, sales, rate )
14   {
15      setBaseSalary( salary ); // validate and store base salary
16   } // end BasePlusCommissionEmployee constructor
17
18   // set base salary
19   void BasePlusCommissionEmployee::setBaseSalary( double salary )
20   {
21      if ( salary >= 0.0 )
22         baseSalary = salary;
23      else
24         throw invalid_argument( "Salary must be >= 0.0" );
25   } // end function setBaseSalary
26
27   // return base salary
28   double BasePlusCommissionEmployee::getBaseSalary() const
29   {
```

Fig. 19.15 | BasePlusCommissionEmployee class that inherits from class CommissionEmployee but cannot directly access the class's private data. (Part 1 of 2.)

```
30        return baseSalary;
31    } // end function getBaseSalary
32
33    // calculate earnings
34    double BasePlusCommissionEmployee::earnings() const
35    {
36        return getBaseSalary() + CommissionEmployee::earnings();
37    } // end function earnings
38
39    // print BasePlusCommissionEmployee object
40    void BasePlusCommissionEmployee::print() const
41    {
42        cout << "base-salaried ";
43
44        // invoke CommissionEmployee's print function
45        CommissionEmployee::print();
46
47        cout << "\nbase salary: " << getBaseSalary();
48    } // end function print
```

Fig. 19.15 | BasePlusCommissionEmployee class that inherits from class
CommissionEmployee but cannot directly access the class's private data. (Part 2 of 2.)

BasePlusCommissionEmployee Member Function *earnings*

Class BasePlusCommissionEmployee's earnings function (Fig. 19.15, lines 34–37) redefines class CommissionEmployee's earnings member function (Fig. 19.14, lines 85–88) to
calculate the earnings of a base-salaried commission employee. Class BasePlusCommissionEmployee's version of earnings obtains the portion of the employee's earnings based
on commission alone by calling base-class CommissionEmployee's earnings function with
the expression CommissionEmployee::earnings() (Fig. 19.15, line 36). BasePlus-
CommissionEmployee's earnings function then adds the base salary to this value to calculate the total earnings of the employee. Note the syntax used to invoke a redefined base-
class member function from a derived class—place the base-class name and the scope resolution operator (::) before the base-class member-function name. This member-function
invocation is a good software engineering practice: Recall from Chapter 17 that, if an object's member function performs the actions needed by another object, we should call that
member function rather than duplicating its code body. By having BasePlusCommission-
Employee's earnings function invoke CommissionEmployee's earnings function to calculate part of a BasePlusCommissionEmployee object's earnings, we avoid duplicating the
code and reduce code-maintenance problems.

Common Programming Error 19.2

*When a base-class member function is redefined in a derived class, the derived-class version
often calls the base-class version to do additional work. Failure to use the :: operator prefixed
with the name of the base class when referencing the base class's member function causes infinite recursion, because the derived-class member function would then call itself.*

BasePlusCommissionEmployee Member Function *print*

Similarly, BasePlusCommissionEmployee's print function (Fig. 19.15, lines 40–48) redefines class CommissionEmployee's print function (Fig. 19.14, lines 91–98) to output the ap-

propriate base-salaried commission employee information. The new version displays part of a `BasePlusCommissionEmployee` object's information (i.e., the string `"commission employee"` and the values of class `CommissionEmployee`'s `private` data members) by calling `CommissionEmployee`'s `print` member function with the qualified name `CommissionEmployee::print()` (Fig. 19.15, line 45). `BasePlusCommissionEmployee`'s `print` function then outputs the remainder of a `BasePlusCommissionEmployee` object's information (i.e., the value of class `BasePlusCommissionEmployee`'s base salary).

Testing the Modified Class Hierarchy
Once again, this example uses the `BasePlusCommissionEmployee` test program from Fig. 19.9 and produces the same output. Although each "base-salaried commission employee" class behaves identically, the version in this example is the best engineered. *By using inheritance and by calling member functions that hide the data and ensure consistency, we've efficiently and effectively constructed a well-engineered class.*

Summary of the CommissionEmployee–BasePlusCommissionEmployee Examples
In this section, you saw an evolutionary set of examples that was carefully designed to teach key capabilities for good software engineering with inheritance. You learned how to create a derived class using inheritance, how to use `protected` base-class members to enable a derived class to access inherited base-class data members and how to redefine base-class functions to provide versions that are more appropriate for derived-class objects. In addition, you learned how to apply software engineering techniques from Chapter 17 and this chapter to create classes that are easy to maintain, modify and debug.

19.4 Constructors and Destructors in Derived Classes

As we explained in the preceding section, instantiating a derived-class object begins a *chain* of constructor calls in which the derived-class constructor, before performing its own tasks, invokes its direct base class's constructor either explicitly (via a base-class member initializer) or implicitly (calling the base class's default constructor). Similarly, if the base class is derived from another class, the base-class constructor is required to invoke the constructor of the next class up in the hierarchy, and so on. The last constructor called in this chain is the one of the class at the base of the hierarchy, whose body actually finishes executing *first*. The most derived-class constructor's body finishes executing *last*. Each base-class constructor initializes the base-class data members that the derived-class object inherits. In the `CommissionEmployee`/`BasePlusCommissionEmployee` hierarchy that we've been studying, when a program creates a `BasePlusCommissionEmployee` object, the `CommissionEmployee` constructor is called. Since class `CommissionEmployee` is at the base of the hierarchy, its constructor executes, initializing the `private` `CommissionEmployee` data members that are part of the `BasePlusCommissionEmployee` object. When `CommissionEmployee`'s constructor completes execution, it returns control to `BasePlusCommissionEmployee`'s constructor, which initializes the `BasePlusCommissionEmployee` object's baseSalary.

Software Engineering Observation 19.6
When a program creates a derived-class object, the derived-class constructor immediately calls the base-class constructor, the base-class constructor's body executes, then the derived class's member initializers execute and finally the derived-class constructor's body executes. This process cascades up the hierarchy if it contains more than two levels.

When a derived-class object is destroyed, the program calls that object's destructor. This begins a chain (or cascade) of destructor calls in which the derived-class destructor and the destructors of the direct and indirect base classes and the classes' members execute in *reverse* of the order in which the constructors executed. When a derived-class object's destructor is called, the destructor performs its task, then invokes the destructor of the next base class up the hierarchy. This process repeats until the destructor of the final base class at the top of the hierarchy is called. Then the object is removed from memory.

Software Engineering Observation 19.7

Suppose that we create an object of a derived class where both the base class and the derived class contain (via composition) objects of other classes. When an object of that derived class is created, first the constructors for the base class's member objects execute, then the base-class constructor body executes, then the constructors for the derived class's member objects execute, then the derived class's constructor body executes. Destructors for derived-class objects are called in the reverse of the order in which their corresponding constructors are called.

Base-class constructors, destructors and overloaded assignment operators (Chapter 18) are *not* inherited by derived classes. Derived-class constructors, destructors and overloaded assignment operators, however, can call base-class versions.

C++11: Inheriting Base Class Constructors

Sometimes a derived class's constructors simply mimic the base class's constructors. A frequently requested convenience feature for C++11 was the ability to *inherit* a base class's constructors. You can now do this by *explicitly* including a using declaration of the form

```
using BaseClass::BaseClass;
```

anywhere in the derived-class definition. In the preceding declaration, *BaseClass* is the base class's name. With a few exceptions (listed below), for each constructor in the base class, the compiler generates a derived-class constructor that calls the corresponding base-class constructor. The generated constructors perform only *default initialization* for the derived class's additional data members. When you inherit constructors:

- By default, each inherited constructor has the *same* access level (public, protected or private) as its corresponding base-class constructor.

- The default, copy and move constructors are *not* inherited.

- If a constructor is *deleted* in the base class by placing = delete in its prototype, the corresponding constructor in the derived class is *also* deleted.

- If the derived class does not *explicitly* define constructors, the compiler generates a default constructor in the derived class—*even* if it inherits other constructors from its base class.

- If a constructor that you *explicitly* define in a derived class has the *same* parameter list as a base-class constructor, then the base-class constructor is *not* inherited.

- A base-class constructor's default arguments are *not* inherited. Instead, the compiler generates *overloaded constructors* in the derived class. For example, if the base class declares the constructor

```
BaseClass( int = 0, double = 0.0 );
```

the compiler generates the following *two* derived-class constructors *without* default arguments

```
DerivedClass( int );
DerivedClass( int, double );
```

These each call the *BaseClass* constructor that specifies the default arguments.

19.5 public, protected and private Inheritance

When deriving a class from a base class, the base class may be inherited through public, protected or private inheritance. We normally use public inheritance in this book. Use of protected inheritance is rare. In some cases, private inheritance is used as an alternative to composition. Figure 19.16 summarizes for each type of inheritance the accessibility of base-class members in a derived class. The first column contains the base-class access specifiers.

Base-class member-access specifier	Type of inheritance		
	public inheritance	**protected** inheritance	**private** inheritance
public	public in derived class. Can be accessed directly by member functions. friend functions and nonmember functions.	protected in derived class. Can be accessed directly by member functions and friend functions.	private in derived class. Can be accessed directly by member functions and friend functions.
protected	protected in derived class. Can be accessed directly by member functions and friend functions.	protected in derived class. Can be accessed directly by member functions and friend functions.	private in derived class. Can be accessed directly by member functions and friend functions.
private	Hidden in derived class. Can be accessed by member functions and friend functions through public or protected member functions of the base class.	Hidden in derived class. Can be accessed by member functions and friend functions through public or protected member functions of the base class.	Hidden in derived class. Can be accessed by member functions and friend functions through public or protected member functions of the base class.

Fig. 19.16 | Summary of base-class member accessibility in a derived class.

When deriving a class with public inheritance, public members of the base class become public members of the derived class, and protected members of the base class become protected members of the derived class. A base class's private members are *never* accessible directly from a derived class, but can be accessed through calls to the public and protected members of the base class.

When deriving a class with `protected` inheritance, `public` and `protected` members of the base class become `protected` members of the derived class. When deriving a class with `private` inheritance, `public` and `protected` members of the base class become `private` members (e.g., the functions become utility functions) of the derived class. `Private` and `protected` inheritance are not *is-a* relationships.

19.6 Software Engineering with Inheritance

Sometimes it's difficult for students to appreciate the scope of problems faced by designers who work on large-scale software projects in industry. People experienced with such projects say that effective software reuse improves the software development process. Object-oriented programming facilitates software reuse, thus shortening development times and enhancing software quality.

When we use inheritance to create a new class from an existing one, the new class inherits the data members and member functions of the existing class, as described in Fig. 19.16. We can customize the new class to meet our needs by redefining base-class members and by including additional members. The derived-class programmer does this in C++ *without* accessing the base class's source code (the derived class must be able to *link* to the base class's object code). This powerful capability is attractive to software developers. They can develop proprietary classes for sale or license and make these classes available to users in object-code format. Users then can derive new classes from these library classes rapidly and without accessing the proprietary source code. The software developers need to supply the headers along with the object code

The availability of substantial and useful class libraries delivers the maximum benefits of software reuse through inheritance. The standard C++ libraries tend to be general purpose and limited in scope. There is a worldwide commitment to the development of class libraries for a huge variety of application arenas.

Software Engineering Observation 19.8

At the design stage in an object-oriented system, the designer often determines that certain classes are closely related. The designer should "factor out" common attributes and behaviors and place these in a base class, then use inheritance to form derived classes.

Software Engineering Observation 19.9

Creating a derived class does not affect its base class's source code. Inheritance preserves the integrity of the base class.

19.7 Wrap-Up

This chapter introduced inheritance—the ability to create a class by absorbing an existing class's data members and member functions and embellishing them with new capabilities. Through a series of examples using an employee inheritance hierarchy, you learned the notions of base classes and derived classes and used `public` inheritance to create a derived class that inherits members from a base class. The chapter introduced the access specifier `protected`—derived-class member functions can access `protected` base-class members. You learned how to access redefined base-class members by qualifying their names with the base-class name and scope resolution operator (`::`). You also saw the order in which constructors and destructors are called for objects of classes that are part of an inheritance hierarchy. Finally, we explained the three types of inheritance—public, protected and private—and the accessibility of base-class members in a derived class when using each type.

In Chapter 20, Object-Oriented Programming: Polymorphism, we build on our discussion of inheritance by introducing polymorphism—an object-oriented concept that enables us to write programs that handle, in a more general manner, objects of a wide variety of classes related by inheritance. After studying Chapter 20, you'll be familiar with classes, objects, encapsulation, inheritance and polymorphism—the essential concepts of object-oriented programming.

Summary

Section 19.1 Introduction
- Software reuse reduces program development time and cost.
- Inheritance (p. 733) is a form of software reuse in which you create a class that absorbs an existing class's capabilities, then customizes or enhances them. The existing class is called the base class (p. 733), and the new class is referred to as the derived class (p. 733).
- Every object of a derived class is also an object of that class's base class. However, a base-class object is not an object of that class's derived classes.
- The *is-a* relationship (p. 733) represents inheritance. In an *is-a* relationship, an object of a derived class also can be treated as an object of its base class.
- The *has-a* relationship (p. 733) represents composition—an object contains one or more objects of other classes as members, but does not disclose their behavior directly in its interface.

Section 19.2 Base Classes and Derived Classes
- A direct base class (p. 735) is the one from which a derived class explicitly inherits. An indirect base class (p. 735) is inherited from two or more levels up the class hierarchy (p. 734).
- With single inheritance (p. 735), a class is derived from one base class. With multiple inheritance (p. 735), a class inherits from multiple (possibly unrelated) base classes.
- A derived class represents a more specialized group of objects.
- Inheritance relationships form class hierarchies.
- It's possible to treat base-class objects and derived-class objects similarly; the commonality shared between the object types is expressed in the base class's data members and member functions.

Section 19.4 Constructors and Destructors in Derived Classes
- When an object of a derived class is instantiated, the base class's constructor is called immediately to initialize the base-class data members in the derived-class object, then the derived-class constructor initializes the additional derived-class data members.
- When a derived-class object is destroyed, the destructors are called in the reverse order of the constructors—first the derived-class destructor is called, then the base-class destructor is called.
- A base class's public members are accessible anywhere that the program has a handle to an object of that base class or to an object of one of that base class's derived classes—or, when using the scope resolution operator, whenever the class's name is in scope.
- A base class's private members are accessible only within the base class or from its friends.
- A base class's protected members can be accessed by members and friends of that base class and by members and friends of any classes derived from that base class.

- In C++11, a derived class can inherit constructors from its base class by including anywhere in the derived-class definition a using declaration of the form

    using *BaseClass*::*BaseClass*;

Section 19.5 public, protected and private Inheritance

- Declaring data members private, while providing non-private member functions to manipulate and perform validity checking on this data, enforces good software engineering.

- When deriving a class, the base class may be declared as either public, protected or private.

- When deriving a class with public inheritance (p. 761), public members of the base class become public members of the derived class, and protected members of the base class become protected members of the derived class.

- When deriving a class with protected inheritance (p. 762), public and protected members of the base class become protected members of the derived class.

- When deriving a class with private inheritance (p. 762), public and protected members of the base class become private members of the derived class.

Self-Review Exercises

19.1 Fill in the blanks in each of the following statements:

a) _____ is a form of software reuse in which new classes absorb the data and behaviors of existing classes and embellish these classes with new capabilities.

b) A base class's _____ members can be accessed in the base-class definition, in derived-class definitions and in friends of the base class its derived classes.

c) In a(n) _____ relationship, an object of a derived class also can be treated as an object of its base class.

d) In a(n) _____ relationship, a class object has one or more objects of other classes as members.

e) In single inheritance, a class exists in a(n) _____ relationship with its derived classes.

f) A base class's _____ members are accessible within that base class and anywhere that the program has a handle to an object of that class or one of its derived classes.

g) A base class's protected access members have a level of protection between those of public and _____ access.

h) C++ provides for _____, which allows a derived class to inherit from many base classes, even if the base classes are unrelated.

i) When an object of a derived class is instantiated, the base class's _____ is called implicitly or explicitly to do any necessary initialization of the base-class data members in the derived-class object.

j) When deriving a class with public inheritance, public members of the base class become _____ members of the derived class, and protected members of the base class become _____ members of the derived class.

k) When deriving a class from with protected inheritance, public members of the base class become _____ members of the derived class, and protected members of the base class become _____ members of the derived class.

19.2 State whether each of the following is *true* or *false*. If *false*, explain why.

a) Base-class constructors are not inherited by derived classes.

b) A *has-a* relationship is implemented via inheritance.

c) A Car class has an *is-a* relationship with the SteeringWheel and Brakes classes.

d) Inheritance encourages the reuse of proven high-quality software.

e) When a derived-class object is destroyed, the destructors are called in the reverse order of the constructors.

Answers to Self-Review Exercises

19.1 a) Inheritance. b) protected. c) *is-a* or inheritance (for public inheritance). d) *has-a* or composition or aggregation. e) hierarchical. f) public. g) private. h) multiple inheritance. i) constructor. j) public, protected. k) protected, protected.

19.2 a) True. b) False. A *has-a* relationship is implemented via composition. An *is-a* relationship is implemented via inheritance. c) False. This is an example of a *has-a* relationship. Class Car has an *is-a* relationship with class Vehicle. d) True. e) True.

Exercises

19.3 *(Composition as an Alternative to Inheritance)* Many programs written with inheritance could be written with composition instead, and vice versa. Rewrite class BasePlusCommissionEmployee of the CommissionEmployee–BasePlusCommissionEmployee hierarchy to use composition rather than inheritance. After you do this, assess the relative merits of the two approaches for designing classes CommissionEmployee and BasePlusCommissionEmployee, as well as for object-oriented programs in general. Which approach is more natural? Why?

19.4 *(Inheritance Advantage)* Discuss the ways in which inheritance promotes software reuse, saves time during program development and helps prevent errors.

19.5 *(Protected vs. Private Base Classes)* Some programmers prefer not to use protected access because they believe it breaks the encapsulation of the base class. Discuss the relative merits of using protected access vs. using private access in base classes.

19.6 *(Student Inheritance Hierarchy)* Draw an inheritance hierarchy for students at a university similar to the hierarchy shown in Fig. 19.2. Use Student as the base class of the hierarchy, then include classes UndergraduateStudent and GraduateStudent that derive from Student. Continue to extend the hierarchy as deep (i.e., as many levels) as possible. For example, Freshman, Sophomore, Junior and Senior might derive from UndergraduateStudent, and DoctoralStudent and MastersStudent might derive from GraduateStudent. After drawing the hierarchy, discuss the relationships that exist between the classes. [*Note:* You do not need to write any code for this exercise.]

19.7 *(Richer Shape Hierarchy)* The world of shapes is much richer than the shapes included in the inheritance hierarchy of Fig. 19.3. Write down all the shapes you can think of—both two-dimensional and three-dimensional—and form them into a more complete Shape hierarchy with as many levels as possible. Your hierarchy should have the base class Shape from which class TwoDimensionalShape and class ThreeDimensionalShape are derived. [*Note:* You do not need to write any code for this exercise.] We'll use this hierarchy in the exercises of Chapter 20 to process a set of distinct shapes as objects of base-class Shape. (This technique, called polymorphism, is the subject of Chapter 20.)

19.8 *(Quadrilateral Inheritance Hierarchy)* Draw an inheritance hierarchy for classes Quadrilateral, Trapezoid, Parallelogram, Rectangle and Square. Use Quadrilateral as the base class of the hierarchy. Make the hierarchy as deep as possible.

19.9 (*Package Inheritance Hierarchy*) Package-delivery services, such as FedEx®, DHL® and UPS®, offer a number of different shipping options, each with specific costs associated. Create an inheritance hierarchy to represent various types of packages. Use class Package as the base class of the hierarchy, then include classes TwoDayPackage and OvernightPackage that derive from Package. Base class Package should include data members representing the name, address, city, state and ZIP code for both the sender and the recipient of the package, in addition to data members that store the weight (in ounces) and cost per ounce to ship the package. Package's constructor should initialize these data members. Ensure that the weight and cost per ounce contain positive values. Package should provide a public member function calculateCost that returns a double indicating the cost associated with shipping the package. `Package`'s `calculateCost` function should determine the cost by multiplying the weight by the cost per ounce. Derived class `TwoDayPackage` should inherit the functionality of base class `Package`, but also include a data member that represents a flat fee that the shipping company charges for two-day-delivery service. `TwoDayPackage`'s constructor should receive a value to initialize this data member. `TwoDayPackage` should redefine member function `calculateCost` so that it computes the shipping cost by adding the flat fee to the weight-based cost calculated by base class `Package`'s `calculateCost` function. Class `OvernightPackage` should inherit directly from class `Package` and contain an additional data member representing an additional fee per ounce charged for overnight-delivery service. `OvernightPackage` should redefine member function `calculateCost` so that it adds the additional fee per ounce to the standard cost per ounce before calculating the shipping cost. Write a test program that creates objects of each type of `Package` and tests member function `calculateCost`.

19.10   *(Account Inheritance Hierarchy)* Create an inheritance hierarchy that a bank might use to represent customers' bank accounts. All customers at this bank can deposit (i.e., credit) money into their accounts and withdraw (i.e., debit) money from their accounts. More specific types of accounts also exist. Savings accounts, for instance, earn interest on the money they hold. Checking accounts, on the other hand, charge a fee per transaction (i.e., credit or debit).

Create an inheritance hierarchy containing base class `Account` and derived classes `SavingsAccount` and `CheckingAccount` that inherit from class `Account`. Base class `Account` should include one data member of type `double` to represent the account balance. The class should provide a constructor that receives an initial balance and uses it to initialize the data member. The constructor should validate the initial balance to ensure that it's greater than or equal to `0.0`. If not, the balance should be set to `0.0` and the constructor should display an error message, indicating that the initial balance was invalid. The class should provide three member functions. Member function `credit` should add an amount to the current balance. Member function `debit` should withdraw money from the `Account` and ensure that the debit amount does not exceed the `Account`'s balance. If it does, the balance should be left unchanged and the function should print the message `"Debit amount exceeded account balance."` Member function `getBalance` should return the current balance.

Derived class `SavingsAccount` should inherit the functionality of an `Account`, but also include a data member of type `double` indicating the interest rate (percentage) assigned to the `Account`. `SavingsAccount`'s constructor should receive the initial balance, as well as an initial value for the `SavingsAccount`'s interest rate. `SavingsAccount` should provide a `public` member function `calculateInterest` that returns a `double` indicating the amount of interest earned by an account. Member function `calculateInterest` should determine this amount by multiplying the interest rate by the account balance. [*Note:* `SavingsAccount` should inherit member functions `credit` and `debit` as is without redefining them.]

Derived class `CheckingAccount` should inherit from base class `Account` and include an additional data member of type `double` that represents the fee charged per transaction. `CheckingAccount`'s constructor should receive the initial balance, as well as a parameter indicating a fee amount. Class `CheckingAccount` should redefine member functions `credit` and `debit` so that they subtract the fee from the account balance whenever either transaction is performed successfully. `CheckingAccount`'s versions of these functions should invoke the base-class `Account` version to perform the updates to an account balance. `CheckingAccount`'s `debit` function should charge a fee only if money is actually withdrawn (i.e., the debit amount does not exceed the account balance). [*Hint:* Define `Account`'s `debit` function so that it returns a `bool` indicating whether money was withdrawn. Then use the return value to determine whether a fee should be charged.]

After defining the classes in this hierarchy, write a program that creates objects of each class and tests their member functions. Add interest to the `SavingsAccount` object by first invoking its `calculateInterest` function, then passing the returned interest amount to the object's `credit` function.

Object-Oriented Programming: Polymorphism

20

Objectives

In this chapter you'll learn:

- How polymorphism makes programming more convenient and systems more extensible.

- The distinction between abstract and concrete classes and how to create abstract classes.

- To use runtime type information (RTTI).

- How C++ implements virtual functions and dynamic binding.

- How virtual destructors ensure that all appropriate destructors run on an object.

20.1 Introduction

We now continue our study of OOP by explaining and demonstrating **polymorphism** with inheritance hierarchies. Polymorphism enables you to "program in the *general*" rather than "program in the *specific*." In particular, polymorphism enables you to write programs that process objects of classes that are part of the *same* class hierarchy as if they were all objects of the hierarchy's base class. As we'll soon see, polymorphism works off base-class *pointer handles* and base-class *reference handles*, but *not* off name handles.

Implementing for Extensibility

With polymorphism, you can design and implement systems that are easily *extensible*—new classes can be added with little or no modification to the general portions of the program, as long as the new classes are part of the inheritance hierarchy that the program processes generally. The only parts of a program that must be altered to accommodate new classes are those that require direct knowledge of the new classes that you add to the hierarchy. For example, if we create class `Tortoise` that inherits from class `Animal` (which might respond to a move message by crawling one inch), we need to write only the `Tortoise` class and the part of the simulation that instantiates a `Tortoise` object. The portions of the simulation that process each `Animal` generally can remain the same.

Optional Discussion of Polymorphism "Under the Hood"

A key feature of this chapter is its (optional) detailed discussion of polymorphism, `virtual` functions and dynamic binding "under the hood," which uses a detailed diagram to explain how polymorphism can be implemented in C++.

20.2 Introduction to Polymorphism: Polymorphic Video Game

Suppose that we design a video game that manipulates objects of many *different* types, including objects of classes Martian, Venutian, Plutonian, SpaceShip and LaserBeam. Imagine that each of these classes inherits from the common base class SpaceObject, which contains the member function draw. Each derived class implements this function in a manner appropriate for that class. A screen-manager program maintains a container (e.g., a vector) that holds SpaceObject *pointers* to objects of the various classes. To refresh the screen, the screen manager periodically sends each object the *same* message—namely, draw. Each type of object responds in a unique way. For example, a Martian object might draw itself in red with the appropriate number of antennae, a SpaceShip object might draw itself as a silver flying saucer, and a LaserBeam object might draw itself as a bright red beam across the screen. The *same* message (in this case, draw) sent to a *variety* of objects has *many forms* of results—hence the term polymorphism.

A polymorphic screen manager facilitates adding new classes to a system with minimal modifications to its code. Suppose that we want to add objects of class Mercurian to our video game. To do so, we must build a class Mercurian that inherits from SpaceObject, but provides its own definition of member function draw. Then, when *pointers* to objects of class Mercurian appear in the container, you do not need to modify the code for the screen manager. The screen manager invokes member function draw on *every* object in the container, *regardless* of the object's type, so the new Mercurian objects simply "plug right in." Thus, without modifying the system (other than to build and include the classes themselves), you can use polymorphism to accommodate additional classes, including ones that were *not even envisioned* when the system was created.

Software Engineering Observation 20.1

Polymorphism enables you to deal in generalities *and let the execution-time environment concern itself with the* specifics. *You can direct a variety of objects to behave in manners appropriate to those objects* without even knowing their types—*as long as those objects belong to the same inheritance hierarchy and are being accessed off a common base-class pointer or a common base-class reference.*

Software Engineering Observation 20.2

Polymorphism promotes extensibility: *Software written to invoke polymorphic behavior is written* independently *of the specific types of the objects to which messages are sent. Thus, new types of objects that can respond to* existing *messages can be incorporated into such a system without modifying the base system. Only client code that instantiates new objects must be modified to accommodate new types.*

20.3 Relationships Among Objects in an Inheritance Hierarchy

Section 19.3 created an employee class hierarchy, in which class BasePlusCommission-Employee inherited from class CommissionEmployee. The Chapter 19 examples manipulated CommissionEmployee and BasePlusCommissionEmployee objects by using the objects' names to invoke their member functions. We now examine the relationships among classes in a hierarchy more closely. The next several sections present a series of examples that demonstrate how base-class and derived-class *pointers* can be aimed at base-class and derived-class objects, and how those pointers can be used to invoke member functions that manipulate those objects.

- In Section 20.3.1, we assign the address of a derived-class object to a base-class pointer, then show that invoking a function via the base-class pointer invokes the *base-class functionality* in the derived-class object—i.e., the *type of the handle determines which function is called.*

- In Section 20.3.2, we assign the address of a base-class object to a derived-class pointer, which results in a compilation error. We discuss the error message and investigate why the compiler does *not* allow such an assignment.

- In Section 20.3.3, we assign the address of a derived-class object to a base-class pointer, then examine how the base-class pointer can be used to invoke only the base-class functionality—*when we attempt to invoke derived-class member functions through the base-class pointer, compilation errors occur.*

- Finally, in Section 20.3.4, we demonstrate how to get polymorphic behavior from base-class pointers aimed at derived-class objects. We introduce virtual functions and polymorphism by declaring a base-class function as virtual. We then assign the address of a derived-class object to the base-class pointer and use that pointer to invoke derived-class functionality—*precisely the capability we need to achieve polymorphic behavior.*

A key concept in these examples is to demonstrate that with public inheritance *an object of a derived class can be treated as an object of its base class.* This enables various interesting manipulations. For example, a program can create an array of base-class pointers that point to objects of many derived-class types. Despite the fact that the derived-class objects are of *different types*, the compiler allows this because each derived-class object *is an* object of its base class. However, *we cannot treat a base-class object as an object of any of its derived classes.* For example, a CommissionEmployee is not a BasePlusCommissionEmployee in the hierarchy defined in Chapter 19—a CommissionEmployee does *not* have a baseSalary data member and does *not* have member functions setBaseSalary and getBaseSalary. The *is-a* relationship applies only from a *derived class* to its *direct and indirect base classes.*

20.3.1 Invoking Base-Class Functions from Derived-Class Objects

The example in Fig. 20.1 reuses the final versions of classes CommissionEmployee and BasePlusCommissionEmployee from Section 19.3.5. The example demonstrates three ways to aim base- and derived-class pointers at base- and derived-class objects. The first two are natural and straightforward—we aim a base-class pointer at a base-class object and invoke base-class functionality, and we aim a derived-class pointer at a derived-class object and invoke derived-class functionality. Then, we demonstrate the relationship between derived classes and base classes (i.e., the *is-a* relationship of inheritance) by aiming a base-class pointer at a derived-class object and showing that the base-class functionality is indeed available in the derived-class object.

```
 1   // Fig. 20.1: fig20_01.cpp
 2   // Aiming base-class and derived-class pointers at base-class
 3   // and derived-class objects, respectively.
 4   #include <iostream>
 5   #include <iomanip>
 6   #include "CommissionEmployee.h"
 7   #include "BasePlusCommissionEmployee.h"
 8   using namespace std;
 9
10   int main()
11   {
12      // create base-class object
13      CommissionEmployee commissionEmployee(
14         "Sue", "Jones", "222-22-2222", 10000, .06 );
15
16      // create base-class pointer
17      CommissionEmployee *commissionEmployeePtr = nullptr;
18
19      // create derived-class object
20      BasePlusCommissionEmployee basePlusCommissionEmployee(
21         "Bob", "Lewis", "333-33-3333", 5000, .04, 300 );
22
23      // create derived-class pointer
24      BasePlusCommissionEmployee *basePlusCommissionEmployeePtr = nullptr;
25
26      // set floating-point output formatting
27      cout << fixed << setprecision( 2 );
28
29      // output objects commissionEmployee and basePlusCommissionEmployee
30      cout << "Print base-class and derived-class objects:\n\n";
31      commissionEmployee.print(); // invokes base-class print
32      cout << "\n\n";
33      basePlusCommissionEmployee.print(); // invokes derived-class print
34
35      // aim base-class pointer at base-class object and print
36      commissionEmployeePtr = &commissionEmployee; // perfectly natural
37      cout << "\n\n\nCalling print with base-class pointer to "
38         << "\nbase-class object invokes base-class print function:\n\n";
39      commissionEmployeePtr->print(); // invokes base-class print
40
41      // aim derived-class pointer at derived-class object and print
42      basePlusCommissionEmployeePtr = &basePlusCommissionEmployee; // natural
43      cout << "\n\n\nCalling print with derived-class pointer to "
44         << "\nderived-class object invokes derived-class "
45         << "print function:\n\n";
46      basePlusCommissionEmployeePtr->print(); // invokes derived-class print
47
48      // aim base-class pointer at derived-class object and print
49      commissionEmployeePtr = &basePlusCommissionEmployee;
50      cout << "\n\n\nCalling print with base-class pointer to "
51         << "derived-class object\ninvokes base-class print "
```

Fig. 20.1 │ Assigning addresses of base-class and derived-class objects to base-class and derived-class pointers. (Part 1 of 2.)

```
52          << "function on that derived-class object:\n\n";
53      commissionEmployeePtr->print(); // invokes base-class print
54      cout << endl;
55  } // end main
```

```
Print base-class and derived-class objects:

commission employee: Sue Jones
social security number: 222-22-2222
gross sales: 10000.00
commission rate: 0.06

base-salaried commission employee: Bob Lewis
social security number: 333-33-3333
gross sales: 5000.00
commission rate: 0.04
base salary: 300.00


Calling print with base-class pointer to
base-class object invokes base-class print function:

commission employee: Sue Jones
social security number: 222-22-2222
gross sales: 10000.00
commission rate: 0.06


Calling print with derived-class pointer to
derived-class object invokes derived-class print function:

base-salaried commission employee: Bob Lewis
social security number: 333-33-3333
gross sales: 5000.00
commission rate: 0.04
base salary: 300.00


Calling print with base-class pointer to derived-class object
invokes base-class print function on that derived-class object:

commission employee: Bob Lewis
social security number: 333-33-3333
gross sales: 5000.00
commission rate: 0.04            ── Notice that the base salary is not displayed
```

Fig. 20.1 | Assigning addresses of base-class and derived-class objects to base-class and derived-class pointers. (Part 2 of 2.)

Recall that each BasePlusCommissionEmployee object *is a* CommissionEmployee that *also* has a base salary. Class BasePlusCommissionEmployee's earnings member function (lines 34–37 of Fig. 19.15) redefines class CommissionEmployee's earnings member function (lines 85–88 of Fig. 19.14) to include the object's base salary. Class BasePlusCommissionEmployee's print member function (lines 40–48 of Fig. 19.15) redefines class CommissionEmployee's version (lines 91–98 of Fig. 19.14) to display the same information *plus* the employee's base salary.

Creating Objects and Displaying Their Contents
In Fig. 20.1, lines 13–14 create a CommissionEmployee object and line 17 creates a pointer to a CommissionEmployee object; lines 20–21 create a BasePlusCommissionEmployee object and line 24 creates a pointer to a BasePlusCommissionEmployee object. Lines 31 and 33 use each object's name to invoke its print member function.

Aiming a Base-Class Pointer at a Base-Class Object
Line 36 assigns the address of base-class object commissionEmployee to base-class pointer commissionEmployeePtr, which line 39 uses to invoke member function print on that CommissionEmployee object. This invokes the version of print defined in base class CommissionEmployee.

Aiming a Derived-Class Pointer at a Derived-Class Object
Similarly, line 42 assigns the address of derived-class object basePlusCommissionEmployee to derived-class pointer basePlusCommissionEmployeePtr, which line 46 uses to invoke member function print on that BasePlusCommissionEmployee object. This invokes the version of print defined in derived class BasePlusCommissionEmployee.

Aiming a Base-Class Pointer at a Derived-Class Object
Line 49 then assigns the address of derived-class object basePlusCommissionEmployee to base-class pointer commissionEmployeePtr, which line 53 uses to invoke member function print. This "crossover" is allowed because an object of a derived class *is an* object of its base class. Despite the fact that the base class CommissionEmployee pointer points to a *derived class* BasePlusCommissionEmployee object, the *base class* CommissionEmployee's print member function is invoked (rather than BasePlusCommissionEmployee's print function). The output of each print member-function invocation in this program reveals that *the invoked functionality depends on the type of the pointer (or reference) used to invoke the function, not the type of the object for which the member function is called*. In Section 20.3.4, when we introduce virtual functions, we demonstrate that it's possible to invoke the object type's functionality, *rather than* invoke the handle type's functionality. We'll see that this is crucial to implementing polymorphic behavior—the key topic of this chapter.

20.3.2 Aiming Derived-Class Pointers at Base-Class Objects

In Section 20.3.1, we assigned the address of a derived-class object to a base-class pointer and explained that the C++ compiler allows this assignment, because a derived-class object *is a* base-class object. We take the opposite approach in Fig. 20.2, as we aim a derived-class pointer at a base-class object. [*Note:* This program reuses the final versions of classes CommissionEmployee and BasePlusCommissionEmployee from Section 19.3.5.] Lines 8–9 of Fig. 20.2 create a CommissionEmployee object, and line 10 creates a BasePlusCommissionEmployee pointer. Line 14 attempts to assign the address of base-class object commissionEmployee to derived-class pointer basePlusCommissionEmployeePtr, but the compiler generates an error. The compiler prevents this assignment, because a CommissionEmployee is *not* a BasePlusCommissionEmployee.

Consider the consequences if the compiler were to allow this assignment. Through a BasePlusCommissionEmployee pointer, we can invoke *every* BasePlusCommissionEmployee member function, including setBaseSalary, for the object to which the pointer points (i.e., the base-class object commissionEmployee). However, the CommissionEmployee object does *not* provide a setBaseSalary member function, *nor* does it provide a baseSalary data member to set. This could lead to problems, because member function setBaseSalary would assume that there is a baseSalary data member to set at its "usual location" in a BasePlusCommissionEmployee object. This memory does not belong to the CommissionEmployee object, so member function setBaseSalary might overwrite other important data in memory, possibly data that belongs to a different object.

```
1   // Fig. 20.2: fig20_02.cpp
2   // Aiming a derived-class pointer at a base-class object.
3   #include "CommissionEmployee.h"
4   #include "BasePlusCommissionEmployee.h"
5
6   int main()
7   {
8       CommissionEmployee commissionEmployee(
9           "Sue", "Jones", "222-22-2222", 10000, .06 );
10      BasePlusCommissionEmployee *basePlusCommissionEmployeePtr = nullptr;
11
12      // aim derived-class pointer at base-class object
13      // Error: a CommissionEmployee is not a BasePlusCommissionEmployee
14      basePlusCommissionEmployeePtr = &commissionEmployee;
15  } // end main
```

Microsoft Visual C++ compiler error message:

```
C:\examples\ch20\Fig20_02\fig20_02.cpp(14): error C2440: '=' :
    cannot convert from 'CommissionEmployee *' to 'BasePlusCommissionEmployee *'
        Cast from base to derived requires dynamic_cast or static_cast
```

Fig. 20.2 | Aiming a derived-class pointer at a base-class object.

20.3.3 Derived-Class Member-Function Calls via Base-Class Pointers

Off a base-class pointer, the compiler allows us to invoke *only* base-class member functions. Thus, if a base-class pointer is aimed at a derived-class object, and an attempt is made to access a *derived-class-only member function*, a compilation error will occur.

Figure 20.3 shows the consequences of attempting to invoke a derived-class member function off a base-class pointer. [*Note:* We're again reusing the versions of classes CommissionEmployee and BasePlusCommissionEmployee from Section 19.3.5.] Line 11 creates commissionEmployeePtr—a pointer to a CommissionEmployee object—and lines 12–13 create a BasePlusCommissionEmployee object. Line 16 aims the base-class commissionEmployeePtr at derived-class object basePlusCommissionEmployee. Recall from Section 20.3.1 that this is allowed, because a BasePlusCommissionEmployee *is a* CommissionEmployee (in the sense that a BasePlusCommissionEmployee object contains all the functionality of a CommissionEmployee object). Lines 20–24 invoke base-class member functions getFirstName, getLastName, getSocialSecurityNumber, getGrossSales and getCommissionRate off the base-class pointer. All of these calls are allowed, because BasePlusCommissionEmployee *inherits* these member functions from CommissionEmployee. We know that commissionEmployeePtr is aimed at a BasePlusCommissionEmployee object, so in lines 28–29 we attempt to invoke BasePlusCommissionEmployee member functions getBaseSalary and setBaseSalary. The compiler generates errors on both of these calls, because they're *not* made to member functions of base-class CommissionEmployee. The handle can be used to invoke *only* those functions that are members of that handle's associated class type. (In this case, off a CommissionEmployee *, we can invoke only CommissionEmployee member functions setFirstName, getFirstName, setLastName, getLastName, setSocialSecurityNumber, getSocialSecurityNumber, setGrossSales, getGrossSales, setCommissionRate, getCommissionRate, earnings and print.)

```
1   // Fig. 20.3: fig20_03.cpp
2   // Attempting to invoke derived-class-only member functions
3   // via a base-class pointer.
4   #include <string>
5   #include "CommissionEmployee.h"
6   #include "BasePlusCommissionEmployee.h"
7   using namespace std;
8
9   int main()
10  {
11     CommissionEmployee *commissionEmployeePtr = nullptr; // base class ptr
12     BasePlusCommissionEmployee basePlusCommissionEmployee(
13        "Bob", "Lewis", "333-33-3333", 5000, .04, 300 ); // derived class
14
15     // aim base-class pointer at derived-class object (allowed)
16     commissionEmployeePtr = &basePlusCommissionEmployee;
17
18     // invoke base-class member functions on derived class
19     // object through base-class pointer (allowed)
20     string firstName = commissionEmployeePtr->getFirstName();
21     string lastName = commissionEmployeePtr->getLastName();
22     string ssn = commissionEmployeePtr->getSocialSecurityNumber();
23     double grossSales = commissionEmployeePtr->getGrossSales();
24     double commissionRate = commissionEmployeePtr->getCommissionRate();
25
26     // attempt to invoke derived-class-only member functions
27     // on derived-class object through base-class pointer (disallowed)
28     double baseSalary = commissionEmployeePtr->getBaseSalary();
29     commissionEmployeePtr->setBaseSalary( 500 );
30  } // end main
```

GNU C++ compiler error messages:

```
fig20_03.cpp:28:47: error: 'class CommissionEmployee' has no member named
   'getBaseSalary'
fig20_03.cpp:29:27: error: 'class CommissionEmployee' has no member named
   'setBaseSalary'
```

Fig. 20.3 | Attempting to invoke derived-class-only functions via a base-class pointer.

Downcasting
The compiler will allow access to derived-class-only members from a base-class pointer that's aimed at a derived-class object *if* we explicitly cast the base-class pointer to a derived-class pointer—this is known as **downcasting**. As you know, it's possible to aim a base-class

pointer at a derived-class object. However, as we demonstrated in Fig. 20.3, a base-class pointer can be used to invoke *only* the functions declared in the base class. Downcasting allows a derived-class-specific operation on a derived-class object pointed to by a base-class pointer. After a downcast, the program *can* invoke derived-class functions that are not in the base class. Downcasting is a potentially dangerous operation. Section 20.8 demonstrates how to *safely* use downcasting.

Software Engineering Observation 20.3

If the address of a derived-class object has been assigned to a pointer of one of its direct or indirect base classes, it's acceptable to cast that base-class pointer back to a pointer of the derived-class type. In fact, this must *be done to call derived-class member functions that do not appear in the base class.*

20.3.4 Virtual Functions and Virtual Destructors

In Section 20.3.1, we aimed a base-class `CommissionEmployee` pointer at a derived-class `BasePlusCommissionEmployee` object, then invoked member function `print` through that pointer. Recall that the *type of the handle* determined which class's functionality to invoke. In that case, the `CommissionEmployee` pointer invoked the `CommissionEmployee` member function `print` on the `BasePlusCommissionEmployee` object, even though the pointer was aimed at a `BasePlusCommissionEmployee` object that has its own custom `print` function.

Software Engineering Observation 20.4

With `virtual` *functions, the type of the object,* not *the type of the handle used to invoke the member function, determines which version of a* `virtual` *function to invoke.*

Why `virtual` *Functions Are Useful*

First, we consider why `virtual` functions are useful. Suppose that shape classes such as `Circle`, `Triangle`, `Rectangle` and `Square` are all derived from base class `Shape`. Each of these classes might be endowed with the ability to *draw itself* via a member function `draw`, but the function for each shape is quite different. In a program that draws a set of shapes, it would be useful to be able to treat all the shapes generally as objects of the base class `Shape`. Then, to draw any shape, we could simply use a base-class `Shape` pointer to invoke function `draw` and let the program determine *dynamically* (i.e., at runtime) which derived-class `draw` function to use, based on the type of the object to which the base-class `Shape` pointer points at any given time. This is *polymorphic behavior*.

Declaring `virtual` *Functions*

To enable this behavior, we declare `draw` in the base class as a **`virtual` function**, and we **override** `draw` in *each* of the derived classes to draw the appropriate shape. From an implementation perspective, *overriding* a function is no different than *redefining* one (which is the approach we've been using until now). An overridden function in a derived class has the *same signature and return type* (i.e., *prototype*) as the function it overrides in its base class. If we do not declare the base-class function as `virtual`, we can *redefine* that function. By contrast, if we declare the base-class function as `virtual`, we can *override* that function to enable *polymorphic behavior*. We declare a `virtual` function by preceding the function's prototype with the keyword `virtual` in the base class. For example,

```
virtual void draw() const;
```

would appear in base class Shape. The preceding prototype declares that function draw is a virtual function that takes no arguments and returns nothing. This function is declared const because a draw function typically would not make changes to the Shape object on which it's invoked—virtual functions do *not* have to be const functions.

Software Engineering Observation 20.5
Once a function is declared virtual, it remains virtual all the way down the inheritance hierarchy from that point, even if that function is not explicitly declared virtual when a derived class overrides it.

Good Programming Practice 20.1
Even though certain functions are implicitly virtual because of a declaration made higher in the class hierarchy, explicitly declare these functions virtual at every level of the class hierarchy to promote program clarity.

Software Engineering Observation 20.6
When a derived class chooses not to override a virtual function from its base class, the derived class simply inherits its base class's virtual function implementation.

Invoking a virtual Function Through a Base-Class Pointer or Reference
If a program invokes a virtual function through a base-class pointer to a derived-class object (e.g., shapePtr->draw()) or a base-class reference to a derived-class object (e.g., shapeRef.draw()), the program will choose the correct derived-class draw function *dynamically* (i.e., at execution time) *based on the object type—not the pointer or reference type*. Choosing the appropriate function to call at execution time (rather than at compile time) is known as **dynamic binding** or **late binding**.

Invoking a virtual Function Through an Object's Name
When a virtual function is called by referencing a specific object by *name* and using the dot member-selection operator (e.g., squareObject.draw()), the function invocation is *resolved at compile time* (this is called **static binding**) and the virtual function that's called is the one defined for (or inherited by) the class of that particular object—this is *not* polymorphic behavior. Thus, dynamic binding with virtual functions occurs only off pointers (and, as we'll soon see, references).

virtual Functions in the CommissionEmployee Hierarchy
Now let's see how virtual functions can enable polymorphic behavior in our employee hierarchy. Figures 20.4–20.5 are the headers for classes CommissionEmployee and BasePlusCommissionEmployee, respectively. We modified these to declare each class's earnings and print member functions as virtual (lines 29–30 of Fig. 20.4 and lines 19–20 of Fig. 20.5). Because functions earnings and print are virtual in class CommissionEmployee, class BasePlusCommissionEmployee's earnings and print functions *override* class CommissionEmployee's. In addition, class BasePlusCommissionEmployee's earnings and print functions are declared **override**.

Error-Prevention Tip 20.1

Apply C++11's override *keyword to every overridden function in a derived-class. This forces the compiler to check whether the base class has a member function with the same name and parameter list (i.e., the same signature). If not, the compiler generates an error.*

Now, if we aim a base-class `CommissionEmployee` pointer at a derived-class `BasePlusCommissionEmployee` object, and the program uses that pointer to call either function `earnings` or `print`, the `BasePlusCommissionEmployee` object's corresponding function will be invoked. There were *no* changes to the member-function implementations of classes `CommissionEmployee` and `BasePlusCommissionEmployee`, so we reuse the versions of Figs. 19.14 and 19.15.

```cpp
1  // Fig. 20.4: CommissionEmployee.h
2  // CommissionEmployee class header declares earnings and print as virtual.
3  #ifndef COMMISSION_H
4  #define COMMISSION_H
5
6  #include <string> // C++ standard string class
7
8  class CommissionEmployee
9  {
10 public:
11    CommissionEmployee( const std::string &, const std::string &,
12       const std::string &, double = 0.0, double = 0.0 );
13
14    void setFirstName( const std::string & ); // set first name
15    std::string getFirstName() const; // return first name
16
17    void setLastName( const std::string & ); // set last name
18    std::string getLastName() const; // return last name
19
20    void setSocialSecurityNumber( const std::string & ); // set SSN
21    std::string getSocialSecurityNumber() const; // return SSN
22
23    void setGrossSales( double ); // set gross sales amount
24    double getGrossSales() const; // return gross sales amount
25
26    void setCommissionRate( double ); // set commission rate
27    double getCommissionRate() const; // return commission rate
28
29    virtual double earnings() const; // calculate earnings
30    virtual void print() const; // print object
31 private:
32    std::string firstName;
33    std::string lastName;
34    std::string socialSecurityNumber;
35    double grossSales; // gross weekly sales
36    double commissionRate; // commission percentage
37 }; // end class CommissionEmployee
38
39 #endif
```

Fig. 20.4 | CommissionEmployee class header declares earnings and print as virtual.

```
 1   // Fig. 20.5: BasePlusCommissionEmployee.h
 2   // BasePlusCommissionEmployee class derived from class
 3   // CommissionEmployee.
 4   #ifndef BASEPLUS_H
 5   #define BASEPLUS_H
 6
 7   #include <string> // C++ standard string class
 8   #include "CommissionEmployee.h" // CommissionEmployee class declaration
 9
10   class BasePlusCommissionEmployee : public CommissionEmployee
11   {
12   public:
13      BasePlusCommissionEmployee( const std::string &, const std::string &,
14         const std::string &, double = 0.0, double = 0.0, double = 0.0 );
15
16      void setBaseSalary( double ); // set base salary
17      double getBaseSalary() const; // return base salary
18
19      virtual double earnings() const override; // calculate earnings
20      virtual void print() const override; // print object
21   private:
22      double baseSalary; // base salary
23   }; // end class BasePlusCommissionEmployee
24
25   #endif
```

Fig. 20.5 | BasePlusCommissionEmployee class header declares earnings and print functions as virtual and override.

We modified Fig. 20.1 to create the program of Fig. 20.6. Lines 40–51 of Fig. 20.6 demonstrate again that a CommissionEmployee pointer aimed at a CommissionEmployee object can be used to invoke CommissionEmployee functionality, and a BasePlusCommissionEmployee pointer aimed at a BasePlusCommissionEmployee object can be used to invoke BasePlusCommissionEmployee functionality. Line 54 aims the base-class pointer commissionEmployeePtr at derived-class object basePlusCommissionEmployee. Note that when line 61 invokes member function print off the base-class pointer, the derived-class BasePlusCommissionEmployee's print member function is invoked, so line 61 outputs different text than line 53 does in Fig. 20.1 (when member function print was *not* declared virtual). We see that declaring a member function virtual causes the program to dynamically determine which function to invoke *based on the type of object to which the handle points, rather than on the type of the handle.* Note again that when commissionEmployeePtr points to a CommissionEmployee object, class CommissionEmployee's print function is invoked (Fig. 20.6, line 40), and when CommissionEmployeePtr points to a BasePlusCommissionEmployee object, class BasePlusCommissionEmployee's print function is invoked (line 61). Thus, the same message—print, in this case—sent (off a base-class pointer) to a variety of objects related by inheritance to that base class, takes on many forms—this is polymorphic behavior.

```cpp
1   // Fig. 20.6: fig20_06.cpp
2   // Introducing polymorphism, virtual functions and dynamic binding.
3   #include <iostream>
4   #include <iomanip>
5   #include "CommissionEmployee.h"
6   #include "BasePlusCommissionEmployee.h"
7   using namespace std;
8
9   int main()
10  {
11     // create base-class object
12     CommissionEmployee commissionEmployee(
13        "Sue", "Jones", "222-22-2222", 10000, .06 );
14
15     // create base-class pointer
16     CommissionEmployee *commissionEmployeePtr = nullptr;
17
18     // create derived-class object
19     BasePlusCommissionEmployee basePlusCommissionEmployee(
20        "Bob", "Lewis", "333-33-3333", 5000, .04, 300 );
21
22     // create derived-class pointer
23     BasePlusCommissionEmployee *basePlusCommissionEmployeePtr = nullptr;
24
25     // set floating-point output formatting
26     cout << fixed << setprecision( 2 );
27
28     // output objects using static binding
29     cout << "Invoking print function on base-class and derived-class "
30        << "\nobjects with static binding\n\n";
31     commissionEmployee.print(); // static binding
32     cout << "\n\n";
33     basePlusCommissionEmployee.print(); // static binding
34
35     // output objects using dynamic binding
36     cout << "\n\n\nInvoking print function on base-class and "
37        << "derived-class \nobjects with dynamic binding";
38
39     // aim base-class pointer at base-class object and print
40     commissionEmployeePtr = &commissionEmployee;
41     cout << "\n\nCalling virtual function print with base-class pointer"
42        << "\nto base-class object invokes base-class "
43        << "print function:\n\n";
44     commissionEmployeePtr->print(); // invokes base-class print
45
46     // aim derived-class pointer at derived-class object and print
47     basePlusCommissionEmployeePtr = &basePlusCommissionEmployee;
48     cout << "\n\nCalling virtual function print with derived-class "
49        << "pointer\nto derived-class object invokes derived-class "
50        << "print function:\n\n";
51     basePlusCommissionEmployeePtr->print(); // invokes derived-class print
```

Fig. 20.6 | Demonstrating polymorphism by invoking a derived-class virtual function via a base-class pointer to a derived-class object. (Part 1 of 2.)

```
52
53     // aim base-class pointer at derived-class object and print
54     commissionEmployeePtr = &basePlusCommissionEmployee;
55     cout << "\n\nCalling virtual function print with base-class pointer"
56        << "\nto derived-class object invokes derived-class "
57        << "print function:\n\n";
58
59     // polymorphism; invokes BasePlusCommissionEmployee's print;
60     // base-class pointer to derived-class object
61     commissionEmployeePtr->print();
62     cout << endl;
63  } // end main
```

```
Invoking print function on base-class and derived-class
objects with static binding

commission employee: Sue Jones
social security number: 222-22-2222
gross sales: 10000.00
commission rate: 0.06

base-salaried commission employee: Bob Lewis
social security number: 333-33-3333
gross sales: 5000.00
commission rate: 0.04
base salary: 300.00


Invoking print function on base-class and derived-class
objects with dynamic binding

Calling virtual function print with base-class pointer
to base-class object invokes base-class print function:

commission employee: Sue Jones
social security number: 222-22-2222
gross sales: 10000.00
commission rate: 0.06

Calling virtual function print with derived-class pointer
to derived-class object invokes derived-class print function:

base-salaried commission employee: Bob Lewis
social security number: 333-33-3333
gross sales: 5000.00
commission rate: 0.04
base salary: 300.00

Calling virtual function print with base-class pointer
to derived-class object invokes derived-class print function:

base-salaried commission employee: Bob Lewis
social security number: 333-33-3333
gross sales: 5000.00
commission rate: 0.04
base salary: 300.00——— Notice that the base salary is now displayed
```

Fig. 20.6 | Demonstrating polymorphism by invoking a derived-class `virtual` function via a base-class pointer to a derived-class object. (Part 2 of 2.)

virtual Destructors

A problem can occur when using polymorphism to process dynamically allocated objects of a class hierarchy. So far you've seen destructors that are not declared with keyword virtual. If a derived-class object with a non-virtual destructor is destroyed by applying the delete operator to a *base-class pointer* to the object, the C++ standard specifies that the behavior is *undefined*.

The simple solution to this problem is to create a public **virtual destructor** in the base class. If a base class destructor is declared virtual, the destructors of any derived classes are *also* virtual and they *override* the base class destructor. For example, in class CommissionEmployee's definition, we can define the virtual destructor as follows:

```
virtual ~CommissionEmployee() { }
```

Now, if an object in the hierarchy is destroyed explicitly by applying the delete operator to a *base-class pointer*, the destructor for the *appropriate class* is called based on the object to which the base-class pointer points. Remember, when a derived-class object is destroyed, the base-class part of the derived-class object is also destroyed, so it's important for the destructors of *both* the derived and base classes to execute. The base-class destructor automatically executes after the derived-class destructor. From this point forward, we'll include a virtual destructor in *every* class that contains virtual functions.

Error-Prevention Tip 20.2

If a class has virtual functions, always provide a virtual destructor, even if one is not required for the class. This ensures that a custom derived-class destructor (if there is one) will be invoked when a derived-class object is deleted via a base class pointer.

Common Programming Error 20.1

Constructors cannot be virtual. Declaring a constructor virtual is a compilation error.

C++11: final Member Functions and Classes

Prior to C++11, a derived class could override *any* of its base class's virtual functions. In C++11, a base-class virtual function that's declared **final** in its prototype, as in

```
virtual someFunction( parameters ) final;
```

cannot be overridden in any derived class—this guarantees that the base class's final member function definition will be used by all base-class objects and by all objects of the base class's direct *and* indirect derived classes. Similarly, prior to C++11, *any* existing class could be used as a base class in a hierarchy. As of C++11, you can declare a class as final to prevent it from being used as a base class, as in

```
class MyClass final // this class cannot be a base class
{
   // class body
};
```

Attempting to override a final member function or inherit from a final base class results in a compilation error.

20.4 Type Fields and switch Statements

One way to determine the type of an object is to use a switch statement to check the value of a field in the object. This allows us to distinguish among object types, then invoke an appropriate action for a particular object. For example, in a hierarchy of shapes in which each shape object has a shapeType attribute, a switch statement could check the object's shapeType to determine which print function to call.

Using switch logic exposes programs to a variety of potential problems. For example, you might forget to include a type test when one is warranted, or might forget to test all possible cases in a switch statement. When modifying a switch-based system by adding new types, you might forget to insert the new cases in *all* relevant switch statements. Every addition or deletion of a class requires the modification of every switch statement in the system; tracking these statements down can be time consuming and error prone.

Software Engineering Observation 20.7

Polymorphic programming can eliminate the need for switch logic. By using the polymorphism mechanism to perform the equivalent logic, you can avoid the kinds of errors typically associated with switch logic.

Software Engineering Observation 20.8

An interesting consequence of using polymorphism is that programs take on a simplified appearance. They contain less branching logic and simpler sequential code.

20.5 Abstract Classes and Pure virtual Functions

When we think of a class as a type, we assume that programs will create objects of that type. However, there are cases in which it's useful to define *classes from which you never intend to instantiate any objects*. Such classes are called **abstract classes**. Because these classes normally are used as base classes in inheritance hierarchies, we refer to them as **abstract base classes**. These classes cannot be used to instantiate objects, because, as we'll soon see, abstract classes are *incomplete*—derived classes must define the "missing pieces" before objects of these classes can be instantiated. We build programs with abstract classes in Section 20.6.

An abstract class is a base class from which other classes can inherit. Classes that can be used to instantiate objects are called **concrete classes**. Such classes define or inherit implementations for *every* member function they declare. We could have an *abstract* base class TwoDimensionalShape and derive such *concrete* classes as Square, Circle and Triangle. We could also have an *abstract* base class ThreeDimensionalShape and derive such *concrete* classes as Cube, Sphere and Cylinder. Abstract base classes are *too generic* to define real objects; we need to be *more specific* before we can think of instantiating objects. For example, if someone tells you to "draw the two-dimensional shape," what shape would you draw? Concrete classes provide the *specifics* that make it possible to instantiate objects.

An inheritance hierarchy does *not* need to contain any abstract classes, but many object-oriented systems have class hierarchies headed by abstract base classes. In some cases, abstract classes constitute the top few levels of the hierarchy. A good example of this is the shape hierarchy in Fig. 19.3, which begins with abstract base class Shape. On the next level of the hierarchy we have two more abstract base classes—TwoDimensionalShape and `ThreeDimensionalShape`. The next level of the hierarchy defines *concrete* classes for two-dimensional shapes (namely, `Circle`, `Square` and `Triangle`) and for three-dimensional shapes (namely, `Sphere`, `Cube` and `Tetrahedron`).

Pure Virtual Functions

A class is made abstract by declaring one or more of its `virtual` functions to be "pure." A **pure `virtual` function** is specified by placing "`= 0`" in its declaration, as in

```
virtual void draw() const = 0; // pure virtual function
```

The "`= 0`" is a **pure specifier**. Pure `virtual` functions typically do *not* provide implementations, though they can. Each *concrete* derived class *must override all* base-class pure `virtual` functions with concrete implementations of those functions; otherwise, the derived class is also abstract. The difference between a `virtual` function and a pure `virtual` function is that a `virtual` function *has* an implementation and gives the derived class the *option* of overriding the function; by contrast, a pure `virtual` function does *not* have an implementation and *requires* the derived class to override the function for that derived class to be concrete; otherwise the derived class remains *abstract*.

Pure `virtual` functions are used when it does *not* make sense for the base class to have an implementation of a function, but you want all concrete derived classes to implement the function. Returning to our earlier example of space objects, it does not make sense for the base class `SpaceObject` to have an implementation for function `draw` (as there is no way to draw a generic space object without having more information about what type of space object is being drawn). An example of a function that would be defined as `virtual` (and not pure `virtual`) would be one that returns a name for the object. We can name a generic `SpaceObject` (for instance, as `"space object"`), so a default implementation for this function can be provided, and the function does not need to be *pure* `virtual`. The function is still declared `virtual`, however, because it's expected that derived classes will override this function to provide *more specific* names for the derived-class objects.

Software Engineering Observation 20.9

An abstract class defines a common public interface for the various classes in a class hierarchy. An abstract class contains one or more pure `virtual` functions that concrete derived classes must override.

Common Programming Error 20.2

Failure to override a pure `virtual` function in a derived class makes that class abstract. Attempting to instantiate an object of an abstract class causes a compilation error.

Software Engineering Observation 20.10

An abstract class has at least one pure `virtual` function. An abstract class also can have data members and concrete functions (including constructors and destructors), which are subject to the normal rules of inheritance by derived classes.

Although we *cannot* instantiate objects of an abstract base class, we *can* use the abstract base class to declare *pointers* and *references* that can refer to objects of any *concrete classes* derived from the abstract class. Programs typically use such pointers and references to manipulate derived-class objects polymorphically.

Device Drivers and Polymorphism

Polymorphism is particularly effective for implementing *layered software systems*. In operating systems, for example, each type of physical device could operate quite differently from the others. Even so, commands to *read* or *write* data from and to devices may have a certain uniformity. The *write* message sent to a *device-driver* object needs to be interpreted specifically in the context of that device driver and how that device driver manipulates devices of a specific type. However, the *write* call itself really is no different from the *write* to any other device in the system—place some number of *bytes* from memory onto that device. An object-oriented operating system could use an abstract base class to provide an interface appropriate for all device drivers. Then, through inheritance from that abstract base class, derived classes are formed that all operate similarly. The capabilities (i.e., the public functions) offered by the device drivers are provided as pure virtual functions in the abstract base class. The implementations of these pure virtual functions are provided in the derived classes that correspond to the specific types of device drivers. This architecture also allows new devices to be *added* to a system easily. The user can just plug in the device and install its new device driver. The operating system "talks" to this new device through its device driver, which has the same public member functions as all other device drivers—those defined in the device driver abstract base class.

20.6 Case Study: Payroll System Using Polymorphism

This section reexamines the CommissionEmployee–BasePlusCommissionEmployee hierarchy that we explored throughout Section 19.3. In this example, we use an abstract class and polymorphism to perform payroll calculations based on the type of employee. We create an enhanced employee hierarchy to solve the following problem:

> *A company pays its employees weekly. The employees are of three types:* Salaried employees *are paid a fixed weekly salary regardless of the number of hours worked,* commission employees *are paid a percentage of their sales and* base-salary-plus-commission employees *receive a base salary plus a percentage of their sales. For the current pay period, the company has decided to reward base-salary-plus-commission employees by adding 10 percent to their base salaries. The company wants to implement a C++ program that performs its payroll calculations polymorphically.*

We use abstract class Employee to represent the general concept of an employee. The classes that derive directly from Employee are SalariedEmployee and CommissionEmployee. Class BasePlusCommissionEmployee—derived from CommissionEmployee—represents the last employee type. The UML class diagram in Fig. 20.7 shows the inheritance hierarchy for our polymorphic employee payroll application. The abstract class name Employee is *italicized*, as per the convention of the UML.

Abstract base class Employee declares the "interface" to the hierarchy—that is, the set of member functions that a program can invoke on all Employee objects. Each employee, regardless of the way his or her earnings are calculated, has a first name, a last name and a social security number, so private data members firstName, lastName and socialSecurityNumber appear in abstract base class Employee.

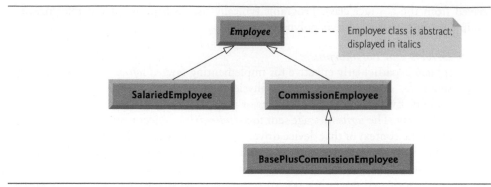

Fig. 20.7 | Employee hierarchy UML class diagram.

Software Engineering Observation 20.11

A derived class can inherit interface and/or implementation from a base class. Hierarchies designed for implementation inheritance tend to have their functionality high in the hierarchy—each new derived class inherits one or more member functions that were defined in a base class, and the derived class uses the base-class definitions. Hierarchies designed for interface inheritance tend to have their functionality lower in the hierarchy—a base class specifies one or more functions that should be defined for each class in the hierarchy (i.e., they have the same prototype), but the individual derived classes provide their own implementations of the function(s).

The following sections implement the Employee class hierarchy. The first five each implement one of the abstract or concrete classes. The last section implements a test program that builds objects of all these classes and processes the objects polymorphically.

20.6.1 Creating Abstract Base Class Employee

Class Employee (Figs. 20.9–20.10, discussed in further detail shortly) provides functions earnings and print, in addition to various *get* and *set* functions that manipulate Employee's data members. An earnings function certainly applies generally to all employees, but each earnings calculation depends on the employee's class. So we declare earnings as pure virtual in base class Employee because *a default implementation does not make sense* for that function—there is not enough information to determine what amount earnings should return. Each derived class *overrides* earnings with an appropriate implementation. To calculate an employee's earnings, the program assigns the address of an employee's object to a base class Employee *pointer*, then invokes the earnings function on that object. We maintain a vector of Employee pointers, each of which points to an Employee object. *Of course, there cannot be Employee objects, because Employee is an abstract class—because of inheritance, however, all objects of all concrete derived classes of Employee may nevertheless be thought of as Employee objects*. The program iterates through the vector and calls function earnings for each Employee object. C++ processes these function calls *polymorphically*. Including earnings as a pure virtual function in Employee *forces* every direct derived class of Employee that wishes to be a *concrete* class to *override* earnings.

Function print in class Employee displays the first name, last name and social security number of the employee. As we'll see, each derived class of Employee overrides function print to output the employee's type (e.g., "salaried employee:") followed by the rest of the employee's information. Function print in the derived classes could also call earnings, even though earnings is a pure-virtual function in base class Employee.

The diagram in Fig. 20.8 shows each of the four classes in the hierarchy down the left side and functions earnings and print across the top. For each class, the diagram shows the desired results of each function. Italic text represents where the values from a particular object are used in the earnings and print functions. Class Employee specifies "= 0" for function earnings to indicate that this is a pure virtual function and hence has *no* implementation. Each derived class overrides this function to provide an appropriate implementation. We do *not* list base class Employee's *get* and *set* functions because they're *not* overridden in any of the derived classes—each of these functions is inherited and used "as is" by each of the derived classes.

	earnings	print
Employee	= 0	*firstName lastName* social security number: *SSN*
Salaried-Employee	*weeklySalary*	salaried employee: *firstName lastName* social security number: *SSN* weekly salary: *weeklySalary*
Commission-Employee	*commissionRate * grossSales*	commission employee: *firstName lastName* social security number: *SSN* gross sales: *grossSales*; commission rate: *commissionRate*
BasePlus-Commission-Employee	*(commissionRate * grossSales) + baseSalary*	base-salaried commission employee: *firstName lastName* social security number: *SSN* gross sales: *grossSales*; commission rate: *commissionRate*; base salary: *baseSalary*

Fig. 20.8 | Polymorphic interface for the Employee hierarchy classes.

Employee Class Header

Let's consider class Employee's header (Fig. 20.9). The public member functions include a constructor that takes the first name, last name and social security number as arguments (lines 11–12); a virtual destructor (line 13); *set* functions that set the first name, last name and social security number (lines 15, 18 and 21, respectively); *get* functions that return the first name, last name and social security number (lines 16, 19 and 22, respectively); pure virtual function earnings (line 25) and virtual function print (line 26).

```
1   // Fig. 20.9: Employee.h
2   // Employee abstract base class.
3   #ifndef EMPLOYEE_H
```

Fig. 20.9 | Employee abstract base class. (Part 1 of 2.)

```
4    #define EMPLOYEE_H
5
6    #include <string> // C++ standard string class
7
8    class Employee
9    {
10   public:
11      Employee( const std::string &, const std::string &,
12         const std::string & );
13      virtual ~Employee() { } // virtual destructor
14
15      void setFirstName( const std::string & ); // set first name
16      std::string getFirstName() const; // return first name
17
18      void setLastName( const std::string & ); // set last name
19      std::string getLastName() const; // return last name
20
21      void setSocialSecurityNumber( const std::string & ); // set SSN
22      std::string getSocialSecurityNumber() const; // return SSN
23
24      // pure virtual function makes Employee an abstract base class
25      virtual double earnings() const = 0; // pure virtual
26      virtual void print() const; // virtual
27   private:
28      std::string firstName;
29      std::string lastName;
30      std::string socialSecurityNumber;
31   }; // end class Employee
32
33   #endif // EMPLOYEE_H
```

Fig. 20.9 | Employee abstract base class. (Part 2 of 2.)

Recall that we declared earnings as a pure virtual function because first we must know the *specific* Employee type to determine the appropriate earnings calculations. Declaring this function as pure virtual indicates that each concrete derived class *must* provide an earnings implementation and that a program can use base-class Employee pointers to invoke function earnings *polymorphically* for *any* type of Employee.

Employee Class Member-Function Definitions
Figure 20.10 contains the member-function definitions for class Employee. No implementation is provided for virtual function earnings. The Employee constructor (lines 9–14) does not validate the social security number. Normally, such validation should be provided.

```
1    // Fig. 20.10: Employee.cpp
2    // Abstract-base-class Employee member-function definitions.
3    // Note: No definitions are given for pure virtual functions.
4    #include <iostream>
5    #include "Employee.h" // Employee class definition
6    using namespace std;
```

Fig. 20.10 | Employee class implementation file. (Part 1 of 2.)

```
7
8    // constructor
9    Employee::Employee( const string &first, const string &last,
10      const string &ssn )
11      : firstName( first ), lastName( last ), socialSecurityNumber( ssn )
12   {
13      // empty body
14   } // end Employee constructor
15
16   // set first name
17   void Employee::setFirstName( const string &first )
18   {
19      firstName = first;
20   } // end function setFirstName
21
22   // return first name
23   string Employee::getFirstName() const
24   {
25      return firstName;
26   } // end function getFirstName
27
28   // set last name
29   void Employee::setLastName( const string &last )
30   {
31      lastName = last;
32   } // end function setLastName
33
34   // return last name
35   string Employee::getLastName() const
36   {
37      return lastName;
38   } // end function getLastName
39
40   // set social security number
41   void Employee::setSocialSecurityNumber( const string &ssn )
42   {
43      socialSecurityNumber = ssn; // should validate
44   } // end function setSocialSecurityNumber
45
46   // return social security number
47   string Employee::getSocialSecurityNumber() const
48   {
49      return socialSecurityNumber;
50   } // end function getSocialSecurityNumber
51
52   // print Employee's information (virtual, but not pure virtual)
53   void Employee::print() const
54   {
55      cout << getFirstName() << ' ' << getLastName()
56         << "\nsocial security number: " << getSocialSecurityNumber();
57   } // end function print
```

Fig. 20.10 | Employee class implementation file. (Part 2 of 2.)

The `virtual` function `print` (lines 53–57) provides an *implementation* that will be *overridden* in *each* of the derived classes. Each of these functions will, however, use the abstract class's version of `print` to print information *common to all classes* in the `Employee` hierarchy.

20.6.2 Creating Concrete Derived Class `SalariedEmployee`

Class `SalariedEmployee` (Figs. 20.11–20.12) derives from class `Employee` (line 9 of Fig. 20.11). The `public` member functions include a constructor that takes a first name, a last name, a social security number and a weekly salary as arguments (lines 12–13); a `virtual` destructor (line 14); a *set* function to assign a new nonnegative value to data member `weeklySalary` (line 16); a *get* function to return `weeklySalary`'s value (line 17); a `virtual` function `earnings` that calculates a `SalariedEmployee`'s earnings (line 20) and a `virtual` function `print` (line 21) that outputs the employee's type, namely, `"salaried employee: "` followed by employee-specific information produced by base class `Employee`'s `print` function and `SalariedEmployee`'s `getWeeklySalary` function.

```
 1   // Fig. 20.11: SalariedEmployee.h
 2   // SalariedEmployee class derived from Employee.
 3   #ifndef SALARIED_H
 4   #define SALARIED_H
 5
 6   #include <string> // C++ standard string class
 7   #include "Employee.h" // Employee class definition
 8
 9   class SalariedEmployee : public Employee
10   {
11   public:
12      SalariedEmployee( const std::string &, const std::string &,
13         const std::string &, double = 0.0 );
14      virtual ~SalariedEmployee() { } // virtual destructor
15
16      void setWeeklySalary( double ); // set weekly salary
17      double getWeeklySalary() const; // return weekly salary
18
19      // keyword virtual signals intent to override
20      virtual double earnings() const override; // calculate earnings
21      virtual void print() const override; // print object
22   private:
23      double weeklySalary; // salary per week
24   }; // end class SalariedEmployee
25
26   #endif // SALARIED_H
```

Fig. 20.11 | `SalariedEmployee` class header.

SalariedEmployee Class Member-Function Definitions
Figure 20.12 contains the member-function definitions for `SalariedEmployee`. The class's constructor passes the first name, last name and social security number to the Employee constructor (line 11) to initialize the private data members that are inherited from the base class, but not directly accessible in the derived class. Function `earnings`

(lines 33–36) overrides pure `virtual` function earnings in Employee to provide a *concrete* implementation that returns the SalariedEmployee's weekly salary. If we did not define earnings, class SalariedEmployee would be an *abstract* class, and any attempt to instantiate a SalariedEmployee object would cause a compilation error. In class SalariedEmployee's header, we declared member functions earnings and print as `virtual` (lines 20–21 of Fig. 20.11)—actually, placing the `virtual` keyword before these member functions is *redundant*. We defined them as `virtual` in base class Employee, so they remain `virtual` functions throughout the class hierarchy. Explicitly declaring such functions `virtual` at every level of the hierarchy promotes program clarity. Not declaring earnings as pure `virtual` signals our intent to provide an implementation in this concrete class.

```
1   // Fig. 20.12: SalariedEmployee.cpp
2   // SalariedEmployee class member-function definitions.
3   #include <iostream>
4   #include <stdexcept>
5   #include "SalariedEmployee.h" // SalariedEmployee class definition
6   using namespace std;
7
8   // constructor
9   SalariedEmployee::SalariedEmployee( const string &first,
10     const string &last, const string &ssn, double salary )
11     : Employee( first, last, ssn )
12  {
13     setWeeklySalary( salary );
14  } // end SalariedEmployee constructor
15
16  // set salary
17  void SalariedEmployee::setWeeklySalary( double salary )
18  {
19     if ( salary >= 0.0 )
20        weeklySalary = salary;
21     else
22        throw invalid_argument( "Weekly salary must be >= 0.0" );
23  } // end function setWeeklySalary
24
25  // return salary
26  double SalariedEmployee::getWeeklySalary() const
27  {
28     return weeklySalary;
29  } // end function getWeeklySalary
30
31  // calculate earnings;
32  // override pure virtual function earnings in Employee
33  double SalariedEmployee::earnings() const
34  {
35     return getWeeklySalary();
36  } // end function earnings
37
38  // print SalariedEmployee's information
39  void SalariedEmployee::print() const
40  {
```

Fig. 20.12 | SalariedEmployee class implementation file. (Part 1 of 2.)

```
41        cout << "salaried employee: ";
42        Employee::print(); // reuse abstract base-class print function
43        cout << "\nweekly salary: " << getWeeklySalary();
44    } // end function print
```

Fig. 20.12 | SalariedEmployee class implementation file. (Part 2 of 2.)

Function print of class SalariedEmployee (lines 39–44 of Fig. 20.12) overrides Employee function print. If class SalariedEmployee did not override print, SalariedEmployee would inherit the Employee version of print. In that case, SalariedEmployee's print function would simply return the employee's full name and social security number, which does not adequately represent a SalariedEmployee. To print a SalariedEmployee's complete information, the derived class's print function outputs "salaried employee: " followed by the base-class Employee-specific information (i.e., first name, last name and social security number) printed by *invoking the base class's print function* using the scope resolution operator (line 42)—this is a nice example of code reuse. Without the scope resolution operator, the print call would cause *infinite recursion*. The output produced by SalariedEmployee's print function also contains the employee's weekly salary obtained by invoking the class's getWeeklySalary function.

20.6.3 Creating Concrete Derived Class CommissionEmployee

Class CommissionEmployee (Figs. 20.13–20.14) derives from Employee (Fig. 20.13, line 9). The member-function implementations (Fig. 20.14) include a constructor (lines 9–15) that takes a first name, last name, social security number, sales amount and commission rate; *set* functions (lines 18–24 and 33–39) to assign new values to data members commissionRate and grossSales, respectively; *get* functions (lines 27–30 and 42–45) that retrieve their values; function earnings (lines 48–51) to calculate a CommissionEmployee's earnings; and function print (lines 54–60) to output the employee's type, namely, "commission employee: " and employee-specific information. The constructor passes the first name, last name and social security number to the Employee constructor (line 11) to initialize Employee's private data members. Function print calls base-class function print (line 57) to display the Employee-specific information.

```
1   // Fig. 20.13: CommissionEmployee.h
2   // CommissionEmployee class derived from Employee.
3   #ifndef COMMISSION_H
4   #define COMMISSION_H
5
6   #include <string> // C++ standard string class
7   #include "Employee.h" // Employee class definition
8
9   class CommissionEmployee : public Employee
10  {
11  public:
12     CommissionEmployee( const std::string &, const std::string &,
13        const std::string &, double = 0.0, double = 0.0 );
```

Fig. 20.13 | CommissionEmployee class header. (Part 1 of 2.)

```
14      virtual ~CommissionEmployee() { } // virtual destructor
15
16      void setCommissionRate( double ); // set commission rate
17      double getCommissionRate() const; // return commission rate
18
19      void setGrossSales( double ); // set gross sales amount
20      double getGrossSales() const; // return gross sales amount
21
22      // keyword virtual signals intent to override
23      virtual double earnings() const override; // calculate earnings
24      virtual void print() const override; // print object
25   private:
26      double grossSales; // gross weekly sales
27      double commissionRate; // commission percentage
28   }; // end class CommissionEmployee
29
30   #endif // COMMISSION_H
```

Fig. 20.13 | CommissionEmployee class header. (Part 2 of 2.)

```
1    // Fig. 20.14: CommissionEmployee.cpp
2    // CommissionEmployee class member-function definitions.
3    #include <iostream>
4    #include <stdexcept>
5    #include "CommissionEmployee.h" // CommissionEmployee class definition
6    using namespace std;
7
8    // constructor
9    CommissionEmployee::CommissionEmployee( const string &first,
10      const string &last, const string &ssn, double sales, double rate )
11      : Employee( first, last, ssn )
12   {
13      setGrossSales( sales );
14      setCommissionRate( rate );
15   } // end CommissionEmployee constructor
16
17   // set gross sales amount
18   void CommissionEmployee::setGrossSales( double sales )
19   {
20      if ( sales >= 0.0 )
21         grossSales = sales;
22      else
23         throw invalid_argument( "Gross sales must be >= 0.0" );
24   } // end function setGrossSales
25
26   // return gross sales amount
27   double CommissionEmployee::getGrossSales() const
28   {
29      return grossSales;
30   } // end function getGrossSales
31
```

Fig. 20.14 | CommissionEmployee class implementation file. (Part 1 of 2.)

```
32   // set commission rate
33   void CommissionEmployee::setCommissionRate( double rate )
34   {
35      if ( rate > 0.0 && rate < 1.0 )
36         commissionRate = rate;
37      else
38         throw invalid_argument( "Commission rate must be > 0.0 and < 1.0" );
39   } // end function setCommissionRate
40
41   // return commission rate
42   double CommissionEmployee::getCommissionRate() const
43   {
44      return commissionRate;
45   } // end function getCommissionRate
46
47   // calculate earnings; override pure virtual function earnings in Employee
48   double CommissionEmployee::earnings() const
49   {
50      return getCommissionRate() * getGrossSales();
51   } // end function earnings
52
53   // print CommissionEmployee's information
54   void CommissionEmployee::print() const
55   {
56      cout << "commission employee: ";
57      Employee::print(); // code reuse
58      cout << "\ngross sales: " << getGrossSales()
59         << "; commission rate: " << getCommissionRate();
60   } // end function print
```

Fig. 20.14 | CommissionEmployee class implementation file. (Part 2 of 2.)

20.6.4 Creating Indirect Concrete Derived Class BasePlusCommissionEmployee

Class BasePlusCommissionEmployee (Figs. 20.15–20.16) directly inherits from class CommissionEmployee (line 9 of Fig. 20.15) and therefore is an *indirect* derived class of class Employee. Class BasePlusCommissionEmployee's member-function implementations include a constructor (lines 9–15 of Fig. 20.16) that takes as arguments a first name, a last name, a social security number, a sales amount, a commission rate *and* a base salary. It then passes the first name, last name, social security number, sales amount and commission rate to the CommissionEmployee constructor (line 12) to initialize the inherited members. BasePlusCommissionEmployee also contains a *set* function (lines 18–24) to assign a new value to data member baseSalary and a *get* function (lines 27–30) to return baseSalary's value. Function earnings (lines 34–37) calculates a BasePlusCommissionEmployee's earnings. Line 36 in function earnings calls base-class CommissionEmployee's earnings function to calculate the commission-based portion of the employee's earnings. This is another nice example of code reuse. BasePlusCommissionEmployee's print function (lines 40–45) outputs "base-salaried", followed by the output of base-class CommissionEmployee's print function (another example of code reuse), then the base salary. The resulting output begins with "base-salaried commission employee: " followed by the rest of the Base-

PlusCommissionEmployee's information. Recall that CommissionEmployee's print displays the employee's first name, last name and social security number by invoking the print function of its base class (i.e., Employee)—yet another example of code reuse. BasePlusCommissionEmployee's print initiates a chain of functions calls that spans *all three levels* of the Employee hierarchy.

```cpp
1   // Fig. 20.15: BasePlusCommissionEmployee.h
2   // BasePlusCommissionEmployee class derived from CommissionEmployee.
3   #ifndef BASEPLUS_H
4   #define BASEPLUS_H
5
6   #include <string> // C++ standard string class
7   #include "CommissionEmployee.h" // CommissionEmployee class definition
8
9   class BasePlusCommissionEmployee : public CommissionEmployee
10  {
11  public:
12     BasePlusCommissionEmployee( const std::string &, const std::string &,
13        const std::string &, double = 0.0, double = 0.0, double = 0.0 );
14     virtual ~CommissionEmployee() { } // virtual destructor
15
16     void setBaseSalary( double ); // set base salary
17     double getBaseSalary() const; // return base salary
18
19     // keyword virtual signals intent to override
20     virtual double earnings() const override; // calculate earnings
21     virtual void print() const override; // print object
22  private:
23     double baseSalary; // base salary per week
24  }; // end class BasePlusCommissionEmployee
25
26  #endif // BASEPLUS_H
```

Fig. 20.15 | BasePlusCommissionEmployee class header.

```cpp
1   // Fig. 20.16: BasePlusCommissionEmployee.cpp
2   // BasePlusCommissionEmployee member-function definitions.
3   #include <iostream>
4   #include <stdexcept>
5   #include "BasePlusCommissionEmployee.h"
6   using namespace std;
7
8   // constructor
9   BasePlusCommissionEmployee::BasePlusCommissionEmployee(
10     const string &first, const string &last, const string &ssn,
11     double sales, double rate, double salary )
12     : CommissionEmployee( first, last, ssn, sales, rate )
13  {
14     setBaseSalary( salary ); // validate and store base salary
15  } // end BasePlusCommissionEmployee constructor
16
```

Fig. 20.16 | BasePlusCommissionEmployee class implementation file. (Part 1 of 2.)

```
17   // set base salary
18   void BasePlusCommissionEmployee::setBaseSalary( double salary )
19   {
20      if ( salary >= 0.0 )
21         baseSalary = salary;
22      else
23         throw invalid_argument( "Salary must be >= 0.0" );
24   } // end function setBaseSalary
25
26   // return base salary
27   double BasePlusCommissionEmployee::getBaseSalary() const
28   {
29      return baseSalary;
30   } // end function getBaseSalary
31
32   // calculate earnings;
33   // override virtual function earnings in CommissionEmployee
34   double BasePlusCommissionEmployee::earnings() const
35   {
36      return getBaseSalary() + CommissionEmployee::earnings();
37   } // end function earnings
38
39   // print BasePlusCommissionEmployee's information
40   void BasePlusCommissionEmployee::print() const
41   {
42      cout << "base-salaried ";
43      CommissionEmployee::print(); // code reuse
44      cout << "; base salary: " << getBaseSalary();
45   } // end function print
```

Fig. 20.16 | BasePlusCommissionEmployee class implementation file. (Part 2 of 2.)

20.6.5 Demonstrating Polymorphic Processing

To test our Employee hierarchy, the program in Fig. 20.17 creates an object of each of the three concrete classes SalariedEmployee, CommissionEmployee and BasePlusCommissionEmployee. The program manipulates these objects, first with *static binding*, then *polymorphically*, using a vector of Employee pointers. Lines 22–27 create objects of each of the three concrete Employee derived classes. Lines 32–38 output each Employee's information and earnings. Each member-function invocation in lines 32–37 is an example of *static binding*—at *compile time*, because we are using *name handles* (not *pointers* or *references* that could be set at *execution time*), the *compiler* can identify each object's type to determine which print and earnings functions are called.

```
1   // Fig. 20.17: fig20_17.cpp
2   // Processing Employee derived-class objects individually
3   // and polymorphically using dynamic binding.
4   #include <iostream>
5   #include <iomanip>
6   #include <vector>
```

Fig. 20.17 | Employee class hierarchy driver program. (Part 1 of 4.)

```
7   #include "Employee.h"
8   #include "SalariedEmployee.h"
9   #include "CommissionEmployee.h"
10  #include "BasePlusCommissionEmployee.h"
11  using namespace std;
12
13  void virtualViaPointer( const Employee * const ); // prototype
14  void virtualViaReference( const Employee & ); // prototype
15
16  int main()
17  {
18     // set floating-point output formatting
19     cout << fixed << setprecision( 2 );
20
21     // create derived-class objects
22     SalariedEmployee salariedEmployee(
23        "John", "Smith", "111-11-1111", 800 );
24     CommissionEmployee commissionEmployee(
25        "Sue", "Jones", "333-33-3333", 10000, .06 );
26     BasePlusCommissionEmployee basePlusCommissionEmployee(
27        "Bob", "Lewis", "444-44-4444", 5000, .04, 300 );
28
29     cout << "Employees processed individually using static binding:\n\n";
30
31     // output each Employee's information and earnings using static binding
32     salariedEmployee.print();
33     cout << "\nearned $" << salariedEmployee.earnings() << "\n\n";
34     commissionEmployee.print();
35     cout << "\nearned $" << commissionEmployee.earnings() << "\n\n";
36     basePlusCommissionEmployee.print();
37     cout << "\nearned $" << basePlusCommissionEmployee.earnings()
38        << "\n\n";
39
40     // create vector of three base-class pointers
41     vector< Employee * > employees( 3 );
42
43     // initialize vector with pointers to Employees
44     employees[ 0 ] = &salariedEmployee;
45     employees[ 1 ] = &commissionEmployee;
46     employees[ 2 ] = &basePlusCommissionEmployee;
47
48     cout << "Employees processed polymorphically via dynamic binding:\n\n";
49
50     // call virtualViaPointer to print each Employee's information
51     // and earnings using dynamic binding
52     cout << "Virtual function calls made off base-class pointers:\n\n";
53
54     for ( const Employee *employeePtr : employees )
55        virtualViaPointer( employeePtr );
56
57     // call virtualViaReference to print each Employee's information
58     // and earnings using dynamic binding
59     cout << "Virtual function calls made off base-class references:\n\n";
```

Fig. 20.17 | Employee class hierarchy driver program. (Part 2 of 4.)

```
60
61       for ( const Employee *employeePtr : employees )
62         virtualViaReference( *employeePtr ); // note dereferencing
63    } // end main
64
65    // call Employee virtual functions print and earnings off a
66    // base-class pointer using dynamic binding
67    void virtualViaPointer( const Employee * const baseClassPtr )
68    {
69       baseClassPtr->print();
70       cout << "\nearned $" << baseClassPtr->earnings() << "\n\n";
71    } // end function virtualViaPointer
72
73    // call Employee virtual functions print and earnings off a
74    // base-class reference using dynamic binding
75    void virtualViaReference( const Employee &baseClassRef )
76    {
77       baseClassRef.print();
78       cout << "\nearned $" << baseClassRef.earnings() << "\n\n";
79    } // end function virtualViaReference
```

```
Employees processed individually using static binding:

salaried employee: John Smith
social security number: 111-11-1111
weekly salary: 800.00
earned $800.00

commission employee: Sue Jones
social security number: 333-33-3333
gross sales: 10000.00; commission rate: 0.06
earned $600.00

base-salaried commission employee: Bob Lewis
social security number: 444-44-4444
gross sales: 5000.00; commission rate: 0.04; base salary: 300.00
earned $500.00

Employees processed polymorphically using dynamic binding:

Virtual function calls made off base-class pointers:

salaried employee: John Smith
social security number: 111-11-1111
weekly salary: 800.00
earned $800.00

commission employee: Sue Jones
social security number: 333-33-3333
gross sales: 10000.00; commission rate: 0.06
earned $600.00

base-salaried commission employee: Bob Lewis
social security number: 444-44-4444
gross sales: 5000.00; commission rate: 0.04; base salary: 300.00
earned $500.00
```

Fig. 20.17 | Employee class hierarchy driver program. (Part 3 of 4.)

```
Virtual function calls made off base-class references:

salaried employee: John Smith
social security number: 111-11-1111
weekly salary: 800.00
earned $800.00

commission employee: Sue Jones
social security number: 333-33-3333
gross sales: 10000.00; commission rate: 0.06
earned $600.00

base-salaried commission employee: Bob Lewis
social security number: 444-44-4444
gross sales: 5000.00; commission rate: 0.04; base salary: 300.00
earned $500.00
```

Fig. 20.17 | Employee class hierarchy driver program. (Part 4 of 4.)

Line 41 creates the vector employees, which contains three Employee pointers. Line 44 aims employees[0] at object salariedEmployee. Line 45 aims employees[1] at object commissionEmployee. Line 46 aims employee[2] at object basePlusCommissionEmployee. The compiler allows these assignments, because a SalariedEmployee *is an* Employee, a CommissionEmployee *is an* Employee and a BasePlusCommissionEmployee *is an* Employee. Therefore, we can assign the addresses of SalariedEmployee, CommissionEmployee and BasePlusCommissionEmployee objects to base-class Employee pointers, even though Employee is an *abstract* class.

Lines 54–55 traverse vector employees and invoke function virtualViaPointer (lines 67–71) for each element in employees. Function virtualViaPointer receives in parameter baseClassPtr the address stored in an employees element. Each call to virtualViaPointer uses baseClassPtr to invoke virtual functions print (line 69) and earnings (line 70). Function virtualViaPointer does *not* contain *any* SalariedEmployee, CommissionEmployee or BasePlusCommissionEmployee type information. The function knows *only* about base-class type Employee. Therefore, the compiler *cannot know* which concrete class's functions to call through baseClassPtr. Yet at execution time, each virtual-function invocation *correctly* calls the function on the object to which baseClassPtr currently points. The output illustrates that *the appropriate functions for each class are indeed invoked* and that each object's proper information is displayed. For instance, the weekly salary is displayed for the SalariedEmployee, and the gross sales are displayed for the CommissionEmployee and BasePlusCommissionEmployee. Also, obtaining the earnings of each Employee polymorphically in line 70 produces the same results as obtaining these employees' earnings via *static binding* in lines 33, 35 and 37. All virtual function calls to print and earnings are resolved at *runtime* with *dynamic binding*.

Finally, lines 61–62 traverse employees and invoke function virtualViaReference (lines 75–79) for each vector element. Function virtualViaReference receives in its parameter baseClassRef (of type const Employee &) a *reference* to the object obtained by *dereferencing the pointer* stored in each employees element (line 62). Each call to virtualViaReference invokes virtual functions print (line 77) and earnings (line 78) via baseClassRef to demonstrate that *polymorphic processing occurs with base-class references as well.*

Each virtual-function invocation calls the function on the object to which baseClassRef refers at runtime. This is another example of *dynamic binding*. The output produced using base-class references is identical to the output produced using base-class pointers.

20.7 (Optional) Polymorphism, Virtual Functions and Dynamic Binding "Under the Hood"

C++ makes polymorphism easy to program. It's certainly possible to program for polymorphism in non-object-oriented languages such as C, but doing so requires complex and potentially dangerous pointer manipulations. This section discusses how C++ can implement polymorphism, virtual functions and dynamic binding internally. This will give you a solid understanding of how these capabilities really work. More importantly, it will help you appreciate the *overhead* of polymorphism—in terms of additional *memory consumption* and *processor time*. This can help you determine when to use polymorphism and when to avoid it. C++ Standard Library classes like array and vector are implemented *without* polymorphism and virtual functions to avoid the associated execution-time overhead and achieve optimal performance.

First, we'll explain the data structures that the compiler builds at *compile time* to support polymorphism at execution time. You'll see that polymorphism is accomplished through three levels of pointers, i.e., *triple indirection*. Then we'll show how an executing program uses these data structures to execute virtual functions and achieve the *dynamic binding* associated with polymorphism. Our discussion explains one *possible* implementation; this is not a language requirement.

When C++ compiles a class that has one or more virtual functions, it builds a **virtual function table** (*vtable*) for that class. The *vtable* contains pointers to the class's virtual functions. Just as the name of a built-in array contains the address in memory of the array's first element, a **pointer to a function** contains the starting address in memory of the code that performs the function's task. An executing program uses the *vtable* to select the proper function implementation each time a virtual function of that class is called. The leftmost column of Fig. 20.18 illustrates the *vtables* for the classes Employee, SalariedEmployee, CommissionEmployee and BasePlusCommissionEmployee.

Employee *Class* vtable
In the Employee class *vtable*, the first function pointer is set to 0 (i.e., nullptr), because function earnings is a *pure* virtual function and therefore *lacks an implementation*. The second function pointer points to function print, which displays the employee's full name and social security number. [*Note:* We've abbreviated the output of each print function in this figure to conserve space.] Any class that has one or more null pointers in its *vtable* is an *abstract* class. Classes without any null *vtable* pointers (such as SalariedEmployee, CommissionEmployee and BasePlusCommissionEmployee) are *concrete* classes.

SalariedEmployee *Class* vtable
Class SalariedEmployee overrides function earnings to return the employee's weekly salary, so the function pointer points to the earnings function of class SalariedEmployee. SalariedEmployee also overrides print, so the corresponding function pointer points to the SalariedEmployee member function that prints "salaried employee: " followed by the employee's name, social security number and weekly salary.

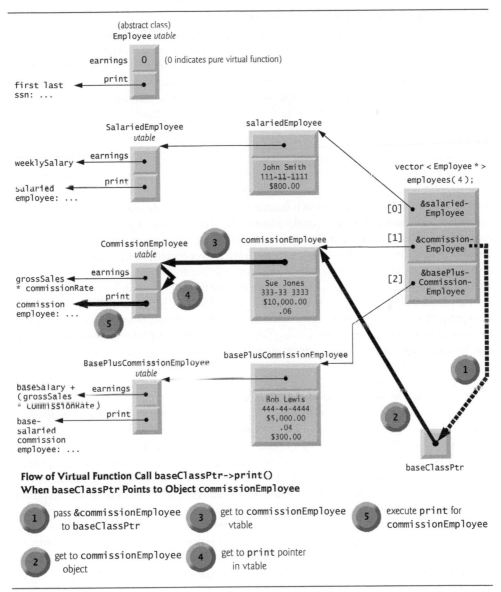

Fig. 20.18 | How virtual function calls work.

CommissionEmployee *Class* vtable

The earnings function pointer in the *vtable* for class CommissionEmployee points to CommissionEmployee's earnings function that returns the employee's gross sales multiplied by the commission rate. The print function pointer points to the CommissionEmployee version of the function, which prints the employee's type, name, social security number, commission rate and gross sales. As in class HourlyEmployee, both functions override the functions in class Employee.

BasePlusCommissionEmployee *Class* vtable

The earnings function pointer in the *vtable* for class BasePlusCommissionEmployee points to the BasePlusCommissionEmployee's earnings function, which returns the employee's base salary plus gross sales multiplied by commission rate. The print function pointer points to the BasePlusCommissionEmployee version of the function, which prints the employee's base salary plus the type, name, social security number, commission rate and gross sales. Both functions override the functions in class CommissionEmployee.

Inheriting Concrete virtual *Functions*

In our Employee case study, each *concrete* class provides its own implementation for virtual functions earnings and print. You've learned that each class which inherits *directly* from abstract base class Employee *must implement* earnings in order to be a *concrete* class, because earnings is a pure virtual function. These classes do *not* need to implement function print, however, to be considered concrete—print is *not a pure* virtual function and derived classes can inherit class Employee's implementation of print. Furthermore, class BasePlusCommissionEmployee does *not* have to implement either function print or earnings—both function implementations can be inherited from concrete class CommissionEmployee. If a class in our hierarchy were to inherit function implementations in this manner, the *vtable* pointers for these functions would simply point to the function implementation that was being inherited. For example, if BasePlusCommissionEmployee did not override earnings, the earnings function pointer in the *vtable* for class BasePlusCommissionEmployee would point to the same earnings function as the *vtable* for class CommissionEmployee points to.

Three Levels of Pointers to Implement Polymorphism

Polymorphism is accomplished through an elegant data structure involving *three levels of pointers*. We've discussed one level—the function pointers in the *vtable*. These point to the actual functions that execute when a virtual function is invoked.

Now we consider the second level of pointers. *Whenever an object of a class with one or more virtual functions is instantiated, the compiler attaches to the object a pointer to the vtable for that class.* This pointer is normally at the front of the object, but it isn't required to be implemented that way. In Fig. 20.18, these pointers are associated with the objects created in Fig. 20.17 (one object for each of the types SalariedEmployee, CommissionEmployee and BasePlusCommissionEmployee). The diagram displays each of the object's data member values. For example, the salariedEmployee object contains a pointer to the SalariedEmployee *vtable*; the object also contains the values John Smith, 111-11-1111 and $800.00.

The third level of pointers simply contains the handles to the objects that receive the virtual function calls. The handles in this level may also be *references*. Fig. 20.18 depicts the vector employees that contains Employee *pointers*.

Now let's see how a typical virtual function call executes. Consider the call baseClassPtr->print() in function virtualViaPointer (line 69 of Fig. 20.17). Assume that baseClassPtr contains employees[1] (i.e., the address of object commissionEmployee in employees). When the compiler compiles this statement, it determines that the call is indeed being made via a *base-class pointer* and that print is a virtual function.

The compiler determines that print is the *second* entry in each of the *vtables*. To locate this entry, the compiler notes that it will need to skip the first entry. Thus, the compiler compiles an **offset** or **displacement** into the table of machine-language object-code pointers to find the code that will execute the `virtual` function call. The size in bytes of the offset depends on the number of bytes used to represent a function pointer on an individual platform. For example, on a 32-bit platform, a pointer is typically stored in four bytes, whereas on a 64-bit platform, a pointer is typically stored in eight bytes. We assume four bytes for this discussion.

The compiler generates code that performs the following operations [*Note:* The numbers in the list correspond to the circled numbers in Fig. 20.18]:

1. Select the ith entry of `employees` (in this case, the address of object `commissionEmployee`), and pass it as an argument to function `virtualViaPointer`. This sets parameter `baseClassPtr` to point to `commissionEmployee`.

2. *Dereference* that pointer to get to the `commissionEmployee` object—which, as you recall, begins with a pointer to the `CommissionEmployee` *vtable*.

3. *Dereference* `commissionEmployee`'s *vtable* pointer to get to the `CommissionEmployee` *vtable*.

4. Skip the offset of four bytes to select the `print` function pointer.

5. *Dereference* the `print` function pointer to form the "name" of the actual function to execute, and use the function call operator () to execute the appropriate `print` function, which in this case prints the employee's type, name, social security number, gross sales and commission rate.

Fig. 20.18's data structures may appear to be complex, but this complexity is managed by the compiler and *hidden* from you, making polymorphic programming straightforward. The pointer dereferencing operations and memory accesses that occur on every `virtual` function call require some additional execution time. The *vtables* and the *vtable* pointers added to the objects require some additional memory.

Performance Tip 20.1

Polymorphism, as typically implemented with `virtual` functions and dynamic binding in C++, is efficient. You can use these capabilities with nominal impact on performance.

Performance Tip 20.2

Virtual functions and dynamic binding enable polymorphic programming as an alternative to `switch` logic programming. Optimizing compilers normally generate polymorphic code that's nearly as efficient as hand-coded `switch`-based logic. Polymorphism's overhead is acceptable for most applications. In some situations—such as real-time applications with stringent performance requirements—polymorphism's overhead may be too high.

20.8 Case Study: Payroll System Using Polymorphism and Runtime Type Information with Downcasting, `dynamic_cast`, `typeid` and `type_info`

Recall from the problem statement at the beginning of Section 20.6 that, for the current pay period, our fictitious company has decided to reward `BasePlusCommissionEmployees` by adding 10 percent to their base salaries. When processing `Employee` objects polymorphically in Section 20.6.5, we did not need to worry about the "specifics." Now, however, to adjust the base salaries of BasePlusCommissionEmployees, we have to determine the *specific type* of each Employee object *at execution time*, then act appropriately. This section demonstrates the powerful capabilities of **runtime type information (RTTI)** and **dynamic casting**, which enable a program to determine an object's type at execution time and act on that object accordingly.[1]

Figure 20.19 uses the Employee hierarchy developed in Section 20.6 and increases by 10 percent the base salary of each BasePlusCommissionEmployee. Line 21 declares three-element vector employees that stores pointers to Employee objects. Lines 24–29 populate the vector with the *addresses* of *dynamically allocated* objects of classes SalariedEmployee (Figs. 20.11–20.12), CommissionEmployee (Figs. 20.13–20.14) and BasePlusCommissionEmployee (Figs. 20.15–20.16). Lines 32–52 iterate through the employees vector and display each Employee's information by invoking member function print (line 34). Recall that because print is declared virtual in *base class* Employee, the system invokes the appropriate *derived-class* object's print function.

```cpp
1   // Fig. 20.19: fig20_19.cpp
2   // Demonstrating downcasting and runtime type information.
3   // NOTE: You may need to enable RTTI on your compiler
4   // before you can compile this application.
5   #include <iostream>
6   #include <iomanip>
7   #include <vector>
8   #include <typeinfo>
9   #include "Employee.h"
10  #include "SalariedEmployee.h"
11  #include "CommissionEmployee.h"
12  #include "BasePlusCommissionEmployee.h"
13  using namespace std;
14
15  int main()
16  {
17     // set floating-point output formatting
18     cout << fixed << setprecision( 2 );
19
20     // create vector of three base-class pointers
21     vector < Employee * > employees( 3 );
22
23     // initialize vector with various kinds of Employees
24     employees[ 0 ] = new SalariedEmployee(
25        "John", "Smith", "111-11-1111", 800 );
26     employees[ 1 ] = new CommissionEmployee(
27        "Sue", "Jones", "333-33-3333", 10000, .06 );
28     employees[ 2 ] = new BasePlusCommissionEmployee(
29        "Bob", "Lewis", "444-44-4444", 5000, .04, 300 );
30
```

Fig. 20.19 | Demonstrating downcasting and runtime type information. (Part 1 of 2.)

---

1. Some compilers require that RTTI be enabled before it can be used in a program. The compilers we used for testing this book's C++ examples—GNU C++, Visual C++ and Xcode LLVM—each enable RTTI by default.

```
31        // polymorphically process each element in vector employees
32        for ( Employee *employeePtr : employees )
33        {
34           employeePtr->print(); // output employee information
35           cout << endl;
36
37           // attempt to downcast pointer
38           BasePlusCommissionEmployee *derivedPtr =
39              dynamic_cast < BasePlusCommissionEmployee * >( employeePtr );
40
41           // determine whether element points to a BasePlusCommissionEmployee
42           if ( derivedPtr != nullptr ) // true for "is a" relationship
43           {
44              double oldBaseSalary = derivedPtr->getBaseSalary();
45              cout << "old base salary: $" << oldBaseSalary << endl;
46              derivedPtr->setBaseSalary( 1.10 * oldBaseSalary );
47              cout << "new base salary with 10% increase is: $"
48                 << derivedPtr->getBaseSalary() << endl;
49           } // end if
50
51           cout << "earned $" << employeePtr->earnings() << "\n\n";
52        } // end for
53
54        // release objects pointed to by vector's elements
55        for ( const Employee *employeePtr : employees )
56        {
57           // output class name
58           cout << "deleting object of "
59              << typeid( *employeePtr ).name() << endl;
60
61           delete employeePtr;
62        } // end for
63     } // end main
```

```
salaried employee: John Smith
social security number: 111-11-1111
weekly salary: 800.00
earned $800.00

commission employee: Sue Jones
social security number: 333-33-3333
gross sales: 10000.00; commission rate: 0.06
earned $600.00

base-salaried commission employee: Bob Lewis
social security number: 444-44-4444
gross sales: 5000.00; commission rate: 0.04; base salary: 300.00
old base salary: $300.00
new base salary with 10% increase is: $330.00
earned $530.00

deleting object of class SalariedEmployee
deleting object of class CommissionEmployee
deleting object of class BasePlusCommissionEmployee
```

Fig. 20.19 | Demonstrating downcasting and runtime type information. (Part 2 of 2.)

Determining an Object's Type with dynamic_cast

In this example, as we encounter a BasePlusCommissionEmployee object, we wish to increase its base salary by 10 percent. Since we process the Employees polymorphically, we cannot (with the techniques you've learned so far) be certain as to which type of Employee is being manipulated at any given time. This creates a problem, because BasePlusCommission-Employee employees *must* be identified when we encounter them so they can receive the 10 percent salary increase. To accomplish this, we use operator **dynamic_cast** (line 39) to determine whether the current Employee's type is BasePlusCommissionEmployee. This is the *downcast* operation we referred to in Section 20.3.3. Lines 38–39 *dynamically downcast* employeePtr from type Employee * to type BasePlusCommissionEmployee *. If employeePtr points to an object that *is a* BasePlusCommissionEmployee object, then that object's *address* is assigned to derived-class pointer derivedPtr; otherwise, nullptr is assigned to derived-Ptr. Note that dynamic_cast rather than static_cast is *required* here to perform type checking on the underlying object—a static_cast would simply cast the Employee * to a BasePlusCommissionEmployee * regardless of the underlying object's type. With a static_cast, the program would attempt to increase *every* Employee's base salary, resulting in undefined behavior for each object that is not a BasePlusCommissionEmployee.

If the value returned by the dynamic_cast operator in lines 38–39 *is not* nullptr, the object *is* the correct type, and the if statement (lines 42–49) performs the special processing required for the BasePlusCommissionEmployee object. Lines 44, 46 and 48 invoke BasePlusCommissionEmployee functions getBaseSalary and setBaseSalary to retrieve and update the employee's salary.

Calculating the Current **Employee**'s *Earnings*

Line 51 invokes member function earnings on the object to which employeePtr points. Recall that earnings is declared virtual in the base class, so the program invokes the derived-class object's earnings function—another example of *dynamic binding*.

Displaying an **Employee**'s *Type*

Lines 55–62 display each employee's *object type* and uses the delete operator to deallocate the dynamic memory to which each vector element points. Operator **typeid** (line 59) returns a *reference* to an object of class **type_info** that contains the information about the type of its operand, including the name of that type. When invoked, type_info member function **name** (line 59) returns a pointer-based string containing the typeid argument's *type name* (e.g., "class BasePlusCommissionEmployee"). To use typeid, the program must include header **<typeinfo>** (line 8).

Portability Tip 20.1
The string returned by type_info *member function* name *may vary by compiler.*

Compilation Errors That We Avoided By Using **dynamic_cast**

We avoid several compilation errors in this example by *downcasting* an Employee pointer to a BasePlusCommissionEmployee pointer (lines 38–39). If we remove the dynamic_cast from line 39 and attempt to assign the current Employee pointer directly to BasePlusCommissionEmployee pointer derivedPtr, we'll receive a compilation error. C++ does *not* allow a program to assign a base-class pointer to a derived-class pointer because the *is-a* relationship does *not* apply—a CommissionEmployee is *not* a BasePlusCommissionEmployee. The *is-a* relationship applies only between the derived class and its base classes, not vice versa.

Similarly, if lines 44, 46 and 48 used the current base-class pointer from employees, rather than derived-class pointer derivedPtr, to invoke derived-class-only functions get-BaseSalary and setBaseSalary, we would receive a compilation error at each of these lines. As you learned in Section 20.3.3, attempting to invoke *derived-class-only functions* through a *base-class pointer* is *not* allowed. Although lines 44, 46 and 48 execute only if commissionPtr is not nullptr (i.e., if the cast *can* be performed), we *cannot* attempt to invoke derived-class BasePlusCommissionEmployee functions getBaseSalary and setBaseSalary on the base-class Employee pointer. Recall that, using a base class Employee pointer, we can invoke only functions found in base class Employee—earnings, print and Employee's *get* and *set* functions.

20.9 Wrap-Up

In this chapter we discussed polymorphism, which enables us to "program in the general" rather than "program in the specific," and we showed how this makes programs more extensible. We began with an example of how polymorphism would allow a screen manager to display several "space" objects. We then demonstrated how base-class and derived-class pointers can be aimed at base-class and derived-class objects. We said that aiming base-class pointers at base-class objects is natural, as is aiming derived-class pointers at derived-class objects. Aiming base-class pointers at derived-class objects is also natural because a derived-class object *is an* object of its base class. You learned why aiming derived-class pointers at base-class objects is dangerous and why the compiler disallows such assignments. We introduced virtual functions, which enable the proper functions to be called when objects at various levels of an inheritance hierarchy are referenced (at execution time) via base-class pointers or references. This is known as dynamic binding or late binding. We discussed virtual destructors, and how they ensure that all appropriate destructors in an inheritance hierarchy run on a derived-class object when that object is deleted via a base-class pointer or reference. We then discussed pure virtual functions and abstract classes (classes with one or more pure virtual functions). You learned that abstract classes cannot be used to instantiate objects, while concrete classes can. We then demonstrated using abstract classes in an inheritance hierarchy. You learned how polymorphism works "under the hood" with *vtables* that are created by the compiler. We used runtime type information (RTTI) and dynamic casting to determine the type of an object at execution time and act on that object accordingly. We also used the typeid operator to get a type_info object containing a given object's type information.

In the next chapter, we discuss many of C++'s I/O capabilities and demonstrate several stream manipulators that perform various formatting tasks.

Summary

Section 20.1 Introduction

- Polymorphism (p. 768) enables us to "program in the general" rather than "program in the specific."
- Polymorphism enables us to write programs that process objects of classes that are part of the same class hierarchy as if they were all objects of the hierarchy's base class.

- With polymorphism, we can design and implement systems that are easily extensible—new classes can be added with little or no modification to the general portions of the program. The only parts of a program that must be altered to accommodate new classes are those that require direct knowledge of the new classes that you add to the hierarchy.

Section 20.2 Introduction to Polymorphism: Polymorphic Video Game
- With polymorphism, one function call can cause different actions to occur, depending on the type of the object on which the function is invoked.
- This makes it possible to design and implement more extensible systems. Programs can be written to process objects of types that may not exist when the program is under development.

Section 20.3 Relationships Among Objects in an Inheritance Hierarchy
- C++ enables polymorphism—the ability for objects of different classes related by inheritance to respond differently to the same member-function call.
- Polymorphism is implemented via virtual functions (p. 776) and dynamic binding (p. 777).
- When a base-class pointer or reference is used to call a virtual function, C++ chooses the correct overridden function in the appropriate derived class associated with the object.
- If a virtual function is called by referencing a specific object by name and using the dot member-selection operator, the reference is resolved at compile time (this is called static binding; p. 777); the virtual function that is called is the one defined for the class of that particular object.
- Derived classes can override a base-class virtual function if necessary, but if they do not, the base class's implementation is used.
- Declare the base-class destructor virtual (p. 782) if the class contains virtual functions. This makes all derived-class destructors virtual, even though they do not have the same name as the base-class destructor. If an object in the hierarchy is destroyed explicitly by applying the delete operator to a base-class pointer to a derived-class object, the destructor for the appropriate class is called. After a derived-class destructor runs, the destructors for all of that class's base classes run all the way up the hierarchy.

Section 20.4 Type Fields and switch Statements
- Polymorphic programming with virtual functions can eliminate the need for switch logic. You can use the virtual function mechanism to perform the equivalent logic automatically, thus avoiding the kinds of errors typically associated with switch logic.

Section 20.5 Abstract Classes and Pure virtual Functions
- Abstract classes (p. 783) are typically used as base classes, so we refer to them as abstract base classes (p. 783). No objects of an abstract class may be instantiated.
- Classes from which objects can be instantiated are concrete classes (p. 783).
- You create an abstract class by declaring one or more pure virtual functions (p. 784) with pure specifiers (= 0) in their declarations.
- If a class is derived from a class with a pure virtual function and that derived class does not supply a definition for that pure virtual function, then that virtual function remains pure in the derived class. Consequently, the derived class is also an abstract class.
- Although we cannot instantiate objects of abstract base classes, we can declare pointers and references to objects of abstract base classes. Such pointers and references can be used to enable polymorphic manipulations of derived-class objects instantiated from concrete derived classes.

Section 20.7 (Optional) Polymorphism, Virtual Functions and Dynamic Binding "Under the Hood"

- Dynamic binding requires that at runtime, the call to a virtual member function be routed to the virtual function version appropriate for the class. A virtual function table called the *vtable* (p. 800) is implemented as an array containing function pointers. Each class with virtual functions has a *vtable*. For each virtual function in the class, the *vtable* has an entry containing a function pointer to the version of the virtual function to use for an object of that class. The virtual function to use for a particular class could be the function defined in that class, or it could be a function inherited either directly or indirectly from a base class higher in the hierarchy.

- When a base class provides a virtual member function, derived classes can override the virtual function, but they do not have to override it.

- Each object of a class with virtual functions contains a pointer to the *vtable* for that class. When a function call is made from a base-class pointer to a derived-class object, the appropriate function pointer in the *vtable* is obtained and dereferenced to complete the call at execution time.

- Any class that has one or more nullptr pointers in its *vtable* is an abstract class. Classes without any nullptr *vtable* pointers are concrete classes.

- New kinds of classes are regularly added to systems and accommodated by dynamic binding.

Section 20.8 Case Study: Payroll System Using Polymorphism and Runtime Type Information with Downcasting, dynamic_cast, typeid and type_info

- Operator dynamic_cast (p. 804) checks the type of the object to which a pointer points, then determines whether the type has an *is-a* relationship with the type to which the pointer is being converted. If so, dynamic_cast returns the object's address. If not, dynamic_cast returns nullptr.

- Operator typeid (p. 806) returns a reference to a type_info object (p. 806) that contains information about the operand's type, including the type name. To use typeid, the program must include header <typeinfo> (p. 806).

- When invoked, type_info member function name (p. 806) returns a pointer-based string that contains the name of the type that the type_info object represents.

- Operators dynamic_cast and typeid are part of C++'s runtime type information (RTTI; p. 804) feature, which allows a program to determine an object's type at runtime.

Self-Review Exercises

20.1 Fill in the blanks in each of the following statements:
  a) Treating a base-class object as a(n) _____ can cause errors.
  b) Polymorphism helps eliminate _____ logic.
  c) If a class contains at least one pure virtual function, it's a(n) _____ class.
  d) Classes from which objects can be instantiated are called _____ classes.
  e) Operator _____ can be used to downcast base-class pointers safely.
  f) Operator typeid returns a reference to a(n) _____ object.
  g) _____ involves using a base-class pointer or reference to invoke virtual functions on base-class and derived-class objects.
  h) Overridable functions are declared using keyword _____.
  i) Casting a base-class pointer to a derived-class pointer is called _____.

20.2 State whether each of the following is *true* or *false*. If *false*, explain why.
  a) All virtual functions in an abstract base class must be declared as pure virtual functions.
  b) Referring to a derived-class object with a base-class handle is dangerous.
  c) A class is made abstract by declaring that class virtual.

d) If a base class declares a pure virtual function, a derived class must implement that function to become a concrete class.

e) Polymorphic programming can eliminate the need for switch logic.

Answers to Self-Review Exercises

20.1 a) derived-class object. b) switch. c) abstract. d) concrete. e) dynamic_cast. f) type_info. g) Polymorphism. h) virtual. i) downcasting.

20.2 a) False. An abstract base class can include virtual functions with implementations. b) False. Referring to a base-class object with a derived-class handle is dangerous. c) False. Classes are never declared virtual. Rather, a class is made abstract by including at least one pure virtual function in the class. d) True. e) True.

Exercises

20.3 *(Programming in the General)* How is it that polymorphism enables you to program "in the general" rather than "in the specific"? Discuss the key advantages of programming "in the general."

20.4 *(Polymorphism vs. **switch** logic)* Discuss the problems of programming with switch logic. Explain why polymorphism can be an effective alternative to using switch logic.

20.5 *(Inheriting Interface vs. Implementation)* Distinguish between inheriting interface and inheriting implementation. How do inheritance hierarchies designed for inheriting interface differ from those designed for inheriting implementation?

20.6 *(Virtual Functions)* What are virtual functions? Describe a circumstance in which virtual functions would be appropriate.

20.7 *(Dynamic Binding vs. Static Binding)* Distinguish between static binding and dynamic binding. Explain the use of virtual functions and the *vtable* in dynamic binding.

20.8 *(Virtual Functions)* Distinguish between virtual functions and pure virtual functions.

20.9 *(Abstract Base Classes)* Suggest one or more levels of abstract base classes for the Shape hierarchy discussed in this chapter and shown in Fig. 19.3. (The first level is Shape, and the second level consists of the classes TwoDimensionalShape and ThreeDimensionalShape.)

20.10 *(Polymorphism and Extensibility)* How does polymorphism promote extensibility?

20.11 *(Polymorphic Application)* You've been asked to develop a flight simulator that will have elaborate graphical outputs. Explain why polymorphic programming could be especially effective for a problem of this nature.

20.12 *(Payroll System Modification)* Modify the payroll system of Figs. 20.9–20.17 to include private data member birthDate in class Employee. Use class Date from Figs. 18.6–18.7 to represent an employee's birthday. Assume that payroll is processed once per month. Create a vector of Employee references to store the various employee objects. In a loop, calculate the payroll for each Employee (polymorphically), and add a $100.00 bonus to the person's payroll amount if the current month is the month in which the Employee's birthday occurs.

20.13 *(**Package** Inheritance Hierarchy)* Use the Package inheritance hierarchy created in Exercise 19.9 to create a program that displays the address information and calculates the shipping costs for several Packages. The program should contain a vector of Package pointers to objects of classes TwoDayPackage and OvernightPackage. Loop through the vector to process the Packages polymorphically. For each Package, invoke *get* functions to obtain the address information of the sender and the recipient, then print the two addresses as they would appear on mailing labels. Also, call each Package's calculateCost member function and print the result. Keep track of the total shipping cost for all Packages in the vector, and display this total when the loop terminates.

20.14 *(Polymorphic Banking Program Using* Account *Hierarchy)* Develop a polymorphic banking program using the Account hierarchy created in Exercise 19.10. Create a vector of Account pointers to SavingsAccount and CheckingAccount objects. For each Account in the vector, allow the user to specify an amount of money to withdraw from the Account using member function debit and an amount of money to deposit into the Account using member function credit. As you process each Account, determine its type. If an Account is a SavingsAccount, calculate the amount of interest owed to the Account using member function calculateInterest, then add the interest to the account balance using member function credit. After processing an Account, print the updated account balance obtained by invoking base-class member function getBalance.

20.15 *(Payroll System Modification)* Modify the payroll system of Figs. 20.9–20.17 to include additional Employee subclasses PieceWorker and HourlyWorker. A PieceWorker represents an employee whose pay is based on the number of pieces of merchandise produced. An HourlyWorker represents an employee whose pay is based on an hourly wage and the number of hours worked. Hourly workers receive overtime pay (1.5 times the hourly wage) for all hours worked in excess of 40 hours.

Class PieceWorker should contain private instance variables wage (to store the employee's wage per piece) and pieces (to store the number of pieces produced). Class HourlyWorker should contain private instance variables wage (to store the employee's wage per hour) and hours (to store the hours worked). In class PieceWorker, provide a concrete implementation of method earnings that calculates the employee's earnings by multiplying the number of pieces produced by the wage per piece. In class HourlyWorker, provide a concrete implementation of method earnings that calculates the employee's earnings by multiplying the number of hours worked by the wage per hour. If the number of hours worked is over 40, be sure to pay the HourlyWorker for the overtime hours. Add a pointer to an object of each new class into the vector of Employee pointers in main. For each Employee, display its string representation and earnings.

Making a Difference

20.16 *(*CarbonFootprint *Abstract Class: Polymorphism)* Using an abstract class with only pure virtual functions, you can specify similar behaviors for possibly disparate classes. Governments and companies worldwide are becoming increasingly concerned with carbon footprints (annual releases of carbon dioxide into the atmosphere) from buildings burning various types of fuels for heat, vehicles burning fuels for power, and the like. Many scientists blame these greenhouse gases for the phenomenon called global warming. Create three small classes unrelated by inheritance—classes Building, Car and Bicycle. Give each class some unique appropriate attributes and behaviors that it does not have in common with other classes. Write an abstract class CarbonFootprint with only a pure virtual getCarbonFootprint method. Have each of your classes inherit from that abstract class and implement the getCarbonFootprint method to calculate an appropriate carbon footprint for that class (check out a few websites that explain how to calculate carbon footprints). Write an application that creates objects of each of the three classes, places pointers to those objects in a vector of CarbonFootprint pointers, then iterates through the vector, polymorphically invoking each object's getCarbonFootprint method. For each object, print some identifying information and the object's carbon footprint.

21

Stream Input/Output: A Deeper Look

Objectives

In this chapter you'll learn:

- To use C++ object-oriented stream input/output.

- To format input and output.

- The stream-I/O class hierarchy.

- To use stream manipulators.

- To control justification and padding.

- To determine the success or failure of input/output operations.

- To tie output streams to input streams.

21.1 Introduction

This chapter discusses a range of capabilities sufficient for performing most common I/O operations and overviews the remaining capabilities. We discussed some of these features earlier in the text; now we provide a more complete treatment. Many of the I/O features that we'll discuss are object oriented. This style of I/O makes use of other C++ features, such as references, function overloading and operator overloading.

C++ uses *type-safe I/O*. Each I/O operation is executed in a manner sensitive to the data type. If an I/O function has been defined to handle a particular data type, then that member function is called to handle that data type. If there is no match between the type of the actual data and a function for handling that data type, the compiler generates an error. Thus, improper data cannot "sneak" through the system (as can occur in C, allowing for some subtle and bizarre errors).

Users can specify how to perform I/O for objects of user-defined types by overloading the stream insertion operator (<<) and the stream extraction operator (>>). This **extensibility** is one of C++'s most valuable features.

Software Engineering Observation 21.1
Use the C++-style I/O exclusively in C++ programs, even though C-style I/O is available to C++ programmers.

Error-Prevention Tip 21.1

C++ I/O is type safe.

Software Engineering Observation 21.2

C++ enables a common treatment of I/O for predefined types and user-defined types. This commonality facilitates software development and reuse.

21.2 Streams

C++ I/O occurs in **streams**, which are sequences of bytes. In input operations, the bytes flow from a device (e.g., a keyboard, a disk drive, a network connection, etc.) to main memory. In output operations, bytes flow from main memory to a device (e.g., a display screen, a printer, a disk drive, a network connection, etc.).

An application associates meaning with bytes. The bytes could represent characters, raw data, graphics images, digital speech, digital video or any other information an application may require. The system I/O mechanisms should transfer bytes from devices to memory (and vice versa) consistently and reliably. Such transfers often involve some mechanical motion, such as the rotation of a disk or a tape, or the typing of keystrokes at a keyboard. The time these transfers take typically is far greater than the time the processor requires to manipulate data internally. Thus, I/O operations require careful planning and tuning to ensure optimal performance.

C++ provides both "low-level" and "high-level" I/O capabilities. Low-level I/O capabilities (i.e., **unformatted I/O**) specify that some number of bytes should be transferred device-to-memory or memory-to-device. In such transfers, the individual byte is the item of interest. Such low-level capabilities provide high-speed, high-volume transfers but are not particularly convenient.

Programmers generally prefer a higher-level view of I/O (i.e., **formatted I/O**), in which bytes are grouped into meaningful units, such as integers, floating-point numbers, characters, strings and user-defined types. These type-oriented capabilities are satisfactory for most I/O other than high-volume file processing.

Performance Tip 21.1

Use unformatted I/O for the best performance in high-volume file processing.

Portability Tip 21.1

Unformatted I/O is not portable across all platforms.

21.2.1 Classic Streams vs. Standard Streams

In the past, the C++ **classic stream libraries** enabled input and output of chars. Because a char normally occupies *one* byte, it can represent only a limited set of characters (such as those in the ASCII character set used by most readers of this book, or other popular character sets). However, many languages use alphabets that contain more characters than a single-byte char can represent. The ASCII character set does not provide these characters; the **Unicode® character set** does. Unicode is an extensive international character set that represents the majority of the world's "commercially viable" languages, mathematical symbols and much more. For more information on Unicode, visit www.unicode.org.

C++ includes the **standard stream libraries**, which enable developers to build systems capable of performing I/O operations with Unicode characters. For this purpose, C++ includes the type **wchar_t**, which among other uses can store Unicode characters. The C++ standard also redesigned the classic C++ stream classes, which processed only chars, as class templates with specializations for processing characters of types char and wchar_t, respectively. We use the char specializations. The size of type wchar_t is not specified by the standard. C++11's new char16_t and char32_t types for representing Unicode characters were added to provide character types with explicitly specified sizes.

21.2.2 iostream Library Headers

The C++ iostream library provides hundreds of I/O capabilities. Several headers contain portions of the library interface.

Most C++ programs include the <iostream> header, which declares basic services required for all stream-I/O operations. The <iostream> header defines the cin, cout, cerr and clog objects, which correspond to the standard input stream, the standard output stream, the unbuffered standard error stream and the buffered standard error stream, respectively. (cerr and clog are discussed in Section 21.2.3.) Both unformatted- and formatted-I/O services are provided.

The <iomanip> header declares services useful for performing formatted I/O with so-called **parameterized stream manipulators**, such as setw and setprecision. The <fstream> header declares services for file processing.

21.2.3 Stream Input/Output Classes and Objects

The iostream library provides many templates for handling common I/O operations. For example, class template **basic_istream** supports stream-input operations, class template **basic_ostream** supports stream-output operations, and class template **basic_iostream** supports both stream-input and stream-output operations. Each template has a predefined template specialization that enables char I/O. In addition, the iostream library provides a set of typedefs that provide aliases for these template specializations. The **typedef** specifier declares synonyms (aliases) for data types. You'll sometimes use typedef to create shorter or more readable type names. For example, the statement

```
typedef Card *CardPtr;
```

defines an additional type name, CardPtr, as a *synonym* for type Card *. Creating a name using typedef does *not* create a data type; it creates only a new type name. Section 10.6 discusses typedef in detail. The typedef **istream** represents a basic_istream<char> that enables char input. Similarly, the typedef **ostream** represents a basic_ostream<char> that enables char output. Also, the typedef **iostream** represents a basic_iostream<char> that enables both char input and output. We use these typedefs throughout this chapter.

Stream-I/O Template Hierarchy and Operator Overloading
Templates basic_istream and basic_ostream both derive through single inheritance from base template **basic_ios**.[1] Template basic_iostream derives through *multiple in-*

heritance from templates `basic_istream` and `basic_ostream`. The UML class diagram of Fig. 21.1 summarizes these inheritance relationships.

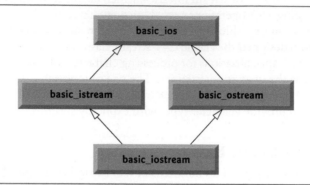

Fig. 21.1 | Stream-I/O template hierarchy portion.

Operator overloading provides a convenient notation for performing input/output. The *left-shift operator (<<)* is overloaded to designate stream output and is referred to as the *stream insertion operator*. The *right-shift operator (>>)* is overloaded to designate stream input and is referred to as the *stream extraction operator*. These operators are used with the standard stream objects `cin`, `cout`, `cerr` and `clog` and, commonly, with stream objects you create in your own code.

Standard Stream Objects `cin`, `cout`, `cerr` and `clog`

Predefined object `cin` is an `istream` instance and is said to be "connected to" (or attached to) the *standard input device*, which usually is the keyboard. The stream extraction operator (>>) as used in the following statement causes a value for integer variable `grade` (assuming that `grade` has been declared as an `int` variable) to be input from `cin` to memory:

```
cin >> grade; // data "flows" in the direction of the arrows
```

The compiler determines the data type of `grade` and selects the appropriate overloaded stream extraction operator. Assuming that `grade` has been declared properly, the stream extraction operator does not require additional type information (as is the case, for example, in C-style I/O). The >> operator is overloaded to input data items of fundamental types, strings and pointer values.

The predefined object `cout` is an `ostream` instance and is said to be "connected to" the *standard output device*, which usually is the display screen. The stream insertion operator (<<), as used in the following statement, causes the value of variable `grade` to be output from memory to the standard output device:

```
cout << grade; // data "flows" in the direction of the arrows
```

The compiler determines the data type of `grade` (assuming `grade` has been declared properly) and selects the appropriate stream insertion operator. The << operator is overloaded to output data items of fundamental types, strings and pointer values.

---

1. This chapter discusses templates only in the context of the template specializations for `char` I/O.

The predefined object cerr is an ostream instance and is said to be "connected to" the *standard error device*, normally the screen. Outputs to object cerr are **unbuffered**, implying that each stream insertion to cerr causes its output to appear *immediately*—this is appropriate for notifying a user promptly about errors.

The predefined object clog is an instance of the ostream class and is said to be "connected to" the *standard error device*. Outputs to clog are **buffered**. This means that each insertion to clog could cause its output to be held in a buffer (that is, an area in memory) until the buffer is filled or until the buffer is flushed. Buffering is an I/O performance-enhancement technique discussed in operating-systems courses.

File-Processing Templates

C++ file processing uses class templates **basic_ifstream** (for file input), **basic_ofstream** (for file output) and **basic_fstream** (for file input and output). As with the standard streams, C++ provides typedefs for working with these class templates. For example, the typedef **ifstream** represents a basic_ifstream<char> that enables char input from a file. Similarly, typedef **ofstream** represents a basic_ofstream<char> that enables char output to a file. Also, typedef **fstream** represents a basic_fstream<char> that enables char input from, and output to, a file. Template basic_ifstream inherits from basic_istream, basic_ofstream inherits from basic_ostream and basic_fstream inherits from basic_iostream. The UML class diagram of Fig. 21.2 summarizes the various inheritance relationships of the I/O-related classes. The full stream-I/O class hierarchy provides most of the capabilities that you need. Consult the class-library reference for your C++ system for additional file-processing information.

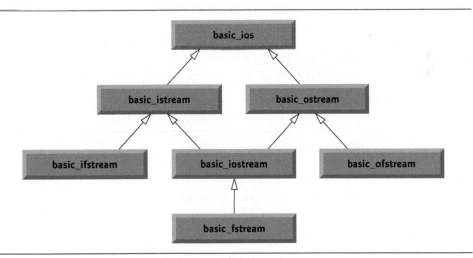

Fig. 21.2 | Stream-I/O template hierarchy portion showing the main file-processing templates.

21.3 Stream Output

Formatted and unformatted output capabilities are provided by ostream. Capabilities include output of standard data types with the stream insertion operator (<<); output of characters via the put member function; unformatted output via the write member function; output of integers in decimal, octal and hexadecimal formats; output of floating-point values with various precision, with forced decimal points, in scientific notation and in fixed notation; output of data justified in fields of designated widths; output of data in fields padded with specified characters; and output of uppercase letters in scientific notation and hexadecimal notation.

21.3.1 Output of char * Variables

C++ determines data types automatically—an improvement over C, but this feature sometimes "gets in the way." For example, suppose we want to print the address stored in a char * pointer. The << operator has been overloaded to output a char * as a *null-terminated C-style string*. To output the *address*, you can cast the char * to a void * (this can be done to any pointer variable). Figure 21.3 demonstrates printing a char * variable in both string and address formats. The address prints here as a hexadecimal (base-16) number—in general, the way addresses print is *implementation dependent*. To learn more about hexadecimal numbers, see Appendix C. We say more about controlling the bases of numbers in Section 21.6.1 and Section 21.7.4.

```
1   // Fig. 21.3: fig21_03.cpp
2   // Printing the address stored in a char * variable.
3   #include <iostream>
4   using namespace std;
5
6   int main()
7   {
8      const char *const word = "again";
9
10     // display value of char *, then display value of char *
11     // after a static_cast to void *
12     cout << "Value of word is: " << word << endl
13        << "Value of static_cast< const void * >( word ) is: "
14        << static_cast< const void * >( word ) << endl;
15  } // end main
```

```
Value of word is: again
Value of static_cast< const void * >( word ) is: 0135CC70
```

Fig. 21.3 | Printing the address stored in a char * variable.

21.3.2 Character Output Using Member Function put

We can use the put member function to output characters. For example, the statement

```
cout.put( 'A' );
```

displays a single character A. Calls to put may be *cascaded*, as in the statement

```
cout.put( 'A' ).put( '\n' );
```

which outputs the letter A followed by a newline character. As with <<, the preceding statement executes in this manner, because the dot operator (.) associates from left to right, and the put member function returns a reference to the ostream object (cout) that received the put call. The put function also may be called with a numeric expression that represents an ASCII value, as in the following statement, which also outputs A:

```
cout.put( 65 );
```

21.4 Stream Input

Now let's consider stream input. Formatted and unformatted input capabilities are provided by istream. The stream extraction operator (>>) normally skips **white-space characters** (such as blanks, tabs and newlines) in the input stream; later we'll see how to change this behavior. After each input, the stream extraction operator returns a *reference* to the stream object that received the extraction message (e.g., cin in the expression cin >> grade). If that reference is used as a condition (e.g., in a while statement's loop-continuation condition), the stream's overloaded void * cast operator function is implicitly invoked to convert the reference into a non-null pointer value or the null pointer based on the success or failure, respectively, of the last input operation. A non-null pointer converts to the bool value true to indicate success and the null pointer converts to the bool value false to indicate failure. When an attempt is made to read past the end of a stream, the stream's overloaded void * cast operator returns the *null pointer* to indicate *end-of-file*.

Each stream object contains a set of state bits used to control the stream's state (i.e., formatting, setting error states, etc.). These bits are used by the stream's overloaded void * cast operator to determine whether to return a non-null pointer or the null pointer. Stream extraction causes the stream's failbit to be set if data of the wrong type is input and causes the stream's badbit to be set if the operation fails. Section 21.7 and Section 21.8 discuss stream state bits in detail, then show how to test these bits after an I/O operation.

21.4.1 get and getline Member Functions

The **get** member function with *no arguments* inputs *one* character from the designated stream (including white-space characters and other nongraphic characters, such as the key sequence that represents end-of-file) and returns it as the value of the function call. This version of get returns EOF when *end-of-file* is encountered on the stream.

*Using Member Functions **eof**, **get** and **put***

Figure 21.4 demonstrates the use of member functions eof and get on input stream cin and member function put on output stream cout. Recall from Chapter 4 that EOF is represented as an int. This program reads characters into the int variable character, so that we can test each character entered to see if it's EOF. The program first prints the value of cin.eof()—i.e., false (0 on the output)—to show that *end-of-file* has *not* occurred on cin. The user enters a line of text and presses *Enter* followed by end-of-file (*<Ctrl> z* on Microsoft Windows systems, *<Ctrl> d* on Linux and Mac systems). Line 15 reads each character, which line 16 outputs to cout using member function put. When end-of-file is encountered, the while statement ends, and line 20 displays the value of cin.eof(), which is now true (1 on the output), to show that end-of-file has been set on cin. This program uses the version of istream member function get that takes no arguments and returns the character being input (line 15). Function eof returns true only after the program attempts to read past the last character in the stream.

```
1   // Fig. 21.4: fig21_04.cpp
2   // get, put and eof member functions.
3   #include <iostream>
4   using namespace std;
5
6   int main()
7   {
8      int character; // use int, because char cannot represent EOF
9
10     // prompt user to enter line of text
11     cout << "Before input, cin.eof() is " << cin.eof() << endl
12        << "Enter a sentence followed by end-of-file:" << endl;
13
14     // use get to read each character; use put to display it
15     while ( ( character = cin.get() ) != EOF )
16        cout.put( character );
17
18     // display end-of-file character
19     cout << "\nEOF in this system is: " << character << endl;
20     cout << "After input of EOF, cin.eof() is " << cin.eof() << endl;
21   } // end main
```

```
Before input, cin.eof() is 0
Enter a sentence followed by end-of-file:
Testing the get and put member functions
Testing the get and put member functions
^Z

EOF in this system is: -1
After input of EOF, cin.eof() is 1
```

Fig. 21.4 | get, put and eof member functions.

The get member function with a character-reference argument inputs the next character from the input stream (even if this is a *white-space character*) and stores it in the character argument. This version of get returns a reference to the istream object for which the get member function is being invoked.

A third version of get takes three arguments—a built-in array of chars, a size limit and a delimiter (with default value '\n'). This version reads characters from the input stream. It either reads *one fewer* than the specified maximum number of characters and terminates or terminates as soon as the *delimiter* is read. A null character is inserted to terminate the input string in the character array used as a buffer by the program. The delimiter is not placed in the character array but *does remain in the input stream* (the delimiter will be the next character read). Thus, the result of a second consecutive get is an empty line, unless the delimiter character is removed from the input stream (possibly with cin.ignore()).

Comparing cin and cin.get
Figure 21.5 compares input using stream extraction with cin (which reads characters until a white-space character is encountered) and input using cin.get. The call to cin.get (line 22) does *not* specify a delimiter, so the *default* '\n' character is used.

```
 1   // Fig. 21.5: fig21_05.cpp
 2   // Contrasting input of a string via cin and cin.get.
 3   #include <iostream>
 4   using namespace std;
 5
 6   int main()
 7   {
 8      // create two char arrays, each with 80 elements
 9      const int SIZE = 80;
10      char buffer1[ SIZE ];
11      char buffer2[ SIZE ];
12
13      // use cin to input characters into buffer1
14      cout << "Enter a sentence:" << endl;
15      cin >> buffer1;
16
17      // display buffer1 contents
18      cout << "\nThe string read with cin was:" << endl
19         << buffer1 << endl << endl;
20
21      // use cin.get to input characters into buffer2
22      cin.get( buffer2, SIZE );
23
24      // display buffer2 contents
25      cout << "The string read with cin.get was:" << endl
26         << buffer2 << endl;
27   } // end main
```

```
Enter a sentence:
Contrasting string input with cin and cin.get

The string read with cin was:
Contrasting

The string read with cin.get was:
 string input with cin and cin.get
```

Fig. 21.5 | Contrasting input of a string via cin and cin.get.

Using Member Function getline

Member function **getline** operates similarly to the third version of the get member function and *inserts a null character* after the line in the built-in array of chars. The getline function removes the delimiter from the stream (i.e., reads the character and discards it), but does *not* store it in the character array. The program of Fig. 21.6 demonstrates the use of the getline member function to input a line of text (line 13).

```
 1   // Fig. 21.6: fig21_06.cpp
 2   // Inputting characters using cin member function getline.
 3   #include <iostream>
 4   using namespace std;
```

Fig. 21.6 | Inputting characters using cin member function getline. (Part 1 of 2.)

```
5
6   int main()
7   {
8      const int SIZE = 80;
9      char buffer[ SIZE ]; // create array of 80 characters
10
11     // input characters in buffer via cin function getline
12     cout << "Enter a sentence:" << endl;
13     cin.getline( buffer, SIZE );
14
15     // display buffer contents
16     cout << "\nThe sentence entered is:" << endl << buffer << endl;
17  } // end main
```

```
Enter a sentence:
Using the getline member function

The sentence entered is:
Using the getline member function
```

Fig. 21.6 | Inputting characters using cin member function getline. (Part 2 of 2.)

21.4.2 istream Member Functions peek, putback and ignore

The **ignore** member function of istream reads and discards a designated number of characters (the default is *one*) or terminates upon encountering a designated delimiter (the default is EOF, which causes ignore to skip to the end of the file when reading from a file).

The **putback** member function places the previous character obtained by a get from an input stream back into that stream. This function is useful for applications that scan an input stream looking for a field beginning with a specific character. When that character is input, the application returns the character to the stream, so the character can be included in the input data.

The **peek** member function returns the next character from an input stream but does not remove the character from the stream.

21.4.3 Type-Safe I/O

C++ offers **type-safe I/O**. The << and >> operators are overloaded to accept data items of *specific* types. If unexpected data is processed, various error bits are set, which the user may test to determine whether an I/O operation succeeded or failed. If operators << and >> have not been overloaded for a user-defined type and you attempt to input into or output the contents of an object of that user-defined type, the compiler reports an error. This enables the program to "stay in control." We discuss these error states in Section 21.8.

21.5 Unformatted I/O Using read, write and gcount

Unformatted input/output is performed using the **read** and **write** member functions of istream and ostream, respectively. Member function read inputs *bytes* to a built-in array of chars in memory; member function write outputs bytes from a built-in array of chars. These bytes are *not formatted* in any way. They're input or output as raw bytes. For example, the call

```
char buffer[] = "HAPPY BIRTHDAY";
cout.write( buffer, 10 );
```

outputs the first 10 bytes of buffer (including null characters, if any, that would cause output with cout and << to terminate). The call

```
cout.write( "ABCDEFGHIJKLMNOPQRSTUVWXYZ", 10 );
```

displays the first 10 characters of the alphabet.

The read member function inputs a designated number of characters into a built-in array of chars. If *fewer* than the designated number of characters are read, failbit is set. Section 21.8 shows how to determine whether failbit has been set. Member function gcount reports the number of characters read by the last input operation.

Figure 21.7 demonstrates istream member functions read and gcount, and ostream member function write. The program inputs 20 characters (from a longer input sequence) into the array buffer with read (line 13), determines the number of characters input with gcount (line 17) and outputs the characters in buffer with write (line 17).

```
1   // Fig. 21.7: fig21_07.cpp
2   // Unformatted I/O using read, gcount and write.
3   #include <iostream>
4   using namespace std;
5
6   int main()
7   {
8       const int SIZE = 80;
9       char buffer[ SIZE ]; // create array of 80 characters
10
11      // use function read to input characters into buffer
12      cout << "Enter a sentence:" << endl;
13      cin.read( buffer, 20 );
14
15      // use functions write and gcount to display buffer characters
16      cout << endl << "The sentence entered was:" << endl;
17      cout.write( buffer, cin.gcount() );
18      cout << endl;
19  } // end main
```

```
Enter a sentence:
Using the read, write, and gcount member functions
The sentence entered was:
Using the read, writ
```

Fig. 21.7 | Unformatted I/O using read, gcount and write.

21.6 Introduction to Stream Manipulators

C++ provides various **stream manipulators** that perform formatting tasks. The stream manipulators provide capabilities such as setting field widths, setting precision, setting and unsetting format state, setting the fill character in fields, flushing streams, inserting a newline into the output stream (and flushing the stream), inserting a null character into the output stream and skipping white space in the input stream. These features are described in the following sections.

21.6.1 Integral Stream Base: dec, oct, hex and setbase

Integers are interpreted normally as decimal (base-10) values. To change the base in which integers are interpreted on a stream, insert the **hex** manipulator to set the base to hexadecimal (base 16) or insert the **oct** manipulator to set the base to octal (base 8). Insert the **dec** manipulator to reset the stream base to decimal. These are all *sticky* manipulators.

A stream's base also may be changed by the **setbase** stream manipulator, which takes an int argument of 10, 8, or 16 to set the base to decimal, octal or hexadecimal, respectively. Because setbase takes an argument, it's called a *parameterized stream manipulator*. Parameterized stream manipulators like setbase require the header <iomanip>. The stream base value remains the same until changed explicitly; setbase settings are sticky. Figure 21.8 demonstrates stream manipulators hex, oct, dec and setbase. For more information on decimal, octal and hexadecimal numbers, see Appendix C.

```cpp
1   // Fig. 21.8: fig21_08.cpp
2   // Using stream manipulators hex, oct, dec and setbase.
3   #include <iostream>
4   #include <iomanip>
5   using namespace std;
6
7   int main()
8   {
9      int number;
10
11     cout << "Enter a decimal number: ";
12     cin >> number; // input number
13
14     // use hex stream manipulator to show hexadecimal number
15     cout << number << " in hexadecimal is: " << hex
16        << number << endl;
17
18     // use oct stream manipulator to show octal number
19     cout << dec << number << " in octal is: "
20        << oct << number << endl;
21
22     // use setbase stream manipulator to show decimal number
23     cout << setbase( 10 ) << number << " in decimal is: "
24        << number << endl;
25  } // end main
```

```
Enter a decimal number: 20
20 in hexadecimal is: 14
20 in octal is: 24
20 in decimal is: 20
```

Fig. 21.8 | Using stream manipulators hex, oct, dec and setbase.

21.6.2 Floating-Point Precision (precision, setprecision)

We can control the **precision** of floating-point numbers (i.e., the number of digits to the right of the decimal point) by using either the setprecision stream manipulator or the **precision** member function of ios_base. A call to either of these sets the precision for all subsequent output operations until the next precision-setting call. A call to member function precision with no argument returns the current precision setting (this is what you need to use so that you can *restore the original precision* eventually after a sticky setting is no longer needed). The program of Fig. 21.9 uses both member function precision (line 22) and the setprecision manipulator (line 31) to print a table that shows the square root of 2, with precision varying from 0 to 9.

```cpp
 1  // Fig. 21.9: fig21_09.cpp
 2  // Controlling precision of floating-point values.
 3  #include <iostream>
 4  #include <iomanip>
 5  #include <cmath>
 6  using namespace std;
 7
 8  int main()
 9  {
10     double root2 = sqrt( 2.0 ); // calculate square root of 2
11     int places; // precision, vary from 0-9
12
13     cout << "Square root of 2 with precisions 0-9." << endl
14        << "Precision set by ios_base member function "
15        << "precision:" << endl;
16
17     cout << fixed; // use fixed-point notation
18
19     // display square root using ios_base function precision
20     for ( places = 0; places <= 9; ++places )
21     {
22        cout.precision( places );
23        cout << root2 << endl;
24     } // end for
25
26     cout << "\nPrecision set by stream manipulator "
27        << "setprecision:" << endl;
28
29     // set precision for each digit, then display square root
30     for ( places = 0; places <= 9; ++places )
31        cout << setprecision( places ) << root2 << endl;
32  } // end main
```

```
Square root of 2 with precisions 0-9.
Precision set by ios_base member function precision:
1
1.4
1.41
1.414
1.4142
1.41421
1.414214
1.4142136
1.41421356
1.414213562
```

Fig. 21.9 | Controlling precision of floating-point values. (Part 1 of 2.)

```
Precision set by stream manipulator setprecision:
1
1.4
1.41
1.414
1.4142
1.41421
1.414214
1.4142136
1.41421356
1.414213562
```

Fig. 21.9 | Controlling precision of floating-point values. (Part 2 of 2.)

21.6.3 Field Width (width, setw)

The **width** member function (of base class ios_base) sets the *field width* (i.e., the number of character positions in which a value should be output or the maximum number of characters that should be input) and *returns the previous width*. If values output are narrower than the field width, **fill characters** are inserted as **padding**. A value wider than the designated width will *not* be truncated—the *full number* will be printed. The width function with no argument returns the current setting.

Common Programming Error 21.1

The width setting applies only for the next insertion or extraction (i.e., the width setting is not sticky); afterward, the width is set implicitly to 0 (that is, input and output will be performed with default settings). Assuming that the width setting applies to all subsequent outputs is a logic error.

Common Programming Error 21.2

When a field is not sufficiently wide to handle outputs, the outputs print as wide as necessary, which can yield confusing outputs.

Figure 21.10 demonstrates the use of the width member function on both input and output. On input into a char array, *a maximum of one fewer characters than the width will be read*, because provision is made for the null character to be placed in the input string. Remember that stream extraction *terminates* when *nonleading white space* is encountered. The setw stream manipulator also may be used to set the field width. [*Note:* When prompted for input in Fig. 21.10, the user should enter a line of text and press *Enter* followed by end-of-file (*<Ctrl> z* on Microsoft Windows systems and *<Ctrl> d* on Linux and OS X systems).]

```
1   // Fig. 21.10: fig21_10.cpp
2   // width member function of class ios_base.
3   #include <iostream>
4   using namespace std;
5
```

Fig. 21.10 | width member function of class ios_base. (Part 1 of 2.)

```
6   int main()
7   {
8       int widthValue = 4;
9       char sentence[ 10 ];
10
11      cout << "Enter a sentence:" << endl;
12      cin.width( 5 ); // input only 5 characters from sentence
13
14      // set field width, then display characters based on that width
15      while ( cin >> sentence )
16      {
17          cout.width( widthValue++ );
18          cout << sentence << endl;
19          cin.width( 5 ); // input 5 more characters from sentence
20      } // end while
21  } // end main
```

```
Enter a sentence:
This is a test of the width member function
This
   is
    a
   test
     of
     the
     widt
        h
      memb
        er
       func
       tion
```

Fig. 21.10 | `width` member function of class `ios_base`. (Part 2 of 2.)

21.6.4 User-Defined Output Stream Manipulators

You can create your own stream manipulators. Figure 21.11 shows how to create and use *new* nonparameterized stream manipulators `bell` (lines 8–11), `carriageReturn` (lines 14–17), `tab` (lines 20–23) and `endLine` (lines 27–30). For output stream manipulators, the return type and parameter must be of type `ostream&`. When line 35 inserts the `endLine` manipulator in the output stream, function `endLine` is called and line 29 outputs the escape sequence \n and the `flush` manipulator (which flushes the output buffer) to the standard output stream `cout`. Similarly, when lines 35–44 insert the manipulators `tab`, `bell` and `carriageReturn` in the output stream, their corresponding functions—`tab` (line 20), `bell` (line 8) and `carriageReturn` (line 14) are called, which in turn output various escape sequences.

```
1   // Fig. 21.11: fig21_11.cpp
2   // Creating and testing user-defined, nonparameterized
3   // stream manipulators.
4   #include <iostream>
5   using namespace std;
```

Fig. 21.11 | User-defined, nonparameterized stream manipulators. (Part 1 of 2.)

```
 6
 7    // bell manipulator (using escape sequence \a)
 8    ostream& bell( ostream& output )
 9    {
10       return output << '\a'; // issue system beep
11    } // end bell manipulator
12
13    // carriageReturn manipulator (using escape sequence \r)
14    ostream& carriageReturn( ostream& output )
15    {
16       return output << '\r'; // issue carriage return
17    } // end carriageReturn manipulator
18
19    // tab manipulator (using escape sequence \t)
20    ostream& tab( ostream& output )
21    {
22       return output << '\t'; // issue tab
23    } // end tab manipulator
24
25    // endLine manipulator (using escape sequence \n and flush stream
26    // manipulator to simulate endl)
27    ostream& endLine( ostream& output )
28    {
29       return output << '\n' << flush; // issue endl-like end of line
30    } // end endLine manipulator
31
32    int main()
33    {
34       // use tab and endLine manipulators
35       cout << "Testing the tab manipulator:" << endLine
36          << 'a' << tab << 'b' << tab << 'c' << endLine;
37
38       cout << "Testing the carriageReturn and bell manipulators:"
39          << endLine << "..........";
40
41       cout << bell; // use bell manipulator
42
43       // use carriageReturn and endLine manipulators
44       cout << carriageReturn << "-----" << endLine;
45    } // end main
```

```
Testing the tab manipulator:
a       b       c
Testing the carriageReturn and bell manipulators:
-----.....
```

Fig. 21.11 | User-defined, nonparameterized stream manipulators. (Part 2 of 2.)

21.7 Stream Format States and Stream Manipulators

Various stream manipulators can be used to specify the kinds of formatting to be performed during stream-I/O operations. Stream manipulators control the output's format settings. Figure 21.12 lists each stream manipulator that controls a given stream's format state. All these manipulators belong to class ios_base. We show examples of most of these stream manipulators in the next several sections.

Manipulator	Description
skipws	*Skip white-space characters* on an input stream. This setting is reset with stream manipulator noskipws.
left	*Left justify* output in a field. *Padding* characters appear to the *right* if necessary.
right	*Right justify* output in a field. Padding characters appear to the *left* if necessary.
internal	Indicate that a number's *sign* should be *left justified* in a field and a number's *magnitude* should be *right justified* in that same field (i.e., *padding* characters appear *between* the sign and the number).
boolalpha	Specify that *bool values* should be displayed as the word true or false. The manipulator noboolalpha sets the stream back to displaying bool values as 1 (true) and 0 (false).
dec	Specify that integers should be treated as *decimal* (base 10) values.
oct	Specify that integers should be treated as *octal* (base 8) values.
hex	Specify that integers should be treated as *hexadecimal* (base 16) values.
showbase	Specify that the *base* of a number is to be output *ahead* of the number (a leading 0 for octals; a leading 0x or 0X for hexadecimals). This setting is reset with stream manipulator noshowbase.
showpoint	Specify that floating-point numbers should be output with a *decimal point*. This is used normally with fixed to *guarantee* a certain number of digits to the *right* of the decimal point, even if they're zeros. This setting is reset with stream manipulator noshowpoint.
uppercase	Specify that *uppercase letters* (i.e., X and A through F) should be used in a *hexadecimal* integer and that *uppercase* E should be used when representing a floating-point value in *scientific notation*. This setting is reset with stream manipulator nouppercase.
showpos	Specify that *positive* numbers should be preceded by a plus sign (**+**). This setting is reset with stream manipulator noshowpos.
scientific	Specify output of a floating-point value in *scientific notation*.
fixed	Specify output of a floating-point value in *fixed-point notation* with a specific number of digits to the *right* of the decimal point.

Fig. 21.12 | Format state stream manipulators from <iostream>.

21.7.1 Trailing Zeros and Decimal Points (showpoint)

Stream manipulator **showpoint** is a sticky setting that forces a floating-point number to be output with its *decimal point* and *trailing zeros*. For example, the floating-point value 79.0 prints as 79 without using showpoint and prints as 79.000000 (or as many trailing zeros as are specified by the current *precision*) using showpoint. To reset the showpoint setting, output the stream manipulator **noshowpoint**. The program in Fig. 21.13 shows how to use stream manipulator showpoint to control the printing of *trailing zeros* and *decimal points* for floating-point values. Recall that the *default precision* of a floating-point number is 6. When neither the fixed nor the scientific stream manipulator is used, the precision represents the number of significant digits to display (i.e., the total number of digits to display), *not* the number of digits to display after decimal point.

```
1   // Fig. 21.13: fig21_13.cpp
2   // Controlling the printing of trailing zeros and
3   // decimal points in floating-point values.
4   #include <iostream>
5   using namespace std;
6
7   int main()
8   {
9      // display double values with default stream format
10     cout << "Before using showpoint" << endl
11        << "9.9900 prints as: " << 9.9900 << endl
12        << "9.9000 prints as: " << 9.9000 << endl
13        << "9.0000 prints as: " << 9.0000 << endl << endl;
14
15     // display double value after showpoint
16     cout << showpoint
17        << "After using showpoint" << endl
18        << "9.9900 prints as: " << 9.9900 << endl
19        << "9.9000 prints as: " << 9.9000 << endl
20        << "9.0000 prints as: " << 9.0000 << endl;
21  } // end main
```

```
Before using showpoint
9.9900 prints as: 9.99
9.9000 prints as: 9.9
9.0000 prints as: 9

After using showpoint
9.9900 prints as: 9.99000
9.9000 prints as: 9.90000
9.0000 prints as: 9.00000
```

Fig. 21.13 | Controlling the printing of trailing zeros and decimal points in floating-point values.

21.7.2 Justification (left, right and internal)

Stream manipulators **left** and **right** enable fields to be *left justified* with *padding* characters to the *right* or *right justified* with *padding* characters to the *left*, respectively. The padding character is specified by the fill member function or the setfill parameterized stream manipulator (which we discuss in Section 21.7.3). Figure 21.14 uses the setw, left and right manipulators to left justify and right justify integer data in a field.

```
1   // Fig. 21.14: fig21_14.cpp
2   // Left and right justification with stream manipulators left and right.
3   #include <iostream>
```

Fig. 21.14 | Left and right justification with stream manipulators left and right. (Part 1 of 2.)

```
4    #include <iomanip>
5    using namespace std;
6
7    int main()
8    {
9       int x = 12345;
10
11      // display x right justified (default)
12      cout << "Default is right justified:" << endl
13         << setw( 10 ) << x;
14
15      // use left manipulator to display x left justified
16      cout << "\n\nUse std::left to left justify x:\n"
17         << left << setw( 10 ) << x;
18
19      // use right manipulator to display x right justified
20      cout << "\n\nUse std::right to right justify x:\n"
21         << right << setw( 10 ) << x << endl;
22   } // end main
```

```
Default is right justified:
    12345

Use std::left to left justify x:
12345

Use std::right to right justify x:
    12345
```

Fig. 21.14 | Left and right justification with stream manipulators `left` and `right`. (Part 2 of 2.)

Stream manipulator **internal** indicates that a number's *sign* (or *base* when using stream manipulator showbase) should be *left justified* within a field, that the number's *magnitude* should be *right justified* and that *intervening spaces* should be *padded* with the *fill character*. Figure 21.15 shows the internal stream manipulator specifying internal spacing (line 10). Note that **showpos** forces the plus sign to print (line 10). To reset the showpos setting, output the stream manipulator **noshowpos**.

```
1    // Fig. 21.15: fig21_15.cpp
2    // Printing an integer with internal spacing and plus sign.
3    #include <iostream>
4    #include <iomanip>
5    using namespace std;
6
7    int main()
8    {
9       // display value with internal spacing and plus sign
10      cout << internal << showpos << setw( 10 ) << 123 << endl;
11   } // end main
```

Fig. 21.15 | Printing an integer with internal spacing and plus sign. (Part 1 of 2.)

+	123

Fig. 21.15 | Printing an integer with internal spacing and plus sign. (Part 2 of 2.)

21.7.3 Padding (fill, setfill)

The **fill member function** specifies the *fill character* to be used with justified fields; *spaces* are used for padding by *default*. The function returns the prior padding character. The **setfill manipulator** also sets the *padding character*. Figure 21.16 demonstrates function fill (line 30) and stream manipulator setfill (lines 34 and 37) to set the fill character.

```
1   // Fig. 21.16: fig21_16.cpp
2   // Using member function fill and stream manipulator setfill to change
3   // the padding character for fields larger than the printed value.
4   #include <iostream>
5   #include <iomanip>
6   using namespace std;
7
8   int main()
9   {
10      int x = 10000;
11
12      // display x
13      cout << x << " printed as int right and left justified\n"
14         << "and as hex with internal justification.\n"
15         << "Using the default pad character (space):" << endl;
16
17      // display x with base
18      cout << showbase << setw( 10 ) << x << endl;
19
20      // display x with left justification
21      cout << left << setw( 10 ) << x << endl;
22
23      // display x as hex with internal justification
24      cout << internal << setw( 10 ) << hex << x << endl << endl;
25
26      cout << "Using various padding characters:" << endl;
27
28      // display x using padded characters (right justification)
29      cout << right;
30      cout.fill( '*' );
31      cout << setw( 10 ) << dec << x << endl;
32
33      // display x using padded characters (left justification)
34      cout << left << setw( 10 ) << setfill( '%' ) << x << endl;
35
36      // display x using padded characters (internal justification)
37      cout << internal << setw( 10 ) << setfill( '^' ) << hex
38         << x << endl;
39   } // end main
```

Fig. 21.16 | Using member function fill and stream manipulator setfill to change the padding character for fields larger than the printed values. (Part 1 of 2.)

```
10000 printed as int right and left justified
and as hex with internal justification.
Using the default pad character (space):
     10000
10000
0x    2710

Using various padding characters:
*****10000
10000%%%%%
0x^^^^2710
```

Fig. 21.16 | Using member function fill and stream manipulator setfill to change the padding character for fields larger than the printed values. (Part 2 of 2.)

21.7.4 Integral Stream Base (dec, oct, hex, showbase)

C++ provides stream manipulators **dec**, **hex** and **oct** to specify that integers are to be displayed as decimal, hexadecimal and octal values, respectively. Stream insertions *default* to *decimal* if none of these manipulators is used. With stream extraction, integers prefixed with 0 (zero) are treated as *octal* values, integers prefixed with 0x or 0X are treated as *hexadecimal* values, and all other integers are treated as *decimal* values. Once a particular base is specified for a stream, all integers on that stream are processed using that base until a different base is specified or until the program terminates.

Stream manipulator **showbase** forces the *base* of an integral value to be output. Decimal numbers are output by default, octal numbers are output with a leading 0, and hexadecimal numbers are output with either a leading 0x or a leading 0X (as we discuss in Section 21.7.6, stream manipulator **uppercase** determines which option is chosen). Figure 21.17 demonstrates the use of stream manipulator **showbase** to force an integer to print in decimal, octal and hexadecimal formats. To reset the showbase setting, output the stream manipulator **noshowbase**.

```
1   // Fig. 21.17: fig21_17.cpp
2   // Stream manipulator showbase.
3   #include <iostream>
4   using namespace std;
5
6   int main()
7   {
8      int x = 100;
9
10     // use showbase to show number base
11     cout << "Printing integers preceded by their base:" << endl
12        << showbase;
13
14     cout << x << endl; // print decimal value
15     cout << oct << x << endl; // print octal value
16     cout << hex << x << endl; // print hexadecimal value
17  } // end main
```

Fig. 21.17 | Stream manipulator showbase. (Part 1 of 2.)

```
Printing integers preceded by their base:
100
0144
0x64
```

Fig. 21.17 | Stream manipulator showbase. (Part 2 of 2.)

21.7.5 Floating-Point Numbers; Scientific and Fixed Notation (scientific, fixed)

The sticky stream manipulators scientific and fixed control the output format of floating-point numbers. Stream manipulator **scientific** forces the output of a floating-point number to display in scientific format. Stream manipulator **fixed** forces a floating-point number to display a specific number of digits (as specified by member function precision or stream manipulator setprecision) to the right of the decimal point. Without using another manipulator, the floating-point-number value determines the output format.

Figure 21.18 demonstrates displaying floating-point numbers in fixed and scientific formats using stream manipulators scientific (line 18) and fixed (line 22). The exponent format in scientific notation might differ across different compilers.

```
 1   // Fig. 21.18: fig21_18.cpp
 2   // Floating-point values displayed in system default,
 3   // scientific and fixed formats.
 4   #include <iostream>
 5   using namespace std;
 6
 7   int main()
 8   {
 9      double x = 0.001234567;
10      double y = 1.946e9;
11
12      // display x and y in default format
13      cout << "Displayed in default format:" << endl
14         << x << '\t' << y << endl;
15
16      // display x and y in scientific format
17      cout << "\nDisplayed in scientific format:" << endl
18         << scientific << x << '\t' << y << endl;
19
20      // display x and y in fixed format
21      cout << "\nDisplayed in fixed format:" << endl
22         << fixed << x << '\t' << y << endl;
23   } // end main
```

```
Displayed in default format:
0.00123457      1.946e+009

Displayed in scientific format:
1.234567e-003   1.946000e+009
```

Fig. 21.18 | Floating-point values displayed in default, scientific and fixed formats. (Part 1 of 2.)

```
Displayed in fixed format:
0.001235          1946000000.000000
```

Fig. 21.18 | Floating-point values displayed in default, scientific and fixed formats. (Part 2 of 2.)

21.7.6 Uppercase/Lowercase Control (uppercase)

Stream manipulator **uppercase** outputs an uppercase X or E with hexadecimal-integer values or with scientific notation floating-point values, respectively (Fig. 21.19). Using stream manipulator uppercase also causes all letters in a hexadecimal value to be uppercase. By *default*, the letters for hexadecimal values and the exponents in scientific notation floating-point values appear in *lowercase*. To reset the uppercase setting, output the stream manipulator **nouppercase**.

```
 1   // Fig. 21.19: fig21_19.cpp
 2   // Stream manipulator uppercase.
 3   #include <iostream>
 4   using namespace std;
 5
 6   int main()
 7   {
 8      cout << "Printing uppercase letters in scientific" << endl
 9         << "notation exponents and hexadecimal values:" << endl;
10
11      // use std:uppercase to display uppercase letters; use std::hex and
12      // std::showbase to display hexadecimal value and its base
13      cout << uppercase << 4.345e10 << endl
14         << hex << showbase << 123456789 << endl;
15   } // end main
```

```
Printing uppercase letters in scientific
notation exponents and hexadecimal values:
4.345E+010
0X75BCD15
```

Fig. 21.19 | Stream manipulator uppercase.

21.7.7 Specifying Boolean Format (boolalpha)

C++ provides data type bool, whose values may be false or true, as a preferred alternative to the old style of using 0 to indicate false and nonzero to indicate true. A bool variable outputs as 0 or 1 by *default*. However, we can use stream manipulator **boolalpha** to set the output stream to display bool values as the strings "true" and "false". Use stream manipulator **noboolalpha** to set the output stream to display bool values as integers (i.e., the default setting). The program of Fig. 21.20 demonstrates these stream manipulators. Line 11 displays the bool value, which line 8 sets to true, as an integer. Line 15 uses manipulator boolalpha to display the bool value as a string. Lines 18–19 then change the bool's value and use manipulator noboolalpha, so line 22 can display the bool value as an integer. Line 26 uses manipulator boolalpha to display the bool value as a string. Both boolalpha and noboolalpha are sticky settings.

Good Programming Practice 21.1

Displaying bool *values as* true *or* false, *rather than nonzero or 0, respectively, makes program outputs clearer.*

```
1   // Fig. 21.20: fig21_20.cpp
2   // Stream manipulators boolalpha and noboolalpha.
3   #include <iostream>
4   using namespace std;
5
6   int main()
7   {
8      bool booleanValue = true;
9
10     // display default true booleanValue
11     cout << "booleanValue is " << booleanValue << endl;
12
13     // display booleanValue after using boolalpha
14     cout << "booleanValue (after using boolalpha) is "
15        << boolalpha << booleanValue << endl << endl;
16
17     cout << "switch booleanValue and use noboolalpha" << endl;
18     booleanValue = false; // change booleanValue
19     cout << noboolalpha << endl; // use noboolalpha
20
21     // display default false booleanValue after using noboolalpha
22     cout << "booleanValue is " << booleanValue << endl;
23
24     // display booleanValue after using boolalpha again
25     cout << "booleanValue (after using boolalpha) is "
26        << boolalpha << booleanValue << endl;
27  } // end main
```

```
booleanValue is 1
booleanValue (after using boolalpha) is true

switch booleanValue and use noboolalpha

booleanValue is 0
booleanValue (after using boolalpha) is false
```

Fig. 21.20 | Stream manipulators boolalpha and noboolalpha.

21.7.8 Setting and Resetting the Format State via Member Function flags

Throughout Section 21.7, we've been using stream manipulators to change output format characteristics. We now discuss how to return an output stream's format to its default state after having applied several manipulations. Member function **flags** without an argument returns the current format settings as an **fmtflags** data type (of class ios_base), which represents the **format state**. Member function flags with an fmtflags argument sets the format state as specified by the argument and returns the prior state settings. The initial settings of the value that flags returns might differ across several systems. The program of Fig. 21.21 uses member function `flags` to save the stream's original format state (line 17), then restore the original format settings (line 25).

```cpp
1   // Fig. 21.21: fig21_21.cpp
2   // flags member function.
3   #include <iostream>
4   using namespace std;
5
6   int main()
7   {
8      int integerValue = 1000;
9      double doubleValue = 0.0947628;
10
11     // display flags value, int and double values (original format)
12     cout << "The value of the flags variable is: " << cout.flags()
13        << "\nPrint int and double in original format:\n"
14        << integerValue << '\t' << doubleValue << endl << endl;
15
16     // use cout flags function to save original format
17     ios_base::fmtflags originalFormat = cout.flags();
18     cout << showbase << oct << scientific; // change format
19
20     // display flags value, int and double values (new format)
21     cout << "The value of the flags variable is: " << cout.flags()
22        << "\nPrint int and double in a new format:\n"
23        << integerValue << '\t' << doubleValue << endl << endl;
24
25     cout.flags( originalFormat ); // restore format
26
27     // display flags value, int and double values (original format)
28     cout << "The restored value of the flags variable is: "
29        << cout.flags()
30        << "\nPrint values in original format again:\n"
31        << integerValue << '\t' << doubleValue << endl;
32  } // end main
```

```
The value of the flags variable is: 513
Print int and double in original format:
1000    0.0947628

The value of the flags variable is: 012011
Print int and double in a new format:
01750   9.476280e-002

The restored value of the flags variable is: 513
Print values in original format again:
1000    0.0947628
```

Fig. 21.21 | `flags` member function.

21.8 Stream Error States

The state of a stream may be tested through bits in class `ios_base`. Earlier in the book, we indicated that you can test, for example, whether an input was successful. Figure 21.22

shows how to test these state bits. In industrial-strength code, you'll want to perform similar tests on your I/O operations.

```cpp
1   // Fig. 21.22: fig21_22.cpp
2   // Testing error states.
3   #include <iostream>
4   using namespace std;
5
6   int main()
7   {
8      int integerValue;
9
10     // display results of cin functions
11     cout << "Before a bad input operation:"
12        << "\ncin.rdstate(): " << cin.rdstate()
13        << "\n    cin.eof(): " << cin.eof()
14        << "\n   cin.fail(): " << cin.fail()
15        << "\n    cin.bad(): " << cin.bad()
16        << "\n   cin.good(): " << cin.good()
17        << "\n\nExpects an integer, but enter a character: ";
18
19     cin >> integerValue; // enter character value
20     cout << endl;
21
22     // display results of cin functions after bad input
23     cout << "After a bad input operation:"
24        << "\ncin.rdstate(): " << cin.rdstate()
25        << "\n    cin.eof(): " << cin.eof()
26        << "\n   cin.fail(): " << cin.fail()
27        << "\n    cin.bad(): " << cin.bad()
28        << "\n   cin.good(): " << cin.good() << endl << endl;
29
30     cin.clear(); // clear stream
31
32     // display results of cin functions after clearing cin
33     cout << "After cin.clear()" << "\ncin.fail(): " << cin.fail()
34        << "\ncin.good(): " << cin.good() << endl;
35  } // end main
```

```
Before a bad input operation:
cin.rdstate(): 0
    cin.eof(): 0
   cin.fail(): 0
    cin.bad(): 0
   cin.good(): 1

Expects an integer, but enter a character: A

After a bad input operation:
cin.rdstate(): 2
    cin.eof(): 0
   cin.fail(): 1
```

Fig. 21.22 | Testing error states. (Part 1 of 2.)

```
     cin.bad(): 0
     cin.good(): 0

After cin.clear()
cin.fail(): 0
cin.good(): 1
```

Fig. 21.22 | Testing error states. (Part 2 of 2.)

The **eofbit** is set for an input stream after *end-of-file* is encountered. A program can use member function **eof** to determine whether end-of-file has been encountered on a stream after an attempt to extract data *beyond* the end of the stream. The call

```
     cin.eof()
```

returns true if end-of-file has been encountered on cin and false otherwise.

The **failbit** is set for a stream when a *format error* occurs on the stream and no characters are input (e.g., when you attempt to read a *number* and the user enters a *string*). When such an error occurs, the characters are *not* lost. The **fail** member function reports whether a stream operation has failed. Usually, recovering from such errors is possible.

The **badbit** is set for a stream when an error occurs that results in the *loss of data*. The **bad** member function reports whether a stream operation *failed*. Generally, such serious failures are nonrecoverable.

The **goodbit** is set for a stream if *none* of the bits eofbit, failbit or badbit is set for the stream.

The **good** member function returns true if the bad, fail and eof functions would *all* return false. I/O operations should be performed only on "good" streams.

The **rdstate** member function returns the stream's *error state*. Calling cout.rdstate, for example, would return the stream's state, which then could be tested by a switch statement that examines eofbit, badbit, failbit and goodbit. The *preferred* means of testing the state of a stream is to use member functions eof, bad, fail and good—using these functions does not require you to be familiar with particular status bits.

The **clear** member function is used to *restore* a stream's state to "good," so that I/O may proceed on that stream. The default argument for clear is goodbit, so the statement

```
     cin.clear();
```

clears cin and sets goodbit for the stream. The statement

```
     cin.clear( ios::failbit )
```

sets the failbit. You might want to do this when performing input on cin with a user-defined type and encountering a problem. The name clear might seem inappropriate in this context, but it's correct.

The program of Fig. 21.22 demonstrates member functions rdstate, eof, fail, bad, good and clear. The actual values output may differ across different compilers.

The **operator!** member function of basic_ios returns true if the badbit is set, the failbit is set or *both* are set. The **operator void *** member function returns false (0) if the badbit is set, the failbit is set or both are set. These functions are useful in file processing when a true/false condition is being tested under the control of a selection statement or repetition statement.

21.9 Tying an Output Stream to an Input Stream

Interactive applications generally involve an istream for input *and* an ostream for output. When a prompting message appears on the screen, the user responds by entering the appropriate data. Obviously, the prompt needs to appear *before* the input operation proceeds. With output buffering, outputs appear only when the buffer *fills*, when outputs are *flushed* explicitly by the program or automatically at the end of the program. C++ provides member function **tie** to synchronize (i.e., "tie together") the operation of an istream and an ostream to ensure that outputs appear *before* their subsequent inputs. The call

```
cin.tie( &cout );
```

ties cout (an ostream) to cin (an istream). Actually, this particular call is redundant, because C++ performs this operation automatically to create a user's standard input/output environment. However, the user would tie other istream/ostream pairs explicitly. To untie an input stream, inputStream, from an output stream, use the call

```
inputStream.tie( 0 );
```

21.10 Wrap-Up

This chapter summarized how C++ performs input/output using streams. You learned about the stream-I/O classes and objects, as well as the stream I/O template class hierarchy. We discussed ostream's formatted and unformatted output capabilities performed by the put and write functions. You learned about istream's formatted and unformatted input capabilities performed by the eof, get, getline, peek, putback, ignore and read functions. We discussed stream manipulators and member functions that perform formatting tasks—dec, oct, hex and setbase for displaying integers; precision and setprecision for controlling floating-point precision; and width and setw for setting field width. You also learned additional formatting iostream manipulators and member functions—showpoint for displaying decimal point and trailing zeros; left, right and internal for justification; fill and setfill for padding; scientific and fixed for displaying floating-point numbers in scientific and fixed notation; uppercase for uppercase/lowercase control; boolalpha for specifying boolean format; and flags and fmtflags for resetting the format state. In the next chapter, we take a deeper look at C++'s rich set of exception handling capabilities.

Summary

Section 21.1 Introduction
• I/O operations are performed in a manner sensitive to the type of the data.

Section 21.2 Streams
• C++ I/O occurs in streams (p. 814). A stream is a sequence of bytes.

• Low-level I/O-capabilities specify that bytes should be transferred device-to-memory or memory-to-device. High-level I/O is performed with bytes grouped into meaningful units such as integers, strings and user-defined types.

- C++ provides both unformatted-I/O and formatted-I/O operations. Unformatted-I/O (p. 814) transfers are fast, but process raw data that is difficult for people to use. Formatted I/O processes data in meaningful units, but requires extra processing time that can degrade the performance.
- The <iostream> header declares all stream-I/O operations (p. 815).
- The <iomanip> header declares the parameterized stream manipulators (p. 815).
- The <fstream> header declares file-processing operations (p. 817).
- The basic_istream template (p. 815) supports stream-input operations.
- The basic_ostream template (p. 815) supports stream-output operations.
- The basic_iostream template supports both stream-input and stream-output operations.
- Templates basic_istream and the basic_ostream each derive from the basic_ios (p. 815) template.
- Template basic_iostream derives from both the basic_istream and basic_ostream templates.
- The istream object cin is tied to the standard input device, normally the keyboard.
- The ostream object cout is tied to the standard output device, normally the screen.
- The ostream object cerr is tied to the standard error device, normally the screen. Outputs to cerr are unbuffered (p. 817)—each insertion to cerr appears immediately.
- The ostream object clog is tied to the standard error device, normally the screen. Outputs to clog are buffered (p. 817).
- The C++ compiler determines data types automatically for input and output.

Section 21.3 Stream Output
- Addresses are displayed in hexadecimal format by default.
- To print the address in a pointer variable, cast the pointer to void *.
- Member function put outputs one character. Calls to put may be cascaded.

Section 21.4 Stream Input
- Stream input is performed with the stream extraction operator >>, which automatically skips whitespace characters (p. 819) in the input stream and returns false after end-of-file is encountered.
- Stream extraction causes failbit (p. 819) to be set for improper input and badbit (p. 819) to be set if the operation fails.
- A series of values can be input using the stream extraction operation in a while loop header. The extraction returns 0 when end-of-file is encountered or an error occurs.
- The get member function (p. 819) with no arguments inputs one character and returns the character; EOF is returned if end-of-file is encountered on the stream.
- Member function get with a character-reference argument inputs the next character from the input stream and stores it in the character argument. This version of get returns a reference to the istream object (p. 819) for which the get member function is being invoked.
- Member function get with three arguments—a character array, a size limit and a delimiter (with default value newline)—reads characters from the input stream up to a maximum of limit − 1 characters, or until the delimiter is read. The input string is terminated with a null character. The delimiter is not placed in the character array but remains in the input stream.
- Member function getline (p. 821) operates like the three-argument get member function. The getline function removes the delimiter from the input stream but does not store it in the string.
- Member function ignore (p. 822) skips the specified number of characters (the default is 1) in the input stream; it terminates if the specified delimiter is encountered (the default delimiter is EOF).

- The putback member function (p. 822) places the previous character obtained by a get on a stream back into that stream.

- The peek member function (p. 822) returns the next character from an input stream but does not extract (remove) the character from the stream.

- C++ offers type-safe I/O (p. 822). If unexpected data is processed by the << and >> operators, various error bits are set, which can be tested to determine whether an I/O operation succeeded or failed. If operator << has not been overloaded for a user-defined type, a compiler error is reported.

Section 21.5 Unformatted I/O Using read, write and gcount

- Unformatted I/O is performed with member functions read and write (p. 822). These input or output bytes to or from memory, beginning at a designated memory address.

- The gcount member function (p. 823) returns the number of characters input by the previous read operation on that stream.

- Member function read inputs a specified number of characters into a character array. failbit is set if fewer than the specified number of characters are read.

Section 21.6 Introduction to Stream Manipulators

- To change the base in which integers output, use the manipulator hex (p. 824) to set the base to hexadecimal (base 16) or oct (p. 824) to set the base to octal (base 8). Use manipulator dec (p. 824) to reset the base to decimal. The base remains the same until changed explicitly.

- The parameterized stream manipulator setbase (p. 824) also sets the base for integer output. setbase takes one integer argument of 10, 8 or 16 to set the base.

- Floating-point precision can be controlled with the setprecision stream manipulator or the precision member function (p. 824). Both set the precision for all subsequent output operations until the next precision-setting call. The precision member function with no argument returns the current precision value.

- Parameterized manipulators require the inclusion of the <iomanip> header.

- Member function width (p. 826) sets the field width and returns the previous width. Values narrower than the field are padded with fill characters (p. 826). The field-width setting applies only for the next insertion or extraction, then input is performed using the default settings. Values wider than a field are printed in their entirety. Function width with no argument returns the current width setting. Manipulator setw also sets the width.

- For input, the setw stream manipulator establishes a maximum string size; if a larger string is entered, the larger line is broken into pieces no larger than the designated size.

- You can create your own stream manipulators.

Section 21.7 Stream Format States and Stream Manipulators

- Stream manipulator showpoint (p. 829) forces a floating-point number to be output with a decimal point and with the number of significant digits specified by the precision.

- Stream manipulators left and right (p. 830) cause fields to be left justified with padding characters to the right or right justified with padding characters to the left.

- Stream manipulator internal (p. 831) indicates that a number's sign (or base when using stream manipulator showbase; p. 833) should be left justified within a field, its magnitude should be right justified and intervening spaces should be padded with the fill character.

- Member function fill (p. 832) specifies the fill character to be used with stream manipulators left, right and internal (space is the default); the prior padding character is returned. Stream manipulator setfill (p. 832) also sets the fill character.

- Stream manipulators oct, hex and dec specify that integers are to be treated as octal, hexadecimal or decimal values, respectively. Integer output defaults to decimal if none of these is set; stream extractions process the data in the form the data is supplied.

- Stream manipulator showbase forces the base of an integral value to be output.

- Stream manipulator scientific (p. 834) is used to output a floating-point number in scientific format. Stream manipulator fixed (p. 834) is used to output a floating-point number with the precision specified by the precision member function.

- Stream manipulator uppercase (p. 829) outputs an uppercase X or E for hexadecimal integers and scientific notation floating-point values, respectively. Hexadecimal values appear in all uppercase.

- Member function flags (p. 836) with no argument returns the current format state (p. 836) as a long value. Function flags with a long argument sets the format state specified by the argument.

Section 21.8 Stream Error States
- The state of a stream may be tested through bits in class ios_base.

- The eofbit (p. 839) is set for an input stream after end-of-file is encountered during an input operation. The eof member function (p. 839) reports whether the eofbit has been set.

- A stream's failbit is set when a format error occurs. The fail member function (p. 839) reports whether a stream operation has failed; it's normally possible to recover from such errors.

- A stream's badbit is set when an error occurs that results in data loss. Member function bad reports whether a stream operation failed. Such serious failures are normally nonrecoverable.

- The good member function (p. 839) returns true if the bad, fail and eof functions would all return false. I/O operations should be performed only on "good" streams.

- The rdstate member function (p. 839) returns the error state of the stream.

- Member function clear (p. 839) restores a stream's state to "good," so that I/O may proceed.

Section 21.9 Tying an Output Stream to an Input Stream
- C++ provides the tie member function (p. 840) to synchronize istream and ostream operations to ensure that outputs appear before subsequent inputs.

Self-Review Exercises

21.1 *(Fill in the Blanks)* Answer each of the following:
   a) Input/output in C++ occurs as _____ of bytes.
   b) The stream manipulators for justification are _____, _____ and _____.
   c) Member function _____ can be used to set and reset format state.
   d) Most C++ programs that do I/O should include the _____ header that contains the declarations required for all stream-I/O operations.
   e) When using parameterized manipulators, the header _____ must be included.
   f) Header _____ contains the declarations required for file processing.
   g) The ostream member function _____ is used to perform unformatted output.
   h) Input operations are supported by class _____.
   i) Standard error stream outputs are directed to the stream objects _____ or _____.
   j) Output operations are supported by class _____.
   k) The symbol for the stream insertion operator is _____.
   l) The four objects that correspond to the standard devices on the system include _____, _____, _____ and _____.
   m) The symbol for the stream extraction operator is _____.

n) The stream manipulators _____, _____ and _____ specify that integers should be displayed in octal, hexadecimal and decimal formats, respectively.

o) The _____ stream manipulator causes positive numbers to display with a plus sign.

21.2   *(True or False)* State whether the following are *true* or *false*. If the answer is *false*, explain why.

a) The stream member function flags with a long argument sets the flags state variable to its argument and returns its previous value.

b) The stream insertion operator << and the stream extraction operator >> are overloaded to handle all standard data types—including strings and memory addresses (stream insertion only)—and all user-defined data types.

c) The stream member function flags with no arguments resets the stream's format state.

d) The stream extraction operator >> can be overloaded with an operator function that takes an istream reference and a reference to a user-defined type as arguments and returns an istream reference.

e) The stream insertion operator << can be overloaded with an operator function that takes an istream reference and a reference to a user-defined type as arguments and returns an istream reference.

f) Input with the stream extraction operator >> always skips leading white-space characters in the input stream, by default.

g) The stream member function rdstate returns the current state of the stream.

h) The cout stream normally is connected to the display screen.

i) The stream member function good returns true if the bad, fail and eof member functions all return false.

j) The cin stream normally is connected to the display screen.

k) If a nonrecoverable error occurs during a stream operation, the bad member function will return true.

l) Output to cerr is unbuffered and output to clog is buffered.

m) Stream manipulator showpoint forces floating-point values to print with the default six digits of precision unless the precision value has been changed, in which case floating-point values print with the specified precision.

n) The ostream member function put outputs the specified number of characters.

o) The stream manipulators dec, oct and hex affect only the next integer output operation.

21.3   *(Write a C++ Statement)* For each of the following, write a single statement that performs the indicated task.

a) Output the string "Enter your name: ".

b) Use a stream manipulator that causes the exponent in scientific notation and the letters in hexadecimal values to print in capital letters.

c) Output the address of the variable myString of type char *.

d) Use a stream manipulator to ensure that floating-point values print in scientific notation.

e) Output the address in variable integerPtr of type int *.

f) Use a stream manipulator such that, when integer values are output, the integer base for octal and hexadecimal values is displayed.

g) Output the value pointed to by floatPtr of type float *.

h) Use a stream member function to set the fill character to '*' for printing in field widths larger than the values being output. Repeat this statement with a stream manipulator.

i) Output the characters '0' and 'K' in one statement with ostream function put.

j) Get the value of the next character to input without extracting it from the stream.

k) Input a single character into variable charValue of type char, using the istream member function get in two different ways.

l) Input and discard the next six characters in the input stream.

m) Use `istream` member function read to input 50 characters into `char` array `line`.

n) Read 10 characters into character array `name`. Stop reading characters if the `'.'` delimiter is encountered. Do not remove the delimiter from the input stream. Write another statement that performs this task and removes the delimiter from the input.

o) Use the `istream` member function `gcount` to determine the number of characters input into character array `line` by the last call to `istream` member function `read`, and output that number of characters, using `ostream` member function `write`.

p) Output 124, 18.376, `'Z'`, 1000000 and `"String"`, separated by spaces.

q) Display `cout`'s current precision setting.

r) Input an integer value into `int` variable `months` and a floating-point value into `float` variable `percentageRate`.

s) Print 1.92, 1.925 and 1.9258 separated by tabs and with 3 digits of precision, using a stream manipulator.

t) Print integer 100 in octal, hexadecimal and decimal, using stream manipulators and separated by tabs.

u) Print integer 100 in decimal, octal and hexadecimal separated by tabs, using a stream manipulator to change the base.

v) Print 1234 right justified in a 10-digit field.

w) Read characters into character array `line` until the character `'z'` is encountered, up to a limit of 20 characters (including a terminating null character). Do not extract the delimiter character from the stream.

x) Use integer variables `x` and `y` to specify the field width and precision used to display the `double` value 87.4573, and display the value.

21.4 *(Find and Correct Code Errors)* Identify the error in each of the following statements and explain how to correct it.

a) `cout << "Value of x <= y is: " << x <= y;`

b) The following statement should print the integer value of `'c'`.
`cout << 'c';`

c) `cout << ""A string in quotes"";`

21.5 *(Show Outputs)* For each of the following, show the output.

a) `cout << "12345" << endl;`
`cout.width( 5 );`
`cout.fill( '*' );`
`cout << 123 << endl << 123;`

b) `cout << setw( 10 ) << setfill( '$' ) << 10000;`

c) `cout << setw( 8 ) << setprecision( 3 ) << 1024.987654;`

d) `cout << showbase << oct << 99 << endl << hex << 99;`

e) `cout << 100000 << endl << showpos << 100000;`

f) `cout << setw( 10 ) << setprecision( 2 ) << scientific << 444.93738;`

Answers to Self-Review Exercises

21.1 a) streams. b) `left`, `right` and `internal`. c) `flags`. d) `<iostream>`. e) `<iomanip>`. f) `<fstream>`. g) `write`. h) `istream`. i) `cerr` or `clog`. j) `ostream`. k) `<<`. l) `cin`, `cout`, `cerr` and `clog`. m) `>>`. n) `oct`, `hex` and `dec`. o) `showpos`.

21.2 a) False. The stream member function `flags` with a `fmtflags` argument sets the `flags` state variable to its argument and returns the prior state settings. b) False. The stream insertion and stream extraction operators are not overloaded for all user-defined types. You must specifically provide the overloaded operator functions to overload the stream operators for use with each user-defined type you create. c) False. The stream member function `flags` with no arguments returns the current format settings as a `fmtflags` data type, which represents the format state. d) True. e) False. To overload the stream insertion operator `<<`, the overloaded operator function must take an `ostream` reference and a reference to a user-defined type as arguments and return an `ostream` reference. f) True. g) True. h) True. i) True. j) False. The `cin` stream is connected to the standard input of the computer, which normally is the keyboard. k) True. l) True. m) True. n) False. The `ostream` member function put outputs its single-character argument. o) False. The stream manipulators `dec`, `oct` and `hex` set the output format state for integers to the specified base until the base is changed again or the program terminates.

21.3
a) `cout << "Enter your name: ";`
b) `cout << uppercase;`
c) `cout << static_cast< void * >( myString );`
d) `cout << scientific;`
e) `cout << integerPtr;`
f) `cout << showbase;`
g) `cout << *floatPtr;`
h) `cout.fill( '*' );`
   `cout << setfill( '*' );`
i) `cout.put( 'O' ).put( 'K' );`
j) `cin.peek();`
k) `charValue = cin.get();`
   `cin.get( charValue );`
l) `cin.ignore( 6 );`
m) `cin.read( line, 50 );`
n) `cin.get( name, 10, '.' );`
   `cin.getline( name, 10, '.' );`
o) `cout.write( line, cin.gcount() );`
p) `cout << 124 << ' ' << 18.376 << ' ' << "Z " << 1000000 << " String";`
q) `cout << cout.precision();`
r) `cin >> months >> percentageRate;`
s) `cout << setprecision( 3 ) << 1.92 << '\t' << 1.925 << '\t' << 1.9258;`
t) `cout << oct << 100 << '\t' << hex << 100 << '\t' << dec << 100;`
u) `cout << 100 << '\t' << setbase( 8 ) << 100 << '\t' << setbase( 16 ) << 100;`
v) `cout << setw( 10 ) << 1234;`
w) `cin.get( line, 20, 'z' );`
x) `cout << setw( x ) << setprecision( y ) << 87.4573;`

21.4
a) *Error:* The precedence of the `<<` operator is higher than that of `<=`, which causes the statement to be evaluated improperly and also causes a compiler error.
   Correction: Place parentheses around the expression `x <= y`.
b) *Error:* In C++, characters are not treated as small integers, as they are in C.
   Correction: To print the numerical value for a character in the computer's character set, the character must be cast to an integer value, as in the following:
   `cout << static_cast< int >( 'c' );`
c) *Error:* Quote characters cannot be printed in a string unless an escape sequence is used.
   Correction: Print the string:
   `cout << "\"A string in quotes\"";`

21.5
a) `12345`
   `**123`
   `123`
b) `$$$$$10000`
c) `1024.988`

d) 0143
    0x63
e) 100000
    +100000
f) 4.45e+002

Exercises

21.6 *(Write C++ Statements)* Write a statement for each of the following:
a) Print integer 40000 left justified in a 15-digit field.
b) Read a string into character array variable state.
c) Print 200 with and without a sign.
d) Print the decimal value 100 in hexadecimal form preceded by 0x.
e) Read characters into array charArray until the character 'p' is encountered, up to a limit of 10 characters (including the terminating null character). Extract the delimiter from the input stream, and discard it.
f) Print 1.234 in a 9-digit field with preceding zeros.

21.7 *(Inputting Decimal, Octal and Hexadecimal Values)* Write a program to test the inputting of integer values in decimal, octal and hexadecimal formats. Output each integer read by the program in all three formats. Test the program with the following input data: 10, 010, 0x10.

21.8 *(Printing Pointer Values as Integers)* Write a program that prints pointer values, using casts to all the integer data types. Which ones print strange values? Which ones cause errors?

21.9 *(Printing with Field Widths)* Write a program to test the results of printing the integer value 12345 and the floating-point value 1.2345 in various-sized fields. What happens when the values are printed in fields containing fewer digits than the values?

21.10 *(Rounding)* Write a program that prints the value 100.453627 rounded to the nearest digit, tenth, hundredth, thousandth and ten-thousandth.

21.11 *(Length of a String)* Write a program that inputs a string from the keyboard and determines the length of the string. Print the string in a field width that is twice the length of the string.

21.12 *(Converting Fahrenheit to Celsius)* Write a program that converts integer Fahrenheit temperatures from 0 to 212 degrees to floating-point Celsius temperatures with 3 digits of precision. Use the formula

```
celsius = 5.0 / 9.0 * ( fahrenheit - 32 );
```

to perform the calculation. The output should be printed in two right-justified columns and the Celsius temperatures should be preceded by a sign for both positive and negative values.

21.13 In some programming languages, strings are entered surrounded by either single or double quotation marks. Write a program that reads the three strings suzy, "suzy" and 'suzy'. Are the single and double quotes ignored or read as part of the string?

21.14 *(Reading Phone Numbers with and Overloaded Stream Extraction Operator)* In Fig. 18.5, the stream extraction and stream insertion operators were overloaded for input and output of objects of the PhoneNumber class. Rewrite the stream extraction operator to perform the following error checking on input. The operator>> function will need to be reimplemented.
a) Input the entire phone number into an array. Test that the proper number of characters has been entered. There should be a total of 14 characters read for a phone number of the form (800) 555-1212. Use ios_base-member-function clear to set failbit for improper input.

b) The area code and exchange do not begin with 0 or 1. Test the first digit of the area-code and exchange portions of the phone number to be sure that neither begins with 0 or 1. Use ios_base-member-function clear to set failbit for improper input.

c) The middle digit of an area code used to be limited to 0 or 1 (though this has changed). Test the middle digit for a value of 0 or 1. Use the ios_base-member-function clear to set failbit for improper input. If none of the above operations results in failbit being set for improper input, copy the parts of the telephone number into the PhoneNumber object's areaCode, exchange and line members. If failbit has been set on the input, have the program print an error message and end, rather than print the phone number.

21.15 *(Point Class)* Write a program that accomplishes each of the following:

a) Create a user-defined class Point that contains the private integer data members xCoordinate and yCoordinate and declares stream insertion and stream extraction over-loaded operator functions as friends of the class.

b) Define the stream insertion and stream extraction operator functions. The stream extraction operator function should determine whether the data entered is valid, and, if not, it should set the failbit to indicate improper input. The stream insertion operator should not be able to display the point after an input error occurred.

c) Write a main function that tests input and output of user-defined class Point, using the overloaded stream extraction and stream insertion operators.

21.16 *(Complex Class)* Write a program that accomplishes each of the following:

a) Create a user-defined class Complex that contains the private integer data members real and imaginary and declares stream insertion and stream extraction overloaded operator functions as friends of the class.

b) Define the stream insertion and stream extraction operator functions. The stream extraction operator function should determine whether the data entered is valid, and, if not, it should set failbit to indicate improper input. The input should be of the form

```
3 + 8i
```

c) The values can be negative or positive, and it's possible that one of the two values is not provided, in which case the appropriate data member should be set to 0. The stream insertion operator should not be able to display the point if an input error occurred. For negative imaginary values, a minus sign should be printed rather than a plus sign.

d) Write a main function that tests input and output of user-defined class Complex, using the overloaded stream extraction and stream insertion operators.

21.17 *(Printing a Table of ASCII Values)* Write a program that uses a for statement to print a table of ASCII values for the characters in the ASCII character set from 33 to 126. The program should print the decimal value, octal value, hexadecimal value and character value for each character. Use the stream manipulators dec, oct and hex to print the integer values.

21.18 *(String-Terminating Null Character)* Write a program to show that the getline and three-argument get istream member functions both end the input string with a string-terminating null character. Also, show that get leaves the delimiter character on the input stream, whereas getline extracts the delimiter character and discards it. What happens to the unread characters in the stream?

Exception Handling: A Deeper Look

22

Objectives

In this chapter you'll learn:

- To use `try`, `catch` and `throw` to detect, handle and indicate exceptions, respectively.

- To declare new exception classes.

- How stack unwinding enables exceptions not caught in one scope to be caught in another.

- To handle `new` failures.

- To use `unique_ptr` to prevent memory leaks.

- To understand the standard exception hierarchy.

22.1 Introduction

An **exception** is an indication of a problem that occurs during a program's execution. **Exception handling** enables you to create applications that can resolve (or handle) exceptions. In many cases, this allows a program to continue executing as if no problem had been encountered. The features presented in this chapter enable you to write **robust** and **fault-tolerant programs** that can deal with problems and continue executing or terminate gracefully.

We begin with a review of exception-handling concepts via an example that demonstrates handling an exception that occurs when a function attempts to divide by zero. We show how to handle exceptions that occur in a constructor or destructor and exceptions that occur if operator new fails to allocate memory for an object. We introduce several C++ Standard Library exception handling classes and show you how to create your own.

Software Engineering Observation 22.1

Exception handling provides a standard *mechanism for processing errors. This is especially important when working on a project with a large team of programmers.*

Software Engineering Observation 22.2

Incorporate your exception-handling strategy into your system from its inception. Including effective exception handling after a system has been implemented can be difficult.

Error-Prevention Tip 22.1

Without exception handling, it's common for a function to calculate and return a value on success or return an error indicator on failure. A common problem with this achitecture is using the return value in a subsequent calculation without first checking whether the value is the error indicator. Exception handling eliminates this problem.

22.2 Example: Handling an Attempt to Divide by Zero

Let's consider a simple example of exception handling (Figs. 22.1–22.2). We show how to deal with a common arithmetic problem—*division by zero*. Division by zero using integer arithmetic typically causes a program to terminate prematurely. In floating-point arithmetic, many C++ implementations allow division by zero, in which case a result of positive or negative infinity is displayed as INF or -INF, respectively.

In this example, we define a function named quotient that receives two integers input by the user and divides its first int parameter by its second int parameter. Before performing the division, the function casts the first int parameter's value to type double. Then, the second int parameter's value is (implicitly) promoted to type double for the calculation. So function quotient actually performs the division using two double values and returns a double result.

Although division by zero is often allowed in floating-point arithmetic, for the purpose of this example we treat any attempt to divide by zero as an error. Thus, function quotient tests its second parameter to ensure that it isn't zero before allowing the division to proceed. If the second parameter is zero, the function *throws an exception* to indicate to the caller that a problem occurred. The caller (main in this example) can then process the exception and allow the user to type two new values before calling function quotient again. In this way, the program can continue executing even after an improper value is entered, thus making the program more robust.

The example consists of two files. DivideByZeroException.h (Fig. 22.1) defines an *exception class* that represents the type of the problem that might occur in the example, and fig22_02.cpp (Fig. 22.2) defines the quotient function and the main function that calls it. Function main contains the code that demonstrates exception handling.

Defining an Exception Class to Represent the Type of Problem That Might Occur

Figure 22.1 defines class DivideByZeroException as a derived class of Standard Library class runtime_error (from header <stdexcept>). Class runtime_error—a derived class of exception (from header <exception>)—is the C++ standard base class for representing runtime errors. Class exception is the standard C++ base class for exception in the C++ Standard Library. (Section 22.10 discusses class exception and its derived classes in detail.) A typical exception class that derives from the runtime_error class defines only a constructor (e.g., lines 11–12) that passes an error-message string to the base-class runtime_error constructor. Every exception class that derives directly or indirectly from exception contains the virtual function what, which returns an exception object's error message. You're not required to derive a custom exception class, such as DivideByZeroException, from the standard exception classes provided by C++. However, doing so allows you to use the virtual function what to obtain an appropriate error message. We use an object of this DivideBy-ZeroException class in Fig. 22.2 to indicate when an attempt is made to divide by zero.

```
1   // Fig. 22.1: DivideByZeroException.h
2   // Class DivideByZeroException definition.
3   #include <stdexcept> // stdexcept header contains runtime_error
4
5   // DivideByZeroException objects should be thrown by functions
6   // upon detecting division-by-zero exceptions
7   class DivideByZeroException : public std::runtime_error
8   {
9   public:
10      // constructor specifies default error message
11      DivideByZeroException()
12         : std::runtime_error( "attempted to divide by zero" ) {}
13   }; // end class DivideByZeroException
```

Fig. 22.1 | Class DivideByZeroException definition.

Demonstrating Exception Handling

Figure 22.2 uses exception handling to wrap code that might throw a DivideByZeroException and to handle that exception, should one occur. The user enters two integers, which are passed as arguments to function quotient (lines 10–18). This function divides its first parameter (numerator) by its second parameter (denominator). Assuming that the user does not specify 0 as the denominator for the division, function quotient returns the division result. If the user inputs 0 for the denominator, quotient throws an exception. In the sample output, the first two lines show a successful calculation, and the next two show a failure due to an attempt to divide by zero. When the exception occurs, the program informs the user of the mistake and prompts the user to input two new integers. After we discuss the code, we'll consider the user inputs and flow of program control that yield *these outputs*.

```cpp
1   // Fig. 22.2: fig22_02.cpp
2   // Example that throws exceptions on
3   // attempts to divide by zero.
4   #include <iostream>
5   #include "DivideByZeroException.h" // DivideByZeroException class
6   using namespace std;
7
8   // perform division and throw DivideByZeroException object if
9   // divide-by-zero exception occurs
10  double quotient( int numerator, int denominator )
11  {
12     // throw DivideByZeroException if trying to divide by zero
13     if ( denominator == 0 )
14        throw DivideByZeroException(); // terminate function
15
16     // return division result
17     return static_cast< double >( numerator ) / denominator;
18  } // end function quotient
19
20  int main()
21  {
22     int number1; // user-specified numerator
23     int number2; // user-specified denominator
24
25     cout << "Enter two integers (end-of-file to end): ";
26
27     // enable user to enter two integers to divide
28     while ( cin >> number1 >> number2 )
29     {
30        // try block contains code that might throw exception
31        // and code that will not execute if an exception occurs
32        try
33        {
34           double result = quotient( number1, number2 );
35           cout << "The quotient is: " << result << endl;
36        } // end try
37        catch ( DivideByZeroException &divideByZeroException )
38        {
```

Fig. 22.2 | Example that throws exceptions on attempts to divide by zero. (Part 1 of 2.)

```
39                cout << "Exception occurred: "
40                    << divideByZeroException.what() << endl;
41            } // end catch
42
43            cout << "\nEnter two integers (end-of-file to end): ";
44        } // end while
45
46        cout << endl;
47    } // end main
```

```
Enter two integers (end-of-file to end): 100 7
The quotient is: 14.2857

Enter two integers (end-of-file to end): 100 0
Exception occurred: attempted to divide by zero

Enter two integers (end-of-file to end): ^Z
```

Fig. 22.2 | Example that throws exceptions on attempts to divide by zero. (Part 2 of 2.)

Enclosing Code in a try *Block*

The program begins by prompting the user to enter two integers. The integers are input in the condition of the while loop (line 28). Line 34 passes the values to function quotient (lines 10–18), which either divides the integers and returns a result, or throws an exception (i.e., indicates that an error occurred) on an attempt to divide by zero. Exception handling is geared to situations in which the function that detects an error is unable to handle it.

As you learned in Chapter 15, try blocks enable exception handling, enclosing statements that might cause exceptions and statements that should be skipped if an exception occurs. The try block in lines 32–36 encloses the invocation of function quotient and the statement that displays the division result. In this example, because the invocation of function quotient (line 34) can *throw* an exception, we enclose this function invocation in a try block. Enclosing the output statement (line 35) in the try block ensures that the output will occur *only* if function quotient returns a result.

 Software Engineering Observation 22.3
Exceptions may surface through explicitly mentioned code in a try block, through calls to other functions and through deeply nested function calls initiated by code in a try block.

Defining a catch *Handler to Process a* DivideByZeroException

You saw in Chapter 15 that exceptions are processed by catch handlers. At least one catch handler (lines 37–41) *must* immediately follow each try block. An exception parameter should *always* be declared as a *reference* to the type of exception the catch handler can process (DivideByZeroException in this case)—this prevents copying the exception object when it's caught and allows a catch handler to properly catch derived-class exceptions as well. When an exception occurs in a try block, the catch handler that executes is the first one whose type *matches* the type of the exception that occurred (i.e., the type in the catch block matches the thrown exception type exactly or is a *direct or indirect* base class of it). If an exception parameter includes an *optional* parameter name, the catch handler can use that parameter name to interact with the caught exception in the body of the catch handler, which is delimited by braces ({ and }). A catch handler typically reports the error to the user, logs it to a file, terminates the program gracefully or tries an alternate strategy to accomplish the failed task. In this example, the catch handler simply reports that the user attempted to divide by zero. Then the program prompts the user to enter two new integer values.

Common Programming Error 22.1

It's a syntax error to place code between a try block and its corresponding catch handlers or between its catch handlers.

Common Programming Error 22.2

Each catch handler can have only a single parameter—specifying a comma-separated list of exception parameters is a syntax error.

Common Programming Error 22.3

It's a compilation error to catch the same type in multiple catch handlers following a single try block.

Termination Model of Exception Handling

If an exception occurs as the result of a statement in a try block, the try block expires (i.e., terminates immediately). Next, the program searches for the first catch handler that can process the type of exception that occurred. The program locates the matching catch by comparing the thrown exception's type to each catch's exception-parameter type until the program finds a match. A match occurs if the types are *identical* or if the thrown exception's type is a *derived class* of the exception-parameter type. When a match occurs, the code in the matching catch handler executes. When a catch handler finishes processing by reaching its closing right brace (}), the exception is considered handled and the local variables defined within the catch handler (including the catch parameter) go out of scope. Program control does *not* return to the point at which the exception occurred (known as the **throw point**), because the try block has *expired*. Rather, control resumes with the first statement (line 43) after the last catch handler following the try block. This is known as the **termination model of exception handling**. Some languages use the **resumption model of exception handling**, in which, after an exception is handled, control resumes just after the throw point. As with any other block of code, *when a try block terminates, local variables defined in the block go out of scope.*

Common Programming Error 22.4

Logic errors can occur if you assume that after an exception is handled, control will return to the first statement after the throw point.

Error-Prevention Tip 22.2

With exception handling, a program can continue executing (rather than terminating) after dealing with a problem. This helps ensure the kind of robust applications that contribute to what's called mission-critical computing or business-critical computing.

If the try block completes its execution successfully (i.e., no exceptions occur in the try block), then the program ignores the catch handlers and program control continues with the first statement after the last catch following that try block.

If an exception that occurs in a try block has *no* matching catch handler, or if an exception occurs in a statement that is *not* in a try block, the function that contains the statement terminates immediately, and the program attempts to locate an enclosing try block in the calling function. This process is called **stack unwinding** and is discussed in Section 22.4.

Flow of Program Control When the User Enters a Nonzero Denominator

Consider the flow of control when the user inputs the numerator 100 and the denominator 7. In line 13, function quotient determines that the denominator is not zero, so line 17 performs the division and returns the result (14.2857) to line 34 as a double. Program control then continues sequentially from line 34, so line 35 displays the division result—line 36 ends the try block. Because the try block completed successfully and did *not* throw an exception, the program does *not* execute the statements contained in the catch handler (lines 37–41), and control continues to line 43 (the first line of code after the catch handler), which prompts the user to enter two more integers.

Flow of Program Control When the User Enters a Denominator of Zero

Now consider the case in which the user inputs the numerator 100 and the denominator 0. In line 13, quotient determines that the denominator is zero, which indicates an attempt to divide by zero. Line 14 throws an exception, which we represent as an object of class DivideByZeroException (Fig. 22.1).

To throw an exception, line 14 in Fig. 22.2 uses keyword **throw** followed by an operand of the type of exception to throw. Normally, a throw statement specifies *one* operand. (In Section 22.3, we discuss how to use a throw statement with *no* operand.) The operand of a throw can be of *any* type (but it must be copy constructable). If the operand is an object, we call it an **exception object**—in this example, the exception object is of type DivideByZeroException. However, a throw operand also can assume other values, such as the value of an expression that does *not* result in an object of a class (e.g., throw x > 5) or the value of an int (e.g., throw 5). The examples in this chapter focus exclusively on throwing objects of exception classes.

Error-Prevention Tip 22.3

In general, you should throw only objects of exception class types.

As part of throwing an exception, the throw operand is created and used to initialize the parameter in the catch handler, which we discuss momentarily. The throw statement in line 14 creates a DivideByZeroException object. When line 14 throws the exception, function quotient exits immediately. So, line 14 throws the exception *before* function quotient can perform the division in line 17. This is a central characteristic of exception handling: *If your program explicitly throws an exception, it should do so before the error has an opportunity to occur.*

Because we enclosed the call to quotient (line 34) in a try block, program control enters the catch handler (lines 37–41) that immediately follows the try block. This catch handler serves as the exception handler for the divide-by-zero exception. In general, when an exception is thrown within a try block, the exception is caught by a catch handler that specifies the type matching the thrown exception. In this program, the catch handler specifies that it catches DivideByZeroException objects—this type matches the object type thrown in function quotient. Actually, the catch handler catches a *reference* to the

DivideByZeroException object created by function quotient's throw statement (line 14), so that the catch handler does *not* make a copy of the exception object.

The catch's body (lines 39–40) prints the error message returned by function what of base-class runtime_error—i.e., the string that the DivideByZeroException constructor (lines 11–12 in Fig. 22.1) passed to the runtime_error base-class constructor.

Good Programming Practice 22.1

Associating each type of runtime error with an appropriately named exception type improves program clarity.

22.3 Rethrowing an Exception

A function might use a resource—like a file—and might want to release the resource (i.e., close the file) if an exception occurs. An exception handler, upon receiving an exception, can release the resource then notify its caller than an exception occurred by **rethrowing the exception** via the statement

```
throw;
```

Regardless of whether a handler can process an exception, the handler can *rethrow* the exception for further processing outside the handler. The next enclosing try block detects the rethrown exception, which a catch handler listed after that enclosing try block attempts to handle.

Common Programming Error 22.5

Executing an empty throw statement outside a catch handler abandons exception processing and terminates the program immediately.

The program of Fig. 22.3 demonstrates rethrowing an exception. In main's try block (lines 29–34), line 32 calls function throwException (lines 8–24). The throwException function also contains a try block (lines 11–15), from which the throw statement in line 14 throws an instance of standard-library-class exception. Function throwException's catch handler (lines 16–21) catches this exception, prints an error message (lines 18–19) and rethrows the exception (line 20). This terminates function throwException and returns control to line 32 in the try...catch block in main. The try block *terminates* (so line 33 does *not* execute), and the catch handler in main (lines 35–38) catches this exception and prints an error message (line 37). Since we do not use the exception parameters in the catch handlers of this example, we omit the exception parameter names and specify only the type of exception to catch (lines 16 and 35).

```
1   // Fig. 22.3: fig22_03.cpp
2   // Rethrowing an exception.
3   #include <iostream>
4   #include <exception>
5   using namespace std;
6
```

Fig. 22.3 | Rethrowing an exception. (Part 1 of 2.)

```
7    // throw, catch and rethrow exception
8    void throwException()
9    {
10       // throw exception and catch it immediately
11       try
12       {
13          cout << "  Function throwException throws an exception\n";
14          throw exception(); // generate exception
15       } // end try
16       catch ( exception & ) // handle exception
17       {
18          cout << "  Exception handled in function throwException"
19             << "\n  Function throwException rethrows exception";
20          throw; // rethrow exception for further processing
21       } // end catch
22
23       cout << "This also should not print\n";
24    } // end function throwException
25
26    int main()
27    {
28       // throw exception
29       try
30       {
31          cout << "\nmain invokes function throwException\n";
32          throwException();
33          cout << "This should not print\n";
34       } // end try
35       catch ( exception & ) // handle exception
36       {
37          cout << "\n\nException handled in main\n";
38       } // end catch
39
40       cout << "Program control continues after catch in main\n";
41    } // end main
```

```
main invokes function throwException
  Function throwException throws an exception
  Exception handled in function throwException
  Function throwException rethrows exception

Exception handled in main
Program control continues after catch in main
```

Fig. 22.3 | Rethrowing an exception. (Part 2 of 2.)

22.4 Stack Unwinding

When an exception is thrown but not caught in a particular scope, the function call stack is "unwound," and an attempt is made to catch the exception in the next outer try...catch block. Unwinding the function call stack means that the function in which the exception was not caught terminates, all local variables that have completed intitialization in that function are destroyed and control returns to the statement that originally invoked that function. If a try block encloses that statement, an attempt is made to catch the exception. If a try block does *not* enclose that statement, stack unwinding occurs again. If no catch handler ever catches this exception, the program terminates. The program of Fig. 22.4 demonstrates stack unwinding.

```cpp
1   // Fig. 22.4: fig22_04.cpp
2   // Demonstrating stack unwinding.
3   #include <iostream>
4   #include <stdexcept>
5   using namespace std;
6
7   // function3 throws runtime error
8   void function3()
9   {
10     cout << "In function 3" << endl;
11
12     // no try block, stack unwinding occurs, return control to function2
13     throw runtime_error( "runtime_error in function3" ); // no print
14   } // end function3
15
16  // function2 invokes function3
17  void function2()
18  {
19     cout << "function3 is called inside function2" << endl;
20     function3(); // stack unwinding occurs, return control to function1
21  } // end function2
22
23  // function1 invokes function2
24  void function1()
25  {
26     cout << "function2 is called inside function1" << endl;
27     function2(); // stack unwinding occurs, return control to main
28  } // end function1
29
30  // demonstrate stack unwinding
31  int main()
32  {
33     // invoke function1
34     try
35     {
36        cout << "function1 is called inside main" << endl;
37        function1(); // call function1 which throws runtime_error
38     } // end try
39     catch ( runtime_error &error ) // handle runtime error
40     {
41        cout << "Exception occurred: " << error.what() << endl;
42        cout << "Exception handled in main" << endl;
43     } // end catch
44  } // end main
```

Fig. 22.4 | Stack unwinding. (Part 1 of 2.)

```
function1 is called inside main
function2 is called inside function1
function3 is called inside function2
In function 3
Exception occurred: runtime_error in function3
Exception handled in main
```

Fig. 22.4 | Stack unwinding. (Part 2 of 2.)

In main, the try block (lines 34–38) calls function1 (lines 24–28). Next, function1 calls function2 (lines 17–21), which in turn calls function3 (lines 8–14). Line 13 of function3 throws a runtime_error object. However, because no try block encloses the throw statement in line 13, stack unwinding occurs—function3 terminates at line 13, then returns control to the statement in function2 that invoked function3 (i.e., line 20). Because no try block encloses line 20, stack unwinding occurs again—function2 terminates at line 20 and returns control to the statement in function1 that invoked function2 (i.e., line 27). Because no try block encloses line 27, stack unwinding occurs one more time—function1 terminates at line 27 and returns control to the statement in main that invoked function1 (i.e., line 37). The try block of lines 34–38 encloses this statement, so the first matching catch handler located after this try block (line 39–43) catches and processes the exception. Line 41 uses function what to display the exception message.

22.5 When to Use Exception Handling

Exception handling is designed to process **synchronous errors**, which occur when a statement executes, such as *out-of-range array subscripts, arithmetic overflow* (i.e., a value outside the representable range of values), *division by zero, invalid function parameters* and *unsuccessful memory allocation* (due to lack of memory). Exception handling is not designed to process errors associated with **asynchronous events** (e.g., disk I/O completions, network message arrivals, mouse clicks and keystrokes), which occur in parallel with, and independent of, the program's flow of control.

Software Engineering Observation 22.4
Exception handling provides a single, uniform technique for processing problems. This helps programmers on large projects understand each other's error-processing code.

Software Engineering Observation 22.5
Exception handling enables predefined software components to communicate problems to application-specific components, which can then process the problems in an application-specific manner.

Exception handling also is useful for processing problems that occur when a program interacts with software elements, such as member functions, constructors, destructors and classes. Such software elements often use exceptions to notify programs when problems occur. This enables you to implement *customized error handling* for each application.

Software Engineering Observation 22.6

Functions with common error conditions should return nullptr, 0 *or other appropriate values, such as* bools, *rather than throw exceptions. A program calling such a function can check the return value to determine success or failure of the function call.*

Complex applications normally consist of predefined software components and application-specific components that use the predefined components. When a predefined component encounters a problem, that component needs a mechanism to communicate the problem to the application-specific component—the *predefined component cannot know in advance how each application processes a problem that occurs.*

C++11: Declaring Functions That Do Not Throw Exceptions

As of C++11, if a function does not throw any exceptions *and* does not call any functions that throw exceptions, you should explicitly state that a function *does not* throw exceptions. This indicates to client-code programmers that there's no need to place calls to the function in a try block. Simply add **noexcept** to the right of the function's parameter list in both the prototype and the definition. For a const member function, place noexcept after const. If a function that's declared noexcept calls another function that throws an exception or executes a throw statement, the program terminates. We say more about noexcept in Chapter 24 of our book *C++ How to Program, 9/e.*

22.6 Constructors, Destructors and Exception Handling

First, let's discuss an issue that we've mentioned but not yet resolved satisfactorily: What happens when an error is detected in a *constructor*? For example, how should an object's constructor respond when it receives invalid data? Because the constructor *cannot return a value* to indicate an error, we must choose an alternative means of indicating that the object has not been constructed properly. One scheme is to return the improperly constructed object and hope that anyone using it would make appropriate tests to determine that it's in an inconsistent state. Another scheme is to set some variable outside the constructor. The preferred alternative is to require the constructor to throw an exception that contains the error information, thus offering an opportunity for the program to handle the failure.

Before an exception is thrown by a constructor, destructors are called for any member objects whose constructors have run to completion as part of the object being constructed. Destructors are called for every automatic object constructed in a try block before the exception is caught. Stack unwinding is guaranteed to have been completed at the point that an exception handler begins executing. If a destructor invoked as a result of stack unwinding throws an exception, the program terminates. This has been linked to various security attacks.

Error-Prevention Tip 22.4

Destructors should catch exceptions to prevent program termination.

Error-Prevention Tip 22.5

Do not throw exceptions from the constructor of an object with static storage duration. Such exceptions cannot be caught.

If an object has member objects, and if an exception is thrown before the outer object is fully constructed, then destructors will be executed for the member objects that have been constructed prior to the occurrence of the exception. If an array of objects has been partially constructed when an exception occurs, only the destructors for the constructed objects in the array will be called.

Error-Prevention Tip 22.6

When an exception is thrown from the constructor for an object that's created in a new expression, the dynamically allocated memory for that object is released.

Error-Prevention Tip 22.7

A constructor should throw an exception if a problem occurs while initializing an object. Before doing so, the constructor should release any memory that it dynamically allocated.

Initializing Local Objects to Acquire Resources

An exception could preclude the operation of code that would normally *release a resource* (such as memory or a file), thus causing a **resource leak** that prevents other programs from acquiring the resource. One technique to resolve this problem is to initialize a local object to acquire the resource. When an exception occurs, the destructor for that object will be invoked and can free the resource.

22.7 Exceptions and Inheritance

Various exception classes can be derived from a common base class, as we discussed in Section 22.2, when we created class DivideByZeroException as a derived class of class exception. If a catch handler catches a reference to an exception object of a base-class type, it also can catch a reference to all objects of classes publicly derived from that base class—this allows for polymorphic processing of related exceptions.

Error-Prevention Tip 22.8

Using inheritance with exceptions enables an exception handler to catch related errors with concise notation. One approach is to catch each type of reference to a derived-class exception object individually, but a more concise approach is to catch pointers or references to base-class exception objects instead. Also, catching pointers or references to derived-class exception objects individually is error prone, especially if you forget to test explicitly for one or more of the derived-class reference types.

22.8 Processing new Failures

When operator new fails, it throws a **bad_alloc** exception (defined in header <new>).In this section, we present two examples of new failing. The first uses the version of new that throws a bad_alloc exception when new fails. The second uses function **set_new_handler** to handle new failures. [*Note:* The examples in Figs. 22.5–22.6 allocate large amounts of dynamic memory, which could cause your computer to become sluggish.]

new *Throwing* bad_alloc *on Failure*

Figure 22.5 demonstrates new *implicitly* throwing bad_alloc on failure to allocate the requested memory. The for statement (lines 16–20) inside the try block should loop 50 times and, on each pass, allocate an array of 50,000,000 double values. If new fails and throws a bad_alloc exception, the loop terminates, and the program continues in line 22, where the catch handler catches and processes the exception. Lines 24–25 print the message "Exception occurred:" followed by the message returned from the base-class-exception version of function what (i.e., an implementation-defined exception-specific message, such as "bad allocation" in Microsoft Visual C++). The output shows that the program performed only four iterations of the loop before new failed and threw the bad_alloc exception. Your output might differ based on the physical memory, disk space available for virtual memory on your system and the compiler you're using.

```
1   // Fig. 22.5: fig22_05.cpp
2   // Demonstrating standard new throwing bad_alloc when memory
3   // cannot be allocated.
4   #include <iostream>
5   #include <new> // bad_alloc class is defined here
6   using namespace std;
7
8   int main()
9   {
10      double *ptr[ 50 ];
11
12      // aim each ptr[i] at a big block of memory
13      try
14      {
15         // allocate memory for ptr[ i ]; new throws bad_alloc on failure
16         for ( size_t i = 0; i < 50; ++i )
17         {
18            ptr[ i ] = new double[ 50000000 ]; // may throw exception
19            cout << "ptr[" << i << "] points to 50,000,000 new doubles\n";
20         } // end for
21      } // end try
22      catch ( bad_alloc &memoryAllocationException )
23      {
24         cerr << "Exception occurred: "
25            << memoryAllocationException.what() << endl;
26      } // end catch
27   } // end main
```

```
ptr[0] points to 50,000,000 new doubles
ptr[1] points to 50,000,000 new doubles
ptr[2] points to 50,000,000 new doubles
ptr[3] points to 50,000,000 new doubles
Exception occurred: bad allocation
```

Fig. 22.5 | new throwing bad_alloc on failure.

new *Returning* nullptr *on Failure*

The C++ standard specifies that programmers can use an older version of new that returns nullptr upon failure. For this purpose, header <new> defines object **nothrow** (of type nothrow_t), which is used as follows:

```
double *ptr = new( nothrow ) double[ 50000000 ];
```

The preceding statement uses the version of new that does *not* throw bad_alloc exceptions (i.e., nothrow) to allocate an array of 50,000,000 doubles.

Software Engineering Observation 22.7

To make programs more robust, use the version of new that throws bad_alloc exceptions on failure.

*Handling **new** Failures Using Function **set_new_handler***

An additional feature for handling new failures is function set_new_handler (prototyped in standard header <new>). This function takes as its argument a pointer to a function that takes no arguments and returns void. This pointer points to the function that will be called if new fails. This provides you with a uniform approach to handling all new failures, regardless of where a failure occurs in the program. Once set_new_handler registers a **new handler** in the program, operator new does *not* throw bad_alloc on failure; rather, it defers the error handling to the new-handler function.

If new allocates memory successfully, it returns a pointer to that memory. If new fails to allocate memory and set_new_handler did not register a new-handler function, new throws a bad_alloc exception. If new fails to allocate memory and a new-handler function has been registered, the new-handler function is called. The new-handler function should perform one of the following tasks:

1. Make more memory available by deleting other dynamically allocated memory (or telling the user to close other applications) and return to operator new to attempt to allocate memory again.

2. Throw an exception of type bad_alloc.

3. Call function abort or exit (both found in header <cstdlib>) to terminate the program. These were introduced in Section 17.7.

Figure 22.6 demonstrates set_new_handler. Function customNewHandler (lines 9–13) prints an error message (line 11), then calls abort (line 12) to terminate the program. The output shows that the loop iterated four times before new failed and invoked function customNewHandler. Your output might differ based on the physical memory, disk space available for virtual memory on your system and your compiler.

```cpp
 1   // Fig. 22.6: fig22_06.cpp
 2   // Demonstrating set_new_handler.
 3   #include <iostream>
 4   #include <new> // set_new_handler function prototype
 5   #include <cstdlib> // abort function prototype
 6   using namespace std;
 7
 8   // handle memory allocation failure
 9   void customNewHandler()
10   {
11      cerr << "customNewHandler was called";
12      abort();
13   } // end function customNewHandler
```

Fig. 22.6 | set_new_handler specifying the function to call when new fails. (Part 1 of 2.)

```
14
15   // using set_new_handler to handle failed memory allocation
16   int main()
17   {
18      double *ptr[ 50 ];
19
20      // specify that customNewHandler should be called on
21      // memory allocation failure
22      set_new_handler( customNewHandler );
23
24      // aim each ptr[i] at a big block of memory; customNewHandler will be
25      // called on failed memory allocation
26      for ( size_t i = 0; i < 50; ++i )
27      {
28         ptr[ i ] = new double[ 50000000 ]; // may throw exception
29         cout << "ptr[" << i << "] points to 50,000,000 new doubles\n";
30      } // end for
31   } // end main
```

```
ptr[0] points to 50,000,000 new doubles
ptr[1] points to 50,000,000 new doubles
ptr[2] points to 50,000,000 new doubles
ptr[3] points to 50,000,000 new doubles
customNewHandler was called
```

Fig. 22.6 | set_new_handler specifying the function to call when new fails. (Part 2 of 2.)

22.9 Class unique_ptr and Dynamic Memory Allocation

A common programming practice is to *allocate* dynamic memory, assign the address of that memory to a pointer, use the pointer to manipulate the memory and *deallocate* the memory with delete when the memory is no longer needed. If an exception occurs after successful memory allocation but *before* the delete statement executes, a *memory leak* could occur. C++11 provides class template **unique_ptr** in header **<memory>** to deal with this situation.

An object of class unique_ptr maintains a pointer to dynamically allocated memory. When a unique_ptr object destructor is called (for example, when a unique_ptr object goes out of scope), it performs a delete operation on its pointer data member. Class template unique_ptr provides overloaded operators * and -> so that a unique_ptr object can be used just as a regular pointer variable is. Figure 22.9 demonstrates a unique_ptr object that points to a dynamically allocated object of class Integer (Figs. 22.7–22.8).

```
1   // Fig. 22.7: Integer.h
2   // Integer class definition.
3
4   class Integer
5   {
```

Fig. 22.7 | Integer class definition. (Part 1 of 2.)

```
6    public:
7       Integer( int i = 0 ); // Integer default constructor
8       ~Integer(); // Integer destructor
9       void setInteger( int i ); // set Integer value
10      int getInteger() const; // return Integer value
11   private:
12      int value;
13   }; // end class Integer
```

Fig. 22.7 | Integer class definition. (Part 2 of 2.)

```
1    // Fig. 22.8: Integer.cpp
2    // Integer member function definitions.
3    #include <iostream>
4    #include "Integer.h"
5    using namespace std;
6
7    // Integer default constructor
8    Integer::Integer( int i )
9       : value( i )
10   {
11      cout << "Constructor for Integer " << value << endl;
12   } // end Integer constructor
13
14   // Integer destructor
15   Integer::~Integer()
16   {
17      cout << "Destructor for Integer " << value << endl;
18   } // end Integer destructor
19
20   // set Integer value
21   void Integer::setInteger( int i )
22   {
23      value = i;
24   } // end function setInteger
25
26   // return Integer value
27   int Integer::getInteger() const
28   {
29      return value;
30   } // end function getInteger
```

Fig. 22.8 | Member function definitions of class Integer.

Line 15 of Fig. 22.9 creates unique_ptr object ptrToInteger and initializes it with a pointer to a dynamically allocated Integer object that contains the value 7. Line 18 uses the unique_ptr overloaded -> operator to invoke function setInteger on the Integer object that ptrToInteger manages. Line 21 uses the unique_ptr overloaded * operator to dereference ptrToInteger, then uses the dot (.) operator to invoke function getInteger on the Integer object. Like a regular pointer, a unique_ptr's -> and * overloaded operators can be used to access the object to which the unique_ptr points.

```
1   // Fig. 22.9: fig22_09.cpp
2   // Demonstrating unique_ptr.
3   #include <iostream>
4   #include <memory>
5   using namespace std;
6
7   #include "Integer.h"
8
9   // use unique_ptr to manipulate Integer object
10  int main()
11  {
12     cout << "Creating a unique_ptr object that points to an Integer\n";
13
14     // "aim" unique_ptr at Integer object
15     unique_ptr< Integer > ptrToInteger( new Integer( 7 ) );
16
17     cout << "\nUsing the unique_ptr to manipulate the Integer\n";
18     ptrToInteger->setInteger( 99 ); // use unique ptr to set Integer value
19
20     // use unique_ptr to get Integer value
21     cout << "Integer after setInteger: " << ( *ptrToInteger ).getInteger()
22        << "\n\nTerminating program" << endl;
23  } // end main
```

```
Creating a unique_ptr object that points to an Integer
Constructor for Integer 7

Using the unique_ptr to manipulate the Integer
Integer after setInteger: 99

Terminating program
Destructor for Integer 99
```

Fig. 22.9 | unique_ptr object manages dynamically allocated memory.

Because ptrToInteger is a local automatic variable in main, ptrToInteger is destroyed when main terminates. The unique_ptr destructor forces a delete of the Integer object pointed to by ptrToInteger, which in turn calls the Integer class destructor. The memory that Integer occupies is released, regardless of how control leaves the block (e.g., by a return statement or by an exception). Most importantly, using this technique can *prevent memory leaks*. For example, suppose a function returns a pointer aimed at some object. Unfortunately, the function caller that receives this pointer might not delete the object, thus resulting in *a memory leak*. However, if the function returns a unique_ptr to the object, the object will be deleted automatically when the unique_ptr object's destructor gets called.

unique_ptr *Notes*
The class is called unique_ptr because only *one* unique_ptr at a time can own a dynamically allocated object. By using its overloaded assignment operator or copy constructor, a unique_ptr can *transfer ownership* of the dynamic memory it manages. The *last* unique_ptr object that maintains the pointer to the dynamic memory will delete the

memory. This makes unique_ptr an ideal mechanism for returning dynamically allocated memory to client code. When the unique_ptr goes out of scope in the *client* code, the unique_ptr's destructor destroys the dynamically allocated object and deletes its memory.

unique_ptr to a Built-In Array

You can also use a unique_ptr to manage a dynamically allocated built-in array. For example, consider the statement

```
unique_ptr< string[] > ptr( new string[ 10 ] );
```

which dynamically allocates an array of 10 strings managed by ptr. The type string[] indicates that the managed memory is a built-in array containing strings. When a unique_ptr that manages an array goes out of scope it deletes the memory with delete [] so that every element of the array receives a destructor call.

A unique_ptr that manages an array provides an overloaded [] operator for accessing the array's elements. For example, the statement

```
ptr[ 2 ] = "hello";
```

assigns "hello" to the string at ptr[2] and the statement

```
cout << ptr[ 2 ] << endl;
```

displays that string.

22.10 Standard Library Exception Hierarchy

Experience has shown that exceptions fall nicely into a number of categories. The C++ Standard Library includes a hierarchy of exception classes, some of which are shown in Fig. 22.10. As we first discussed in Section 22.2, this hierarchy is headed by base-class exception (defined in header <exception>), which contains virtual function what that derived classes can override to issue appropriate error messages.

Immediate derived classes of base-class exception include runtime_error and **logic_error** (both defined in header <stdexcept>), each of which has several derived classes. Also derived from exception are the exceptions thrown by C++ operators—for example, bad_alloc is thrown by new (Section 22.8), **bad_cast** is thrown by dynamic_cast (Chapter 20) and **bad_typeid** is thrown by typeid (Chapter 20).

Common Programming Error 22.6

Placing a catch handler that catches a base-class object before a catch that catches an object of a class derived from that base class is a logic error. The base-class catch catches all objects of classes derived from that base class, so the derived-class catch will never execute.

Class logic_error is the base class of several standard exception classes that indicate errors in program logic. For example, class **invalid_argument** indicates that a function received an invalid argument. (Proper coding can, of course, prevent invalid arguments from reaching a function.) Class **length_error** indicates that a length larger than the maximum size allowed for the object being manipulated was used for that object. Class **out_of_range** indicates that a value, such as a subscript into an array, exceeded its allowed range of values.

Class runtime_error, which we used briefly in Section 22.4, is the base class of several other standard exception classes that indicate execution-time errors. For example, class

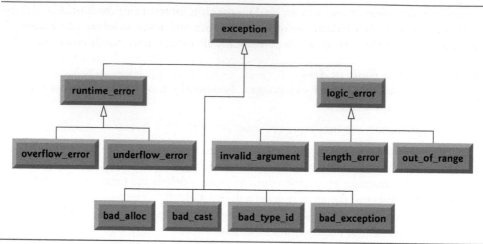

Fig. 22.10 | Some of the Standard Library exception classes.

overflow_error describes an **arithmetic overflow error** (i.e., the result of an arithmetic operation is larger than the largest number that can be stored in the computer) and class **underflow_error** describes an **arithmetic underflow error** (i.e., the result of an arithmetic operation is smaller than the smallest number that can be stored in the computer).

Common Programming Error 22.7

Exception classes need not be derived from class exception, *so catching type* exception *is not guaranteed to* catch *all exceptions a program could encounter.*

Error-Prevention Tip 22.9

To catch *all exceptions potentially thrown in a try block, use* catch(...). *One weakness with catching exceptions in this way is that the type of the caught exception is unknown. Another weakness is that, without a named parameter, there's no way to refer to the exception object inside the exception handler.*

Software Engineering Observation 22.8

The standard exception *hierarchy is a good starting point for creating exceptions. You can build programs that can* throw *standard exceptions, throw exceptions derived from the standard exceptions or throw your own exceptions not derived from the standard exceptions.*

Software Engineering Observation 22.9

Use catch(...) *to perform recovery that does not depend on the exception type (e.g., releasing common resources). The exception can be rethrown to alert more specific enclosing* catch *handlers.*

22.11 Wrap-Up

In this chapter, you learned how to use exception handling to deal with errors in a program. You learned that exception handling enables you to remove error-handling code from the "main line" of the program's execution. We demonstrated exception handling in the context of a divide-by-zero example. We reviewed how to use try blocks to enclose code that may throw an exception, and how to use catch handlers to deal with exceptions that may arise. You learned how to throw and rethrow exceptions, and how to handle the exceptions that occur in constructors. The chapter continued with discussions of processing new failures, dynamic memory allocation with class unique_ptr and the standard library exception hierarchy. In the next chapter, you'll learn how to build your own custom class templates.

Summary

Section 22.1 Introduction
- An exception (p. 850) is an indication of a problem that occurs during a program's execution.
- Exception handling (p. 850) enables you to create programs that can resolve problems that occur at execution time—often allowing programs to continue executing as if no problems had been encountered. More severe problems may require a program to notify the user of the problem before terminating in a controlled manner.

Section 22.2 Example: Handling an Attempt to Divide by Zero
- Class exception is the standard base class for exceptions classes (p. 851). It provides virtual function what (p. 851) that returns an appropriate error message and can be overridden in derived classes.
- Class runtime_error (p. 851), which is defined in header <stdexcept> (p. 851), is the C++ standard base class for representing runtime errors.
- C++ uses the termination model (p. 854) of exception handling.
- A try block consists of keyword try followed by braces ({}) that define a block of code in which exceptions might occur. The try block encloses statements that might cause exceptions and statements that should not execute if exceptions occur.
- At least one catch handler must immediately follow a try block. Each catch handler specifies an exception parameter that represents the type of exception the catch handler can process.
- If an exception parameter includes an optional parameter name, the catch handler can use that parameter name to interact with a caught exception object (p. 855).
- The point in the program at which an exception occurs is called the throw point (p. 854).
- If an exception occurs in a try block, the try block expires and program control transfers to the first catch in which the exception parameter's type matches that of the thrown exception.
- When a try block terminates, local variables defined in the block go out of scope.
- When a try block terminates due to an exception, the program searches for the first catch handler that matches the type of exception that occurred. A match occurs if the types are identical or if the thrown exception's type is a derived class of the exception-parameter type. When a match occurs, the code contained within the matching catch handler executes.
- When a catch handler finishes processing, the catch parameter and local variables defined within the catch handler go out of scope. Any remaining catch handlers that correspond to the try block are ignored, and execution resumes at the first line of code after the try...catch sequence.

- If no exceptions occur in a try block, the program ignores the catch handler(s) for that block. Program execution resumes with the next statement after the try...catch sequence.

- If an exception that occurs in a try block has no matching catch handler, or if an exception occurs in a statement that is not in a try block, the function that contains the statement terminates immediately, and the program attempts to locate an enclosing try block in the calling function. This process is called stack unwinding (p. 855).

- To throw an exception, use keyword throw followed by an operand that represents the type of exception to throw. The operand of a throw can be of any type.

Section 22.3 Rethrowing an Exception

- The exception handler can defer the exception handling (or perhaps a portion of it) to another exception handler. In either case, the handler achieves this by rethrowing the exception (p. 856).

- Common examples of exceptions are out-of-range array subscripts, arithmetic overflow, division by zero, invalid function parameters and unsuccessful memory allocations.

Section 22.4 Stack Unwinding

- Unwinding the function call stack means that the function in which the exception was not caught terminates, all local variables in that function are destroyed and control returns to the statement that originally invoked that function.

Section 22.5 When to Use Exception Handling

- Exception handling is for synchronous errors (p. 859), which occur when a statement executes.

- Exception handling is not designed to process errors associated with asynchronous events (p. 859), which occur in parallel with, and independent of, the program's flow of control.

- As of C++11, if a function does not throw any exceptions and does not call any functions that throw exceptions, you should explicitly declare the function noexcept (p. 860).

Section 22.6 Constructors, Destructors and Exception Handling

- Exceptions thrown by a constructor cause destructors to be called for any objects built as part of the object being constructed before the exception is thrown.

- Each automatic object constructed in a try block is destructed before an exception is thrown.

- Stack unwinding completes before an exception handler begins executing.

- If a destructor invoked as a result of stack unwinding throws an exception, the program terminates.

- If an object has member objects, and if an exception is thrown before the outer object is fully constructed, then destructors will be executed for the member objects that have been constructed before the exception occurs.

- If an array of objects has been partially constructed when an exception occurs, only the destructors for the constructed array element objects will be called.

- When an exception is thrown from the constructor for an object that is created in a new expression, the dynamically allocated memory for that object is released.

Section 22.7 Exceptions and Inheritance

- If a catch handler catches a reference to an exception object of a base-class type, it also can catch a reference to all objects of classes derived publicly from that base class—this allows for polymorphic processing of related errors.

Section 22.8 Processing **new** Failures

- The C++ standard document specifies that, when operator new fails, it throws a bad_alloc exception (p. 861), which is defined in header <new>.

- Function set_new_handler (p. 861) takes as its argument a pointer to a function that takes no arguments and returns void. This pointer points to the function that will be called if new fails.
- Once set_new_handler registers a new handler (p. 863) in the program, operator new does not throw bad_alloc on failure; rather, it defers the error handling to the new-handler function.
- If new allocates memory successfully, it returns a pointer to that memory.

Section 22.9 Class *unique_ptr* and Dynamic Memory Allocation
- If an exception occurs after successful memory allocation but before the delete statement executes, a memory leak could occur.
- The C++ Standard Library provides class template unique_ptr (p. 864) to deal with memory leaks.
- An object of class unique_ptr maintains a pointer to dynamically allocated memory. A unique_ptr's destructor performs a delete operation on the unique_ptr's pointer data member.
- Class template unique_ptr provides overloaded operators * and -> so that a unique_ptr object can be used just as a regular pointer variable is. A unique_ptr also transfers ownership of the dynamic memory it manages via its copy constructor and overloaded assignment operator.

Section 22.10 Standard Library Exception Hierarchy
- The C++ Standard Library includes a hierarchy of exception classes. This hierarchy is headed by base-class exception.
- Immediate derived classes of base class exception include runtime_error and logic_error (both defined in header <stdexcept>), each of which has several derived classes.
- Several operators throw standard exceptions—operator new throws bad_alloc, operator dynamic_cast throws bad_cast (p. 867) and operator typeid throws bad_typeid (p. 867).

Self-Review Exercises

22.1 List five common examples of exceptions.

22.2 Give several reasons why exception-handling techniques should not be used for conventional program control.

22.3 Why are exceptions appropriate for dealing with errors produced by library functions?

22.4 What's a "resource leak"?

22.5 If no exceptions are thrown in a try block, where does control proceed to after the try block completes execution?

22.6 What happens if an exception is thrown outside a try block?

22.7 Give a key advantage and a key disadvantage of using catch(...).

22.8 What happens if no catch handler matches the type of a thrown object?

22.9 What happens if several handlers match the type of the thrown object?

22.10 Why would you specify a base-class type as the type of a catch handler, then throw objects of derived-class types?

22.11 Suppose a catch handler with a precise match to an exception object type is available. Under what circumstances might a different handler be executed for exception objects of that type?

22.12 Must throwing an exception cause program termination?

22.13 What happens when a catch handler throws an exception?

22.14 What does the statement throw; do?

Answers to Self-Review Exercises

22.1   Insufficient memory to satisfy a new request, array subscript out of bounds, arithmetic overflow, division by zero, invalid function parameters.

22.2   (a) Exception handling is designed to handle infrequently occurring situations that often result in program termination, so compiler writers are not required to implement exception handling to perform optimally. (b) Flow of control with conventional control structures generally is clearer and more efficient than with exceptions. (c) Problems can occur because the stack is unwound when an exception occurs and resources allocated prior to the exception might not be freed. (d) The "additional" exceptions make it more difficult for you to handle the larger number of exception cases.

22.3   It's unlikely that a library function will perform error processing that will meet the unique needs of all users.

22.4   A program that terminates abruptly could leave a resource in a state in which other programs would not be able to acquire the resource, or the program itself might not be able to reacquire a "leaked" resource.

22.5   The exception handlers (in the catch handlers) for that try block are skipped, and the program resumes execution after the last catch handler.

22.6   An exception thrown outside a try block causes a call to terminate.

22.7   The form catch(...) catches any type of exception thrown in a try block. An advantage is that all possible exceptions will be caught. A disadvantage is that the catch has no parameter, so it cannot reference information in the thrown object and cannot know the cause of the exception.

22.8   This causes the search for a match to continue in the next enclosing try block if there is one. As this process continues, it might eventually be determined that there is no handler in the program that matches the type of the thrown object; in this case, the program terminates.

22.9   The first matching exception handler after the try block is executed.

22.10   This is a nice way to catch related types of exceptions.

22.11   A base-class handler would catch objects of all derived-class types.

22.12   No, but it does terminate the block in which the exception is thrown.

22.13   The exception will be processed by a catch handler (if one exists) associated with the try block (if one exists) enclosing the catch handler that caused the exception.

22.14   It rethrows the exception if it appears in a catch handler; otherwise, the program terminates.

Exercises

22.15   *(Exceptional Conditions)* List various exceptional conditions that have occurred throughout this text. List as many additional exceptional conditions as you can. For each of these exceptions, describe briefly how a program typically would handle the exception, using the exception-handling techniques discussed in this chapter. Some typical exceptions are division by zero, arithmetic overflow, array subscript out of bounds, exhaustion of the free store, etc.

22.16   *(Catch Parameter)* Under what circumstances would you not provide a parameter name when defining the type of the object that will be caught by a handler?

22.17   *(**throw** Statement)* A program contains the statement

```
throw;
```

Where would you normally expect to find such a statement? What if that statement appeared in a different part of the program?

22.18 *(Exception Handling vs. Other Schemes)* Compare and contrast exception handling with the various other error-processing schemes discussed in the text.

22.19 *(Exception Handling and Program Control)* Why should exceptions *not* be used as an alternate form of program control?

22.20 *(Handling Related Exceptions)* Describe a technique for handling related exceptions.

22.21 *(Throwing Exceptions from a **catch**)* Suppose a program throws an exception and the appropriate exception handler begins executing. Now suppose that the exception handler itself throws the same exception. Does this create infinite recursion? Write a program to check your observation.

22.22 *(Catching Derived-Class Exceptions)* Use inheritance to create various derived classes of runtime_error. Then show that a catch handler specifying the base class can catch derived-class exceptions.

22.23 *(Throwing the Result of a Conditional Expression)* Throw the result of a conditional expression that returns either a double or an int. Provide an int catch handler and a double catch handler. Show that only the double catch handler executes, regardless of whether the int or the double is returned.

22.24 *(Local Variable Destructors)* Write a program illustrating that all destructors for objects constructed in a block are called before an exception is thrown from that block.

22.25 *(Member Object Destructors)* Write a program illustrating that member object destructors are called for only those member objects that were constructed before an exception occurred.

22.26 *(Catching All Exceptions)* Write a program that demonstrates several exception types being caught with the catch(...) exception handler.

22.27 *(Order of Exception Handlers)* Write a program illustrating that the order of exception handlers is important. The first matching handler is the one that executes. Attempt to compile and run your program two different ways to show that two different handlers execute with two different effects.

22.28 *(Constructors Throwing Exceptions)* Write a program that shows a constructor passing information about constructor failure to an exception handler after a try block.

22.29 *(Rethrowing Exceptions)* Write a program that illustrates rethrowing an exception.

22.30 *(Uncaught Exceptions)* Write a program that illustrates that a function with its own try block does not have to catch every possible error generated within the try. Some exceptions can slip through to, and be handled in, outer scopes.

22.31 *(Stack Unwinding)* Write a program that throws an exception from a deeply nested function and still has the catch handler following the try block enclosing the initial call in main catch the exception.

23

Introduction to Custom Templates

Objectives

In this chapter you'll:

- Use class templates to create groups of related classes.

- Distinguish between class templates and class-template specializations.

- Learn about nontype template parameters.

- Learn about default template arguments.

- Learn about overloading function templates.

23.1 Introduction

The C++ Standard Library contains many prepackaged templatized data structures and algorithms. Function templates (which were introduced in Chapter 15) and **class templates** enable you to conveniently specify a variety of related (overloaded) functions—called **function-template specializations**—or a variety of related classes—called **class-template specializations**, respectively. This is called **generic programming**. Function templates and class templates are like *stencils* out of which we trace shapes; function-template specializations and class-template specializations are like the separate tracings that all have the same shape, but could, for example, be drawn in different colors and textures. In this chapter, we demonstrate how to create a custom class template and a function template that manipulates objects of our class-template specializations.

23.2 Class Templates

It's possible to *understand* the concept of a stack (a data structure into which we insert items *only* at the *top* and retrieve those items *only* from the *top* in *last-in, first-out order*) *independent of the type of the items* being placed in the stack. However, to *instantiate* a stack, a data type must be specified. This creates a nice opportunity for software reusability. Here, we define a stack *generically* then use *type-specific* versions of this generic stack class.

Software Engineering Observation 23.1
Class templates encourage software reusability by enabling a variety of type-specific class-template specializations to be instantiated from a single class template.

Class templates are called **parameterized types**, because they require one or more *type parameters* to specify how to customize a generic class template to form a *class-template specialization*. To produce many specializations you write only one class-template definition (as we'll do shortly). When a particular specialization is needed, you use a concise, simple notation, and the compiler writes the specialization source code. One Stack class template, for example, could thus become the basis for creating many Stack class-template specializations (such as "Stack of doubles," "Stack of ints," "Stack of Employees," "Stack of Bills," etc.) used in a program.

Common Programming Error 23.1

To create a template specialization with a user-defined type, the user-defined type must meet the template's requirements. For example, the template might compare objects of the user-defined type with < to determine sorting order, or the template might call a specific member function on an object of the user-defined type. If the user-defined type does not overload the required operator or provide the required functions, compilation errors occur.

Creating Class Template **Stack<T>**

The Stack class-template definition in Fig. 23.1 looks like a conventional class definition, with a few key differences. First, it's preceded by line 7

```
template< typename T >
```

All class templates begin with keyword **template** followed by a list of **template parameters** enclosed in **angle brackets** (< and >); each template parameter that represents a type *must* be preceded by either of the *interchangeable* keywords **typename** or **class**. The type parameter T acts as a placeholder for the Stack's element type. The names of type parameters must be *unique* inside a template definition. You need not specifically use identifier T—any valid identifier can be used. The element type is mentioned generically throughout the Stack class-template definition as T (lines 12, 18 and 42). The type parameter becomes associated with a specific type when you create an object using the class template—at that point, the compiler generates a copy of the class template in which all occurrences of the type parameter are replaced with the specified type. Another key difference is that we did *not* separate the class template's interface from its implementation.

Software Engineering Observation 23.2

Templates are typically defined in headers, which are then #included in the appropriate client source-code files. For class templates, this means that the member functions are also defined in the header—typically inside the class definition's body, as we do in Fig. 23.1.

```
1   // Fig. 23.1: Stack.h
2   // Stack class template.
3   #ifndef STACK_H
4   #define STACK_H
5   #include <deque>
6
7   template< typename T >
8   class Stack
9   {
10  public:
11     // return the top element of the Stack
12     T& top()
13     {
14        return stack.front();
15     } // end function template top
```

Fig. 23.1 | Stack class template. (Part 1 of 2.)

```
16
17      // push an element onto the Stack
18      void push( const T &pushValue )
19      {
20          stack.push_front( pushValue );
21      } // end function template push
22
23      // pop an element from the stack
24      void pop()
25      {
26          stack.pop_front();
27      } // end function template pop
28
29      // determine whether Stack is empty
30      bool isEmpty() const
31      {
32          return stack.empty();
33      } // end function template isEmpty
34
35      // return size of Stack
36      size_t size() const
37      {
38          return stack.size();
39      } // end function template size
40
41  private:
42      std::deque< T > stack; // internal representation of the Stack
43  }; // end class template Stack
44
45  #endif
```

Fig. 23.1 | Stack class template. (Part 2 of 2.)

Class Template Stack<T>'s Data Representation

The C++ Standard Library's prepackaged stack adapter class can use various containers to store its elements. Of course, a stack requires insertions and deletions *only* at its *top*. So, for example, a vector or a deque could be used to store the stack's elements. A vector supports fast insertions and deletions at its *back*. A deque supports fast insertions and deletions at its *front* and its *back*. A deque is the default representation for the Standard Library's stack adapter because a deque grows more efficiently than a vector. A vector is maintained as a *contiguous* block of memory—when that block is full and a new element is added, the vector allocates a larger contiguous block of memory and *copies* the old elements into that new block. A deque, on the other hand, is typically implemented as list of fixed-size, built-in arrays—new fixed-size built-in arrays are added as necessary and none of the existing elements are copied when new items are added to the front or back. For these reasons, we use a deque (line 42) as the underlying container for our Stack class.

Class Template Stack<T>'s Member Functions

The member-function definitions of a class template are *function templates*, but are not preceded with the template keyword and template parameters in angle brackets (< and >) when they're defined within the class template's body. As you can see, however, they do use the class template's template parameter T to represent the element type. Our Stack class template does *not* define it's own constructors—the *default constructor* provided by the compiler will invoke the deque's default constructor. We also provide the following member functions in Fig. 23.1:

- top (lines 12–15) returns a reference to the Stack's top element.
- push (lines 18–21) places a new element on the top of the Stack.
- pop (lines 24–27) removes the Stack's top element.
- isEmpty (lines 30–33) returns a bool value—true if the Stack is empty and false otherwise.
- size (lines 36–39) returns the number if elements in the Stack.

Each of these member functions *delegates* its responsibility to the appropriate member function of class template deque.

Declaring a Class Template's Member Functions Outside the Class Template Definition

Though we did *not* do so in our Stack class template, member-function definitions can appear *outside* a class template definition. If you do this, each must begin with the template keyword followed by the *same* set of template parameters as the class template. In addition, the member functions must be qualified with the class name and scope resolution operator. For example, you can define the pop function outside the class-template definition as follows:

```
template< typename T >
inline void Stack<T>::pop()
{
    stack.pop_front();
} // end function template pop
```

Stack<T>:: indicates that pop is in the scope of class Stack<T>. The Standard Library's container classes tend to define all their member functions *inside* their class definitions.

Testing Class Template Stack<T>

Now, let's consider the driver (Fig. 23.2) that exercises the Stack class template. The driver begins by instantiating object doubleStack (line 9). This object is declared as a Stack<double> (pronounced "Stack of double"). The compiler associates type double with type parameter T in the class template to produce the source code for a Stack class with elements of type double that actually stores its elements in a deque<double>.

Lines 16–21 invoke push (line 18) to place the double values 1.1, 2.2, 3.3, 4.4 and 5.5 onto doubleStack. Next, lines 26–30 invoke top and pop in a while loop to remove the five values from the stack. Notice in the output of Fig. 23.2, that the values do pop off in *last-in, first-out order*. When doubleStack is empty, the pop loop terminates.

```
1   // Fig. 23.2: fig23_02.cpp
2   // Stack class template test program.
3   #include <iostream>
4   #include "Stack.h" // Stack class template definition
```

Fig. 23.2 | Stack class template test program. (Part I of 3.)

```cpp
5   using namespace std;
6
7   int main()
8   {
9      Stack< double > doubleStack; // create a Stack of double
10     const size_t doubleStackSize = 5; // stack size
11     double doubleValue = 1.1; // first value to push
12
13     cout << "Pushing elements onto doubleStack\n";
14
15     // push 5 doubles onto doubleStack
16     for ( size_t i = 0; i < doubleStackSize; ++i )
17     {
18        doubleStack.push( doubleValue );
19        cout << doubleValue << ' ';
20        doubleValue += 1.1;
21     } // end while
22
23     cout << "\n\nPopping elements from doubleStack\n";
24
25     // pop elements from doubleStack
26     while ( !doubleStack.isEmpty() ) // loop while Stack is not empty
27     {
28        cout << doubleStack.top() << ' '; // display top element
29        doubleStack.pop(); // remove top element
30     } // end while
31
32     cout << "\nStack is empty, cannot pop.\n";
33
34     Stack< int > intStack; // create a Stack of int
35     const size_t intStackSize = 10; // stack size
36     int intValue = 1; // first value to push
37
38     cout << "\nPushing elements onto intStack\n";
39
40     // push 10 integers onto intStack
41     for ( size_t i = 0; i < intStackSize; ++i )
42     {
43        intStack.push( intValue );
44        cout << intValue++ << ' ';
45     } // end while
46
47     cout << "\n\nPopping elements from intStack\n";
48
49     // pop elements from intStack
50     while ( !intStack.isEmpty() ) // loop while Stack is not empty
51     {
52        cout << intStack.top() << ' '; // display top element
53        intStack.pop(); // remove top element
54     } // end while
55
56     cout << "\nStack is empty, cannot pop." << endl;
57  } // end main
```

Fig. 23.2 | Stack class template test program. (Part 2 of 3.)

```
Pushing elements onto doubleStack
1.1 2.2 3.3 4.4 5.5

Popping elements from doubleStack
5.5 4.4 3.3 2.2 1.1
Stack is empty, cannot pop

Pushing elements onto intStack
1 2 3 4 5 6 7 8 9 10

Popping elements from intStack
10 9 8 7 6 5 4 3 2 1
Stack is empty, cannot pop
```

Fig. 23.2 | Stack class template test program. (Part 3 of 3.)

Line 34 instantiates int stack intStack with the declaration

```
Stack< int > intStack;
```

(pronounced "intStack is a Stack of int"). Lines 41–45 repeatedly invoke push (line 43) to place values onto intStack, then lines 50–54 repeatedly invoke top and pop to remove values from intStack until it's empty. Once again, notice in the output that the values pop off in last-in, first-out order.

23.3 Function Template to Manipulate a Class-Template Specialization Object

Notice that the code in function main of Fig. 23.2 is *almost identical* for both the double-Stack manipulations in lines 9–32 and the intStack manipulations in lines 34–56. This presents another opportunity to use a function template. Figure 23.3 defines function template testStack (lines 10–39) to perform the same tasks as main in Fig. 23.2—push a series of values onto a Stack<T> and pop the values off a Stack<T>.

```
1   // Fig. 23.3: fig23_03.cpp
2   // Passing a Stack template object
3   // to a function template.
4   #include <iostream>
5   #include <string>
6   #include "Stack.h" // Stack class template definition
7   using namespace std;
8
9   // function template to manipulate Stack< T >
10  template< typename T >
11  void testStack(
12     Stack< T > &theStack, // reference to Stack< T >
13     const T &value, // initial value to push
14     const T &increment, // increment for subsequent values
15     size_t size, // number of items to push
16     const string &stackName ) // name of the Stack< T > object
17  {
```

Fig. 23.3 | Passing a Stack template object to a function template. (Part 1 of 2.)

```
18        cout << "\nPushing elements onto " << stackName << '\n';
19        T pushValue = value;
20
21        // push element onto Stack
22        for ( size_t i = 0; i < size; ++i )
23        {
24           theStack.push( pushValue ); // push element onto Stack
25           cout << pushValue << ' ';
26           pushValue += increment;
27        } // end while
28
29        cout << "\n\nPopping elements from " << stackName << '\n';
30
31        // pop elements from Stack
32        while ( !theStack.isEmpty() ) // loop while Stack is not empty
33        {
34           cout << theStack.top() << ' ';
35           theStack.pop(); // remove top element
36        } // end while
37
38        cout << "\nStack is empty. Cannot pop." << endl;
39     } // end function template testStack
40
41     int main()
42     {
43        Stack< double > doubleStack;
44        const size_t doubleStackSize - 5;
45        testStack( doubleStack, 1.1, 1.1, doubleStackSize, "doubleStack" );
46
47        Stack< int > intStack;
48        const size_t intStackSize = 10;
49        testStack( intStack, 1, 1, intStackSize, "intStack" );
50     } // end main
```

```
Pushing elements onto doubleStack
1.1 2.2 3.3 4.4 5.5

Popping elements from doubleStack
5.5 4.4 3.3 2.2 1.1
Stack is empty, cannot pop

Pushing elements onto intStack
1 2 3 4 5 6 7 8 9 10

Popping elements from intStack
10 9 8 7 6 5 4 3 2 1
Stack is empty, cannot pop
```

Fig. 23.3 | Passing a Stack template object to a function template. (Part 2 of 2.)

Function template testStack uses T (specified at line 10) to represent the data type stored in the Stack<T>. The function template takes five arguments (lines 12–16):

- the Stack<T> to manipulate

- a value of type T that will be the first value pushed onto the Stack<T>
- a value of type T used to increment the values pushed onto the Stack<T>
- the number of elements to push onto the Stack<T>
- a string that represents the name of the Stack<T> object for output purposes

Function main (lines 41–50) instantiates an object of type Stack<double> called doubleStack (line 43) and an object of type Stack<int> called intStack (line 47) and uses these objects in lines 45 and 49. The compiler infers the type of T for testStack from the type used to instantiate the function's first argument (i.e., the type used to instantiate doubleStack or intStack).

23.4 Nontype Parameters

Class template Stack of Section 23.2 used only a type parameter (Fig. 23.1, line 7) in its template declaration. It's also possible to use **nontype template parameters**, which can have default arguments and are treated as constants. For example, the C++ standard's array class template begins with the template declaration:

```
template < class T, size_t N >
```

(Recall that keywords class and typename are *interchangeable* in template declarations.) So, a declaration such as

```
array< double, 100 > salesFigures;
```

creates a 100-element array of doubles class-template specialization, then uses it to instantiate the object salesFigures. The array class template encapsulates a *built-in array*. When you create an array class-template specialization, the array's built-in array data member has the type and size specified in the declaration—in the preceding example, it would be a built-in array of double values with 100 elements.

23.5 Default Arguments for Template Type Parameters

In addition, a type parameter can specify a **default type argument**. For example, the C++ standard's stack *container adapter* class template begins with:

```
template < class T, class Container = deque< T > >
```

which specifies that a stack uses a deque *by default* to store the stack's elements of type T. The declaration

```
stack< int > values;
```

creates a stack of ints class-template specialization (behind the scenes) and uses it to instantiate the object named values. The stack's elements are stored in a deque<int>.

Default type parameters must be the *rightmost* (trailing) parameters in a template's type-parameter list. When you instantiate a template with two or more default arguments, if an omitted argument is not the rightmost, then all type parameters to the right of it also must be omitted. As of C++11, you can now use default type arguments for template type parameters in function templates.

23.6 Overloading Function Templates

Function templates and overloading are intimately related. In Chapter 15, you learned that when overloaded functions perform *identical* operations on *different* types of data, they can be expressed more compactly and conveniently using function templates. You can then write function calls with different types of arguments and let the compiler generate separate *function-template specializations* to handle each function call appropriately. The function-template specializations generated from a given function template all have the same name, so the compiler uses overload resolution to invoke the proper function.

You may also *overload* function templates. For example, you can provide other function templates that specify the *same* function name but *different* function parameters. A function template also can be overloaded by providing nontemplate functions with the same function name but different function parameters.

Matching Process for Overloaded Functions

The compiler performs a matching process to determine what function to call when a function is invoked. It looks at both existing functions and function templates to locate a function or generate a function-template specialization whose function name and argument types are consistent with those of the function call. If there are no matches, the compiler issues an error message. If there are multiple matches for the function call, the compiler attempts to determine the *best* match. If there's *more than one* best match, the call is *ambiguous* and the compiler issues an error message.[1]

23.7 Wrap-Up

This chapter discussed class templates and class-template specializations. We used a class template to create a group of related class-template specializations that each perform identical processing on different data types. We discussed nontype template parameters. We also discussed how to overload a function template to create a customized version that handles a particular data type's processing in a manner that differs from the other function-template specializations.

---

1. The compiler's process for resolving function calls is complex. The complete details are discussed in Section 13.3.3 of the C++ standard.

Summary

Section 23.1 Introduction
• Templates enable us to specify a range of related (overloaded) functions—called function-template specializations (p. 875)—or a range of related classes—called class-template specializations (p. 875).

Section 23.2 Class Templates
• Class templates provide the means for describing a class generically and for instantiating classes that are type-specific versions of this generic class.

- Class templates are called parameterized types (p. 875); they require type parameters to specify how to customize a generic class template to form a specific class-template specialization.

- To use class-template specializations you write one class template. When you need a new type-specific class, the compiler writes the source code for the class-template specialization.

- A class-template definition (p. 875) looks like a conventional class definition, but it's preceded by `template<typename T>` (or `template<class T>`) to indicate this is a class-template definition. T is a type parameter that acts as a placeholder for the type of the class to create. The type T is mentioned throughout the class definition and member-function definitions as a generic type name.

- The names of template parameters must be unique inside a template definition.

- Member-function definitions outside a class template each begin with the same `template` declaration as their class. Then, each function definition resembles a conventional function definition, except that the generic data in the class always is listed generically as type parameter T. The binary scope-resolution operator is used with the class-template name to tie each member-function definition to the class template's scope.

Section 23.4 Nontype Parameters
- It's possible to use nontype parameters (p. 882) in a class or function template declaration.

Section 23.5 Default Arguments for Template Type Parameters
- You can specify a default type argument (p. 882) for a type parameter in the type-parameter list.

Section 23.6 Overloading Function Templates
- A function template may be overloaded in several ways. We can provide other function templates that specify the same function name but different function parameters. A function template can also be overloaded by providing other nontemplate functions with the same function name, but different function parameters. If both the template and non-template versions match a call, the non-template version will be used.

Self-Review Exercises

23.1 State which of the following are *true* and which are *false*. If *false*, explain why.
   a) Keywords `typename` and `class` as used with a template type parameter specifically mean "any user-defined class type."
   b) A function template can be overloaded by another function template with the same function name.
   c) Template parameter names among template definitions must be unique.
   d) Each member-function definition outside its corresponding class template definition must begin with `template` and the same template parameters as its class template.

23.2 Fill in the blanks in each of the following:
   a) Templates enable us to specify, with a single code segment, an entire range of related functions called _____, or an entire range of related classes called _____.
   b) All template definitions begin with the keyword _____, followed by a list of template parameters enclosed in _____.
   c) The related functions generated from a function template all have the same name, so the compiler uses _____ resolution to invoke the proper function.
   d) Class templates also are called _____ types.
   e) The _____ operator is used with a class-template name to tie each member-function definition to the class template's scope.

Answers to Self-Review Exercises

23.1 a) False. Keywords `typename` and `class` in this context also allow for a type parameter of a fundamental type. b) True. c) False. Template parameter names among function templates need not be unique. d) True.

23.2 a) function-template specializations, class-template specializations. b) `template`, angle brackets (< and >). c) overload. d) parameterized. e) scope resolution.

Exercises

23.3 *(Operator Overloads in Templates)* Write a simple function template for predicate function `isEqualTo` that compares its two arguments of the same type with the equality operator (==) and returns `true` if they are equal and `false` otherwise. Use this function template in a program that calls `isEqualTo` only with a variety of fundamental types. Now write a separate version of the program that calls `isEqualTo` with a user-defined class type, but does not overload the equality operator. What happens when you attempt to run this program? Now overload the equality operator (with the operator function) `operator==`. Now what happens when you attempt to run this program?

23.4 *(Array Class Template)* Reimplement class `Array` from Figs. 18.10–18.11 as a class template. Demonstrate the new `Array` class template in a program.

23.5 Distinguish between the terms "function template" and "function-template specialization."

23.6 Explain which is more like a stencil—a class template or a class template specialization?

23.7 What's the relationship between function templates and overloading?

23.8 The compiler performs a matching process to determine which function-template specialization to call when a function is invoked. Under what circumstances does an attempt to make a match result in a compile error?

23.9 Why is it appropriate to refer to a class template as a parameterized type?

23.10 Explain why a C++ program would use the statement

```
Array< Employee > workerList( 100 );
```

23.11 Review your answer to Exercise 23.10. Explain why a C++ program might use the statement

```
Array< Employee > workerList;
```

23.12 Explain the use of the following notation in a C++ program:

```
template< typename T > Array< T >::Array( int s )
```

23.13 Why might you use a nontype parameter with a class template for a container such as an array or stack?

C and C++ Operator Precedence Charts

Operators are shown in decreasing order of precedence from top to bottom (Figs. A.1–A.2).

C Operator	Type	Associativity
()	parentheses (function call operator)	left to right
[]	array subscript	
.	member selection via object	
->	member selection via pointer	
++	unary postincrement	
--	unary postdecrement	
++	unary preincrement	right to left
--	unary predecrement	
+	unary plus	
-	unary minus	
!	unary logical negation	
~	unary bitwise complement	
(*type*)	C-style unary cast	
*	dereference	
&	address	
sizeof	determine size in bytes	
*	multiplication	left to right
/	division	
%	modulus	
+	addition	left to right
-	subtraction	
<<	bitwise left shift	left to right
>>	bitwise right shift	
<	relational less than	left to right
<=	relational less than or equal to	
>	relational greater than	
>=	relational greater than or equal to	

Fig. A.1 | C operator precedence chart. (Part 1 of 2.)

C Operator	Type	Associativity
==	relational is equal to	left to right
!=	relational is not equal to	
&	bitwise AND	left to right
^	bitwise exclusive OR	left to right
|	bitwise inclusive OR	left to right
&&	logical AND	left to right
||	logical OR	left to right
?:	ternary conditional	right to left
=	assignment	right to left
+=	addition assignment	
-=	subtraction assignment	
*=	multiplication assignment	
/=	division assignment	
%=	modulus assignment	
&=	bitwise AND assignment	
^=	bitwise exclusive OR assignment	
|=	bitwise inclusive OR assignment	
<<=	bitwise left shift assignment	
>>=	bitwise right shift with sign	
,	comma	left to right

Fig. A.1 | C operator precedence chart. (Part 2 of 2.)

C++ Operator	Type	Associativity
::	binary scope resolution	left to right
::	unary scope resolution	
()	parentheses (function call operator)	left to right
[]	array subscript	
.	member selection via object	
->	member selection via pointer	
++	unary postincrement	
--	unary postdecrement	
typeid	runtime type information	
dynamic_cast<*type*>	runtime type-checked cast	
static_cast<*type*>	compile-time type-checked cast	
reinterpret_cast<*type*>	cast for nonstandard conversions	
const_cast<*type*>	cast away const-ness	

Fig. A.2 | C++ operator precedence chart. (Part 1 of 3.)

C++ Operator	Type	Associativity
++	unary preincrement	right to left
--	unary predecrement	
+	unary plus	
-	unary minus	
!	unary logical negation	
~	unary bitwise complement	
(*type*)	C-style unary cast	
sizeof	determine size in bytes	
&	address	
*	dereference	
new	dynamic memory allocation	
new[]	dynamic array allocation	
delete	dynamic memory deallocation	
delete[]	dynamic array deallocation	
.*	pointer to member via object	left to right
->*	pointer to member via pointer	
*	multiplication	left to right
/	division	
%	modulus	
+	addition	left to right
-	subtraction	
<<	bitwise left shift	left to right
>>	bitwise right shift	
<	relational less than	left to right
<=	relational less than or equal to	
>	relational greater than	
>=	relational greater than or equal to	
==	relational is equal to	left to right
!=	relational is not equal to	
&	bitwise AND	left to right
^	bitwise exclusive OR	left to right
|	bitwise inclusive OR	left to right
&&	logical AND	left to right
||	logical OR	left to right
?:	ternary conditional	right to left

Fig. A.2 | C++ operator precedence chart. (Part 2 of 3.)

C++ Operator	Type	Associativity
=	assignment	right to left
+=	addition assignment	
-=	subtraction assignment	
*=	multiplication assignment	
/=	division assignment	
%=	modulus assignment	
&=	bitwise AND assignment	
^=	bitwise exclusive OR assignment	
|=	bitwise inclusive OR assignment	
<<=	bitwise left shift assignment	
>>=	bitwise right shift with sign	
,	comma	left to right

Fig. A.2 | C++ operator precedence chart. (Part 3 of 3.)

ASCII Character Set

	0	1	2	3	4	5	6	7	8	9
0	nul	soh	stx	etx	eot	enq	ack	bel	bs	ht
1	lf	vt	ff	cr	so	si	dle	dc1	dc2	dc3
2	dc4	nak	syn	etb	can	em	sub	esc	fs	gs
3	rs	us	sp	!	"	#	$	%	&	'
4	(	)	*	+	,	-	.	/	0	1
5	2	3	4	5	6	7	8	9	:	;
6	<	=	>	?	@	A	B	C	D	E
7	F	G	H	I	J	K	L	M	N	O
8	P	Q	R	S	T	U	V	W	X	Y
9	Z	[	\	]	^	_	'	a	b	c
10	d	e	f	g	h	i	j	k	l	m
11	n	o	p	q	r	s	t	u	v	w
12	x	y	z	{	|	}	~	del		

Fig. B.1 | ASCII Character Set.

The digits at the left of the table are the left digits of the decimal equivalent (0–127) of the character code, and the digits at the top of the table are the right digits of the character code. For example, the character code for "F" is 70, and the character code for "&" is 38.

Number Systems

C

Objectives

In this appendix, you'll learn:

- To understand basic number systems concepts such as base, positional value and symbol value.

- To understand how to work with numbers represented in the binary, octal and hexadecimal number systems

- To be able to abbreviate binary numbers as octal numbers or hexadecimal numbers.

- To be able to convert octal numbers and hexadecimal numbers to binary numbers.

- To be able to convert back and forth between decimal numbers and their binary, octal and hexadecimal equivalents.

- To understand binary arithmetic and how negative binary numbers are represented using two's complement notation.

C.1 Introduction

In this appendix, we introduce the key number systems that programmers use, especially when they are working on software projects that require close interaction with machine-level hardware. Projects like this include operating systems, computer networking software, compilers, database systems and applications requiring high performance.

When we write an integer such as 227 or –63 in a program, the number is assumed to be in the **decimal (base 10) number system**. The **digits** in the decimal number system are 0, 1, 2, 3, 4, 5, 6, 7, 8 and 9. The lowest digit is 0 and the highest digit is 9—one less than the **base** of 10. Internally, computers use the **binary (base 2) number system**. The binary number system has only two digits, namely 0 and 1. Its lowest digit is 0 and its highest digit is 1—one less than the base of 2.

As we'll see, binary numbers tend to be much longer than their decimal equivalents. Programmers who work in assembly languages and in high-level languages like C that enable programmers to reach down to the machine level, find it cumbersome to work with binary numbers. So two other number systems—the **octal number system (base 8)** and the **hexadecimal number system (base 16)**—are popular primarily because they make it convenient to abbreviate binary numbers.

In the octal number system, the digits range from 0 to 7. Because both the binary number system and the octal number system have fewer digits than the decimal number system, their digits are the same as the corresponding digits in decimal.

The hexadecimal number system poses a problem because it requires 16 digits—a lowest digit of 0 and a highest digit with a value equivalent to decimal 15 (one less than the base of 16). By convention, we use the letters A through F to represent the hexadecimal digits corresponding to decimal values 10 through 15. Thus in hexadecimal we can have numbers like 876 consisting solely of decimal-like digits, numbers like 8A55F consisting of digits and letters and numbers like FFE consisting solely of letters. Occasionally, a hexadecimal number spells a common word such as FACE or FEED—this can appear strange to programmers accustomed to working with numbers. The digits of the binary, octal, decimal and hexadecimal number systems are summarized in Figs. C.1–C.2.

Each of these number systems uses **positional notation**—each position in which a digit is written has a different **positional value**. For example, in the decimal number 937 (the 9, the 3 and the 7 are referred to as **symbol values**), we say that the 7 is written in the ones position, the 3 is written in the tens position and the 9 is written in the hundreds position. Each of these positions is a power of the base (base 10) and these powers begin at 0 and increase by 1 as we move left in the number (Fig. C.3).

Binary digit	Octal digit	Decimal digit	Hexadecimal digit
0	0	0	0
1	1	1	1
	2	2	2
	3	3	3
	4	4	4
	5	5	5
	6	6	6
	7	7	7
		8	8
		9	9
			A (decimal value of 10)
			B (decimal value of 11)
			C (decimal value of 12)
			D (decimal value of 13)
			E (decimal value of 14)
			F (decimal value of 15)

Fig. C.1 | Digits of the binary, octal, decimal and hexadecimal number systems.

Attribute	Binary	Octal	Decimal	Hexadecimal
Base	2	8	10	16
Lowest digit	0	0	0	0
Highest digit	1	7	9	F

Fig. C.2 | Comparing the binary, octal, decimal and hexadecimal number systems.

Positional values in the decimal number system			
Decimal digit	9	3	7
Position name	Hundreds	Tens	Ones
Positional value	100	10	1
Positional value as a power of the base (10)	10^2	10^1	10^0

Fig. C.3 | Positional values in the decimal number system.

For longer decimal numbers, the next positions to the left would be the thousands position (10 to the 3rd power), the ten-thousands position (10 to the 4th power), the hundred-thousands position (10 to the 5th power), the millions position (10 to the 6th power), the ten-millions position (10 to the 7th power) and so on.

In the binary number 101, the rightmost 1 is written in the ones position, the 0 is written in the twos position and the leftmost 1 is written in the fours position. Each position is a power of the base (base 2) and these powers begin at 0 and increase by 1 as we move left in the number (Fig. C.4). So, $101 = 1 * 2^2 + 0 * 2^1 + 1 * 2^0 = 4 + 0 + 1 = 5$.

Positional values in the binary number system			
Binary digit	1	0	1
Position name	Fours	Twos	Ones
Positional value	4	2	1
Positional value as a power of the base (2)	2^2	2^1	2^0

Fig. C.4 | Positional values in the binary number system.

For longer binary numbers, the next positions to the left would be the eights position (2 to the 3rd power), the sixteens position (2 to the 4th power), the thirty-twos position (2 to the 5th power), the sixty-fours position (2 to the 6th power) and so on.

In the octal number 425, we say that the 5 is written in the ones position, the 2 is written in the eights position and the 4 is written in the sixty-fours position. Each of these positions is a power of the base (base 8) and that these powers begin at 0 and increase by 1 as we move left in the number (Fig. C.5).

Positional values in the octal number system			
Decimal digit	4	2	5
Position name	Sixty-fours	Eights	Ones
Positional value	64	8	1
Positional value as a power of the base (8)	8^2	8^1	8^0

Fig. C.5 | Positional values in the octal number system.

For longer octal numbers, the next positions to the left would be the five-hundred-and-twelves position (8 to the 3rd power), the four-thousand-and-ninety-sixes position (8 to the 4th power), the thirty-two-thousand-seven-hundred-and-sixty-eights position (8 to the 5th power) and so on.

In the hexadecimal number 3DA, we say that the A is written in the ones position, the D is written in the sixteens position and the 3 is written in the two-hundred-and-fifty-sixes position. Each of these positions is a power of the base (base 16) and these powers begin at 0 and increase by 1 as we move left in the number (Fig. C.6).

For longer hexadecimal numbers, the next positions to the left would be the four-thousand-and-ninety-sixes position (16 to the 3rd power), the sixty-five-thousand-five-hundred-and-thirty-sixes position (16 to the 4th power) and so on.

Positional values in the hexadecimal number system			
Decimal digit	3	D	A
Position name	Two-hundred-and-fifty-sixes	Sixteens	Ones
Positional value	256	16	1
Positional value as a power of the base (16)	16^2	16^1	16^0

Fig. C.6 | Positional values in the hexadecimal number system.

C.2 Abbreviating Binary Numbers as Octal and Hexadecimal Numbers

The main use for octal and hexadecimal numbers in computing is for abbreviating lengthy binary representations. Figure C.7 highlights the fact that lengthy binary numbers can be expressed concisely in number systems with higher bases than the binary number system.

Decimal number	Binary representation	Octal representation	Hexadecimal representation
0	0	0	0
1	1	1	1
2	10	2	2
3	11	3	3
4	100	4	4
5	101	5	5
6	110	6	6
7	111	7	7
8	1000	10	8
9	1001	11	9
10	1010	12	A
11	1011	13	B
12	1100	14	C
13	1101	15	D
14	1110	16	E
15	1111	17	F
16	10000	20	10

Fig. C.7 | Decimal, binary, octal and hexadecimal equivalents.

A particularly important relationship that both the octal number system and the hexadecimal number system have to the binary system is that the bases of octal and hexadecimal (8 and 16 respectively) are powers of the base of the binary number system (base 2). Consider the following 12-digit binary number and its octal and hexadecimal equivalents. See if you can determine how this relationship makes it convenient to abbreviate binary numbers in octal or hexadecimal. The answer follows the numbers.

Binary number	Octal equivalent	Hexadecimal equivalent
100011010001	4321	8D1

To see how the binary number converts easily to octal, simply break the 12-digit binary number into groups of three consecutive bits each and write those groups over the corresponding digits of the octal number as follows:

100	011	010	001
4	3	2	1

The octal digit you have written under each group of three bits corresponds precisely to the octal equivalent of that 3-digit binary number, as shown in Fig. C.7.

The same kind of relationship can be observed in converting from binary to hexadecimal. Break the 12-digit binary number into groups of four consecutive bits each and write those groups over the corresponding digits of the hexadecimal number as follows:

1000	1101	0001
8	D	1

The hexadecimal digit you wrote under each group of four bits corresponds precisely to the hexadecimal equivalent of that 4-digit binary number as shown in Fig. C.7.

C.3 Converting Octal and Hexadecimal Numbers to Binary Numbers

In the previous section, we saw how to convert binary numbers to their octal and hexadecimal equivalents by forming groups of binary digits and simply rewriting them as their equivalent octal digit values or hexadecimal digit values. This process may be used in reverse to produce the binary equivalent of a given octal or hexadecimal number.

For example, the octal number 653 is converted to binary simply by writing the 6 as its 3-digit binary equivalent 110, the 5 as its 3-digit binary equivalent 101 and the 3 as its 3-digit binary equivalent 011 to form the 9-digit binary number 110101011.

The hexadecimal number FAD5 is converted to binary simply by writing the F as its 4-digit binary equivalent 1111, the A as its 4-digit binary equivalent 1010, the D as its 4-digit binary equivalent 1101 and the 5 as its 4-digit binary equivalent 0101 to form the 16-digit 1111101011010101.

C.4 Converting from Binary, Octal or Hexadecimal to Decimal

We're accustomed to working in decimal, and therefore it's often convenient to convert a binary, octal, or hexadecimal number to decimal to get a sense of what the number is "really" worth. Our tables in Section C.1 express the positional values in decimal. To convert a number to decimal from another base, multiply the decimal equivalent of each digit by its positional value and sum these products. For example, the binary number 110101 is converted to decimal 53, as shown in Fig. C.8.

Converting a binary number to decimal					
Postional values:	32	16	8	4	2	1
Symbol values:	1	1	0	1	0	1
Products:	1*32=32	1*16=16	0*8=0	1*4=4	0*2=0	1*1=1
Sum:	= 32 + 16 + 0 + 4 + 0 + 1 = 53					

Fig. C.8 | Converting a binary number to decimal.

To convert octal 7614 to decimal 3980, we use the same technique, this time using appropriate octal positional values, as shown in Fig. C.9.

Converting an octal number to decimal			
Positional values:	512	64	8	1
Symbol values:	7	6	1	4
Products	7*512=3584	6*64=384	1*8=8	4*1=4
Sum:	= 3584 + 384 + 8 + 4 = 3980			

Fig. C.9 | Converting an octal number to decimal.

To convert hexadecimal AD3B to decimal 44347, we use the same technique, this time using appropriate hexadecimal positional values, as shown in Fig. C.10.

Converting a hexadecimal number to decimal			
Postional values:	4096	256	16	1
Symbol values:	A	D	3	B
Products	A*4096=40960	D*256=3328	3*16=48	B*1=11
Sum:	= 40960 + 3328 + 48 + 11 = 44347			

Fig. C.10 | Converting a hexadecimal number to decimal.

C.5 Converting from Decimal to Binary, Octal or Hexadecimal

The **conversions** in Section C.4 follow naturally from the positional notation conventions. Converting from decimal to binary, octal, or hexadecimal also follows these conventions.

Suppose we wish to convert decimal 57 to binary. We begin by writing the positional values of the columns right to left until we reach a column whose positional value is greater than the decimal number. We do not need that column, so we discard it. Thus, we first write:

Positional values:	64	32	16	8	4	2	1

Then we discard the column with positional value 64, leaving:

Positional values:	32	16	8	4	2	1

Next we work from the leftmost column to the right. We divide 32 into 57 and observe that there is one 32 in 57 with a remainder of 25, so we write 1 in the 32 column. We divide 16 into 25 and observe that there is one 16 in 25 with a remainder of 9 and write 1 in the 16 column. We divide 8 into 9 and observe that there is one 8 in 9 with a remainder of 1. The next two columns each produce quotients of 0 when their positional values are divided into 1, so we write 0s in the 4 and 2 columns. Finally, 1 into 1 is 1, so we write 1 in the 1 column. This yields:

Positional values:	32	16	8	4	2	1
Symbol values:	1	1	1	0	0	1

and thus decimal 57 is equivalent to binary 111001.

To convert decimal 103 to octal, we begin by writing the positional values of the columns until we reach a column whose positional value is greater than the decimal number. We do not need that column, so we discard it. Thus, we first write:

Positional values:	512	64	8	1

Then we discard the column with positional value 512, yielding:

Positional values:	64	8	1

Next we work from the leftmost column to the right. We divide 64 into 103 and observe that there is one 64 in 103 with a remainder of 39, so we write 1 in the 64 column. We divide 8 into 39 and observe that there are four 8s in 39 with a remainder of 7 and write 4 in the 8 column. Finally, we divide 1 into 7 and observe that there are seven 1s in 7 with no remainder, so we write 7 in the 1 column. This yields:

Positional values:	64	8	1
Symbol values:	1	4	7

and thus decimal 103 is equivalent to octal 147.

To convert decimal 375 to hexadecimal, we begin by writing the positional values of the columns until we reach a column whose positional value is greater than the decimal number. We do not need that column, so we discard it. Thus, we first write:

Positional values:	4096	256	16	1

Then we discard the column with positional value 4096, yielding:

Positional values:	256	16	1

Next we work from the leftmost column to the right. We divide 256 into 375 and observe that there is one 256 in 375 with a remainder of 119, so we write 1 in the 256 column. We divide 16 into 119 and observe that there are seven 16s in 119 with a remainder of 7 and write 7 in the 16 column. Finally, we divide 1 into 7 and observe that there are seven 1s in 7 with no remainder, so we write 7 in the 1 column. This yields:

Positional values:	256	16	1
Symbol values:	1	7	7

and thus decimal 375 is equivalent to hexadecimal 177.

C.6 Negative Binary Numbers: Two's Complement Notation

The discussion so far in this appendix has focused on positive numbers. In this section, we explain how computers represent negative numbers using **two's complement notation**. First we explain how the two's complement of a binary number is formed, then we show why it represents the **negative value** of the given binary number.

Consider a machine with 32-bit integers. Suppose

```
int value = 13;
```

The 32-bit representation of value is

```
00000000 00000000 00000000 00001101
```

To form the negative of value we first form its **one's complement** by applying C's **bitwise complement operator** (~):

```
onesComplementOfValue = ~value;
```

Internally, ~value is now value with each of its bits reversed—ones become zeros and zeros become ones, as follows:

```
value:
00000000 00000000 00000000 00001101
```

```
~value (i.e., value's ones complement):
11111111 11111111 11111111 11110010
```

To form the two's complement of value, we simply add 1 to value's one's complement. Thus

```
Two's complement of value:
11111111 11111111 11111111 11110011
```

Now if this is in fact equal to −13, we should be able to add it to binary 13 and obtain a result of 0. Let's try this:

```
 00000000 00000000 00000000 00001101
+11111111 11111111 11111111 11110011
-------------------------------------
 00000000 00000000 00000000 00000000
```

The carry bit coming out of the leftmost column is discarded and we indeed get 0 as a result. If we add the one's complement of a number to the number, the result would be all 1s. The key to getting a result of all zeros is that the twos complement is one more than the one's complement. The addition of 1 causes each column to add to 0 with a carry of 1. The carry keeps moving leftward until it's discarded from the leftmost bit, and thus the resulting number is all zeros.

Computers actually perform a subtraction, such as

```
x = a - value;
```

by adding the two's complement of value to a, as follows:

```
x = a + (~value + 1);
```

Suppose a is 27 and value is 13 as before. If the two's complement of value is actually the negative of value, then adding the two's complement of value to a should produce the result 14. Let's try this:

```
a (i.e., 27)        00000000 00000000 00000000 00011011
+(~value + 1)      +11111111 11111111 11111111 11110011
                   ------------------------------------
                    00000000 00000000 00000000 00001110
```

which is indeed equal to 14.

Summary

- An integer such as 19 or 227 or −63 in a program is assumed to be in the decimal (base 10; p. 892) number system. The digits in the decimal number system are 0, 1, 2, 3, 4, 5, 6, 7, 8 and 9. The lowest digit is 0 and the highest digit is 9—one less than the base of 10.

- Internally, computers use the binary (base 2; p. 892) number system. The binary number system has only two digits, namely 0 and 1. Its lowest digit is 0 and its highest digit is 1—one less than the base of 2.

- The octal number system (base 8; p. 892) and the hexadecimal number system (base 16; p. 892) are popular primarily because they make it convenient to abbreviate binary numbers.

- The digits of the octal number system range from 0 to 7.

- The hexadecimal number system (p. 892) poses a problem because it requires 16 digits—a lowest digit of 0 and a highest digit with a value equivalent to decimal 15 (one less than the base of 16). By convention, we use the letters A through F to represent the hexadecimal digits corresponding to decimal values 10 through 15.

- Each number system uses positional notation (p. 892)—each position in which a digit is written has a different positional value (p. 892).

- A particularly important relationship of both the octal number system and the hexadecimal number system to the binary system is that the bases of octal and hexadecimal (8 and 16 respectively) are powers of the base of the binary number system (base 2).

- To convert (p. 897) an octal to a binary number, replace each octal digit with its three-digit binary equivalent.

- To convert a hexadecimal number to a binary number, simply replace each hexadecimal digit with its four-digit binary equivalent.

- Because we're accustomed to working in decimal, it's convenient to convert a binary, octal or hexadecimal number to decimal to get a sense of the number's "real" worth.

- To convert a number to decimal from another base, multiply the decimal equivalent of each digit by its positional value and sum the products.

- Computers represent negative numbers using two's complement notation.

- To form the negative of a value in binary, first form its one's complement by applying C's bitwise complement operator (~; p. 899). This reverses the bits of the value. To form the two's complement (p. 899) of a value, simply add one to the value's one's complement.

Self-Review Exercises

C.1   Fill in the blanks in each of the following statements:
   a) The bases of the decimal, binary, octal and hexadecimal number systems are _____, _____, _____ and _____ respectively.
   b) The positional value of the rightmost digit of any number in either binary, octal, decimal or hexadecimal is always _____.
   c) The positional value of the digit to the left of the rightmost digit of any number in binary, octal, decimal or hexadecimal is always equal to _____.

C.2   State whether each of the following is *true* or *false*. If *false*, explain why.
   a) A popular reason for using the decimal number system is that it forms a convenient notation for abbreviating binary numbers simply by substituting one decimal digit per group of four binary bits.
   b) The highest digit in any base is one more than the base.
   c) The lowest digit in any base is one less than the base.

C.3   In general, the decimal, octal and hexadecimal representations of a given binary number contain (more/fewer) digits than the binary number contains.

C.4   The (octal / hexadecimal / decimal) representation of a large binary value is the most concise (of the given alternatives).

C.5   Fill in the missing values in this chart of positional values for the rightmost four positions in each of the indicated number systems:

decimal	1000	100	10	1
hexadecimal	...	256	...	...
binary	...	...	...	...
octal	512	...	8	...

C.6   Convert binary 110101011000 to octal and to hexadecimal.

C.7   Convert hexadecimal FACE to binary.

C.8   Convert octal 7316 to binary.

C.9   Convert hexadecimal 4FEC to octal. [*Hint:* First convert 4FEC to binary, then convert that binary number to octal.]

C.10   Convert binary 1101110 to decimal.

C.11   Convert octal 317 to decimal.

C.12   Convert hexadecimal EFD4 to decimal.

C.13   Convert decimal 177 to binary, to octal and to hexadecimal.

C.14   Show the binary representation of decimal 417. Then show the one's complement of 417 and the two's complement of 417.

C.15   What is the result when a number and its two's complement are added to each other?

Answers to Self-Review Exercises

C.1   a) 10, 2, 8, 16. b) 1 (the base raised to the zero power). c) The base of the number system.

C.2   a) False. Hexadecimal does this. b) False. The highest digit in any base is one less than the base. c) False. The lowest digit in any base is zero.

C.3   Fewer.

C.4   Hexadecimal.

C.5

decimal	1000	100	10	1
hexadecimal	4096	256	16	1
binary	8	4	2	1
octal	512	64	8	1

C.6   Octal 6530; Hexadecimal D58.

C.7   Binary 1111 1010 1100 1110.

C.8   Binary 111 011 001 110.

C.9   Binary 0 100 111 111 101 100; Octal 47754.

C.10   Decimal 2 + 4 + 8 + 32 + 64 = 110.

C.11   Decimal 7 + 1 * 8 + 3 * 64 = 7 + 8 + 192 = 207.

C.12   Decimal 4 + 13 * 16 + 15 * 256 + 14 * 4096 = 61396.

C.13   Decimal 177
to binary:

```
256 128 64 32 16 8 4 2 1
128 64 32 16 8 4 2 1
(1*128)+(0*64)+(1*32)+(1*16)+(0*8)+(0*4)+(0*2)+(1*1)
10110001
```

to octal:

```
512 64 8 1
64 8 1
(2*64)+(6*8)+(1*1)
261
```

to hexadecimal:

```
256 16 1
16 1
(11*16)+(1*1)
(B*16)+(1*1)
B1
```

C.14   Binary:

```
512 256 128 64 32 16 8 4 2 1
256 128 64 32 16 8 4 2 1
(1*256)+(1*128)+(0*64)+(1*32)+(0*16)+(0*8)+(0*4)+(0*2)+(1*1)
110100001
```

One's complement: 001011110
Two's complement: 001011111
Check: Original binary number + its two's complement

```
110100001
001011111
---------
000000000
```

C.15   Zero.

Exercises

C.16   Some people argue that many of our calculations would be easier in the base 12 number system because 12 is divisible by so many more numbers than 10 (for base 10). What is the lowest digit in base 12? What would be the highest symbol for the digit in base 12? What are the positional values of the rightmost four positions of any number in the base 12 number system?

C.17   Complete the following chart of positional values for the rightmost four positions in each of the indicated number systems:

	1000	100	10	1
decimal	1000	100	10	1
base 6	...	...	6	...
base 13	...	169	...	...
base 3	27	...	...	...

C.18   Convert binary 100101111010 to octal and to hexadecimal.

C.19   Convert hexadecimal 3A7D to binary.

C.20   Convert hexadecimal 765F to octal. (*Hint:* First convert 765F to binary, then convert that binary number to octal.)

C.21   Convert binary 1011110 to decimal.

C.22   Convert octal 426 to decimal.

C.23   Convert hexadecimal FFFF to decimal.

C.24   Convert decimal 299 to binary, to octal and to hexadecimal.

C.25   Show the binary representation of decimal 779. Then show the one's complement of 779 and the two's complement of 779.

C.26   Show the two's complement of integer value −1 on a machine with 32-bit integers.

D

Sorting: A Deeper Look

Objectives

In this appendix, you'll:

- Sort an array using the selection sort algorithm.

- Sort an array using the insertion sort algorithm.

- Sort an array using the recursive merge sort algorithm.

- Learn about the efficiency of searching and sorting algorithms and express it in "Big O" notation.

- Explore (in the exercises) additional recursive sorts, including quicksort and a recursive selection sort.

- Explore (in the exercises) the high performance bucket sort.

D.1 Introduction

As you learned in Chapter 6, sorting places data in order, typically ascending or descending, based on one or more sort keys. This appendix introduces the selection sort and insertion sort algorithms, along with the more efficient, but more complex, merge sort. We introduce **Big O notation**, which is used to estimate the worst-case run time for an algorithm—that is, how hard an algorithm may have to work to solve a problem.

An important point to understand about sorting is that the end result—the sorted array of data—will be the same no matter which sorting algorithm you use. The choice of algorithm affects only the run time and memory use of the program. The first two sorting algorithms we study here—selection sort and insertion sort—are easy to program, but inefficient. The third algorithm—recursive merge sort—is more efficient, but harder to program.

The exercises present two more recursive sorts—quicksort and a recursive version of selection sort. Another exercise presents the bucket sort, which achieves high performance by clever use of considerably more memory than the other sorts we discuss.

D.2 Big O Notation

Suppose an algorithm is designed to test whether the first element of an array is equal to the second element. If the array has 10 elements, this algorithm requires one comparison. If the array has 1,000 elements, the algorithm still requires one comparison. In fact, the algorithm is completely independent of the number of elements in the array. This algorithm is said to have a **constant run time**, which is represented in Big O notation as $O(1)$ and pronounced "order 1." An algorithm that is $O(1)$ does not necessarily require only one comparison. $O(1)$ just means that the number of comparisons is *constant*—it does not grow as the size of the array increases. An algorithm that tests whether the first element of an array is equal to any of the next three elements is still $O(1)$ even though it requires three comparisons.

An algorithm that tests whether the first element of an array is equal to *any* of the other elements of the array will require at most $n-1$ comparisons, where n is the number of elements in the array. If the array has 10 elements, this algorithm requires up to nine comparisons. If the array has 1,000 elements, this algorithm requires up to 999 comparisons. As n grows larger, the n part of the expression "dominates," and subtracting 1 becomes inconsequential. Big O is designed to highlight these dominant terms and ignore terms that become unimportant as n grows. For this reason, an algorithm that requires a total of $n-1$ comparisons (such as the one we described earlier) is said to be $O(n)$. An $O(n)$ algorithm is referred to as having a **linear run time**. $O(n)$ is often pronounced "on the order of n" or more simply "order n."

Suppose you have an algorithm that tests whether *any* element of an array is duplicated elsewhere in the array. The first element must be compared with every other element in the array. The second element must be compared with every other element except the first—it was already compared to the first. The third element must be compared with every other element except the first two. In the end, this algorithm will end up making $(n - 1) + (n - 2) + \ldots + 2 + 1$ or $n^2/2 - n/2$ comparisons. As n increases, the n^2 term dominates, and the n term becomes inconsequential. Again, Big O notation highlights the n^2 term, leaving $n^2/2$. But as we'll soon see, constant factors are omitted in Big O notation.

Big O is concerned with how an algorithm's run time grows in relation to the number of items processed. Suppose an algorithm requires n^2 comparisons. With four elements, the algorithm will require 16 comparisons; with eight elements, the algorithm will require 64 comparisons. With this algorithm, doubling the number of elements quadruples the number of comparisons. Consider a similar algorithm requiring $n^2/2$ comparisons. With four elements, the algorithm will require eight comparisons; with eight elements, the algorithm will require 32 comparisons. Again, doubling the number of elements quadruples the number of comparisons. Both of these algorithms grow as the square of n, so Big O ignores the constant and both algorithms are considered to be $O(n^2)$, which is referred to as **quadratic run time** and pronounced "on the order of n-squared" or more simply "order n-squared."

When n is small, $O(n^2)$ algorithms (running on today's billion-operation-per-second personal computers) will not noticeably affect performance. But as n grows, you'll start to notice the performance degradation. An $O(n^2)$ algorithm running on a million-element array would require a trillion "operations" (where each could actually require several machine instructions to execute). This could require a few hours to execute. A billion-element array would require a quintillion operations, a number so large that the algorithm could take decades! $O(n^2)$ algorithms, unfortunately, are easy to write, as you'll see in this appendix. You'll also see an algorithm with a more favorable Big O measure. Efficient algorithms often take a bit more cleverness and work to create, but their superior performance can be well worth the extra effort, especially as n gets large and as algorithms are combined into larger programs.

D.3 Selection Sort

Selection sort is a simple, but inefficient, sorting algorithm. The first iteration of the algorithm selects the smallest element in the array and swaps it with the first element. The second iteration selects the second-smallest element (which is the smallest of those remaining) and swaps it with the second element. The algorithm continues until the last iteration selects the second-largest element and swaps it with the second-to-last, leaving the largest element as the last. After the ith iteration, the smallest i positions of the array will be sorted into increasing order in the first i positions of the array.

As an example, consider the array

34	56	4	10	77	51	93	30	5	52

A program that implements selection sort first determines the smallest element (4) of this array which is contained in the third element of the array (i.e., element 2 because array subscripts start at 0). The program swaps 4 with 34, resulting in

4	56	34	10	77	51	93	30	5	52

The program then determines the smallest of the remaining elements (all elements except 4), which is 5, contained at array subscript 8. The program swaps 5 with 56, resulting in

4	5	34	10	77	51	93	30	56	52

On the third iteration, the program determines the next smallest value (10) and swaps it with 34.

4	5	10	34	77	51	93	30	56	52

The process continues until after nine iterations the array is fully sorted.

4	5	10	30	34	51	52	56	77	93

After the first iteration, the smallest element is in the first position. After the second iteration, the two smallest elements are in order in the first two positions. After the third iteration, the three smallest elements are in order in the first three positions.

Figure D.1 implements the selection sort algorithm on the array array, which is initialized with 10 random ints (possibly duplicates). The main function prints the unsorted array, calls the function sort on the array, and then prints the array again after it has been sorted.

```c
 1  // Fig. D.1: figD_01.c
 2  // The selection sort algorithm.
 3  #define SIZE 10
 4  #include <stdio.h>
 5  #include <stdlib.h>
 6  #include <time.h>
 7
 8  // function prototypes
 9  void selectionSort(int array[], size_t length);
10  void swap(int array[], size_t first, size_t second);
11  void printPass(int array[], size_t length, unsigned int pass, size_t index);
12
13  int main(void)
14  {
15     int array[SIZE]; // declare the array of ints to be sorted
16
17     srand(time(NULL)); // seed the rand function
18
19     for (size_t i = 0; i < SIZE; i++) {
20        array[i] = rand() % 90 + 10; // give each element a value
21     }
22
23     puts("Unsorted array:");
24
25     for (size_t i = 0; i < SIZE; i++) { // print the array
26        printf("%d  ", array[i]);
27     }
28
29     puts("\n");
30     selectionSort(array, SIZE);
31     puts("Sorted array:");
```

Fig. D.1 | The selection sort algorithm. (Part 1 of 3.)

```
32
33      for (size_t i = 0; i < SIZE; i++) { // print the array
34         printf("%d ", array[i]);
35      }
36   }
37
38   // function that selection sorts the array
39   void selectionSort(int array[], size_t length)
40   {
41      // loop over length - 1 elements
42      for (size_t i = 0; i < length - 1; i++) {
43         size_t smallest = i; // first index of remaining array
44
45         // loop to find index of smallest element
46         for (size_t j = i + 1; j < length; j++) {
47            if (array[j] < array[smallest]) {
48               smallest = j;
49            }
50         }
51
52         swap(array, i, smallest); // swap smallest element
53         printPass(array, length, i + 1, smallest); // output pass
54      }
55   }
56
57   // function that swaps two elements in the array
58   void swap(int array[], size_t first, size_t second)
59   {
60      int temp = array[first];
61      array[first] = array[second];
62      array[second] = temp;
63   }
64
65   // function that prints a pass of the algorithm
66   void printPass(int array[], size_t length, unsigned int pass, size_t index)
67   {
68      printf("After pass %2d: ", pass);
69
70      // output elements till selected item
71      for (size_t i = 0; i < index; i++) {
72         printf("%d ", array[i]);
73      }
74
75      printf("%d* ", array[index]); // indicate swap
76
77      // finish outputting array
78      for (size_t i = index + 1; i < length; i++) {
79         printf("%d ", array[i]);
80      }
81
82      printf("%s", "\n                    "); // for alignment
83
```

Fig. D.1 | The selection sort algorithm. (Part 2 of 3.)

```
84       // indicate amount of array that is sorted
85       for (unsigned int i = 0; i < pass; i++) {
86           printf("%s", "--  ");
87       }
88
89       puts(""); // add newline
90    }
```

```
Unsorted array:
72   34   88   14   32   12   34   77   56   83

After pass  1: 12   34   88   14   32   72*  34   77   56   83
               --

After pass  2: 12   14   88   34*  32   72   34   77   56   83
               --   --

After pass  3: 12   14   32   34   88*  72   34   77   56   83
               --   --   --

After pass  4: 12   14   32   34*  88   72   34   77   56   83
               --   --   --   --

After pass  5: 12   14   32   34   34   72   88*  77   56   83
               --   --   --   --   --

After pass  6: 12   14   32   34   34   56   88   77   72*  83
               --   --   --   --   --   --

After pass  7: 12   14   32   34   34   56   72   77   88*  83
               --   --   --   --   --   --   --

After pass  8: 12   14   32   34   34   56   72   77*  88   83
               --   --   --   --   --   --   --   --

After pass  9: 12   14   32   34   34   56   72   77   83   88*
               --   --   --   --   --   --   --   --   --

After pass 10: 12   14   32   34   34   56   72   77   83   88*
               --   --   --   --   --   --   --   --   --   --

Sorted array:
12   14   32   34   34   56   72   77   83   88
```

Fig. D.1 | The selection sort algorithm. (Part 3 of 3.)

Lines 39–55 define the selectionSort function. Line 43 declares the variable smallest, which stores the index of the smallest element in the remaining array. Lines 42–54 loop length - 1 times. Line 43 assigns to smallest the index i—representing the first index of the unsorted portion of the array. Lines 46–50 loop over the remaining elements in the array. For each of these elements, line 47 compares the current element's value to the value of the element at index smallest. If the current element is smaller, line 48 assigns the current element's index to smallest. When this loop finishes, smallest contains the index of the smallest element in the remaining array. Line 52 calls function swap (lines 58–63) to place the smallest remaining element in the next spot in the array.

The output of this program uses dashes to indicate the portion of the array that is guaranteed to be sorted after each pass. An asterisk is placed next to the position of the element that was swapped with the smallest element on that pass. On each pass, the element to the left of the asterisk and the element above the rightmost set of dashes were the two values that were swapped.

Efficiency of Selection Sort
The selection sort algorithm runs in $O(n^2)$ time. The selectionSort method in Fig. D.1—which implements the algorithm—contains two for loops. The outer for loop (lines 42–

54) iterates over the first $n - 1$ elements in the array, swapping the smallest remaining item into its sorted position. The inner for loop (lines 46–50) iterates over each item in the remaining array, searching for the smallest element. This loop executes $n - 1$ times during the first iteration of the outer loop, $n - 2$ times during the second iteration, then $n - 3$, ... , 3, 2, 1. This inner loop iterates a total of $n(n - 1) / 2$ or $(n^2 - n)/2$. In Big O notation, smaller terms drop out and constants are ignored, leaving a Big O of $O(n^2)$.

D.4 Insertion Sort

Insertion sort is another simple, but inefficient, sorting algorithm. The first iteration of this algorithm takes the second element in the array and, if it's less than the first element, swaps it with the first element. The second iteration looks at the third element and inserts it into the correct position with respect to the first two elements, so all three elements are in order. At the ith iteration of this algorithm, the first i elements in the original array will be sorted.

Consider as an example the following array [*Note:* This array is identical to the one used in the discussions of selection sort and merge sort.]

| 34 | 56 | 4 | 10 | 77 | 51 | 93 | 30 | 5 | 52 |

A program that implements the insertion sort algorithm will first look at the first two elements of the array, 34 and 56. These two elements are already in order, so the program continues (if they were out of order, the program would swap them).

In the next iteration, the program looks at the third value, 4. This value is less than 56, so the program stores 4 in a temporary variable and moves 56 one element to the right. The program then checks and determines that 4 is less than 34, so it moves 34 one element to the right. The program has now reached the beginning of the array, so it places 4 in element 0. The array now is

| 4 | 34 | 56 | 10 | 77 | 51 | 93 | 30 | 5 | 52 |

In the next iteration, the program stores the value 10 in a temporary variable. Then the program compares 10 to 56 and moves 56 one element to the right because it's larger than 10. The program then compares 10 to 34, moving 34 right one element. When the program compares 10 to 4, it observes that 10 is larger than 4 and places 10 in element 1. The array now is

| 4 | 10 | 34 | 56 | 77 | 51 | 93 | 30 | 5 | 52 |

Using this algorithm, after the ith iteration, the first $i + 1$ elements of the original array are sorted with respect to one another. They may not be in their final locations, however, because smaller values may be located later in the array.

Figure D.2 implements the insertion sort algorithm. Lines 38–55 define the insertionSort function. The variable insert (line 43) holds the element you're going to insert while you move the other elements. Lines 41–54 iterate over the items in the array from index 1 through the end. In each iteration, line 42 initializes the variable moveItem, which keeps track of where to insert the element, and line 43 stores in insert the value that will be inserted into the sorted portion of the array. Lines 46–50 loop to locate the position where the element should be inserted. The loop terminates either when the program reaches the front of the array or when it reaches an element that is less than the value to be inserted. Line 48 moves an element to the right, and line 49 decrements the position at which to insert the next element. After the loop ends, line 52 inserts the element into place. The output of this program uses dashes to indicate the portion of the array that is sorted after each pass. An asterisk is placed next to the element that was inserted into place on that pass.

```c
1   // Fig. D.2: figD_02.c
2   // The insertion sort algorithm.
3   #define SIZE 10
4   #include <stdio.h>
5   #include <stdlib.h>
6   #include <time.h>
7
8   // function prototypes
9   void insertionSort(int array[], size_t length);
10  void printPass(int array[], size_t length, unsigned int pass, size_t index);
11
12  int main(void)
13  {
14     int array[SIZE]; // declare the array of ints to be sorted
15
16     srand(time(NULL)); // seed the rand function
17
18     for (size_t i = 0; i < SIZE; i++) {
19        array[i] = rand() % 90 + 10; // give each element a value
20     }
21
22     puts("Unsorted array:");
23
24     for (size_t i = 0; i < SIZE; i++) { // print the array
25        printf("%d  ", array[i]);
26     }
27
28     puts("\n");
29     insertionSort(array, SIZE);
30     puts("Sorted array:");
31
32     for (size_t i = 0; i < SIZE; i++) { // print the array
33        printf("%d  ", array[i]);
34     }
35  }
36
37  // function that sorts the array
38  void insertionSort(int array[], size_t length)
39  {
40     // loop over length - 1 elements
41     for (size_t i = 1; i < length; i++) {
42        size_t moveItem = i; // initialize location to place element
43        int insert = array[i]; // holds element to insert
44
```

Fig. D.2 | The insertion sort algorithm. (Part 1 of 3.)

```
45          // search for place to put current element
46          while (moveItem > 0 && array[moveItem - 1] > insert) {
47              // shift element right one slot
48              array[moveItem] = array[moveItem - 1];
49              --moveItem;
50          }
51
52          array[moveItem] = insert; // place inserted element
53          printPass(array, length, i, moveItem);
54      }
55  }
56
57  // function that prints a pass of the algorithm
58  void printPass(int array[], size_t length, unsigned int pass, size_t index)
59  {
60      printf("After pass %2d: ", pass);
61
62      // output elements till selected item
63      for (size_t i = 0; i < index; i++) {
64          printf("%d  ", array[i]);
65      }
66
67      printf("%d* ", array[index]); // indicate swap
68
69      // finish outputting array
70      for (size_t i = index + 1; i < length; i++) {
71          printf("%d  ", array[i]);
72      }
73
74      printf("%s", "\n                    "); // for alignment
75
76      // indicate amount of array that is sorted
77      for (size_t i = 0; i <= pass; i++) {
78          printf("%s", "-- ");
79      }
80
81      puts(""); // add newline
82  }
```

```
Unsorted array:
72  16  11  92  63  99  59  82  99  30

After pass  1: 16* 72  11  92  63  99  59  82  99  30
               --  --
After pass  2: 11* 16  72  92  63  99  59  82  99  30
               --  --  --
After pass  3: 11  16  72  92* 63  99  59  82  99  30
               --  --  --  --
After pass  4: 11  16  63* 72  92  99  59  82  99  30
               --  --  --  --  --
After pass  5: 11  16  63  72  92  99* 59  82  99  30
               --  --  --  --  --  --
```

Fig. D.2 | The insertion sort algorithm. (Part 2 of 3.)

```
After pass  6: 11   16   59* 63   72   92   99   82   99   30
               --   --   --  --   --   --
After pass  7: 11   16   59  63   72   82* 92   99   99   30
               --   --   --  --   --   --   --
After pass  8: 11   16   59  63   72   82   92   99   99* 30
               --   --   --  --   --   --   --   --
After pass  9: 11   16   30* 59   63   72   82   92   99   99
               --   --   --  --   --   --   --   --   --   --
Sorted array:
11   16   30   59   63   72   82   92   99   99
```

Fig. D.2 | The insertion sort algorithm. (Part 3 of 3.)

Efficiency of Insertion Sort

The insertion sort algorithm also runs in $O(n^2)$ time. Like selection sort, the insertion-Sort function uses nested loops. The for loop (lines 41–54) iterates SIZE - 1 times, inserting an element into the appropriate position in the elements sorted so far. For the purposes of this application, SIZE - 1 is equivalent to $n - 1$ (as SIZE is the size of the array). The while loop (lines 46–50) iterates over the preceding elements in the array. In the worst case, this while loop requires $n - 1$ comparisons. Each individual loop runs in $O(n)$ time. In Big O notation, nested loops mean that you must multiply the number of iterations of each loop. For each iteration of an outer loop, there will be a certain number of iterations of the inner loop. In this algorithm, for each $O(n)$ iterations of the outer loop, there will be $O(n)$ iterations of the inner loop. Multiplying these values results in a Big O of $O(n^2)$.

D.5 Merge Sort

The **Merge sort** algorithm is efficient, but conceptually more complex than selection sort and insertion sort. The merge sort algorithm sorts an array by splitting it into two equal-sized subarrays, sorting each subarray, then merging them into one larger array. With an odd number of elements, the algorithm creates the two subarrays such that one has one more element than the other.

The implementation of merge sort in this example is recursive. The base case is an array with one element. A one-element array is, of course, sorted, so merge sort immediately returns when it's called with a one-element array. The recursion step splits an array of two or more elements into two equal-sized subarrays, recursively sorts each subarray, then merges them into one larger, sorted array. [Again, if there are an odd number of elements, one subarray is one element larger than the other.]

Suppose the algorithm has already merged smaller arrays to create sorted arrays A:

4	10	34	56	77

and B:

5	30	51	52	93

Merge sort combines these two arrays into one larger, sorted array. The smallest element in A is 4 (located in the element zero of A). The smallest element in B is 5 (located in the zeroth index of B). To determine the smallest element in the larger array, the algorithm compares 4 and 5. The value from A is smaller, so 4 becomes the first element in the merged array. The algorithm continues by comparing 10 (the second element in A) to 5 (the first element in B). The value from B is smaller, so 5 becomes the second element in the larger array. The algorithm continues by comparing 10 to 30, with 10 becoming the third element in the array, and so on.

Figure D.3 implements the merge sort algorithm, and lines 35–38 define the merge-Sort function. Line 37 calls function sortSubArray with 0 and length - 1 as the arguments (length is the array's size). The arguments correspond to the beginning and ending indices of the array to be sorted, causing sortSubArray to operate on the entire array. Function sortSubArray is defined in lines 41–64. Line 44 tests the base case. If the size of the array is 1, the array is sorted, so the function simply returns immediately. If the size of the array is greater than 1, the function splits the array in two, recursively calls function sortSubArray to sort the two subarrays, then merges them. Line 58 recursively calls function sortSubArray on the first half of the array, and line 59 recursively calls function sortSubArray on the second half of the array. When these two function calls return, each half of the array has been sorted. Line 62 calls function merge (lines 67–114) on the two halves of the array to combine the two sorted arrays into one larger sorted array.

```c
1   // Fig. D.3: figD_03.c
2   // The merge sort algorithm.
3   #define SIZE 10
4   #include <stdio.h>
5   #include <stdlib.h>
6   #include <time.h>
7
8   // function prototypes
9   void mergeSort(int array[], size_t length);
10  void sortSubArray(int array[], size_t low, size_t high);
11  void merge(int array[], size_t left, size_t middle1,
12     size_t middle2, size_t right);
13  void displayElements(int array[], size_t length);
14  void displaySubArray(int array[], size_t left, size_t right);
15
16  int main(void)
17  {
18     int array[SIZE]; // declare the array of ints to be sorted
19
20     srand(time(NULL)); // seed the rand function
21
22     for (size_t i = 0; i < SIZE; i++) {
23        array[i] = rand() % 90 + 10; // give each element a value
24     }
25
26     puts("Unsorted array:");
27     displayElements(array, SIZE); // print the array
28     puts("\n");
29     mergeSort(array, SIZE); // merge sort the array
30     puts("Sorted array:");
```

Fig. D.3 | The merge sort algorithm. (Part 1 of 5.)

```
31        displayElements(array, SIZE); // print the array
32     }
33
34     // function that merge sorts the array
35     void mergeSort(int array[], size_t length)
36     {
37        sortSubArray(array, 0, length - 1);
38     }
39
40     // function that sorts a piece of the array
41     void sortSubArray(int array[], size_t low, size_t high)
42     {
43        // test base case: size of array is 1
44        if ((high - low) >= 1) { // if not base case...
45           size_t middle1 = (low + high) / 2;
46           size_t middle2 = middle1 + 1;
47
48           // output split step
49           printf("%s", "split:    ");
50           displaySubArray(array, low, high);
51           printf("%s", "\n          ");
52           displaySubArray(array, low, middle1);
53           printf("%s", "\n          ");
54           displaySubArray(array, middle2, high);
55           puts("\n");
56
57           // split array in half and sort each half recursively
58           sortSubArray(array, low, middle1); // first half
59           sortSubArray(array, middle2, high); // second half
60
61           // merge the two sorted arrays
62           merge(array, low, middle1, middle2, high);
63        }
64     }
65
66     // merge two sorted subarrays into one sorted subarray
67     void merge(int array[], size_t left, size_t middle1,
68        size_t middle2, size_t right)
69     {
70        size_t leftIndex = left; // index into left subarray
71        size_t rightIndex = middle2; // index into right subarray
72        size_t combinedIndex = left; // index into temporary array
73        int tempArray[SIZE]; // temporary array
74
75        // output two subarrays before merging
76        printf("%s", "merge:    ");
77        displaySubArray(array, left, middle1);
78        printf("%s", "\n          ");
79        displaySubArray(array, middle2, right);
80        puts("");
81
```

Fig. D.3 | The merge sort algorithm. (Part 2 of 5.)

```
82      // merge the subarrays until the end of one is reached
83      while (leftIndex <= middle1 && rightIndex <= right) {
84         // place the smaller of the two current elements in result
85         // and move to the next space in the subarray
86         if (array[leftIndex] <= array[rightIndex]) {
87            tempArray[combinedIndex++] = array[leftIndex++];
88         }
89         else {
90            tempArray[combinedIndex++] = array[rightIndex++];
91         }
92      }
93
94      if (leftIndex == middle2) { // if at end of left subarray ...
95         while (rightIndex <= right) { // copy the right subarray
96            tempArray[combinedIndex++] = array[rightIndex++];
97         }
98      }
99      else { // if at end of right subarray...
100        while (leftIndex <= middle1) { // copy the left subarray
101           tempArray[combinedIndex++] = array[leftIndex++];
102        }
103     }
104
105     // copy values back into original array
106     for (size_t i = left; i <= right; i++) {
107        array[i] = tempArray[i];
108     }
109
110     // output merged subarray
111     printf("%s", "            ");
112     displaySubArray(array, left, right);
113     puts("\n");
114  }
115
116  // display elements in array
117  void displayElements(int array[], size_t length)
118  {
119     displaySubArray(array, 0, length - 1);
120  }
121
122  // display certain elements in array
123  void displaySubArray(int array[], size_t left, size_t right)
124  {
125     // output spaces for alignment
126     for (size_t i = 0; i < left; i++) {
127        printf("%s", "   ");
128     }
129
130     // output elements left in array
131     for (size_t i = left; i <= right; i++) {
132        printf(" %d", array[i]);
133     }
134  }
```

Fig. D.3 | The merge sort algorithm. (Part 3 of 5.)

```
Unsorted array:
 79 86 60 79 76 71 44 88 58 23

split:    79 86 60 79 76 71 44 88 58 23
          79 86 60 79 76
                        71 44 88 58 23

split:    79 86 60 79 76
          79 86 60
                  79 76

split:    79 86 60
          79 86
                60

split:    79 86
          79
             86

merge:    79
             86
          79 86

merge:    79 86
                60
          60 79 86

split:          79 76
                79
                   76

merge:          79
                   76
                76 79

merge:    60 79 86
                76 79
          60 76 79 79 86

split:                71 44 88 58 23
                      71 44 88
                               58 23

split:                71 44 88
                      71 44
                            88

split:                71 44
                      71
                         44

merge:                71
                         44
                      44 71
```

Fig. D.3 | The merge sort algorithm. (Part 4 of 5.)

```
merge:                        44 71
                                    88
                              44 71 88

split:                              58 23
                                    58
                                       23

merge:                              58
                                       23
                                    23 58

merge:                        44 71 88
                                       23 58
                              23 44 58 71 88

merge:            60 76 79 79 86
                                 23 44 58 71 88
                     23 44 58 60 71 76 79 79 86 88

Sorted array:
 23 44 58 60 71 76 79 79 86 88
```

Fig. D.3 | The merge sort algorithm. (Part 5 of 5.)

Lines 83–92 in function merge loop until the program reaches the end of either subarray. Line 86 tests which element at the beginning of the arrays is smaller. If the element in the left array is smaller, line 87 places it in position in the combined array. If the element in the right array is smaller, line 90 places it in position in the combined array. When the while loop completes, one entire subarray is placed in the combined array, but the other subarray still contains data. Line 94 tests whether the left array has reached the end. If so, lines 95–97 fill the combined array with the elements of the right array. If the left array has not reached the end, then the right array must have reached the end, and lines 100–102 fill the combined array with the elements of the left array. Finally, lines 106–108 copy the combined array into the original array. The output from this program displays the splits and merges performed by merge sort, showing the progress of the sort at each step of the algorithm.

Efficiency of Merge Sort

Merge sort is a far more efficient algorithm than either insertion sort or selection sort (although that may be difficult to believe when looking at the rather busy Fig. D.3). Consider the first (nonrecursive) call to function sortSubArray. This results in two recursive calls to function sortSubArray with subarrays each approximately half the size of the original array, and a single call to function merge. This call to function merge requires, at worst, $n - 1$ comparisons to fill the original array, which is $O(n)$. (Recall that each element in the array is chosen by comparing one element from each of the subarrays.) The two calls to function sortSubArray result in four more recursive calls to function sortSubArray, each with a subarray approximately one quarter the size of the original array, along with two calls to function merge. These two calls to the function merge each require, at worst, $n/2 - 1$ comparisons, for a total number of comparisons of $O(n)$. This process continues, each call to sortSubArray generating two additional calls to sortSubArray and a call to merge, until the algorithm has split the array into one-element subarrays. At each level, $O(n)$ comparisons are required to merge the subarrays. Each level splits the size of the arrays in half, so doubling the size of the array requires one more level. Quadrupling the size of the array requires two more levels. This pattern is logarithmic and results in $\log_2 n$ levels. This results in a total efficiency of $O(n \log n)$.

Figure D.4 summarizes many of the searching and sorting algorithms covered in this book and lists the Big O for each of them. Figure D.5 lists the Big O values we've covered in this appendix along with a number of values for n to highlight the differences in the growth rates.

Algorithm	Big O
Insertion sort	$O(n^2)$
Selection sort	$O(n^2)$
Merge sort	$O(n \log n)$
Bubble sort	$O(n^2)$
Quicksort	Worst case: $O(n^2)$
	Average case: $O(n \log n)$

Fig. D.4 | Searching and sorting algorithms with Big O values.

n	Approximate decimal value	$O(\log n)$	$O(n)$	$O(n \log n)$	$O(n^2)$
2^{10}	1000	10	2^{10}	$10 \cdot 2^{10}$	2^{20}
2^{20}	1,000,000	20	2^{20}	$20 \cdot 2^{20}$	2^{40}
2^{30}	1,000,000,000	30	2^{30}	$30 \cdot 2^{30}$	2^{60}

Fig. D.5 | Approximate number of comparisons for common Big O notations.

Summary

Section D.1 Introduction
- **Sorting** involves arranging data into order.

Section D.2 Big O Notation
- One way to describe the efficiency of an algorithm is with **Big O notation** (*O*; p. 905), which indicates how hard an algorithm may have to work to solve a problem.
- For searching and sorting algorithms, Big O describes how the **amount of effort** of a particular algorithm varies, depending on how many elements are in the data.
- An algorithm that is $O(1)$ is said to have a **constant run time** (p. 905). This does not mean that the algorithm requires only one comparison. It just means that the number of comparisons does not grow as the size of the array increases.
- An $O(n)$ algorithm is referred to as having a **linear run time** (p. 905).

- Big O is designed to highlight dominant factors and ignore terms that become unimportant with high values of n.
- Big O notation is concerned with the growth rate of algorithm run times, so constants are ignored.

Section D.3 Selection Sort
- **Selection sort** (p. 906) is a simple, but inefficient, sorting algorithm.
- The first iteration of selection sort selects the smallest element in the array and swaps it with the first element. The second iteration of selection sort selects the second-smallest element (which is the smallest of those remaining) and swaps it with the second element. Selection sort continues until the last iteration selects the second-largest element and swaps it with the second-to-last, leaving the largest element as the last. At the ith iteration of selection sort, the smallest i elements of the whole array are sorted into the first i positions of the array.
- The selection sort algorithm runs in $O(n^2)$ time (p. 909).

Section D.4 Insertion Sort
- The first iteration of **insertion sort** (p. 910) takes the second element in the array and, if it's less than the first element, swaps it with the first element. The second iteration of insertion sort looks at the third element and inserts it in the correct position with respect to the first two elements. After the ith iteration of insertion sort, the first i elements in the original array are sorted. Only $n - 1$ iterations are required.
- The insertion sort algorithm runs in $O(n^2)$ time (p. 913).

Section D.5 Merge Sort
- The **merge sort algorithm** (p. 913) is faster, but more complex to implement, than selection sort and insertion sort.
- The merge sort algorithm sorts an array by **splitting** the array into two equal-sized **subarrays**, sorting each subarray and **merging** the subarrays into one larger array.
- Merge sort's base case is an array with one element, which is already sorted, so merge sort immediately returns when it's called with a one-element array. The merge part of merge sort takes two sorted arrays (these could be one-element arrays) and combines them into one larger sorted array.
- Merge sort performs the merge by looking at the first element in each array, which is also the smallest element. Merge sort takes the smallest of these and places it in the first element of the larger, sorted array. If there are still elements in the subarray, merge sort looks at the second element in that subarray (which is now the smallest element remaining) and compares it to the first element in the other subarray. Merge sort continues this process until the larger array is filled.
- In the worst case, the first call to merge sort has to make $O(n)$ comparisons to fill the n slots in the final array.
- The merging portion of the merge sort algorithm is performed on two subarrays, each of approximately size $n/2$. Creating each of these subarrays requires $n/2-1$ comparisons for each subarray, or $O(n)$ comparisons total. This pattern continues, as each level works on twice as many arrays, but each is half the size of the previous array.
- This halving results in $\log n$ levels, each level requiring $O(n)$ comparisons, for a total efficiency of $O(n \log n)$ (p. 919), which is far more efficient than $O(n^2)$.

Self-Review Exercises

D.1 Fill in the blanks in each of the following statements:
a) A selection sort application would take approximately _____ times as long to run on a 128-element array as on a 32-element array.
b) The efficiency of merge sort is _____.

D.2   The Big O of the linear search is $O(n)$ and of the binary search is $O(\log n)$. What key aspect of both the binary search (Chapter 6) and the merge sort accounts for the logarithmic portion of their respective Big Os?

D.3   In what sense is the insertion sort superior to the merge sort? In what sense is the merge sort superior to the insertion sort?

D.4   In the text, we say that after the merge sort splits the array into two subarrays, it then sorts these two subarrays and merges them. Why might someone be puzzled by our statement that "it then sorts these two subarrays"?

Answers to Self-Review Exercises

D.1   a) 16, because an $O(n^2)$ algorithm takes 16 times as long to sort four times as much information. b) $O(n \log n)$.

D.2   Both of these algorithms incorporate "halving"—somehow reducing something by half on each pass. The binary search eliminates from consideration one-half of the array after each comparison. The merge sort splits the array in half each time it's called.

D.3   The insertion sort is easier to understand and to implement than the merge sort. The merge sort is far more efficient—$O(n \log n)$—than the insertion sort—$O(n^2)$.

D.4   In a sense, it does not really sort these two subarrays. It simply keeps splitting the original array in half until it provides a one-element subarray, which is, of course, sorted. It then builds up the original two subarrays by merging these one-element arrays to form larger subarrays, which are then merged, and so on.

Exercises

D.5   (*Recursive Selection Sort*) A selection sort searches an array looking for the smallest element in the array. When that element is found, it's swapped with the first element of the array. The process is then repeated for the subarray, beginning with the second element. Each pass of the array results in one element being placed in its proper location. This sort requires processing capabilities similar to those of the bubble sort—for an array of n elements, $n - 1$ passes must be made, and for each subarray, $n - 1$ comparisons must be made to find the smallest value. When the subarray being processed contains one element, the array is sorted. Write a recursive function `selectionSort` to perform this algorithm.

D.6   (*Bucket Sort*) A bucket sort begins with a one-dimensional array of positive integers to be sorted, and a two-dimensional array of integers with rows subscripted from 0 to 9 and columns subscripted from 0 to $n - 1$, where n is the number of values in the array to be sorted. Each row of the two-dimensional array is referred to as a bucket. Write a function `bucketSort` that takes an integer array and the array size as arguments.

The algorithm is as follows:

    a) Loop through the one-dimensional array and place each of its values in a row of the bucket array based on its ones digit. For example, 97 is placed in row 7, 3 is placed in row 3 and 100 is placed in row 0.

    b) Loop through the bucket array and copy the values back to the original array. The new order of the above values in the one-dimensional array is 100, 3 and 97.

    c) Repeat this process for each subsequent digit position (tens, hundreds, thousands, and so on) and stop when the leftmost digit of the largest number has been processed.

On the second pass of the array, 100 is placed in row 0, 3 is placed in row 0 (it had only one digit so we treat it as 03) and 97 is placed in row 9. The order of the values in the one-dimensional array is 100, 3 and 97. On the third pass, 100 is placed in row 1, 3 (003) is placed in row zero and 97

(097) is placed in row zero (after 3). The bucket sort is guaranteed to have all the values properly sorted after processing the leftmost digit of the largest number. The bucket sort knows it's done when all the values are copied into row zero of the two-dimensional array.

The two-dimensional array of buckets is ten times the size of the integer array being sorted. This sorting technique provides far better performance than a bubble sort but requires much larger storage capacity. Bubble sort requires only one additional memory location for the type of data being sorted. Bucket sort is an example of a space–time trade-off. It uses more memory but performs better. This version of the bucket sort requires copying all the data back to the original array on each pass. Another possibility is to create a second two-dimensional bucket array and repeatedly move the data between the two bucket arrays until all the data is copied into row zero of one of the arrays. Row zero then contains the sorted array.

D.7 (*Quicksort*) In the examples and exercises of Chapter 6 and this appendix, we discussed various sorting techniques. We now present the recursive sorting technique called Quicksort. The basic algorithm for a one-dimensional array of values is as follows:

a) *Partitioning Step:* Take the first element of the unsorted array and determine its final location in the sorted array (i.e., all values to the left of the element in the array are less than the element, and all values to the right of the element in the array are greater than the element). We now have one element in its proper location and two unsorted subarrays.

b) *Recursive Step:* Perform *Step a* on each unsorted subarray.

Each time *Step a* is performed on a subarray, another element is placed in its final location of the sorted array, and two unsorted subarrays are created. When a subarray consists of one element, it must be sorted; therefore, that element is in its final location.

The basic algorithm seems simple enough, but how do we determine the final position of the first element of each subarray? As an example, consider the following set of values (the element in bold is the partitioning element—it will be placed in its final location in the sorted array):

37   2   6   4   89   8   10   12   68   45

a) Starting from the rightmost element of the array, compare each element with **37** until an element less than **37** is found. Then swap **37** and that element. The first element less than **37** is 12, so **37** and 12 are swapped. The new array is

12   2   6   4   89   8   10   **37**   68   45

Element 12 is in italic to indicate that it was just swapped with **37**.

b) Starting from the left of the array, but beginning with the element after 12, compare each element with **37** until an element greater than **37** is found. Then swap **37** and that element. The first element greater than **37** is 89, so **37** and 89 are swapped. The new array is

12   2   6   4   **37**   8   10   *89*   68   45

c) Starting from the right, but beginning with the element before 89, compare each element with **37** until an element less than **37** is found. Then swap **37** and that element. The first element less than **37** is 10, so **37** and 10 are swapped. The new array is

12   2   6   4   *10*   8   **37**   89   68   45

d) Starting from the left, but beginning with the element after 10, compare each element with **37** until an element greater than **37** is found. Then swap **37** and that element. There are no more elements greater than **37**, so when we compare **37** with itself, we know that **37** has been placed in its final location in the sorted array.

Once the partition has been applied to the array, there are two unsorted subarrays. The subarray with values less than 37 contains 12, 2, 6, 4, 10 and 8. The subarray with values greater than 37 contains 89, 68 and 45. The sort continues by partitioning both subarrays in the same manner as the original array.

Write recursive function `quicksort` to sort a one-dimensional integer array. The function should receive as arguments an integer array, a starting subscript and an ending subscript. Function `partition` should be called by `quicksort` to perform the partitioning step.

E

Multithreading and Other C11 and C99 Topics

Objectives

In this appendix, you'll:

- Learn various additional C99 and C11 features.

- Initialize arrays and structs with designated initializers.

- Use data type bool to create boolean variables whose data values can be true or false.

- Perform arithmetic operations on complex variables.

- Learn about preprocessor enhancements.

- Learn which headers were new in C99 and C11.

- Use C11's multithreading features to improve performance on today's multi-core systems.

E.1 Introduction

C99 (1999) and C11 (2011) are revised standards for the C programming language that refine and expand the capabilities of Standard C. Not every C compiler implements every C99 and C11 feature. Before using the features shown in this appendix, check that your compiler supports them. Our goal is to introduce these capabilities and provide resources for further reading.

We discuss compiler support and include links to several free compilers and IDEs that provide various levels of C99 and C11 support. We explain with complete working code examples and code snippets some of these key features that were not discussed in the main text, including designated initializers, compound literals, type `bool`, implicit `int` return type in function prototypes and function definitions (not allowed in C11) and complex numbers. We provide brief explanations for additional key C99 features, including restricted pointers, reliable integer division, flexible array members, generic math, `inline` functions and `return` without expression. Another significant C99 feature is the addition of `float` and `long double` versions of most of the math functions in `<math.h>`.

We discuss capabilities of the C11 standard, including improved Unicode support, the `_Noreturn` function specifier, type-generic expressions, the `quick_exit` function, memory alignment control, static assertions, analyzability and floating-point types. Many of these capabilities have been designated as optional. We include an extensive list of Internet resources to help you locate appropriate C11 compilers and IDEs, and dig deeper into the technical details of the language.

Multithreading

A key feature of this appendix is the introduction to multithreading (Section E.9.2). In today's multicore systems, the hardware can put multiple processors to work on different parts of your task, thereby enabling the tasks (and the program) to complete faster. To take advantage of multicore architecture from C programs you need to write multithreaded applications. When a program splits tasks into separate threads, a multicore system can run those threads in parallel. Section E.9.2 first demonstrates long-running calculations performed in sequence, then shows that by separating those calculations into multiple threads, we can significantly improve performance on a multicore system.

Compiler Flags for C99 and C11 on GNU gcc for Linux[1]
GNU supports many C99 and C11 features (but not C11's multithreading). To compile for C99, you must use the compiler flag -std=c99 as in

```
gcc -std=c99 YourProgram.c -o YourExecutableName
```

Similarly, for C11 you must used the flag -std=c11 (as we showed in Section 1.10.2):

```
gcc -std=c11 YourProgram.c -o YourExecutableName
```

On Windows, you can install GCC to run C99 or C11 programs by downloading either Cygwin (www.cygwin.com) or MinGW (sourceforge.net/projects/mingw). Cygwin is a complete Linux-style environment for Windows, while MinGW (Minimalist GNU for Windows) is a native Windows port of the compiler and related tools.

E.2 New C99 Headers

Figure E.1 lists alphabetically the standard library headers added in C99 (three of these were added in C95). All of these remain available in C11. We'll discuss the new C11 headers later in Section E.9.1.

Standard library header	Explanation
<complex.h>	Contains macros and function prototypes for supporting *complex numbers* (see Section E.6). [C99 feature.]
<fenv.h>	Provides information about the C implementation's *floating-point environment and capabilities*. [C99 feature.]
<inttypes.h>	Defines several new *portable integral types* and provides *format specifiers for defined types*. [C99 feature.]
<iso646.h>	Defines *macros* that represent the equality, relational and bitwise operators; an *alternative to trigraphs*. [C95 feature.]
<stdbool.h>	Contains macros defining bool, true and false, used for *boolean variables* (see Section E.4). [C99 feature.]
<stdint.h>	Defines *extended integer types and related macros*. [C99 feature.]
<tgmath.h>	Provides *type-generic macros* that allow functions from <math.h> to be used with a variety of parameter types (see Section E.8). [C99 feature.]
<wchar.h>	Along with <wctype.h>, provides *multibyte and wide-character input and output support*. [C95 feature.]
<wctype.h>	Along with <wchar.h>, provides *wide-character library support*. [C95 feature.]

Fig. E.1 | Standard library headers added in C99 and C95.

---

1. For the C99 and C11 features that Xcode LLVM and Microsoft Visual C++ support, no additional compiler flags are required.

E.3 Designated Initializers and Compound Literals

[This section can be read after Section 10.3.]

Designated initializers allow you to initialize the elements of an array, union or struct explicitly by subscript or name. Figure E.2 shows how we might assign the first and last elements of an array.

```
1   // Fig. E.2: figE_02.c
2   // Assigning elements of an array prior to C99
3   #include <stdio.h>
4
5   int main(void)
6   {
7      int a[5]; // array declaration
8
9      a[0] = 1; // explicitly assign values to array elements...
10     a[4] = 2; // after the declaration of the array
11
12     // assign zero to all elements but the first and last
13     for (size_t i = 1; i < 4; ++i) {
14        a[i] = 0;
15     }
16
17     // output array contents
18     printf("The array is\n");
19
20     for (size_t i = 0; i < 5; ++i) {
21        printf("%d\n", a[i]);
22     }
23  }
```

```
The array is
1
0
0
0
2
```

Fig. E.2 | Assigning elements of an array prior to C99.

In Fig. E.3 we show the program again, but rather than *assigning* values to the first and last elements of the array, we *initialize* them explicitly by subscript, using **designated initializers**.

```
1   // Fig. E.3: figE_03.c
2   // Using designated initializers
3   // to initialize the elements of an array in C99
4   #include <stdio.h>
5
```

Fig. E.3 | Using designated initializers to initialize the elements of an array in C99. (Part 1 of 2.)

```
 6   int main(void)
 7   {
 8      int a[5] =
 9      {
10         [0] = 1, // initialize elements with designated initializers...
11         [4] = 2 // within the declaration of the array
12      }; // semicolon is required
13
14      // output array contents
15      printf("The array is \n");
16
17      for (size_t i = 0; i < 5; ++i) {
18         printf("%d\n", a[i]);
19      }
20   }
```

```
The array is
1
0
0
0
2
```

Fig. E.3 | Using designated initializers to initialize the elements of an array in C99. (Part 2 of 2.)

Lines 8–12 declare the array and initialize the specified elements within the braces. Note the syntax. Each initializer in the initializer list (lines 10–11) is separated from the next by a comma, and the end brace is followed by a semicolon. Elements that are not explicitly initialized are *implicitly* initialized to zero (of the correct type). This syntax was not allowed prior to C99.

In addition to using an initializer list to declare a variable, you can also use an initializer list to create an unnamed array, struct or union. This is known as a **compound literal**. For example, if you wanted to pass an array equivalent to a in Fig. E.3 to a function without having to declare it beforehand, you could use

```
demoFunction((int [5]) {[0] = 1, [4] = 2});
```

Consider the more elaborate example in Fig. E.4, where we use designated initializers for an array of structs.

```
 1   // Fig. E.4: figE_04.c
 2   // Using designated initializers to initialize an array of structs in C99
 3   #include <stdio.h>
 4
 5   struct twoInt // declare a struct of two integers
 6   {
 7      int x;
 8      int y;
 9   };
```

Fig. E.4 | Using designated initializers to initialize an array of structs in C99. (Part 1 of 2.)

```
10
11    int main(void)
12    {
13        // explicitly initialize elements of array a
14        // then explicitly initialize two elements
15        struct twoInt a[5] =
16        {
17            [0] = {.x = 1,  .y = 2},
18            [4] = {.x = 10, .y = 20}
19        };
20
21        // output array contents
22        printf("x\ty\n");
23
24        for (size_t i = 0; i < 5; ++i) {
25            printf("%d\t%d\n", a[i].x, a[i].y);
26        }
27    } //end main
```

```
x       y
1       2
0       0
0       0
0       0
10      20
```

Fig. E.4 | Using designated initializers to initialize an array of structs in C99. (Part 2 of 2.)

Lines 17 and 18 each use a *designated initializer* to explicitly initialize a struct element in the array. Then, within that initialization, we use another level of designated initializer, explicitly initializing the x and y members of the struct. To initialize struct or union members we list each member's name preceded by a *period*.

Compare lines 15–19 of Fig. E.4, which use designated initializers, to the following executable code, which does not use designated initializers:

```
struct twoInt a[5];

a[0].x = 1;
a[0].y = 2;
a[4].x = 10;
a[4].y = 20;
```

Using initializers rather than runtime assignments improves program startup time.

E.4 Type bool

[This section can be read after Section 3.6.]
The C99 **boolean type** is _Bool, which can hold only the values 0 or 1. Recall C's convention of using *zero* and *nonzero* values to represent *false* and *true*—the value 0 in a condition evaluates to *false*, while *any* nonzero value in a condition evaluates to *true*. Assigning *any* nonzero value to a _Bool sets it to 1. C99 provides the **<stdbool.h>** header file which defines macros representing the type bool and its values true and false. These macros re-

place true with 1, false with 0 and bool with the keyword _Bool. Figure E.5 uses a function named isEven (lines 29–37) that returns a bool value of true if the function's argument is even and false if it's odd.

```
1   // Fig. E.5: figE_05.c
2   // Using the type bool and the values true and false in C99.
3   #include <stdio.h>
4   #include <stdbool.h> // allows the use of bool, true, and false
5
6   bool isEven(int number); // function prototype
7
8   int main(void)
9   {
10      // loop for 2 inputs
11      for (int i = 0; i < 2; ++i) {
12         printf("Enter an integer: ");
13         int input; // value entered by user
14         scanf("%d", &input);
15
16         bool valueIsEven = isEven(input); // determine if input is even
17
18         // determine whether input is even
19         if (valueIsEven) {
20            printf("%d is even \n\n", input);
21         }
22         else {
23            printf("%d is odd \n\n", input);
24         }
25      }
26   }
27
28   // isEven returns true if number is even
29   bool isEven(int number)
30   {
31      if (number % 2 == 0) { // is number divisible by 2?
32         return true;
33      }
34      else {
35         return false;
36      }
37   }
```

```
Enter an integer: 34
34 is even

Enter an integer: 23
23 is odd
```

Fig. E.5 | Using the type bool and the values true and false in C99.

Line 16 declares a bool variable named valueIsEven. Lines 13–14 in the loop prompt for and obtain the next integer. Line 16 passes the input to function isEven (lines 29–37).

Function isEven returns a value of type bool. Line 31 determines whether the argument is divisible by 2. If so, line 32 returns true (i.e., the number is *even*); otherwise, line 35 returns false (i.e., the number is odd). The result is assigned to bool variable valueIs-Even in line 16. If valueIsEven is true, line 20 displays a string indicating that the value is *even*. If valueIsEven is false, line 23 displays a string indicating that the value is *odd*.

E.5 Implicit int in Function Declarations

[**This section can be read after Section 5.5.**]
Prior to C99, if a function does not have an *explicit* return type, it *implicitly* is assumed to return an int. In addition, if a function does not specify a parameter type, that type implicitly becomes int. Consider the program in Fig. E.6.

```
 1  // Fig. E.6: figE_06.c
 2  // Using implicit int prior to C99
 3  #include <stdio.h>
 4
 5  returnImplicitInt(); // prototype with unspecified return type
 6  int demoImplicitInt(x); // prototype with unspecified parameter type
 7
 8  int main(void)
 9  {
10     // assign data of unspecified return type to int
11     int x = returnImplicitInt();
12
13     // pass an int to a function with an unspecified type
14     int y = demoImplicitInt(02);
15
16     printf("x is %d\n", x);
17     printf("y is %d\n", y);
18  }
19
20  returnImplicitInt()
21  {
22     return 77; // returning an int when return type is not specified
23  }
24
25  int demoImplicitInt(x)
26  {
27     return x;
28  }
```

Fig. E.6 | Using implicit int prior to C99.

When this program is run in compilers that are not C99 compliant, no compilation errors or warning messages occur and the program executes correctly. C99 *disallows* the use of the implicit int, requiring that C99-compliant compilers issue either a warning or an error. On C99-compliant compilers this program generates warnings or errors. Figure E.7 shows the warning messages from GNU gcc 4.9.2.

```
test.c:5:1: warning: data definition has no type or storage class
 returnImplicitInt(); // prototype with unspecified return type
 ^
test.c:5:1: warning: type defaults to 'int' in declaration of 'returnImplic-
itInt'
test.c:6:1: warning: parameter names (without types) in function declaration
 int demoImplicitInt(x); // prototype missing a parameter name type
 ^
test.c:20:1: warning: return type defaults to 'int'
 returnImplicitInt()
 ^
test.c: In function 'demoImplicitInt':
test.c:25:5: warning: type of 'x' defaults to 'int'
 int demoImplicitInt(x)
     ^
```

Fig. E.7 | Warning messages for implicit int produced by gcc.

E.6 Complex Numbers

[This section can be read after Section 5.3.]
The C99 standard introduced support for complex numbers and complex arithmetic. The program of Fig. E.8 performs basic operations with complex numbers. We compiled and ran this program on the LLVM compiler in Apple's Xcode 6.[2]

```
1  // Fig. E.8: figE_08.c
2  // Using complex numbers in C99
3  #include <stdio.h>
4  #include <complex.h> // for complex type and math functions
5
6  int main(void)
7  {
8     double complex a = 32.123 + 24.456 * I; // a is 32.123 + 24.456i
9     double complex b = 23.789 + 42.987 * I; // b is 23.789 + 42.987i
10    double complex c = 3.0 + 2.0 * I; // c is 3.0 + 2.0i
11
12    double complex sum = a + b; // perform complex addition
13    double complex pwr = cpow(a, c); // perform complex exponentiation
14
15    printf("a is %f + %fi\n", creal(a), cimag(a));
16    printf("b is %f + %fi\n", creal(b), cimag(b));
17    printf("a + b is: %f + %fi\n", creal(sum), cimag(sum));
18    printf("a - b is: %f + %fi\n", creal(a - b), cimag(a - b));
19    printf("a * b is: %f + %fi\n", creal(a * b), cimag(a * b));
20    printf("a / b is: %f + %fi\n", creal(a / b), cimag(a / b));
21    printf("a ^ b is: %f + %fi\n", creal(pwr), cimag(pwr));
22 }
```

Fig. E.8 | Using complex numbers in C99. (Part 1 of 2.)

---

2. In GNU gcc, the function cpow (line 13 in Fig. E.8) is not supported. Microsoft Visual C++ supports the complex-number features defined by the C++ standard, not those from C99.

```
a is 32.123000 + 24.456000i
b is 23.789000 + 42.987000i
a + b is: 55.912000 + 67.443000i
a - b is: 8.334000 + -18.531000i
a * b is: -287.116025 + 1962.655185i
a / b is: 0.752119 + -0.331050i
a ^ b is: -17857.051995 + 1365.613958i
```

Fig. E.8 | Using complex numbers in C99. (Part 2 of 2.)

For C99 to recognize complex, we include the <complex.h> header (line 4). This will expand the macro complex to the keyword _Complex—a type that reserves an array of exactly two elements, corresponding to the complex number's *real part* and *imaginary part*.

Having included the header file in line 4, we can define variables as in lines 8–10 and 12–13. We define each of the variables a, b, c, sum and pwr as type double complex. We also could have used float complex or long double complex.

The arithmetic operators also work with complex numbers. The <complex.h> header also defines several math functions, for example, cpow in line 13. You can also use the operators !, ++, --, &&, ||, ==, != and unary & with complex numbers.

Lines 17–21 output the results of various arithmetic operations. The *real part* and the *imaginary part* of a complex number can be accessed with functions creal and cimag, respectively, as shown in lines 15–21. In the output string of line 21, we use the symbol ∧ to indicate exponentiation.

E.7 Additions to the Preprocessor

[This section can be read after Chapter 13.]

C99 adds features to the C preprocessor. The first is the **_Pragma** operator, which functions like the #pragma directive introduced in Section 13.6. _Pragma ("*tokens*") has the same effect as #pragma *tokens*, but is more flexible because it can be used inside a macro definition. Therefore, instead of surrounding each usage of a compiler-specific pragma by an #if directive, you can simply define a macro using the _Pragma operator once and use it anywhere in your program.

Second, C99 specifies three standard pragmas that deal with the behavior of floating-point operations. The first token in these standard pragmas is always STDC, the second is one of FENV_ACCESS, FP_CONTRACT or CX_LIMITED_RANGE, and the third is ON, OFF or DEFAULT to indicate whether the given pragma should be *enabled, disabled,* or set to its *default value,* respectively. The FENV_ACCESS pragma is used to inform the compiler which portions of code will use functions in the C99 <fenv.h> header. On modern desktop systems, floating-point processing is done with 80-bit floating-point values. If FP_CONTRACT is enabled, the compiler may perform a sequence of operations at this precision and store the final result into a lower-precision float or double instead of reducing the precision after each operation. Finally, if CX_LIMITED_RANGE is enabled, the compiler is allowed to use the standard mathematical formulas for complex operations such as multiplying or dividing. Because floating-point numbers are *not* stored exactly, using the normal mathematical definitions can result in *overflows* where the numbers get larger than the floating-point type can represent, even if the operands and result are below this limit.

Third, the C99 preprocessor allows passing *empty arguments* to a macro call—in the previous version, the behavior of an empty argument was *undefined*, though gcc acts according to the C99 standard even in C89 mode. In many cases, it results in a syntax error, but in some cases it can be useful. For instance, consider a macro PTR(type, cv, name) defined to be type * cv name (where cv means const or volatile). In some cases, there is no const or volatile declaration on the pointer, so the second argument will be empty. When an empty macro argument is used with the # or ## operator (Section 13.7), the result is the empty string or the identifier the argument was concatenated with, respectively.

A key preprocessor addition is *variable-length argument lists for macros*. This allows for macro wrappers around functions like printf—for example, to automatically add the name of the current file to a debug statement, you can define a macro as follows:

```
#define DEBUG(...) printf(__FILE__ ": " __VA_ARGS__)
```

The DEBUG macro takes a variable number of arguments, as indicated by the ... in the argument list. As with functions, the ... must be the *last* argument; unlike functions, it may be the *only* argument. The identifier **__VA_ARGS__**, which begins and ends with *two* underscores, is a *placeholder* for the variable-length argument list. When a call such as

```
DEBUG("x = %d, y = %d\n", x, y);
```

is preprocessed, it's replaced with

```
printf("file.c" ": " "x = %d, y = %d\n", x, y);
```

As mentioned in Section 13.7, strings separated by whitespace are *concatenated* during preprocessing, so the three string literals will be combined to form the first argument to printf.

E.8 Other C99 Features

Here we provide brief overviews of some additional C99 features. These include keywords, language capabilities and standard library additions.

E.8.1 Compiler Minimum Resource Limits

[This section can be read after Section 14.5.]
Prior to C99 the standard required implementations of the language to support identifiers of no less than 31 characters for identifiers with *internal linkage* (valid only within the file being compiled) and no less than six characters for identifiers with *external linkage* (also valid in other files). For more information on internal and external linkage, see Section 14.5. The C99 standard increases these limits to 63 characters for identifiers with internal linkage and to 31 characters for identifiers with external linkage. These are just *lower* limits. Compilers are free to support identifiers with *more* characters than these limits. Identifiers are now allowed to contain national language characters via Universal Character Names (C99 Standard, Section 6.4.3) and, if the implementation chooses, directly (C99 Standard, Section 6.4.2.1). [For more information, see C99 Standard Section 5.2.4.1.]

In addition to increasing the identifier length that compilers are required to support, the C99 standard sets *minimum* limits on many language features. For example, compilers are required to support at least 1,023 members in a struct, enum or union, and at least

127 parameters to a function. For more information on other limits set by the C99 Standard, see C99 Standard Section 5.2.4.1.

E.8.2 The `restrict` Keyword

[This section can be read after Section 7.5.]
The keyword `restrict` is used to declare *restricted pointers*. We declare a **restricted pointer** when that pointer should have *exclusive* access to a region of memory. Objects accessed through a restricted pointer cannot be accessed by other pointers except when the value of those pointers was derived from the value of the restricted pointer. We can declare a restricted pointer to an `int` as:

```
int *restrict ptr;
```

Restricted pointers allow the compiler to optimize the way the program accesses memory. For example, the standard library function `memcpy` is defined in the C99 standard as follows:

```
void *memcpy(void *restrict s1, const void *restrict s2, size_t n);
```

The specification of the `memcpy` function states that it should not be used to copy between *overlapping* regions of memory. Using restricted pointers allows the compiler to see that requirement, and it can *optimize* the copy by copying multiple bytes at a time, which is more efficient. Incorrectly declaring a pointer as restricted when another pointer points to the same region of memory can result in *undefined behavior*. [For more information, see C99 Standard Section 6.7.3.1.]

E.8.3 Reliable Integer Division

[This section can be read after Section 2.5.]
In compilers prior to C99, the behavior of integer division varies across implementations. Some implementations *round a negative quotient toward negative infinity*, while others *round toward zero*. When one of the integer operands is negative, this can result in different answers. Consider dividing –28 by 5. The exact answer is –5.6. If we round the quotient toward zero, we get the integer result of –5. If we round –5.6 toward negative infinity, we get an integer result of –6. C99 removes the ambiguity and *always* performs integer division (and integer modulus) by *rounding the quotient toward zero*. This makes integer division reliable—C99-compliant platforms all treat integer division in the same way. [For more information, see C99 Standard Section 6.5.5.]

E.8.4 Flexible Array Members

[This section can be read after Section 10.3.]
C99 allows us to declare an *array of unspecified length* as the *last* member of a `struct`. Consider the following:

```
struct s {
    int arraySize;
    int array[];
};
```

A **flexible array member** is declared by specifying empty square brackets (`[]`). To allocate a `struct` with a flexible array member, use code such as:

```
int desiredSize = 5;
struct s *ptr;
ptr = malloc(sizeof(struct s) + sizeof(int) * desiredSize);
```

The `sizeof` operator ignores flexible array members. The `sizeof(struct s)` phrase is evaluated as the size of all the members in a `struct s` *except* for the flexible array. The extra space we allocate with `sizeof(int) * desiredSize` is the size of our flexible array.

There are many restrictions on the use of flexible array members. A flexible array member can be declared only as the *last* member of a `struct`—so each `struct` may contain at most *one* flexible array member. Also, a flexible array cannot be the *only* member of a `struct`. The `struct` must also have *one or more* fixed members. Furthermore, any `struct` containing a flexible array member *cannot* be a member of another `struct`. Finally, a `struct` with a flexible array member cannot be *statically* initialized—it must be allocated *dynamically*. You cannot fix the size of the flexible array member at compile time. [For more information, see C99 Standard Section 6.7.2.1.]

E.8.5 Relaxed Constraints on Aggregate Initialization
[This section can be read after Section 10.3.]
In C99, it's no longer required that aggregates such as arrays, structs, and unions be initialized by constant expressions. This enables the use of more concise initializer lists instead of using many separate statements to initialize members of an aggregate.

E.8.6 Type Generic Math
[This section can be read after Section 5.3.]
The `<tgmath.h>` header is new in C99. It provides type-generic macros for many math functions in `<math.h>`. For example, after including `<tgmath.h>`, if x is a `float`, the expression `sin(x)` will call `sinf` (the `float` version of `sin`); if x is a `double`, `sin(x)` will call `sin` (which takes a `double` argument); if x is a `long double`, `sin(x)` will call `sinl` (the `long double` version of `sin`); and if x is a complex number, `sin(x)` will call the appropriate version of the `sin` function for that complex type (`csin`, `csinf` or `csinl`). C11 includes additional generics capabilities which we mention later in this appendix.

E.8.7 Inline Functions
[This section can be read after Section 5.5.]
C99 allows the declaration of *inline functions* (as C++ does) by placing the keyword `inline` before the function declaration, as in:

```
inline void randomFunction();
```

This has *no effect* on the logic of the program from the user's perspective, but it can *improve performance*. Function calls take time. When we declare a function as `inline`, the program might no longer call that function. Instead, the compiler has the option to replace every call to an inline function with a copy of the code body of that function. This improves the run-time performance but it may increase the program's size. Declare functions as `inline` *only* if they are short and called frequently. The `inline` declaration is only *advice* to the compiler, which can decide to ignore it. [For more information, see C99 Standard Section 6.7.4.]

E.8.8 Return Without Expression

[This section can be read after Section 5.5.]
C99 adds tighter restrictions on returning from functions. In functions that return a non-void value, we are no longer permitted to use the statement

```
return;
```

In compilers prior to C99 this is allowed but results in *undefined behavior* if the caller tries to use the returned value of the function. Similarly, in functions that do not return a value, we are no longer permitted to return a value. Statements such as:

```
void returnInt() {return 1;}
```

are no longer allowed. C99 requires that compatible compilers produce warning messages or compilation errors in each of the preceding cases. [For more information, see C99 Standard Section 6.8.6.4.]

E.8.9 __func__ Predefined Identifier

[This section can be read after Section 13.9.]
The __func__ predefined identifier is similar to the __FILE__ and __LINE__ preprocessor macros—it's a string that holds the *name of the current function*. Unlike __FILE__, it's not a string literal but a real variable, so it cannot be concatenated with other literals. This is because string literal concatenation is performed during preprocessing, and the preprocessor has no knowledge of the semantics of the C language proper.

E.8.10 va_copy Macro

[This section can be read after Section 14.3.]
Section 14.3 introduced the <stdarg.h> header and facilities for working with variable-length argument lists. C99 added the **va_copy** macro, which takes two va_lists and copies its second argument into its first argument. This allows for multiple passes over a variable-length argument list without starting from the beginning each time.

E.9 New Features in the C11 Standard

C11 refines and expands the capabilities of C. At the time of this writing, most C compilers that support C11 implement only a *subset* of the new features. In addition, various new features are considered *optional* by the C11 standard. Microsoft Visual C++ provides only partial support for features that were added in C99 and C11. Figure E.9 lists C compilers that have incorporated various C11 features.

Compiler	URL
GNU GCC	https://gcc.gnu.org/gcc-4.9/
Clang/LLVM	clang.llvm.org/docs/ReleaseNotes.html
IBM XL C	http://www.ibm.com/software/products/en/ccompfami
Pelles C	www.smorgasbordet.com/pellesc/

Fig. E.9 | C11-compliant compilers.

A pre-final draft of the standard document can be found at

> www.open-std.org/jtc1/sc22/wg14/www/docs/n1570.pdf

and the final standard document can be purchased at

> webstore.ansi.org/RecordDetail.aspx?sku=INCITS%2FISO%2FIEC+9899-2012

E.9.1 New C11 Headers

Figure E.10 lists the new C11 standard library headers.

Standard library header	Explanation
`<stdalign.h>`	Provides type alignment controls.
`<stdatomic.h>`	Provides uninterruptible access to objects, used in multithreading.
`<stdnoreturn.h>`	Nonreturning functions
`<threads.h>`	Thread library
`<uchar.h>`	UTF-16 and UTF-32 character utilities

Fig. E.10 | New C11 standard library header files

E.9.2 Multithreading Support

Multithreading is one of the most significant improvements in the C11 standard. Though multithreading has been around for decades, interest in it is rising quickly due to the proliferation of multicore systems—even smartphones and tablets are typically multicore now. Most new processors today have at least two cores, with three, four and eight cores now common. The number of cores will continue to grow. In multicore systems, the hardware can put multiple cores to work on different parts of your task, thereby enabling the tasks (and the program) to complete faster. To take the fullest advantage of multicore architecture you need to write multithreaded applications. When a program splits tasks into separate threads, a multicore system can run those threads in parallel.

Standard Multithreading Implementation

Previously, C multithreading libraries were nonstandard, platform-specific extensions. C programmers often want their code to be portable across platforms. This is a key benefit of standardized multithreading. C11's `<threads.h>` header declares the new (optional) multithreading capabilities that enable you to write more portable multithreaded C code. At the time of this writing, very few C compilers provide C11 multithreading support. For the examples in this section, we used the *Pelles C compiler* (Windows only), which you can download from www.smorgasbordet.com/pellesc/. In this section, we introduce the basic multithreading features that enable you to create and execute threads. At the end of the section we introduce several other multithreading features that C11 supports.

Running Multithreaded Programs

When you run a program on a modern computer system, your program's tasks compete for the attention of the processor(s) with the operating system, *and* with other programs and other activities that the operating system is running on your behalf. All kinds of tasks are typically running in the background on your system. When you execute the examples in this section, the time to perform each calculation will vary based on your computer's processor speed, number of processor cores and what's running on your computer. It's not unlike a drive to the supermarket—the time it takes can vary based on traffic conditions, weather and other factors. Some days the drive might take 10 minutes, but during rush hour or bad weather it could take longer. The same is true for executing applications on computer systems.

There is also overhead inherent in multithreading itself. Simply dividing a task into two threads and running it on a dual-core system does not run it twice as fast, though it will typically run faster than performing the thread's tasks in sequence.

Performance Tip E.1

As you'll see, executing a multithreaded application on a single-core processor can actually take longer than simply performing the thread's tasks in sequence.

Overview of This Section's Examples

To provide a convincing demonstration of the power of multithreading on a multicore system, this section presents two programs:

- One performs two compute-intensive calculations sequentially.

- The other executes the same compute-intensive calculations in parallel threads.

We executed each program on single-core *and* dual-core Windows computers to demonstrate the performance of each program in each scenario. We timed each calculation and the total calculation time in both programs. The program outputs show the time improvements when the multithreaded program executes on a multicore system.

Example: Sequential Execution of Two Compute-Intensive Tasks

Figure E.11 uses the recursive `fibonacci` function (lines 37–46) that we introduced in Section 5.15. Recall that, for larger Fibonacci values, the recursive implementation can require significant computation time. The example sequentially performs the calculations `fibonacci(50)` (line 16) and `fibonacci(49)` (line 25). Before and after each `fibonacci` call, we capture the time so that we can calculate the total time required for the calculation. We also use this to calculate the total time required for both calculations. Lines 21, 30 and 33 use function `difftime` (from header `<time.h>`) to calculate the number of seconds between two times.

```
1   // Fig. E.11: figE_11.c
2   // Fibonacci calculations performed sequentially
3   #include <stdio.h>
4   #include <time.h>
5
6   unsigned long long int fibonacci(unsigned int n); // function prototype
7
```

Fig. E.11 | Fibonacci calculations performed sequentially. (Part 1 of 3.)

```
 8    // function main begins program execution
 9    int main(void)
10    {
11       puts("Sequential calls to fibonacci(50) and fibonacci(49)");
12
13       // calculate fibonacci value for 50
14       time_t startTime1 = time(NULL);
15       puts("Calculating fibonacci(50)");
16       unsigned long long int result1 = fibonacci(50);
17       time_t endTime1 = time(NULL);
18
19       printf("fibonacci(%u) = %llu\n", 50, result1);
20       printf("Calculation time = %f minutes\n\n",
21          difftime(endTime1, startTime1) / 60.0);
22
23       time_t startTime2 = time(NULL);
24       puts("Calculating fibonacci(49)");
25       unsigned long long int result2 = fibonacci(49);
26       time_t endTime2 = time(NULL);
27
28       printf("fibonacci(%u) = %llu\n", 49, result2);
29       printf("Calculation time = %f minutes\n\n",
30          difftime(endTime2, startTime2) / 60.0);
31
32       printf("Total calculation time = %f minutes\n",
33          difftime(endTime2, startTime1) / 60.0);
34    }
35
36    // Recursively calculates fibonacci numbers
37    unsigned long long int fibonacci(unsigned int n)
38    {
39       // base case
40       if (0 == n || 1 == n) {
41          return n;
42       }
43       else { // recursive step
44          return fibonacci(n - 1) + fibonacci(n - 2);
45       }
46    }
```

a) Output on a Dual-Core Windows Computer

```
Sequential calls to fibonacci(50) and fibonacci(49)
Calculating fibonacci(50)
fibonacci(50) = 12586269025
Calculation time = 1.366667 minutes

Calculating fibonacci(49)
fibonacci(49) = 7778742049
Calculation time = 0.883333 minutes

Total calculation time = 2.250000 minutes
```

Fig. E.11 | Fibonacci calculations performed sequentially. (Part 2 of 3.)

b) Output on a Single-Core Windows Computer

```
Sequential calls to fibonacci(50) and fibonacci(49)
Calculating fibonacci(50)
fibonacci(50) = 12586269025
Calculation time = 1.566667 minutes

Calculating fibonacci(49)
fibonacci(49) = 7778742049
Calculation time = 0.883333 minutes

Total calculation time = 2.450000 minutes
```

c) Output on a Single-Core Windows Computer

```
Sequential calls to fibonacci(50) and fibonacci(49)
Calculating fibonacci(50)
fibonacci(50) = 12586269025
Calculation time = 1.450000 minutes

Calculating fibonacci(49)
fibonacci(49) = 7778742049
Calculation time = 0.883333 minutes

Total calculation time = 2.333333 minutes
```

Fig. E.11 | Fibonacci calculations performed sequentially. (Part 3 of 3.)

The first output shows the results of executing the program on a dual-core Windows computer on which every execution produced the same results, though this is not guaranteed. The second and third outputs show the results of executing the program on a single-core Windows computer on which the results varied, but execution always took longer, because the processor was being shared between this program and all the others that happened to be executing on the computer at the same time.

Example: Multithreaded Execution of Two Compute-Intensive Tasks

Figure E.12 also uses the recursive fibonacci function, but executes each call to it in a *separate thread*. The first two outputs show the multithreaded Fibonacci example executing on a dual-core computer. Though execution times varied, the total time to perform both Fibonacci calculations (in our tests) was always less than for sequential execution in Fig. E.11— because our program split into two threads and used two cores, rather than just one. The last two outputs show the example executing on a single-core computer with the same speed as the dual-core computer. Again, times varied for each execution, but the total time was *more* than the sequential execution due to the overhead of sharing *one* processor among the program's threads and the other programs executing on the computer at the same time.

```
1   // Fig. E.12: figE_12.c
2   // Fibonacci calculations performed in separate threads
3   #include <stdio.h>
```

Fig. E.12 | Fibonacci calculations performed in separate threads. (Part 1 of 4.)

```
 4    #include <threads.h>
 5    #include <time.h>
 6
 7    #define NUMBER_OF_THREADS 2
 8
 9    int startFibonacci(void *nPtr);
10    unsigned long long int fibonacci(unsigned int n);
11
12    typedef struct ThreadData {
13       time_t startTime; // time thread starts processing
14       time_t endTime; // time thread finishes processing
15       unsigned int number; // fibonacci number to calculate
16    } ThreadData; // end struct ThreadData
17
18    int main(void)
19    {
20       // data passed to the threads; uses designated initializers
21       ThreadData data[NUMBER_OF_THREADS] =
22          { [0] = {.number = 50},
23            [1] = {.number = 49}};
24
25       // each thread needs a thread identifier of type thrd_t
26       thrd_t threads[NUMBER_OF_THREADS];
27
28       puts("fibonacci(50) and fibonacci(49) in separate threads");
29
30       // create and start the threads
31       for (size_t i = 0; i < NUMBER_OF_THREADS; ++i) {
32          printf("Starting thread to calculate fibonacci(%d)\n",
33             data[i].number);
34
35          // create a thread and check whether creation was successful
36          if (thrd_create(&threads[i], startFibonacci, &data[i]) !=
37             thrd_success) {
38
39             puts("Failed to create thread");
40          }
41       }
42
43       // wait for each of the calculations to complete
44       for (size_t i = 0; i < NUMBER_OF_THREADS; ++i)
45          thrd_join(threads[i], NULL);
46
47       // determine time that first thread started
48       time_t startTime = (data[0].startTime < data[1].startTime) ?
49          data[0].startTime : data[1].startTime;
50
51       // determine time that last thread terminated
52       time_t endTime = (data[0].endTime > data[1].endTime) ?
53          data[0].endTime : data[1].endTime;
54
```

Fig. E.12 | Fibonacci calculations performed in separate threads. (Part 2 of 4.)

```
55       // display total time for calculations
56       printf("Total calculation time = %f minutes\n",
57          difftime(endTime, startTime) / 60.0);
58    }
59
60    // Called by a thread to begin recursive Fibonacci calculation
61    int startFibonacci(void *ptr)
62    {
63       // cast ptr to ThreadData * so we can access arguments
64       ThreadData *dataPtr = (ThreadData *) ptr;
65
66       dataPtr->startTime = time(NULL); // time before calculation
67
68       printf("Calculating fibonacci(%d)\n", dataPtr->number);
69       printf("fibonacci(%d) = %lld\n",
70          dataPtr->number, fibonacci(dataPtr->number));
71
72       dataPtr->endTime = time(NULL); // time after calculation
73
74       printf("Calculation time = %f minutes\n\n",
75          difftime(dataPtr->endTime, dataPtr->startTime) / 60.0);
76       return thrd_success;
77    }
78
79    // Recursively calculates fibonacci numbers
80    unsigned long long int fibonacci(unsigned int n)
81    {
82       // base case
83       if (0 == n || 1 == n) {
84          return n;
85       }
86       else { // recursive step
87          return fibonacci(n - 1) + fibonacci(n - 2);
88       }
89    }
```

a) Output on a Dual-Core Windows Computer

```
fibonacci(50) and fibonacci(49) in separate threads
Starting thread to calculate fibonacci(50)
Starting thread to calculate fibonacci(49)
Calculating fibonacci(50)
Calculating fibonacci(49)
fibonacci(49) = 7778742049
Calculation time = 0.866667 minutes

fibonacci(50) = 12586269025
Calculation time = 1.466667 minutes

Total calculation time = 1.466667 minutes
```

Fig. E.12 | Fibonacci calculations performed in separate threads. (Part 3 of 4.)

b) Output on a Dual-Core Windows Computer

```
fibonacci(50) and fibonacci(49) in separate threads
Starting thread to calculate fibonacci(50)
Starting thread to calculate fibonacci(49)
Calculating fibonacci(50)
Calculating fibonacci(49)
fibonacci(49) = 7778742049
Calculation time = 0.783333 minutes

fibonacci(50) = 12586269025
Calculation time = 1.266667 minutes

Total calculation time = 1.266667 minutes
```

c) Output on a Single-Core Windows Computer

```
fibonacci(50) and fibonacci(49) in separate threads
Starting thread to calculate fibonacci(50)
Starting thread to calculate fibonacci(49)
Calculating fibonacci(50)
Calculating fibonacci(49)
fibonacci(49) = 7778742049
Calculation time = 1.683333 minutes

fibonacci(50) = 12586269025
Calculation time = 2.183333 minutes

Total calculation time = 2.183333 minutes
```

d) Output on a Single-Core Windows Computer

```
fibonacci(50) and fibonacci(49) in separate threads
Starting thread to calculate fibonacci(50)
Starting thread to calculate fibonacci(49)
Calculating fibonacci(50)
Calculating fibonacci(49)
fibonacci(49) = 7778742049
Calculation time = 1.600000 minutes

fibonacci(50) = 12586269025
Calculation time = 2.083333 minutes

Total calculation time = 2.083333 minutes
```

Fig. E.12 | Fibonacci calculations performed in separate threads. (Part 4 of 4.)

struct ThreadData

The function that each thread executes in this example receives a ThreadData object as its argument. This object contains the number that will be passed to fibonacci and two time_t members where we store the time before and after each thread's fibonacci call. Lines 21–23 create an array of the two ThreadData objects and use designated initializers to set their number members to 50 and 49, respectively.

thrd_t

Line 26 creates an array of thrd_t objects. When you create a thread, the multithreading library creates a *thread ID* and stores it in a thrd_t object. The thread's ID can then be used with various multithreading functions.

Creating and Executing a Thread

Lines 31–41 create two threads by calling function thrd_create (line 36). The function's three arguments are:

- A thrd_t pointer that thrd_create uses to store the thread's ID.

- A pointer to a function (startFibonacci) that specifies the task to perform in the thread. The function must return an int and receive a void pointer representing the argument to the function (in this case, a pointer to a ThreadData object). The int represents the thread's state when it terminates (e.g., thrd_success or thrd_error).

- A void pointer to the argument that should be passed to the function in the second argument.

Function thrd_create returns thrd_success if the thread is created, thrd_nomem if there was not enough memory to allocate the thread or thrd_error otherwise. If the thread is created successfully, the function specified as the second argument begins executing in the new thread.

Joining the Threads

To ensure that the program does not terminate until the threads terminate, lines 44–45 call thrd_join for each thread that we created. This causes the program to *wait* until the threads complete execution before executing the remaining code in main. Function thrd_join receives the thrd_t representing the ID of the thread to join and an int pointer where thrd_join can store the status returned by the thread. After the threads terminate, lines 48–57 calculate and display the total execution time by determining the time difference between the time the first thread started and the second thread ended.

Function startFibonacci

Function startFibonacci (lines 61–77) specifies the task to perform—in this case, to call fibonacci to recursively perform a calculation, to time the calculation, to display the calculation's result and to display the time the calculation took (as we did in Fig. E.11). The thread executes until startFibonacci returns the thread's status (thrd_success, line 76), at which point the thread terminates.

Other C11 Multithreading Features

In addition to the basic multithreading support shown in this section, C11 also includes other features such as _Atomic variables and atomic operations, thread local storage, conditions and mutexes. For more information on these topics, see Sections 6.7.2.4, 6.7.3, 7.17 and 7.26 of the standard and the following blog post and article:

```
http://blog.smartbear.com/software-quality/bid/173187/
    C11-A-New-C-Standard-Aiming-at-Safer-Programming
http://lwn.net/Articles/508220/
```

E.9.3 `quick_exit` function

In addition to `exit` (Section 14.6) and `abort`, C11 now also supports function `quick_exit` (header `<stdlib.h>`) for terminating a program. Like `exit`, you call `quick_exit` and pass it an *exit status* as an argument—typically `EXIT_SUCCESS` or `EXIT_FAILURE`, but other platform-specific values are possible. The exit status value is returned from the program to the calling environment to indicate whether the program terminated successfully or an error occurred. When called, `quick_exit` can, in turn, call up to at least 32 other functions to perform clean-up tasks. You register these functions with the `at_quick_exit` function (similar to `atexit` in Section 14.6) and are called in the *reverse* order from which they were registered. Each registered function must return `void` and have a `void` parameter list. The motivation for functions `quick_exit` and `at_quick_exit` is explained at

```
http://www.open-std.org/jtc1/sc22/wg14/www/docs/n1327.htm
```

E.9.4 Unicode® Support

Internationalization and localization is the process of creating software that supports *multiple spoken languages* and *locale-specific requirements*—such as displaying monetary formats. The Unicode® character set contains characters for many of the world's languages and symbols.

C11 now includes support for both the *16-bit (UTF-16)* and *32-bit (UTF-32)* Unicode character sets, which makes it easier for you to internationalize and localize your apps. Section 6.4.5 in the C11 standard discusses how to create Unicode string literals. Section 7.28 in the standard discusses the features of the new Unicode utilities header (`<uchar.h>`), which include the new types `char16_t` and `char32_t` for UTF-16 and UTF-32 characters, respectively. At the time of this writing, the new Unicode features are *not* widely supported among C compilers.

E.9.5 `_Noreturn` Function Specifier

The *`_Noreturn` function specifier* indicates that a function will *not* return to its caller. For example, function `exit` (Section 14.6) terminates a program, so it does *not* return to its caller. Such functions in the C Standard Library are now declared with `_Noreturn`. For example, the C11 standard shows function `exit`'s prototype as:

```
_Noreturn void exit(int status);
```

If the compiler knows that a function does *not* return, it can perform various *optimizations*. It can also issue error messages if a `_Noreturn` function is inadvertently written to return.

E.9.6 Type-Generic Expressions

C11's new `_Generic` keyword provides a mechanism that you can use to create a macro (Chapter 13) that can invoke different type-specific versions of functions based on the macro's argument type. In C11, this is now used to implement the features of the type-generic math header (`<tgmath.h>`). Many math functions provide separate versions that take as arguments `float`s, `double`s or `long double`s. In such cases, there is a macro that automatically invokes the corresponding type-specific version. For example, the macro `ceil` invokes the function `ceilf` when the argument is a `float`, `ceil` when the argument is a `double` and `ceill` when the argument is a `long double`. Section 6.5.1.1 of the C11 standard discusses the details of using `_Generic`.

E.9.7 Annex L: Analyzability and Undefined Behavior

The C11 standard document defines the features of the language that compiler vendors must implement. Because of the extraordinary range of hardware and software platforms and other issues, the standard specifies in a number of places that the result of an operation is *undefined behavior*. These can raise security and reliability concerns—every time there's an undefined behavior something happens that could leave a system open to attack or failure. The term "undefined behavior" appears approximately 50 times in the the C11 standard document.

The people from CERT (`cert.org`) who developed C11's optional Annex L on analyzability scrutinized all undefined behaviors and discovered that they fall into two categories—those for which compiler implementers should be able to do something reasonable to avoid serious consequences (known as *bounded undefined behaviors*), and those for which implementers would not be able to do anything reasonable (known as *critical undefined behaviors*). It turned out that most undefined behaviors belong to the first category. David Keaton (a researcher from the CERT Secure Coding Program) explains the categories in the following article:

```
http://blog.sei.cmu.edu/post.cfm/improving-security-in-the-latest-
    c-programming-language-standard-1
```

The C11 standard's Annex L identifies the critical undefined behaviors. Including this annex as part of the standard provides an opportunity for compiler implementors—a compiler that's Annex L compliant can be depended upon to do something reasonable for most of the undefined behaviors that might have been ignored in earlier implementations. Annex L still does not guarantee reasonable behavior for critical undefined behaviors. A program can determine whether the implementation is Annex L compliant by using conditional compilation directives (Section 13.5) to test whether the macro `__STDC_ANALYZABLE__` is defined.

E.9.8 Memory Alignment Control

In Chapter 10, we discussed the fact that computer platforms have different boundary alignment requirements, which could lead to `struct` objects requiring more memory than the total of their members' sizes. C11 now allows you to specify the boundary alignment requirements of any type using features of the `<stdalign.h>` header. `_Alignas` is used to specify alignment requirements. Operator `alignof` returns the alignment requirement for its argument. Function `aligned_alloc` allows you to dynamically allocate memory for an object and specify its alignment requirements. For more details see Section 6.2.8 of the C11 standard document.

E.9.9 Static Assertions

In Section 13.10, you learned that C's `assert` macro tests the value of an expression at execution time. If the condition's value is false, `assert` prints an error message and calls function `abort` to terminate the program. This is useful for debugging purposes. C11 now provides `_Static_assert` for compile-time assertions that test constant expressions after the preprocessor executes and at a point during compilation when the types of expressions are known. For more details see Section 6.7.10 of the C11 standard document.

E.9.10 Floating-Point Types

C11 is now compatible with the IEC 60559 floating-point arithmetic standard, though support for this is optional. Among its features, IEC 60559 defines how floating-point arithmetic should be performed to ensure that you always get the same results, whether the calculations are performed by hardware, software or both, and across implementations (whether in C or in other languages that support this standard). You can learn more about this standard at:

```
http://www.iso.org/iso/iso_catalogue/catalogue_tc/
    catalogue_detail.htm?csnumber=57469
```

E.10 Web Resources

C99 Resources

`http://www.open-std.org/jtc1/sc22/wg14/`
Official site for the C standards committee. Includes defect reports, working papers, projects and milestones, the rationale for the C99 standard, contacts and more.

`http://blogs.msdn.com/b/vcblog/archive/2007/11/05/iso-c-standard-update.aspx`
Blog post of Arjun Bijanki, the test lead for the Visual C++ compiler. Discusses why C99 is not supported in Visual Studio.

`http://www.ibm.com/developerworks/linux/library/l-c99/index.html`
Article: "Open Source Development Using C99," by Peter Seebach. Discusses C99 library features on Linux and BSD.

`http://www.informit.com/guides/content.aspx?g=cplusplus&seqNum=215`
Article: "A Tour of C99," by Danny Kalev. Summarizes some of the new features in the C99 standard.

C11 Standard

`http://webstore.ansi.org/RecordDetail.aspx?sku=INCITS%2FISO%2FIEC+9899-2012`
Purchase the ANSI variant of the C11 standard.

`http://www.open-std.org/jtc1/sc22/wg14/www/docs/n1570.pdf`
This is the last *free* draft of the C11 standard before it was approved and published.

What's New in C11

`http://en.wikipedia.org/wiki/C11_(C_standard_revision)`
The Wikipedia page for the new C11 standard describes what's new since C99.

`http://progopedia.com/dialect/c11/`
This page includes a brief listing of the new features in C11.

`http://www.informit.com/articles/article.aspx?p=1843894`
The article, "The New Features of C11," by David Chisnall.

`http://www.drdobbs.com/cpp/c-finally-gets-a-new-standard/232800444`
The article, "C Finally Gets a New Standard," by Tom Plum. Discusses concurrency, keywords, the `thread_local` storage class, optional threads and more.

`http://www.drdobbs.com/cpp/cs-new-ease-of-use-and-how-the-language/240001401`
The article, "C's New Ease of Use and How the Language Compares with C++," by Tom Plum. Discusses some of the new C11 features that match features in C++, and a few key differences in C11 that have no corresponding features in C++.

http://www.i-programmer.info/news/98-languages/3546-new-iso-c-standard-c1x.html
The article, "New ISO C standard—C11," by Mike James. Briefly discusses some of the new features.

http://www.drdobbs.com/cpp/the-new-c-standard-explored/232901670
The article, "The New C Standard Explored," by Tom Plum. Discusses the C11 Annex K functions, fopen() safety, fixing tmpnam, the %n formatting vulnerability, security improvements and more.

http://www.sdtimes.com/link/36892
The article, "The thinking behind C11," by John Benito, the convener of the ISO working group for the C programming language standard. The article discusses the C programming language standard committee's guiding principles for the new C11 standard.

Improved Security

http://blog.smartbear.com/software-quality/bid/173187/C11-A-New-C-Standard-Aiming-at-Safer-Programming
The blog, "C11: A New C Standard Aiming at Safer Programming," by Danny Kalev. Discusses the problems with the C99 standard and new hopes with the C11 standard in terms of security.

http://www.amazon.com/exec/obidos/ASIN/0321822137/deitelassociatin
The book, *Secure Coding in C and C++, Second Edition*, by Robert Seacord. Discusses the security benefits of the Annex K library.

http://blog.sei.cmu.edu/post.cfm/improving-security-in-the-latest-c-programming-language-standard-1
The blog, "Improving Security in the Latest C Programming Language Standard," by David Keaton of the CERT Secure Coding Program at Carnegie Mellon's Software Engineering Institute. Discusses bounds checking interfaces and analyzability.

http://blog.sei.cmu.edu/post.cfm/helping-developers-address-security-with-the-cert-c-secure-coding-standard
The blog, "Helping Developers Address Security with the CERT C Secure Coding Standard," by David Keaton. Discusses how C has handled security issues over the years and the CERT C Secure Coding Rules.

Bounds Checking

http://www.securecoding.cert.org/confluence/display/seccode/ERR03-C.+Use+runtime-constraint+handlers+when+calling+the+bounds-checking+interfaces
Carnegie Mellon's Software Engineering Institute's post, "ERR03-C. Use runtime-constraint handlers when calling the bounds-checking interfaces," by David Svoboda. Provides examples of noncompliant and compliant code.

Multithreading

http://stackoverflow.com/questions/8876043/multi-threading-support-in-c11
The forum discussion, "Multi-Threading support in C11." Discusses the improved memory sequencing model in C11 vs C99.

http://www.t-dose.org/2012/talks/multithreaded-programming-new-c11-and-c11-standards
The slide presentation, "Multithreaded Programming with the New C11 and C++11 Standards," by Klass van Gend. Introduces the new features of both the C11 and C++11 languages and discusses how far gcc and clang are implementing the new standards.

http://www.youtube.com/watch?v=UqTirRXe8vw
The video, "Multithreading Using Posix in C Language and Ubuntu," with Ahmad Naser.

http://fileadmin.cs.lth.se/cs/Education/EDAN25/F06.pdf
The slide presentation, "Threads in the Next C Standard," by Jonas Skeppstedt.

http://www.youtube.com/watch?v=gRe6Zh2M3zs
A video of Klaas van Gend discussing multithreaded programming with the new C11 and C++11 standards.

Compiler Support

http://www.ibm.com/developerworks/rational/library/support-iso-c11/support-iso-c11-pdf.pdf
The whitepaper, "Support for ISO C11 added to IBM XL C/C++ compilers: New features introduced in Phase 1." Provides an overview of the new features supported by the compiler including complex value initialization, static assertions and functions that do not return.

Appendices on the Web

The following appendices are available as PDF documents from this book's Companion Website (www.pearsonhighered.com/deitel/):

- Appendix F, Using the Visual Studio Debugger
- Appendix G, Using the GNU gdb Debugger
- Appendix H, Using the Xcode Debugger

These files can be viewed in Adobe® Reader® (get.adobe.com/reader).

Index

C++ Reviewer Comments (Content Selected from the Deitels' *C++ How to Program, 9/e* Textbook)

"Gets you into C++ programming quickly with relevant and important tips, excellent exercises, gradual progression towards advanced concepts and comprehensive coverage of C++11 features." —**Dean Michael Berris, Google, Member ISO C++ Committee**

"The examples are accessible to CS, IT, software engineering and business students." —**Thomas J. Borrelli, Rochester Institute of Tech.**

"An excellent 'objects first' coverage of C++ accessible to beginners." —**Gavin Osborne, Saskatchewan Inst. of App. Sci. and Tech.**

"As an instructor, I appreciate the thorough discussion of the C++ language, especially the use of code examples and demonstration of best coding practices. For my consulting work I use the Deitel books as my primary reference." —**Dean Mathias, Utah State University**

"Extensive coverage of the new C++11 features: list-initialization of scalar types and containers, nullptr, range for-loops, scoped enumerated types, inheritance control keywords (override and final), auto declarations and more. Code tested meticulously with three leading, industrial-strength compilers." —**Danny Kalev, C++ expert, Certified System Analyst and former member of C++ Standards Committee**

"Just when you think you are focused on learning one topic, suddenly you discover you've learned more than you expected." —**Chad Willwerth, U. Washington, Tacoma**

"The virtual function figure and corresponding explanation in the Polymorphism chapter is thorough and truly commendable." —**Gregory Dai, eBay**

"The Object-Oriented Programming: Inheritance chapter is well done. Excellent introduction to polymorphism." —**David Topham, Ohlone College**

"Thorough and detailed coverage of exceptions from an object-oriented point of view." —**Dean Mathias, Utah State University**

"Good use of diagrams, especially of the activation call stack." —**Amar Raheja, California State Polytechnic University, Pomona**

"Terrific discussion of pointers—the best I have seen." —**Anne B. Horton, Lockheed Martin**

"I especially value the code examples and diagrams. Great coverage of OOP. Nice detail in Intro to Classes—students can learn so much from it; I love that every line of code is explained and that UML class diagrams are given. Good visuals provided for what's going on in memory [for pass-by-value and pass-by-reference]. The Inheritance examples nicely reinforce the concepts. I love the description of [a possible] polymorphic video game." —**Linda M. Krause, Elmhurst College**

"The Introduction to Classes, Objects and Strings examples are solid." —**Dean Michael Berris, Google, Member ISO C++ Committee**

"The pointers chapter manages to explain something that's quite difficult to teach: the elusive nature of pointers. The Operator Overloading chapter explains the topic clearly and builds a convincing, realistic Array class that demonstrates the capabilities of OOD and C++." —**Danny Kalev, C++ expert, Certified System Analyst and former member of C++ Standards Committee**

"I like the idea of std::array [not built-in arrays] by default. Exception Handling is accurate and to the point." —**James McNellis, Microsoft Corporation**

"Novices and advanced programmers will find this book an excellent tool for learning C++. Really fun and interesting exercises." —**José Antonio González Seco, Parliament of Andalusia**

"I really like the Making a Difference exercises. The dice and card games get students excited." —**Virginia Bailey, Jackson State University**

"Provides a complete basis of fundamental instruction in all core aspects of C++." —**Peter DePasquale, The College of New Jersey**

"Great coverage of polymorphism and how the compiler implements polymorphism 'under the hood.'" —**Ed James-Beckham, Borland**

"Will get you up and running quickly with the smart pointers library." —**Ed Brey, Kohler Co.**

"Replete with real-world case studies. Code examples are extraordinary!" —**Terrell Hull, Logicalis Integration Solutions**

C Reviewer Comments Begin on the Back Cover

Additional Comments from Recent Editions Reviewers

"An excellent introduction to the C programming language, with many clear examples. Pitfalls of the language are clearly identified and concise programming methods are defined to avoid them." **—John Benito, Blue Pilot Consulting, Inc., and Convener of ISO WG14—the working group responsible for the C Programming Language Standard**

"An already excellent book now becomes superb. This new edition focuses on secure programming and provides extensive coverage of the newest C11 features, including multi-core programming. All of this, of course, while maintaining the typical characteristics of the Deitels' *How to Program* series—astonishing writing quality, great selection of real-world examples and exercises, and programming tips and best practices that prepare students for industry." **—José Antonio González Seco, Parliament of Andalusia**

"A very nice selection of exercises in Chapter 3 Structured Program Development in C—good job." **—Alan Bunning of Purdue University**

"I like the structured programming summary (in Chapter 4, Program Control) with instruction on how to form structured programs by using the flow chart building blocks; I also like the range and variety of questions at the end of the chapter and the Secure C Programming section." **—Susan Mengel, Texas Tech University**

"The descriptions of function calls and the call stack will be particularly helpful to beginning programmers learning the semantics of how functions work—plenty of function exercises." **—Michael Geiger, University of Massachusetts, Lowell**

"The examples and end-of-chapter programming projects are very valuable. This is the only C book in the market that offers so many detailed C examples—I am pleased to be able to have such a resource to share with my students. Coverage of the C99 and C11 standards is especially important. For one of my classes the starting language is C and the course includes an introduction to C++—this book provides both. I feel confident that this book prepares my students for industry. Overall a great book. I always enjoy lecturing the Arrays chapter; examples are perfect for my CE, EE and CSE students—this chapter is one of the most important in my class; I find the examples to be very relatable for my students. Chapters 8 and above are used for my Data Structures class, which is taught to students majoring in Electrical Engineering and Computer Engineering; Chapter 10 plays a big role for them to understand bitwise operations—this is the only textbook that covers bitwise operations in such detail." **—Sebnem Onsay, Special Instructor, Oakland University School of Engineering and Computer Science**

"A great book for the beginning programmer. Covers material that will be useful in later programming classes and the job market." **—Fred J. Tydeman, Tydeman Consulting, Vice-Chair of J11 (ANSI C)**

"An excellent introductory C programming text. Clearly demonstrates important C programming concepts. Just the right amount of coverage of arrays. The Pointers chapter is well-written and the exercises are rigorous. Excellent discussion of string functions. Fine chapters on formatted input/output and files. I was pleased to see a hint at Big O running time in the binary search example. Good information in the preprocessor chapter." **—Dr. John F. Doyle, Indiana U. Southeast**

"I have been teaching introductory programming courses since 1975, and programming in the C language since 1986. In the beginning there were no good textbooks on C—in fact, there weren't any! When Deitel, C How to Program, 1/e, came out, we jumped on it—it was at the time clearly the best text on C. The new edition continues a tradition—it's by far the best student-oriented textbook on programming in the C language—the Deitels have set the standard—again! A thorough, careful treatment of not just the language, but more importantly, the ideas, concepts and techniques of programming! 'Live code' is also a big plus, encouraging active participation by the student. A great text!" **—Richard Albright, Goldey-Beacom College**

"I like the quality of the writing. The book outlines common beginner mistakes really well. Nice visualization of binary search. The card shuffling example illustrates an end-to-end solution to the problem with nice pseudocode, great coding and explanation. Card and maze exercises are very involving." **—Vytautus Leonavicius, Microsoft Corporation**

"Introduces C programming and gets you ready for the job market, with best practices and development tips. Nice multi-platform explanation [running Visual C++ on Windows, GNU C on Linux and Xcode on Mac OS X]." **—Hemanth H.M., Software Engineer at SonicWALL**

"Control statements chapters are excellent; the number of exercises is amazing. Great coverage of functions. The discussions of secure C programming are valuable. The C Data Structures chapter is well written, and the examples and exercises are great; I especially like the section about building a compiler. Explanation of the sorting algorithms is excellent." **—José Antonio González Seco, Parliament of Andalusia**

"The live-code approach makes it easy to understand the basics of C programming. I highly recommend this textbook as both a teaching text and a reference." **—Xiaolong Li, Indiana State University**

"An exceptional textbook and reference for the C programmer." **—Roy Seyfarth, University of Southern Mississippi**

"An invaluable resource for beginning and seasoned programmers. The authors' approach to explaining the concepts, techniques and practices is comprehensive, engaging and easy to understand. A must-have book." **—Bin Wang, Department of CS and Engineering, Wright State Univ.**

C++ Reviewer Comments on the Back of This Page